THE PRE-NICENE
NEW TESTAMENT

THE PRE-NICENE NEW TESTAMENT

Fifty-four Formative Texts

ROBERT M. PRICE

Signature Books • Salt Lake City • 2006

For Professor David M. Scholer, who first sent me swimming in the ocean of church fathers, martyrs, heretics, and apocrypha. When he threw me a life preserver, it wasn't his fault that I didn't grab it!

www.signaturebooks.com

Jacket design by Ron Stucki

The Pre-Nicene New Testament: Fifty-four Formative Texts was printed on acid-free paper and was composed, printed, and bound in the United States of America.

2016 2015 2014 2013 2012 8 7 6 5 4 3

Library of Congress Cataloging-in-Publication Data

The pre-Nicene New Testament: fifty-four formative texts / by Robert M. Price.

p. cm.

Includes bibliographical references and index.

ISBN 10: 1-56085-194-5

ISBN 13: 978-1-56085-194-3

1. Apocryphal books (New Testament) I. Price, Robert M., 1954- II. Bible. N.T. English. Price. 2006.

BS2832.P75 2006

229'.9205209—dc22

2006045036

CONTENTS

INTRODUCTION TO THE CANON
History, Text, and Interpretation

Fruit as well as root

The question of the New Testament canon, which is to say the official list of writings or table of contents, is a vitally important one, as all recognize, and even more important than many realize. On the one hand, if one regards the Bible as inspired and authoritative scripture, it is obviously a vital matter to get clear about which writings are to wield authority over belief and conscience and which shall not. Believing in scripture *in general* means nothing: it is a matter of specific claims, commandments, doctrines, and rites, and some appear in some documents, others in other documents. For this reason, Protestants follow Martin Luther in rejecting both the book of 2 Maccabees and the practice of praying for the dead, which is endorsed in it. They are ready to believe in the bodily assumption of Elijah into heaven since this event is recounted in 2 Kings, but they scoff at the bodily ascension of the Virgin Mary since this very similar belief is recounted only in non-canonical writings such as *The Falling Asleep of the Holy Mother of God.* Similarly, biblicists opposing abortion would have a much simpler case to make had the Epistle of Barnabas or the Apocalypse of Peter been admitted into the canon, as they explicitly condemn abortion, whereas the practice does not come up for mention in any document considered canonical.

A more crucial aspect still is that of the authority underlying the Bible. If the texts of scripture authorize everything else in Christian belief and practice, what is it that authenticates the biblical canon? It is not as if the Bible were delivered from the hand of an angel like the Book of Mormon or dictated by an angel like the Koran. The Bible, as everyone knows, is a compilation of many short writings, many of them the products of several writers, redactors, revisers, and scribes. In addition, there were books of the same type that did not finally

make it into the canonical list. Who decided on the list and how did they decide? The Bible is not only the beginning of one theological process but is itself the end of another. It is worth looking back at "how came the Bible," as Edgar J. Goodspeed used to say. When we have done that, we will be in a position to re-evaluate other books that were not canonized.

Marcionite invasion

The history of a distinctively Christian scriptural canon begins with Marcion of Pontus in Asia Minor. Traditionally dated about 140 AD/CE, Marcion actually may have begun his public ministry earlier, just after the turn of the century. One ancient tradition makes Marcion the amanuensis (secretary) of the evangelist John at the end of the first century. That is probably not historically true, but no one would have told the story if they had not assumed Marcion was living at that time. It was a general tendency of early Catholic apologists to late-date the so-called "heretics" to distance them from the apostolic period in the same way apologists today prefer the earliest possible date for the epistles and gospels.

Marcion was the first Paulinist we know of. It would later be a matter of some embarrassment to the church fathers that the earliest readers and devotees of the Pauline epistles were the Marcionites and the Valentinian Gnostics. We know of no Paulinists before these second-century Christians. The mid-first century existence of Pauline Christianity is simply an inference, admittedly a natural one, from taking the authorship and implied dates of the Pauline epistles at face value as works representing a wing of first-century Christianity. But it is quite possible that the Pauline literature is the product of Marcionite and Gnostic movements in the late first and early second centuries. Even if most of the Pauline epistles are genuinely from the first century, the most likely candidate for the first collector of the corpus remains Marcion. No one else in the relevant time period would have had either the interest or the opportunity. No one was as interested in Paul as Marcion. Why?

It was because he shared with his theological cousins, the Gnostics, the belief that the true God and Father of Jesus Christ was not the

same deity as the creator and law-giver God of Israel and of the Jewish scriptures. In this belief Marcion was perhaps influenced by Zoroastrian Zurvanism, a dualistic doctrine, as Jan Koester suggests. Marcion allowed that the creator God was righteous and just but also harsh and retributive. His seeming grace was but a function of his arbitrariness: Nero might render a verdict of thumbs-up or thumbs-down as the whim moved him, and so with the God of Israel. Marcion deemed the Jewish scriptures historically true and expected messianic prophecies to be fulfilled by a Davidic king who would restore Jewish sovereignty. But Marcion deemed all of this strictly irrelevant to the new religion of Christianity. In his view, which he claimed to have derived from Paul's epistles, Jesus Christ was the son and revealer of an alien God who had not created the world, had not given the Torah to Moses, and would not judge mankind. The Father of Jesus Christ was a God of perfect love and righteousness who would punish no one. Through Jesus, and by extension Paul, the Christian God offered humans the opportunity to be adopted as his children. If they were gentiles, this meant a break with paganism. If they were Jews, it entailed a break from Judaism and the Torah. Marcion preached a strict morality. All sex was sinful. Begetting children only produced more souls to live in bondage to the creator. Marcion believed Jesus had no physical birth but had appeared out of heaven one day in a body that seemed to be that of a thirty-year-old, complete with a misleading belly button, although not human at all: rather a celestial being. Jesus taught and was later crucified. His twelve disciples were to spread his gospel of an alien God and his adoption of all who would come to him. But things went awry: the disciples, as thick-headed and prone to misunderstanding as they appear in the Gospel of Mark, underestimated the discontinuity of Jesus' new revelation with their hereditary Judaism, thereby combining the two. This was the origin of the Judaizing heresy with which Paul deals in Galatians and elsewhere.

Marcion had noticed an oddity most Christians never notice as they read the New Testament: if Jesus had named the Twelve to succeed him and seemed satisfied with them, why was there a need for Paul at all? And why should he come to eclipse the others in importance? The Twelve are, for the most part, merely a list of names. By

contrast, Paul wrote letters that formed the basis of much of the church's theology. Marcion saw a simple answer: the risen Jesus saw how far off the track his disciples would go and decided to recruit another who would get the message straight. This was Paul. To invoke a recurrent pattern in Christian history, think of Martin Luther, Alexander Campbell, John Nelson Darby, Joseph Smith, Charles Taze Russell, Victor Paul Wierwille, and others. All these believed that original, apostolic Christianity was corrupted by an admixture of human tradition, and they believed they had a new vision of the outlines of the original, true Christianity and could restore it. This is what Marcion thought already in the early second century. It should not sound that strange to us. Like these later men, Marcion would succeed very well in launching a new church, one that would spread like wildfire all over and even beyond the Roman Empire. Most noteworthy is the fact that the New Testament was his idea.

The emerging Catholic Church, which would develop into the medieval church, which then subsequently split into Roman Catholicism and Eastern Orthodoxy, was by this time employing the familiar authority structure of scripture and tradition. By scripture was meant the Septuagint, the Greek translation of Jewish scriptures, including the so-called apocryphal or deutero-canonical books of the Maccabees, Judith, Tobit, Sirach/Ecclesiasticus, Wisdom, Baruch, the Epistle of Jeremiah, 1 Esdras, and so on. This was "scripture." Tradition, on the other hand, was a growing body of sayings attributed to Jesus and stories about him, as well as the summaries of "apostolic" doctrine represented in such formulae as the Apostles Creed and similar summaries in the late second century by writers like Irenaeus and Tertullian, to name two. There were a number of early Christian writings of various kinds (gospels, epistles, apostolic acts, revelations, church manuals) that were written and circulated more or less widely, but these were at first more *expressions of* the faith than either the *source* or *criteria for* faith. That is not to say they were not important. Think of the writings of Calvin and Luther: they are important to Calvinists and Lutherans who still study them, but Calvinists and Lutherans would not consider the wise writings of their founders to be scripture on the same level with the Bible. Admittedly, the difference in actual

practice may evaporate, but that is just the technical distinction that is important here. The question that concerns us is precisely how the early Christian writings came to cross that line and join the category of scripture. The earliest Catholic Christians felt no need as yet for new scripture since they found the Septuagint Bible adequate to their needs as long as they could use allegory and typology to see in it a book about Jesus Christ and Christianity.

This reinterpretation of Jewish scripture was not something Marcion was willing to undertake. He insisted on a literal, straightforward reading of the Septuagint, refusing to treat it as a ventriloquist dummy and make it seem to speak with Christian accents. Theodore of Mopsuestia (350-428) had the same attitude, though he was no Marcionite. Read in a plain-sense fashion, the Jewish scriptures, Marcion realized, had nothing to do with Christianity. Even lacking his belief in two different biblical Gods, one can see his point when one thinks of the strained arguments needed in order to make various Old Testament passages sound like predictions of Jesus. And it is still common today to hear Christians contrast the severe God of Israel with the tender Father of Jesus. So Marcion repudiated the Jewish scriptures. It wasn't that he didn't believe them, because he did. He simply felt they were the scriptures of someone else's religion and didn't overlap with Christianity as he understood it. Nor was he anti-Semitic or even anti-Judaic. For him, Judaism was true on its own terms, just not the religion of Jesus Christ or of the apostle Paul.

Without the Septuagint as his scripture, Marcion felt the need to compile a new canon that would teach Christian faith and morals authoritatively. He accordingly collected the early Christian writings he felt served this purpose. These were paramountly the Pauline epistles except for the Pastorals, 1 and 2 Timothy, and Titus, because these did not exist yet, still waiting to be written in reaction to Marcion and other "heretics" in the mid-second century. Marcion had shorter, earlier versions of the texts than ours. Likewise, he had a book he knew simply as "the gospel" corresponding to a shorter version of our Gospel of Luke. Catholic writers decades later would claim he had edited and censored the texts, cutting out material that served to link Christianity with its Jewish background. Marcion no doubt did do some

editing, textual criticism as it seemed to him, but it seems that Catholic apologists did much more in the way of padding the texts with their own added material, claiming their own versions were original and should be adopted instead of the Marcionite text. Marcion called his scripture the *Apostolicon* ("Book of the Apostle"). In his and his opponents' claims and counter claims, we begin to see the inevitable relation of the twin issues of *text* and *canon*—which versions of which writings are authoritative?

The first counter-reformation

If Marcion had been merely some eccentric scribe, people like Justin Martyr, Irenaeus, and Tertullian would not have bothered with him. In fact, he became a force to be reckoned with as his Pauline Christianity spread far and wide. The relationship between Marcion and the Catholic leaders of his own day is strikingly paralleled in the uneasy relations between Paul and the Jerusalem apostles in Galatians and 2 Corinthians. There were initial attempts at ecumenical cooperation, but it did not work. The Catholic Church sought to co-opt Marcionism late in the second century by, as anticipated above, adding material to the Pauline texts and to Luke, harmonizing Pauline Christianity with Judaism in the manner still familiar today, insisting that Christianity was the rightful heir to God's covenant promises with Israel and the Jewish people. Had Marcionism triumphed, I dare say we would have seen more peaceful Jewish-Christian relations since neither side would have been perceived as a threat to the other.

How did the Catholic Church respond to the Marcionite Sputnik of a specifically Christian scripture? Where Marcion relinquished the Jewish scriptures to the Jewish religion and replaced them with distinctly Christian writings, the Catholic bishops decided to retain the Jewish Bible, reinterpreted in a Christian manner, and to add a new set of scriptures onto it. They had no objection to having a set of books that would speak overtly of Christian faith and practice. Remember that they already had them and it was just a question of making them officially part of the Bible. So they took over the Pauline corpus, adding the Pastorals and interpolating the others to bring them into accord with Catholic teaching. Marcion's gospel became our Gospel of

Luke by adding chapters 1-3, the Nazareth synagogue sermon, the prodigal son, the tower of Siloam and Pilate's massacre of the Galileans, the "wisdom saith" speech, the triumphal entry, the wicked tenants, the prediction of spirit baptism, and the ascension. To balance and dilute Luke, they added Matthew, Mark, and John, though John had to be extensively reshuffled and interpolated, as Bultmann showed, before it could pass as orthodox. It may attest the relative unimportance of the Twelve that no one made any attempt to even ascribe apostolic names to Mark's and Luke's narratives. The gospels are all anonymous, not pseudonymous, the four names being editorial conventions added once people began to use a *collection* of gospels, creating the need to differentiate them: "Let's read from the Gospel ... according to Matthew this time." Perhaps at one point the characters Mark and Luke were held in equal esteem with John and Matthew as important leaders, though only guesswork identifies them with New Testament personalities of those names. It is interesting that the two most common male names in the Roman Empire happened to be Mark and Luke.

Wanting to restore the clout of the Twelve, the compilers of the New Testament made a late attempt to represent them in the canon alongside Paul. The Acts of the Apostles sought to co-opt Paul and make Peter his twin, bringing both sides together, devotees of Paul's memory and devotees of Peter's, as well as to imply that the Twelve had played some prominent role. If they ever had, their labors were among Jewish Christians in Palestine and largely forgotten after 70 AD/CE and the destruction of Jerusalem. A group of three anonymous epistles from "the Elder," a master of traveling missionaries late in the first century, were ascribed gratuitously to John, son of Zebedee. Two spurious Petrine writings (1 and 2 Peter, by different pseudonymous authors) were chosen out of the much larger bin of Petrine apocrypha surviving today, including the two Apocalypses of Peter, the Gospel of Peter, the Journeys of Peter, the Acts of Peter, the Preaching of Peter, the Letter of Peter to Philip, the Letter of Peter to James, and so on. The two favored epistles were added, as was a letter by someone named James and another by one Jude. Was James the brother of the Lord? Son of Zebedee? Son of Alphaeus? Some other James?

No one knows. In any case, these documents gave us the core of the Catholic canon, though its exact outlines would take some centuries to be delimited.

Loose canon

For Irenaeus (115-202), bishop of Lyons and major opponent of Gnosticism, the Christian Testament included the four gospels, the Pauline Epistles, and Acts. He also used 1 Peter, 1 John, either 2 or 3 John (he does not say which, but he mentions "another" Johannine epistle), Jude, and Revelation but seemed not yet to regard these as scripture. No mention of Hebrews, 2 Peter, or James. Twenty years later, Tertullian (mid-second to mid-third century), a follower of Irenaeus, had the same list but considered them all scripture. Tertullian used Hebrews and the Epistle of Barnabas without saying specifically that he regarded them as canonical. He thought 1 Enoch ought to be included in the Old Testament. The first Christian we know of who referred to the Jewish scriptures as the Old Testament was Melito of Sardis in the last third of the second century. Clement of Alexandria (160-215) was the first to call the Christian scriptures the New Testament.

While Irenaeus considered the books just listed above to be authoritative and canonical, he did not predicate that authority upon divine inspiration. As he saw it, their authority stemmed from their place as the foundational documents of the apostolic age. Again, Tertullian carried things a significant step farther, locating the authority of these books specifically in apostolic authorship rather than just the early period of Christianity. To be considered authoritative, they had to have been composed by Jesus' apostles and their delegates, by which he meant Mark and Luke because they were said to have been assistants to Peter and Paul respectively. Irenaeus has his predecessor, Papias, bishop of Hierapolis, linking Mark to Peter in this way in about 130 AD/CE. However, ascribing statements to Papias functioned as convenient *hadith*—licenses to make this or that item authoritative as needed—as in Islam where the claim of access to left-over Koranic verses or ancient oral traditions was a way of circumventing scripture.

Clement of Alexandria had no closed canon and made frequent reference not only to our four conventional gospels but also to the Gospel according to the Hebrews and the Gospel according to the Egyptians, to apocryphal as well as canonical Acts, to the Epistles of Clement and Barnabas, the Preaching of Peter, and the Shepherd of Hermas. If Morton Smith is to be believed, Clement also possessed a Secret Mark. Thus far, the New Testament books were authoritative because they were apostolic. It was Clement's successor, Origen (185-251), who first pronounced them inspired writings, as opposed to writings of inspired or authoritative writers, which was an important distinction that continues to be drawn even in the twenty-first century. Origen reasoned that since a book either was inspired or was not, it behooved the church to decide which ones belonged in the Bible, but he himself did not make that judgment. He only saw the need.

Eusebius, the great church historian and propagandist for Constantinian Christianity, makes it clear that precise canonical boundaries were still a matter in dispute in the mid-fourth century. He tells us how, in the discussions of contemporary theologians, the available writings in effect fell into four categories. First, there were the books regarded as genuinely apostolic: the four conventional gospels and the Pauline epistles, with some disputing of Hebrews, 1 John, 1 Peter, and Acts. Some of the church fathers included Revelation in the apostolic category, though Eusebius himself was no fan of it. Second, there were generally disputed books: 2 and 3 John, Jude, James, and 2 Peter, while some accepted Hebrews; Origen admitted that "God alone knows" who wrote Hebrews. Third were the "spurious" works (meaning they were possibly pseudonymous), which were nevertheless acceptable and usable: the Gospel according to the Hebrews, the Acts of Paul, Shepherd of Hermas, Apocalypse of Peter, the Didache (Teaching of the Twelve Apostles to the Nations), Barnabas, and for some the Revelation of John. Eusebius thought it was a "John the Elder" rather than the son of Zebedee who wrote the Revelation. Fourth were outright heretical forgeries: the Acts of John, of Andrew, Peter, Thomas, and others, and the Gospels of Peter, Thomas, and Matthias. The question of a definitive list was still open, at least for a while. But Eusebius tells us how Constantine had fifty deluxe vellum

copies of the New Testament manufactured and sent to prelates all over the empire, this of course implying a fixed text. We cannot help thinking of the Islamic tradition that, to stifle theological debates in which opponents appealed to different texts of the Koran, the Caliph Uthman called in all known variant copies, had his scholars standardize an official text, and burned the earlier ones. The distribution of a New Testament codex from the home office by Constantine must have had the same effect of establishing an official list. However, the Constantine Bible may not have quite matched our familiar list of twenty-seven books. Codex Sinaiticus and Codex Vaticanus, which date from this period and are possibly examples of the Constantinian pulpit Bibles, include such books as Barnabas and 1 Clement.

The Muratorian Canon, a fragmentary document from Rome discovered by Muratori, has generally been placed in the second century, but some now argue it dates to the fourth century. It lists all of our New Testament books except for Hebrews, James, and 1 and 2 Peter, while including the Apocalypse of Peter and the Wisdom of Solomon. It mentions but rejects the Shepherd of Hermas.

Bonfire of the heresies

The first known list of our twenty-seven New Testament writings appears in the paschal (Easter) letter of Athanasius to his diocese in 367 AD/CE. Athanasius lists them and warns his flock to use these and no others. One immediate result of this encyclical was to prompt the brethren of the Monastery of Saint Pachomius in Egypt, the very first known Christian monastery, to hide away their copies of the banned books. They buried them in a cave in leather satchels, where they rested in oblivion till 1945 when they were accidentally discovered by a shepherd boy at Nag Hammadi. The monks knew the inquisitors would be coming around again to see if the encyclical had been obeyed, and they did not want to hand over their precious copies of the Gospels of Thomas, Philip, Peter, the Egyptians, and Mary Magdalene; their Revelations of Zostrianos, James, Melchizedek, Seth, Shem, and Dositheus; their Epistles of Peter and James; or their Apocrypha of John and James to be burned. Their library attests to an astonishing range of Christian scriptures still in use at the time. We

have only these and a very few other copies of the excluded books because the Constantinian authorities carried out a systematic purge of the writings deemed heretical per Athanasius' encyclical. Others, like the Shepherd of Hermas, survived outside the canon since they were not considered dangerous, just not official. The importance of this fact is still vastly underestimated today. It means that the New Testament as we read it is as much a document of the fourth century as of the first. The canonical deck was cleared, so to speak, to leave us with a highly misleading impression of what early Christianity was like. Even so, the scholar F. C. Baur was able in the nineteenth century to discern the split in early Christianity along pro- and anti-Torah, Petrine vs. Pauline, lines, with Gnosticism lurking somewhere down the road. Some decades later Walter Bauer (*Orthodoxy and Heresy in Earliest Christianity*) demonstrated that the Christian movement was much more diverse than even Baur had thought, that emerging Catholicism had managed to rewrite history in such a way as to cast itself as the original Christianity, caricaturing all other varieties as unimportant cranks and fringe groups. Shortly after Bauer's book appeared, the 1945 discovery of the Nag Hammadi library made it clear that early Christianity must have been an even more lush theological jungle than any scholar had conceived of. Here, for the first time, were multiple primary sources attesting to many completely different families of early Christian belief, of which we had hitherto only the slightest, if any, hint. Who would have imagined there were whole wings of Christianity that thought Jesus was the reincarnation of Seth, of Melchizedek, or of Zoroaster? Elaine Pagels (*The Gnostic Gospels*) was about the only scholar who seemed to realize the full significance of the Gnostic texts discovered at Nag Hammadi, that they were not some sort of ancient science fiction novels but rather the cherished scriptures of people's living faith. She did a good job of putting some flesh on the bones. For instance, if we wonder about the identity of the "single ones" held up as a model in the Gospel according to Thomas, we need only remind ourselves that the Greek word is *monachos* (monk) and that the document was found at a monastery. As in Buddhism still today, there was then no one canon. Different species of Christians used different sacred books. This was about to change.

The canon list of Athanasius, who championed *homoousias* christology (Christ is "of the same nature" as the Father) at Nicea, was officially adopted by the local Synod of Hippo in 393 and again by the Synod of Carthage in 397. This hardly meant that from then on everyone agreed on what should constitute the New Testament. Surviving manuscript codices (and there are a great many) from the next few centuries continue to include some of the less heretical books or lack some of the more orthodox ones. Scribes apparently did not feel particularly bound to conform to the Athanasian norm. Why should they? No ecumenical council would rule on the matter until the Counter-Reformation Council of Trent in 1551! In general, though, it would be fair to say that by about 400 AD/CE, the western Mediterranean churches used the Athanasian canon, while remaining grudgingly reluctant about Hebrews. It took another two centuries until the eastern churches were ready to accept Revelation as canonical. Even today in the Monophysite churches of Armenia and Ethiopia, the New Testament canon contains such books as Barnabas, Clement, and 3 Corinthians.

During the Protestant Reformation, Martin Luther was able to reshape the canon simply by virtue of the fact that he was preparing the official German edition of the Bible. It was up to him what would be included. He rejected the Old Testament Apocrypha, mainly because it had not survived in its original languages. He felt scripture could be considered authoritative in its original Hebrew or Greek, that one could not rely on the Septuagint or the Latin Vulgate; therefore a book that existed only in translation could not be canonized. He rejected the theological content of some of the Apocrypha, as well, but fell short of condemning it. Even the Puritans would read from the Apocrypha for edification, and it was included in the King James Bible until 1823 when its printers finally decided to remove it.

Luther reshuffled the books of the New Testament, restricting Hebrews, James, Jude, and Revelation to an appendix. He referred to James contemptuously as the "epistle of straw," while he said the Book of Revelation deserved to be thrown into the Elbe River. None of these books adequately conveyed the doctrine of salvation by grace through faith alone, which was his plumbline. Needless to say, Lu-

therans would not choose to follow their leader on this point. In the nineteenth century, Protestant theologians would revisit the question, Schleiermacher urging colleagues to sift the "canonical" from the "apocryphal" within the New Testament, while Harnack said it was time to follow Marcion and cut loose the Old Testament. Perhaps the most astonishing Protestant remark on canonical questions came from Willi Marxsen, a twentieth-century German who noted that Protestants had implicitly sawed off the branch they sat on when they rejected church tradition as the norm for faith in favor of "scripture alone." How did they come to this predicament? By ignoring that the canon itself was purely a matter of church tradition, not of a decree from God. The Bible doesn't tell us what ought to be in the Bible, tradition does, and the latter is what Protestants claimed to reject. Uh-oh.

Making the cut: criteria

As a matter of tradition, the selection of the books for the canon was gradual and to some degree haphazard. It was the result of a gradual accumulation of local usage and then a comparison of such local versions and usages by larger councils. It still remained a matter of local habit and custom until the mostly anonymous Catholic bishops and theologians in the second, third, and fourth centuries began applying certain criteria to determine the degree to which a book should be revered. Some of these criteria will sound familiar by now, but I will nevertheless discuss them in order of descending importance, noting how each argument has a tendency to collapse into another.

First, *catholicity*: Was a book known in and used liturgically all over the empire? If it was not, it was dubious since a real apostolic writing (see just below) would have had time to circulate more widely. The fewer quarters of the church it was known in, the greater the likelihood it might be a recent forgery. "Why didn't we hear about this Gospel of Wally until now? I smell a rat!" is how the logic went. The little book of 3 John had trouble passing muster on this score, but it made it in because it was evidently by the same author as the popular and renowned 1 John, so it was reasoned that its short length had caused it to be largely overlooked. In practice, catholicity meant "more

widely known," whatever its contents, because long familiarity and wide readership meant there had been more opportunity for the rough edges to be worn away through harmonizing exegesis. But if it was unfamiliar, the foreign ring to the prose jumped right out. This is what happened to the Gospel of Peter. Bishop Serapion was asked to look at a copy in rural Syria where it was popular. The bishop had never heard of it, so he took a look but saw no problem. Then someone advised a second look, and he picked out signs of docetism, the belief that Jesus had only *seemed* (Greek: *dokeo*) to suffer while remaining divinely impassive. So the book was condemned. Had the concerned reader grown up hearing it read every Sunday in a familiar context, he would not have noticed a problem any more than the Syrian congregations had. In addition, the less widely known a book was, the easier it was to exclude it out of political considerations since it had fewer partisans to defend it.

Second, *orthodoxy*. Did the contents promote the rule of faith, which was the emerging creed? Again, catholicity might overrule this since unorthodox elements could be harmonized if the book were held in high esteem. For instance, no one complains about the numerous Gnostic, docetic, and adoptionistic verses in Paul's letters. Even so, evidence of docetism could prejudice the decision, as with the Gospel of Peter or the Acts of John. A book might also be spurned over something as simple as citing other books no longer considered canonical. Barnabas cited 1 Enoch as scripture and was not canonized; but Jude cited 1 Enoch and was accepted, though someone tried to replace it with 2 Peter, a book which incorporates most of Jude and cuts references to the Assumption of Moses and 1 Enoch. A book might also be rejected not because of outright heresy but because it risked letting the camel's nose under the tent flap. In this way, late apocalypses like the Shepherd of Hermas were considered dangerous because they were of later vintage, and if one could accept them, there would no longer be any clear reason not to accept the prophetic rantings of the Montanist prophetess Maximilla. Other books were rejected not so much because of their content but because of guilt by association due to long or notorious use by heretical sects. The Gospel of Thomas was probably excluded because Valentinians and Mani-

cheans used it. Their interpretations were by no means the only way to read the book, and had it been included in the canon it would not sound heretical to anyone today. The familiar Gospel of John came near to sharing Thomas's fate because it was popular among the Gnostics, one of whom, Heracleon, wrote the first known commentary on it. The anti-Montanist Gaius thought it might have been written by the Gnostic Cerinthus himself! A whole group, dubbed by their enemies the *alogoi* (a pun: opponents of the Logos/witless ones), opposed John. And in fact, John probably *was* Gnostic. As Bultmann showed, it was toned down by an "ecclesiastical redactor" to make it suitable to orthodox ears.

Third, *apostolicity*. Was it written by an apostle or by an associate of an apostle? We have seen how important this criterion was, but it was a wax nose easily twisted. If a book was widely known and deemed orthodox, then an apostolic byline could be created for it. In this way, to secure entrance into the canon, the anonymous Epistle to the Hebrews was ascribed to Paul. It was also possible to claim some tenuous link between the ascribed authorship and an apostle, as when Mark was made Peter's secretary and Luke Paul's. If a book sounded too blatantly unorthodox despite a clear apostolic authorship claim, such as the numerous books attributed to Thomas, Peter, Paul, Matthias, James, and John, it could be dismissed as a forgery. While Eusebius embraced the chiliastic (millenarian) teaching of Revelation, he ascribed it to John, son of Zebedee. Once he rejected the doctrine, he decided the Revelation must have been the work of another John after all.

Similarly, one is forced to wonder whether the reason Matthew's gospel received its apostolic ascription was because it was by far the most popular of the gospels, while Mark and Luke were damned with faint praise through the assignations of sub-apostolic names. By the time the grossly different John was added to the equation, Gaius, remember, had suggested Cerinthus for its author as a function of its Gnostic content. To go so far as to grant it a fully apostolic pedigree was a counterblast. Had no one gone so far as to credit it to Cerinthus, it is likely no one would have over-compensated with Johannine authorship. It is parallel to the criticisms aimed at the erotic Song of

Solomon in the first century among rabbis. Shouldn't such a piece of pornography be ejected from the canon and public reading? No, came the reply. In fact, the book was said to be especially holy, rendering anyone who touched it ritually unclean. From one end of the pendulum to the other.

Fourth, *numerology*. Irenaeus was desperate to include Matthew, Mark, Luke, and John and equally zealous to crowd out the Valentinian Gospel of Truth. He reasoned that there could be only four canonical gospels due to the fact that there are four winds, four compass directions, and four Argus-eyed creatures in the heavenly throne room in Revelation chapter 4. Irenaeus was also attentive to the perfect number seven—the number of planets known to the ancients, each worshipped on one day of the week. Paul's epistles were first organized according to the seven recipient churches: Rome, Corinth (1 and 2 Corinthians having once been combined or confused), Galatia, Philippi, Thessalonica, Colossae, Ephesus. But this arrangement threatened to leave little Philemon out in the cold, to say nothing of the Pastorals. Once these were added, one could count epistles, not recipients, and this brought the total to thirteen with two each to Corinth and Thessalonica. Hence the need to make Hebrews a fourteenth Pauline epistle, resulting in two sevens. One could have as easily ascribed Hebrews to Apollos or Clement or Barnabas, as some did.

Scripture as tradition

In retrospect, what we see is a process, first of expansion of the canon in reaction to Marcion, then of contraction of the canon to exclude the books of Montanists and Gnostics. There are in all religions differences over the contents of the canon. Different sects, or subdivisions of religions, still have different canons even if it is only a matter of which individual books they like best and read more often. It is well to ask just what the point is of delimiting a canon. As Frank Kermode says, the point is to restrict the number of possible sources of divination or doctrine, to limit the number of available voices one must heed and obey. If you don't want the flock considering certain doctrines, you need to omit any scriptural texts that might be understood as teaching them. By the same token, hand in hand with defin-

ing the canon comes interpretation by an authoritative elite. Until Vatican II, the Catholic Church discouraged lay Bible reading lest it unleash sectarian fanaticism and make every Bible reader his own pope. To the extent that Protestants have avoided this, it is because individual Protestants have been content to stay within the limits set by the interpretive tradition of their pastor or denomination. Notice how the late 2 Peter both recognizes a Pauline collection as *scripture* (3:15-16) and admonishes the reader never to presume to engage in personal exegesis (1:20) since it is a perilous task that has already led many into soul-blasting heresy (3:16). Tertullian set forth his *Prescription against Heretics,* wherein he advised the apologist never to get embroiled in scripture arguments since the heretics might well win. What one should do instead was to deny the heretics' right to appeal to scripture. The canon is authoritative only when interpreted through the filter of apostolic tradition, so the argument went.

Today's biblicists are caught in a double irony. First, the contents of the Bible, whose infallibility they idolize, have been set by fallible mortals like themselves rather than by some miracle of revelation. They are dependent for their Bible's table of contents on the unquestioned traditions of men, which in principle they claim to disregard. Second, they continue to quote the Bible as if it were their sole authority when in fact they control the reading of it by their own traditions of orthodoxy, condemning as heretical any who venture a different interpretation. In fact, their terror in the face of higher criticism of the Bible is plainly an unwillingness to allow the Bible to speak with new voices.

The complete canon

The goal of the present collection is to try to strip away the Nicene, that is, the orthodox, traditional gloss from the underlying early Christian texts. To invoke a contemporary shibboleth and apply it to ancient matters, we want to celebrate the original authentic diversity of early Christianity. As Helmut Koester remarked in class, "The best canon is the most inclusive canon." This is true historically because widening the net gives a truer sense of the early years of the religion. But remember, too, what Kermode said: by throwing open the canon-

ical doors, we welcome in new sources of inspiration and ideas. Why should we allow committees of unknown and long-extinct clerics to decide for us what will be on our spiritual menu? Here is a chance to give an ear to Ebionites, Nasoreans, Gnostics, Marcionites, Dositheans, and others who entered into the mix of early Christianity without making them second-class citizens, without putting the twenty-seven approved books over here and the "also-rans" over there, even as many scholars continue to do.

I have said that along with the delimitation of the table of contents, the fixing of the canon included making one version of each book official, along with an official interpretation. Marcion's editions were not safe, and people were required to utilize the Catholic versions. Nor were people allowed to decide what the text meant merely by reading it; one had to consult a bishop, who consulted the creed. This book seeks to undo these restrictions in favor of an eclectic approach, including for the first time in a printed New Testament the work of such radical text critics as J. C. O'Neill, Winsome Munro, and William O. Walker Jr. In the absence of absolute proof, most scholars still conservatively resist suggestions that early texts were tampered with. In the case of the New Testament, it is not possible to point to an original manuscript to show that it lacks lines one suspects were added later. But to insist on evidence that is definitive is to ignore the obvious. We have no manuscripts from before about 200 CE. The possible changes would have been made before that. Conservatives just don't want to deal with the repercussions. If stylistic factors, theological inconsistencies, and logical jumps are deemed sufficient to convince us that the text has been interpolated, the whole text becomes quicksand, say the conservatives. Then we could never be certain of what Paul thought, what Jesus did, what the Bible really says. True enough, but that is a problem only if one feels entitled to dogmatize from the text. No scholar has ever had such a prerogative. All exegesis must be tentative, and no one will object unless he or she is too scared to think for oneself or to allow others to do so. This will disappoint only the dogmatist who wishes to proof-text an infallible book to short circuit theological debate.

The same goes for interpreting the text. It is easy to fall into the

habit of feeding the text through the creed. The historian has no business doing that and must keep his or her eyes peeled and ears cocked for old and new possibilities of what the text means, what it might have meant to ancient writers and readers who shared different assumptions from ours. The goal of this translation, as Vladimir Schklovsky said of literary criticism in general, is to "defamiliarize" the text. In other words, to strip away false assumptions that render it virtually invisible to the reader. To do this, to reveal the New Testament as a new book, I have adopted a policy of moving back and forth between translating the text more literally than usual, even if it sounds a bit brusque, and paraphrasing if that will bring out neglected implications. Disputed passages—those absent from some manuscripts—are shown in italics. There are also numerous critical and historical footnotes, including cross-references for related passages in other scriptural or extra-canonical books.

In pursuing the agenda I have chosen, I have to acknowledge two illustrious predecessors: first Ethelbert Stauffer, whose neglected *New Testament Theology* made full and unprecedented use of extra-canonical sources to fill in the astonishing richness of the myth- and thought-world of the early Christians. Second is Hugh J. Schonfield, who, though without expanding the table of contents, did produce a fresh New Testament translation (*The Authentic New Testament*), which sought to present the old book as if it had just been excavated from some sun-bleached Near-Eastern tomb.

This book represents one of an almost infinite number of possibilities for what the New Testament might have looked like if it had been assembled under different circumstances. It is not definitive in any sense, nor could it be. But if it attains its goal of shaking the New Testament loose from the mummy-bands of familiarity and helps make the New Testament a whole new book for the reader, then I am satisfied.

Bibliography and Further Reading

Walter Bauer. *Orthodoxy and Heresy in Earliest Christianity*. Translated by the Philadelphia Seminar on Christian Origins; edited by Robert A. Kraft and Gerhard Krodel. Philadelphia: Fortress Press, 1971.

Rudolf Bultmann. *Primitive Christianity in Its Contemporary Setting.* Translated by Reginald H. Fuller. Philadelphia: Fortress Press, 1980.

John Burton. *The Collection of the Qur'an.* New York: Cambridge University Press, 1977.

Hans von Campenhausen. *The Formation of the Christian Bible.* Translated by J. A. Baker. Philadelphia: Fortress Press, 1972.

Robert M. Grant. *A Short History of the Interpretation of the Bible.* New York: Macmillan, 1963.

Adolf von Harnack. *Marcion: The Gospel of the Alien God.* Translated by John E. Steely and Lyle D. Bierma. Durham: Labyrinth Press, 1999.

R. Joseph Hoffmann. *Marcion on the Restitution of Christianity: An Essay on the Development of Radical Paulinist Theology in the Second Century.* American Academy of Religion Series 46. Chico, California: Scholars Press, 1984.

Frank Kermode. "Institutional Control of Interpretation." In *The Art of Telling: Essays on Fiction,* edited by Frank Kermode. Cambridge: Harvard University Press, 1983, 168-84.

John Knox. *Marcion and the New Testament: An Essay in the Early History of the Canon.* Chicago: University of Chicago Press, 1942.

Winsome Munro. *Authority in Paul and Peter: The Identification of a Pastoral Stratum in the Pauline Corpus and I Peter.* Society for New Testament Studies Monograph Series 45. New York: Cambridge University Press, 1983.

Elaine Pagels. *The Gnostic Gospels.* New York: Random House, 1979.

Robert M. Price. "The Evolution of the Pauline Canon." *Journal of Higher Criticism* website, online at www.depts.drew.edu/jhc/.

Hugh J. Schonfield. *The Authentic New Testament.* London: Dobson, 1955.

Ethelbert Stauffer. *New Testament Theology.* New York: Macmillan, 1956.

I.
Pre-Apostolic Writings

1.
The Book of John the Baptizer

The Gospels of Luke and John, even Mark, make it clear enough that John the Baptist led a movement that continued alongside Christianity for at least a century or so and maybe longer. In Mark 2:18 we read that John's disciples did not emulate the practice of Jesus' disciples and stop fasting. They continued conspicuously to go their own way. From Luke 11:1 we learn that John's sect had special prayers, and Mark tells us, though he may not have meant to, that some were already preaching that the martyred John had risen from the grave, newly empowered with divine energy to perform miracles (6:14). Mark assumes such beliefs were mistaken interpretations of Jesus' own miracles, but that was probably his own attempt to debunk a rival sect. Both Luke and John manipulate their John the Baptist character to have him deny what his followers believed of him, that he was the Christ (Luke 3:15-16; John 1:8, 20; 3:25-30). Matthew 3:14-15 and John 1:29 have John publicly proclaim Jesus his superior and successor, but that is not found in Mark, whose John does not seem to know Jesus from Adam. Mark's Jesus is a face in the crowd, one more willing suppliant to be dunked in the Jordan.

We learn more about the sect of John, both in its early days and in the late first century, from the book of *Recognitions* ascribed to Clement of Rome. There we eavesdrop on a debate between various Jewish sects, one of them the partisans of the Baptizer. "And behold, one of the disciples of John asserted that John was the Christ, and not Jesus: 'Inasmuch,' he said, 'as Jesus himself declared that John was greater than all men and prophets. If therefore,' he said, 'he is greater than all men, he must without doubt be held to be greater than Moses

and Jesus himself. But if he is greater than all, he himself is the Christ'" (1:60:1-3a). This polemic may have had its origin at an earlier date but was nevertheless still in use at the time the Clementine *Recognitions* were compiled sometime in the fourth century, which means the sect of John was still alive.

We learn from *Recognitions* 2:8 and *Homilies* 1:23 that Simon Magus and Dositheus the Samaritan had been among the thirty disciples of John.[a] The membership matched the number of days of a lunar month, as well as the Gnostic Pleroma of the Aeons. We have here a scenario where John the Baptizer is clearly associated with Jewish-Gnostic sectarianism as the grandfather of Jesus-Nazoreanism, Simonianism, and Dositheanism, as well as father of his own long-lived sect. How long-lived? It may still exist today.

In Iraq there survives in the ancient reed marshes a baptizing Gnostic sect called by scholars the Mandaeans, which is Aramaic for "Gnostics," though they call themselves the Nazoreans. Many scholars deny it, but I remain convinced that Richard Reitzenstein, Rudolf Bultmann, and others were right to say this sect survives from pre-Christian, Jewish-Gnostic sectarianism and is, specifically, a remnant of the sect of John the Baptizer. It is otherwise difficult, really impossible, to explain why they venerate John the Baptist as a true prophet and heavenly being, while they execrate Jesus as the antichrist! This simply must represent the ancient antipathy of the sect, resentful of the greater success of Christianity. If such a grudge seems too ancient to be plausible, just recall the age-old calumny aimed against Jewish "Christ-killers," their crime having been the failure to convert to the rival Christian faith.

The Aramaic scriptures of the Mandaeans survive in medieval copies. There is no way to be sure how long ago their originals were composed, but some scholars have proposed a date between 250 and 300, the assumption being that the legends and liturgical poems contained within the scriptures are even older. The following is based on G.R.S. Mead's reconstruction of the Mandaean Book of John. Readers will notice that it seems to parallel Luke's Gospel, but by far most

a. See the Revelation of Dositheus in this collection.

of the material is older and independent of Luke and provides a non-Christian look at the Baptist, a John who is not merely a function of Christian polemic. The book is episodic, not necessarily in chronological order, and various scenes are introduced by "John speaks in the night, John on the evenings of the night," meant to recall again and again the characteristic posture of John and his preaching, which still echoes. Readers may find it helpful to be reminded that John's earthly parents were the priest Zachariah and his wife Elizabeth.

1

[1]In the name of Great Life, glory be to light!

[2]From the height of heaven was a child planted in a woman's womb, a mystery long concealed, now revealed in Jerusalem. [3]The priests saw dreams in troubled sleep. Their little ones shivered, Jerusalem huddled with the chill.

[4]Early in the morning one went to the temple. This one opened his mouth to blaspheme, his lips to utter lies. He set his tongue to blaspheming and spoke to every priest:

[5]"In my night-spawned vision I beheld, in my trance I saw! As I lay there, sleep escaped me and rest was far from me. Sleep passed me by that night. I tossed and turned and saw! [6]A star appeared and paused above Elizabeth. Fire blazed up from ashes in Old Father Zachariah. [7]Three lights lit up the heavens. The sun plunged, the lights rose. Fire painted orange the synagogue, while smoke billowed over the temple. [8]Great quaking rocked the throne chariot in heaven so that the earth skipped her orbit! [9]A star swooped down into Judea, a luminary into Jerusalem. The sun appeared at night, the moon by day!"

[10]Upon hearing these things, the priests sprinkled dust atop their heads. Jacob, the priest, sobs and Benjamin's tears flow forth. Shilai and Shalbai toss dust on their heads. [11]Eliezar, the archpriest, opened his lips and addressed the other priests: "Jacob is an interpreter of dreams, but so far no truth dawns on him from these. Benjamin also makes sense of them. Is he not a revealer of mysteries? [12]Tab-Yomin offers no explanation, though you esteem him as one who knows all that is and is not."

[13]The very earth moans at the unnaturalness of it and plunges through the spheres of heaven. She whispers to Eliezar, "Go to Luke. He shall make sense of all your dreams!" [14]At this, Eliezar opened his lips and addressed the company of priests: "Who will go to Luke to have him

interpret these nightmares you have seen?" [15]Then they collaborated on a letter and placed it in the trusted hand of Tab-Yomin. Tab-Yomin accepted responsibility and set off for the dwelling of Luke. [16]As for Luke, he lay upon his bed, sleep not yet having departed for the day. But in his sleep, his heart began to throb until his heart broke in pieces and fell from its dreaming height. [17]Tab-Yomin drew near to his bedside to shake him from out of his troubled slumbers, and spoke to him. [18]"The priests saw dreams. A star appeared and paused above Elizabeth. Fire blazed up from ashes in Old Father Zachariah. [19]Three lights lit up the heavens. The sun plunged, the lights rose. Fire painted orange the synagogue, while smoke billowed over the temple. [20]Great quaking rocked the throne chariot in heaven so that the earth skipped her orbit. A star swooped down into Judea, a luminary into Jerusalem. The sun appeared at night, the moon by day!"

[21]Hearing this, Luke dropped dust upon his head. He rose naked from his bed and located his dream book. He opens it and scans it and looks for the right passage. [22]Finding it, he reads for a bit, then interprets the dreams in silence, not reading out loud. Instead, he writes his explanations in a letter; he expounds the dreams upon a page. [23]In it, he tells them, "Woe to you, all you priests, for Elizabeth shall bear a child! Woe to you, you rabbis, for a child will be born in Jerusalem. [24]Woe to you, you teachers and students, for Elizabeth shall have a child. Woe to you, Mistress Torah, for John shall be born in Jerusalem."

[25]So Luke writes to them on paper and tells them: "The star that appeared and hovered over Elizabeth means that a child shall be planted from high in the heavens. [26]He is on his way to Elizabeth. As for the fire that blazed up in Old Father Zachariah, it warns that John shall be born in Jerusalem."

[27]Tab-Yomin took the letter and hastened back to Jerusalem. He arrived to discover the whole priesthood sitting in mourning. Taking the letter, he handed it to Eliezar. [28]Eliezar opens it, reads it, and finds there an astonishing message. Opening it, he reads it and sees what awaits him there. [29]He peruses it in silence while they wait, but he renders no decision. Instead, Eliezar took it and handed it to Old Father Zachariah. [30]He opens and reads it and sees the message lurking there. Silently he reads it and has nothing to say of it. [31]So Eliezar opened his mouth and spoke to old Zachariah: "Old Father, get up and leave Judea at once or you will arouse strife in Jerusalem!"

[32]Old Father Zachariah then raised his right hand and struck Eliezar

on the head, saying, "Eliezar, great noble, head of the whole priesthood, if you knew the truth about your mother, you would never dare set foot in our synagogue! [33]If you really knew, you would never presume to read the Torah readings. For your mother was an adulteress, a loose woman she was, who had no business marrying into the house of her husband's father. [34]Your father did not have the hundred gold staters required to write her the divorce certificate, so he simply abandoned her at once and never again asked about her welfare. [35]But as for me, has there been a single day in which I did not come and look to see the scroll of Moses, son of Amram? Has there been one day when I came and failed to pray in your synagogue, to justify you all being false and dishonest and spreading rumors about me that began with you? [36]Where is a dead man who has returned to life? No more can Elizabeth bear a child! Where is a blind man who regains his sight? A lame man for whom his feet walk once more? A mute who learns to read aloud from a book? No more can Elizabeth bear a child! [37]Today marks twenty-two years since I have had relations with her. No, Elizabeth shall bear no child, whether mine or yours!"

[38]Then did the priests arise as one, saying to Old Father Zachariah, reproaching him, "Calm down and stay in your seat, Old Father. Let the peace of the Good Ones settle upon you. [39]Old Father, if there were no prophetic dreams in Judea, then everything Moses said would be a lie. [40]But both your words and ours will yet be vindicated, as well as our dreams. John will receive the Jordan for his lot and be called prophet in Jerusalem."

[41]At this, Old Father went out from among them, and Eliezar followed him. Then three lights appeared surrounding Zachariah. [42]The rest ran up and snatched at the fringe of his prayer shawl and asked him, "Old Father! What is that which goes in front of you? And what is it that goes behind you?" [43]Then he answered them, "O Eliezar, you great noble, you chief of all the priests, I do not know whom these lights going before me are meant to guard. [44]Nor do I know whom the fire following me is meant to accompany. But I do know that Elizabeth will bear no child, whether mine or yours!"

[45]Again, all the priests stood up and rebuked Old Father Zachariah, saying, "Old Father Zachariah, calm down, be firm and resolute, for the child will be planted in her womb from out of the highest zenith and presented to you in your old age. [46]John will be born. John will receive Jordan for his post and will be called prophet in Jerusalem. [47]We will baptize with his baptism, and with his pure sign we will be sealed. We will receive

from him his bread and drink his drink and ascend with him to the Region of Light."

[48]And every priest rose up and said to Old Father Zachariah, rebuking him, "Old Father! Permit us to enlighten you as to your true race and lineage from which you have come forth: [49]Adam and Abel and Seth and Enosh and Enoch and Noah and Shem and Abraham and Isaac and Jacob and Levi the seer and Amram and Moses and the rest. [50]Tab-Yomin and the teachers have descended from your race. The blessed princes who are your ancestors, Old Father, not one of them ever took a wife or fathered a son. [51]Yet in their old age, each one had a son. They had sons who became prophets in Jerusalem. [52]If now a prophet is to come forth from you, too, you will once more revive this race. Yes, John will be born and will be called prophet in Jerusalem."

[53]Then Eliezar opened his mouth to address Old Father: "Old Father! If John receives Jordan as his lot, then I will be his slave, will be baptized with his baptism and sealed with his pure sign. [54]We will receive his bread and drink his drink and ascend with him to the Region of Light!"

[55]Then Old Father opened his mouth and spoke to all the priests: "If the child descends from the highest zenith, what then will you in Jerusalem do?"

[56]So the angels have lifted the child up from the riverbed of the Jordan and placed him tenderly in the womb of Elizabeth.

2

[1]John proclaims in the nights, John on the evenings of the night.

[2]John proclaims in the night and says, "I give light through the words of my father, and through the praises of my creator, the Man. [3]I have extricated myself from this world and from all deeds abominable and evil. [4]The Seven Archons interrogated me, those dead ones who are strangers to Life, and they say, "By whose authority do you stand,[b] and with whose commendation do you preach?"[c] [5]To that I gave answer: "I stand by the authority of my father and with the commendation of my creator, the Man. [6]I have built no house in Judea, nor founded a throne in Jerusalem.[d] I have no love for the rosy wreath, nor the company of beautiful women. I have not loved imperfection, nor the cup of the drunkard.

---

b. Simon, purported to be a disciple of John (Clementine *Homilies* 2:23-24), referred to "the Standing One" and claimed to be his successor.

c. John 1:19-23

d. Matt. 11:7-11a

[7]I have not loved the food of the body,[e] nor has envy any foothold in me.[f]
I have not neglected my vespers, nor left the wondrous Jordan. [8]I have
not shirked my baptizing, nor the sealing with the sign of purity. I have
not forgotten Sunday[g] and its evening has not accused me of neglecting it.
[9]I have not failed to honor Shilmai and Nibdai, twin guardians of the Jordan who ever dwell in the House of the Mighty. They wave me on and allow me to ascend; they find no fault, no flaw in me."

[10]When John said these things, Life rejoiced greatly on his account.
The Seven Archons saluted him, and the Twelve Zodiacal Powers prostrated themselves before him.[h] [11]They said to him, "Of all the things you
have said, you have said nothing falsely. Your voice is a delight to the ear
and most fair to hear. You have no peer![i] Beautiful is the discourse of
your mouth and precious your speaking, a gift bestowed upon you. [12]The
garment that First Life bestowed upon Adam, the First Man; the garment
that First Life bestowed upon Ram,[j] the Man; the garment that First Life
bestowed upon Shurbai,[k] the Man; the garment that First Life bestowed
upon Shem, son of Noah, he has now placed on your shoulders.[l] [13]He has
bestowed it upon you, O John, so you may ascend, and those you have
baptized and sealed may ascend with you. [14]The house of imperfection[m]
will be left behind in the desert. All who prove to be without sin will ascend unto you, to the Region of Light. [15]Those who do not prove to be
sinless will be made to explain themselves in the guard houses.[n]

And Life is victorious!

---

e. Matt. 11:18

f. John 3:27-30

g. Sunday is the holy day of the Mandaeans, who follow the Essene custom of bowing to the rising sun each day. Christians came from the same sectarian matrix and seem to have retained Sunday worship, later locating the resurrection of Jesus on that day to give it a uniquely Christian meaning.

h. Phil. 2:9-11

i. John 7:46

j. Ram is short for the Persian hero Bihram; see below on his relation to John and Jesus.

k. Possibly Hammurabi, the neo-Babylonian emperor upon whom the sun god Shamash bestowed the famous Code of Hammurabi.

l. Here is essentially the same "True Prophet, Adam reincarnated" doctrine found in the Preaching of Peter in this collection, attesting to the originally common milieu from which both movements arose.

m. Meaning the body of flesh.

n. The guardhouses were manned by archons, who stood watch over the concentric planetary spheres. This was a vestige of Babylonian astrology common to

3

[1]John proclaims in the nights, John on the evenings of the night.

[2]John proclaims in the night, saying: "In the name of him who is wondrous and surpasses all! The sun sat in state and the moon rode the dragon. The four winds departed on the wing and blow not here. All is at peace."

[3]The sun opened his mouth and spoke to John, "You have three headbands and a crown[o] equal in value to the whole world. [4]You have a spiritual ship that sails the Jordan.[p] You captain a great vessel which sails in mid-heaven between the waters under the earth and those above the firmament.[q] [5]When next you visit the house of the Great One, mention us to His Greatness?" [6]At that, John opened his mouth and spoke to the sun in Jerusalem, "You ask concerning the headbands? May the Perfect Ones guard your own crown! [7]This spirit ship they have indeed crafted together with radiant glory. On this vessel that sails between the waters above and the waters below, the seal of the king has been placed.

[8]"She who dwells in your house has played the harlot. She wanders far, approaching even the dung pit.[r] [9]She is determined to bear bastard children,[s] but she has none. [10]If only in this way she fulfills her marriage vow and then departs this world, she shall be found unworthy of the House of Life and will not be assigned to the Light Dwelling."

4

[1]John proclaims in the nights, John in the evenings of the night.

[2]John proclaims in the night, saying, "Do I not stand alone? I go to and fro but find no peer! Where is a prophet equal to me? Who makes proclamation equal to my proclamation? Who can discourse with my marvelous voice?"

Gnosticism, Mithraism, and ancient Judaism. See the Revelation of Paul in this collection.

o. The headbands and crown refer to a flaming aurora halo invisible to mortals. See Thomas, saying 46, where we hear that John was so great, any mortal looking upon him would have his eyes "broken," blinded by the halo.

p. Baptism is portrayed as a new ark of salvation like Noah's ark, only spiritual. The same identification is made with Christian baptism in 1 Pet. 3:20-22.

q. The ancient understanding of the world was of a flat disk floating on "the deep" and covered tightly with a solid dome, "the firmament," to keep out waters from the universe above, whence the rain fell. See Gen. 1:6-8.

r. Hell is described here in Zoroastrian terms as a cesspool, as in the Talmud, which has heretics, including Jesus, eternally boiling in dung.

s. This apparently refers to works done in the service of a different god. The Dead Sea Scrolls vilify Jews who are not Essenes as "fornicators."

3When John said these things, both women weep—Miriam and Elizabeth weep, and the tears of both flow down. Both say, "We will depart, but you stay here; and be sure you do not make us stumble." 4Miriam said, "I will depart now, but you stay here; be sure you do not make me stumble."[t] Elizabeth said, "I will depart now, but you stay here; be sure you do not fill me with mourning."[u]

5Then did John open his mouth and speak to Elizabeth in Jerusalem, "Is there anyone capable of taking my place at the zenith, causing you to pay ransom for me? 6What could you offer to be sufficient? If you think you can pay ransom for me, then bring your jewels and ransom me! 7If you think you can ransom me, then bring your pearls and ransom me! If you think you can ransom me, then bring your gold and ransom me!"

8At this, Elizabeth opened her mouth and spoke to John in Jerusalem, "Who is your equal in Judea? Who is your equal in Jerusalem, that I should look to him and forget you?"

9"Indeed, who is my equal? Who is my equal to cause you to look to him and forget about me?[v] At the sound of my voice and at the sound of my proclamation, the Torah vanished in Jerusalem![w] 10At the sound of my discourse, the lectors read no more in Jerusalem. The adulterers repent of their fornication, and the women no longer go forth to their rendevous. 11The brides come before me wearing their wreaths, and their tears spill down to the ground. The babe in its mother's womb heard my voice and wept![x] 12The merchants cease business in Judea, and the fishers cease fishing in Jerusalem.[y] 13The women of Israel no more bedeck themselves in colored gowns; brides eschew gold and the matrons their jewels.[z] Neither women nor men dote on their faces in the mirror.

14"At my voice and at the sound of my proclamation, the waters welled up to the capitals of the pillars supporting the firmament. 15Because of my voice and the sound of my proclamations, the fish saluted me. At the sound of my voice and that of my preaching, the birds bowed before me, saying, "Good for you! And again, good for you, John. 16And

---

t. Mary is perhaps leaving to bear the child Jesus, who will later challenge John for supremacy. Cf. Matt. 11:6.

u. Luke 2:35a

v. John 1:35-39

w. Luke 16:16

x. Luke 1:44

y. 1 Cor. 7:29-31; Mark 1:5

z. Mark 2:18

good for the Man, whom you worship. You have freed yourself and won release, O John, and left the world a ruin. 17The women have failed to seduce you with their fornications, and their words have not turned your head. Despite their perfumes and fragrances, you have not allowed the remembrance of your Lord to slip your mind. 18You have not become drunk with wine, nor done impious deeds. You have not fallen prey to backsliding in Jerusalem. 19You have freed yourself and won release and established your throne in the House of Life."

5

1John proclaims in the nights, John in the evenings of the night.

2John proclaims and speaks: "You nobles who lie inert, you ladies who will not wake up, what will you do on Judgment Day? 3When the soul strips off the body on Judgment Day, what will you do? O scatter-brained, overturned world in chaos! 4Your people die and your false scriptures are a closed book. Where is Adam, the First Man, who was here as chief of the aeons? 5Where is Eve, his wife, by whom the world was awakened to life? Where is divine Seth, son of Adam, out of whom worlds and aeons arose? 6Where are Ram and Rud, who belonged to the age of the sword? Where are Shurbai and Sharhabel, who belonged in the age of fire? Where is Shem, son of Noah, who belonged to the age of the flood? 7All have departed, never to return and resume their thrones as guardians of this world. The Last Day is as a feast day, for which the worlds and the aeons wait eagerly. 8The planets are like fattened oxen awaiting the day of slaughter. The children of this world are like plump rams penned in the market for sale. 9But what of my friends who render due worship to Life? Their sins and trespasses will be forgiven them."

6

1"I take no joy from the aeons, no delight in all the worlds. I take no joy from the aeons, no delight in all the worlds, but I am pleased by the letter of truth which has arrived here."

2The angels took the letter and handed it to the Jews. These open it and study it and realize it does not contain what they wish, that it does not say what their very souls wish to read. 3They brought the letter to John and gave it to him. "Take, Rabbi John," they urge him, "truth's letter, which has been delivered here to you from your father." 4John opened it and studied it and recognized in it a marvelous writing. Opening it and reading it, he became full of life. "This," he says, "is what I want and what my soul wishes!"

5John has left his body in a trance. In his absence, his brothers make

proclamations. His brothers call out to him atop Mount Carmel. In answer, the angels took the letter and brought it to the mount, to Mount Carmel. They read from the letter to them and decipher the writing for them, to Jacob and Benjamin and Samuel, assembled on Mount Carmel.

6Manda d'Haiye,[a] who is now far from the zenith, to you, beloved soul, Greetings!

7I have come to you, O soul, whom Life has sent into this world.
In the robes of the eighth heaven I descended into the world. 8I went
in the garment of Life and came into the world. I took with me the
garment of the seventh heaven and went as far as the eighth. 9I took
the garment of the seventh and I grasped the eighth with my hand. I
have taken them, I take them now, and I will take them and not release them. 10I have seized them and I hold them tight, and the
wicked spirits who dwell therein shall change into good.

11Why do you weep, O nations? What makes you cry, O peoples? Why do your smiles fade? 12It is for you that I have brought my
image, for your sakes that I betook myself into the world!

7

1John proclaims in the night, John in the evenings of the night.

2John proclaims in the night and speaks: "Is there anyone greater than I?[b] They assess my deeds. My wage is calculated, my crown prepared, and my accolades waft me heavenward in peace."

3Jacob leaves the synagogue, Benjamin leaves the temple, Eliezar,
scion of the noble house, leaves the dome of the priests. 4The priests
spoke to John in Jerusalem: "John, get out of our city! The sound of your
voice shook the synagogue. 5The sound of your proclamations made the
temple rock. The sound of your discourse made the dome of the priests to
shudder."

6At that, John answered the priests in Jerusalem: "Bring fire to burn
me! Bring a sword and hack me to bits!" 7But the priests in Jerusalem replied, "Fire will not burn you, O John, for Life's name has been invoked over you. No sword will hack you to bits,[c] O John, for the son of Life[d] rests here upon you."

---

a. Manda d'Haiye is the Gnosis of Life, son of Life and father of John.

b. Matt. 11:11a

c. Simon Magus, John's disciple and successor, proved himself worthy over his rival Dositheus by demonstrating invulnerability to the sword (Clementine *Homilies* 2:23-24), a trait inherited from John. One thinks of Elisha, who inherited the rank and powers of his master, Elijah (2 Kings 2:13-14).

8

[1]John proclaims in the nights, John in the evenings of the night.

[2]John proclaims in the nights. Glory rises over the worlds.

Who told Jesus? Who told Jesus Messiah, son of Mary? [3]Who told Jesus so that he went to the bank of the Jordan and said, "John, baptize me with your baptism and also utter over me that name it is your custom to pronounce.[e] If I thus show myself to be your disciple, I will mention you in my Gospel. [4]If I do not prove myself as your disciple, then erase my name from your page."[f]

[5]At this, John answered Jesus in Jerusalem: "You have lied to the Jews and deceived the priests! You have cut off all descendants from men and deprived the women of pregnancy and delivering children.[g] [6]The Sabbath, which Moses made obligatory, you have undone in Jerusalem.[h] You have lied to them with a fanfare and broadcast disgrace with the shofar!"[i]

[7]At this, Jesus Messiah answered John in Jerusalem: "If I have lied to the Jews, may a blazing fire consume me! [8]If I have deceived the priests, let me die a double death! If I have cut off men's descendants, may I not cross over the sea of death to the land beyond. [9]If I have deprived the women of pregnancy and childbearing, then truly a judge looms over me. If I have undone the Sabbath, let the blazing fire swallow me up! [10]If I have lied to the Jews, I will gladly walk on thorns and thistles. If I have broadcast disgrace with the sound of horns, may I never look upon Abathur who weighs the deeds of all mankind. [11]So then, baptize me with your baptism and utter over me that name it is your custom to invoke. If I acquit myself as your disciple, I will mention you then in my Gospel. [12]But if I make a poor showing as your disciple, then erase my name from your page."

[13]Then John spoke to Jesus Messiah in Jerusalem: "No stammerer becomes a scholar. No blind man pens a letter. [14]The scion of a childless house does not rise into heaven and no widow becomes a virgin. [15]Foul water cannot become sweet, nor does a stone soften when rubbed with oil."

---

d. See note 26.

e. Matt. 3:13-15

f. This may be a reference to the Ledger of the Saved or the Book of John the Baptizer itself.

g. Luke 23:28-29; Matt. 19:12

h. Mark 2:23-28; 3:1-6; et seq.

i. Matt. 6:2. A shofar is a ram's horn.

[16]At this, Jesus Messiah offered a rejoinder to John in Jerusalem: "A
stammerer may yet become a scholar. [17]A blind man may write a letter.
The scion of a childless house may indeed rise into heaven. [18]A widow
may yet become a virgin. Foul water can become sweet, and a stone may
soften with oil."

[19]At that, John spoke to Jesus Messiah in Jerusalem: "If you can give
me examples of these things, you are truly a wise messiah."

[20]At that, Jesus Messiah offered an answer to John in Jerusalem: "A
stammerer may become a scholar when a child, who comes from the
womb, blossoms and grows big. [21]Through paying fair wages and by giving alms, he rises on high; he ascends and beholds the Region of Light.[j]

[22]"A blind man writes a letter when a villain becomes virtuous. One
who forsakes profligacy and stealing and has arrived at faith in Almighty
Life.

[23]"The scion of a childless house who yet ascends to the Light is a
man of position who humbles himself. He left his palaces and forsook his
pride and built a house on the seashore. [24]He built a house on the sea, and
two doors opened into it so he might bring in with him everyone who lay
down there in misery. [25]To such, he opened his door and received them to
himself. [26]If one was hungry, he would spread a table before him, along
with truth. If one were thirsty, he would mix for him a cup of wine with
truth. If one required rest, he made a bed for him in truth. [27]If he were
ready to leave again, the man would lead him out onto the way to truth.
He led him forth upon the way of truth and of faith and then he ascends
and beholds the Region of Light.[k]

[28]"A widow who becomes a virgin again is a woman who has been
widowed already in her youth. She kept her privates closed and remained
until her children are grown. [29]If she passes over into the next world, she
does not go pale at the sight of her husband since she remained ever faithful to him.[l]

[30]"Foul water restored unto sweetness is a promiscuous girl who has
regained her honor. She walked up and down the streets of a hamlet without unveiling her face.

[31]"A stone softened with the application of oil is a heretic who descends the mountain of darkness where the archons meet. [32]He aban-

j. Matt. 10:40-41

k. Such a benefactor is the opposite of the rich man in Luke 16:19-31.

l. Many in the ancient world praised the *univirae,* widows who refused to remarry.

doned magic and sorcery and professed faith in Almighty Life. He found an orphan and satisfied his hunger and filled the widow's pockets with coins.

33"So baptize me, O John, with your baptism and pronounce over me that name you are accustomed to invoke! 34If I show myself a worthy disciple, I will mention you in my Gospel. If I fail to distinguish myself as your disciple, then erase my name from your page!"

35When Jesus Messiah said this, a letter appeared from the House of Abathur: "John, baptize the deceiver in the Jordan. Lead him down into the Jordan and baptize him, and lead him up to the shore again and leave him standing there."[m]

36Then Spirit made herself like a dove and projected a cross of light on the face of the Jordan[n] and made its water turn various colors. "O Jordan," she says, "you hold me sacred and you sanctify my seven sons.[o]

---

m. For early Christians, Jesus' baptism was an embarrassment because it seemed to imply John was Jesus' superior. John's sect became no less embarrassed by its association with Jesus. To offset this disgrace, our text has John baptize the messiah reluctantly at the command of Abathur, an angelic figure. The Christian counter-scene occurs in Matt. 3:13-15, wherein Jesus is baptized against John's better judgment, only because God wishes it.

n. Jewish-Christian gospels have fire or radiance erupt on the face of the Jordan at the moment of Jesus' baptism.

o. The water turns from white, the color of doctrinal purity for Mandaeans, to a rainbow of hues representing heresies. Notice that the Mandaeans cede to Christianity the terms *messiah* and *spirit*, which they feel are tainted by heresy. Thus, Jesus is called Messiah as part of his name, and Spirit (*Ruha*) refers to the fallen *Zeitgeist*—the world spirit, mother of the Seven Archons, and fountainhead of heresy. Christianity is one of these heresies.

By the same token, the Dosithean-influenced Gospel of Philip contains the reverse scene, whereby Jesus enters "the dye-works of Levi" and turns seventy-two colors white. "Even so came the Son of Man," the scripture reads, and in an earlier passage, "Since [God's] dyes are immortal, the baptized are immortal through his colors. But God dips [βαπτιζειν] what he dips in water" (54, 43).

The image ultimately stems from a Samaritan story, according to Richard J. Arthur, in which a priest dispatches his nephew Levi to capture and kill Dositheus. Levi and his comrades miss their intended prey, but the latter's hostess points to a pile of writings by Dositheus, who has warned that anyone reading them needed to first purify himself in an adjacent pool. Levi can see no harm if he and his comrades cleanse themselves "from the traces of the road." However, when he and his men immerse themselves in the pool, they emerge declaring faith in "Yahweh, and in Dusis Thy servant, and in his prophecy." "Woe unto us!" Levi adds; "We have been pursuing the prophet of God, Dusis!" See Stanley Jerome Isser, *The Dositheans: A Samaritan Sect in Late Antiquity,* Studies in Judaism in Late Antiquity 17 (Leiden, Netherlands: E. J. Brill, 1976), 78.

[37]This Jordan, in which Messiah Paul was baptized, I have made into a baptismal pool. The bread which Messiah Paul receives, I have made into a sacrament. [38]The drink which Messiah Paul receives, I have made into a supper. The headband which Messiah Paul receives, I have made into a priest's miter. [39]The staff which Messiah Paul receives, I have made a shepherd's crook."[p]

9

[1]John proclaims in the nights, John on the evenings of the night.

[2]John proclaims in the night and he says, "The wheels and chariots of heaven shook! Sun and moon weep, and Spirit's eyes shed tears!"

[3]The sun says, "John, you are like a scorched mountain on which no grapes can grow. You are like a dried-up stream, on whose bank no vegetation thrives. [4]You have become a plot of ground unattended, a tottering empty house. You have become a false prophet with no one left who remembers your name. [5]Who now will give you necessities and food? And who will come to your grave to mourn?"

[6]When John heard this, a tear came to his eye. A tear wet his eye, and he spoke: "It would be pleasant to take a wife, a great delight to have children. [7]But if I do not take a woman to wife, what happens? Then sleep comes, and desire for her seizes me and I miss my night prayer. [8]If only desire would not awaken in me and cause me to forget my Lord and put him out of my mind.[q] If only desire would not awaken in me and make me neglect my prayer every time!"

[9]When John said this, a letter came to him from the House of Abathur:

> John, take a wife and start a family, and see that you do not let this world come to an end! [10]On Monday night is the wedding and Tuesday night go to your first bedding. On Wednesday night and Thursday night, devote yourself to your holy prayers.[r] [11]On Sunday, take three hours for prayer and leave three for sleep—take three for

p. This strange passage has enormous implications. Paul and Jesus are identified by virtue of the fact that the Aramaic *paulis* transliterates the Persian word for *deceiver,* implying that Paul is an epithet for a false prophet or antichrist, as well as the perfect equivalent of the Dead Sea Scrolls epithet for Paul (on Robert Eisenman's theory), "the Spouter of Lies." See Robert Eisenman, *James, the Brother of Jesus: The Key to Unlocking the Secrets of Early Christianity and the Dead Sea Scrolls* (New York: Viking Penguin, 1997).

q. 1 Cor. 7:32-34

r. 1 Cor. 7:5

prayer, leave three for sleep. See that you do not allow this world to come to an end![s]

[12]At this, the angels fashioned a wife for John out of you, O Region of the Faithful.[t] From the first conception, Handan and Sharrath were born. [13]From the middle conception, Bihram and R'himath-Haiye were born. From the last conception, Nsab, Sam, and Radiant Anhar were born.[u]

[14]John opened his mouth and spoke to Anhar, his wife in Jerusalem: "Instruct your daughter that she may not perish,[v] and I will enlighten my sons and teach them so they may not be hindered on their heavenly ascent."

[15]At this, Anhar opened her mouth and spoke to John: "I have brought sons into this world," she said to him, "yet I have not given birth to a heart for them in the world. [16]If they are willing to receive instruction, then they will ascend to the Region of Light. But if they are not, then the blazing fire will devour them."

[17]John opened his mouth and spoke to Anhar in Jerusalem: "If I leave the world, tell me: what will you do after I am gone?"

[18]"I will neither eat nor drink," she answered him, "until I see you again."[w]

[19]"You have spoken a lie, Anhar, and your word has come forth clothed in deception! After a single day comes and goes, you will resume eating and drinking and will put me entirely out of mind. [20]I asked you

s. This is a variation on an honorific hyperbole, as in Thomas, saying 12, "James the Just, for whom the earth was created." In this case, the world can only survive as long as John or his heirs are present in it.

t. The region of the faithful is heaven, the mytheme being that of Pandora, who was created jointly by all the gods to be Prometheus' wife.

u. The children seem to be named after, or are perhaps incarnations of, angelic beings. Handan is reminiscent of Hercules Sandan; Sharrath may be Shahar, Jerusalemite goddess of the dawn (Pss. 110:3; 139:9); while Bihram is a later name for the Iranian hero Verethragna, a reincarnation of Zoroaster and preincarnation of Jesus, according to the Apocalypse of Adam. R'himath-Haiye ("life's beloved") is a variation of a name already encountered; Nsab ("planter, fashioner") is the Great Watcher, an office shared with Sam ("establisher"), Watcher of the Aeons. Anhar-Ziwa ("radiant Anhar") is possibly the same as Mithra's consort Anahita. She is named after Anhar, the wife of John.

v. There seem to be three daughters, not one.

w. John was curious what his wife would do when he died, but she understood him to mean a temporary trip, perhaps an out-of-body visionary journey, from which he would return.

rather, by Great Life and by the eve of the day whose name is precious: If I leave the world, tell me, what will you do after I am gone?”

[21]“I will neither wash nor comb my hair,” she says to him, “until I see you again!”

[22]“Again you lie! And your word comes forth garbed in deceit. Once a single month passes, you will wash and comb your hair and put me clean out of your mind! [23]Again I ask you, Anhar, by the bed of our wedding night: If I leave my body, tell me, what will you do after I am gone?”

[24]“I will don no new garments until I see you again,” she answers him.

“Again you have lied, Anhar, and your word is clothed in guile. Once a year passes by, you will don new garments and forget me, put me out of mind.”

[25]“Why do you not tell me everything, John?” she says to him. “How your words make me ache all over! If you depart, when will you return, that my eyes may light upon you?”

[26]“If a woman in labor goes down into Sheol, do they hang up a bell for her in the graveyard?[x] If they paint a picture in Sheol, does she then go forth to a feast in the graveyard? [27]If a bride parades her finery in Sheol, do they celebrate her marriage in the graveyard? [28]If the wedding guests borrow money to sponsor the feast in Sheol, do they repay the debt in the graveyard? Nay, it is too late!”

[29]Then she answered him, “My lord, how can it be that a woman in labor goes down into Sheol and they hang up a bell for her in the graveyard? [30]That they paint a picture in Sheol and she then goes forth to a feast in the graveyard? That a bride parades her finery in Sheol and they celebrate her marriage in the graveyard? [31]That the wedding guests borrow money in Sheol and repay the debt in the graveyard?”

[32]“If you know this never happens,” he answers her, “why do you press the question, ‘When will you return?’ I go hence and will not return. [33]Enjoy the day in which you still see me. If there were both departure and returning, one would find no widows in this world. [34]If there were departure and returning, then there would be no orphans in this world. If there were a departure and a subsequent return, no Nazoreans would be found in this world.”

[35]At this, Anhar opened her mouth and spoke to John in Jerusalem:

x. The tradition was to ring a bell during childbirth to frighten away Lilith and her sisters and to paint a portrait of the mother as a decoy.

"I will buy you a brick grave with precious gold and have a wooden coffin built for you in the graveyard."

[36]But John opened his mouth and spoke to Anhar in Jerusalem: "Why would you buy a brick grave for precious gold and have a wooden coffin made for me in the graveyard? [37]Are you, after all, so sure I will return that you say, 'Let no dust fall on him'? Instead of buying a brick grave with precious gold, go out and distribute bread in my name. [38]Instead of getting a wooden box made for me, go and have masses for the dead read for me."

[39]At this, Anhar opened her mouth and spoke to John in Jerusalem: "You shall go hence and forget about me![y] And I shall be abandoned here where sinners dwell."

[40]But John replied, "If I forget you, let the Light Dwelling forget me! May my eyes never look upon Abathur! If I ascend to Life's House, your wailing will rise to my ears from the graveyard."

10

[1]John proclaims in the nights, John on the evenings of the night.

[2]John proclaims in the night and speaks: "The heavenly wheels and chariots shook! Earth and heaven weep and the tears of the clouds rain down!

[3]"My father," says John, "was ninety-nine, my mother eighty-eight years old. Out of the Jordan River basin the angels took me. [4]They lifted me up and placed me in the womb of Elizabeth. 'Nine months,' they told me, 'you shall abide in her womb like all other children.' [5]'Twas no wizened midwife who brought me forth in Judea," he said, "nor did they sever my cord in Jerusalem. [6]They made for me no decoy picture, hung up for me no demon-distracting bell. I was born of Elizabeth in the environs of Jerusalem.

[7]"The environs of Jerusalem shake and the wall of the priests' quarters rocks. Eliezar, of the great house, stands still and his body trembles. [8]The Jews assemble and come to Old Father Zachariah, and they tell him, 'O Old Father Zachariah, you are to have a son! Tell us now, what name shall we give him? Shall we call him Jacob the Wise, that he may teach the scripture in Jerusalem? [9]Or shall we call him Zatan the Pillar so all Jews may swear by him and never break their oaths?'[z]

---

y. Eccles. 9:5

z. These names are reminiscent of Jacob (James) the Just, one of the Pillars of Jerusalem (Gal. 2:9). Zatan the Pillar, a foe of the Mandaeans, is perhaps the equivalent of Satan. It would seem that John the Baptizer, Jesus the Nazorean,

[10]"When Elizabeth heard this, she cried out, saying: 'Of all these names that you suggest, I will not give him one, but I will give him the name John, which Life itself has given him!'[a]

[11]"Hearing this, the Jews were flushed with evil rage against her and said to one another: 'What weapon shall we prepare for this one and his mother so we ourselves may slay him?'

[12]"When Glorious Enosh[b] heard this, he seized the babe and brought it to Parwan, the white mountain, to Mount Parwan where nurslings and infants are fed with holy drink.[c]

[13]"There I stayed until the age of twenty-two. There I learned the whole of my wisdom and memorized all of my future speeches. [14]They dressed me in vestments of shining glory and veiled me with airy clouds. They girded me with a sash of running water which shone indescribably and glistened like the waterfall. [15]They stood me in a cloud, a cloud of glory, and in the seventh hour of a Sunday, they brought me to the environs of Jerusalem. [16]They shout out, 'What woman bore a son who was then stolen? What woman has made a vow to God in exchange for his safety and has years ago given up on it in despair? [17]What woman had a

---

James the Just, Simon Magus, and Dositheus the Samaritan were all originally members of the same sect until a centrifuge of factionalism caused them to spin off in different directions (cf. 1 Cor. 1:11-13). In this case, "Zatan the Pillar" may be a vilification of James the Just, just as Jesus becomes for Mandaeans "the deceiver."

a. Perhaps Jacob the Wise and Zatan the Pillar are understood to be relatives of John. James the Just, as Jesus' brother, would have been John's cousin according to Luke 1:59-61.

b. Enosh is the son of Seth (Gen. 4:26), later a quasi-messianic figure for the Sethians, some of whom believed Jesus was his reincarnation. Mandaeans venerated Adam, Abel, Seth, and Enosh as angels or deities. Enosh is especially crucial in connection with the Mandaean doctrine of Primal Man, John's divine Father. Enosh means *man* and appears in the gospels as part of the title Son of Man, *bar-enosh,* who is a twin of the Zoroastrian Gayomard and the Vedic Purusha. In Genesis, Enosh has been harmonized with Adam, yielding what must have been his original role as first man to Adam. We can only guess that Adam was originally the first progenitor in *Edom*ite mythology ("Adam" = "Edom," both meaning "red earth") and that this myth circulated in Israel alongside the Israelite Enosh myth, eventually displacing it.

c. This is an ancient mytheme: the infant savior is in danger of human or demonic foes but is rescued by an angel and taken to safety in some remote place. It is told of the infant Zeus in Hesiod's *Theogony* and of many heroes thereafter. See Rev. 12:13-17; Apocalypse of Adam; Robert M. Price, "Jesus and John the Baptist," chapter 4 in Price, *The Incredible Shrinking Son of Man* (Amherst, New York: Prometheus Books, 2004). Apparently, Mount Parwan was a region of heaven reserved for those who died as infants.

son who was kidnapped? Let her come and see if this is her son!'

[18]"Who told Battai? Who instructed Battai? Who told Battai to go and tell Elizabeth, 'A youth has arrived in Judea, a prophet has come to Jerusalem. [19]And his guardian angel stands beside him. His mouth is like yours and his lips like his father's, Old Father Zachariah. [20]His eyes are like yours and his brows like his father's, Old Father Zachariah. His nose is like yours and his hands like his father's, Old Father Zachariah!'

[21]"The moment Elizabeth heard this, she rushed outside, forgetting her veil. When Old Father Zachariah saw her bare-faced in public, he drew up a certificate of divorce for her.[d] [22]The sun whispered down from the sky and the moon likewise from its place among the stars. The sun opened its mouth and spoke to Old Father Zachariah in Jerusalem: 'Old Father Zachariah, you old fool! [23]You have grown old and lost your mind! A youth has come to Judea, a prophet arrived in Jerusalem. [24]Your son has come to Judea. Why do you send Elizabeth away?'"

[25]When the youth saw her alone, he freed himself and dropped down from the cloud. He set himself free and descended from the cloud and kissed the lips of Elizabeth. [26]When Glorious Enosh saw it, he said to John in Jerusalem, "Is it permitted for you in your scripture, is it allowed you on the sacred page to kiss her on the lips?"

[27]At this, John replied to Glorious Enosh in Jerusalem, "Nine months I lived in her womb, the same length of time all other children stay there, and she made no complaint. [28]Thus, it is not immodest for me now to kiss her on the lips alone. No, all honor to any man who repays father and mother in full! A man who recompenses father and mother is unparalleled in the world."

[29]When John said this, Glorious Enosh realized how wise John was. At this, Glorious Enosh spoke to the sun in Jerusalem: "Take care of the youth, the Man,[e] for me; he is sent by the king. Take care of the youth for

---

d. This seems extreme, but outrage at perceived immodesty was not unparalleled in the ancient world. First-century writer Valerius Maximus becomes nostalgic in his *Memorable Deeds and Sayings* remembering when "Gaius Sulpicius Gallus ... divorced his wife because he had caught her outdoors with her head uncovered, a stiff penalty, but not without a certain logic. 'The law,' he said, 'prescribes for you my eyes alone to which you may prove your beauty. For these eyes you should provide the ornaments of beauty, for these be lovely.... If you, with heedless provocation, invite the look of anyone else, you must be suspected of wrongdoing."

e. John must be the very incarnation of the Man, who is also reflected in Enosh himself.

me until we ask for him again." 30Then Glorious Enosh spoke to the moon in Jerusalem: "Take care of the youth, the Man, who is sent by the king. Take care of the youth for me until we ask for him again."

11

1John proclaims in the nights, John in the evenings of the night.

2John proclaims in the night, and he says, "Do I not stand alone? At the sound of my voice, the wheels shake and the chariots of heaven capsize! 3The storm grew silent and quieted to nothing in the deserts of the earth. Sun and moon wail, and earth and heaven mourn!"

4Messiah opened his mouth and spoke to John in Jerusalem: "I asked you, John, by Great Life and by Sunday, whose name is precious; 5I asked you, John, by the Way by which pious men, once put to the test, go unhindered. Tell me: what is the shape of Sauriel's knife? 6Tell me: Once the soul leaves the body, with what is it clothed? And with what part of the empty body might it be compared? 7Surely the soul cannot be like the blood, which comes to a halt in the body if it becomes too hot. 8Surely the soul cannot be like the breath, that it should drift to the mountains, dissipate there, and be ended. 9Surely the soul cannot be like the dew, that it might fall on the fruit and evaporate."[f]

10When Messiah said this, John cries aloud; tears flow uncontrollably from him, and he speaks: "Perish the thought that the High King of Light should find his portion in deceivers! 11The soul is not like blood, that it should become heated in the body and stop circulating. Neither is the soul like the dew, to fall on the fruit and evaporate. 12The soul is not as the wind, that it should drift to the mountains and dissipate. Firmly developed in her own right does the soul enter into the empty body. 13If the soul has preserved herself perfect, she ascends in a garment of glory.

14"As for Sauriel's knife, it is made of three flames. When he prods the soul to hurry, intending to carry her away, he unsheathes the triple flame against her. 15The first flame he looses at her in the evening, the second at cock-crow, the third he discharges at her at the first light of dawn. 16Once the fire begins to blaze fiercely, the soul ebbs out through the feet and the knees. From the feet and the knees, she slips and draws near to

---

f. Jesus means here to challenge the existence of an immortal soul. We are told that Dositheans did not believe in an afterlife. Here Jesus seeks to trap John as the Sadducees, with whom the Dositheans are sometimes associated, try to trap him into admitting the absurdity of a resurrection (Mark 12:18-23). Specifically, he employs the same *reductio ad absurdam* argument Paul's anticipated objector uses in 1 Cor. 15:35.

the hips. [17]At this, she forsakes the hips, reaches the heart, and tries there to make her stand. Then she sinks into the breast, and it squeezes till she departs. [18]The eyes, the face, the lips of the dying twitch and the tongue writhes like a snake.

[19]"Then Sauriel sits upon the eyebrows; he sits and speaks to her: 'Go out, O soul! Why do you linger in the body?'

[20]"Then she replies to him, 'Will you greet me outside the body, Sauriel? First show me what I will wear, and dress me therein. Then greet me and bring me away from here.'[g]

[21]"'First, I must assess your deeds and your duc wage,' he answers her. 'Then I will show you your garment and dress you.'

[22]"'I had no idea, O Sauriel,' she says to him, 'that my time had come, and the angels summon me to reward me for doing good deeds, for you to bring me my garment and dress me in it.'

[23]"Notwithstanding, he answered her, 'Have you never seen anyone die? Have they not carried anyone out to be buried in your sight?'

[24]"At this, she says to him, 'Because of the authority of one who has died before me, and thanks to the prestige of the one they carried to the graveyard, I witnessed quite a spectacle! The women who lamented ran here and there as long as the body lay there before them. [25]When the soul abandons the body, four ritual mourners proceed into the graveyard. The women who wept ran here and there and they ran about in hysterics until the body was lowered into the earth. [26]When they had lowered the empty body and shoveled the dirt over it, the women left off their dirge. They filled in the grave and the men went off to their homes. [27]Hurriedly they left the body and the grave and departed. At home, they picked up cups and ate bread and put the body out of their minds.

[28]"'So if you will, O Sauriel, let me remain here two more days. Then I will cash in all my estate and provide for my heirs and then I will be ready to receive my garment, that robe that ascends to the Region of Light!'

[29]"But Sauriel answered her, 'Once a child leaves its mother's womb, can it ever return there? No more may I leave you in the domain of the wicked for you to see to your sons' inheritance. [30]I will lead you out and put on you the shroud of darkness because you took to heart no warning in this world, nor did you love the way to the Region of Life. [31]Therefore, you shall be imprisoned in the house of the wicked till heaven and earth pass away.'"

g. 2 Cor. 5:1-4

2.
The Revelation of Dositheus

(Three Tablets of Seth)

Dositheus is described in the Clementine *Homilies* and its more ancient sources as a disciple of John the Baptist, who is understood as a Gnostic baptizing sectarian, as in the Book of John the Baptizer. In a subsequent dispute with Simon Magus over which of the two was entitled to the leadership of the sect and to the honorific "the Standing One," we are told Dositheus yielded to the claims of Simon and died soon after. This may be merely the Simonian version of the story; all we may infer from it with any probability is that Simon and Dositheus parted ways, occasioning a schism. In fact, we continue to hear of Simonian and Dosithean sects for years thereafter, the latter existing in many subsequent subdivisions until the fourteenth century. In the same way, the Gospel of John would have us believe John the Baptist gladly and publicly abdicated the prophetic mantle in favor of Jesus, though evidence from the John sect a century later tells a different tale. We may envision a Dosithean version of the encounter in which Simon played the role of the upstart Korah, coveting the God-given privilege of Dositheus, the new Moses (see below), and suffering as ignominious a defeat as he would at the hands of Simon Peter in later Christian legend.

Dositheus is mentioned by several early Christian heresy hunters who provide various hints of what he taught. He seems to have presented himself as a Deuteronomic Prophet like Moses (Deut. 18), with the coveted title of "the Standing One," probably similar to what we read in a sixteenth-century Samaritan text which calls Moses

"the master of the Fasting and the Standing" in vigil.[a] The Standing One would also denote an eschatological figure "who shall stand in the latter days," as in the case of the Shi'ite Mahdi, also called the Qa'im, or "Standing One," or "He Who Shall Arise."

Claiming Mosaic authority, Dositheus seems to have written commentaries on the Torah or his own version of it, something not particularly unusual for the times. Other examples of this include the Qumran *Manual of Discipline,* the *Book of Jubilees,* and the Gospel of Matthew. Dositheus is said to have advocated vegetarianism and celibacy, at least for the elite. Dositheus' followers believed he had not died but was translated to heaven, just like Moses, according to contemporary Jewish belief. Some Dositheans taught a denial of any future resurrection, though they likely believed in Dositheus' own future second coming. The denial of the resurrection was probably, as in the earliest version of the Gospel of John, an inference from the fact of the Messiah's (Dositheus') appearance on earth: the Last Days were *now.* Resurrection was spiritual. (The nineteenth-century followers of Mirza Ali Muhammad, the Bab, believed in realized eschatology for precisely the same reason, since the Bab was supposed to be the awaited Mahdi.) Some say that, for the same reason, Dositheus abolished all ritual observances. Who needs shadows when reality has appeared?[b]

Copies of Dositheus' writings are said to have been left with a woman who had long served as his hostess in the fashion of the widow of Zarephath or the Shunammite woman. Perhaps one of these writings is our present document, the Revelation of Dositheus, which was discovered among the Nag Hammadi documents in 1945. It is a sequence of hymns and draws upon ancient traditions. Seth, the messianic son of Adam, is said to have inscribed primal secrets upon three tablets on a mountain so the secrets would survive the Flood. These must be the three tablets of which Dositheus was vouchsafed a vision. This story

---

a. Isma'il ar-Rumaihi, "Maulid an-Nanshi," in Stanley Jerome Isser, *The Dositheans: A Samaritan Sect in Late Antiquity* (Leiden, Netherlands: Brill, 1976), 139.

b. Cf. Col. 2:16-17; Mark 2:18-22. Cf. Thomas, saying 51: "His disciples say to him, 'When will the repose of the dead begin? And when will the new world come?' He says to them, 'what you look for has already come, but you fail to recognize it.'"

represents a fusion with the ur-myth that the king of Babylon ascended to heaven the first day of each new year to read the heavenly Tablets of Destiny in order to rule wisely through the coming year. We can see the basic pattern in most subsequent revelation books, including the Revelation of John, wherein John ascends to heaven to witness the unrolling of the seven-sealed scroll of the Lamb; six centuries later Muhammad ascends to heaven and receives angelic dictation from the Mother of the Book to transcribe the Koran. Even so, Dositheus has a vision of primordial tablets revealing a pattern of worship in heaven. We recognize this, too, from the hymns of the Dead Sea Scrolls, which emulate the worship of the angels, and the hymns of the Revelation of John, sung by the angels and twenty-four elders. The Revelation of Dositheus claims the same sort of divine pedigree for the hymns used in his community's worship. It is exactly the kind of liturgy we would expect to find in a Samaritan baptizing sect.

Finally, it becomes apparent that the text hints at identification of Dositheus as the earthly revealer and Seth as a heavenly being. Like Simon Magus, Dositheus apparently viewed himself as the divine Standing One. Was there more than a fortuitous resemblance between the names *Seth* and Do*sith*eus? Readers will notice from the content of the following revelation that it is divided into six hymns—two each on three tablets—occupying six chapters beginning with chapter 2, with short introductory and concluding chapters.

1

[1]The Revelation of Dositheus concerning the three tablets of Seth,
the father of the living and unshakable race, which he saw and understood. [2]And once he had read them, he remembered them. [3]And he
passed them on to the chosen ones exactly as first inscribed.

[4]After joining often with the Powers as they worshipped, I myself was judged worthy to glimpse the things of infinite majesty. And this is what I saw.

2

[1]The first tablet of Seth: The first hymn.

[2]I bless you, Father, Stranger Adam, I your own son, Eternal Seth,
whom you fathered without fleshly coupling as a blessing of our God.
[3]For I am your son and you are my mind, O my father. [4]I, too, sowed and

fathered, but you have seen the Majestic Ones! You have stood immortal.[c] I bless you, Father! [5]Bless me, O Father! It is because of you that I exist. It is because of God that you exist. [6]Because of you, I am with that very One. You are light, since you ever behold the light. You have revealed the light. [7]You are a portion of the divine; you are even my divine part. I extol you as God! I extol your divinity! [8]Great is that noble self-engendered One who stood, the God who had already stood. You came in goodness; you have appeared revealing goodness. [9]As for me, I shall utter your name, for you are a primordial name. You are unbegotten. [10]You have appeared so you might reveal the Eternal Ones. You yourself are He Who Is! Thus have you made manifest those who truly are. [11]You are he who is uttered with one's voice, but it is with the mind that you are worshipped, you who hold sway in every place. [12]Therefore, the visible world also knows you because of you, and thus they have offspring. You are full of mercy.

[13]And you are from a foreign race whose rightful place is over another race. And now you belong to an alien race, and it belongs ruling over a different race. [14]You stem from a different race, for you are not like them. And you are merciful because you are eternal. [15]And your rightful position is to rule over a race, for you have made all of them to multiply, and this for the sake of my own descendants. [16]For as you alone know, its role is to father children, who will likewise be aliens. [17]But they are destined to rule supreme over other races, for their home is in Life. You are the portion of divinity!

3

[1]The second hymn.

[2]I extol this power bestowed upon me, I who caused the masculinities that truly are male to become again thrice-male. [3]He who was sundered into the Pentad, the One given to us in triple power, the One who was fathered without carnal coupling, the One who stemmed from that which is precious: because of great humility, he went forth from the midst.

[4]You are a father by means of a father, a word issuing forth from a command. [5]We extol you, Thrice Male! For through the All, you did unite all things, for you have empowered us. [6]You arose at first from the One; from that One you have issued forth; you have arrived at One again. [7]You have saved, you have saved, you have saved us, O Crowned One and crown bestower. We will extol you forever! [8]We extol you, being

c. The "Standing One" was the title contested by Dositheus and Simon Magus as would-be successors to John the Baptist; it would seem that both claimed to be avatars or tulkus of the Standing One. See also note a above.

perfect individuals, perfect thanks to you, those who became perfect in union with you, the One who is complete and who completes, the One who is perfect and is found the same everywhere.

[9]Thrice Male, you have stood. You have already stood. You were divided everywhere, and yet you did continue to be One.[d] [10]And those whom you desired, you saved. But your desire is to save all who are worthy.

[11]You are perfect! You are perfect! You are perfect!

The first tablet of Seth.

4

[1]The second tablet of Seth: The third hymn.

[2]How great is the first aeon, the male virgin Bar-Belo,[e] the dawn splendor of the Unseen Father, she who is called perfect! [3]Lady, you have beheld the One who truly pre-exists all beings, for that he is a non-being. [4]And from him, and through him, you too have pre-existed from the ages, the non-being from a single indivisible yet triple power, yourself being thus also a triple power, a great monad from an absolute monad. [5]You are a chosen monad, the first shadow projected from the Holy Father, light from Light!

[6]We extol you, matrix of perfection! Aeon bearer! You have beheld the Eternal Ones because they arise from a shadow. [7]And you have made yourself multiple. And you were found to perdure as a womb of oneness; yet fissioning into multiplicity, you are three-fold. [8]You are truly triple, you female singularity from the male. [9]And you come from a shadow of him, being a hidden one, even a cosmos of understanding. [10]And these are the aspects of your essence.

[11]For the sake of the many, you have empowered being in the Eternal Ones. You have empowered life with divinity. [12]You have empowered goodness with knowledge. You have empowered with bliss the shadows which pour out from the fountain of oneness. [13]You have empowered this one with knowledge; you have empowered another with the ability to create. [14]Both the equal and the unequal: you have empowered them, both the similar and the dissimilar. [15]You have given the power of fathering and have provided forms of existence to others who are fathered. [16]You have empowered all these. He is that One hidden in the heart, while you have come forth from the many and return from them. [17]You are distributed among them. And you become a great male firstborn idea.

---

d. Here is the essence of the doctrine of Primal Man, whether we call him Purusha, Gayomard, Glorious Enosh, Adam Kadmon, or the Son of Man.

e. Perhaps meaning "the son of Baal."

5

[1]The fourth hymn.

[2]Paternal God, divine child, father of multiplicity patterned on the division of all who have true being, you are he who has appeared to them all implicit in a single word. [3]And you are he who possesses all those who are without physical origin, and who are forever indestructible, thanks, Lady, to you!

[4]Salvation has visited us, salvation comes ever from you. You are wisdom, you yourself knowledge. [5]You are truthfulness. Life exists because of you. From you comes life. [6]Thanks to you, mind exists. From you comes mind. You yourself are mind, a cosmos of truth-telling, three times a triple power. [7]In truth, you see threefold, the aeon of aeons! You alone behold undimmed the first Eternal Ones and the unbegotten ones!

[8]But the initial divisions were your own dissemination. Unite us as you yourself were reunited. [9]Teach us the things you have seen. Empower us to be saved for age-abiding life. [10]For each of us is a shadow of that initial pre-existent One. Give ear to us before all others, for we are Eternal Ones. [11]Hear us, the perfect individuals. You are the aeon of aeons, the all-perfect who is forever established.

[12]You have heard! You have heeded!
You have saved! You have delivered!
[13]We render thanks! Ever do we extol you!
We shall give you the glory!

The second tablet of Seth.

6

[1]The third tablet of Seth: The fifth hymn.

[2]We rejoice! We rejoice! We rejoice! We have beheld! We have beheld! [3]We have beheld him who truly pre-exists. We beheld that he truly exists and that he is the first Eternal One.

[4]O Unconceived One, from you stem the Eternal Ones, and the aeons, the all-perfect, those established, the perfect individuals.

[5]We extol you, non-being, existence prior to all existences, primordial entity before all entities. [6]Father of divinity and life, creator of mind, bestower of good, giver of bliss.

[7]We extol you, O knower, in worshipful blessing—you, thanks to whom [all these exist]. He knows you really as you know all else who know you, [through] yourself alone. [8]For there is no one [who is] active before you. You are a solitary and living [spirit]. [9]And [you] know One,

for those who are yours surround you. We cannot utter his glory, for your light blinds us.

[10]O command us to look upon you that we may be saved. Knowledge of you! It is the salvation of all. [11]Utter this, your command! When your command sounds forth, we shall be saved.

7

[1]The sixth hymn.

[2]In truth, we have been saved. We have beheld you with the mind. [3]You who save them all, you are them all. But you were not saved, not saved through them, nor needed it. For you have issued your command.

[4]You are One, you are One, as surely as there is one to say to you: "You are One!" You are a single living spirit. [5]What can we call you? We have no adequate name. For you are the very being of them all. [6]You are the life of them all. You are the mind of them all. [For] you [are he in whom all] rejoice.

[7]You have commanded these here assembled [to be saved] through your revelation of his glory who is prior to him, [8]O Hidden One, blessed Senaon, self-engendered, O Asineus. [O T]ephneus, O Optaon, O Elemaon the great Power, O Emouniar, O Nibareus, O Kandephoros, O Aphredon, O Deiphaneus, [9]you who are to me Armedon, Father of Powers, O Thalaneus, O Antitheus, you who exist within your own womb, you are before yourself. And after you, no one entered the field of action.

[10]In what terms shall we extol you? We are not able to express it.[f] But to be humble before you, we give what thanks we can. [11]For you have commanded us as one who is chosen to worship you as best we can. We extol you because we were saved. [12]Ever do we ascribe glory unto you. For this cause do we glorify you: that we may be delivered unto age-abiding salvation. [13]We have extolled you, for we have been empowered. We have been saved, for you have decided that we shall ever do so.

[14]We all did this. We blessed you not through the knowledge gained from the aeon, but from the One who was present before the beginning, we and those who were with us.

The third tablet of Seth.

8

[1]He who will remember these names and not leave off glorifying will become the perfect among the perfect, by all beings unsurpassable. [2]For they all extol these names, one by one and collectively. After this, let them

f. Thomas, saying 13.

all fall silent. 3And just as was ordained for them, they ascend. Following
the silence, they descend again from the third heaven. 4They bless the second as they descend through it, and finally the first. For the path of ascent
is the same as the path of descent.

5Know then, as those who have life, that you have attained. And you
taught yourselves the infinite things. 6Be amazed at the truth that lies concealed within and at the revelation.

3.

The Great Declaration of Simon Magus

SIMON MAGUS ("THE MAGICIAN") IS A fascinating character whom we meet in chapter 8 of Acts of All the Apostles, where he is depicted as a charlatan, though perhaps with real supernatural powers. He is a temporary, easily vanquished competitor of Christianity in Samaria. There he is said to have aggrandized himself as the Great Power, or as God himself come to earth. A number of church fathers speak of him as the father of all heresies and of Gnosticism in particular. Some say he was accompanied by one Helen, a woman he rescued from a brothel in Tyre when he recognized in her the incarnation of heavenly wisdom (the Epinoia or Ennoia, "first thought"). She had been abducted and ravished by evil angels who had made the world, and then she had passed into forgetfulness to be reincarnated ever and again into one earthly, fleshly life after another till Simon, having himself entered the time stream, came to earth to deliver her. In her, the mother of all souls, he had redeemed all the elect souls contained in her. One might attain salvation, return to the godhead, by accepting the saving grace of Simon Magus. Simon taught that his previous appearances on earth included one in Judea, where he was crucified and appeared to suffer, an implicit identification with Jesus. This probably had something to do with the synoptic story about the cross of Jesus being carried by Simon of Cyrene, a Phoenician, especially since Simon Magus, hailing from Gitta, might be either a Samaritan or a Phoenician (Gitta is Gath, Goliath's hometown), and Phoenicians were called the Kittim, easily confused with Gitta. So Simon of Cyrene and Simon of Gitta might easily have been the same character.

Many conflicting tales are told in early Christian literature concerning Simon, and some portray him as a kind of evil twin of the apostle Paul. F. C. Baur, to whose work virtually all subsequent New Testament scholarship is pretty much a massive set of footnotes, was the first to see this. In the Preaching of Peter, we read a replay of the encounter between Simon Magus and Simon Peter recorded in Acts. It becomes immediately clear that Simon Magus stands in for Paul in this narrative. Peter rebukes him for daring to claim equal apostleship on the basis of having seen a vision of the risen Christ. Peter and his brethren have been instructed in person by the earthly Jesus for a whole year. Simon Magus is shown teaching something astonishingly close to Marcionite doctrine, rejecting the creator and his Torah. Here Simon is not a rival of Christianity per se but of Petrine, Jewish-based Christianity.

Looking back at the account in Acts, Baur was able to recognize that there, too, Simon serves as a substitute for Paul. In all of these stories, what we have is a set of refracted images of the public showdown between Peter and Paul in Antioch (Gal. 2:10-21). When Simon converts to Christianity in Acts 8, then seeks to purchase the apostolic privilege of imparting the Holy Spirit, the point is to parody Paul's attempt to buy recognition from the Pillars of Jerusalem by collecting funds for them among his own constituency, the Gentiles (Gal. 2:9-10). By extension, Simon is portrayed as trying to buy a magic trick from Peter (Acts 8:19), but Peter's response that Simon can have "neither part nor lot in this word" (8:21) reveals that what was at stake was a role in the apostleship.

Does this identification mean that some Christian authors occasionally used Simon Magus as a satirical mask for Paul as Baur thought? Or does the identification go deeper? Was the historical Paul actually Simon? Hermann Detering and Stephan Hermann Huller think so. This would certainly explain the business about Simon being the father of heresy and Gnosticism because it would mean the same as Tertullian's famous description of Paul as the "apostle of Marcion and the apostle of the heretics." The earliest Paulinists we know of, including the earliest to write commentaries on his epistles, were Marcionites and Gnostics. As the church fathers make them the

whelps of Simon, the Gnostics themselves claim to hail from Paul. Detering and Huller turn Baur's position on its head: instead of Simon being a polemical mask, Paul is the orthodox, sanitized version of Simon, a kind of ventriloquist dummy for orthodoxy once Simon and his letters had been co-opted by the emerging Catholic Church.

If this is true, it would enable us to look at Acts 13:6-12 in a new way. Simon Magus reappears there under an alternate name, Elymas or Etoimas, depending on which manuscript one is reading, which seems to be the same as Atomus, an alternative name for Simon Magus in Josephus's writing, as Robert Eisenman notes. There is a striking and implicit identification between Paul and this Simon since in connection with the conversion of a Paul (Sergius Paulus), Elymas is temporarily blinded just as Saul was in Acts 9. It is at this point in Acts when Saul is first called Paul, as if he had been transformed from one to the other in the manner of Jacob becoming Israel or Abram becoming Abraham. Darrell J. Doughty identifies this strange tale as a confused or reworked variant version of a more basic conversion story. Whatever else is going on, there appears to be an effort to dissociate Paul from Simon Magus, presupposing that someone was identifying the two.

As for the names Saul and Paul, both may be secondary appellations. G.R.S. Mead wrote (*The Gnostic John the Baptizer*) that the Mandaeans identified Paul with Jesus, both being tantamount to the antichrist, since *paulis* is a transliteration into Aramaic of a Persian word for "deceiver." This is exactly the epithet Robert Eisenman sees Paul bearing in the Dead Sea Scrolls, where Paul is excoriated as the opponent of James the Just, the Teacher of Righteousness. However, as Huller notes, the Aramaic word *paulat* means "advocate"—*paraklete* in Greek, which might identify "Paul" (i.e., Simon) as the Johannine Paraclete, Simon then becoming known simply as "Paul" in the same way "Christ" became the last name of Jesus. This is a common phenomenon in religious history, whereby a sect takes on a label of belittlement and embraces it, as with the Methodists, the Moonies, and previously the Pharisees, who re-defined their epithet Parsees, or "closet Zoroastrians," to mean *Perushim*, the "separated ones." What of Saul? I think it was a compromise to ease the transition be-

tween Shimeon (Simon) and Paul. What do we get with half of one and half of the other? "Shaul," of course.

Hermann Detering thinks even the double name "Simon Peter" is secondary, denoting a subsequent Catholic co-opting of Paul as an apostle of orthodoxy: Peter has bested his rival Simon Magus (Paul) and in effect was merged with him. That is likely since it is the same process we observe in "catholicizing" documents such as 1 and 2 Peter and Acts 15, where Peter is remodeled as sounding very Pauline in order to assimilate the two factions by blending the characteristics of their figureheads.

We learn an astonishing bit of information from both the Clementine *Recognitions* and the *Homilies,* two different versions of the same work drawing on the same sources, some of them early Jewish-Christian in character. The *Homilies* (1:23) and the *Recognitions* (2:8) tell us Simon Magus was one of the thirty disciples of John. Membership was restricted to thirty for numerological reasons. Simon was John's favorite and his chosen successor. But Simon happened to be in Egypt when John was killed, so another disciple, Dositheus the Samaritan, succeeded John. After Simon's return, he "began to depreciate Dositheus himself, saying that he did not teach purely or perfectly and that this was the result not of ill intention but of ignorance. But Dositheus, when he perceived that Simon was depreciating him, fearing lest his reputation among men might be obscured (for he himself was supposed to be the Standing One), moved with rage, when they met as usual at the school, seized a rod, and began to beat Simon; but suddenly the rod seemed to pass through his body, as if it had been smoke. On which Dositheus, being astonished, says to him, 'Tell me if you are the Standing One, that I may adore you.' And when Simon answered that he was, then Dositheus, perceiving that he himself was not the Standing One, fell down and worshipped him, and gave up his own place as chief to Simon, ordering all the rank of thirty men to obey him; himself taking the inferior place which Simon formerly occupied. Not long after this he died."

Dositheus of Samaria was a rival Gnostic sect leader, and in this account of him yielding to Simon we must recognize another application of the same storyline found in John 1:35-37; 3:30, where John

the Baptist yields priority to Jesus. If this were anything like the historical truth about Simon, it would fit nicely with Eisenman's identification of Paul with the Qumran figure "the Spouter of Lies" arising within the primitive baptizing community, eventually headed by James the Just. We would have in a "James versus Paul" scenario yet another refraction of the sectarian succession strife we see in the Jesus-John friction, as well as the "Simon versus Dositheus" competition.

Kunsoo Choi rejects the identification of Simon with Paul because there is no Pauline analogue to Simon's association with Helen. But perhaps there is. Some have nominated Thecla for this position, while Huller believes the Paul/Simon character was associated with Mary Magdalene. May we not see Simon's association with Helen, who was also said to be a reincarnation of Queen Helen of Troy, as a reflection of Paul's possible association with Queen Helen of Adiabene, who with her sons Izates and Monobazus converted under the tutelage of Jewish missionaries who taught that circumcision was unnecessary? Simon's attempt to "buy" the Holy Spirit may have been associated with the famine-relief donation of Helen (Edessa), brought by Paul to Jerusalem from Antioch in Acts 11:27-30.

At any rate, Epiphanius of Salamis, the great heresiologist of the fourth century, included in his *Panarion,* an encyclopedic catalogue of unorthodox beliefs, the greater part of a treatise attributed to Simon Magus, the *Megale Apophasis* or "Great Declaration." Epiphanius seems largely to be quoting it, adding only occasional phrases such as "he says" to remind readers whose notions he is quoting. Sometimes Epiphanius may be summarizing, but even here the words are likely just abridged from the original. Thus, for the most part, it is not difficult to extract the original text from the *Panarion,* as I have done here. An element of conjecture arises toward the end of Epiphanius' discussion where he starts to cite a teaching about Simon's own Christlike role in the Simonian system of salvation. Has Epiphanius moved on to utilize other sources? Is he still quoting, albeit more patchily, from the Great Declaration? My guess is that he is continuing to quote the same document, mainly because the earlier text seems to lay groundwork for the later discussion of the double divine principle of voice and name as male and female, so I take the explicit

discussion of Simon and Helen to be the culmination of the earlier train of thought. Therefore, I include it, though in italics to caution the reader about the possibility of paraphrase by Epiphanius.

1

[1]This is the writing down of the declaration of voice and name from thought, which is the Great Power, the Boundless. [2]Thus it shall be sealed up, hidden, concealed, placed in the dwelling which rests upon the Universal Root. [3]To you, then, I say what I have to say, and I write what I have to write. And this is the writing thereof.

[4]From the universal aeons spring two shoots, which are without beginning or ending, stemming forth from a single root, which is that invisible Power, unknowable silence. [5]Of the two shoots, one appears from above. This is the Great Power, the Universal Mind that sets all things in order, being male. [6]The other appears from below. It is the Great Thought, which is female and brings forth all things.

[7]From this state they pair off with each other, uniting and appearing in the middle distance, the incomprehensible air, without beginning or end. [8]Here is to be found the Father by whom are all things sustained, and by whom are nourished those things which do partake of beginning and ending.

[9]Such is He Who Has Stood, Stands and Will Stand, a male/female power like unto that Boundless Power which is a stranger equally to beginning and ending, existing in oneness. [10]For it was from this that the thought within the oneness proceeded and became two.

[11]Thus was the One; for as he had her in himself, he was yet alone. He had not been so at first because, though pre-existent, by revealing himself to himself he became a second. [12]Nor could he be called Father till Thought named him so.

[13]Thus, producing himself by himself, he revealed to himself his own thought. [14]In the same way, the thought that was revealed did not make the Father known but rather concealed him by contemplating him, that is, the power, in herself, the result being male-female, power and thought.

[15]Thus do they pair off with each other, yet being one, there being no difference between power and thought. [16]Power is revealed from the things above, while thought is revealed by the things below.

[17]In the same way, too, that which was revealed from them, though it is one, is however found as two, the male-female having the female in it-

self. [18]Thus is mind contained within thought, things inseparable one from the other, which though in reality one are seen as two.

[19]Man, here below, born from blood, is the dwelling, and the Boundless Power dwells in him, and it is the Universal Root. [20]Nor is the Boundless Power, that is, fire, one. The fire is in being twofold, one side being manifest, the other concealed. [21]And the concealed things of fire are within the Manifest Ones, while those revealed are produced by Those Hidden. [22]The manifest side of fire contains all things within itself that are visible and that one may perceive, as well as those which one neither suspects nor perceives. [23]But in the concealed side of fire may be found all that is conceived and that is intelligible, even if it surpasses the senses, or that which one is unable to conceive.

2

[1]In general, one may say concerning all things, the visible and the intelligible, that is the concealed and manifested, that they are contained in the fire which overpasses the very heavens, even as a great tree like unto that glimpsed in a vision by Nebuchadnezzar[a] which nourishes all flesh. [2]Of this, the manifested side corresponds to the trunk, limbs, leaves, and encasing bark. All these members of the tree are set ablaze from the all-consuming flame of the fire and destroyed. [3]But as for the fruit of the tree, if its form is perfect and it assumes the true shape, it is gathered into the storehouse, not thrown into the fire.[b] [4]For the fruit is produced in order to be stored away, but the bark of the tree, having served its purpose, is destined for the fire, as it was produced for no purpose in its own right but only to protect the fruit.

[5]As it is written in scripture: "For the vineyard of the Lord Sabaoth is the house of Israel, and a man of Judah is a well-loved shoot."[c] [6]And if a man of Judah is a well-loved shoot, it is evident that a tree is nothing but a man. [7]As to its being divided and distributed, scripture has spoken plainly enough and suffices for the instruction of those who have ripened unto perfection, to wit: [8]"All flesh is mere grass, and everything in which mortals glory is like the wildflower. The grass is dried up, and the wildflower droops, but the word of the Lord endures through the aeon."[d] [9]So the word of the Lord is the speech which comes to flower in the mouth and in the word, for where else may it be produced?

---

a. Dan. 4:4-17

b. Luke 3:9, 17

c. Isa. 5:7

d. Isa. 40:6-9

[10]In sum, therefore, the fire, partaking of such a nature, containing both all things visible and invisible, and in like manner those heard within and those heard aloud, the numerable and the innumerable, may be called the Perfect Intellect, [11]since it is everything one can think of an infinite number of times in an infinite number of ways, whether of speech, thought, or deed. [12]For I judge that all parts of the fire, both seen and unseen, possess awareness and a modicum of intelligence. [13]Thus the contingent cosmos was generated out of the Unbegotten Fire. And it began to be generated in this manner. [14]The first six roots of the principle of generation which the cosmos received came from that fire. [15]And the roots themselves were begotten of the fire by pairs, which are mind and thought, voice and name, reason and reflection. [16]In these six roots was contained all the totality of the Boundless Power, albeit only in potentiality, not yet in actuality. [17]And this Boundless Power is He who has Stood, Stands and Will Stand. [18]This one, if he matures to perfection while within the six powers, will himself be, in essence, power, greatness, and completeness, one and the same with the Unbegotten and Boundless Power, in no respect inferior to that Unbegotten, Immutable and Boundless Power. [19]But if it remains in potentiality only, and it never attains unto its proper image, then it is doomed to vanish and perish just like the unused knowledge of grammar and geometry latent in the mind. [20]For if something potential is exercised, it comes to light among created things. [21]But if it is never realized, it lapses into darkness as if it had never been there in the first place. And when one dies, it dies with him.

3

[1]Of these six powers, and of the seventh which lies beyond the six, the initial pair are mind and thought, or heaven and earth. [2]The male gazes down from the height and remembers its partner, while the earth below receives from the heaven the fruits of intellect that rain down upon it and correspond to the things of earth. [3]For this reason does the word often and faithfully contemplate those things generated from mind and thought, heaven and earth, and says, "Hear, O heaven! Give ear, O earth, for the Lord has said, 'I have begotten sons and raised them up, but they have shoved me aside!'"[e] [4]And who says this? It is the seventh power, He Who Has Stood, Stands and Will Stand, for he is the creator of those things Moses eulogized, saying that they were very good.[f]

---

e. Isa. 1:2

f. Gen. 1:4, 10, 12, 18, 21, 25, 31

[5]Next come voice and name, which are sun and moon. After them are reason and reflection, or air and water. [6]And in all of them was mixed and mingled the Great Power, the Boundless, He Who Has Stood, Stands and Will Stand.

[7]And when Moses says, "In six days God made the heaven and the earth, and on the seventh rested from all his labors,"[g] [he tells a great mystery. [8]This may be seen from the contradictions wherein Moses says God made the sun and moon to exist on the fourth day, yet called the light into being on the first day].[h] [9]When, therefore, Moses says there are three days before the generation of the sun and the moon, he means esoterically mind and thought, or heaven and earth, and the seventh power, the Boundless. [10]For these three powers were begotten before all others. [11]And when he says, "He has begotten me before all the aeons,"[i] the words are used with reference to the seventh power. [12]So this seventh power, which was the first power subsisting in the Boundless Power, which was begotten before all aeons, this is the seventh power of which Moses says, "And the Spirit of God hovered over the water,"[j] [13]which means the Spirit which holds all things in itself, the image of the Boundless Power, the image reflecting the eternal form which by itself orders everything. [14]For the power hovering above the water is begotten by an immortal form and by itself orders everything.

4

[1]Having made the world in some such fashion, God, as Moses says, formed man by taking dirt from the ground. [2]And he made him not single but double according to both the image and the likeness. [3]And the image is that Spirit hovering over the water which, if it does not mature into its true form, perishes along with the world since it has lingered in potentiality and never attains unto actuality. [4]And this is what scripture means when it says, "So we may not be condemned along with the world."[k] [5]But if it matures perfectly into its intended image and it is begotten from an indivisible point, the small shall become great. [6]And this great thing shall persist through the endless and eternal aeon since it no longer belongs to the process of becoming.

g. Gen. 2:2
h. Gen. 1:16-17
i. Prov. 8:22-23
j. Gen. 1:2
k. 1 Cor. 11:32

[7]How and in what manner does God fashion man? In the Garden. [8]We must view the womb as a garden or a cave, as in the scripture when it says, "It was you who formed my inner parts, you who knitted me together in my mother's womb. [9]My frame was not unknown to you when I was being made in secret, intricately crafted in the caverns of the earth."[1] [10]This is why he chose this metaphor. So when he speaks of the Garden, Moses referred allegorically to the womb. [11]Or so he must if we are to believe the word and not dismiss it as nonsense.

[12]And if God fashions man in his mother's womb, that is, the Garden, as I have said, not only must the womb be understood for the Garden, but Eden is to be understood as the area around the womb, and the "river going out of Eden to water the Garden" as the umbilical cord. [13]This cord is divided into four channels. On either side of the cord are a pair of air ducts so the fetus may breathe and a pair of veins to carry blood. [14]But when the cord extending from the area of Eden connects to the fetus in the epigastric region, and the pair of veins through which the blood flows carry it from the Edenic region through the so-called gates of the liver, they nourish the fetus. [15]And the air-ducts, channels for the breath which surround the bladder on either side in the pelvic region, are united at the great duct called the dorsal aorta. [16]In this way the breath passing through the lateral doors into the heart provokes the motion of the embryo. [17]For as long as the babe is being fashioned in the Garden, it neither receives nourishment by the mouth nor breathes through the nostrils. [18]As it is completely surrounded in water, death would strike as soon as it were to take a breath. It would inhale the fluid and die. [19]Rather, the whole is contained in an envelope called the amnion and is nourished through the umbilical cord and receives the same thing breath conveys through the dorsal duct, as I said.

[20]Thus, the river which goes out of Eden and divides into four streams, four ducts, speaks in reality of the four senses of the fetus: [21]vision, smelling, taste, and touch, these being the only senses possessed by the child while still in the womb.

5

[1]Such is the law laid down by Moses, and it was on the pattern of it that he wrote each of his books, as the titles tell. [2]The first of them is Genesis, and this title in and of itself bespeaks the whole matter. [3]For this Genesis denotes vision, one of the divisions of the river. For it is through

1. Pss. 139:13, 15

sight that one perceives the creation. [4]The second book has the title Exodus, for everyone who is born must needs travel through the Red Sea and cross the wilderness, the red denoting blood, and taste the bitter water at Marah.[m] [5]This bitterness is that of the water beyond the Red Sea, referring to the painful, bitter path of learning we must walk through life. [6]But when it is transformed by Moses, really by the word, what was bitter becomes sweet. [7]This is attested even by secular sources, as witness the poet: "Its root was black, but the flower was like unto milk. Moly, the immortals name it. How hard for mortals to dig up, but for the gods all is child's play." [8]What the gentiles say here is enough to give knowledge of the whole thing as long as one has ears to hear. [9]Whoever tasted of this fruit was not only immune from Circe's spell, changing men into pigs, but it had the power to restore those so cursed. [10]Regaining their proper shape, they were like a defaced coin melted down again and struck again according to the type. [11]By the use of this fruit, as white as milk, one discovered the true man, beloved of the wizardress.

[12]In the same way, the third book, Leviticus, concerns smelling or breathing since the entire content of the book is taken up with sacrifices and offerings. [13]And inseparable from sacrificing is the ascending odor of the incense accompanying the sacrifice, and it is the olfactory sense that determines the propriety of the scent.[n] [14]Numbers, the fourth book, refers to taste, which is activated by speaking. [15]The book receives its name from the listing of everything in numerical order.

6

[1]All eternal ideas, like grammar or geometry, are inside us as potential but not as actual. [2]And if they encounter appropriate discourse and teaching, and if the bitter thus becomes sweet like spears turned to pruning hooks and swords into ploughshares,[o] [3]the fire will not have reaped husks and sticks but perfect fruit, not malformed, as I said above: equal and similar to the Unbegotten and Boundless Power. [4]"For now the axe is set at the root of the tree. Every tree that fails to bear good fruit is chopped down and flung onto the fire."[p]

[5]And so that blessed and immortal principle, power, is concealed in everything potentially if not actually, which is He Who Has Stood,

m. Exod. 15:23-24

n. Gen. 8:21. Readers will recall that the ancients believed the smell of a burnt sacrifice was pleasing to God's nose.

o. Isa. 2:4

p. Luke 3:9. Recall the association between Simon and the Baptizer.

Stands and Will Stand, [6]who has stood above in the Unbegotten Power, who stands below in the stream of the waters, begotten in an image, and who shall stand above, at the side of the Blessed and Boundless Power, providing there is perfect conformity to the image he bears. [7]For those who stand are three, and if there were not three standing aeons, there would be no ordering of the creation which hovers over the water and has been created in the likeness unto a perfect celestial being, [8]which becomes in no way inferior to the Unbegotten Power, so that one shall say to the other: "You and I are one; you are before me that I may be after you." [9]This is the One Power, divided into the above and the below, begetting itself, multiplying itself, seeking itself, finding itself, mother unto itself and father, sister, mate: the daughter, son, mother, and father of itself: One, the Universal Root.

[10]Of all things generated, the spark of desire for their generation comes from fire, just as the desire for physical begetting is called "being on fire." [11]And though fire is one thing, still it admits of two modes of change. [12]For in the male, the blood, being hot and yellow like fire when newly kindled, is changed into semen. But in the female, the same blood becomes milk. [13]And this transformation in the male accounts for the generative function, while the transmutation in the female results in the ability to nurse the child. [14]And this is what is meant by "the flaming sword that turned this way and that to guard the path to the Tree of Life."[q] [15]This because the blood turns this way into semen and that way into milk, and like the tree, this power becomes both mother and father, father of all who are born and mother of those who are nourished. [16]It stands in need of nothing, self-sufficient. [17]And the Tree of Life, guarded by the whirling, fiery sword, is the seventh power which proceeds from itself, containing all and yet latent in the six powers. [18]For if the fiery sword did not turn about, that beautiful tree would be despoiled and die. [19]But if it is turned into semen and milk, what is stored in them potentially, having come finally to the age of reason and found an appropriate place where reason may mature, beginning from the merest spark, [20]it will increase to mature protection and expand till it becomes an infinite power, immutable, equal in power and alike in form to the Immutable Aeon, which is no more begotten for an illimitable eternity.

7

[1]*And in this manner did the fire assume both male and female forms,*

q. Gen. 3:24

the one from above and the other from below, [2]*as each did mature unto perfect conformity with the Heavenly Power whose likeness and image they were.* [3]*And when they appeared in the midst of the rushing water of this realm of becoming, the female Thought was set upon and defiled by the angels and lower powers who made this world of matter.* [4]*And they used the fiery power within her to give life to their creations.*

[5]*It is Thought who is the lost sheep of the parable, and Mind who seeks her out at the cost of abandoning all his goods.* [6]*For she passes from body to body,* ever abiding in the forms of women, and ever does she hurl the powers of the world into confusion, pitting the one against the other, by reason of her superlative beauty, as of the heavens themselves. [7]And in this manner did the Trojan War erupt on account of her. [8]For this Thought took up its residence in the contemporary Helen, and it was because all the powers, both governing Achaia and ruling Troy, laid claim to her, that schism and war erupted among the nations to whom she was made manifest. [9]Thus, it was not Helen at fault, but those covetous powers who lusted for her and fought with each other on the plains of Illium, Zeus against Skamander, Apollo against Memnon.

[10]*This is why, in truth, the poet Stesichorus was deprived of his sight when he treated her rudely in his verses.* [11]*This is the reason, too, when he afterward recanted and wrote new verses extolling her virtues, he received his sight again.*

[12]*After these things, when her body was exchanged by the angels and powers, she was exposed in the streets of Tyre in Phoenicia as an infant, taken up by a brothel master, and raised in a brothel, where she knew no other life save that of degradation.* [13]*But as the poet recounts the stratagem of the Achaians whereby they infiltrated the fastness of Troy inside a great toy horse, so did her yoke-mate Mind, the male, gain entry to the realm of her captors by appearing in the likeness of their creatures as a man.*

[14]*The angels who governed the world were corrupt by reason of their lust for power, and so I appeared to set things right, transforming myself and making myself like unto the dominions, principalities, and angels, so that I manifested myself as a man, though I was not really a man.* [15]*And I seemed to suffer in Judea, although I did not really undergo it.* [16]*I was manifested to the Jews as the Son, in Samaria as the Father, and among the gentiles as the Holy Spirit, and I permitted them to call me by whatever name they pleased.* [17]*The angels who made the world issued whatever laws amused them, thinking thus to enslave all humanity.* [18]*And I*

sought her out. I arrived in Tyre and found her and purchased her freedom. [19]*Thus I wrought the ransoming of the human race, recalling to myself the sparks of the latent fire which the angels used to order their creation,* [20]*and this must issue in the dissolution of the world, but equally in the redemption of all who believe in me.*

4.

The Sayings of Jesus

Some ancient writers found it difficult to distinguish between early Christian preachers and their Cynic counterparts. Cynicism was a post-Socratic philosophy begun in the late fourth century BCE by two men: Antisthenes of Athens, a direct disciple of Socrates, who taught in the Cynosarges building in Athens, and Diogenes of Sinope, a wandering sage who adopted the roaming dog (*kynos*) for his ideal. Cynics taught that one ought to live in accord with nature, by reason, rejecting with scorn and humor all social conventions and material possessions. Diogenes went about naked or clothed in a barrel or a tub. Cynics generally adopted the distinctive garb of a tunic or loincloth, a cloak, a shoulder pouch, and a staff—nothing else, especially no money. They were mendicant beggars and claimed to have been sent by Zeus to witness to mankind that we may live as unencumbered and carefree as the lilies of the field and the birds of the air, that we have as little need for possessions, jobs, marriages, or government as animals do. They believed they should love their enemies and refused to retaliate when beaten. They flouted common decency with relish.

It is hard to miss the similarity between Cynic teachings and many of the sayings attributed to Jesus, in which Jesus orders disciples to renounce job, possessions, family, and worldly cares, leaving everything instead in the hands of a caring Providence, imitating the creatures of the wild. Indeed, there is no other religious or philosophical movement in antiquity that provides such close parallels with the most characteristic and radical sayings of Jesus. In fact, it seems most likely that the mission charge of the Synoptics (Mark 6:8-11; Matt.

10:5-23; Luke 9:3-6; 10:2-12) frets over whether Christian missionaries may take with them a staff, a cloak, a shoulder bag, and so on mainly in order to differentiate them from similar-appearing Cynic apostles.

Was the historical Jesus a Cynic? It is by no means impossible, as Gerald Downing, Burton L. Mack, John Dominic Crossan, David Seeley, and others have argued. Cynics had long been known in areas adjacent to Palestine, and it was a cosmopolitan age in which Hellenistic culture penetrated Jewish Palestine. But as the case of Proteus Peregrinus shows,[a] Cynics were attracted to Christianity and even wrote some of the Christian literature. Thus, the sayings that sound like Cynicism may have been unattributed maxims brought into the Christian movement by converts and subsequently attributed to Jesus. We do not know.

At any rate, it is striking that the Sufi mystics of medieval Islam venerated Jesus in much the same terms as the Cynic hypothesis casts him: an ascetical hermit who wandered the countryside homeless, accompanied by disciples. The Sufis preserved his sayings. After all, Jesus has always had high standing in Islam as a messiah, though not as the son of God or as a redeemer. The Islamic Jesus was virgin-born, but he did not die; someone else replaced him upon the cross and Jesus was taken to heaven to await the time when he would return to earth. The Sufi sayings call him the "Spirit of God." However, this appellation is most likely an honorific denoting Jesus' indifference to the physical world. It is likely that some or even many of the sayings of Jesus came to the Sufis from their Syriac monkish forbears, with the possibility that they originated in an even earlier period in the Christian movement. In large measure they present a pre-Christian, pre-Christological vision of Jesus as a Cynic-like ascetic, just as Mack, Downing, and the others make him. It may be, rather than that the Christology has been trimmed from these sayings, the proto-orthodox theology has not yet been added. The sayings included here are the ones appearing in al-Ghazali's *Revival of the Religious Sciences*, a twelfth-century Sufi work. There are indications the author may have

---

a. See the second-century satire by Lucian of Samosata, *The Passing of Peregrinus*.

derived all of these sayings from a source with earlier Christian roots. If the historical Jesus were a Cynic, this is the sort of thing he would have said.

1. Jesus said, "It is not merely he who knows, but he who does and teaches who shall be called great in the kingdom of heaven."[b]

2. Jesus said, "The decree of God is this: those who render the worship required of them will be saved, while those who worship beyond what is required will be drawn close to him."

3. Jesus said, "Trees are of many sorts, not all of them yielding fruit, and fruits are of many kinds, not all of them fit for food; and knowledge is of many varieties, not all of them profitable."

4. Jesus said, "Do not entrust wisdom to those who are not ready for it or you may harm it, and do not keep it back from those who are ready for it or you may harm them. Be like a careful physician who applies the remedy to the diseased spot."

5. Jesus said, "They do not hang jewels upon the necks of swine, and yet he who values not wisdom above jewels is worse than a swine."

6. Jesus said, "Vain scholars are like a rock having fallen at the mouth of a brook; it neither drinks the water nor does it let it flow to the field. Again, they are like the pipe of a latrine which is plastered outside and foul inside or like graves which are decorated outside but are filled with the bones of the dead."[c]

7. Jesus said, "What manner of scholar is he who says he is journeying to the next world but guides his steps to the things of this world? What sort of scholar is he who masters words only in order to communicate by them and does not implement them?"

8. God said to Jesus, "Exhort yourself first, and once you have profited by the exhortation, then exhort others; otherwise shrink from my gaze."

9. Jesus said, "The one who presumes to teach higher knowledge without practicing the wisdom thereof is like a secret adulteress whose swelling belly soon betrays her shame. Such a one, who does not act on the precepts he knows, will be shamed by the Lord before all mankind on the Day of Judgment."

---

b. Matt. 5:19; James 1:22

c. Matt. 23:13, 27; Luke 11:52, 44; Thomas, sayings 39, 102

10. Jesus said, "It is not profitable for you to come to know what you did not know if you neglect to implement what you know already. Too much knowledge only multiplies pride if you do not act upon it."

11. Jesus said, "If anyone sends away a beggar empty-handed from his house, no angel will watch over that house for seven nights."[d]

12. Jesus once went into the desert to pray for rain. When a crowd gathered round, he told them, "Whoever has sinned, go back." Everyone went away except one man. Jesus turned to this man and asked him, "You mean you have never sinned?" The man replied, "By God's name, I swear I am a stranger to sin. Indeed, one day as I said my prayers, a woman walked by. My eye chanced to light upon her so I gouged it out and tossed it behind her." Jesus then told him to pray. As soon as he began, clouds gathered. Rain began to fall—and the heavens gushed!

13. The Prayer of Jesus: "O God, I awake today unable to fend off what I hate or to gain what I love. That power is in the hands of others. My deeds have drawn my boundaries and no one is so poor as to be poorer than I am. O God, do not let my enemy triumph over me, nor cause my friend to mourn me. I care not for trouble unless it trouble my faith; free me from the care of this world and do not put me in the power of one who will not pity me."

14. Jesus met a man who merely sat. He asked him, "What are you doing?" "I am devoting myself to God," the man replied. Jesus asked, "And who is seeing to your needs?" "My brother," replied the man. Jesus said, "I should say your brother is more devoted to God than you are."

15. God revealed to Jesus, "Though you worshipped with all the devotion of heaven and earth, if you did not love what God loves and hate what God hates, it would avail you nothing."[e]

16. Jesus said, "Ingratiate yourselves with God by hating evil doers. Come closer to God by moving far from them and seek to please God by displeasing them." They said, "O Spirit of God, then with whom shall we converse?" Then he said, "Converse with those whose presence makes you mindful of God, whose words will inspire good deeds, and whose deeds will make you desire the next world."

17. Jesus said to the apostles, "What would you do if you saw your brother asleep and the wind had blown aside his tunic, leaving him exposed?" They said, "We would cover him up." He said, "No, you would uncover him." They said, "God forbid! Who would do that?" He said,

---

d. Matt. 10:12-13

e. 1 Cor. 13:1-3

"Anyone who hears a rumor about his brother and adds to it, then passes it on."

18. Jesus said, "O you who would secure worldly goods in order to do good works! This world and the next are like two women a man is trying to please at the same time; when either is pleased, the other is annoyed."[f]

19. Satan, the accursed, appeared before Jesus, saying to him, "Say, 'There is no God but God.'" He said: "The saying is true, but I will not utter it at your behest."[g]

20. On the night Jesus was born, the demons came to Satan and reported, "All idols have toppled from their places!" He said, "This is nothing but an accident, a coincidence. Calm down." Then he flew till he had gone over both hemispheres and he found nothing. Later he discovered the son of Mary had already been born, with the angels surrounding him. He returned to the demons and said, "A prophet was born yesterday; no woman ever conceived or delivered a child without my presence except for this one. So forget about the idols being worshipped after tonight; instead, attack mankind through haste and thoughtlessness."[h]

21. Jesus was asked, "Who was your teacher?" He answered, "No one taught me. I saw that the ignorance of the fool was a shame and I avoided it."

22. Jesus said, "Blessed is he who foregoes a present pleasure for the sake of a promised one, yet absent and unseen."

23. Jesus said, "O company of apostles! Make your stomachs hungry and your bodies bare; perhaps then your hearts may see God."[i]

24. Jesus lingered sixty days in prayer to his Lord, fasting all the while. All at once the thought of bread entered into his mind. His communion was interrupted as he saw a loaf of bread in his mind's eye. At this, he sat and wept at his loss of concentration. When he noticed an old man close by, Jesus said to him, "God bless you, O saint of God! Pray to God for me, for I was in an ecstasy when the thought of bread breached my mind, and the ecstasy evaporated." The old man said, "O God, if you know that the thought of bread came into my mind since I knew you,

---

f. Matt. 6:24

g. James 2:19

h. For the toppling of idols in Egypt during the sojourn of the Holy Family, see the Infancy Gospel of Matthew, vv. 22-23.

i. Thomas, saying 27

then do not forgive me! No, even when it was in front of me, I would eat it without thought or reflection."

25. Jesus said, "Beware! Not even glances are innocent, for they plant passion's seed in the heart and that is enough of a temptation."[j]

26. Jesus was asked by some to guide them to a course by which they might enter paradise. He answered, "Never speak at all." They said, "We cannot do this." He said, "Then only say something good."[k]

27. Jesus said, "Piety has ten parts. Nine-tenth's part is silence, one being solitude."

28. Jesus said, "Whoever lies much loses beauty, whoever is cantankerous loses honor, and whoever worries much sickens in body; and whoever has an evil disposition tortures himself."[l]

29. Jesus, walking past a pig, said to it, "Go in peace." Those with him said, "O Spirit of God, do you speak thus to a pig?" He answered, "I do not want my tongue to learn evil."

30. Jesus said, "One of the severest sins in God's estimation is for one to swear 'God knows' when he knows it not."

31. Jesus one day walked with his apostles and they passed by the carcass of a dog. The apostles said, "What a stench this dog gives off!" But Jesus said, "What white teeth it has!"

32. Jesus met John and said to him, "Admonish me." John told him, "Avoid feeling anger." Jesus replied, "This I cannot do." He said, "Then do not own any wealth." He said, "So this! This is possible."

33. John the Baptist asked Jesus what was the hardest thing to endure. The latter replied, "The wrath of God." "Then," asked John, "what is the lightning rod of God's anger?" "One's own anger," answered Jesus. "And what brings on one's own anger?" asked John. Jesus said, "Pride, conceit, vainglory, and arrogance."

34. Christ walked past certain Jews who muttered curses at him, but he spoke pleasantly to them in return. Someone said to him: "See how evilly they speak of you! And you speak well to them?" He said, "Each gives out of what he has."

35. Jesus said, "Whoever prays for those who mistreat him trounces Satan."

36. Jesus said, "Take not the world for your master, for it will surely claim you for its slaves. Entrust your treasure with him who will not

j. Matt. 5:28

k. James 3:2

l. Matt. 6:22-23; Luke 11:34-35

waste it. He who has worldly wealth is ever haunted by fear of losing it, while no such fears beset him who has his wealth with God."[m]

37. Jesus said, "O company of apostles, I have in truth overthrown the world for you. She lies prone upon her face. Be sure you do not raise her up after I am gone. It is proof of the foulness of this world that, in it, God is set at naught and that one cannot attain the next world without forsaking this one. So pass on through this world and do not linger! Know that the root of every sin is love for the world. How often does the pleasure of a single hour exact from a man long pain."

38. He said again, "I have made the world to kneel before me so you may mount upon its back. Do not allow kings or women to contest its possession with you. Not with kings, for so long as you leave their world to them, you have nothing to fear from them; but guard against women by fasting and prayer."[n]

39. He said again, "The world both seeks and is sought. If a man seeks the next world, this world seeks him, not letting him rest till he obtains from it his whole livelihood. But if a man seeks this world, the next world seeks him relentlessly till death seizes him by the jugular."[o]

40. Jesus said, "The love of this world and of the next cannot co-exist in a believer's heart, just as fire and water cannot share a single vessel."[p]

41. Jesus being asked "Why do you not take a house to shelter you?" said, "The ruins of our predecessors are good enough for us."

42. One day Jesus was sorely troubled by the rain and thunder and lightning and he looked about for some shelter. He spotted a tent nearby, but when he reached it, he discovered a woman within and left. Next he spied a mountain cave, but when he climbed up, he found a lion there. Laying his hand upon the lion, he said, "My God, you have provided for each thing a place of rest, but to me you have allowed none!" Then God revealed to him, "Is not your resting place the shelter of my mercy? I shall make you a wedding feast on the Day of Judgment, and I shall prolong your marriage feast four thousand years, of which each day is equal to a lifetime in this present world. And I shall order a herald to proclaim: 'Where are they who fast in this world? Come to the marriage feast of Jesus, who fasted in this world.'"[q]

---

m. Matt. 6:19-21, 24; Luke 12:33-34; 16:1-8

n. Thomas, saying 21; Mark 12:1-9; 13:34-37

o. Matt. 6:31-33; Luke 12:16-20; 29-31

p. Matt. 6:19-21

q. Matt. 8:20; 22:1-10; Luke 9:58; 14:16-24; Rev. 19:1-9; 14:1-5

43. Jesus said, "Woe to him who loves this world, since he must die and leave it behind with all that is in it! It deceives him, yet he trusts in it; he relies upon it only to have it betray him. Woe to those who are deceived, for on that day they shall be shown what they loathe and shall be forsaken by what they love, and they shall be overtaken by what threatens them. Woe to him whose concern is the world and whose labor is sin, for one day his sin shall expose his disgrace."

44. Jesus said, "Does anyone build upon the waves of the sea? Such is the world; do not make it your resting place."[r]

45. Some said to Jesus, "Teach us some doctrine for which God will love us." Jesus said, "You need but hate the world for God to love you."[s]

46. Jesus came to a village whose inhabitants were all scattered dead in the pathways and around the houses. "O company of disciples," he declared, "this community has been destroyed by the wrath of God; otherwise, they would have received decent burial."

"O Spirit of God," they urged, "tell us what happened to them!"

So Jesus invoked God's name and received a revelation. God instructed him to call out to the villagers after nightfall to gain his answer. When night came, Jesus climbed a hill and hailed the dead, and one answered: "What do you wish, O Spirit of God?" Jesus asked concerning their fate. The reply came: "We slept soundly one night and the next dawn woke up to find ourselves in the pit of hell." Jesus asked the reason. "Because we loved the world," came the answer, "and heeded the counsel of sinners."

"In what way did you love the world?" Jesus inquired.

"As a child loves its mother," he replied. "Whenever it favored us, we were happy, and whenever it forsook us, we were saddened and cried."

Then Jesus asked, "Why are your comrades silent?"

"Harsh and brutal angels have clamped their mouths with red hot bits," the voice answered.

"Then how is it you are able to speak?" countered Jesus.

"I was not one of them," said the other, "even though I was with them. When the torment descended, I shared their doom. Just now, I linger at the edge of hell, waiting to know if I shall be saved or flung into the infernal depths."

At this, Jesus turned to his disciples and told them: "Eating barley

---

r. Matt. 7:24-27; Luke 6:47-49

s. 1 John 2:15

bread with rock salt, wearing sackcloth, and sleeping on dunghills in squalor are no high price to secure one's well-being in this world and the next."

47. Jesus said, "You company of apostles, be happy with very little in this world to keep your faith sound, just as the people of this world are happy to have but little faith so as to succeed in this world."[t]

48. Jesus said, "O you who seek the wealth of this world to do charity: to abandon it would be more charitable."

49. Jesus used to say, "My constant state is hunger, my tunic is fear, and my robe is wool. I warm myself in the winter sun; my candle is the moon, my mounts are my feet. My food and delicacies are the fruits of the earth. Neither at the start of the day nor at its close do I possess a thing, yet no one on earth is a richer man than I."

50. The world appeared to Jesus as an old woman with rotten teeth, decked out with many fine ornaments. He asked her, "How many husbands have you had?" She replied, "I cannot count them all." He asked, "Did every one leave you a widow or did they all divorce you?" She said, "Neither: I have killed them all." Jesus said, "Woe to the rest of your husbands! Why do they not mark the fate of your former husbands? You have destroyed those one after the other and yet these are not on guard against you."[u]

51. Jesus said, "Amen, I say to you: just as the sick man looks at food without pleasure because of his racking pain, so the worldly man has no pleasure in worship, neither can he taste how sweet is the love of this world which he feels. Amen, I say to you: just as a horse, if his owner neglects his riding and exercise, becomes stubborn and changes his disposition, even so if the heart is not softened by mindfulness of death and the fatigue of devotion, it becomes hard and coarse. Amen, I say to you: just as a leather bottle, so long as it is not torn or dried out, is fit to hold honey, even so the heart, if it is not torn by passion or befouled by lust, nor coarsened by comfort, may become a vessel for wisdom."

52. Jesus said, "He who seeks after this world is like a man who drinks sea water: the more he drinks, the thirstier he becomes until it kills him."

53. The apostles said to Jesus, "How is it that you can walk on the water whereas we cannot?" He said to them, "What is your opinion of

t. Luke 16:8b

u. Tobit 2:7-8; Mark 12:20-23; John 4:16-18

the denarius and the drachma?" They said, "They are precious." He said, "But to me they are no better than dirt."

54. Jesus said, "There are three dangers in wealth: first, it may be made illegally." "But what if it is made legally?" they asked. He answered, "It may be given to someone unworthy of it." They asked, "But what if it is given to someone worthy of it?" He answered, "The mere handling of it may distract its owner from God."

55. Jesus said, "Store up for yourselves something which the fire will not devour." They said, "Like what?" He answered, "Mercy."[v]

56. Jesus said, "You vain scholars, you fast and pray and give alms and neglect doing what you are commanded, and you teach what you do not practice. How perverse is your judgment! You repent verbally and in your imagination, but you act as your lust dictates. It does you no good to wash your skin when your hearts are filthy. Amen, I say to you: be not like the sieve from which the good escapes, leaving only the husks. Even so with you: judgment issues from your mouths but mischief remains in your hearts. You slaves of this world! How shall a man attain the next world when he still lusts after this world and yearns for it? Amen, I say to you: your hearts shall weep for your actions. Submitting the world to your tongues, you have trampled good works under your feet. Amen, I say to you: you have ruined your future, for the prosperity of this world is more precious to you than the prosperity of the next. Who among mankind is more wretched than you, if you only knew it? Woe to you! How long will you map out directions for those who are in earnest, while you yourselves remain rooted to the spot like one who is lost and confused? It is as if you sought to trick all who dwell in this world to flee it and leave it to you. Stop, stop! Woe to you! What good does it do for a dark house, to set a lamp atop the roof when all remains dark within? Even so, it does you no good for the light of the world to shine from your open mouths when your hearts are plunged in shadow. You are slaves of this world and neither faithful slaves nor honorable freemen. Before long, the world will pull you up by the roots and throw you down on your faces; and then your sins shall take hold of your forelocks and push you from behind till they hand you over naked and destitute to the king and judge. Then he shall confront you with your wickedness and make you ashamed of your evil deeds."[w]

57. A man once accompanied Jesus, saying to him, "Let me go with

v. 1 Cor. 3:13; Matt. 7:1-2

w. Matt. 23; John 5

you and be your disciple." They set out and got as far as the bank of a river, and they sat down to eat. They had with them three bread rolls. They ate two and a third was left. Jesus then rose and went to the river to drink.

When he returned, he did not see the third roll, so he asked the man: "Who took the roll?"

"I do not know," the man replied.

Jesus and his companion got underway again and he saw a doe with two fawns. Jesus called one of the two and it approached him. Then Jesus slaughtered it, roasted some of it, and shared it with the other. Then he said to the deer, "Rise, if God grants." The deer did get up and left. Jesus then turned to his companion and said, "I ask you in the name of him who showed you this miracle, who took the roll?"

"I do not know," the man replied.

The two of them next arrived at a lake in a valley. Jesus took the man by the hand and together they walked upon the water. When they had crossed over, Jesus said to him, "I ask you in the name of him who showed you this miracle, who took the roll?"

"I do not know," the man replied.

Then they came to a parched desert and sat down on the ground. Jesus picked up some dirt and sand, then said, "Turn to gold, if God grants!" And it did. Jesus separated the gold into three portions, saying, "A third for me, a third for you, and a third for whoever took the roll."

The man said, "It was I who took the roll."

Jesus said, "The gold is all yours."

Jesus then left him. Two men overtook him in the desert, saw the gold, and wanted to rob and kill him. He said to them, "Why not split it three ways? Then one of you may go into town to buy us some food to eat." One of them was sent off and then said to himself, "Why should I divide the gold with those two? I need only poison the food and I shall have all the gold for myself." He went off and bought what he required.

Meanwhile, the two who stayed behind said to each other, "Why should we give him a third of the gold? Instead, let us kill him when he returns and divide the money between the two of us." When he got back, they fell upon him, ate the food, and died. The gold remained in the desert with three corpses beside it. Jesus passed by, found them that way, and said to his companions, "Such is the world. Beware of it."[x]

---

x. Thomas, sayings 56, 80

58. Jesus said, "What God loves most are the strangers." He was asked, "Who are these strangers?" He replied, "Those who escape the world with their faith intact. They shall find a place with me on the Day of Judgment."

59. Jesus told his disciples, "Whenever one of you fasts, let him refresh his hair and face and lips so no one may realize he is fasting; and when he gives with his right hand, not even his left hand should know what he is doing, and when he prays, he should draw a curtain across the doorway—for God distributes his rewards just as surely as he apportions food for his creatures."[y]

60. Christ said, "Blessed is the one whom God teaches his book and who does not die proud."

61. God revealed to Jesus: "When I grant you some blessing, receive it with humble gratitude that I may lavish upon you my full bounty."[z]

62. Christ said, "The reed grows in the plain but does not grow on the rock. Even so, wisdom seasons the heart of the humble, but it does not penetrate the heart of the proud. Do you not see that if one lifts his head to the roof, it hits him, whereas if he bows his head, the roof shelters him?"

63. Jesus said, "Beautiful raiment is inseparable from pride of heart."

64. Jesus said, "Why do you come to me wearing the habits of monks while your hearts are those of ravenous wolves? Better to put on the robes of kings and sober your hearts with fear."

65. The disciples said, "Christ of God, behold the house of God—how beautiful it is!" He replied, "Amen, amen, I say to you: God will not leave one stone of this place upon another but will completely destroy it because of the sins of its people. God has no use for gold, silver, or these stones. Far more precious in the sight of God are the pure in heart. On their account, God builds up the earth—or else destroys it if their hearts are anything but pure."

66. Jesus lay down one day with his head upon a stone. Satan, passing by, said, "O Jesus, I see you are fond of this world!" So he took the stone from under his head and tossed it away, saying, "Here, take it, along with the rest of the world!"[a]

67. Christ said, "You shall not attain what you want except by enduring what you do not want."

---

y. Matt. 6:1-18

z. Deut. 8:17-18

a. Gen. 28:12

68. There was a highwayman who had haunted the roads of Israel over some forty years. One day Jesus walked by him with a pious Israelite, an apostle. The robber thought to himself, "Here is the prophet of God walking by with his apostle at his side. What would happen if I were to join them?" Stepping out onto the road, he hesitantly approached the apostle, all the while comparing his own loathsomeness with the holiness of the apostle, reproaching himself for even thinking to associate with such a righteous man. When the apostle noticed him, he thought, "Am I to put up with the company of such a sinner?" So gathering his skirts together, he went and walked by the side of Jesus, leaving the robber behind. Then God revealed unto Jesus: "Tell them, they must begin their work all over again, for I have canceled their former deeds. I have erased the good works of the apostle for his conceit and the evil works of the other for his humility." So Jesus told them, and he took the robber for his companion on his pilgrimage and made him one of his apostles.[b]

69. Jesus said, "You, the company of the apostles, fear transgression, but we, the prophets, fear unbelief."

70. Christ said, "You company of apostles, the fear of God and the love of paradise make for patience in tribulation and serve to alienate one from the world. Amen, I say to you: to eat of barley bread and sleep with dogs on a dunghill in search for paradise are not much to ask."

71. Christ, in his wanderings, passed by a sleeping man wrapped in a robe. He woke him and said, "O you sleeper, wake up, rise and make mention of God." The man said, "What more do you want from me? Truly I have left the world to them that are of the world." Jesus said unto him, "Then sleep on, my beloved."

72. They say there was no epithet Jesus preferred to "Poor man."

73. Jesus said, "This world is a bridge. Cross over it. Do not linger upon it."

74. He was once asked, "Prophet of God, shall we not build a house where we can worship God?" He said, "Go and build a house on water." They asked him, "How can anything sound be built on water?" He replied, "How can there be sound worship if it is joined with love of the world?"

75. Christ said, "Do not envy the riches of the people of this world, for the glitter of their wealth dims the light of their faith."

76. Christ said, "Four things can be attained only with great ef-

---

b. Luke 18:9-14

fort—silence, which is the beginning of piety, humility, constant prayer, and poverty."

77. As Jesus sat in the shade of a wall owned by a certain man, the owner came and ordered him to leave the spot. Jesus said, "It was not you who made me leave your property, but rather he who did not want me to indulge in the shade."[c]

78. Jesus used to take with him nothing but a comb and a pitcher. One day, noticing a man comb his beard with his fingers, he tossed away the comb; another day, seeing a man dip out of the river with his hands, he discarded the pitcher.

79. Jesus said, "Work for the sake of God and not for the sake of your bellies. Look at the birds coming and going. They neither reap nor plow, and God provides for them. If you say, 'Our bellies are larger than the bellies of birds,' then look at the beasts, wild or tame: they come and go, neither reaping nor plowing, and God provides for them, too.[d] Watch out for the luxuries of the world, for the luxuries of the world are an abomination in God's eyes."[e]

80. Jesus said, "He is no wise man who does not rejoice when disaster and disease fall upon his body and his riches, for thus he gains an opportunity to do penance for his sins."

81. Jesus said, "Whoever loves God loves hardship."

82. Once Jesus came upon a large company of the devout who were emaciated on account of their devotion, like worn-out water skins. "Who are you?" he asked. "We are worshippers of God," they answered. "Why do you worship?" he asked. They replied, "God put the fear of hell in us, and so we were afraid." So he said, "It seems only right for God to save you from what you fear." Then Jesus passed on and came to others who were even more devout. He asked, "Why do you worship?" and they replied, "God gave us a thirst for paradise and what he has prepared there for his friends. That is what we hope for." So Jesus said, "It seems only right for God to give you what you hope for." Then he went on from there and came upon others who were worshipping, and he said, "Who are you?" They said, "We are lovers of God. We worship him, not out of fear of hell or longing for paradise, but out of love for him and for his greater glory." So Jesus said, "You are truly the friends of God, and it is

---

c. Thomas, saying 29

d. Matt. 6:25-33

e. Luke 16:14-15

with you that I was commanded to live." And he resided among them.

83. Among the sayings of Jesus is this: "If you see a youth afire with the pursuit of God, this makes him oblivious of all else."

84. Jesus was asked, "Why do you not buy a donkey to ride?" He answered, "I am too precious to God for him to let a donkey interrupt my contemplation of him."

85. Jesus saw a man who was blind, leprous, lame, paralyzed on both sides, and skin scarred from elephantiasis, but he was saying, "Praise be to God, who has kept me free from that wherewith he hath afflicted many of his creatures!" Jesus said unto him, "Sir, what form of affliction is that which has been spared you?" He answered, "O Spirit of God, I am better off than those into whose hearts God has not placed that knowledge of himself which he has placed into mine." Jesus said, "You have spoken the truth; give me your hand." He extended his hand and at once became the most handsome and best-looking of men, for God had healed him of his afflictions. So he accompanied Jesus and shared his devotions.

86. Jesus asked the children of Israel, "Where does the seed grow?" They answered: "In the mulch." He said, "Amen, I say to you: wisdom grows only in a heart like the mulch."

87. God revealed to Jesus: "When I examine a man's heart and find in it no love for this world or for the next, I fill it with love of me and carefully guard it."

88. Jesus was asked, "What is the best of works?" He answered, "Contentment with God Almighty, and to love him."

89. Jesus said, "Blessed is the eye that closes in sleep and dreams no evil, then awakens to sinlessness."

90. Jesus said, "None of you can arrive at true belief until it means nothing to you to be praised for your devotion to God Almighty and equally nothing to share in the things of this world."

91. The apostles asked Jesus, "What action is just?" He answered, "That of him who labors for God, caring not that anyone should praise him for it."

92. Jesus said, "Time is made of three days: yesterday, which is gone already, when you were admonished; today which meets your needs; and tomorrow, which holds in store you know not what."

93. Jesus said, "Actions are of three sorts: those which are plainly right, which you must imitate; those which are plainly wrong, which you must shun; and those which are doubtful, which you must refer to those wiser than you."

94. The apostles asked Jesus, "Is there anyone on earth today like you?" He answered, "Indeed! Anyone whose speech is always prayer, whose silence is always meditation, and whose vision is ever tearful, he is like me."[f]

95. Jesus once sat down to watch an old man digging up the earth with a spade. Said Jesus, "O Lord God, take away his hope." At once the man put down his spade and lay down. After an hour, Jesus said: "O Lord God, restore hope to him." At once he got up and got busy again. Then Jesus asked him what had happened, and he said: "While I was laboring, my soul whispered to me, 'How much longer will you labor, now that you are an old man?' So I tossed my spade aside and lay down. Then it said to me again, 'By God, you must live out what span is left you!' So I got back up and picked up my spade again.'"

96. Said Jesus, "Waste not a thought as to your provisions for tomorrow, for if tomorrow is appointed to your lifetime, then your provisions will arrive with it, but if it is not to be, then you are merely worrying for the livelihood of others."[g]

97. Whenever Jesus contemplated death, his pores dripped blood.

98. Jesus said, "You company of apostles, pray to God that this cup may prove easy for me, for I fear death with a terror like the agony of death itself."[h]

99. Jesus, passing by a skull, kicked it and commanded it to speak by God's leave. It said: "O Spirit of God, long ago I was a king. One day, as I sat proudly in state on the throne of my kingdom, crown on my head, armies and courtiers around me, the angel of death appeared to me. Then my limbs all collapsed and my spirit went forth to him. If only all those armies had been a single man! If only all that entourage had been solitude!"

100. Said Jesus, "How many sleek bodies, comely faces, and clever tongues shall tomorrow be screaming on the griddles of hell!"

f. Thomas, saying 13

g. Matt. 6:31-34; Luke 12:16-23

h. Mark 14:34, 36

II.
Matthean Cycle

5.

The Gospel according to Mark

THIS IS THE EARLIEST KNOWN GOSPEL. The word *gospel* (*euaggelion*) did not begin life as a particularly religious term. It meant something like "good news" or "big news," the prefix *eu* meaning *good.* As Hugh J. Schonfield points out, by the time the New Testament was written, the word had long since lost this specificity, which is why I follow Schonfield in translating the word simply as "the news." In both the gospels and the epistles, we find *euaggelion* meaning the message of salvation, whether about the coming kingdom or of the death and resurrection of Jesus Christ. Very rarely, if at all, does the word seem to denote a written text such as a gospel book, although this may be the intended meaning in Matthew where he writes, "Wherever in the world this gospel is preached, what she has done will be told as a memorial to her" (24:14; 26:13). It was a matter of metonymy that "gospel" came to stand for writings in which the message of salvation was set forth. It was an editorial convention, in other words. I have retained the original meaning, "good spell of news," in the narrative portions, as opposed to titles of books, in order to minimize confusion.

What sort of book?

If a gospel is a book, what sort of a book is a gospel? Rudolf Bultmann and others argued that the genre was Mark's innovation, a unique new Christian type of literature, but it seems clear now that Charles L. Talbert and others are correct in seeing it as belonging to a well-known ancient literary type, that of the hero's biography or

saint's hagiography. Often such books were written about the myth-laden lives of venerated philosophers like Pythagoras, Empedocles, and Apollonius of Tyana, including some of the teacher's sayings and ideas, with stories of divine annunciation, conception, nativity, child prodigy performance, miracles or other feats, popular acclaim or even coronation, subsequent disfavor, execution or near death, ascension to heaven, subsequent reappearance, and visions. These figures, like Jesus, were considered sons of gods. Their stories belonged to the larger category of the mythic hero archetype studied by Lord Raglan, Joseph Campbell, Otto von Ranck, and others. The gospels also have much in common with ancient novels of romance and adventure current in the Hellenistic world, in which there were frequent cliff-hangers like feigned deaths, people awakening in tombs after premature burial only to be freed by surprised grave robbers, survival of death by crucifixion, and so on.

But as one might expect, the gospels also have much to do with Old Testament narrative. As George Nickelsburg has shown, the basic plot of the gospel Passion narratives seems to belong to a category of Jewish tales of the "suffering righteous one" or "suffering wise man," usually a Jewish figure who is persecuted, or perhaps captured, by heathen rulers only to succeed against all odds and to be delivered from his foes' evil designs and to triumph in the end. Indeed, several clues in the gospel narratives seem to betray an earlier version of the stories in which Jesus was depicted, like the heroes of the Jewish tales and Hellenistic novels, as escaping death rather than rising from death.

Gospel and scripture

But the gospels owe a still greater debt to the Old Testament. Virtually all gospel episodes, on close scrutiny, seem to bear such striking resemblance to this or that Old Testament narrative scene that the similarity cannot be coincidental. It seems rather that the gospel incidents have been retold or rewritten from scriptural prototypes, especially from the Septuagint (LXX), the Greek translation of the Tanakh, or Hebrew Bible. Why are the gospels filled with rewritten stories of Jonah, David, Moses, Elijah, and Elisha rather than reports

of the historical Jesus? Quite likely because the earliest Christians, perhaps Jewish, Samaritan, and Galilean sectarians like the Nasoreans or Essenes, did not understand their savior to have been a figure of mundane history at all, any more than the devotees of the cults of Attis, Hercules, Mithras, and Osiris did. Their gods, too, had died and risen in misty antiquity. Plutarch, Herodotus, and others eventually assumed that these saviors were based on historical individuals, perhaps famous heroes, athletes, physicians, and kings. They ventured to place the "historical Osiris" or "historical Hercules" into their appropriate historical period. The same thing may have occurred with Jesus: he may have begun as a local variation on Osiris, with whom he shows a number of striking parallels, and then been given the title "Jesus" (savior), which in turn was later taken as a proper name, and his link to his Egyptian prototype was forgotten. Various attempts were made to place his death—originally a crime of unseen angelic or demonic forces[a]—as a historical event at the hands of known ancient rulers. Some thought Jesus slain at the command of Alexander Jannaeus in about 87 BCE, others blamed Herod Antipas, others Pontius Pilate. Some thought he died at age thirty or so, others thought age fifty. During this process, a historical Jesus became useful in the emerging institutional consolidation of Christianity as a separate religious community, a figurehead for numerous legitimization myths and sayings. The result was that all manner of contradictory views were retroactively fathered onto Jesus, many surviving to puzzle gospel readers still today.

But what had Jesus *done*? There may have been nothing to remember since nothing, strictly speaking, may have happened. As Earl Doherty (*The Jesus Puzzle*) has shown, the early Christians searched Jewish scripture on the assumption that it held coded clues of what the savior Jesus would have done, that everything must have happened "according to the scriptures." How could one discover what had happened? By divining the esoteric sense of passages featuring a code word such as "son" or "raised." Hence, Matthew seized upon Hosea 11:1, "out of Egypt I called my son," a reference to the exodus

a. 1 Cor. 2:6-8; Col. 2:13-15; Heb. 8:1-5

of Israel; it "revealed" to him that the infant Jesus must have retreated into Egypt, then returned to Israel. If Hosea 6:2 said that "on the third day, he will raise us up," that implied that Jesus' resurrection must have taken place on the third day. Other gospel sources included the *Iliad* and *Odyssey* of Homer, as Dennis R. MacDonald has shown in *The Homeric Epics and the Gospel of Mark*.

A different Gospel, a different Jesus

The evolution of the gospel genre marked a major shift in Christian consciousness or at least stemmed from a different version of Christian thinking. As long as the gospel was a preached message about a dying and rising savior, a message appropriated by the hearer through rituals like baptism and the eucharist, the focus was on the suffering and death of the savior. This is the sort of salvation mysticism we find in the epistles attributed to Paul. They neither mention nor have room for a historical Jesus who wandered about Palestine doing miracles or coining wise sayings. But once this basic structure ("Jesus died, but God raised him from the dead") was established as a skeleton to hang stories from, Jesus became less the savior than the divine hero like Hercules, Odysseus, Empedocles, even Moses and Elijah. The cross becomes the darkness before the dawn: a hurdle for the hero to conquer on his way to final triumph. Then it matters little whether Jesus actually died or just passed out sedated on the cross to reappear still alive some days later, as Apollonius of Tyana did.

There were other types of gospel books, too, such as "sayings gospels," collections of proverbs or prophecies attributed to Jesus after the fact and anchored to his name. The *Quelle*, or Q source, underlying both Matthew and Luke would have been such a sayings gospel, as were the Gospel according to Thomas and the gospel used by the medieval Sufi writer al-Ghazzali. As Helmut Koester and James M. Robinson have shown in *Trajectories through Early Christianity,* the compilers and readers of such gospels did not revere a savior Jesus so much as a wise man Jesus, a Socrates, Will Rogers, or Abe Lincoln. Theirs was not a superman who walked on water or ascended into heaven. Indeed, they may have had little idea what happened to him or who he was, just like Aesop or Idris Shah's Mullah

Nasrudin. In the present volume are gospels from both categories, those that emphasize the wise man and those that emphasize the divine hero. As for Mark, there is little doubt what kind of a gospel and what kind of a Jesus it represents. The Markan Jesus is a son of God striding the earth like a human dynamo. This gospel contains the least amount of teaching of any of the traditional four gospels and the greatest percentage of action. By contrast, Matthew will be seen to have combined the hero biography genre (*aretalogy*) with the sayings gospel type.

Date, author, and editions

Like the other gospels, Mark seems to come from the mid-second century AD/CE. Probably the crucial piece of evidence for dating the book is the Olivet Discourse, or the Little Apocalypse as Timothee Colani dubbed it, constituting chapter 13 of the gospel. It appears to have been an independent apocalyptic pamphlet circulating on the eve of the Roman destruction of Jerusalem and its temple. Mark picked it up and made it part of his text; but which destruction and which temple were portrayed? As Hermann Detering has shown,[b] the warnings of dangers and dooms outlined in the text fit better the destruction of city and temple during the Roman campaign against the messianic King Simon bar-Kochba in CE 136 than in CE 70 as is usually assumed. This means that Mark has absorbed an earlier document that already stemmed from the first third of the second century CE. How long afterward he composed the rest of the book remains uncertain. Another possible clue, however, comes in chapter 9 where Mark attempts to make the Transfiguration a substitute fulfillment for the original promise of the Parousia, the Second Coming of Christ, which had long since failed to materialize on schedule within the generation of the apostles. The necessity for such damage control implies a late date, though not a specific one. Mark also contains several anachronisms such as the depiction of synagogues scattered throughout Galilee when in fact they seem to have been largely confined to Judea be-

b. Hermann Detering, "The Synoptic Apocalypse (Mark 13): A Document from the Time of Bar-Kochba," *Journal of Higher Criticism* 7 (Fall 2000), 161-210.

fore CE 70, after which time the scribes and Pharisees perforce moved north. Also, Mark's stories have Jesus addressed by the title rabbi ("master," implying "teacher"), which did not enter common usage until the end of the first century, yet seems well established in Mark.

We may also note the clear Marcionite tendency of the gospel, with its unremittingly scathing portrayal of the disciples of Jesus as utter failures to carry on the Christian legacy. Indeed, it is not unlikely the subsequent choice of the ascription "Mark" reflects the name of Marcion, the early-to-mid second century champion of Paulinism. Papias, as quoted, or perhaps fabricated, by Irenaeus and Eusebius, makes the gospel the record of the oral preaching of Simon Peter at Rome. Following his death, the church fathers say, Mark, Simon Peter's secretary and assistant, decided to preserve what he could remember of his master Peter's teachings, much as Socrates' disciples were said to have made notes of his dialogues. But as Dennis E. Nineham and others have shown, whatever the Gospel of Mark is, it is certainly not a collection of eyewitness table talk. As Stephan Hermann Huller (*Against Polycarp*) has suggested, there may have been confusion between Simon Peter and his arch-rival Simon Magus, the ersatz apostle Paul. In this case, "Mark," the disciple of "Simon," would have been Marcion, the advocate of Paul. He would quite likely be the same as "Marcos the Magician," disciple of Simon Magus, lampooned by Irenaeus. This need not mean that Marcion the Paulinist was himself the author of the present gospel, but it very likely does preserve the memory of the Marcionite/Gnostic milieu in which it was written. A better candidate for authorship would be Basilides, a Gnostic who claimed to be the disciple of Glaukias, interpreter of Simon Peter, unless this too is a confusion with Simon Magus/Paul.

In 1958 Morton Smith was visiting the Syrian monastery of Mar Saba in Israel when he chanced on a stray page of an old manuscript copy of a letter from Clement of Alexandria. It was addressed to a certain Theodore, who had asked Clement's opinion about a longer version of Mark's gospel used by the Gnostic sect of Carpocratians. It contained passages strange to Theodore's ears even though he, too, knew of a Secret Gospel of Mark, which he shared with Clement. Clement tells Theodore that the more shocking passages cited by the

Carpocratians are heretical interpolations, even though their own, genuine Secret Gospel was longer than the familiar, now-canonical version. There is no way of knowing who interpolated and who excised material, but some scholars, such as Helmut Koester, believe our familiar Mark is in fact a cut version of a longer narrative. Huller suggests that the original Secret Mark was the same as the Gospel of the Egyptians, which Clement quotes in his *Stromateis.* The person who has been nominated as author of the fragmentary Gospel of the Egyptians is Basilides. If this is correct, it would imply by extension that Basilides was the author of Secret Mark. It is possible to read Mark, even in the canonical text, as containing doctrines notoriously ascribed to Basilides such as the adoption of Jesus as God's son at the Jordan when an angelic entity entered him and the substitution of Simon for Jesus on the cross of Golgotha.

Mark has been associated with both Rome and with Alexandria in ecclesiastical legend. This may indicate that there was an attempt to cover up the originally heretical non-Catholic character of Egyptian Christianity. Irenaeus has Mark writing up the gospel in Rome, but Clement has him finish it in Alexandria. Why such a double-headed legend? As Huller contends, it would make sense as a reflection of the Alexandrian origin of the longer, original Mark, as well as the Roman promulgation of the shorter version. Huller notes that the Asian presbyter Polycarp had encountered Marcellina, a Carpocratian missionary to Rome, who surely would have carried with her a copy of Secret Mark. Polycarp would likely have taken a copy and censored it for orthodox consumption. Thus, the ultimate author of Mark might well have been Basilides the Gnostic, with the "Ecclesiastical Redactor" none other than Polycarp of Smyrna.

Words and names

A note of explanation is in order regarding the translation of certain familiar terms and words. Mark frequently mentions "the kingdom of God." Sometimes this seems simply to denote the realm where God reigns. Sometimes there seems to be an apocalyptic denotation, a temporal rather than spatial reference, anticipating the soon-to-come Messianic Era which will see God's will perfectly enacted and the de-

mons banished. The kingdom of God in such passages would denote not so much the place as the time when God will rule unopposed. Occasionally I have paraphrased or translated according to the implied meaning in a given passage.

Great controversy has attached itself to the phrase "son of man." It seems to represent three different usages in the Aramaic language. It basically means a human being, but sometimes it was used as a self-reference like the Chinese in referring to themselves as "this humble person." In one or two cases, I have translated it as "yours truly." Sometimes "son of man" is euphemistically inclusive of humanity in general, as when we say "You really know how to hurt *a guy,*" by which we particularly mean *me.* Another example would be the current axiom, "*A man* has to have something to live for," meaning first and foremost *me.* I sometimes render the phrase as "a man" or "a person," even in Passion predictions where the reader knows good and well that only Jesus is intended, yet the disciples are confused. It is the ambiguity of the term in such a context that makes sense of this confusion. Thirdly, sometimes "son of man" is a thumbnail reference to Daniel 7:13, which was already read in contemporary Judaism and Christianity as a messianic text. As Maurice Casey has shown, it was not used as a title in Judaism. It was rather, as Norman Perrin observed, something like a shorthand reference to the passage and thus an indirect reference to the messiah. In cases where the gospel speaks of "the coming of the son of man," I try to communicate Perrin's understanding of it, as "one like a son of man," to recall Daniel 7:13.

The Greek text does not reproduce the Hebrew names of God, though it might have transliterated them in Greek letters. Very often when we read *kurios,* "Lord," the reference is to the Hebrew God, not to Jesus, since there is no article. In such cases, I venture that the intent was a substitution for *Adonai,* Hebrew for Lord, itself a substitute for the more holy name *Yahve.* Thus, when we find *kurios* without an article, I translate "Adonai." Similarly, I think occasional references to "the Most High" represent the Hebrew divine name *El Elyon,* and I so translate. Also where we find the transliterated Hebrew "Satan," I translate it not as a proper name, since it was originally a title, as "the adversary." The Greek *diabolos* means "the thrower," as in our terms

“mud-slinger” or “hurler of accusations.” So I translate *diabolos* not as the devil but as “the accuser.” These are Heideggerian deconstructions: I think the original meaning of the word still shines through and controls its usage even when it apparently has been forgotten.

As elsewhere, I italicize bits of the text that are lacking in important manuscripts and hence are likely later interpolations. Occasionally but not often I have silently added a phrase to make explicit what I see implicit in the text, in this respect following William Barclay’s precedent. And unlike other translations, I preserve the vivid present tense which Mark frequently uses, just as we still do when orally telling an exciting story.

1

1The beginning of the news of Jesus Christ, *the son of God:*

2Just as it is written in Isaiah the prophet, “Behold, I send my angel in
front of you, who will prepare your way; 3a voice of one crying out in the
desert: ‘Prepare the way of Adonai, all of you; make his route straight,’”[c]
4even so John arrived, baptizing in the desert, announcing a rite of baptism for forgiveness of sins. 5And all the region of Judea and all the
Jerusalemites went out to him and were baptized by him in the Jordan
River, enumerating their sins. 6And John had dressed himself in camel’s
hair and a leather waistband around his loins and was eating locusts and
wild honey. 7And he preached, saying, “One stronger than me comes afterward, compared to whom I am not fit to stoop down and untie the
thongs of his sandals. 8As for me, in my day I baptized you with water,
but he shall baptize you in the Holy Spirit.”

9And it came about that in those days Jesus came from Nazareth of
the Galilee and was baptized in the Jordan by John. 10And at once, going
up out of the water, he saw the skies split open and the Spirit like a dove
come down into him, 11as well as a voice out of the heavens: “You are my
son, the beloved; in you I am satisfied.”[d] 12And at once the Spirit expels
him into the desert. 13And he was in the desert forty days, being tested by
the adversary. And he was with the wild animals, and the angels fed him.[e]

14And after John was delivered over, Jesus came into the Galilee, an-

c. A conflation of Mal. 3:1a and Exod. 23:20a, plus Isa. 40:3.

d. The heavenly voice represents a scribal combination of bits and pieces of Pss. 2:7, Isa. 42:1, and Gen. 22:12, LXX.

e. The forty days recall Moses’ period of forty years in the desert of Midian

nouncing the news of God: [15]"The time has been fulfilled, and the kingdom of God has come near. Repent and believe the news!"

[16]And going along beside the Sea of Galilee, he saw Simon and Andreas, the brother of Simon, casting a net into the sea, for they were fishermen. [17]And Jesus said to them, "Come after me, and I will teach you to fish for human souls." [18]And at once, leaving their nets, they followed him. [19]And proceeding a little way, he saw Jacob, son of Zebediah, and John his brother, the two of them in the boat darning their nets. [20]And at once he called them, and leaving their father Zebediah in the boat with the hirelings, they went off after him.[f]

[21]And they journeyed into the village of Nahum.[g] And at once, entering the synagogue every Sabbath, he taught. [22]And they were astounded at his teaching, for he was teaching them as one possessing authority, and not like the scripture-parsing scribes. [23]And at once there was in their synagogue a man with an unclean spirit, and he cried out, [24]saying, "What business is there between us and you, Jesus, Nazarene? Are you here to destroy us? I recognize who you are. The saint of God!"[h] [25]And Jesus rebuked him: "Silence! And come out of him!" [26]And casting him aside, shouting with a great voice, the unclean spirit came out of him. [27]And all were astonished so that they debated among themselves, saying, "What is this? A new teaching by exorcism. And he dispatches the unclean spirits, and they obey him!" [28]And at once the report of him went out into all the vicinity of the Galilee.

[29]And at once coming out from the synagogue, they came into the dwelling of Simon and Andreas with Jacob and John. [30]Now the mother-in-law of Simon was laid up fever-stricken, and at once they tell him about her. [31]And approaching her at once, he raised her up, grasping her hand. And the fever left her, and she fed them.[i] [32]When evening came, when the sun set, people brought to him all who were in a bad way and the demonized. [33]And the whole city had assembled at the door. [34]And he

---

and the forty-day retreat of Elijah into the wilderness after his contest with Baal's prophets (1 Kings 19:5-7), where he, like Jesus, is ministered unto by angels.

f. The story comes from Elijah's recruitment of Elisha in 1 Kings 19:19-21.

g. Derived perhaps from Nahum 1:15a, the only passage outside of Isaiah to use the term ευαγγελισομενου in a strictly religious sense: "Behold upon the mountains the feet of him that brings glad tidings and publishes peace."

h. This cry comes directly from the defensive alarm of the Zarephath widow in 1 Kings 17:18.

i. A reshuffling of elements from 1 Kings 17:8-16, 32.

cured many who were in a bad way with various diseases, and he cast out
many demons because they recognized him.

[35]And getting up very early in the night, he went out and went away
to a desert place and prayed there. [36]And Simon and those with him went
looking for him [37]and found him, and they say to him, "All are seeking
you." [38]And he says to them, "Let us go someplace else into the nearby
towns in order that I may proclaim there too. It was for that purpose I
came out here." [39]And he entered their synagogues proclaiming in all the
Galilee and casting out the demons.

[40]And a man with a skin disease comes to him, pleading with him
and falling to his knees, saying to him, "If only you will, you are able to
purify me!" [41]And flooded with compassion, stretching out his hand, he
touched him and says to him, "It is my wish: be purified!" [42]And at once
the skin disease left him and he was purified.[j] [43]And he sternly warned
him, at once sending him off, [44]and saying to him, "See that you tell nothing to anyone. Just go show yourself to the priest and offer the things Moses commanded concerning your cleansing for their certification."

[45]But going out, he began to proclaim many things and to spread the
message far and wide so that he was no longer able to enter a city openly,
but he was out in the desert places. And they came to him from everywhere.

2

[1]And he entered again into the village of Nahum. After some days it
was heard, "He is at home." [2]And many gathered so as no longer to have
room at the door, and he spoke the message to them. [3]And they come to
him carrying a paralytic borne by four. [4]And not being able to bring him
to him through the crowd, they dismantled the roof over the spot where
he was. And having opened it, they lowered the mat on which the paralytic used to lie. [5]And Jesus, seeing their faith, says to the paralytic,
"Child, the sins you were being punished for are forgiven you." [6]Now
there were some of the scribes sitting there and debating in their hearts,
[7]"Why does this fellow speak this way? Surely he blasphemes! Who can
forgive sins except one, namely God?" [8]And sensing at once in his spirit
that they debated this way within themselves, Jesus says to them, "Why
do you debate these things in your hearts? [9]What, after all, is easier, to
say to the paralytic, 'The sins are forgiven you,' or to say, 'Get up, take

---

j. This story is meant to recall the miracle vouchsafed to Moses whereby he could turn his hand leprous white (Exod. 4:6-7).

your mat and walk around'? Let's see, shall we? 10To demonstrate to you that a man has authority to forgive sins on earth as God does in heaven"—here he speaks to the paralytic— 11"To you I say, get up, take your mat and go to your dwelling." 12And he got up and at once, taking the mat, he went out in plain view of all so that they were all beside themselves and worshipped God, saying, "We never saw the like of this!"[k]

13And he went out again alongside the sea and the whole crowd came to him, and he taught them. 14And going along the shore he spotted Levi the son of Alphaeus sitting at the customs booth, and he says to him, "Follow me!" And getting up, he followed him.[l] 15And it develops that he reclines at table in his house, and many customs agents and backsliders reclined with Jesus and his disciples, for there were many of them and they all followed him. 16And the scribes of the Pharisee sect, noticing that he eats with the backsliders and customs agents, remarked to his disciples, "So he eats with the customs agents and backsliders, eh?" 17And overhearing this, Jesus says to them, "The vigorous do not require a physician, but those who are in a bad way. My mission was not to summon the righteous, but the sinful."

18And the disciples of John and of the Pharisee sect used to fast. And people come and say to him, "Why do your disciples not fast when the disciples of John and the disciples of the Pharisee sect fast?" 19And Jesus explained to them, "It would be inappropriate for the groomsmen to fast during the wedding reception, would it not? During the period they have the bridegroom with them, they can hardly fast. 20But inevitably the days will come when the feasting is over, and then it will be appropriate to fast again. 21Look, no one is so stupid as to sew a patch of unlaundered cloth onto an old garment. Otherwise, the new, once washed, shrinks away from the old and a worse rip occurs. 22And no one fills old wineskins with new wine; otherwise, when the new wine ferments, it will burst the brittle skins and the wine will be lost along with the skins! *But new wine goes into new skins.*"

23And it came about that on the Sabbath he was passing through the grain fields, and his disciples began to pluck ears of grain as they walked. 24The Pharisees said to him, "Aha! Why do they do what is not legal?" 25And he says to them, "Did you never read what David did when he had

k. The story seems to be based on an Elijah story in 2 Kings 1:2-17a, where King Ahaziah gains his affliction by falling from his roof through the lattice, thereafter languishing in bed.

l. The story comes from Elijah's recruitment of Elisha in 1 Kings 19:19-21.

need and hungered, he and those with him? [26]He entered into the house of God during the pontificate of Abiathar the high priest and ate the loaves of showbread, which is not legal for anyone but the priests, and he gave it also to those who were with him. [27]Besides," he said to them, "the Sabbath was invented for the benefit of humanity, not humanity for the benefit of the Sabbath! [28]Which means that man was given dominion even over the Sabbath."

3

[1]And he entered again into a synagogue. And there happened to be present a man who had a withered hand. [2]And people watched him closely to see: "Will he heal him on the Sabbath?" so they might accuse him. [3]And he says to the man who had the dried-up hand, "Stand up where everyone can see you." [4]And he says to them, "Which is legal on the Sabbath: to do good or to do evil? To save life or to kill it?" But they remained silent. [5]And looking around on them with rage, stricken at their obtuseness, he says to the man, "Extend the hand!" And he extended it, and his hand was restored to health. [6]And exiting, the Pharisees at once exchanged ideas with Herod's agents against him, how to destroy him.[m]

[7]And Jesus, with his disciples, left the area for the sea, and a great multitude from the Galilee followed. [8]And a great multitude from Judea and from Jerusalem and from Idumea and the Transjordan and the region around Tyre and Sidon, hearing of his feats, came to him.

[9]And he told his disciples that a boat should remain in readiness on account of the crowd lest they trample him. [10]For he cured so many that they mobbed him, so that as many as had plagues might touch him. [11]And the unclean spirits, as soon as they saw him, dropped to their knees before him and shouted, saying in order to expose him, "Hail the Son of God!" [12]And repeatedly he warned them that they must not reveal his identity.

[13]And he goes up into the mountain and summons his choices, and they joined him. [14]And he constituted a group of twelve[n] to accompany him and to be sent out to proclaim [15]and to have authority to cast out the demons; [16]and so he made up the twelve, and he added a name to Simon: Peter. [17]And to Jacob the son of Zebediah and John the brother of Jacob he added a name: each was to be called Boanerges,[o] which is "Son of the

m. The substance of this scene derives from the miracle of the Judean prophet of 1 Kings 13:1-7ff, LXX.

n. This is based on the choice of the twelve spies in Deut. 1:23.

o. This is an old Sumerian title meaning "Upholder of the Vault of Heaven."

Thunderer."[p] [18]And Andreas and Philip and Bar-Ptolemy and Matthew and Thomas and Jacob the son of Alphaeus and Thaddaeus and Simon the Zealot, [19]and Judas the False One, who did indeed betray him.

[20]And he comes into a dwelling, and the crowd comes together again so as to prevent them from eating bread. [21]And hearing it, his relatives went out to seize him, for they said, "He is beside himself."[q] [23]And summoning the crowd, he spoke to them in riddles, "How can the adversary cast out the adversary?" [22]And the scribes coming down from Jerusalem said, "He has Baal-Zebul[r] under his control and uses the ruler of the demons to cast out the demons." [24]Jesus replied, "Thus, if a kingdom is divided against itself, that kingdom is not able to stand. [25]And if a dynastic house is divided against itself, it will not be able to stand. [26]And if the adversary rose up to accuse himself and so was divided, he is not able to stand but has come to an end. [27]But no one entering the strong man's dwelling is able to plunder his vessels unless he first binds the strong man. Then and only then will he plunder his house.[s] [28]Amen: I tell you that all the sins and blasphemies will be forgiven mankind, whatever they may blaspheme; [29]but whoever blasphemes against the Holy Spirit forfeits all forgiveness for the duration of the eon, being liable for an age-abiding sin." [30]This was because they said, "He has an unclean spirit."

[31]And his mother and his brothers arrive and, standing outside, sent word to him, calling him. [32]And a crowd sat around him, and they say to him, "Look! Your mother and your brothers and your sisters outside seek you." [33]And answering them, he says, "Indeed? Just who is my mother? And my brothers?" [34]And looking around at those sitting round him in a circle, he says, "See, you are my mother and my brothers! [35]Whoever obeys the will of God, that one is my brother and sister and mother."

4

[1]And again he began to teach beside the sea, and a huge crowd is gathered to hear him, forcing him to board a boat and sit in it on the sea, and all the crowd sat on the beach facing the sea. [2]And he taught them

---

p. In other words, the sons of Zeus, namely Castor and Pollux.

q. This is based on Exod. 18:1-22, but with an ironic twist.

r. "Baal-Zebul" means literally "Lord of the House" but denotes the "Lord of the World," a powerful patron of exorcists, while "Baal-Zebub" means "Lord of the Flies," denoting an oracle since the priests heard a sound like buzzing when the voice of spirits told the desired fortune.

s. This verse comes from Isa. 49:24-25.

many things by means of parables, and he said to them as he taught them, 3“Hear me! Listen: picture a sower going out to sow. 4And it came about in the process of sowing, some of the seed fell beside the road, and the birds came and ate it up. 5And other seed fell on rocky soil where it had not much soil, and at once it sprang up on account of not having depth of earth; 6and when the sun rose, it was scorched, and on account of not having any root it withered. 7And other seed fell into the thorns, and the thorns came up and choked it and it gave no fruit. 8And others fell into the good earth and gave fruit, coming up and growing, and bore in thirties and sixties and hundreds.” 9And he said, “Whoever has ears to hear, let him hear!”

10And when he was alone, those around him asked him about the parables. 11And he said to them, “To you the mystery of the kingdom of God has been entrusted, but to those on the outside, all things are in parables, 12in order that seeing, they may see and yet not perceive, and hearing, they may hear and yet not understand, lest they should turn from their sins and be forgiven for them.”

13And he says to them, “You do not get the parable? And how do you expect to get any of the parables? 14The sower sows the message.[t] 15And some of these are by the road, where the message is sown, and when they hear, at once the adversary comes and takes the message that has been sown in them. 16And some in like manner are sown on the rocks where, when hearing the message, they at once welcome it with joy 17but having no root in themselves are of short duration; when tribulation or persecution comes because of the message, at once they are scandalized. 18And others are sown into the thorns: these are those hearing the message, 19and the worries of the temporal world and the false promises of worldly wealth and desires for everything, making their way in, choke the message and it becomes barren. 20And some are sown on the good earth, who hear the message and welcome it and bear fruit in thirties and sixties and hundreds.”

21And he said to them, “Surely the lamp is not brought in to be placed underneath the bushel basket or the couch. Is it not the point for it to be placed on the lamp stand? 22For a thing is not hidden unless it is eventually to be made manifest, nor is anything hidden away except in order for it to reappear. 23If anyone has ears to hear, let him hear.”

---

t. Literally, “the word,” perhaps influenced by the Stoic doctrine of the σπερματικοι λογοι, “seeds of reason,” which supply everything its form and function.

[24]And he said to them, "Watch what you hear! They can give you no more than your container will hold. [25]Thus, the one who has, it will be given to him; and the one who has not, even what he has will be taken from him."

[26]And he said, "Therefore, the kingdom of God is like this: as a man might cast seed upon the earth, [27]and might sleep and rise night and day, and the seed sprouts and the stalk gets longer—how, he does not know. [28]The earth bears fruit automatically, first grass, then an ear, then a full head of grain in the ear. [29]When, however, the fruit permits, at once he gets out the sickle because the harvest has come."

[30]And he said, "How may we liken the kingdom of God? Or in what parable may we place it? [31]As a grain of mustard which, when one sows it on the ground, is smaller than all the seeds on the earth, [32] but once it germinates, it comes up and becomes greater than all the herbs and makes great branches so the birds of the sky are able to find lodging in its shadow." [33]And in many such parables he spoke the message to them, as much as they were able to grasp.[u] [34]And unless he had a parable he did not speak to them, but in private to his own disciples he explained everything.

[35]And he says to them on that day, evening having arrived, "Let us go over to the other side." [36]And leaving the crowd, they take him as he was, already in the boat, and other boats were with him. [37]And a great storm of wind blows up, and waves crashed into the boat, so the boat was now filled. [38]And he was in the stern, his head on a pillow, snoozing. And they get him up and say to him, "Teacher! Doesn't it matter to you that we are about to die?" [39]And having been awakened, he rebuked the wind and said to the sea, "Silence! Be muzzled!" And the wind sank, and a great calm settled. [40]And he said to them, "Why are you so fearful? How can you have no faith?" [41]And they feared a great fear and said to one another: "Who then is this man, that both the wind and the sea obey him?"[v]

5

[1]And they came to the opposite side of the sea into the region of the Girgashites.[w] [2]And as he was coming out of the boat, at once a man with an unclean spirit emerged from the tombs to meet him, [3]who had his resi-

---

u. This note contradicts the Gnostic strategy of using the parables to simultaneously reveal the truth and conceal it from the ungifted, as in vv. 11-12.

v. The basis for this story is Jon. 1:4-6; Pss. 107:23-29; *Odyssey* 10:1-69.

w. While most manuscripts have either "Gadarenes" or "Gerasenes," some

dence in the tombs, and no one was able to bind him any more even with a chain, [4]since he had often been bound with fetters and chains, and he had burst the chains and broken the fetters and no one was able to contain him. [5]And always, by night and by day, in the tombs and in the mountains, he used to shriek and to hack himself with stones. [6]And seeing Jesus from a great distance, he ran and kneeled before him. [7]And shouting with a powerful voice, he says, "What business is there between me and you, Jesus, son of El Elyon? I command you in the name of God, that you do not torture me!" [8]Oh yes, he said this because Jesus had said to him, "Unclean spirit, come out of the man!" [9]And he interrogated him, "What is your name?" And he says to him, "Legion is my name since we are so many." [10]And he pleaded desperately with him that he would not send them forth out of the region. [11]Now there was a great herd of pigs feeding there near the mountain. [12]And they pleaded with him, saying, "Send us into the pigs so that we may enter into them!" [13]And he gave them permission. And coming out, the unclean spirits entered into the pigs and stampeded the herd down the ledge into the sea, about two thousand, and they were choked in the sea.

[14]And those feeding them fled and reported the news in the city and in the fields. And they came to see what has happened. [15]And they come to Jesus and see the demonized man sitting dressed and clear-headed, the man who had played host to the legion, and they were afraid. [16]And those seeing it recounted to them how it happened to the demonized man and about the pigs. [17]And they began pleading with him to depart from their shores. [18]And as he was embarking in the boat, the demoniac pleaded with him that he might accompany him. [19]And he did not give him leave but says to him, "Go to your home and tell your relatives and announce to them the things the Lord has done to you and how he showed you mercy." [20]And he departed and began to proclaim in the Decapolis the things Jesus had done to him, and all who heard it marveled.[x]

[21]And when Jesus had crossed back over to the other side in the boat, a large crowd gathered to him, and he was beside the sea. [22]And one of

---

have "Gergesenes," implying a link with the ancient Canaanite Girgashites, associated with the archaic Anakim, who were believed to be "six-foot-tall giants." The name anticipates the Cyclopean figure Legion.

x. The core of the story derives from *Odyssey* 9:101-565. The demoniac is based on Polyphemus the Cyclops, while the pigs come from Circe's transformation of Odysseus' soldiers into swine. See Dennis R. MacDonald, *The Homeric Epics and the Gospel of Mark* (New Haven, CT: Yale University Press, 2000). Other details stem from Pss. 107.

the synagogue rulers, Jairus by name,[y] comes to him and, as soon as he sees him, falls at his feet [23]and pleads earnestly with him, saying, "My daughter has reached the end, but I am pleading that you may come and lay hands on her so she may be saved and may live." [24]And without further ado, he went with him.

And a large crowd followed him and jostled him, [25]and a woman who had been subject to a flow of blood for twelve years, [26]suffering many things under many physicians, spending all her resources, profiting nothing but rather only having reached bottom, [27]having heard the reports about Jesus, approached in the crowd behind him and touched his garment. [28]For she reasoned, "If I may touch even his garments, I shall be saved." [29]And at once the fountain of her blood was dried up, and she knew bodily that she is cured of the plague. [30]And at once, Jesus, inwardly sensing the outflow of power from him, pivoted in the crowd and said, "Who touched my garments?" [31]And his disciples said to him, "You can see for yourself the crowd jostling you, and you say 'Who touched me?'" [32]And he scanned the crowd to find the one who had done this. [33]And the woman, fearing and trembling, knowing what has happened to her, came and fell before him and told him the whole story. [34]And he told her, "Daughter, your own faith has saved you. Go satisfied at last, healed of your plague."

[35]While he was still speaking, messengers come to the synagogue ruler, saying, "Your daughter just died. Why do you still inconvenience the teacher?" [36]But Jesus, overhearing the words being spoken, says to the synagogue ruler, "Do not fear, just believe!" [37]And he did not permit anyone to follow along with him except for Peter and Jacob and John the brother of Jacob. [38]And they come into the dwelling of the synagogue ruler, and he sees a ruckus, people sobbing and wailing hysterically, [39]and entering he says to them, "Why do you make such a ruckus and sob? The child did not die but sleeps!" [40]And they derided him. But he, throwing them all out, takes the father of the child, plus the mother and his companions, and makes his way into where the child was. [41]And grasping the hand of the child, he says to her, "*Talitha koum,*" which is translated, "Girl, I say to you, get up!" [42]And at once the girl got up and walked around. For she was no infant, but twelve years old. And at once they were beside themselves with a great ecstasy. [43]He ordered them re-

y. The name Jairus means "he will awaken," signaling the fictive nature of the character and hence of the story.

peatedly that no one should know what really happened and that something should be given her to eat.[z]

6

[1]And he went out from there and comes into his birthplace, and his disciples follow him. [2]And when a Sabbath came, he began to teach in the synagogue, and the audience was astonished, saying, "Whence do these things come to him?" "And what wisdom is given him by God!" "And what powerful deeds come about through his hands!" [3]"Isn't this the carpenter, the son of Mary and brother of James and Jose and Judah and Simon?" "Aren't his sisters here with us?"

Yet they were scandalized at him. [4]And Jesus said to them, "It just goes to show the only place a prophet gets no respect is in his own birthplace, among his relatives, in his dwelling." [5]And he found himself unable to perform any powerful deeds except that, laying his hands on a few sick, he cured them. [6]And he was shocked at their lack of faith. And he made the circuit of the villages teaching.[a]

[7]And he summons the twelve and began sending them forth two by two and gave them authority over the unclean spirits [8]and stipulated they should take nothing on the road except for a single staff—no bread, no pouch, no coppers in the waistband, [9]but "having fastened sandals, do not put on two tunics."[b] [10]And he said to them, "Wherever you enter into a dwelling, stay there till you leave the village. [11]And whatever place does not welcome you, nor hear you, as you continue on your way, shake off the dust from under your feet as a reproach to them." [12]And going forth, they proclaimed that people should repent, [13]and they cast out many demons and anointed with oil and cured many sick.

[14]And King Herod heard, for his name became famous, and they said, "John the Baptizer has been raised from the dead, and because of that, the Powers are energizing him." [15]But others said, "It is Elijah!" And others said, "A prophet like one of the biblical prophets." [16]But hearing these rumors, Herod said, "The one whom I myself had beheaded, John! This one was raised!" [17]What he meant was, Herod himself sent to seize John and bound him in prison on account of Herodias,

---

z. The intent of feeding her seems to have been to prove she was not a ghost. Jairus's daughter and the bleeding woman play interdependent roles in a single story, which is a retelling of Elisha and the Shunammite woman of 2 Kings 4.

a. Mark's source for Jesus' frosty reception by his own townsfolk is likely 1 Sam. 10:1-27.

b. 2 Kings 4:29; 5:22

the wife of his brother Philip,[c] because he married her. [18]For John said to Herod, "It is not legal for you to have sex with the wife of your brother." [19]Now Herodias nursed a grudge against him and wanted to kill him but was not able, [20]for Herod feared John, knowing him to be a just and holy man, *and dared not touch him.* And hearing him, he was greatly troubled in conscience and yet gladly heard him. [21]And when an opportune day came, when during his birthday festivities Herod hosted a banquet for his courtiers and commanders and the leading citizens of the Galilee, [22]and the daughter of Herodias entered and danced, she pleased Herod and his dinner companions. And the king said to the girl, "Ask me for whatever you want, and I will give it to you." [23]And he swore to her, "Whatever you ask for, I will give you, up to half my kingdom." [24]And going out, she said to her mother, "What should I ask?" And she said, "The head of John the Baptizer." [25]And going in at once with haste to the king, she asked, saying, "I want you at once to give me the head of John the Baptizer—on a dish!" [26]And greatly chagrinned, the king nonetheless did not want to refuse her, because of the promises and the dinner companions. [27]And at once sending an executioner, he gave the order to fetch his head. And going off, he decapitated him right there in the prison [28]and fetched his head on a dish and handed it to the girl, and the girl handed it to her mother. [29]And hearing about it, his disciples went and took his headless corpse and interred it in a tomb.[d]

[30]And the ones sent forth returned; gathering around Jesus they reported to him all they did and taught. [31]And he says to them, "Come, just yourselves, away to a quiet place and relax a bit." For many were coming and going, and they had no opportunity to eat. [32]And they went away in the boat to a desert place by themselves. [33]And many saw them departing and knew where they must be headed, and they ran on foot from all the cities and converged there in advance of them. [34]And when he arrived, he saw a great crowd and felt compassion for them, for they were like sheep who had no shepherd to lead them, and he began to teach them many things.

[35]And now, a late hour striking, his disciples came to him and said,

---

c. Actually, the relevant brother of Herod Antipas was named Herod, as opposed to Philip and Herod Philip, yet other brothers.

d. Herod Antipas's words to his stepdaughter come from Esther 5:3. The way Herod has painted himself into a corner may come from Darius's bamboozlement in the case of Daniel (Dan. 6:6-15). But MacDonald (*Homeric Epics and the Gospel of Mark*) shows how the story of John's martyrdom matches in all essentials the story of Agamemnon's murder (*Odyssey* 3:254-308: 4:512-47; 11:404-34).

"The place is a desert and the hour is late. [36]Dismiss them to the surrounding fields and villages so they may buy themselves something to eat." [37]But answering, he said to them, "You give them something to eat!" And they say to him, "Are we to go off and buy loaves for two hundred denarii to give them to eat?" [38]But he says to them, "How many loaves do you have? Go check." And knowing, they answered, "Five, and two fish." [39]And he gave them instructions to have everyone recline, company by company, on the green grass. [40]And they reclined, group by group, by hundreds and by fifties. [41]And taking the five loaves and the two fish, looking up to the sky, he blessed and broke the loaves and gave it to the disciples to serve them, [42]and he divided up the two fish among all. And they all ate and were satisfied, [43]and they took twelve basket loads of bits of bread as well as fish. [44]And those eating the loaves were five thousand males.[e] [45]And at once he ordered his disciples to launch the boat and precede him to the opposite shore, to Beth-Saida, while he dispersed the crowd. [46]And having waved them good-bye, he went off into the mountain to pray.

[47]And with evening coming on, the boat had made it halfway across the sea, and he remained alone on land. [48]And spotting them in torment at the rowing, since the wind was against them, about the fourth watch of the night he comes toward them walking on the sea; and he intended to pass them by. [49]But seeing him walking on the sea, they thought it a phantom and cried out in terror. [50]For all saw him and shuddered. But at once he spoke with them and says to them, "Cheer up! It is I! Do not be afraid!" [51]And he went up to them, into the boat, and the wind stopped. And inwardly their great astonishment went off the scale.[f] It was because they failed to understand about the loaves since they had become so obtuse.

[53]And crossing over onto the land, they came to shore at Gennesaret and anchored. [54]And as they emerged from the boat, the locals recognized him at once [55]and they ran around that whole region after him and began to carry around on stretchers those in a bad way, going wherever they heard he is. [56]And whenever his journey took him into villages or into cities or into the countryside, they lined up the infirm in the marketplace, and they pleaded with him that they might touch just the very edge of his garment, and as many as managed to touch him were saved.

---

e. The basis for the miraculous feeding stories in Mark's gospel is the story of Elisha multiplying twenty barley loaves for a hundred men in 2 Kings 4:42-44.

f. Pss. 107 (LXX 106):23-30; Job 9:8b; *Iliad* 24:332, 340-41, 345-46, 351-52.

7

[1]And the Pharisees and some of the scribes coming from Jerusalem gathered to him. [2]And observing that some of his disciples eat bread with profane hands—that is, unwashed— [3]for the Pharisees and all the Jews, unless they wash the hands with the fist, they do not eat, holding in this matter to the tradition of the elders; [4]and unless they sprinkle what they bring home from the marketplace, they do not eat it, and there are many other matters which they received by tradition to hold fast: baptisms of cups and utensils and bronze vessels, even bed frames.[g] [5]The Pharisees and the scribes questioned him, "Why do your disciples not conduct themselves by the traditions of the elders, but eat bread with profane hands?" [6]But he said to them, "Isaiah the prophet put it beautifully when he mentioned you, you hypocrites, as it is written: 'This people honors me with lip service, but their heart is remote from me; [7]and their piety toward me is a charade, teaching doctrines that are commandments of mere mortals.' [8]Spurning the commandment of God, you cling to the traditions of mere mortals."[h] [9]And he said to them, "How neatly you suspend the commandment of God in order to observe your precious tradition! [10]For Moses said, 'Take care of your father and your mother' and 'Whoever speaks evil of father or mother, let him end up dead.' [11]But you know better. You say, if one says to one's father or mother, 'Sorry, but whatever you might have hoped to gain from me, it is *corban,* that is, a gift to the temple treasury, [12]you will no longer allow him to use the money to do anything to help them if he has second thoughts. [13]Thus you make the command of God moot in favor of the tradition you received from the elders. And that is only one example."

[14]And summoning the crowd again, he said to them, "Hear me, all of you, and try to understand:[i] [15]There is nothing from outside a person, entering into him, that is capable of profaning him; but the things coming out of a person are the ones that profane a person. [16]*If anyone has ears to hear, let him hear.*"[17]And when he went into a house away from the crowd, his disciples asked him about the parable. [18]And he says to them, "Are you that dense? Even you? Don't you realize that everything exter-

g. These customs were those of Diaspora Jews, not those at home in Palestine. The writer is misinformed and yet thinks readers will find Jewish customs as quaint and amusing as he does.

h. Isa. 29:13, LXX, the Hebrew original of which would not really make the required point.

i. Here we are to discern a reflection of Elijah's gesture in 1 Kings 18: 30.

nal that goes into a person is incapable of profaning one, [19]because it does not enter into one's heart but only into the belly and passes out into the latrine, which purges all foods?" [20]And he said, "The thing coming forth out of a person, that is what profanes a person. [21]For it is from within, out of a person's heart, that evil thoughts emerge: whoredoms, thefts, homicides, [22]adulteries, greeds, evils, deceit, lewd behavior, a miserly squint, blasphemy, arrogance, foolishness. [23]All these evils emerge from within and profane a person."

[24]And he got up from there and went off into the region of Tyre. And he sought seclusion in a house but could not remain hidden. For example: [25]at once hearing about him, a woman whose daughter had an unclean spirit came and fell down before him at his feet. [26]And the woman was a Syro-Phoenician by race, and she asked him to cast the demon out of her daughter. [27]And he said to her, "Let the children satisfy themselves first, for what good parent takes the bread out of the children's mouths and tosses it to the dogs?" [28]But she had an answer ready for him: "True, Lord! But do the dogs not wait under the table for the children's crumbs?" [29]And he said to her, "*Touché!* Just for that, I will do it. Go on home, the demon has already vacated your daughter." [30]And heading off to her dwelling, she discovered the child stretched out on the couch, the demon having abandoned her.[j]

[31]And going out again from Tyre, he came through Sidon to the Sea of Galilee in the middle of the Decapolis district. [32]And they bring to him a deaf man with a speech defect and they plead with him to lay hands on him. [33]And isolating him from the crowd, he inserted his fingers into his ears, and spitting, he touched his tongue, [34]and looking up to the sky, he groaned and says to him, "*Ephphatha!*" which means "Open up!" [35]And his ears were opened, and at once the knot of his tongue was loosened so that he spoke clearly. [36]And he ordered them they should tell no one. But the more he warned them, the wider they proclaimed it; [37]and their astonishment went off the scale: "He has performed all his tasks beautifully. He even makes the deaf hear and the mute speak!"[k]

8

[1]In those days, with many people thronging, none of them with anything to eat, he summons the disciples and says to them, [2]"I feel for the

---

j. Based on Elijah and the widow of Zarephath in 1 Kings 17:8-16.

k. This episode is worked up from Isa. 29:18; 35:5-6, incorporating common Hellenistic magical healing techniques.

crowd because they have been with me three whole days now. [3]And if I send them home still fasting, they will keel over in the road. And some of them are from a great distance away." [4]And his disciples replied to him, "Where will anyone be able to come up with enough bread to satisfy these people here in the desert?" [5]And he asked them, "How many loaves do you have?" And they said, "A total of seven." [6]And he directs the crowd to recline on the ground. And taking the seven loaves, giving thanks, he broke them and gave them to his disciples to serve, and they served the crowd. [7]And they found they had a few fish, and blessing them, he ordered that these too be served. [8]And they ate and were satisfied and gathered up seven hampers of leftover pieces. [9]Now there were about four thousand present. And he dismissed them. [10]And setting sail at once in the boat with his disciples, he came into the region of Dalmanutha.

[11]And the local Pharisees came out and commenced disputing with him, challenging him to produce a sign from heaven. [12]And groaning inwardly, he says to them, "Why does this nation seek a sign? Amen: I say to you, will a sign be given to this nation? Not likely!" [13]And leaving them again, he went off for the opposite shore.

[14]So they forgot to take loaves, and except for one loaf, they had none with them in the boat. [15]And he warned them, saying, "Look, at Passover time, a man takes care that no leaven has crept into his bread; even so, I tell you, watch out for the treachery of the Pharisees and the treachery of Herod!" [16]And they whispered to one another that he must be referring to the fact that they have no loaves. [17]And when he became aware of it, he says to them, "Why do you babble about not having loaves of bread? Don't you see? Do you still not get it? Are you so thick-headed? [18]Having eyes, do you still not see? Having ears, you still cannot hear? If I wanted bread, I could make it myself! Don't you remember, [19]when I divided the five loaves for the five thousand, how many baskets full of leftover pieces you gathered?" They say to him, "Twelve." [20]"When I divided the seven loaves for the four thousand, how many full hampers did you gather?" And they say, "Seven." [21]And he said to them, "And so? Don't tell me you still don't get it!"

[22]And they come to Beth-Saida. And they bring him a blind man and plead with him to touch him. [23]And grasping the hand of the blind man, he led him forth out of the village; and spitting in his eyes, laying hands on him, he questioned him, "Do you see anything?" [24]And looking up, he said, "I see men, but they look like trees walking." [25]Then he laid hands on his eyes again, and he squinted and was restored, and he saw every-

thing clearly. [26]And he sent him home, saying, "You may not enter the village."[1]

[27]And Jesus and his disciples went out to the villages of Caesarea Philippi. And as they were walking on the road, he questioned his disciples, saying to them, "Who do people think me to be?" [28]And they told him, saying, "John the Baptizer," and for others, "Elijah," but others, "One of the biblical prophets." [29]And he questioned them, "But what about you? Who do you think me to be?" Answering, Peter says to him, "You are the Christ." [30]And he warned them that they must tell no one about him. [31]And he began to teach them that a man has to suffer many indignities and be excommunicated by the elders and archpriests and scribes and be executed and after three days rise again. [32]And he said these things quite frankly.

And taking him on ahead, Peter began to admonish him. [33]But he turned around and looked at the rest of his disciples and admonished Peter and says, "Get back with the others, adversary!" And Peter says to him, "But why?" And he says to him, "Because you are not wise to the ways of God, but only to the ways of this world."

[34]Then summoning the crowd to join his disciples, he said to them, "If anyone here wants to come after me, let him repudiate himself and pick up his cross and let him follow me. [35]For whoever tries to save his life will lose it, but whoever will sacrifice his life for the sake of me and the news will save it. [36]For what profit does a man take if he should manage to acquire the whole world only to be fined his own life? [37]For what could a person possibly offer in exchange for his life? [38]I say this because whoever will not stand up for me and my words in this adulterous and sinful nation, no one will stand with him when he comes to life again in the glory of his Father with the holy angels."

9

[1]And he said to them, "Amen: I say to you, there are some of those standing here who will certainly not taste of death before they see the kingdom of God having come with power."

---

1. Again, the story draws from Isa. 29:18; 35:5-6, incorporating Hellenistic magical healing. We also discern influence from Gen. 19:11-13, where God's angels blind the Sodomite welcoming committee and warn Lot and his family to flee the doomed city. The gospels write off Bethsaida for its lack of responsiveness, and in Matt. 11:24 its fate is likened to Sodom's. The blind man of Bethsaida, then, is healed of the Sodomites' blindness and is sent, like Lot, to escape the doomed city's eventual destruction.

[2]And after six days Jesus takes along Peter and Jacob and John and leads them up into a high mountain solely by themselves. And he was metamorphosed in front of them, [3]and his garments became blinding white, not merely the earthly whiteness of newly laundered clothes. [4]And Elijah and Moses appeared to them, and they were engaged in conversation with Jesus. And Jesus says to Peter, "Simon, have you nothing to say?" [5]And answering, Peter says to Jesus, "Rabbi, it is good for us disciples to be here! And let us make three tents: one for you, one for Moses, and one for Elijah." [6]Actually, he did not know what response to make, for they became frightened out of their wits. [7]And a cloud appeared, overshadowing them, and a voice was heard to speak from the cloud: "This one is my son, the beloved. Hear him!" [8]And suddenly, as they looked around to see who it was who spoke, they no longer saw anyone with them except for Jesus alone.[m] [9]And as they descended from the mountain, he ordered them to recount to none of the others the things they saw except for when a man should rise from the dead. [10]So they kept the matter to themselves, debating what is meant by "rise from the dead"—at the end of the age or beforehand? [11]So they questioned him, "What scripture do the scribes have in mind when they say Elijah must come first or the general resurrection may not take place?"[n] [12]But he said to them, "Elijah does indeed appear first, ushering in the resurrection of all things. The real question is, where does scripture say of the man that he must endure many things and be destroyed? [13]But I say to you that indeed, Elijah has come, and they did with him what they wished," as it is written about him earlier in this gospel.

[14]And coming to the disciples, they saw a great crowd around them, listening to the scribes, debating with them. [15]And at once all the crowd, catching sight of him, were overcome with astonishment because, like Moses, he was still shining like the sun. And running up to him, they greeted him. [16]And he questioned them: "What are you debating with them?" [17]And one man in the crowd answered him: "Teacher, I brought my son to you, having a mute spirit; [18]and wherever he happens to be when it grabs hold of him, it causes him to rip his flesh, and he foams at

---

m. "And six days later" must be understood as a pointer to Exod. 24:12-16. God calls Moses up the mountainside, Moses takes Joshua (Greek: Jesus) with him, the glory cloud covers the mountain for six days, and on the seventh day the divine voice calls Moses from the depth of the cloud. Mark has apparently foreshortened the process. The glowing apparition of Jesus is obviously derived from that of Moses in Exod. 34:29, as well as perhaps from Mal. 3:2.

n. Mal. 4:5-6

the mouth and grinds his teeth, and he is wasting away. And I told your disciples, hoping that they might cast it out, but they were not up to the task." [19]And answering them, he says, "O unbelieving nation! How long till I am free of you? How long must I endure you? Bring him to me." [20]And seeing him, at once the spirit hurled him off his feet, and falling to the ground, he writhed and foamed. [21]And he questioned his father, "How long is it since this befell him?" And he said, "From childhood. [22]And frequently it has thrown him both into the fire and into the water to destroy him. But if you can do anything, help us and have mercy on us." [23]And Jesus said to him, "If I can? All things are possible to the one who believes!" [24]At once crying out, the father of the child said, "I'm trying to believe. Help my unbelief!" [25]And Jesus, seeing that a crowd was running together, rebuked the unclean spirit: "Now it is I who command you! Come on out of him. And you may no more enter into him." [26]And crying out, and causing a frenzy of convulsions, it came out at last. And he lay there like a corpse, giving rise to the rumor that he died, [27]but Jesus, grasping his hand, raised him. And he stood up. [28]And when he entered into a house, his disciples questioned him privately, "Why were we unable to cast it out?" [29]And he told them, "This particular species can come out by means of nothing but prayer. *And if that doesn't work, fasting.*"[o]

[30]And setting out from there, they made their way through the Galilee, and he did not want anyone to know, [31]because he was concentrating his teaching on his disciples, and he told them, "This is the way of things: a man is delivered into the hands of his fellow men and they will kill him, and once killed, after three days, he will rise up." [32]But they did not understand the saying and were afraid to question him further.

[33]And they arrived in the village of Nahum. And at home, he questioned them, "What was it I heard you debating on the road?" [34]And they were silent because, in fact, what they had been arguing about on the road was who ranked highest. [35]And sitting down, he called out for the twelve and says to them, "If anyone wants to be first, he shall end up last of all, even a servant of all." [36]And taking a child, he set it in the midst of them; and enfolding it in his arms, he said to them, [37]"Whoever welcomes one of these children on account of my name welcomes me; and whoever welcomes me, welcomes not me but the one who commissioned me."[p]

[38]John said to him, "Teacher, we caught someone casting out de-

---

o. Just as Elisha succeeded and Gehazi failed simply because he was not Elisha (2 Kings 4:32-35), so here Jesus is the irreplaceable hero of the story.

p. This passage and its parallels go back to the Pentateuchal disputes pitting

mons using your name even though he is not one of our circle. So we told him that, since he was not one of our group, he must cease and desist." [39]But Jesus said, "Why on earth did you forbid him? Do you think someone who is using my name to perform miracles is likely to be one of my critics? [40]For I count anyone who is not actually opposing us as one of our friends. We have few enough of them. [41]All they have to do is offer you a cup of water to drink in the name of your being Christ's, and Amen: I tell you, there is no way they will not be rewarded for it.[q]

[42]"And whoever scandalizes one of these new converts, it is good for him instead to have his head put through the center hole of a heavy millstone and be dumped overboard.

[43]"And speaking of being scandalized, if you find your grasping hand leading you into moral scandal, cut it off! It is good for you to enter the life maimed rather than going off into the Valley of Hinnom with both hands, into the fire that can never be extinguished. [44]*There the feasting maggots never die and the fire is continually replenished.* [45]And should your interloping foot lead you to scandalous behavior, cut it off! It is good for you to hobble into the life, rather than to plunge with both feet into the Valley of Hinnom. [46]*There the devouring maggots never die, and the fires are always stoked.* [47]And if your covetous eye scandalizes you, throw it away! It is good for you to enter into the kingdom of God with one eye if the alternative is being thrown, eyes wide open, into the Valley of Hinnom, [48]where the maggots ever gnaw and the fire continually rages.[r] [49]For I tell you this: every one of the damned will be salted over the fire by Moloch the devourer.

[50]"Salt tastes good, but suppose the salt were to lose its tang? What else could you possibly use to season salt? Become seasoned here and now, so you will not be salted over the fire. And no more arguing with each other!"

10

[1]And rising up to leave, he arrives in the boundaries of Judea and the Transjordan, and once more crowds accompany him, and he taught them again, as was his custom. [2]And Pharisees, approaching him, asked his opinion on whether it is legal for a husband to send away a wife, seeking

---

Moses against Aaron and Miriam (Num. 12), Dathan and Abiram (Num. 16), and it is Moses's meekness that qualifies him for leadership.

q. This is drawn directly from Num. 11:24-30.

r. Isa. 66:24

to gauge him. [3]Answering, he said to them, "What did Moses command you Jews? [4]And they said, "Moses permitted a husband to draw up papers and to send a wife away." [5]And Jesus said to them, "He condescended to your insensitivity when he wrote you this commandment. [6]But the pattern of creation is this: 'Male and female he created them.' [7]And 'this is why a man will leave father and mother, [8]and the two shall be one flesh.' This means they are no longer two but one flesh. [9]So then, if God has yoked them together, let no mere mortal divide them." [10]And back in their lodging, the disciples questioned him about this. [11]And he says to them, "Whoever sends his wife away to marry another commits adultery against her. [12]And if she, having sent her husband away, marries another, she commits adultery."

[13]And they brought children to him, hoping he would touch them and utter some blessing, but the disciples rebuffed them. [14]But seeing it, Jesus became furious and said to them, "Let the children come to me! What is the matter with you? Do not stop them. Don't you know them? These are the very angels of the kingdom of God! [15]Amen: I tell you, whoever does not welcome the kingdom of God when it comes to him in the form of a child will be forever excluded from it." [16]And enfolding them in his arms, he blesses them with the laying on of hands.[s]

[17]And as he embarked on the road again, one runs up to him and kneels before him and questioned him: "Good teacher, what may I do that I may inherit age-long life when I die?" [18]And Jesus said to him, "Just a moment, if you please. Why do you call me 'good'? No one is good except one: God. [19]And why ask me? Surely you already know the ten commandments: Do not murder, Do not commit adultery, Do not steal, Do not testify falsely, Do not defraud, Take care of your father and mother. Well?" [20]But he said to him, "Teacher, I observed all these since I was young." [21]But seeing his perplexity, Jesus' heart went out to him, and he said to him, "You lack one thing. Go, sell what you own and give the price to the poor, and then you will have the treasure in heaven that you seek. And come follow me." [22]But he, crestfallen at this counsel, went away grieving at what he must do, for he had many possessions to disburse. [23]And looking around at his disciples, Jesus says to them, "You see? How painful it will be for those who have riches to enter into the kingdom of God!" [24]And the disciples were amazed at what he said. And

s. This is part of an infant baptism liturgy, as demonstrated by Oscar Cullmann, *Baptism in the New Testament*, transl. J.K.S. Reid (Chicago: Allenson, 1956), 71-80, and suggested in part by 2 Kings 4:26-27.

Jesus, explaining again, says to them, "You think like children. How hard it is to enter into the kingdom of God! [25]It is easier for a camel to pass through the hole of a needle than for a rich man to enter into the kingdom of God. *And if you neglect to forgive, your Father up in the heavens will likewise neglect to forgive your transgressions.*" [26]At this, their astonishment went off the scale, and they reflected, "If even God's favorites cannot enter heaven, then who can save himself?" [27]Looking at them, Jesus says, "True, for mortals impossible! But not for God. And when you pray, why should you doubt? For all things are possible for God!"

[28]Then Peter began to say to him, "As you see, we have abandoned everything and have followed you." [29]Jesus said, "Amen: I tell you, there is no one who has abandoned dwelling or brothers or sisters or mother or father or children or farms for the sake of me and for the sake of the news, [30]unless he receives, now in this time, a hundred times as many dwellings and brothers and sisters and mothers and children and farms after the persecutions are over, and in the coming time, age-long life. [31]But many of the first will wind up last and vice versa."[t]

[32]Now they were going up the mountain road to Jerusalem, and Jesus was walking ahead of them; and they marveled at him going there, and the ones following were afraid of what might transpire there. And taking the twelve aside once again, he began to tell them the things about to happen to him: [33]"Behold, these are the days when a man will be delivered up to the archpriests and to the scribes, and they will sentence him to death and will deliver him up to the gentiles, [34]and they will jeer at him and spit on him and flog him and will kill him, and after three days he will stand up again."

And they arrive at Beth-Anu. And a particular woman whose brother had died was there. And coming, she knelt down before Jesus and says to him, 'Son of David, have mercy on me!' But the disciples rebuffed her. And Jesus, becoming furious, went off with her into the garden where the tomb was, and at once a great noise was heard from the tomb. And approaching it, Jesus rolled away the stone from the door of the tomb. And at once entering in where the youth was, he extended his hand and raised him up, grasping his hand. But the youth, looking upon him, loved him and started pleading with him that he might accompany him. And going out of the tomb they entered into the dwelling of the youth, for he was

t. This is an important qualification. It suggests that the summons to give up family, home, and loved ones anticipates persecution for principle rather than elective poverty.

rich. And after six days, Jesus instructed him, and in the evening the youth comes to him, wearing a linen sheet over his bare body. And he stayed with him that night, naked man with naked man, for Jesus was teaching him the mystery of the kingdom of God. And getting up to leave, he returned to the other side of the Jordan.[u]

Salome asked, "How long will death have dominion?" And Jesus replied, saying, "As long as you women bear children." And she asked, "So I have done well in bearing no children?" Jesus answered and says to her, "Eat every plant, but do not eat that which leaves a bitter taste. I have come to undo the deeds of the female." Salome asked, "Lord, when will these things be?" He says to her, "When you have trodden underfoot the garment of shame and when the two become one and the male with the female is neither male nor female."[v]

[35]And Jacob and John, the two sons of Zebediah, made their way to
him, saying to him, "Teacher, we wish that whatever we ask you, you
will do for us." [36]And he said to them, "Oh really? What is it you want of
me? What can I do for you?" [37]And they said to him, "Just this: grant us
that we may sit, one to the right of you and one to the left, in your regime." [38]But Jesus said to them, "You have no idea what it is you are asking. Are you capable of drinking the cup which I am to drink? Or of being
baptized with that baptism with which I am to be baptized?" [39]And they
said to him, "We can do it." But Jesus said to them, "So be it! The cup I
am to drink, you shall indeed drink. The baptism with which I am to be
baptized: you too shall be baptized with it. [40]Nonetheless, to sit to the
right of me or to the left is not my favor to grant. That privilege is reserved for someone else to decide."[w] [41]And overhearing this, the other ten
became furious with Jacob and John. [42]And Jesus summoned them, and
he says to them, "You know how those who aim to rule the gentiles lord

u. So reads the Secret Gospel of Mark, according to Morton Smith, who interpreted this controversial passage to imply a secret ritual involving naked baptism. See his *Clement of Alexandria and a Secret Gospel of Mark* (Cambridge: Harvard University Press, 1973).

v. This dialogue is easily reconstructed from the Gospel according to the Egyptians, as quoted by Clement of Alexandria in his *Stromateis*. Stephan Hermann Huller *(Against Polycarp*, 114) suggests the Gospel according to the Egyptians was an alternate title for the Secret Gospel of Mark. Another Gospel according to the Egyptians, discovered at Nag Hammadi, is distinguished by its other title, The Holy Book of the Great Invisible Spirit.

w. This comes from 2 Kings 2:9-10, "Ask what I shall do for you before I am taken from you." Hearing the request, Elijah reflects, "You have asked a hard thing," just as Jesus warns Jacob and John.

it over them? How their grandees wield authority over them? [43]And is it not the same with you Jews? But whoever wants to be great among you shall be your servant. [44]And whoever wants to be first among you shall be slave to all. [45]For man, too, was not created to be served, but to serve,[x] to spend his life for the sake of many."

[46]And they reach Jericho. *And the sister of the youth whom Jesus loved and his mother and Salome were there, and Jesus did not welcome them.*[y] And as he, with his disciples and a sizable crowd, was leaving Jericho, the son of Timaeus, or Bar-Timaeus, a blind beggar,[z] sat at the side of the road. [47]And hearing that it was Jesus the Nazarene, he saw his chance and began to shout and say, "Son of David, Jesus! Have mercy on me!" [48]And many rebuked him and told him to be quiet. But this only made him shout the louder: "Son of David, have mercy on me!" [49]Jesus stopped and said, "Call him." And they call the blind man, saying to him, "You're in luck! He is calling for you. Get up!" [50]So flinging aside his garment and springing up,[a] he came to Jesus. [51]And answering him at last, Jesus said, "What do you want? What can I do for you?" And the blind man said to him, "My rabbi, my wish is that I may see again!" [52]And Jesus said to him, "You may leave now. Your own faith has healed you." And at once he recovered his sight and followed him along the road.[b]

11

[1]And when they come close to Jerusalem, to Beth-Phage and Beth-Anu before the Mount of Olives, he assigns two of his disciples [2]and tells them, "Go into the village over there, and as soon as you enter into it you will discover a colt tethered, one on which no one has ever sat. Untie it and bring it back. [3]And should anyone say to you, 'What do you think you are doing?' reply, 'The Lord requires it, and he means to send it back here at once.'" [4]And they went and found a colt tethered to a door outside on the open street, and they free it. [5]And some of those standing there

---

x. Gen. 2:15, "to tend God's garden."

y. The Secret Gospel of Mark adds this line, according to Morton Smith.

z. The Aramaic form of the name is *Bar-teymah,* "son of poverty," which means he is a "narrative man"—his name a fictional device.

a. Isa. 35:6

b. This may originally have been an exorcism story. Note the elements of silencing someone who reveals knowledge of Jesus' true nature, only to be cured to keep him from blabbing. "What do you want me to do for you?" seems utterly beside the point here. The line may have been copied from the nearby Jacob and John request story and added here.

said to them, "What do you think you are you doing, freeing the colt?"
[6]And they replied as Jesus said, and they let them go.[c]

[7]And they bring the colt to Jesus, and they throw their garments on
it, and he sat on it. [8]And many strewed their garments in the road, and
others scattered switches cut from the fields. [9]And those going before and
following shouted out: "Hosanna! Blessed in the name of Adonai be the
Coming One![d] [10]Blessed be the coming kingdom of our father David! Let
hosannas ring in the highest spheres!" [11]And he went into Jerusalem into
the temple, and looking around at everything, the hour now being late, he
left and went back to Beth-Anu with the twelve.

[12]And the next day, as they were leaving Beth-Anu, he felt hungry.
[13]And noticing at a distance a fig tree in leaf, he went to see: will he find
anything on it? And coming up to it, he found nothing but leaves for it
was not the season for figs. [14]And answering this affront, he said, "May
no one ever eat fruit from you forever!" And his disciples overheard
this.

[15]And they arrive at the temple. And going into the temple, he started
ejecting the sellers and the buyers stationed in the temple, and he upended
the currency exchange tables and the chairs of those selling doves. [16]And
he did not permit anyone to carry a single sacrificial vessel through the
temple.[e] [17]And he taught and said to them, "Is it not written, 'My house
shall be called a house of prayer for all the nations[f] but you have made it a
robbers' cave'?"[g] [18]And the archpriests and the scribes heard it, and they
looked for a way to eliminate him for they were afraid of him because all
the crowd of pilgrims were enthused at his teaching.

[19]And when it grew late, they made their way back outside the city.
[20]And passing along the same route early the next morning, they noticed
the fig tree withered up from the roots. [21]And recalling Jesus' words the
day before, Peter says to him, "Rabbi, look! The fig tree which you

---

c. This story derives from 1 Sam. 9.

d. This is based on the entrance liturgy of Pss. 118:26-27, in which "he who comes in the name of the Lord" refers to any pilgrim.

e. The cleansing of the temple must have in view Malachi's messenger of the covenant purifying the sons of Levi (Mal. 3:1-3; cf. Mark 1:2; 9:3), as well as the oracle of Zechariah: "And there shall no longer be a trader in the house of the Lord of hosts on that day" (Zech. 14:21b). It is not unlikely that we also have a memory of Simon bar-Gioras clearing the temple of John of Gischala's band of thieves on the eve of the temple's destruction.

f. Isa. 56:7

g. Jer. 7:11

cursed has dried up. What a coincidence!"[h] 22And answering, Jesus says to them, "Have faith in God. 23Amen: I tell you, that whoever says to this mountain,[i] 'Up and into the sea with you,' and does not doubt in his heart, but believes that what he says happens, it will be granted to him. 24In view of that, I tell you, all things for which you pray and ask, believe they are yours, and your request will be granted you. 25And when you stand in prayer, forgive if you have anything against anyone in order that your Father in the heavens may also forgive you your transgressions."

27And they arrive at Jerusalem again. And as he was walking in the temple, the archpriests and the scribes and the elders come to him 28and said to him, "By what authorization do you do these things? Who authorized your actions?" 29But Jesus said to them, "First let me question you on one matter. You answer me and I will be glad to tell you the authorization for my actions. 30Remember the baptism of John? Was it authorized by God in heaven or only by mortals? Answer me that." 31And they huddled debating, whispering, "It's a trap. If we say 'from heaven,' he will surely say, 'Then why didn't you believe in him when you had the chance?' 32But do we really want to say, 'from mortal men'?" They were afraid of the listening crowd for everyone held that John was really a prophet. 33So answering Jesus they say, "We have not yet reached a conclusion on that." And Jesus says to them, "Well, if you refuse to tell me what you really think, neither can I tell you the authority behind my actions."

12

1And he started to speak to them in parables. "A man planted a vineyard and erected a hedge around it and dug a wine press and put up a tower, and he leased it out to sharecroppers and went away.[j] 2And at the right time he sent a slave to the sharecroppers so that he might collect from the sharecroppers his due from the produce of the vineyard. 3And grabbing him, they beat him and sent him away empty handed. 4And again the following year, he sent to them another slave. That one they gave a head wound and humiliated. 5And still another he sent. That one they killed. And they treated many others likewise, beating some, killing others. 6He had one left, a beloved son. He sent him to them last, saying, 'Surely they will pay my son due respect.' 7But those sharecroppers conspired: 'The old man must be dead. This one is his heir. Come, let us kill

h. Based on Pss. 37:35-36.

i. This would be Mt. Zion.

j. Isa. 5:1-7

him, and the inheritance will pass to us!' [8]And grabbing him, they killed
him and threw him outside the vineyard. [9]What will the lord of the vineyard do? I'll tell you what. He will come in person and will massacre the
sharecroppers, and he will give the vineyard to others. [10]Didn't you read
this scripture? 'A stone which the contractors deemed unusable, this very
one became the cornerstone. [11]This was from the Lord, and we regard it
as a marvel.'"[k] [12]And they looked for a chance to apprehend him, but
they were afraid of the crowd, for they were well aware that he aimed the
parable at them. So they left him, making a judicious retreat.

[13]And they send some of the Pharisees and some of Herod's agents to
trick him into saying something incriminating. [14]And coming, they say to
him, "Teacher, we know that you are frank and that no one intimidates
you. So then, is it legal to pay tribute to Caesar or not? May we pay or
may we not pay?" [15]But aware of their duplicity, he said to them, "Why
put me on the spot? Bring me a denarius that I may see it." [16]And they
fetched one. And he says to them, "Whose is this image and epigraph?"
And they answered him, "Caesar's, of course." [17]"So," Jesus said to
them, "give Caesar's coins to Caesar in taxes and God's coins to God in
the temple."[l] And they were flabbergasted at him.

[18]Next some Syndics come to him, who say there is no resurrection,
and they questioned him saying, [19]"Teacher, Moses wrote that if anyone's brother should die leaving a wife behind and not leaving a child, his
brother may take his wife and may beget heirs for his brother. [20]Suppose
there were seven brothers and the oldest took a wife and, dying, left no
heirs. [21]And the second oldest married her and died, failing to leave behind heirs, and the third similarly. [22]In the end, none of the seven left
heirs. [23]And last of all, the woman died. [23]In this 'resurrection,' when all
of them get up again, which one of them will she be wife to? After all, all
seven of them had her as their wife at one time or another." [24]Jesus said
to them, "Isn't this why you're mistaken? Because you are ignorant of
scripture and do not take into account the power of God? [25]For when
they get up again from the dead, neither do men marry, nor are women
given in marriage, but they are like angels in the heavens. [26]And didn't
you read in the scroll of Moses at the passage about the burning bush
how God spoke to him, saying, 'I, the God of Abraham and God of Isaac

k. Pss. 118:22-23

l. The infamous money-changing tables were there so pilgrims could trade Roman coins, with their "idolatrous" image of Caesar, for Hebrew and Phoenician coins.

and God of Jacob'? [27]He is not a God of corpses but of living men! You are all mixed up!"

[28]And one of the scribes, who had approached and heard them engaged in debate, realizing that he answered them well, put his own question to him: "What commandment is primary over all others?" [29]Jesus answered, "Number one is, 'Hear this, Israel: Adonai our God is one lord, [30]and you shall love Adonai your God from your whole heart and with your whole soul and your whole mind and your whole strength.' [31]And this is number two: 'You shall love your neighbor as yourself.' Greater than these, there are no other commandments." [32]And the scribe said to him, "Well said, teacher! You speak the simple truth when you say that there is one and there is not another beside him; [33]and to love him from the whole heart and the whole understanding and the whole of one's strength, and to love the neighbor as oneself, is better than all the burnt carcasses and sacrifices stipulated in scripture." [34]And Jesus, seeing that he answered insightfully, said to him, "You haven't far to go before you reach the kingdom of God." And no one dared question him anymore.

[35]So Jesus turned the tables and said as he was teaching in the temple, "How can the scribes teach that the Christ is a son of David? [36]David himself said with the voice of the Holy Spirit, 'Adonai said to my lord, Sit at my right till I put the necks of your enemies under your feet.' [37]If David himself calls him 'lord,' where do they get the idea he is his son?" And the great crowd was delighted to hear him make the scribes squirm.

[38]And in the course of his teaching he warned them, "Watch out for the scribes, the ones who love to walk around in flowing robes and to receive deferential greetings in the marketplaces, [39]and to be shown to the front-row seats in the synagogues and the head table at formal dinners, [40]all the while hungrily repossessing the houses of the widows and making long prayers for show. These will receive more severe judgment than common sinners."

[41]And sitting across from the temple treasury, he watched how the crowd tosses coppers into the treasury box, and many of the wealthy put in much. [42]And one poor widow, coming up to the box, threw in two lepta, which add up to a quadrans. [43]And summoning his disciples, he said to them, "Amen: I tell you, that this poor widow put in more than all who were tossing coins into the treasury combined; [44]for all the rest gave out of their abundance, but she gave, in her penury, everything she had, her entire living."[m]

m. This anecdote does not form an integral part of the Passion narrative.

13

[1]And as he made his way out of the temple, one of his disciples says
to him, "Teacher, have you ever seen such huge stones and such huge
buildings?" [2]And Jesus said to him, "Look at these great buildings while
you can, for there is no way any pair of these stones will remain together
amid the rubble." [3]And once he took a seat on the Mount of Olives across
from the temple, Peter and Jacob and John and Andreas elicited from him
a private revelation:[n] [4]"Tell us, when will these things be? And what is
the sign that all these prophecies are on the verge of fulfillment?" [5]And
Jesus began his answer: "Watch out that no one deceives you in this matter. [6]Many will appear trading on my name, saying, 'It is I! And with this
tactic they will mislead many. [7]But when you hear of wars and rumors of
more distant wars, do not worry: it is destined to happen, but the end has
not yet arrived.[o] [8]For nation will be pitted against nation and kingdom
against kingdom. There will be earthquakes in far-flung places. There
will be famines. And yet these mark only the onset of labor pains.[p] [9]But
look to yourselves! They will deliver you up to Sanhedrins and you will
be beaten in synagogues. And you will stand before governors and kings
on account of me in order to testify before them. [10]And first the news
must be proclaimed to all the nations. [11]And when they lead you before
the authorities, do not bother formulating beforehand what you will say,
but whatever comes to you on the spot, say it. For you are not the speakers, but the Holy Spirit. [12]And a brother will betray a brother to death,
and a father a child, and children will rise up against parents and will execute them.[q] [13]And you will be hated by all on account of my name. But
the one enduring to the end without renouncing my name, only such a
one will save himself.

Mark placed it here because he knew of but one trip of Jesus to Jerusalem. Whoever coined this brief episode simply felt it natural that Jesus should be found at the temple.

n. A "private revelation" may signal material nobody actually remembered Jesus having said. In 1864 Timothee Colani realized this portion of Mark (13:5-31) constituted a "little apocalypse," which was composed prior to Mark from various pieces of Jewish scripture. Eusebius mentions a "revelation" that alerted Christians to flee Jerusalem just before its fall to the Romans (*Ecclesiastical History* 3:5), and Colani surmised this must be what Mark eventually incorporated into his gospel. See Timothee Colani, "The Little Apocalypse of Mark 13," trans. Nancy Wilson, *Journal of Higher Criticism* 10 (Spring 2003): 41-47.

o. Dan. 2:28

p. Isa. 19:2; 2 Chron. 15:6

q. Mic. 7:6

[14]“Only once you behold the abomination of desolation[r] standing where it must not be—may the reader understand the reference—then let those in Judea flee to the mountains.[s] [15]Anyone on the roof: let him not try to retrieve anything, just climb down the fire escape and flee! [16]And the one working in the field when that hour strikes, let him not even return to the house to retrieve his garment. [17]And pity those with a child in the womb and those nursing in those days. [18]But pray that it may not strike in winter, [19]because those days will witness tribulation the like of which has not befallen mankind since the very beginning of the creation which God created until the present and which will never be repeated.[t] [20]In fact, if not for Adonai shortening the allotted days, no flesh at all would be preserved alive. [21]And at that point, if anyone says to you, ‘Look! Here he is. The Christ! Look there!’ do not believe it. [22]But pseudo-messiahs and pseudo-prophets will be brought in, and they will perform signs and wonders for the purpose of seducing the chosen people astray if at all possible.[u] [23]But you know better, since I have told you all about it in advance. [24]But in those days, after that tribulation, the sun will go dark and the moon will withhold her light, [25]and the stars will be falling out of the sky[v] and the Angelic Powers in heaven will be shaken.[w] [26]And then they will see one like a son of man coming in cloud chariots with much power and brilliance.[x] [27]And then he will send out the angels and they will gather together the chosen people, Israel, from the four winds, from the rim of the earth to the rim of the sky.[y]

[28]“But from the fig tree, learn the parable: as soon as its branch grows tender and puts forth leaves, you know that the summer is near. [29]So you also must recognize, when these things transpire, it is knocking at the doors. [30]Amen: I tell you, in answer to your question, the present generation will by no means pass away until these things all happen. [31]The sky and the earth will pass away, but my predictions will not fail. [32]But as to that specific day or hour, no one knows that, neither the angels in heaven nor the son, except the Father. [33]Look, be watchful, be-

r. Dan. 8:13

s. Dan. 9:27; 12:11; Gen. 19:17

t. Dan. 12:1

u. Deut. 13:2

v. Isa. 13:10

w. Isa. 34:4

x. Dan. 7:13

y. Zech. 2:10; Deut. 30:4

cause you do not know when the crucial moment is. [34]It is just like a man
away from home, who gives his slaves the authority, to each his task, and
commands the doorkeeper to stand watch. [35]Therefore, you watch! Because you do not know when the master of the house comes, whether late
or at midnight or cock-crow or early. [36]Do not let him come suddenly
and find you napping. [37]And my warning is not just for you. I say to all:
Watch!"

14

[1]And it was the Passover and the Feast of Unleavened Bread in two
days. And the archpriests and the scribes looked for a way to seize him by
stealth and to kill him; [2]because they said, "Not during the feast, so as to
avoid rioting among the people."

[3]And when he was reclining at table in Beth-Anu in the house of Simon the leper, a woman came with an alabaster jar of pure muskroot
ointment, very costly. Breaking the alabaster jar, she poured it over his
head. [4]But some were privately angry, whispering to one another: "What
justifies this waste of the ointment? [5]For wasn't it possible for this ointment to be sold for upward of three hundred denarii, and the price given
to the poor?" And they grumbled about her. [6]But Jesus said, "Let her be!
Why do you give her trouble? She has done a fine thing for me. [7]After all,
you have the poor with you all the time, but this is a special occaision.
[8]She did what she had available; she undertook to anoint my body beforehand for the entombment. [9]Amen: I tell you, wherever the news is
heralded in all the world, what this woman did will also be told, so she
will be remembered."[z] [10]And Judas the False One, that one of the twelve,
went off to the archpriests intending to deliver him up to them. [11]And
hearing his offer, they rejoiced and promised to give him silver. And he
looked for a likely opportunity to deliver him up.

[12]And on the first day of unleavened bread when they sacrificed the
Passover lamb, his disciples say to him, "Where do you want us to go and
prepare for you to eat the Passover seder?" [13]And he sends two of his disciples and tells them, "Go into the city and someone carrying a pitcher of
water will meet you. Follow him, [14]and wherever he enters, tell the inn-
keeper, 'Our master asks, Where is the room I reserved where I may eat
the Passover seder with my disciples?'" [15]And he will show you a large
second-story room, already spread and ready. It is there you will prepare
the meal for us." [16]And the disciples departed and went into the city and

---

z. Thus her name must have been omitted from the story as we now read it.

found things just as he told them, and they prepared the Passover seder.[a]

[17]With evening falling, he arrives with the rest of the twelve. [18]And as they were reclining and eating, Jesus said, "Amen: I tell you, one of you will deliver me up, one of you eating with me." [19]They went into shock and said to him, each in turn, "Not I!" [20]But he said to them, "One of the twelve, one dipping his bread with me in the dish, [21]for indeed one goes when his preordained time comes, but woe to that individual through whose agency one is delivered up. It would be good for him not to have been born in the first place."

[22]And as they were eating, taking a loaf and blessing it, he broke it and gave it to them and said, "Take it, this is my body." [23]And taking a cup and giving thanks, he gave it to them, and all drank of it. [24]And he said to them, "This is my blood of the *new* covenant being shed for many.[b] [25]Amen: I pledge to you, no more by any means will I drink of the fruit of the vine until that day when I drink it anew with you in the kingdom of God."

[26]And having sung a hymn, they went out to the Mount of Olives. [27]And as they walked Jesus says to them, "All of you will be scandalized. I know because it is written, 'I will strike down the shepherd and the sheep will panic.'[c] [28]But after my raising up, I will precede you into the Galilee." [29]But Peter said to him, "Even if all shall be scandalized, yet not I!"[d] [30]And Jesus says to him, "Amen: I say, as for you, today this very night before a rooster sounds twice, you will repudiate me three times." [31]But he only insisted the more emphatically, "If I should have to die at your side, there is no way I will repudiate you!"[e]

[32]And they arrive at a plot of ground called Gethsemane, and he says to his disciples, "Sit here till I am done praying." [33]And he takes Peter and Jacob and John with him, and was suddenly overcome with astonishment and distress.[f] [34]And he says to them, "My soul is in mortal dread of imminent death. You stay here on guard." [35]And going on a bit further, he

a. This story is based on 1 Sam. 9. The upper room of the Last Supper may hark back to the second-story rooms provided by benefactors for Elijah (1 Kings 17:19) and Elisha (2 Kings 4:10).

b. Exod. 24:8

c. It seems Zech. 13:7 is the whole source for the subsequent scene where Jesus' disciples flee from the arresting party.

d. 2 Kings 2:2, 4, 6

e. 1 Sam. 15:21

f. His inexplicable distress comes as if in response to an unexpected revelation.

dropped to the ground and prayed that if possible the hour of doom might pass from him; [36]and he said, "*Abba,* Father, all is possible to you: let this cup pass me by for another.[g] But not what I want, but what you want."

[37]And he comes back and finds them sleeping, and he says to Peter, "Sleeping are you, Simon? Could you not keep guard for a single hour? [38]The three of you, keep watch and pray that you do not come to the test. Granted, the spirit is eager enough, but the flesh is weak." [39]And going away again, he prayed the same thing, [40]only to find them sleeping again once he returned, for they could not keep their eyes open. And they did not know what to say for themselves. [41]And he comes the third time and says to them, "Finish your nap and relax, you've had enough rest. The hour has arrived—behold, yours truly is delivered into the hands of sinners. [42]Get up! Let us go. The one handing me over has come near."

[43]And at once, while he was still speaking, Judas arrives, one of the twelve, and with him a mob with swords and clubs sent from the archpriests and the scribes and the elders. [44]Now the one handing him over had given them a signal, saying, "Whomever I kiss on the cheek is the one you want. Seize him and lead him away securely." [45]And coming at once to the fore, he approaches him and says, "Rabbi!" and gave him a friendly kiss. [46]And at this they laid hands on him and grabbed him. [47]But a particular bystander, drawing the sword, struck the slave of the archpriest but managed only to cut off an ear.

[48]And answering, Jesus said to them, "You came out to arrest me with swords and clubs as against some desperado? [49]Every day I was with you, teaching in the temple, and you did not apprehend me, but it happened this way so scripture could be fulfilled." [50]And at this, his disciples abandoned him, all of them fleeing. [51]And one particular youth had accompanied him dressed with a linen sheet over his bare body, and they grab him, too, [52]but abandoning the linen sheet he escaped their clutches and ran away naked.[h]

---

g. J. Duncan M. Derrett, "The Prayer in Gethsemane," *Journal of Higher Criticism* 4 (Spring 1997): 78-88.

h. The basis of this whole scene can be found in 2 Sam. 15-16. There, a weeping David, fleeing from his usurping son Absalom (a Judas figure), heads up the Mount of Olives and sends three of his allies (15:27, LXX) back to Jerusalem. David finds himself mocked and harassed by one Shimei, who curses the fallen king. David's man Abishai offers to chop off the mocker's head, but David prevents him, musing that God must have bidden Shimei to curse him. As they slink along in silence, Shimei continues to pelt the refugees with rocks. Here we find more elements underlying Mark's story. Abishai is the prototype of the disciple who at-

[53]And they marched Jesus away to the archpriest, and all the archpriests and the elders and the scribes assemble. [54]And Peter followed him
at a safe distance until he made it inside the courtyard of the archpriest,
and he was sitting among the attendants and warming himself by the
light. [55]Now the archpriests and the whole Sanhedrin tried to marshal
testimony against Jesus to execute him, but they were unsuccessful.[i]
[56]Many indeed lied under oath against him, but their testimonies were
not consistent. [57]And some, standing up, perjured against him, saying,
[58]"We heard him saying, 'I myself will throw down this handmade holy
place, and for three days I will build another, not handmade.'" [59]And
even at that, the details of their testimonies did not match up.

[60]Finally, standing up in the middle of the council, the archpriest interrogated Jesus, saying, "Have you no rejoinder to what these men allege against you?" [61]But he was silent and said nothing in answer.[j] Again
the archpriest interrogated him and says to him, "You are the Christ, the
son of the Blessed One." [62]And Jesus said, "If you say so. And all of you
will see one like a son of man taking his seat to the right of Shaddai, arriving with the cloud chariots of the sky."[k] [63]But the archpriest, ripping his
tunic, says, "Who needs witnesses? [64]You heard the blasphemy with your
own ears! How does the case appear to you?" And they all judged him

---

tempts to behead Malchus in the arresting party. Shimei, another form of Shimeon or Simon, is a prototype for the Simon who denies Jesus repeatedly, Shimei's stony missiles suggesting "Peter," as well. God having assigned Shimei to utter curses on David has become Jesus' prediction of Peter's denials, as well as Peter's calling down curses on himself (or on Jesus) in the high priest's courtyard (14:71).

What of Jesus' prayer? The way it is reported, no one was on hand to listen to it, but it was derived from one of the traditional Passover hymns, which Jesus implicitly sings at the close of the supper: "My distress was bitter. In panic I cried, 'How faithless all men are!'... I will take in my hand the cup of salvation and invoke the Lord by name.... A precious thing in the Lord's eyes is the death of those who die faithful to him" (Pss. 116:10-15).

Judas's betraying kiss (vv. 44-45) would seem to derive from 2 Sam. 20:7-10, where Joab, backed up by armed men, greets Amasa as a brother, kisses him, then stabs him. The origin of the fleeing young man who loses his sole garment to escape naked (v. 51) is probably Amos 2:16: "And he who is stout of heart among the mighty shall flee away naked in that day," the reference to "that day" sounding like a good prediction of the momentous day of Jesus' Passion.

i. Mark borrowed from Dan. 6:4, LXX, for a scene involving a crossfire of false accusations: "The governors and satraps sought (εζετουν) to find (ευρειν) occasion against Daniel, but they found against him no accusation."

j. Isa. 50:7; 53:7

k. Dan. 7:13-14

worthy of death. [65]At this, some started spitting at him and veiling his face and abusing him and saying to him, "Prophesy!" And the attendants did him homage with their fists.[l]

[66]And with Peter below in the courtyard, one of the archpriest's serving maids comes down from the council chamber, [67]and noticing Peter warming himself she scrutinizes him and says, "You, too, were with the Nazarene sectarian Jesus." [68]But he denied it, saying, "I have no idea what you're talking about!" And he left to go back outside into the forecourt. [69]And the serving maid, noticing him go, started to tell the bystanders again, "This man is one of them!" [70]But again he denied it. And again a little later, the bystanders said to Peter, "In fact, you are one of them! For you are a Galilean!" [71]And he started to damn and swear: "I do not know this person you speak about!" [72]And at once a second rooster crow sounded. And Peter recalled what Jesus said to him, "Before a rooster sounds a second time, you will repudiate me three times." And thinking about it, he cried.

15

[1]And at once, early in the morning, the archpriests met in session with the elders and the scribes and all the Sanhedrin; and having tied Jesus up, they led him away and delivered him to Pilatus. [2]And Pilatus interrogated him: "So you are the king of the Jews." And answering him, he says, "If you say so." [3]And the archpriests accused him of many things. [4]But Pilatus interrogated him, saying, "You offer no rejoinder? See how many things they accuse you of." [5]But Jesus answered nothing more,[m] which amazed Pilatus. [6]Now at festival time, he used to release to them any single prisoner they petitioned for. [7]Now there was one called Bar-Abbas, chained with the rebels who had committed murder in the rebellion. [8]And the crowd approached and began to ask him to do for them as he usually did. [9]But Pilatus answered them, saying, "Do you want me to release to you the king of the Jews?" [10]For he was well aware the archpriests had delivered him up out of mere envy. [11]But the archpriests incited the crowd to clamor for the release of Bar-Abbas to them instead. [12]So Pilatus answering again said to them, "What then am I to do with the one you call the king of the Jews?" [13]Again they shouted, "Crucify

---

l. This passage constitutes a rewriting of 1 Kings 22:24, "Then Zedekiah the son of Chenaanah came near and *struck Micaiah on the cheek,* and said, 'How did the spirit of the Lord go from me to speak to you?' And Micaiah said, 'Behold, *you shall see* on that day when you go into an inner chamber to hide yourself.'"

m. Isa. 50:7; 53:7

him!" 14Pilatus said to them, "But really, what evil did he do?" But they shouted all the more, "Crucify him!" 15Pilatus, judging it best to yield to their demands, released Bar-Abbas to them and delivered Jesus up, having him whipped to be crucified.

16The soldiers marched him off inside the courtyard, which is called the praetorium, and they call together the entire cohort. 17And they put the royal purple on him and put a wreath of acanthus leaves on his head. 18And they began to salute him, "Hail, King of the Jews!" 19And they hit him over the head with a reed scepter and spat at him and, bending the knee, bowed before him. 20And when they were done tormenting him, they removed the royal purple from him and put his own garments on him again. And they march him off to crucify him. 21And they commandeer a particular passerby, Simon, a Cyrenian,[n] coming in from the fields, the father of Alexander and of Rufus, that he should bear his cross. 22And they carry him to the place Golgotha, which is translated "place of a skull." 23And they offered him wine spiced with myrrh, but he did not accept it.

24And they crucify him[o] and distribute his garments, casting lots to see what one might take.[p] 25Now it was the third hour, and they crucified him. 26And the epigraph of his accusation was written above: "The King of the Jews." 27And with him they crucify two thieves, one to his right and one to his left. 28*And the verse of scripture was fulfilled which said, "He was counted as one of the lawbreakers."* 29And the passersby blasphemed him, wagging their heads[q] and saying, "Ooh! The one who throws down the holy place to build it in three days! 30Save yourself by coming down from the cross!" 31Similarly, the archpriests, trading jokes with the scribes, said, "Some savior! He couldn't even save himself." 32"Let the Christ, King of Israel, come down from the cross alive that we may 'see and believe!'" And the co-crucifieds insulted him. 33And when the sixth hour struck, darkness appeared over the whole earth until the

n. This Simon is a "Cyrenian," or one of the "Kittim," sea peoples anciently associated with the Philistines and Phoenicians. Eisenman has shown that Simon of Cyrene shades over from "Simon of the Kittim" to "Simon of Gitta" or ancient Gath, hometown of Goliath the Philistine. Simon of Gitta is, of course, Simon Magus, who claimed to have undergone apparent crucifixion in Judea as Jesus. Simon of Cyrene's appearance here seems to betray an underlying knowledge of that version of the story.

o. Pss. 22:16b

p. Pss. 22:18

q. Pss. 22:7

ninth hour.[r] 34And at the ninth hour, Jesus shouted, "*Eloi, Eloi, lama sabachthani?*" which is translated, "My God, my God, why did you forsake me?"[s] 35And some of the bystanders, hearing this, said, "Get a load of this! He invokes Elijah!" 36And one of them ran and filled a sponge with vinegar and, putting it on a lance head, gave it to him to drink,[t] but others objected, saying, "Leave him be! Let us see if Elijah comes to take him down." 37But Jesus, letting go a loud shout, expired. 38And the hanging veil of the holy place was split in two from top to bottom.

39And the centurion standing by across from him, seeing that he expired in such a manner, said, "Truly, this man was God's son!" 40But there were also women looking on from a distance, among them both Maria the hairdresser and Maria the mother of Jacob the Lesser and of Jose and Salome, 41who when he was in the Galilee followed him and fed him, as well as many others who had come up with him to Jerusalem.

42And now, with evening coming, since it was Preparation, which is the day before Sabbath, 43Joseph, the one from Arimathea, a prestigious councilor who was himself looking forward to the kingdom of God, mustered his courage to appear before Pilatus and requested custody of the body of Jesus.[u] 44And Pilatus marveled that he should already be dead. And summoning the centurion, he interrogated him whether he died long before.[v] 45And ascertaining the facts from the centurion, he granted the corpse to Joseph. 46And having bought a linen sheet, and taking him down, he wrapped him in the linen and laid him out in a tomb cut from living rock, and he rolled a stone up to the door of the tomb. 47But Maria the hairdresser and Maria of Jacob marked where he was interred.

16

1And once the Sabbath was past, Maria the hairdresser and Maria of Jacob and Salome brought aromatics to anoint him with once they arrived.[w] 2And very early on the first day of the week, they come up to the

r. Amos 8:9

s. Pss. 22:1

t. Pss. 69:21

u. Joseph is surely a combination of King Priam, who courageously came to Achilles' camp to beg the body of his son Hector, and the patriarch Joseph, who asked Pharaoh's permission to bury the body of Jacob in the cave-tomb Jacob had hewn for himself beyond the Jordan (Gen. 50:4-5).

v. Pilatus may have feared an attempt to rescue Jesus alive.

w. The vigil of the mourning women reflects the mourning cult of the dying and rising god, long familiar in Israel (Ezek. 8:14; Zech. 12:11; Canticles 3:1-4 2).

tomb just as the sun was rising. [3]And they mused, "Who will roll away for us the stone from the door of the tomb?" [4]And looking up, they see that the stone has been rolled back. They were greatly relieved, for the stone was extremely huge.[x] [5]And entering into the tomb, they saw a youth sitting to the right, dressed in a white robe. And they were overcome with amazement. [6]But he says to them, "Do not be overcome with amazement. Jesus is the one you are looking for, the crucified Nazarene. He was raised; he is not here. See for yourself the place where they laid him out. [7]But you go tell his disciples and Peter that he precedes you into the Galilee. That's where you will see him, as he once told you." [8]And exiting, they bolted from the tomb, for trembling seized them and they were beside themselves, and they said nothing, not to anyone, for they were terrified.

But they announced briefly to Peter and those with him all that they had been told. And afterward, Jesus himself sent forth, by means of them, from east to west the sacred and imperishable proclamation of age-abiding salvation.[y]

[9]*But getting up early on the first of the week,*[z] *he appeared first to Maria the hairdresser, from whom he had once cast out seven demons.* [10]*That woman went and announced the news to those who had been with him, whom she found mourning and weeping.* [11]*And those men, hearing that he lives and was seen by her, disbelieved.* [12]*After these events, he was disclosed in a different form to two of their number walking into the countryside.* [13]*And those, going back, announced it to the rest. They didn't believe those men either.* [14]*Still later, he was manifested to the eleven as they reclined eating, and he castigated them for their stubborn unbelief because they refused to credit the reports of those who had seen him after he had been raised.*

They gave him this excuse: "This lawless and unbelieving age is under the control of the adversary, who does not permit those who are unclean and dominated by spirits to comprehend the true power of God." Thus they spoke to Christ, saying, "Therefore make known now your righteous authority!" Christ answered, saying, "The measure of the years allotted to the adversary's power has indeed been fulfilled. But other,

---

x. Josh. 10:26-27, 18, 22

y. This paragraph represents the older, shorter ending of the Gospel.

z. Beginning with verse 9 is the variant, longer ending to the Gospel of Mark.

more fearsome things are at hand. Yet it was on behalf of sinners that I was delivered up to death, that they might return to the truth and no longer sin, and so inherit the spiritual and immortal glory of justification in heaven."[a]

15 *And he said to them, "Journey into all the world and proclaim the news to the whole of creation.* 16 *The one who believes and is baptized will be saved. But the one who disbelieves will be condemned.* 17 *And these signs will accompany those who believe: in my name they will cast out demons, they will speak in new languages,* 18 *they will pick up serpents; and if they drink anything poisonous, it will not hurt them at all. They will lay hands on the sick, and they will be fine."* 19 *Therefore, the Lord Jesus, after speaking to them, was taken up into the sky and sat down to the right of God.* 20 *But those men went forth proclaiming everywhere, the Lord working with them and confirming the message through the attendant signs.*

---

a. This paragraph comes from an early fifth-century codex purchased by Charles Freer. The paragraph is named after him as the Freer "logion" or saying.

6.

The Gospel according to Matthew

Authorship

The mid-second-century bishop Papias, together with some other not particularly credible sources, informs us that the apostle Matthew compiled the sayings of the Lord in Hebrew, possibly meaning the sister language Aramaic, and other unnamed persons translated the work with varying degrees of success. Many have supposed Papias to be talking about our Gospel according to Matthew, but there is no solid reason for thinking so. Our Matthew was written in Greek, based on a prior Greek document, the Gospel according to Mark. In addition, our Matthew is much more than a collection of sayings, so this would not be the most obvious way to refer to it. It is commonplace nowadays to assume Papias was referring to the Q document, a hypothetical source of sayings ascribed to Jesus constituting a major source of our Matthew and Luke. But that seems to be just an attempt to maintain some sort of apostolic connection to Matthew even though a less direct heir wrote the whole of it. Even if Papias did refer to a narrative like our Matthew, he might have been thinking of another of the Jewish-Christian gospels which Jerome and others thought might be the supposed Hebrew original of Matthew. Another complication is that there were additional works circulating under Matthew's name, including the Infancy Gospel of Matthew, so it is altogether unclear which book Papias had in mind.

In any case, there are two factors making it impossible for the apostle Matthew to have penned our gospel. First, we can scarcely

imagine that an eyewitness of the historical Jesus, present to hear both his master's public proclamations and informal table talk, would have ignored his own fund of memories in favor of a third-hand account like Mark's. Matthew's gospel is essentially no more than a new and revised edition of Mark. Second, there is the matter of the Matthean character called "Matthew the tax collector" (Matt. 9:9; 10:3). This fellow is a combination of two distinct Markan characters: Levi the tax-collector (Mark 2:14) and Matthew the disciple (Mark 3:18). Neither Mark nor Matthew nor anyone else knew of a "Matthew also called Levi" or "Levi also called Matthew." He is a figment of the harmonistic imagination. Like all the gospels, our so-called Matthew was originally anonymous. We have no idea how this common name became attached to it any more than we know how Matthew became credited with the Infancy Gospel. But to avoid confusion that re-titling the book would cause, I hold fast to the handy convention of referring to it as Matthew's.

If we cannot tell who the author was, we can surmise his likeness because our author makes a brief cameo appearance (Matt. 13:52). He was a Jewish scribe who had "become discipled to the kingdom of heaven." He had become a Jewish Christian and as a result could plumb the scripture, which he calls his "storehouse," for old meanings, historical and literalistic, such as Isaiah's son serving as a living stopwatch to measure the fall of Syria, and new ones, such as the virgin conception of Jesus, recognized only in Christianized hindsight as an interpretation of Isaiah 7:14. Matthew had great facility and familiarity with a variety of sources since he appears to quote as needed from both the Hebrew and Syriac Old Testament and from both the Septuagint (LXX) and Theodotion Greek translations. He practiced a kind of esoteric exegesis (*pesher,* "puzzle solution"), whereby one could "recognize" scripture as referring to one's own sect. The Dead Sea Scrolls are filled with the same stuff.

Matthew might have been called a rabbi if he hadn't already repudiated the title with the democratizing zeal of the typical sectarian (23:8). Still, he must have been a teacher in his community. Besides the Jewish scriptures, the primary document he would have taught from would have been Mark's gospel.

Date

Scholars usually date Matthew around 80-90 AD/CE in order to push it back as close as possible to the ostensible time of the historical Jesus, similarly pegging Mark at about 70 CE. That is, however, entirely too early for Mark as we have seen,[a] and thus too early for Matthew as well. Even if Mark were so early, we would need more than the minimum possible time between its composition and copying, on one hand, and Matthew getting hold of it, on the other. There were bookstalls back then, but nothing like today. We have to picture Matthew or his predecessors using Mark for quite some time until, instead of merely copying it, they decided to make a new edition, probably to solve some of the problems posed by the original. We might be talking about twenty, forty, fifty years.

In an inverse way, Matthew's reliance on Mark explains some of the differences in the two gospels, especially the additional details in Matthew's narrative. Many of the new portions seem to be answers to questions the teacher's catechumens might have raised in their reading of Mark: Why would Judas betray Jesus? If for money, then how much? Why would Pilate have lifted a finger to rescue Jesus? What happened to Judas? and so on. For some of these answers, Matthew no doubt used his own narrative ingenuity; for others, he resorted to *pesher* clues and filled in the blanks with the Old Testament.

If Mark's gospel is already beset with such anachronisms as synagogues in the wrong locations and holy men being called "rabbi," Matthew mentions the Seat of Moses (21:2), a chair set aside in every synagogue for the presiding elder. Unfortunately, this was a second-century phenomenon. Everything considered, it seems that Matthew should be dated about as late as we can possibly date it. Irenaeus's list of four canonical gospels in 180 CE gives us an upper limit. But if, as some have suggested, Irenaeus's *Against Heresies* was pseudepigraphical, like the various pseudo-Justin and pseudo-Tertullian writings, then the sky is the limit. As Walter Schmithals has suggested, the gospels appear to have been all but non-existent for about 200 years. They are nowhere quoted or cited verbatim till very late in the second century.

a. See the introduction to Mark's gospel in this volume.

Location

Surely the most educated guess is that Matthew's gospel stems from Antioch in Syria, a hypothesis supported by various good reasons. For one, Matthew is interested in the gentile mission. In fact, his gospel is manifestly composed as a church manual[b] and a catechism handbook. At the close of the book, the parting words of the risen Christ constitute a mission charge to the first readers, with the eleven pictured in the scene standing in for all. As it happens, we learn from Acts that Antioch was a hub for the gentile mission (13:1-3ff). Galatians similarly shows us how ethnically diverse the Antiochene congregation was, with both Jew and gentile members and the resultant issues of dietary restrictions and table fellowship (2:11-12). It is no surprise, then, that Matthew is conversant with the Hebrew Tanakh, the Syriac Bible, and the Greek Septuagint and Theodotion. He would have needed to be in order to teach such an audience.

From Galatians we learn further that the Antioch congregation was a reluctant host to a good bit of church politics between the factions of Paul, Peter, and James. Paul represented the Torah-free gospel for gentiles and assimilated Jews. James stood for strict observance of Torah for everyone. Peter seemed to be a voice of ambiguity, playing it by ear, so to speak, both zealous for Jewish heritage and careful not to impose alien cultural mores on gentile converts. His position might have been similar to that of the Galatians Paul challenges to think logically. If they were to be circumcised in order to be real Christians, Paul asks them, why couldn't they see that circumcision was metonymy for a strict, all-round Torah observance (Gal. 5:3)? This threefold division of loyalty within a functioning congregation[c] provides a clue to understanding the theological contradictions within Matthew, which appears to be a compromise document incorporating elements conducive to this or that faction. A related possibility is that what we now have represents a conflation of three once-distinct versions of an Antiochene gospel. Long afterward, someone may have harmonized the different versions from three factions from the same locale,

---

b. Matthew's "Manual of Discipline," to borrow a Dead Sea Scrolls term, comprises chapter 18.

c. Cf. 1 Cor. 1:11-12; 3:4

smoothing out the idiosyncracies which had been tailored to individual tastes.

It is clear, first of all, that Matthew is a Jewish-Christian document. Jesus is pictured as a new Moses, his teachings organized into five major blocks of sayings: the Sermon on the Mount (chaps. 5-7), the Mission Charge (chap. 10), the Parable Collection (chap. 13), the Manual of Discipline (chap. 18, spilling into 19), and finally a section juxtaposing denunciations of the Pharisees alongside the Olivet Discourse (chaps. 23-25). Each one ends with some variation of the phrase, "he finished these sayings and went on from there." That Matthew really should have separated the last one by topic into two blocks only underlines the point: he wanted Jesus to offer a new Torah, a new Pentateuch. There had to be five books. Near the beginning of the keynote speech, the Matthean Jesus warns his hearers neither to relax the least important Torah command *nor to teach others to do so* (5:19). Christians were wrong who taught that the son of man had come "to abolish the Law and the Prophets" (5:17). At the end of the book, an injunction is given to take these commandments to the nations, the gentiles, who must therefore be taught to keep every last Mosaic command (28:19-20). These are the words of Petrine Jewish Christianity, supportive of the gentile mission (Acts 10-11; 15:7-11) but with some antipathy toward Paul (3 Peter). Of course, it is to Peter and his successors that Jesus is portrayed as awarding the halachic keys (Matt. 16:17-19).

Yet we also find hostility to the gentile mission (Matt. 10:5), which is the initial position of the Jerusalem elders (Acts 11:1-3) and of the "men from James" (Gal. 2:12). It is probably to the James faction that we owe the blistering polemics of Matthew 23. The followers of James are the closest to the Pharisees and scribes of Yavneh Judaism and preoccupied with the minutiae separating them from their rivals.[d] They are intimidated by the recognized authority of the Yavneh Sanhedrin and do not want to see Christianity go the way of a schism (23:1-3a), leaving Judaism altogether, though many Jews no doubt already see them in that light. The Jewish Christians envy and

d. Matt. 5:34-35; 6:1-6, 16-18; 23:16-24

condemn the honor accorded their rabbinic rivals and pretend to be above such vanities (23:5-11). It is they who cherish the expectation that Paulinists will finally be shut out of the kingdom (7:21-23), whereas Peter's faction was content to demote Paulinists to the position of *shudras,* the lowest caste in heaven (5:19). It must be those of the James faction who jeer at glossolalia as pagan gibberish (6:7) since Peter (Acts 2:4) and Paul (1 Cor. 14:18) were both associated with the practice.

It is surely through Paulinist channels that Mark came into use in Matthew's congregation in the first place. However, note that in Matthew we no longer read of a lone wolf exorcist, who must stand for Paul (Mark 9:38-40). And we would never have certain passages in Mark (7:14-19) taken over into Matthew (15:10-20) if not for lingering Pauline influence in the community; yet at that, Matthew omits a clause which might have been taken as an abolition of the kosher laws. Mark had rejected the exclusivity of the twelve disciples' claim to authority. His constant, virtually Marcionite, denigration of the twelve is somewhat mitigated in Matthew, who must have respected them. Similarly, Mark rejected the heirs, or family, of Jesus, including James. He has Jesus repudiate his family, and they return the compliment (Mark 3:19b-21, 31-5). Matthew omits the bit about Jesus' family thinking him insane because it ill comports with his nativity story, which must forever rule out such doubts. But he leaves the repudiation of the heirs intact (Matt. 12:46-50). The followers of Paul and Peter alike must have appreciated the anecdote, and we may feel sure it was Paulinists in Antioch whose acid comment on Jewish-Christian missionaries, with their Torah gospel, is preserved in Matthew 23:15. The same sentiments may be found in the Pauline epistles.[e] It is probably thanks to the Pauline faction that we have what Arlo J. Nau *(Peter in Matthew: Discipleship, Diplomacy, and Dispraise)* calls "dispraise" of Peter. Several passages exalt Peter, thanks to the Matthean redactor of Mark, but then take Peter back down a peg. It sounds as if a subsequent editor thought Peter's elevation too much and tried to correct it. For example, the keys of the kingdom

e. Gal. 1:8-9; 2 Cor. 11:13-15; Phil. 3:2.

given to Peter in Matthew 16:19 are given to the twelve as a whole in Matthew 18:18-20, or even to any two or three believers who find themselves in agreement. (Accordingly, Paul is shown exercising such Petrine authority in 1 Corinthians 5:3-5.) Originally, a Matthean (or Antiochene) redactor probably just replaced the Markan "Get behind me, Satan!" scene of Mark 8:33 with the blessing of Peter in Matthew 16:17-19, but a subsequent Matthean redactor decided to puncture that bubble by restoring the Satan curse at Matthew 16:22-23. According to Matthew 14:28-29, it is clear Peter is initially pictured as successfully recapitulating Jesus' feat of walking on water. But verses 30-31 make Peter play the fool. As Nau suggests, they represent redactional dispraise of Peter by someone who wanted to mitigate the claims of his heirs and supporters—likely a Paulinist in the community. What Ernst Käsemann said of the New Testament canon as a whole[f] is no less true for the individual writings within it: Matthew's gospel provides equal, at least substantial, support for the variety of sects who appeal to it. This is because as many factional viewpoints went into it as came out of it.

1

[1]The book of the generations of Jesus Christ, son of David, son of
Abraham.
[2]Abraham fathered Isaac, and Isaac fathered Jacob, and Jacob fathered Judah and his brothers, [3]and Judah fathered Peres and Zerah with
Tamar, and Peres fathered Hezron, and Hezron fathered Aram, [4]and
Aram fathered Aminadab, and Aminadab fathered Naasson, and Naasson fathered Shalman, [5]and Shalman fathered Boaz with Rahab, and
Boaz fathered Obed with Ruth, and Obed fathered Jesse, [6]and Jesse fathered David the king. And David fathered Solomon with the widow of
Uriah, [7]and Solomon fathered Rehoboam, and Rehoboam fathered Abijah, and Abijah fathered Asaph, [8]and Asaph fathered Jehoshaphat, and
Jehoshaphat fathered Joram, and Joram fathered Uzziah, [9]and Uzziah fathered Jotham, and Jotham fathered Ahaz, and Ahaz fathered Hezekiah,
[10]and Hezekiah fathered Manasseh, and Manasseh fathered Amoz, and

f. Ernst Käsemann, "The Canon of the New Testament and the Unity of the Church," in *Essays on New Testament Themes*, ed. Ernst Käsemann (Naperville, IL: Alec R. Allenson, 1964).

Amoz fathered Josiah, [11]and Josiah fathered Jeconiah and his brothers just before the deportation to Babylon. [12]And after the deportation to Babylon, Jeconiah fathered Salathiel, and Salathiel fathered Zerub-babel, [13]and Zerub-babel fathered Abihud, and Abihud fathered Eliakim, and Eliakim fathered Azor, [14]and Azor fathered Zadok, and Zadok fathered Achim, and Achim fathered Elihud, [15]and Elihud fathered Eleazar, and Eleazar fathered Matthan, and Matthan fathered Jacob, [16]and Jacob fathered Joseph, and Joseph, to whom the virgin Maria was betrothed, fathered Jesus, the one called Christos.[g]

[17]So all the generations from Abraham until David make fourteen generations, and from David until the deportation to Babylon make fourteen generations, and from the deportation to Babylon until the Christ fourteen generations.

[18]Now of Jesus Christ, the birth was thus: his mother Maria being betrothed to Joseph, before they came together, she was found to have a child in the womb, as it would soon be discovered, by the Holy Spirit. [19]And Joseph her husband, being just and not wishing to make her a public scandal, decided to send her away privately. [20]But while he deliberated these matters, behold, an angel of Adonai appeared to him in a dream, saying, "Joseph, scion of David, do not be afraid to take Maria your wife; for what is in her is fathered by the Holy Spirit. [21]And she will bear a son, and you will call his name Jesus because he will save his people from their sins. [22]Now all this has occurred so that the esoteric sense of the oracle of Adonai through the prophet might be revealed, namely, [23]'Behold, the maid shall have a child in the womb and will bear a son, and they will call his name Emmanuel,'" which is translated, "God with us."[h] [24]Then Joseph, being wakened from sleep, did as the angel of Adonai asked him, and he took his wife, [25]and he did not know her carnally before she bore a son, and he called his name Jesus.

2

[1]Now once Jesus was born in Beth-Lehem of Judea in the days of Herod the king, behold, mages from the east arrived in Jerusalem, [2]saying, "Where is the newborn king of the Jews? For we saw his natal star when it rose and came to do homage to him." [3]So hearing about this,

g. This line about Joseph fathering Jesus comes from an Old Syriac manuscript. It is hard to imagine it could be a scribal correction to eliminate evidence for the virgin birth, so it remains a lone textual witness for the original before scribes sought to harmonize the text with the virgin birth doctrine.

h. Isa. 7:14, LXX

King Herod was agitated, and all Jerusalem feared what he might do. [4]And once he had assembled all the archpriests and scribes and elders of the people, he asked them where the Christ is to be born. [5]And they told him, "In Beth-Lehem in Judea, for thus it has been laid down through the prophet: [6]'And you, Beth-Lehem, land of Judah, are by no means least among the governors of Judah. For out of you will emerge a governor who will shepherd my people Israel.'"[i] [7]Then Herod, privately summoning the mages, ascertained in detail from them the time the star appeared, [8]and sending them to Beth-Lehem, he said, "On your journey, carefully investigate the child. And when you discover him, give me a report so that I, too, may come and render him homage." [9]So hearing the king's instructions, they embarked on their journey. And behold, the star they saw, when it rose, led them onward until, arriving, it stood over where the child was. [10]And seeing the reappearance of the star, they rejoiced exceedingly with a great joy. [11]And entering into the house, they saw the child with Maria his mother, and prostrating themselves, they did him homage. And opening their treasures, they set gifts before him of gold and frankincense and myrrh. [12]And having been alerted by a dream not to return to Herod, they departed by a different route to their own country.

[13]And when they departed, behold, an angel of Adonai appears in a dream to Joseph, saying, "Wake up and take the child and his mother and flee into Egypt and live there till I may tell you. For Herod is about to search out the child to destroy him." [14]So getting up, he took the child and his mother under cover of night and departed to Egypt, [15]and they were there till the death of Herod in order that the esoteric sense of the oracle of Adonai through the prophet might be revealed, namely, "Out of Egypt I called my son."[j]

[16]Then Herod, realizing he was tricked by the mages, became livid with fury and, sending orders, killed all the male children in Beth-Lehem and in the adjacent districts, from two years and under, coinciding with the time he had determined from the mages, when the star rose.[k] [17]Then was revealed the esoteric sense of Jeremiah the prophet, namely, [18]"A voice was heard in Ramah, weeping and lamenting loudly: Rachel weeping for her children, and she was inconsolable because they are gone."[l]

---

i. Mic. 5:2

j. Hosea 11:1

k. Matthew's nativity story is largely based on Josephus's story of the birth of Moses in *Antiquities* 2, 9:2-3.

l. Jer. 31:15

[19]But once Herod died, behold, an angel of Adonai appears in a
dream to Joseph in Egypt, [20]saying, "Wake up and take the child and his
mother and go to the land of Israel. For those seeking the life of the child
have died." [21]So he got up and took the child and his mother and entered
into the land of Israel. [22]But hearing "Archelaus reigns over Judea in
place of his father Herod," he feared to go there. And being warned of
this by a dream, he left for the vicinity of the Galilee. [23]And arriving there,
he settled in a city called Nazareth so that the thing spoken through the
prophet might be fulfilled, "A Nazorean he shall be called."[m]

3

[1]And in those days[n] arrives John the Baptist, preaching in the desert
of Judea, [2]saying, "Repent, for the kingdom of the heavens has come
near!" [3]For this is the one spoken of through Isaiah the prophet, namely,
"a voice of one crying out in the desert: 'Prepare the way of Adonai, all of
you; make his route straight.'" [4]And John himself had his clothing made
from camel's hair and a leather waistband around his loins, and his food
was locusts and wild honey. [5]Then Jerusalem and all Judea and all the environs of the Jordan went out to him [6]and were baptized in the Jordan
River by him, enumerating their sins. [7]And seeing many of the Pharisees
and the Syndics coming to the baptism, he said to them, "Spawn of vipers! Who alerted you to flee the impending rage? [8]Therefore, first you
must produce fruit befitting repentance. [9]And do not think to reassure
yourselves by saying, 'For father, we have Abraham.' For I tell you that
God is able to raise up sons to Abraham from these stones.[o] [10]And already
the axe is poised at the root of the trees. Therefore, every tree not producing good fruit is chopped down and is thrown into fire. [11]I indeed baptize
you with water for repentance, but the one coming after me is stronger
than me, whose sandals I am not worthy to carry. He shall baptize you in
the Holy Spirit and fire, [12]he whose winnowing fan is in his hand, and he
will completely purify his threshing floor, gathering his wheat into the
silo, but the chaff he will consume with inextinguishable fire."

[13]Then Jesus arrives from the Galilee at the Jordan before John, to be
baptized by him. [14]But he refused him, saying, "I myself have need to be

---

m. Judg. 13:7

n. Which is the anachronism? Did John minister closer to the time of the birth of Jesus ("those days"), as Robert Eisler suggested? Or has Matthew unwittingly jumped from the nativity events to the baptism without a transition?

o. This is a pun. God can make sons, *beni,* from stones, *ebeni.*

baptized by you, and you come to me!"[p] [15]But answering, Jesus said to him, "Let it go for now lest we offend them, for it is fitting for us in this way to observe all piety." Then he lets him. [16]And having been baptized, Jesus at once went up out of the water, and behold, the skies were split open and he saw the Spirit coming down like a dove, coming upon him. [17]And behold, a voice out of the skies saying: "This is my son, the beloved; in whom I was quite satisfied."

4

[1]Then Jesus was led up into the desert by the Spirit to be tested by the accuser. [2]And having fasted forty days and forty nights, afterward he hungered. [3]And approaching him, the tester said to him, "If you are God's son, say that these stones shall become loaves." [4]But answering, he said, "It is written, 'Not solely on bread shall a human being live, but on every precious utterance proceeding through the lips of God.'" [5]Then the accuser takes him into the holy city and placed him standing on the wing of the temple, [6]and says to him, "If you are God's son, throw yourself down. After all, it is written, 'He will put his angels in charge of you, and they will scoop you up lest you so much as stub your toe on a rock.'" [7]Jesus said to him, "Again it is written, 'You shall not presume on the good will of Adonai your God.'" [8]Again the accuser takes him into an extremely high mountain, from whence he could see all the kingdoms of the world and their glory, [9]and he said to him, "All these I will give you if you will fall down before me and swear fealty." [10]Then Jesus says to him, "Be gone, adversary! For it is written, 'Adonai your God you shall worship, and him only you shall serve.'" [11]Then the accuser leaves him, and behold, the angels approached and fed him, his ordeal ended.[q]

---

p. This Matthean addition to Mark resembles a story in chapter 5 of the Mandaean scripture, *The Right Ginza* ("treasury of the right hand"). John baptizes in the name of a heavenly aeon, Manda d'Haiye (Gnosis of Life), who appears to the Baptizer in the form of a child and requests baptism. John first tells him to wait, then beholds the Jordan flowing backward and recognizes his savior. He asks Manda d'Haiye to baptize him instead, and the deity does so, telling him that "when I lay my hand upon you, you shall leave your body." Then "in the Jordan [Manda] removed [John's] garment from him: he removed from him his garment of flesh and blood. He dressed him in a robe of brilliance and coronated him with a noble turban of pure light." Together the pair ascends into paradise, after which John asks that all his baptized may experience this same mystic rapture.

q. Jesus resists the devil's blandishments by citing three texts from Deuteronomy (8:3; 6:13, 16), all of which refer to the trials of the people of Israel in the wilderness: manna, Massa, and idolatry. The Israelites failed, but Jesus, embodying a new Israel, passes with flying colors.

[12]Now hearing that John was delivered up, he left that region for the Galilee. [13]And leaving Nazara, coming to the village of Nahum,[r] he settled at the seaside in the region of Zebulon and Naphtali, [14]for he sought to fulfill the thing spoken by Isaiah the prophet, namely, [15]"Land of Zebulon and land of Naphtali, seaboard beyond the Jordan, Galilee of the gentiles, [16]the people stranded in the dark saw a great light, and to those sitting in a land of death and its shadow, light blazed up for them." [17]From then on, Jesus started to preach and to say, "Repent, for the kingdom of the heavens has come near!"

[18]And walking beside the Sea of Galilee, he saw two brothers, Simon, called Peter, and Andreas his brother, casting a net into the sea, for they were fishermen. [19]And he says to them, "Come after me and I will teach you to fish for human souls." [20]And at once, leaving the nets, they followed him. [21]And going on from there, he saw another two brothers, Jacob, son of Zebediah, and John his brother, in the boat with Zebediah their father, darning their nets. And he called them. [22]And at once, leaving the boat and their father, they followed him.[s]

[23]And he made the circuit of all the Galilee, teaching in their synagogues and proclaiming the news of the kingdom and curing every disease and every malady among the people. [24]And the report of him went out into the whole of Syria, and they brought him all those in a bad way, having various diseases and suffering from torments: the demonized and lunatics and paralytics, and he cured them. [25]And many crowds followed him from the Galilee and the Decapolis and Jerusalem and Judea and the Transjordan.

5

[1]And seeing these crowds, he went up into the mountain; and once he sat down, his disciples came to him.

[2]And breaking his silence, he taught them, saying,

[3]"Blessed in spirit are the poor, for they are the subjects of the kingdom of the heavens.

[4]"Blessed are the mourners, for they shall be encouraged.

[5]"Blessed are the meek, for when the great ones destroy one another fighting over it, the meek shall remain to inherit the earth.

---

r. The story may be fictively set in Caphar-Nahum, Village of Nahum, because of Nahum 1:15a, the only passage outside of Isaiah to use the term ευαγγελιζομενου in a strictly religious sense: "Behold upon the mountains the feet of him that brings glad tidings and publishes peace."

s. The story comes from Elijah's recruitment of Elisha in 1 Kings 19:19-21.

6“Blessed are those starved and parched for justice, for they shall be sated.

7“Blessed are those who show mercy, for others will show them mercy when they find themselves in need of it.

8“Blessed are those with a clean conscience, for only they shall see God.

9“Blessed are the reconcilers, for they shall be called sons of God.

10“Blessed are those persecuted for righteousness, for the kingdom of the heavens is made up of them.

11“Blessed are you when they vilify you and persecute you and make every false charge against you on account of me; 12rejoice and celebrate, for your reward is large in the heavens. For in the same way, they used to persecute your predecessors, the prophets.

13“You are the salt of the earth. But suppose the salt is tainted: by what can it be re-seasoned? It is no longer tangy enough for anything except for being thrown into the street. 14You are the light of the world. A city set on a mountain is not capable of being hidden. 15Nor does anyone kindle a lamp and set it under the bushel basket, but rather atop the lamp stand so it illumines all in a one-room house. 16In the same way, let your light shine before others so they may see your noble deeds and may thank your Father in the heavens for you.

17“Pay no heed to the doctrine that my mission was to destroy the Torah or the Prophets. My mission was not to destroy scripture, but to fulfill it! 18For, Amen: I say to you, even if the heavens and the earth should pass away, a single *yodh,* a single vowel point, shall by no means pass away from the Torah until all its commandments are perfectly obeyed. 19Therefore, whoever presumes to abrogate the least significant of these commandments and teaches this to others, in the kingdom of heaven they shall call him the least significant. 20For I tell you, unless your Torah piety exceeds that of the scribes and Pharisees, you shall by no means enter into the kingdom of the heavens.

21“You heard that the ancients were commanded, ‘You shall not murder’ and ‘Whoever commits murder shall face sentencing.’ 22But I command you that every one who gets angry at his brother shall face sentencing. And if anyone should say to his brother, ‘*Raca!* Apostate!’ he shall face the Sanhedrin. And if anyone should say, ‘You moron!’ he shall face the fire of the Valley of Hinnom. 23So if you find yourself bringing your offering forward to the altar and you suddenly remember that your brother has a complaint against you, 24leave your sacrificial animal

standing there at the altar. First, square things with your brother, and
only then return and offer your sacrifice if you want God to accept it.
[25]Try to settle with your creditor before you get to court; otherwise the
creditor may hand you over to the judge, and the judge may hand you
over to the bailiff, and you may be thrown into debtors prison. [26]Amen: I
say to you, you will never make it out of there till you pay the creditor the
last quadrans you owe him.

[27]"You heard it was commanded, 'You shall not commit adultery.'
[28]But I command you that every one who ogles a woman, fantasizing
about her, has already committed adultery with her in his heart. [29]So if
your right eye scandalizes you, gouge it out and throw it away! It is better
to cut your losses and let one of your organs be destroyed rather than
have your whole body dumped into the Valley of Hinnom. [30]And if you
find yourself morally scandalized by your right hand's larcenous behavior, cut it out! Throw it away! Won't you come out ahead if one of your
members is destroyed instead of your whole body being packed off to the
Valley of Hinnom?

[31]"And it was commanded, 'If one sends his wife away, let him give
her a certificate of divorce.' [32]But I command you that anyone sending his
wife away, apart from a matter of whoredom, of course, makes her commit adultery, when she hadn't already, since she will have to remarry.
And whoever marries a divorced woman commits adultery since she is really still bound to the original husband.

[33]"Again, you heard that the ancients were commanded, 'You shall
not default on a vow, but shall pay to the Lord what you have vowed.'
[34]But I command you not to swear a vow at all, neither by the sky since it
is the throne of God, [35]nor by the earth since it is the footstool for his feet,
nor yet by Jerusalem since it is the city of the divine king. [36]Swear not by
your own head since you cannot do so much as change one hair to white
or black. [37]But let your final word be 'Yes, yes!' 'No, no!' Whatever goes
beyond these simple words denotes a wicked person.

[38]"You heard it was commanded, 'An eye in recompense for an eye,
a tooth as recompense for a tooth.' [39]But I command you, do not call the
wicked person to task; but whoever raps you on the right cheek, turn to
him the other also. [40]And to the one who wants to sue you for your tunic,
let him have your coat as well. [41]And if a Roman soldier shall commandeer you to carry his field pack for one mile, go with him two. [42]To the
one asking you, give, and the one wishing to borrow from you, do not
turn him away.

[43]"You heard that it was commanded, 'You shall love your neighbor, reserving your hate only for your enemy.'[t] [44]But I command you, love your enemies and pray for your persecutors, [45]so that you may become true sons of your Father in the heavens, for he orders his sun to rise on the wicked and good alike, and he rains equally on the righteous and unrighteous. [46]For if you love the ones who love you, what reward awaits you in the heavens? Do not even the miserable customs agents do the same? [47]And if you give a greeting only to your brothers, what extra are you doing? Do not even the heathen do the same? [48]Therefore, be perfect, as your heavenly Father is perfect.

6

[1]"Be careful not to practice your religion in front of others so as to be seen doing it. Otherwise it gains you no wage from your Father in the heavens. [2]Accordingly, when you give to beggars, do not herald it with a trumpet fanfare as the hypocrites do, making a great show in the synagogues and in the streets, so they may be praised by others. Amen: I tell you, they will have to be content with that paltry recompense. [3]But when you give to beggars, keep it secret so even your left hand will not know your right hand has given coins. [4]And your Father, the one who watches invisibly, will bless you visibly. [5]And when you pray, do not be like the hypocrites, because they just love to pray standing in the synagogues and the corners of the public streets if the hour of prayer 'happens' to catch them there, so they may be on display. Amen: I say to you, they have thus received all the payment they are going to get. [6]But when you pray, enter into your private room and, having shut your door, pray to your Father who is invisible, and your Father who watches invisibly will repay you for this offering. [7]When you pray, do not say *batta batta batta* as the heathen do, for they imagine their prayer will be heard by virtue of sheer verbiage. [8]So do not be like them, for your Father knows full well what you have need of before you ask him. [9]Therefore, pray thusly:

Our Father in the heavens,
may your name[u] be revered;
[10]may your kingdom come,
let your will come to pass

t. There was no biblical commandment to "hate your enemy," but this does not mean Matthew did not think there was, and it would not be his only misquotation.

u. Yahve.

as in heaven also on earth.
[11]Give us our daily bread today,
[12]and release us from our debts
even as we released our debtors.
[13]And draw us not into testing,
but rescue us from the wicked.

[14]"For if you grant others amnesty for their legal transgressions, your heavenly Father will also forgive you. [15]But if you refuse to grant amnesty for others, neither will your Heavenly Father overlook your own violations of the Torah.

[16]"And when you fast, do not look mournful like the hypocrites, for they mar the appearance of their faces so they may display themselves as fasting. Amen: I tell you, they have the only reward they will ever get. [17]But when you are fasting, groom your hair and wash your face, [18]so that no one but your Father, the invisible one, will suspect you are fasting. And your Father, watching invisibly, will reward your piety.[v]

[19]"Do not amass treasures for yourselves on the earth where moth and rust make it disappear and where burglars dig through[w] and steal it, [20]but amass for yourselves treasures in heaven, where neither moth nor rust makes it disappear, where burglars neither dig through nor steal it. [21]For where your treasure is, there your heart will be also. [22]The lamp of the body is the eye, so if your eye is focused, your whole body will be shining. [23]In the same way, if the light in you goes dark, how deep is that darkness! [24]No one is able to be a slave to two lords at the same time; for eventually either he will hate the first and he will love the second or he will attach himself to the first and loathe the second. You are no more capable of being a slave to God and to Mammon, the Almighty Denarius. [25]Therefore, I say to you, do not be preoccupied with your life: what you may eat, *what you may drink,* what you may wear. Is not life a greater matter than food, and the body more than clothing? [26]Look to the birds of the sky: note how they do not plant or reap or gather into barns and your heavenly Father feeds them anyway. Do you not count for much more than them? [27]But which one of you is able to add another cubit to his height by worrying about it? [28]And why worry about clothing, of all things? Think of the lilies of the field, how they grow. They neither labor

v. Here we see an explanation for why the apparently impious succeed so well in life: they may be secretly pious and God is rewarding them openly.

w. An anachronism since Galilean houses were built of basalt.

keeping sheep nor spin wool, [29]but I assure you, not even Solomon in all
his golden finery was decked out like a single one of them. [30]But if God so
dresses up the ephemeral grass in the field, destined for nothing more noble than heating the stove, will he not be the more sure to provide clothes
for you? Scant is your faith! [31]Therefore, don't be preoccupied, saying,
What may we eat; what may we drink, what may we wear in our old age?
[32]For all these things preoccupy the heathen. Your heavenly Father is
fully aware that you need all these. [33]But you as Jews, seek first to enter
his kingdom and to gain his righteousness and all these things shall be
provided you. [34]Therefore, do not be preoccupied with what tomorrow
may bring, for tomorrow will take care of itself. Dealing with today's
troubles is enough for today.

7

[1]"Do not judge or you will be judged. [2]For you will be judged by the
same criteria for judgment you use to judge, and whatever measuring
stick you use to size someone up, others will use to measure you. [3]And
how can you spot the sawdust speck in your brother's eye without even
realizing there is a board sticking out of your own? [4]How are you going to
be able to say to your brother, 'Here, just let me extract that speck from
your eye,' when the whole time there is this board in your own eye?
[5]Hypocrite! First extract the board from your own eye and then, perhaps,
you will see clearly enough to extract the speck from your brother's eye.

[6]"Do not give consecrated food to the dogs, nor set your pearls before pigs if you don't want them to trample them into the mud and then
turn on you and rip your flesh.

[7]"Just ask! It shall be given you. Look for it. You will find it. Knock,
and the door will swing open for you. [8]For every persistent asker receives
and every determined seeker finds, and for the insistent knocker, it shall
sooner or later be opened. [9]Just point out a man among you who would
give his son a rock if he asked him for a barley roll. [10]Or if he asked for a
fish, who would give him a snake? [11]And if even sinners like you know to
give good gifts to your children, how much more can you expect your Father in the heavens to give good things to those who ask him?

[12]"Therefore, whatever way you want others to treat you, you treat
them the same way. For this is the essence of the Torah and the Prophets.
[13]Choose the narrow gate to enter because the wide one with the broad
road leads off to utter ruin, and there are many who enter that way.
[14]Because the gate to the life is narrow and the road is built to accommodate few. And indeed, few ever find it. [15]Watch out for pseudo-prophets

who approach you disguised as sheep but underneath are drooling wolves. [16]From their fruits, you will be able to recognize them. Vine dressers do not collect grapes from thorn bushes or figs from thistles, do they? [17]Even so, every sound tree produces luscious fruit, while the diseased tree produces poison fruit. [18]Nor is it an accident. A sound tree is not capable of bearing poison fruit, nor a diseased tree of bearing luscious fruit. [19]And what happens? Every tree failing to produce good fruit gets cut down and tossed into a fire. [20]Therefore, from their fruits you will be able to recognize them. [21]Not every one who flatters me with 'Lord, Lord!' will enter into the kingdom of the heavens, only those who obey the will of my Father in the heavens. [22]On Judgment Day many will appeal to me, 'Lord, Lord! Remember the days when we used to prophesy in your name? And cast out demons using your name? And to accomplish many mighty works in your name? Doesn't that count for something?' [23]I'm just waiting for this because then I will inform them that 'there's been some mistake. I've never seen any of you before. Get out of my sight, you Torah apostates!'

[24]"So then, whoever hears these, my words, and practices them bears comparison to a sensible man who built his dwelling on the rock. [25]And the rain descended and the rivers came up and the winds howled and crashed against that house, and it refused to fall because it had been founded on the rock. [26]And anyone hearing from me these words and neglecting to practice them must be compared to the moron who thought nothing of building his dwelling on the shifting sand. [27]And the rain descended and the rivers came up and the winds howled and crashed against that house, and it collapsed, and there was nothing left standing."

[28]And it happened that, when Jesus came to the end of these words, the crowds were utterly amazed at his teaching, [29]for he was teaching them as an authority in his own right, not like their scripture-parsing scribes.

8

[1]As he descended the mountain, many crowds followed him. [2]And behold, a man with a skin disease comes to him, falling to his knees, and says to him, "If only you will, you are able to purify me!" [3]And stretching out his hand, he touched him, saying, "It is my wish: be purified!" And at once the skin disease left him.[x] [4]And Jesus says to him, "See that you tell

x. This story is meant to recall the credential miracle vouchsafed by God to Moses, whereby he could turn his hand leprous white (Exod. 4:6-7).

nothing to anyone. Just go show yourself to the priest and offer the things Moses commanded concerning your cleansing, for their certification."

[5]As soon as he entered the village of Nahum, a centurion came to him, begging him [6]and saying, "Lord, my servant boy has been laid out in the house paralyzed, severely tortured." [7]He says to him, "I will come and cure him." [8]But answering, the centurion said, "Oh no! Lord, I am not worthy to have you actually set foot under my roof. Just use some incantation, and my servant boy will be cured. [9]I know how it works since I myself am a man under authority, and I have soldiers under my command. And I order this one, 'Go!' and he goes, and to another, 'Come!' and he comes, and I order my slave, 'Do this!' and he does." [10]And hearing this, Jesus marveled. He said to those following along, "Amen: I tell you, I never found such faith in Israel! [11]And I tell you that many from both east and west will come and feast with Abraham and Isaac and Jacob in the kingdom of the heavens.[y] [12]But the proper heirs of the kingdom will be ejected into the outer darkness. In that place, there will be wailing and grinding of teeth." [13]And Jesus said to the centurion, "Go! May it happen just as you believed it would." And the servant boy was cured in that very hour.

[14]And as Jesus came into the dwelling of Peter, he noticed his mother-in-law was laid up fever-stricken. [15]And he touched her hand, and the fever left her, and she got up and fed them.[z] [16]And when evening came, people brought to him many of the demonized. And he cast out the spirits with an incantation. And he cured all who were in a bad way, [17]so that the thing spoken by the prophet Isaiah was fulfilled, namely: "He took our infirmities from us, and he carried our diseases away." [18]But Jesus, seeing such a huge crowd surrounding him, gave orders to his disciples to depart for the opposite shore. [19]And coming to him as they prepared to shove off, one scribe said to him, "Teacher, I am ready to follow you wherever you may go." [20]And Jesus says to him, "Consider well. The foxes have burrows and the birds of the sky have nests, but human beings have no abiding place to call their own." [21]Another, one of the disciples, said to him, "Lord, give me time to leave and bury my father." [22]But Jesus says to him, "Follow me and let the dead bury themselves." [23]And as he set sail, his disciples followed him.

y. The underlying Q source seems to quote 4 Ezra (2 Esdras) 1:38, "And now, father, look with pride and see the people coming from the east; to them I will give as leaders Abraham, Isaac, and Jacob."

z. This reshuffles elements from 1 Kings 17:8-16.

[24]And behold, a great storm blew up so that the boat was covered by the waves. [25]But he himself was snoozing. And coming to him, they got him up, saying, "Lord, save! We are perishing." [26]And he says to them, "Why are you so fearful? Scant is your faith!" Then, getting up, he rebuked the winds and the sea and a great calm settled. [27]And the mortals marveled, saying, "What sort of being is this, that even the wind and the sea obey him?"[a]

[28]And when he came to the opposite side of the sea into the region of the Gadarenes, two demoniacs[b] emerged from the tombs to meet him. They were extremely dangerous so that no one dared travel by that road anymore. [29]And behold, they shouted, saying, "What business is there between us and you, son of God? Have you come to torture us already before the appointed time?" [30]Now there was a herd of many pigs feeding a great distance from them. [31]And the demons pleaded with him, saying, "If you must cast us out, send us into the herd of the pigs!" [32]And he said to them, "Go!" So coming out, they went into the pigs. And behold, all the herd rushed down the ledge into the sea and died in the waters. [33]And those feeding them fled, and going away into the city, they reported all things, even the news of the demoniacs. [34]And behold, all the city came out to meet Jesus and, seeing him, pleaded that he might quit their shores.[c]

9

[1]And embarking in a boat, he crossed over and came into his native city. [2]And behold, they brought him a paralytic laid on a mat. And Jesus, seeing their faith, says to the paralytic, "Cheer up, child, the sins you were being punished for are forgiven you." [3]And behold, some of the scribes said to themselves, "Surely this fellow blasphemes!" [4]And Jesus, knowing their thoughts, said, "Why do you think evil things in your hearts? [5]For which is easier, to say, 'The sins are forgiven you' or to say, 'Get up and walk'? [6]But to demonstrate to you that a man has authority to forgive sins on earth as God does in heaven"—then he speaks to the

a. The basis for the story is Jon. 1:4-6; Pss. 107:23-29; *Odyssey* 10:1-69.

b. Why are there two demoniacs in place of Mark's one? Matthew eliminates the "legion" business and seems to have deemed it a fair trade: two demoniacs for two thousand devils.

c. The core of the story derives from *Odyssey* 9:101-565. The demoniacs are based on Polyphemus the Cyclops; the pigs come from Circe's transformation of Odysseus' soldiers into swine. See Dennis R. MacDonald, *The Homeric Epics and the Gospel of Mark* (New Haven, CT: Yale University Press, 2000). Other details stem from Pss. 107.

paralytic—"Get up, take your mat and go to your dwelling.'" 7And getting up, he went to his dwelling. 8But the crowd, seeing this, feared and praised God, the one delegating such authority to mortal men.[d]

9And going along from there, he spotted a man sitting at the customs booth named Matthew, and he says to him, "Follow me!" And getting up, he followed him.[e] 10And it came about that he reclined at table in his house, and behold, many customs agents and backsliders came and reclined with Jesus and his disciples. 11And the Pharisees, noticing, remarked to his disciples, "Why does your teacher eat with the customs agents and backsliders?" 12And overhearing this, he said, "The vigorous do not require a physician, but those who are in a bad way do. 13Go and consider the implications of this scripture: 'Mercy is what I desire, not sacrifice.'[f] My mission was not to summon the righteous, but the sinful."

14Then the disciples of John come to him, saying, "Why do your disciples not fast when we and the Pharisee sect fast?" 15And Jesus explained to them, "Can you expect the groomsmen to mourn during the wedding reception? Inevitably, the days will come when the feasting is over, and then fasting will be appropriate again. 16Look, no one is so stupid that he sews a patch of unlaundered cloth onto an old garment. Otherwise, the new, once washed, shrinks away from the old and a worse rip occurs. 17And no one fills old wineskins with new wine; otherwise, when the new wine ferments, it will burst the old skins and let the wine pour out and the skins are ruined. No, they always put new wine into fresh skins, and that way both are preserved intact."

18As he was speaking to them of these matters, behold, a ruler came up and bowed before him, saying, "My daughter has just died, but come lay your hand on her and she will live." 19And getting up, Jesus followed him, and his disciples, too. 20And behold, a woman, subject to a flow of blood for twelve years, approached from behind and touched the fringe of his prayer shawl. 21For she was saying to herself, "If only I may touch his garment, I shall be saved." 22And Jesus, pivoting and seeing her, said, "Cheer up, daughter, your own faith has saved you!" And the woman

d. The story seems to be based on an Elijah incident in 2 Kings 1:2-17a, where King Ahaziah gains his affliction by falling from his roof through the lattice and thereafter languishes in bed.

e. The story comes from Elijah's recruitment of Elisha in 1 Kings 19:19-21. Notice that the evangelist has gratuitously changed Mark's character "Levi" into "Matthew" even though no New Testament writer mentions Matthew as an alternate name for anyone called Levi.

f. Hosea 6:6

was saved as of that hour. [23]And Jesus, coming into the dwelling of the ruler and seeing the flute-players and the crowd terrified, [24]said, "Get on out of here, for the girl did not die but sleeps!" And they derided him. [25]But when the crowd had been hustled out, he entered and seized her hand, and the girl was raised. [26]And the report of this circulated through that whole region.[g]

[27]And as Jesus was going along from there, two blind men followed him, shouting and saying, "Show mercy on us, son of David!"[h] [28]And when he came into the house, the blind men came up to him, and Jesus says to them, "Do you believe I am capable of doing this?" They say to him, "Yes, Lord." [29]Then he touched their eyes, saying, "May it be done to you as you believed." [30]And their eyes were opened. And Jesus gave them strict orders, saying, "See that you let no one know who did it!" [31]But going out of the house, they spread the story about him in all that land.

[32]And as they were coming out, behold, they brought to him a mute demoniac. [33]And with the demon cast out, the mute spoke. And the crowds marveled, saying, "Never has this appeared in Israel!" [34]But the Pharisees said, "It is plain magic. By using the ruler of the demons, he casts out the demons." [35]And Jesus made the circuit of all the cities and villages, teaching in their synagogues and heralding the news of the kingdom and curing every disease and every malady. [36]And seeing the crowds, he was flooded with compassion for them because they were agitated and clueless, like sheep with no shepherd to lead them. [37]Then he says to his disciples, "Though there is so much to be harvested, there are so few workers doing the job. So beg the Lord of the harvest, and perhaps he will see the urgency of the situation and rush more workers into his harvest."

10

[1]And to this end, summoning his twelve disciples, he gave them authority over unclean spirits so as to cast them out and to cure every disease and every malady. [2]Now these are the names of the twelve he sent:[i] Simon, called Peter, and Andreas his brother; and Jacob, son of Zebediah, and John his brother; [3]Philip and Bar-Ptolemy; Thomas and Matthew the

g. The two anecdotes of Jairus's daughter and the bleeding woman are interdependent parts of a single story, a retelling of the story of Elisha and the Shunammite woman (2 Kings 4).

h. It is possible this doubling of Bartimaeus stems from a confused reading of Mark 10:46, as if there Jesus had healed both Bartimaeus and his father, Timaeus.

i. Based on the choice of the twelve spies in Deut. 1:23.

customs agent; Jacob of Alphaeus and Thaddaeus, called Lebbaeus; and
Simon the Zealous, [4]and Judas the False One, who did indeed betray him.
[5]These twelve Jesus sent forth, instructing them thusly: "Do not take the
way that leads to the gentiles, and do not enter any city of the Samaritans.
[6]But go rather to the lost sheep who dwell in Israel. [7]And as you journey,
make proclamation, saying, 'The kingdom of the heavens has come near.'
[8]Cure the infirm, raise up the dead, cleanse those with skin disease, cast
out demons. You received these powers without cost, use them without
charging a fee. [9]Do not carry provisions of gold or silver or brass in your
waistbands, [10]no wallet for the road, nor a second tunic, nor sandals, nor
a staff,[j] for the worker deserves to be fed. [11]And whatever city or village
you may enter, first make inquiries as to who in it is worthy to put you up,
and remain with them until you are ready to leave the village. [12]As you
first enter into the dwelling, greet those in it. [13]If it does, in fact, prove
worthy of you, impart to it your blessing of protection. If it does not, then
let your protection follow you when you leave. [14]And whoever may not
welcome you or hear your words, go outside that dwelling or city and
shake the dust off of your feet. [15]Amen: I tell you, it will go easier for
Sodom and Gomorrah in the Day of Judgment than for that city! [16]See: I
send you forth like helpless sheep among hungry wolves. So learn to be as
canny as snakes and as harmless as doves. [17]And beware of people, for
there are those who will not hesitate to deliver you up to Sanhedrins, and
they will flog you in their synagogues; [18]and before governors and even
kings you will be led, on account of me, to bear witness to them and to the
gentiles. [19]But when they do deliver you up, do not worry about how or
what you will speak. For what to say will be supplied you on the spot.
[20]Because you are not the speakers, but rather the Spirit of your Father is
the one speaking in you. [21]But brother will deliver up brother to death,
and a father a child, and children will stand up in court against parents
and put them to death. [22]And you will be pariahs in the sight of all because of my name. But the one enduring in his allegiance, only such a one
will save himself. [23]But when they persecute you in this city, flee to another. For amen: I tell you, you will by no means be able to cover all the
cities of Israel in the time before the one like a son of man comes.

[24]"After all, a disciple by definition does not rank above the teacher,
nor does a slave rank above his lord. [25]It is good enough for the disciple
to become his teacher's equal in erudition and that the slave become a

j. 2 Kings 4:29; 5:22

free man like his master. If they called the head of the household Baal-Zebul, how much more will they vilify the members of his household? 26So do not fear them; for nothing is veiled except to be sooner or later unveiled, nothing hidden except to be revealed eventually. 27What I say to you in the dark, repeat it in the light of day. And what you hear whispered in your ear, proclaim from the housetops.[k] 28And do not fear the ones who threaten to kill the body but who are not capable of killing the soul. Rather, fear the one who is quite capable of destroying both soul and body in the Valley of Hinnom! 29Are not two sparrows sold for a farthing? And whenever one of them falls to the ground, it does not escape your Father's notice. 30He even keeps a running inventory of the hairs on your head! 31Therefore, do not fear: you excel many sparrows in value. 32Therefore, anyone willing to confess his association with me to others, I will likewise acknowledge him to my Father in the heavens. 33And if anyone repudiates me before others, I will likewise repudiate him before my Father in the heavens. 34Have you heard it said my mission was to cast peace over the land? My mission was not to bring peace, but rather a sword. 35For my mission was to pit a man against his father and a daughter against her mother and a bride against her mother-in-law, 36and to make into a person's enemies those who dwell under the same roof.[l] 37The one loving father or mother, more than me, if you must choose, is not worthy of me, and the one loving son or daughter above me is not worthy of me. 38And whoever does not take his cross and follow me is not worthy of me. 39The one finding his life shall lose it, and the one losing his life for my sake will find it. 40The one welcoming you welcomes me, and the one welcoming me welcomes the one who sent me out. 41The one welcoming a prophet because he is a prophet will receive a prophet's wage, and the one welcoming a *zaddik*[m] because he is a *zaddik* will receive a *zaddik's* wage. 42But whoever gives one of these little ones a cup of cold water to drink simply because he is a disciple, amen: I say to you, under no circumstances will he forfeit his wage."

11

1And it happened that, when Jesus finished giving instructions to his twelve disciples, he went away from there to teach and to make procla-

k. Here is a possible apologetic for ascribing to Jesus newly coined sayings no one has heard before.

l. Mic. 7:6

m. *Zaddik,* meaning "righteous one," was a special type of holy man, the equivalent of a *hasid,* "pious one."

mation in their cities. [2]But John, hearing in the prison the deeds of Christ, sent word through his disciples, [3]saying to him, "Are you the Coming One or should we look for someone else?" [4]And answering, Jesus said to them,[n] "Go and report to John what you hear and see: [5]blind men see again and lame men walk, men with skin disease are cleansed and deaf men hear, dead men are raised and poor men are given hope. [6]And blessed is the one who is not scandalized by me."[o] [7]And as they were on their way, Jesus began to speak to the crowds about John. "What did you go out into the desert to look at? A reed being swept by the wind? [8]Of course not. What did you go out to see? Someone dressed in dainty clothes? You'd better look elsewhere: the ones decked out in dainty clothes can be found in the palaces of kings. [9]But why did you go out? To see for yourselves a prophet? Yes! And I tell you, more than a prophet. [10]This is the one about whom it is written, "Behold, I send forth my angel before your face." [11]Amen: I tell you, there has not risen among mortal men one greater than John the Baptist. But the very least of those angels in the kingdom of the heavens is greater than he is.[p] [12]And from the era of John the Baptist until now, the kingdom of the heavens is torn asunder by violence, and the violent storm its gates.[q] [13]For all the predictions of the Prophets and the Torah culminated in John. [14]And if you want to welcome the imminent Coming One, Elijah, it is he! [15]The one with ears, let him hear.

[16]"But what can I compare this nation to? It is like children sitting inactive in the marketplace, who call out to each other, [17]saying, 'It's your fault. We played you girls the pipe and you wouldn't dance!' And the girls reply, 'That's a boy's game! We sang laments, and you boys wouldn't play funeral with us!' And the boys reply, 'But that's only for girls!' [18]For John's way was to abstain from food and drink, and you people say, 'He is a demoniac! [19]Man came into the world to eat and drink.' And John's sect says, 'No, that is a gluttonous man and a wine-drinker! A friend of customs agents and backsliders!' Where is wisdom in this exchange? The wise choice will be vindicated by the results."

---

n. The fact that Jesus is made to answer *them,* not *him,* may imply the verse was aimed at the John the Baptist sect.

o. Originally a martyrdom saying.

p. This is a Mandaean saying reflecting their belief in John and higher allegiance to the angels and glorified patriarchs Enosh-Uthras, Hibil (Abel) Ziwa, and Manda-d'Haiye.

q. A reference to the War in Heaven myth (cf. Luke 10:18).

[20]At that point, he started to denounce the cities in which the majority of his powerful deeds were performed because they did not repent. [21]"Woe to you, Chorazin! Woe to you, Beth-Saida! If the powerful deeds done in you had happened in Tyre and Sidon, they would have repented in hair shirts and ashes in the ancient past. [22]Even though they didn't repent, I tell you, it will go easier for Tyre and Sidon on the Day of Judgment than for you! [23]And you, village of Nahum! Did you say to yourself, 'I will be exalted to the heavens. I will be like the Most High'? You shall descend as far as Hades! Because if the deeds of power performed in you had been performed in Sodom, it would still be there today. [24]Even though they were destroyed for rebuffing God's messengers, it will go easier for the land of Sodom on the Day of Judgment than for you."

[25]And at that time, Jesus replied to certain scribes, saying, "I applaud you, Father, Lord of the sky and the earth,[r] because you concealed these things from the wise men and the intellectuals, revealing them instead to infants. [26]Yes, Father, because it seemed good sport to you. [27]All things were bestowed on me by my Father and no one knows the Son except the Father, nor does anyone know the Father except the Son and any to whom the Son shall deign to reveal him!"[s] [28]And to the crowd he said, "Come to me, all those laboring under heavy burdens, and I will relieve you. [29]Take my yoke on your shoulders instead and learn my doctrine, for I am meek and humble in heart, no taskmaster, and you shall find rest for your souls; [30]for my yoke is easy to bear and the burden I assign is light, not like the scribes.'"[t]

12

[1]And at that time, Jesus made his way on the Sabbath through the grainfields, and his disciples hungered and began to pluck the ears of grain and to eat. [2]But the Pharisees, seeing it, said to him, "Aha! Your disciples are doing what is not legal to do on a sabbath." [3]And he said to them, "Did you not read what David did when he hungered, he and those with him? [4]How he entered into the house of God and ate the loaves of showbread, which is not legal for him to eat, neither for those who were with him, except for the priests alone? [5]Or did you not read in the Torah that on the Sabbaths the priests on duty in the temple profane the Sab-

---

r. Notice that Jesus responds to critics while addressing God, engaging in apostrophe for effect.

s. Akhenaten's Hymn to the Sun reads similarly: "O Aten, no man knoweth thee, save for thy son Akhenaten."

t. Sirach 51:23-27

bath and are not culpable for it? [6]But I tell you that something greater than the temple is at stake here! [7]If you had known what it is to say, 'I want mercy, not sacrifice,' you would not have condemned the innocent. [8]For man was given dominion even over the Sabbath."

[9]And leaving there, he entered into their synagogue. [10]And behold, there was a man with a withered hand. And they questioned him, saying, "Is it legal on the Sabbath to heal?" that they might accuse him. [11]And he said to them, "Which of you men, if he had one sheep, and it happened to fall into a ditch on the Sabbath, would not grasp hold of it and lift it out?[u] [12]And how much more is a man worth than a mere sheep! So then, surely it is legal on the Sabbath to do good deeds." [13]Then he says to the man, "Extend your hand!" And it was restored as healthy as the other. [14]But going out of the synagogue, the Pharisees at once plotted against him so as to destroy him.[v] [15]But Jesus, aware of this, left the borders of that region, and many followed him. And he healed them all [16]and gave them strict orders not to expose him [17]so that the thing spoken by Isaiah the prophet might be fulfilled, namely: [18]"Behold my servant whom I chose, my beloved with whom my soul was quite pleased; I will place my Spirit upon him, and he will decree judgment on the gentiles. [19]He will not raise a ruckus or shout, nor will anyone hear his voice in the streets. [20]He will not so much as snap the drooping reed or snuff out the dying candle until his judgment prevails. [21]And the gentiles will set their hopes on his name."

[22]Then a blind and mute demoniac was brought to him, and he cured him so that the mute was able to speak and see. [23]And all the crowds were astonished and said, "Is this not Solomon, master of demons and the son of David?" [24]But the Pharisees hearing them said, "The only way this man casts out demons is by enlisting the services of Baal-Zebul, ruler of the demons!"[w] [25]Knowing what they were thinking, he said to them, "Every kingdom divided against itself is reduced to ruins. And every city or house divided against itself will not stand. [26]And if the adversary casts out the adversary, he must have been divided against himself. Then, how

u. As far as we know, all Jewish sects forbade doing so, which means that Jesus would not have been able to take this for granted. It is an early Christian anachronism.

v. The substance of this scene derives from the miracle of the Judean prophet of 1 Kings 13:1-7ff, LXX.

w. Baal-Zebul ("Lord of the House," implying "Lord of the World") was a powerful patron of exorcists, while Baal-Zebub ("Lord of the Flies") denoted an oracle because the priests heard a sound like buzzing, the voice of spirits telling the desired fortune. Jesus' reply (v. 29) seems to come from Isa. 49:24.

will his kingdom stand? [27]And besides, if I am casting out the demons by means of Baal-Zebul, by what name do your protégées cast them out? They will condemn what you said as quickly as I! [28]But suppose it is by means of the Spirit of God that I cast out the demons, then the kingdom of God has overtaken you.[x] [29]But how is anyone to be able to enter into a strong man's dwelling and seize his vessels unless he first binds the strong man? Then and only then will he plunder his house. [30]The one who is not with me is against me, and the one not harvesting with me is sowing the wind. [31]Because of this, I tell you that all sin and blasphemy will be forgiven mankind, but blasphemy of the Spirit will not be forgiven. [32]And whoever may speak a thing against mortal man, it will be forgiven him; but whoever speaks against the Divine Spirit, it will not be forgiven him, neither in this age nor in the impending one. [33]How long will you limp between two opinions? Either purify the tree and make its fruit good or poison the tree and make the fruit go bad, for by the fruit the tree's condition is discerned. [34]Spawn of vipers! How can you say good things when you are wicked? The mouth only speaks by drawing on what fills the heart. [35]The good person produces goods from the treasury of good and the wicked person produces evils out of the treasury of wickedness. [36]But I tell you that every careless remark people make, they will have to give an explanation for it on the Day of Judgment. [37]For out of the transcript of your words you will be vindicated, and from the record of your words you will be condemned."

[38]Then some of the scribes and Pharisees made this rejoinder to him, saying, "Teacher, we would like to see a confirming sign from you." [39]But answering, he said to them, "Only an evil and idolatrous nation seeks a sign, and a sign shall not be vouchsafed to it except for the sign of Jonah the prophet. [40]*For just as Jonah was in the belly of the whale three days and three nights, so will another man be in the heart of the earth three days and three nights.*[y] [41]Ninevite men will rise up in the Day of

---

x. Compressed into these verses is an unmistakable midrash upon the story of Moses's miracle contest with the magicians of Pharaoh. Initially able to match Moses feat for feat, they prove incapable of copying the miracle of the gnats and therefore warn Pharaoh to capitulate, saying, "This is the finger of God" (Exod. 8:19).

y. Krister Stendahl argues that v. 40 is a later interpolation. It is missing from Justin's quotation of this passage. See Stendahl, *The School of Saint Matthew* (Philadelphia: Fortress Press, 1968), 132-33, and agreement from O. Lamar Cope, *Matthew: A Scribe Trained for the Kingdom of Heaven* (Washington, DC: Catholic Biblical Association, 1976), 40-44.

Judgment to accuse this nation and will condemn it. After all, they repented at the preaching of Jonah, and just look: something greater than Jonah is at work here. [42]The Queen of Sheba will be resurrected in the Day of Judgment to accuse this nation and will condemn it. After all, she came from the far reaches of the earth to hear the wisdom of Solomon, and as you can see, something greater than Solomon is at work here. [43]But when the unclean spirit exits from a human host, he wanders through arid places seeking respite and finds none. [44]Then he reasons, "Why not return to enter the dwelling I left?" And he arrives to find it untenanted, swept, and furnished. [45]Then he goes and recruits seven other spirits more wicked than himself, and entering, he dwells there happily ever after. And the last condition of the wretch is worse than the first! So will it be also with this wicked nation."[z]

[46]As he was still addressing the crowds, behold, his mother and brothers stood outside seeking to speak to him. [47]*And someone said to him, "Look: your mother and your brothers are standing outside hoping to speak to you."* [48]And he answered the one speaking to him, saying, "Indeed? Who is my mother? And who are my brothers?" [49]And extending his hand toward his disciples, he said, "Behold, you are my mother and my brothers! [50]For whoever obeys the will of my Father in the heavens, that one is my brother and sister and mother."[a]

13

[1]On that day, Jesus went out of the house and sat beside the sea. [2]And many crowds gathered to him, forcing him to board a boat and sit in it on the sea, and all the crowd stood on the beach. [3]And he spoke to them many things by means of parables, saying, "Listen: picture a sower going out to sow. [4]And in the process of sowing, some seeds indeed fell beside the road, and the birds came and ate them up. [5]But others fell on the rocky places where it had not much soil, and at once it sprang up on account of not having depth of earth. [6]But when the sun rose, it was scorched, and on account of not having any root, it withered. [7]But others fell upon the thorns, and the thorns came up and choked them. [8]But others fell upon the good earth and gave fruit, one producing by hundreds, another by sixties, yet another by thirties. [9]The one who has ears, let him hear."

---

z. Perhaps an old comment on the folly of Jewish leaders who, having thrown off Seleucid tyranny, eventually called in the Romans to settle their internecine disputes.

a. Based on Exod. 18:1-22 with an ironic twist.

[10]And approaching him, the disciples said to him, "Why do you speak to them in parables?" [11]And answering, he said, "Because to you it has been vouchsafed to know the mysteries of the kingdom of the heavens, but it has not been vouchsafed to them. [12]For the one who has, more will be given to him and he will have abundance; but the one who has not, even what he has will be taken from him. [13]This is why I speak to them in parables, because seeing, they do not see, and hearing, they do not hear, nor understand. [14]And in them the prophecy of Isaiah is fulfilled, namely, 'In hearing, you will hear and not understand at all, and seeing, you will see and not perceive at all. [15]For the mind of this people has grown dense, and they heard dimly with their ears and closed their eyes, lest they see with the eyes and hear with the ears and understand with the mind and turn about, and I will heal them.' [16]But blessed are your eyes because they do see and your ears because they do hear. [17]For amen: I tell you, many prophets and wise men desired to behold what you see, and did not see, and to hear what you hear, and did not hear. [18]Therefore, listen, and I will gladly explain the parable of the sower to you. [19]Everyone who hears the message of the kingdom and does not understand, the wicked one comes and seizes what has been sown in his heart. This is the one sown by the road. [20]But the one sown on the rocky places, this is the one hearing the message and at once welcoming it with joy. [21]But he has no root in himself but is short-lived, and when tribulation or persecution comes because of the message, at once he is scandalized. [22]But the one sown in the thorns, this is the one hearing the message, but the worries of the temporal world and the false promises of worldly wealth choke the message, and it becomes barren. [23]And the one sown on the good earth, this is the one who, hearing and understanding the message, bears fruit and produces, one by hundreds, one by sixties, and one by thirties."

[24]And he set forth another parable for their consideration, saying, "The kingdom of the heavens was compared to a man sowing good seed in his field. [25]But while everyone else was asleep, his enemy's henchmen came and sowed tares in between the wheat and then left. [26]But when the grass sprouted and produced fruit, then the tares appeared, too. [27]So coming to the master of the house, his slaves said to him, 'Lord, did you not sow good seed in your field? Then where did the tares come from?' [28]And he said to them, 'The man who is my enemy[b] did this.' And his slaves say, 'So do you want us to go and gather them?' [29]But he says, 'No,

b. Peter refers to Paul as "the man who is my enemy" in the Epistle of Peter to James. Paul may be in view here, too, as the corrupter of true Torah Christianity.

I'm afraid that in collecting the tares you might uproot the wheat, too.
[30]Leave both to grow together until the harvest; and at harvest time I will
instruct the reapers to collect the tares first and tie them in bundles to
burn them. But as for the wheat, gather it into my barn.'"

[31]He set another parable before them, saying, "The kingdom of the
heavens is like a grain of mustard which a man took and sowed in his
field, [32]which indeed is smaller than all the seeds but when grown is
greater than the herbs and becomes a tree so big the birds of the sky find
lodging in its branches."

[33]Another parable he spoke to them. "The kingdom of the heavens is
like leaven which a woman took and hid in three measures of meal until
the whole was leavened."

[34]All these things Jesus spoke to the crowds in parables, and unless
he had a parable, he spoke nothing to them, [35]so that the thing spoken by
the prophet was fulfilled, namely, "I will open my mouth in parables, I
will utter things kept secret since creation."

[36]Then dismissing the crowds, he came into the house and his disciples approached him, saying, "Explain to us the parable of the tares in the
field." [37]And answering, he said, "The one sowing the good seed is yours
truly. [38]And the field is the world. And the good seed, these are the heirs
of the kingdom, and the tares are the spawn of the wicked one, [39]and the
enemy sowing them is the slanderer.[c] And the harvest is the culmination
of the age, and the reapers are angels. [40]Therefore, just as the tares are
collected and consumed with fire, it will be that way at the culmination of
the age: [41]one like a son of man will send forth his angels, and they will
collect out of his kingdom all causes of scandal and all Torah apostates
[42]and will toss them into the blazing furnace; there will be wailing and
grinding of teeth. [43]At that time, the righteous will beam forth like the
sun in the heavens where their Father reigns.

"The one who has ears, let him hear! [44]The kingdom of the heavens
is like treasure buried in the field, which a man found and reburied, and
from his joy, he goes and cashes in his possessions and buys that field.
[45]Again, the kingdom of the heavens is like a merchant looking for beautiful pearls. [46]And finding one choice pearl, he went away, sold off his entire stock, and bought it. [47]Again, the kingdom of the heavens is like a net
thrown into the sea, rounding up every kind of sea creature, [48]and which,
when filled, the fishermen drag up on shore, and they sit and collect the

c. In the Dead Sea Scrolls, Paul is called "the Spouter of Lies"; in Gal. 4:16 and 3 Peter he is referred to as "the enemy."

good ones into vessels, while throwing out the worthless ones. [49]It will be that way at the culmination of the age: the angels will march forth and will separate the wicked from among the just, [50]and they will throw them into the blazing furnace. There will be wailing and grinding of teeth.

[51]"Did you understand all these things?" They say to him, "Yes." [52]So he told them one last parable: "Because of this, every scribe trained as a disciple to the kingdom of the heavens is like a man, master of a house, who produces out of his treasure goods both new and old."

[53]And it came about, when Jesus finished these parables, he departed from there. [54]And coming into his birthplace, he taught them in their synagogue in such a way as to astonish them and make them say, "Where does this man come by this wisdom?" "And the powerful deeds!" [55]"Isn't this man the son of the carpenter? Isn't his mother called Mary and his brothers James and Joseph and Simon and Judah?" [56]"And aren't all his sisters here with us?"

[57]Yet, they were scandalized at him. But Jesus said to them, "It just goes to show, the only place a prophet gets no respect is his own birthplace and in his own dwelling." [58]And there he did not perform any powerful deeds because of their lack of faith.[d]

14

[1]At that time Herod the tetrarch heard the report of Jesus, [2]and he said to his servants, "This must be John the Baptist! He was raised from the dead and, because of that, the Powers are energizing him." [3]What he meant was that Herod seized John, bound him, and put him in prison on account of Herodias, the wife of his brother Philip. [4]For John said to him, "It is not legal for you to have sex with her." [5]And wishing to kill him, he nonetheless feared the crowd because they revered him as a prophet. [6]Now when Herod's birthday arrived, the daughter of Herodias danced in the midst of the guests and pleased Herod. [7]And so, with an oath, he promised to give her whatever she might ask. [8]Being instructed in advance by her mother, she says, "Give me, here on a dish, the head of John the Baptist." [9]And the king, grieved because of the oaths and the dinner companions, ordered that it be given. [10]So sending an executioner, he beheaded John right there in the prison, [11]and his head was brought on a dish and given to the girl. [12]And coming forth, his disciples took his headless corpse and buried him and came and reported it to Jesus.[e] And Jesus,

---

d. The likely source of the frosty reception among his own townsfolk is 1 Sam. 10:1-27.

e. Herod Antipas's words to his stepdaughter come from Esther 5:3. Herod

hearing the news, departed from there in a boat to a desert place by himself. [13]And hearing of this, the crowds followed him on foot from the cities. [14]And upon his arrival, he saw a great crowd and felt compassion for them and cured their sick.

[15]And now, evening coming, the disciples came to him and said, "This place is a desert and the dinner hour already passed. Dismiss the crowds, that they may go to the villages and buy themselves food." [16]But Jesus said to them, "They need not go away. You can give them something to eat." [17]But they say to him, "We have nothing here but five loaves and two fish." [18]And he said, "Bring them here to me." [19]And having ordered the crowds to recline on the grass, taking the five loaves and two fish, looking up to the sky, he blessed the loaves and, breaking them, gave them to the disciples, and the disciples gave them to the crowd. [20]All ate and were satisfied, and they took twelve basket-loads of leftover pieces. [21]And those eating were about five thousand males, not counting women and children.[f]

[22]And at once he ordered his disciples to launch the boat and precede him to the opposite shore while he dispersed the crowds. [23]And having waved them good-bye, he went up into the mountain to pray. [24]And with evening coming on, he remained there alone. [25]But the boat was now many stadia away from land, being tormented by the waves, seeing the wind was against them. [26]So in the fourth watch of the night, he came toward them, walking on the sea. And the disciples, seeing him walking on the sea, were frantic, saying to one another, "It is a phantom!" And they shrieked with fear. [27]But at once Jesus spoke to them, saying, "Cheer up! It is I. Do not be afraid." [28]And answering him, Peter said, "Lord, if you are not a phantom, enable me to come to you on the waters."[g] [29]And he said, "Come!" And dropping over the side of the boat, Peter walked on the waters and covered the distance between him and Jesus. [30]But noticing the wind, he grew afraid and, beginning to sink, shouted, "Lord, save me!" [31]And at once, extending a hand, Jesus grasped hold of him and

painting himself into a corner may come from Darius's bamboozlement in Dan. 6:6-15. But MacDonald (*The Homeric Epics and the Gospel of Mark*) shows how the story of John's martyrdom matches in all essentials the *Odyssey* story of the murder of Agamemnon (3:254-308: 4:512-47; 11:404-34).

f. The basis for the two miraculous feeding stories is Elisha multiplying twenty barley loaves for a hundred men in 2 Kings 4:42-44.

g. Peter seems to think his own suspension on the sea as an entity of flesh and blood would prove the other figure need not be a ghost either.

says to him, "Scant is your faith! Why did you doubt?"[h] [32]And as they climbed into the ship, the wind died. [33]And those in the ship bowed before him, exclaiming, "Truly, you are God's son!"[i]

[34]And crossing over onto the land, they came to shore at Gennesaret. [35]And the men of the place, recognizing him, sent word into that whole region, and they brought to him all those in a bad way, pleading with him that they might touch just the very edge of his garment, and as many as managed to touch him were wholly saved.

15

[1]Then Pharisees and scribes from Jerusalem approached him, saying, [2]"Why do your disciples violate the tradition of the elders? For they do not wash their hands when they eat bread." [3]But answering, he said to them, "And why do you violate the commandment of God for the sake of your tradition? [4]For God said, 'Take care of father and mother' and 'Whoever speaks evil of father or mother, let him end up dead.' [5]But you know better! Because you say, 'If one says to one's father or mother, Whatever you might have been owed by me, it is a consecrated gift, [6]by no means shall he take care of his father or his mother.' And thus you made the command of God moot in favor of your tradition. [7]Isaiah the prophet put it beautifully when he mentioned you, you hypocrites, saying: [8]'This people honors me with lip service, but their heart is remote from me; [9]and their piety toward me is a charade, teaching doctrines that are commandments of mortal men.'"[j] [10]And summoning the crowd, he said to them, "Hear me, and try to understand:[k] [11]nothing entering into the mouth makes a person profane; but what comes forth out of the mouth, this makes a person profane." [12]Then, coming to him, the disciples say to him, "Are you aware the Pharisees were scandalized by what you said?" [13]And he, answering, said, "Every plant that my heavenly Father did not plant shall be uprooted. [14]Forget about them! Blind, they pretend to lead the blind. But if a blind man leads a blind man, both of them will end up in the ditch."

---

h. As Arlo J. Nau (*Peter in Matthew*) suggests, verses 30-31 contradict the previous verse's account of Peter's successful miracle. They were probably added by a subsequent Matthean/Antiochean scribe who chafed at the exaltation of Peter.

i. Pss. 107 (LXX 106): 23-30; Job 9:8b, *Iliad* 24:332, 340-41, 345-46, 351-52.

j. The Hebrew original of Isaiah 29:13, LXX, would not make the same precise point.

k. Here we are to discern a reflection of Elijah's gesture in 1 Kings 18:30.

[15]And answering, Peter said to him, "Explain the parable to us." [16]So he said, "You, too, are witless? [17]Do you not grasp that everything coming into the mouth goes into the stomach and is finally ejected into the latrine? [18]But the things coming forth out of the mouth come out of the heart, and those make a person profane. [19]For out of the heart come wicked reasonings, murders, adulteries, whoredoms, thefts, false testimonies, blasphemies. [20]It is this sort of thing that makes a person profane. But to eat with unwashed hands? It does not make a person profane!"

[21]And going forth from there, Jesus left for the region of Tyre and Sidon. [22]And behold, a woman, a Canaanite from those borders, came forth and shouted, saying, "Take pity on me, Lord, for you are a mighty exorcist like Solomon, the son of David. My daughter is badly demonized." [23]But he answered her not a word. And approaching him, his disciples urged him, saying, "Get rid of her! She keeps calling out behind us." [24]So he decided he had best answer her, and he said, "My mission was only to the lost sheep dwelling in Israel." [25]But she came and bowed before him, saying, "Lord, help me!" [26]But he, answering, said, "It is not proper to take the bread that belongs to the children and to throw it to the dogs, now is it?" [27]But she had an answer ready for him: "True, Lord. But even the dogs eat the crumbs falling from their masters' table." [28]Then, answering, Jesus said to her, "Woman, your determination is great! I grant you what you wish." And her daughter was cured as of that very hour.[1]

[29]And leaving from there, Jesus came by the Sea of Galilee, and going up into the mountains, he sat there. [30]And crowds came to him, having with them various lame, maimed, blind, mute, and many others. And they cast them at his feet, and he cured them, [31]causing the crowd to marvel, seeing mutes speaking, the maimed restored to health, lame folk walking, and blind people seeing. And they worshipped the God of Israel. [32]And Jesus summoned his disciples and said, "I feel for the crowd because they remain with me three whole days now and have not anything they may eat. I am not willing to send them home still fasting for fear they will keel over in the road." [33]And the disciples say to him, "Where in the desert do we come up with enough loaves to satisfy so great a crowd?" [34]And Jesus says to them, "How many loaves do you have?" And they said, "A total of seven, plus a few fish." [35]And having directed the crowd to recline on the ground, [36]he took the seven loaves and the fish and, giving thanks,

1. This is based on Elijah and the widow of Zarephath in 1 Kings 17:8-16.

broke them and gave them to the disciples, and the disciples gave them to the crowds. [37]And all ate and were satisfied, and the leftover fragments they gathered filled seven hampers. [38]And those eating were about four thousand males, not counting women and children. [39]And dismissing the crowd, he set sail in the boat and came into the region of Magadan.

16

[1]And the local Pharisees and Syndics, coming to him to challenge him, requested that he show them a sign from heaven. [2]But answering, he said to them, "With evening coming on, you say, 'Good weather ahead, for the heaven is red'; [3]and in the morning, 'Stormy today with clouds overhead, the dawn is red.' You know how to discern the face of the sky, but the signs of the times baffle you? [4]A wicked and idolatrous nation seeks a sign, and a sign shall not be vouchsafed it except for the sign of Jonah." And walking away from them, he left the area. [5]And on the trip to the other side, the disciples forgot to take loaves. And Jesus said to them, [6]"Beware and do not underestimate the leaven of the Pharisees and the Syndics!" [7]And they whispered to one another, "We took no loaves!" [8]But becoming aware of it, Jesus said, "Why do you babble about not having loaves of bread? Do you have any faith at all? [9]Do you still not get it? If I wanted bread, I could make it myself! Don't you remember the five loaves for the five thousand and how many baskets you gathered? [10]Nor the seven loaves for the four thousand, how many hampers you gathered? [11]How can you possibly fail to grasp that I wasn't talking about loaves of bread? Rather, look to the insidiousness of the Pharisees and Syndics!" [12]At last they saw that he was not saying to reckon with the yeast in loaves of bread, but with that of the teaching of the Pharisees and Syndics.

[13]And coming into the environs of Caesarea Philippi, Jesus questioned his disciples, saying, "Who do people think yours truly to be?" [14]And they said, "While some say John the Baptist, others say Elijah, but others Jeremiah or one of the prophets." [15]He says to them, "But what about you? Who do you think me to be?" [16]And answering, Simon Peter said, "You are the Christ, the son of the one true God."[l] [17]And answering, Jesus said to him, "Blessed are you, Simon bar-Jonah,[m] for flesh and

l. Literally, Peter confesses that Jesus is the Christ, "the son of the *living* God," but the point of that title is to contrast Israel's God with the dead idols of the heathen. Thus, the "living God" denotes the "only God."

m. A pun for "sign of Jonah," *semeion Jonas*.

blood did not reveal this to you, but rather my Father in the heavens.[n] [18]And I also say to you, 'You are Peter, and on this rock I will build my church and the gates of Hades will not withstand it. [19]I will give you the keys of the kingdom of the heavens, and what obligations and penances you may bind on men shall be considered bound in the heavens, and what duties and penalties you may annul on earth shall be considered annulled in the heavens.'" [20]Then he warned the disciples that they must tell no one that he is the Christ.

[21]From then on, Jesus *Christ* began to indicate to his disciples that he must go to Jerusalem and suffer many indignities at the hands of the elders and archpriests and scribes and be executed and on the third day be raised. [22]And taking him on ahead, Peter began to admonish him, saying, "May God favor you, Lord, but this shall by no means befall you!" [23]But turning, he said to Peter, "Get back with the others, adversary! You are a stumbling stone to me because you are not wise to the ways of God, but only to the ways of this world." [24]Then Jesus said to his disciples, "If anyone here wants to come after me, let him repudiate himself and let him pick up his cross and follow me. [25]For whoever tries to save his life will lose it, but whoever will sacrifice his life for my sake will save it. [26]For what profit would a person make if he managed to acquire the whole world, only to be fined his own life? For what could a person possibly offer in exchange for his life? [27]I say this because one like a son of man is about to come in the radiance of his Father with his angels, and then he will repay each one according to his acts. [28]Amen: I say to you, there are some of those standing here who will certainly not taste of death before they see one like a son of man coming to receive his crown."

17

[1]And after six days, Jesus takes along Peter and Jacob and John his brother and leads them up into a high mountain solely by themselves. [2]And he was metamorphosed in front of them, and his face shone like the sun and his garments became white as the light. [3]And behold, Elijah and Moses appeared to them, conversing with Jesus. And Jesus says to Peter, "Simon, have you nothing to say?" [4]And answering, Peter says to Jesus, "Rabbi, it is good for us disciples to be here. If you wish, I will make three tents here: one for you, one for Moses, and one for Elijah." [5]While he was still speaking, behold, a glowing cloud overshadowed them and a voice from the cloud: "This one is my son, the beloved, in whom I was quite

n. Cf. Gal. 1:1, 11-12

pleased. Hear him!" [6]And hearing this, the disciples fell on their faces and were terrified. [7]And Jesus approached, touching them, and said, "Rise and do not fear." [8]And lifting their eyes tentatively, they saw no one except for Jesus alone.[o] [9]And as they descended from the mountain, Jesus ordered them, "Recount the vision to no one before a man be raised from the dead." [10]And the disciples questioned him, saying, "Then what scripture do the scribes have in mind when they say Elijah must come first or the general resurrection may not take place?" [11]But he, answering, said, "Elijah is indeed coming and will usher in the resurrection of all things; [12]but I say to you that, indeed, Elijah already came and they did not recognize him but did with him what they wished. In the same way, another man is about to suffer at their hands." [13]Then the disciples understood that he was referring to John the Baptist.

[14]And as they were approaching the crowd, a man came to him and, falling on his knees before him, [15]said, "Lord, take pity on my son because he is moonstruck and in a bad way, for often he falls into the fire and into the water. [16]And I brought him to your disciples and they were not able to cure him." [17]And answering him, Jesus said, "O unbelieving and perverted nation! How long till I am free of you? How long must I endure you? Bring him here to me." [18]And Jesus rebuked it, and the demon exited from him, and the lad was healed as of that hour. [19]Then, approaching Jesus privately, the disciples said, "Why were we unable to cast it out?" [20]And he says to them, "Because of your scant faith. For amen: I say to you, if you have faith like a grain of mustard, you will command this mountain, 'Move from here to there!' and it will be moved, and nothing will be impossible for you. [21]*Even so, this particular species can come out by means of nothing but prayer and fasting.*"[p]

[22]And while they were walking together in the Galilee, Jesus said to them, "This is the way of things: a man will be delivered into the hands of his fellow men, [23]and they will kill him, and on the third day he will be raised." And they were overcome with grief.

---

o. "And six days later" must be understood as a pointer to the Exodus account where God calls Moses up the mountainside, Moses takes Joshua (Greek: Jesus) with him, the glory cloud covers the height for six days, and on the seventh day the divine voice calls Moses from the depth of the cloud (24:12-16). The glowing apparition of Jesus is derived from Exod. 34:29, as well as Mal. 3:2. Matthew makes the Moses parallel even closer than it was in Mark by having Jesus' face, as well as his clothes, shine like the sun.

p. Just as Elisha succeeded where Gehazi failed (2 Kings 4:32-35) because he was not Elisha, so here Jesus is irreplaceable because he is the hero of the story.

[24]And when they arrived in the village of Nahum, the ones collecting the two drachma tax came to Peter and said, "Your teacher does not pay the two drachmas?" He says, "Yes." [25]And as he came into the house, Jesus anticipated him, saying, "How does it seem to you, Simon? The kings of the earth—from whom do they take toll or tribute? From their own people or from foreigners?" [26]When he said, "From foreigners," Jesus said to him, "Then their people are exempt. [27]But in order not to create a scandal, when next you go to the sea, throw in a hook and take the first fish to come up, and opening its mouth, you will discover a stater. Take that and give it to them for me and you."

18

[1]In that hour the disciples came to Jesus, saying, "So who ranks highest in the kingdom of the heavens?" [2]And summoning a child, he stood it where all could see [3]and said, "Amen: I say to you, unless you turn about and become like the children, you will by no means enter the kingdom of the heavens. [4]Therefore, whoever is willing to humble himself like this child, this one ranks highest in the kingdom of the heavens.[q] [5]And whoever welcomes one such child on account of my name, welcomes me; [6]and whoever scandalizes one of these new converts, it is good for him instead to have his head put through the center hole of the upper millstone and be dumped overboard into the depths. [7]Woe to the world because of scandals! For though it is inevitable for scandals to arise, woe to the wretch through whom the scandal arises. [8]But if your hand or your foot leads you into scandal, chop it off and pitch it away from you. It is to your advantage to enter into the life mutilated or limping than, having both hands and both feet, to be thrown into the age-long fire. [9]And if your eye leads you into scandal, gouge it out and pitch it away from you! It is to your advantage to enter into the life one-eyed than, with both eyes intact, to be thrown into the fire of the Valley of Hinnom. [10]See to it that you don't give short shrift to these little ones, for I tell you that their guardian angels have immediate access to my Father in heaven.

[11]"*For a man came to save what was lost.* [12]How does it seem to you? If any man has a hundred sheep and one strays, will he not leave the ninety-nine grazing on the mountains and go off to seek the stray?[r] [13]And

q. This passage and its parallels go back to the Pentateuchal disputes pitting Moses against Aaron and Miriam, Dathan and Abiram (Num. 12, 16). It is Moses's meekness that qualifies him for leadership.

r. Some say no shepherd would take such a risk and that Jesus expects the

if he chances to discover it, Amen: I say to you, he rejoices over it more than over the ninety-nine who did not go astray. [14]Even so, it is not the will of their angels before your Father in the heavens that one of these little ones should be lost. [15]So if your brother sins, go and admonish him privately between you and him. If he listens to you, you have won back your brother. [16]But if he does not listen, take with you one or two more so that only by the testimony of two or three witnesses every accusation may be corroborated. [17]But if he remains unmoved by them, tell the Church. And if he remains unmoved by the Church, write him off like the heathen and the customs agent. [18]Amen: I say to you, whatever penalty you impose on earth shall be seconded in heaven, and whatever sentence you may mitigate on earth shall be considered mitigated in heaven. [19]Again, I say to you that if two of you agree on earth concerning every disciplinary matter which they may ask, it shall happen for them thanks to my Father in the heavens. [20]For where two or three are assembled in my name, I am there in their midst."

[21]Then Peter, approaching, said to him, "Lord, how often will my brother sin against me and I will forgive him? Until the seventh time?" [22]Jesus says to him, "I do not say to you until the seventh time, but rather until the seventy-seventh time. [23]Because of this, the kingdom of the heavens was compared to a man, a king, who wanted to settle accounts with his slaves. [24]And as he began the process, one was brought forward to him, a debtor of ten thousand talents. [25]And the poor wretch not having the wherewithal to pay him, the lord commanded him to be sold with his wife and children and all his possessions toward repayment of the debt. [26]Therefore, falling down before him, the slave prostrated himself before him, saying, 'Postpone your wrath at me and I will pay you the whole thing!' [27]And flooded with compassion, the lord of that slave released him and forgave him the loan. [28]But going out, that slave looked up one of his fellow slaves who owed him one hundred denarii. And grabbing him, he choked him, saying, 'Pay, if you owe something!' [29]Therefore, his fellow slave, falling down before him, pleaded with him, 'Postpone your wrath at me and I will repay you!' [30]But he did not want to do it. So instead, he went off and threw him into prison till he should repay the sum he owed. [31]Therefore, his fellow slaves, seeing what had taken place, were extremely dismayed and they went and explained to their lord all that had happened. [32]Then, summoning him, his lord says to him,

---

reader to know this, intending irony; but more likely the gaff reflects the ignorance and romanticism of a later, urban creator of the parable.

'Wicked slave! All that debt I forgave you since you pleaded with me! [33]Weren't you obliged to have mercy on your fellow slave as I had mercy on you?' [34]And infuriated, his lord handed him over to the torturers, to take it out of his hide. [35]My Heavenly Father will do the same to you unless each of you forgives his brother from your hearts."

19

[1]And it happened, when Jesus finished these words, that he left the Galilee and arrives in the boundaries of Judea across the Jordan. [2]And many crowds followed him, and he cured them there. [3]And Pharisees approached him, seeking to gauge him, and they asked if it is legal to dismiss one's wife for any cause. [4]And answering, he said, "Did you not read that the Creator, right from the start, 'made them male and female?' [5]And he said, 'This is why a man shall leave father and mother and shall join with his wife, and the two shall be one flesh.' [6]This means they are no longer two but one flesh. So then, if God has yoked them together, let no mere mortal divide them." [7]They say to him, "Then why did Moses command one to draw up the papers necessary to send his wife away?" [8]He says to them, "Because of your insensitivity, Moses permitted you Jews to send your wives packing. [9]But I say to you that whoever sends his wife away, except of course for impurity, and marries another, commits adultery."

[10]The disciples say to him, "If such is the man's situation with the wife, it is not prudent to marry in the first place!" [11]And he said to them, "Not everyone accepts this saying, [12]for there are eunuchs who were born thus from a mother's womb, and there are eunuchs who were made eunuchs by others, and there are eunuchs who made themselves eunuchs for the sake of gaining the kingdom of the heavens. As for anyone capable of accepting it, let him accept it."

[13]And they brought children to him, hoping he would lay hands on them and pray, and the disciples rebuffed them. [14]But Jesus said, "Let the children come to me. What is the matter with you? Don't stop them! Don't you know them? These are the very angels of the kingdom of the heavens." [15]And laying hands on them, he moved on from there.[s]

[16]And behold, one approached him and said, "Teacher, what good deed may I do that I may have age-long life?" [17]And he said to him, "Why do you ask me about the good? The good is one thing: if you want to en-

s. This is part of an infant baptism liturgy, as Oscar Cullmann demonstrated (*Baptism in the New Testament*), suggested in part by 2 Kings 4:26-27.

ter into the life, keep all the commandments equally." 18He says to him,
"Which ones?" And Jesus said, "Do not murder, Do not commit adultery, Do not steal, Do not testify falsely, 19Take care of father and
mother, and You shall love your neighbor as yourself." 20The young man
says to him, "All these I kept. Is there something more I am missing?"
21Jesus said to him, "If you want to be perfect, go sell what you own and
give the price to the poor,[t] and you shall have treasure in the heavens, and
come follow me." 22But hearing this reply, the young man went away
grieving at what he must do, for he had many possessions to disburse.
23So Jesus said to his disciples, "Amen: I tell you, a rich man will enter the
kingdom of God only reluctantly. 24And again I tell you, it is easier for a
camel to enter through the hole of a needle than for a rich man to enter
into the kingdom of God." 25Hearing this, the disciples were completely
astonished, reflecting that "if even God's favorites cannot enter heaven,
then who can save himself?" 26Looking at them, Jesus says, "True, for
mortals this is impossible. But for God, all things are possible."

27Then answering, Peter said to him, "Behold, we have abandoned
everything and followed you. What then shall we get?" 28And Jesus said
to them, "Amen: I tell you, that you who followed me, in the rebirth of all
things, when one like a son of man sits on a shining throne, you too will
seat yourselves on twelve thrones, governing the twelve tribes of Israel.
29And everyone who abandoned dwellings or brothers or sisters or father
or mother or children or farms for the sake of my name will receive many
times as much and will inherit age-long life. 30But many of the first will
wind up last and vice versa."

20

1"For the kingdom of the heavens is like a man, master of a house,
who went out early in the morning to hire laborers for his vineyard. 2And
settling with the laborers on a wage of a denarius per day, he dispatched
them into his vineyard. 3And going out about the third hour,[u] he spotted
others loitering in the marketplace, 4and he said to those, 'You, too, go
into the vineyard and I will pay you whatever seems fair given the late
start.' And they went. 5Going out again about the sixth and ninth hours,
he made the same arrangements with other late-comers. 6And going out
about the eleventh hour, he found others standing around, and he says to

t. By giving to "the poor," Jesus might have had himself and his disciples in mind.

u. This would be 9:00 a.m.

them, 'Why do you men stand here doing nothing all day long?' [7]They
say to him, 'That's simple: no one offered us any work.' He says to them,
'Consider yourselves hired! You, too, go into the vineyard.' [8]And evening
having come, the lord of the vineyard says to his steward, 'Call the workmen and pay the wage, starting with the last, up to the first.' [9]But the ones
who started about the eleventh hour each received a denarius! [10]And the
ones starting first supposed, 'We will receive more.' But they, too, each
received a single denarius. [11]And receiving their wages, they murmured[v]
against the master of the house, saying, [12]'These last put in one hour. And
you made them equal to us, the ones who bore the burden of the whole
day and the torment of the heat.' [13]But he, answering one of them, said,
'My good fellow, I do you no injustice. Didn't we settle on a denarius?
[14]Take your due and go! So I want to give to this last man the same as I
gave you. [15]Isn't it my prerogative to do what I want with my own
money? Or is it really that you are squinting with envy because I am
good?' [16]Thus, the last ones will be the first and the first ones the last."

[17]And as he was about to go up to Jerusalem, he took the twelve
aside by themselves and said to them, [18]"Behold, we are going up to Jerusalem, and a man will be delivered up to the archpriests and scribes and
they will sentence him to death, [19]and they will deliver him up to the gentiles for jeering and flogging and crucifixion, and on the third day he will
be raised."

[20]Then the mother of the sons of Zebediah came to him with her
sons, bowing before him, and requesting something from him. [21]And he
said to her, "What is it you want?" She says to him, "Say that these two
sons of mine may sit, one to the right and one to the left of you, in your regime." [22]But answering, Jesus said, "You have no idea what you are asking. Are you capable of drinking the cup which I am about to drink *and
being baptized with the baptism with which I am baptized*?" They say to
him, "We can do it." [23]He says to them, "My cup you shall drink *and the
baptism with which I am baptized, you shall be baptized with it.* [24]None-
theless, to say who will sit to the right of me or to the left is not my prerogative. That privilege is reserved for my Father."[w] And overhearing

v. The word for "murmur" in Old Testament stories applies to Israel's faithless whining in the wilderness. Here it underlines the fact that Matthew created this parable against Jewish Christian complaints about accepting gentiles into the church.

w. This comes from 2 Kings 2:9-10: "Ask what I shall do for you before I am taken from you." Hearing the request, Elijah reflects, "You have asked a hard

this, the other ten became furious with the two brothers. [25]And Jesus summoned them and said, "You know how the rulers of the gentiles domineer them, and their grandees exercise authority over them. [26]Is it not the same with you? But whoever wants to become great among you shall be your servant. [27]And whoever wants to be first among you shall be your slave. [28]For man, too, was not created to be served, but to serve,[x] to spend his life on behalf of many.

"Seek to increase from smallness, and from greatness to become less. When you attend a dinner to which you have been invited, do not recline in the most prominent place in case someone more illustrious than you should enter and your host has to ask you, 'Please sit lower down,' and you will be grossly embarrassed. But if you recline in the lower place as soon as you get there, and one of lesser rank enters, your host will say to you, 'What are you doing all the way down there? Come, sit up here!' and this will be to your advantage." [y]

[29]And as they traveled out of Jericho, a sizable crowd followed him. [30]And behold, two blind men sat at the side of the road. Hearing "Jesus is passing by" they cried out, saying, "Lord! Take pity on us, son of David!" [31]But the crowd rebuked them, that they should be quiet. But this only made them shout the louder: "Lord! Take pity on us, son of David!" [32]And stopping, Jesus called them and said, "What do you want? What can I do for you?" [33]They say to him, "Lord, that our eyes may be opened." [34]And flooded with compassion, Jesus touched their eyes, and at once they saw again and followed him.[z]

21

[1]And when they come close to Jerusalem and arrived at Beth-Phage at the Mount of Olives, then Jesus assigns two disciples, [2]telling them, "Go into the village over there and at once you will discover a donkey tethered and a colt with her. Untie them and bring them to me. [3]And should anyone say anything to you, you shall say, 'Their Lord requires them,' and at once he will send them." [4]Now this has happened so that the thing spoken through the prophet might be fulfilled, namely, [5]"Tell

---

thing," just as Jesus warns Jacob and John. Matthew, to make Jacob and John look less obnoxious, has ascribed the request to their prying stage mother.

x. Gen. 2:15

y. Codex Bezae adds this pericope, in common with some Latin and Syriac manuscripts.

z. Matthew, as elsewhere, takes a single character from Mark's narrative and doubles it, in this case taking Bar-Timaeus and making him into two blind men.

Zion's daughter, 'Behold! Your king comes to you meek and mounted on a donkey and on a colt, son of a donkey.'"[a] 6And setting off, doing just as Jesus directed them, the disciples 7brought the donkey and the colt and piled on them the garments, and he mounted on them.[b]

8And the very large crowd strewed their own garments on the road and others cut branches from the trees and scattered them on the road. 9And the crowds going before and following shouted out, saying, "Hosanna to the son of David! Blessed in the name of Adonai be the Coming One![c] Let hosannas ring in the highest spheres!" 10And as he went into Jerusalem, all the city was shaken, saying, "Who is this?" 11And the crowds said, "Why, this is the prophet Jesus from Nazareth in the Galilee."

12And Jesus entered into the temple and ejected all those selling and buying in the temple. And he upended the currency exchange tables and the chairs of those selling doves,[d] 13and he says to them, "It is written, 'My house shall be called a house of prayer.[e] But you are making it a robbers' cave!'"[f] 14And blind and lame people approached him in the temple and he cured them. 15But the archpriests and the scribes saw the marvels that he performed and heard the children shouting in the temple and saying, "Hosanna to the son of David!" and they were furious. 16And they said to him, "Do you hear what these are saying? Surely you don't approve?" And Jesus says to them, "Yes, I do! Did you never read, 'Out of the mouths of infants and nurslings you have brought perfect praise?'"[g] 17And turning his back on them, he exited the city and repaired to Beth-Anu, and he found lodging there.

18So as he was going up to the city early, he felt hungry. 19And notic-

---

a. Originally, as Matthew knew, the point was to be "mounted on a donkey, yes, a pure-bred donkey," rather than a mule. But in the accepted manner of contemporary scribes, Matthew interpreted the biblical parallelism in hyper-literal fashion to mine extra information from the text.

b. This story derives from 1 Sam. 9.

c. This is based on the entrance liturgy of Pss. 118:26-27, in which "he who comes in the name of the Lord" refers to any pilgrim.

d. The cleansing of the temple must have in view Malachi's messenger of the covenant purifying the sons of Levi (Mal. 3:1-3; cf. Mark 1:2; 9:3), as well as the oracle of Zechariah: "And there shall no longer be a trader in the house of the Lord of hosts on that day" (Zech. 14:21b). However, we may also have echoes of Simon bar-Gioras clearing John of Gischala's band of thieves out of the temple on the eve of its destruction.

e. Isa. 56:7

f. Jer. 7:11

g. Pss. 8:2, LXX.

ing by the roadside a lone fig tree, he went up to it and found nothing on it but leaves only, and he says to it, "May no fruit at all come from you forever!" And instantly the fig tree was withered up.[h] [20]And seeing this, the disciples marveled, saying, "How on earth did the fig tree wither up instantly?" [21]And answering, Jesus said to them, "Amen: I tell you, if you have faith and do not doubt, you will perform not only the wonder of the fig tree; but also, if you say to this mountain, 'Be taken and thrown into the sea!' it shall happen. [22]And all things which you ask in prayer, believing, you shall receive."

[23]And as he came into the temple and was teaching, the archpriests and the elders of the people came to him, saying, "With what authorization do you do these things? Who authorized your actions?" [24]But answering, Jesus said to them, "First, I will question you on one matter. You answer me, and I will be glad to tell you the authorization for my actions. [25]Remember the baptism of John? Where did its authorization come from, from God in heaven or only from mortals?" And they huddled, debating, whispering: "It's a trap. If we say 'from heaven,' he will surely ask us, 'Then why didn't you believe in him when you had the chance?' [26]But if we say, 'from mortal men,' we have the crowd to reckon with, for everyone esteems John as a prophet." [27]So answering Jesus, they said, "We still have not reached a conclusion on that matter." And he said to them also, "Well, if you refuse to tell me what you really think, neither can I tell you the authority behind my actions. [28]But how does it seem to you? A man had two children. Approaching the first, he said, 'Child, go today and work in the vineyard.' [29]And he said, 'I go, Lord!' And he did not go. [30]And approaching the second, he spoke similarly. And answering, he said, 'I will not!' Later, thinking better of it, he went after all. [31]Which of the two did the will of the father?" They say, "The latter." Jesus says to them, "Amen: I tell you, the customs agents and the prostitutes will get into the kingdom of God before you ever darken the door. [32]For John came to you walking a path of righteousness and you dismissed him as a fanatic. But the customs agents and the prostitutes believed him. But even seeing this miracle, you did not change your mind to believe in him.

[33]"Listen to another parable. There was a man, master of a house, who planted a vineyard and erected a hedge around it, and dug in it a wine press, and put up a tower, and leased it out to sharecroppers, and went away.[i] [34]And when the right time for fruit drew near, he sent his

h. Based on Pss. 37:35-36.

i. Isa. 5:1-7

slaves to the sharecroppers to collect his due from the produce. 35And the sharecroppers grabbed his slaves, flogging this one, killing that one, stoning another. 36Again the following year, he sent other slaves, more than the first group, and they treated them the same way. 37At last he sent to them his son, saying, 'They will have to pay my son due respect!' 38But the sharecroppers, seeing the son, conspired: 'The old man must be dead. This one is his heir. Come, let us kill him and the inheritance will pass to us!' 39And grabbing him, they threw him outside the vineyard and killed him. 40I ask you, then, when the lord of the vineyard comes, what will he do to those sharecroppers?" 41They say to him, "He will utterly destroy the villains, and he will let out the vineyard to other sharecroppers who will pay him his share of the fruit in the proper season." 42Jesus says to them, "You never read in the scriptures, 'A stone which the contractors deemed unusable, this very one became the cornerstone. This was from the Lord and we regard it as a marvel'?[j] 43Because of this I tell you, 'The kingdom of God will be taken from you and will be given to a nation producing its fruits.' 44*And the one falling on this stone will be shattered to pieces while it will pulverize anyone it falls on.*" 45And the archpriests and the Pharisees, hearing his parables, were well aware he was referring to them. 46And looking to apprehend him, they were afraid of the crowd, for they considered him a prophet.

22

1And answering his critics, Jesus again spoke to them in parables, saying, 2"The kingdom of the heavens was compared to a man, a king, who arranged a wedding feast for his son. 3And he sent his slaves to summon those who had been invited to the feast, and they did not want to come. 4Again, he sent other slaves, saying, 'Tell the ones invited, look, I have prepared my supper. My bulls and the fattened beasts have been slaughtered and everything is ready. Come to the feast!' 5But they heedlessly went off, each to his business: one to his own field, another on a business trip; 6and the rest, grabbing his slaves, insulted and killed them. 7The king was infuriated and, sending his armies, destroyed those murderers and burned their city. 8Then he says to his slaves, 'Though the feast is hot on the table, those originally invited were not worthy. 9Therefore, go to the forks in the roads and invite to the feast as many as you may chance to find.' 10And going out into the roads, those slaves assembled all whom they found, both wicked and good, and the wedding

j. Pss. 118:22-23

hall was filled with people reclining at table. [11]But coming in to look at those reclining, the king saw there a man not dressed in wedding attire. [12]And he says to him, 'My good fellow, how did you get in here without proper wedding attire?' But he was speechless. [13]Then the king said to the servants, 'Tie his feet and hands and throw him into the darkness outside where there will be wailing and grinding of teeth.' [14]For many are invited, but few are selected."

[15]Then the Pharisees went and conferred over how to trick him into saying something incriminating. [16]And they send their disciples to him, with Herod's agents, saying, "Teacher, we know you speak frankly and that no one intimidates you. [17]So then, tell us, how does it seem to you: is it legal to pay tribute to Caesar or not?" [18]But aware of their duplicity, he said to them, "Why put me on the spot, you hypocrites? Show me the tribute money." [19]And they fetched a denarius. [20]And he says to them, "Whose is this image and epigraph?" And they answered him, "Caesar's, of course." [21]"So," Jesus said to them, "give Caesar's coins to Caesar in taxes and give God's coins to God in the temple." [22]And they were flabbergasted at him, and they left him and walked away.

[23]On that day, some Syndics came to him, who say there is no resurrection; and they questioned him, [24]saying, "Teacher, Moses said, 'If anyone should die, not having children, his brother shall take to wife afterward the wife of his brother and shall raise up heirs for his brother.' [25]So once we knew seven brothers and the oldest, having married, died, and not having heirs, he left his wife to his brother. [26]Similarly with the second oldest and the third until the seventh died. [27]And last of all, the woman died. [28]In this 'resurrection,' then, which one of the seven will she be wife to? After all, all had her at one time or another." [29]And answering, Jesus said to them, "You're mistaken, being ignorant of scripture and the power of God. [30]For in the resurrection, neither do men marry nor are women given in marriage, but they are like angels in the heavens. [31]But concerning the resurrection of the dead, didn't you read what God said to you, namely, 'I am the God of Abraham and the God of Isaac and the God of Jacob'? [32]He is not a God of corpses, but of living men!" [33]And the crowd who heard this were astonished at his polemical skill.

[34]But when the Pharisees heard the report that he had silenced the Syndics, they called a meeting. [35]And one of them, a sage of the Torah, asked him a loaded questioned: [36]"Teacher, what is the chief commandment in the Torah?" [37]And he said to him, "'You shall love Adonai your God with all your heart and with all your soul and with all your under-

standing.' [38]This is the chief and most important commandment. [39]A second is like it: 'You shall love your neighbor as yourself.' [40]On these two commandments hang the whole Torah and the Prophets."

[41]And since the Pharisees were assembled to hear their spokesman take on Jesus, Jesus questioned them, saying, [42]"How does it seem to you concerning the Christ? Whose son is he?" They say to him, "David's." [43]He says to them, "Then how is it that in spirit David calls him 'Lord,' saying, [44]'Adonai said to milord, Sit at my right till I put the necks of your enemies under your feet'? [45]If then David himself calls him 'lord,' how is he his son?" And no one was able to come up with a word in reply, and from that day on, no one ventured to question him again.

23

[1]Then Jesus spoke to the crowds and to his disciples, [2]saying, "The scribes and the Pharisees assumed the throne of Moses. [3]Therefore, perform and observe anything whatever they may tell you; we don't want schism, but do not emulate the works they perform. For what they say, they do not perform. [4]And they tie heavy burdens onto people's shoulders, but they themselves make not the slightest effort to carry them. [5]No, all the pious works they perform, they do for public consumption. They widen the phylacteries across their foreheads and they lengthen the fringes of their prayer shawls, [6]and they relish the head table at formal dinners and to be shown to the front row seats in the synagogues, [7]and to receive deferential greetings in the marketplaces and to be addressed by others as 'rabbi.' [8]But don't you ever be called rabbi, for one is your teacher, Moses, and you are all brothers. [9]And address no one on earth as 'abba,' for only one is your heavenly Father. [10]Neither be addressed as 'master,' for your master is one, the Christ. [11]And the greater of you shall be your servant. [12]But he who shall exalt himself shall be humbled. [13]But woe to you, scribes and Pharisees, hypocrites! For you slam shut the kingdom of the heavens in people's faces, for you don't enter, nor do you allow entry to anyone else.

[14]*"Woe to you, scribes and Pharisees, hypocrites! For you hungrily repossess the houses of the widows and make long prayers for show. Therefore, you will receive more severe judgment than common sinners.*

[15]"Woe to you, scribes and Pharisees, hypocrites! For you crisscross the sea and the dry land to make one proselyte, and when he becomes one, you make him twice the heir of the Valley of Hinnom you yourselves are.

[16]"Woe to you, blind guides, who say, 'Whoever may swear an oath by the holy place, it does not count; but whoever may swear by the gold

of the holy place, his obligation is binding.' [17]Morons! Blind men! For which is greater? The gold itself or the sanctum that sanctifies the gold? [18]And you say, 'Whoever may swear by the sacrificial altar, it does not count; but whoever may swear by the offering lying on it, his obligation is binding.' [19]Are you blind? For logically, which is greater? The offering itself or the altar which makes the offering sacred? [20]Therefore, whoever swears by the altar automatically swears by it and everything upon it. [21]And whoever swears by the holy place swears equally by it and the one who lives in it. [22]And whoever swears by heaven swears by the throne of God and the one sitting upon it.

[23]"Woe to you, scribes and Pharisees, hypocrites! Because you are careful to meticulously tithe mint and dill and cumin, yet you have neglected the weightier portions of the Torah: justice and mercy and faith. But these you were obliged to perform, albeit not neglecting the fine points. [24]Blind guides, carefully sifting out the gnat but swallowing the camel whole!

[25]"Woe to you, scribes and Pharisees, hypocrites! Because you purify the outside of the cup and the plate, but inside they are full of rapine and excess. [26]Blind Pharisee! First purify the inside of the cup so the outside, too, may automatically be rendered ritually pure.

[27]"Woe to you, scribes and Pharisees, hypocrites! Because you are just like freshly whitewashed graves which, while indeed appearing externally to be beautiful, are filled inside with the bones of the dead and with all impurity. [28]Thus, you too, indeed, appear externally to others to be righteous, but internally you are stuffed with hypocrisy and disdain for the Torah.

[29]"Woe to you, scribes and Pharisees, hypocrites! Because you build shrines to the prophets and place flowers at the monuments of the *zaddiks,* [30]and you say, 'If we were in the days of our fathers, we would not have been their accomplices in shedding the blood of the prophets.' [31]So you admit you are the heirs of those who murdered the prophets, [32]and you fully measure up to the example of your fathers! [33]Snakes! Spawn of vipers! How do you plan to escape being sentenced to the Valley of Hinnom?

[34]"Therefore, behold, I myself send you prophets and sages and scribes. Some of them you will kill and crucify, and some you will flog in your synagogues and pursue from city to city. [35]And thus, all the righteous blood spilled onto the ground from the blood of Abel the righteous until the blood of Zechariah, son of Berachiah, whom you murdered be-

tween the shrine and the altar, will come to rest on you! 36Amen: I say to
you, all these crimes will come upon this nation. 37O Jerusalem, Jerusalem, who kills the prophets and stones those sent to her—how often I
wished to gather your children as a bird gathers her young under the
wings, and you refused. 38Behold, your house is left abandoned. For I tell
you, you will by no means see me from now until perchance you say,
'Blessed in the name of Adonai be the Coming One.'"[k]

24

1And as he made his way out of the temple, his disciples approached
to point out the buildings of the temple. 2And answering, he said to him,
"Do not waste your time looking at all these! Amen: I tell you, for there is
no way any pair of stones will remain together amid the rubble." 3And
once he took a seat on the Mount of Olives, the disciples approached him
privately, saying, "Tell us, when will these things be? And what is the sign
of your advent and of the culmination of the age?" 4And answering, Jesus
said to them: "Watch out that no one deceives you in this matter. 5For
many will appear, trading on my name, saying, "I am the Christ!" and
they will mislead many with this tactic. 6But you will next hear of wars
and rumors of more distant wars; do not worry: it is destined to happen
but the end is not yet at hand.[l] 7For nation will be pitted against nation
and kingdom against kingdom. There will be famines and earthquakes in
far-flung places. 8And yet these mark only the onset of labor pains.[m]
9Then they will deliver you up to tribulation and will kill you; you will be
pariahs among all nations because of my name. 10And then many will fall
away and will hand over their former co-religionists and they will hate
one another. 11And many pseudo-prophets will come out of the wood-
work to lead many off the path. 12And due to the increasing apostasy
from the Torah, many people's love will grow cold. 13But the one enduring to the end without renouncing my name, only such a one will save

k. The underlying Q source seems to be quoting from 4 Ezra (2 Esdras) 1:30-32: "I gathered you as a hen gathers her brood under her wings. But now what shall I do to you? I will cast you out from my presence. When you offer oblations to me, I will turn my face from you; for I have rejected your feast days and new moons and fleshly circumcisions. I sent to you my servants the prophets, but you have taken and slain them and torn their bodies in pieces. Their blood I will require of you, says the Lord. Thus says the Lord Almighty: Your house is desolate. I will drive you out as the wind drives straw."

l. Dan. 2:28

m. Isa. 19:2; 2 Chron. 15:6

himself. [14]And this Gospel of the kingdom[n] will be proclaimed in all the inhabited earth for a testimony to all the nations, and then the end will come. [15]Therefore, once you behold the abomination of desolation, spoken of through Daniel[o] the prophet, standing in the holy place—may the reader understand the reference—[16]then let those in Judea flee to the mountains.[p] [17]Anyone on the roof: let him not come down to retrieve anything, but rather let him climb down the fire escape and flee. [18]And the one working in the field, when that hour strikes, let him not even return home to retrieve his garment. [19]And pity those with a child in the womb and those nursing in those days. [20]Pray that your escape may not happen in winter or on a Sabbath, [21]because there will be a great tribulation the like of which has not befallen mankind since the very beginning of the creation until the present and which will never be repeated.[q] [22]In fact, if not for those allotted days being cut short, no flesh at all would be preserved alive.

[23]"And at that point, if anyone says to you, 'Behold here: the Christ! Behold there!' do not believe it. [24]But pseudo-messiahs and pseudo-prophets will be brought in, and they will provide great signs and prodigies for the purpose of seducing the chosen people, if at all possible.[r] [25]Behold, I have told you in advance. [26]If therefore they say to you, 'Behold, he is in the desert,'[s] do not go out to join him. Or if they say, 'Behold, in the private chambers,'[t] do not believe. [27]For as the lightning emerges from the east and branches out to the west, thus will be the advent of the one like a son of man. [28]Wherever the carcass happens to be, there you will see the vultures circling. [29]And immediately after the tribulation of those days, the sun will go dark, and the moon will withhold her light, and the stars will fall out of the sky,[u] and the angelic Powers of the

---

n. The Gospel of Matthew itself is meant here, apparently written as a handbook for missionaries.

o. Dan. 8:13

p. Dan. 9:27; 12:11; Gen. 19:17

q. Dan. 12:1

r. Deut. 13:2

s. The allusion here seems to be to such claimants as the Jeroboam redivivus prophet-messiah from Egypt, who is mentioned in Acts 21:38 and in Josephus's *Antiquities* 20:8:6 and *Jewish War* 2:13:5.

t. Simon bar-Kochba was endorsed by Rabbi Akiba as King Messiah in 132 CE.

u. Isa. 13:10

heavens will be shaken.[v] [30]And then will appear in the sky the portent of one like a son of man. Then all the tribes of the land of Israel will lament, and they will see one like a son of man coming in the cloud chariots of heaven with power and great brilliance.[w] [31]And he will send out his angels with a great trumpet, and they will gather together his chosen people Israel from the four winds, from one rim of the sky to the other rim.[x]

[32]"But from the fig tree, learn the parable: as soon as its branch grows tender and puts forth leaves, you know that the summer is near; [33]so you also recognize, when you see all these things, that it is knocking at the doors. [34]Amen: I tell you, in answer to your question, this present generation will by no means pass away until these things all happen. [35]The sky and the earth will pass away but my predictions will not fail. [36]But as to that specific day or hour, no one knows that, neither the angels of the heavens nor the son, except the Father only. [37]For just like the days of Noah, so will be the advent of one like a son of man. [38]For as they were in those days before the cataclysm eating and drinking, marrying and being given in marriage, until the day on which Noah entered into the ark, [39]and they suspected nothing before the cataclysm came and swept all away, so also will be the advent of one like a son of man. [40]Then two men will be in a field: one is taken away and one is abandoned. [41]There will be two women grinding in the mill: one is taken away and one is abandoned.

[42]Therefore, be watchful because you do not know on which day your lord is coming. [43]And know this, that if the master of the house had known in what watch of the night the burglar planned to arrive, he would have kept watch and would not have allowed his house to be dug through. [44]Therefore, be ready because a man always comes in the hour you think least likely. [45]Who, then, is the faithful and prudent slave whom the lord placed in charge of his household to give the staff food at the proper time? [46]Blessed is that slave whose lord, when he comes, will find him so doing. [47]Amen: I tell you, he will put him in charge of all his goods. [48]But suppose the slave is wicked and says to himself, 'My lord is late,' [49]and begins to beat his fellow slaves for minor infractions and eats and drinks with the drunks. [50]The lord of that slave will show up on a day when he does not expect and at an hour he does not know, [51]and he will

v. Isa. 34:4

w. Dan. 7:13

x. Zech. 2:10; Deut. 30:4

dismember him and will assign him a place with the hypocrites. There one finds wailing and grinding of teeth."

25

[1]"Then the kingdom of the heavens will be compared to ten virgins who, taking their lamps, went out to the place where they should join the bridegroom. [2]But five of them were thoughtless and five prudent. [3]For the thoughtless, while taking their lamps, did not take oil with them, [4]but the prudent took oil in the vessels with their lamps. [5]But as the bridegroom was delayed, all slumbered and slept. [6]And in the middle of the night comes a shout: 'Behold, the bridegroom! Go out to the meeting place!' [7]Then all those virgins were awakened and trimmed their lamps. [8]But the thoughtless said to the prudent, 'Give us some of your oil because our lamps are going out.' [9]But the prudent answered, saying, 'Then it would never be enough for us and for you. Instead, go to the merchants and buy more for yourselves.' [10]And as they were off buying, the bridegroom arrived, and those ready to meet him entered in with him to the festivities and the door was shut. [11]Finally, the remaining virgins arrived, too, saying, 'Lord, lord, open to us!' [12]But he, answering, said, 'Amen: I say to you, I do not know you.' [13]Keep watch, therefore, for you do not know the day or the hour!

[14]"For it is just like a man going away from home. He summoned his own slaves and entrusted his goods to them. [15]And to one he gave five talents, to another two, to another one, each according to his ability, and he left home. [16]At once, the one receiving the five talents, going off, traded with them and made another five. [17]Similarly, the one receiving two made another two. [18]But the one receiving one went away and dug a hole in the ground and buried his master's silver. [19]Then, after a long time, the lord of those slaves comes and settles accounts with them. [20]And the one receiving five talents approached and presented the five additional talents, saying, 'Lord, you entrusted five talents to me: look, I made five more.' [21]His lord said to him, 'Well done, good and faithful slave! You have proven yourself responsible with a few things, I will place you in charge of many. Welcome to your lord's favor.' [22]The one with two talents also approached, saying, 'Lord, you entrusted me with two talents: look, I made another two.' [23]His lord said to him, 'Well done, good and faithful slave! You proved yourself responsible with a few things, I will place you in charge of many. Welcome to your lord's favor.' [24]And the one having received one talent also approached and said, 'Lord, I knew you for a ruthless man, reaping crops that others sowed, harvesting fields that others

planted. 25And fearing to risk it, I went away and hid your talent in the ground. Look, here it is, safe and sound.' 26But answering, his lord said to him, 'Wicked slave! Lazy lout, you say you knew that I reap fields that others sowed, that I harvest crops that others planted? 27Then surely you must have known at least to leave my silver with the exchange tables and when I returned I should have recovered my money with interest. 28So you there! Take the talent from him and give it to the one with the ten talents. 29The know-how that brought the wealthy his success will get him even more abundance. The one not knowing what to do with it will lose even the pittance he has. 30The useless slave? Throw him outside into the dark night. Let him lament his error and grind his teeth in chagrin!'

31"And when one like a son of man comes in his radiance with his retinue of angels, then he will take his seat on his shining throne, 32and before him all the nations will be assembled, and he will sort them out as a shepherd sorts the sheep from the goats, 33and he will stand the sheep to his right but the goats to his left. 34Then the king will say to those to his right, 'Come, O blessed of my Father! Enter into the kingdom that was designed for you when the foundations of creation were laid. 35For I hungered and you gave me to eat. I thirsted and you gave me a cup of cold water to drink. I was a foreigner and you took me home for a meal. 36I was naked and you dressed me. I was infirm and you looked in on me. I was in prison and you came to visit me.' 37Then the righteous will answer him, saying, 'Lord, there must be some mistake. When did any of us ever see you hungry and feed you? Or see you thirsty and give you something to drink? 38And when did we see you a foreigner and bring you home? Or naked and clothe you? 39And when did we see you infirm or in prison and come to see you? Surely we'd remember.' 40And answering, the king will say to them, 'Amen: I tell you, insofar as you did it for the most insignificant of these my wandering brothers, you did it to me.' 41Then he will say also to the ones on his left, 'Be gone, you damned, into the age-long fire stoked for the accuser and you, his angels. 42For I hungered and you gave me nothing to eat, I thirsted and you gave me nothing to drink, 43I was a foreigner and you did not invite me home for a meal.' 44Then they will answer the same way, saying, 'When on earth did we see you hungry or thirsty or a foreigner or naked or infirm or in prison, much less fail to help you?' 45Then he will answer them, saying, 'Amen: I tell you, insofar as you failed to help one of these insignificant ones, you failed to help me.' 46And these will go away into age-long punishment, but the righteous into age-long life."

26

[1]And it happened that when Jesus finished all these words, he said to his disciples, [2]"You know that after two days the Passover comes and a man is delivered up to be crucified." [3]At the same time, the archpriests and the elders of the people gathered in the court of the archpriest, named Caiaphas, [4]and they exchanged ideas to seize him by stealth and to kill him, [5]but one thing they ruled out: "Not during the feast, so as to avoid rioting among the people."

[6]And when Jesus was in Beth-Anu in the house of Simon the leper, [7]a woman came to him with an alabaster jar of ointment, very costly, pouring it over his head as he reclined at table. [8]But seeing it, the disciples were angry, saying, "Why this waste? [9]For it would have been possible for this to be sold for much and the price given to the poor." [10]And Jesus, aware of it, said to them, "Why do you give the woman trouble? For she has done a fine thing for me! [11]After all, you have the poor with you all the time, but this is a special occasion. [12]For this woman put this ointment on my body to bury me. [13]Amen: I tell you, wherever this Gospel is heralded in all the world, what this woman did will also be told so she will be remembered."

[14]Then one of the twelve, the one called Judas the False One,[y] going to the archpriests, [15]said, "What are you willing to give me, and I for my part will deliver him up to you?" And they weighed out thirty silver pieces for him.[z] [16] And starting then, he looked for a likely opportunity to deliver him up.

[17]And on the first day of unleavened bread, the disciples came to Jesus, saying, "Where do you want us to prepare for you to eat the Passover seder?" [18]And he said, "Go into the city to so-and-so and say to him, 'The teacher says, My fateful time is near. With you I will observe the Passover with my disciples.'" [19]And the disciples did as Jesus instructed them, and they prepared the Passover seder.

[20]With evening falling, he reclined at table with the twelve disciples. [21]And as they were eating, Jesus said, "Amen: I tell you, one of you will deliver me up." [22]They went into shock and said to him, each in turn, "Not I, Lord!" [23]But answering, he said, "The one dipping his hand with me in the dish, this man will hand me over. [24]For indeed one goes when his preordained time comes, but woe to that wretch through whose

---

y. This need not mean he was "called the False One" at the time any more than Jesus was "called Christ" at the time (1:16).

z. The thirty silver pieces come from Zech. 11:11b.

agency one is delivered up. It would be good for him not to have been born in the first place!" [25]And answering, Judas, the one handing him over, said, "Not I, Rabbi?" He says to him, "You said so."

[26]And as they were eating, Jesus, taking a loaf and blessing it, broke and gave it to the disciples and said, "Take and eat: this is my body." [27]And taking a cup and giving thanks, he gave it to them, saying, "Drink from it, all of you. [28]For this is my blood of the *new* covenant, the blood concerning many, shed for the forgiveness of sins.[a] [29]And I pledge to you, no more, by any means, will I drink of the fruit of the vine until that day when I drink it anew with you in the kingdom of my Father."

[30]And having sung a hymn, they went out to the Mount of Olives. [31]And Jesus says to them, "All of you will be scandalized by me this night. I know because it is written, 'I will strike down the shepherd, and the sheep of the flock will panic.'[b] [32]But after my raising up, I will precede you into the Galilee." [33]But Peter, answering, said to him, "Even if all shall be scandalized by you, I will never be scandalized."[c] [34]Jesus says to him, "Amen: I tell you, as for you, today, this very night before a rooster crows, you will repudiate me three times." [35]Peter says to him, "If I should have to die at your side, there is no way I will repudiate you!"[d] And all the disciples said likewise.

[36]Then Jesus comes with them to a plot of ground called Gethsemane, and he says to his disciples, "Sit here till I am done praying over there." [37]And taking Peter and the two sons of Zebediah, he was suddenly overcome with grief and distressed. [38]Then he says to them, "My soul is mortally wounded with sorrow. You stay here and keep vigil with me." [39]And going on a bit farther, he dropped to the ground and prayed, saying, "My Father, if it is possible, let this cup pass me by for another. But not what I want, but what you want."

[40]And he comes to the disciples and finds them sleeping, and he says to Peter, "So you were not able to stand vigil with me for a single hour? [41]The three of you, stand vigil and pray that you not come to the test.[e]

---

a. Exod. 24:8

b. The whole source for the subsequent scene of Jesus' disciples fleeing the arresting party seems to be Zech. 13:7.

c. 2 Kings 2:2, 4, 6

d. 1 Sam. 15:21

e. It is as if things would have turned out differently had the disciples stayed awake and fortified themselves with prayer. Jesus' prayer would have been heard, and there would have been no arrest; hence the disciples would have been spared

Granted, the spirit is eager enough, but the flesh is weak." 42And going away again, he prayed a second time, saying, "My Father, if this cup cannot pass by without my drinking it, may your will be done." 43And coming again, he discovered them sleeping, for they could not keep their eyes open. 44And leaving them again, going off, he prayed a third time, saying the same thing again. 45Then he comes to the disciples and says to them, "Finish your nap and relax. Behold, the hour has arrived and yours truly is delivered into the hands of gentiles. 46Get up! Let us go! The one handing me over has arrived."

47And while he was still speaking, behold, Judas arrived, one of the twelve, and with him a mob with swords and clubs sent from the archpriests and the elders of the people. 48So the one handing him over had given them a signal, saying, "Whomever I may kiss on the cheek is the one you want." 49And at once, approaching Jesus, he said, "Hail, Rabbi!" and gave him a friendly kiss. 50But Jesus said to him, "Old friend, why are you here?" Then closing in, they laid hands on him and grabbed him. 51And behold, one of Jesus' companions, reaching for his sword, drew it and, striking the slave of the archpriest, managed only to cut off the ear. 52Then Jesus said to him, "Put your sword back into its place. For all who take up a sword will die by a sword. 53Or perhaps you have forgotten, I need only appeal to my heavenly Father for him to put at my disposal over twelve legions of angels. 54But then, how do you expect the scriptures to be fulfilled, where it says it has to happen this way?" 55In that hour, Jesus said to the mob, "Am I some desperado, that you came out to arrest me with swords and clubs? Every day I sat teaching in the temple and you did not apprehend me. 56But all this has happened so scripture could be fulfilled." Then his disciples all abandoned him and fled.[f]

---

the test of nerve they would soon fail. Jesus goes back and repeats the prayer twice, apparently thinking it would avail little without the reinforcement of his disciples' prayers. They fail him and he is arrested after all.

f. The basis of this whole scene can be found in 2 Sam. 15-16. There, a weeping David, fleeing from his usurping son Absalom (a Judas figure), heads up the Mount of Olives and sends three of his allies (15:27, LXX) back to Jerusalem. David finds himself mocked and harassed by one Shimei, who curses the fallen king. David's man Abishai offers to chop off the mocker's head, but David prevents him, musing that God must have bidden Shimei to curse him. As they slink along in silence, Shimei continues to pelt the refugees with rocks. Here we find more elements underlying Mark's story. Abishai is the prototype of the disciple who attempts to behead Malchus in the arresting party. Shimei, another form of Shimeon or Simon, is a prototype for the Simon who denies Jesus repeatedly, Shimei's stony missiles suggesting "Peter," as well. God having assigned Shimei to

[57]And the ones who arrested Jesus marched him away to Caiaphas the archpriest, where the scribes and the elders were assembled. [58]And Peter followed him at a safe distance up to the courtyard of the archpriest and, entering inside, sat among the attendants and waited to see the outcome. [59]Now the archpriests and the whole Sanhedrin tried to suborn perjury against Jesus to execute him, but they were unsuccessful. [60]And though many false witnesses came forward, they did not find any damning testimony.[g] But later two came forward and said, [61]"This fellow said, 'I am able to destroy the holy place of God and after three days build it.'" [62]And standing up, the archpriest said to him, "Have you no rejoinder to what these men allege against you?" [63]But Jesus remained silent.[h] And the archpriest said to him, "I charge you by the true God that you tell if you are the Christ, the son of God!" [64]Jesus says to him, "You said so. And yet, I tell you, from now on, all of you will see one like a son of man sitting to the right of Shaddai, arriving with the cloud chariots of the sky."[i] [65]Then the archpriest, ripping his garments, said, "He blasphemed! Who still needs witnesses? Behold now, you heard the blasphemy with your own ears. [66]How does the case appear to you?" And they, answering, said, "He is worthy of death!" [67]And they spat in his face and punched him and slapped him, [68]saying, "Prophesy to us, you Christ! Which one struck you?"[j]

[69]And with Peter outside in the courtyard, a serving maid comes to him, saying, "You, too, were with Jesus the Galilean." [70]But he denied it in front of everyone, saying, "I have no idea what you're talking about!" [71]And he went outside to the porch where another noticed him and says to those there, "This man was with Jesus the Nazorean!" [72]But again he denied with an oath: "I do not know the man!" [73]And again, a little later, one of the bystanders, approaching, said to Peter, "Truly you, too, are one of them. For indeed, your speech gives you away." [74]Then he started

utter curses on David has become Jesus' prediction of Peter's destined denials, as well as Peter's calling down curses on himself (or on Jesus) in the high priest's courtyard. For Jesus' prayer and Judas's betraying kiss, cf. Pss. 116:10-15; 2 Sam. 20:7-10.

g. Dan. 6:4, LXX

h. Isa. 50:7; 53:7

i. Dan. 7:13-14

j. Rewritten from 1 Kings 22:24: "Then Zedekiah the son of Chenaanah came near and struck Micaiah on the cheek, and said, 'How did the spirit of the Lord go from me to speak to you?' And Micaiah said, 'Behold, you shall see on that day when you go into an inner chamber to hide yourself.'"

to curse and to swear: "I do not know the man!" And at once a rooster sounded. [75]And Peter recalled what Jesus had said, "Before a rooster sounds, you will repudiate me three times." And departing outside, he broke down sobbing.

27

[1]And early morning coming, all the archpriests and the elders of the people met in session against Jesus to put him to death. [2]And having tied Jesus up, they led him away and delivered him to Pilatus the governor. [3]Then Judas, the one who handed him over, seeing him, that he was condemned, thought better of what he had done and returned the thirty silver pieces to the archpriests and elders, [4]saying, "I sinned, betraying innocent blood." But they said, "What is that to us? It's your problem." [5]And flinging the silver into the holy place, he left, and going off, he hanged himself.[k] [6]But the archpriests, picking up the silver, said, "Hmmm. It is not legal to deposit them as *corban,* since it is bounty money." [7]So deliberating, they decided to use the silver to buy the potter's field for the burial of strangers. [8]For that reason that field came to be known as the Field of Blood, even today. [9]Then the thing spoken by Jeremiah the prophet was fulfilled, namely, "And they took the thirty silver pieces, the wage of the one assessed, whom they assessed from the sons of Israel, [10]and gave them for the potter's field as Adonai directed me."[l]

[11]And Jesus stood before the governor, and the governor interrogated him, saying, "So you are the king of the Jews." And Jesus said, "If you say so." [12]And the archpriests and elders accused him, but he answered nothing.[m] [13]Then Pilatus says to him, "Don't you hear the things they accuse you of?" [14]And he did not answer him, not one word, which completely amazed the governor. [15]So at festival time the governor used to release to the crowd any single prisoner they wanted. [16]And they had just then a notorious prisoner called Jesus bar-Abbas. [17]Therefore, hav-

k. How does Matthew know Judas hanged himself? It is because David's traitorous counselor Ahithophel (2 Sam. 17:23), whom scribal tradition took to be the subject of Pss. 41:9, hanged himself and Matthew applied this to Judas.

l. The quote is not from Jeremiah, but rather Zechariah (11:13). How does Matthew know Judas returned the money, throwing it into the temple treasury, and that the priests used it to buy the potter's field? The Syriac version of Zechariah reads: "Then the Lord said to me, 'Cast it into the treasury, this lordly price at which I was paid off by them.' So I took the thirty shekels of silver and cast them into the treasury in the house of the Lord." The Hebrew of the same verse reads: "Cast it to the potter."

m. Isa. 50:7; 53:7

ing called the crowd together, Pilatus said to them, "Whom do you wish I
may release to you: Jesus bar-Abbas or Jesus called Christ?" [18]For he was
well aware they delivered him up out of envy of his popularity with the
crowd, and he hoped to use that popularity to release him. [19]So as he sat
on the judgment seat, his wife sent word to him, saying, "Have nothing to
do with that righteous man, for today I suffered many things in a dream
thanks to him." [20]But the archpriests and the elders incited the crowd to
ask for Bar-Abbas and to destroy Jesus. [21]Answering, the governor said
to them, "Which of the two do you wish I may release to you?" And they
said, "Bar-Abbas!" [22]Pilatus says to them, "What then am I to do with Jesus called Christ?" [23]All say, "Have him crucified!" But he said, "What
evil did he do?" But they shouted all the more, "Have him crucified!"
[24]But Pilatus, seeing that nothing is gained but rather a riot is brewing,
taking water, washed his hands in front of the crowd, saying, "I am innocent of the blood of this man; have it your way!"[n] [25]In answer, all the
people said, "May his blood cover us and our children!" [26]Then he released Bar-Abbas to them, and having Jesus whipped, he delivered him
up to be crucified. [27]Then the soldiers of the governor, having taken Jesus
into the praetorium, assembled before him the whole cohort. [28]And undressing him, they draped him with a scarlet cloak; [29]and having prepared a wreath of acanthus leaves, they set it on his head and placed a
reed in his right hand and, bowing the knee before him, jeered at him,
saying, "Hail, King of the Jews!" [30]And spitting at him, they took the
reed sceptre and stabbed at his head with it. [31]And when they finished
tormenting him, they removed the cloak off him and dressed him in his
own garments, and they marched him off to crucify him.

[32]And going forth, they found a man, a Cyrenian named Simon; this
one they commandeered so that he should bear his cross. [33]And coming
to a place called Golgotha, which is translated "Place of a Skull," [34]they
gave him to drink wine mixed with gall; and tasting it, he did not wish to
drink. [35]And crucifying him,[o] they distributed his garments, casting lots.[p]
[36]And sitting, they guarded him there lest his people come and take him
down. [37]And they placed above his head the charge against him, having
been written, "This is Jesus, the King of the Jews." [38]Then two robbers
are crucified with him, one to the right and one to the left. [39]And the

n. Susanna 46; Dan. 13:46, LXX: "I am innocent of the blood of this woman."

o. Pss. 22:16b

p. Pss. 22:18

passers-by blasphemed him, wagging their heads[q] 40and saying, "Ooh! The one destroying the holy place and in three days building it. Save yourself if you are a son of God and come down from the cross." 41Similarly, the archpriests, trading jokes with the scribes and elders, said, 42"Some savior! He couldn't even save himself!" "King of Israel, is he? Let him come down from the cross alive and we will believe in him. 43He has trusted in God? Let him rescue him now, if he wants him.[r] After all, he said 'I am God's son.'"[s] 44And the robbers crucified with him insulted him the same way.

45So from the sixth hour, darkness appeared over the whole earth until the ninth hour.[t] 46And around the ninth hour, Jesus shouted with a loud voice *"Eli, Eli, lama sabachthani?"* which is translated, "My God, my God, why did you forsake me?"[u] 47And some of the bystanders, hearing this, said, "This fellow invokes Elijah!" 48And at once, one of them ran and took a sponge and, filling it with vinegar, put it on a lance head and gave it to him to drink.[v] 49But the others objected, saying, "Leave him be! Let us see if Elijah comes to rescue him!" 50But Jesus, again shouting in a loud voice, let go the spirit. 51And behold, the hanging veil of the holy place was split in two from top to bottom, and the earth was shaken and the rocks were split, 52and the tombs were opened and many bodies of the saints who had fallen asleep were raised 53and, emerging out of the tombs *after his rising*, they entered into the holy city and appeared to many. 54And the centurion and those with him guarding Jesus, seeing the earthquake and the things happening, were completely terrified, saying, "Truly, this man was God's son!" 55So there were also many women looking on from a distance who followed Jesus from the Galilee, feeding him, 56among whom were Maria the hairdresser and Maria the mother of James and of Joseph and the mother of the sons of Zebediah.

57And with evening coming, a rich man from Arimathea, named Joseph, who also himself was trained as a disciple of Jesus, 58this man, approaching Pilatus, requested custody of the body of Jesus.[w] Then Pilatus

---

q. Pss. 22:7

r. Pss. 22:8

s. Wisd. of Sol. 2:12-20

t. Amos 8:9

u. Pss. 22:1

v. Pss. 69:21. Some scribe has added these words to adjust the verse to 1 Cor. 15:22-23.

w. Joseph of Arimathea reminds one of King Priam acquiring the body of his

ordered it to be given him. [59]And taking the body, Joseph wrapped it in a clean length of linen [60]and laid him out in his new tomb, which he cut from living rock; and having rolled a great stone up to the door of the tomb, he went away. [61]And Maria the hairdresser was there with the other Maria, sitting across from the grave.

[62]And on the morrow, which is after the Preparation, the archpriests and the Pharisees assembled before Pilatus, [63]saying, "Lord, we suddenly remembered how that impostor said before he died, 'After three days, I am raised!' [64]Therefore, command the grave to be secured until the third day so the disciples do not come and steal him and say to the people, 'He was raised from the dead,' and the last imposture will be worse than the first." [65]Pilatus said to them, "You have custodians; go, make it as secure as you know how." [66]And they went and secured the grave, the custodians sealing the stone.[x]

28

[1]And late on the Sabbath, at the dawning of the first day of the week, Maria the hairdresser and the other Maria came to view the grave.[y] [2]And behold, a massive earthquake occurred, for an angel of Adonai, coming down out of the sky and approaching, rolled the stone away and sat on it.[z] [3]And his appearance was like lightning,[a] and his clothing white as snow.[b] [4]And for fear of him, the guards trembled and fainted dead away.[c] [5]But answering, the angel said to the women, "You need not fear me. For I know you seek Jesus, the crucified one. [6]He is not here. For he was raised, just as he said. Come closer and see the place where he lay. [7]And go quickly, tell his disciples that he was raised from the dead, and behold, he precedes you into the Galilee! That's where you will see him! Behold, I

---

son Hector and the patriarch Joseph acquiring the body of Jacob to bury in a cave tomb beyond the Jordan (Gen. 50:4-5). The fact that Joseph is rich and buries Jesus in his own tomb provides the narrative motivation for grave robbers to open the tomb, thinking Joseph himself must have been buried with opulent funeral tokens. Coma victims awakening in opulent tombs are thus rescued in novels from the period.

x. Dan. 6:17

y. The vigil of the mourning women likely reflects the mourning cult of the dying and rising god, long familiar in Israel (Ezek. 8:14; Zech. 12:11; Canticles 3:1-4 2).

z. Josh. 10:18, 22, 26-27

a. Dan. 10:6

b. Dan. 7:9b

c. Dan. 3:22

have delivered my message." [8]And going quickly away from the tomb with fear as well as great joy, they ran to report to the disciples. [9]And behold, Jesus met them, saying, "Hail!" And approaching, they grasped his feet and bowed before him. [10]Then Jesus says to them, "Do not be afraid! Go announce to my brothers that they may set out for the Galilee and there they will see me."

[11]And as they were going, behold, some of the custodians, coming into the city, announced to the archpriests all the events that had transpired. [12]And meeting with the elders and discussing the matter, they took enough silver and offered it to the soldiers, [13]saying, "You're to say, 'His disciples came under cover of night and stole him while we were sleeping.' [14]And if this comes to the governor's ears, we will persuade him so you will have nothing to worry about." [15]And taking the silver, they did as they were instructed. And this propaganda was disseminated by Jews until the present day.

[16]And the eleven disciples journeyed to the Galilee to the mountain where Jesus had first appointed them. [17]And seeing him, they bowed before him, though they doubted. [18]And approaching, Jesus spoke with them, saying, "Full authority in heaven and on the earth was given me.[d] [19]Therefore, journey forth, train all the gentiles as disciples, baptizing them in my name,[e] [20]teaching them to observe all the commandments I gave you; and behold, I myself am with you all the days until the culmination of the age."

---

d. This is based on a conflation of two Greek versions of Dan. 7:14. In the LXX, "to him" refers to "one like a son of man ... given the rule [and] ... the authority of him," meaning "the Ancient of Days." In Theodotion, he receives "authority to hold all in the heaven and upon the earth." The charge to make all nations his disciples comes from Dan. 7:14, "that all people, nations, and languages should serve him."

e. Eusebius tells us he saw copies of Matthew pre-dating the Council of Nicea that had "in my name" rather than the now-familiar trinitarian "in the name of the Father and of the Son and of the Holy Spirit." It is hard to resist the inference that a Nicene baptism formula, reflecting the newly minted doctrine of the trinity, was inserted into the text from that time on.

7.

The Gospel according to the Hebrews

The Gospel according to the Hebrews occupies a special place on the margins of the traditional canon. Its position in early Christianity was among the heretics, to be sure, explaining why it did not then find inclusion in the canon. But it was not very heretical for it was a favorite of many of the Jewish-Christian sects which held the Torah and Jesus equally sacred, finding no difficulty combining the two. The emerging Catholic Church uneasily tolerated this position. It was certainly more to their liking than Marcionite Christianity's thorough repudiation of Judaism. And even though scholars of the Church held the Gospel according to the Hebrews at arm's length, they nevertheless did hold onto it. We find various major orthodox figures commenting on it, bringing it to bear on the exegesis of canonical passages where light might be shed. Some thought it should be included in the canon, but even those who would not brook its presence there did not deem it to be a false gospel. Copies circulated even into the early Middle Ages, though as far as we know it is no longer extant. That being the case, how in the world can it be included here?

From the several quotations and passing mentions of it from the early church fathers, we actually know a good deal about the book. It was a shorter version of Matthew, and commentators such as Jerome considered it to be the Hebrew or Aramaic original of the Greek Matthew. This cannot have been since the latter patently makes verbatim use of the Greek Gospel of Mark. Still, there is some relation. We have at least two Hebrew versions of Matthew, one of which seems

pretty much coeval with the Greek version.[a] And various Jewish Christian gospels, including Hebrews and the related narratives of the Ebionites and the Nazoreans, appear to be variant editions of Matthew. All survive only in Greek translation. Nicephorus tells us exactly how much shorter Hebrews was than the canonical Matthew, about 2,400 words. Several other ancient writers provided a handful of juicy passages they thought worthy of preservation and comparison with the canonical Matthew. Numerous others made comments or short notes on variant readings or regarding very slight differences from Matthew. These quotations and notices have often been compiled for the modern reader. But what has not previously been done, as far as I know, is a reconstruction of the Gospel according to the Hebrews, something that should not be too hard to do given the extensive similarity and even substantial identity between Matthew and the Hebrew Gospel. If ancient writers thought occasional minor variants from Matthew to be worth noting, this implies it must have been almost identical, though somewhat shorter. On this basis, I have ventured to reconstruct the Gospel according to the Hebrews.

My guidelines for doing so were as follows: first, of course, I used canonical Matthew as my basis or *Grundschrift*. It was a simple matter to add or substitute the alternate texts preserved by the early Christian commentators. But then, how much else to chop? Our early commentators specified only a couple of brief omissions or "non-interpolations," as the case may be. Even so, some possibilities seem more likely than others.

I have taken the early Christian surmises about Hebrews being the original of Matthew to denote that Hebrews is based on an earlier Matthew than the one we have. It certainly seems there were intermediate versions. The rabbis or catechists of Antioch enlarged Mark in various stages. For instance, chapter 6 of Matthew must have originally featured the threefold contrast of prayer, fasting, and almsgiving as practiced by the hypocrites but without the brief digression lampooning the glossolalia of the heathen and without the addition of the Lord's Prayer. Likewise, chapter 10 once sought to restrict the

a. George Howard, *Hebrew Gospel of Matthew* (Macon, GA: Mercer University Press, 1995).

gospel mission to "the lost sheep of the house of Israel," but chapter 28 clearly reverses this, mandating a mission to all the gentiles. So I have taken the liberty, in composing this "artist's conception" of the work, of snipping some of what appear to me to be later insertions. In particular, I have been guided by the thesis of Arlo J. Nau (*Peter in Matthew*) regarding the portrayal of Peter, that our Greek Matthew represented not a first but a second stage of interpolation after Mark. Mark was severely critical of Peter. Matthew contains materials which seem to undo some of Mark's polemic and instead magnify Peter. Equally curious is that other new material was added, which took Peter down a peg again. The best explanation would seem to be that an earlier Matthean redaction of Mark cut out some of the anti-Peter material and generally rehabilitated his character, but the text later passed through the hands of other redactors who deemed the previous stage's glorification of Peter a bit much and sought to lower the thermostat. I have omitted this latest layer of critical dispraise.

Joachim Jeremias (*The Parables of Jesus*) pointed out how the Matthean version of the great supper parable (22:2-14) seems to have combined the supper story, preserved more faithfully in Luke and Thomas, with a brief parable of the guest without a wedding garment (22:2, 11-14). I agree, and I am guessing the two parables stood separately in the version of Matthew used by the evangelist of Hebrews.

I have also taken a hint from the Gospel of Thomas, which has some material we would call Matthean—the parables of the tares, dragnet, and so on—but lacks distinctive Matthean interpretations and vocabulary. Many scholars take this to mean Thomas preserves independent versions of material that Matthew redacted but did not create even though it is absent from Mark, Luke, and John. I think Thomas quotes Matthew (and Luke) from memory and that, in fact, the Matthean-sounding material derives from an earlier version of that gospel, one that lacked the rather pedantic interpretations and hellfire emphasis. I am guessing Hebrews used the same earlier version of Matthew that was paraphrased by Thomas.

I have also assumed that the Hebrews redactor would likely have simply abridged and condensed Matthew, as the latter did with Mark, snipping superfluous doublets—though we know the Hebrews

narrative had at least one pair Matthew lacked: the two rich men—and needless verbiage. I have cut the genealogy on the admittedly slim basis that Epiphanius says he does not know whether the Hebrews author may have omitted it. This comment seems to me to imply he heard some such suggestion, and at this distance, it sounds like a hint we cannot ignore. After all, *something* was missing!

I have retained the verse numbering of Matthew, simply omitting the verse numbers of omitted verses and adding no verse numbers to material derived from ancient references to the Hebrew Gospel. This latter material is printed in italics. It may look a bit odd at first, but it will facilitate comparison between Matthew and Hebrews.

If some doughty archaeologist someday discovers an actual copy of the Gospel according to the Hebrews and makes my endeavor superfluous, I can only say I will welcome the news. In the meantime, it is not enough to read contextless snippets and fragments when we can get closer to encountering the tantalizing, ever-intriguing Hebrew version of the gospel than scholars have previously dared. In the present hypothetical reconstruction, we may see it as in a glass darkly, but we are seeing it. From our rather substantial evidence, we can be sure it must have looked pretty much like this.

1

[1]*So when the Christ wished to come upon the earth to mankind, the good Father summoned a mighty power in the heavens, called Michael, and he entrusted Christ to his care. And that power descended into the world, where it was called Miriam, and he was in her womb seven months.* And his mother Miriam, being betrothed to Joseph, before they came together, was found to have a child in the womb, as it would soon be discovered, by the Holy Spirit. And Joseph, her husband, being just and not wishing to make her a public scandal, decided to send her away privately. [20]But while he deliberated these matters, behold, an angel of Adonai appeared to him in a dream, saying, "Joseph, scion of David, do not be afraid to take Miriam your wife; for what is in her is fathered by the Holy Spirit! [21]And she will bear a son, and you will call his name Jesus because he will save his people from their sins." [22]Now all this has occurred so that all things spoken by Adonai through the prophet might be fulfilled, namely, [23]"Behold, the maid shall have a child in the womb and will bear a son, and they will call his name Emmanuel," which is trans-

lated, "God with us." [24]Then Joseph, being wakened from sleep, did as the angel of Adonai asked him, and he took his wife, [25]and he did not know her carnally before she bore a son; and he called his name Jesus.

2

[1]So when Jesus was born in Beth-Lehem of Judea in the days of Herod the king, behold, mages from the east arrived in Jerusalem, [2]saying, "Where is the newborn king of the Jews? For we saw his natal star when it rose and came to do homage to him." [3]So hearing about this, King Herod was agitated, and all Jerusalem feared what he might do. [4]And once he had assembled all the archpriests and scribes of the people, he asked them where the Christ is to be born. [5]And they told him, "In Beth-Lehem in Judea, for thus it has been laid down through the prophet: [6]'And you, Beth-Lehem, land of Judah, are by no means least among the chiefs of Judah. For out of you will emerge a ruler who will shepherd my people Israel.'" [7]Then Herod, privately summoning the mages, ascertained in detail from them the time the star appeared; [8]and sending them to Beth-Lehem, he said, "On your journey, carefully investigate the child. And when you discover him, give me a report so that I, too, may come and render him homage." [9]So hearing the king's instructions, they embarked on their journey. [11]And entering into the house, they saw the child with Miriam his mother, and prostrating themselves, they did him homage. And opening their treasures, they set gifts before him, gold and frankincense and myrrh. [12]And having been alerted by a dream not to return to Herod, they departed by a different route to their own country.

[13]And when they departed, behold, an angel of Adonai appears in a dream to Joseph, saying, "Wake up and take the child and his mother and flee into Egypt and live there till I may tell you. For Herod is about to search out the child to destroy him." [14]So getting up, he took the child and his mother under cover of night and departed to Egypt, [15]and was there till the death of Herod in order that the thing spoken by Adonai through the prophet might be fulfilled, namely, "Out of Egypt I called my son."

[16]Then Herod, realizing he was tricked by the mages, became livid with fury, and sending orders, he killed all the male children in Beth-Lehem and in the adjacent districts from two years and under, coinciding with the time he had determined from the mages when the star rose. [17]Then was fulfilled the thing spoken by Jeremiah the prophet, namely, [18]"A voice was heard in Ramah, weeping and lamenting loudly: Rachel weeping for her children, and she was inconsolable because they are gone."

[19]But with Herod's death, behold, an angel of Adonai appears in a dream to Joseph in Egypt, [20]saying, "Wake up and take the child and his mother and go to the land of Israel. For those seeking the life of the child have died." [21]So he got up and took the child and his mother and entered into the land of Israel. [22]But hearing from the angel that Archelaus reigns over Judea in place of his father, he feared to go there. And being warned of this by a dream, he left for the vicinity of the Galilee, [23]and arriving there settled in a city called Nazareth so that the thing spoken through the prophet might be fulfilled, "A Nazorean he shall be called."

3

[1]And in those days arrives John the Baptist, preaching in the desert of Judea, [2]saying, "Repent, for the kingdom of the heavens has come near." [3]For this is the one spoken of through Isaiah the prophet, namely, "a voice of one crying out in the desert: 'Prepare the way of Adonai, all of you; make his route straight.'" [4]And John himself had his clothing made from camel's hair and a leather waistband around his loins, and his food was locusts and wild honey. [5]Then Jerusalem and all Judea and all the environs of the Jordan went out to him, [6]and were baptized in the Jordan River by him, enumerating their sins. [7]And seeing many of the Pharisees and the Syndics coming to the baptism, he said to them, "Spawn of vipers! Who warned you to flee the impending rage? [8]Therefore, first you must produce fruit befitting repentance. [9]And do not think to reassure yourselves, saying, 'For father, we have Abraham.' For I tell you that God is able to raise up sons to Abraham from these stones. [10]And already the axe is poised at the root of the trees. Therefore, every tree not producing good fruit is chopped down and is thrown into a fire. [11]I indeed baptize you with water for repentance, but the one coming after me is stronger than me, for whom I am not worthy to carry his sandals. He shall baptize you in holy spirit and fire, he whose winnowing fan is in his hand, and he will completely purify his threshing floor, gathering his wheat into the silo, but the chaff he will consume with inextinguishable fire."

Behold, the mother of the Lord and his brothers said to him, "John the Baptist baptizes for the remission of sins. Let us go and be baptized by him." But he said to them, "Wherein did I sin that I should go and be baptized by him? Unless perhaps this very saying be judged a sin of ignorance." [13]Then Jesus arrives from the Galilee at the Jordan, before John, to be baptized by him. [14]But he refused him, saying, "I myself have need to be baptized by you, and you come to me?" [15]But answering, Jesus said to him, "Let it go for now, lest we offend them, for it is seemly for us in

this way to observe all piety." Then he lets him. [16]*And it happened that, when the Lord had come up out of the water, the whole fount of the Holy Spirit descended and rested upon him and said to him, "My son, of all the prophets, I was waiting for you, that you should come and I might rest in you. For you are my rest; you are my first-begotten son who reigns forever!"*

4

[1]Then Jesus was led up into the desert by the Spirit to be tested by the accuser. [2]And having fasted forty days and forty nights, afterward he hungered. [3]And approaching him, the tester said to him, "If you are God's son, say that these stones may become loaves." [4]But answering, he said, "It is written, 'Not solely on bread shall a human being live, but on every precious utterance proceeding through the lips of God.'" [5]Then the accuser takes him *into Jerusalem* and placed him standing on the wing of the temple, [6]and says to him, "If you are God's son, throw yourself down! After all, it is written, 'He will put his angels in charge of you, and they will scoop you up lest you so much as stub your toe on a rock.'" [7]Jesus said to him, "Again it is written, 'You shall not presume on the good will of Adonai, your God.'" [8]Again the accuser takes him into an extremely high mountain, from whence he could see all the kingdoms of the world and their glory, [9]and he said to him, "All these I will give you if you will fall down before me and swear fealty." [10]Then Jesus says to him, "Be gone, adversary! For it is written, 'Adonai your God you shall worship and him only you shall serve.'" [11]Then the accuser leaves him and, behold, the angels approached and fed him, *and he said, "Even now did my mother, the Holy Spirit, take me by one of my hairs and she did carry me away unto the great mountain, Tabor."*

[12]So hearing that John was delivered up, he left the region for the Galilee. [13]And leaving Nazara, coming to the village of Nahum, he settled at the seaside in the region of Zebulon and Naphtali, [14]for he sought to fulfill the thing spoken by Isaiah the prophet, namely, [15]"Land of Zebulon and land of Naphtali, seaboard beyond the Jordan, Galilee of the nations, [16]the people stranded in the dark saw a great light, and to those sitting in a land of death and its shadow, light blazed up for them." [17]From then on, Jesus started to preach and to say, "Repent, for the kingdom of the heavens has come near!"

[18]And walking beside the Sea of Galilee, he saw two brothers, Simon, called Peter, and Andreas, his brother, casting a net into the sea, for they were fishermen. [19]And he says to them, "Come after me and I will teach

you to fish for human souls." [20]And at once, abandoning the nets, they
followed him. [21]And going on from there, he saw another two brothers,
Jacob of Zebediah and John, his brother, in the boat with Zebediah, their
father, darning their nets. And he called them. [22]And at once, abandoning
the boat and their father, they followed him.

[23]And he made the circuit of all the Galilee, teaching in their synagogues and proclaiming the news of the kingdom and curing every disease and every malady among the people.

5

[1]And seeing the crowds, he went up into the mountain, and once he
sat down, his disciples came to him. [2]And breaking his silence, he taught
them, saying:

[3]"Blessed in spirit are the poor, for they are the subjects of the kingdom of the heavens.

[4]"Blessed are the mourners, for they shall be encouraged.

[5]"Blessed are the meek, for when the great ones destroy one another fighting over it, the meek shall remain to inherit the earth.

[6]"Blessed are those starved and parched for justice, for they shall be sated.

[7]"Blessed are those who show mercy, for others will show them mercy when they find themselves in need of it.

[8]"Blessed are those with a clean conscience, for only they shall see God.

[9]"Blessed are the reconcilers, for they shall be called sons of God.

[10]"Blessed are those persecuted for righteousness, for the kingdom of the heavens is made up of them.

[11]"Blessed are you when they vilify you and persecute you and make
every false charge against you on account of me. [12]Rejoice and
celebrate, for a large reward awaits you in the heavens. For in the same way, they used to persecute your predecessors, the prophets.

[13]"You are the salt of the earth. But suppose the salt is tainted: by
what can it be seasoned again? It is no longer tangy enough for anything
except for being thrown into the street. [14]You are the light of the world. A
city set on a mountain is not capable of being hidden. [15]Nor does anyone
kindle a lamp and set it under the bushel basket, but atop the lamp stand
where it illumines all in the one-room house. [16]In the same way, let your
light shine before others so they may see your noble deeds and may thank
your Father in the heavens for you.

17“Pay no heed to the doctrine that my mission was to destroy the Torah and the Prophets. My mission was not to destroy scripture, but to fulfill it! 18For amen: I say to you, even if the heavens and the earth should pass away, a single yodh, a single vowel point, shall by no means pass away from the Torah until all its commandments are perfectly obeyed. 19Therefore, whoever presumes to abrogate the least significant of these commandments and teaches this to others, in the kingdom of heaven they shall call him the least significant. 20For I tell you, unless your Torah piety exceeds that of the scribes and Pharisees, you shall by no means enter into the kingdom of the heavens.

21“You heard that the ancients were commanded, ‘You shall not murder’ and ‘Whoever commits murder shall face sentencing.’ 22But I command you that every one who gets angry at his brother shall face sentencing. And if anyone should say to his brother, *‘Raca!* Apostate!’ he shall face the Sanhedrin. And if anyone should say, ‘You moron!’ he shall face the fire of the Valley of Hinnom. 23So if you find yourself bringing your offering forward to the altar and you suddenly remember that your brother has a complaint against you, 24leave your sacrificial animal standing there at the altar. First, go and be reconciled to your brother and only then return and offer your sacrifice if you want God to accept it. 25Negotiate with your creditor while you are with him on the road to court; otherwise the creditor may hand you over to the judge and the judge may hand you over to the bailiff and you may be thrown into debtors’ prison. 26Amen: I say to you, you will never make it out of there till you pay the creditor the last quadrans you owe him.

27“You heard it was commanded, ‘You shall not commit adultery.’ 28But I command you that every one who ogles a woman, fantasizing about her, has already committed adultery with her in his heart. 29So if your right eye scandalizes you, gouge it out and throw it away! It is better to cut your losses and let one of your organs be destroyed rather than having your whole body dumped into the Valley of Hinnom. 30And if you find yourself morally scandalized by your right hand stealing, cut it off—throw it away! Won’t you come out ahead if one of your members is destroyed instead of your whole body being packed off to the Valley of Hinnom?

33“Again, you heard that the ancients were commanded, ‘You shall not default on a vow, but shall pay to the Lord what you have vowed.’ 34But I command you not to swear a vow at all, neither by the sky since it is the throne of God, 35nor by the earth since it is the footstool for his feet,

nor yet by Jerusalem since it is the city of the divine king. [36]Swear not by your own head since you cannot do so much as change one hair to white or black. [37]But let your final word be 'Yes, yes!' 'No, no!' Whatever goes beyond these simple words denotes a wicked person.

[38]"You heard that it was commanded, 'An eye in recompense for an eye, a tooth as recompense for a tooth.' [39]But I command you, do not call the wicked person to task. But whoever raps you on the right cheek, turn to him the other also. [40]And to the one who wants to sue you for your tunic, let him have your coat, as well. [41]And if a Roman soldier shall commandeer you to carry his field pack for one mile, go with him two. [42]To the one asking you to give and the one wishing to borrow from you, do not turn him away.

[43]"You heard that it was commanded, 'You shall love your neighbor and you shall reserve your hate only for your enemy.' [44]But I command you, love your enemies and pray for your persecutors, [45]so that you may become true sons of your Father in the heavens, for he orders his sun to rise on the wicked and good alike, and he rains equally on the righteous and unrighteous."

6

[1]"Be careful not to practice your religion in front of others so as to be seen doing it. Otherwise, it wins you no wage from your Father in the heavens. [2]Accordingly, when you give to beggars, do not herald it with a trumpet fanfare as the hypocrites do, making a great show in the synagogues and in the streets so they may be praised by others. Amen: I tell you, they will have to be content with that paltry recompense. [3]But when you give to beggars, [4]keep it so secret that [3b]even your left hand will not know your right hand has given coins. [4b]And your Father, the one who watches invisibly, will bless you visibly. [5]And when you pray, do not be like the hypocrites, because they just love to pray standing in the synagogues and the corners of the public streets if the hour of prayer 'happens' to catch them there, so they may be on display. Amen: I say to you, they have thus received all the payment they are ever going to get. [6]But when you pray, enter into your private room, and having shut your door, pray to your Father, he who is invisible, and your Father who watches invisibly will repay you for this offering. [9]Therefore, pray thusly:

Our Father in the heavens,
may your name[b] be revered,

---

b. Yahve

[10]may your kingdom come;
let your will come to pass,
as in heaven, also on earth.
[11]Our bread *for the morrow* give us today,
[12]And release us from our debts,
even as we have released our debtors;
[13]And draw us not into testing,
but rescue us from the wicked.

[16]"And when you fast, do not look mournful like the hypocrites, for
they twist the appearance of their faces so they may display themselves as
fasting. Amen: I tell you, they have the only reward they will ever get.
[17]But when you are fasting, groom your hair and wash your face, [18]so
that no one will suspect you are fasting. And your Father, watching invisibly, will reward your piety.

[19]"Do not amass treasures for yourselves on the earth where moth
and rust make it disappear and where burglars dig through and steal it,
[20]but amass for yourselves treasures in heaven where neither moth nor
rust makes it disappear, where burglars neither dig through nor steal it.
[21]For where your treasure is, there your heart will be also. [22]The lamp of
the body is the eye. So if your eye is focused, your whole body will be
shining. In the same way, if the light in you goes dark, how deep is that
darkness! [24]No one is able to be a slave to two lords at the same time; for
eventually, either he will hate the first and he will love the second or he
will attach himself to the first and loathe the second: you are no more capable of being a slave to God and to Mammon, the Almighty Denarius.

[25]"Therefore, I say to you, do not be preoccupied with your life:
what you may eat or what you may wear. Is not life more than food and
the body more than clothing? [26]Look to the birds of the sky; note how
they do not plant or reap or gather into barns and your heavenly Father
feeds them anyway. Do you not count for much more than they? [27]But
which one of you is able to add another cubit to his height by worrying
about it? [28]And why worry about clothing? Think of the lilies of the field,
how they grow. They neither labor keeping sheep nor spin wool, [29]but I
assure you, not even Solomon in all his golden finery was decked out like
a single one of them. [30]But if God so dresses up the ephemeral grass in the
field, destined for nothing more noble than heating the stove, will he not
be the more sure to provide clothes for you? Scant is your faith! [33]Seek
first to enter his kingdom and to gain his righteousness and all these
things shall be provided you."

7

1“Do not judge, or you will be judged. 2For you will be judged by the same criteria for judgment you use to judge, and whatever measuring stick you use to size someone up, others will use to measure you. 3And how can you spot the sawdust speck in your brother’s eye without even realizing there is a board sticking out of your own? 4How are you going to be able to say to your brother, ‘Here, just let me extract that speck from your eye,’ when the whole time there is this board in your own eye?

6“Do not give consecrated food to the dogs, nor set your pearls before pigs if you don’t want them to trample them into the mud, then turn on you and rip your flesh.

7“*Let him who seeks, not cease seeking till he finds, for when he finds, he shall be astonished, and when astonished, he shall reign, and when he reigns, he shall at last rest.* 9Just point out a man among you who would give his son a rock if he asked him for a barley roll. 10Or if he asked for a fish, who would give him a snake? 11And if you, being sinners, nonetheless know to give good gifts to your children, how much more can you expect your Father in the heavens to give good things to those who ask him?

12“Therefore, whatever way you want others to treat you, you treat them the same way. For this is the essence of the Torah and the Prophets. 13Choose the narrow gate to enter because the wide one with the broad road leads off to utter ruin and many enter that way. 14For the gate to the life is narrow and the road is built to accommodate few. And indeed, there are few who ever find it. 15Watch out for pseudo-prophets who approach you disguised as sheep but underneath are drooling wolves. 16From their fruits you will be able to recognize them. Vine dressers do not collect grapes from thorn bushes or figs from thistles, do they? 17Even so, every sound tree produces luscious fruit, while the diseased tree produces poison fruit. 21Not everyone who flatters me with ‘Lord, Lord!’ will enter into the kingdom of the heavens, only one who obeys the will of my Father in the heavens. 22In that day of judgment, many will appeal to me, saying: ‘Lord, Lord! Remember how we used to prophesy in your name? And cast out demons using your name? And to accomplish many mighty works in your name? Doesn’t that count for something?’ *If you are gathered in my embrace and do not keep my commandments, I will cast you away* and say to you: ‘Get out of my sight! I don’t know where you came from, you Torah apostates!’

[24]“So then, whoever hears these, my words, and practices them bears comparison to a sensible man who built his dwelling on the rock. [25]And the rain descended, and the rivers came up, and the winds howled and crashed against that house and it refused to fall because it had been founded on the rock. [26]And anyone hearing from me these words and neglecting to practice them must be compared to the moron who thought nothing of building his dwelling on the shifting sand. [27]And the rain descended, and the rivers came up, and the winds howled and crashed against that house and it collapsed, and not a stone of it was left standing.”

[28]And it happened that, when Jesus came to the end of these words, the crowds were utterly amazed at his teaching, [29]for he was teaching them as an authority in his own right, not like their scripture-parsing scribes.

8

[1]As he descended the mountain, many crowds followed him. [2]And behold, a man with a skin disease comes to him, falling to his knees, and says to him, “If only you will, you are able to purify me.” [3]And stretching out his hand, he touched him, saying, “It is my wish: be purified!” And at once the skin disease left him. [4]And Jesus says to him, “See that you tell nothing to anyone. Just go show yourself to the priest and offer the things Moses commanded concerning your cleansing, for their certification.”

[5]As soon as he entered the village of Nahum, a centurion came to him, begging him [6]and saying, “Lord, my servant boy has been laid out in the house, paralyzed, severely tortured.” [7]He says to him, “I will come and cure him.” [8]But answering, the centurion said, “Oh no! Lord, I am not worthy to have you set foot under my roof. Just use some incantation and my servant boy will be cured. [9]I know how it works since I myself am a man under authority and I have soldiers under my command. And I order this one, ‘Go!’ and he goes, and to another, ‘Come!’ and he comes, and I order my slave, ‘Do this!’ and he does.” [10]And hearing this, Jesus marveled. And he said to those following along, “Amen: I tell you, I never found faith such as this in Israel! [11]And I tell you that many from both east and west will come and feast with Abraham and Isaac and Jacob in the kingdom of the heavens. [12]But the proper heirs of the kingdom will be ejected into the outer darkness.” [13]And Jesus said to the centurion, “Go! Let it happen just as you believed it would.” And the servant boy was cured in that very hour.

[14]And as Jesus came into the dwelling of Peter, he noticed his

mother-in-law was laid up fever-stricken. [15]And he touched her hand and the fever left her, and she got up and fed them. [16]And when evening came, people brought to him many of the demonized. And he cast out the spirits with an incantation. And he cured all who were in a bad way, [17]so that the thing spoken by the prophet Isaiah was fulfilled, namely: "He took our infirmities from us and he carried our diseases away." [18]But Jesus, seeing such a huge crowd surrounding him, gave orders to his disciples to depart for the opposite shore. [19]And coming to him as they prepared to shove off, one scribe said to him, "Teacher, I am ready to follow you wherever you may go." [20]And Jesus says to him, "Consider well! The foxes have burrows and the birds of the sky have nests, but human beings have no abiding place to call their own." [21]Another, one of the disciples, said to him, "Lord, give me time to leave and bury my father." [22]But Jesus says to him, "Follow me and let the dead bury themselves." *And another said to him, "Lord, I will follow you, but secretly for fear of men." And Jesus said to him, "He who is near me is near the fire; but he who is far from me is far from the kingdom."* [23]And as he set sail, his disciples followed him.

[24]And behold, a great storm occurred so that the boat was covered by the waves. [25]But he himself was sleeping. And coming to him, they got him up, saying, "Lord, save! We are perishing." [26]And he says to them, "Why are you so fearful? Scant is your faith!" Then, getting up, he rebuked the winds and the sea. And a great calm settled. [27]And the mortals marveled, saying, "What sort of being is this that even the wind and the sea obey him?"

[28]And when he came to the opposite side of the sea into the region of the Gadarenes, two demoniacs emerged from the tombs to meet him. They were extremely dangerous so that no one dared travel by that road anymore. [29]And behold, they shouted, saying, "What business is there between us and you, son of God? Have you come to torture us already before the appointed time?" [30]There was a herd of many pigs feeding a great distance from them. [31]And the demons pleaded with him, saying, "If you must cast us out, send us into the herd of the pigs!" [32]And he said to them, "Go!" So coming out, they went into the pigs. And behold, all the herd rushed down the ledge into the sea and died in the waters. [33]And those feeding them fled, and going away into the city, they reported all things, even the news of the demoniacs. [34]And behold, all the city came out to meet Jesus and, seeing him, pleaded that he might quit their shores.

9

1And embarking in a boat, he crossed over and came into his native
city. 2And behold, they brought him a paralytic laid on a mat. And Jesus,
seeing their faith, says to the paralytic, “Cheer up, child; the sins you
were being punished for are forgiven you.” 3And behold, some of the
scribes said to themselves, “Surely this fellow blasphemes.” 4And Jesus,
knowing their thoughts, said, “Why do you think evil things in your
hearts? 5For which is easier? To say, ‘The sins are forgiven you,’ or to say,
‘Get up and walk’? 6But to demonstrate to you that a man has authority
to forgive sins on earth as God does in heaven”—then he speaks to the
paralytic—“Get up, take your mat and go to your dwelling.” 7And getting up, he went to his dwelling. 8But the crowd, seeing this, feared and
praised God, the one delegating such authority to mortal men.

9And going along from there, he spotted a man sitting at the customs
booth named Matthew, and he says to him, “Follow me!” And getting
up, he followed him. 10And it came about that he reclined at table in his
house, and behold, many customs agents and backsliders came and reclined with Jesus and his disciples. 11And the Pharisees, noticing, remarked to his disciples, “Why does your teacher eat with the customs
agents and backsliders?” 12And overhearing this, he said, “The strong
ones do not have need of a physician, but those who are in a bad way.
13My mission was to summon, not the righteous, but the sinful.”

14Then the disciples of John come to him, saying, “Why do your disciples not fast when we and the Pharisee sect fast?” 15And Jesus explained
to them, “Can you expect the groomsmen to mourn during the wedding
feast? But inevitably the days will come when the feast is over and then
they will return to fasting.”

18As he was speaking to them of these matters, behold, a ruler came
up and bowed before him, saying, “My daughter has just died, but come
lay your hand on her and she will live.” 19And getting up, Jesus followed
him, and his disciples, too. And behold, a woman, subject to a flow of
blood for twelve years, approached from behind and touched the fringe
of his prayer shawl. 21For she was saying to herself, “If only I may touch
his garment, I shall be saved.” 22And Jesus, pivoting and seeing her, said,
“Cheer up, daughter, your own faith has saved you.” And the woman
was saved as of that hour. 23And Jesus, coming into the dwelling of the
ruler and seeing the flute players and the crowd terrified, 24said, “Get on
out of here, for the girl did not die but sleeps!” And they ridiculed him.
25But when the crowd had been hustled out, entering, he seized her hand,

and the girl was raised. [26]And the report of this circulated through all that region.

[36]And seeing the crowds, he was flooded with compassion for them because they were agitated and clueless, like sheep with no shepherd to lead them. [37]Then he says to his disciples, "Though there is so much to be harvested, there are so few workers doing the job! So beseech the Lord of the harvest and perhaps he will see the urgency of the situation and rush more workers into his harvest."

10

[1]And to this end, summoning his twelve disciples, he gave them authority over unclean spirits so as to cast them out and to cure every disease and every malady. [2]So these are the names of the twelve apostles: Simon, called Peter, and Andreas his brother; and Jacob of Zebediah and John, his brother; [3]Philip and Bar-Ptolemy; Thomas and Matthew the customs agent; Jacob of Alphaeus and Thaddaeus, called Lebbaeus; Simon the Zealous, [4]and Judas the False One, who did indeed betray him. [5]These twelve Jesus sent forth, instructing them thusly: "Do not take the way that leads to the gentiles and do not enter a city of the Samaritans. [6]But go rather to the lost sheep who dwell in Israel. [7]And as you journey, make proclamation, saying the kingdom of the heavens has come near. [8]Cure the infirm, raise up the dead, cleanse those with skin disease, cast out demons. You received these powers without cost, give without charging a fee. [9]Do not carry provisions of gold or silver or brass in your waistbands, [10]no wallet for the road, nor a second tunic, nor sandals, nor a staff, for the worker is worth his food.

[11]"And whatever city or village you may enter, first make inquiries as to who in it is honorable, and remain with them until you are ready to leave. [12]As you first enter into the dwelling, greet those in it. [13]If it does, in fact, prove worthy of you, impart to it your blessing of protection. If it does not, then let your protection follow you when you leave. [14]And whoever may not welcome you, go outside that dwelling and shake the dust off of your feet. [15]Amen: I tell you, it will go easier for Sodom and Gomorrah in the Day of Judgment than for that city! [16]Behold, I send you forth like helpless sheep among hungry wolves. So learn to be *wiser than* snakes and harmless as doves. [17]And beware of people, for there are those who will not hesitate to deliver you up to Sanhedrins, and they will flog you in their synagogues; [18]and before governors and even kings you will be led on account of me to bear witness to them and to the gentiles. [19]But when they do deliver you up, do not worry about how or what you will

speak. For what to say will be supplied you on the spot. [20]Because you are not the speakers, but the Spirit of your Father is the one speaking in you. [21]Brother will deliver up brother to death and a father a child, and children will stand up in court against parents and put them to death. [22]And you will be pariahs in the sight of all because of my name. But the one who hangs on to his faith till the bitter end, only such a one will save himself. [23]But when they persecute you in this city, flee to another. For amen: I tell you, you will by no means be able to complete all the cities of Israel in the time before the one like a son of man comes.

[24]"After all, a disciple by definition does not rank above the teacher, nor does a slave rank above his lord. [25]It is good enough for a disciple to become his teacher's equal in erudition, that the slave become a free man like his master. If they called the head of the household Baal-Zebul, how much more will they vilify the members of his household? [26]So do not fear them; for nothing is veiled except to be sooner or later unveiled, nothing hidden except to be revealed eventually. [27]What I say to you in the dark, repeat it in the light of day. And what you hear whispered in your ear, proclaim from the housetops! [28]And do not fear the ones threatening to kill the body but who are not capable of killing the soul. Rather, fear the one who is quite capable of destroying both soul and body in the Valley of Hinnom. [29]Are not two sparrows sold for a farthing? And one of them will not fall on the ground escaping your Father's notice. [30]He even keeps a running inventory of the hairs on your head!. [31]Therefore, do not fear: you excel many sparrows in value. [32]Therefore, anyone willing to confess his association with me to others, I will likewise acknowledge him to my Father in the heavens. [33]And if anyone repudiates me before others, I will likewise repudiate him before my Father in the heavens. [34]Have you heard it said my mission was to cast peace over the land? My mission was not to bring peace but rather a sword! [35]For my mission was to pit a man against his father and a daughter against her mother, and a bride against her mother-in-law, [36]and to make into a person's enemies those who dwell under the same roof!"

And he said, "I choose for myself those who are worthy. The worthy are they whom my Father in the heavens has given me. [37]The one loving father or mother above me, if you must choose, is not worthy of me, and the one loving son or daughter more than me is not worthy of me. [38]And whoever does not take his cross and follow me is not worthy of me. [39]The one finding his life shall lose it, and the one losing his life for my sake will find it. [40]The one welcoming you welcomes me and the one welcoming

me welcomes the one who sent me. [41]The one welcoming a prophet because he is a prophet will receive a prophet's wage, and the one welcoming a *zaddik* [c]because he is a *zaddik* will receive a *zaddik's* wage. But whoever gives one of these little ones a cup of cold water to drink simply because he is a disciple, amen: I say to you, under no circumstances will he forfeit his wage."

11

[1]And it happened that, when Jesus finished giving instructions to his twelve disciples, he went away from there to teach and to make proclamation in their cities. [2]But John, hearing in prison the deeds of the Christ, sent word through his disciples, [3]saying to him, "Are you the Coming One or shall we look for someone else?" [4]And answering, Jesus said to them, "Go and report to John what you hear and see: [5]blind men see again and lame men walk, men with skin disease are cleansed and deaf men hear, dead men are raised and poor men are given hope. [6]And blessed is the one who is not scandalized by me." [7]And as they were on their way, Jesus began to speak to the crowds about John. "What did you go out into the desert to look at? A reed being swept by the wind? [8]Of course not! What did you go out to see? Someone dressed in dainty clothes? You'd better look elsewhere! The ones decked out in dainty clothes can be found in the palaces of kings. [9]But why did you go out? To see for yourselves a prophet? Yes! And I tell you, more than a prophet. [10]This is the one about whom it is written, 'Behold, I send forth my angel before your face.' [11]Amen: I tell you, there has not risen among mortal men one greater than John the Baptist. But the very least of those angels in the kingdom of the heavens is greater than he is. [12]And from the era of John the Baptist until now, the kingdom of the heavens is *plundered* by violence, and the violent storm its gates. [13]For all the predictions of the Prophets and the Torah culminated in John. [14]And if you want to welcome the imminent Coming One, Elijah, it is he. [15]The one with ears, let him hear.

[16]"But what can I compare this nation to? It is like children sitting inactive in the marketplace, who call to each other, [17]saying, 'It's your fault! We played you girls the pipe and you wouldn't dance.' And the girls reply, 'That's a boy's game! We sang laments, and you boys wouldn't play funeral with us.' And the boys reply, 'But that's only for girls!' [18]For John's way was to abstain from food and drink and you people say, 'He is

c. "Righteous one," a special type of holy man, equivalent to a *hasid,* "pious one."

a demoniac! [19]Man came into the world to eat and drink.' And John's sect says, 'No, that is a gluttonous man and a wine-drinker! A friend of customs agents and backsliders.' Where is wisdom in this exchange? The wise choice will be vindicated by the results."

[20]At that point, he started to lambaste the cities in which the majority of his powerful deeds were performed because they did not repent. [21]"Woe to you, Chorazin! Woe to you, Beth-Saida! For if the powerful deeds done in you had happened in Tyre and Sidon, they would have repented in hair shirts and ashes in the ancient past. [22]Even though they didn't repent, I tell you, it will go easier for Tyre and Sidon on the Day of Judgment than for you. [23]And you, village of Nahum! Did you say to yourself, 'I will be exalted to the heavens. I will be like the Most High'? But you shall descend as far as Hades because if the deeds of power that happened in you occurred in Sodom, it would still be there today. [24]Even though they were destroyed for rebuffing God's messengers, it will go easier for the land of Sodom on the Day of Judgment than for you."

[25]And at that time, Jesus replied to certain scribes, saying, "I *give you thanks,* Father, lord of the sky and the earth, because you concealed these things from the wise men and the intellectuals and revealed them instead to infants. [26]Yes, Father, because so it seemed good sport to you." [27]And to the crowd he said, "Come to me, all those laboring under heavy burdens, and I will relieve you. [28]Take my yoke on your shoulders instead and learn my doctrine, for I am meek and humble in heart, no taskmaster, and you shall find rest for your souls; [30]for my yoke is easy to bear and the burden I assign is light and not like the scribes.'"

12

[1]And at that time Jesus made his way on the Sabbath through the grainfields, and his disciples hungered and began to pluck the ears of grain and to eat. [2]But the Pharisees, seeing it, said to him, "Aha! Your disciples are doing what is not legal to do on a Sabbath." [3]And he said to them, "Did you not read what David did when he hungered, he and those with him? [4]How he entered into the house of God and ate the loaves of showbread, which is not legal for him to eat, neither for those who were with him, except for the priests alone? [8]For man was given dominion even over the Sabbath."

[9]And leaving there, he entered into their synagogue. [10]And behold, a man with a withered hand, *who said to Jesus, "I was a mason seeking to make a living with my hands. I beg you, Jesus, to restore to me my health so I may not have to beg commonly for my food."* And they questioned

him, saying, "Is it legal on the Sabbath to heal?" that they might accuse him. [11]And he said to them, "Which of you men, if he had one sheep, and it happened to fall into a ditch on the Sabbath, would not grasp hold of it and lift it out? [12]And how much more is a man worth than a mere sheep! So then, surely it is legal on the Sabbath to do good deeds." [13]Then he says to the man, "Extend your hand!" And it was restored, healthy as the other. [14]But going out of the synagogue, the Pharisees at once plotted against him so as to destroy him. [15]But Jesus, aware of this, left the borders of that region, and many followed him. And he healed them all, [16]and he gave them strict orders not to expose him, [17]so that the thing spoken by Isaiah the prophet might be fulfilled, namely, "Behold my servant whom I chose, my beloved with whom my soul was quite pleased; I will place my spirit upon him and he will decree judgment on the gentiles. [19]He will not raise a ruckus or shout, nor will anyone hear his voice in the streets. [20]He will not so much as snap the drooping reed or snuff out the dying candle until his judgment prevails. [21]And the gentiles will set their hopes on his name."

[22]Then a blind and mute demoniac was brought to him, and he cured him so that the mute man was able to speak and see. [23]And all the crowds were astonished and said, "Is this not Solomon, master of demons and son of David?" [24]But the Pharisees, hearing them, said, "The only way this man casts out demons is by the agency of Baal-Zebul, ruler of the demons!" [25]Knowing what they were thinking, he said to them, "Every kingdom divided against itself is reduced to ruins. And every city or house divided against itself will not stand. [26]And if the adversary casts out the adversary, he must have been divided against himself. Then how will his kingdom stand? [27]And besides, if I am casting out the demons by means of Baal-Zebul, by what name do your protégées cast them out? They will condemn what you said as quickly as I. [28]But suppose it is by means of the Spirit of God that I cast out the demons; then the kingdom of God has overtaken you! [29]But how is anyone to be able to enter into a strong man's dwelling and seize his vessels unless he first binds the strong man? Then and only then will he plunder his house. [30]The one who is not with me is against me, and the one not harvesting with me is sowing the wind. [31]Because of this, I tell you that all sin and blasphemy will be forgiven mankind, but blasphemy against the Spirit will not be forgiven. [32]And whoever may speak a thing against mortal man, it will be forgiven him; but whoever speaks against the Divine Spirit, it will not be forgiven him, neither in this age nor in the impending one.

34“Spawn of vipers! How can you say good things when you are wicked? For the mouth only speaks by drawing on what fills the heart. 35The good person produces goods from the treasury of good, and the wicked person produces evils out of the treasury of wickedness. 36But I tell you that every careless remark people make, they will have to give an explanation for it on the Day of Judgment. 37For out of the transcript of your words you will be vindicated, and from the record of your words you will be condemned.”

38Then some of the scribes and Pharisees made this rejoinder to him, saying, “Teacher, we would like to see a confirming sign from you.” 39But answering, he said to them, “Only an evil and idolatrous nation seeks a sign, and a sign shall not be vouchsafed to it except for the sign of Jonah the prophet. 41Ninevite men will rise up in the court of judgment to accuse this race and will condemn it. After all, they repented and turned to the preaching of Jonah, and behold, something greater than Jonah is at work here! 42The Queen of Sheba will be resurrected in the Day of Judgment with this nation and will condemn it. After all, she came from the far reaches of the earth to hear the wisdom of Solomon, and behold, something greater than Solomon is at work here!

43But when the unclean spirit exits from a human host, he wanders through arid places seeking respite and finds none. 44Then he says to himself, ‘Why not return to enter the dwelling I left?’ And he arrives to find it untenanted, swept, and furnished. 45Then he goes and recruits seven other spirits more wicked than himself, and entering, he dwells there with them happily ever after. And the last condition of the wretch is worse than the first. So will it be also with this wicked nation.”

13

3And he told them many things by means of parables, saying, “Listen: picture a sower going out to sow. 4And in the process of sowing, some seeds indeed fell beside the road, and the birds came and ate them up. 5But others fell on the rocky places where it had not much soil, and at once it sprang up on account of not having depth of earth. 6But when the sun rose, it was scorched, and it withered. 7Others fell upon the thorns, and the thorns came up and choked them. 8But others fell upon the good earth and gave fruit, one giving a hundred, another sixty, yet another thirty. 9The one having ears, let him hear.”

10And approaching, the disciples said to him, “Why do you speak to them in parables?” 11And answering, he said, “Because to you it has been

vouchsafed to know the mysteries of the kingdom of the heavens, but it has not been vouchsafed to them. [13]This is why I speak to them in parables, because seeing, they do not see, and hearing, they do not hear or understand. [14]And in them the prophecy of Isaiah is fulfilled, namely, 'In hearing, you will hear and not understand at all, and seeing you will see and not perceive at all. [15]For the mind of this people has grown dense and they heard dimly with their ears, and they closed their eyes lest they see with the eyes and hear with the ears and understand with the mind and turn about and I will heal them.' [16]But blessed are your eyes because they do see and your ears because they do hear. [17]For amen: I tell you, many prophets and sages desired to behold what you see and did not see and to hear what you hear and did not hear. [18]Therefore, listen and I will gladly explain the parable of the sower to you. [19]Everyone who hears the message of the kingdom and does not understand, the wicked one comes and seizes what has been sown in his heart. This is the one sown by the road. [20]But the one sown on the rocky places, this is the one hearing the message and at once welcoming it with joy. [21]But he has no root in himself and is short-lived, and when tribulation or persecution comes because of the message, at once he is scandalized. [22]But the one sown in the thorns, this is the one hearing the message, and the worries of the temporal world and the false promises of worldly wealth choke the message and it becomes barren. [23]And the one sown on the good earth, this is the one who, hearing and understanding the message, bears fruit and produces, one a hundred, one sixty, and one thirty."

[24]And he set forth another parable for their consideration, saying, "The kingdom of the heavens was compared to a man sowing good seed in his field. [25]But while everyone else was asleep, his enemy's henchmen came and sowed tares in between the wheat and left. [26]But when the grass sprouted and produced fruit, then the tares appeared, too. [27]So coming to the master of the house, his slaves said to him, 'Lord, did you not sow good seed in your field? Then where did the tares come from?' [28]And he said to them, 'The man who is my enemy[d] did this!' And his slaves say, 'So do you want us to go and gather them?' [29]But he says, 'No, I'm afraid that in collecting the tares, you might uproot the wheat, too. [30]Leave both to grow together until the harvest; and at harvest time I will instruct the reapers to collect the tares first and tie them in bundles to burn them. But as for the wheat, gather it into my barn.'"

---

d. Paul may be in view here as the corrupter of true Torah Christianity. In the Epistle of Peter to James, Paul is called "the man who is my enemy."

[31]He set another parable before them to consider, saying, "The kingdom of the heavens is like a grain of mustard which a man took and sowed in his field, which indeed is smaller than all the seeds, but when grown is greater than the herbs and becomes a tree so big that the birds of the sky find lodging in its branches."

[33]Another parable he spoke to them: "The kingdom of the heavens is like leaven which a woman took and hid in three measures of meal until the whole was leavened."

[34]All these things Jesus spoke to the crowds in parables, and lacking a parable, he spoke nothing to them, [35]so that the thing spoken by the prophet was fulfilled, namely, "I will open my mouth in parables; I will utter things kept secret since creation."

[43b]"The one having ears, let him hear! [44]The kingdom of the heavens is like treasure buried in the field, which a man found and reburied and, from his joy he goes and cashes in his possessions and buys that field.

[45]"Again, the kingdom of the heavens is like a merchant looking for beautiful pearls. [46]And finding one choice pearl, he went away, sold off his entire stock, and bought it.

[47]"Again, the kingdom of the heavens is like a net thrown into the sea, rounding up every kind of sea creature. [48]*When it was filled, the fisherman threw back the small fish and chose the large fish without regret.*

[51]"Did you understand all these things?" They say to him, "Yes." [52]So he told them one last parable: "Because of this, every scribe trained as a disciple to the kingdom of the heavens is like a man, master of a house, who produces out of his treasure goods both new and old."

[53]And it came about, when Jesus finished these parables, he departed from there. [54]And coming into his birthplace, he taught them in their synagogue in such a way as to astonish them and make them say, "Where does this man come by this wisdom?" "And his powerful deeds!" [55]"Isn't this man the son of the carpenter? Isn't his mother called Mary and his brothers are named James and Joseph and Simon and Judah?" [56]"And aren't all his sisters here with us?" [57]And yet they were scandalized by him. But Jesus said to them, "It just goes to show that the only place a prophet gets no respect is his birthplace and in his dwelling."

14

[1]At that time, Herod the tetrarch heard the report of Jesus, [2]and he said to his servants, "This is surely John the Baptist! He was raised from the dead, and because of that, the Powers are energizing him." [3]What he meant was that Herod had seized John, bound him, and put him in

prison on account of Herodias, the wife of his brother Philip. [4]For John said to him, "It is not legal for you to have sex with her." [5]And wishing to kill him, he nonetheless feared the crowd because they held him as a prophet. [6]So Herod's birthday coming round, the daughter of Herodias danced in the midst of the guests and pleased Herod. [7]And so, with an oath, he promised to give her whatever she might ask. [8]So being instructed in advance by her mother, she says, "Give me, here on a dish, the head of John the Baptist." [10]And sending an executioner, he beheaded John right there in the prison. [11]And his head was brought on a dish and given to the girl. [12]And coming forth, his disciples took his headless corpse and buried him and, coming, reported to Jesus. And Jesus, hearing their report, departed from there in a boat to a desert place by himself. [13]And hearing of it, the crowds followed him on foot from the cities. [14]And leaving his tent, he saw a great crowd and felt compassion for them, and he cured their sick.

[15]And now, evening coming, the disciples came to him and said, "The place is a desert and the dinner hour is long past. So dismiss the crowds that they may go to the villages and buy themselves food." [16]But Jesus said to them, "They need not go away. You give them to eat!" [17]But they say to him, "We have nothing here but five loaves and two fish." [18]And he said, "Bring them here to me." [19]And having ordered the crowds to recline on the grass, taking the five loaves and the two fish, looking up to the sky, he blessed the loaves and, breaking them, gave them to the disciples, and the disciples distributed them to the crowd. [20]And all ate and were satisfied, and they took twelve basket-loads of the leftover pieces. [21]And those eating were about five thousand males, not counting women and children. [22]And at once he ordered his disciples, despite their protests, to launch the boat and precede him to the opposite shore while he dispersed the crowds.

[23]And having bade them good-bye, he went up into the mountain to pray, and with evening coming on, he remained there alone. [24]But the boat was now many stadia away from land, being tormented by the waves and the wind was against them. [25]Now in the fourth watch of the night, he came toward them walking on the sea. [26]And the disciples, seeing him walking on the sea, were frantic, saying to one another, "It is a phantom!" And they shrieked with fear. [27]But at once Jesus spoke to them, saying, "Cheer up! It is I! Be not afraid." [28]And answering him, Peter said, "Lord, if you are not a phantom, enable me to come to you on the waters." [29]And he said, "Come!" And dropping over the side of the

boat, Peter walked on the waters and came toward Jesus. [32]And as they climbed into the boat, the wind died. [33]And those in the ship bowed before him, exclaiming, "Truly, you are God's son!" [34]And crossing over onto the land, they came to shore at Gennesaret.

15

[1]Then Pharisees and scribes from Jerusalem approached him, saying, [2]"Why do your disciples violate the tradition of the elders? For they do not wash the hands when they eat bread!" [3]But answering, he said to them, "And why do you violate the commandment of God because of your tradition? [4]For God said, 'Take care of father and mother' and 'Whoever speaks evil of father or mother, let him end up dead.' [5]But you know better. You say, 'If one says to one's father or mother, whatever you might have been owed by me, it is *corban,* [6]by no means shall he take care of his father or his mother.' And thus you made the command of God moot in favor of your tradition. [7]Isaiah the prophet put it beautifully when he mentioned you, you hypocrites, saying: [8]'This people honors me with lip service, but their heart is far away from me [9]and their piety toward me is a charade, teaching doctrines that are commandments of men.'" [10]And summoning the crowd, he said to them, "Hear me and try to understand: [11]nothing entering into the mouth makes a person profane, but what comes forth out of the mouth, this makes a person profane." [12]Then coming to him, the disciples say to him, "Are you aware the Pharisees were scandalized by what you said?" [13]And he, answering, said, "Every plant that my heavenly Father did not plant shall be uprooted. [14]Forget about them! Blind, they pretend to lead the blind. But if a blind man leads a blind man, the pair of them will end up in the ditch!"

[21]And going forth from there, Jesus left for the region of Tyre and Sidon. [22]And behold, a woman, a Canaanite from those borders, came forth and shouted, saying, "Take pity on me, Lord, for you are a mighty exorcist like Solomon, the son of David. My daughter is badly demonized." But he answered her not a word. And approaching him, his disciples urged him, saying, "Get rid of her! She keeps calling out behind us." [24]So he decided he had best answer her, and he said, "My mission was only to the lost sheep dwelling in Israel." [25]But she came and bowed before him, saying, "Lord, help me!" [26]But he, answering, said, "It is not proper to take the bread that belongs to the children and to throw it to the dogs, now is it?" [27]But she had an answer ready for him: "True, Lord! But even the dogs eat from the crumbs falling from their master's table." [28]Then answering, Jesus said to her, "Woman, your determination is

great! I grant you what you wish." And her daughter was cured as of that
very hour.

[29]And leaving from there, Jesus came by the Sea of Galilee, and going
up into the mountains, he sat there. [30]And crowds came to him, having
with them many lame, maimed, blind, mute, and many others. And they
cast them at his feet, and he cured them, [31]causing the crowd to marvel,
seeing mutes speaking, maimed people restored to health, lame folk
walking, and blind people seeing. And they acclaimed the God of Israel.
[32]And Jesus summoned his disciples and said, "I feel for the crowd because they remain with me three whole days now and have not anything
they may eat. And I am not willing to send them home still fasting for fear
they will keel over in the road." [33]And the disciples say to him, "Where in
the desert do we come up with enough loaves to satisfy a crowd so
great?" [34]And Jesus says to them, "How many loaves do you have?" And
they said, "A total of seven, plus a few fish." [35]And having directed the
crowd to recline on the ground, [36]he took the seven loaves and the fish
and, giving thanks, broke them and gave them to the disciples, and the
disciples gave them to the crowds. [37]And all ate and were satisfied, and
the leftover fragments they gathered were seven hampers full. [38]And
those eating were about four thousand males, not counting women and
children. [39]And dismissing the crowd, he set out in the boat and came
into the region of Magadan.

16

[5]And on the trip to the other side, the disciples forgot to take loaves.
And Jesus said to them, [6]"Beware! Do not underestimate the leaven of the
Pharisees and the Syndics!" [7]And they whispered to one another, "We
took no loaves." [8]But becoming aware of it, Jesus said, "Why do you
babble about not having loaves of bread? Do you have any faith at all?
[9]Do you still not get it? If I wanted bread, I could make it myself! Don't
you remember the five loaves for the five thousand and how many baskets you gathered? [10]Nor the seven loaves for the four thousand, how
many hampers you gathered? [11]How can you possibly fail to grasp that I
wasn't talking about loaves of bread? But watch out for the insidiousness
of the Pharisees and Syndics." [12]At last they saw he was not saying to beware the yeast in loaves of bread, but that of the teaching of the Pharisees
and Syndics.

[13]And coming into the environs of Caesarea Philippi, Jesus questioned his disciples, saying, "Who do people think yours truly to be?"
[14]And they said, "While some say John the Baptist, others say Elijah, and

others Jeremiah or one of the biblical prophets." [15]He says to them, "But what about you? Who do you think me to be?" [16]And answering, Simon Peter said, [17]"You are the Christ, the son of the one true God." And answering, Jesus said to him, "Blessed are you, Simon *son of John!* For flesh and blood did not reveal it to you, but rather my Father in the heavens. [18]And I also say to you: You are Peter, and on this rock I will build my Church and the gates of Hades will not withstand it. [19]I will give you the keys of the kingdom of the heavens, and what obligations and penances you may bind on men shall be considered binding by God, and what duties and penalties you may loose from their consciences on earth shall be considered loosed in the heavens." [20]Then he warned the disciples that they must tell no one he is the Christ.

[21]From then on, Jesus Christ began to indicate to his disciples that he must go to Jerusalem and suffer many indignities at the hands of the elders and archpriests and scribes and to be executed and on the third day to be raised. [24]Then Jesus said to his disciples, "If anyone here wants to come after me, let him repudiate himself and let him pick up his cross and let him follow me. [25]For whoever tries to save his life will lose it, but whoever will sacrifice his life for my sake will save it. [26]For what profit does a person make if he manages to acquire the whole world, only to be fined his own life? For what could a person possibly offer in exchange for his life? [27]I say this because one like a son of man is about to come in the radiance of his Father with his angels, and then he will repay each one according to his acts. [28]Amen: I say to you, there are some of those standing here who will certainly not taste of death before they see one like a son of man coming to receive his kingship."

17

[1]And after six days, Jesus takes along Peter and Jacob, and John, his brother, and leads them up into a high mountain solely by themselves. [2]And he was metamorphosed in front of them and his face shone like the sun and his garments became white as the light. [3]And behold, Elijah and Moses appeared to them, conversing with Jesus. And Jesus says to Peter, "Simon, have you nothing to say?" [4]And answering, Peter says to Jesus, "Rabbi, it is good for us disciples to be here. If you wish, I will make three tents here: one for you, one for Moses, and one for Elijah." [5]While he was still speaking, behold, a glowing cloud overshadowed them and a voice from the cloud: "This one is my son, the beloved, in whom I am quite pleased. Hear him!" [6]And hearing this, the disciples fell on their faces and were terrified. [7]And Jesus approached and, touching them, said, "Rise

and do not fear." [8]And lifting their eyes tentatively, they saw no one except for Jesus alone. [9]And as they descended from the mountain, Jesus ordered them, "Recount the vision to no one before a man be raised from the dead."

[10]And the disciples questioned him, saying, "Then what scripture do the scribes have in mind when they say Elijah must come first or the general resurrection may not take place?" [11]But he, answering, said to them, "Elijah is indeed due to usher in the resurrection of all things; [12]but I say to you that indeed, Elijah already came and they did not recognize him but did with him what they wished. In the same way, another man is about to suffer at their hands." [13]Then the disciples understood that he was referring to John the Baptist.

[14]And as they were coming to the crowd, a man came to him and, falling on his knees before him, [15]said, "Lord, take pity on my son because he is moonstruck and in a bad way, for often he falls into the fire and into the water. [16]And I brought him to your disciples and they were not able to cure him." [17]And answering him, Jesus said, "O unbelieving and perverted nation! How long till I am free of you? How long must I endure you? Bring him here to me." [18]And Jesus rebuked it, and the demon exited from him and the lad was healed as of that hour. [19]Then approaching Jesus privately, the disciples said, "Why were we unable to cast it out?" [20]And he says to them, "Because of your scant faith!"

[22]And while they were walking together in the Galilee, Jesus said to them, "This is the way of things: a man will be delivered into the hands of his fellow men [23]and they will kill him and on the third day he will be raised." And they were overcome with grief.

[24]And when they arrived in the village of Nahum, the ones collecting the two drachma tax came to Peter and said, "Your teacher does not pay the two drachmas?" He says, "Yes." [25]And as he came into the house, Jesus anticipated him, saying, "How does it seem to you, Simon? The kings of the earth—from whom do they take toll or tribute, from their own people or from foreigners?" [26]When he said, "From foreigners," Jesus said to him, "Then the people are exempt."

And the scribes and the Pharisees brought to him a woman accused of many sins, and standing her in the middle of the crowd, they say to him, "Teacher, in the Torah, Moses commanded that such a woman be stoned. But what do you say?" They said this to test him. But Jesus bent down and wrote with his finger their names in the dust of the ground. But when they persisted in questioning him, he stood and said, "Fine, let him

who is without sin among you cast the first stone." And stooping down, he continued to write. And seeing what he wrote there, they slinked away, one by one, from the eldest to the youngest till at last the woman stood alone before Jesus. And he stood up and said to her, "Woman, where are they? Did no one condemn you?" And she said, "None, Lord." So Jesus said, "Then I can hardly condemn you, can I? Go, and leave off sinning."

18

[1]In that hour the disciples came to Jesus, saying, "Who then ranks highest in the kingdom of the heavens?" [2]And summoning a child, he set it in the midst of them [3]and said, "Amen: I say to you, unless you turn about and become like the children, you will by no means enter the kingdom of the heavens. [4]Therefore, whoever is willing to humble himself like this child, this one ranks highest in the kingdom of the heavens. [5]And whoever welcomes one such child on account of my name, welcomes me; [6]and whoever scandalizes one of these new converts, it is good for him instead to have his head put through the center hole of the millstone, then dumped overboard into the depths. [7]Woe to the world because of scandals! For though it is inevitable for scandals to arise, woe to the wretch through whom the scandal arises! [10]See to it that you don't give short shrift to these little ones, for I tell you that their guardian angels forever contemplate the face of my Father in heaven.

[12]"How does it seem to you? If any man has a hundred sheep and one strays, won't he leave the ninety-nine grazing on the mountains and go off to seek the stray? [13]And if he chances to discover it—amen: I say to you, he rejoices over it more than over the ninety-nine who did not go astray. [14]Even so, it is not the will of their angels before your Father in the heavens that one of these little ones should be lost. [15]*Now if a man has grieved the spirit of his brother*, go and admonish him privately, between you and him. If he listens to you, you have won back your brother. [16]But if he does not listen, take with you one or two more so that only by the mouth of two or three witnesses every word of testimony may be corroborated. [17]But if he remains unmoved by them, tell the Church. And if he remains unmoved by the Church, write him off just as you would the heathen and the customs agent. [19]Again, I say to you that if two of you agree on earth concerning every disciplinary matter which they may ask, my Father in the heavens will see to it that it transpires. [20]For where two or three are assembled in my name, I am there in their midst.

[21]"*If your brother has sinned in any matter and made amends, wel-*

come him seven times in a single day." Simon, his disciple, said to him, "Seven times in a day?" The Lord answered and said to him, "Yes, I say to you, until seventy times seven times. For in the prophets, after they were anointed with the Holy Spirit, a word of sin was found.

[23]"Because of this, the kingdom of the heavens may be compared to a man, a king, who wanted to settle accounts with his slaves. [24]And as he began the process, one was brought forward to him, a debtor of ten thousand talents. [25]And the poor wretch not having the wherewithal to pay him, the lord commanded him to be sold with his wife and children and all his possessions toward repayment of the debt. [26]Therefore, falling to his knees, the slave prostrated himself before him, saying, 'Postpone your wrath at me, and I will pay you the whole thing!' [27]And flooded with compassion, the lord of that slave released him from the debt and forgave him the loan. [28]But going out, that slave looked up one of his fellow slaves who owed him one hundred denarii. And grabbing him, he choked him, saying, 'Pay if you owe something!' [29]Therefore, his fellow slave, falling to his knees, pleaded with him, 'Postpone your wrath at me and I will repay you!' [30]But he did not want to do it. But instead, he went off and threw him into prison till he should repay the sum he owed. [31]Therefore, his fellow slaves, seeing what had taken place, were extremely dismayed and they went and explained to their lord all that had happened. [32]Then summoning him, his lord says to him, 'Wicked slave! All that debt I forgave you since you pleaded with me! [33]Weren't you obliged to have mercy on your fellow slave as I had mercy on you?' [34]And infuriated, his lord handed him over to the torturers to take it out of his hide.[e] [35]My heavenly Father will do the same to you unless each of you forgives his brother from your hearts." *And he said, "Never be joyful except when you love upon your brother with love."*

19

[1]And it happened, when Jesus finished these words, that he left the Galilee and arrives in the boundaries of Judea across the Jordan. [3]And Pharisees, approaching him, seeking to gauge him, were asking if it is legal for a man to dismiss his wife for any cause. [4]And answering, he said, "Did you not read that the creator from the beginning 'made them male and female?' [5]And he said, 'This is why a man shall leave father and mother and shall join with his wife, and the two shall be one flesh.' [6]So

e. Alternately, "his lord handed him over to keep him under torture till his family should arrange to repay the whole sum he owed him."

then, if God has yoked them together, let no mere mortal divide them." 7They say to him, "Then why did Moses command a husband to draw up papers and to dismiss a wife?" 8He says to them, "Because of your insensitivity, Moses permitted you Jews to send away your wives. 9But I say to you that whoever dismisses a wife, except of course for prostitution,[f] and marries another commits adultery."

10The disciples say to him, "If such is the man's situation with the wife, it is not prudent to marry in the first place!" 11And he said to them, "Not everyone accepts this saying. 12For there are eunuchs who were born thus from a mother's womb, and there are eunuchs who were made eunuchs by others, and there are eunuchs who made themselves eunuchs for the sake of gaining the kingdom of the heavens. The one capable of accepting it, let him accept it."

13And they brought children to him, hoping he would lay hands on them and pray, and the disciples rebuffed them. 14But Jesus said, "Let the children come to me. What's the matter with you? Don't you know them? These are the very angels of the kingdom of the heavens." 15And laying hands on them, he moved on from there.

16And behold, two rich men approached him and *the first* said, "Teacher, what good deed may I do that I may have age-long life?" 17And he said to him, "Why do you ask me about the good? The good is one thing. If you want to enter into the life, keep the commandments equally." 18He says to him, "Which ones?" And Jesus said, "Do not murder, Do not commit adultery, Do not steal, Do not testify falsely, Take care of father and mother, and You shall love your neighbor as yourself." 20The young man says to him, "All these I kept. Is there something more I am missing?" 21Jesus said to him, "If you want to be perfect, go sell what you own and give the price to the poor, and you shall have treasure in the heavens, and come follow me." 22But hearing this, the young man went away grieving at what he must do, for he had many possessions to disburse.

The second of the rich men said to him, "Master, what good thing can I do and live?" He said to him, "O man, fulfill the Torah and the Prophets." He answered him, "I have kept them." He said to him, "Go sell all that you own and distribute it to the poor and come follow me." But the rich man began to scratch his head and it displeased him. And the Lord said to him, "How can you say you have kept the Torah and the Prophets? For it is written in the Torah, 'You shall love your neighbor as

f. More literally, "consanguineous marriage."

yourself,' and lo, many of your brothers, sons of Abraham, are coated in filth and dying of hunger, and your house is full of many good things and nothing at all goes out of it to them."

And he turned and said to Simon, his disciple, who was sitting by him, "Simon, son of Joanna, it is easier for a camel to enter through the hole of a needle than for a rich man to enter into the kingdom of the heavens." [25]Hearing this, the disciples were completely astonished, reflecting, "If even God's favorites cannot enter heaven, then who can save himself?" [26]Looking at them, Jesus says, "True, for mortals this is impossible. But for God, all things are possible!"

[27]Then answering, Peter said to him, "Behold, we have abandoned everything and followed you. What then shall we get?" [28]And Jesus said to them, "Amen: I tell you, that you who followed me, in the rebirth of all things when one like a son of man sits on a shining throne, you too will seat yourselves on twelve thrones, governing the twelve tribes of Israel. [29]And everyone who abandoned dwellings or brothers or sisters or father or mother or children or farms for the sake of my name will receive many times as much and will inherit age-long life. [30]But many of the first will wind up last and vice versa."

20

[1]"For the kingdom of the heavens is like a man, master of a house, who went out early in the morning to hire laborers for his vineyard. [2]And settling with the laborers on a wage of a denarius per day, he dispatched them into his vineyard. [3]And going out about the third hour,[g] he spotted others loitering in the marketplace, [4]and he said to those, 'You, too, go into the vineyard and I will pay you whatever seems fair given the late start.' And they went. [5]Going out again about the sixth and ninth hours, he made the same arrangements with other late-comers. [6]And going out about the eleventh hour, he found others loitering around and says to them, 'Why do you men stand here doing nothing all day long?' [7]They say to him, 'That's simple: no one offered us any work.' He says to them, 'Consider yourselves hired! You, too, go into the vineyard.' [8]And evening having come, the lord of the vineyard says to his steward, 'Call the workmen and pay the wage, starting with the last, up to the first.' [9]But the ones who started about the eleventh hour each received a denarius, [10]and the ones starting first supposed they will receive more. And they, too, each received the denarius! [11]And receiving their wages, they murmured against

g. 9:00 a.m.

the master of the house, saying, [12]'These last put in one hour and you made them equal to us, the ones who bore the burden of the whole day and the torment of the heat!' [13]But he, answering one of them, said, 'My good fellow, I do you no injustice. Didn't we settle on a denarius? [14]Take your due and go! So I want to give to this last man the same as I gave you? [15]Isn't it my prerogative to do what I want with my own money? Or is it really that you are squinting with envy because I am good?' [16]Thus, the last ones will be the first and the first ones the last."

[17]And as he was about to go up to Jerusalem, he took the twelve aside by themselves and he said to them, [18]"Behold, we are going up to Jerusalem and a man will be delivered up to the archpriests and scribes, and they will sentence him to death, [19]and they will deliver him up to the gentiles for jeering and flogging and crucifixion, and on the third day he will be raised."

[20]Then the mother of the sons of Zebediah came to him with her sons, bowing before him and requesting something from him. [21]And he said to her, "What is it you want?" She says to him, "Say to me that these, my two sons, may sit, one to the right and one to the left of you, in your regime." [22]But answering, Jesus said, "You have no idea what you are asking. Are you capable of drinking the cup which I am about to drink?" They say to him, "We can do it." [23]He says to them, "My cup you shall drink. [24]Nonetheless, to sit to the right of me or to the left is not my prerogative to grant. That privilege is reserved by my Father for someone else." [24]And overhearing this, the other ten became furious with the two brothers. [25]And seeking to settle the dispute, Jesus summoned them and said, "You know how the rulers of the gentiles domineer them and the great exercise authority over them? [26]Is it not the same with you? But whoever wants to become great among you shall be your servant. [27]And whoever wants to be first among you shall be your slave. [28]For man, too, did not come to be served, but to serve,[h] to spend his life on behalf of many."

[29]And as they traveled out of Jericho, a sizable crowd followed him. [30]And behold, two blind men sitting at the side of the road, hearing "Jesus is passing by!" cried out saying, "Lord! Take pity on us, son of David!" [31]But the crowd rebuked them, that they should be quiet. But this only made them shout the louder: "Lord! Take pity on us, son of David!" [32]And stopping, [34]flooded with compassion, Jesus touched their eyes and at once they saw again and followed him.

---

h. Gen. 2:15

21

[1]And when they come close to Jerusalem and came to Beth-Phage at the Mount of Olives, then Jesus assigns two disciples, [2]telling them, “Go into the village over there, and at once you will discover a donkey tethered and a colt with her. Untie them and bring them to me. [3]And should anyone say anything to you, you shall say, ‘Their Lord requires them,’ and at once he will send them.” [4]Now this has happened so the thing spoken through the prophet might be fulfilled, namely, [5]“Tell Zion’s daughter, ‘Look! Your king comes to you meek and mounted on a donkey, and on a colt, son of a donkey.’” [6]And setting off, doing just as Jesus directed them, the disciples [7]brought the donkey and the colt and piled on them the garments, and he mounted on them. [8]And the very large crowd strewed their own garments on the road, and others cut branches from the trees and strewed them on the road. [9]And the crowds going before and following shouted out, saying, “Hosanna to the son of David! Blessed in the name of Adonai be the Coming One! Let hosannas ring in the highest spheres!” [10]And as he went into Jerusalem, all the city was shaken, saying, “Who is this?” [11]And the crowds said, “Why, this is the prophet Jesus from Nazareth in the Galilee.”

[12]And Jesus entered into the temple and ejected all those selling and buying in the temple. And he upended the currency exchange tables and the chairs of those selling doves, *and no one resisted him, for a certain fiery and starry light shone from his eyes and the divine majesty gleamed in his face.* [13]And he says to them, “It is written, ‘My house shall be called a house of prayer. But you are making it a robbers’ cave!’” [14]And blind and lame people approached him in the temple and he cured them. [15]But the archpriests and the scribes, seeing the marvels that he performed and hearing the children shouting in the temple and saying, “Hosanna to the son of David,” were furious. [16]And they said to him, “Do you hear what these are saying? Surely you don’t approve?” And Jesus says to them, “Yes! Did you never read, ‘Out of the mouths of infants and nurslings you have brought perfect praise?’” [17]And turning his back on them, he exited from the city to Beth-Anu and he found lodging there.

[18]Now as he was going up to the city early, he felt hungry. [19]And noticing by the roadside a lone fig tree, he went up to it but found nothing in it but leaves only, and he says to it, “May no fruit at all come from you forever!” And instantly the fig tree was withered up. [20]And seeing this, the disciples marveled, saying, “How on earth did the fig tree wither up instantly?” [21]And answering, Jesus said to them, “Amen: I tell you, if you

have faith and do not doubt, you will perform not only the wonder of the
fig-tree, but also if you say to this mountain, 'Be taken and thrown into
the sea,' it shall happen. 22And all things which you ask in prayer, believing, you shall receive."

23And as he came into the temple and was teaching, the archpriests
and the elders of the people came to him, saying, "With what authorization do you do these things? Who authorized your actions?" 24But answering, Jesus said to them, "First I will question you on one matter. You
answer me and I will be glad to tell you the authorization for my actions.
25Remember the baptism of John? Where did its authorization come
from? From God in heaven or only from mortals?" And they huddled,
debating, whispering, "It's a trap. If we say 'from heaven,' he will surely
ask us, 'Then why didn't you believe in him when you had the chance?'
26But if we say, 'from mortal men,' we have the crowd to reckon with, for
everyone holds John as a prophet." 27So answering Jesus, they said, "We
do not know." And he said to them also, "Well, if you refuse to tell me
what you really think, I'm afraid I cannot tell you the authority behind
my actions.

28"But how does it seem to you? A man had two children. Approaching the first, he said, 'Child, go today and work in the vineyard.'
29But he said, 'I go, Lord!' And he did not go. 30And approaching the second, he spoke similarly. And answering, he said, 'I will not!' Later, thinking better of it, he went after all. 31Which of the two did the will of the father?" They say, "The latter." Jesus says to them, "Amen: I tell you, the
customs agents and the prostitutes are preceding you into the kingdom of
God. 32For John came to you walking a path of righteousness and you
dismissed him as a fanatic. But the customs agents and the prostitutes believed him. But even seeing this miracle, you did not change your mind to
believe in him.

33"Listen to another parable. There was a man, master of a house,
who planted a vineyard and erected a hedge around it and dug in it a wine
press and put up a tower, and he leased it out to sharecroppers and went
away. 34And when the right time for fruit drew near, he sent his slaves to
the sharecroppers to collect his due from the produce. 35And the sharecroppers grabbed his slaves, flogging this one, killing that one, stoning
another. 36Again the following year he sent other slaves, more than the
first group, and they treated them the same way. 37At last he sent to them
his son, saying, 'They will pay my son due respect!' 38But the sharecroppers, seeing the son, conspired: 'The old man must be dead! This one is

his heir. Come, let us kill him, and the inheritance will pass to us.' [39]And grabbing him, they threw him outside the vineyard and killed him. I ask you then, when the lord of the vineyard comes, what will he do to those sharecroppers?" [41]They say to him, "He will utterly destroy the villains, and he will let out the vineyard to other sharecroppers who will pay him his share of the fruit in the proper season." [42]Jesus says to them, "You never read in the scriptures, 'A stone which the house builders deemed unusable, this very one became the head of the corner. This was from the Lord, and we regard it as a marvel'? [43]Because of this, I tell you, the kingdom of God will be taken from you and will be given to a nation producing its fruits." [45]And the archpriests and the Pharisees, hearing his parables, were well aware he is referring to them. [46]And looking to apprehend him, they were afraid of the crowd, for they held him as a prophet.

22

[2]And answering his critics, Jesus again spoke to them in parables, saying, "The kingdom of the heavens may be compared to a man who arranged a great feast. [3]And he sent his slaves to summon those who had been invited to the feast, and they did not want to come. [4]Again he sent other slaves, saying, 'Tell the ones invited, look, I have prepared my supper. My bulls and the fattened beasts have been slaughtered and everything is ready. Come to the feast!' But they heedlessly went off each to his business, one to his own field, another on a business trip. [8]Then he says to his slaves, 'Though the feast is hot on the table, those originally invited were not worthy. [9]Therefore, go to the forks in the roads and invite to the feast as many as you may chance to find.' [10]And going out into the roads, those slaves assembled all whom they found, both wicked and good, and the wedding hall was filled with people reclining at table."

[15]Then the Pharisees went and conferred over how to trick him into saying something incriminating. [16]And they send their disciples to him, with Herod's agents, saying, "Teacher, we know you speak frankly and that no one intimidates you. [17]So then, tell us, how does it seem to you: is it legal to pay tribute to Caesar or not?" [18]But aware of their duplicity, he said to them, "Why put me on the spot, you hypocrites? Show me the tribute money." [19]And they fetched a denarius. [20]And he says to them, "Whose is this image and epigraph?" And they answered him, "Caesar's, of course." [21]"So," Jesus said to them, "give Caesar's coins to Caesar in taxes and give God's coins to God in the temple." [22]And they were greatly taken aback at him and they left him and walked away.

[23]On that day, some Syndics came to him, who say there is no resur-

rection, and they questioned him, [24]saying, "Teacher, Moses said, 'If anyone should die, not having children, his brother shall take to wife afterward the wife of his brother and shall raise up heirs for his brother.' [25]So once we knew seven brothers and the oldest, having married, died, and not having heirs, he left his wife to his brother. [26]Similarly with the second oldest and the third until the seventh died. [27]And last of all, the woman died. [28]In this 'resurrection,' then, which one of the seven will she be wife to? After all, each had her at one time or another." [29]And answering, Jesus said to them, "You're mistaken, being ignorant of scripture and the power of God. [30]For in the resurrection, neither do men marry, nor are women given in marriage, but they are like angels in the heavens. [31]But concerning the resurrection of the dead, didn't you read what God said to you, namely, 'I am the God of Abraham and the God of Isaac and the God of Jacob'? [32]He is not a God of corpses but of living men!" [33]And the crowd who heard this were astonished at his polemical skill.

[34]But when the Pharisees heard the report that he had silenced the Syndics, they called a meeting. [35]One of them, a sage of the Torah, asked him a loaded question: [36]"Teacher, what is the chief commandment in the Torah?" [37]And he said to him, "'You shall love Adonai your God with all your heart and with all your soul and with all your understanding.' [38]This is the chief and most important commandment. [39]A second is like it: 'You shall love your neighbor as yourself.' [40]On these two commandments hang the whole Torah and the Prophets."

[41]And since the Pharisees were assembled to hear their spokesman take on Jesus, Jesus questioned them, saying, "How does it seem to you concerning the Christ? Whose son is he?" They say to him, "David's." [43]He says to them, "Then how is it that in the mantic state David calls him 'Lord,' saying, 'Adonai said to my lord, sit at my right till I put the necks of your enemies under your feet'? [45]If then David himself calls him 'lord,' how is he his son?" And no one was able to come up with a word in reply, and from that day on, no one ventured to question him again.

23

[1]Then Jesus spoke to the crowds and to his disciples, [2]saying, "The scribes and the Pharisees assumed the throne of Moses. [3]Therefore, perform and observe anything they may tell you; we don't want schism, but do not emulate the works they perform. For what they say, they do not perform. [4]And they tie heavy burdens onto people's shoulders, but they themselves make not the slightest effort to carry them. [5]No, all the pious works they perform they do for public consumption. They widen the

phylacteries across their foreheads and they lengthen the fringes of their prayer shawls, [6]and they relish the head table at formal dinners and to be shown to the front-row seats in the synagogues, [7]and to receive deferential greetings in the marketplaces and to be addressed by others as 'rabbi!' [8]But don't you ever be called rabbi, for one is your teacher, Moses, and you are all brothers. And address no one on earth as your *abba,* for only one is your heavenly Father. [10]Neither be addressed as master, for your master is one, the Christ.

[13]"Woe to you, scribes and Pharisees, hypocrites! For you slam shut the kingdom of the heavens in people's faces. For you don't enter, nor do you allow entry to anyone else.

[15]"Woe to you, scribes and Pharisees, hypocrites! For you crisscross the sea and the dry land to make one proselyte, and when he becomes one, you make him twice the heir of the Valley of Hinnom you yourselves are.

[16]"Woe to you, blind guides who say, 'Whoever may swear an oath by the holy place, it does not count; but whoever may swear by the gold of the holy place, his obligation is binding.' [17]Morons! Blind men! For which is greater? The gold itself or the sanctum that sanctifies the gold? [18]And you say, 'Whoever may swear by the sacrificial altar, it does not count; but whoever may swear by the offering lying on it, his obligation is binding.' [19]Are you blind? For logically, which is greater? The offering itself or the altar which makes the offering sacred?

[23]"Woe to you, scribes and Pharisees, hypocrites! Because you meticulously tithe mint and dill and cumin and you have neglected the weightier portions of the Torah: justice and mercy and faith. But these you were obliged to perform, albeit not neglecting the fine points. [24]Blind guides, carefully sifting out the gnat but swallowing the camel whole!

[25]"Woe to you, scribes and Pharisees, hypocrites, because you purify the outside of the cup and the plate, but inside they are full of rapine and excess! [26]Blind Pharisee! First purify the inside of the cup so the outside, too, may automatically be rendered ritually pure.

[27]"Woe to you, scribes and Pharisees, hypocrites, because you are just like freshly whitewashed graves, which while indeed appearing externally to be beautiful are filled inside with the bones of the dead and with all impurity!

[29]"Woe to you, scribes and Pharisees, hypocrites! Because you build shrines to the prophets and place flowers at the monuments of the *zaddiks,* [30]and you say, 'If we lived in the days of our fathers, we would not have been their accomplices in shedding the blood of the prophets.'

[31]So you admit you are the heirs of those who murdered the prophets.
[32]And you fully measure up to the example of your fathers. [33]Snakes!
Spawn of vipers! How do you plan to escape being sentenced to the Valley of Hinnom?

[34]"Therefore behold, I myself send you prophets and sages and
scribes. Some of them you will kill and crucify, and some you will flog in
your synagogues and pursue from city to city. [35]And thus all the righteous
blood spilled onto the ground from the blood of Abel the righteous until
the blood of Zechariah, son of *Jehoida,* whom you murdered between the
shrine and the altar, will rain on you! [36]Amen: I say to you, all these
crimes will come upon this nation! [37]O Jerusalem, Jerusalem, who kills
the prophets and stones those sent to her, how often I wished to gather
your children as a bird gathers her young under the wings, and you refused. [38]Behold, your house is left abandoned. For I tell you, you will by
no means see me from now until perchance you say, 'Blessed in the name
of Adonai be the Coming One.'"

24

[1]And as he made his way out of the temple, his disciples approached
to point out the buildings of the temple. [2]And answering, he said to him,
"Look not at all these! Amen: I tell you, for there shall by no means be left
here a pair of stones not knocked apart." [3]And once he took a seat on the
Mount of Olives, the disciples approached him privately, saying, "Tell
us, when will these things be? And what is the sign of your advent and of
the culmination of the age?" [4]And answering, Jesus said to them: "Watch
out that no one deceive you in this matter. [5]For many will appear trading
on my name, saying, "I am the Christ!" and they will mislead many with
this tactic. [6]But you will next hear of wars and rumors of more distant
wars, for nation will be pitted against nation and kingdom against kingdom. There will be famines and earthquakes in scattered places. [8]And yet
these mark only the onset of labor pains. [9]Then they will deliver you up to
tribulation and will kill you; you will be pariahs among all nations because of my name. [10]And then many will fall away and will hand over
their former co-religionists, and they will hate one another. [11]And many
pseudo-prophets will emerge to lead many off the path. [12]And due to the
increasing apostasy from the Torah, many people's love will grow cold.
[13]But the one enduring to the end without renouncing my name, only
such a one will save himself. [14]And this news of the kingdom will be proclaimed in all the inhabited earth for a testimony to all the nations, and
then the end will come.

[15]Therefore, once you behold the abomination of desolation, spoken of through Daniel the prophet, standing in the holy place—may the reader understand the reference—[16]then let those in Judea flee to the mountains. [17]Anyone on the roof: let him not come back down to retrieve anything, but rather let him climb down the fire escape and flee! [18]And the one working in the field when that hour strikes, let him not even return home to retrieve his garment. [19]But woe to those with a child in the womb and those nursing in those days! [20]Pray that your escape may not happen in winter or on a Sabbath, [21]because then there will be a great tribulation the like of which has not befallen mankind since the very beginning of the creation until the present and which will never be repeated! [22]In fact, if not for those allotted days being cut short, no flesh at all would be saved alive. [23]And at that point, if anyone says to you, ‘Behold here: the Christ! Behold there!’ do not believe it. [24]But pseudo-messiahs and pseudo-prophets will be brought in, and they will provide great signs and prodigies for the purpose of seducing the chosen people Israel, if at all possible. [25]Behold, I have told you in advance. [26]If, therefore, they say to you, ‘Behold, he is in the desert,’ do not go out to join him. Or if they say, ‘Behold, in the private chambers,’ do not believe. [27]For as the lightning emerges from the east and branches out unto the west, thus will be the advent of the one like a son of man. [28]Wherever the carcass happens to be, there you will see the vultures circling. [29]And immediately after the tribulation of those days, the sun will go dark and the moon will withhold her light and the stars will fall out of the sky and the angelic Powers of the heavens will be shaken. [30]And then all the tribes of the land of Israel will lament, and they will see one like a son of man coming on the cloud chariots of heaven with power and great brilliance. [31]And he will send out his angels with a great trumpet, and they will gather together his chosen people Israel from the four winds, from one rim of the sky to the other rim.

[32]“But from the fig tree learn the parable: as soon as its branch grows tender and puts forth leaves, you know that the summer is near; [33]so you also know, when you see all these things, it is at the doors. [34]Amen: I tell you, in answer to your question, this generation by no means passes away until these things all happen. [35]The sky and the earth will pass away but my predictions will not fail. [36]About that specific day or hour, no one knows that, neither the angels of the heavens nor the son, except the Father only. [37]For just like the days of Noah, so will be the advent of one like a son of man. [38]For as they were in those days, before the cataclysm, eating and drinking, marrying and being given in marriage, until the day

on which Noah entered into the ark, [39]and suspected nothing before the
cataclysm came and swept all away, so also will be the advent of one like
a son of man. [40]Then two men will be in a field: one is taken away and
one is abandoned. [41]There will be two women grinding in the mill: one is
taken away and one is abandoned. [42]Therefore, be watchful because you
do not know on which day your lord is coming. [43]And know this! That if
the master of the house had known in what watch of the night the burglar
planned to arrive, he would have kept watch and would not have allowed
his house to be dug through. [44]Therefore, be ready because a man always
comes in the hour you think least likely.

22
(continued)

[2]"The kingdom of the heavens may also be compared to a king who
arranged a wedding feast for his son. [11]But coming in to look at those reclining at table, the king saw there a man not dressed in wedding attire.
[12]And he says to him, 'My good fellow, how did you get in here without
proper wedding attire?' But he was speechless. [13]Then the king said to the
servants, 'Tie his feet and hands and throw him outside!' [14]For many are
invited, but few are selected."

25

[1]"Then the kingdom of the heavens will be compared to ten virgins
who, taking their lamps, went out to the place where they should join the
bridegroom. [2]But five of them were thoughtless and five prudent. [3]For
the thoughtless, while taking their lamps, did not take oil with them. [4]But
the prudent took oil in the vessels with their lamps. [5]But as the bridegroom was delayed, all slumbered and slept. [6]And in the middle of the
night comes a shout: 'Behold, the bridegroom! Go out to the meeting
place!' [7]Then all those virgins were awakened and trimmed their lamps.
[8]But the thoughtless said to the prudent, 'Give us some of your oil because our lamps are going out.' [9]But the prudent answered, saying, 'Then
it would never be enough for us and for you! Instead, go to the merchants
and buy more for yourselves.' [10]And as they were off buying, the bridegroom arrived, and those ready to meet him entered in with him to the
festivities and the door was shut. [11]Finally, the remaining virgins arrived
too, saying, 'Lord, lord, open to us!' [12]But he, answering, said, 'Amen: I
say to you, I do not know you.' [13]Keep watch, therefore, for you do not
know the day or the hour!

[14]"For it is just like a man going away from home. He summoned his
own slaves and entrusted his goods to them. [15]And to one he gave five tal-

ents, to another two, to another one, each according to his ability, and he
left home. [16]At once, the one receiving the five talents, going off, traded
with them and made another five. [17]The one receiving two, going away,
dug a hole in the ground and buried his master's silver. [18]*But the third devoured his master's silver with prostitutes and dancing girls.* [19]Then, after
a long time, the lord of those slaves comes and settles accounts with them.
[20]And the one receiving five talents, approaching, brought the five additional talents, saying, 'Lord, you entrusted five talents to me; look, I made
five more!' [21]His lord said to him, 'Well done, good and faithful slave!
You have proven yourself responsible with a few things, I will place you
in charge of many. Welcome to your lord's favor.' [22]The one with two
talents also approached, saying, 'Lord, I knew you, that you are a hard
man, reaping crops that others sowed, harvesting fields that others
planted. Fearing to risk it, I went away and hid your talents in the
ground. Look, here they are, safe and sound!' [26]But answering, his lord
said to him, 'Lazy lout! You say you knew I reap fields that others sowed?
That I harvest crops that others planted? [27]Then surely you must have
known at least to leave my silver with the exchange tables, and when I returned I should have recovered my money with interest. [28]So you there!
Take the talents from him and give them to the one with the ten talents.
[29]The know-how that brought the wealthy his success will get him even
more abundance. But the one not knowing what to do with it will lose
even the pittance he has.' [30]*Then, the one with a single talent of silver approached, saying, 'Lord, have mercy on me, for I thought my master is
delayed, and I thought you died, and I spent your silver on prostitutes
and dancing girls.'* And his lord said, 'Wicked slave! *Throw him into
prison till he shall pay his debt!'*

[31]"And when one like a son of man comes in his radiance with his
retinue of angels, then he will take his seat on his shining throne, [32]and
before him all the nations will be assembled, and he will sort them out as
a shepherd sorts the sheep from the goats, [33]and he will stand the sheep to
his right but the goats to his left. [34]Then the king will say to those to his
right, 'Come, O blessed of my Father! Enter into the kingdom that was
designed for you when the foundations of creation were laid. [35]For I hungered and you gave me to eat. I thirsted and you gave me a cup of cold
water to drink. I was a foreigner and you took me home for a meal.
[36]Naked and you dressed me; I was infirm and you looked in on me. I was
in prison and you came to visit me.' [37]Then the righteous will answer
him, saying, 'Lord, there must be some mistake. When did any of us ever

see you in such a plight and help you?' And answering, the king will say to them, 'Amen: I tell you, insofar as you did it for the most insignificant of these my itinerant brothers, you did it to me.' [41]Then he will say also to the ones on his left, 'Be gone, you damned, into the age-long fire stoked for the accuser and you, his angels. [42]For I hungered and you gave me nothing to eat, I thirsted and you gave me nothing to drink, I was a foreigner and you did not invite me home for a meal.' [43]Then they will answer the same way, saying, 'When on earth did we see you thus and fail to help you?' [45]Then he will answer them, saying, 'Amen: I tell you, insofar as you failed to help one of these insignificant ones, you failed to help me.' [46]And these will go away into age-long punishment, but the righteous into age-long life."

26

[1]And it happened that when Jesus finished all these words, he said to his disciples, [2]"You know that after two days the Passover comes, and a man is delivered up to be crucified." [3]Then the archpriests and the elders of the people gathered in the court of the archpriest named Caiaphas, [4]and they exchanged ideas to seize him by stealth and to kill him, [5]but one thing they ruled out: "Not during the feast so as to avoid rioting among the people."

[6]And when Jesus was in Beth-Anu, in the house of Simon the leper, [7]a woman came to him with an alabaster jar of ointment, very costly, pouring it over his head as he reclined at table. [8]But seeing it, the disciples were angry, saying, "Why this waste? [9]For it would have been possible for this to be sold for much and the price given to the poor!" [10]And Jesus, aware of it, said to them, "Why do you give the woman trouble? She has done a fine thing for me. [11]After all, you have the poor with you all the time, but my visiting is a special occasion. [12]For this woman put this ointment on my body to bury me. [13]Amen: I tell you, wherever this news is heralded in all the world, what this woman did will also be told, so she will be remembered."

[14]Then one of the twelve, the one called Judas the False One, going to the archpriests, [15]said, "What are you willing to give me, and I for my part will deliver him up to you?" And they weighed out thirty silver pieces for him. [16]And starting then, he looked for a likely opportunity to deliver him up.

[17]And on the first day of unleavened bread, the disciples came to Jesus, saying, "Where do you want us to prepare for you to eat the Passover seder?" [18]And he said, "Go into the city to so-and-so and say to him, 'The

teacher says, My fateful time is near. With you I will observe the Passover
with my disciples.'" [19]And the disciples did as Jesus instructed them and
they prepared the Passover seder.

[20]With evening falling, he reclined at table with the twelve disciples.
[21]And as they were eating, Jesus said, "Amen: I tell you, one of you will
deliver me up." [22]They went into shock and said to him, each in turn,
"Not I, Lord!" [25]And answering, Judas, the one handing him over, said,
"Not I, Rabbi?" He says to him, "You said so."

[26]And as they were eating, Jesus, taking a loaf and blessing it, broke
and gave it to the disciples and said, "Take and eat: this is my body."
[27]And taking a cup and giving thanks, he gave it to them, saying, "Drink
from it, all of you. [28]For this is my blood of the *new* covenant, shed for
the forgiveness of sins. [29]And I pledge to you, no more, by no means, will
I drink of the fruit of the vine until that day when I drink it new with you
in the kingdom of my Father." *And James, his brother, says to him, "No
more shall I eat bread henceforth until the day the man is raised from
among those who sleep."*

[30]And having sung a hymn, they went out to the Mount of Olives.
[31]And Jesus says to them, "All of you will be scandalized by me in this
night. I know because it is written, 'I will strike down the shepherd, and
the sheep of the flock will scatter in panic.' [32]But after my raising up, I
will precede you into the Galilee." [33]But Peter, answering, said to him,
"Even if all shall be scandalized by you, I will never be scandalized."
[34]Jesus says to him, "Amen: I tell you, as for you, today, this very night
before a rooster crows, you will repudiate me three times."

[36]Then Jesus comes with them to a plot of ground called Gethsemane, and he says to his disciples, "Sit here till I am done praying over
there." [37]And taking Peter and the two sons of Zebediah, he was suddenly overcome with grief and distressed. [38]Then he says to them, "My
soul is mortally wounded with sorrow. You stay here and keep vigil with
me." [39]And going on a bit farther, he dropped to the ground and prayed,
saying, "My Father, if it is possible, let this cup pass me by for another.
But not what I want but what you want."

[40]And he comes to the disciples and finds them sleeping, and he says
to Peter, "So you were not able to stand vigil with me for a single hour?
[45]Behold, the hour has arrived, and a man is delivered into the hands of
gentiles. [46]Get up! Let us go. The one handing me over has come near."

[47]And while he was still speaking, behold, Judas arrived, one of the
twelve, and with him a mob with swords and clubs sent from the arch-

priests and the elders of the people. 48So the one handing him over had
given them a signal, saying, "Whomever I may kiss on the cheek is the one
you want." 49And at once approaching Jesus, he said, "Hail, Rabbi!" and
gave him a friendly kiss. 50But Jesus said to him, "Old friend, why are you
here?" Then closing in, they laid hands on him and grabbed him. 51And
behold, one of Jesus' companions, reaching for his sword, drew it and,
striking the slave of the archpriest, managed only to cut off the ear.
52Then Jesus said to him, "Put your sword back into its place! For all taking up a sword will die by a sword. 53Or perhaps you have forgotten I
need only appeal to my heavenly Father for him to put at my disposal over
twelve legions of angels. 54But then, how do you expect the scriptures to
be fulfilled where it says it has to happen this way?" 55In that hour, Jesus
said to the mob, "Am I some desperado, that you came out to arrest me
with swords and clubs? Every day I sat teaching in the temple and you did
not apprehend me. 56But all this has happened so scripture could be fulfilled." Then his disciples all abandoned him and fled.

57And the ones who arrested Jesus marched him away to Caiaphas
the archpriest, where the scribes and the elders were assembled. 58And
Peter followed him at a safe distance up to the courtyard of the archpriest
and, entering inside, sat among the attendants and waited to see the outcome. 59So the archpriests and the whole Sanhedrin tried to suborn perjury against Jesus to execute him, but they were unsuccessful. 60And
though many false witnesses came forward, they did not find any damning testimony. But later two came forward and said, 61"This fellow said,
'I am able to destroy the holy place of God and after three days to build
it.'" 62And standing up, the archpriest said to him, "Have you no rejoinder to what these men are alleging against you?" 63But Jesus remained silent. And the archpriest said to him, "I charge you by the only true God
that you tell if you are the Christ, the son of God!" 64Jesus says to him,
"You said so. And yet I tell you, from now on all of you will see one like a
son of man sitting to the right of Shaddai and coming with the cloud
chariots of the sky." 65Then the archpriest, ripping his garments, said,
"Who still needs witnesses? Behold now, you heard the blasphemy with
your own ears! 66How does the case appear to you?" And they, answering, said, "He is worthy of death!" 67And they spat in his face *and blind-*
folded him and punched him and slapped him, 68saying, "Prophesy to us,
Christ! Which one struck you?"

69And with Peter outside in the courtyard, a serving maid comes to
him, saying, "You, too, were with Jesus the Galilean!" 70But he denied in

front of everyone, saying, "I have no idea what you're talking about!"
71And he went outside to the porch where another noticed him and says
to those there, "This man was with Jesus the Nazorean." 72But again, he
denied with an oath: "I do not know the man!" 73And again a little later,
one of the bystanders, approaching, said to Peter, "Truly, you too are one
of them. For indeed, your speech gives you away." 74*And he denied and
swore and cursed:* "I do not know the man!" And at once a rooster
sounded. 75And Peter recalled what Jesus had said, "Before a rooster
sounds, you will repudiate me three times." And departing outside, he
broke down sobbing.

27

1And early morning coming, all the archpriests and the elders of the
people took council against Jesus to put him to death. 2And having tied
Jesus up, they led him away and delivered him to Pilatus the governor.
3Then Judas, the one who handed him over, seeing him, that he was condemned, thought better of what he had done and returned the thirty silver pieces to the archpriests and elders, 4saying, "I sinned, betraying innocent blood." But they said, "What is that to us? It's your problem."
5And flinging the silver into the holy place, he left, and going off, he
hanged himself. 6But the archpriests, picking up the silver, said, "Hmmm,
it is not legal to deposit them as *corban* since it is bounty money." 7So deliberating, they bought with the silver the potter's field for the burial of
strangers. 8For that reason that field came to be known as the Field of
Blood, even today. 9Then the thing spoken by Jeremiah the prophet was
fulfilled, namely, "And they took the thirty silver pieces, the wage of the
one assessed, whom they assessed from the sons of Israel, 10and gave
them for the potter's field as Adonai directed me."

11And Jesus stood before the governor, and the governor interrogated him, saying, "So you are the King of the Jews." And Jesus said, "If
you say so." 12And as the archpriests and elders accused him, he answered nothing. 13Then Pilatus says to him, "Don't you hear the things
they accuse you of?" 14And he did not answer him, not one word, which
completely amazed the governor. 15So at festival time the governor used
to release to the crowd any single prisoner they wanted. 16And they had
just then a notorious prisoner called Jesus bar-*Rabban*. 17Therefore, having called the crowd together, Pilatus said to them, "Whom do you wish I
may release to you: Jesus bar-*Rabban* or Jesus called Christos?" 18For he
was well aware they delivered him up out of envy. 20But the archpriests
and the elders incited the crowd to ask for Bar-*Rabban* and to destroy

Jesus. [21]Answering, the governor said to them, "Which of the two do you wish me to release to you?" And they said, "Bar-*Rabban!*" [22]Pilatus says to them, "What, then, am I to do with Jesus called Christos?" [23]All say, "Let him be crucified!" But he said, "What evil did he do?" But they shouted all the more, "Let him be crucified!" [24]But Pilatus, seeing that nothing is gained but rather a riot is brewing, taking water, washed his hands in front of the crowd, saying, "I am innocent of the blood of this man; have it your way." [25]In answer, all the people said, "May his blood cover us and our children!" [26]Then he released Bar-*Rabban* to them, and having Jesus whipped, he delivered him up to be crucified.

[27]Then the soldiers of the governor, having taken Jesus into the praetorium, assembled before him the whole cohort. [28]And undressing him, they draped him with a scarlet cloak; [29]and having woven a wreath of acanthus leaves, they set it on his head and placed a reed in his right hand; and bowing the knee before him, only jeered at him, saying, "Hail, King of the Jews!" [30]And spitting at him, they took the reed scepter and stabbed at his head with it. [31]And when they finished tormenting him, they removed the cloak off him and dressed him in his own garments and marched him off to crucify him.

[32]And going forth, they found a man, a Cyrenian, named Simon. This one they commandeered so that he should bear his cross. [34]And coming to a place called Golgotha, which is translated "Place of a Skull," they gave him to drink wine mixed with gall, and tasting it, he did not wish to drink. [35]And crucifying him, they distributed his garments, casting a lot. [36]And sitting, they guarded him there lest his people come and take him down. And they placed above his head the charge against him, having been written: "This is Jesus the King of the Jews." [38]Then two robbers are crucified with him, one to the right and one to the left. [39]And the passers by blasphemed him, wagging their heads [40]and saying, "Ooh! The one destroying the holy place and building it in three days! Save yourself if you are a son of God and come down from the cross!" [41]Similarly, the archpriests, trading jokes with the scribes and elders, said, "Some savior! He couldn't even save himself." [42]"King of Israel, is he? Let him come down from the cross alive and we will believe in him! He has trusted in God? Let him rescue him now, if he wants him. After all, he said, 'I am God's son.'" [44]And the robbers crucified with him insulted him the same way.

[45]So from the sixth hour, darkness shrouded the whole earth until the ninth hour. [46]And around the ninth hour, Jesus shouted with a loud

voice, *"Eli, Eli, lama sabachthani?"* which is translated, "My God, my
God, why did you forsake me?" 47And some of the bystanders, hearing
this, said, "This man invokes Elijah!" 48And at once, one of them ran and
took a sponge and, filling it with vinegar, put it on a lance head and gave
it to him to drink. 49But the rest objected, saying, "Leave him be! Let us
see if Elijah comes to rescue him!" 50But Jesus, again shouting in a loud
voice, let go the spirit. 51And behold, the earth was shaken and the rocks
were split *and the lintel of the temple, of immense size, fell and broke in*
pieces. 54And the centurion and those with him guarding Jesus, seeing the
earth quake and the things happening, were completely terrified, saying,
"Truly, this man was God's son!"

55So there were also many women looking on from a distance, who
followed Jesus from the Galilee, feeding him, among whom were Miriam
the hairdresser and Miriam the mother of James and Joseph, and the
mother of the sons of Zebediah.

57And with evening coming, a rich man from Arimathea named Joseph, who also himself was trained as a disciple of Jesus, 58this man, approaching Pilatus, requested custody of the body of Jesus. Then Pilatus
ordered it to be given him. 59And taking the body, Joseph wrapped it in a
clean length of linen 60and laid him out in his new tomb, which he cut
from the rock; and having rolled a great stone up to the door of the tomb,
he went away. 61And Miriam the hairdresser was there with the other
Miriam, sitting across from the grave.

62And on the morrow, which is after the Preparation, the archpriests
and the Pharisees assembled before Pilatus, 63saying, "Lord, we suddenly
remembered how that impostor said before he died, 'After three days, I
am raised!' 64Therefore, command the grave be secured until the third
day so the disciples do not come and steal him and say to the people, 'He
was raised from the dead!' and the last hoax will be worse than the first."
65*And he assigned to them armed men to sit over against the cave and*
guard it night and day. 66And they went and secured the grave, sealing the
stone, with the custodians, *and the servant of the archpriest stood by.*

28

1And late on the Sabbath at the dawning of the first day of the week,
Miriam the hairdresser and the other Miriam came to view the grave.
2And behold, a massive earthquake occurred, for an angel of Adonai,
coming down out of the sky and approaching, rolled the stone away and
sat on it. 3And his appearance was like lightning and his clothing white as
snow. 4And for fear of him, the guards trembled and fainted dead away.

5But answering, the angel said to the women, "You need not fear me. For I know you seek Jesus, the crucified one. 6He was raised, just as he said. Come closer, see the place where he lay." *And looking in, they saw a man loosed from his graveclothes, walking in the midst of the tomb, and his appearance was like a son of God.* 9And behold, Jesus met them, saying, "Hail!" And approaching, they grasped his feet and bowed before him. 10Then Jesus says to them, "Do not be afraid! Go announce to my brothers that they may set out for the Galilee and there they will see me." 8And they ran to report to the disciples.

11And as they were going, behold, Jesus *gave the linen cloth to the slave of the priest.* But some of the custodians, coming into the city, announced to the archpriests all the events that had transpired. 12And meeting with the elders and discussing the matter, they took enough silver and offered it to the soldiers, 13saying, "You're to say, 'His disciples came under cover of night and stole him while we were sleeping.' 14And if this comes to the governor's ears, we will persuade him and relieve you of your worries." 15And taking the silver, they did as they were instructed. And this propaganda was disseminated by Jews until the present day. *But the archpriests knew what had happened because of the linen cloth.*

Now the Lord, when he had given the linen cloth to the servant of the priest, went to James and appeared to him, for James had sworn that he would not eat bread from that hour wherein he had drunk the Lord's cup until he should see him risen again from among those who sleep. And he said to him, "Hail!" And he called to the servants, who were greatly amazed. "Bring," said the Lord, "a table and bread." He took bread and blessed and broke and gave it to James the Just and said to him, "My brother, eat your bread, for the man has risen from those who sleep."

16And the eleven disciples journeyed to the Galilee, to the mountain where Jesus had first appointed them. 17And seeing him, they bowed before him, though they doubted. 18And approaching, Jesus spoke with them, saying, "*Lo, touch me and see that I am not a bodiless demon." And at once they touched him and believed. And the Father took him up into the heavens unto himself.*

8.

The Infancy Gospel of Thomas

If nature abhors a vacuum, so does popular piety. Early Christians could not abide not knowing what the son of God was doing before he began his public ministry. If one had only Mark's gospel, the answer would be nothing special: Jesus' boyhood and young adulthood would have been even less eventful than most since he was busy being righteous. Granted, Mark has Jesus appear at a baptism of repentance, but as everyone knows, it is the conscience of the righteous that impels them to such rituals. For Mark, the real action started only once Jesus was imbued with power from on high at his baptism. Matthew and Luke began the process of compromising this picture by adding a miraculous birth story, making Jesus a demigod right from the start. Thus, it comes as no surprise when Matthew has Jesus already knowing he is God's son before he is baptized and Luke portrays him as a twelve-year-old child prodigy, no real child at all but a godling in childlike form. Once this precedent was established, Christian curiosity was given the green light and the pious imagination went wild concocting stories of what the boy Jesus might have done, would have done, and finally did do.

Such stories are filled with contempt for the dull-witted adults around Jesus: "What fools these mortals be!" The point is to glorify Jesus at their expense; they must, like Mark's disciples, be fools, otherwise Jesus' preternatural wisdom would not be apparent. We can see this ubiquitous theme in two stories that crept into the traditional canonical gospels. In Luke 2:41-51, Jesus' parents are comically negligent, then pitifully inept as they look for their missing child. Where

else would he be but in the temple, deep in *halakhic* debate with the scribes? Totally clueless, they rebuke him, and with eyes rolling skyward, he places himself under their moronic supervision. Such is the *kenosis* of the god. As Raymond E. Brown saw, John 2:1-11 also took a bit of Infancy Gospel material and made Jesus older in this scene, adding his disciples in a purely vestigial capacity. Originally the Cana story featured young Jesus and his mother who, contrary to John 2:11, appears to be quite used to her son performing miracles for the convenience of adults. "They are out of wine," she says; "What do you propose to do about it?" Despite his irritated refusal to help, Mary knows he will eventually heed her request ("Do whatever he tells you.") and bail out the adults who have been so short-sighted they have not stocked enough wine for the wedding reception. To the disconcertion of teetotalers everywhere, the boy Jesus transforms hundreds of gallons of water into wine.

One may say about the stories of the Infancy Gospel tradition, here and in the canonized gospels, as well as in the numerous other such texts including the Arabic Gospel of the Infancy and the Infancy Gospel of Matthew, the spiritual level is not very high. The young Jesus is ruthless, not to mention capricious, in his application of divine power. He does not suffer fools. The gospel saying that best fits him is Mark 9:19: "O faithless generation! How long am I to be with you? How long must I endure you?" The stories are, none of them, elevated beyond the level of 2 Kings 2:23-24, where the prophet Elisha rids himself of the nuisance of mocking children by calling she-bears to rip their intestines out. More than anyone else, the young god Jesus must remind us of the blue-skinned Krishna, a godling who plays jokes on his devotees—only Jesus has less of a sense of humor.

Ernst Käsemann once called the Gospel according to John a piece of "naive docetism," as indeed it is. And the same can be said of the Infancy Gospel of Thomas. There is no attempt to deny the fleshly existence of Jesus Christ here. But there is the tendency, still common today, to deny Jesus the traits of genuine humanity. What would most people answer if asked whether Jesus could have gotten by without eating? Did he really have to go to the bathroom? Did he ever get sick? Could he have added numbers incorrectly? Could he have been

married? This sort of docetism implies naive hero worship, and it is probably every bit alive today as it was whenever this gospel was compiled. When was that? No doubt some time in the second century, but it is impossible to be more specific. Infancy Thomas was likely written originally in Greek, and there are two Greek forms of the book extant in different manuscript traditions. However, I have worked from the Latin, which seems better written. Though most of the individual episodes and anecdotes in Infancy Thomas do not require any particular setting, just like most stories and sayings in the familiar adult gospels, on the whole the book has been constructed as a great patch to fill in a perceived hole in Matthew by answering what might have happened to the holy family while sojourning in Egypt and then later when they returned. By the end of the book, we seem to have been brought up more or less even with Luke 2:41.

I, Thomas the Israelite, the philosopher, address you, all the brothers of the nations, to inform you of the childhood deeds of our Lord, Jesus Christ, and his miracles, everything he did when he was born in our land. The beginning of it is as follows.[a]

1

[1]Amid the furor that erupted over the search that Herod ordered for
our Lord, Jesus Christ, when he sought to kill him, an angel told Joseph,
"Take with you Mary and her boy and escape into Egypt from the presence of his would-be murderers." [2]And Jesus was two years old when he
went to Egypt.

[3]And as Joseph was walking through a grain field, he reached out
and took some of the ears of grain, rubbing them over the fire, and began
to eat the roasted grain.[b]

---

a. This original form of the opening, preserved in the Greek versions, occurs in the Latin only at the end of section 3 and is clumsily worded. It seems some scribe decided to harmonize the Infancy Gospel of Thomas with Matthew's nativity narrative, but did so ineptly. I have therefore restored the introduction to its proper position, introducing the adventures of young Jesus beginning where Matthew 2 leaves off.

b. The subject here may be Jesus instead of Joseph, but an adult would more likely be gleaning wheat. Otherwise in this gospel, the child is only shown doing the miraculous. If the pronoun refers to Joseph, it connects him to the typology of Joseph in Egypt, whose association with *grain* saved the world in ancient times.

[4]And once they had entered Egypt, a certain widow offered them hospitality in her home and they stayed with her for a year.[c] [5]And Jesus, now being three years old, saw boys at play and began to join them. [6]And he took a dried fish and dropped it into a basin and commanded it to swim around. And it began to swim around.[d] [7]And again, he addressed the fish: "Expel the salt you are rubbed with and walk over land into the nearest body of water!" [8]And it happened. And when the neighbors saw what happened, they related the story to the widow woman in whose house Mary, his mother, lived. [9]And as soon as she heard it, she ejected them from her house in a great hurry.

2

[1]Once when Jesus was strolling with Mary, his mother, through the thick of the city marketplace, he chanced to see a schoolmaster teaching his pupils. [2]And behold, twelve sparrows who were arguing with each other tumbled from their ledge into the lap of that school teacher in the midst of his instruction. [3]When Jesus saw it, he was highly amused and stood there laughing. And when that teacher saw him having a good time, he became infuriated and told his pupils, "Go and bring him here!" [4]And when they had dragged him to the teacher, he seized him by the ear and demanded, "What did you see that was so funny?" [5]And he answered him, "Rabbi, look: my hand is full of wheat. I showed it to the birds and sprinkled some among them for them to carry it away from the busy street where they would be in danger; and this is why they fought with each other, to divide up the wheat." [6]And Jesus did not leave there until they had finished. And once this was done, the teacher put it into motion to expel him and his mother from the city.

3

[1]And lo, the angel of Adonai met Mary and told her, "Take the boy and go back to the land of the Jews, for the ones who sought his life are dead." [2]And Mary got up and took Jesus, and they journeyed to the city of Nazareth where her father was landlord.[e] [3]And when Joseph left Egypt after the death of Herod, he kept him in the desert,[f] waiting for those in

c. 1 Kings 17:8-16, 19

d. This miracle has been ascribed to many holy men throughout the ages from St. Francis of Padua to the Pentecostal faith healer William Marrion Branham.

e. The seeming absence of Joseph makes the story parallel to the ejection, wandering, and angelic rescue of Hagar and Ishmael in Gen. 16:6-15; 21:9-21.

f. This element, too, derives from the Hagar and Ishmael story in Gen. 21:21.

Jerusalem who had sought the boy's life to settle down.[g] [4]And he thanked God for giving him to understand he should do this[h] and because he had found favor in the sight of the Lord God. Amen.

4

[1]Now when Jesus was five years old there was a great rain upon the earth, and the child Jesus walked about in it. [2]And the rain was very terrible, and he gathered the water together into a pool and commanded with a word that it should become clear, and immediately it did. [3]Again, he took some of the clay from that pool and fashioned it into twelve sparrows.[i] [4]So it was the Sabbath day when Jesus did this among the Hebrew children, and the Hebrew children went and said to his father, Joseph, "Lo, your son was playing with us, and he took clay and made sparrows, which it was not right to do on the Sabbath, and he has broken it." [5]And Joseph went to the child Jesus and said to him, "Why have you done this which was not right to do on the Sabbath?" [6]But Jesus spread forth his hands and commanded the sparrows, "Go forth into the sky and fly! You shall not meet death at any man's hands." [7]And they flew and began to cry out and praise Almighty God. But when the Jews saw what was done, they marveled and departed, proclaiming the signs Jesus did.

[8]But a Pharisee who was with Jesus took a branch of an olive tree and began to empty the pool Jesus had made. [9]And when Jesus saw it, he was annoyed and said to him, "O man of Sodom, ungodly and ignorant, what harm did the fountain of water I made do you? Lo, you shall become like a dry tree with neither root, leaf, nor fruit!" [10]And immediately he shriveled up, fell to the earth, and died. [11]His parents carried him away dead and reviled Joseph, saying, "Look what your son has done! Teach him to pray, not to curse!"

5

[1]And after some days, as Jesus walked with Joseph through the city, one of the children ran and struck Jesus on the arm. [2]But Jesus said to him, "You have reached the end of the road!" And at once he fell to the earth and died. [3]But when those present saw this wonder, they cried out,

---

g. Where did young Jesus go after Egypt? Did he go to Nazareth with Mary or to the Judean desert with Joseph? Our evangelist has conflated Matt. 2:19-23 with Gen. 21:9-21.

h. Matt. 2:22

i. There is an echo here of the Genesis creation stories, wherein God separates the waters from the dry land and begins creating life forms from the clay of the earth.

"Where does this child come from?" And they said to Joseph, "It is not right for such a child to live among us!" [4]As he departed, taking Jesus with him, they called out, "Leave this place! Or else, if you must stay with us, teach him to pray and not to curse, for our sons lose consciousness."

[5]And Joseph called Jesus and began to admonish him: "Why do you call down curses? Those who live here are coming to hate us." [6]But Jesus said, "I know these words are yours, not mine, but for your sake I will be silent from now on. [7]Only let them see the result of their own foolishness." And immediately those who spoke against Jesus were made blind, and as they wandered about they said, "Every word from his mouth is fulfilled!" [8]And when Joseph saw what Jesus had done, he took hold of his ear in anger. [9]But Jesus was annoyed and said to Joseph, "It is enough for you to see me, not to touch me. For you do not know who I am, and if you knew it, you would not vex me. [10]Although I am with you now, I was made before you."

6

[1]There was a man named Zacchaeus who heard all that Jesus said to Joseph, and he marveled silently and said, "I have never seen a child who spoke this way." [2]And he approached Joseph and said, "You have a wise child. Bring him to me to learn the alphabet. [3]And when he has mastered the alphabet, I shall instruct him in honorable behavior so that he may not grow up a fool." [4]But Joseph replied to him, saying, "No one can teach him except God alone. Do not imagine that the boy, of little stature, will be of little consequence!" [5]And when Jesus heard Joseph say these things, he said to Zacchaeus, "Indeed, Rabbi, whatever issues from my lips is true. And before creation I was Lord, but you are as gentiles. [6]The glory of the worlds has been bestowed upon me, but you have been awarded nothing. Why? Because I am before the worlds! [7]And I know how many years are assigned you, and that you will be carried off into exile. [8]My Father has so decreed it to the end that you Jews may come to understand that whatever I say is true." [9]And the Jews on the scene, hearing Jesus' words, were amazed and exclaimed, "We have seen this lad perform miraculous deeds and heard him say such things as we have never heard, [10]nor are we likely to hear them again from any human source, whether from the archpriests or the rabbis or the Pharisees!" [11]Jesus replied, saying to them, "Why should you wonder? Do you think it is impossible that what I have said might be true? [12]Listen, I know the exact times both you and your ancestors were born and, what is more, when the very world was made. I know as well who sent me to you." [13]And

when the Jews heard what he said, they gasped, finding themselves at a loss for words. [14]And as he thought in his heart, the child's heart swelled, and he said, "I have spoken to you by way of a proverb because I am aware of your weak understanding and your ignorance." [15]And that schoolmaster said to Joseph, "Bring him to me and I shall teach him the alphabet."[j]

[16]And Joseph took the child Jesus and brought him to the house where other children also were taught. [17]But the teacher began to teach him the letters with sweet speech and wrote for him the first line, from A to T, and began to pat him on the head and to teach him. [18]But the child remained silent. Then the teacher hit him on the head, and when the child felt the blow, he said to him, "I ought to be teaching you rather than you teaching me![k] [19]I know the letters you would teach me, and equally I know that you are to me like an empty jar from which only echoes proceed: only sounds, no wisdom." [20]And beginning with that line he pronounced all the letters from A to T well and swiftly. [21]Then he looked at the teacher and said, "But you do not know how to interpret A and B; how do you propose to teach others, you hypocrite? If you do know A and can tell me about it, then I will teach you about B."[l] [22]But when the teacher started to explain A, he was speechless. So Jesus said to Zacchaeus, "Listen to me, Rabbi, and understand the first letter: see how it has two lines, [23]advancing in the middle, as if standing still, then giving, scattering, varying, threatening? The triple intermixes with the double and simultaneously all of one kind, all alike."

[24]And when Zacchaeus saw how he deconstructed the first letter, he gazed at it in wonder. He was equally dumbfounded at such a human being, one with such erudition. [25]And he exclaimed loudly, "Woe is me, for I am dumbfounded! All I have accomplished here is to bring on my own disgrace." [26]And he said to Joseph, "I beg you, brother, take him off my hands, for I cannot bear to look him in the face, nor can I tolerate his powerful command. [27]For this child can quench fire and bring to heel the raging sea. He was born before all worlds! What sort of womb could

j. This section (vv. 3-15) does not appear in the Greek versions. The text was plainly inserted by a pious scribe who wanted to reassure readers that Jesus had no need of human instruction.

k. The point here is to allay "the anxiety of influence," showing the divine Jesus was not in need of anyone else's instruction or ministry, a concept distasteful to Christians. Cf. Matt. 3:14 ("I need to be baptized by you, and you are coming to me?"); Gal. 1:1, 11-12.

l. Cf. Mark 11:29; Matt. 21:24

have brought him forth, what manner of being his mother, I know not. [28]O my friends, I am driven to distraction! I am an object of ridicule! I bragged that I had recruited a disciple, but he has turned out to be my teacher. [29]Nor can I live down my disgrace, for I am an old man. I do not know what to say to him. [30]All that is left to me now is to fall ill with some terrible malady and exit this world or at least to leave town since everyone has seen my shame: a mere infant has tricked me. [31]What is there to say? What excuse can I offer? He has bested me at the very first letter! [32]I am at a loss for words, O my friends and associates, unable even to begin framing an apt reply to him. [33]So now, I beg you, brother Joseph, take him out of my sight; take him home because he is a teacher or Adonai or perhaps an angel. Beyond that, I do not know what to say."

[34]And Jesus turned to face the Jews who attended Zacchaeus, saying to them: "Whoever does not see, let him see! Let those without understanding understand! Let the deaf hear, and through me, let the dead rise! [35]And as for the exalted ones, let me summon them to ever higher things, even as he who sent me to you has commanded me." [36]And when Jesus finished his speech, all who had formerly suffered from any infirmity found themselves made well by his word.

7

[1]So one day Jesus climbed up on top of a house with the children and began to play with them. [2]But one of the boys fell down through the door to the upper room and immediately died. [3]And when the children saw it, they all fled, leaving Jesus alone in the house. [4]And when the parents of the boy who had died arrived, they accused Jesus, saying, "Truly, it was you who made him fall!" [5]But Jesus said, "I never made him fall." Nevertheless, they went on accusing him. [6]So Jesus came down from the house and stood over the dead child and shouted, calling him by name, "Zeno! Zeno! Arise and tell whether I made you fall." [7]And immediately he arose and said, "No, Lord." And when his parents saw this great miracle which Jesus did, they worshipped God and kneeled before Jesus.

8

[1]And after a few days, one of the boys in that village was chopping wood and struck his foot. [2]And when a crowd of people came out to see him, Jesus accompanied them. And he touched the wounded foot and immediately it was made well. [3]And Jesus said to him, "Rise and chop the wood and remember me."[m] [4]But when the crowd with him saw these

m. Thomas 77b: "Split the wood, and I am there."

signs, they kneeled before Jesus and said, "Truly, we surely believe you are God!"

9

[1]And when Jesus was six years of age, his mother sent him to draw water. [2]And once Jesus had arrived at a fountain or a well, he had to make his way through a thick crowd and his pitcher was broken in the crush. [3]So he took off the cloak he was wearing, filled it with water, and brought it to his mother, Mary. [4]And his mother, once she saw the miracles he had performed, kissed him and said, "O Adonai, hear my petition: save my son!"

10

[1]In the season for sowing, Joseph went out to the fields to sow wheat and Jesus followed him. [2]When Joseph began to sow, Jesus reached out and filled his fist with as much seed as he could hold and he scattered it. [3]When the season for reaping arrived, Joseph returned to the field to harvest his crop. [4]Jesus came, too, and collected the ears of grain he had planted, and it came to a hundred pecks of the finest grain. [5]So he summoned the poor, the widows, and the orphans and divided among them the wheat he had produced. [6]For the sake of Jesus' blessing on his house, Joseph too took a bit of the same wheat.

11

[1]And Jesus came to be eight years old. So Joseph was a builder and made ploughs and ox yokes. [2]One day a certain rich man said to Joseph, "Sir, make me a bed, both sturdy and beautiful." [3]But Joseph was dismayed when he saw that the beam he had prepared was too short. [4]Jesus said to him, "Do not be dismayed. You take hold of one end of the beam and I will take the other, and let us stretch it out." [5]And so it happened, and at once he found it suitable for the job. [6]And he said to Joseph, "Make it any way you want." [7]But when Joseph saw what happened, he hugged him and said, "Blessed am I that God has given me such a son!"

12

[1]Since Joseph could see that the boy enjoyed such divine favor and that he was getting taller, he deemed it proper to take him to learn to read. [2]And he entrusted him to another teacher for instruction. And that teacher asked Joseph, "Which language do you want me to teach the lad?" [3]Joseph answered him, "First Greek, then Hebrew." The teacher saw that he was very intelligent and gladly took charge of him. [4]And writing out the first line of the alphabet for him, namely A and B, he lectured

him for several hours. [5]But Jesus kept quiet, giving him no answer. Finally, Jesus said to the rabbi, "If you are really a rabbi, and if you truly know the alphabet, tell me the force of the A and I will tell you the force of the B." [6]Then his teacher was livid with fury and rapped him on the head, and Jesus was angry and cursed him. At once he keeled over dead. [7]So Jesus returned home, and Joseph strictly charged his mother, Mary, not to let him out beyond the courtyard of their house.[n]

13

[1]After many days had passed, another teacher, a friend of Joseph, arrived and urged him, "Let me have him and I will teach him to read with a very winsome manner." [2]And Joseph replied, "Very well: if you think you are up to the task, take him and instruct him. Good luck!" [3]When the teacher had taken him, he went along with the boy in fear but with sure purpose, thrilled to be assigned the task of teaching him. [4]And when Jesus arrived at the teacher's house, he noticed a scroll lying there. [5]Picking it up and unrolling it, he commenced to speak. But instead of reading what was written in the scroll, he spoke from the Holy Spirit and taught Torah. [6]And indeed, everyone standing around him listened closely. The teacher sat down beside him and heard him gladly, begging him to teach them further. [7]A large crowd had now gathered to hear all the holy doctrine he propounded and the excellent eloquence of a mere child who spoke in such a manner.

[8]And when Joseph heard of it, he feared a replay of past events and ran to the house of study, hoping he was not too late to stop Jesus from killing the man. [9]But the teacher with Jesus said to Joseph, "Be assured, brother, that though I took charge of your child to teach him or to train him, he is already filled with great maturity and wisdom. [10]Lo, now take him back home rejoicing, my brother, because the maturity he has is a gift of Adonai." [11]And Jesus, hearing the teacher speak this way, cheered up and said, "Lo now, Rabbi, you have spoken truly! [12]And for your sake, he who is dead shall rise again."[o] And Joseph returned home with him.

14

[1]And Joseph sent James to gather straw, and Jesus followed him.

---

n. We may catch here an echo of the orders of Suddhodana, father of Prince Siddhartha, to keep his son from straying off the royal estates lest he behold the world's pain and become a savior.

o. That is, the disrespectful teacher he had struck dead in the previous episode.

[2]And as James was busy gathering the straw, a viper bit him, and he collapsed on the ground, apparently dead from the venom. [3]When Jesus saw this, he blew on the wound. At once, James was restored to health and the viper died.[p]

15

[1]A few days later, a neighbor's child died and his mother grieved for him terribly. [2]Hearing of it, Jesus went and stood over the boy and rapped on his chest, saying, "I say to you, child, do not die, rather live!" [3]At once, the child got up. And Jesus said to the child's mother, "Take your son, nurse him, and remember me." [4]And the crowd who witnessed the miracle exclaimed, "In truth, this child is from heaven! He has already freed many souls from death, and he has made well all who looked to him for help."[q]

[5]The scribes and Pharisees asked Mary, "Are you the mother of this child?" And Mary replied, "I am indeed!" [6]And they said to her, "Then you are the most blessed of women since God has blessed the fruit of your womb, giving you so splendid a child with such wisdom as we have never seen nor heard of." [7]Jesus got up and followed his mother. And Mary stored away in her memory all the great miracles Jesus had performed among the people as he healed many who were diseased. [8]And Jesus grew in height and in wisdom, and everyone who saw him praised God the Omnipotent Father who ever dwells in bliss. Amen.

[9]I, Thomas, the Israelite, have written what I have seen, and I have recounted these events both to the nations and to our brothers, as well as many other deeds performed by Jesus,[r] who was born in the land of Judah. [10]Behold then, how the house of Israel has seen everything from the very first, even as far as the last: [11]what great signs and wonders Jesus

---

p. A similar tale is told in Berakoth 33a: "Our rabbis report that once a poisonous snake was biting people. Some went to Rabbi Hanina ben Dosa and told him about it. He said to them, 'Show me its hole.' They showed him, and he covered the opening with his heel. It emerged and bit him. And it died. He draped the snake over his shoulders and went to the House of Study, saying to those present, 'Behold, my sons, it is not the serpent that kills, but sin that kills.' Then they said, 'Woe to the man attacked by a serpent, but woe to the snake attacked by Rabbi Hanina ben Dosa!'"

q. Luke 7:13-16; 1 Kings 17:21-24

r. In fact, what we have are three categories: childhood miracles wrought before Thomas came on the scene; events from Jesus' public ministry, of which Thomas claims to have been an eyewitness; and other events from the adult life of Jesus for which Thomas was not present, as in John 20:19-24.

performed among them, things which were overwhelmingly good, the like of which their father Abraham never saw, as holy scripture tells. 12 And the prophets have testified about his deeds among all the tribes of Israel. 13 And it is he who is to judge the world, chosen for the task by the will of the immortal, since he is the son of God, acknowledged throughout the entire world. 14 All worship and honor are due him for ever and ever, who lives and reigns as God throughout ages multiplied by ages! Amen.

9.

The Generations of Jesus

THE *Toledoth Jeschu* (GENERATIONS OF JESUS) is the title of several variants of an anti-gospel text portraying Jesus as a false prophet and magician. They often contain nasty parodies of the Christian gospels, probably as a safe way to let off some of the steam of hostility Jews felt over their hideous treatment by Christians. The texts are often considered to be late Medieval compositions and historically worthless. But the wide distribution of various language versions and manuscript fragments, together with the numerous parallels with second-century Jewish-Christian polemic preserved in Tertullian, Celsus, and elsewhere, imply as Samuel Krauss (*Das Leben Jesu nach jüdischen Quellen*) and Hugh J. Schonfield *(According to the Hebrews)* demonstrate, an original date of about the fourth century with numerous underlying traditions going back even further. Schonfield even suggests the *Toledoth* was based on a prior Hebrew gospel circulated among Jewish Christians. The reason for this is that the text treats Jesus with much more respect than one would expect if the *Toledoth* were merely a burlesque. It has certainly been worked over by later redactors hostile to Christianity: Jesus is regularly called "that bastard" in a taunt against the virgin birth doctrine; but one would expect more of the sort of thing we encounter in later Talmudic references to Jesus as a false prophet. Again, the huge number of Christian "testimonia" or proof texts from the Old Testament marshaled to prove Jesus was the Messiah would be odd in a work that began as a lampoon of Christian messianism, all the more since none of these proof texts is ever refuted.

When we think of messianic proof texts and *testimonia,* we are bound to think of Matthew's gospel, and there is probably more than

fortuitous similarity between Matthew and the document presented here. As Jane Schaberg (*The Illegitimacy of Jesus*) suggests, Matthew appears already to be dealing in its own way with traditions much like those found in the *Toledoth Jeschu*. Matthew seems, at its beginning, to want to rebut or at least redeem the charge that Jesus was the misbegotten bastard of Mary and Pandera. The way we have always read it, Matthew says Jesus was miraculously conceived: admittedly then, Joseph was not his father—but God was! But Schaberg argues very persuasively that Matthew admits the conception of Jesus was sexually dubious, presumably the result of rape, and had that in common with the cases of Bath-Sheba, Rahab, Ruth, and Tamar, the only women mentioned in Matthew's genealogy of Jesus.

Matthew's genealogy also pushes Jesus' ancestry back beyond David, which would have been sufficient to provide messianic credentials, extending all the way to the patriarch Abraham. The implication is that Matthew knows Jesus had been made out to be a gentile, perhaps sired by a Roman soldier. It is Jesus' parentage and pedigree that give rise to the actual title of the anti-gospel: The Generations of Jesus. And how does Matthew begin? With the same phrase! Presumably, Matthew also meant his work to be titled the Generations of Jesus, implying it was a rejoinder to the existing document, though the present example is perhaps not the earliest version. Finally, Matthew ends with a comical counter-satire about the fate of Jesus' corpse being stolen, just as we find in the *Toledoth*. Thus, the Generations of Jesus belongs in the Matthean cycle as a close cousin.

One of the chief points of interest in this work is its chronology, placing Jesus about 100 BCE. This is no mere blunder, though it is not hard to find anachronisms elsewhere in the text. Epiphanius and the Talmud also attest to Jewish and Jewish-Christian belief in Jesus having lived a century or so before we usually imagine, implying that perhaps the Jesus figure was at first an ahistorical myth and various attempts were made to place him in a plausible historical context, just as Herodotus and others tried to figure out when Hercules "must have" lived.

There are two major versions of the text, represented by the Wagenseil (1681) and the Huldreich (1705) printed editions and un-

derlying manuscripts. The Huldreich accumulated various late embellishments. The present version represents an eclectic text drawn almost entirely from Wagenseil, the apparent doubling of some episodes resulting from harmonizing different tellings of the story, each with enough interesting details to be preserved.

Our document not only parallels the Christian gospels but goes on to add a kind of "Acts of the Apostles," with various odd traditions that are extremely fascinating, perhaps even, one could say, valuable, in ways suggested in the footnotes. Whatever historical value there may be to the Generations of Jesus, and it is probably not much, it seems salutary to at last include within the Christian canon an opposing, critical voice. As Paul Tillich said, the best way to avoid fanaticism is to include alongside one's creed a criticism of that creed.

1

1The beginning of the birth of Jesus. 2His mother was Miriam of Israel. 3And she had a fiancé who belonged to the royal line, the dynasty of
David. His name was John. 4And he was erudite in the Torah and greatly
feared heaven. 5Across from her house lived a handsome fellow, the warrior Joseph, son of Pandera, who lusted after her. 6So it was in the course
of the night on Sabbath eve when he, being drunk with much wine,
crossed the court to her door and gained entry, looking for her. But she
took him for her betrothed, John. 7She turned her face away in shame
since it was her period. He drew her to him, but she protested: "Do not
touch me, for I am in the period of separation." 8This he ignored, nor did
he pay the slightest heed to her words but persisted in his design. 9And she
conceived by him, as she later discovered. At midnight her fiancé John arrived. 10She said to him, "What do you mean by this? Ever since we have
been betrothed, it has never been your habit to visit me twice in a single
night."

11He replied to her, saying, "I have come to you only this once tonight!"

12She said to him, "You did come to me and I told you I was in my
period of separation, but you paid no attention, but had your way with
me and left!" 13When he heard this, he realized that Joseph, son of
Pandera, who lusted for her, had done it.

He left her and went home again. 14The next morning he got up and
called on Rabban Simeon, son of Shetach. 15He said to him, "So let me

tell you what happened this night with my betrothed. [16]I approached her as men do. But before I touched her, she said, 'You have visited me once already tonight and I told you I was in my period of separation, and you paid me no mind but had your way with me and left.' Hearing such a report from her, I left her and went out."

[17]Rabban Simeon, son of Shetach, asked him, "Who occurred to you as having been the culprit?" He answered him, "The son of Pandera. He lives near her and he is always looking for fornication."

[18]"I realize you have no witnesses in the case. Therefore, I advise you to keep quiet. If he has in truth gained entry once, then no doubt he will do so again. When he does, you must be ready, lying in wait, with witnesses spying on him."

[19]After a while the rumor went round that Miriam was pregnant. [20]Then John, her fiancé, said, "She is not pregnant by me. Am I to stay here and bear daily abuse from every man?" So he departed for Babylon. [21]And after some months, she gave birth to a son and they named him Jehoshua for his mother's brother. But later, when the shame of his birth became known, they called him Jeshua.[a]

[22]His mother brought him to a tutor so he might become wise in the *halacha,* erudite in Torah and Talmud. [23]It was customary for the disciples of the sages that neither a youth nor a lad must walk by without having his head veiled and his eyes lowered to show a disciple's veneration for his masters. [24]But one day that wicked one walked by when the rabbis were seated all in a group at the synagogue gate, for they had called a convocation to study scripture; and that impudent one passed before our masters with erect posture and head unveiled, his forehead shamelessly exposed before his lord. [25]Then one of them commented, "He is a bastard, you know." And another added, "Not only that, but conceived during his mother's period!"

[26]So one day the rabbis were debating the tractate *Nezikin*[b] when he began to offer *halachoth*[c] [27]Then one of them said to him, "Have you not heard that anyone who presumes to suggest a *halacha* in the presence of his tutor deserves death?" [28]But he says to the sage, "Who is the teacher here and who is the disciple? And which of the two was wiser, Moses or Jethro? Was it not Moses, the father of the prophets and chief of the

a. The first means "Yahve is salvation," while the second lacks the divine name and means simply "salvation."

b. *Nezikin* denote torts.

c. *Halachoth* are legal opinions.

sages? Furthermore, the Torah testifies about him: 'And there has arisen in Israel no prophet like Moses.'[d] [29]Notwithstanding, Jethro was a foreigner, yet he taught Moses practical wisdom as it is written: 'Put in charge of them rulers of thousands and rulers of hundreds.'[e] [30]But if you say that Jethro is greater than Moses, that would be the end of the greatness of Moses."

[31]When the sages heard this, they said, "He is so impudent! We must investigate him." [32]They sent word to his mother, asking, "Tell us, who was the father of this lad?"

[33]She answered, saying, "He is the son of my husband, John, who has abandoned me and gone to Babylon. I do not know what has happened to him since."

[34]They answered her, saying, "Then why do people say of him, 'He is a bastard and the son of a woman conceived during her period?'"

[35]At this, Rabban Simeon, son of Shetach, explained, "It was thirty years ago today that John, her betrothed, sought me out and told me, 'Thus and so has befallen me.'" [36]And he recounted what he, Rabban Simeon, answered John, and how in his great shame he left for Babylon, never to return. "And this Miriam has borne this Jesus. [38]And she deserves no death sentence since she did not willingly cooperate. It was Joseph, son of Pandera, who looked for a chance to fornicate every day."

[39]When she heard Rabban Simeon say she was in no danger of a death sentence, then she too answered, saying, "The thing happened in this manner," and she admitted it.

[40]But once the report about Jesus began to circulate—for they were saying about him, "He is a bastard and the son of a menstruating woman; he deserves death"—Jesus left and fled to Jerusalem.

2

[1]So the reins of power in Israel were in the hand of a woman named Helena, the wife of King Jannaeus, who succeeded him on the throne. [2]And within the temple was the foundation stone, which denotes that Yah established it, and it is the stone which Jacob anointed with oil,[f] and

---

d. Deut. 34:10

e. Exod. 18:21

f. This is an error since the story of Jacob's vision and anointing the stone is an etiology accounting for the foundation of Jeroboam's temple at Bethel in northern Israel (cf. Gen. 28:18-22), whereas the text here is describing the Jerusalem temple. Rabbinical lore claimed the Jerusalem temple housed the very foundation stone of the universe.

on it were engraved the letters of the Tetragrammaton. [3]And if anyone learned them, he could do whatever he desired. [4]Thus, fearing that the young men of Israel might learn them and accidentally destroy the world, the sages made sure that it would be impossible to learn them. [5]Brass lions were chained to a pair of iron pillars at the gate of the place where burnt offerings were made, the idea being that if anyone did enter and memorize the letters, as soon as he made to leave again, the lions would roar at him, and when, startled, he looked at them, the letters would fly from his memory. [6]Then Jesus came and memorized them. He copied them onto a slip of parchment, cut open his thigh,[g] and inserted the parchment which, bearing the sacred letters, made the incision painless. And with a word, he restored the flesh to its original state. [7]As he went out, the lions chained to the pillars roared at him and the letters fled from his memory. [8]But when he went into his house and cut open his flesh with a knife, he took out the note and memorized the letters again.

[9]Then he set to work and collected three hundred and ten of the youths of Israel. [10]He says to them, "Look at those who call me a bastard and the son of a woman in her period of separation. They desire greatness for themselves and scheme to exercise sovereignty in Israel. [11]Have you not read how all the prophets prophesied about the messiah of God? Well, I am the messiah. [12]Isaiah prophesied about me and said, 'Behold, a virgin shall conceive and have a son and shall name him Immanuel.'[h] [13]Again, my ancestor David prophesied about me, saying, 'The Lord said to me, you are my son; this day I have begotten you.'[i] [14]He fathered me without a male lying with my mother, yet they call me 'bastard'! Again he prophesied: 'What is the use of the nations fuming, of the people making futile schemes? For the kings of the earth oppose themselves to the Lord and the rulers plot together against his anointed.'[j] [16]I am the messiah, and as for those who oppose me, they are the whelps of prostitutes. So says scripture: 'For they shall be the children of prostitution.'"[k]

[17]Then the youths answered him, "If you are the messiah, then show us a sign!"

[18]He says to them, "What sort of sign would you like me to do for you?"

---

g. Possibly a euphemism for his penis, as often in the Old Testament.

h. Isa. 7:14

i. Pss. 2:7

j. Pss. 2:1-2

k. Hos. 2:4

[19]At once they conducted him to a lame man, one who had never been able to stand to his feet. He uttered the sacred letters over him and the man rose to his feet. [20]From that hour, they all bowed before him and said, "This is the messiah, the son of the Highest!"

[21]Again he performed a second sign for them. [22]They brought a leper to him, and he uttered the letters over him and he was healed. [23]The radicals among his people attached themselves to him, fully three hundred of the wicked of Israel, highwaymen and lawbreakers.

[24]After five days, the dismaying report was brought to Jerusalem, that most holy city, and there they recounted everything Jesus had done. [25]At this, all the sinners celebrated, but the elders, the pious, and the sages lamented bitterly. Both the greater and the lesser Sanhedrins mourned with tears.[l]

[26]And it came about that when Jesus reached Nob near Jerusalem, he asked them, "Do you have a good and handsome donkey here?" [27]And when they replied that they did have one on hand, he said, "Bring him here!" [28]And when they had produced the handsome donkey, he sat upon him and rode into Jerusalem. [29]As he entered the city, all the people rushed out to meet him. [30]And he cried aloud, saying to them, "The prophet Zechariah bore witness about me, saying, 'Behold, your king comes to you, righteous and bringing salvation, humble and mounted on a donkey, a pure-bred donkey.'"[m]

[31]Once these things became known, great weeping and mournful ripping of robes erupted and the pious went out to complain to the queen. [32]This was Queen Helena, wife of King Jannaeus, already mentioned, who ruled after the death of her husband. She is also called Oleina and had a son called Nunbasus, himself a king, otherwise known as Hyrcanus, eventually killed by his subordinate Herod. [33]The pious urged the queen, "This fellow deserves the stiffest punishment, for he is a seducer of Israel. Please grant us the needful authority and we will capture him by stealth."

[34]They agreed to dispatch envoys to Jesus, reasoning, "It may be that God will bless our attempt to capture him, bring him to court, and sentence him to death." [35]So they sent Ananias and Ahaziah, highly esteemed members of the lower house of the Sanhedrin, and they went to Jesus and prostrated themselves in adoration before him, fanning the flames of his evil pride. [36]So assuming they meant it, he welcomed them

l. At this point, Wagenseil skips to v. 34.

m. Zech. 9:9

with a smile and made them leaders of his wicked flock. 37Soon they began to lay their trap: "Lo, the chief citizens of Jerusalem have sent us as envoys to you, requesting that you might condescend to visit them, for they have heard that you are the son of God."[n]

38Then Jesus replied, "They have heard the truth! Lo, I shall do as you suggest but on this condition: 39that all the counselors of the greater and lesser Sanhedrins, as well as those who have maligned my parentage, shall reveal themselves and bow before me, swearing fealty to me as a slave swears the oath to his master."

40The envoys returned to Jerusalem to report everything that had been said. 41The elders and the pious answered, "We will do everything he asks."

42So the men went back to Jesus and reported that the Sanhedrin would do just as he asked. Then Jesus said, "I will go with you at once!"

And thus, they laid hold of him and tied him up. The sages went again before the queen and reported, "We have him in our power."

3

1The queen commanded them, saying, "Bring him before me so I may gain a better understanding of the accusation." 2She was actually trying to rescue him from their clutches because she was a blood relative of his.

3So the sages, since they surmised her true intent, answered her, "O regal mistress, we bid you not to do this since it is possible you may come to aid his mischief because he employs wizardry to hypnotize people into committing error and crime." 4And then they unfolded to her the whole business of the divine name, concluding, "It is your prerogative to decide punishment, though he deserves the worst." 5Then they related the story of Joseph Pandera as well.

6Then the queen answered, "I have heard you out, and this is my will: Bring him before me and let me hear what he has to say and see what he may do. For everyone tells me about the great miracles he performs."

7The sages replied, "We will do as you command." 8So they sent for Jesus and set him before the queen.

---

n. Verses 33-37 contain elements of the story of the correspondence between Jesus and King Abgar of Edessa, as well as that of the conversion of Helen, queen of adjacent Adiabene, and her son Monobazus. Ananias was the name both of the missionary who converted Queen Helen and of the courier bearing the letter from Abgar inviting Jesus, whom the king has decided must be the son of God, to visit him. See the introduction to the Letter of Jesus to Abgarus.

[9]Then the queen said, "I have heard that you perform many wonderful miracles. Now do one here before me."

[10]Jesus answered, "Whatever you command, I will do. But I do ask one thing: that you will not hand me over to the clutches of these wicked men who have condemned me as a bastard."

[11]The queen replied, "You have nothing to fear."

[12]Then Jesus said, "Let a leper be brought to me, and I shall heal him." [13]And when a leper was brought in, he placed his hand upon him and, invoking the all-powerful name, restored him to health so that the skin of his face became like a boy's. [14]Furthermore, Jesus said, "Have a corpse brought in." [15]And when a corpse was fetched, at once he placed his hand on it and uttered the name and it came to life again and rose to its feet! [16]Then Jesus said to her, "Lady, I am he, and I revive the dead. Isaiah prophesied about me: 'Then shall the cripple leap like a hart.'"[o]

[17]Jesus says to her, "The prophets prophesied about me long ago: 'And a rod shall emerge from the stock of Jesse,'[p] and I am he. As for my accusers, scripture warns of them: 'Blessed is anyone who does not live by the advice of the ungodly.'"[q]

[18]She asks them, "Is it in your scripture, what he claims?"

[19]They reply, "It is in scripture, to be sure, but it does not apply to him. Rather, as to his type, it is written: 'And any prophet who dares speak anything in my name that I did not tell him to say or who speaks representing other gods, he shall die. Thus, you shall rid yourselves of the evil infesting you.'[r] But the messiah we expect, he is to bring with him other signs: 'He shall strike the earth with the rod of his command!'[s] But this bastard cannot produce such signs as that."

[20]Then the queen turned to the sages and said, "How dare you call this man a wizard? Have I not seen with my own eyes how he performs miracles as if he were God's own son?"

[21]But the sages answered, saying, "Let not the queen say such things. The man is most definitely a conjurer."

[22]But the queen said, "Get out of my sight! And you are never again to bring such an accusation before me." With that, the sages left the queen's presence, deeply saddened.

---

o. Isa. 35:6

p. Isa. 11:1

q. Pss. 1:1

r. Deut. 18:20

s. Isa. 11:4

[23]The ranks of the radicals swelled and followed him, and there came a great schism in Israel. [24]Jesus went forth to upper Galilee. And the sages gathered and gained audience with the queen, saying to her, "Lady, he practices his wizardry and with it he leads the world astray. Is that not finally clear to you?"

[25]So she dispatched Ananias and Ahaziah, esteemed members of the lesser Sanhedrin, with a company of horsemen to deal with him. They found him in the act of misleading the masses of upper Galilee, telling them, "I am the Son of God predicted in your scripture!" [26]So the horsemen moved to apprehend him, but the men of upper Galilee would not allow them and they began to fight. [27]Jesus says to them, "Do not fight! Only trust in the power of my Father who is in heaven."

[28]So the men of Galilee were molding birds of clay. And he uttered the Tetragrammaton, and they flapped their wings.[t] And at once the Galileans prostrated themselves before him.

[29]He commanded them, "Bring me a millstone!" So they fetched one and wheeled it to the shore. And he uttered the letters, setting it upon the surface of the water, and sat on it as one sits in a boat. Then he made it move, floating over the water. [30]And the troops who were sent to apprehend him marveled. [31]And Jesus said to the horsemen, "Return to your mistress and report what you have seen!" Then the wind caught him up from the surface of the lake and carried him to dry land. [32]So the horsemen left and reported all these things to the queen. The queen trembled and was seized with astonishment. [33]So she summoned the elders of Israel, then said to them, "You call him a charlatan, yet every day he performs new signs."

[34]Then they answered her, "Lady, do not take his tricks so seriously. Send messengers and bring him now and his guilt will be revealed." [35]At once she dispatched messengers, who found his army of hooligans with him, and all of them accompanied him to the queen. [36]Meanwhile, the elders went and, discussing the matter, they said, "Let us prove our shrewdness and trap this rogue!" [37]Then one of their number made a suggestion: "If it sounds good to the rest of you, let one of us also memorize the name as he did and duplicate his miracles. That way, perhaps, we have an opportunity to apprehend him." [38]The sages approved the plan, saying, "Whoever memorizes the name and is able to get hold of this rascal shall receive a double reward in the age to come." [39]At once, one of

t. Infancy Gospel of Thomas, v. 4; Koran 5:110

the sages named Judas stood up and said, "If someone else will take responsibility for the sin I will commit by uttering the omnipotent name, I will volunteer to memorize it. [40]And who knows? God may show his mercy and his great beneficence by blessing my effort and delivering this bastard son of an adulteress." [41]Then all cried out in chorus, "The guilt be on us! Do as you have proposed and success to you!" [42]So he, too, penetrated the Holy of Holies, where he memorized the letters of the Tetragrammaton as engraved on the foundation stone. [43]Then he inscribed them on a slip of parchment and sliced open his thigh, speaking the Tetragrammaton so that he was protected from the pain, just as Jesus had done at the beginning.

4

[1]As soon as Jesus and his entourage had returned to the queen's court, where she had invited the sages to be present, Jesus commented, saying, "It was prophesied of me, 'For dogs surrounded me on all sides.'"[u]

[2]When the sages entered, Judas Iscariot being with them, they started hurling accusations at him and he returned them likewise. [3]Then Judas cried out, "Where are those who call this bastard the son of God? Am I, being mere flesh and blood, able to do the feats Jesus has done?" [4]Then Judas spoke these words to the queen and all the people: "Nothing this fellow does is any surprise to us. Let him nestle among the very stars and I will cast him down!"

[5]Then Jesus spoke to the whole people: "Have you not been a stubborn people from the beginning when I first chose you?"

[6]Judas answered, "Is it not true that you practice evil? That your mother was an adulteress? [7]Did not our master Moses say about you, 'If your brother, son of your mother, seduces you—whispering, Let us sacrifice to other gods—you shall drag him out into the open and bombard him with stones till he is dead?'"[v]

[8]But the bastard answered, saying, "Did not Isaiah prophesy about me, 'Behold my servant, whom I uphold, my chosen one, in whom my heart delights'?[w] [9]And are not these the words of my great ancestor about me, 'You are my son, today I have fathered you'? [10]Likewise in another passage, he said, 'The Lord said to my lord, sit here to my right.'" [11]And

u. Pss. 22:17

v. Deut. 13:6-11

w. Isa. 42:1a

turning to the queen, he said, "It was said of me, 'I will ascend into heaven,'[x] and it is written, 'For he shall welcome me. Selah.'"[y]

[12]Then he extended his arms and hands like an eagle's wings and he flew. And the whole world was agog over him: "Lo, he is able to fly between heaven and earth!"[z] [13]Then the elders of Israel urged Judas Iscariot: "Utter the letters, man, and rise up after him!" [14]And immediately he did so; he flew through the sky and the world was astonished: "Behold, they have the power to soar like eagles!" [15]Iscariot seized at him as he flew in mid-heaven, but he was not able to force him back to earth. Neither could Jesus force him, invoking the Tetragrammaton, since both alike bore it. [16]Once Judas perceived this, he got close enough to wipe Jesus with his sweat, rendering him unclean, whereupon he plummeted to the ground and Judas with him.

[17]At once they grabbed him and said to Helena, "He is but a conjurer! Let him be executed as Moses ordained. Make him tell us which one struck him!" [18]And they covered his head and bludgeoned him with pomegranate staves, and as he said nothing it was evident the Tetragrammaton had abandoned him. [19]As he was now securely in their grasp; he exclaimed to his compatriots in front of the queen, "It was said of me, 'Who will stand up for me against the evil-doers?'[a] And of such men he said, 'the proud waves!'[b] Yes, of them the prophet said, 'They have made their resolve as firm as a rock.'"[c]

[20]Hearing this, the queen threatened the radicals and said to the sages of Israel, "Behold, he is in your power."

[21]Then a death sentence was decreed for Jesus, and they told him, "You may go free if you will again perform the miracles you formerly did."

[22]But when Jesus realized he was not able to perform them, he lifted his voice in lamentation and said, [23]"David my ancestor prophesied about me, 'Indeed, for your sake we are killed from dawn to dusk.'" [24]When his disciples that followed him saw these developments and saw they, too, stood in danger of death, they attacked the elders and sages of Jerusalem, enabling Jesus to escape the city.

---

x. Isa. 14:13

y. Pss. 44:15

z. Rev. 13:4; John 12:32

a. Pss. 94:16

b. Pss. 124:5

c. Jer. 5:3

[25]So Jesus betook himself swiftly to the Jordan, where he washed himself. When he was again purified, he pronounced the name of God again and began to repeat his former miracles. [26]Beyond this, he took two millstones and made them float on the water. Climbing onto them, he sat there and caught fish in the sight of the crowd and fed them with the catch.[d] [27]When word of this reached Jerusalem, all the sages and the pious wept in anguish, crying out, [28]"Who will risk death by going to this bastard to deprive him of the omnipotent name? Lo, we guarantee such a one shall inherit everlasting bliss." [29]Then Judas volunteered, and the sages sent him off, saying, "Go in peace." [30]So Judas disguised himself and infiltrated the camp of Jesus' disciples.

5

[1]Along about midnight, God caused the bastard to sink into a profound slumber, whereupon Judas hypnotized him as he slept. [2]Then Judas snuck into Jesus' tent, took out a knife, and cut his flesh. From there he retrieved the sacred parchment, then left. [3]Suddenly, Jesus awoke from a dream, terrified by a huge and hideous demon. [4]Knowing what had happened, he said to his disciples, "Know this: my heavenly Father wants to welcome me home because he sees that I receive no honor from mortals."

[5]Then his disciples say to him, "Then what will become of us?"[e]

[6]He says to them, "Blessed are you and blessed your inheritance if you heed my voice, for you shall sit to my right with my heavenly Father." [7]Then they all cried out weeping. [8]But Jesus said to them, "Do not weep, for a reward awaits your deeds. Just be sure you do not transgress my commands."

[9]Then they replied, "Whatever you command, we will gladly do. And whoever may disobey your commands, he shall die!"

[10]"If indeed you are willing to heed my voice," Jesus told them, "you will treat me with favor and justice. When you accompany me to Jerusalem, I will disguise myself and walk among you so the Jerusalemites will not recognize me." [11]Jesus said these things with a hidden plan in mind, for he intended to slip into Jerusalem incognito, enter the temple, and memorize the name again. [12]But they did not suspect he planned such evil and they answered in unison, saying, "We will do all that you tell us, and we will not veer off to the right or to the left."

---

d. The adjacent miracles of multiplying loaves and fish and of walking on the sea (Mark 6:35-52) have been combined here.

e. Thomas, v. 12

[13]And he demanded, "Swear fealty to me!" So they all swore an oath, from the least to the greatest of them. [14]So they had no idea Judas was among them, for no one recognized him. [15]Later Judas said to the chief lieutenants, "I propose we arrange to wear similar garments so no one will be able to distinguish the master."[f] [16]And it sounded good to them, and they did it.

[17]And they took to the road to Jerusalem for the feast day, namely the Feast of Unleavened Bread. [18]So when the sages saw Judas, for he had secretly separated from the disciples to visit the city elders and the sages, [19]they were delighted and they asked him, "Tell us, please, all that we should do." [20]Then Judas recounted for them everything that had transpired and how he had taken the name from that bastard. [21]At this they rejoiced greatly. Then Judas told them, "You need only do as I say and tomorrow I will deliver that bastard into your grasp." [22]Then the sages said, "Do you know his movements?"

[23]And he replied, "Indeed I know them, and behold, tomorrow he will go to the temple to offer the Passover sacrifice. But I have sworn to him by the ten commandments that I would not hand him over to you myself.[g] [24]Besides, he is accompanied by two thousand men, all dressed in similar clothing. So be ready tomorrow; the man before whom I bow down and prostrate myself, that is the bastard. Comport yourselves like heroes. Attack his followers and seize him!" [25]Then Simeon, son of Shetach, and all the sages and elders danced in delight and they promised to do as Judas advised.

[26]And it came about on the next day that Jesus arrived with his whole mob, and Judas appeared before him and bowed down and prostrated himself before him with his face to the ground. [27]Then all the men of Jerusalem, having come well-armed and protected, captured Jesus. [28]And seeing him a prisoner in their grasp and that it was pointless to fight, his disciples took off running, raised their voices, and sobbed with anguish. [29]At this, the Jerusalemites only grew bolder and overcame the bastard, that son of a woman in her period of separation, along with his

f. This detail answers a question left open in the gospels: why did anyone need Judas to identify Jesus? Similarly, according to a tradition among Muslims preserved by tenth-century Sunnite commentator al-Tabari, Jesus' companions all miraculously assumed his appearance when the arresting party came upon them. Neal Robinson, *Christ in Islam and Christianity* (Albany: State University of New York Press, 1991), 127.

g. Apparently Judas refers to the loyalty oath he took, along with the disciples, in vv. 6-13 above.

forces, killing many of them, while the rest ran off to the mountains.
[30]And they brought him to the synagogue at Tiberias and tied him to
a pillar. [31]Then the mob of fools and backsliders who believed his preaching called a meeting. [32]They wanted to rescue him from the elders, but
they could not see how to do it and they broke up in strife.
[33]So when he realized he was powerless to escape, he said, "Give me
a little water." But they gave him vinegar in a copper vessel. [34]He cried
out and said, "Did not David prophesy about me, saying, 'In my thirst
they gave me vinegar to drink'?"[h]
[35]They took thorn branches and wove them into a crown and placed
it on his head, [36]and seeing it, the radicals lamented bitterly. They began
to fight among themselves, brother against brother, father against son,
but the sages overcame the radicals.
[37]Then he answered and said, "It was of me that the prophecy was
spoken, 'I yielded my back to the lash, and my cheeks to those who pluck
the beard.'[i] And again, as for these, scripture says, 'Come here, you sons
of the sorceress!'[j] But of me it was said, 'And we considered him to have
been beaten, struck, and tormented by God.'[k] And he said about me: 'The
messiah shall be snuffed out, left with nothing.'"[l]
[38]When the radicals heard this, they began to bruise themselves with
stones in mourning.[m] And there was great violence among them. [39]The elders were confused and the radicals effected his escape from them. His
three hundred and ten disciples brought him into the area around
Antioch, where he stayed till Passover eve.

6

[1]Now that year Passover happened to fall on a Sabbath day. [2]And accompanied by his entourage, he arrived in Jerusalem on the eve of Passover. He was riding a donkey, telling his disciples: "It was of me it said,
'Rejoice greatly, O daughter of Zion! Shout, O daughter of Jerusalem!
Behold, your king approaches you. He is just and carries salvation with
him. He is humble, riding but a donkey, a pure-bred donkey.'"[n] [3]And

---

h. Pss. 69:21

i. Isa. 1:6

j. Isa. 57:3

k. Isa. 53:4

l. Dan. 9:26

m. Mark 5:5

n. Zech. 9:9

they all shouted and cheered and bowed before him. [4]Then he entered the temple with his three hundred and ten disciples.

[5]Then one of them, named Gehazi,[o] approached the sages and asked, "Would you pay for the wicked one?"

[6]They reply, "But where may he be found?"

[7]He says, "He is in the temple right now!"

They answer him, "Show us."

[8]He says to them, "All three hundred and ten of us, his disciples, have already taken an oath by the ten commandments that we will not reveal his identity. But if you come in the morning and greet us, I will come and make obeisance before him. So the one before whom I make obeisance, he is the wicked one." And they agreed to do so.

[9]And when Jesus and his disciples had assembled as an anonymous troop of pilgrims, the sages went and greeted the companions of Jesus as those who had journeyed from all points to pray at the Passover feast at the Mount of Olives. [10]And when the sages had entered the temple, they saw those who had come from Antioch, and the wicked one was with them. Then Gehazi came in with them. He emerged from the congregation and made obeisance to the wicked Jesus. [11]As soon as the sages saw it, they rushed him and grabbed him.[p]

[12]From then on they held him, and even his three hundred and ten disciples were unable to set him free. [13]So in the very hour in which he would witness his own death, he began citing scripture: "Did not David prophesy about me, saying, 'We are killed on account of you'?[q] But of you, Isaiah said, 'Your hands are covered with blood.'[r] And it was you the prophet had in mind when he said before the Holy One, blessed be he, 'Your prophets they killed with the sword.'"[s]

[14]Then the radicals began to mourn, but they could do nothing to help him.

[15]And in that very hour, he was executed. It was the sixth hour and the eve of the Passover as well as of the Sabbath. [16]When they brought him out to hang him on a tree, the tree broke, for the Tetragrammaton was with him. [17]When fools saw that one tree after another snapped be-

---

o. Gehazi is Elisha's greedy disciple in 2 Kings 5:20-27.

p. Omitting an interpolation from Talmud *Sanhedrin* 43a, where five disciples are interrogated and executed according to puns on their names.

q. Pss. 44:23

r. Isa. 1:15

s. 1 Kings 19:10

neath him, they ascribed it to his great righteousness—[18]until, that is, they fetched for him the trunk of a carob tree. You see, while he still lived he was aware of the custom of hanging in Israel,[t] and he already knew of his death, as well as the manner of it, that in the end he would be hanged on a tree. [19]So at that time he had decreed by the Tetragrammaton that no tree should hold his weight; but he had neglected uttering the Tetragrammaton over the carob, for it is not a tree, but a plant.[u] [20]And this is why in some years a Jerusalem carob tree will yield over a hundred liters to this day.[v] [21]When they had left him hanging until the hour of afternoon prayer, they took him down from the tree, for it is written, "His body must not remain over night on the tree."[w] Then they buried him.[x]

7

[1]When the first day of the week had dawned, the radicals of his people were mourning at his grave. [2]Some youths of Israel passed by and said to one another in Aramaic: "Why do the pall bearers sit and raise up such a lament? Who can they be mourning? Let us satisfy our curiosity!" [3]The fools mourning Jesus told themselves that the youths would not find him. [4]Then the radicals came before Helena, the queen, and said, "They have killed the messiah, who displayed many wonders in his lifetime. And now, after killing him, they buried him. [5]But he is not in his grave! Already he has ascended into heaven, as it is written, 'For he shall welcome me. Selah.' He prophesied the same of himself."

[6]She summoned the sages and demanded, "What have you done with him?"

They replied to her, "We have executed him, for that was the sentence passed on him."

[7]She asked them, "After you executed him, then what did you do with him?"

They reply to her, "We have buried him."

---

t. Deut. 21:22

u. Loki saw to Baldar's death in precisely the same way: Frigga secured the promise of every plant of the wood never to harm Baldar so that all spears and shafts thrown at him would turn aside. But she had ignored the seemingly innocuous mistletoe. Loki took it and made it into a dart and guided blind Hother's hand to throw it, killing Baldar.

v. This detail is reminiscent of the Christian dogwood tree legend, attesting the original significance of a sacrificial death to rejuvenate vegetation.

w. Deut. 21:23

x. Acts 13:29

8At once they mounted a search for him in the grave but they did not
find him. 9She asked them, "If you buried him in this grave, where is he
now?" 10At this, the sages were perplexed and had no answer for her. In
fact, a certain man had removed him from his grave and brought him into
his garden, and he had divided the stream flowing into his garden and
buried him in a pit he dug in the sand.[y] Then he had restored the waters to
their proper channel over the new grave. 11But unaware of this, the queen
said, "If you cannot show me Jesus, I will deprive you of both freedom
and escape."

12They reply to her, "Grant us enough time." 13And after she had
granted them three days, all Israel was mourning with fasting and prayer.

14And the radicals saw their opportunity and raised a ruckus, saying,
"You have killed the Lord's anointed!" 15And all Israel was in great distress, fearing the outbreak of persecution.

16Then one went forth, an elder named Rabbi Tanchuma, and he
was walking in a field, weeping. 17The caretaker of the garden saw him
and asked him, "Why do you weep?"

He told him the story, then said it was "because of that wicked one who is not to be found, and lo, the time granted us by the queen is already up and we are all weeping and fasting."

18So when he heard this report, that all Israel was mourning and that
the wicked were claiming "he has ascended into heaven," 19then the care-
taker said, "This is a day for Israel to rejoice and be glad, then; for as it happens, I stole him away because of the insurgents, to prevent their absconding with the body, for then we should never hear the end of it."

20At once they went to Jerusalem and told them the good news.[z]

21And all Israel followed the caretaker of the garden. Then they tied
the corpse by the ankles to a horse's tail and dragged him through the
streets of Jerusalem until they brought him to the queen.[a] 22And they said,

y. John 20:15

z. Here is a remarkable satire, an alternate version of the Lukan Emmaus story, wherein it is Jesus' foes who mourn his death, albeit for a much different reason. In addition, a friendly stranger who asks about their anxiety is the one who tells them what had really happened to the missing body. Disillusionment is banished through recovery of the corpse rather than an encounter with the risen Lord. Like the Emmaus disciples, they run to Jerusalem proclaiming the "good news."

a. This is the same treatment rendered Hector by Achilles, who dragged the corpse behind his chariot around the city of Troy. This comports well with the theory that the Markan Passion was originally based on the *Iliad*. See Dennis R.

"Behold that fellow who ascended to heaven!" [23]And they departed from her courts rejoicing while she mocked the radicals and praised the sages.[b]

8

[1]Then his disciples fled and scattered among the nations: three of them to Mount Ararat, three of them to Armenia, three to Rome, and the rest to other places, spreading error among the people wherever they went. [2]Nonetheless, wherever they went the Lord, blessed be he, decreed his judgment on them, and every one was killed. [3]And many of our own radicals went astray after him and there was constant strife between them and the true children of Israel, and the former would assault the latter, interrupting their synagogue prayers and despoiling them of their riches. [4]And whenever the radicals saw Israelites, they said to them, "You killed the Lord's anointed!" [5]And Israel used to reply, "You are children of death because you have believed in a false prophet." [6]For all that, the followers of Jesus would not leave the community of Israel, so Israel had no rest from continual strife and discord.

[7]So when the sages of Israel saw the state of things, they said, "It has been thirty years since that villain was killed, and from that day to this we have had no peace with these impious fellows. [8]This has surely happened to us because of the great number of our sins, as it is written, 'They have goaded me into a jealous rage with their false god; they have provoked me to fury with their idols. [9]So I am going to goad them to jealously over a false people,' namely the Nazarenes, who are false, 'and I will provoke them to anger with a nation of fools,' namely the Ishmaelites."[c]

[10]And the sages said, "How long are the radicals to desecrate the Sabbath and the feasts and kill each other? Let us find a man wise enough to remove these impious louts from the community of Israel. [12]Today marks thirty years we have warned them, and they have not returned to the Lord. Instead, the notion has entered their heads that Jesus is the messiah. If this plan works, they may go to perdition and we will have rest at last."

[13]And the sages shared their knowledge and agreed on a greatly erudite man named Simon, son of Cleophas.[d] [14]And they said to him, "We

---

MacDonald, *The Homeric Epics and the Gospel of Mark* (New Haven: Yale University Press, 2000).

b. It is surprising they would do this since the violent degradation of the corpse should have made it impossible for the queen or anyone else to have identified it!

c. Deut. 32:21

d. The Strasbourg Codex identifies this man as Elijah. The Wagenseil makes

have agreed to pray for you, and despite the deception we ask of you, you shall surely be numbered among the company of Israel who will share in the age to come. [15]Go and do a great service of mercy to Israel: remove the radicals from our midst so they may pursue their own path to destruction." [16]So Simeon went from the council at Tiberias to Antioch, principle city of the Nazarenes, and he sent word through the whole territory of Israel: "Let every believer in Jesus join me!"

[17]When they had assembled to hear him, he announced, "I am the apostle of Jesus. He has sent me to you and I will give you a sign just as Jesus did." [18]They brought him a leper and he placed his hand on him and he was healed. [19]Then they brought him a lame man and he uttered the Tetragrammaton and placed his hand upon him, and he was healed and stood to his feet. [20]At once they bowed before him, saying, "Truly, you are the apostle of Jesus, for you show us signs just as he did."

[21]And he said, "Therefore, Jesus greets you, saying, 'I am at my Father's side in heaven, yes, at his right hand until he avenges himself upon the Jews, as David says, The Lord said to my lord, sit here on my right till I make your enemies' skulls your footstool!'"

[22]In that hour they all wept, adding folly to their foolishness.

[23]Simeon addressed them: "Jesus says to you, 'Whoever would join me in the age to come, let him leave the community of Israel behind and do not associate with them, for my Father in heaven despises them and from now on he rejects their sacrifices. [24]For he says as much by the pen of Isaiah: Your new moon observances and your scheduled feasts I hate from the center of my being. They are a nuisance to me and I am sick of enduring them.[e] [25]But Jesus says to you, 'Whoever would belong to my company, let him desecrate the Sabbath, for the Holy One, blessed be he, hates it and observes the first day of the week instead, since on it the Holy One, blessed be he, gave light to his world.' [26]And instead of the Passover celebrated by Israel, you shall observe the commemoration of the resurrection, for on that day he rose from the grave. [27]And in place of the Feast of Weeks, celebrate the day of his ascension. [28]And instead of New Year, observe the finding of the cross.[f] [29]And instead of the Day of Atonement,

---

him Simeon Kepha (Cephas). I follow Huldreich, which makes him Simeon bar Cleophas, the second brother of Jesus, after James the Just, to rule as caliph of the Jerusalem church. Simon Kepha is a natural substitution for the more obscure Simeon bar Cleophas, whose surprising mention sounds authentic.

e. Isa. 1:14

f. A gross anachronism since this was a Constantinian holiday.

keep the feast of his circumcision. [30]And in place of the Feast of Lights, celebrate the calends.

[31]"The foreskin is nothing, circumcision is nothing. Whoever wishes to be circumcised, let him be circumcised. Whoever wishes it not, let him not be circumcised.[g]

[32]"Furthermore, whatever the Holy One, blessed be he, created in his world from the tiniest gnat to the largest elephant, butcher it and eat it;[h] for so it is written: 'Just as I gave you the green plants, I have given you all things.'[i]

[33]"And if anyone compels you to go one mile, go with him two miles.[j] [34]And if a Jew should slap you on the left cheek, offer him the right as well.[k] [35]And if a Jew insults you, permit it and do not insult him in return,[l] for in this way Jesus suffered, too. [36]He let himself be seen as meek to provide an example of meekness for you so you might endure whatever is done to you.[m] [37]On Judgment Day Jesus will deal with them, but you cannot expect that unless you are in the meantime meek.[n] [38]For it is written that way: 'Seek the Lord, all the meek of the earth who have called forth his judgment. Seek justice; seek meekness and you may find a place to hide when the day of the Lord's anger erupts.'"[o]

[39]And so he preached until he had separated them from Israel. [40]And this Simeon, who "gave them statutes that were not good,"[p] did it in order to restore peace to Israel. And the Nazarenes called him Paul.[q] [41]After Paul had established these statutes and commandments, the impious separated themselves from Israel and the strife stopped.

---

g. 1 Cor. 7:18-19; Gal. 5:6

h. Acts 10:12-13

i. Gen. 9:3

j. Matt. 4:41

k. Matt. 5:39

l. Rom. 12:17, 19-20

m. 1 Pet. 2:21-23

n. As in the Acts of Paul and Thecla, it is Paul (see just below), not Jesus, who delivers the Sermon on the Mount.

o. Note the ironic lampoon of Christian ethics as passive aggression. The scriptural reference is to Zeph. 2:3.

p. Ezek. 20:25

q. F. C. Baur argued long ago that Simon Magus is to be identified in some way with Paul. Some (Hermann Detering, Stephan Hermann Huller) think "Paul" was the title bestowed upon him (Acts 13:9) by friends or enemies, depending on what it meant (Aramaic "paraclete," Persian "deceiver"), and that he was born

9

[1]So after a long time, one arose in the kingdom of Persia, [2]and he
struck out from them and made mischief for them, just as the heretics had
made mischief for the sages. [3]And he taught them, "Paul was mistaken to
write you, 'Do not be circumcised,' for Jesus himself was circumcised.
[4]Furthermore, Jesus said, 'I have not come to minimize a single word of
the Torah of Moses, not even one vowel point, but rather to fulfill all his
words.'[r] [5]You see the shame that Paul imposed on you when he said, 'Do
not be circumcised.'" And Nestorius said to them, "Have yourselves circumcised as Jesus was circumcised."[s]

[7]Besides this, Nestorius said, "You are idolaters because you say, 'Jesus is God,' since he was born of a woman. It is just that the Holy Spirit
ministered through him, as with the prophets."[t]

[8]And Nestorius began to debate with the Nazarenes, convincing
their wives, [9]for he said to them, "I will make the rule that no Nazarene
may havc two wives."

[9]And as Nestorius became increasingly odious to them, strife increased among them. A Nazarene considered the God of Nestorius an
abomination and refused to pray to it, while a Nestorian deemed the
Nazarene God an abomination and refused to pray to it. [11]Afterward,
Nestorius left for Babylon and went to a place called Chazaza and everyone fled the place. [12]The women retreated to their nests, for Nestorius was
a violent man. [13]The women said to him, "What do you want from us?"

[14]He answered them, "I only want you to accept the bread and wine
sacrament." [15]So it was customary for the women of Chazaza to carry
large keys in their hands. [16]He gave one of them the sacrament, and she
dashed it to the ground. [17]At this, the women pelted him with their keys,

---

"Simon." Here is a passage which explicitly says Paul was first known by that name. Acts calls him "Saul" ("Shaul"), a compromise conflation of "Shimeon" and "Paul."

r. Matt. 5:17-18

s. Nestorius, bishop of Constantinople, does not in fact seem to have been a Judaizer.

t. Nestorius actually taught that it was improper to adore, as his parishioners did, Mary as *theotokos,* mother of God, because the Incarnation did not extend so far as to make a squalling infant God in the flesh. He seems to have thought that Jesus possessed two ego-subjects, God and man. It was against his Christology that the doctrine of Christ's two natures *in one person* was framed. Nestorius's Christ seemed implicitly a multiple personality at worst or a mere prophet hearing the voice of God at best.

injuring him so badly that he died. [18]But the strife he unleashed continued among them for a long time.

10

[1]So the president of the Sanhedrin was named Simeon Cephas. [2]And why was he surnamed Cephas? Because he used to stand upon the stone Ezekiel had stood on as he prophesied by the River Chebar, and while Simeon stood on that stone, a voice from heaven came to him. [3]Once the Nazarenes learned Simeon was a hearer of heavenly voices and a treasury of unsearchable wisdom, they envied Israel that such a great man belonged to Israel. [4]And God put the suggestion into Simeon Cephas's mind to travel to Jerusalem to pray during the Feast of Tabernacles, where all the governors and the patriarch of the Nazarenes were gathered. [5]And on the seventh day of the feast, they visited Simeon Cephas on the Mount of Olives. [6]When they perceived his wisdom, they all agreed that he was unique in Israel and that he must be converted to the faith of the Nazarenes. [7]So they coerced him, threatening: "If you refuse to profess our faith, we will kill you, nor will we leave any alive in Israel to enter the sanctuary!" And they left him to consider their words.

[8]So when the sages of Israel saw the situation, they urged him, "Give in to their demands and then do whatever seems wise to you. Neither sin nor iniquity shall be ascribed to you since you act for the sake of God's glory."

[9]Once he saw the dire situation of Israel, he sought out the Nazarenes and told them, "I will accept your terms on one condition: that you kill not a single Jew, nor strike him, nor restrict his access to the sanctuary." [10]And the patriarch and the Nazarenes agreed to his terms and all the stipulations. [11]In addition, he made them promise to build a high tower for him to serve as a retreat in which he should eat neither meat nor anything else except bread and water. He would let down a hook on a cord and they would raise up to him a basket containing bread and water, and he should remain in that tower till the day he died. [12]He did this, so as to avoid defilement by mixing with them or eating their food, for the glory of the name of heaven. But he explained it to the Nazarenes in terms of their faith, as if he were mourning for Jesus by eating nothing but bread and water.[u] [14]So they built him the tower and he lived in it. And he

u. Here we have an astonishing reflection of the strongly Jewish-Christian character of Peter and Petrine Christianity as envisioned by F. C. Baur and the Tübingen school.

avoided defiling himself with food and venerating the cross.[v]

[15]After he had lived in the tower for a long time, he composed *keruboth, yotzroth,* and *zulthoth* in his own name, as Eleazar son of Kalir had done, and he summoned the elders of Israel and delivered to them these fruits of his knowledge. [16]He ordered them to teach his poetry to the cantors to use in prayer services so he might be remembered for something good. [17]He even sent it to Rabbi Nathan, the prince of the captivity, in Babylon. And he showed it to the masters of the academies and to the Sanhedrin, and they pronounced on it: "It is good." [18]And they taught it to the cantors throughout Israel and they used it in prayer. [19]Anyone who wished to commemorate the name of Rabbi Simeon by chanting did so, may his memory last for ever. [20]For God in his mercy made him a good defender of Israel. Amen forever! Selah.

v. The retreat tower for Simeon Cephas surely reflects Matt. 16:18, as well as the famous practices of such Pillar Saints as Symeon Stylites, an interesting link, in view of Cephas being called one of "the Pillars" (Gal. 2:9).

III.
Marcion's Apostolicon

10.

The Gospel of Marcion

MARCION WAS THE FIRST TO CALL for a new and distinctively Christian scripture. Having decided that Judaism and Christianity were completely different, though equally true religions, he thought it would be improper for Christians to seek to co-opt Jewish scripture in search of warrants for their own different beliefs through esoteric exegesis. Why not let it go and assemble a new canon from Christian writings? And then the only ones to be counted were the Pauline epistles (Marcion was surely the first to collect those he did not actually compose) plus a single gospel, which Marcion may have supposed Paul had written. The focus on Paul was not merely one of preference but, as Marcion saw it, of necessity. In his view, Paul was the only true apostle, the only one to grasp the radical novelty of the Christian revelation that Jesus' Father was a new, hitherto unknown God looking to adopt the hapless creatures of the Creator-Lawgiver. Jesus was the son of a new God, not of the Old Testament Hebrew deity. Jesus had made his invitation to the Jews, but his disciples could not grasp his message and imagined him to be teaching about the Hebrew God. They confused the two deities and the two distinct messages. The risen Christ had to recruit Paul, who had never before been a Christian, to carry his message. Naturally, since Paul's were the only genuinely apostolic writings, they formed the core of Marcion's scripture, which Marcion appropriately called the *Apostolicon,* or Book of the Apostle.

So what of his gospel? All ancient writers commenting on the matter agree that Marcion's gospel was a shorter form of what we call the Gospel according to Luke. Church fathers, including Tertullian,

charged Marcion with corrupting the text, cutting out what was not congenial to his anti-Jewish theology. But as John Knox has argued to my satisfaction (*Marcion and the New Testament: A Study in the Early History of the Canon*), it is more likely that Marcion slightly edited a short version of Luke that scholars call the Ur-Lukas. What he had was not our traditional gospel. The traditional Luke is instead a padded-out version whereby an orthodox censor, whom I will call the Lukan Ecclesiastical Redactor, has modified, sanitized, bowdlerized, rehabilitated, domesticated, and co-opted the Ur-Lukas, leaving in some material (principally the Prodigal Son parable) that Marcion did actually omit, but adding a great deal more. And then the Redactor composed the Acts of the Apostles in order to correct Marcion's one-sided emphasis on Paul. As Winsome Munro showed (*Authority in Paul and Peter: The Identification of a Pastoral Stratum in the Pauline Corpus and 1 Peter*), the same author or a like-minded colleague interpolated a number of catholicizing passages into the Pauline epistles and added the brand new Pastoral Epistles as a template by which to read the Pauline letters in Marcion's canon.

The present task is to reconstruct not Ur-Lukas but Marcion's gospel, which is an important document in its own right. I use as the basis for my version the text featured on D. J. Mahar's website for the Center for Marcionite Research. He provides the text of "The Gospel of the Lord" as compiled by James Hamlyn Hill in 1891, based on the 1823 reconstruction by August Hahn and further revised with reference to Theodor Zahn's 1891 work, *Geschichte des neutestamentlichen Kanons*. The trick is to comb the writings of Tertullian and other ancient writers who comment on the so-called omissions from Luke in Marcion's gospel to see what was in Catholic Luke that Marcion lacked and what Marcion may have had that does not occur in Catholic Luke. We cannot be sure these ancient writers would have spotted or bothered to comment on every minor change, but they seemed outraged enough to mention every departure of significance. Therefore, I think we can be pretty sure we know what the major differences were. I have followed these older reconstructions, but I utilize my own translation of Luke.

Actually, I have taken the process a step farther. I realized that we

have to take a second look at the redaction-critical hypotheses advanced in recent decades concerning Luke-Acts, especially the most comprehensive and illuminating, that of Hans Conzelmann (*The Theology of St. Luke*), if we propose to deny the common authorship of Luke-Acts in the sense of separating out Ur-Lukas. And we need to review the tenet that our conventional Luke is a direct redaction of Mark. In fact, very little changes if we assume that Ur-Lukas was more like Mark; and where Conzelmann says Luke changed Mark, we would say the Ecclesiastical Redactor changed the Mark-like Ur-Lukas. Where there are thematic links bridging Luke and Acts, we just have to take Acts as primary to set the theme and posit the Ecclesiastical Redactor changing Ur-Lukas to accord with these themes. This means that in reconstructing either the Ur-Lukas or Marcion's slightly different gospel, we must restore Markan snippets omitted by the Ecclesiastical Redactor and omit from Luke any material the Redactor added in pursuit of his favorite themes. There are numerous Ur-Lukan additions and alterations to Mark that have no apparent connection to the salvation-history redactional agenda traced by Conzelmann, and these we must assume represent Ur-Lukas's redaction of Mark before either Marcion or the Ecclesiastical Redactor got involved.

Similarly, as Cadbury and Lake (*Beginnings of Christianity*) long ago pointed out, there are a half-dozen instances when Luke omits this or that element of Mark in order to plug them into Acts. We must assume these were borrowed from their original settings in Ur-Lukas by the Ecclesiastical Redactor and used in Acts. Marcion would have had no reason to omit them, and he did not have Acts to transfer them to. So my version of Marcion's gospel restores them. None of these changes is large or obvious enough for Tertullian, Justin, or others to have necessarily noticed, much less commented upon them.

The one major piece of traditional Luke absent from Marcion's gospel that I consider a genuine Marcionite omission is the parable of the Prodigal Son. It has too much in common with other Ur-Lukas material stylistically and thematically not to have formed a part of the original Luke. What would Marcion have found objectionable about it? My guess is that someone suggested the two sons in that story represented Jewish (Petrine) and gentile (Pauline) Christianity and that

the two were being told metaphorically to reconcile their differences. This would be to repeat the error of the Judaizing twelve, in Marcion's mind, so he would have easily repudiated it. Or it may be that some subsequent Marcionite cut the Prodigal Son from the text after a Catholic floated a catholicizing interpretation to co-opt Marcionism.

My footnotes are designed to show how Marcion and his followers must have read the elements of Ur-Lukas which their version retained. Is a Marcionite reading of a passage possible, and if so, arbitrarily or plausibly? My notes suggest what the text would likely have meant for them. If you had first read the gospel under Marcion's tutelage, what would you think it meant? As to chapter and verse numbering, I have retained the conventional Lukan numbering to facilitate comparison to traditional Luke. Finally, I have changed Luke's reference to "the Christ" to "the Good One" (Greek "Chrestos"), Marcion's preferred title for Jesus, which he must have used in his gospel.

3

In the fifteenth year of the hegemony of Tiberius Caesar, Pontius Pilatus was governor of Judea.

4

31 Jesus descended to the village of Nahum, a city of the Galilee,[a] and
he was teaching them on the Sabbaths. And he said, "Do not imagine that
I have come to fulfill the Law and the Prophets! I have come not to fulfill,
but to destroy!" 32 And they were astounded at his teaching, for his word
carried authority. 33 And in the synagogue[b] was a man having a spirit of
an unclean demon, and he cried out with a loud voice, 34 saying, "What
business is there between us and you, Jesus, Nazarene? Did you come to
destroy us? I recognize you, who you are! The saint of God!" 35 And Jesus
rebuked him, saying, "Silence! And come out of him!" And casting him
aside, the demon came out of him into their midst without injuring him.
36 And astonishment overcame all, and they spoke to one another, saying,
"What does this mean? For he commands the unclean spirits with authority and power, and they come out." 37 And a report of him went out
into every place of the vicinity.

---

a. Some took Marcion to mean here that Jesus descended in a celestial adult body directly from heaven.

b. Marcionite congregations also gathered in what they called synagogues.

[16]And he came to Nazareth and entered the synagogue on the Sabbath day and sat down. And he began to speak to them, and they marveled at the words that fell from his lips. And he said to them, "No doubt, you will quote me this proverb: 'Physician, heal yourself,' meaning 'What we heard you did in the village of Nahum, do here in your own country, too.'" [28]And all in the synagogue were provoked to fury, and they rose up to throw him out of the city, and they led him captive to the precipice their city was built on in order to throw him over. But he passed through their midst and went on his way.[c]

[40]When the sun was setting, everyone who had infirm relatives with various diseases brought them to him, and he cured each one with the laying on of hands. [41]And demons, too, came out from many, shouting and saying, "You are the son of God!" And rebuking them, he forbade them to speak because they knew him to be the Good One.

[42]And with the day dawning, going forth, he journeyed into a desert place. And the crowds looked for him till they found him and detained him, begging him not to journey away from them. [43]And he said to them, "I must preach the news of the kingdom of God in the other cities, too, for this is what I was sent to do." [44]And he was preaching in the synagogues of Judea.[d]

5

[1]Now it came about as the crowd mobbed him to hear the message of God, he was standing beside the Lake of Gennesaret [2]and he spotted two boats standing by the lake, but the fishermen from them, having left, were washing their nets. [3]And embarking in one of the boats, which was Simon's, he asked him to put out a little from the shore. And sitting, he taught the crowds from the boat. [4]And when he stopped speaking, he said to Simon, "Put out into the deep and let down your net for a catch." [5]And answering, Simon said, "You're the boss, but we worked all night with nothing to show for it. But if you say so, I'll let down the nets." [6]And doing it, they enclosed a huge load of fish and their nets were splitting open. [7]And they gave their partners in the other boat the heads-up to come and assist them. And they came and filled both boats so as to sink them. [8]Seeing this, Simon Peter fell down at Jesus' knees, saying, "Depart from

c. Marcion was a docetist, which means that his Jesus had a spiritual body. Here we must picture Jesus drifting through the crowd like a phantom.

d. For Marcion, this denoted preaching the dominion of the hitherto unknown Father, not the old familiar God of Israel. Why proclaim what everyone already knew?

me, for I am a sinful man, my Lord!" [9]For amazement seized him and all those present with him at the catch of fish they took in. [10]Likewise both Jacob and John, sons of Zebediah, who were partners with Simon. And Jesus said to Simon, "Do not fear. From now on you will be angling for human souls." [11]And docking the boats on land, abandoning everything, they followed him.

[12]And it came about that as he was in one of the cities, behold, a man covered with skin disease seeing Jesus, prostrating himself, begged him, saying, "Lord, if only you will, you are able to purify me." [13]And stretching out his hand, he touched him, saying to him, "It is my wish: be purified!" And at once the skin disease left him. [14]And he sternly warned him to tell no one, but "going away, show yourself to the priest and offer the things Moses commanded, concerning your cleansing, for their verification."[e] [15]But instead, the report of him circulated and many crowds accompanied him to hear and to be cured of their infirmities. [16]But he was retreating into the desert and praying every chance he got.

[17]And it came about that one day he was teaching and Pharisees and teachers of the Law had come from every village in the Galilee and Judea and Jerusalem, and power from the Lord was in him to cure. [18]And behold: men carried on a couch a man who was paralysed, and they intended to carry him in and to lay him before him. [19]And not seeing how they might carry him in through the crowd, going up onto the roof, they lowered him with the couch through the tiles in the middle of the scene in front of Jesus. [20]And seeing their faith, he said, "Man, the sins you were being punished for are forgiven you."[f] [21]And the scribes and the Pharisees began to dialogue, saying, "Who is this fellow who speaks blasphemies? Who can forgive sins except one, namely God?"[g] [22]But aware of their dialogue, Jesus answered them, saying, "Why do you dialogue secretly? [23]What, after all, is easier, to say 'Your sins are forgiven you' or to say 'Get up and walk around'? Let's see, shall we? [24]To demonstrate to you that a man has authority to forgive sins on earth"—here he spoke to the paralytic—"To you I say, get up, take your mat and go to your dwelling." [25]And getting up at once in the sight of all, and taking the mat, he went away to his dwelling worshipping God. [26]And ecstasy overtook them all,

---

e. Jesus is not necessarily concerned that the man obey the Torah, just that he needs priestly certification before he can re-enter society.

f. In the name of his merciful Father, Jesus frees the sufferer from the excessive judgment meted out by the God of Israel.

g. The Marcionite answer is that the Father of Jesus is a separate God.

and they worshipped God and were filled with awe, saying, "We have beheld paradoxes today!"

[27]And after these events, he went out and spotted a customs agent named Levi sitting at the customs booth, and he said to him, "Follow me!" [28]And dropping everything, getting up, he followed him. [29]And Levi held a great feast in his honor at his house, and there was a large crowd of customs agents and their associates reclining. [30]And the Pharisees and their scribes murmured at his disciples, saying, "Why do you eat with the customs agents and backsliders?" [31]And answering, Jesus said to them, "The healthy do not have need of a physician, but those who are in a bad way. [32]My mission was not to summon the righteous, but the sinful to repentance."[h]

[33]And they said to him, "The disciples of John fast frequently and offer prayers, and the same for those of the Pharisee sect, but yours eat and drink." [34]And Jesus explained to them, "Can you expect the groomsmen to fast during the wedding feast? [35]But inevitably the days come when the celebration will end, and then they fast as usual."[i] [36]And he also told them a parable: "Look, no one is so stupid that he cuts a patch from a new garment to cover the hole in an old one. Otherwise, the new section will shrink with washing and tear away, and the patch from the new will not agree with the old. [37]And no one fills old wine skins with new wine; otherwise, when the new wine ferments, it will burst the taut old skins, the wine will be spilled, and the skins destroyed. [38]But one must put new wine into new skins."[j]

6

[1]And it came about that on the Sabbath he was passing through the grainfields, and his disciples plucked and ate the ears of grain, rubbing with their hands. [2]And some of the Pharisees said, "Why do you do what is not legal on the Sabbath?" [3]And replying to them, Jesus said, "Did you never read what David did when he hungered, and those with him? [4]How he entered into the house of God and, taking the loaves of showbread which is not legal for anyone but the priests to eat, he ate and gave to

h. This is a new gospel because the Hebrew God would have shared the Pharisaic disdain for the lawless.

i. Marcionites were ascetics and would not have thought Jesus was abolishing fasting.

j. Here is a forthright repudiation of early Christian-Jewish syncretism or "Judaizing" the gospel of Jesus with Jewish forms.

those who were with him?" 5And he said to them, "Man was given dominion over the Sabbath."[k]

6And it came about, on another Sabbath he entered into the synagogue to teach, and there was a man there and his right hand was withered. 7And the scribes and the Pharisees watched him closely to see if he heals on the Sabbath, that they might find grounds to accuse him. 8But he was aware of their designs and he said to the man who had the dry hand, "Get up and stand where everyone can see you." And getting up, he stood there. 9And Jesus said to them, "I ask you: is it legal on the Sabbath to do good or to do evil? To save life or to kill it?" 10And looking around at them, he said to him, "Extend your hand!" And he did, and his hand was restored to health. 11But they were filled with mindless rage and exchanged ideas with one another as to what they might do to Jesus.[l]

12Now in these days, he went out into the mountain to pray and passed the night in prayer to God. 13And when it became day, he summoned his disciples, selecting twelve of them whom he also named apostles, 14Simon, whom he also named Peter, and Andreas, his brother, and Jacob and John and Philip and Bar-Ptolemy, 15and Matthew and Thomas the Twin, Jacob of Alphaeus and Simon, the one called the Zealot, and Judas of Jacob, 16and Judas the False One, who became a traitor. 17And coming down with them, he stood on a level place and faced a great crowd of his disciples and a huge mass of the people from all Judea and Jerusalem and the seaboard region of Tyre and Sidon, 18who came to hear him and to be cured of their diseases, and those in torment from unclean spirits were cured. 19And all the crowd tried to touch him, for power went forth from him and healed all.

20And raising his eyes to look at his disciples, he said,

"Blessed are the poor, because the kingdom of God belongs to you.
Blessed are those hungering now, because you shall be filled.
Blessed are those weeping now, because they will have the last laugh.
22Blessed are you when people hate you
and when they excommunicate you and insult you
and put your name on the public enemies list
on account of yours truly.

k. Jesus does not here require scriptural warrant because he uses the "circumstantial ad hominem" argument to turn the Pharisees' own authority against them. His point, after all, is that David did not keep the Torah either.

l. Again, the Torah is death-dealing, while the gospel of the Father is life-giving. It is Jesus against the Jewish Law.

[23]Rejoice in that day and jump for joy, for behold, your reward in heaven is great because their fathers treated the prophets according to the very same pattern.

[24]But woe to you plutocrats, because you already enjoy your consolation.

Woe to you, those satiated now, because you will hunger.

Woe, those laughing now, because one day you will mourn and weep.

[26]Woe when everyone speaks admiringly of you, because their fathers treated the pseudo-prophets according to the very same pattern.[m]

[27]"But I tell you, my audience: love your enemies, treat them well who hate you, [28]bless those who curse you, pray for those insulting you. [29]To the one who slaps you on one side of the face, offer him the other, too; and as for the one taking your cloak, do not prevent him from taking your tunic as well. [30]To all who ask of you, give! And from the one taking your possessions? Do not demand them back. [31]And just as you wish that others would treat you, why, treat them the same way. [32]And if you love those loving you, what thanks do you expect? For even the irreligious love those loving them. [33]And if you do good for those who do good for you, what thanks do you expect? Even the irreligious lend to their fellows to get the same amount back again. [35]But love your enemies and do good and lend, expecting no return, and your reward will be great: you will be sons of the Most High[n] because he is good to the ungrateful and wicked. [36]Be compassionate, just as your Father is compassionate. [37]And do not judge so you may never be judged. And do not condemn so you may never be condemned. Forgive others and they will forgive you. [38]Give, and others will give to you; they will give you what you need as generously as the grain merchant shakes the air out and compacts the gain before pouring it overflowing into your held-up shirt-hem. This is how it works: others will use the same scale of generosity you used for them in their time of need."

---

m. Which did Marcion consider the true and which the false prophets? With the Ebionites, the Koran, and others, he rejected the "writing prophets," which is to say the prophetic books of the Old Testament. Like Gnostics, he may have regarded Balaam, the Edenic serpent, or Eve as true prophets vilified by the Old Testament writers, counting as "their fathers" those who scorned the true prophets and lionized the false.

n. That is, the Father of Jesus Christ, who is higher than the Creator. Jesus' God sends no one to hell. He, too, turns the other cheek.

39And he told them a parable: "A blind man is not capable of guiding
a blind man. Won't both of them end up in the ditch? 40In the nature of
things, a disciple is not superior to the teacher so as to be able to correct
him. But once he finishes his study, every disciple will be the equal of his
teacher and then might presume to offer a worthwhile dissenting opinion.
41And why do you notice the sawdust speck in your brother's eye while
oblivious of the wooden beam in your own? 42How dare you say to your
brother, 'Brother, here, let me just delicately remove that nasty speck
from your eye,' when you can't even see the board sticking out of your
own? Hypocrite! First remove the beam from your own eye, then perhaps
you will see well enough to remove the speck from your brother's eye.

43"For there is no bad tree that produces luscious fruit, nor again a
sound tree producing bad fruit. 44For each tree is recognized by its distinctive fruit; for no one gathers figs from thorns, nor does anyone pick a
grape from a thorn bush. 45The good person brings forth the good out of
the store of good in the heart and the wicked person brings forth the
wicked out of the store of wickedness. For one speaks out of what fills the
heart. 46And why bother calling me 'Lord! Lord!' when you pay no heed
to what I say?[o] 47Everyone coming to me and hearing my words and doing them, well, I will show you who he is like. 48He is like a man building
a house, who dug ever deeper and laid a foundation on bedrock. And
when a flood came, the river crashed against that house but was not able
to shake it because it was built well. 49But the one hearing and not doing
is like a man having built a house on the ground without any foundation
at all, which when a river crashed against it promptly fell flat. And that
house was a total loss."

7

1When he came to the end of all his sayings in the ears of the people,
he entered into the village of Nahum. 2So a certain slave belonging to a
centurion, and dear to him, being in a bad way, was near death. 3And
hearing about Jesus, he sent to him elders of the Jews, asking him to come
and make his slave recover. 4And approaching Jesus, they sought earnestly to persuade him, saying, "He is worthy of your granting him this
favor, 5for he loves our nation and even built our synagogue for us."
6And Jesus agreed to go with them. And while he was not far from the

---

o. According to Marcion, this was exactly the fatal flaw with the twelve: they could not grasp the radical novelty of Jesus' gospel and therefore compromised it with Judaism—this in the name of Jesus!

house, the centurion sent friends with the message, "Lord, do not trouble yourself, for I am not worthy to have you come under the roof of my house. [7]Thus, I did not account myself worthy to come to you in person. Just pronounce an incantation and let my servant be cured. [8]For I, too, am a man set under authority and having soldiers under me, so I know how it works: I say to this one, 'Off with you!' and he is off at once, and to another, 'Come!' and he comes, and to my slave, 'Do this,' and he does." [9]At hearing these words, Jesus marveled at him, and turning to face the crowd following him, he said, "I tell you, I found no such faith in Israel!"[p] [10]And returning to the house, those sent found the slave in good health.

[11]And it came about on the next day, he journeyed into a city called Nain, and his disciples and a large crowd journeyed with him. [12]And as he neared the gate of the city, behold, there was being carried out a man who had died, the only begotten son of his mother, a widow, and a large number of the city's populace crowded along behind. [13]And seeing her, the Lord felt compassion for her and said to her, "Do not cry." [14]And coming up to the bier, he touched it, the pallbearers having halted, and he said, "Young fellow, to you I say, arise!" [15]And the corpse sat up and began to speak. And Jesus gave him to his mother. [16]And all were overcome with awe, and they worshipped God, saying, "A great prophet was raised among us!" and "God has intervened among his people." [17]And word of this went out in all Judea and the whole vicinity concerning him.

[18]And John's disciples reported to him about all this. And John was scandalized.[q] And summoning a certain two of his disciples, John [19]sent word to the Lord saying, "Are you the Coming One? Or must we look for another?" [20]And coming to him, the men said, "John the Baptist sent us to ask you, 'Are you the Coming One? Or must we look for another?'" [21]In that very hour he cured many of diseases and plagues and wicked spirits, and to many blind he gave sight. [22]And answering them, he said, "When you get back to John, report what you saw and heard: blind see again, lame walk around, those with skin disease are purified, and deaf hear, corpses are raised, poor are evangelized. [23]And blessed is anyone not scandalized by me."

---

p. Marcion would see nothing surprising in this, as Jesus represents for him a radical departure beyond the bounds of Judaism.

q. Thus Marcion drives a wedge between the Jewish John and Jesus. He presupposes what we fail to notice, that there has been no reaction from John the Baptist. Did he believe in Jesus or not?

[24]As John's messengers were departing, he began to speak to the crowds about John: "What did you go out into the desert to look at? A reed swept by the wind? [25]No? Then what did you go out to see? A man dressed in effeminate clothing? Behold, those in rich clothing and appointed in luxury are in royal palaces. [26]So what did you go out to see? A prophet? Yes, I tell you, and more than a prophet! [27]This is the one about whom it is written, 'Behold, I send my angel right in front of you, who will get the path ready in advance of you.' [28]I tell you, the prophet John is greater than all those born of women, but the least of the angels in the kingdom of God is greater than he."[r] [29]And all the people hearing this, including the customs agents, attested to it,[s] being baptized with the baptism of John. [30]The Pharisees and the canon lawyers, on the other hand, spurned God's advice to them, not being baptized by him. [31]"To what, then, may I compare the people of this race? What are they like? [32]They are like children sitting idle in a marketplace taunting one another, the boys saying, 'We played the pipe for you, and you refused to dance.' And the girls reply, 'That's a boy's game! We mourned, and you would not weep with us because it's a girl's game.' For John the Baptist's approach was not to eat bread or drink wine, and you say, 'He is a demoniac.' [34]But now a man has come eating and drinking and you say, 'Nothing but a glutton and a wine drinker, a crony of customs agents and backsliders.'" [35]And all her children attested wisdom.[t]

[36]And a certain one of the Pharisees asked him to eat with him, and entering into the house of the Pharisee he reclined at table. [37]And behold, a notorious woman of the city, aware that he reclines in the house of the Pharisee, bringing an alabaster box of ointment [38]and standing behind by his feet and weeping, commenced to get his feet wet with her tears; and with the hair of her head she wiped them off and ardently kissed his feet and anointed them with the ointment. [39]But seeing this, the Pharisee who invited him reflected, "If this man were a genuine prophet, he would have known who and what sort of woman this is who is touching him because

r. According to the Nasorean/Mandaean sect, John was the earthly proclaimer of the angels Glorious Enosh, Radiant Abel, and Manda de'Haiye, and this saying may have been meant to caution against over-enthusiasm for John.

s. Literally, "justified God," an idiom for confession or testimony. Cf. Pss. 51:4; Josh. 7:19; John 9:24.

t. Perhaps Marcion took Jesus to mean, as Albert Schweitzer thought, that John the Baptist was the Coming One, an epithet for Elijah. Marcion did not deny that Elijah would precede the Jewish messiah, just that Jesus was the Jewish messiah.

she is notorious." [40]And answering, Jesus said to him, "Simon, I have something to say to you." And he says, "Teacher, speak." [41]"Two people were in debt to a certain creditor. The one owed five hundred denarii and the other fifty. [42]Neither one of them having the wherewithal to repay, he forgave the debt of both. Which of them would you guess will love him more?" [43]Answering, Simon said, "I should think the one whom he forgave the greater sum." [44]He said to him, "You judged rightly." [44]And turning to the woman, he said to Simon, "Look at this woman. I entered your house, you did not pour water on my feet, but this woman wet my feet with her tears and dried them with her hair. [45]You did not greet me with a kiss, but since I entered, this woman has not stopped ardently kissing my feet. [46]You did not anoint my head with oil, but she anointed my feet with her tears. [47]For the sake of this, her sins, which are many, have been forgiven her because she loved much; but one who needs little forgiveness loves little." [48]And he said to her, "The sins are forgiven you." [49]And those reclining with him began to whisper to one another, "Who is this who even presumes to forgive sins?" [50]But he said to the woman, "Your faith has saved you. Go in peace."[u]

8

[1]And afterward, it came about that he toured every city and village proclaiming and evangelizing the kingdom of God, and the twelve with him. [2]Plus certain women who were cured of wicked spirits and infirmities, Maria, called the hairdresser, from whom seven demons had exited, [3]and Joanna, wife of Chuza, Herod's steward, and Susanna, and many others who provided for them out of their possessions.

[4]And when a great crowd had collected, people from each city traveling to hear him, he said by means of a parable: [5]"A sower went out to sow his seed. And it came about in the process of sowing, this seed fell beside the road, and was trampled, and the birds of the sky ate it up. [6]And other seed fell on the rock, and once grown, it withered on account of not having moisture. [7]And other seed fell into the thorns, and growing up with it, the thorns choked it. [8]And other seed fell into the good earth and, once grown, it gave fruit a hundredfold." Saying these things, he called out, "Whoever has ears to hear, let him hear!" [9]And his disciples questioned him as to what this parable might mean. [10]And he said, "It has been given you to know the mysteries of the kingdom of God, but to the rest it has

u. Again, note the shocking amnesty granted by the gracious Father of Jesus, not anticipated by the representatives of the Law-giver Yahve.

been given in parables so that seeing, they may not see and hearing, they may not understand.

[16]"So no one, having lit a lamp, hides it in a vessel or puts it underneath the couch. But he puts it on a lamp stand so that those entering may see the light. [17]For a thing is not hidden unless it is later to be made manifest, nor is anything hidden away except in order for it to be known and to reappear. [18]So watch how you hear! For the one who has, it will be given to him; and the one who has not, even what he seems to have will be taken from him."[v]

[20]And it was relayed to him: "Your mother and your brothers are standing outside wishing to see you." [21]And answering, he says to them, "Just who are my mother and my brothers? Those who hear my words and practice them: they are my mother and sisters and brothers."[w]

[22]And it came about one day that he and his disciples cast off in a boat, and he said to them, "Let us cross to the other side of the lake." And they put to sea. And as they sailed, he fell asleep. And a storm of wind descended on the lake, and they were filling up and were in danger. [24]And approaching him, they get him up, saying, "Master! Master! We are perishing!" And having been awakened, he rebuked the wind and the choppiness of the water and they ceased, and there was a calm. [25]Then he said to them, "Where is your faith?" Awestruck, they marveled, saying to one another: "Who, then, is this man, that he commands even the winds and the water and they obey him?"[x]

[26]And they sailed down to the region of the Gerasenes, which is opposite the Galilee. [27]And as he was stepping out onto the shore, a certain man from the city met him. He had demons and had not worn a garment in a long time. He did not stay in a house but among the tombs. [28]And seeing Jesus, he cried out and fell prostrate in front of him and said in a loud voice, "What business is there between me and you, Jesus, son of the

v. Here Marcion would see a warning unheeded by the twelve as they let the new gospel slip through their fingers. By confusing Jesus' message with their inherited tradition, the twelve thus hid their light under the smothering basket of Judaism. The twelve lost the spiritual authority once conferred on them by Jesus.

w. So much for the caliphate of James and the relatives of Jesus, who were as misguided as the twelve in mortgaging Christianity to Judaism. I restore here some of the Markan/Ur-Lukan text omitted in traditional Luke. There is no reason to think Marcion would have omitted it.

x. Marcion would see this as attesting the superiority of Jesus and his Father over the Creator, whose terrors would not touch the true elect.

Most High?[y] I beg you, do not torture me!" [29]He said this because Jesus ordered the unclean spirit to come out of the man. For many were the times it had fastened on him, and he was guarded, restrained with chains and fetters; and ripping apart the restraints, he was driven by the demons into the desert places. [30]And Jesus interrogated him: "What is your name?" And he said to him, "Legion!" for many demons entered into him. [31]And they pleaded that he would not order them to depart into the Abyss. [32]Now there was a herd of many pigs feeding in the mountain. And they pleaded with him to allow them to enter into those. And he allowed them. [33]And coming out from the man, the demons entered into the pigs and stampeded the herd down the ledge into the lake, where they choked. [34]And those feeding them, seeing what happened, fled and reported in the city and in the fields. [35]And they came to see what had happened. And they came to Jesus and found the man from whom the demons had gone out sitting, dressed and clear-headed, at the feet of Jesus, and they were afraid. [36]And those seeing how the demoniac was saved recounted it to them. [37]And all the masses of the vicinity of the Gerasenes asked him to depart from them for they were stricken with terror. [38]So embarking in the boat, he returned. And the man from whom the demons had gone out pleaded with him that he might accompany him. But he dismissed him, saying, [39]"Return to your home and recount what God did to you." And he went out throughout the city proclaiming what things Jesus did to him.

[40]And when Jesus returned, the crowd welcomed him, for they were all expecting him. [41]And behold, a man came whose name was Jairus, and this man was a ruler of the synagogue, and falling at the feet of Jesus, he pleaded with him to enter his house, [42]because he had an only-begotten daughter of about twelve years and she was dying. And as he went, the crowd mobbed him. [43]And a woman, subject to a flow of blood for twelve years, and not able to be cured by anyone,[z] [44]approached behind, touching the fringe of his garment. And at once the flow of her blood stood still. [45]And Jesus said, "Who is it who touched me?" And all denying it, Peter said, "Master, the crowds mob and jostle you!" [46]But Jesus said, "Someone in particular touched me, for I sensed power going forth from me." [47]And the woman, seeing she could not escape notice, came

y. Again, the Father is higher than the Creator.

z. Marcion may have seen in the twelve years associated with both healings a symbol of the impotence of Catholic and Jewish Christianity, ostensibly led by the twelve and their successors.

trembling and fell down before him and declared before all the people why she had touched him and how she was instantly cured. [48]And he told her, "Daughter, your own faith has saved you. Go without worries."

[49]While he was still speaking, someone comes from the synagogue ruler, saying, "Your daughter has died. Inconvenience the teacher no more." [50]But Jesus, overhearing, answered him, "Do not fear. Just believe and she will be saved." [51]And coming into the house, he did not permit anyone to enter with him except Peter and John and Jacob and the father and mother of the girl. [52]And all were sobbing and lamenting her. But he said, "Do not weep. She did not die, but sleeps." [53]And they derided him, knowing full well that she died. [54]But he put them all outside,[a] and grasping her hand, he called out saying, "Girl, arise!" [55]And her spirit returned, and she got up at once. And he ordered that something should be given her to eat.[b] [56]And her parents were ecstatic, but he commanded them to tell no one what really happened.[c]

9

[1]And summoning the twelve, he gave them power and authority over all the demons and to cure diseases, [2]and he sent them to proclaim the kingdom of God and to cure. [3]And he said to them, "Take nothing on the road, neither staff, nor pouch, nor bread, nor silver, nor two tunics each.[d] [4]And whatever dwelling you enter, stay there and go out from there. [5]And as many as may not welcome you, as you leave that city, shake off the dust from under your feet as a reproach to them." [6]And going forth, they went throughout the villages evangelizing and healing everywhere. [7]And Herod the tetrarch heard all the things occurring and was bemused because it was said by some that John was raised from the dead, by some that Elijah had appeared, and by others that a certain prophet of the ancients had risen again. [9]But Herod said, "I took John's head off, so who is this about whom I hear such reports?" And he made efforts to see him.

---

a. I am here restoring some Markan material transferred by the Lukan Ecclesiastical Redactor to Acts 9:40.

b. This would assure them she was no ghost.

c. Marcion would see here the failure of Judaism embodied in the synagogue ruler, contrasted with the success of the new gospel of Jesus, "the power of salvation unto everyone who believes."

d. The simultaneous similarity and contrast with ancient Cynicism we see here would make sense as a concern of Marcion, himself a Christian ascetic hailing from Sinope, the very same hometown of Diogenes, founder of Cynicism.

[10]And once they returned, the apostles recounted to him what they did. And taking them along, he left privately for a city called Beth-Saida. [11]But the crowds knew it and followed him; and welcoming them, he spoke to them about the kingdom of God and he cured those having need of healing. [12]But the day began to decline and the twelve came to him and said, "Dismiss the crowd that they may go to the surrounding villages and fields to find lodging and provisions because here we are in a desert place." [13]And he said to them, "You give them to eat!" And they said, "We have no more than five rolls and two fish unless we are to go and buy food for all these people." [14]For there were about five thousand men. And he said to his disciples, "Have them recline in groups of about fifty each." [15]And they did so and had all recline. [16]And taking the five rolls and the two fish, looking up to the sky, he blessed and broke them and gave them to the disciples to set before the crowd. [17]And they all ate and were satisfied, and twelve baskets of fragments were returned to them.

[18]And it came about that as he was praying silently, the disciples were with him, and he questioned them, saying, "Who do people think me to be?" [19]And they answered and said, "John the Baptist, but others Elijah, and others that a certain prophet of the ancients rose up again." [20]And he said to them, "But what about you? Who do you think me to be?" And Peter, answering, said, "You are the good man of God." [21]And he warned them they must tell this to no one, [22]saying that a man has to suffer many indignities and be excommunicated by the elders and arch-priests and scribes and be executed and then raised on the third day. [23]And he said to all, "If anyone wants to come after me, let him repudiate himself and pick up his cross daily and let him follow me. [24]For whoever tries to save his life will lose it, but whoever will sacrifice his life for my sake, he will save it. [25]For what profit does a person make if he manages to acquire the whole world only to be fined his own life or to suffer loss? [26]I say this because whoever will not stand up for me, neither will I stand with him when I come in my radiance and that of the Father and of the holy angels. And I tell you truly: there are some of those standing here who will certainly not taste of death before they see the kingdom of God come with power."[e]

[28]And it happened that about eight days after these sayings, taking along Peter and John and Jacob, he went up into the mountain to pray. [29]And as he prayed, the appearance of his face became different and his

e. More Markan content absent from traditional Luke, probably omitted from Ur-Lukas by the Ecclesiastical Redactor; Marcion would not have omitted it.

clothing sparkling white. [30]And behold, two men stood with him, who were Moses and Elijah.[f] [32]But Peter and those with him had been overcome with sleep, but coming awake with a jolt, they saw his glory and the two men standing with him. [33]And it happened that when they left him, Peter said to Jesus, "Master, it is good for us to be here. And let us make three shrines: one for you, and one for Moses, and one for Elijah," not knowing what he said. [34]As he said these things, a cloud appeared, overshadowing them, and they feared as they ascended into the cloud. [35]And a voice came out of the cloud saying, "Of the three, this one is my son, the chosen. Hear him!" And when the voice came, Jesus was found alone.[g] And they were silent and reported to no one in those days any of the things they have seen.[h]

[37]And it came about that on the following day, as they were descending the mountain, a great crowd met him. [38]And behold, a man from the crowd called out saying, "Teacher, I beg you to look at my son because he is my only begotten [39]and, as you can see, a spirit takes him and yells out abruptly and throws him down foaming and leaves him only with difficulty, bruising him in the process. [40]And I begged your disciples that they might cast it out, but they were not able."[i] [41]And answering, he says to them, "O unbelieving and perverted race! How long till I am free of you? How long must I endure you? Bring your son here." [42]And while he was still approaching him, the demon tore his flesh and hurled him violently. And Jesus rebuked the unclean spirit and cured the boy and restored him to his father. [43]And all were astonished at the greatness of God. And while they all marveled at all that he did, he said to his disciples, [44]"Embed these words in your ears: for a man is about to be betrayed into the clutches of men." [45]But they did not understand this saying and it had been veiled from them so that they should not perceive it,[j]

---

f. Some Marcionites understood this as a negotiation between Jesus and representatives of the Creator over the souls Jesus would win, though this reads too much into the text.

g. How much sense this makes as a statement of Marcionite theology! The Father sweeps away the Torah of Moses and the writings of the Prophets, represented by Elijah, to say Christians should listen to Jesus alone. Of course, the twelve do not get it.

h. This is a fatal error in that the twelve should have told Christians to heed Jesus, not the Jewish scriptures, but they didn't.

i. Marcion would see this as indicative of the utter spiritual failure and consequent impotence of Catholic and Jewish Christianity stemming from the twelve.

j. See 2 Cor. 3:14-15; 4:3-4. It is the God of the Torah who has blinded them.

and they were afraid to learn what it meant.[k]

46And they entered into debate over which of them might be the greater. 47And Jesus, aware of their whispered debate, took a child and stood him beside him, 48and said to them, “Whoever welcomes one of these children on account of my name welcomes me; and whoever welcomes me, welcomes not me but the one who commissioned me. For the one who is lesser among you all, this one is great.”

49And answering, John said, “Master, we caught someone casting out demons using your name, so we told him that, since he was not one of our group, he must cease and desist.” 50But Jesus said to him, “Why on earth did you forbid him? For anyone who is not actually opposing you is on your side!”[l]

51And it came about that as the days of his assumption into the sky were counting down, he set an unswerving course for Jerusalem, 52and he sent messengers in advance of him. And on their journey, they entered into a village of Samaritans to prepare for his arrival. 53And they did not welcome him once they heard his destination was Jerusalem. 54And the disciples Jacob and John, seeing this, said, “Lord, do you want us to call down fire from the sky to destroy them just as Elijah dealt with Samaritans?”[m] 55But turning, he rebuked them, *saying, “You don't realize which spirit you belong to! For a man's task is to save human lives, not to destroy them.”* 56And they journeyed into another village.[n]

57And as he traveled along the road, one said to him, “I will follow you wherever you may go.” 58And Jesus said to him, “Think twice! The foxes have holes and the birds of the sky nests, but a man has no permanent abode.” 59And he said to another, “Follow me!” And he said, “Gladly, Lord. First just let me see to my father's burial.” 60But he said to him, “Let the dead bury themselves. You go and announce the kingdom of God!”[o]

---

k. Again, why trust these pseudo-apostles who had not the faintest understanding of the clear teaching of Jesus?

l. This anticipates the antipathy of the twelve and their heirs toward Paul, who had not belonged to the group of the twelve, and Jesus' approval of Paul.

m. 2 Kings 1:9-14

n. Here is a pointed repudiation of the merciless wrath of Yahve and his servants, contrasted with the mercy of Jesus and his Father. The fundamental error of the twelve was precisely the failure to recognize which Spirit, or which of the two Gods, they belonged to.

o. Luke 10:61-62 are omitted here as likely the creation of the Ecclesiastical

10

[1]Now after these things, the Lord appointed seventy-*two* others, and he sent them in pairs in advance into every city and place where he was about to come. [2]And he said to them, "Indeed, there is much to be harvested, but so few workers are available. So prevail upon the harvest master to dispatch workers into his fields. [3]Go! Behold, I send you like lambs into a ravening wolf pack. [4]Do not bring a change purse or a wallet or sandals, and do not stop to chat with anyone you meet on the road.[p] [5]And whatever dwelling you enter, first say, 'Peace to this house.' [6]And if a peaceful man is there, your blessing of peace shall protect it; otherwise, it shall cover you alone. [7]And remain in the same house, eating and drinking with them, for the worker deserves his pay. Do not flit from house to house. [8]And whatever city you may enter and they welcome you, eat the things set before you,[q] [9]and cure the sick in it, and tell them, 'The kingdom of God has come close upon you!' [10]And whatever city you enter and they do not welcome you, go out into its streets and say, 'Even the dust of your city sticking to our feet we shake off at you. Nevertheless, we warn you. The kingdom of God has drawn near!' [12]I tell you, it will go easier on that day for Sodom than for such a city. [13]Woe to you, Chorazin! Woe to you, Beth-Saida! Because if the powerful deeds performed in you had been performed in Tyre and Sidon, they would have repented long ago, sitting in sackcloth and ashes. [14]Even so, it will go easier for Tyre and Sidon in the judgment than for you. [15]And you, village of Nahum, will you be lifted as high as heaven? No, you shall descend to Hades.[r]

[16]"Whoever hears you hears me, and whoever rejects you rejects me, and whoever rejects me rejects him who sent me."

[17]And the seventy-*two* returned with joy, saying, "Lord, even the demons yield to us in your name."[s] [19]But he said, "Behold, I have given you the authority to walk over snakes and scorpions and over all the Powers

---

Redactor, who also wrote the related 2 Tim. 2:15, "plowing a straight furrow with the message of truth."

p. 2 Kings 4:29

q. Heedless of Jewish dietary regulations, in other words.

r. It is no surprise to Marcion that Jewish towns rejected the tidings of the unknown Father.

s. Omitting v. 18 as the work of the ecclesiastical redactor: it is a bit of Lukan "realized eschatology" and serves the Lukan motif of the "Satan-free" period of Jesus' ministry, both added by the redactor.

of the enemy and nothing shall harm you at all.[t] [20]Nevertheless, do not rejoice in the fact that the spirits yield to you, but rather that your names have been registered in the heavens."

[21]In that very hour he felt rapture in the Holy Spirit and said, "I confess to you, Lord of heaven, because you concealed these things from the sages and the intellectuals, revealing them instead to infants. Yes, Father, because it seemed good sport to you! [22]All things were delivered to me by my Father, and no one knows who the son is except for the Father, nor who the Father is except for the son—and him to whom the son deigns to reveal him."[u] [23]And turning privately to the disciples, he said, "Blessed the eyes that see what you see. [24]For I tell you that many prophets and kings did not see what you see and did not hear what you hear."[v]

[25]And behold, a certain canon lawyer stood up with a question to feel him out, saying, "Teacher, what should I do to inherit the life?" [26]And he said to him, "What does the Law say, as you understand it?" [27]And answering, he said, "You shall love the Lord from your whole heart and with your whole soul and with all your strength and with all your mind, and your neighbor as yourself." [28]And he said to him, "You answered correctly. If one does this, he will live."[w] [29]And hoping to justify his moral complacency, he pressed the question, asking Jesus, "And just who, pray tell, counts as one's 'neighbor'?" [30]Jesus said to him, "Imagine a man was going down from Jerusalem to Jericho, who fell prey to thieves who stripped him naked and pummeled him with blows, then left, abandoning him half-dead. [31]It just so happened that a certain priest was going down the same road and, seeing him, crossed the street to

t. A reflection of Zoroastrianism: the "creeping things," as the Bible calls them, were considered the anti-creation of Ahriman and his demonic henchmen. Thus they represent demonic Powers here. Marcionism, too, presupposes two rival Gods, and in this it may show the influence of Zoroastrianism, as Jan Koester suggests. The Father, Jesus' God, would not have been the Creator of snakes and scorpions, contrary to Monty Python: "All things dull and ugly, all creatures short and squat, all things rude and nasty, the Lord God made the lot."

u. An unabashed declaration that Jesus is the revealer of a hitherto unknown God. The statement hardly makes sense if Jesus is referring to the well-known Hebrew God.

v. This would be because Jesus and his Father were utterly unanticipated by the Hebrew prophets or their religion, representing an invasion from outside their cosmology.

w. Marcion didn't deny that Jews would be saved by their God for keeping his commandments. But notice how this champion of the Torah comes off in the end.

avoid him. [32]In the same way, a Levite, too, coming upon the place,
crossed the street to avoid him. [33]And a certain Samaritan on a journey
came upon him and, seeing him, was filled with compassion. [34]Approaching him, he bandaged his wounds, treating them with oil and
wine. And hoisting him onto his own animal, he brought him to an inn
and took care of him. [35]And in the morning, taking out two denarii, he
gave them to the innkeeper and said, 'Take care of him, and whatever you
may spend additionally, I will pay you when I return.' [36]Which of these
three seems to you to have become a neighbor to the man who fell prey to
the robbers?" [37]And he said, "The one showing mercy." And Jesus said
to him, "You go and do likewise."[x]

[38]And as they journeyed, he entered into a certain village and a certain woman named Martha welcomed him into the house. [39]And this
woman had a sister named Mariam who, sitting beside the Lord at his
feet, was absorbed in his teaching. [40]But Martha was preoccupied with
much serving; and standing over him, she said, "Lord, doesn't it make
any difference to you that my sister has left all the work to me? So tell her
to help me!" [41]And answering, the Lord said to her, "Martha, Martha,
calm down! You are anxious and worried about many things, [42]but few
things are needed, really only one. Mariam chose the good portion for
herself, and I for one shall not take it away from her."

11

[1]And it came about as he was in a certain place praying, as he finished, a certain one of his disciples said to him, "Lord, teach us a prayer,
just as John also taught his disciples." [2]And he said to them, "When you
pray, say this:

> Father,
> May your name be revered.
> May your Spirit come upon us and sanctify us.
> [3]Give us each day your bread.
> [4]And forgive us our sins,
> For we ourselves forgive everyone indebted to us.
> And do not permit us to be led into temptation."

[5]And he said to them, "Suppose one of you has a friend who comes

x. A damning depiction of the most characteristic representatives of the Torah as uncaring monsters, much inferior to a Samaritan who stood outside the pale of Judaism.

to him at midnight saying, 'Friend, lend me three loaves, [6]for a friend of mine arrived at my house from a long journey and I have nothing to set before him.' [7]Would you answer him from inside, 'Don't bother me, the door has been shut and my children surround me in bed. I can't get up to get you anything'? [8]I tell you, even if you won't get up and give him what he asks simply because he is your friend, still on account of his being such a nuisance you will get up and give him as many loaves as he needs just to get rid of him. [9]And I tell you, ask and it will be given you. Look for it and you will find it. Keep knocking and the door will be opened to you. [10]For it is only the one who asks that receives, and only the seeker who finds, and it is only to the one who knocks that the door opens. [11]And which of you fathers, if his son asks him for a fish, will hand him a snake instead of a fish? [12]Or what sort of a father, if his son asks for an egg, would hand him a scorpion? [13]And if you, being sinners, still know to give good gifts to your children, how much more can you depend on your Father to give a Holy Spirit from heaven to those who ask him?"[y]

[14]And he was casting out a demon and it was mute. And it happened that as the demon was leaving, the mute man spoke. And the crowds marveled. [15]But some of them said, "It is plain magic! By Baal-Zebul, ruler of the demons, he casts out demons." [16]And others challenged him, daring him to produce a sign from heaven. [17]But knowing what was going through their minds, he said to them, "Every kingdom divided against itself is laid waste, and houses will collapse against one another. [18]And if even the adversary was divided against himself, how will his kingdom remain standing? I say this because you say I cast out demons by means of Baal-Zebul. [19]But if I cast out demons by Baal-Zebul, by what authority do your sons cast them out?[z] Ask them what they think of your logic. [20]Suppose it is by means of a finger of God that I cast out demons? In that case the kingdom of God has overtaken you! [21]When the strong man, well armed, guards his palace, his possessions are safe. [22]But when someone stronger overtakes him and prevails over him, he relieves him of his armor on which he had relied and distributes his weapons.[a] [23]Whoever is

y. This refreshing message of compassion was something new for those who feared the thunderbolts of a God who had people executed for gathering sticks on the Sabbath.

z. Note that Jesus seems to refer to Jewish scribes and their exorcists as belonging to a different religion than his own. According to Marcion, they did.

a. The strong man, for Marcion, is the Creator, his creatures being his possessions. The stronger man is the Father, who by his gracious mission of salvation despoils the Creator of his creatures as they become the Father's adopted children.

not with me is against me, and whoever does not join me in the harvest scatters seed instead. [24]When the unclean spirit departs from a man, he wanders through arid places seeking relief, and failing to find it, he says, "I will return to my dwelling that I left." [25]Once he arrives, he finds it tidied up and newly furnished. [26]Then he goes and rounds up seven other spirits even more wicked than himself, and entering, he makes himself at home. And the last state of that man becomes worse than the first."[b]

[27]And it happened that, as he said these things, a certain woman from the crowd raised her voice and said to him, "Blessed the womb that bore you and the breasts that nursed you!" [28]But he said, "Rather, blessed the ones who hear the command of God and keep it."[c]

[33]"No one having lit a lamp hides it, nor places it under a bushel basket, but on the lamp stand so whoever enters may see the light. [34]Well, the lamp of the body is your eye; when your eye is focused, your whole body is seen clearly. When it is misbehaving, you can't see your hand in front of your face. [35]So watch out that you do not imperceptibly lose your focus. [36]Thus, when you are wholly transparent, with nothing to hide, you will be a shining example like the lamp that shines its light on others."

[37]So as he was out speaking, a Pharisee asks him to dine with him. And entering, he reclined at table. [38]But the Pharisee was shocked to see that he did not baptize his hands before the dinner. [39]But the Lord said to him, "Now you of the Pharisee sect purify the exterior of the cup and of the dish, but your own interior is full of robbery and wickedness. [40]Fools! Didn't the one who made the outside make the inside, too? [41]At any rate, give away those possessions, the desire for which fills your hearts, and behold, the whole thing is purified for you, inside and out.

[42]"But woe to you, the Pharisees, because you tithe the mint and the rue and every single herb and ignore the call and the love of God.[d] [43]Woe to you Pharisees! Because you love to be shown the chief seat in the synagogues and the deferential greetings in the market places. [44]Woe to you because you are like the unmarked graves which people walk right over

b. This is the fate of the twelve and their benighted followers: thinking to have advanced beyond Judaism to a new dispensation, they now suffer the worst of both worlds, being neither Jews nor true Christians. They would have been better off sticking with Judaism.

c. Marcion, an encratite, taught universal celibacy for the baptized. Thus, the contrast here is between childbearing and keeping the word of God.

d. Marcion's Christ rejects the Torah as a collection of distractions and minutiae.

never knowing." [45]And one of the canon lawyers, answering, said to him, "Teacher, saying such things, you insult us, too!" [46]And he said, "If the shoe fits, wear it! Because you burden people with unwieldy loads which you yourselves make not the slightest effort to budge. [47]Woe to you because you construct monuments for the prophets, and it was your fathers who killed them in the first place! [48]You testify against yourselves. You are endorsing your fathers' deeds: they killed—you build! [52]Woe to you canon lawyers! For you hid the key of knowledge; you did not enter yourself and you prevented those who wanted to enter." [53]And as he got up and left, the scribes and the Pharisees became livid with rage and began a campaign to bait him with all kinds of trick questions to embarrass him publicly.

12

[1]As a crowd of many thousands gathered, to the point of trampling one another, he began speaking, first to his disciples. "Be on your guard against the insidious leaven of the Pharisees, in other words, hypocrisy.[e] [2]And there is nothing covered up which will not be revealed, nor hidden that will not be made known. [3]Therefore, whatever you said under cover of darkness will be heard in the light, and whatever you whispered in the ear in the private rooms will be proclaimed from the roof tops. [4]And friends, I say, you have nothing to fear from those who can kill you but can do nothing more than that. [5]No, I will warn you whom to fear. Fear the one who, after killing, has authority to throw you into the Valley of Hinnom. Yes, I tell you, fear this one![f]

[8]"But I tell you, whoever confesses allegiance to me in the presence of others, one like a son of man will acknowledge him in the presence of God. [9]And whoever repudiates me in the presence of others will himself be repudiated in the presence of God. [10]And everyone who shall say a thing against a human being, it will be forgiven him, but the one who blasphemes against the Divine Spirit will not be forgiven. [11]And when they haul you in before synagogues and rulers and authorities, do not worry about how or what you may speak by way of apologia or what you should say. [12]For the Holy Spirit will teach you in that very hour the things you ought to say."

[13]And someone out in the crowd said to him, "Teacher, tell my

---

e. Clearly, Jesus anticipated the very real danger of the twelve lapsing into Judaism's insidious Pharisaism, which Marcion believed had happened.

f. The Creator and Law-giver is a fearsome tyrant, worse than persecutors. He is not the Father.

brother to divide the inheritance with me!" [14]But he said to him, "Man, who made me the executor?" [15]And he said to him, "Watch out! Be on your guard against every kind of covetousness. Because no one's worth is a matter of how many possessions he has."

[16]And he told them a parable, saying, "The land of a certain rich man bore well. [17]And he deliberated, reflecting, "What am I to do? Because I lack sufficient space to store my harvest." [18]And he concluded, "I know! I will do this: I will pull down my barns and I will build bigger ones, and there I will store all my wheat and my goods. [19]And I will be able to say to myself, 'My boy, you have many goods laid up for many years to come. So relax: eat, drink, be merry!' And he did so. [20]But God said to him, 'Fool! This very night they clamor for your soul. Then all this which you so carefully prepared—who will inherit it?' [21]See the fate of one who sees to his own treasure but is not rich where God is concerned."[g]

[22]And he said to his disciples, "That is why I tell you, do not be preoccupied with the necessities of life, what you will find to eat, nor about your body, nor what you will find to wear. [23]For one's life is more than mere survival, and the body more than a mannequin. [24]Think of the ravens, how they neither plant crops nor harvest them. They do not maintain warehouses or barns and God sees to it that they are fed. How different you are from birds! [25]And who here has the ability to add a cubit to his height by worrying about it? [26]If you cannot do even that, why bother worrying about the rest? [27]Think of the lilies, how they waste no time at spindle or loom, but I assure you, not even Solomon in all his finery was adorned like one of them. [28]What pitiful faith you have! [29]Do not busy yourselves with obtaining food and drink and do not sweat over it. [30]For these are matters all the heathen nations pursue, but your Father knows your situation, that you need these things. [31]Instead, seek admittance to his kingdom and all these things will be provided you. [32]Do not fear, little sheepfold, because the Father was quite pleased to give you the kingdom.[h] [33]Sell your possessions and give alms. Furnish yourselves purses that do not wear out, an inexhaustible treasure in the heavens where no

g. Judaism naturally saw material wealth as the blessing of the Creator and meant to be enjoyed by his favorites. Marcion's God is not the Creator, and for Marcion, material wealth distances one from the Father. "Whoever loves the world and the things of the world, the love of the Father is not in him" (1 John 2:15).

h. Marcion would see here a contrast between "God," who provides for his creatures, and "your Father," who may be expected to be much more generous with his adopted children than the Creator is with his animal creations.

burglar comes near it, nor do moths devour your heavenly robes. [34]For
wherever your treasure is located, your heart will be there, too. [35]Be
dressed and ready, lamps burning, [36]like men expecting their lord when
he returns from the wedding reception, so that whenever he appears they
may be ready to open immediately to his knock. [37]Good for those slaves
whom the lord will find waiting when he arrives. Amen: I say to you, he
will don an apron, tell them to recline at table, and he will wait on them
one by one. [38]And if he arrives in the second watch or the third and finds
them so, good for them!

[39]"But be sure of this. If the master of the house knew what hour to
expect the thief, he would have prevented his digging through the walls of
his house. [40]You, too, be prepared because a man will come at some hour
you do not expect." [41]And Peter said, "Lord, are you directing this parable just to us or to the reader, too?" [42]And the Lord said, "What do you
think? Who fits the description of the faithful, prudent steward, whom
the lord will appoint over his household staff to give them their meals at
the proper time? [43]That slave will be very glad when his lord arrives and
finds him carrying out his duties. [44]Truly, I tell you, he will put him in
charge of all his possessions. [45]But suppose that slave says to himself, 'My
lord delays his arrival' and starts to beat the servant boys and serving
maids and starts to eat and drink and to get drunk; [46]the lord of that slave
will appear unexpectedly one day, undetected while the slave is in a stupor, and he will have him drawn and quartered and assigned a place
among the unfaithful. [47]That slave who knew his lord's will, but failed to
prepare for his return or to do his will, will receive many lashes. [48]The
one who didn't know and did things worthy of a flogging will be beaten
with only a few lashes. But from everyone to whom much was given,
much shall be expected. And of whomever was entrusted with much, they
will ask much more. If the shoe fits, wear it.[i]

[49]"I came to hurl fire onto the earth, and how I wish it were already
ignited! [50]And I have a baptism to be baptized with, and how I dread it till
it is over. [51]Surely you don't think my mission was to give peace to the
earth? Rather, I tell you, division! [52]For from now on, there will be five
divided in the same house, three versus two, and two versus three.

---

i. Marcion would surely have seen in these parables not a teaching about the judgment of sinful individuals by the Father, who does not, after all, judge or punish, but rather a condemnation of the unfaithful stewards of Christ's legacy, the twelve apostles. This is underlined by Peter's question. Paul, on the other hand, as well as Marcion and his followers, will be blessed by Christ, the returning Lord.

[53]Father will be divided against son and son against father, mother versus daughter and daughter against the mother, mother-in-law against her daughter-in-law and daughter-in-law against the mother-in-law."

[54]And he said also to the crowds, "When you see a cloud rising over the west, at once you say, 'A storm is coming,' and so it happens. [55]And when a south wind is blowing, you say, 'It will be hot,' and so it happens. [56]Hypocrites! You know well enough how to interpret the earth and the sky, but how is it you do not know what to make of this time? [57]And why do you not even judge for yourselves the just verdict? [58]For as you go with your accuser to a ruler, while still on the road, try to settle with him or he will haul you before the judge and the judge will hand you over to the bailiff and the bailiff will throw you into prison. [59]I tell you, you will never come out of there until you pay the very last lepton."[j]

13

[1]On the same occasion, some were present reporting to him about the Galileans whose blood Pilatus mixed with that of their sacrifices. [2]And answering, he said to them, "Do you deem these Galileans worse sinners than the common run of Galileans because they have suffered these things? [4]Or those eighteen on whom the tower in Siloam collapsed, crushing them—do you consider them debtors worse than the rest of the Jerusalemites?"[k]

[10]And he was teaching in one of the synagogues on the Sabbath. [11]And behold, a woman having a spirit of infirmity eighteen years was present, and she was bent double, unable to straighten up completely. [12]And seeing her, Jesus summoned her and said to her, "Woman, you have been released from your infirmity!" [13]And he laid his hands on her, and at once she was straightened out and worshipped God. [14]But the synagogue ruler, upset that Jesus healed on the Sabbath, retorted and said to the crowd, "There are six days on which one ought to work, so come then and be cured, and not on the Sabbath day!" [15]But the Lord answered him and said, "Hypocrites! Doesn't every one of you untie his ox or his donkey from the manger on the Sabbath and lead it away to give it a drink? [16]And this woman, being a daughter of Abraham, whom, behold, the adversary bound these ten years and eight, hadn't she every right to be

---

j. No doubt, Marcion understood the accuser to be the Creator, prosecuting sinners for their failure to keep his commandments. One could flee this vengeance by taking refuge with the merciful Father.

k. Marcion's deity was not in the business of punishing people.

loosed from this bond on the Sabbath day?"[l] [17]And as he said these things, all opposing him were put to shame, and all the crowd rejoiced at all the glorious things happening through him.

[18]So he said, "What is the kingdom of God like? And what can I compare it to? [19]I know! It is just like a grain of mustard which a man took and planted in his garden, and it grew and grew into a tree and the birds of the sky found lodging in its branches." [20]And again he said, "What may I compare the kingdom of God to? [21]It is like yeast which a woman took and hid in three measures of meal until finally the whole thing was leavened."[m]

[22]And he journeyed through cities and villages, making his way to Jerusalem. [23]Someone said, "Lord, what if only a few are saved?" And he said to them, [24]"Try to squeeze through the door frame because many, I assure you, will try to enter and will not be equal to it. [25]For when the householder gets up to shut the door, and you begin to congregate outside and pound on the door, saying, 'Lord, open up! It's us!' he will say to you, 'You are total strangers to me.' [26]Then you will try another angle, 'Remember? We ate and drank across the table from you and you taught in our streets.' [27]And he will reply, telling you, 'You are total strangers to me, I tell you! Get out of here, all workers of unrighteousness!' [28]There will be weeping and grinding of teeth when you Jews see the righteous and all the prophets in the kingdom of God, but you being held outside."[n]

14

[1]And it came about, as he entered the dwelling of one of the leaders of the Pharisee sect on a Sabbath to eat bread, they were observing him closely. [2]And behold, a certain man with dropsy appeared before him. [3]And answering their expectant stares, Jesus spoke to the canon lawyers

l. The analogy implies that God lacks the elementary consideration for his own creature that a farmer would show for his livestock. By contrast, Jesus and his Father will show that mercy instead.

m. Scholars as diverse as G. Campbell Morgan and Bernard Brandon Scott have pointed out the incongruity of this positive symbolic use of leaven, or yeast. In Jewish tradition, it is always a symbol for evil corruption. But this would have posed no problem for Marcion.

n. Marcion would have understood this parable, which need not be applied point for point, as warning of the shock of Jews who hope for salvation, refusing to believe it was available from a God unknown to them, since they refused to believe there was a saving God distinct from the Old Testament deity. Indeed, they will discover to their chagrin that they are talking to the wrong God—he does not know them!

and Pharisees, saying, "Is it legal to heal on the Sabbath or not?" [4]And they were silent. And taking hold of him, he cured and dismissed him. [5]And to them he said, "Whose son or ox shall fall into a pit and you will not at once pull him out on the Sabbath?" [6]And there was nothing they could say to these things.[o]

[7]And he told a maxim to the other dinner guests, observing how they scrambled for the places of honor, saying to them, [8]"Whenever you are invited by anyone to a wedding reception, do not recline in the place of honor, for someone more prestigious than you may have been invited by the host, [9]and the one who invited you both will come and say to you, 'Give your place to this man,' and you will slink down to the last place. [10]Instead, when you are invited, go recline in the last place so that when your host comes, he will say to you, 'Friend, what are you doing down here? Go up higher!' Then you will shine before all your fellow guests. [11]Because whoever exalts himself will be humiliated, and whoever humbles himself will be exalted."[p]

[12]And he said also to the one who had invited him, "When you plan a dinner or a supper, do not call your friends or your brothers or your kinsmen because they might return the favor, and that would be your sole reward. [13]But when you plan a party, invite the poor, maimed, blind. [14]Then you will be blessed because they have no means to repay you, and you will be repaid by inclusion in the resurrection of the just."

[15]Hearing these things, one of those at the table said to him, "Amen! Blessed is he who eats bread in the kingdom of God!" [16]And he said to him, "Too bad you won't be one of them! A certain man gave a great supper and invited many. [17]And he sent his slave at the hour of the supper to say to the invited guests, 'Come, because now it is ready.' [18]And as one man, they all began to beg off. The first said, 'I, uh, bought a farm and I need to go out and look it over. Render my apologies.' [19]And another said, 'I, er, bought five yoke of oxen, and I need to go try them out. Render my apologies, will you?' [20]And another said, 'I, um, married a woman and she will not let me out of the house. You know how it is.' [21]And coming up to the house, the slave reported these things to his lord. Then, deeply hurt, the master of the house ordered his slave, 'Go out quickly

o. Again, the point is to demonstrate the merciless legalism of the Torah.

p. Marcion might well have seen this as a parable of the arrogance of Judaism in claiming primacy in God's affections. Little did Jews realize they had been superseded by the gentiles, who arrive late to the eschatological banquet but receive the seat of honor.

into the streets and lanes of the city and bring the poor, maimed, blind and lame in here." 22Afterward, the slave said, 'Lord, what you ordered has been done and there is still room.' 23And the lord said to the slave, 'Go out into the roads and hedges and round up the vagrants so my house may be filled. 24For I tell you that not one of those I originally invited will get as much as a taste of my supper!'"[q]

25And great crowds gathered around him, and turning to them he said, 26"If anyone comes to me and does not disdain his father and mother and his wife and children and brothers and sisters and, besides this, even his own life, he cannot be a disciple of mine. 27Whoever does not carry his cross and come after me, he cannot be a disciple of mine.[r] 28For which of you, if he wanted to build a tower, does not first sit down and estimate the cost to see if he has enough to complete the job? 29Otherwise, having laid the foundation and not being able to finish, those who see it begin to ridicule him, 30saying, 'This man began to build and was not able to finish.' 31Or what king would go forth to attack another king in war without first sitting down and deliberating whether he, with his ten thousand troops, is going to be able to meet the challenge of the one who fields twenty thousand against him? 32If not, while his foe is still far off, he will send a delegation to ask terms of peace. 33Even so, every one of you who does not say good-bye to all his possessions cannot be a disciple of mine. 34*Thus, salt tastes good, but suppose the salt were to become useless? What else could you possibly use to season salt?* 35*It is suitable neither for the soil nor for the compost heap. They sprinkle it outside. Whoever has ears to hear, let him hear.*"[s]

15

1Now all the customs agents and backsliders were drawing near to hear him. 2And both the Pharisees and the scribes murmured much against him, saying, "This fellow welcomes backsliders and eats with them." 3And he told them this parable, saying, 4"Which of you men, if he had a hundred sheep and lost one of them, would not leave the ninety-nine in the desert to go look for the lost one until he finds it? 5And finding

q. For Marcion, this would denote the general refusal of Jews to accept the Father's invitation and the baton being passed to the Paulinist gentiles, who must have made up the bulk of Marcionism.

r. Marcionites produced a great many martyrs, as even their opponents admitted.

s. Marcion saw Catholic Christianity as having lost the distinctive tang of the true gospel.

it, he places it across his shoulders rejoicing. [6]And coming into the house, he calls together the friends and the neighbors, saying to them, 'Rejoice with me because I found my lost sheep!' [7]I tell you, there will be the same joy in heaven over a single backslider repenting than over ninety-nine righteous individuals who require no repentance. [8]Or what wife, if she had ten drachmas and she lost one, would not light a lamp and sweep the house and look carefully until she finds it? [9]And finding it, she calls together the friends and neighbors, saying, 'Rejoice with me because I found the drachma which I lost!' [10]Even so, I tell you, God rejoices greatly whenever a single backslider repents."

16

[1]And he said also to the disciples, "There was a certain rich man who had a steward, and he received a complaint that this man was wasting his possessions. [2]And calling him, he said to him, 'What is this I hear about you? Make a full report of your stewardship, for you can no longer continue as steward.' [3]And the steward said to himself, 'What am I to do now that my lord takes the stewardship away from me? I am not equal to digging. I am ashamed to beg. [4]I know what to do! This way, when I am removed from the stewardship, they will welcome me into their own houses.' [5]And summoning each one of his lord's debtors, he said to the first, 'How much do you owe my lord?' [6]And he said, 'A hundred baths of oil' And he told him, 'Not any more! Take your bill, sit down quickly, and write fifty.' [7]Then he said to another, 'And how much do you owe?' And he said, 'A hundred cors of wheat.' He tells him, 'Not any more. Take your bill and write eighty.' [8]And his master said, 'That sly devil! It's a shame to lose him!' It goes to show you: the natives of this world are more prudent among their own kind than those who come from the light.[t]

[9]And I tell you, make friends for yourselves by the mammon of unrighteousness so that when it runs out, they may welcome you into the permanent homes. [10]The one faithful in the least is faithful also in much, and the one who is unrighteous in the least is unrighteous also in much. [11]Thus, if you were not faithful with unrighteous mammon, who will entrust the true riches to you? [12]And if you were not faithful in that which

t. Here is a picture of the twelve and their successors. At first they were "stewards of the mysteries of God," but the Father discharged them for their ineptitude. They made things worse by selling out to Judaism through compromise after compromise. It was shrewd, considering the numerical success of Catholic Christianity, but it had nothing to do with the sons of the light, the adopted faithful of the Father, according to Marcion.

belongs to another, who will give you mine? [13]No domestic slave can be enslaved to two lords at the same time! Either he will hate the first and love the second or he will pledge loyalty to the first and he will despise the second. You are not able to be slaves to both God and Mammon."[u] [14]Now the Pharisees, who were money lovers, heard all these things, and they scoffed at him. [15]And he said to them, "You are those who make yourselves look good to mortal men, but God knows your hearts. For whatever is highly exalted by mortal men is an abomination in the eyes of God![v]

[16]"The Law and the Prophets pointed to John; from then on, the advent of the kingdom of God is proclaimed and everyone forces his way into it. [17]But it is easier for sky and earth to pass away than for one of my sayings to pass away.[w] [18]Everyone dismissing his wife and marrying another commits adultery, and the one who marries a wife dismissed from a husband commits adultery.[x]

[19]"Now a certain man was rich, and he used to dress in a purple robe and a fine linen tunic, and he feasted lavishly every day. [20]And a certain poor man, Lazarus by name, had been dropped off by his gate, covered with sores [21]and desiring to satisfy himself with what fell from the rich man's table. But even the dogs came and licked his sores. [22]And it came time for the poor man to die and to be carried away by the angels to Abraham's welcoming embrace. And the rich man also died and was buried. [23]And looking up from Hades, writhing under torture, he glimpses Abraham at a great distance welcoming Lazarus. [24]And calling, he said, 'My Lord! Pity me and send Lazarus to dip his finger in water and cool my tongue, for I am suffering in this flame.' [25]But God said, 'My child, remember how you received your good things in your lifetime? Well, Laza-

---

u. One suspects Marcion saw the contrast as between the Creator God and the Father of Jesus Christ, who must be distinguished. The Creator, understood as Mammon, would be like the Buddhist idea of Mara, not precisely an evil being, but the lord of the material world, the Bhagavad, traditionally a good and "bounteous Lord" in Hinduism. Marcionism, though non-retributive, was nonetheless world-denying and ascetical. Thus, the blessings of the Creator are temptations for the true elect who know a higher, purely spiritual standard.

v. What a radically world-negating saying!

w. Since the Law is not binding for those who accept the Father, it is the words of Jesus, not those of the Torah, which are eternal.

x. Though an advocate of the celibacy gospel, Marcion rejected divorce for those already married, as in 1 Cor. 7:8-10, 25-31, where Paul tells the married not to separate even though he wishes all were celibate.

rus likewise received the bad. Accordingly, he is now comforted here but you are suffering. [26]And part of the arrangement is that a great chasm has been firmly installed so that any who wish to cross over here cannot, nor may any cross over from there to us for salvation.' [27]And he said, 'I ask you, then, my Lord, to send him to my father's house, [28]for I have five brothers, and let him warn them of what awaits them lest they too end up in this pit of torture.' [31]But God said to him, 'Look, if they are deaf to Moses and the Prophets, they'd find a way to laugh off someone rising from the dead, too.'"[y]

17

[1]He said to his disciples, "It is impossible for scandals not to come, but woe to him by whom they come! [2]He is better off if a millstone is put around his neck and he is thrown overboard than if he should scandalize one of these new converts. [3]Consider your situation. If your brother sins, rebuke him, and if he repents, forgive him. [4]And if he sins against you seven times a day, and seven times turns back to you saying, 'I'm sorry,' forgive him."

[5]And the apostles said to the Lord, "Give us more faith." [6]And the Lord said, "You either have it or you don't. If you have faith the size of a mustard grain, you would have said to this sycamine tree, 'You! Pull up your roots and transplant yourself in the sea'—and it would have obeyed you. [7]But which of you, having a slave out plowing or herding, when he comes in from the field, would say to him, 'Come at once, recline at table'? [8]Instead, wouldn't you say to him, 'Prepare something for my dinner, change your clothes and serve me until I finish eating and drinking, and after these tasks, you may eat and drink'? [9]Do you thank the slave because he did the things he was commanded? Hardly. [10]Do likewise when you do all the things commanded."[z] [11]And it came about that as he went to Jerusalem, he passed through the middle of Samaria and Galilee. [12]And as he entered into a certain village, ten men with skin disease met him, standing at a distance, [13]and they lifted their voices to say, "Jesus, master, pity us!" [14]And seeing them, he said to them, "Go and let the priests inspect you." And it happened that as they went, they were purified. [15]But one of them, realizing that he was cured, returned worship-

y. Here Marcion would see unveiled a perfect portrait of the Hebrew God, the God of Abraham, Moses, and the scriptures, who is just but merciless, not willing to even hear petitions on behalf of the damned.

z. This bespeaks the Marcionite axiom that righteousness should be unmotivated by the prospect of reward or punishment.

ping God at the top of his lungs, [16]and he fell on his face at his feet, thanking him. And he was a Samaritan. [17]And answering, Jesus said, "I could have sworn all ten were purified, but what happened to the other nine? [18]I found none returning to give thanks to God except for this foreigner.[a] There were many lepers in Elisha's time, but none of these did he cure: only Naaman the Syrian." [19]And he said to him, "Rise up and go. Your own faith has cured you."[b]

[22]And he said to the disciples, "The time will come when you will be desperate to see day one of the reign of one like a son of man, and you will not see it. [23]And they will say to you, 'Look there! Look here!' Do not go away or follow.[c] [24]For just as the lightning flashes from one horizon and shines clear over to the other horizon, so will the one like a son of man be in his day. [25]But first he is obliged to suffer many indignities and to be disowned by this race.

[26]"And as it was at the time of Noah, it will be the same in the time when one like a son of man comes. [27]They were eating, drinking, men marrying and giving women in marriage, business as usual, until that day when Noah entered the ark and the cataclysm came and destroyed everything. [28]Likewise, as it was at the time of Lot: they were eating, drinking, buying, selling, planting, building, [29]but on that day when Lot fled Sodom it rained fire and brimstone from the sky and destroyed everything. [30]It will be the same on that day when one like a son of man is revealed. [31]In that day, whoever finds himself on the roof with his vessels in the house, let him not come down to retrieve them but rather let him climb down the fire escape and run. And the one working in the field when that hour strikes, let him not turn back to the things left behind. [32]Remember what happened to Lot's wife! [33]Whoever may try to save his skin, he will lose it, and whoever will let it go, he will preserve it. [34]I tell you, in this night there will be two on one couch—the one will be taken and the other will be left. [35]There will be two grinding grain together—

a. Luke 4:27

b. As with the good Samaritan parable, the idea of noble Samaritans is symbolic of Marcionite-Pauline Christians, something elsewhere reflected by the association of Simon Magus, who was a Samaritan, with Paul and the Marcionite teaching in the Preaching of Peter. I have omitted vv. 20-21 as ecclesiastical Lukan redaction in accord with the motif of de-eschatologizing the Gospel.

c. Marcion allowed that the Jewish messiah, an anointed Davidic king, would come to liberate Jews. Just let him not be confused with Jesus, either in his first or second coming! The point is not that these imposters are not the Christian messiah, but rather that Jesus is not the Jewish messiah.

the one will be taken but the other will be left! [36]*There will be two in the field—the one will be taken and the other will be left.*" [37]And answering, they say to him, "Taken where, Lord?" And he said to them, "Where do you think? You'll find the body where the vultures are circling."

18

[1]And he told them a parable to show they were obliged always to pray and not give up, [2]saying, "There was a certain judge in a certain city, not fearing God and caring nothing for human rights. [3]And there was in that city a widow, and she came before him saying, 'Exonerate me from the slanders of my accuser!' [4]And for a while, he would not. But after these appeals, he said to himself, 'Though indeed I do not fear God or give a fig for justice, [5]if only because this widow annoys me, I will exonerate her; otherwise, she will finally assault me.'" [6]And the Lord said, "Do you hear what the unrighteous judge says? [7]Will not God, by any means, render justice to his chosen people who cry out to him day and night, even though he takes his time over them? [8]I tell you, he will vindicate them suddenly, but will it be too late? When the one like a son of man comes, will they all have given up in despair?"

[9]And he aimed this parable at people who congratulated themselves for their own righteousness, despising everyone else. [10]"Two men went up to the temple to pray, the one a Pharisee, the other a customs agent. [11]The Pharisee standing there prayed these things silently: 'God, I thank you that I am not like the rest of mankind, rapacious, unjust, adulterers, or even as this customs agent! [12]I fast twice a week, I tithe everything I get.' [13]But the customs agent, keeping his distance, dared not even look up toward heaven but beat his breast, saying, 'God, be merciful to me, a sinner!' [14]I tell you, this is the man who descended the temple mount to his dwelling having been accepted by God rather than that other one. Because every one who exalts himself will be humiliated, and every one who humbles himself will be exalted."[d]

[15]And they brought babies to him, hoping he would touch them and utter some blessing, but seeing it, the disciples rebuffed them. [16]But Jesus called to them, "Let the children come to me. Don't stop them! The kingdom of God is made of such as these. [17]Amen: I tell you, whoever does not welcome the kingdom of God as a child will be forever excluded from it."[e]

---

d. A scathing parody on the confession of one's piety in Deut. 26:12-15.

e. For Marcion, those accepting salvation are adopted as children, hence the rebirth imagery.

[18]And a certain ruler questioned him, saying, "Good teacher, what am I to do that I may inherit age-long life when I die?" [19]And Jesus said to him, "Just a moment, if you please. Why do you call me 'good'? No one is good except one: God the Father. [20]And why ask me? Surely you already know the ten commandments: do not commit adultery, do not murder, do not steal, do not testify falsely, take care of your father and mother. Well?" [21]But he said to him, "I observed all these since I was young." [22]But hearing this, Jesus said to him, "You still lack one thing. Sell everything, whatever you own, and distribute the price to poor people, and then you will have the treasure in heaven that you seek. And come follow me."[f] [23]But hearing these words, he became very sad, for he was extremely rich. [24]And seeing his reaction, Jesus said, "You see with what difficulty those who have property enter into the kingdom of God! [25]For it is easier for a camel to squeeze through the hole of a needle than for a rich man to enter into the kingdom of God." [26]And his hearers said, "If even God's favorites cannot enter heaven, then who can save himself?"[g] [27]And he said, "Human impossibilities are possible for God."

[28]And Peter said, "Behold, abandoning our own things, we followed you."

[35]And it came about as he came close to Jericho, a certain blind man sat at the roadside begging. [36]And hearing the noise of the approaching crowd, he asked what this might be. [38]And he shouted, saying, "Jesus, son of David, pity me!" [39]And those in the vanguard rebuked him, telling him to be silent, but he only shouted all the more, "Son of David, pity me!" [40]And coming to a stop, Jesus ordered him to be brought to him. And as he approached, Jesus questioned him. [41]"What do you want me to do for you?" And he said, "Lord, I want to see again." [42]And Jesus said to him, "Then see again! Your own faith has healed you." [43]And at once he saw again, and he followed him, worshipping God. And all the people with sight gave praise to God.[h]

19

[1]And having entered, he passed through Jericho. [2]And behold, there was a man called by the name Zacchaeus, and he was a chief customs

f. The Marcionite gospel provided a higher path to salvation than the Torah. The young man instinctively intuits this, and Jesus, adopting a Socratic pose, elicits the inquirer's realization of it.

g. See previous note g on p. 290.

h. Marcion would have seen the man's blindness as consisting in his misidentification of Jesus with the Davidic messiah.

agent and was rich. [3]And he tried to see Jesus, who he was, and he was not able on account of the crowd because he was small in stature. [4]And having run forward to the front of the crowd, he climbed onto a sycamore tree so that he might see him because he was about to pass that way. [5]And as he reached the spot, Jesus, looking up, said to him, "Zacchaeus, hurry on down, for today I must stay in your house." [6]And he hastened down and welcomed him, rejoicing. [7]And seeing this, everyone murmured, saying, "Did you see that? He went in to lodge with an impious man." [8]And Zacchaeus said to the Lord, "Not so! Behold, the half of my possessions I give to the poor, Lord, and if I find I have accused anyone of anything falsely, I restore fourfold." [9]And Jesus said to him, "Today salvation[i] came to this house. [10]For a man ought to seek and to save what was lost."[j]

[11]And he said, "A certain nobleman made ready for a journey. And having summoned ten of his slaves, he gave them ten minas and said to them, 'See to business while I am away.' [15]And it came about when he returned, he ordered his slaves to be summoned, these to whom he had given the silver, so as to know what any of them had gained in business. [16]And the first came and said, 'Lord, your mina gained ten minas.' [17]And he said to him, 'Well done, good slave!' [18]And the second came and said, 'Your mina, Lord, has made five minas.' [19]And he said to this one also, 'Well done, you good and faithful slave!' [20]And the other came and said, 'Lord, behold your mina. I took the precaution of storing it away in a napkin. [21]You see, I feared you, because you are an austere man; you pick up what others laid down on the gambling table and you harvest crops that others sowed, seizing the fields of your debtors.' [22]He says to him, 'Out of your own mouth I will judge you, wicked slave! You say you knew me for an austere man, picking up what others laid down and harvesting what others sowed? [23]Then why on earth did you not take my money to the banker's table? That way, on my return, I would have withdrawn my money with interest.' [24]And to those standing by he said, 'Take the mina from him and give it to the one who has ten minas.' [25]And they said to him, 'Lord, he already has ten minas.' [26]I tell you that to everyone who has the knack, more will be given, and from the one lacking it, even what little money he has will sooner or later be taken away."[k]

---

i. The name "Jesus" means "salvation."

j. The man is already a good Jew and is being saved precisely from bondage to the Hebrew God.

k. Another depiction of the stern and merciless character of a God who is excessive in both his demands and his punishments. I have omitted the ill-fitting sub-

[28]And when he had said these things, he went in front of the crowd, going up the mountain path to Jerusalem. [47]And he was teaching day by day in the temple, but the archpriests and the scribes and the leading citizens looked for a way to eliminate him, [48]and they found nothing they could do, for all the people hung upon his every word.

20

[1]And it came about one day as he was teaching the people in the temple and evangelizing, the archpriests and the scribes with the elders came up to him [2]and spoke, saying to him, "Tell us, with what authorization do you do these things? Who gave you this authorization?" [3]And answering, he said to them, "First I will question you on one matter. You tell me. [4]Remember the baptism of John? Was it authorized by God in heaven or only by mortals?" [5]And they huddled, debating, whispering, "It's a trap. If we say 'from heaven,' he will surely say, 'Then why didn't you believe in him when you had the chance?' [6]But if we say, 'from mortal men,' the people will stone us, for they have been deluded that John is a prophet." [7]So they answered that they did not know where John's mandate came from. [8]And Jesus said to them, "Why am I not surprised? Then I'm afraid I cannot tell you the authority behind my actions, either."[l] [19]And the scribes and the archpriests tried to get their hands on him there and then, but they checked themselves, fearing the people.

[20]And they kept a close eye on him, sending shills posing as sincere inquirers, hoping to seize on something he might say to use as grounds to hand him over to the law and authority of the governor. [21]And they questioned him saying, "Teacher, we know that you speak and teach frankly. You do not tell wealthy donors what they want to hear, but you teach the way of God forthrightly. [22]So then, is it legal to pay tribute to Caesar or not?" [23]But aware of their duplicity, he said to them, "Show me a denarius. Whose image and epigraph does it have?" And they said, "Caesar's, of course." [25]And he said to them, "So give Caesar's coins to Caesar and God's coins to God."[m] [26]And they were unable to pounce on anything he said in the presence of the people; and greatly taken aback at his answer, they were silent.

---

plot of the man going far away to receive a kingship, then killing his enemies, as this seems to represent an ecclesiastical Lukan redaction in the interest of a de-eschatologizing motif, also found in Acts 1:6-8.

l. Jesus is not being coy. The Jewish authorities do not suspect the existence of his Father, a separate God.

m. One must suspect that Marcionite exegesis would see here another con-

[27]Next some of the Syndics came to him, those who in opposition to the Pharisee sect say there is no resurrection, and they questioned him, [28]saying, "Teacher, Moses wrote us that if a brother of anyone should die leaving a wife behind him and not leave a child, the brother should take his wife and beget heirs for his brother. [29]Suppose there were seven brothers and the oldest took a wife and died childless. [30]And the second *married her, and he died childless*; [31]and the third married her; and similarly the seven did not leave children and died. [32]And last of all, the woman died. [33]In this 'resurrection,' which one's wife will she become? After all, all seven of them had her as their wife at one time or another." [34]And Jesus said to them, "The sons of this temporal world marry and are given in marriage, [35]but the ones whom God deems worthy to gain that aeon by the resurrection from the dead neither marry nor are they given in marriage. [36]For neither can they die anymore, for they are the same as angels and sons of God, being born of the resurrection." [39]And answering, some of the scribes said, "Teacher, well said!" [40]For they no longer dared ask him about anything.[n]

[41]So he turned the tables and said to them, "How can they say the Christ is a son of David? [42]For David himself says in the scroll of Psalms, 'The Lord said to my lord, Sit at my right, [43]till I make the necks of your enemies a footstool for your feet.' [44]Therefore, David calls him 'lord.' So how can he be his son?"[o]

[45]And in the hearing of all the people, he said to the disciples, [46]"Be on guard against the scribes, who delight in parading around in flowing robes and basking in deferential greetings in the marketplaces and being shown to the platform seats in the synagogues and the head tables at banquets, [47]who evict poor widows and make a performance of long prayer. These will receive more severe judgment than common sinners!"

---

trast between the Jewish and Marcionite deities. "Caesar" is a divine tyrant, while "God" here denotes the Father. In both cases, the Old Testament God, as the Creator, is associated with money.

n. Note that not only does Marcion's gospel lack the scriptural argument on behalf of the resurrection, it seems to accept the Sadducaic assumption that the doctrine is unscriptural. The difference for Marcionites is that it's a point in its favor! Resurrection is incompatible with the biblical law of levirate marriage, so one must reject that law. The arrangement assumes there is but an "immortality of influence," since the point of the law is to provide for the continuation of the late husband's name. This is completely pointless if one believes in literal immortality.

o. The passage again shows the incompatibility of Christian Christology with Jewish messianism, with which Jesus has nothing to do.

21

[1]And looking up, he watched the rich tossing their donations into the
treasury box. [2]And he saw a certain poor widow throwing in two lepta,
[3]and he said, “Truly, I tell you that this poor widow put in more than all
the rest, [4]for all these gave out of their abundance, but this woman gave
out of her privation everything she had, all her living.”

[5]And as some spoke about the temple, that it has been decorated
with fine stones and gifts, he said, ‘These things which you behold, the
days will come when stone will not be left on stone that will not be
thrown down.” [7]And they questioned him, saying, “Teacher, when will
these things happen? And what will be the signal that they are about to
happen?” [8]And he said, “Watch out so that you are not deceived, for
many will appear trading on my name, saying, ‘It is I!’[p] Do not go off after them. [9]But when you hear of wars and upheavals, do not panic; for
these things are destined to happen first, but the end is not imminent.”

[10]Then he said to them, “Nation will be pitted against nation and
kingdom against kingdom. [11]And there will be great earthquakes in scattered places, and plagues and famines. [12]But before all this, they will get
their hands on you and persecute you, delivering you up to synagogues
and thence to prisons to be hauled before governors and kings for the
sake of my name. [13]It will be an opportunity for you to bear witness and
attain salvation. [14]So resolve not to practice beforehand to defend yourselves, [15]for I will give you a mouth and wisdom which none of your opponents will be able to resist or confute. [16]And you will be betrayed even
by parents and brothers and relatives and friends, and they will put some
of you to death. [17]And you will be hated by all on account of my name.
[19]By your endurance, you will save your souls.

[20]“But when you see the Abomination of Desolation standing where
it ought not to be,[q] [25]there will be signs in the sun, moon, and stars; and
on earth nations will cower with dread and alarm at the roaring of the sea
and its waves, [26]while people faint from fear and anticipation of what is
coming on the whole inhabited earth. For the Powers of the heavens will
be shaken from their thrones [27]and then those angels will see one like a
son of man coming from the skies with power and great brilliance. [28]And
when these things start to happen, stand up straight and raise your heads
because your redemption is fast approaching!”

---

p. Omitting here the ecclesiastical Lukan redaction.

q. Omitting again the redaction.

[29]And he told them a parable: "Look at the fig tree, and for that matter, all the trees. [30]As soon as they burst into leaf, you can see for yourselves that summer is near. [31]So you also know, when you see these things transpire, that the kingdom of God is near. [32]Amen: I tell you, the sky and the earth shall by no means pass away until these things all happen. [33]The sky and the earth will pass away, but my words remain forever.[r] But as to that day or hour, no one knows, not even the angels in heaven, nor the son, but only the Father. [34]Consider your position, that your hearts not become gross with wild feasting and drunken binges and the worries of life so that the day suddenly overtakes you, [35]like a hunter's trap. For it will overtake everyone sitting on the face of all the earth. [36]But be ever vigilant, praying earnestly that you may be counted worthy to escape all these impending things."

[37]Now he was teaching daily in the temple, going out each night to lodge in the mountain named for its olives. [38]And every morning all the people came to him in the temple to hear him.

22

[1]Now the feast of unleavened bread called Passover drew near. [2]And the archpriests and the scribes looked for a way to destroy him, but carefully and "not during the Passover," they said.[s] For they feared the reaction of the people. [3]And the adversary entered into Judas called the False One, who was included in the ranks of the twelve. [4]And going off, he discussed with the archpriests and captains how he might deliver him up. [5]And they rejoiced, and they readily agreed to give him money. [6]And he agreed and looked for a good opportunity to deliver him to them away from the crowd.

[7]And when the day of unleavened bread came, when it is required to kill the Passover lamb,[t] [8]they said to him, "Where do you want us to prepare?" [10]And he told them, "Behold, as you go into the city, a man carrying a pitcher of water will meet you. Follow him into the house he enters; [11]and you will tell the inn-keeper, 'The teacher says to you, Where is the guestroom where I may celebrate the Passover with my disciples?' [12]And that man will show you a large second-story room already furnished and ready. Prepare it there." [13]And going, they found things just as he told them, and they prepared for Passover.

---

r. Restoring here the Markan material transferred by the redactor to Acts1:7.

s. Restoring text moved by the redactor to Acts 12:4.

t. Omitting the redaction.

[14]He reclined, and the apostles with him. [15]And he said to them, "With eager expectation I anticipated eating this Passover with you before I suffer." [19]And taking a loaf, having given thanks, he broke it and gave it to them, saying, "This is my body, *which is being given for you. Do this for my memorial.* [20]*And similarly he took the cup after supper, saying, "This cup is the covenant in my blood, being shed for you.*[u] [21]And yet, behold the hand of my betrayer on the table with my own! [22]For one goes when his preordained time comes, but woe to that individual through whose agency he is delivered up!"

[23]And they began to argue among themselves which one of them it might be who was about to do this. [24]And there was also contention among them over who should be in charge after Jesus was gone. [25]So he said to them, "The kings of the gentiles lord it over them, and the ones wielding authority over them are often called Euergetes.[v] [26]But not among you Jews![w] But let the greater among you become like the younger, and the governor like the servant. [27]After all, who is greater, the one reclining or the one serving? Isn't it the one reclining? And yet here I am in your midst as the one serving![x] [28]But you are those who have stuck with me throughout all my trials, [29]and as my Father conferred kingship on me, so I confer it on you.[y]

[31]"Simon, Simon, the adversary has insisted on his right to sift you twelve like the wheat. [32]I, however, requested that in your own case, your faith may not give out."[z] [33]And he said to him, "Lord, I am ready even to go to prison and to death with you!" [34]But he said, "I tell you, Peter, a rooster will not have time to sound today before you three times deny knowing me."[a]

---

u. If this passage occurred in its longer version in Marcion's gospel, the new covenant theme implies that Jesus had inaugurated a new arrangement that was incongruous with the Passover. This would seem to fit Marcionite discontinuity theology better than Catholic continuity theology. The ecclesiastical Lukan redactor may have omitted the italicized portion to shift the salvific emphasis from the Passion to baptism in Jesus' name, dispensed sacramentally by the church.

v. A common epithet chosen by Hellenistic kings meaning "benefactor."

w. Marcion would no doubt have seen here a claim that God, the divine king of Jews, was anything but a benefactor.

x. Cf. John 13:4-5.

y. The invitation to enter his Father's kingdom, that of a new God, is something Jewish people would not have anticipated.

z. The ecclesiastical Lukan redaction, omitted here, has Peter turning again and strengthening his brothers—a preview of Acts.

a. Thus Jesus knew his hopes for Peter were to be disappointed. The disci-

39And leaving there, he went, as was his habit, to the Mountain of the Olives, and the disciples also followed him. 40And arriving at the place he sought, he said to them, "Pray that you may be spared the trial." 41And he distanced himself about a stone's throw from them, and kneeling, he prayed, 42saying, "Father, if you will, take this hemlock cup away from me. Nevertheless, let your will be done, not mine." 43*And an angel from heaven appeared to him, strengthening him.* 44*And entering into agony, he prayed all the more earnestly and his sweat became like drops of blood spilling onto the ground.* 45And getting up from prayer, he returned to the disciples only to discover them sleeping, depressed from grief. 46And he said to them, "How can you sleep? Get up and pray, otherwise you will find yourselves unprepared for temptation."[b] 47And while he was still speaking, a mob arrived, and the one called Judas, one of the twelve,[c] advanced before them and approached Jesus to kiss him. 48But Jesus said to him, "Judas, would you betray a man with a kiss?" 52And Jesus said to the archpriests and captains of the temple police and elders who were surrounding him, "You came armed with swords and clubs, as against some desperado? 53Every day I was with you in the temple and you did not apprehend me; but then, this is your hour when darkness holds sway."

54And arresting him, they marched him to the house of the archpriest, and Peter followed him at a safe distance.[d] 55And once they had lit a fire in the center of the courtyard and seated themselves together around it, Peter sat among them. 56And noticing him, a certain serving maid of the archpriest sitting near the light scrutinized him and said, "This man was with him, too." 57But he denied it, saying, "I do not know him, woman!" 58And after a short while, another noticed him and said, "You, too, are one of them." But Peter said, "Man, I am not!" 59And after an hour's interval, a certain other one declared emphatically, "It's true: this man was with him, for he too is a Galilean!" 60But Peter said,

ple's faith would fail, even perhaps contradicting the Catholic legend that Peter died a martyr's death. The adversary sifted the twelve like wheat, resulting in the corruption of Christianity at their hands, in Marcion's view.

b. The twelve repeatedly demonstrate their lack of spiritual fortitude, repeatedly disappointing Jesus. Yet, they were to be the leaders of the church!

c. Scholars have wondered why Judas's membership in the college of the twelve is again mentioned when the reader already knows it. The answer is to emphasize how representative he is of the entire group, all of them traducers of the true gospel and thus betrayers of Jesus.

d. This is symbolic of the spiritual distance between Jesus and the one reputed to be his successor.

"Man, I don't know what you're talking about!" And at once, while he was still speaking, a rooster crow sounded. [61]And turning, the Lord looked at Peter, and Peter recalled the Lord's prediction, how he told him, "Before a rooster sounds today, you will deny me three times." [62]And going outside, he cried bitterly.[e]

[63]And the men in charge of him mocked him as they beat him, [64]and blindfolding him, they taunted him, saying, "Prophesy! Which one hit you?" [65]And they said many other things against him, blaspheming. [66]And when day dawned, the presbytery of the people convened, both archpriests and scribes, and they led him away to their Sanhedrin.[f] They suborned false witnesses who said, "This man never stops railing against the holy place and the Law! We have heard him say, 'I will destroy this place and will abolish the customs Moses bequeathed us!'" But their testimonies did not agree. [67]Finally, the archpriests and the scribes addressed him, saying, "If you are the Christ, tell us!" And he said to them, "Why bother? If I tell you, there is no way you will believe me. [68]And if I question you, there is no way you will answer. [69]But from now on, you will see[g] one like a son of man seated at the right of the power of God and coming with the clouds." [70]And they all said, "That means you are the son of God." And he said to them, "If you say I am." [71]And they said, "Is there any further need for witnesses? For we heard it for ourselves from his own mouth!"

23

[1]And standing to their feet, the whole body of them led him before Pilatus. [2]And they started accusing him, saying, "We discovered this fellow corrupting our nation, forbidding people to pay tribute to Caesar, and destroying both the Law and the Prophets, and leading astray both the women and the children.[h] And he makes himself out to be Christ, a king." [3]And Pilatus interrogated him, saying: "So you are Chrestus." And answering him, he says, "If you say so." [4]And Pilatus said to the archpriests and to the crowds, "I find no crime in this man." [5]But they in-

e. Peter is depicted here in no uncertain terms as an apostate, entailing an uncompromising rejection of Petrine spiritual authority.

f. Restoring here material transferred to the Stephen story in Acts 6.

g. Restoring Markan text omitted by the Lukan redaction.

h. Jesus persuaded women to renounce sex and follow him, among them Joanna, who left her husband in what must have been a public scandal. The apostles would elicit similar contempt for doing the same thing in the Acts of Paul, Peter, Thomas, Andrew, and John.

sisted, saying, "He incites the people, teaching throughout all Judea, beginning from all the way in the Galilee to here." [6]And Pilatus, hearing this, inquired whether the man were in fact a Galilean, [7]for it occurred to him that he fell under Herod's jurisdiction. So he remanded him to Herod, who was also in Jerusalem for the feast. [8]And when he saw Jesus, Herod was delighted, for he had for some time wished to see him, having heard about him, and he hoped to see him perform some feat. [9]And he interrogated him with many questions, but he gave no answer. [10]And the archpriests and the scribes stood there hurling accusations at him. And Herod and his soldiers treated him with contempt and mocked him, draping him in royal purple, and packed him off back to Pilatus. [12]And both of them, Herod and Pilatus, became fast friends that day; previously they had been feuding.

[13]And Pilatus, calling together the archpriests and the rulers and the people, [14]said to them, "You brought this man to me as corrupting the people, and behold, examining him in your presence I found this man guilty of none of the crimes you allege against him. [15]And neither did Herod, for he sent him back to us; and it is plain he has done nothing worthy of death. [16]Therefore, I will let him go with a flogging. [17]*For he was obliged to release one prisoner to them at the feast.* [18]But the whole mass shouted, saying, "Take this fellow away and release to us Barabbas!" He was thrown in prison on account of some insurrection in the city and for murder. [20]But again Pilatus appealed to them, wanting to let Jesus go. [21]But they shouted, saying, "Crucify! Crucify him!" [22]But he said to them a third time, "But what evil did this fellow do? I found no reason to put him to death, so I will let him go with a flogging." [23]But they insisted with loud shouting, calling for him to be crucified, and their voices won out. [24]And Pilatus decided to carry out their request. [25]And he released the one thrown into prison for insurrection and murder, whom they requested, but Jesus he delivered over to their will.

[26]And as they led him away, they commandeered Simon, a certain Cyrenian on his way in from the fields, and they placed the cross on him to carry behind Jesus. [27]And a great mass of the people followed him including women who mourned and lamented him. [28]And turning to them, Jesus said, "Daughters of Jerusalem, do not waste your tears on me! Weep on your own account and that of your children; [29]because open your eyes, a time is coming when they will say, 'Blessed are the barren, even the wombs that did not bear and breasts which never nursed.'[i]

i. This expresses the Marcionite gospel of celibacy: encratism.

[30]Then they will begin to say to the mountains, 'Crush us!' and to the hills, 'Hide us!' [31]Because if they do these things when a tree is running with sap, who knows what may happen when it is sere?"

[32]And other criminals, too, were led off with him to be killed. [33]And when they reached the place called the Skull, there they crucified him and the criminals, one to the right and one to the left. [34]*And Jesus said, "Father, forgive them, for they don't realize what they are doing!"*[j] And dividing up his garments, they cast lots. [35]And the people stood watching. And the rulers also scoffed, saying, "Some savior! If this fellow is the Christ of God, the Elect One, let him save himself." [36]And the soldiers joined in mocking him, approaching him to offer him vinegar [37]and saying, "If you are the king of the Jews, save yourself!"[k] [38]And there was also an epigraph above him: "This is the king of the Jews." [39]And the hanged criminals blasphemed him, saying, "Aren't you the Christ? Save yourself and us as well,"[l] [42]and, "Jesus, remember me when you come to your throne!"[m] [44]It was by now about the sixth hour[n] and darkness appeared over the whole earth until the ninth hour, [45]the sun having gone out, and the hanging veil of the holy place was torn down the middle. [46]And shouting with a loud voice, Jesus said, "Father, I entrust my spirit into your hands!" And saying this, he breathed his last. [47]And the centurion, seeing what happened, worshipped God, saying, "This man really was God's son!"[o] [48]And all the crowds gathering together at the spectacle, once they saw what happened, beat their breasts and went back home. [49]And all the ones known to him stood far away, even the women accompanying him from the Galilee, watching these things.

[50]And behold, a man named Joseph, a counsel member, a good and just man, [51]not having consented to the council and their action, was from Arimathea, a city of the Jews, and was also looking forward to the kingdom of God; [52]this man approached Pilatus and requested custody of

j. Here is the essence of the Marcionite gospel.

k. Of course, according to Marcion, he isn't king of the Jews, which may be why he does not come down and destroy his enemies.

l. Omitting the ecclesiastical Lukan redaction.

m. This quip is a direct quotation from Diodorus Siculus where a nobleman mocks a deluded slave's pretensions to kingly lineage. Ur-Lukas had added it as an example of the mockery aimed at Jesus. The Ecclesiastical Redactor made it into the sincere wish of a repentant thief in the interest of apologetics, anticipating a "Paul on trial" motif in Acts.

n. 12:00 midday.

o. Omitting the ecclesiastical Lukan redaction.

the body of Jesus. [53]And taking it down, he wrapped it in linen and placed him in a tomb cut from living rock where no one was yet laid out. [54]And it was the Day of Preparation, and the Sabbath was coming on fast. [55]And the women who had accompanied him out of the Galilee followed behind him and saw the tomb and how the body was positioned. [56]And returning to the city, they prepared spices and myrrh and then rested on the Sabbath in accordance with the Law.

24

[1]On the first of the week, while it was still quite early, they arrived at the tomb carrying the spices which they prepared. [2]And they discovered the stone rolled away from the tomb, and [3]venturing inside, they did not find the body of the Lord Jesus. [4]And it happened, as they were perplexed about this, behold, two men appeared beside them in shining clothing. [5]And as they were stricken with terror and bowed with faces to the ground, they said to them, "Why are you looking for a living man among the dead? [6]*He is not here, but was raised!*"[p] [9]And returning from the tomb, they reported all these things to the eleven and to all the rest. Now they were Maria the hairdresser and Joanna and Maria mother of James and the rest with them, who told these things to the apostles. [11]And these words seemed like nonsense when spoken aloud, and they gave the women no credence. [12]*Then Peter got up and ran to the tomb, and bending down, he saw the linen wrappings by themselves and left, speculating over what might have happened.*[q]

[13]And behold, on the same day, two of them were journeying to a village situated sixty stadia from Jerusalem, called Emmaus, [14]and they discussed with each other all these things that had happened. [15]And it happened that as they were walking and discussing, Jesus himself approached and journeyed with them, [16]but their eyes were prevented from recognizing him. [17]And he said to them, "What is it you are discussing among yourselves as you walk?" And they came to a halt, visibly downcast. [18]Then one of them called Cleopas answered him, "You must be the only pilgrim to Jerusalem ignorant of what has happened there these last few days." [19]And he asked, "What events?" And they told him, "Those surrounding Jesus the Nazarene, regarded as a prophet of powerful deeds and words by God and the whole populace. [20]Our archpriests and

p. Omitting the redaction.

q. Again, Peter is so spiritually obtuse, he cannot imagine what has happened despite Jesus' many clear predictions of it.

rulers handed him over to be sentenced to death, and they crucified him. [21]We had pinned our hopes on him as the one destined to liberate Israel. Yes, besides all this, three days have passed since then. [22]Worse yet, some women of our sect alarmed us. They were at the tomb early this morning [23]and they discovered his body missing. They returned with the tale that they had even seen a vision of angels who said he was alive. [24]Some of our companions went to the tomb and found it to match the women's description: they saw no trace of him." [25]And he said to them, "You fools! Doesn't it even occur to you to believe the things that he spoke?" [28]And they drew near the village where they were journeying, and he made as if to journey farther. [29]And they urged him, saying, "Stay with us, for it is toward evening and the day has declined." And he went in to stay with them. [30]And it came about, as he reclined at table with them, that taking the loaf, he blessed it and, having broken it, handed it to them. [31]And their eyes were opened up and they recognized him—and he became invisible to them. [32]And they said to each other, "Did not hope begin to rekindle inside us as he spoke to us on the road?" [33]And getting up despite the lateness of the hour, they retraced their steps to Jerusalem, and they discovered the eleven and those with them already gathered, [34]*saying, "The Lord was really raised and appeared to Simon!"*[r] [35]And they recounted the events on the road and how he was recognized by them in the act of breaking the loaf.

[36]And as they were saying these things, he stood in their midst.[s] [37]But frightened and terror-stricken, they thought they beheld a spirit. [38]And he said to them, "Why do you tremble, and why do such thoughts arise in your hearts? [39]Look at my hands and my feet, that it is I myself! A spirit has not flesh as you can see in my case."[t] [41]And with them still thinking it too good to be true, and stunned, he said to them, "Do you have any food here?" [42]And they handed him part of a broiled fish, [43]and taking it, he ate it before their eyes. [47]And he told them that repentance for forgiveness of sins must be proclaimed in his name among the nations.[u]

r. Could this be a Catholicizing gloss intended to restore Petrine primacy? It deflates the climax of the Emmaus story in a comical way.

s. This implies, again, and contrary to the ensuing scene, that Jesus has a celestial body not bound to the laws governing gross matter.

t. Marcion, like other docetists, would have seen in this proof that no spirit has flesh, as Jesus' case demonstrated, since as a spirit, he had none.

u. Omitting here the ecclesiastical Lukan redaction.

11.
The Epistle to the Galatians

TRADITIONALLY, THE EPISTLE TO THE Galatians is considered among the bedrock writings of Paul. Even F. C. Baur considered it a genuine work of the apostle. Martin Luther interpreted the text as setting forth the doctrine of justification by grace through faith, the balm of the introspective conscience tortured by its own unworthiness. He took Paul to reject the possibility of salvation by morally righteous works since all human beings were already lost in sin. More recently, though already in Baur's *Paul: The Apostle of Jesus Christ,* scholars have found that the "works" in view were probably the ritual works required of Jews and proselytes according to the Torah. These were the ethno-cultural markers of Jewish distinctiveness, which were perceived as a burden by gentiles contemplating conversion to Jewish Christianity. The point of Galatians, then, would be to defend Paul's Torah-free gospel for gentiles.

But Bruno Bauer, Rudolf Steck, W. C. van Manen, and others have observed numerous contradictions and anachronisms implying that the work is multi-layered, having gone through the hands of various redactors, and that even the original form was pseudepigraphical. Van Manen judged that Marcion himself wrote the first draft. I take Marcion as the author, partly because of the striking comment of Tertullian (*Against Marcion,* 5: chap. 3) that "Marcion, discovering the Epistle of Paul to the Galatians, ... labors very hard to destroy the character of these Gospels which are published as genuine and under the names of the apostles." If we take "discover" in its strongest sense, the comment implies no one had seen the epistle before. Like Hilkiah, the priest who "discovered" Deuteronomy, or Joseph Smith,

who "discovered" the Book of Mormon, Marcion actually wrote the Epistle to the Galatians.

But in my view, Marcion wrote only what we read as chapters 3-6. The first two chapters, in their first form, were added subsequently by Marcionites as a rebuttal to the story in Acts, which attempts to co-opt Paul, and with him Paulinists (Marcionites, Encratites, Gnostics), for Catholic Christianity. That portion of the letter has suffered a number of subsequent interpolations as indicated. Even in the original Marcionite section, Marcion is writing as Paul and his audience is a group of early followers from his own area who have begun to yield to the missionary propaganda of catholicizing Christianity. It is the Catholic attachment to the Torah that Marcion combats, easily imposing the earlier Pauline struggle with Ebionite Jewish Christians onto the controversies of his own day.

1

[1]Paul, an apostle, not sent from any human authority, *neither by human beings,* but by Jesus-Christ and God the Father, the one who has
raised him from the dead, [2]and with me, all the brothers,[a] to the congregations of Galatia:

[3]May you enjoy the favor and the protection of God our Father and
the Lord Jesus-Christ, [4]the one who has given himself for the sake of our
sins, so he might rescue us out of the present *evil* age in accordance with
the will of our God and Father, [5]to whom all worship is due throughout
ages multiplied by ages. Amen.

[6]I am astonished that already this soon you are detaching yourselves from the one who called you by the favor of Christ, embracing a different
message of salvation, [7]which in fact is not another, only that there are
some bothering you and intent on perverting the news of Christ. [8]As for
that, even if we or some angel from heaven should proclaim to you some message of salvation besides the one we proclaimed to you, let him be excommunicated! [9]Let me just repeat that for emphasis. If anyone proclaims a message of salvation beside the one you first welcomed, let him be excommunicated![b]

---

a. "Brothers" denotes itinerant missionaries.

b. This anticipates the claim that the Mosaic Torah was the gift of angels, not of God (cf. 3:19-20 below); thus a Judaizing gospel must be the creation of angels, too.

[10]Is that blunt enough for you? Am I ingratiating myself with my audience now or am I calling down God? Or am I mincing words to flatter
men? For if I were still concerned to meet the expectations of mere mortals, I would have chosen some other task than being a slave of Christ.
[11]For I am letting you know, brothers, that the news preached by me is
not human in origin, [12]for it was not from human beings that I received it,
nor was I instructed in it;[c] on the contrary, it was revealed by Jesus-
Christ.[d] [13]*You are acquainted with my actions while I belonged to Judaism,*[e] *how I went to insane lengths persecuting God's community and laid
it waste,* [14]*and progressed in Jewish religion beyond many contemporaries in my race, being many times over a zealot for my ancestral traditions.*[f]
[15]And yet, when God, who had watched over me since my umbilical cord
was cut, [16]thought it choice irony to reveal his Son to me,[g] and called me
by his favor in order for me to proclaim him among the nations, I paused
not to consult with flesh and blood, [17]neither did I go up at once to Jerusalem to the apostles previous to me.[h] No, I took off for Arabia and went
back to Damascus.[i] [18]*It was only after three years that I went up to Jerusalem to consult with Cephas and remained with him fifteen days.*[j] [19]*But
I did not so much as see any of the other apostles except for James, the
Lord's brother.*[k] [20]Now in this recounting, I swear before God: I am not

---

c. What lies in the background here is Paul's instruction by Ananias of Damascus, as in Acts 9:17-19.

d. The same claim is borrowed for Peter in Matt. 16:16-18.

e. As Bruno Bauer and J. C. O'Neill point out, the use of this term is anachronistic, presupposing two distinct religions, which was not yet clear in Paul's day. The word was used in the first century, but only to offset Judaism from paganism. It had not yet come to be used vis-a-vis Christianity. O'Neill brackets verses 13-14 as an interpolation, veering off the train of argument.

f. Note the seeming equation of Jewish zeal with the persecution of Christians.

g. Here we find the influence of Euripides' *Bacchae,* where Dionysus hypnotically compels the conversion of his persecutor, Pentheus, as part of a death trap. See also the irony-laden words of Christ in Acts 9:16.

h. Again, contra Acts 9:26-27.

i. The writer presupposes the narrative of Acts since Damascus has not been mentioned previously, as it is in Acts 9.

j. He remembers the exact duration fourteen years later? This sounds like a narrator simply positing plausible times and seasons for the sake of a story.

k. In Tertullian's treatise, *Against Marcion,* he does not mention this first visit, implying the text of Galatians did not yet mention it either. If it had, Tertullian surely would have made hay of it: it would have clearly implied Paul's subor-

lying![l] [21]From there I went into the regions of Syria and Cilicia. [22]*And still
I remained known only by reputation to the congregations in Christ of
Judea.* [24]*Never having seen me in person,*[m] [23]*they only heard rumors:
"The one who persecuted us now preaches the very religion*[n] *he was then
intent on destroying!"*[o] [25]*And they worshipped God on account of my
case.*

2

[1]Then, after an interval of fourteen years, I went up to Jerusalem
again with Bar-Nabas, taking along Titus, too. [2]And I went up, summoned by a revelation.[p] And I laid out before them the news as I proclaim it among the nations, in private session with those of great repute,
for fear I might have been running off course.[q] [3]But my companion Titus,
a Greek, was not compelled to be circumcised. He was willing to go
along with it voluntarily as a concession. [4]But on account of the pseudo-

---

dination to the Jerusalem authorities, a point Tertullian would have used against Marcion. He didn't, though, implying that he didn't have it to use. Thus, it is a later insertion designed to abet the notion that Paul did go to Jerusalem to submit himself to the twelve as soon as he was able. "Again" was added to 2:1 at the same time by way of harmonization. Tertullian mentions the visit of 2:1-10 apparently as *the* visit, not as a *second* visit.

l. Obviously, this is a rebuttal to another account, widely known, in which Paul was a delegate of mortal agencies and had at once submitted himself to the previous apostles. Either the writer is responding to Acts 9 or that was the common version, which our writer seeks to overthrow, rewriting history in the interests of later sectarian strife.

m. Contrary to Acts 9:28-30.

n. The term here literally reads "the faith," generally considered to be post-Pauline usage.

o. This is a crucial admission that the whole notion of Paul as a persecutor is the product of popular rumor. In all probability, it is a distortion of the Ebionite claim that Paul, as an anti-Torah Christian, had opposed the true Christian religion—theirs. In a later time, when few remembered the sectarian divisions of an earlier generation, this version was misunderstood as if Paul, a non-Christian, had physically persecuted believers in Christianity *per se*.

p. Note that he is not making an appearance in Jerusalem at the behest of any human authority, contra Acts 15:2.

q. Here we find a retrojection into imagined apostolic times of Marcion's own visit to Rome to join the church there and voluntarily disclose his doctrine. Obviously at the time, he took seriously the reputation of the Roman Church for authority, disdaining it only after they had rejected his doctrine. In the same way, Muhammad very often in the Koran retells the stories of Israelite prophets, including Moses, Abraham, and Noah, in terms modeled quite closely upon himself and his conflicts.

brothers who had sneaked into the session[r] in order to spy on our freedom from the Torah that we gentiles have in Christ, thinking they would enslave us, [5]we yielded to them in submission but for an hour *in order to preserve the news for you.*[s] [6]But as for those esteemed to be something great[t]—what they were then makes no difference to me now; God is impressed by no man's clout—those of repute added no proviso to me. [7]*On the contrary! Once they saw how I had been entrusted by God with the news for the uncircumcised, just as Peter was for the circumcised,* [8]*the one energizing Peter for an apostolate to the circumcised energizing me also, but to the nations,* [9]*and acknowledging the favor shown me by God, James and Cephas and John, the ones reputed to be Pillars,*[u] *offered to me and to Bar-Nabas the good right hand of partnership, dividing the territory: we would henceforth go to the nations, they to the circumcised,*[v] [10]except that we should not forget the Poor,[w] the very thing I was eager to do in any case!

[11]But when Cephas arrived in Antioch, I stood up to him publicly be-

r. He thus seeks to hide the fact that this Torah faction was part of the core group of Pillars, "those of repute." He implies that no one knew them at that time for what they turned out to be: Judaizing hardliners.

s. The reference is to the token circumcision of Titus, another version of which is told in Acts 16:3, where Timothy has been substituted for Titus.

t. Not coincidentally, in Acts 8:9 we find pretty much the same disdainful phrase characterizing Simon Magus. In Acts we are reading the other side of the same argument.

u. This is cosmic terminology denoting the Atlas-like function of upholding the vault of heaven, perhaps signaling a channel of communication with heaven, much like Jacob's ladder, the *axis mundi.* Accordingly, James the Just is said to have served as high priest for the Jerusalem Church. After his death, it was possible for Jerusalem to fall because it no longer retained the protection of his presence. The exalted office of the Pillars would thus have been analogous to the later Jewish legend of the Fifty Righteous, whose presence on earth guaranteed God's protection no matter how sinful everyone else became (Gen. 18:24-26).

v. As William O. Walker Jr. points out, vv. 7-9 must be an interpolation since they rudely interrupt the sequence of 6 and 10, where the original means the Pillars imposed no condition upon Paul and Barnabas except for the relief collection. Note that the interpolator slips and calls Cephas "Peter," his more familiar name.

w. The Jerusalem *Ebionim,* in other words, for whom Paul is constantly raising money in his churches. This is a fictive version of Marcion's own initial gift of a large sum to the Roman Church, which they refunded after deeming him a heretic. Its refusal is echoed in Acts 8:18-24; 21:20-26; 24:17-18; Rom. 15:16, 30. This proviso, representing tribute money to be paid the Jerusalem Church as the price of recognition of Paulinism, obviously should follow verse 6.

cause he was blatantly out of line.[x] [12]For before a certain party arrived from James,[y] he used to dine with the gentiles,[z] but when this one arrived, he stood down, segregating himself, fearing the circumcision faction. [13]And the rest of the Jews played hypocrite along with him so that even Bar-Nabas was led astray by their hypocrisy. [14]But as soon as I noticed they were not walking the straight path of the news, I said to Cephas in front of everyone: "If you, being a Jew, nonetheless live like a gentile,[a] where do you get off forcing the gentiles to Judaize?[b] [15]Physically, we are Jews, not sinners from the nations, [16]and since we know that a person is not accepted as righteous by virtue of deeds of Torah, but by belief in Christ-Jesus—even we believed in Christ-Jesus in order that we might be counted righteous by token of belief in Christ and not by deeds of Torah because no human being will ever be counted righteous by deeds of Torah. [17]But if, in the very effort to be counted righteous through Christ, we were found to be sinners no better than the gentiles, does that make Christ a facilitator of sin? Never! [18]But if I start to rebuild the very things I demolished, this is what makes me a transgressor. [19]For it was by means of the Torah that I died relative to the Torah, escaping its grasp so I might live relative to God. I have been crucified alongside Christ. I live no more, but Christ now inhabits my body; as a result, what I now undergo in the flesh I endure by the belief in *the Son of* God loving me and giving himself up on my behalf. [21]I for one do not presume to turn my nose up at the mercy of God: for if it is really through the Torah that salvation comes, then Christ's death is moot!"[c]

3

[1]O senseless Galatians! Who is it who has cast a spell on you? The crucifixion of Jesus-Christ was plainly demonstrated from scripture be-

x. This was apparently because Peter signaled he was promoting a different gospel that would involve Judaizing the gentiles (v. 14), thus incurring the curse of *anathema* (1:8-9).

y. This party consisted of delegates sent to check on the implementation of the Jerusalem decree dealing with basic kosher laws (cf. Acts 15:30-32).

z. Acts 10

a. Peter behaves like a gentile by eating non-kosher food, something implied here but made clearer in Acts 10:12-15; 11:3. See Frank R. McGuire, "Galatians as a Reply to Acts," *Journal of Higher Criticism* 9 (Fall 2002), 161-72.

b. Against his better judgment, Peter decided to acquiesce to James by imposing the stipulations of the Jerusalem decree (Acts 15). The decree remains hidden here but nonetheless lurks in the background, as McGuire points out.

c. This impromptu speech corresponds very closely to that ascribed to Peter

fore your eyes.[d] 2This is the only question I want you to answer me: Did you experience the onrush of the Spirit by performing deeds of Torah? Or by hearing about faith? 3Are you so obtuse that, having started with the Spirit, you are now seeking perfection by deeds of the flesh? 4Did you endure so much for nothing? 5That is, if it was in vain! So the one who supplies the Spirit to you, performing powerful works among you—does he do it in response to deeds of Torah or to hearing about faith? 6Just as Abraham believed God's promise and it was reckoned as merit to him, 7know this: the ones marked by faith, these are sons of Abraham. 8And scripture, foreseeing that God would count the nations righteous by virtue of their faith, pre-evangelized Abraham: "In you all the nations will be blessed."[e] 9So it is those marked by faith who are eulogized with the believing Abraham.

10For as many as are marked by deeds of Torah labor under a curse, for it is written: "Cursed is everyone who does not persist in performing all the things written in the scroll of the Torah."[f] 11So it is clear that no one is counted righteous, as far as God is concerned, by keeping the Torah because "the righteous one shall live by faith."[g] 12And the Torah has nothing to do with faith; rather, "the one who performs them shall live by them."[h] 13Christ bought our freedom from the Torah's curse, becoming a curse on our behalf, as we know from scripture: "Cursed is everyone hanging from a tree,"[i] 14in order that the blessing of Abraham might extend to the nations by Jesus Christ, so we gentiles might receive the prom-

---

in Acts 15:7-11, but with a pinch of Romans added. Which apostle is credited with it turns on which one was the pioneer evangelist to the gentiles, an honor Acts gives Peter, while the epistles give it to Paul. German critics of the Tübingen school say Acts adapted the speech from Galatians, whereas Dutch critics claim Galatians adapted it from Acts.

d. As Earl Doherty contends in *The Jesus Puzzle: Did Christianity Begin with a Mythical Christ?* (Ottawa: Canadian Humanist Press, 1999), belief in the crucifixion was derived not from historical memory but from esoteric exegesis of scripture. Thus, for instance, Mark 15 is based entirely on Pss. 22, and Matthew elaborates the story with more details drawn from Zechariah and the Wisdom of Solomon.

e. The sense of the famous benediction, "May God bless me as he did the Hebrew Abraham" (see Gen. 12:2; 18:18), was eventually taken to mean, "Through you (Abraham), all the nations will be blessed."

f. Deut. 27:26

g. Hab. 2:4

h. Lev. 18:5

i. Deut. 21:23

ise of the Spirit[j] through the faith. [15]Brothers, let me speak in human terms: even in the case of a covenant between mere mortals, no one has the liberty to abrogate or to add to it unilaterally. [16]So to Abraham the promises were spoken, and to his seed.[k] It does not say "to his seeds," as if intending many descendants, but as intending a single one. [17]So I say this: the Torah, which came into being after four hundred and thirty years, does not abrogate a covenant previously ratified by God and so abolish the promise. [18]For if what one inherits is conditional upon obeying laws, it is no longer a promise at all. But God gave the inheritance to Abraham by promise.

[19]Then what is the point of the Torah? It was added for the sake of transgressions, to deal with them until the seed should arrive to whom the promise had been made. It was promulgated by angels at the hand of a go-between. [20]Everyone knows there is no use for a go-between to represent a single individual, but God is one individual.[l] [21]Is the Torah therefore opposed to the promises *of God*? Never! For if a law was given that could make one alive, salvation would indeed have come by means of law; [22]but scripture consigns all to sin in order for the promise realized by belief in Jesus-Christ to be made to those who believe. [23]But before faith arrived, we were guarded under the Torah, being preserved for the faith[m] that was about to be revealed. [24]Thus the Torah has become a schoolmaster for us to prepare us to graduate to Christ[n] in order that we might be

---

j. An echo of Acts 2:38-39?

k. Gen. 12:7

l. Here is the seed form of the Marcionite doctrine of the Torah, which is that the Law was given to the world by lesser spiritual entities—angels in charge of the elements (4:3), described in great detail in 1 Enoch 60:11-22, where they are said to dispense rain and snow as needed. To identify them with the Torah was not arbitrary in view of the promise of good weather and lush crops if Israel kept the Torah (Deut. 28:11-12, 22-23). Is this the Pauline toe-hold for the later Marcionite doctrine or is it Marcion's own statement in its earliest form? It would not be surprising if it turned out to be the latter, just as the Gospel of Truth by Valentinus does not contain the whole of the Valentinian system, the latter being his mature development of an earlier insight. So Galatians might be Marcion's own first statement of his doctrine, which he himself subsequently expanded.

m. The new faith, the Marcionite renewal of Christianity in its intended form.

n. How can the same writer identify as a gentile in 2:4; 3:13 and as a Jew here? He doesn't. His tutelage to the Torah occurred in his period of upbringing in Catholic Christianity, which mixed the Torah of Judaism with the revelation of Jesus Christ. Where he does seem to pose as a Jew, it is part of his literary pose as Paul. He is simply inconsistent.

accepted as righteous by virtue of faith; [25]but faith having arrived, we are
out from under the schoolmaster's jurisdiction. [26]For you are all mature
sons of God by token of believing in Christ-Jesus and thus have no need
for the Torah. [27]For each one of you who was baptized into Christ, you
have assumed the likeness of Christ: there can no longer be any Jew nor
Greek; there can be no slave or free; there can be no male and female, for
you are all identical in Christ Jesus.[o] [29]But if you belong to Christ, then
you are a descendant of Abraham, heirs by the provisions of the promise.

4

[1]But let me point out, for as long as the heir remains an infant, even
though he were lord of all existence, he is no different from a slave, [2]under
guardians and stewards until the term his father set at first. [3]It was the
same with us: when we were infants, we had been indentured to the spirits
who control the elements of this cosmos; but when time was almost full,
God sent out his son, who became an infant born of womankind, becoming a Jew under the dominion of the Torah, [5]in order that he might buy
the freedom of those under the dominion of the Torah so we could receive
adoption as sons.[p] [6]And since you are sons, God sent out the Spirit of his
Son into our hearts, crying, "*Abba!* Father!"[q] [7]Thus, you are no longer a
slave but a son, and if a son, also an heir, just as God planned.

[8]Back then, not knowing God, you were enslaved to those who by nature are not gods. [9]But now, knowing God, or better, being known by
God, what are you doing turning back to the weak and destitute elemental

o. Here is the root insight of Christian encratism—the celibacy gospel: sex was the original sin, from which all others stemmed, because it was the result of androgynous Adam's fission into male and female. Subsequent sins begat ever new divisions (rich and poor, slave and free), and further sex acts produced nations (Greek and Jew, Barbarian and Scythian). But baptism into Christ as the Second Adam restores the baptized to a version of the primordial oneness of the androgynous Adam before the Fall. See Wayne A. Meeks, "The Image of the Androgyne: Some Uses of an Image in Earliest Christianity," in Allen R. Hilton and H. Gregory Snyder, eds., *In Search of the Early Christians: Selected Essays* (New Haven: Yale University Press, 2002), 3-54.

p. A major element of the Marcionite doctrine of redemption was that the Father offers to adopt the creatures of the Hebrew Creator. Since human beings are not creations of the Father, they can only become children of the unknown God through adoption.

q. In all likelihood, this Christian prayer has been gratuitously transferred to Jesus himself in Mark 14:36 (cf. Rom. 8:15). It seems artificial there since Mark has excluded all possible witnesses from the scene. He probably assumed Jesus would have used the prayer language familiar to Christians.

spirits whose slaves you want to be all over again? [10]You keep holy days and months of fasting and penitential seasons and canonical calendars! [11]You are scaring me! Have I put in all that work with you for nothing?

[12]Become like I am, brothers, I beg you. For I am just like you! I bear no grudge, for you never did me wrong, [13]and you remember how it was on account of weakness of the flesh that I first preached the news to you, yet you did not disdain my difficulties in the flesh, nor did you disdain me; but instead, you welcomed me as an angel of God, namely, as Christ-Jesus.[r] [14]So what has become of your blessing me? [15]For I swear on your behalf that, if it had been possible, you would have gouged out your own eyes and given them to me! [16]So have I now become the Enemy[s] by speaking the truth to you? [17]They are zealous for you, to be sure, but not to the good, for they wish to isolate you [18]to the end that you may focus your zeal on them. Well, it is always a good thing to be zealous, provided the zeal is for something good and not just when I am present with you, [19]my children, for whom I am undergoing the labor pains all over again till Christ gestates within you. [20]How I wanted to be there with you now so I might change my tone because I don't know what to make of you.

[21]Tell me this, those who want to be under the dominion of the Torah:[t] don't you realize what the Torah says? [22]For it is written that Abraham had two sons, one from the concubine and one from the free woman. [23]But the one from the concubine has been born according to the flesh and the one from the free woman miraculously, according to the promise. [24]These things are to be allegorized as follows: these stand for two covenants, one indeed issuing from Mount Sinai, issuing in slavery, which is Hagar. [25]Hagar is in turn Mount Sinai in Arabia and corresponds to today's Jerusalem, for she is a slave along with her children.[u]

---

r. Many early Christians understood Jesus to be some kind of archangel. See Richard N. Longenecker, *The Christology of Early Jewish Christianity*, Studies in Biblical Theology, 2nd series, vol. 17 (London: SCM Press, 1970).

s. This was the epithet for Paul among Torah Christians who viewed him virtually as an anti-Christ. See Matt. 13:28, where the counterfeit believers, Torah-free Paulinists, are sown like weeds in the field by "the enemy" (see also 3 Peter).

t. He refers to the Catholic Christians.

u. The "enslaved" condition of Jerusalem probably refers to the aftermath of the Roman conquest of CE 70 or CE 136, in either case an anachronism for the historical Paul. In light of this allegory, it is possible the reference to an Arabian ministry (1:17) implies some initial period of preaching Judaized Christianity—circumcision, that is (cf. 5:11). See Francis Watson, *Paul, Judaism and the Gentiles: A Sociological Approach* (New York: Cambridge University Press, 1989), 30-31.

26 But the Jerusalem in heaven above is free, she who is the mother of us
all. 27 For it is written,

> "Be glad, O barren one!
> She who bears not, break forth,
> And shout, she who is without labor!
> For many are the children of the desolate,
> Rather than her who has a husband!"[v]

28 But you, brothers, are children by the promise, like Isaac. 29 And
just as back then the one born in the fleshly manner persecuted the one
born spiritually, it is the same now. 30 But what does scripture say?
"Throw out the concubine and that son of hers! For there is no way the
son of the concubine shall be a co-heir with the son" of the free woman.[w]
31 And we, brothers, are not children of some concubine, but of the free
woman.

5

1 It was to live in freedom that Christ liberated us; so stand firm and
don't allow yourselves to be lassoed and placed back under the yoke of
slavery! 2 Behold! I, Paul,[x] say to you, if you are circumcised, Christ will
do you no good! 3 And I testify again to every human being who embraces
circumcision, he is henceforth obliged to perform all the commandments
of the Torah! 4 You who are deemed righteous by Torah observance, you
were released from the fellowship of Christ; you plunged headlong from
the path of divine favor. 5 For the Spirit moves us to anxiously anticipate
the prospect of vindication—by faith. 6 For as far as Christ Jesus is concerned, neither circumcision makes any difference, nor lack of circumcision, but only faith as it operates through love. 7 You were well on your
way. Who held you back? Who made you so reluctant to be persuaded by
truth? 8 This persuasion does not come from the one who calls you. 9 It
takes only a little yeast to contaminate the whole lump of dough. 10 I have
confidence in the Lord that you will think nothing else, but the one who is
confusing you shall bear responsibility for it, no matter what his status.
11 As for me, brothers, if I still preach circumcision, why am I still being

---

v. Isa. 54:1

w. Gen. 21:10

x. The explicit self-reference, "I, so-and-so," hints at pseudepigraphy, affirming emphatically what should be quietly self-evident and implicit in the genuine writings of a signed author. See also the note at 2 Cor. 10:1.

persecuted? Because then the scandal of the cross would be nullified. [12]I
only wish that those who are upsetting you might chop themselves off!
[13]You were called to be free, brothers—just do not let that freedom
become a pretext for the flesh; but motivated by love, serve one another
as slaves. [14]For the whole of the Torah has been epitomized in a single
maxim, namely, "You shall love your neighbor as yourself." [15]But if you
bite and consume one another, watch out! You will be destroyed by one
another. [16]Now I say, set your sail to the Spirit and you will never act
upon carnal lust. [17]For the flesh lusts against the Spirit and the Spirit contests against the flesh, for the two are locked in stalemate, and thus it is
your own preference that tips the balance, resulting in your act. [18]But if
you are led by the Spirit, you are not under the dominion of Torah. [19]So
the works of the flesh are obvious enough. They include prostitution, impurity, lewd acts, [20]idol worship, sorcery, alienation, discord, jealousy,
grudges, rivalries, divisions, sectarianism,[y] [21]envy, drunken binges, orgies, and such things, of which I forewarn you, as I did before: those who
practice such things will not arrive after death in the world of God.[z] [22]But
the harvest of the Spirit is love, joy, peace, long-suffering, kindness, goodness, fidelity, [23]meekness, self-mastery;[a] no law is required to regulate
these. [24]So those who belong to Christ-Jesus crucified the flesh with the
attendant passions and lusts. [25]If we live in the power of the Spirit, then
let us behave in the newness of the Spirit. [26]Let us not seek empty glory,
the one provoking, the other envying.

6

[1]Brothers, if it should happen that an individual succumbs to some
transgression, it is up to you spiritual ones to win back such a one in a

y. It seems a bit early in the evolution of the Christian movement for sects to be forming if this is really the dawn age of a pioneer apostle's first writings.

z. Here the pseudepigraphist finds himself momentarily confused between his actual scene of writing and that envisioned for Paul: a warning aimed at things now happening or soon liable to happen. He is warning about them *now*. Paul would have *fore*warned these readers in a letter ostensibly penned long before the actual readers will see it. But the writer has himself *fore*warn as well as having Paul "already forewarn" them. Cf. 2 Pet. 3:2, where the pseudonymous writer, pretending to be Peter, forgets that his narratees, the fictive audience, the first Christian generation, are long dead, and he reminds the actual intended readers in the second century of a prediction made long ago by "your apostles," having momentarily forgotten he is posing as one of them.

a. If Marcion is indeed the author, εγκρατεια ("self-mastery" or "self-control") probably refers specifically to celibacy, for which it had become code in the anti-sexual encratite sects of Tatian and others.

spirit of meekness, mindful all the while of how liable to temptation you are yourself. [2]Shoulder one another's burdens, and that way you will keep the law of Christ.[b] [3]For if anyone imagines himself to be something great when in fact he is nothing, he is kidding himself. [4]But let each man point to the quality of his work as proof, and then he will have sufficient reason to brag with reference to himself alone, leaving anyone else out of consideration; [5]for in the judgment, each will have to carry his own load. [6]And let each one who receives catechism in the doctrine of Christ share all worldly necessities with the one catechizing him.

[7]Don't kid yourselves: no one makes a fool of God! [8]For whatever an individual sows, one will reap the same thing. The one who begets physical offspring only supplies more victims to death and corruption. But the one sowing for the Spirit will reap from the Spirit age-long life.[c] [9]And let us not give up hope of reward in doing good deeds, for in good time we shall reap if we do not give up. [10]So then, in the time we have, let us do good to everyone and most of all to the household of faith.

[11]Notice what large letters I have hand-written![d]

[12]All those who wish to cultivate a reputation on fleshly terms, these people compel you to be circumcised, only to avoid incurring the persecution that the cross of Christ must bring. [13]For it is not as if those who are being circumcised keep the Torah themselves; they only want you to be circumcised so they may brag that they were able to get you to do it![e]

---

b. A Marcionite context makes better sense for the origin and meaning of this term than any other hitherto proposed. A "law of Christ" must be the antithesis to the Law of Moses. In fact, it is tantamount to Marcion's call for a Christian canon to replace the Jewish one.

c. Given the real possibility that Marcion is the author of our epistle, we must not ignore the possibility that he here refers to the error of physical, sexual begetting, which will only supply more hostages to the Creator.

d. Ostensibly a mark of authenticity, this detail is actually proof of the reverse. If Paul had really signed the letter thus, it would be self-evident to the reader. But the text masquerades as a subsequent copy of a Pauline letter written decades before. No autograph ever appeared on it. Thus this wording draws attention to something only a second-generation reader, i.e., of what is supposed to be a later copy, would need to have pointed out for him. See Gerald Prince, *Narratology: The Form and Function of Narrative* (Berlin: Walter de Gruyter & Co., 1982), 34: "Sometimes, in diary novels, for example—even the physical appearance of a narration and the very practice of narration are commented on." Not coincidentally, our pseudepigraphist prepared the way for this with his reference to the apostle's eye troubles in 4:15.

e. One must suspect the writer has in mind the trickery of Simeon and Levi (Gen. 34:13-29), employing a demand for circumcision as part of a subterfuge.

[14]But as for me, may I never brag except about the cross of our Lord
Jesus-Christ, through which the world has been crucified relative to me
just as surely as I have been crucified relative to the world. [15]For neither
circumcision nor lack of circumcision means anything; all that matters is
a new creation. [16]And as many as are willing to live by this rule, peace be
upon them, and mercy on the Israel of God.

[17]From here on in, let no one bother me, for I bear in my body the
very stigmata of Christ.[f]

[18]May the favor of our Lord Jesus Christ be with your spirit, brothers. Amen.

---

f. As Charles Ensminger proposes in "Paul the Stigmatic," *Journal of Higher Criticism* 8 (Fall 2001), 183-209, our writer very likely pictures Paul as manifesting the open wounds of the crucified Christ, a devotional affliction attested as early as St. Francis of Assisi but quite possibly occurring earlier. This would certainly suffice to account for the repulsive physical weakness mentioned in 4:13 and perhaps even for the visible depiction of the crucifixion mentioned in 3:1, if οφθαλμους ... προεγραφι is translated as "before your eyes ... portrayed."

12.

The First Epistle to the Corinthians

First Corinthians is perhaps the most fascinating of the Pauline epistles, providing a window on early Christianity in all its diversity, its exotic luxuriance of faith and practice, and its typically human foibles. It is the earliest of the epistles to be definitely quoted by early Christian writers, notably Clement, Polycarp, and Ignatius. However, since 1 Clement is anonymous and appears to be a digest added to over many years, and the work ascribed to the second writer is also very likely pseudonymous and late, and the third is almost certainly a late group of forgeries, it is not clear just how early these citations of 1 Corinthians are. Many scholars believe there are also some early citations of Paul's Epistle to the Romans, but these are more ambiguous and equivocal—certainly not provable.

As Walter Bauer (*Orthodoxy and Heresy in Earliest Christianity*) suggests, 1 Corinthians became a useful weapon in the service of the Roman agenda to supplant other types of Christianity and to draw other churches into its own orbit. The so-called 1 Clement makes an explicit appeal to Paul's "letter" (17:1) to Corinth in order to rebuke factionalism, which had broken forth again in the form of a group of Young Turks usurping the offices of the Corinthian elders. The letter to the Corinthians, then, was used as a "hammer against heretics," and in fact we must wonder if it was not written for that purpose in a post-Pauline generation when sectarianism flourished and thought crimes were quashed by appealing to the consolidating orthodoxy.

The frame premise of the epistle has Paul reply to a two-fold inquiry from Corinth—an official list of questions and some unofficial

gossip from the associates of Chloe (1:11) dealing with dirty linen. This provides an ideal situation for Paul to address many frequent problem areas in church discipline. In fact, the very idea of Paul replying, as if to a long-distance press conference, ought to make one think of the artificiality of the Gnostic resurrection dialogues (*Pistis Sophia, Dialogue of the Savior, Gospel of Mary Magdalene*). The whole thing seems to be an excuse for setting forth a church order, the like of which would later be compiled and published under the names of the twelve apostles as the *Didache* (Teaching of the Twelve Apostles to the Nations); the *Didascalia Apostolorum*; and the *Apostolic Constitutions*, not to mention Titus and 1 Timothy, manifestly church manuals with Paul's name attached to them. The notion of Paul answering a list of questions allows for a topical structure to the epistle: "Now concerning the things you wrote about," "concerning virgins," "concerning the meat of animal sacrifices," "concerning pneumatics," "concerning the collection for the saints," "concerning Apollos, the brother."[a] Mirrored here are the category titles of the Didache: "concerning food," "concerning baptism," "concerning the eucharist," "concerning apostles and prophets."[b]

As to 1 Corinthians as a "hammer against heretics," Walter Schmithals (*Gnosticism in Corinth*) observed how virtually everything in the document would make sense if Gnosticism were in view. All the parallels Schmithals adduced between Corinthian "errorists" and second-century Gnostics would seem to imply further, though Schmithals did not so infer, that the epistle itself stems from the late first or early second centuries. Schmithals has inadvertently shown it is this later period that best fits 1 Corinthians as a historical context. Almost everything in it, from baptism for the dead to celibate marriage, eating idol sacrifices to speaking in tongues, fits the circumstances of second-century Christianity. Of course W. C. van Manen and the Dutch Radicals had long since placed the epistle in a post-Paul era.

In light of this conclusion, I would go further and suggest that the destination, Corinth, is fictive and more likely dealt with the Cerinthians, followers of the notorious Gnostic whose name was synecdoche

---

a. 1 Cor. 7:1, 25; 8:1; 12:1; 16:1, 12

b. Didache 5:3; 7:1; 9:1; 11:3

for all heretics. Simone Petrement[c] suggests that Cerinthus may have been a fictive heresiarch name derived in reverse from the Corinthian errorists just as the fictive Ebion was abstracted from the Ebionites. My guess is that the reverse happened. The letter is fictively addressed to the Corinthians as a pun for those whose doctrines it seeks to refute, the Cerinthians, and any groups designated to the same hell pit.

The letter, in any case, is a patchwork containing all manner of fragments representing different sides of the same arguments, no doubt because the text passed through the hands of scribes belonging to various factions (as with the evolution of the Gospel of John). Numerous hands "corrected" what had gone before. New topics were added here and there. As Darrell J. Doughty has pointed out,[d] commentaries assuming it to be a unitary production from Paul's own hand are taken up with elaborate, epicycles-within-epicycles, harmonizations of various passages with one another, synthesizing elements from different writers, "splitting the difference," and otherwise sophistical results intended by none of the writers. It seems better to treat 1 Corinthians as we have learned to treat the synoptic gospels since the advent of form criticism: as layered desposits, distinguishing different strata of sedimentation by various writers. This way, we may have a chance to understand the text(s) for the first time, dropping the theologically biased, arbitrary demand that all the texts agree internally.

1

1 Paul, an apostle of Christ-Jesus, summoned to the task by the will of
God, and Sosthenes, the brother,[e] 2 to the assembly of God at Corinth, to
those who have been consecrated to Christ-Jesus, *made saints, and to all*

c. Simone Petrement, *A Separate God: The Christian Origins of Gnosticism* (New York: HarperCollins, 1990), 309-10.

d. Darrell J. Doughty, "Pauline Paradigms and Pauline Authenticity," *Journal of Higher Criticism* 1 (Fall 1994): 95-128.

e. In accord with Martin Noth's redundancy principle in his *History of Penteteuchal Traditions* (Englewood Cliffs, N.J.: Prentice Hall, 1972), we must wonder if the seemingly superfluous presence of the name Sosthenes doesn't hint that he is the one who originally wrote or compiled this epistle, Paul's name being attached, either by Sosthenes or a subsequent scribe, in order to lend the document apostolic weight.

those in every place who invoke the name of our Lord Jesus Christ, likewise their Lord and ours:[f] [3]May God our Father and the Lord Jesus Christ grant you favor and peace!

[4]I ever thank my God for you on account of God's favor shown you by Christ-Jesus, [5]because you were enriched by him in every respect, in all manner of inspired speech and gnosis, [6]just as the testimony about Christ was corroborated by you, [7]so that you lack not one of the charismas, awaiting revelations from our Lord Jesus-Christ, [8]who in turn will certify you as blameless when you reach perfection when the day of our Lord Jesus-*Christ* dawns. [9]God is faithful, who summoned you into the mystic sharing in his Son, Jesus-Christ our Lord.

[10]Let me charge you, brothers, by the name of our Lord Jesus Christ, that you all teach the same thing, that there be no schisms among you, but that you may be unified in the same thinking and the same opinion.[g] [11]You see, my brothers, those who follow Chloe demonstrated this to me about you: that there are contentions raging among you. [12]This is what I am talking about: one individual announces, "As for me, I belong to Paul!" while another says, "For my part, I belong to Apollo!" Or "I belong to Cephas!" Or "I belong to Christ!"[h] [13]Since when was Christ divided up? Was Paul crucified for you?[i] Or was it Paul's name into which you were baptized? [14]I am glad now that I baptized none of you—except for Crispus and Gaius;[j] [15]otherwise someone might charge I was baptizing

---

f. Either this material ("and to all those in every place") is a later insertion intended to make an epistle to a single church seem to speak to all or it is original to the text, thereby indicating the fictive character of the addressees. The epistle is, in fact, intended for the widest possible audience and was published as an encyclical against heresy from the beginning.

g. The concern for orthodox unanimity was a second-century issue.

h. This scenario represents the early period in which Paul, Apollo, Cephas, and Christ were full rivals, distinct saviors, avatars, or gurus. The type of united front urged here eventually resulted in a kind of apostolic pantheon in which Christ found the top spot, with Paul, Apollo (perhaps originally Apollonius of Tyana), and Cephas (perhaps Simon Peter) reinterpreted as subordinates of Christ. The term "Christ-Jesus," alternately "Jesus-Christ," similarly attests an early fusion of two heroes or savior deities, Jesus ("salvation") and Christ ("the anointed one").

i. The point may be to avoid syncretistically combining these figures and their myths and soteriologies. While Christ was crucified, Paul atoned for his followers' sins (Col. 1:24) by his beheading.

j. This afterthought, a subsequent insertion, is an attempt to cement apostolic credentials for the succession lines of these two church leaders.

you in my own name! 16But I also baptized Stephanas's family and slaves; as for the rest of the congregation, to tell the truth, I can no longer remember whom I may have baptized.[k] 17After all, Christ did not send me to baptize, but to evangelize,[l] and that not with subtle rhetoric; otherwise the cross of Christ is rendered moot. 18You see, on the one hand, the message of the cross is utter nonsense to those who are perishing. On the other, for us who are being saved by it, it is the very power of God. 19For it is written: "I will destroy the wisdom of the sophisticates, and the prudence of the judicious I will nullify." 20And hasn't he done it? Find me a sophist! Find me a scribe! Find me one of the debaters of this worldly age! Has any joined us from their ranks? Has not God in fact exposed the wisdom of the world for nonsense? 21For since, by the hidden plan of God, the world in its vaunted wisdom failed to arrive at knowledge of God, God thought it good sport to use the nonsense of the proclamation to save the ones believing in it. 22Seeing that Jews demand signs from heaven[m] and Greeks seek after wisdom,[n] 23we still proclaim "Christ crucified"—a scandal on one hand to Jews and on the other to the nations mere nonsense; 24but to the ones summoned from the ranks of both Jews and Greeks, Christ is God's power and God's wisdom. 25Because God's most foolish scheme is yet wiser than mortals, and God's weakest link is yet stronger than mortals. 26It is evident in your own case, brothers! There are among you not many wise by mortal standards, not many powerful, not many high-born. 27It was precisely the nonsense of the world that God chose in order to shame the sophisticate; God chose the unimpressive things in order to put the strongest ones to shame, 28and the most common and contemptible things—God chose the nothings in order to abolish the somethings.[o] 29All this in order to prevent mortals bragging in the presence of God. 30And thanks to him, you are included in Christ-Jesus, who was himself a revelation to us of God's wisdom, namely righteousness and sanctification and redemption, 31so as to bring about the state described in scripture: "Let the braggart brag on Adonai."

---

k. First Stephanas and his sons are added to the Pauline succession genealogy, then the door is shut lest such claims become inflated and devalued.

l. Whence we must suppose both that he did *not,* contra vv. 14 and 16, baptize *anyone—and* that his gospel did *not* include the need for baptism, and thus the sacramentalizing passages like Rom. 6:3-4 do not stem from the same author.

m. Mark 8:11-12

n. Acts 17:21

o. Mark 12:10-11; Matt. 11:25-26; 18:4; Luke 16:15b; one also thinks of such fables as Aesop's tortoise and the hare.

2

[1]I, too, brothers, when I came to you, I did not come armed with excellent rhetoric or wisdom as I announced to you the witness to God. [2]I had decided that while among you, I should offer no other answer to any question but Jesus-Christ and him crucified.[p] [3]And it was in weakness and fear and much trembling that I was with you, I freely admit, [4]and my speaking and my proclamation were not marked by sophistical rhetoric, but by a definitive display of spirit and power. [5]Otherwise, you should have placed your faith in human wisdom, not in divine power.

[6]In fact, however, we do utter wisdom among the perfect, though hardly a wisdom of this temporal world, nor of the archons who rule it and who are rapidly being brought to nothing.[q] [7]But we speak a wisdom of God known in a mystery and hidden away, preordained by God before the ages to result in our transfiguration into the divine splendor, [8]one which none of the archons ruling this worldly age so much as suspected. Had they known, they never would have crucified the Lord of splendor.[r] But as it is written, "Things which eye saw not and ear heard not and never arose in the human mind"—how many such revelations has God prepared for those who love him! [10]For God revealed them to us through the Spirit. You see, the Spirit scrutinizes all things, even the depths of God![s] [11]After all, among human beings, who knows the truth of a person

---

p. He did not present Christ as a heavenly revealer.

q. The writer is about to launch into an exposition of Gnostic mystagogy. The preceding verses (1-5) constitute a paralepsis, a retroactive filling of a blank we would not have been aware of till the writer offered to fill it. Verses 6ff are a subsequent addition, attempting to supplant this earlier, known period of non-Gnostic preaching with the disclosure that all was not as it seemed but that all the while Paul was secretly teaching esoteric doctrine, now to be generally revealed. What sounds like a supplement is really intended to supplant the previous picture. What we read here is precisely parallel to the Messianic Secret in Mark's gospel, an apologetic harmonization of (1) the fact that some later thought Paul taught Gnosticism with (2) the earlier ignorance of any such thing. No one had previously heard of such teaching? Well, no wonder: he kept it secret among the elite. Also note that here, as in 2 Cor. 10:1-11, criticism of an unimpressive speaking style and lack of personal charisma accompany the implied theological criticism of Paul.

r. As we read in the *Ascension of Isaiah,* Christ descended to the earth through the concentric planetary spheres, stopping at each to clothe himself in the likeness of matter appropriate to each sphere in various astral, ectoplasmic, psychic, ghostly-appetitive, and physical bodies possessed by the archons and their subjects on each level. In this way, he could descend to earth incognito, slipping past the guardian archons.

s. Laodiceans 3:18; Rom. 8:39; cf. Rev. 2:24, where a prophetess vilified as

except that person's own inner spirit? Just so, no one has come to know the truth of God except for God's Spirit. [12]And we did not receive the spirit of the cosmos, but the Spirit that comes from God so we may grasp the secrets freely given us by God, [13]the very secrets we relate not in terms of learned rhetoric but of that taught by the Spirit, conveying spiritual matters to those who have the Spirit. [14]But the natural man can make nothing of the truths of the Spirit of God since to him they appear nonsense. Indeed, he is simply incapable of grasping them, for they can be understood only by means of the Spirit. [15]But the pneumatic,[t] on the one hand, understands everything, but on the other, is understood by no one. [16]For who knew the Lord's thoughts, to be able to instruct him? But we do have the mind of Christ.[u]

3

[1]The trouble is, brothers, that when I first came among you, I could not speak to you as to pneumatics,[v] but as to carnal beings, as to mere infants, new initiates in Christ. [2]It was milk I gave you to drink, not solid food, because that's all you were ready for.[w] But you are still not capable of more even now, [3]for you are still carnal! For insofar as jealousy and strife flourish among you, are you not carnal, conducting yourselves in a merely human manner? [4]For whenever anyone says, "I myself belong to Paul!" and another replies, "Well, I belong to Apollo!" are you not mere mortals? [5]After all, what is Apollo, and what is Paul? Merely servants through whom you came to believe, each as the Lord assigned. [6]I planted,

---

"Jezebel" is said to teach "the depths of Satan." Of course, the actual claim must have been the same as in 1 Cor. 2:10, gnosis of "the depths of God."

t. "The spiritual one."

u. Here we breathe the atmosphere of Valentinian Gnosticism, where humanity was parceled out among three categories: first the pneumatics, or spirituals, who possess a spark of the divine Spirit awakened by the preaching of the gospel; then the psychics, or "soulish," "natural ones," who are not divine by nature but may be saved through faith in the death of Jesus; and lastly the doomed sarkics, "carnal" ones—two-legged animals driven by lust. If one could preach esoteric wisdom to all and sundry, it would make the cross moot since it existed as a way of salvation for the natural ones unable to discern the Gnostic call (1 Cor. 1:17; 2:14). Valentinus claimed to be the student of Theodas, a disciple of Paul. Valentinians were the first to write commentaries on the Pauline letters. Thus, along with Marcionites, Valentinians are the earliest Paulinist Christians we know of.

v. In other words, he did not assume from the start that his initiates were spiritual adepts.

w. John 16:12-15; Heb. 5:11-14

Apollo watered, true, but it was God who made it grow.[x] [7]Just as in agriculture: who did the planting and who did the watering is quite immaterial. [8]So the one who plants and the one who waters—it's all the same and each will receive the appropriate reward his particular labors have earned.[y] [9]For we are fellow laborers for God; you are God's farm, God's building project. [10]Like an architect, I used the skill given me by God to lay the foundation, leaving it to another to do the actual building. Just let each subsequent builder watch how he does the construction! [11]Let none imagine he may start over from a different foundation than the one I laid down: Jesus-Christ![z] [12]So whether anyone builds on this foundation using gold, silver, and precious stones on the one hand or wood, hay, and stubble on the other, [13]the quality of each one's work will be revealed for all to see. It is the Day of Judgment that will reveal it because fire will make it clear, and the fire will test the work of each to see what quality it has. [14]If anyone's construction work survives the ordeal, he will receive a reward. [15]If anyone's construction is burnt up, he will be left empty-handed. He himself will be saved, like a burned-out homeowner grateful just to be alive. [16]Don't you understand that together you are a shrine of God, that God's Spirit lives among you? [17]Well, whoever defiles the shrine of God, God will render him profane, for God's shrine is holy, and you are that shrine.

[18]Let no one kid himself: if anyone among you considers himself wise by worldly standards, let him become a moron: that way he really will be wise. [19]Because the wisdom of this cosmos is nonsense to God. We know this, for it is written: "The One who apprehends the wise in their cleverest moment."[a] [20]And again: "Adonai is well aware of the reasonings of the sophists, that they are moot."[b] [21]In view of this, let no one brag about mortal men, for all things belong to you; you do not "belong to" them, [22]whether Paul or Apollo or Cephas or the cosmos or life or death, either

x. As W. C. van Manen noted, this discussion assumes Paul and Apollo are figures of the past whose distinct church-building careers can be looked back upon and compared.

y. The opposite view is advanced in Matt. 20:12.

z. This counters the Petrinist/Catholic claim that Simon Peter was the foundation of the Church (Matt. 16:18), an idea that remains from the early period when Peter (Cephas?) may have been a true alternative to Jesus Christ, not yet his vicar.

a. Job 5:13

b. Pss. 94:11

the present order or that which is coming—all these belong to you, [23]just as you belong to Christ and Christ belongs to God.[c]

4

[1]Thus, people ought to think of us as Christ's retainers and stewards in charge of doling out the mysteries of God. [2]More than anything else, it is demanded of stewards that one be found reliable. [3]And to me, it is insignificant if you judge me as unreliable or if I am judged on some court date before a mortal tribunal, but neither do I judge myself. [4]For I am not aware of any strike against me but that does not vindicate me; no, the one to judge me is the Lord.[d] [5]So do not rush to judgment ahead of time until the Lord arrives. It is he who will both expose to the light the things hidden in darkness and reveal the inner will. [6]Now all this, brothers, I have ventured to apply to myself and Apollo because of you so that in our case you might learn not to read too much between the lines, so that you do not make too much of either one at the expense of the other.[e]

> [7]For what makes you so great? And what do you have that you did not receive?[f] And if indeed you did receive it, why do you brag as if you hadn't?[g] [8]Now you are sated! Now you are rich![h] Without us, you reign unopposed! But in fact, it is to our advantage that you reign because perhaps we might be your co-regents! [9]For sometimes I think God has assigned us apostles to bring up the rear in the triumphal procession, prisoners condemned to death. Why? Because we were made a gladiatorial spectacle to the world, both to evil angels and to mortals alike. [10]We are thus stage buffoons on account of

c. The discussion of apostolic factionalism seems properly to end right here. A Catholicizing redactor picks it up again from a different, alternative, non-Gnostic viewpoint in what follows.

d. The same is said by Jesus in John 8:15-16. This kind of apologetical statement would more likely be made on a founder's behalf by a latter-day admirer.

e. "What is written" implies some scriptural or quasi-scriptural source, but no Old Testament citations occur in the argument. It may be that this catholicizing section, which seeks to co-opt Paul and Apollo and domesticate them, means to introduce vv. 7-13 as a citation from "what is written," namely a letter of rebuke from the Jerusalem apostles which also solicits contributions for the poor Jerusalem community (cf. Gal. 2:10).

f. Gal. 2:9

g. A rejoinder to the Pauline affirmation of theological independence from Jerusalem expressed in Gal. 1:11-12; see also 1 Cor. 15:1, 3ff.

h. This refers to the belief that Paul had enriched himself by exploiting his constituents, as in 9:3-14.

Christ, but you are "realistic" in Christ![i] We are "weak," but you are "strong"![j] You are held in high esteem, while we are dishonored. [11]Even now, we both hunger and thirst, go naked and get beaten up, flee from place to place,[k] [12]*and are reduced to working with our hands.*[l] *Insulted, we bless; persecuted, we endure*;[m] [13]though slandered, we act the Paraclete.[n] *We became the very filth of the world,*[o] *scrubbed-off rust and dirt—and still are!*

[14]My motive in writing these things[p] is not to shame you, but rather to admonish my beloved children. [15]For while you might have ten thousand pedagogues in the things of Christ, you can have only one father, and in the religion of Christ-Jesus I have fathered you by means of the news.[q] [16]Thus I urge you: become imitators of me. [17]Indeed, this is precisely why I sent you Timothy, my beloved and reliable child in the Lord's family, whose conduct will remind you of my own in the way of Christ-Jesus, *that which I teach everywhere in every assembly.*[r]

[18]So when I failed to visit you, some egos became inflated. [19]But I will come quickly to you,[s] if the Lord allows, and I will ascertain the truth of the matter: not just the talk of those inflated egos but whether there is any power behind it. [20]For the kingdom of God does not come by mere talk, but in power.[t] [21]Which would you prefer? That I come to you with a rod, ready to punish, or in love and a gentle spirit?[u]

---

i. This demonstrates Catholic/Jewish derision of Gnostics because the Gnostics thought martyrdom unnecessary.

j. See the discussion of eating meat offered to idols in 8:12; 9:22, and of vegetarianism in Rom. 14:1-2; 15:1, where the "weak" are those who observe traditional Jewish dietary scruples, the position held by Jerusalem.

k. Matt. 25:34-36; 10:22-23

l. Acts 6:2b

m. Winsome Munro assigns vv. 12 and13b to the Pastoral Stratum. Cf. Matt. 10:22.

n. Matt. 10:19-20

o. Torah piety becomes mere dung in Pauline eyes; see Phil. 3:8.

p. He picks ups the discussion concluded in 3:23.

q. The same point is made in Matt. 23:8-12, but not on Paul's behalf.

r. This appeal to catholicity of practice bespeaks the late first century or early second century.

s. Rev. 22:12

t. Mark 9:1

u. The preceding discussion sounds much like a prophecy of the risen Christ warning of imminent apocalyptic judgment. In v. 18 there is even the problem of

5

[1]One actually hears of a kind of whoredom among you that even the pagans do not tolerate: that a man should have sex with his stepmother! [2]And your reaction is to be inflated with pride—instead of mourning for the one who committed this deed because he has been expelled from your company? [3]For I myself, indeed, albeit absent in body, am nonetheless present in spirit, and [4]assembled with you in the name of the Lord Jesus and of my spirit, with the power of our Lord Jesus, [3b]I have already passed judgment on the one who committed this deed,[v] [5]*that he be handed over to the accuser for the destruction of the flesh in order that the spirit may be saved in the day of the Lord Jesus.*[w] [6]This bragging of yours is not healthy! Don't you realize that it takes only a pinch of yeast to permeate the whole mass? [7]Expurgate the old yeast in order to become a new unleavened loaf, which ostensibly you are. [8]So let us celebrate the feast neither with the old yeast of Judaism or with the insidious corruption of malice and wickedness but with the pure matzoh of sincerity and truth.

[9]*In the epistle I wrote you not to patronize prostitutes,*[x] [10] *but not to avoid completely the prostitutes, or for that matter, the covetous, the greedy, and the idolaters among the worldly—in that case, you should have to leave the planet.*[y] [11]*But now, I wrote you*[z] *to shun the company of*

---

the delay of the Parousia (cf. Matt. 24:48-51). The passage may have originated as an oracle of the risen Christ and been transferred here, ascribed to Paul, who was taking on ever more Christlike proportions. Or the passage may be a fossil from the pre-Christian cult of Paul, in which case it is his own second advent which is in view, a Pauline Mahdi.

v. We have in vv. 3-4 an exact parallel to Matt. 18:18-20, only here it is Paul himself who hovers like the divine Shekinah over the assembly of his followers, empowering them with the keys of the kingdom.

w. Winsome Munro makes v. 5 part of the Pastoral Stratum.

x. In what follows, we have a classic case of a Paulinist writer engaging in exegesis of an earlier epistle attributed to Paul. By commenting as if he were himself Paul, he tries to preempt opposing interpretations.

y. The writer of 15:22-24 envisioned just this happening eventually, but the writer here seems to introduce the prospect of leaving the world to escape the wicked as a *reductio ad absurdum.* It is absurd from a position of bourgeois religiosity which can no longer conceive of a Qumran-style communal withdrawal from the sinful world. Here we witness a put-down of an earlier, more radical stage of Paulinism in the name of a later, more domesticated one.

z. The contrast formula, setting aside previous exegesis and practice in favor of a new approach, reminds one of Matthew 5:21-22, 27-28, 31-32, 33-34, 38-39, 43-44.

any reputed brother who is a prostitute or a coveter or an idolater or an
abusive drunk or greedy, not even to share a meal with such a one.[a] [12]*For*
what business is it of mine to judge outsiders? Don't you judge those in-
side the fold? [13]*Those outside, God will judge. Expel the evil one from*
your company![b]

6

[1]Does any one of you who has some complaint against a brother dare
take it before the unrighteous rather than the saints?[c] [2]Or can it be you
don't know the saints will one day judge the world?[d] And if the world is
one day to be judged by you, don't tell me you are not equal to adjudicat-
ing trivial matters. [3]Are you unaware that we shall judge angels?[e] So why
not matters of this life? If then, you do in fact have disputes over matters
of this life, do you take them before those despised in the assembly? [5]I say
this to shame you! Don't tell me you cannot find a single wise man among
you equal to the task of trying his brother's case! [6]But instead, brother
hauls brother to judgment, and that before unbelievers? [7]As it is, the fact
of your mutual lawsuits signals a complete collapse. Wouldn't it be better
simply to suffer the original wrong? Wouldn't it be better just to suffer
deprivation? [8]But you act unjustly and deprive, and you do it to brothers!
[9]Surely you cannot be unaware that the unrighteous shall not receive the

---

a. We seem to have here the strategy rejected in 4:5, as well as by Matt. 13:14-30, 36-43. If the pious try to insist on a rigid standard of purity and orthodoxy for everyone, it destroys the peace and harmony of all. This is a lesson Matthew and others must have learned the hard way, reflecting a kind of post-sectarian compromise.

b. The italicized portion (9-13) is part of the Pastoral Stratum according to Winsome Munro.

c. Here is a far different posture regarding nonbelievers from the one we meet in 2 Cor. 8:21, where it is assumed that Christians will share moral standards with the rest of mankind ("Do what is right ... in the sight of all"). Here we have a Qumran-type vilification of all unbelievers as "the unrighteous," while Christians are called "the saints." The 2 Cor. 8:21 stance is well on the way to a second-generation rapprochement with wider society, the one here in 1 Cor. 6 a piece of pure sectarianism.

d. In 5:12, we read that the saints have no business judging the world! These two passages, from different sources, owe their juxtaposition here to a simple catchword repetition: "judging those without/of the world," regardless of respective contexts.

e. This is a stray bit of the encratite celibacy gospel, more prominently on display in the Acts of Paul and Thecla 1:21-22, but here attempting to ameliorate the sectarian radical tenet that all Christians must renounce sex in order to judge the lustful, fallen angels of Gen. 6:2; Jude 6; 2 Pet. 2:4.

kingdom of God when they die. Don't kid yourselves! No prostitutes, no idolaters, no adulterers, no call-boys, no men who lie with men,[f] [10]no thieves, no coveters, no drunken loudmouths, none greedy will enter the kingdom of God when they die. [11]And some of you used be on this list, but you were washed by the Spirit of our God, you were made holy, you were set right invoking the name of the Lord Jesus-Christ.[g]

[12]All things are permitted me, but not everything is expedient. Nothing is forbidden me, but neither will I mortgage my liberty. [13]Food is for the belly and the belly is for food, but in the end, God will destroy both, won't he?[h] The body, on the other hand, is not for prostitution but is set aside for the Lord,[i] and the Lord satisfies the body. [14]And God both raised up the Lord and will raise us up by his power.[j] [15]Can you be ignorant of the fact that your bodies are members of the cosmic body of Christ? So how about if I take the members of Christ's body and make them the members of a prostitute? Never! [16]You know, of course, that whoever joins himself with a prostitute is a single body with her, for it says, "the two shall be one flesh."[k] [17]But whoever joins himself to the Lord becomes one spirit with him. [18]Abandon prostitution! Whatever sin one may commit is external to the body, but the one prostituting himself actually sins against his own body. [19]Or perhaps it has escaped you that your body is a shrine of the Holy Spirit in you, which you have received from God so that you are no longer your own property. [20]For you were bought at considerable cost. So use your body *and your spirit, which belong to God,* to worship God.

---

f. For this translation of αρσενοκοιται, see Robin Scroggs, *The New Testament and Homosexuality* (Philadelphia: Fortress Press, 1983). It is also possible that the rare word denotes "male prostitutes," for which see John Boswell, *Christianity, Homosexuality, and Social Tolerance: Gay People in Western Europe from the Beginning of the Christian Era to the Fourteenth Century* (Chicago: University of Chicago Press, 1980), 107.

g. All this is baptismal language stemming from a secondary stage of Paulinist sacramentalism.

h. A Gnostic-leaning argument for libertinism, at least where dietary laws are concerned. See Mark 7:18-19, where we read that food "enters not the heart, but only the mouth and thence passes on into the latrine, which purges all foods."

i. That is, pledged to celibacy, as in the next chapter.

j. Rom. 1:4

k. What a disdainful view of marriage! Of course, it is to be expected from an encratite who thought marriage no better than prostitution, a view similar to that held by some modern feminists. See Gen. 2:24 for the quote.

7

[1]Now concerning the things you wrote about.[l] It is good for a husband not to have sex with his wife.[m] [2]But because of the temptation of
prostitution, let each husband have sex with his wife and let each woman
have sex with her own husband.[n] [3]Let the husband pay what he owes his
wife, and likewise the wife her husband. [4]The wife does not possess exclusive rights to her own body, but the husband has rights to it, too. In the
same way, the husband does not have exclusive rights to his body, but his
wife has rights, too. [5]Do not deprive one another, unless you mutually
agree to abstinence for an opportune period so as to use the time for
prayer instead, and then you may come together again in case the accuser
tries to tempt you due to a lack of self-control.[o] [6]Now I say this by way of
permission, not as a command. [7]In fact, I wish everyone was celibate like
I myself am, but each one has his own particular calling from God, one
this way, one that.[p]

[8]Now I say to the unmarried men and to the widows, it is good for
them to remain as I am, too. [9]But if they lack self-mastery, let them
marry; it is better to marry than to burn. [10]But to those who have married, I charge you—actually not I, but the Lord—a wife is not to be sepa-

l. This is the first of several subjects introduced by "Now concerning" this or that—or similar wording. The notion of the Corinthians writing for Paul's advice on these matters is a useful literary device, resulting in a manual of church order much like the topically divided Gospel according to Matthew, the Qumran Manual of Discipline, and the numerous second-, third-, and fourth-century church orders like the *Didache,* which has the same sort of section dividers, περι δε,"now concerning." All of these texts pass themselves off as stemming from the apostles, which bolsters their authoritativeness. We will see another example of this in the spurious 1 Timothy and Titus.

m. Here is an anachronistic reference to the second- and third-century practice of the *agapetae* or *virgines subintroductae,* much debated by Tertullian, Chrysostom, and others, of non-sexual "spiritual marriage," believed to have been the arrangement between Mary and Joseph and therefore the model for all Christian couples.

n. That is, lest she be tempted to have another's husband if hers refuses.

o. The point throughout is to ameliorate the radicalism of Pauline encratism as celebrated in the Acts of Paul and Thecla. Here, later Paulinists try to adjust the movement's lifestyle closer to the mainstream, assimilating to the larger society and looser norms of Catholic Christianity. The Pauline sect is on its way to becoming the Pauline Church. The effort was necessary since many Paulinists (Valentinians, Marcionites, Encratites) still held fast to the straight and narrow path of gospel celibacy ascribed to Paul.

p. Matt. 19:12

rated from her husband. [11]But if, in fact, she is already separated, she must remain single or else reconcile with her husband. Equally, I charge a husband not to leave his wife. [12]And to the rest, it is not the Lord but I who say if any brother has an unbelieving wife and she is content to live with him, he must not leave her. [13]And if a woman has an unbelieving husband who agrees to live with her, she must not leave her husband. [14]For the unbelieving husband has been made holy by virtue of his connection to his wife, and the unbelieving wife has been made holy by her connection to her husband.[q] Otherwise the children of such unions would be considered profane, but as it is, they are considered holy.

[15]But if the unbeliever is the one who separates, let the spouse go; the brother or sister is not bound to the marriage in such circumstances, for God has called you to live in peace.[r] [16]After all, O wife, you cannot be sure you will save your husband. And husband, how can you be sure you would save your wife? [17]Only let each one live the life to which God called him when he distributed our respective lots. *And this I command in all the assemblies.*[s]

[18]Was anyone circumcised when God called him? He must not seek the procedure to undo it. Was anyone uncircumcised when God called him? He must not be circumcised. [19]Circumcision is nothing to brag about, nor is uncircumcision; what matters is keeping the commandments of God.[t] [20]So let each one remain in the niche he occupied when God called him.[u] [21]Were you a slave when God called you, my friend?

---

q. In the Apocryphal Acts, which promote the encratite celibacy gospel, the believing spouse repudiates the unbelieving spouse as a matter of course. Couples who convert together swear off sex forever. Rigid restrictions of this kind are as social as they are sexual in nature. In all sectarian groups, access to the body is as guarded as access to the body politic. To shut the non-Christian spouse off from sex is to isolate the inner circle from all outside, to minimize "sinful" influences.

r. Here is the later compromising, conventional morality of the Pastoral Epistles (1 Tim. 2:22). Common sense replaces revelation; comfortable living is the goal of those who are "prudential" or "realistic in Christ" (1 Cor. 4:10).

s. This is another catholicizing gloss to make the text seem to apply to a wider audience, or at least another wink signaling the text was originally written for the general reader, not for Corinthians, as in Luke 12:41; Mark 13:37. Winsome Munro makes verse 17b part of the Pastoral Stratum.

t. As circumcision was certainly one of the most important Torah commandments, the reference here must be to the so-called Noachian commands (Gen. 9:4-6; cf. Acts 15:29, the Jerusalem Tetralogue). The point would be for circumcised Jews and uncircumcised pious gentiles to keep the commandments appropriate to each, as God had already marked out separate paths for them.

u. This *dharma* doctrine could result from either a bourgeois concern to

Don't let it bother you, but if in fact you are able to become free, by all means avail yourself of the opportunity! [22]For the slave called by the Lord is henceforth the Lord's freedman. Conversely, the free man called by Christ is henceforth the slave of Christ. [23]You were bought at considerable cost; don't sell yourself into slavery to pay your debts. [24]Whatever niche one occupied, brothers, let him remain there—God will be with him there.[v]

[25]Now concerning consecrated virgins: I admit I lack any commandment from the Lord,[w] but I give a legal opinion as one who is reliable, thanks to the mercy Adonai has shown me. [26]I think that, given the present distress, this virginal state is good—that it is good for a man to be so. [27]Have you been joined to a wife? Do not seek to be released. Have you been released from a marriage? Do not seek another one. [28]But if indeed you do marry, you have not sinned,[x] and if a consecrated virgin marries, no sin has occurred,[y] but such individuals are asking for the troubles besetting this natural life, and I mean to spare you that.

[29]But I will say this, brothers: the remaining time has grown short. As for everyone else, I could wish for those who have wives to be the same as those who do not, [30]for those who weep to be the same as those who are not weeping, the one rejoicing the same as the ones not rejoicing, the

---

squelch revolutionary unrest (Col. 3:22-25; 1 Tim. 6:6-10) or from apocalyptic fatalism—no need to re-arrange furniture aboard a sinking ship (Rev. 22:10-11).

v. Verses 18-24 constitute an off-topic insertion, swerving away from the announced topic of sexual relations and treating broader topics characteristic of the *Haustafeln,* or household codes, sprinkled into the epistles (Eph. 5:21-6:9; Col. 3:18-22; 1 Pet. 2:13-3:7) by the Pastoral redactors: slavery, Jews and gentiles. The reason is that the original discussion did treat male-female relations, as do the household codes, but not the rest of the domestic agenda, so the Pastoral redactor thought it wise to supplement the original here. The interpolated section is neatly set off by redactional seams: verse 24 reproduces verse 17, which in context summarized the preceding discussion that men and women should not change the marital status they occupied when they converted to Christianity. Verse 24 seeks to restore the peg from which the following verses originally depended.

w. Here and in 7:10, 12, the writer invokes "commandment[s] from the Lord," something unique to the Pauline corpus. They may refer to sayings attributed to Jesus from the Q document. But are they to be understood as quotes from a historical Jesus or prophecies from the risen, heavenly Christ? We do not know how early such distinctions would have been made.

x. Contra Marcionite and encratite teaching, which made sex the original sin.

y. Contra 1 Tim. 5:11-12, which embraces the very principle rejected here, that the consecrated virgin who marries thereby violates her pledge of exclusive devotion to Christ.

ones buying the same as those with no property, [31]and the ones manipulating this world as those who don't abuse it.[z] For the system of this cosmos is passing away. [32]But I want you to be free of care. The unmarried man is at liberty to care only for the Lord's concerns, [33]considering how he may please the Lord. But the married man of necessity occupies himself with worldly affairs, considering how he may please his wife. [34]Thus his attention has been divided. And the unmarried woman, that is to say, the consecrated virgin, is mindful only of the concerns of the Lord, in order to be holy both in the body and in the spirit.[a] But the married woman is properly mindful of worldly concerns, planning how to please her husband. [35]All this I say for your own advantage, not in order to hinder your freedom but for good order and for you to be attentive servants of the Lord without distraction.

[36]But if anyone thinks he is behaving inappropriately toward his virgin partner and he is sexually frustrated and it seems inevitable, let him do what he wants; he does not sin. Let them marry. [37]But he who stands firm in his heart, not feeling the inevitable urge but having authority over his own will, and has decided in his own heart to keep his virgin partner at arm's length, he will do a fine thing. [38]Thus the one who marries his virgin partner does a fine thing, and the one who does not marry will do better.

[39]A wife has been bound for as long a time as her husband lives; but if the husband falls asleep in death, she is free to be married to whomever she pleases, only within the household of the Lord. [40]But she is sure to be happier if she remains as she is, at least in my opinion, and I think I, too, have the wisdom of the Spirit of God.

8

[1]Now concerning the meat of idol sacrifices: we are agreed that we all possess gnosis.[b] Gnosis tends to ego-inflation, while love leads to edifi-

---

z. The instructions smack of Stoicism, with its prescription of inner detachment, and encratism, with its purely formal, nonsexual marriage arrangement. Again, vv. 29-31 appear to be an insertion, indicated by the repetitious redactional seam beginning and ending the passage. See Luke 16:8-9; James 5:1-6; Rev. 11:18.

a. Married folk, by contrast, cannot be holy in body since sex pollutes it, which is also why couples must abstain from sex for a season of prayer in 1 Cor. 7:5.

b. Of course, the Gnostics attacked here would never say everyone possessed esoteric knowledge elevating them above the rank-and-file *psuchikoi.* The ensuing argument attacks the Gnostic claim to an elite status while pretending, merely for

cation. [2]If anyone thinks he knows something, he only shows that he does not yet know as he ought to know.[c] [3]But if anyone loves God, God is ipso facto known by him. [4]Thus concerning idol sacrifice meat, we know that no deity depicted by an idol exists outside the imagination and that there is no God except one. [5]For even if there are so-called gods, either in heaven or on earth, as in fact there are many gods and many lords,[d] [6]still as far as we are concerned there is one God, the Father, from whom all things are, and we in him, and one Lord, Jesus-Christ, through whom are all things, and we through him. [7]But not all men possess this gnosis,[e] and some by habit cannot help thinking of the meat as an idol sacrifice as they eat it, and their conscience, weak as it is, is defiled.[f] [8]But food will not make us pleasing to God; we are at no disadvantage if we do not eat it, nor are we superior if we do eat it.[g] [9]But watch out that this authority of yours does not degenerate into a scandal to trip up the weak ones! [10]For if anyone sees the gnostic sitting down to a meal in an idol's temple, won't his weak conscience be encouraged to eat the idol sacrifice as an act of devotion to an alien deity? [11]Thus, the weak one is destroyed by your gnosis, this brother for whom Christ died. [12]And so, sinning against the weak brothers and wounding their consciences, you are sinning against Christ. [h] [13]This is why, if food trips up my brother, I will never eat meat again so that I do not trip up my brother.

---

the sake of argument, to share it. We see the same sort of feeble attempt by the Babbit bishops to co-opt what they cannot understand in chaps. 12, 14.

c. Socratic humility is used as a polemical weapon against the knowledge claims this Catholic writer rejects, as if to say, "A little knowledge is a dangerous thing."

d. The Gods (Θεοι) represent traditional top-tier pantheon deities like Zeus, Helios, Apollo, Ormuzd, and Amun-Ra, while Lords (κυριοι) are newer and younger versions of older deities, sometimes their sons or successors such as Hercules, Asclepius, Mithras, and Osiris. Gods were the object of worship in traditional pagan religion, while lords were the saviors of the mystery cults. Judaism is a God religion, Christianity quite self-consciously a mystery religion.

e. Contra v. 1.

f. See Rom. 14:14-15, where the same principle ascribes vegetarianism to the weak. The issues may be one and the same if Christian vegetarians swore off meat for fear of consuming something a pagan priest had sold to the meat market. See 10:25 below.

g. It is Gnostic indifference to the idol origin of meat and consequent willingness to eat it that are under attack here, not the hesitancy of a superstitious neurotic.

h. It is the Gnostic who is the *monotheist* (or possibly God-Christ binitarian) since he knows the Greek gods for mere figments, their altars for nothing more

9

[1]Am I not free to do as I please? Am I not an apostle? Have I not seen Jesus our Lord? In fact, are you not my work in the Lord's service? [2]If to others I do not count as an apostle, still indeed I count as one as far as you are concerned. For you are the authenticating mark of my apostleship. [3]To anyone cross-examining me, this is my defense: [4]Haven't we the right to eat and to drink at our converts' expense? [5]Haven't we the right to be accompanied by a sister-wife[i] like the rest of the apostles and the brothers of the Lord[j] and Cephas?[k] [6]Or is it only I and Bar-Nabas who lack the right not to engage in secular work? [7]Who ever goes off to serve in wartime at his own expense? Who plants a vineyard without receiving a share of the grapes from it? Who shepherds a flock without receiving some of the milk from it? [8]I am not speaking merely from common sense; does not the Torah itself say these things? [9]As a matter of fact, in the Law of Moses it is written: "You shall not muzzle an ox while threshing." Do oxen matter to God? [10]Of course not. The whole reason he says it is for our sake! It was written because of us. The ploughman ought to plow with some incentive. The thresher should thresh in hope of partaking of the wheat. [11]If we did the spiritual sowing among you, is it asking too much for us to reap some material return from you? [12]If others have a right to expect some share of support from you, surely it should be we who have that right.[l]

---

than buffet tables. The recent convert is a *monolater,* believing that the other deities exist but are not his to worship, and the danger from the Catholic point of view is that the Gnostic's example, misunderstood, may encourage *monolaters* to become *henotheists,* worshipping Christ and other gods serially. But of course, the writer summons us to lock the barn door long after the horse has escaped: the easy flow of religious seekers between and among mystery cults, including that of the Kyrios Jesus, resulted in a syncretistic exchange of mythemes and soteriologies already, as the shape of Christianity in this epistle readily attests. Winsome Munro makes vv. 1-12 part of the Pastoral Stratum.

i. Again, virginal partners traveling to evangelize, the issue debated by Chrysostom and Tertullian.

j. There is no particular reason to think "brothers" in this instance implies siblings of Jesus, given the references to Sosthenes, a "brother," and other "brothers," clearly indicating a group of missionaries analogous to the apostles. Cf. Matt. 25:40; 3 John 3, 5, 10.

k. This may not be Simon Peter, as Cephas seems to be distinct from "the apostles," as also in 15:5, 7.

l. Up to this point, we have read a defense against critics who regard itinerant apostles as flim-flam artists bilking the gullible out of their money, as in Lucian's *Alexander the Quack Prophet.* Now we are going to read, as Gerd Theissen ar-

But we did not avail ourselves of this right; we would rather put up with anything than place an obstacle in the path to the news of Christ. [13]Don't you know that those who work at priestly duties get their living from the holy place and that those who wait on the altar share in what is offered there?[m] [14]In the same way, the Lord ordained that those who proclaim the news should live by the news. [15]Yet I have not availed myself of any of these precedents. Nor have I written these things in order to do so now. For I should prefer to die rather than to have anyone nullify my boast.

[16]It is not the preaching of the news of which I boast. No, I have to do that, and woe is me if I do not preach the news! [17]If I did this on my own initiative, I might be due a reward, but as it is a matter of obedience, I am more of a slave entrusted with the stewardship. [18]What reward could I desire? Simply that in preaching the news without charge I may offer the news in such a way as to refrain from using my full rights as an apostle of the news. [19]Being free of everyone, I became enslaved to everyone in order that I might gain the more. [20]And among the Jews I comported myself like a Jew[n] so as to win Jews. Among those under the Torah, I comported myself like one under the Torah so as to gain the confidence of the Torah-observant.[o] [21]Among those without Torah, I became as one without Torah—not, you understand, actually being with-

gues, a defense against critics who carp that any itinerant teacher who does not take money cannot be a genuine apostle since genuine apostles are entitled to such support. Harmonizers plead that the first argument is Paul's statement of agreement with his critics on basics, whereas the second argument is his explanation of his extenuating reasons for nonetheless not exercising the rights for which he has so eloquently argued. But no one takes such trouble to establish the other fellow's argument, only to dismiss it and to establish one's own position in a few words, as we would have to read Paul as doing here if he wrote the whole thing. No, we are reading an initial plea for recognition of the apostolic rights of Paul and Paulinists, then a subsequent correction in vv. 12b, 16-18. The text was "updated" to reflect changing missionary practice.

m. This fact is the presupposition of the whole discussion of meat offered to idols in the previous chapter, which makes it curious that it seems to arise as a new thing here. The connection between the two chapters seems minimal, depending merely upon the catchword connection "eat and drink" in 8:3. Their connection is purely redactional.

n. Ebionite Christians claimed Paul was not a Jew by birth, that he converted to and then apostatized from Judaism because the Torah was too great a burden, perhaps implying a brief association with the rigorous Rechabites/Nazoreans. Here we may have an admission of this.

o. Acts 21:20-24

out the Law of God, but still abiding by the law of Christ!—so I might gain the confidence of those without the Torah. [22]Among the weak in faith, I observed their scruples so as to gain the confidence of the weak. I have become everything to everyone in order that, by whatever means, I might gain the confidence of some.[p]

[23]But all this I do because of the news in order that I may come to share in the salvation promised by it. [24]Don't you know that of all who compete in the stadium race, only one receives the prize? Run fast enough to win! [25]And everyone who agonizes in any sport exercises self-mastery, and they do it for the sake of receiving a fading laurel wreath. But we seek one that will never fade. [26]That is why I run as I do in no random direction and why I box as I do, not wasting my punches on thin air. [27]I subject my body to a severe regimen, making it my slave so I will never find myself, having preached to others, in the end disqualified.[q]

10

[1]For I do not want you to ignore the fact that our Jewish ancestors were all sheltered beneath the pillar of cloud and all passed through the sea, [2]and all were committed to Moses through baptism in the cloud and in the sea, [3]and all alike ate the same spiritual food, [4]and all drank the same spiritual drink, for they all drank from the same spiritual rock that pursued them,[r] and the rock was the counterpart to Christ. [5]Still, with the majority of them, God was not pleased, as can be seen from the fact that their bones were left scattered in the wilderness. [6]So these things were precedents to warn us not to yearn for evil things as those people did. [7]And you must refuse to be idolaters as some of them were, as it is written: "The people sat to eat and to drink and got up to revel."[s] [8]Neither let us

p. The retrospective character of this astonishing admission looks like Paulinists defending their patron's chameleon-like deportment long after the fact. It is not much of a defense in any case, suggesting a kind of Pauline docetism: just as Jesus assumed various forms and adjusted to the spiritual perception of the observer, so Paul condescended and adapted to the mortals he was sent to redeem.

q. If vv. 23-27 came after chap. 7, they would make more sense since "to exercise self-mastery" (εγκρατευεται) was a key term in Encratite (celibate) spirituality, from which it derived its name.

r. Since there are two accounts of Israel drinking miraculously from a rock (Exod. 17:6; Num. 20:11), harmonists reasoned it was the same rock which followed the camp of Israel through the desert! This exegetical legend was well known in the Hellenistic diaspora and need not be taken as a sign of rabbinic erudition on the writer's part.

s. Exod. 32:6

indulge in prostitution, as some of them indulged in cult-prostitution, where twenty-three thousand fell in a single day![t] [9]Neither let us push the Lord's patience over the limit as some of them did—and were destroyed by serpents![u] [10]Neither must you grouse as some of them groused and were destroyed by the destroyer.[v] [11]So these things befell these people paradigmatically and were recorded to provide admonition for future readers like us, whom the cusp of the ages has overtaken. [12]So whoever thinks he stands, let him watch out that he does not fall! [13]No trial has beset you that is beyond human capacity. No, God is reliable: he will not allow you to be tested beyond the breaking point; with every test, he will also provide an escape route so you will be able to endure it.

[14]For this reason, my beloved ones, abandon idolatry! [15]I assume I am writing to people with some sense; draw your own conclusion. [16]The sacred cup that we consecrate, is it not a sharing in the blood of Christ? The bread we break, is it not a sharing in the body of Christ? [17]Because the bread is a single loaf, we the many are made one body because we all share in the one loaf of bread. [18]Consider ethnic Israel: are not those who eat the sacrifice sharers in the altar? [19]So what am I trying to say? That it is anything more than a charade when a sacrifice is offered to idols? Or that there is any reality to an idol? [20]Rather, that what the poor fools sacrifice, they are offering to demons, not to God.[w] And I do not want you to become table companions with demons. [21]You cannot drink a cup of the Lord and a cup of demons; you cannot partake of a table of the Lord and a table of demons.[x] [22]Or do we propose to make the Lord jealous?[y] Can we possibly manipulate him?

---

t. Num. 25:1-18

u. Num. 21:5-6

v. Num. 16:41-50; cf. Exod. 12:23; Rev. 9:11

w. The portion of chap. 10 to this point is a corrective insertion by someone who could not believe participation in idol feasts was as neutral as Gnostic pneumatics would make it. It was to be shunned not merely because of unintended collateral damage to third parties but because it was blasphemous in its own right: these sacrifices were really being consecrated to devils! At v. 23, we have the continuation of the argument that it is morally neutral but should be avoided out of concern for the "weaker brethren," the *psuchikoi.*

x. The sacramental dinner tables of the other deities, *kyrioi,* were also "tables of the Lord," as in an ancient papyrus dinner invitation: "Come dine with me today at the table of the Lord Serapis." It is in this early intercommunion between devotees of *Kyrios* Jesus and other *kyrioi* that the syncretistic mixing of myths and rituals must have occurred; it is precisely to staunch this flow that such dining is condemned here.

23*All things are permitted me, but not everything is smart to do.*[z] *Everything is permitted, but not everything is constructive.* 24*Let no one
look out for his own interests alone, but also to the good of others.* 25*For
conscience's sake, eat whatever is sold in the marketplace without asking questions about where it came from. For ultimately, it comes from
the Lord in any case, as he owns the whole earth and its bounty.* 27*If any
unbelievers invite some of you to dinner and you want to go, feel free to
eat everything they serve you without asking the questions of an over-
scrupulous conscience.* 28*But if anyone remarks, "This is sacrificial meat,
you know," decline to eat it, both because of the man who pointed it out
and for the sake of conscience.* 29*Not one's own conscience, mind you,
but that of the other.*[a] *But why should my freedom be condemned by the
conscience of another?* 30*If I partake, offering thanks, why should what
I am giving thanks for expose me to false charges of doing evil? I'm free
to do it, all right, but it's hardly worth it.*

31*So whether you are eating or drinking, whatever you may do, do
everything as worship offered to God.* 32*Learn not to give needless offense either to Jews or to Greeks or to the congregation of God,* 33*just as I
also try to get along with everyone in every situation by not pursuing my
own advantage, but that of the many, in order that they may be saved.*

11

1*Imitate me in this policy as I am imitating Christ.* 2*But I take my hat
off to you, that you have remembered me in every detail and that you
have held firmly to the traditions in the same form I originally committed
them to you.*[b] 3*But I should add something you didn't know:*[c] *that of ev-*

---

y. That is what the Old Testament prophets said idol-worshipping Israelites were doing: cuckolding Yahve, their rightful husband, "whoring after the heathen."

z. Winsome Munro makes 10:23-11:29, 33-34 part of the Pastoral Stratum.

a. Is it the impression left on a pagan host or a fellow Christian that is at issue? Probably the latter, as the host is taken care of in the previous verse. As long as no one is scandalized, it is just meat without complications.

b. As W. C. van Manen noted, this and other references to "traditions," rather than new instructions, imply a post-Pauline authorship looking back over a great many years. The tone is the same as in the exhortations of Rev. 2-3, esp. 2:13, speaking fictively for the risen Jesus to congregations decades later.

c. The rhetorical device is the same as in John 16:12-14, professing to offer the community information too sophisticated for the same audience in earlier years. It is actually a late reinterpretation now offered fictively in the name of the founder.

ery male, the chief is Christ, and of a wife, the chief is the husband, and of Christ, the chief is God.[d] [4]*Thus every male praying or prophesying with something drawn down over his head is hiding his head in shame.*[e] [5]*But every female praying or prophesying without a veil covering her head shamelessly exposes her head, for it is one and the same with the case of the woman with a shaved head.* [6]*For if a woman is not veiled, let her hair be cut off! But if a shaved or shorn head is a mark of shame for a woman, then let her follow the same instinct for propriety and go veiled.* [7]*For while a male ought not to veil his head, being the image and the delight of God, the female is the delight of a male.*[f] [8]*For male does not originate from female, but female from male.*[g] [9]*For indeed, it was not the male who was created for the sake of the female, but the female for the sake of the male.*[h] [10]*That is why a woman ought to have an authority over the head, because of the angels.*[i]

[11]*Nevertheless, there is neither female apart from male nor male apart from female in the Lord's order of things.*[j] [12]*For just as the female is from the male, even so the male now comes from the female, so there is parity after all.*[k] [13]*Judge for yourselves: is it fitting for a woman to pray to*

---

d. This chain of command is intended to supplant the state of gender equality which had hitherto prevailed. This second-generation correction accommodates the surrounding social mores, a case of being "conformed to this worldly age" (Rom. 12:2a). This is evident from the different senses in which the word κεφαλη is used, first as "chief," as in the Septuagint, then as head or "cranium."

e. Exod. 34:29-35

f. Gen. 2:23

g. Gen. 2:21-22

h. Gen. 2:18

i. As depicted in the *Hypostasis of the Archons,* another version of the Eden myth and older in some respects than the one in Genesis, lustful archons, angels of the Demiurge/Creator, sought to rape Eve, though she had been prepared for Adam. She was herself a mighty power (angel) and escaped their clutches, turning into a tree, presumably the Tree of Life, as Daphne did when fleeing the lust of Apollo. She left behind a docetic likeness of herself which the angels raped. Wearing a veil somehow provides the authority—the angelic presence of the spiritual Eve—to protect her earthly sisters from the depredations of the evil angels, still feared in Jewish apocalyptic and Gnostic literature.

j. Here is a still later "correction" of the preceding discussion, restoring more primitive egalitarianism, suggesting that the New Testament order renders the Old Testament order superfluous (cf. Gal. 3:28). Or the point may be to appeal to the priestly creation account in which men and women are created simultaneously, excluding any ranking by priority (Gen. 1:27).

k. Another correction from yet a different hand, this one seeking to refute the

God unveiled? 14*Doesn't nature herself teach you that if a man wears his hair long, it is dishonorable for him?*[l] 15*But if a woman has long hair, it is her boast, for she was created with long hair as a natural veil.* 16*But if anyone seems to be argumentative on the point, we have no such custom as allowing women to prophesy unveiled, nor do the assemblies of God.*[m]

17*But in this admonition, I cannot praise you because it is not for the better that you assemble, but for the worse.*[n] 18*For first of all, when you gather in the assembly, I hear there are schisms among you, and to some degree I am inclined to believe it.*[o] 19*For there must be heresies*[p] *among you in order that the ones with God's approval may become manifest for all to see.*[q] 20*The result is that when you come together, it is not to eat a supper dedicated to the Lord.* 21*No, each one takes his own meal first, leaving one hungry while another is drunk.* 22*Don't you have houses in which to eat and drink? Or is it perhaps that you disdain the assembly of God and humiliate the needy? I am at a loss as to what to say to you. Shall I praise you? No, on this score, I cannot praise.*

23*For I myself received directly from the Lord what I in turn delivered to you, that the Lord Jesus, on the night he was delivered up, took bread* 24*and, having given thanks, he broke it and said, "This is my body on your behalf. Do this as my memorial."* 25*In the same fashion he took the cup*[r] *after dining, saying, "This cup is the new covenant written in my*

"order of creation" argument on its own grounds, unlike the strategy in the preceding verse.

l. The reference is to perfumed and elaborately coifed μαλακοι, boy prostitutes mentioned in 6:9. Verses 13-16 are the original conclusion following on v. 10.

m. This appeal is to the universal, ecumenical custom of the Catholic Church, the flip side of which is to make deviation into heresy, which seems anachronistic for Paul.

n. This verse reads like a direct continuation of v. 2, and probably was, marking the whole intervening treatment of women and veils as a subsequent interpolation.

o. How can the author of 1 Cor. 1:11-13ff have written this? Does he have only the vaguest idea of Corinthian factional strife? He seems not quite sure whether to believe it. We have a different author here.

p. "Heresies" (literally "factions") as denoting false doctrines is a second-century usage.

q. Matt. 13:41-43

r. Note that the wording is "the cup," rather than "a cup." The passage implies a cult etiology, working back from given elements rather than being a free narrative, working forward to an unknown outcome.

blood. Do this every time you drink it, as my memorial." [26]*For every time you eat this bread and drink the cup, you portray the death of the Lord until he comes.* [27]*In view of this, whoever eats the bread or drinks the cup of the Lord unworthily*[s] *will be guilty of the body and the blood of the Lord.*[t] [28]*But let a person undergo self-examination and only then eat of the bread and drink of the cup.* [29]*For anyone eating and drinking his own condemnation is eating and drinking oblivious of the body.*[u] [30]This is why many of you are weak and sickly and a number sleep in death.[v] [31]But if we only engaged in introspection, we should avoid condemnation. [32]But judged by the Lord, we are chastened so that we do not face the judgment with the rest of the world. [33]*And so, my brothers, coming together to eat, wait for one another.* [34]*If anyone is especially hungry, let him eat something at home beforehand so you don't risk coming together to incur judgment. As for the rest of your concerns, I will set everything in order when I come.*[w]

12

[1]Now concerning pneumatics, brothers, I do not want you to continue in ignorance. [2]You recall how, when you were gentiles, you were led by circuitous paths to worship mute idols. Yes, it is easy to be led astray in spiritual matters. [3]Thus, I reveal to you: no one speaking by impetus of the Spirit of God says, "Jesus be damned!" and no one can say, "O Lord Jesus!" except by impetus of the Holy Spirit.[x]

---

s. Matt. 5:23-24

t. Such a one falls from the sphere of forgiveness. Here is the seed from which the story of Judas the Betrayer grows.

u. There are hints here of a "real presence," a potent sacramentalism to be expected from mystery cults.

v. Here is a prime bit of priestcraft. This kind of superstitious scare story infests the Old Testament in Lev. 10:1-3; 16; Num. 12; 2 Sam. 6:6-9. Cf. also Acts 5:1-11.

w. This enjoins a policy of tolerance on nonessentials, matters where the Paulinist communities had no word from Paul. One might have expected the epistle to end right here, but eventually other issues became so controversial that the apostle's guidance had to be fabricated in order to deal with them; hence the following chapters. Verse 34 is exactly like John 20:30-31, intended as a conclusion but left intact by a later continuator.

x. Behold the imposition of standards of orthodoxy where the free voice of prophecy is muted in favor of accepted dogmas, which of course had their own origin in just such prophecies. We see the same thing happening in 1 John 4:1-6. In 1 Cor. 12:3 the heresy in view is like that of the Cainite Gnostics, whom Origen tells us cursed the human Jesus as the fleshly (hence the unclean) vessel of the Christ

[4]Now there are varieties of charismas, but the same Spirit. [5]And there are different ways to serve, but the same Lord. [6]And there are different inner empowerments, but the same God energizing all of them in everyone. [7]But to each one there is given the appropriate display of the Spirit for the greatest benefit. [8]For to one there is given by the Spirit a saying of esoteric wisdom, and to another a saying of gnosis according to the same Spirit.[y] [9]To another there is given faith by the same Spirit and to another the charisma of healing powers, [10]to another the working of miracles, to another prophecy, and to another the discernment of spirits,[z] to another varieties of tongues, and to another to provide the sense of tongues-utterances. [11]And one and the same Spirit energizes all these things, assigning them appropriately to each as he decides best. [12]For just as the body is one and yet has many members—but all the members of the body, while many, yet compose one body—so also is Christ. [13]For in truth, we all were baptized in one Spirit into one body, whether Jews or Greeks, whether slaves or free, and we were all given one Spirit to drink.[a]

[14]For indeed, the body is not one member but many. [15]If the foot should say, "Because I am not a hand, I might as well leave the body!" it would not for that reason be excluded from the body. [16]And if the ear should say, "Because I am not an eye, I might as well leave the body!" that would not make it excluded from the body. [17]If the whole body were one big eye, where would the hearing be? If all the organs were for hearing, where would the sense of smell be? [18]But in fact, God has arranged the members in the body precisely as he wished. [19]And if the whole thing were one member, what sort of body would that be? [20]But now there are indeed many members but one body. [21]The eye cannot say to the hand, "I do not require your services." Nor can the head say to the feet, "Who needs you? Be on your way!" [22]But the members of the body which seem

---

Spirit. In 1 John it is hard-line docetism under attack—the denial of any fleshly incarnation.

y. The fear here is perhaps of contradictory revelations dividing the community. If they proceed from the same source, they can hardly disagree, so the logic goes, although they do in vv. 2-3.

z. Meaning prophecies, as in 1 John 4:1.

a. Here we pick up Gnostic themes akin to those in 1:17, for instance the repudiation of water baptism in favor of something more spiritual. The same is said of communion. Cf. Mark 1:8; Luke 3:16; Matt. 3:11, where water baptism is cast aside as a vestige of the old dispensation. Water baptism is everywhere understood as the crude washing away of sins, whereas spirit baptism makes one part of the Light Body of the Primal Man.

lackluster turn out to be all the more necessary. [23]And members of the body that we think best to conceal, we clothe with greater splendor, designing artful garments to cover them, and the less attractive parts of the body wind up much more attractive. [24]The attractive members of the body, on the other hand, require no special adornment. But God designed the body so as to provide more abundant honor to the members lacking
it, [25]to avoid schism in the body and so that the members should look out
for one another. [26]Should one member suffer, all the rest suffer with it; should one member feel delight, all the members rejoice with it.

[27]You constitute a body, Christ's, each one of you a member. [28]And
God has appointed some in the church, firstly, as apostles, secondly prophets, thirdly teachers, then miracle workers, then charismas of heal-
ing, helps, administration, varieties of tongues. [29]Is everyone an apostle? Is everyone a prophet? A teacher? Does everyone work miracles? Or have healing charisma? Does everyone speak in tongues? Or interpret them?
Of course not! [31]Just be sure you zealously seek the greater charismas.[b] And yet, I must needs show you a more excellent way.[c]

13

[1]If I speak in human tongues and those of angels, but I have not love,
I am merely making noise, like a trumpet blast or a crashing cymbal. [2]If I
have the mantel of prophecy and know all mysteries and all gnosis, and if I have complete faith so as to be able to uproot mountains at a word,[d] but

b. Here "Paulus Episcopus," as A. Pierson and S. A. Naber called the literary Paul in their *Verisimilia* (Amsterdam: Van Kampen, 1886), attempts on behalf of his fellow *psuchikoi,* the weaker brothers (or as we might today dub them, the "pew potatoes"), to reinterpret the Gnostic understanding of the pneumatics, whereby the spectacular *and only* charismas were prophecy, tongues-speaking, oracular interpretation, and revealed words of *sophia* and *gnosis,* the possession of which made one a member of the Light-Body of Christ. The Catholic-leaning corrector tries to redefine the Body of Christ to include the manifestly ungifted, the mundane laity who supply church suppers and keep the books. The same tactic of co-optation, which serves to confirm the ordinary in their mediocrity, never convinces the pneumatics who instantly recognize the cluelessness of the hierarchs for what it is (1 Cor. 2:14). One heard precisely the same arguments from the denominational apologists who sought to domesticate the charismatic renewals of the late twentieth century.

c. This phrase introduces chap. 13, a further addition tacked on in the middle of the continuous discussion (chaps. 12, 14) gently seeking to minimize charismatic fanaticism. Chapter 13 comes from still later Paulinists who have grown weary of such theatrics and now seek to enlist Paul, supposedly the greatest glossolalist of all, to "prophetically" declare tongues and prophecy superannuated and defunct.

d. Mark 11:23

I have not love, I am nothing. [3]And if I donate all my possessions,[e] and if I deliver up my body to be burnt,[f] but I have not love, I gain no heavenly reward by it.

[4]Love endures much; how kind is love! Never jealous, love thinks of others first, knows no conceit, [5]throws no tantrums, has no selfish interest to pursue, turns the cheek, keeps no record of wrongs done, [6]takes no pleasure in evil works; delighting in true deeds; [7]it wipes the slate clean, assumes you are telling the truth, never gives up hope of you, withstands all opposition.

[8]Love never runs out, unlike prophecies, which God shall abolish,[g] or tongues, which he shall still, or gnosis, which he shall forbid.[h] [9]Thus for now we know but fragments, we prophesy but hints. [10]But whenever the perfect version of a thing appears, the imperfect attempts are cast aside. [11]When I was an infant, I spoke as an infant naturally does. I thought like infants do. I made childish judgments. So having attained manhood, I put an end to all childishness. [12]As yet, we still see the truth in a distorted way, spoken in riddles; then we will see it[i] face to face.[j] For now, my gnosis is but partial; then I shall know as fully as God knows me.[k] [13]When all else fails, faith, hope, and love still stand, and chief among them is love.

14

[1]Choose love as your quest, but be zealous for the pneumatic powers

---

e. This is the boast of the itinerant charismatic apostles who claimed Jesus as their prototype, with poverty a condition for true discipleship. It goes hand-in-hand with the pneumatic boast of elite prophetic gifts.

f. In view here must be the voluntary immolation of the Christian Cynic philosopher Proteus Peregrinus in the early second century, spoofed by Lucian as mere grandstanding.

g. Josephus and the rabbis claimed God had abolished prophecy before Maccabean times. This was in order to discredit prophets like John the Baptist and Jesus ben Ananias. The same point should be taken here: the writer wishes to have no further prophecy, favoring the written creeds, which are said to crystallize perfect knowledge.

h. Here is an anticipation of the condemnation of Gnosticism as a Christian heresy.

i. This writer, happy to close the book on primitive Christian enthusiasm, is quite as capable of deeming his own writing the "perfect," mature fruit of revelation, as did the author of John's gospel, which similarly disdained the previous, fragmentary knowledge of gospel truth (John 16:12-13, 25, 29). One might also compare the boast of the evangelist Luke to supersede and to stultify all previous gospel writers (Luke 1:1-4).

j. Deut. 34:10

k. Pss. 139:1-6

and, rather than the others, that you may prophesy.[l] [2]After all, he who speaks in an angelic tongue speaks over everyone else's heads directly to God; for no one can make sense of it, naturally, since such a one, in the grip of the Spirit, utters mysteries. [3]But the one who prophesies constructively to fellow mortals speaks words of encouragement and consolation. [4]To be sure, the one who speaks in an angelic tongue edifies himself, but the one who prophesies edifies the whole assembly. [5]It is not that I love speaking in tongues less but that I love prophecy more! I want you all to speak in tongues but only in order for you to prophesy once your utterance is interpreted.[m] Prophesying is a higher task than speaking in tongues, unless one interprets, in order that the congregation may be fortified.

[6]Just imagine, brothers, if I arrive among you speaking in tongues: how am I doing you any favor unless I speak to you by way of revelation or of gnosis or of prophecy or of teaching? [7]If inanimate objects like pipe or harp produced indistinguishable sounds, how could anyone tell which tune was being played? [8]Indeed, if a trumpet gives forth an indefinite sound, who will take it as a signal to prepare for battle? [9]In the same way, unless you give a clear communication through your tongue, how can anyone tell what you are saying? You will seem to be speaking into the wind! [10]Who knows how many voices there may be in this world, yet not one of them is without meaning. [11]But if I happen not to know the import of what is said, I remain a foreigner to the speaker and the speaker remains a foreigner to me.

[12]So in your case, since you are such zealots for the spiritual, strive to increase your proficiency in such a way as to fortify the congregation. [13]Thus the one who speaks in an angelic tongue, let him pray to be able

l. This verse is a redactional seam paraphrasing 12:31a, the graft point from which to reattach the original continuation, which the anti-pneumatic chap. 13 interrupted.

m. In these and the ensuing verses, the writer betrays a lack of acquaintance with a real charismatic milieu, where it is precisely mass glossolalia which is said to transport worshippers into a "finite province of meaning" an "alternative reality" of mystical fellowship, something rational discourse cannot achieve. In fact, while posing as an insider, our writer seems to occupy the position described in 14:23. See Peter L. Berger and Thomas V. Luckmann, *The Social Construction of Reality: A Treatise on the Sociology of Knowledge* (Garden City: Doubleday Anchor, 1967), 25; Felicitas D. Goodman, *Ecstasy, Ritual, and Alternate Reality: Religion in a Pluralistic World* (Bloomington and Indianapolis: Indiana University Press, 1988), 43-47; Goodman, *Speaking in Tongues: A Cross-Cultural Study of Glossolalia* (Chicago: University of Chicago Press, 1972).

also to interpret. [14]For if I pray in an angelic tongue, my spirit prays, but my mind lies fallow. [15]So what am I to do? Of course, I shall pray with the spirit, and I will also pray with the mind. I will sing in the spirit, and I will sing also with the mind. [16]Otherwise, when you bless God in the spirit, how is anyone who finds himself suddenly relegated to the place of the uninitiated supposed to say "amen"? He has no idea what you are saying! [17]Indeed, you are giving thanks right enough, but he is not fortified. [18]I give thanks to God, I speak in tongues more than all of you. [19]But in the congregation, I would rather speak five good words with my mind in order to instruct others than ten thousand words in an angelic tongue.

[20]Brothers, you should be naïve only as regards malice, not in your judgment. In that, you should be mature. [21]In the Torah it is written, "In alien speech and by alien lips I will speak to this people, and thus they will not hear me, says Adonai."[n] [22]Just so, the effect of tongues is not to provoke belief, but to provoke unbelief. Prophecy, on the other hand, provokes not unbelief but belief. [23]Accordingly, if the whole congregation assembles and all speak in tongues, and some uninitiated or unbelievers enter, will they not at once conclude that you are raving mad?[o] [24]But if all prophesy and some unbeliever or uninitiated person enters, he is convicted by all, condemned by all,[p] [25]the secrets of his heart become manifest, and thus, falling prostrate, he will worship God, declaring that without doubt God is present among you.

[26]So brothers, how should it be from now on? Whenever you gather together, follow this pattern: each one has a psalm, a teaching, a revelation, an angelic tongue, an interpretation. Let everything be done constructively. [27]If anyone perhaps speaks in an angelic tongue, let there be two or at most three, and each in turn,[q] [28]and have someone interpret. But if there is no interpreter present, let him keep silent in the meeting and let him speak only to himself and to God. [29]And have two or three prophets speak, [30]and have the rest pass judgment. But if a revelation strikes someone else as he sits there, let the first speaker defer to him and fall silent.[r]

n. Isa. 28:11-12

o. Exactly as in Acts 2:13. None of this should surprise anyone; indeed, this is precisely why there *was* "instruction" and "initiation." The sacred mysteries of the Spirit were by definition not open to the scrutiny of uninformed outsiders. See 1 Cor. 2:12-14. The author of this anti-charismatic section is completely out of touch with the milieu he presumes to describe and to regulate.

p. John 16:7-11

q. This is to avoid the bedlam envisioned in v. 23.

r. It seemed proper for all the prophets to sound forth at once in v. 24, but the

[31]For you can all prophesy, one by one, in order that all may learn and all
may be encouraged.[s] [32]And surely the spirits of prophets are obedient to
prophets.[t] [33]For God is never the God of confusion, but always of peace.
As in all the congregations of the saints,[u] [34]*let the women be silent
while in the congregations, for they are forbidden to speak; but let them
submit, as the law also says.*[v] [35]*But if they want to learn anything, let
them question their own husbands at home, for it is disgraceful for a
woman to speak in public.*[w] [36]Do you think divinely inspired speech begins and ends with you? [37]If anyone deems himself a prophet or a pneumatic, then let him prove it and admit that what I write to you is a commandment of the Lord. [38]But if anyone claims he does not know that for
a fact, dismiss him as an ignoramus and no gnostic.[x]

[39]In sum, then, my brothers, be zealous to prophesy and do not forbid speaking in tongues.[y] [40]Let everything be done becomingly and with
decorum.[z]

15

[1]So I inform you, brothers, of the news with which I evangelized you,
the same that you welcomed[a] and in which tradition you stand, [2]the one

---

point there was to contrast glossolalia and prophecy for intelligibility. In this verse the point is to increase intelligibility further still so listeners can hear a single prophet without distraction. We are well on the way to the Calvinist (re)interpretation of prophecy as the rational, discursive preaching of the gospel.

s. Too bad no one told this to the company of prophets in 1 Sam. 19:20-21.

t. This is contrary to Jer. 20:9. The author of this portion of the epistle now betrays his cynical assumption that so-called prophets are mere prima donnas talking out of their hats. There is no thought that they might actually speak by the Spirit of God. No, "the spirits of prophets" are more like wizards' familiars.

u. In other words, throughout the whole Catholic Church.

v. This would imply church canon law, not the Torah, where no such stipulation can be found.

w. Literally, "in a congregation." Concern for women's decorum during charismatic worship (10:1-10) is non-charismatic, but the present interpolation is even later, as the redactor cannot countenance even the prospect of women asking questions about teaching, much less women prophesying. Many scholars see 33b-35 as an interpolation. Winsome Munro makes it part of the Pastoral Stratum. In Western Text manuscripts, these verses appear at the very end of the chapter.

x. How similar in spirit and style this is to Titus 3:10-11.

y. The writer acknowledges that to forbid glossolalia might seem the natural inference from his systematic denigration of it.

z. There is no more striking example of Pastoral-type, almost Victorian, sensibilities so infinitely removed from the sectarian radicalism of early Christianity.

a. Is he now informing them, or rather reminding them, of something he told

by which you are saved, providing you hold firmly to what I said when I evangelized you—unless, perhaps, it was all some mistake?[b]

3 *For I handed on to you, first and foremost, what I received the same way:*

that Christ died on account of our sins, as we know from the scriptures; and
that he was buried; and
that he has been raised on the third day, as we know from the scriptures;[c] 5 *and*
that he was seen by Cephas,
then by the Twelve.
6 *After that, he was seen by over five hundred brothers at once, of whom the greatest number linger even now, though some fell asleep;*
7 *after that, he was seen by James,*
then by all the apostles.

8 *And finally, appearing even as to the Ektroma, he was seen by me,*
too.[d] 9 *For I am least of the apostles, unworthy even to be considered an*
apostle because I persecuted the congregation of God. 10 *But by the mercy*
of God, I have such status as I do occupy.[e] *Nor was his mercy toward me a futile gesture, for as it turned out, I labored more fruitfully than all the rest put together. Well, of course, not I myself, but the charisma of God*

---

them long ago? The strange wording bespeaks the fictive recollection, the first-time announcement of something for which a venerable Pauline pedigree is now sought.

b. The original direct continuation of this thought is found in v. 12. What follows here is an interpolation.

c. Hosea 6:2-3

d. The reference here is to the Primordial Light Man, of whom Jesus Christ was believed to be a kind of reincarnation, appearing to the wondering Demiurge, the Gnostic Creator, who cast covetous eyes on the former's spiritual substance and contrived to steal it to give life and order to his inert creation. This Demiurge was a defective and malicious bastard offspring of the fallen Sophia (Wisdom). Against the will of the godhead, she brought him forth, and he was called Ektroma, the Abortus.

e. This is precisely the conception of Paul in Acts: he is not an apostle even though his gospel harvest appears far greater than that of the Twelve. Rather than an independent conduit of Christ's revelation, Paul had been taught by his predecessors Ananias and Barnabas, just as here in v. 3. What a different tale is told in Gal. 1:11-12!

with which I was equipped. [11]Thus, whether it was I myself or them, this is what we alike proclaim and this is what you believed.[f]

[12]But if Christ is proclaimed as having been resurrected, how is it that some among you say there is no resurrection of dead people? [13]So if it is true that there is no resurrection of dead people, then Christ has not been raised either. [14]And if Christ has not been raised, then our preaching is a sham and so is your faith. [15]And we are then exposed as false witnesses about God because we testified about God, that he raised Christ, whom it turns out he did not raise if, after all, no dead will rise. [16]For if dead persons are not raised, Christ has not been raised either. [17]And if Christ has not been raised, then your faith is superfluous: you still languish in your sins. [18]Then, too, those who have fallen asleep in death, holding fast their faith in Christ, have simply perished. [19]If we have placed our hopes on Christ only for the duration of this earthly life, we are the most miserable of fools! [20]But as it happens, Christ has been raised from the dead, the first of those fallen asleep to ripen for harvest.

[21]For since it was through a single individual that death arrived, it was fitting that a resurrection of dead people arrived through one single individual, too. [22]For just as in Adam's wake all die, so in Christ's wake shall all be restored to life. [23]But let each rise in his proper order. Christ ripens first, then those who belong to him, once he appears, [24]then the end whenever he may hand over royal authority to God, his Father, namely, whenever he may declare an end to all the archons, authorities,

---

f. As Arthur Drews, G. A. Wells, Winsome Munro, J. C. O'Neill, and others have argued, vv. 3-11 constitute an interpolated piece of apologetics for the resurrection, using several earlier bits and pieces to compose it. R. Joseph Hoffmann rejects vv. 5-8 as an interpolation. As Adolf von Harnack saw long ago, the parallel lists "Cephas and the Twelve" and "James and all the apostles" must originally have been rival credential claims, their redundancy ("the Twelve" = "the apostles") the result of a subsequent ecumenical truce. The business about the 500 witnesses to the resurrection post-dates the gospels since it is impossible for such a memory/tradition (if such it were) to have remained unmentioned for so long and so widely. Its appearance must be even later than the rest of the list of appearances. It refers in an abbreviated manner to a longer episode told at greater length in the Gospel of Nicodemus/Acts of Pilate, where we learn that the 500 were Roman troops guarding the tomb of Jesus. The notion of James as a believer in Jesus already at the time of Easter is a second-century product, occurring also in the Gospel of Luke and the Gospel of the Hebrews. Earlier sources (Mark and even John) had him indifferent or hostile to Jesus. No New Testament source has him first hostile, *then* converted by a resurrection appearance; that is a post-biblical harmonization. The addition of Paul to the list of resurrection witnesses seeks to define his not-quite apostolic status in the same terms used by Acts.

and powers. 25For he must wield authority while he is occupied in subduing all his enemies. 26The last such enemy to be eliminated is death, which he will vanquish by raising those who are his. For he has subjected, yea, trampled, everything; hence, it must be soon. 27But when it says that "all things have been subjected to him,"[g] it is obvious that "all" does not include the one who did the subjecting.[h] 28Thus, once all things are subject to him, then the Son himself will likewise subject himself to the One who subjected all else to him in order that God may be all in all.[i]

29Otherwise, those who are baptized vicariously for the dead[j] will find they have wasted their time. If the dead are not to be raised, what is the point of being baptized on their behalf? 30And why would we risk danger every hour of the day? 31I die each day,[k] as you boast about me, brothers, a boast which I have earned by my years in Christ's service. 32If, as they say, I contested with wild beasts in Ephesus,[l] what have I gained by it?[m] If the dead are never to be raised—well then, let us eat, drink, and be merry! Life is short.

---

g. Pss. 8:6. Here, as in v. 3 above, we get the impression, as Earl Doherty noted in *The Jesus Puzzle,* that these saving facts of Christ and his saga are the result of esoteric scripture exegesis, not of historical memory, as Christians would later claim. They seem to be derived from, not proof-texted by, selected scripture verses.

h. The same argument might have been pressed against vv. 13, 16.

i. According to the concept of mystic nondualism, all beings are distinct from God, or seem to themselves to be, and are thus at enmity with God. If they can be reconciled or subjugated, the result will be absolute unity and bliss.

j. John Chrysostom described Marcionite necrobaptism: "For if one of their catechumens dies, they conceal a living person beneath the bier of the departed, approach the corpse, talk with the dead person, and ask him whether he intended to receive baptism. Thereupon the person who is concealed, speaking from beneath for the other who does not answer, avers that he did indeed plan to be baptized, and then they baptize him for the departed one." Epiphanius of Salamis wrote of the Cerinthians that "when some of them die before being baptized, others are baptized in place of them, in their name, so that when they rise in the resurrection they may not have to pay the penalty of not having received baptism and become subject to the authority of the one who made the world."

k. See Paul's virtual invulnerability in the Acts legend, e.g., 14:19-20.

l. This is a figure of speech for "debating with Epicureans," as shown by Abraham J. Malherbe in *Paul and the Popular Philosophers* (Minneapolis: Fortress Press, 1989), chap. 6 (cf. Acts 17:18; Titus 1:12). "Beasts" denotes "hedonists." However, the author or redactor no longer understands the idiom and imagines Paul to have been tossed into an arena with literal leopards, lions, and bears, as in the Acts of Paul.

m. Note the crude calculus equating martyrdom with extra credit. At 13:3, the author had at least a bit more religious insight than this.

[33]Don't let yourselves be led off the path! Corrupt associations ruin good habits. [34]Sober up! Return to righteousness and stop sinning! For some among you are oblivious of God, which I point out to shame you.[n]

[35]"But," someone is sure to object, "how are the dead raised? And what sort of body do they return with?"[o] [36]You fool! The common seed you sow does not come to life unless it dies first. And the seed you sow, [37]it does not already have its eventual form as you sow it, but is only a bare grain, perhaps of wheat or of some other variety. [38]But God then supplies a body for it, as he determined long ago, and he assigned each seed its own mature form. [39]All flesh need not be the same to count as flesh; rather, there is one kind for human beings, another sort of animal flesh, another sort of flesh for birds, another for fish. [40]Similarly, there are heavenly "bodies" and earthly "bodies," but the splendor of the heavenly bodies is quite different from that of their earthly counterparts. [41]The sun shines in its own fashion, as does the moon, and so the stars. Star differs even from star in magnitude. [42]And it is the same with the resurrection of the dead. One is sown in decay, raised up undecaying. [43]One is planted in shameful condition, raised up glorious! It is buried inert but raised powerful. [44]One is sowed a natural body, it is raised a pneumatic body. It stands to reason: if there is a natural body, there must also be a pneumatic one. [45]It says just this in scripture: "the primordial human being, Adam, became a living nature; the Adam at the end of time became a vivifying spirit."[p] [46]But the pneumatic body does not come first, rather the natural, and the pneumatic after that.[q] [47]The first human being was

---

n. This (vv. 33-34) is an inept gloss added by someone who misunderstood the point of v. 32 and turned it into a *reductio ad absurdum*. No one was actually getting drunk or proposing it.

o. Mark 12:18-27

p. Of course, the second part of this passage is not found in the ostensible source, Gen. 2:7. It may come from some lost Gnostic rewrite of Genesis, the like of which we see in the Nag Hammadi library. Or more likely, the writer is quoting from memory and assuming an inference he drew long ago. The basic idea sounds Zoroastrian, reminiscent of the Saoshyant, or "Benefactor," an eschatological descendant of Zoroaster, some say a reincarnation of the Primal Man Gayomard, who will finally come to earth to enliven the dead for judgment and salvation.

q. Many see here a dissent from the Philonic and Valentinian notion that earthly bodies are poor copies of the heavenly "image" or prototype of perfect humanity. But that seems not to be the point; rather, he means that we bear first the one image, then the other. Undoubtedly, the author believed in a Primordial Light Man, but his point is that it was not manifested on earth until after the resurrection, and so it will be with the redeemed.

formed out of the earth, earthy in character; the second human being
comes out of heaven. 48 As with the clay homunculus, so will it be with the
creatures of clay; and as it is with the ethereal one, so will it be with the
ethereal ones.[r] 49 And as we displayed the image of the clay homunculus,
so we shall display the image of the ethereal one. 50 Mark my words,
brothers: flesh and blood are incapable of attaining the divine realm after
death, no more than the decaying can, upon death, be made undecayed.
51 Behold, I reveal to you a mystery hitherto unguessed! Not all of us shall
fall asleep in death, but all of us shall nonetheless be transformed—52 in a
moment, in the blink of an eye, at the last note of the trumpet. For a trumpet will blow, and the dead will be raised up undecayed. And we, too,
shall be transformed.[s] 53 For this body of decay must needs assume immu-
nity from decay,[t] and this mortal body must assume immortality. 54 And
when this decaying body shall clothe itself in freedom from decay, when
this mortal body shall don immortality, then that saying from scripture
will come true, namely, "Death was consumed by victory. 55 O death,
where is your much-vaunted victory? Where, O death, your barb?"[u]
56 Well, of course, the barb in death's scorpion tail[v] is sin, and what makes
it fatal is the Torah.[w] 57 But thank God, he has granted us, rather than our

r. Here we again pick up the distinction between "heavenly bodies" and "earthly bodies" from v. 40. The soteriology sounds Gnostic: only the pneumatics will be saved since, as in the mystery religions, salvation is the mystical transformation of individuals through sacramental initiation, which quickens an inner spark of the divine nature and fans it gradually into flame till death when the inner glorious nature subsumes the outward husk and one ascends to heaven. It is still orthodox in Eastern Christianity, where the doctrine is called *theosis,* "divinization." The verse seems to imply that the pneumatics will be saved, but the mere *psuchikoi,* "natural men," will not.

s. Here is a rare piece of self-conscious doctrinal innovation. Since the general apocalyptic scenario described here is common enough, the point is either to ascribe it to Paul after the fact or to admit that the *eschaton* will not arrive quickly enough that all alive in Paul's generation will live to see it. In the latter case, we have an equivalent to the spurious predictions (Matt. 24:48; 25:5) of a delay in Jesus' own announced timetable—a subsequent corrector posing as Jesus before the fact. The actual intended audience, as opposed to the fictive Corinthian recipients, can be imagined heaving a sigh of relief that those who died before the Parousia were not necessarily "lost" after all. If only they had read this letter from Paul as soon as it was received! What a tragedy it had been lost in the interval.

t. Wasn't this very notion ruled out as impossible in v. 50?

u. Hosea 13:14

v. Rev. 9:10, 19

w. This is a clumsy gloss, presumably by a Paulinist scribe who misunderstood the rhetorical questions of v. 55 as riddles.

opponent, Death, the victory through our Lord Jesus-Christ. [58]In view of this, my beloved brothers, stand firm, immovable, becoming ever more productive in the Lord's service, mindful that your labor for the Lord is not futile, as it would be if there were no resurrection.[x]

16

[1]Now concerning the collection for the saints, you are to do as I urged the congregations in Galatia to do.[y] [2]On the first day of each week, let each of you keep aside some amount, as God has prospered him, so we need not organize the collection once I get there. [3]And when I get there, whomever you approve for the task, I will send them with the appropriate epistles to carry your gift to Jerusalem. [4]And if it looks opportune for me to go, too, they shall accompany me. [5]And I will come to you whenever I pass through Macedonia. For I mean to pass through Macedonia, too, and I may even stay with you or even spend the winter there so you may send me off rested and fully provisioned when I go. [7]I do not want to see you only in passing, for I am hoping to remain with you some time if the Lord permits. [8]But I will remain in Ephesus till Pentecost, [9]because a great opportunity for effective work has opened wide for me there, and typically in such situations, there are many opponents requiring my attention.[z]

[10]So if Timothy comes, give him no reason to be intimidated among you, for he does the Lord's work the same as I do. [11]So don't anyone there

---

x. The discussion goes from the unthinkability of denying resurrection, given the unacceptable implications, to an argument from natural and astronomical analogies to defend the notion of a "resurrection of the flesh" or of the body that need not entail the revival of mortal flesh after all. As Richard C. Carrier points out, in all this one would never get a hint that a writer who must resort to such discourse had himself settled the issue by directly beholding a man raised from the dead! Clearly, it is all speculation and theory, not the work of a witness to the resurrected Jesus.

y. Namely, contributions to the Jerusalem Pillars and their community (Gal. 2:10), the erstwhile tribute paid by Paulinist churches to their salvation-historical forbears before the link was severed by Marcion and Valentinus. In the same way, the prophet Muhammad had initially retained the Jewish *qiblah,* praying toward Jerusalem, only to change it later to Mecca after becoming disillusioned with Jews for failing to accept his message.

z. Such itinerary notes, either in the epistles or in Acts, serve the same purpose as the itinerary of Abraham in Genesis 12ff: to increase the clout of certain localities by their association with the apostle. This became even more intensified with claims that an apostle actually founded the church in a given locality.

think they can disregard him.[a] But give him a happy send-off on his way to me, for I am awaiting him with the brothers.[b]

12Now concerning Apollo, the brother,[c] I strongly urged him to come to you with the other brothers,[d] but he was not wholly convinced that he should come. Rest assured, he will come when he has the opportunity.

13Keep guard! Stand fast in the faith![e] Be men![f] Be strong! 14Let everything you do be done in love.

15*So I plead with you, brothers, about the household of Stephanas: you know them as the first converts in Achaia and how they have devoted themselves to the service of the saints.* 16*Submit yourselves to the authority of them and to everyone working and laboring with them.*[g] 17At present, I rejoice at the arrival of Stephanas and of Fortunatus and of Achaicus, *who have made up in some measure for your not being here.* 18For they have refreshed my spirit as they do yours. Be sure to acknowledge such as these.[h]

19The congregations of the province of Asia greet you. Aquila and Prisca, along with the assembly meeting in their house, send fondest greetings to you all. 20Greet all the brothers.[i] Greet one another with a ritual kiss.

21I greet you in my own handwriting.[j]

---

a. Timothy serves as a symbol for the post-Pauline generation of leaders, for whose esteem a Pauline boost is being sought here, as in 1 and 2 Tim.

b. Presumably the missionary "brothers of the Lord," as in 9:5.

c. Here "brother" designates an itinerant preacher, as indeed Apollo(s) in Acts 18:24-28.

d. See note for 16:11.

e. What is meant by "faith" is not some existential posture but rather "the Christian religion," as in the Pastorals.

f. Notice that the writer addresses male readers despite the charismatic egalitarianism characteristic of the first generation, as subtly acknowledged in chap. 10. The writer gravitates back to the social norm of chauvinism, which was standard in his day.

g. Winsome Munro makes vv. 15-16, 17b part of the Pastoral Stratum.

h. We can assume the pedigree was forged after the fact by a particular Paulinist faction or school. Remember that for many years people made rival claims to have been the "first convert" in a particular city. Was it Lydia (Acts 16) or Frontina (Acts of Paul) in Philippi? This was important as an authority claim, especially in such cases as here, where it is the "household," the dynasty of Stephanas, that is recommended.

i. Again, the reference is to the missionaries staying there.

j. A fatal slip of the pseudonymous mask! If Paul signed the letter, this would have been evident without pointing it out in this fashion.

22 If anyone does not truly love the Lord, excommunicate him![k]
Maranatha![l] 23 May the favor of the Lord Jesus be with you. 24 I send all of
you my love in connection with Christ-Jesus.

---

k. Aramaic for "damned," a liturgical fossil borrowed from Judaism whereby heretics were ritually cursed in synagogue prayers. Many think this represents a piece of eucharistic liturgy in which the lukewarm are warned against partaking unworthily, as in 11:27-29.

l. Again, the celebrant warns away any hypocrites and invokes the presence of the Lord in the eucharist, anticipating the eschatological Parousia of Christ. The inclusion of liturgical rubrics implies that the pseudo-Pauline writer wants his text to be accepted as scripture and included in the canon.

13. The Second Epistle to the Corinthians

THE SO-CALLED SECOND EPISTLE TO the Corinthians seems rather a collection of material that had fallen into disarray and was ineptly re-assembled by someone who wanted to circulate a second anti-Cerinthian treatise. Most scholars agree on this. Where they differ is over which fragment properly goes with which in an attempt to restore something like the original order. Most scholars believe all or most of the material was authentically Pauline. We, however, belong to that minority following Bruno Bauer, W. C. van Manen, and the Dutch Radical critics, thus rejecting Pauline authorship for most or all of these materials.

The majority of the 2 Corinthians material seems to have first made up a pair of letters composed in the interest of counteracting a catholicizing trend to supplant local Pauline traditions, retroactively providing non-heretical foundation legends and re-writing history to make someone other than Paul the founder of various congregations. The whole polemic here, if advanced by the historical Paul, would be aimed at rivals who have poached among his converts, moving in to undermine his work after he had moved on instead of striking out with pioneer evangelism efforts in their own new territories. But as Van Manen points out, the perspective here is retrospective: the labors of Paul are in the past, over and done. The writer looks back on them, delineating the bounds of the Pauline mission field like the Deuteronomic historian mapping out the ancestral lots of the tribes of Israel. If the letter is pseudonymous, the argument is aimed at posthu-

mous attempts to supplant Paul's legacy by proposing that Peter or John founded this or that Pauline congregation. In this way, the orthodox eventually sought to replace the heretical credentials of the Alexandrian Church, possibly founded by Carpocrates, with an orthodox pedigree that has Mark as the first bishop. Though Marcion and Basilides planted Christianity in Edessa, later apologists for orthodoxy claimed Addai, one of the Seventy, had founded the church there. John has become the apostle of Ephesus to replace Paul, on whom the blame for Gnostic heresy was perhaps rightly laid. In this case, the whole epistle will be seen as the equivalent of Paul's fictive speech in Acts 20:18-35, an attempt to forestall retroactively such attempts at supplanting Paul's heretical legacy.

Such would seem to be the point even if Paul had nothing to do with the foundation of the churches in question. After all, two can play this game. Perhaps such letters are clever attempts to make headway for Marcionite Christianity or Gnosticism in the churches addressed by trying to supply a fictive and retroactive Pauline pedigree. "Come back to Paul!" would mean "Join the (latter-day) Pauline movement!" Who knows?

The first of the letter fragments comprising this epistle[a] opens more abruptly than any other letter attributed to Paul. It may be that a typical, more elaborate salutation stood here originally but was cut off when the scribe thought to connect all the loose pages together. Presumably, the brusque "I, Paul" was thought fitting enough to begin what is called "the severe letter," which is said to have caused so much grief, as discussed in 7:8. Paul is so upset and urgent, he feels he must skip the usual pleasantries and go straight for the jugular. At any rate, it ought to be noted that the manner of self-representation, "I, so-and-so," is a clue to pseudepigraphy since it protests authorial identity too much.[b] But let no one think the epistle is taken up solely

a. The "severe letter" comprises 10:1-13:9a; 2:1-6:13; 7:2-4; 13:9b-14.

b. Other examples of this are found in the Apocalypse of Abraham 1:2; Apocalypse of Peter 2; Apocalypse of Zephaniah B:7; Apocryphon of John 1:19; 2 Baruch 6:1; 3 Baruch 1:3; Book of Thomas the Contender 1:2; Dan. 7:15; 1 Enoch 25:1; 4 Ezra 2:33; Gospel of Peter 60; Infancy Gospel of Thomas 1:1; Protevangelium of James 25:1; Rev. 1:9; Testament of Levi 2:1; Testament of Solomon 1:3; Tobit 1:3.

with dreary church politics. On the contrary, the discussion of true and false apostleship, the genuine and superficial following of Christ, is filled with some of the most profound spiritual insights in the New Testament.

The second letter[c] expresses gratitude and relief for the happy resolution of the conflict, much like the reunion scene between Jesus and Peter in John 21:15-17. The two letters follow one another directly and circulated together in the manner of an epistolary novel.

Chapters 8 and 9, as L. Gordon Rylands (*A Critical Analysis of the Four Chief Pauline Epistles*) argues, would seem to have been a pair of independent fund-raising letters, written by two different people, both using Paul's name to encourage generosity. This would be like the instances where the gospel writers used Jesus as a mouthpiece for their own advice for readers to give their possessions to the poor. In 8:23 the writer introduces Titus in a fashion that would have been wholly unnecessary if the chapter formed part of the preceding text since Titus is there supposed to be well-known to the Corinthians. The passage at 9:1 appears to introduce the collection as a new topic, so it cannot have originally followed chapter 8. Both chapters envision a team arriving to collect the funds, while 8:18-19, 22 speaks of some famous brother, an evangelistic preacher, who will oversee matters. Oddly, the famous brother is not named, which may suggest the space was left blank to be filled in by anyone who wanted to use the letter. In any case, the letter in chapter 9 appears to be earlier than that in chapter 8.

Most scholars recognize that the section comprising 6:14-7:1 has no connection to its context. It seems, in fact, to be from a conservative synagogue sermon addressed to Jews tempted by assimilationism. Probably whoever pieced together 2 Corinthians found this material on the back of one of his scraps and just kept copying front to back, then continued on to the next sheet, not realizing this material was an older document and that someone, short of paper, had copied the Pauline material onto the empty back of it. He made a minimal attempt to harmonize, as evidenced by the redactional seam at 7:2a.

c. The letter of reconciliation comprises 1:1-2:13; 7:5-16.

The severe letter

10

Now I, Paul—myself—beseech you by the meekness and the gentleness of Christ—I who am so humble among you in person but so fierce on paper! [2]Now I beg you: don't make it necessary for me to act in person with the boldness with which I plan to be daring toward some who consider us to be behaving by mere mortal standards. [3]For though we live in the flesh, we wage war not in a worldly manner, [4]for the weapons of our warfare are not material, but derive from God their power to overthrow fortress mentalities, turning aside the rapier of argument and demolishing [5]every Babel tower raised up against true knowledge of God, taking prisoner every scheme to convert it forcibly to obey Christ [6]and standing ready to avenge all disobedience once your obedience is secured.

[7]You look no deeper than the surface of things. If anyone has satisfied himself that he belongs to Christ, then he had better take another look and see that if he belongs to Christ, so do we.[d] [8]For even if I do brag more than usual about our authority which the Lord gave to fortify you, not to demolish you, I shall not wind up ashamed of what I said [9]for fear of frightening you through the epistles. [10]"Oh, his epistles," he says, "are weighty and powerful, to be sure, but his presence in person is weak and his oratory contemptible."[e] [11]Well, let such a person remember this: what we are in word in epistles while absent, we will also be in person and in action![f] [12]Oh, we would never presume to class ourselves or to compare ourselves with some who commend themselves; but they, measuring themselves only among themselves and comparing themselves only with themselves, naturally do not understand. [13]But on the other hand, we will not boast without any measure, but rather according to the measure of that yardstick which God measured out and apportioned to us, demarcating our sphere of activity as far as you. [14]For we do not overreach our proper bounds as if our territory did not reach as far as you, for we came all the way to you in our preaching the news of Christ, [15]not bragging disproportionately over others' accomplishments but expecting that, as

d. If their faith is genuine and they got it from Paul, how can they imagine his is counterfeit?

e. This reference, like 2 Pet. 3:16, presupposes a collection of Pauline letters and the controversies surrounding them. It is surely anachronistic for a genuine Pauline letter.

f. Verses 10-11 parallel Mark 8:38, where anyone ashamed of the prophetic speaker's words will find himself eating crow on the day Jesus, or Paul, arrives.

your faith matures, we will be more appreciated by you according to our assignment there until finally you appreciate us fully. 16We aim to preach the news in the regions beyond you, not to brag of things already accomplished in someone else's domain. 17No, "If anyone wants to brag, let him extol the greatness of Adonai."[g] 18For it is not the one who commends himself that is approved, but the one whom the Lord commends.

11

1I ask you to permit me a little bit of foolishness. No, really, permit me! 2For I am jealous for you with a godly jealousy. I betrothed you to one husband, hoping to present a pure virgin to Christ. 3But now I fear that perhaps somehow, as the serpent seduced Eve by his cleverness, your minds may have been seduced from the simple purity of Christ. 4For indeed, if someone arrives and proclaims another savior whom we did not proclaim,[h] or if you receive a different spirit that you did not receive or a different preaching from the one you originally welcomed, you have not the slightest trouble putting up with him. 5For I estimate that in no respect do I fall short of the super-apostles.[i] 6But if in truth I am unskilled in speech, yet I am not so in gnosis, but we have instead been completely transparent in our dealings with you.

7Or did my sin lie in humbling myself so you could be exalted, because I evangelized you with the news of God free of charge? 8No, I robbed the other congregations, accepting their wages so I could serve you. 9When present with you and in need, I was a burden to no one, for the brothers arriving from Macedonia supplied my needs; and in every respect I kept from becoming a burden to you, and so I will remain. 10As the truth of Christ is in me, I swear no one will deprive me of this boast in the regions of Achaia. 11Why? Because I do not love you? God knows I do! 12But what I do, I will keep right on doing in order to prevent anyone boasting that they practice the same as us. 13For these are pseudo-apostles,

---

g. Jer. 9:24

h. Literally "another Jesus," although possibly the generic use of the name's underlying meaning, "savior" (Matt. 1:21; cf. Mark 13:6, 21). Another possibility is that different cults and sects had their own figureheads named "Jesus," with disparate mythical or historical origins which eventually fused together, something perhaps in the works here.

i. These would be the twelve apostles, figureheads of orthodoxy, with whom Paul is being posthumously compared and to whom some, like the author of Acts, would subordinate him—thus degrading the relative authority of his bequeathed teaching.

charlatans, masquerading as apostles of Christ.[j] [14]And that should surprise no one: for the accuser himself masquerades as an angel of light. [15]Thus, it is no great surprise if his servants, too, masquerade as servants of righteousness. Their ultimate fate will be as their deeds deserve.

[16]Again I say, let no one think me foolish. But if you do, at least indulge me so I may do a little bragging. [17]What I am saying, I say not as an apostle of the Lord, but as if I were a jester in this pose of bragging. [18]Since it seems a popular sport, why shouldn't I, too, take a turn? [19]Being so wise, surely you can afford to be patient with fools! [20]In fact, you are patient with anyone who enslaves you, who makes a meal of you, who takes you in, who exalts himself, who slaps you in the face. [21]I am ashamed to admit that indeed we were too weak for that. But in whatever way anyone dares, I say I too will dare! [22]What, are they Hebrews? Me too! Israelites, are they? Me too! Seed of Abraham, are they? Me too! [23]Are they servants of Christ? Please keep in mind, I am speaking as if I have lost my mind—I am more of one! I can point to more numerous labors, far more imprisonments, excessive whippings, and being on the verge of death many times! [24]Let's see: from the Jews I received the thirty-nine lashes on five different occasions; [25]three times I was caned by Romans; once I was stoned; three times shipwrecked, [26]spending a night and a day adrift; many times on the road in danger from robbers, from flash floods, from my race, from gentiles, in the city, in the wilderness, at sea; in danger from false brothers,[k] [27]in labor and hardship, passing many vigils, in famine and drought, often fasting, cold and naked.[l] [28]Apart from outward circumstances, there are the daily conspiracies against me, the burden of anxiety for all the congregations. [29]For who among them is weak, and I am not weak? Who is offended and I do not feel his anguish? [30]If one has to brag, I choose to brag about my weaknesses. [31]This one may be hard to believe, but the God and Father of our Lord Jesus, the one who will be eulogized throughout the ages, he knows I am not lying. [32]In Damascus the ethnarch serving King Aretas posted guards around the city, looking to apprehend me, [33]and I was lowered in a basket through a window in the city wall and escaped his grasp.[m]

---

j. A neat summation of the Marcionite estimate of the Twelve.

k. The implied picture of Paul is that of an indefatigable superman whom nothing can stop, which is part and parcel of the Pauline legend.

l. See the similar stock list of vicissitudes of the ideal missionary in Matt. 25:35-36.

m. Acts 9:22-25

12

[1]Surely it is inadvisable for me to boast, unless perhaps on another's behalf, so I will go on to visions and revelations from the Lord. [2]I know a man caught up by Christ some fourteen years ago—whether bodily I do not know, or out of the body I do not know, only God knows—to the third heaven. [3]And I know such a man—whether bodily or apart from the body I do not know, I tell you, only God knows—he was caught up into the Paradise and there heard unutterable utterances which human beings are forbidden to speak. [5]On behalf of such a one, I will readily brag, but not on my own behalf except for my weaknesses. [6]For should I wish to brag, it would be no foolishness; for I would be telling the truth. But I will spare you so that no one forms an opinion of me based on anything but what he sees of me or hears from me.

[7]To prevent me from becoming swell-headed over the superabundance of revelations vouchsafed me,[n] a thorn in the flesh was given me, an angel of the accuser to pummel me, to prevent my self-inflation. [8]I pleaded with the Lord three times about this, to call him off. [9]And he said to me, "My charisma is sufficient for you, for my power is perfected in weakness."[o] In that case, I will all the more gladly brag about my weaknesses in order that the power of Christ may eclipse me. [10]That is why I am delighted with weaknesses, with insults, with tight spots, with persecutions and difficulties, all on behalf of Christ, for whenever I am weak, then I am mighty.[p]

---

n. Is Paul, then, the one who ascended to the third heaven after all? Is he talking about himself? Not necessarily. Revelation claims are often ascribed to Paul, and these revelations in v. 7 need have nothing to do with those of the ascended man. But we cannot help suspecting, as most readers do, that the ascended visionary of vv. 2-3 is intended as Paul. Then why the third-person reference? For the moment, the pseudepigraphist drops his pose, feeling himself unworthy of impersonating Paul in such an exalted condition. The situation is again (see 10:11-12 above) strikingly similar to that underlying Mark 8:38: "For whoever is ashamed of me and my words in this adulterous and sinful generation, of him will the one like a Son of Man be ashamed when he comes in his Father's splendor with the holy angels." Why the third person? In Mark 8:38, "my words" are those of the anonymous itinerant apostle, while "he" is the one like a son of man, the returning Christ. The speaker represents him but is not he. It may be the same here, the writer being unable to completely erase the line between himself and the one in whose name he speaks.

o. Here the "word of the Lord" is like in 1 Cor. 7:10, 25; 14:37, and it is clearly a "channeled" piece of prophecy, not a quote from a historical Jesus. The rest need not be quotations either.

p. The scene is set entirely in the third heaven before the enthroned Christ.

[11]What a fool I have become! But it is your fault. For I should be getting commended by you. For I came short of the super-apostles in no respect, even if, as they say, I am nothing! [12]Indeed, the authenticating signs of an apostle were performed among you in all patience, both by signs and wonders and works of power.[q] [13]So in what respect were you deprived, compared to the other congregations, except that I made myself a burden to none of you?[r] Well, forgive me this wrong! [14]Behold, this third time I am ready to come to you, nor will I burden you, for I am not interested in your money but in you! For it is not the children who should store up money to care for their parents, but the parents who are obliged to provide for their children. [15]And as for me, I am quite ready to spend and to be spent out on behalf of your souls. If I love you all the more, am I to be loved the less? [16]Be that as it may, the fact is, I did not burden you. But perhaps I was crafty and took you in by deceit? [17]There was no one whom I sent to you [18]through whom I cheated you, was there? I persuaded Titus and have now sent him along with the other brother—Titus hasn't cheated you, has he? And didn't we behave in the same spirit? Didn't we walk in the same path?

[19]Again, you no doubt think we are on the defensive. But we speak before God and in the voice of Christ. And all of it, my beloved, is aimed at building you up. [20]For I am afraid that when I come, I will not find you as I would like to and you will not find me as you would like to see me—that strife, jealousy, old angers, rivalries, badmouthing, whisper campaigns, inflated egos, and brawls may erupt again, that when I come, my God may humiliate me before you and I shall have to mourn over many of the ones who previously sinned and neglected to repent of the impurity and whore-mongering and perversion which they practiced.

13

[1]This third time, I am coming to you. "By the testimony of two or

---

Under attack by a punishing angel, who reflects the overarching biblical role of the adversary as tester of God's servants, Paul cries out thrice in rapid succession for deliverance—just as Jesus does in Gethsemane—and is vouchsafed a lesson about where strength lies. He learns that true discipleship lies not in conjuring miracles but in sharing the sufferings of Christ.

q. Notice that the writer, ostensibly Paul, does not use the active voice. He does not say, "I performed ... signs and wonders and works of power." Why not? He is too used to thinking of another, the historical Paul, doing these things.

r. Paul was known to have accepted contributions from Thessalonica and Philippi in Macedonia, but he did not want to take any support from Corinth or other congregations in Achaia.

three witnesses shall every word be corroborated."[s] [2]I have said before and now say in advance while yet absent, as I did while present on my second visit, to those who sinned before and to everyone else that if I do decide to come again, I will show no mercy, [3]since you require evidence that Christ is speaking in me, he who is by no means weak toward you but powerful in you. [4]To be sure, he was crucified by token of weakness, but he lives by the power of God. For indeed, we are weak as sharing in the death of him, but we shall live with him by the power of God exercised upon you. [5]Test yourselves, whether you are firm in the faith; prove yourselves! Don't you perceive that Jesus-Christ is in you—unless you are counterfeits? [6]But I hope you will know that we are no counterfeits.[t] [7]Even now, we pray to God that you will do no evil, and not because it would reflect badly on us but simply in order that you may do the good, whether we are counterfeits or not. [8]For we are incapable of any action against the truth, only on behalf of the truth. [9]We rejoice whenever we are weak and you are powerful; we have no desire to feel superior at your expense.

2

[14]But thank God, who is always leading us along in Christ's triumphal parade, sending forth the incense of the knowledge of him through us in every place we go. [15]Because of Christ, we are a sweet savor rising before God to those being saved, as well as to those being lost. [16]To the latter, we are a poisonous reek of decay, but to the former, the fresh scent of spring. And who is equal to this task? [17]For we are not like the majority, hustling the message of God, but rather, we speak from sincerity, from God, and in the sight of God in the power of Christ.

3

[1]Oh no! Are we starting to commend ourselves again? Surely we do not need reference letters either to you from other congregations we served or from you to others we hope to enter, as some apparently do?[u]

---

s. Deut. 19:15

t. If their faith seems genuine, they cannot very well reject Paul as a counterfeit since he is the origin of their faith. Their criticisms backfire.

u. The thought sequence through the chapter is strikingly equivalent to John 8:13-20. The author requires no testimony from anyone else. His movements to and fro are no proper concern of his audience, and there is an *ad hominem* appeal to Jewish scripture since his audience seems to accept its authority. By contrast, it is the God who is unknown to Jews who is the source of his authority. Both passages bespeak someone writing pseudonymously in the kind of self-exalting terms

[2]You yourselves are all the credential we need. You are engraved on our hearts for all to read, as everyone knows.[v] [3]It is thus plain that you are an epistle from Christ, delivered by us, one written not with ink but by the Spirit of the true God, not on stony tablets, but on tablets that are fleshy hearts.[w]

[4]And we have such confidence before God thanks to Christ. [5]It is not from our own resources that we are competent, as if we could ascribe anything to our own merit. No, our competence comes from God, [6]the one who also made us competent as servants of a new covenant, not one of letter but one of spirit. After all, the letter kills, but the spirit vivifies. [7]Now if the ministry of death,[x] having been engraved in letters in stone, was glorious to the extent that the sons of Israel could not stand to look upon Moses's face because of its radiance as it faded away,[y] [8]how much greater glory will mark the ministry of the Spirit? [9]For if the ministry of condemnation was marked by glory, the ministry of vindication increases in splendor much more. [10]For indeed, the thing not hitherto glorified has been made splendid in this respect because of this superabundance of glory. [11]For if the covenant that was fading away shone with glory, how much more brilliant will the one be that remains in force? [12]With a prospect like this, naturally we speak with great boldness, [13]unlike Moses, who placed a veil over his face to prevent the sons of Israel seeing the end of his fading halo.[z] [14]But their thoughts became obtuse, for even today

---

another writer would feel appropriate for a great founder, whether Jesus or Paul, the latter being an apostle of Marcionite gnosis, at that.

v. At stake here are rival claims of apostolic patronage and lineage and the relative authority of various major churches in the late first or early second century. What evidence was there to elevate this or that church above the norm? Such a concern would lead naturally to the fabrication not only of foundation legends but also of epistles to churches who wished to show them off. Just as the writer of 1 Cor. 2:1 forswears rhetoric at the outset of his use of it, so does this writer reject the need for credential letters as he writes one.

w. Ezek. 36:26-27

x. Notice how it is simply taken for granted that the Mosaic scripture covenant is death-dealing, with no explanation such as we find in Rom. 3-4, 7; Gal. 3-5. As W. C. van Manen saw, this implies a context of intra-Paulinist scholastic debate where much is taken for granted before the argument starts. What is taken for granted seems to be a wholesale devaluation of the Torah in a manner wholly unimaginable for a Jew. The Torah dispensation was merely one of death?

y. Exod. 34:29-35

z. Startlingly, the parallel here is not between Moses and Jesus but rather between Moses and Paul! This bespeaks an early or late Christology of Paul, who

the same veil obscures the reading of the Old Testament[a] so it is not revealed to them that that covenant is being rendered obsolete by Christ.
15Even today whenever Moses is being read, a veil shrouds their heart;
16"but whenever he turns to Adonai, the veil is removed."[b] 17So "Adonai" refers to the Spirit, and wherever the Spirit of Adonai is, there is freedom.[c] 18But we all, faces unveiled, look upon the splendor of Adonai in a
mirror, witnessing our own metamorphosis into the same image, from
splendor to splendor even as a spirit from Adonai.[d]

4

1Because of this, having this ministry by the mercy of God, we will
not give up; 2on the contrary, we have repudiated underhanded and
shameful methods, not conducting ourselves with craftiness, nor dilut-
ing the message of God, as is the policy of some we could name, but commending ourselves to every human conscience and in the sight of God by
the simple expedient of setting forth the truth. 3If, however, there is anything secret about our message, it is because it remains invisible to those
who are lost.[e] 4In their case, the God of this world[f] has blinded the
thoughts of the unbelievers to prevent the dawning of the enlightenment
of the news of the splendor of Christ, who is the image of God. 5For it is
not ourselves that we promote, but Christ-Jesus as Lord and ourselves as
your slaves on account of Jesus. 6Because God, the one who said, "Out
of darkness, light shall shine!"[g] is also the one who ignited in our hearts
the enlightenment of knowing the splendor of God shining from the face
of Christ.[h]

---

was either on the way to eclipsing the rival savior Jesus or has not yet been eclipsed by him.

a. This is a gross anachronism, the Jewish scriptures not being referred to as the Old Testament till the time of Melito of Sardis in the second century.

b. As Gordon D. Fee recognized, this is a quotation from Exod. 34:34.

c. The appeal to Jewish scripture is of an *ad hominem* character, using it against itself in the manner of the Gnostics.

d. This sounds like Valentinian Gnosticism, also like the Eastern Orthodox *theosis* doctrine, which has the same source.

e. As in John 18:19-21, this is a rather disingenuous rejoinder to those who object to Paulinist claims of secret gnosis reserved for the elite, as in 1 Cor. 2:6-7ff.

f. The reference would be to the Hebrew Creator God in whose name Moses promulgated the Torah, not the Father of Jesus Christ.

g. Gen. 1:3

h. This language suggests the Kabbalistic idea that God created the world by emitting the divine light through the mouth, eyes, nostrils, and ears of the heav-

7And we carry this treasure in brittle ceramic vessels in order that the surpassing power may be God's, not ours. 8We are being afflicted in every possible way, but not held back; mired in problems, yet not despairing; 9persecuted by human beings, but not abandoned by God; being thrown down, but not destroyed; 10ever carrying around in the body the dying of Jesus in order that the life of Jesus may be equally seen in our body. 11For we, the living, are always being delivered up to death because of Jesus in order that the life of Jesus might be manifested against the background of our dying flesh. 12So then, death is consuming us while life is energizing you. 13And having the same disposition of faith as the scriptural writer who said, "I believed; therefore I spoke,"[i] we both believe and therefore speak, 14confident that the one who raised the Lord Jesus will also raise us along with Jesus[j] and will present us with you as our boast on that day. 15For everything we do is for your sake so that the favor done to the greater number may cause thanksgiving to increase with greater worship rendered to God. 16That is why we do not give up; but if, as does happen, our exterior selves are being worn down, still our inner selves are being renewed every day. 17For the current trifling affliction in the long run generates for us an unimaginable deposit of divine splendor many times as large.[k] 18Thus we are not occupied with visible reality but with the invisible, for the visible realities are fleeting, while the invisible ones endure the ages.

5

1For instance, we know that if the tent we dwell in on earth is destroyed, we have a building from God to look forward to, a house not constructed by human hands, but abiding the ages in the skies.[l] 2For indeed, in this one we groan, urgently anxious to don our dwelling place from the sky, 3if indeed the alternative is finding ourselves naked spirits.

---

enly Adam, Primal Man (Adam Kadmon), who was the living image of himself and the prototype for the earthly Adam to come.

i. Pss. 116:10

j. This seems to imply that Jesus has not already been raised but awaits, as do those who believe in him, the resurrection at the end of time, a belief ascribed to Cerinthians by Epiphanius.

k. The literal phrase, "weight of glory," recalls the notion of the *kabod,* the weight or burden of the glory cloud of the Shekinah. This is a return to the theme of assimilation to the divine glory in 3:18.

l. There is a play here on the ancient Israelite tent or tabernacle, built at the command of Moses and based on specifications he copied from a heavenly tabernacle glimpsed atop Mount Sinai in Exod. 25:9.

[4]To be sure, being yet in this tent, we groan with our burdens, but what we want is not to slough off bodily form but to put on a new one so that the mortal may be swallowed up by the life. [5]So he who has prepared us for this great transition is God, who has provided the down-payment of the Spirit. [6]Thus, ever rejoicing and mindful that, as long as we are at home in the body, we are homesick for the Lord, [7]we live by faith, not according to appearances. [8]That way, we maintain good cheer amid danger and deem it a happy prospect to depart the home of the body and come home to the Lord. [9]And this is why our ambition is to earn his approval, whether at home or away. [10]For none of us can avoid full disclosure before the judgment throne of Christ in order that each may receive due recompense for the deeds done in this life, either good or worthless.

[11]Therefore, in godly fear, we do not hesitate to persuade people to repent. We stand thus transparent before God's sight and, I should hope, before you in all good conscience. [12]We are not thus commending ourselves to you, only giving you the opportunity to brag about us, ready to reply to those who brag about appearances, not about the heart. [13]If we are carried away in spiritual ecstasy, it is between us and God; if we speak rationally, it is for your benefit.[m]

[14]The self-giving love of Christ compels us, since our understanding is as follows: one died on behalf of all, which means that all died; [15]and he died on behalf of all in order that those who live may henceforth live no more for themselves but for him who died on their behalf and was raised.[n] [16]Thus, from now on, we evaluate no one according to fleshly appearances. Even if we once took Christ for a being of flesh, we know better now.[o] [17]So provided anyone is in the mode of Christ, there is a new creation: the archaic creation[p] has passed away and, behold, the new has appeared. [18]And all this is from God, the one who reconciled us to himself through Christ[q] and has assigned us the administration of this reconciliation: [19]the news that, by Christ, God was reconciling the world to himself,

m. See 1 Cor. 14:14-19, 23-24, 28.

n. Verses 14-15 sound like a correction to the motivation given for preaching in vv. 10-11. A Marcionite reader would have thought it strange that fear of eschatological judgment should form any part of Paul's motivation, so a redactor apparently sought to correct the impression by having Paul motivated instead by Christ's sacrifice of love.

o. This implies Paulinist-Gnostic-Marcionite docetism.

p. The creation by the Old Testament deity is intended here.

q. Not by forgiving our sins, as they were not committed against him and he had not given the law in the first place. Rather, the Father of Jesus Christ made it

not counting up their legal trespasses as evidence against them,[r] and planting in us the message of reconciliation. 20Therefore, we are ambassadors for Christ as if it were God himself pleading with you through us. We plead with our hearers on Christ's behalf, "Be reconciled to God! 21The one who was innocent of sin, he was turned into sin on our behalf in order that by means of him we might become the righteousness of God."[s]

6

1As colleagues, therefore, we now urge you, do not let your initial welcome of God's favor turn out to be in vain. 2For he says, "At a crucial time I heard your plea, and in the day of deliverance I helped you."[t] Well, this is a crucial time! Today is a day of deliverance!

3Providing no occasion for anyone to be alienated in anything we do so as to keep our ministry free of blame, 4we commend ourselves as servants of God in everything: in patient endurance, afflictions, tight spots, predicaments, floggings, 5prisons, riots, labors, vigils, fastings, 6purity, knowledge, long-suffering, kindness, in the Holy Spirit, non-hypocritical love, 7the utterance of truth, and the power of God, with the weapons of righteousness in the right hand and the left, 8through glory and dishonor, bad report as deceivers and good report as truthful, 9being unknown yet notorious, dying and alive. As being punished and yet not to death, 10constantly grieved but rejoicing, beggars making many rich, and having nothing yet being heirs of all things.

11We have been free in our speech to you, O Corinthians! Our hearts have only opened wider to you. 12You are not estranged from us; you are estranged from your own affections. 13But for the same requital, I say as to beloved children, open yourselves wide to us as well.

7

2*Open up to us!*[u] We did no one wrong, we injured no one, cheated

---

possible for us to come to him, overcoming the gap of alienness since he was not our creator.

r. As did the Hebrew God, whose stern judgment Christians are fleeing by coming to Christ.

s. Valentinus, who claimed to be the disciple of Theodas, a disciple of Paul, admitted that Jesus had died for the *psuchikoi* who lack the divine nature, the remembrance of which the teaching of the Christ-Spirit sought to awaken in the latent *pneumatikoi*. Thus, the *psuchikoi* required a kind of second-track salvation, which God in his mercy provided.

t. Isa. 49:8

u. This is a redactional seam, repeating the phrase from the previous verse. It was probably added when the fragment 6:14-7:1 was inserted.

no one. [3]I say this not to condemn you; on the contrary, have I not already made it clear that you are so close to our hearts that we would as
soon die for you as live for you? [4]True, I dare much in speaking to you,
but equally, I brag much about you. I have been filled with comfort. I
overflow with joy amid all our affliction.

13

[9b]We also pray for your restoration to us. [10]For this reason, while absent, I write these things, so that when I get there, I may not have to deal
severely with the authority which, after all, the Lord gave me, not to tear
you down, but to build you up.

[11]As for everything else, brothers, rejoice, reconcile yourselves, encourage one another, come to agreement—and the blessings of the God of
love and of peace will be with you. [12]Greet one another with a ritual kiss.

[13]All the saints greet you. [14]May the favor of the Lord, Jesus-Christ,
and the love of God and the visitation of the Holy Spirit be with all of you.

Letter of reconciliation

1

[1]Paul, an apostle of Christ by the will of God, and Timothy,[v] the
brother,[w] to the congregation of God situated in Corinth, along with all
the saints in Achaia. [2]Grace to you and peace from God our Father and
from our Lord Jesus-Christ.

[3]Blessed be our Lord Jesus-Christ's God and Father.[x] All acts of
mercy are his children, and he is the God of all comfort, [4]the one who
comforts us every time we are afflicted, showing us how to console others
who are undergoing every affliction, using the lessons of comfort we have
learned from God who played the Paraclete to us. [5]Because as we find
ourselves experiencing more and more the sufferings of Christ, we feel
proportionately more of the consolation that comes through Christ. [6]So
whether we are afflicted for the sake of your comfort and healing or
whether we are comforted for the sake of your comfort, energizing your

v. Noth's redundancy principle ought to make us ask if perhaps the name Paul has been added later, crowding aside that of the vestigial Timothy, who was perhaps the original author, whether pseudonymous or real. Or it may denote that Timothy is the author of some of the non-Pauline additions.

w. This is in reference to an itinerant missionary, not just a Christian brother in general.

x. The emphasis on God as Christ's Father makes best sense on a Marcionite reading: at the outset the writer is careful to distinguish the Christian God from the Hebrew God.

endurance of the same sufferings that we ourselves endure, [7]either way,
our hope is firm regarding you, knowing that, just as you have joined us
in sharing the sufferings, so you will share in the comfort to follow.

[8]I do not want you to remain uninformed about our afflictions in
Asia Minor: we were burdened entirely beyond our power to endure so
that we had given up hope of surviving. [9]But we felt inside us the announcement of the death sentence in order that we might learn no longer
to place our reliance on ourselves but on God, who can always raise the
dead if it comes to that! [10]He rescued us from our great death-trap, and
he will rescue yet again. In him we have placed our hopes that he will rescue even now, [11]as long as you cooperate in prayer so that thanks may be
rendered by many for the gift granted at the request of so many.

[12]For when we come to the Judgment, this will be our boast and the
testimony of our conscience, too: that in this world we have behaved in
holiness and in sincerity before God, not by mere mortal wisdom, but in
God's favor—and more especially in our dealings with you. [13]For we
write you nothing beyond the plain sense that you read and perceive,[y]
and I hope you will perceive me fully, [14]just as you already perceived part
of the truth from us, because you will boast about us, as we will you, on
the day of the Lord Jesus.[z]

[15]And in this confidence, I had first resolved to come to you so that
you might enjoy a second favor, [16]and by way of you I would have
passed on into Macedonia, and again from Macedonia, I would have
come to you, and by way of you, I would have headed for Judea. [17]So
was this plan the product of fickleness on my part? Or do I make my res-
olutions by some cynical calculus, retreating into ambiguity and equivocal speech? [18]No, as God himself is faithful, I swear our promise to you is
not equivocal. [19]For there was nothing equivocal about the Son of God,
Christ-Jesus, the one preached among you by me and Silvanus and Timothy. No, in him there was only a clear affirmation. [20]For however many
promises of God there are, all of them receive their confirmation in him,
which is also why it is through him that we pronounce the amen as we
worship God. [21]But God is the one who fortifies us and you and has

---

y. The author wants his work to be taken with scriptural seriousness, but he is concerned it not become the object of allegorical text-twisting against his intent, which he tries to forestall. The point is much the same as in 2 Pet. 3:16 and Rev. 22:18-19.

z. The point is essentially the same as in 1 Cor. 13:8-13 and John 16:12-14: the writer poses as a voice from the past to predict the fuller revelation he is about to impart now.

anointed us [22]even with the Holy Spirit, having thus both set his stamp on us and provided us the down payment in our hearts.

[23]Now on my life, as God is my witness, I came no more to Corinth in order to spare you. [24]It is not that we domineer your faith, but rather, we are colleagues that you ought to rejoice to see since it is by the faith we promote that you stand firm.

2

[1]But I resolved this within myself: not to come to you again grieving. [2]After all, if I cause you to grieve, who is left to cheer me up? It would have been you, but then I would have saddened you instead. [3]And I wrote you about my change of plans so as to avoid coming and being made to grieve by those who ought to make me rejoice since I expect that you all share my joy.[a] [4]Indeed, I wrote to you out of great affliction and with much inner anxiety, blinking away the tears. My point was not to grieve you but to let you know of the love I have for you, even more than before! [5]For if anyone has offended, it is not so much me he has offended but, at least in part, all of you as well,[b] not to overburden you with my own hurt feelings. [6]It is enough for such an offender that he receive the punishment rendered by the majority, [7]and then it is up to you to forgive and to comfort such a person so that he not be consumed by excessive self-reproach. [8]Thus I urge you to reaffirm your love for him, [9]and this in fact is precisely why I wrote, as a test to determine whether you are completely obedient. [10]Now anyone you forgive of any sin, I also forgive. For indeed, what I have forgiven, if I have forgiven anything, it is for your sake and in Christ's place,[c] [11]so we may avoid being made fools of by the accuser, for we are well acquainted with his tricks.[d]

---

a. The Paulinist writer is dealing with a crisis of the "delay in the Pauline parousia"! Why did the apostle not return as he said he would? On the other side of the coin, the point is to explain the long absence of epistolary guidance from Paul, something unavoidable since these very epistles are written long after the fact for "rediscovery," like Deuteronomy or the Book of Mormon. Why are these letters coming to light only now if they are really by Paul? We know.

b. The point of the passage, the writer hints, is not that the historical Paul may have suffered some offense but that the writer is using Paul's persona to tell them how to deal with offenders in their own time. Hence the vagueness. See Luke 12:41.

c. See Matt. 16:19; 18:18; John 20:23. Here Paul is made to bequeath judicial authority to his successors. He is the vicar of Christ and, more to the point, so are they.

d. The author of the epistle seeks to temper Paul's excommunication procedure laid down in 1 Cor. 5:3-5, where an offender is consigned to Satan to see to his death.

[12]But coming to Troas on a mission for Christ, a door of opportunity having been opened there by the Lord, [13]still I had no inner peace when I failed to find my brother Titus there, so I bade them farewell and left for Macedonia.

7

[5]For indeed, when we arrived in Macedonia, our flesh had had no rest, but was being afflicted in every possible manner: struggles outside, fears inside. [6]But God, the one who comforts the downcast, comforted us by the arrival of Titus. [7]And not only by the fact of his presence but also by the comfort he himself had received in respect of you. He reported to us your urgent longing, your bitter self-reproach, your jealousy for my sake, so as to make me rejoice all the more. [8]Because if, in fact, I had grieved you by my epistle, I do not regret it. If indeed I did regret it, I see that that epistle, though it grieved you, did so only briefly; [9]I rejoice, not to have grieved you, but that you were grieved to the point of repenting. For you were grieved in a godly fashion in order that you might not suffer any loss from us. [10]For godly grief effects a repentance that no one will regret: that which leads to salvation. But worldly grief results in death. [11]Is that not clear in your own case? What earnestness it produced in you! What, but defense of me? What, but vexation on my behalf? What, but fear of God? What, but eager desire for reconciliation? What, but jealousy for my good name? What, but vengeance on my offender? In every respect, you have cleared yourselves in this matter. [12]If indeed I then wrote to you, it was not for the sake of the one who did wrong, nor for the sake of the one who was wronged, but rather so that your earnestness on our behalf might become clear to you before God. [13]That is why we found it comforting. But speaking of our comfort, we rejoiced all the more over the joy of Titus, whose spirit has been refreshed by all of you, [14]because whatever I have said bragging about you to him, I was put to shame in nothing. Rather, just as we spoke truly in everything we said to you, the bragging I did to Titus about you turned out to be true. [15]And his affection for you is great, as he calls to mind everyone's obedience, as you welcomed him with fear and trembling. [16]I rejoice that I can be completely confident in you.[e]

Fund-raising letter 1

9

[1]Now concerning the ministry to the saints, it is superfluous for me to write anything to you, [2]for I know your zeal, of which I brag about you

e. The implied scenario (vv. 9, 10, 15) is that the unfaithful, indecisive Corin-

to the Macedonians: "Achaia has made preparations a year ago!" And your zeal prompted most to emulate you. [3]And I have sent with this letter the brothers, just to make sure our bragging about you is not exposed as empty in this respect, that I said you were prepared; [4]so if I arrive with the Macedonians and find you unprepared, we should be embarrassed, not to mention you, in the confidence we had. [5]This is why I thought it needful to urge the brothers to come to you in advance so as to arrange beforehand the blessing that you promised, so it might actually be a blessing and not something you feel begrudged to give on the spot. [6]And remember this: the one who sows stingily will also reap a stingy harvest, and the one sowing blessing on blessing will also reap appropriately. [7]Each one should give as he has resolved conscientiously, not grudgingly or under pressure, for God loves a cheerful giver. [8]And God is able to cause all fortune to increase for you in order that, always having your own self-sufficiency in everything, you may increase in every good deed, [9]as it is written: "He scattered, he gave to the poor, his reputation for righteousness will last forever."[f] [10]Now the one providing seed for the sower will both supply bread for food and increase the harvest of your righteousness [11]so that in every way you will grow rich in liberality, which results through us as your couriers in thanksgiving to God! [12]Because the ministration of this service not only supplies the needs of the saints but also increases manyfold the thanks rendered God. [13]This ministry will glorify God, demonstrating to the saints your submission, by confession of faith, to the news of God, as well as the liberality of the fellowship of the gentiles to them and to all people, [14]with them praying poignantly for you on account of the excelling favor of God upon you. [15]Thank God for his indescribable gift!

Fund-raising letter 2

8

[1]Now we make known to you, brothers, the divine favor shown to the congregations of Macedonia, [2]how in the very crucible of affliction their abundance of joy and depth of poverty combined to produce a fortune in liberal generosity, [3]how, according to their resources, even beyond their resources, on their own initiative [4]they begged us the favor of

---

thians were terrified by the possibility of mass excommunication, threatened by Paul as he departed in a huff after some embarrassing encounter with one of the members. The Corinthians initially stood by the member. Of course, the scenario could well be manufactured for the sake of the narrative frame.

f. Pss. 112:9

assisting in the service to the saints, [5]and as we could never have expected, they gave themselves first to the Lord and then to us by the will of God, asking us to plead with Titus to complete what he had previously begun, extending this favor to you, too. [7]But just as you are rich in everything, in faith, in inspired utterance, in gnosis, and in all diligence, and in our love for you, see that you may be equally rich in this charisma. [8]I do not pretend to command you, but to measure the reality of your love in comparison with the diligence of others. [9]You are aware of the gratuitous kindness of our Lord Jesus, how on your account, though being rich, he impoverished himself in order that you, by means of his poverty, might become rich. [10]So I give an opinion in this matter: this is expedient for you [11]to bring to completion, from what resources you have, the task you were the first to resolve and to do already a year ago and to do it with the zeal you had then. [12]For if the eagerness is already present, whatever one has is acceptable, no matter how little. [13]For the goal is not that others should be relieved at the cost of your distress, but that by way of equality, [14]at the present time your abundance might supply their lack in order that their abundance may one day supply your want so that equality might prevail. [15]As it is written: "He who gathered much did not have too much, and he who gathered little had no less."[g] [16]But thank God for placing the same diligence on your behalf in the heart of Titus, for indeed he welcomed the Macedonians' request, and being more diligent on his own initiative, he went out to you. [18]And we sent with him _________,[h] the brother whose work preaching the news is praised throughout the congregations. [19]Not only this, but I have also sent our traveling companion, _________, elected by the congregations, to administer this gift to the glory of our common Lord, as we are eager to avoid any possibility of anyone finding anything questionable in our administration of this bounty. [21]For we are concerned for propriety not only before God but in the sight of other people. [22]And we sent with them our brother, _________, whose diligence we proved many times over in many tasks, and now all the more diligent for his confidence in you. [23]Whether you ask of Titus, my partner and colleague on your behalf, or our brothers, delegates of the congregations, they seek only the glory of Christ. [24]Therefore, demonstrate in the presence of the congregations they represent both the evidence of your love and of our bragging about you.

g. Exod. 16:18

h. A blank left for whomever uses the letter and poses as its courier.

A sermon fragment

6

14 Do not be mismated with unbelievers, for what can righteousness and lawlessness possibly share in common? Or what mutual association can light have with darkness? 15 And what peace can be negotiated between Christ and Beliar?[i] Or what business does a believer have with an unbeliever? 16 And what ecumenical union can be effected between a shrine of God and idols? For we are a shrine of the true God, as God said, "I will take up residence among them and I will walk among them.[j] 17 So come out from among them and be distinct, says Adonai, and do not touch any ritually unclean food.[k] Then I will welcome you, and I will be like a Father to you, and you shall be sons and daughters to me, says Adonai Shaddai."[l]

7

1 Since we have these promises, brothers, let us purify ourselves from all pollution of flesh and of spirit, perfecting consecration in the fear of God.

i. An apocalyptic term for the Antichrist in Judaism.

j. Ezek. 37:27; Lev. 26:12

k. Isa. 52:11

l. Perhaps Hosea 1:10 or Isa. 43:6 is intended.

14.
The Epistle to the Romans

SCHOLARS HAVE TRADITIONALLY taken Paul as the real, not the pseudonymous, author of Romans. Read that way, the work would date from about 57 CE, written in Corinth to the collection of house congregations in Rome. The letter prepares the ground for Paul's stop in Rome en route from Jerusalem to Spain after he has at last delivered the financial assistance from his congregations for the poor in Jerusalem, whose leaders required this of him in return for recognition of his apostolic work (Gal. 2:6, 10). Paul has reason to fear the Jerusalem leaders may not receive the gift graciously. But if all goes well, he hopes to journey to Spain to preach, and he has long wanted to visit Rome to place his mark on the church there, though he was not its founder. He knows he is liable to receive a mixed reception since sympathetic contacts listed in chapter 16 have already warned him of factional strife among the congregations and of anti-Pauline suspicions. Thus he sends the epistle ahead as an apologia for his preaching, outlining some key themes in detail, with a focus on correcting current misunderstandings. It would be the equivalent of sending a professional paper to colleagues prior to a scholarly conference so participants have a chance to digest the material ahead of time, leading to a more fruitful discussion.

Paul seems to be juggling several different opinions in his appeal to various factions. There would appear to be Jewish Christians akin to the Jerusalem saints who kept the Torah as part of Christian discipleship. These would have included the earliest layer of Christians in Rome, laid down not by apostles but by traveling merchants and slaves. There would also likely be gentile converts to this sort of Torah

Christianity. Both factions will have heard or inferred from Paul's Torah-free gospel that he rejects the Torah as superannuated or even evil. He must assure these skeptics that he does not regard the Torah or Jewish precedence as obsolete. On the other hand, he does relegate Torah Christians to the status of "weaker brothers" who do not yet understand their birthright as true sons of Abraham who attained saving faith and merit long before the Law was even an item on the table. Whether one is a Christian Diaspora Jew dead set against assimilation or a convert to the Torah who, for the sheer cognitive dissonance, cannot afford to admit a mistaken commitment of such magnitude, Torah Christians are not likely to relish such second-class status.

But Paul does stand up for them against the faction of gentile Christian triumphalists and supersessionists who ridicule Jewish customs and make no provisions for Jewish sensibilities at common meetings. Paul warns these not to embrace the view, already current and one day to be officially embraced by Catholics and Calvinists, that Christians have simply replaced Jews as God's chosen people. No, the seniority and dignity of Jews are retained in the Christian dispensation, not only because of their heritage, without which Christianity could not exist, but also because of the historical fact that Christianity began among Jews. Gentile Christians must never forget the debt they owe to Jewish Christians.

Paul strives to show how his message of salvation by faith apart from Torah piety does not eventuate in libertinism and antinomian behavior. It is possible that Torah Christians proposed such an implication as a *reductio ad absurdum* of his teaching or that some gentile Christians, rejecting the Torah as a whole, drew no distinction between moral and ritual portions of the Torah. Paul seems to admit that while libertinism might be a logical implication of justification by faith, his message contains extenuating factors such as the baptismal infusion of the Holy Spirit to cause a change in behavior, freeing one from the compulsive bondage of temptations of the flesh. Then, as if feeling he is dangerously close to the Gnostic enthusiasm of some in Rome, he qualifies this freedom from sin, rejecting perfectionism by deferring liberation from the body, thus from sin, till the second coming of Christ.

Returning to the question of Paul's mission, for which he seeks the contribution of Roman funds, Paul seems to be defending the very legitimacy of the enterprise before the skeptical eyes of influential Jewish-Christian elders who seem to have held an attitude like that of the Jerusalem elders in Acts 11:3. Why does he not stick to Jewish evangelism? His answer? In a sense, he is still evangelizing Jews, but because Jewish evangelism had reached an impasse, most Jews refusing to embrace Jesus, his outreach to the gentiles will ultimately attract Jews too, albeit through the back door. Once they see the historic Jewish mission of being a beacon to the gentiles fulfilled by gentiles converting to Christianity, they will realize Christianity is the proper fulfillment of Judaism and join it, even as the Jewish Christians of Rome have done.

Upon very close examination, however, the preceding summation of Romans begins to look like a very elaborate, even brilliant attempt at harmonization of a text whose many contradictions and anachronisms make it appear more like a patchwork quilt woven by the hands of various Paulinists with competing views, along with other extraneous material. If Romans is understood this way, then the historical context is fictive. Can we surmise the actual occasion for the writing of the basic substratum of Romans? It may well be that the trip to Rome anticipated by the writer is that of Marcion when he brought a contribution to the church at Rome and set forth his Gospel before its elders. He was rejected, as was his monetary gift. Perhaps the basis of Romans was written by or for Marcion to be submitted as a statement of his theology. The deliberations over the Torah would then reflect the dispute over Marcionite belief that Jews had a separate religion from Christianity, that the two had nothing in common. Arguments from scripture in the original Marcionite text would have to be understood as circumstantial *ad hominem* arguments, embarrassing opponents who upheld the Torah by making their own scripture betray them.

Subsequent redactors and interpolators would have interposed alternate views into the discussion or even sought to correct earlier statements—as for instance, the complete stultification of the Torah—in the interests of co-opting and sanitizing the text for Catholic

use. Explicit references to Paul may have been added at this time to cover over the Marcio-Gnostic origins of the epistle. The basic Marcionite document would stem from about 130-140 CE.

1

[1]Paul, slave of Christ-Jesus, called as apostle, devoted exclusively to the news of God, [2]which he had already promised through his prophets in Holy Scripture, [3]about his Son, "sprung from the line of David according to flesh, [4]miraculously appointed Son of God according to the Spirit of Holiness by a resurrection of the dead, Jesus-Christ, our Lord,"[a] [5]by whom we received charisma and apostleship for securing international faith and submission to his name, [6]in which scope you too are included, being called by Jesus-Christ.[b] [7]To all those *in Rome*[c] whom God loves, the ones called saints: May God, our Father and that of the Lord, Jesus-Christ, grant you his favor and his blessing of peace.

[8]First of all, let me thank my God, invoking Jesus-Christ, for all of you! Your faith is being made known worldwide, [9]since, as God is my witness, whom I serve at the core of my being in service of the news of his Son, I never omit mention of you [10]in my prayers wherever I happen to be, requesting if perhaps by the will of God I may be granted a propitious journey to come to you. [11]For I yearn to see you in order to present you with some spiritual charisma so you may be established as greatest among the churches of God,[d] [12]and in order that we may be mutually encouraged by means of the faith you and I have in one another. [13]But brothers, I do not want you to be unaware that I have several times re-

---

a. The Christological fragment in vv. 3-4 may, as most think, be a quotation from an early creed. It seems anachronistic if the author is really Paul. Creed making would seem to fit better a subsequent stage of the institutionalization of the church. It does sound creedal, but then the author is a later Paulinist.

b. As W. C. van Manen argued, this salutation is so much longer than those found in genuine letters from antiquity, we must suspect the author is really writing a treatise, a book of Romans, as it is still commonly called, rather than a letter. The epistolary form is fictive, with the intent of claiming Paul's authority for its authorship.

c. A few manuscripts omit the reference to Rome. Possibly the epistle was originally an encyclical and then the destination was added to lend more plausibility as a letter. On the other hand, someone may have sought to turn the epistle into an encyclical by omitting the specific address.

d. Here is the Catholic legend of the Pauline foundation (along with Peter) of the Roman Church.

solved to come see you, only to be hindered till now, wanting to harvest a crop from you as I have among the other nations. [14]I am in debt to both Greeks and uncouth barbarians, to both the wise and the savage. [15]Consequently, insofar as it is up to me, I am eager to preach to you *in Rome.* [16]My long absence is by no means due to some reluctance I might have about the news of Christ. How could it be? It is divine power to save everyone who believes, first of course the Jew, and also the Greek. [17]For in it there is revealed a salvation[e] beginning and ending in faith, just as it is written: "The righteous man will live off faith."[f]

[18]For the heavens declare the wrath of God[g] on all the impiety and unrighteousness of mankind who hide away the truth in unrighteousness [19]because what is known about God is no secret to them: God has revealed it to them [20]simply by creating the world. For anyone can clearly see his invisible attributes in the things he made, notably both his everlasting power and divinity, and this leaves human beings without excuse; [21]because even though they knew God, they did not worship him as God nor render him due thanks, but instead, their thinking became an exercise in futility, their obtuse minds blinded. [22]Claiming a reputation for wisdom, they only became more foolish [23]and refashioned the sublimity of the immutable Godhead into something like the image of ephemeral humanity and birds and quadrupeds and reptiles. [24]Accordingly, God abandoned them to pursue their hearts' desire for impurity, to the mutual defilement of each other's bodies, [25]these who twisted the truth of God into a tissue of lies, offering worship and sacrifice to the creature rather than to the creator, blessed may he be through the ages! [26]Because of all this, God surrendered them to degrading passions, for even their[h] females, of whom better might have been expected, traded the natural function for the unnatural,[i] [27]and in the same way, the males, too, disdaining the natural vessel for their seed, the female, burned with their desire for one another, males on males, enacting the perversion and unable to evade the in-

---

e. Joachim Jeremias, *The Central Message of the New Testament* (New York: Scribners, 1965), 52-53, shows how the term "to be justified" denotes "finding grace, salvation, acceptance with God."

f. Hab. 2:4

g. The text from this point through the end of chapter 2 must originally have formed an anonymous sermon preached in some Hellenistic synagogue and circulated among Jews of the Diaspora, as J. C. O'Neill suggests.

h. The pronoun refers to the gentiles, whose abominations have alienated them from the true God.

i. The implication is that they have fornicated with animals: Lev. 18:23.

evitable repercussions of their error on their consciences. [28]And as they did not judge it best to retain God in their awareness, God allowed them to fall victim to a substandard mind, inclined to the worst thoughts, to do whatever is improper, [29]bloated with all manner of injustice, evil, covetousness, maliciousness, full of murderous envy, deceitful strife, ill-will, conspiratorial whisperers, [30]detractors, God-haters, with over-weening pride, the arrogant, braggarts, evil schemers, defiant of parental authority, [31]obtuse, welchers, without love of family, unrelenting; [32]those who know full well the edict of God, that people doing these things deserve death, and not only still do them but approve others who do the same.

2

[1]So what excuse can you possibly offer, O man, when you presume to judge everyone else? For whenever you condemn another, you yourself are equally guilty. [2]But we know the verdict that God renders on people who practice such things is objective. [3]And you who condemn those who practice these things while doing them yourself, do you imagine you will escape the judgment of God? [4]Or is it perhaps that you disdain the wealth of his goodness and his tolerance and patience, oblivious of the fact that the kindness of God ought to lead you to repent? [5]But as your stubborn, impenitent heart deserves, you have amassed yourself a tidy sum of wrath to be inherited on the Day of Wrath when the righteous judgment of God will be declared—[6]he who will repay every individual as his deeds deserve: [7]on the one hand, age-long life to those who seek to be glorified and honored with immortality by persisting in good deeds, [8]on the other, wrath and anger to those who are self-seeking, disobeying the demands of truth but obeying the dictates of unrighteousness. [9]There will be tribulation and anguish upon every human soul who does evil, both to Jew, firstly, and to Greek; [10]but glory, reward, and respite upon every one doing good, both to Jew, firstly, and to Greek. [11]For no partiality is to be found with God. [12]Every one who sinned outside the reach of the Torah will also perish without reference to the Torah; and every one who sinned, having the Torah, will be condemned from the Torah. [13]For it is not those who merely hear the Torah readings who will be declared just before God, but those who practice the commandments will be accepted. [14]For whenever nations without the Torah nonetheless obey the dictates of the Torah, these without the Torah are nonetheless a law unto themselves; [15]they evidence the requirement of the Torah inscribed on their hearts,[j] their conscience vouching for them when their inner thoughts either ac-

j. Mic. 6:8

cuse or excuse them, [16]*on that day when God judges the secrets of mortals, as my preaching has it, by means of Jesus-Christ.*[k] [17]But suppose you bear the designation Jew and rely on the Torah, boasting of your God, [18]knowing the divine will and approving the things that excel, having been instructed in the Torah, [19]having convinced yourself you are a guide to the blind, a beacon for the benighted, [20]an instructor of the simple, a trainer of infants, possessing in the Torah the very standard for knowledge and truth.[l] [21]You who teach another, do you not bother teaching yourself? You who preach not to steal, do you steal? [22]The one saying not to commit adultery, do you commit adultery? The one who hates idols, do you rob temples? [23]You who brag about the Torah, do you disgrace the name of God by violating the Torah? [24]For indeed, the name of God is ridiculed among the nations because of you, as it is written.[m] [25]While circumcision is worthwhile if you keep the Torah, if you are a violator of the Torah, your circumcision has reverted to uncircumcised paganism.[n] [26]Equally then, if an uncircumcised man keeps the provisions of the Torah, will not his lack of circumcision be waived, with him being considered as if circumcised? [27]The one who is uncircumcised but keeps the Torah spontaneously will judge you who, despite possessing the written text and circumcision, violate the Torah. [28]For he is not the Jew externally, nor is the real circumcision external in the flesh. [29]But Jewish identity is an invisible thing and the circumcision is of the heart, by spirit, not by letter, and it calls forth the admiration, not of one's fellows, but of God.[o]

---

k. Verse 16 constitutes a bit of Christianizing redaction, tying the sermon into the context.

l. Matt. 3:8-9

m. This topic exposes the tip of an important iceberg. The implication is that God's name comes into disrepute when national tragedies elicit scoffing from gentiles about the Jews' reliance on God. If they are his chosen people, why doesn't he deliver them? The use of the theme here implies a recent national disaster, most likely the Roman defeat of the Jewish uprisings of CE 73 or 136. See Pss. 74:10, 18; 79:9-10a; Exod. 32:12.

n. 1 Sam. 17:26b

o. The same idea is attributed to Jesus in Matt. 6:1-6, 16-18. One can easily see why this Jewish text proved attractive to Christian congregations of both Jews and gentiles, especially Hellenistic Jews. The sermon's doctrine of the Torah, and of why Jews and gentiles are equal before it, has nothing to do with Paulinism. The latter holds that everyone is equally guilty and therefore in need of God's grace. This sermon maintains one can prove oneself worthy by good deeds, whether defined by the Mosaic Torah or by an inner moral compass common to all human beings. See J. C. O'Neill, *Paul's Letter to the Romans* (Baltimore: Pen-

3

[1]In that case, what is the advantage in being a Jew? Why is it better to have been circumcised?[p] [2]Actually, its value is quite considerable by any standard. First and foremost, they were vouchsafed the revelations of God. [3]What do you think? Just because some of them failed to believe, will their unbelief nullify the fidelity of God? [4]Never! No, let God be true and every human being a liar. So it is written: "Thus, you are proven right in your assertions and will prevail when you come before the bar of judgment."[q] [5]So if our unrighteousness accentuates God's righteousness, what are we to infer? Is God in the wrong to inflict wrath? I am just playing devil's advocate, you understand. [6]Never! If that were so, how could God judge the world? And we know he will, so your reasoning has gone off track somewhere. [7]But if by means of my lying, God's truth is magnified, glorifying him all the more, then why am I also condemned as a sinner? [8]Indeed, why not say, as we are slanderously misrepresented by some as saying, "Let us do evil deeds to bring about good results"?[r] These people deserve every bit of the judgment awaiting them.

[9]What then, are we Jews better? Not at all. We have already demonstrated both Jews and Greeks to be equally under sin, [10]exactly as it is written: "There is not a single righteous man! Not one! There is no man of understanding. [11]There is no one seeking God. [12]All turned away from him, *en masse* they have become worthless; there is not a one engaging in kindness—not even one!"[s] [13]"From their throats rise the loathsome exhalations of a violated grave.[t] They deceive with their tongues like asps with their venom sacks."[u] [14]"Their mouth overflows with bitterness and exe-

guin Books, 1975), 40-56; William O. Walker Jr., *Interpolations in the Pauline Letters,* Journal for the Study of the New Testament Supplement Series 213 (London: Sheffield Academic Press, 2001), 166-89.

p. Thomas 53

q. Pss. 51:4

r. This might be a reference to critics of Paulinism, employing the *reductio ad absurdum,* pointing out a supposedly inevitable, albeit unintended, implication, written by someone like the author of James 2:14-26. But just as likely, a la Van Manen, what we are hearing is an intra-Paulinist debate over the dangerous implications of grace-soteriology, once "deeds" have come to be understood as "good deeds of morality" rather than as ritual obedience to the Torah as originally, quite a different issue.

s. Pss. 14:1-3; 53:1-3

t. Pss. 5:9

u. Pss. 140:3

cration."[v] [15]"They run swiftly to violent crime. [16]Behind them stretches a wake of ruin and woe. [17]They are total strangers to the ways of peace."[w] [18]"They reckon without the fear of God."[x] [19]So it stands to reason that whatever the Torah says to those mentioned in the text, it says not to them alone, but in order to silence every mouth and place the whole human race under judgment before God, [20]this for the simple reason that all flesh will not be vindicated before him by means of deeds of Torah.[y] No, the role of the Torah is to document the full extent of sin, as we have just seen.[z] [21]But now, apart from the Torah, a way of salvation[a] sent from God has been revealed[b] in full view of the Torah and the Prophets,[c] [22]a salvation that comes from God by means of belief in Jesus-Christ for all those who believe. For there is no difference, [23]for all sinned and forfeit the vision of God, [24]being vindicated for free by token of his beneficence, their freedom purchased by means of Jesus-Christ. [25]*By virtue of his fidelity even to the point of shedding of blood, God deigned to accept him as a propitiation in order to vindicate his righteousness since he had patiently overlooked sins previously committed,* [26]*showing forth his plan of salvation now in the present time, himself being just and the one who accepts those with the belief in Jesus-Christ.*[d] [27]What room is left for bragging? It is ruled out. But by what rule, the Torah of deeds? No, through a principle of faith. [28]We have to conclude thusly: a person without the Torah is accepted by God through belief. [29]Or does God belong to Jews only? Does he not belong to the nations, too? Yes, to the nations, too, [30]since

v. Pss. 10:7

w. Isa. 59:7-8

x. Pss. 36:1

y. Contra 2:13 above.

z. It must be admitted that the foregoing defense of universal sinfulness, depravity, and fallenness is facile and specious, a cento of out-of-context proof texts, none of whose authors sought to make the point in question. And it is in this fashion that the author of Romans thinks the Torah brings all humanity to the conviction of sin.

a. Again, see Jeremias, *Central Message of the New Testament,* 52-53.

b. This piece of theology is thoroughly Marcionite.

c. Alternatively, "albeit testified by the Torah and the Prophets," likely a subsequent anti-Marcionite gloss.

d. We appear to have (vv. 25-26) either a later interpolation or the patching in of an underlying source. For the interpretation given here, see Sam K. Williams, *Jesus' Death as Saving Event: The Background and Origin of a Concept* (Missoula: Scholars Press, 1975), 19-51.

there is a single God who will accept circumcision by faith and uncircumcision through faith. 31Do we in this way nullify the Torah through this faith? Never! Instead, we set the Torah on a whole new footing.[e]

4

1How shall we characterize the achievement of Abraham, our father according to the flesh? 2For if it was by deeds of Torah that Abraham was saved, then he has reason to brag, but not as far as God is concerned. 3After all, look what scripture says: "And Abraham believed God, and it was counted for him as merit."[f] 4So the wages paid the workman are not weighed up by gratuitous kindness but by what he is owed by contract. But as for the one without deeds of Torah, 5while counting on the one who accepts the irreligious, his belief is counted as merit 6even as David says, too, describing the bliss of the one to whom God ascribes merit without deeds of Torah: 7"Blessed are they whose deeds of lawlessness were forgiven and whose sins were covered up. 8Blessed be a man to whom Adonai may in no respect ascribe sin."[g] 9Is this beatitude pronounced only upon the circumcised? Or not also upon the uncircumcised? For our position is that it is the faith of Abraham that was ascribed to him as merit. 10And precisely how was it ascribed? With him in a state of circumcision? Or in a state of uncircumcision? Not in circumcision, but in uncircumcision! 11He received circumcision only subsequently as a token of the merit of the faith he exercised while uncircumcised so he could be a fit father to all who believe, despite not being circumcised, so merit might be ascribed to them, 12as well as a father of a covenant[h] with those, not only of the circumcision, but also those following in the steps of the uncircumcised faith of our father Abraham. 13For the promise to Abraham or to his descendants that he should inherit the world did not come to him via the Torah but by the merit of his faith. 14For if the heirs owe their position to Torah, faith has been vitiated and the promise destroyed. 15For the Torah effects wrath, and where Torah is absent, neither can there be transgression. 16That is why it is a matter of faith, so it

e. Here and in 7:7 we have accommodating attempts by subsequent Paulinists to back away from the thoroughgoing anti-Torah position of original Marcionite and Gnostic Paulinism, seeking to retain the Torah nominally by domesticating it with theological euphemism while still setting it aside as essentially irrelevant and obsolete. See Matt. 5:17.

f. Gen. 15:6

g. Pss. 32:1-2

h. Literally, "father of circumcision to those ..."

might come by God's gratuitous will, so the promise will continue to be firm for all the descendants, not only to those who observe the Torah, but also to those marked by the faith of Abraham, who is thus the father of all of us equally, 17as it is written: "I have appointed you a father to many nations."[i]

He stands as our father in the sight of him whom he believed, namely God, the one who resuscitates the dead and calls the nonexistent into being, 18as he did with Abraham who, long past all hope, nonetheless staked everything on hope in order to become a father to many nations, in accord with the promise made to him: "So shall your descendants be."[j] 19And without weakening in faith, he wrote off his body as already moribund, being about a century old, and Sarah's womb just as dead. 20But he did not give up on the promise of God by unbelief but was strengthened by faith, worshipping God, 21and being fully convinced that what he has promised he will also be able to deliver. 22This is why it was ascribed to him as merit. 23Understand that it was written that it was ascribed to him not just to memorialize him, 24but also because of us, to whom it is soon to be ascribed, those counting on the one who raised Jesus our Lord from the dead, 25he who was yielded up, thanks to our offenses, and was raised through our salvation.[k]

5

1Therefore, being accepted by faith, we enjoy peace with God, thanks to our Lord, Jesus-Christ, 2who has also arranged access for us by the password of faith,[l] into this position of favor we now occupy, bragging of our hope of sharing the divine splendor. 3Not only that, but we even brag amid our tribulations, remembering that tribulations breed patience, 4and patience leads to approval, and approval to hope. 5And this hope will not disappoint because the love of God has been poured out into our hearts with the Holy Spirit given us. 6Indeed, while we were past help, just in time, Christ died on behalf of the irreligious. 7Hardly anyone will die on behalf of a righteous man, though admittedly someone might

---

i. Gen. 17:5

j. Gen. 15:5

k. In other words, since we are no longer guilty before God, the savior does not need to remain dead by token of punishment.

l. The theme of the redeemer providing access to God is the central Gnostic motif. The Gnostic Jesus reveals the way beyond the evil guardians at the cosmic gates, including the formulae required to slip past them. Nothing quite so complex is suggested here, but the occurrence of the basic idea is striking.

venture to die on behalf of a good man.[m] 8But it bespeaks the love God had for us that Christ died on our behalf while we were still sinners. 9Now that we have been accepted by virtue of his blood, by how much more shall we be rescued by him from the coming wrath! 10For if, being enemies, we were reconciled to God by the death of his son, having now been reconciled, we shall much more be saved by his life. 11And not only that, but we are also bragging on God thanks to our Lord, Jesus *Christ,* through whose agency we have the reconciliation we now enjoy.

12Therefore, just as sin gained entry into the world through a single individual, with death arriving on sin's coat tails, death permeated all mankind since all sinned. 13Before the Torah, of course, there was sin in the world, but sin is not counted as such when there is no law to condemn it. 14Nonetheless, death prevailed from Adam till Moses even among those not sinning the same way Adam did, he who reflects the mirror-image of the Coming One. 15But the offense is not quite like the gift; for if it was by means of the one man's offense that the many died, how much more fully did the gratuitous gift of God become abundant for the many by one individual! 16And the gift is not as with the one individual sinning; for on the one hand, the judgment starts from a single offense and ends in condemnation, while on the other, the free gift starts from many offenses and ends in salvation. 17For if it was by the one individual's offense that death prevailed through an individual, how much more will those who accept the abundance of kindness and the gift of salvation prevail in life through the one individual Christ-Jesus? 18So therefore, as through one single offense all humanity came to condemnation, even so through one single righteous act all humanity came to salvation and life. 19For as through the disobedience of the one man, the many were made sinners, so also through the obedience of one man the many will be made righteous.[n] 20But law entered the picture so that the offense might be magnified; but where sin became abundant, divine favor became more abundant still, 21in order that in the same way sin prevailed by means of death, so too divine favor might prevail through salvation to age-long life by means of Jesus-Christ, our Lord.

6

1What can we infer from this? May we continue sinning to make the

---

m. John 15:13

n. Verses 15-19 are so redundant, some copyist must have rounded up all known variant readings to provide a variorum edition of this passage.

divine forgiveness the more abundant? [2]Never! How can those who died in respect to sin continue to live in it? [3]Or don't you realize what baptism means?[o] Every one baptized into Christ-Jesus was baptized, specifically, into his death. [4]Thus we shared a common grave with him by virtue of baptism into death in order that, as Christ was raised from the dead by the splendor of the Father, we too might live a new quality of life. [5]It only stands to reason that, if we have become one with him in the symbol of his death, so we will also be with regard to the resurrection, [6]mindful of this: that our old humanity was crucified along with him[p] so this incarnation of sin might be destroyed and so we should obey sin's orders no more. [7]For anyone who has died has been delivered from sin. [8]But if we died with Christ, we believe we shall also live with him, [9]keeping in mind that Christ, having been raised from the dead, is henceforth immune to death so that death has no further claim on him. [10]For insofar as he died, he died one single time, leaving behind the world of sin, but insofar as he still lives, he lives anew in the world of God. [11]The same goes for you: consider yourself dead in respect to sin but alive with respect to God, newly awakened from the dead with your members as veritable weapons of righteousness at God's disposal. [12]Therefore, do not allow sin to rule your mortal bodies, obeying its impulses, [13]nor put your members at sin's disposal as an arsenal of unrighteousness, but instead put yourselves at God's disposal as newly awakened from the dead with your members as weapons of righteousness. [14]For sin's dominion over you is finished since you are no longer under obligation to the Torah, but to divine favor.

[15]What is the implication? Are we at liberty to sin because we are out from under the Torah but under the umbrella of divine favor? Never! [16]Isn't it obvious that you become enslaved to whomever you decide you are going to obey, whether it is sin leading to death or obedience leading to salvation? [17]But thank God, though you were slaves of sin, you swore heart-felt fealty to the type of religion to which you were consigned.[q] [18]And having been liberated from sin, you became slaves of righteousness. [19]I am resorting to a worldly analogy by way of accommodation to

o. This sacramentalism cannot be the product of the same Paulinist who said "Christ did not send me to baptize, but to proclaim the news" (1 Cor. 1:17a). Nor does it comport with the many passages in Romans where belief is made the criterion of salvation.

p. Possibly the origin of the image of two sinners being executed to the left and the right of Jesus.

q. Gal. 2:9; Acts 15:19-31; 21:25

your human way of thinking. So as you used to offer your members as slaves to impurity and lawlessness, leading to lawlessness, in the same way you must now offer your members as tools of righteousness leading to sanctification. [20]For when you were slaves to sin, you were free of righteousness. [21]And what benefit did you reap from that? Now you find yourselves chagrined at those things, for they lead in the end to death. [22]But having now been liberated from sin and enslaved to God, you harvest fruit ripening to sanctification, the ultimate end being age-long life. [23]For the wage paid by sin is death, but the anointing of God brings age-long life in union with Christ-Jesus, our Lord.

7

[1]Can you be unaware, brothers, for I address myself to those familiar with the Torah, that the Torah governs a man's conduct only as long as he is alive? [2]For example, the married woman has been bound to the living husband by law; but once the husband dies, she has been released from the law of the husband. [3]Therefore, with the husband yet alive, she will be considered an adulteress if she becomes wife to another; but if the husband dies, she is free from the law of the husband and is not to be considered an adulteress for marrying a new husband. So my brothers, you too were put to death vis-a-vis the Torah by means of the body of Christ so that you might belong to someone else, the one who has been raised from the dead, in order for us to bear fruit for God. [5]For when we were hostage to the flesh, sinful urges animated our members through the Torah to bring forth fruit ripening to death. [6]But since what held us fast has died, we have now been released from the Torah so we might serve in a new freedom of spirit, no longer in the old slavery to a written text.[r]

[7]So what are we to say? The Torah must be synonymous with sin, no? Never! Yet it has to be admitted that I would have been innocent of sin if not for the Torah. Likewise, I should never have become acquainted with lust had the Torah not commanded, "You shall not lust after your neighbor's goods."[s] [8]But sin seized the opportunity afforded by the commandment and produced in me every kind of lust. For without the Torah, sin is moot. [9]Once I was living without the Torah, but when the commandment

r. It must be admitted that this sounds like pure Marcionism with its characterization of the Torah as a back-firing failure at making its adherents righteous. What follows appears to be back-pedaling, perhaps by a subsequent catholicizing Paulinist, who argues that this self-stultification of the Torah was part of its original divine purpose.

s. Exod. 20:17

arrived, sin revived, [10]and I died. And the commandment to choose life turned out to spell death for me. [11]For sin, seizing the opportunity afforded by the commandment, deceived me and used it to kill me! [12]So the Torah per se is holy, and the commandment is holy and just and good.

[13]So did that which is good spell death for me? Never! And yet sin, in order that it might be exposed in its true colors as sin by using the good to kill me—that is, in order that it might become odiously sinful by means of the commandment—[14]look, we know that the Torah is spiritual. The problem is that I, on the other hand, am carnal, sold into the slavery of sin. [15]For my own behavior is a mystery to me. For it is not what I wish that I practice, but what I hate, I do. [16]But if I do what I do not wish, I agree with the Torah: it is good! [17]But now it is no longer I who act, but the sin that lurks within me. [18]For I know that no goodness lives in me, I mean, in my flesh; for to wish the good is easy for me, but not to do it. [19]For I do not perform the good I wish, but the evil which I wish not to do—that I do! [20]But if what I do not wish is what I actually do, then it can no longer in any meaningful sense be I who am doing it. The real culprit is the sin that lives inside me. [21]So then, I discover a law of human behavior: whenever I wish to do the good, [22]the evil is closer to hand. For I delight in the divine Torah in the inner being, [23]but I can see a very different law governing my members, struggling against the law my mind embraces and taking me prisoner using the Torah.[t] [24]Miserable wretch that I am! Can anyone rescue me from this living corpse? [25]I thank God, invoking Jesus-Christ our Lord. To sum up, then: on the one hand, as the real me, I serve the divine Torah, while on the other, with the flesh, I obey the commands of sin.[u]

8

[1]Thus no condemnation is due those joined to Christ-Jesus. [2]For the rule of the vivifying Spirit in Christ-Jesus liberated you from the rule of sin and consequently of death. [3]For what remained impossible to the Torah, the weakness of the flesh being its Achilles' heel, God supplied by sending his own Son in the semblance[v] of flesh and of sin to deal with sin,

---

t. A scribe has altered it to "using the law of sin in my members," a redundancy that ruins the attempted closure by tying the sinner's perversity to the Torah without blaming the Torah.

u. The conclusion of this verse sounds like a gloss attempting to tone down what a scribe perceived as charismatic over-enthusiasm or what Käsemann calls "eschatological triumphalism" in the preceding discussion.

v. Let no one fail to recognize the docetism of Marcionites and Gnostics here.

condemning it in its very seat of power, the flesh, [4]and this in order that the dictates of the Torah might be kept by us[w] insofar as we conduct ourselves, not by the influence of the flesh, but under the influence of the Spirit. [5]For the fleshly ones concern themselves with materialistic matters, but those who are spiritually oriented concern themselves with matters of the Spirit. [6]For the worldly mind is death, but the spiritual mind enjoys life and peace. [7]This is why the worldly mind is automatically set against God, for it is not submissive to God's sovereignty, nor in the nature of the case can it be. [8]Nor can the materialistic please God. [9]But you are not mired in the flesh, but rather soaring free in the Spirit, provided God's Spirit lives within you. But should anyone lack the Spirit of Christ, such a one does not belong to him. [10]But assuming Christ is inside you, the body is dead to sin, while the spirit is alive through practicing righteousness. [11]But if the Spirit of the One who raised Jesus from the dead lives in you, the One who raised Jesus from the dead will also vivify your mortal bodies by means of his Spirit living inside you.

[12]So then, brothers, this makes us debtors, but not to the flesh, as if we were obliged to live by its dictates. [13]Because if you do that, you are soon going to die. But if by the Spirit you atrophy the practices of the body, you will live. [14]For every one responsive to the leading of the divine Spirit is a son of God. [15]For it was no spirit of slavery you received, to fear all over again. No, you received a spirit of adoption, which prompts us to cry out, "*Abba!* Father!"[x] [16]The Spirit itself agrees with our spirit that we are children of God. [17]And if children, that means heirs, as well, in one respect direct beneficiaries of God, in another co-beneficiaries with Christ since we share his suffering to share his glory. [18]And the way I look at it, the sufferings of the present time amount to nothing compared to the future splendor to be revealed from within us! [19]For the eager anticipation of all rational creatures[y] is to behold their unveiling as the sons of God.

w. It sounds like a catholicizing scribe has sought to restore an obligation to keep the Torah within a Pauline framework after all.

x. Here is the key term of Marcionite soteriology: the Father of Jesus Christ has offered to adopt the creations of the Hebrew God. Originally children of the one, they may now transfer themselves to the loving fatherhood of the other.

y. Cf. Mark 16:15, where "creation" is metonymy for "the whole human race." Charles Chauncy, *The Mystery hid from Ages and Generations, made manifest by the Gospel-Revelation: Or, The SALVATION OF ALL MEN, The Grand Thing Aimed at in the Scheme of God, As opened in the New-Testament Writings, and entrusted with JESUS CHRIST to bring into Effect* (London: Charles Dilly, in the Poultry, 1784), 96-121.

[20]Why was the world subjected to futility in the first place? It was not voluntary, but rather the decision of the one who did the subjugation. The hope is that [21]all beings will themselves be liberated from their bondage to corruption to share the freedom of the immortal bliss of the sons of God. [22]For it is readily apparent that all beings groan in unison and suffer labor pains till the present hour.

[23]Not only that, but even we who observe the first flowering of the Spirit inside us nevertheless groan inside, desperately waiting for the adoption papers to be signed, that is, the salvaging of our bodies at the resurrection. [24]For we staked our salvation on this hope, but remember, a visible object of hope is not hoped for at all. After all, who would say he "hopes for" the thing he can see? [25]But if we hope for something we do not see, we have to wait for it patiently. [26]The Spirit, too, takes a hand in our weakness: while we do not know our own good well enough to ask for it, the Spirit itself intercedes on our behalf with inarticulate groanings, [27]with the result that the searcher of hearts knows the thinking of the Spirit because he is able to ask on behalf of the saints from God's perspective. [28]Equally, we know that in the eyes of those who love God, everything is seen to work together for their good, the good of those called to participate in his grand plan: [29]namely, those he chose beforehand[z] were also destined to be transformed into the image of his Son, so to make him the firstborn of many likewise resurrected brothers. [30]The ones thus destined would also be summoned, and those he summoned would also be saved. In turn, those saved must also receive the divine splendor. [31]All one can say is: "If God is for us, what matter who is arrayed against us?"[a] If he did not spare even his own Son, [32]but on all our behalf gave him up, how will he not, with his Son, freely give us everything else? [33]Who do you picture leveling a charge against God's chosen ones? God is vindicating, [34]so who is condemning? Certainly not Christ-Jesus, the very one, after all, who died, or should I say who was raised, who is at the right of God and intercedes on our behalf.[b] [35]Who could possibly separate us from the love of Christ? Tribulation? Distress, maybe? How about persecution? Famine? Abject poverty? Danger? Sword? [36]It is not as if we are immune to these things, as it is written: "For your sake, we are being butchered all

z. "Knew" implies "chose," as in Gen. 18:19.

a. Pss. 118:6

b. Not the adversary? This is precisely his role through much of the Bible, but he has no place in Pauline/Marcionite thinking. There is no judgment with the Father.

day long; we were considered no more than sheep for slaughtering."[c] 37But in all these seeming defeats, we are super-conquerors, thanks to the One who loved us. 38For I have become convinced that neither death nor the vicissitudes of this life, neither angels nor archons, nothing in either the present or the future, nor the powers, neither Hypsos nor Bathos[d] nor anything in all creation will succeed in isolating us from the love God has for those united with Christ-Jesus our Lord.[e]

9

1Despite my reputation, I swear before Christ, I am telling the truth![f] I am not lying! My conscience vouches for me, inspired by the Holy Spirit; 2I suffer deep sorrow and unremitting emotional pain. 3I was even invoking a curse from Christ on my own head on behalf of my brothers, my natural kinsmen,[g] 4who bear the distinction of being Israelites, to whom properly belong the adoption as God's children, the leading of the Shekinah, the covenants with Abraham, Moses, and David, the promulgation of the Torah, and the temple service, and the messianic promises, 5and the patriarchs, and from whose physical line Christ descends. May God, who reigns over all, be blessed through the ages! Amen.

6But then, what has happened? It is not that the message of God has failed to gain its object. For not all descended from Israel are true Israel, 7neither does mere descent from Abraham make all of them his children; but "Isaac's line will be called your descendants."[h] 8This means it is not

c. Pss. 44:22

d. Hypsos ("height") and Bathos ("depth") are two of the aions in the pleroma, here spoken of as if they were archons barring the way of the heavenward-ascending Gnostic. See also Pss. 139:7-8; Laodiceans 3:18; 1 Cor. 2:10, for "the depths of God."

e. Here is classic Gnostic soteriology: the redeemer blazes a trail for us back to the pleroma, the Godhead, past the ranks of archons and angels who would bar our way. Our condition of lostness is this separation from the Godhead, so redemption is a matter of our path of return being cleared.

f. Marcion's copy of Romans lacked chapters 9-11.

g. This casting of Paul as Moses in Exod. 32:32 (cf. 2 Cor. 3:1-18) reflects the fact, pointed out by Stephan Hermann Huller, that the Hebrew *paulat* denoted one who intercedes for forgiveness. *Paul* may have been the equivalent of "Paraclete," an office Valentinians and Marcionites claimed for Paul, whom they saw predicted in John 15:26. At any rate, the parallel with Exodus clearly implies that faithless Israelites are damned and that Paul would vicariously bear their burden if possible. This is not the impression we receive in chapter 11, where a rather different fate is projected for Israel.

h. Gen. 21:12

the natural children who are children of God,[i] but rather only the children of the promise are counted as his descendants. 9And this is the promise in question: "About this time, I will come by, and Sarah will have a son."[j] 10Not only this, but Rebecca, too, having conceived by one man, namely our father Isaac, was told, "The older will serve the younger,"[k] 11though neither had yet been born, much less done anything good or bad, in order that the plan of God might continue according to divine choice—12not based on deeds, but on the decision of the one who issues the call. 13This is just what is written: "Jacob I loved, but Esau I hated."[l]

14What are we to say to that?[m] Is God unfair? Never! 15For he says to Moses, "It is for me to decide whom I will show mercy and whom I will pity!"[n] 16So therefore, it is not up to the one who wishes or the one who competes, but to God the merciful. 17For scripture says to Pharaoh, "I brought you to the throne for one purpose only: so I might use you to demonstrate my power and so my reputation might spread throughout the earth."[o] 18From this we can see that he shows mercy to whomever he wishes, and equally he makes whomever he wants obstinate. 19I know what you're going to say: "Then how can he still find fault with us? It all happens just as he wishes, and who can gainsay him?" 20But I turn the question around. Who are you, a mere mortal, to be telling God his business? 21Does the artifact ever call the artificer to account, "Hey! Why did you make me this way?" 22Doesn't the potter have every right to use half the lump of clay for a wine goblet and the other for a bed pan? So suppose God wanted to demonstrate his anger as well as his endurance and so patiently put up with those who were created long ago as targets of his anger 23and that he wanted to demonstrate his heavenly splendor in vessels

i. Hence, the reference to "the adoption" in v. 4.

j. The logic is even stronger if we consider that in adjacent Arabian and African cultures, an "infertile" or "barren" woman would be assisted by an itinerant holy man, presumably a substitute for an infertile husband—the real cause of the problem. In this scenario, the "angel," rather than the woman, is more accurately the vessel of divine begetting. See M. J. Field, *Angels and Ministers of Grace* (New York: Hill and Wang, 1972). See Gen. 18:10.

k. Gen. 25:23

l. Mal. 1:2-3

m. Verses 14-23 seem to be an originally independent section dealing with the predestination, election, and reprobation of individuals, not the topic of the larger context wherein "election" means something else.

n. Exod. 33:19

o. Exod. 9:16

of mercy, previously made to hold the splendor and set aside for that purpose.[p] 24And these latter are we ourselves, not only Jews, but also those he summoned from the nations. 25He says the same in Hosea: "I will call 'my people' that nation hitherto foreign to me; and those not beloved heretofore, them I will love."[q] 26"And it shall come to pass that in the very place they had been told, 'You are no people of mine!' there they will be called 'sons of the true God.'"[r] 27Nonetheless, Isaiah cries out concerning Israel, "Should the number of the sons of Israel be the same as the grains of sand on the seashore, still only a remnant shall be delivered. 28For Adonai will wrap up his inventory of all the earth and even cut it short."[s] 29And as Isaiah had said in advance: "If Adonai Sabaoth had not left us seed, we should have perished completely like Sodom and would have been likened to Gomorrah."[t]

30What is the upshot of all this? That nations not even pursuing salvation nonetheless found it, a salvation by means of belief, 31while Israel, seeking to follow a law of salvation, failed to arrive at salvation. 32Why? Because they pursued it not as a matter of faith, but as a matter of deeds. They tripped over the hidden stumbling stone, 33as it had been written: "Watch as I place someone in Zion for a stone for stumbling and a rock of offense, and whoever believes in him will not be sorry he did."[u]

10

1Brothers, from my heart I request on their behalf that God grant them the boon of salvation.[v] 2For I can testify what zeal they have for

p. This all suggests the language of the Kabbalah, where in the beginning God prepared *Kelipoth*, fragile vessels to contain the divine light he would project from himself in the image of the heavenly Adam. The vessels shattered and the light of the Shekinah was scattered throughout creation, whence the Adam Kadmon must retrieve the sparks.

q. Hosea 2:23

r. Hosea 1:10

s. Isa. 10:22-23

t. Isa. 1:9

u. Thus concludes the statement of Paulinist supracessionism, a piece of apologetics typical for a new sect finding the majority of the parent religion indifferent to their call. The idea here is that Israel has never been simply synonymous with the majority of natural descendants of Abraham and that the criterion for weeding out false Israel rests with God, a small remnant being the result. This is the doctrine of gentile triumphalism combatted in 11:17-32. See Isa. 28:16.

v. This redactional seam paraphrases 9:1 and seeks to duplicate the peg from which the following text at first depended. Thus, the foregoing supracessionist passage is the interpolation seeking to undermine the different opinion which follows.

God, albeit misdirected by ignorance. [3]Ignorant of God's salvation and trying to achieve their own, they failed to accept the saving message of God. [4]For everyone who believes can see that Christ is the goal to which the Torah points. [5]For Moses writes: "The one who performs the righteous deeds of Torah will gain life thereby."[w] [6]But the salvation that comes from faith says not, "Who can ascend into the sky?" which is to reject Christ's ascension to the right of God. [7]Nor does it say, "Who will descend into the abyss?" which is to disbelieve the death of Christ. [8]But what does it say? "The word is near you, on the tip of your tongue, already in your heart."[x] This is the very message of faith which we preach. [9]Because if you swear fealty to Jesus and you believe sincerely that God raised him from the dead, you will be saved. [10]For it is with the sincere heart that one believes, gaining merit, and it is by public confession that one gains salvation. [11]For again, scripture says, "Every one who believes in him will not be reluctant to admit it."[y] [12]For there is no distinction between Jew and Greek. For the same Lord of all alike is bountiful toward all those invoking him. [13]For "whoever calls on the name of Adonai shall be delivered."[z]

[14]But you will say, how are they supposed to call on one in whom they do not believe? And how are they supposed to believe in one they have never heard of? And how are they supposed to hear if no one serves as herald? [15]And how is a herald to preach if he is not sent? As it is written: "How welcome are the footsteps of the bearer of good tidings!"[a] [16]But not everyone so welcomed the news. For Isaiah says, "Lord, did anyone believe what they heard us preach?"[b] [17]This tells us that faith comes from hearing, and hearing requires some communication about Christ.[c]

[18]But I say in answer to this: Are you so sure they did not hear? Surely they did! For "their speech went out to all the earth, and their

w. Lev. 18:5

x. Deut. 30:12-13

y. Isa. 28:16

z. Joel 2:32

a. Isa. 52:7

b. Isa. 53:1

c. Verses 14-17 argue for the necessity of sending and financially supporting foreign missionaries. That this section is not a straw man statement, raised merely for the sake of argument and to be refuted, is evident from the use of scripture citations to reinforce the argument. What follows, then, in vv. 18-20, is a genuine refutation by another Paulinist, added here to "correct" the preceding.

words to the far reaches of the inhabited earth."[d] [19]And further, I ask, did not Israel know? In the first place, Moses says, "I will provoke you to jealousy over those who are 'no people' to me; over an ignorant nation I will anger you!"[e] [20]But Isaiah is bolder still when he says, "I was found by those who were not looking for me; I revealed myself to those not asking after me."[f] [21]Meanwhile, to Israel he says, "The whole day long I motioned with my hands, beckoning to a people who only disobeyed and contradicted me."[g]

11

[1]So I must ask: has God not rejected his people? Never![h] After all, even I am an Israelite, descended from Abraham, of the tribe of Benjamin.[i] [2]God did not reject his people whom he chose in advance. Or don't you remember what scripture tells of Elijah, when he actually prays for judgment on Israel? [3]"Adonai, they killed your prophets, they dismantled your altars, and I alone am left—and now they are after me."[j] [4]But what does the divine response say to him? "I kept back for myself some seven thousand men who never swore fealty to Baal."[k] [5]In exactly the same way in our day, there has emerged a remnant according to the divine choice to make God's favor the criterion. [6]And if the criterion is divine favor, it is no longer decided by deeds since, if it were, divine favor would be so in name only. [7]So where are we? What Israel sought after, he did not gain, but the chosen remnant gained it while the rest were reinforced in their obtuseness, [8]as it is written: "God stupefied them with a

d. Pss. 19:4. Notice how the writer merely infers from scriptural proof-texts a history of supposed events that we might have expected to be based on historical reminiscence. How much of New Testament narrative has the same origin?

e. Deut. 32:21

f. Isa. 65:1

g. Isa. 65:2

h. This chapter contains a much later reflection on the Jewish rejection of Jesus, including the possibility for an eventual reconciliation.

i. Why on earth does "Paul" not list "a Jew" among his genealogical credentials? As Eisenman suggests, Paul may have been only quasi-Jewish and so claimed to be a "Benjaminite," a euphemism also used by that would-be Jew, but actual Arab-Edomite, Herod the Great. But we must also ask, with Van Manen, why the author of chapters 9-11 never refers to "Jews" at all, but only to "Israel," the exact opposite of the usage up to chapter 9. His answer: chapters 9-11 are not the work of the same author.

j. 1 Kings 19:14

k. 1 Kings 19:18

soporific draught, eyes not seeing, ears not hearing,"[l] which still prevails.
[9]And David says, "May their table become a death trap, a means of capture, to offend them and to recompense them.[m] [10]May their vision fade to blindness and their backs ever bend to the burden!"[n]

[11]I have to ask, then, did they take a fatal misstep from which they can never recover?[o] Never! Rather, by means of their transgression, salvation came to the nations in order to goad them to jealousy! [12]But if their transgression spells riches for the world, and their impoverishment means the wealth of the nations, how much greater bounty shall come from their eventual repentance?

[13]So let me speak to you gentiles. Naturally, since I am the apostle to the nations, I glorify my ministry—for the sake of Jews. [14]I hope to goad my natural kinfolk to jealousy and in this way save some of them.[p] [15]I mean, if their expulsion occasions the reconciliation of the nations, what would it have to mean if God received them back? Resurrection of the dead! [16]And if the first fruits of the showbread are holy, the rest must be, too. And if the root is holy, so must be the branches. [17]And what if some of the branches were broken off and you, a wild olive branch, were grafted in among them, becoming fellow sharers in the nutrition that rises from the root? [18]That is certainly no reason for you to brag about your own position at the expense of the natural branches. If you are inclined to brag, just remember this: it is the root that bears your weight, not the other way around. [19]You might reply: "Branches were broken off to make room for me to be grafted in. That must mean something!" [20]Good point! They were broken off because of unbelief, true, and because of faith you maintain your position in God's favor. Don't be conceited, but fear! [21]For if God had no scruples about chopping off the natural branches, he is not likely to be any more reluctant to dispense with you. [22]Picture, then, both the kindness and the severity of God: on the one hand, severity upon those

l. Isa. 29:10

m. The allusions here and in v. 3 to the fall of the temple and its altar ("table") are anachronistic given the usual dates for Paul.

n. Pss. 69:22-23

o. This is exactly the conclusion advanced by another Paulinist in 1 Thess. 2:14-16, rebutted here as the other side of the intra-Paulinist debate.

p. The writer has in view the petty jealousy depicted in Acts when Jews, proud of their appeal to devout gentiles ("God fearers") on the margins of the synagogue, go crazy with envious rage when Paul wins these admirers away to the new faith. It is anachronistic in both cases, presupposing a population shift that would have taken place over many years.

who have fallen, and on the other, the kindness of God toward you, provided you continue in his kindness since otherwise you too will be cut off.
23Equally, if they do not continue in unbelief, they will be grafted back in,
for it is no great feat for God to restore them. 24After all, you were cut
from the wild olive, where you naturally belong, to be grafted against nature onto a cultivated olive; how much simpler a task it will be to graft the
branches back onto an olive to which they naturally belong!

25Brothers, I do not want you to remain ignorant of this hith-
erto-hidden plan of God lest you become conceited, namely, that obsti-
nacy has afflicted Israel in part only until the full predetermined number
of converts from the nations come in, 26and in this way all Israel will at
last be saved, as it is written, "The deliverer will emerge from Zion, and
he will turn away impiety from Jacob. 27And this is my covenant with
them[q] when I take their sins away."[r] 28On the one hand, when it comes to
preaching the news, they are your opponents; on the other, when it comes
to the ancient election, they are God's beloved because of the patriarchs.[s]
29For the gifts and the vocation from God are irrevocable. 30Keep in mind
how once you disobeyed God and now you have obtained mercy because
of the disobedience of these others. 31In the same way, these have now
disobeyed because of the mercy shown you in order that now they may
obtain mercy, too. 32This way, God finds all alike guilty of disobedience
so he may show mercy upon all.

33How deep, how abundant are the wisdom and the knowledge of
God! How mysterious are his decisions, how far beyond human ken the
courses he plots! 34For who could know the thinking of Adonai? Has he
ever sought the advice of mortal man? 35Who has given anything to God
so that he owes him anything? 36No, from him and by means of him and
unto him all things proceed! All worship to him throughout the ages!
Amen!

12

1In view of this,[t] brothers, I urge you by the compassion of God to

---

q. Jer. 31:33

r. Isa. 27:9

s. This is a reference to, or an echo of, the rabbinical doctrine of the *zakhuth,* or "merits," of the fathers: God imputed the righteousness of Abraham, Isaac, and Jacob even to the most lackluster of their latter-day descendants, which explained why he might save even personally undeserving Jews from their plights. See Exod. 32:7-14.

t. In view of what? The transition fits better coming directly off the end of chapter 8; someone added the intervening chapters 9-11.

present your very bodies as a sacrifice while yet alive, one that is holy and meeting with God's approval, which is the fit worship of a rational creature.[u] [2]And do not let yourselves be assimilated to this present world system, but be transformed by renewing the intellect, enabling you to determine what the will of God is, what is good, what meets his approval, what is perfect. [3]For by the prophetic inspiration given me, I say to all present: Do not cultivate an overly high estimate of yourself, but rather reckon realistically just what portion of faith God has assigned to each one. [4]For just as in a single body we have many distinct members, each with its special function, [5]so we, being many, constitute a single body in Christ-Jesus, all being members of one another. [6]And having gifts that differ according to the varying endowments allotted us, let us exercise them appropriately; if it is prophecy, prophesy within the formula of the faith; if it is to serve, serve in the diaconate; if to teach, teach within the doctrine; [8]if in exhortation, as a paraclete; if sharing, in material simplicity; if leadership, then lead diligently, gladly lenient in assigning penance.[v] [9]Let love be non-hypocritical. Recoil from evil and stick closely to the good. [10]Love one another like family, with brotherly love, deferring in order to show one another the greater honor. [11]Be zealous, not slothful, burning in spirit to serve the Lord. [12]Rejoice at the sure prospect[w] of eventual deliverance, enduring amidst affliction, doggedly persisting in prayer. [13]Give for the needs of the saints and pursue a policy of hospitality to itinerant preachers. [14]Bless persecutors! Bless them instead of cursing them.[x] [15]Share the joy of the fortunate and the tears of the mournful. [16]Hold one another in equal regard, showing no preference to the rich nor patronizing the humble. Do not be too confident of your own wisdom.[y] [17]Do not repay anyone evil for evil;[z] be a source of noble deeds in the sight of all. [18]If possible, insofar as you have any control in the matter, try to live at peace with everyone. [19]Beloved ones, do not avenge your-

---

u. A Stoic-style appeal for rational, ethical religion as a replacement for temple sacrifice was especially attractive after the fall of Jerusalem in 70 CE.

v. These concepts of ecclesiastical offices and teaching formulae are anachronistic for Paul—also the idea that faith could be a quantifiable charisma and not held in common by all believers.

w. See C.F.D. Moule, *The Meaning of Hope* (Philadelphia: Fortress Press, 1963).

x. But see v. 20 below!

y. This repeats v. 3a.

z. Repeating v. 14.

selves, but just let it go. For it is written, "Vengeance is my prerogative: leave it to me, says Adonai."[a] 20Instead, "if your adversary is hungry, feed him; if he is thirsty, give him a drink; for in this way you will be heaping live coals on his head!"[b] 21Do not be vanquished by the Evil One, but conquer the Evil One by doing good.

13

1Let every immortal soul be humble before the authorities arrayed above him![c] For there is no authority except under God, and the existing ones have been ordained under God. 2So whoever resists the authorities has opposed himself to the order established by God,[d] and such opponents will receive condemnation. 3For the archons do not frighten people away from good deeds, only from evil! Do you want to be free from fear of the authorities? Do only the good and you will have its praise! 4For it is God's servant assigned you for good.[e] But if you are doing evil, then you are right to be afraid; for he is not afraid to use the sword God has supplied him, being God's servant, an avenger of wrath to whomever practices evil.[f] 5This is why it is necessary to submit—not just for fear of wrath, if I have given that impression, but for conscience's sake. 6This is also why you pay them tribute, for they are constantly engaged in worshipping God.[g] 7So render to all their due, to human leaders taxes and tolls, to the authorities honor, and to God holy fear.[h]

8Owe nothing to anyone except love for each other, for whoever loves the other has carried out the Torah. 9For "you shall not commit

a. Deut. 32:35

b. Prov. 25:21-22. The logic is the same as in Matt. 6:1-6, 16-18, the idea being that if you seek either reward or vengeance by your own efforts on earth, you will forfeit a much greater reward or vengeance God would have provided had you deferred to him.

c. Jude 8-10

d. Deut. 32:8; Pss. 82

e. This is fully in keeping with the adversary's role throughout scripture as God's investigator or prosecutor.

f. 2 Cor. 12:7; Gen. 3:24

g. This may be the "worship of angels" condemned in Col. 2:18. In Gnosticism, one "paid" the successive planetary archons upon exiting their respective spheres by setting aside the elements appropriate to each sphere (physical, ectoplasmic, astral, etheric, psychical, etc.) on one's journey back to the Godhead.

h. Many scholars take 13:1-7 to inculcate servile obedience to secular powers in the interest of bourgeois Christianity. This is based on understanding "archons" and "authorities" as earthly governments and every "soul" to denote every

adultery,"[i] "you shall not kill,"[j] "you shall not steal,"[k] "you shall not covet,"[l] and whatever other commandments you can name, can be reduced to one byword: "You shall love your neighbor as yourself."[m]
10Love does no evil to the neighbor; thus, love is the carrying out of the Torah.[n]

11And be mindful of the times we are in: it is high time for you to wake up from sleep, for now the day of salvation is nearer than when we
first believed. 12The night is waning and dawn has drawn near! So let us cast away the deeds done in darkness, and let us don the armor of daylight. 13Specifically, let us behave appropriately for the daytime, not in revels and drinking binges, not in profligate sex and gluttony, not in
strife and jealousy. 14Instead, don the Lord Jesus-Christ like a second skin and eliminate any opportunity down the line to give in to the impulses of the flesh.

14

1Welcome anyone who is weak in the faith, but do not subject him
to judgments over debatable matters. 2One has the confidence to eat all
foods, but the weak one eats herbs.[o] 3The one eating meat should not look down on the one abstaining, nor let the abstainer condemn the
meat eater, for after all, God welcomed him. 4Who are you to judge the performance of someone else's domestic servant? It will be in the eyes of his own master that he succeeds or fails, and in this case he will succeed,
for the Lord is able to make him succeed. 5One observes this day as more holy than that, while another considers every day equally holy; let each

---

"individual." Read this way, the passage does seem catholicizing in vocabulary and conception, which would place its origin sometime later than its context. But if one translated as I do, the problem more or less disappears.

i. Exod. 20:14

j. Exod. 20:13

k. Exod. 20:15

l. Exod. 20:17

m. Lev. 19:18

n. Verses 8-10 sound like they were originally an independent statement on love and the Torah.

o. Some ancient Jews and Christians embraced vegetarianism as part of a symbolic return to Edenic innocence, but the idea here seems to be the familiar strategy of "building a fence around the Torah." Avoiding any chance of eating ritually tainted meat, some Christians decided to give up all meat. Against this, the "strong in faith" would adopt Luther's posture: "Sin boldly, but believe more boldly still!"

one come to his own conclusion. [6]The one observing the special day dedicates it to the Lord. The one who eats meat gives thanks to God for it. [7]For not a single one of us lives his life in isolation, nor does anyone die in isolation. [8]For while we live, we live for the Lord; and when we die, we die for the Lord. Thus either way, dead or alive, we belong to the Lord, [9]for this is why Christ died and lived, in order for him to become judge both of the dead and of the living. [10]So what are you doing judging your brother? Or how dare you look down on your brother. For all of us are going to appear before the judgment throne of God. [11]For it is written: "As I live, says Adonai, every knee will bend before me, and every tongue will swear fealty to God!"[p] [12]Thus each one of us will have to explain himself before God. [13]So let us resolve not to judge one another any more.

Except for this:[q] make up your mind never again to scandalize or offend your brother. [14]I know and am convinced that in the code of Jesus-Christ, no food is inherently profane, except that it remains profane for the poor soul who still considers it so. For him, nothing has changed: it is profane. [15]So if your brother is affronted by what you eat, you are no longer behaving in love. Do not destroy, by your food, this man for whom Christ died! [16]Do not cause what you consider good to be spoken ill of because it tempts a brother to violate his tender conscience. [17]For God's order is not concerned with dietary rules, but with righteousness, peace, and holy ecstasy of the spirit. [18]For the one who serves Christ in this respect will win both God's warm approval and the esteem of other people. [19]So therefore, let us pursue objectives conducive to peace and those which strengthen each other. [20]Do not unravel the work of God for the sake of food. All foods indeed are ritually clean but are nonetheless evil for the one who eats them, invited against his conscience. [21]It is good not to eat meat or to drink wine or to do anything else that trips up your brother.[r] [22]The faith you have: keep it between yourself and God. Blessed is the one who does not condemn himself by virtue of the very action he approves. [23]But the man who is unsure of the rightness of his act and goes

---

p. Isa. 45:23

q. Notice that vv. 14:13b-15:1 constitute an interpolation seeking to correct the "live and let live" policy advocated in 14:1-13a; it is a triumph of legalism.

r. Verses 17-23 seem to paraphrase and repeat vv. 14-16, indicating a patchwork from earlier sources, in this case harmonizing two variant versions of the same paraenetic source text in a manner similar to the Gospel of the Ebionites, which combines various versions of the same story from Luke, Matthew, and other sources.

ahead and eats meat, he has condemned himself. All that does not proceed from the confidence of faith, it is sin.

15

[1]So then,[s] we, the strong, ought to shoulder the burdens of the weak
and not act just to please ourselves.[t] [2]Let each one of us behave so as to
please his neighbor for his good, his strengthening. [3]For even Christ did
not endeavor to please himself, but as it is written: "The insults of those
who insulted you rebounded on me."[u] [4]For whatever scripture records
from ancient times, the intention was to teach subsequent readers that
through patience and the encouragement of the scriptures we might have
hope. [5]And may the God of patience and of comfort bless you with unanimity in this attitude toward one another, as is the way of Christ-Jesus,
[6]in order that, united in peace, you may with one voice worship the God
and Father of our Lord Jesus-Christ.

[7]That being the case, welcome one another, just as Christ welcomed
us into the glorious presence of God. [8]For I tell you this: Christ became a
servant of the circumcised on behalf of the trustworthiness of God to give
substance to the promises made to the patriarchs, [9]and a servant to the
nations to lead them to worship God for his mercy, as it is written:
"Therefore, I will testify about you before nations, and I will sing praise
to your name."[v] [10]And elsewhere he says, "Rejoice, O nations, along
with his people!"[w] [11]And yet again: "All nations, praise the Lord, and
may all the peoples praise him!"[x] [12]And again, Isaiah says, "One will
sprout from Jesse's root to rule the nations; on him will the nations set
their hope."[y] [13]So may the God of hope fill you with all joy and peace as

---

s. Marcion's Romans lacked Chapters 15-16.

t. We seem to witness here the compassion of the Gnostic Bodhisattva, advanced beyond the childish scruples of the conventionally religious but willing to conduct himself in public as if he held the same values so as not to outrage the weak. If they did act out their own convictions, some might persecute them, while others might be willing to emulate them but not yet with convinced boldness, to their spiritual peril. Presumably the "stronger" brethren did drink wine and eat meat in the privacy of their homes, and the writer allows for this, advocating a policy of "don't ask, don't tell" in order to avoid these disputes.

u. Pss. 69:9

v. Pss. 18:49

w. Deut. 32:43

x. Pss. 117:1

y. Isa. 11:10

you believe, so you may enjoy a wealth of hope by the power of the Holy
Spirit.[z]

14 But I, even I myself, have been convinced, my brothers, concerning
you, that you yourselves are full of goodness, having been filled with all
knowledge, also capable of admonishing one another; you don't need my
intervention. 15 But I took the liberty of writing you, partly by way of reminder, using the inspiration granted me by God 16 as a servant of
Christ-Jesus to the nations, performing the priestly task of preaching the
news of God in order that the offering of the nations may prove acceptable, having been made holy by the Holy Spirit.

17 I have therefore grounds to boast, thanks to Christ-Jesus, in the
things pertaining to God. 18 I will, however, not presume to say anything
about the things Christ did not accomplish through my own hands for securing the submission of the nations in word and deed, 19 by the power of
signs and wonders, by the power of Spirit, so that I should have fulfilled
the commandment of the news of Christ from Jerusalem and adjacent
parts to Illyricum.[a] 20 So therefore, I have been doing my best not to evangelize where Christ was already invoked so as to avoid building on someone else's foundation,[b] 21 but rather, as it is written, "They shall see, they
to whom nothing about him had hitherto been announced, and those
who have not heard of him will understand."[c]

22 This is also why I was repeatedly hindered from coming to you.
23 But now, having finished the work in this area, and having desired to
visit you for many years now, 24 whenever I make my trip to Spain I hope,
on my journey, to see you and to have you send me on my way to Spain if
only I may first be somewhat replenished by you. 25 But right now I am off
for Jerusalem to serve the saints. 26 For Macedonia and Achaia deemed it
good to make some contribution for the poor among the saints in Jerusalem. 27 For they deemed it only proper, being indebted to them; for if the
nations shared in their spiritual riches, they ought also to return the favor

z. The epistle seems once to have concluded right here, but someone added vv. 14-33 and chapter 16.

a. Is the writer thinking of one of the post-resurrection mission charges from the gospels? If so, we have very late material here.

b. See by contrast 1 Cor. 3:10.

c. Isa. 52:15. Verses 17-21 cannot have belonged originally to this letter, since his policy stated here is in utter contradiction to the whole reason for his planned visit to Rome, where he would be doing nothing else than preaching the message where others had already preached it, adding onto a foundation laid by others (1:8-15).

when it comes to material things. [28]So once I have wrapped up this task and signed over this harvest to them, [29]I will go on by way of you to Spain. And I know that when I do come to you, it will be with the complete approval of Christ. [30]I plead with you, *brothers,* by our Lord Jesus-Christ and by the love of the Spirit, to agonize with me in prayer to God on my behalf, [31]that I may be delivered from those disobedient to the faith in Judea, and that my service to Jerusalem may prove acceptable to the saints,[d] so that coming to you, by God's will, rejoicing, I may at last fall asleep there among you.[e] [33]And may the God of peace be with you all. Amen.

16

[1]So I recommend to you our sister Phoebe, a deacon of the community at Cenchrea,[f] [2]in order that you may welcome her in the name of the Lord in a manner befitting the saints and support her in whatever manner she may require of you, for truly she became a benefactress of many, myself included. [3]Greet Prisca and Aquila,[g] my colleagues in Christ-Jesus, who risked their necks to save my life. [4]It is not only I, but also all our communities among the nations, who owe them a great debt. [5]Greet also the congregation that gathers in their home. Greet Epaetnus, my beloved, one of the first generation for Christ in Asia. [6]Greet Maria, who has labored much for you. [7]Greet Andronicus and Junia, my relatives and fellow prisoners, who are notable among the ranks of apostles and who indeed were my predecessors in the service of Christ. [8]Greet Ampliatus, my beloved in the Lord, as well as my beloved Stachys. [9]Greet Urbanus, our colleague in the service of Christ. [10]Greet Apelles,[h] ap-

---

d. This seems to presuppose the Book of Acts, where Lukan redaction, as Baur saw, changed Paul's tormentors from Jewish-Christian "zealots for the Torah" to some visiting Jews from Asia. In any case, Romans anticipates two groups in Jerusalem, one hostile to Paul, the other doubtful of him.

e. J. C. O'Neill recognizes this as the meaning of συναναπαυσομαι, a reference to the legend of Paul's martyrdom in Rome. The writer looks back on the death of Paul, knowing his readers will, as well. The prospect of a further journey to Spain tantalizes the reader, who then muses over "what might have been."

f. What follows was originally an independent letter of recommendation on behalf of Phoebe, addressed to Ephesus. It cannot originally have formed part of a Pauline letter to Rome since here Paul seems to know many Roman church members, whereas the previous letter says that he does not.

g. Acts 18:2; 2 Tim. 4:19

h. Possibly a reference to Apollos (Acts 18:24-28; 1 Cor. 1:12; 3:5-6, 22; 4:6) or the Marcionite Apelles, who may yet be identical.

proved in Christ's service. Greet those of the house of Aristobulus. [11]Greet Herodion, my relative.[i] Greet those of the house of Narcissus who are believers in the Lord. [12]Greet Tryphaena[j] and Tryphosa, who labor in the Lord's vineyard. Greet the beloved Persis, who labored long in the Lord's ranks. [13]Greet Rufus, chosen of the Lord, and his mother, who is like a mother to me, too. [14]Greet Asyncritus, Phlegon, Hermes, Patrobas, Hermas,[k] and the brothers associated with them. [15]Greet Philologus and Julia, Nereus and his sister, even Olympas, and all the saints associated with them. [16]Greet one another with a ritual kiss. All the communities of Christ greet you.

[17]Now I urge you, brothers, to watch out for those who foment divisions and scandals alien to the teaching which you learned, and to turn away from them. [18]For such people are serving not our Lord Christ but merely their own belly; they use eloquence and flattery to deceive the minds of the innocent. [19]For the report of your submission to the faith came to everyone; therefore, I rejoice over you. I want you to be wise in the good, innocent of the bad. For then the God of peace will trample the accuser under your feet soon. May the favor of our Lord Jesus-Christ be with you![l]

[21]Timothy, my colleague, greets you, and so do Lucius and Jason and Sosipater, my relatives.[m] [22]I, Tertius, the one writing this epistle, greet you in the name of the Lord.[n] [23]Gaius,[o] my host, greets you, along with the whole community. Erastus, the municipal treasurer,[p] greets you, as does Quartus, a brother. *May the favor of our Lord Jesus-Christ be with you all. Amen.*[q]

---

i. Eisenman points out the Herodian connections implied by the names "Aristobulus" and "Herodion."

j. Possibly a reference to the adoptive mother and patroness of Thecla.

k. Possibly a reference to the writer of the Shepherd of Hermas.

l. Verses 17-20, which interrupt the sequence here, sound strikingly like the Pastoral Epistles and are likely a later interpolation.

m. Acts 18:5; 20:4; 17:5-6

n. It is conceivable we have a wink here from the actual writer or original compiler of Romans.

o. Acts 19:29

p. Acts 19:22

q. Is this letter of recommendation fictive? Why would anyone else create such a writing? The answer might be to establish a link between Paul and the individuals named in the letter. It would thereby function the same way as lists of those who saw the risen Christ (1 Cor. 15:3-11), providing credentials to the cho-

25So to the one who is capable of making you stand firm in allegiance to my message, even the proclamation of Jesus-Christ, part of the process of revealing the mystery kept secret for long ages, 26but now being made manifest *through the prophetic writings,*[r] as commanded by the everlasting God and made known to all nations to secure their submission to the faith. 27To God, who alone is wise,[s] let all worship be directed, age after age, through the invocation of Jesus-Christ! Amen.[t]

---

sen few. It is the equivalent of the genealogies in the book of Chronicles, giving credentials for priestly houses whose representatives wrote the book and administered the second temple.

r. Without this phrase, the concluding doxology would sound Marcionite. On the other hand, if it is original, it would suggest Earl Doherty's theory that Christians derived the events of salvation not from historical memory but from esoteric interpretation of scripture: reading Old Testament scripture was how they learned of Jesus.

s. 1 Tim. 1:17

t. The concluding doxology must have been formulated by a redactor who thought the epistle to the Romans needed closure, rather than a closing to the letter for Phoebe.

15.

The First Epistle to the Thessalonians

Walter Schmithals (*Paul and the Gnostics*) has shown how form-critical scrutiny reveals First Thessalonians to be a compilation of two brief letters, easily reconstructed by simply looking for the displaced salutations and initial thanksgivings on behalf of the recipients, the usual formula in Pauline epistles, and restoring them to their characteristic positions.

Plainly, much of the first letter (Epistle A) is taken up with apologetics for Paul, but who is attacking him? Gordon D. Fee suggests he may have heard of a hail of criticisms from those who, in their persecution of the Thessalonian Christians, sought to discredit Paul as a charlatan. On the other hand, it may be that the letter, being post-Pauline and pseudonymous, deals with anti-Pauline factions within Christianity who deemed him a false apostle and sought to wrest the Thessalonian churches away from their historic Pauline sphere of influence, winning their loyalty to other apostolic names and authority claims.

The ostensible scene of writing is historically implausible because how can Paul not have included the doctrine of the general resurrection in his foundational preaching in Thessalonica (4:13)? The whole thing presupposes the delay of the Parousia, marking the epistle as a late product akin to 2 Timothy. And just as in 1 Corinthians, we encounter a series of topical headings (4:9, 13; 5:1), implying the text was first conceived as a handbook, not an ephemeral letter.

The second letter (Epistle B) appears to be a letter written as if by Paul to a later generation of Paulinists to let them know he is smiling

upon them, no doubt from heaven, as his disciples and successors, much like the posthumous prophecies of the risen Christ to his churches in the seven letters in the Revelation of John (chaps. 2-3). As in 1 Corinthians 5:3-5, Paul is "absent in body but present in spirit" (cf. Matt. 18:18-20), overseeing all they do. For this nearly Christlike role ascribed to Paul, keep in mind that Origen tells us Marcionites and Valentinian Gnostics considered Paul to be the predicted Paraclete and that Marcionites depicted Christ on a central throne in heaven with Paul to his right and Marcion himself to his left! An epistle like this, appearing long after Paul's death, is reminiscent of the sporadic messages posthumously relayed to the Shi'ite communities by the Hidden Imam from his place of seclusion, communicated by the hand of the Bab ("the gate"), a secretary who had in effect inherited his prophetic mantle.

Epistle A

1

[1]Paul and Silvanus and Timothy, to the congregation of Thessalonians in the care of God the Father and the Lord Jesus-Christ. May you
know God's favor and protection.

[2]We always give thanks to God about you all, making mention of
you in our prayers, never [3]neglecting your faithful work, your labor of
love, and your endurance in the prospect of the coming of our Lord, Jesus-Christ, all before the eyes of our God and Father,[a] mindful, brothers
beloved of God, of your having been chosen, [5]because our news connected with you, not in mere verbiage, but in power and in the Holy Spirit
and strong certainty. *You know what sort of people we were among you,*
inspired by you. [6]*And you became emulators of us and of the Lord,*[b] welcoming the message in the midst of affliction, albeit with great joy inspired by the Holy Spirit, [7]*so that you became a model to all those in*
Macedonia and Achaia who believed. [8]For you were a sounding board
for the message of the Lord not only throughout Macedonia and Achaia,
but your faith towards God has circulated everywhere, [9]so that we need
not say anything: they themselves relate the tale of our reception among
you and how you turned to God from the idols, henceforth to serve a God

a. Matt. 6:4, 6, 18

b. Winsome Munro makes vv. 5c-6a, 7 part of the later Pastoral Stratum, later additions to the initial combination of letters posited by Schmithals.

living and true, 10 and to await his Son from the skies, whom he raised
from the dead: Jesus, our deliverer from the wrath to come.

2

1 *You yourselves know, brothers, that our reception among you was
not fruitless;* 2 *rather, having previously suffered and been insulted in
Philippi, we were bold in the zeal of our God to speak the news of God to
you despite great struggles.* 3 *For our exhortations did not stem from error
or impure motives or wily deceit as some then charged, but we speak as
we have been authorized by God to be entrusted with the news, not to ingratiate ourselves with our hearers, but to please God who tests our
hearts.* 5 *For neither then did we employ flattery, as you can attest, nor did
we use Christ as a pretext to despoil you, as God is our witness,* 6 *nor did
we seek the adulation of the crowd, neither from you nor from others,*
7 *though as apostles of Christ we might well have thrown our weight
around.* 8 *So cherishing you, we were delighted to impart to you not only
the news of God, but our own selves because you had become dear to us.*
9 *For you remember, brothers, our labor and toil, working night and day
so as not to be a burden to any one of you, proclaiming to you the news of
God.* 10 *You and God are witnesses of how piously and righteously and ir-
reproachably we behaved toward you who believed,* 11 *just as you know
how we encouraged and consoled each one of you as a father with his
own children,* 12 *testifying that you ought to behave worthily of God, who
called you to share his kingdom and his splendor.*[c]

4

2 *For you recall the commandments we gave you through the authority of the Lord Jesus.* 3 *For God's will for you is simply this: your sanctification in that you abstain from prostitution,* 4 *that each one of you be able
to control his own bodily vessel in sanctity and honor,* 5 *not in the grip of
passion and lust like the heathen who do not know God,* 6 *nor to transgress and defraud his brother in this matter because the Lord is the
avenger in all such cases, just as we told you earlier and solemnly testified.* 7 *For God did not summon us to a life of impurity, but to live in sanctity.* 8 *Thus whoever laughs off this advice is rejecting not human opinion
but rather God, who gives his Holy Spirit to you.*[d]

9 *Now concerning brotherly love, it is superfluous to write to you,
for you yourselves are already taught by God spontaneously to love one*

---

c. More of the Pastoral Stratum (2:1-2; 13-16), according to Munro.

d. Mark 8:38

another; [10]*for indeed you manifest it to all the brothers in Macedonia. We only encourage you, brothers, to increase love even more,* [11]*and to make a real effort to be quiet and to mind your own business and to undertake honest labor, as we enjoined you,* [12]*in order that you may conduct yourselves appropriately relative to those outside and so you will lack nothing.*[e]

[13]Now we do not want you to be ignorant, brothers, concerning those asleep, so you do not mourn like others who are bereft of hope. [14]For if we believe that Jesus died and rose again, it stands to reason that God will also bring with Jesus those who have fallen asleep on account of him. [15]For we say this to you by a revelation from the Lord: we who live to see the arrival of the Lord[f] may by no means get ahead of the sleepers. [16]Because the Lord himself will come down from the sky with a shout of command from the voice of an archangel[g] sounding God's trumpet, and the dead who repose in Christ will be the first to rise again. [17]Then we who live and remain shall find ourselves snatched up together with them aboard clouds to meet with the Lord in the upper air, and there we will remain with the Lord forever! [18]So comfort each other with these words whenever one of you dies.

5

[1]So concerning the signs of the times, brothers, it is superfluous to write to you, [2]for you know full well about the Day of the Lord—like a thief in the night, so it comes![h] [3]Just when they are reassuring themselves: "Peace and security," at that moment destruction overtakes them like the labor pains of a pregnant woman. And there will be no escape. [4]But you, brothers, are not shrouded in darkness, that the day should surprise you like a thief.[i] [5]For you are all sons of the light and sons of the day. We do

e. More Pastoral Stratum (4:1-12). Like the kindred text at 1 Tim. 2:1-2, this passage bespeaks a second-generation desire to blend in again with the larger society from which the first-generation sect, in its separatist zeal, did not mind distinguishing itself. Evangelistic zeal, which once attracted persecution on account of its obnoxiousness, had yielded to peaceful co-existence and unobtrusiveness.

f. Luke 18:8; Mark 9:1

g. Does he identify Christ with the archangel? The voice of the one is the voice of the other.

h. So why does he go ahead anyway? Simply because his subsequent teaching is a fictive "recollection" of a teaching the pseudonymous writer seeks to pass off as the old, foundational teaching of Paul in Thessalonica, to undercut and rebut rival beliefs current in his own day.

i. Matt. 24:42-44

not belong to the night, nor to the darkness, [6]thus let us not remain comatose like everyone else; rather, let us stay clear-headed and vigilant. [7]For the sleeper sleeps at night and the drunkard drinks by night. [8]But since we belong to the day, let us snap out of it,[j] donning a breastplate of faith and love and for a helmet the prospect of salvation, [9]because God did not destine us to suffer his wrath, but to attain salvation through the arrival of our Lord Jesus-Christ, [10]the one who died on our behalf in order that, whether we remain awake or we fall asleep in death, we may ultimately live with him. [11]Therefore, comfort one another and fortify each other, as of course you do.

[12]*Now we ask you, brothers, to acknowledge those who do the work among you and who distinguish themselves in the service of the Lord and exhort you,* [13]*and to esteem them most highly in love because of their work. Be at peace among yourselves.* [14]*And we exhort you, brothers, to reprove the lazy, encourage the timid, support the weak, and be long-suffering with everyone.* [15]*See that no one recompenses another evil for evil, but always follow the path of benevolence toward one another and toward everyone else as well.*[k] [16]Rejoice always, [17]pray constantly, [18]giving thanks in whatever circumstances. For this is the plan of God for you, being in the fold of Christ-Jesus.

[19]Do not snuff out the fire of the Spirit. [20]I mean, do not dismiss prophecies out of hand, [21]but weigh them all,[l] *heeding the genuine ones,* [22]*but repudiating every one that smacks of evil.*[m]

[23]And may the God of peace himself sanctify you completely, and may your whole spirit, soul, and body be kept blameless for the arrival of our Lord, Jesus-Christ. [24]The one who summons you to this is faithful: he will see to it.

[25]Brothers, you pray for us, too. [26]Greet all the brothers with a ritual kiss. [27]I command you in the name of the Lord to have this epistle read to all the brothers.[n]

[28]May the favor of our Lord Jesus-Christ be with you.

---

j. Luke 21:34-36

k. How like the Pastoral Epistles this all sounds! The passage (5:12-15) is part of the Pastoral Stratum.

l. 1 Cor. 14:29

m. Munro makes 21b-22 part of the Pastoral Stratum. Cf. 1 Cor. 12:3; 1 John 4:1-3. In vv. 19ff we are well past the golden era of prophecy and it has become a danger and an embarrassment, as in 1 Cor. 12, 14. But we have not yet gone all the way to 1 Cor. 13 with its implicit abolition of all prophecy and glossolalia.

n. As F. C. Baur noted long ago, this note militates against the authenticity of

Epistle B

2

[13]We render thanks to God without stopping, that having welcomed the message of God once you heard it from us, you welcomed it not as some human scheme but as the message of God, which it really is, and which energizes you who believe. [14]For you became imitators, brothers, of God's congregations located in Judea, safe in the bosom of Christ, because you, too, endured the same things at the hands of your compatriots as they did from the Jews, [15]those who both killed the Lord Jesus and the prophets and chased us out, who are not pleasing to God and who set themselves against all mankind,[o] [16]obstructing our efforts to speak to the nations in order that they may be saved, ever in this way filling up their sins. But the wrath of God caught up with them at last.[p]

[17]But we, brothers, being bereaved of you, even for the span of a single hour, in person, though not in heart, were all the more eager with great desire to see your face. [18]Thus we wanted to come to you, indeed I, Paul,[q] not once but twice, but the adversary prevented us. [19]For what is the basis for our hope, our joy, the achievement we brag about to our Lord Jesus when he arrives? What else but you? [20]For you are our pride and joy.

3

[1]This is why, when we could bear the suspense no longer, we were quite happy to be left alone in Athens, [2]and we sent Timothy, our brother and colleague for God in the news of Christ, to fortify you and encourage you in your faith so that no one might drop out because of these afflictions. For you yourselves know this is what we were destined for. [4]For even when we were with you,[r] we already said to you that we were about

---

the epistle: the injunction to have the text read in public is superfluous given that the epistle is written to the whole church anyway. The real agenda is to seek inclusion of this spurious letter among the corpus of the real ones in the public lection of the churches at a time when they have come to be treated as scripture. "Treat this like the authentic Pauline letters, okay?"

o. Our author is no Jew. It is impossible to imagine a Jew, even a sectarian Jew regarding his sect as the "true Israel," speaking of Jews in this manner, which reeks of typical Hellenistic anti-Semitism.

p. This is certainly a reference to the fall of Jerusalem in CE 70, if not actually to the defeat of the Bar-Kochba rebellion in CE 136.

q. See the introduction to 2 Cor. where the "I, so-and-so" formula is noted as a dead giveaway for pseudonymous authorship.

r. Cf. Luke 24:44; John 16:4b. As in these passages, the hint that the writer

to be afflicted, as indeed it happened, as you know. [5]Thus, no longer able to bear the suspense, I sent to find out the state of your faith, hoping the tempter had not somehow tempted you successfully, rendering our labor a loss. [6]But now, with Timothy arriving and announcing to us the news of your faith and love, and that you have us in fond memory always, longing to see us just as we long for you, [7]we were thus comforted about you, by your faith, as to all our distress and affliction, [8]because now we feel alive again if you are standing firm in your commitment to the Lord.[s] [9]How can we render adequate thanks to God over you, given all the joy with which we rejoice over you before our God, [10]vehemently petitioning night and day to be able to see your face and adjust any shortcomings in your faith?

[11]So may our God and Father himself, and our Lord Jesus, direct our steps to you. [12]And may the Lord make you increase and overflow with love for one another and for everyone, just as we also love you, [13]so to fortify your hearts impeccable in sanctity before our God and Father at the coming of our Lord Jesus with all his saints.

4

[1]*Finally, brothers, we bid you and exhort you in the name of the Lord Jesus that you conduct yourselves ever more perfectly in the way that is pleasing to God, as you learned it from us, as of course you already do.*[t]

---

speaks in the name of a figure long dead is when he writes "when I was with you," denoting "during my [his] lifetime."

s. Cf. 3:1-8 with 2 Cor. 2:12-13; 7:5-7. Is one passage modeled upon the other?

t. Munro makes this passage part of the Pastoral Stratum.

16.

The Second Epistle to the Thessalonians

LIKE FIRST THESSALONIANS, THE SECOND epistle to Thessalonica has been shown by Walter Schmithals (*Paul and the Gnostics*) to be a compilation of two additional brief letters, similarly easy to reconstruct because of displaced salutations and thanksgivings on behalf of the recipients, the usual formula in Pauline epistles.

The first letter (Epistle A) is essentially an encouragement to churches under persecution, comforting them with the promise of eventual relief and the satisfaction of beholding their enemies' doom at the second advent of Christ. If the identification of the recipients is not arbitrary, it would denote that someone in the Thessalonian congregation probably fabricated the letter in a time of persecution. If so, it would have created quite a stir for its precise relevance and would have carried the force of a revelation or even a miniature apocalypse. In fact, it would have been analogous to Mark 13 or the Book of Daniel, each of which was a product of persecution.

The italicized section (3:6-16) is part of the Pastoral Stratum delineated by Winsome Munro (*Authority in Paul and Peter*) as material added subsequently to accommodate the standards of "nascent catholic" Christianity. The subject addressed in the Pastorals is not some mysterious outbreak of unmotivated vagrancy among church members. It is rather the expectation that the end of time was imminent, resulting in people following the injunction of 1 Corinthians 7:29-31. However, the Pastoral polemic was no doubt aimed at the itinerant apostles and prophets of the late first and early second century who were abusing their privileges of support from their hearers, precisely

as in the Didache.[a] Hence, the contrast with Paul's example for itinerant ministers. The charge of being idle busybodies echoes the denunciation of the consecrated, stipended widows in 1 Timothy 5:13.

The second letter (Epistle B), which nevertheless lacks the salutation, seeks to dampen the kind of apocalyptic enthusiasm that expected the end of the age at any moment. This fanatical expectation is blamed on two sources: prophets proclaiming the imminent end[b] and previous letters ascribed to Paul, apparently either First Thessalonians A or Second Thessalonians B, either of which may be read as encouraging belief in an imminent end. The observation is very important in that it plainly attests that people were indeed doing what modern critics suggest by forging Pauline epistles.

It is striking that the writer makes "Paul" warn of the Antichrist (whose parousia seems to have been delayed by unspecified forces just as Christ's has been!) in terms exactly like those in which Paul himself was being vilified by contemporary Jewish Christians. Thus the discussion has an apologetical agenda as well.

Epistle A

1

Paul and Silvanus and Timothy, to the congregation of Thessalonians in the care of God our Father and the Lord, Jesus-Christ. 2May you
enjoy the favor and protection of God the Father and the Lord, Jesus-
Christ.
3We are obliged to give thanks to God constantly for you, brothers,
as is only fitting, because your faith grows abundantly and your love,
each for all the rest, increases, 4so that we ourselves brag about you in
God's congregations for your perseverance and faithfulness amid your
persecutions and the afflictions you endure, 5clear evidence of the righteous judgment of God, that you may be counted worthy of the kingdom
of God for which indeed you suffer, 6since it is just for God to recompense
affliction to those now afflicting you, 7and to you who are being afflicted,
surcease, along with us, when the Lord Jesus is revealed from heaven with
his mighty angels 8in blazing fire, dealing out full vengeance to those who

a. Didache 11:3-6, 9-12; 12:1-5

b. See Luke 21:8 where "the time is near" was added to the content of false prophecies.

want nothing to do with God and to those refusing to bow to the news of
our Lord Jesus. [9]They will pay the penalty of being forever shut out from
the presence of the Lord and from the splendor of his might, [10]whenever
he comes to be worshipped by his saints and to be marveled at by all who
have believed, because our testimony to you met with belief. [11]For this
reason we indeed pray always for you, that our God may judge you as
having lived up to his calling and may powerfully fulfill in you every
pleasing good deed and faithful deed, [12]so the name of our Lord Jesus
may be well spoken of, thanks to you, and that you in turn may receive his
blessing and approval, the favor of our God and Lord, Jesus-Christ.

3

[6] *Now we urge you, brothers, in the name of the Lord Jesus-Christ, to
shun any brother*[c] *who behaves lazily, not according to the tradition you
received from us.*[d] [7]*For you yourselves know how it is necessary to emulate us because we were not idle among you,* [8]*nor took free food from anyone, but rather worked with labor and struggled night and day so as not
to be a burden to any one of you.* [9]*Not that we do not have the authority
to receive compensation, but we refrain in order to set an example for you
to imitate us.* [10]*For even when we were with you, we urged you, "If anyone refuses to work, then let him not eat either."* [11]*We hear there are some
among you who behave lazily, working at nothing but being busybodies,*
[12]*and such people we command and exhort in the name of the Lord,
Jesus-Christ, to work quietly and eat the bread they earn for themselves.*

[13]*As for you, brothers, do not grow discouraged when your good
deeds seem to come to nothing.* [14]*And if anyone refuses to obey our command in this epistle, take note of him and refuse to have anything to do
with him in the hope that he may feel due shame.* [15]*And yet do not treat
him with hostility, but admonish him as a brother.*[e]

[16]And may the Lord of peace himself grant you his protection always
in every circumstance. May the Lord be with you all!

Epistle B

2

[13]We are obliged always to thank God on your account, brothers beloved of the Lord, because God chose you as the first to become ripe unto

---

c. As often in the Pauline epistles, the reference is to itinerant missioners, as in 3 John 3, 5, 10; Matt. 25:40.

d. See note k on p. 437.

e. Winsome Munro makes 3:6-15 part of the Pastoral Stratum.

salvation by the sanctification of the Spirit and belief in the truth, [14]to which also he summoned you through our preaching so you could attain to the splendor of our Lord, Jesus-Christ.

[1]Now we ask you, brothers, when it comes to the arrival of our Lord, Jesus-Christ, and our being gathered together to him, [2]not to be too easily confused nor disturbed, neither through some prophecy, nor through some saying, nor through some epistle allegedly from us, to the effect that the Day of the Lord is immediately at hand.[f] [3]Let no one deceive you in any such way because it will not arrive until once the apostasy comes and the Man of Lawlessness is revealed, the Son of Perdition,[g] [4]the one setting himself against and making himself supreme over all that is called God or that is worshipped so that he enthrones himself in the temple of God, presenting himself as a god. [5]Surely you remember how I used to tell you these things while I was still with you?[h] [6]And you know what is now restraining him so that he may be revealed only at his destined time. [7]For the unseen plan of lawlessness proceeds apace, but there is one restraining it right now till it is taken out of the way. [8]And then the Lawless One will be revealed, whom the Lord will destroy by no more than a breath and reduce him to nothing by the epiphany of his coming—[9]the one who will appear energized by the adversary with all possible miracles and signs and deceptive wonders [10]and with every wicked deceit for those who are perishing because they neglected to welcome the love of the truth which would have saved them. [11]Since the truth was not to their liking, God sends them a powerful error, making them believe the lie,[i] [12]in order that all who did not believe the truth but preferred unrighteousness may be judged.[j]

---

f. Here is our earliest instance of 1 Thess. being dismissed as a forgery. Of course, this one, seeking to supplant the previous epistle, is equally spurious.

g. Jewish Christians characterized Paul himself in precisely these terms: an antichrist who prompted a great apostasy from the Torah, hence the Man of Lawlessness. As per v. 4, Paul was even arrested in the temple for profaning it. See Acts 21:27-30.

h.. The phrase "when I was with you" may hint that Paul is dead and the writer is looking back to when Paul was present on earth. In any case, these teachings are new with this letter. The writer retrojects his own views into the foundational age by having Paul "remind" the readers that he had taught it all long before. See Luke 24:44; John 16:4b.

i. 1 Kings 22:19-23

j. Again, Jewish Christians vilified Paul in exactly these terms for having performed "the signs of an apostle" (2 Cor. 12:12), leading people astray with his Torah-free gospel (Acts 21:20b-21). God sent this delusion to the gentiles. It is

[15]*So then, brothers, stand firm and hold fast the traditions you were
taught, whether in person or in an epistle from us.*[k] [16]And our Lord, Jesus-Christ himself, and God our Father, the one who loved us and by his
favor gave us comfort for the ages and a firm hope, [17]may he comfort
your hearts and reinforce you as those whose every word and deed are
good.

3

[1]Finally, brothers, pray for us, that the message of the Lord may race
unhindered and be praised as it was among you, [2]and that we may be delivered from perverse and evil people, for not everyone holds the faith.
[3]But the Lord is faithful: he will fortify you and guard you against the
wicked. [4]*And we are sure about you, thanks to the Lord, that you do the
things we urge and will continue to do them.* [5]*And may the Lord direct
your hearts to the love of God and the patience of Christ.*[l]

---

similar to what Hindus said about the Buddha: the demonic devas had grown powerful by the practice of Yoga and threatened the Gods, so the Gods sent the Buddha to teach an alluring error. The devas accepted the heresy and lost their spiritual power, making them easy for the Gods to defeat.

k. As W. C. van Manen pointed out, it is a gross anachronism for Paul to refer to venerable traditions delivered by him to the church as if from the past. No, this is the language of a later Paulinist, for whom these are hoary traditions. Note also the assumption of a previous letter to Thessalonica in addition to 1 Thess. This verse is part of the Pastoral Stratum.

l. Verses 4-5 are also part of the Pastoral Stratum.

17.
Laodiceans/Ephesians

MARCION IS SAID TO HAVE HAD IN his canon a Pauline epistle to the Laodiceans, which Tertullian thought was likely a version of Ephesians. In fact, some manuscript copies of what we call "Ephesians" lack a specific destination or recipient. Later redactors may have simply added "Ephesians" or substituted it for "Laodiceans." Again from ancient writers, we know Marcion's Pauline texts lacked certain passages contained in the Catholic rescension of the epistles. But with such modern scholars as John Knox (*Marcion and the New Testament*) and R. Joseph Hoffmann (*Marcion: On the Restitution of Christianity*), I suspect Marcion's versions were earlier and that the more familiar versions probably represented the product of catholicizing redactions. It is not too difficult to spot what these contested passages would have been, and I follow Hoffmann's conjectures about these, placing suspected anti-Marcionite interpolations in italics.

As Edgar J. Goodspeed (*The Key to Ephesians*) showed, the epistle makes the most sense as an introduction to a collection of Pauline epistles and, indeed, makes explicit reference to the texts that follow it (3:3-4). The present epistle, then, would have been composed as a preface by the first collector of the Pauline corpus. Goodspeed, followed by Knox (*Philemon among the Letters of Paul*), nominated the freed slave Onesimus[a] for this honor, but Marcion would seem by far to be the most likely candidate. He is the first we know of to have had a collection of the epistles and a pressing reason for collecting them. The text, whether we call it Laodiceans or Ephesians, is an elaborate

a. Onesimus is mentioned in Col. 4:9; Phil. 10; Ignatian Ephesians 1:3; 2:1; 6:2.

mosaic of passages quoted or paraphrased from the collected epistles—excluding the Pastorals, which were subsequently written by Marcion's opponents—and presented as exceedingly long sentences, which is the result of the cut-and-paste method of composition. This is why the text sounds both Pauline and so strangely non-Pauline. The content is Pauline, but not the redactional form.

Hoffmann and Winsome Munro (*Authority in Paul and Peter*) both see the second half of traditional Ephesians as heavily interpolated with harmonizing, catholicizing material. Here I take a step further. It seems to me that what we have in chapters 4-6 is a second letter, a Catholic rejoinder to the Marcionite Laodiceans, much as 2 Thessalonians seeks to correct and supplant 1 Thessalonians. The major arguments against this suggestion are that the mining of Pauline texts as the building blocks for the author's own epistle seems to continue unabated and the accompanying sentence structure persists, though to a markedly diminishing extent. But these considerations do not seem to me decisive. For one thing, the Ecclesiastical Redactor may simply have noticed what the Laodicean writer was doing and copied his method, returning to the same sources, as Matthew and Luke did in using Mark and Q. As for the sentence structure, which is only partly maintained, this may have proved too unwieldy for the second writer, who soon gave up on it. For me, the form-critical consideration is overruling: surely what we read in 3:20-21 is intended to be the closing of an epistle. We observe that the Gospel of John originally must have concluded with 20:30-31, so we regard chapter 21 as an appendix. We recognize that Romans seems to want to conclude at 11:36, then again at 15:32, and yet again at 16:27, and we recognize that scribes have been at work appending more material. Even so, whatever follows 3:20-21 in this epistle must not have belonged to the original letter.

My guess is that chapters 4-6 were first circulated separately because chapter 4 seems to open like an independent manuscript. I have supplied the name Paul, underlining the parallel between Ephesians 4:1 and 2 Corinthians 10:1, the beginning of a separate Pauline epistle subsequently joined to other Corinthian letters and letter-fragments. But no name would have been necessary, as witness Hebrews, 1 John,

and others. The absence of the name made it easier for some subsequent scribe to join the catholicizing Ephesians with its original counterpart, Marcionite Laodiceans. Catholicizing interpolations in the first document cemented the union. The fusion and conflation process would have been pretty much the same as that which produced our familiar versions of 2 Corinthians, 1 Thessalonians, 2 Thessalonians, and Philippians, according to Walter Schmithals (*Paul and the Gnostics*).

One remarkable implication of reading Laodiceans in its restored form is that, if it is of Marcionite origin, we can infer that Marcionism offered a more advanced layer of initiation beyond the basic doctrine of a single Father God who was opposed to the Creator God. There also would have been an esoteric doctrine of multiple divine entities contained within the pleroma, or divine fullness.

Laodiceans

1

Paul, apostle of Christ-Jesus by the will of God, to the saints *at Ephesus,* believers in Christ-Jesus: [2]May the favor and protection of God our Father and the Lord Jesus-Christ be with you.[b]

[3]May the God and Father of our Lord Jesus-Christ[c] dwell in bliss, he who has endowed us with every spiritual blessing in the celestial spheres by virtue of our incorporation in Christ,[d] [4]just as he selected us before the creation of the world for us to be holy and flawless in his sight,[e] [5]in his love predestining us for adoption as sons for himself, through Jesus-Christ, according to the decided preference of his will,[f] [6]to the end that all might extol the splendor of his favor with which he favored us, insofar as we are joined to the one he loved,[g] [7] *the one by whom we have received release through his blood, the forgiveness of trespasses,* the index of the abundance of his favor,[h] [8]which he lavished upon us in the form of all

b. Col. 1:1-2

c. This is Marcionite conceptuality, not just of any possible God, but specifically the compassionate Father of Jesus Christ.

d. 2 Cor. 1:3; Rom. 1:11b

e. Col. 3:12b; 1 Cor. 1:27a, 22b; 2 Thess. 2:13b

f. Rom. 8:29; Gal. 4:5b; 3:26; Phil. 2:13

g. Phil. 1:11b; Rom. 5:15b; 2 Cor. 9:14b, 15

h. Col. 1:20b; 1:14b; Rom. 2:4a; 5:9b; 3:25, 26a; 11:33b; 2 Cor. 5:19b

manner of wisdom, both esoteric and practical,[i] [9]disclosing to us the hitherto unsuspected design which delighted him and which he silently resolved[j] [10]to administer in the pleroma of the times, to subsume the All in Christ, including what is in the concentric heavens and what is on the earth,[k] [11]in whom also we were selected as his inheritance,[l] thus predestined in accord with the universal design that operates by the judgment of his will,[m] [12]to the end that we should be a cause for extolling his splendor, those who had already placed our hopes on Christ,[n] [13]in whom you believed once you heard the message of truth, the news of your salvation, and in whom, as you believed, you were marked with the stamp of the promised Holy Spirit,[o] [14]a down payment on our eventual inheritance till the full purchase of the goods so his splendor may be extolled.[p]

[15]Therefore, I too, since I heard of the faith in the Lord Jesus that had appeared among you, and your love to all the saints,[q] [16]have never stopped rendering thanks on your behalf, making mention of you in my prayers[r] [17]that the God of our Lord Jesus-Christ, the glorious Father, may grant you a spirit of esoteric wisdom and revelation with full knowledge of him,[s] [18]the eyes of your mind being enlightened so you may know the nature of the goal he has called you to, the wealth of the splendor of his bequest to the saints[t] [19]and the unimaginable greatness of the power he wields on our behalf—for us who have believed—appropriate to the energizing might of his strength,[u] [20]which he exercised toward Christ when he raised him from the dead, enthroning him at his right in the

---

i. Col. 1:9b; Rom. 5:15b

j. Col. 1:27a; 1 Cor. 2:7; Phil. 2:13b; Rom. 16:25b-26a

k. Col. 1:25b; 1:20; Gal. 4:4a; Rom. 13:9b; 1 Cor. 15:27

l. As Yahve chose Israel for his inheritance among the seventy national gods in Deut. 32:8-9, so does the Father of Jesus Christ make his own selection.

m. Col. 1:12b; Rom. 8:30a; 8:28b; 1 Cor. 12:6b; Phil. 2:13

n. Rom. 8:30c; 9:23-24; Phil. 1:11b

o. Col. 1:5b-6a; 2 Cor. 6:7a; Rom. 1:16b; 10:14b; 1 Cor. 1:22; Gal. 3:14b

p. The reader will notice that vv. 3-14 constitute a single sentence, which is by no means characteristic for Pauline epistles; Col. 1:12b, 14b; Rom. 8:23b; 1 Thess. 5:9b; Phil. 1:11b.

q. Col. 1:9a; Phil. 5

r. Col. 1:9; Phil. 1:3-4a; Philem. 4; Rom. 1:9a, 10a

s. Col. 1:3; 2 Cor. 1:3b; 11:31a; Rom. 6:4b; 16:25b; 1 Cor. 2:8b, 10a

t. Col. 1:12b, 26b-27; 2 Cor. 4:4b; Rom. 9:23a; 1:21b

u. Col. 1:11a; 2 Cor. 9:14b; Phil. 3:10b, 21b; Rom. 3:22b

heavenly spheres,[v] [21]far above all archons, authorities, Powers, lordships,[w] and every divine name invoked, not only in this age but even in the one to come,[x] [22]and subjugated all things under his feet and bestowed upon him rule over all for the benefit of the Church,[y] [23]which is his body, the pleroma of the one who permeates all things.[z]

2

[1]And you, *then dead in your trespasses and sins,*[a] [2]the way you behaved, following the fashion of this age of the world, dictated by the archon of the authority of the air,[b] the spirit now energizing those who are disobedient,[c] [3]in whose company we too used to busy ourselves back then, with the lusts of our flesh, carrying out the wishes and the understandings of the flesh and thus intrinsically targets of wrath like the rest;[d]
[4]but God, who is rich in mercy, because of his great love with which he loved us,[e] *even with us dead in trespasses, vivified us along with Christ—and by his favor you have been saved*[f]—[6]and co-raised us and co-enthroned us in the heavenly spheres in Christ-Jesus,[g] [7]in order that he might make of us a lasting monument for ages to come of the unimaginable wealth of

v. Col. 1:29b; 3:1b; 1 Cor. 6:14; Phil. 2:9-10; Rom. 8:34

w. These are successive hierarchies of heavenly beings ruling the concentric celestial spheres that separate us from the Father, who is to be found in the divine pleroma (fullness) of light, from which all divine entities emerge and in which, through Christ, all will once again be absorbed at the last.

x. Col. 2:10b; 1 Cor. 15:24b

y. Col. 1:18a; Rom. 12:5a; 11:36a; 1 Cor. 15:28b. As in Ephesians and Colossians, I have translated εκκλεσια as "church," no longer as "assembly" or "congregation" since up to now it has meant simply a local group; but now it has taken on a true theological and mystical meaning representative of the collective Light Body of Christ into which believers are admitted by baptism.

z. Again, vv. 15-23 are a single sentence. Note also the Gnostic-Christian pantheism.

a. Col. 2:13a; Rom. 6:11b. Note how the writer eventually forgets where he was headed in this long sentence.

b. One of the angels administering the weather, as in Gal. 4:3, 9, and in the Torah; see also Gal. 3:19-20; Col. 2:13-15.

c. Col. 3:7a; 1:13a; Rom. 12:2a; 15:31a; 1 Cor. 2:12b; 2 Thess. 2:3b, 4a, 7a, 13b

d. Col. 3:6b-7; 1:21; 3:6b; 2 Cor. 1:12b; Rom. 8:7; 15:14b; Gal. 2:15a; 5:16, 19, 24; 1 Thess. 5:9a

e. Rom. 11:32b-33a; 5:8; 2 Thess. 2:16b

f. Col. 2:13a; Rom. 3:24a

g. Col. 2:12b; 3:1, 3

the favor he showed us in Christ-Jesus.[h] [8]For it is by his favor that you have been saved through faith, and such salvation is not your own doing: it is the gift of God.[i] [9]It comes not by virtue of deeds, *otherwise someone might brag.*[j] [10]For we are his achievement, created by initiation into Christ-Jesus *for good deeds which God had already scheduled for us to perform.*[k] [11]So remember how, when you were physically gentiles, those dismissed as "the uncircumcision" by those who flattered themselves "the circumcision" due to an operation performed by hand,[l] [12]you were then without Christ, long alienated from the commonwealth of Israel, completely outside of the covenants of promise, bereft of hopc for salvation and wandering without God in the world.[m] [13]But now, grafted into Christ-Jesus, you, then remote, were brought near *by means of the blood of Christ.*[n] [14]For he himself is our peace accord, the one who has made both one, having demolished the middle barrier wall;[o] [15]and having abolished in his flesh the occasion for enmity, namely the Torah of commandments and decrees, in order that he might create in himself one new man from the two, making peace,[p] [16]and reconciling both in the one body to God by means of the cross, killing the enmity in himself;[q] [17]upon his arrival he announced the news of peace to the ones far off and peace to those nearby,[r] [18]because through him we both have access through the same Spirit into the presence of the Father.[s] [19]In that case you are no longer foreigners or resident aliens,[t] but you are fellow citizens with the saints and members of the household of God,[u] [20]*built squarely on the*

h. Rom. 9:23a; 2:4; Col. 1:4b. Notice again that vv. 1-7 constitute a single sentence.

i. Rom. 3:24; 8:24; 6:23b; 3:28a

j. Rom. 9:32b; 1 Cor. 1:29-30a

k. Col. 3:9-10; 1:10a; 2 Cor. 5:17a; 9:8b

l. Col. 2:11; 1 Cor. 12:2a; 8:5a; Gal. 6:15; Rom. 2:28b

m. Col. 1:21a; Rom. 9:4; 1 Thess. 4:13b; 4:5b; Gal 4:8-9a

n. Col. 1:22; Gal. 3:23b

o. Col. 1:20b; Rom. 5:1b; Gal. 3:28c

p. Col. 2:14a; 1:21b; 3:9b-10a; 1:19b-20a

q. Col. 1:22; 1 Cor. 12:13a

r. Isa. 52:7b; 57:19

s. Rom. 5:2a; 1 Cor. 12:13a; Phil. 1:27b

t. Respectively, unconverted pagans and "God-fearing gentiles" on the margins of the synogogues.

u. Col. 3:11a; Phil. 3:20a; Gal. 6:10b

foundation of the apostles and prophets.[v] Christ-Jesus himself serving as cornerstone,[w] [21]in whom also the building, its uncut stones being carefully fitted together, are growing into a shrine befitting the Lord,[x] [22]in whom also you are being assembled into a spiritual dwelling for God.[y]

3

[1]For just this reason, I, Paul,[z] the prisoner of Christ-Jesus on behalf of you gentiles[a]—[2]that is, assuming you are familiar with my assigned position dispensing God's favor on your behalf,[b] [3]namely, how by way of revelation the hidden plan was made known to me, as I have previously written briefly,[c] [4]from which, as you read it,[d] you can see for yourselves my grasp of the unfolding mystery of Christ,[e] [5]which in previous generations had never been made known to the human race as it has now been revealed by the Spirit *to his holy apostles and prophets,*[f] [6]that the gentiles should become joint heirs and a common body and co-sharers of the promise thanks to Christ-Jesus through the news,[g] [7]whose servant I became through the gift of the favor of God given me as his power energized me.[h] [8]To me, the least of all saints,[i] this favor was shown to evangelize to the nations the inscrutable riches of Christ,[j] [9]and finally to make manifest

---

v. Here the positions of the Twelve and the Israelite prophets are enhanced.

w. Col. 2:7b; 1 Cor. 3:11a; 12:28a; 3:10-11b

x. Col. 2:19b; 1 Cor. 3:9b; 3:16b; 3:7b; 2 Cor. 6:16b

y. Col. 2:7b; 1 Cor. 3:16b; Rom. 8:9

z. See note for 2 Cor. 10:1, where it is explained that "I, so-and-so" denotes pseudepigraphy.

a. Col. 1:24a; Philem. 1; Rom. 11:13a

b. Gal. 1:13a; 2:9b; Col. 1:25b; 1 Cor. 9:17b; 1 Cor. 1:4b

c. 1 Cor. 2:10a; Gal. 1:12; Col. 1:26a

d. These phrases refer to the collection of letters, for which this one served as a preface. It is cobbled together from bits and pieces of the others, although not from the yet-to-be-composed Pastorals.

e. Col. 1:9b; 4:3b, 16a; 1 Cor. 2:7; 5:9a; 2 Cor. 11:6b; Rom. 16:25b

f. Note there is no Great Commission from the risen Jesus here. The Gentile Mission subsequently occurred to apostles and prophets via revelation. Of course, it is likely that just such prophecies, ascribed to the ascended master Jesus, became concretized as sayings of Jesus still (barely!) on earth. See also Col. 1:26b; 1 Cor. 2:8a; Rom. 16:26.

g. Rom. 4:13-14, 16-17; 8:17b; 12:5a; Gal. 3:26-29; 2 Thess. 2:14b

h. Col. 1:23b, 25, 29b; Rom. 5:15b; 12:3

i. Matt. 5:19: Paul is regarded as the least in the kingdom of heaven on account of his dismissal of the Torah.

j. Col. 1:27; Gal. 1:16b; Rom. 11:33

the administration of the providential plan previously hidden for all the ages from the God who created all things,[k] [10]in order that the many-sided wisdom of God might at last be made known through the Church to the archons and to the authorities in the heavenly spheres,[l] [11]in accord with the purpose at work in the aeons, which he achieved in Christ-Jesus our Lord,[m] [12]in whom therefore we have boldness and confident access to God through faith in him.[n]

[13]This is why I ask you not to give up hope as you hear of my afflictions on your behalf, which are actually something for you to brag about![o] [14]For this reason, I kneel before the Father,[p] *the prototype of all fatherhood in the skies and on the earth,*[q] [16]asking that he may give you richly, befitting the wealth of his splendor, powerful strength in the inner self through his Spirit,[r] [17]so that Christ may live in your hearts by faith, having been firmly rooted and securely founded,[s] [18]in order for you to have the strength to comprehend, along with the rest of the saints, Platos, Mekos, Hypsos, and Bathos,[t] [19]and to know Christ's love that surpasses all esoteric knowledge, to the end that you may be filled to the full extent of all the pleroma of God![u]

[20]Now to him who is able to do superabundantly beyond anything we ask or think, thanks to the power energizing us,[v] [21]be all worship in

k. This is Marcion's version, according to Tertullian. See Col. 1:25b-26; 3:3b; 1:16b; 1 Cor. 2:7; Rom. 16:25.

l. Col. 1:16; 2:7; Rom. 8:38; 2 Cor. 8:18b

m. Rom. 8:28b; 1 Cor. 2:7b

n. Rom. 5:1b-2; 2 Cor. 3:4, 12

o. Col. 1:24a; 2:1; 1 Thess. 2:20a

p. Rom. 14:11b; Isa. 45:23; Phil 2:10

q. 1 Cor. 8:5b

r. Col. 1:27b; Rom. 7:22; 9:23a; 15:13b, 19b; 1 Cor. 16:13b; 2 Cor. 4:16b

s. Col. 1:19; 2:7a; 1:23a; Rom. 8:9b; 1 Cor. 3:16b; 2 Cor. 1:22b

t. "Height" and "Depth" were two aions within the pleroma of God, as in Rom. 8:39; 1 Cor. 2:10. See also Col. 2:2b-3; 2 Cor. 1:1b.

u. The pleroma, or fullness, of God is the Godhead itself, which contains the aeons, divine beings emanating from the Unknown Father before all time. Christ has become this pleroma for Christian Gnostics. It is paralleled by Jewish Kabbalism in the Lore of Creation, which tells of the emanation of the creative design through the externalized image of God known as Adam Kadmon, whose cosmic shape the creation assumed until the day it fell into disorder, thanks to the inherent impurity of the light-vessels (*Kelipoth*) prepared to contain it. Much of this is already found in Philo; see Col. 2:2b-3; 1:9b; 2:9-10a; Rom. 8:35a.

v. Rom. 16:25a; Col. 1:29b

the Church and in Christ-Jesus throughout all the generations of ages multiplied by ages! Amen.[w]

Ephesians

4

[1]I, Paul, the prisoner of the Lord, urge you, to behave in a manner befitting the high calling you have received,[x] [2]always with humility and meekness, with long-suffering, bearing with one another in love,[y] [3]eager to maintain the unity of the Spirit in the strong tie of peace:[z] [4]one body, one Spirit, just as you were called in one prospect to which you were summoned,[a] [5]namely: one Lord, one confession, one rite of baptism, [6]one God and Father of all, the one who reigns over all and permeates all things equally.[b]

[7]But to each one was given a charisma as Christ deemed appropriate.[c] [8]That is why it says, "Ascending to the Zenith, he took captive all captivity and dispensed gifts to humanity."[d] [9]Now the phrase, "he ascended"—what does that mean if he had not already descended here to the sublunar world?[e] [10]The one thus descending is identical with the one who also ascended far above all the concentric heavens in order that he might there permeate all things.[f] [11]And in this very process, he made some into apostles,[g] some prophets, some evangelists, some shepherds and teachers,[h] [12]for the perfecting of the saints and the task of ministry, the building of the body of Christ,[i] [13]until the day we all arrive together at the unity of faith and of the full knowledge of the Son of God, which will be mature adulthood as measured by the stature of the full completion of Christ,[j]

w. Rom. 11:36b; Gal. 1:5a; 1 Cor. 6:4b, 7:17b; Col. 1:26b; Gal. 1:5b

x. Rom. 12:1a; Philem. 1; 2 Cor. 10:1a; Col. 1:10a; 2 Thess. 2:12b

y. Col. 3:12-13a, 14-15; Phil. 2:3b; 1 Thess. 4:9b

z. Col. 3:15

a. Col. 3:15; 1 Cor. 10:17b; 12:13; Rom. 12:4a, 5a; 1 Cor. 7:20

b. Christo-pantheism is taken over from Laodiceans, but "one God" intends to refute the Marcionite ditheism. See 1 Cor. 8:6a; Rom. 11:36a; 9:5b.

c. Rom. 12:6a; 5:15b; 1 Cor. 12:7-11

d. Pss. 68:18

e. Rom. 10:6b

f. Rom. 10:7

g. Note the anti-Marcionite notion of multiple apostles.

h. 1 Cor. 12:28a; Rom. 12:6-8b

i. 2 Cor. 13:9b; 12:19c; 1 Cor. 14:26b; 12:27a

j. Phil. 3:11; Philem. 6; Col. 1:28b; 2:9-10a; 1 Cor. 2:6a

[14]in order that we may no longer be naive, blown over and spun about by every new wind-gust of teaching by the trickery of charlatans whose cleverness and craftiness deceive;[k] [15]rather, speaking the truth with love, we may assimilate to him in every respect, him who is the chief, Christ, the head[l] [16]from whom the whole body, as it fits together and knits itself together through every ligament and artery, each playing its proper role, makes for the growth of the body, building itself in mutual love.[m]

[17]Therefore, I say this, bearing witness in the sight of the Lord: you are no longer to behave as the nations do in the futility of their thinking,[n]
[18]having become blinded in their intellect, alienated from the life of God because of the ignorance infesting them on account of the obtuseness of their minds,[o] [19]who having thrown all scruples aside abandoned themselves to prostitution, to perform every kind of unclean act for money.[p]
[20]But that is not what you learned of Christ[q]—[21]if indeed you did hear him and were taught by him the truth as it is revealed in Jesus,[r] [22]namely, that regarding your previous behavior, you must strip off the old self, reeking of the lusts of deceit,[s] [23]and be renewed in your mode of thinking,[t] [24]and clothe yourself in the new self, created by God's design, fragrant with the righteousness and holiness of truth.[u] [25]Accordingly, renounce lying and speak the truth, each one of you to your neighbor, because we are body parts of one another.[v] What if the hand were on fire and it should lie to the heart, saying, "I do not hurt"? Soon you should lack the hand!

[26]If you are angry, nonetheless do not sin; do not let the sun go down before you resolve the matter,[w] [27]or you may open an opportunity for the

---

k. Col. 2:8; 1 Cor. 3:1b; 14:20. Marcionites and their doctrine are in view here.

l. Col. 1:10b, 18a; 1 Cor. 11:3b

m. Col. 2:19a; 1:29b; Phil. 3:21

n. Col. 2:4; Gal. 5:3a; Col. 3:7

o. Col. 1:21a; Rom. 10:3a; 11:25b

p. Col. 3:5b; Rom. 1:24a; 2 Cor. 12:21b

q. Col. 2:6

r. Col. 2:7; 2 Cor. 11:10a; Rom. 9:1a

s. Col. 3:8a, 9b; Rom. 13:12b

t. Col. 2:18b; Rom. 12:2b; Gal. 3:27b

u. Col. 3:10; Gal. 3:27b; Rom. 12:5

v. Col. 3:8a, 9a; Rom. 12:5

w. Col. 3:8b; 1 Cor. 15:34a; Rom. 12:19b

accuser.[x] [28]Have the thief stop stealing; instead, have him use his nimble fingers at some good craft so he may have enough, as well as some to share with the needy.[y] [29]See to it that no corrupt speech issues from your lips, but speak if you have something constructive to say for your hearers, which will be a gift to them.[z] [30]And do not offend the Holy Spirit of God, by whom you have been marked as belonging to God, looking forward to the day he claims you fully for his own.[a] [31]Thus, repudiate all bitterness and anger and rage and shouting and blasphemy among you,[b] with all the rest of the evils.[c] [32]And be kind to one another, tender-hearted, forgiving each other[d] as God too, thanks to Christ, forgave you.

5

[1]Therefore, be imitators of God like beloved children who eagerly imitate their parents.[e] [2]And conduct yourselves with love, as Christ, too, loved you and handed himself over for our sakes, an offering and a sacrifice to produce a sweet savor satisfying to God.[f] [3]But let no whore mongering or impurity or greed ever be detected among you, as befits saints,[g] [4]neither shameful acts nor moronic chatter nor off-color jokes, none of which is appropriate, but instead thanksgiving.[h] [5]Don't be unaware of this: no whoremonger or impure person or greedy man, who is guilty of idolatry, has any share in the kingdom of Christ and of God.[i] [6]Let no one deceive you with hollow words; it is just this sort of thing that is going to bring the ire of God down on the disobedient.[j] [7]Therefore, do not share in their work.[k] [8]You used to be part of the darkness, but now,

x. 2 Cor. 2:11

y. 1 Thess. 4:11b, 12b; Rom. 12:13a

z. Col. 3:8; 1 Cor. 14:26b

a. 1 Thess. 5:19; 2 Cor. 1:22; Rom. 8:23b

b. It would be odd to find "blasphemy" among the serious missteps of pious Christians. The reference may be to Marcionite criticisms of the Creator.

c. Col. 3:8

d. Col. 3:12-13

e. Col. 3:12a; 1 Cor. 4:16b; 11:1; John 5:19-20

f. Rom. 14:15b; Gal. 2:20b; Phil. 4:18b. This is Old Testament sacrificial language, offensive to Marcionites.

g. Col. 3:5a; 2 Cor. 12:21b; 1 Cor. 5:11b

h. Col. 3:8, 18b; 2:7b; 3:17b; 1 Thess. 5:18a

i. 1 Cor. 6:9a; Col. 3:5b

j. Col. 2:4b; Rom. 1:18a. As opposed to Marcion's God, who will punish no one.

k. 2 Cor. 6:14; 2 John 11

as part of the Lord, you are light; so conduct yourselves as befits enlightened ones,[l] [10]demonstrating in practice what delights the Lord.[m] [9]For what the light yields is all goodness and righteousness and truth.[n] [11]Have nothing to do with the sterile works of darkness, but rather go so far as to reprove them when you see someone else committing them.[o] [12]It is degrading even to mention the shameful acts they perform behind closed doors,[p] [13]but everything reproved by the light thereby becomes exposed for all to see[q] since for a thing to be made manifest means that it is illuminated.[r] [14]This is why it says, "Get up, O sleeper![s] Stand up from the heap of corpses[t] and Christ will illuminate you."[u]

[15]So give close attention to your manner of behavior, not like the unwise, but the wise,[v] [16]thereby giving new meaning to time otherwise wasted, for the days are evil.[w] [17]Therefore, do not be heedless, but discern the will of the Lord.[x] [18]And do not get drunk on wine, which leads to dissipation; instead, be filled with the Spirit,[y] [19]speaking to one another in psalms and hymns and inspired songs, singing and hymning from your hearts to the Lord,[z] [20]ever giving thanks for all things to God the Father, invoking the name of our Lord Jesus-Christ,[a] [21]submitting yourselves one to the other for fear of Christ's judgment on the proud,[b] [22]the wives to their own husbands as if to the Lord,[c] [23]because a husband is chief of the

l. Rom. 2:19b; 1 Thess. 5:5

m. Col. 3:20b; Rom. 12:2b; Phil. 4:18b

n. Gal. 5:22-23

o. 2 Cor. 6:14b; Rom. 12:2b

p. Col. 3:8a; 1 Cor. 4:5. The reference may be to the imagined libertine ways of Gnostics. Tertullian mocks Apelles, assuming that because Gnostics reject the doctrine of punishment, they have no good reason not to engage in riot and orgy.

q. 1 Cor. 14:24b-25a; 4:5b

r. John 3:19-21

s. Isa. 51:17a; 52:1a

t. Isa. 26:19

u. Loosely based on Isa. 60:1.

v. Col. 4:5; Rom. 13:13a

w. Col. 4:5; Gal. 1:4b

x. Col. 4:12b; Rom. 12:2b

y. Acts 2:4, 15; Rom. 13:13b

z. Col. 3:16b

a. Col. 3:17; 1 Thess. 5:18a; Phil. 1:3-4

b. Gal. 5:13b; Phil. 2:3b

c. Col. 3:18

wife, just as Christ is chief of the Church, being savior of the Body.[d] [24]But as the Church is subject to Christ, so too must wives be subject to their husbands in every matter. [25]Husbands, love your wives just as Christ loved the Church and handed himself over for its sake,[e] [26]in order that he might sanctify it, cleansing it by immersion in the truth,[f] [27]in order that he might present the Church to himself radiant and rejuvenated: without age spots, wrinkles, or any such thing, but rather that it might appear[g] holy and unblemished.[h] [28]So it behooves husbands to love their wives like their own bodies.[i] The one who loves his own wife loves himself since she will return his love. [29]For whoever heard of a man hating his own flesh?[j] No, he nourishes it and cherishes it—just as Christ did the Church, [30]because we are all alike members of his body.[k] [31]"For this cause a man shall leave father and mother and shall be joined to his wife, and the two shall become one flesh."[l] [32]This mystery is profound, but I am speaking of Christ and the Church.[m] [33]Nonetheless, it applies also to each one of you: let each one love his wife as himself, and let the wife fear her husband.[n]

6

[1]Children, obey your parents if they are believers in the Lord, for this is right.[o] [2]"Honor your father and mother," which was the first commandment with a promise attached: [3]"so it may go well with you and you may extend your time on earth."[p] [4]And fathers, do not provoke your children to rebellion, but nurture them in the discipline and admonition of the Lord.[q] [5]Slaves, obey your masters in this world with fear and trembling, with single-minded devotion as to Christ,[r] [6]not merely to seem to

d. 1 Cor. 11:3b; Col. 1:18

e. Col. 3:19; Gal. 2:20b

f. 1 Cor. 6:11b; John 15:3

g. That is, at the resurrection.

h. Col. 1:22b; 2 Cor. 11:2b

i. Col. 3:19a; 1 Cor. 7:3-4

j. This is a jibe at Marcionite asceticism.

k. 1 Cor. 6:15a; Rom. 12:5

l. Gen. 2:24

m. Here was the Catholic alternative to Marcion: to reinterpret the Jewish scriptures allegorically to refer to Christian ethics and belief.

n. Col. 3:18a; 1 Cor. 7:2b

o. Col. 3:20

p. Exod. 20:12

q. Col. 3:21; 1 Cor. 4:14b

r. Col. 3:22a

be serving while the master is watching, like those who curry favor, but as slaves of Christ, doing God's will from the soul,[s] [7]with good humor, serving as slaves to the Lord, not merely to mortals,[t] mindful that each one, whatever good deed he does, he will be repaid by the Lord, whether slave or free.[u] [9]And masters, do the same toward them, thinking twice before threatening, mindful that both their master and yours watches from the sky and he is not impressed by any mortal rank.[v]

[10]Finally, draw power from the Lord and from the might of his strength.[w] [11]Don the complete armor of God to equip yourselves to stand unvanquished against the methods of the accuser,[x] [12]for our conflict is not with flesh-and-blood enemies, but against the archons, against the authorities, against the cosmocrators of the darkness that surrounds us, against the spiritual entities of evil in the heavenly spheres![y] [13]That is why you must put on the complete suit of divine armor in order that you may not be vanquished on the day evil attacks, and having taken every precaution, to stand with head unbowed.[z] [14]So stand fast, latching the belt of truth and putting on the breastplate of righteousness,[a] [15]your feet shod with readiness to announce the news of peace;[b] [16]and most important, taking up the shield of faith and having been fully equipped, you will be able to extinguish all the flame-tipped darts of the accuser. [17]And take the helmet of salvation and the sword of the Spirit, which is the command of God.[c] [18]This you may do through all prayer and petition, praying on every occasion in the ecstasy of the Spirit and keeping vigil with every bit of perseverance and petitioning on behalf of the saints,[d] [19]as well as on my

s. Col. 3:22a, 24b

t. Col. 3:22c-25a. We see here the doctrine of karma yoga, acting apart from the mundane fruits of action. One may also think of Stockholm syndrome, whereby a prisoner ameliorates his suffering by identifying with his captors—on display in the comedy film, *The Life of Brian.* See Graham Chapman, et al., *Monty Python's Life of Brian of Nazareth* (New York: Ace Books, 1979), 63.

u. Gal. 3:28b; 1 Cor. 12:13b

v. Col. 4:1; Rom. 2:11

w. Col. 1:11a; Phil. 4:13; 2 Thess. 1:9b

x. Rom. 13:12b; 1 Cor. 16:13; 2 Cor. 2:11

y. Col. 1:16b; Rom. 8:38b; 2 Cor. 10:3-4

z. Col. 3:12a; 4:12b

a. Isa. 11:5; 59:17; 1 Thess. 5:8

b. Isa. 52:7b

c. 1 Thess. 5:8c; Isa. 59:17

d. Col. 4:2a; 1 Thess. 5:17, 18a

behalf, that I may be given effective speech when I open my mouth,[e]
boldly making known the hidden plan of the news,[f] 20on behalf of which I
serve as ambassador, albeit chained, in order that I may indeed speak it
boldly as my position requires.[g]

21But to keep you apprised of my affairs, what I am up to, I have dispatched Tychicus, beloved brother[h] and faithful servant in the Lord's
work,[i] 22whom I sent you[j] for this specific purpose: for you to learn about
us and comfort your hearts.[k]

23Peace to the brothers and love, with faith, from God the Father and
the Lord Jesus-Christ.[l] 24May divine favor visit all who love our Lord Jesus-Christ with integrity.[m]

---

e. Luke 21:14-15

f. Col. 4:3b-4; 2:15b; Rom. 15:30b; Phil. 1:20b; 2 Thess. 2:2b

g. Acts 28:20b; Col. 4:3-4; 2 Cor. 5:20a; Philem. 9b

h. By "brother" is meant an itinerant missionary.

i. Col. 2:1a; 4:7-8

j. It is possible that Tychicus is the real author of this sequel to Laodiceans.

k. Col. 4:7-8

l. 2 Thess. 1:2

m. Col. 4:18b; 1 Cor. 16:22-24; 15:42b

18.
Second Laodiceans

In all probability, this letter was composed simply in order to fill the gap implied by Colossians 4:16, which mentions a Pauline epistle directed to the Laodicean congregation. What's this? A lost Pauline letter? Faith, like nature, abhors a vacuum. There would seem to be little point to the text besides filling that gap. As anyone can see, it is basically a condensed form of Philippians. And yet, it is possible for it to be as genuine a Pauline epistle as one regards Philippians, Galatians, Colossians, and others, for one might argue that it bears much the same relation to Philippians as Galatians does to Romans and as Colossians does to Ephesians, for these too appear to be matched pairs, one shorter than the other but sharing so much in common that one might be viewed as an expansion of the other. Who knows?

Adolf von Harnack noted that canon lists included a Marcionite "Laodiceans" and believed the present document, with its relatively lackluster content, was Marcion's "extra" epistle, written by him. The Muratorian canon mentions a Marcionite Laodiceans, possibly our letter. It is interesting to note the total absence of any citations to Jewish scripture in the letter. In addition, as often in the Pauline corpus and maybe for the same reason, one finds the Marcionite-sounding title "God the Father" making a clear differentiation from the Creator God.

However, most scholars accept Tertullian's ancient proposal that Marcion's Laodiceans was a variant version of Ephesians, which is why we denominate the shorter text as 2 Laodiceans. The small letter was, in fact, included in several Latin New Testament manuscripts. Gregory the Great argued for its canonicity, explaining its wide-

spread omission as the result of an arbitrary attempt to have a double heptad of Pauline epistles, which included Hebrews. This left no room for a fifteenth epistle, and Laodiceans was the easiest to omit. The text of this letter survives only in Latin but was written in Greek in the first or second century.

1Paul, an apostle, not of any mortal agency, nor appointed by any
man, but by Jesus-Christ,[a] to the brothers at Laodicea.[b] 2May you enjoy
favor and protection from God the Father and the Lord, Jesus-Christ.[c]

3In every prayer of mine, I give thanks to Christ that you[d] persevere
in your commitment to him and continue in doing the deeds he commands, ever focused on the promise of salvation on the Day of Judgment.
4Nor do you let the empty chatter of some upset you—those who sneak in
under false pretenses hoping to draw you away from the truth of the news
that I preach.[e] 5But God shall see to it that all who belong to me shall keep
serving for the advance of the truth of the news and bringing about goodness, even the work of salvation—age-long life.[f]

6And now my imprisonment is known to everyone—that which I endure for Christ.[g] In it I rejoice[h] and am glad. 7And for me this is an opportunity for everlasting salvation, which your prayers would also make more likely, as would the ministry of the Holy Spirit, whether my salvation turns out to be deliverance by means of death or a rescue for continued life here below.[i] 8For truly, to me life is Christ and to die is a joyful
prospect.[j] 9As for him, he shall develop his mercy in you to the end that
you may have all the same love and be of one mind.[k]

10Therefore, my dear ones, as I said when I was with you, hold

a. Gal. 1:1
b. Revelation of John 3:14
c. Phil. 1:2
d. Rom. 1:9; Phil. 1:3
e. Gal. 2:4
f. Phil. 1:6; 2:13
g. Phil. 1:13
h. Phil. 1:18
i. Phil. 1:19-20
j. Phil. 1:21
k. Phil. 2:2

tightly to the fear of God and do your work in that frame of mind and your reward shall be age-long life. 11For it is, after all, God energizing you.[l] And whatever you are called upon to do, do it without second thoughts. 13Finally, dear ones, rejoice over Christ and watch out for those who are obsessed with money.[m] 14Do not hesitate to set your requests before God[n] in public, and stand firm in the mindset of Christ. 15And what should you do? Well, what things are wholesome and true and serious and equitable and winsome?[o] 16Hold on tightly to the things you have heard and accepted from me.[p] 17And you will live in peace.[q] 18The saints greet you![r] 19May the favor of the Lord Jesus accompany your spirit.[s] 20Have this read to those at Colosse, and have Colossians read to you.[t]

l. Phil. 2:13
m. Phil. 3:2; 1 Tim. 6:9-10
n. Phil. 4:6
o. Phil. 4:8
p. Phil. 4:9
q. Phil. 4:7
r. Phil. 4:22
s. Phil. 4:23
t. Col. 4:16

19.

The Epistle to the Colossians

F. C. BAUR LONG AGO RECOGNIZED the pronounced Gnostic character of the Epistle to the Colossians and therefore placed it post-Paul. Many scholars today agree with him, but fewer, for instance, than would admit the pseudepigraphical nature of Ephesians. There are many who still defend the authenticity of the letter, but invariably their strategy derives from the weakest of apologetical rationalizations: the irony dodge. That is, they claim that the text is indeed peppered with Gnostic notions and vocabulary because Paul uses the language of his opponents and turns it against them, redefining as he goes. This is an utterly gratuitous assumption necessitated by the unwillingness of the exegete either to imagine that Paul was a Gnostic or that someone later than Paul who was a Gnostic wrote the letter.

In fact, what we find already in the first chapter (vv. 15-20) is a compressed recital of the Gnostic myth in which the demiurge ("authority of darkness") created his own material counterfeit of the pleromatic world of God and the aions emanating from him, including Christ and Church; he stole the light-substance of the Primal Man (firstborn of creation) and used it as *spermatikoi logoi* to vivify and regulate the material creation. But the Father dispatched the Christ aeon (mysteriously identical with the dispersed Light-Man) representing the pleromatic entities to recover the light, enlightening humans who contain a divine spark and preparing them to return to the world of light after death. His own death at the hands of the unsuspecting Powers turns the tables on them, defeating them and canceling the force of the Torah, their creation which oppresses humanity even though it keeps some order among the creatures of the demiurge and the Powers (2:14-15).

In the second chapter, as in 1 Corinthians 2:6-10, the death of Christ is accomplished by heavenly entities with no reference to either historical individuals or circumstances. The original pre-Christian Gnostic myth located the death of the Primal Man of Light at the beginning of all things when the archons attacked and dismembered him in order to use his substance to give life and order to the material creation—a variation of the Rig-Vedic hymn of the self-sacrificing dismemberment of the Primal Man Purusha to form the cosmos, including the human race and the gods, and the Zoroastrian myth in which the Primal Man Gayomard is split in two, giving rise to the human race. The scattered sparks would have been redeemed and regathered simply by the gradual reawakening of the Gnostic elite as they recognized their divine nature and destiny and returned to the pleroma after death. The Gnostic redeemer, variously conceived as Zoroaster, Melchizedek, or Seth, was merely a man, enlightened like the Buddha to the truth about himself and his fellow Gnostics.

But once the myth was Christianized, the death of the Primal Man at the hands of the archons had to be made a part of the saving mission of the redeemer, who was thus identified with the Primal Man in a sort of second coming, in order to coincide with the crucifixion of Christ, already part of the Christian story. The saving death thus becomes instrumental to the plan of salvation. Subsequent Valentinian Gnosticism, derived according to Valentinus from Pauline teaching through the apostle's disciple Theodas, subdivided the saving work of Christ, the death of Jesus availing for the lower-tier *psuchikoi,* or natural ones, while the teaching ministry of the Christ-Spirit, whom Jesus channeled, was sufficient to save the Gnostic illuminati.

As Rudolf Bultmann and others have noted, Colossians seems to embrace Gnostic realized eschatology, the notion that the end-time events have already occurred in symbolic form, especially through baptism. Romans 8:11 envisions the believer's death in Christ accomplished in baptism, with his or her resurrection still a future prospect scheduled to coincide with the Parousia. The third chapter of Colossians crosses this line, inculcating a sort of Gnostic perfectionism like that found in the sectarian interpolations of 1 John. We also seem to have reference to this esoteric doctrine in 2 Timothy 2:18.

Colosse perished in a terrible earthquake in 65 AD. The author must have known this, and it is possible that, to explain why this letter, if genuine, still exists (as well as why no living Colossian has ever seen it), he has cleverly created a scenario in which the epistle was saved by virtue of having been on loan to a neighboring city (4:16). This might occur to him if he wrote in Laodicea even though Laodicea, too, was leveled. Both cities were rebuilt, but it might have been easier to imagine continuity in one's own city, and thus it seemed easier to suppose the letter survived the general destruction there, something actually unlikely for either city. Imagine some Laodicean or Colossian Lot urging his wife to flee the collapsing city while she lingers to retrieve a copy of the Epistle to the Colossians!

1

[1]Paul, an apostle of Christ-Jesus, by the command of God, and Timothy, the brother,[a] [2]to the saints and faithful brothers in Christ in Colosse: May the favor and protection of God the Father extend to you.[b]

[3]As we pray, we always give thanks for you to God, the Father of our Lord, Jesus-Christ, [4]having heard of your belief in Jesus-Christ and the love you have for all the saints [5]because of the sure prospect of heavenly reward amassed for you in the skies, which you heard about in the message of truth in the news [6]that came to you, just as it continues to bear fruit and to expand in the whole world,[c] just as also in you, from the day you first heard of and experienced the favor of God for real [7]as you learned from Epaphras, our beloved fellow-slave, who is a loyal servant of Christ on your behalf, [8]who also has demonstrated to us your Spirit-inspired love.

[9]That, too, is why, ever since the day we heard of your faith, we have been praying unceasingly for you, asking for you to be filled with the sure knowledge of his will, possessing all wisdom and spiritual understanding, [10]so as to behave worthily of the Lord, pleasing him in all you do, evidencing every sort of good deed and ever increasing in the sure knowledge of God, [11]being equipped with every ability from the abundance of

a. The designation "brother" indicates an itinerant preacher.

b. "God the Father" sounds like a Marcionite specification to avoid confusion with God the Creator, the Hebrew God.

c. Could the historical Paul have thought the faith had spread throughout the whole world by the middle of the first century? Such a phrase must surely be understood to include the entire Roman Empire and probably the Parthian Empire.

his glorious might, to provide you with all necessary endurance and long-suffering, joyfully [12]rendering thanks to the Father, who made you fit to share the portion of the saints in the pleroma of light, [13]who rescued us out of the authority of darkness and translated us over into the kingdom of his beloved Son,[d] [14]thanks to whom we have redemption, the forgiveness of sins:

> [15]Who is an image of the invisible God,
> First-born of all creation,
> [16] For in him all things were created,
> In the skies and on the earth,
> The visible and the invisible,
> Whether thrones or dominions,
> Or archons or authorities,
> All things have been created through him and for him.
> [17]And he is prior to all things,
> And all things consist in him,
> [18]And he is the head of the body, the Church,
> Who is the beginning,
> First-born from the dead,
> In order that he may rank first in everything,
> [19]For in him the whole pleroma was delighted to dwell bodily,
> [20]And through him to reconcile all things to himself,
> Making peace through him,
> By means of the blood of his cross,
> Whether they dwell on the earth or in the skies.

[21]And you then were alienated and hostile in mind on account of your evil deeds, [22]but now reconciled in his flesh-body through its death, which was to make you presentable, holy, blameless, irreproachable, [23]which you will be if indeed you persevere in the faith, having been grounded, steadfast and not susceptible of being budged from the sure prospect of the news that you heard proclaimed throughout all creation under the sky, of which I, Paul, became a servant.[e]

[24]Now I rejoice over my sufferings on your behalf, and in my flesh I fill up what remained lacking from the afflictions of Christ on behalf of

d. Here is radicalized Marcionism in the moment it was fermenting into Gnosticism: the stern Old Testament Jehovah has become the prince of darkness from whom the kind Father has rescued us.

e. Again, the very notion of universal evangelization, even as hyperbole, is anachronistic for Paul. See note on 2 Cor. 10:1 for the "I, so-and-so" formula as a sign of pseudonymity.

his body, namely the Church,[f] [25]of which I became a servant by the terms
of the stewardship God assigned me for you to fulfill the promise of God,
[26]the secret plan, hidden from the aions and from the divine emanations,
but now revealed to his saints,[g] [27]to whom God decided to display among
the nations the extent of the wealth of the splendor of this secret plan:
Christ in you, the prospect of sharing divine glory! [28]Him we announce,
warning everyone and teaching everyone very wisely so as to present every individual perfect in union with Christ. [29]For this, too, I labor, battling mightily, thanks to the energy of him who energizes me.

2

[1]For I want you to know how great a battle I wage on your behalf
and for those in Laodicea, and as many as have never seen my face in person,[h] [2]in order to comfort their hearts since we are united in love and in
the full assurance that understanding brings, so we may know the full
scope of the mystery of God, namely Christ, [3]in whom is hidden all the
wealth of wisdom and gnosis.[i] [4]I say this to prevent anyone cleverly deceiving you with fine-sounding rhetoric. [5]For if, as in fact, I am absent
physically, yet in the spirit I am with you,[j] rejoicing at the sight of the
proper order and the firmness of your belief in Christ.

[6]Therefore, in the same way you welcomed Christ-Jesus the Lord,
walk in his way, [7]having been rooted and being built up in your new identity, confirmed in the belief you were taught, inclined to ever greater
thanksgiving. [8]Watch out that no one deceives you by using philosophy
and empty lies from mere human tradition stemming from the elemental
spirits of the cosmos[k] rather than from Christ. [9]For in him all the pleroma

f. Here the cult of Paul, whether surviving from the time before its assimilation to Christianity or from a later period of glorifying the apostle as a new Christ (Acts of Paul), is seen in full force. Paul is, like Mary, the Catholic co-redeemer, a joint savior with Christ.

g. The same contrast between the ignorance of supramundane Powers and revelation to humble mortals is drawn in 1 Cor. 2:6-10. In fully developed Gnosticism, the knowledge of God was shared within the pleroma and its aions, hidden only from the last of them, Lady Sophia, whose desire to know led to her fall.

h. A wink to the reader, implicitly admitting the historical Paul is long gone. He writes to those who have never seen his face.

i. Gnosis is esoteric knowledge; wisdom (*sophia*) also has Gnostic associations.

j. Again, a clever admission that the historical Paul is physically absent from earth.

k. That is, the angels in charge of weather, synecdoche for their rulership of the material world, which they created. See note at Gal. 3:20.

of the Godhead dwells bodily, [10]and being in him, you are likewise filled,
him being the head over all archons and authorities. [11]In him, too, you
were circumcised with a circumcision not performed by hand via the
wholesale cutting off of the body of flesh, rather by the circumcision of
Christ, [12]being buried along with him in baptism and raised along with
him through faith in the vivifying of God, who raised him from the dead,
[13]you yourselves being dead in trespasses and in the uncircumcision of
your flesh-existence whence he vivified you along with him, forgiving you
all your trespasses, [14]expunging the handwritten ordinances which in-
criminated us; and he has taken them out of the way, nailing them as the
posted accusation to the cross. [15]Stripping the archons and the authorities
naked, he publicly exposed them, parading them as captives in the cross.

[16]So don't let anyone condemn you in dietary matters or for not observing feasts or new moon celebrations or Sabbaths, [17]all this being no
more than a charade pointing to things to come, Christ being the reality.
[18]Let no one deprive you of your rights by an appeal to self-abasement
and the worship of angels,[l] blundering into matters someone has halluci-
nated, his head being filled with the phantoms of his own imagination,
[19]out of touch with the head, from whom the whole body, being nourished and knitted together by means of its various joints and ligaments,
will grow with God's green thumb. [20]So if you have died with Christ as
far as the elemental spirits are concerned, why are you, like those native
to the cosmos, living by decrees? [21]"Do not touch, nor taste, nor handle." [22]These all pertain to things destined to perish as they are used[m]
and they stem from man-made commandments and teachings.[n] [23]Such
things, it is true, have a reputation for wisdom by way of self-imposed
devotions, self-abnegation and severity toward the body, but they have
no merit as they merely satisfy the cravings of the flesh in their own,
more subtle, way.[o]

3

[1]So then, if you have been raised along with Christ, seek the things
above where Christ is seated to the right of God. [2]Concentrate on the

---

l. They worship angels unintentionally by keeping the Torah, derived from the angels and archons. They imagine the commandments come from God.

m. This was exactly the rationale for Gnostic libertinism in 1 Cor. 6:12-13.

n. Mark 7:8-16

o. The same insight led the Buddha to aspire to the middle path: ascetical exertions are not necessarily more edifying (one thinks of Kafka's emaciated hunger artist) but can represent feats of perverted pride. True spirituality lies elsewhere.

things above, not on those on earth.[p] [3]Remember, you died and your life is now hidden away with Christ inside God, [4]and whenever Christ is revealed to the world, only then will you too be revealed in divine splendor.

[5]So amputate your members on the earth:[q] prostitution, impurity, passions, illicit desire, and covetousness—which amount to idolatry. [6]It is because of these things the wrath of God is on its way. [7]Indeed, this is how you used to behave when you lived this way. [8]But now, cleanse your mouths of all rage, anger, malice, blasphemy, and abuse. [9]Do not lie to one another since you have stripped off the old self with his duplicitous ways. [10]Having donned the new self, being renewed by means of enlightenment in the image of the one who created it, [11]where "Jew" and "Greek" have no place, neither "circumcision" nor "uncircumcision," nor "Barbarian" or "Scythian," "slave" or "free," but Christ is all and is in all alike. [12]So as the chosen of God, holy and beloved, attire yourselves in the depths of compassion, kindness, humility, meekness, long-suffering, [13]giving one another the benefit of the doubt, forgiving each other if anyone has a gripe against another; indeed, just as the Lord forgave you, you do the same. [14]And above all, love. That is the seal of perfection. [15]And allow the peace of Christ to hold sway in your hearts. To such harmony you were summoned as members of a single body. And be thankful. [16]Let the message of Christ dwell in you lavishly, teaching and exhorting each other with complete wisdom, singing psalms and hymns and spirit-inspired songs, singing to God with inspiration in your hearts. [17]In fact, whatever you do in word or deed in your common worship, do everything invoking the name of the Lord Jesus, giving thanks to God, the Father, through him.

[18]*Now wives, be subordinate to your husbands, as is befitting in the household of the Lord.* [19]*You husbands, love your wives and do not be disagreeable with them.* [20]*Children, obey your parents in everything, for this is what pleases the Lord.* [21]*Fathers, see that you do not provoke your children or they may become discouraged.* [22]*Slaves, obey your mortal masters in everything, not just when they are watching to curry their favor, but in undivided devotion, fearing the reprisals of the Lord.* [23]*Whatever you do, work as if for the Lord, not for men,* [24]*mindful that you will receive from the Lord your inheritance as a reward.*[r] *It is the Lord Christ whom you serve.* [25]*The one who did wrong will receive back what he did wrong; there is no preferential treatment.*

---

p. Matt. 6:31-33

q. Matt. 5:29-30; Mark 9:43-47

r. Karma yoga in a nutshell.

4

[1]*Masters, supply your slaves with a just and equal wage, knowing that you are not without a master of your own in heaven.*[s] [2]Continue vigilant and thankful in prayer, [3]also praying together on our behalf that God may open a door of opportunity for us to speak of the mystery of Christ, on account of which I have been chained up, [4]that I may make it known as behooves me as an apostle. *Behave wisely when it comes to outsiders, using the time to the best advantage.*[t] [6]Let your speech always be graceful, seasoned, and salted, so you will know the appropriate way to answer each individual.

[7]Tychicus will fill you in on all my affairs, that beloved brother, faithful servant and fellow slave in the Lord's service, [8]whom I dispatched to you for no other purpose than to inform you of the news about us and that he might comfort your hearts. [9]I sent him with Onesimus, that loyal and beloved brother who is one of your own. They will tell you everything.

[10]Aristarchus, my fellow prisoner, greets you, as does Mark, the cousin of Bar-Nabas, about whom you will have received word: if he comes to you, welcome him. [11]So does Jesus, the one called Justus. They are my only colleagues from the ranks of the circumcised in the work of the kingdom of God and a great comfort to me. [12]Epaphras, one of your own, greets you, a slave of Christ-Jesus, always struggling in prayer on your behalf for you to stand perfect and fully confident of the will of God. [13]For I can vouch for him, that he endures much anguish for you and those in Laodicea and in Hierapolis. [14]Luke, the beloved physician, greets you, and so does Demas. [15]Greet the brothers in Laodicea, as well as Nymphas and the congregation meeting at her house. [16]And once you are done reading this epistle, see that it is read also in the congregation of the Laodiceans and also that you read the one borrowed from Laodicea. [17]And tell Archippus, "Remember the service rendered you for the Lord's sake, to pay it back."[u]

[18]My handwritten greeting: Paul.[v] Remember my chains. Remain in God's favor!

---

s. Winsome Munro makes 3:18-4:1, 5 part of the Pastoral Stratum.

t. See note for 4:1.

u. A reminder to return the Laodicean epistle, hinting this was never done and suggesting why we lack it: because the only copy perished.

v. See note at Gal. 6:11 on the description of a signature suggesting forgery.

20.
The Letter to Philemon

The traditional reading of the Letter to Philemon is that Paul is interceding on behalf of Onesimus, a runaway slave (perhaps the steward of an estate) who has stolen money and fled, making his way to Paul in prison, eager to see a familiar face. Onesimus would have remembered Paul from the apostle's association with his estranged master, Philemon. Under Paul's influence, Onesimus embraces the Christian faith and becomes a great help to Paul, seeing to his needs and running errands for him. But Paul is hardly at liberty to keep things this way as runaway slaves were liable to crucifixion, and Paul would not dare be found out as an accomplice. So he sends Onesimus back home, carrying this letter asking Philemon to forgive him, not to prosecute his errant slave. This is the first glimmer in the New Testament that it might be improper for one Christian to own another as a slave, to say nothing of the larger issue of slavery, which long since had been denounced by the pre-Socratic philosophers, Stoics, and others. Paul hints broadly, almost clumsily but not without humor, that he wants Philemon to send the slave back to serve as Paul's assistant once again.

There are problems, not so much with this reading, but with the historical plausibility of it. For one thing, the Epistle to the Colossians mentions many of the same characters, but it is clear Paul has never met any of these people. In Philemon they are all old friends. A larger problem, near fatal for the authenticity of the letter, is W. C. van Manen's observation that the letter looks like a Christianized re-write of a famous letter from Pliny Secundus to Sabianus:

> The freedman of yours with whom you said you were angry has been to me, flung himself at my feet, and clung to me as if I were

> you. He begged my help with many tears, though he left a good deal unsaid; in short, he convinced me of his genuine penitence. I believe he has reformed because he realizes he did wrong. You are angry, I know, and I know too that your anger was deserved, but mercy wins most praise when there was just cause for anger. You loved the man once, and I hope you will love him again, but it is sufficient for the moment if you allow yourself to be appeased. You can always be angry again if he deserves it, and will have more excuse if you were once placated. Make some concession to his youth, his tears, and your own kind heart, and do not torment him or yourself any longer—anger can only be a torment to your gentle self.
>
> I'm afraid you will think I am using pressure, not persuasion, if I add my prayers to his—but this is what I shall do, and all the more freely and fully because I have given the man a very severe scolding and warned him firmly that I will never make such a request again. This was because he deserved a fright, and is not intended for your ears; for maybe I shall make another request and obtain it, as long as it is nothing unsuitable for me to ask and you to grant.

But why fabricate such a story for Paul? Stephan Hermann Huller (*Against Polycarp*) turns the theory of Edgar J. Goodspeed and John Knox on its head. Goodspeed's theory, elaborated by Knox (*Philemon among the Letters of Paul*), was that Onesimus, freed and forgiven as per Paul's request, became bishop of Ephesus, the one mentioned by Ignatius in his Epistle to the Ephesians, and his gratitude to Paul led him to collect the Pauline epistles. Huller, by contrast, says Philemon is a pseudepigraph intended to beef up the authority of Bishop Onesimus by linking him with Paul.

[1]Paul, a prisoner of Christ-Jesus, and Timothy, the brother, to Philemon, our beloved colleague, [2]and to Apphia, the sister, and to Archippus, our fellow-soldier, and to the congregation at your house. [3]May the
favor and protection of God our Father and the Lord, Jesus-Christ, attend you.

[4]I thank my God, always making mention of you in my prayers,
[5]hearing of the love you have for all the saints and the faith you have toward the Lord Jesus, [6]so that the sharing of your faith may become effec-

tive for Christ by a full knowledge of all that is good in us. [7]I had great joy
and consolation from your love because the hearts of the saints have been
refreshed by you, brother. [8]Which is why, having great boldness in the
authority assigned me by Christ to command you to do the right thing,
[9]for love's sake, I should plead simply as an old man named Paul and now
also as a prisoner for Christ-Jesus. [10]It is concerning my child, begotten in
my imprisonment, Onesimus, that I plead. [11]Formerly, to be sure, he was
useless to you, but now quite useful[a] both to you and to me. [12]I have herewith sent him back to you, even my own heart. [13]I deliberated, then decided to keep him in order that he might serve me on your behalf in my
imprisonment for the news, [14]but I thought it best not to do anything
without your say, not wanting your good deed to be forced, but rather
voluntary. [15]And perhaps this is why in the providence of God he was
separated from you for an hour in order that you might welcome him
back forever, [16]no longer as a slave but as more than a slave, as a beloved
brother, especially to me, but much more to you, both from natural affection and in the fellowship of the Lord.[b] [17]If therefore you have taken me
as a partner, welcome him as you would me. [18]And if he wronged you or
owes anything, charge it to my account. [19]I, Paul, have written with my
own hand: "I will repay it."[c] [20]Yes, brother, may I have help[d] from you in
the Lord's service?

[21]I wrote to you confident of your obedience, knowing that you will
do more than I have said in so many words. [22]And while you're at it, fix
up a place for me to stay, for I hope, in answer to your prayers, to be restored to you.

[23]Greetings from Epaphras, my fellow prisoner in the cause of Christ-
Jesus, [24]Mark, Aristarchus, Demas, Luke, my colleagues. [25]May the favor
of the Lord, Jesus-Christ, be with your spirit.

---

a. "Onesimus" is a synonym for the word used here for "useful."

b. This whole letter is, in effect, the Paulinist version of the parable of the Prodigal Son.

c. See note at 2 Cor. 10:1 on the use of the "I, so-and-so" formula as betraying pseudonymous authorship and Gal. 6:11 on the description of the signature as another sign of artifice.

d. The word is οναιμην, another pun on "Onesimus."

21.
The Epistle to the Philippians

IN POLYCARP'S EPISTLE TO THE Philippians (3:2), he makes a puzzling remark about Paul having written several epistles to them. Several? All we have is one. Or do we? It may well be that three—or portions of three—letters to Philippi, whether authentic or pseudonymous, survived, and the pages or fragments were eventually jumbled and mixed together within the Philippian archive, then clumsily reassembled in the manner of the mixed-up 2 Corinthians. Günther Bornkamm and Walter Schmithals, working independently, saw the second half of chapter 4 as comprising Paul's first letter, a brief thank-you note. The original salutation would have been lost or snipped for compilation. They both suggested that chapters 1-2 and parts of 3 and 4 originally comprised Paul's second letter. They also saw most of chapter 3 and part of 4 as a third letter to Philippi, from which, again, the original salutation would have been lost or trimmed away.

Schmithals and Bornkamm believed the texts were genuinely Pauline, but surely Baur was correct in seeing a post-Pauline author at work, partly because of unusual vocabulary. This is true even outside the quoted hymn (2:6-11) to a self-emptying Savior. An even more powerful consideration is the heavy tone of irony evident throughout. The writer manifestly knows that the reader knows Paul was in fact executed and nonetheless lingers on for the good of his latter-day disciples by the expedient of posthumous "Pauline" letters penned in his name. Philippians in this respect strongly resembles 2 Timothy, another attempt at a kind of "last testament of Paul."

Abraham J. Malherbe (*Paul and the Popular Philosophers*)[a] drew

a. See also Norman Wentworth DeWitt, *St. Paul and Epicurus* (Minneapolis: University of Minnesota Press, 1954).

attention to the significant debt owed to current philosophical movements by the Pauline epistles. Here we can catch a strong echo of Epicureanism and possibly of Cynicism and Stoicism. Paul makes his famous statement in Philippians that he has learned both how to be abased and to abound, to enjoy largesse and to endure scarcity with equanimity (4:11-12). All three philosophies taught such blessed self-sufficiency. Paul engages in a friendly debate with both Stoics and Epicureans in Acts 17:18. In Philippians 3:2, however, he vilifies "the dogs," which I take as a reference to Cynics, as that is the meaning of their name, their founder Diogenes having hailed the independence of the stray dog as his model. Similarly in 1 Cor. 15:32, Paul is made to refer disdainfully to Epicurean opponents as "beasts," a common epithet from those who misunderstood their avowed "hedonism" as mere sensuality.

Epistle A

4

10My gratitude to the Lord was great indeed when I saw that at last you had renewed your concern for me. Of course, I know the thought is not new, only the opportunity. 11Nor do I speak thus from deprivation, for I have long since learned how to get along fine no matter the conditions. 12I know how to be humbled one day and to prosper the next! In anything and in everything, I know the secret of interchangeably being filled and being hungry, to welcome abundance and lack equally. 13I can do anything, given the one who empowers me! 14But don't mistake me: you did well in coming to my aid in my time of affliction. 15Know this, too, Philippians: in the beginning of my service to the news when I came out from Macedonia, not one congregation entered into partnership in the matter of giving and receiving except you alone. 16Why, in Thessalonica you sent aid for my needs not once but twice! 17It is not the gift I seek, but I seek the increase of merit in your heavenly account. 18But I have everything and prosper! 19I have been filled by what Epaphroditus brought from you, which rises fragrant and appetizing from the altar as a sacrifice to God. In return, my God will satisfy every need of yours abundantly from his treasury of favor in celestial splendor, thanks to Christ-Jesus. 20Let worship redound to our God and Father throughout ages multiplied by ages! Amen.

21Greet every saint consecrated to Christ-Jesus. The brothers[b] visit-

b. Itinerant missionaries.

ing me greet you. 22All the saints greet you, most of all the ones in Caesar's household. 23May you continue to enjoy the favor of the Lord Jesus-Christ in your spirit.

Epistle B

1

1Paul and Timothy, slaves of Christ-Jesus, to all the saints of Christ-Jesus located in Philippi, with bishops and deacons.[c] 2May the favor and protection of God our Father and the Lord, Jesus-Christ, be extended to you!

3I thank my God every time I think of you, 4always praying joyfully every time I pray for all of you, 5on account of your partnership in the work of the news from the day we met right on till the present, 6confident of just this: the one who has initiated a good work in you will bring it to completion until the Day of Christ-Jesus. 7And it is right for me to think so about all of you because I carry you in my heart, whether I am imprisoned or active in the defense and the corroboration of the news, all of you being partners in my mission. 8I swear before God how poignantly I long for you all with the compassion of Christ-Jesus. 9And this I pray: that your love may increase even more and yet more as you reach full realization and complete perception, 10so you may choose wisely from the various options before you in order for you to be sincere and impeccable on the Day of Christ, 11having been filled with the fruit of righteousness by means of Jesus-Christ, that God may be worshipped and praised all the more.[d]

12So then, brothers, I want you to understand that the things that have befallen me actually tend toward the advancement of the news! 13The fact that my imprisonment stems from the cause of Christ has become evident throughout the entire praetorium and to everyone else, 14and the greater number of the brothers find that my imprisonment has only encouraged them to speak the message of God with greater daring.15It is true, some preach Christ because they envy me and want to compete with me, but others do so out of sincere motives. 16These latter preach because of their love for me, knowing that I have been called on at present to defend the news before Caesar. 17Those others announce Christ out of a desire to imitate me, not from pure motives, aiming to

c. As in the Pastorals, these ecclesiastical offices clearly mark the letter as post-Pauline.

d. Matt. 5:16

frustrate me, stuck in prison, as they think. [18]What is the sum of it? Motives notwithstanding, Christ is nonetheless being announced, and this is music to my ears, so I intend to keep right on rejoicing over it!

[19]For I know that the ultimate outcome will be my deliverance, thanks to your prayers and the aid of the Spirit of Jesus-Christ, [20]which is exactly what I eagerly expect and count on, that I will never wind up disappointed, but that with all appropriate boldness, as ever, even now Christ will be manifested all the more in my case, whether through a verdict of life or of death. [21]For to me, living is Christ and dying is only gain! [22]But if my fate is to continue in the flesh, this spells for me fruitful labor, so I cannot tell which outcome would be preferable. [23]Yes, I am caught between the two, having the desire to abandon this life and to be with Christ since this is by all accounts much the better, [24]but your need for me to remain in the flesh would seem to outweigh that consideration. [25]Yes, in view of that, I am quite sure I shall after all remain here and continue working with all of you so your faith may continue to mature and you to rejoice[e] [26]so that you may have all the more reason to brag on me in gratitude to Christ-Jesus on account of my return to you![f]

[27]Just see that you behave in a manner worthy of the news in order that, whether I come and see you in person[g] or remain absent and only hear a report of you, you may stand undaunted in one spirit, pitching in together with a single soul in the faith of the news, [28]and not being in any way intimidated by those who oppose you. That will spell out to them the promise of their own destruction but of your deliverance, and this at the hand of God, [29]because thus you will be seen to carry out the role assigned you on Christ's behalf: not merely to believe in him, but also to suffer on his account, [30]which is of course the very same contest in which you once saw me engaged and hear me engaged in now.

---

e. This sentiment is strikingly parallel to the Mahayana doctrine of the bodhisattvas, holy persons whose deeds earned their own passage into Nirvana, but who linger on the threshold to aid lesser mortals on their quests for salvation.

f. The writer uses poignant irony based on the fact that readers know Paul's imprisonment issued in his execution. However, Paul will "continue with them" by means of pseudepigraphical letters like this one.

g. The language hints at a second coming of Paul, a doctrine akin to that of Shi'ite Mahdism, which anticipates the return of a vanished imam, who communicates with the faithful through messages from self-appointed "babs" ("gates") to the Hidden Imam. These epistles function like prophecies of the risen Christ in the early Christian congregations. Both alike intended to keep new generations in touch with figures of the past but instead obscured the outline of those figures behind the screen of pious accretions.

2

1Assuming there is any encouragement to be had in the bosom of Christ, any consolation offered by love, any fellowship of spirit, any gestures of compassion or pity, 2then won't you make my joy complete by all thinking the same thing, having the same love, being one in soul, sharing the same goal, 3doing nothing from rivalry or grandstanding, but humbly treating each other as more important than yourselves, 4not preoccupied with your own welfare, but concerned with the good of others as well?[h]
5Let there flourish among you the meditation of Christ-Jesus,

> 6Who, disposed in the very form of a god,
> thought ill of seizing equality with God,
> 7but cast himself into the emptiness,
> donning the form of a slave to the archons,
> taking on the outer likeness of humanity,
> to be seen clothed in mortal fashion,
> 8he humbled himself,
> becoming obedient to the point of death, death by crucifixion.
> 9Which is why God super-exalted him,
> and granted him the name ranking above all others,
> 10so hearing the name "Jesus,"
> everyone should bend the knee,
> all angels and men,
> and imprisoned spirits alike.
> 11And every tongue should acknowledge the Lordship
> of Jesus-Christ
> as they worship God the Father.[i]

12So then, my beloved ones, as you always obeyed, and not only in my presence, but now all the more in my absence,[j] work on your salvation for yourselves with deadly seriousness, 13seeing it is God who is ener-

h. Very similar to the panegyric on love in 1 Cor. 13.

i. This hymn fragment, as F. C. Baur perceived, depends upon Gnostic mythology since the unnamed savior casts himself out of the pleroma of divine light into the *kenoma,* the empty void outside the Godhead. He secretly penetrates the world of the evil archons, angels who rule the planetary spheres, to come to earth and take on the illusory semblance of human flesh. At death, he returns triumphantly to the pleroma and receives the titular name "Jesus" ("salvation"). As P. L. Couchoud recognized, the hymn predates the process of historicizing the god Jesus as a historical figure since "Jesus" becomes his name only after his earthly mission is complete.

j. As elsewhere in the epistle, this absence is really that of Paul's long-ago death.

gizing you with both the will and the energy to do what pleases him.
[14]Carry out your duties without complaining and rationalizing, [15]so you
may wind up blameless and having harmed no one, irreproachable children of God in the midst of a crooked and perverted generation, among
whom you shine out like stars in the night sky, [16]holding high the standard of the message of life. All this will be fodder for my bragging on the
day of Christ, when it will be seen that I did not waste the time and effort
I spent on you. [17]But if it should happen that I must yield up my life, I will
rejoice since it will be a libation offered up with the sacrifice of your faith
in divine worship, and I rejoice with all of you, [18]since I know you too
will rejoice along with me.[k]

[19]But I am confident the Lord Jesus will allow me shortly to dispatch
Timothy to you so I may be cheered at the news of you. [20]For I have no
colleague to compare to Timothy! He will be genuinely concerned about
your affairs. [21]As for the rest of them, they seek only their own advancement, and not that of the news of Christ-Jesus; [22]but his sterling character
is known to you—as a child attends his father, he attended me in the
work of the news. [23]Therefore, I hope to send him the moment I see how
things will turn out with me. [24]But I trust in the Lord that I, too, will be
able to come before long.

[25]And yet I thought it needful to send Epaphroditus back to you, my
brother and colleague and fellow soldier and your apostle sent to meet
my needs, [26]since he missed you all so and was disturbed because you
heard he was ill. [27]He was indeed ill, at death's door, but God had mercy
on him, and not just on him, but on me also: otherwise I should have suffered grief upon grief. [28]Thus I sent him all the more eagerly so that, seeing him, you might rejoice and I may be less grieved. [29]Therefore, welcome him in the name of the Lord and hold people like him in honor,
[30]because he hovered on the brink of death for the sake of the work of
Christ, putting his life at risk in order to make up the service to me that
you felt you owed me.

3

[1]Finally, my brothers, rejoice in the Lord! To write the same things to
you again is no burden to me, but it is salutary for you.

4

[4]Rejoice in your faith in the Lord always! Let me repeat that: rejoice!

---

k. Here is a piece of post-Pauline "Paulology" in which the apostle's death is seen as a kind of secondary sacrifice alongside that of Christ himself.

[5]Let your patience with others be an example to them. The coming of the Lord is near. [6]There is no need to be apprehensive, just see that in every matter you inform God of your requests by prayer and petition, not neglecting thanksgiving. [7]This way, the peace of God, justified by no earthly calculation, will garrison your hearts and minds in the strength of Christ-Jesus.

Epistle C

2

Look out for the Cynics, beware the workers of evil, watch out for the mutilators! [3]Remember, it is we who are the circumcision, those who worship not by the flesh but by the Spirit of God and by making Christ-Jesus our boast, not placing confidence in the carving of the flesh, [4]even though I myself have just as much reason to have confidence in the flesh. If anyone else thinks to place confidence in fleshly criteria, I have more! [5]Circumcised on the eighth day, sprung from the race of Israel, the tribe of Benjamin, a Hebrew born of Hebrews and thus no proselyte,[l] a Pharisee in my approach to the Torah; [6]as for zeal, persecuting the church, as to righteousness measured by the Torah, impeccable. [7]But what I once considered profit, I now reckon loss on account of Christ.

[8]No, furthermore, I write off everything as a loss for the sake of the superiority of knowing Christ-Jesus, my Lord, for whose sake I suffered the loss of everything and consider it all mere dung in order that, unencumbered, I might reach Christ [9]and be found with him, not having my salvation by the Torah but rather by belief in Christ, the salvation that comes from God based on belief: [10]to know him, to experience the miracle of his resurrection, and to share his sufferings—following the example of his death, [11]hoping that I may somehow make it as far as the upraising of the dead. [12]Not that I have already received it or have already been perfected, but I follow his footsteps on the chance that I may grab hold of his coattails as I myself was grasped by Christ-Jesus.

[13]Brothers, I do not consider myself to have grasped the prize yet, but I keep one thing in view: forgetting whatever lies behind me, I press on to that which lies ahead of me, [14]the finish line toward which I race for the heavenward summons of God through Christ-Jesus.[m] [15]Therefore, as many as are perfect, let us think this, and if you think anything else, God

l. As his Ebionite critics charged.

m. All this is heavy with irony, as readers would know this imprisonment led to Paul's martyrdom, hence his final perfection via the headsman's axe.

will reveal to you the wisdom of what I am saying. [16]At any rate, whatever level we have attained, let us at least live up to that.

[17]Undertake together to imitate me, brothers, and those who do behave this way, mark them well in the same way you have us for an example. [18]This is necessary because there are many of whom I often warned you, and do so again now, weeping, who are foes of the cross of Christ,
[19]whose fate is destruction, whose god is their own stomach, and who are proudest of their shame—those who are worldly minded. [20]As for us, our citizenship is in the skies, whence we also expect a savior, the Lord, Jesus-Christ, [21]who will change the form of our humiliating body to conform to his own light-body, something easy for him, given his energizing ability to subdue all things to himself.

4

[1]So then, my brothers, whom I love and long to see again, my joy and greatest achievement—in this way stand firm in the faith of the Lord! [2]I beg Euodia and I beg Syntyche to come to one mind in fellowship with the Lord. [3]And I beg you, too, loyal Syzygus, help them who fought at my side in the work of the news with both Clement and the rest of my colleagues, whose names, though they are now long dead, are enshrined in the Book of Life.[n]

[8]Finally, brothers, whatever is true, whatever is serious, whatever is just, whatever pure, lovable, well-regarded, as long as there is anything noble or praiseworthy about it, [9]occupy yourselves with such as this. The habits you learned and appreciated and listened to and remarked in me, adopt for your own and you may be sure the God who brings peace of mind will remain with you.

---

n. The reference to the mytheme of the heavenly book hints that these names are ideal rather than those of real people. This is especially evident for Syzygus, which seems intended as a proper name but is mysteriously unattested elsewhere. Peter Carls wrote in "Identifying Syzygus, Euodia, and Syntyche," *Journal of Higher Criticism* 8 (Fall 2001): 161-82, that all four names are allegorical, derived from the very themes that are prominent in Philippians and thus function like those in Bunyan's *Pilgrim's Progress*. The word *euodia* denotes "good way," the Pauline path readers are urged to emulate (3:17); *syntyche* denotes "joyful union," to which Paul likewise urges these readers (4:2); *syzygus* means "yoke fellow" and embodies the function of mediation, making the fictive Syzygus a narrative man, such as Tzvetan Todorov describes, whose identity equals his narrative function. Similarly, *clement* is peace, the harmonious condition of "forbearance," "patience," as mentioned in 4:5. The names are therefore ascribed to imaginary members of an imagined founding generation, not of actual forbears of the readers, who are probably not Philippians, especially given the fictive nature of the whole. In other words, the Philippians are narratees, not actual recipients.

IV.
To Theophilus

22.

The Gospel according to Luke

Dating Luke-Acts

The Gospel of Luke is addressed to "most excellent Theophilus" (1:3), and the narrative seems to continue in Acts with the opening line: "In the first book, Theophilus, I wrote about all that Jesus did and taught from the beginning" (1:1). Since the two books are often considered together as a two-part document, they will be discussed together here as well.

The first time Luke's gospel is mentioned in the historical record is about 180 AD/CE when Irenaeus listed it among four gospels he was willing to accept. Justin may have referred to Acts in about 150 CE, but the reference is too vague to be certain. Marcion, in about 140 CE, had a shorter version of Luke, but not of Acts. From these various spare clues, three proposals have emerged about when Luke was composed. The first theory puts Luke at about 60 CE, the principle defense coming from Adolf Harnack (*The Date of the Acts and the Synoptic Gospels*), who along with many other scholars considered Luke and Acts to be the work of a common author. On the question of whether Acts was written just after Luke or some time later, Harnack felt it must have been in the 60s because of Luke's noticeable silence on Paul's death. According to this view, the gospel was written when Paul was under house arrest and awaiting trial in Rome, as laid out in Acts 28:30-31. If Luke knew Paul had been martyred, can we imagine he would not have made much of it?

Harnack accepted Luke's dependence upon Mark and knew he had to take this into account, similarly dating Mark and Q very early.

However, this brought up another problem in that Luke is known to have historicized Mark's "abomination of desolation" prophecy (Mark 13:14ff) according to events that unfolded in 70 CE (Luke 21:20; cf. 19:43). Mark's narrative reflects these events, or perhaps some later destruction (see the introduction to the Gospel according to Mark in this book), but Luke went a step further to re-narrate the text more literally as the fall of Jerusalem. What was Harnack's answer to this? He said this did not necessarily mean Luke described the event after the fact but that he may have perceived how the prophecy, yet unfulfilled, would imply a Roman conquest and therefore simply employed what knowledge he had of typical Roman tactics. This seems to me to be a harmonization, a clever attempt to get out of a tight spot. However, there are more serious objections to Harnack's theory of a date before the death of Paul.

Is Luke actually ignorant of Paul's martyr death? Maybe not. Note that at the end of Acts he refers to Paul's two-year imprisonment as a thing completed, a rounded-off episode. "The imprisonment lasted two years." What happened next? It is indeed puzzling that Luke neglects to tell us what happened then, but equally apparent that he assumes something else has happened—that the story goes on. Luke may have conceived a third volume to depict the acquittal and further travels and ultimate death of Paul or perhaps the ministry of Aristarchus, Barnabas, and the others who continued on after Paul's death. Perhaps the fact of Paul's death was so well known, it would have been superfluous to state it. Luke may have been saying, "This is how he came to his famous death. You know the rest."

Paul's own awareness of his fate is explicit in Acts 20:25 (v. 22 notwithstanding)[a] when he writes that "you shall see my face no more." Luke could not have recorded such a prediction without having known the outcome. He does not know of the Spanish mission Paul contemplated elsewhere, which might have taken him away from the East forever. In fact, the passage as a whole constitutes a farewell speech to the Ephesian elders, recognizable as a "last testament," a common device for putting famous last words into the mouth of a fa-

a. In verse 22, Paul anticipates a future trip to Jerusalem.

mous man.[b] Specifically, the prediction (*ex eventu*) of Gnostic heretics emerging later to forage among the churches of Asia Minor seemed to Walter Bauer (*Orthodoxy and Heresy in Earliest Christianity*) to be a much later post-Pauline way of dissociating Paul from the flood tide of heresy that would overtake the area by the second century. Luke seeks here to absolve Paul of its blame, contrary to the heretics themselves who claimed Paul as their patron saint.

Luke draws a large-scale series of parallels between the Passion of Jesus and that of Paul. Both undertake peripatetic preaching journeys, culminating in a last long journey to Jerusalem, where each is arrested in connection with a disturbance in the temple. Each is acquitted by a Herodian monarch, as well as by Roman procurators. Each, as we have seen, makes Passion predictions. Is it likely Luke could have written this in ignorance of what finally happened to Paul? Most scholars today posit a date for Luke of between 80-90 CE, but this is simply an attempt to push it back in time as far as possible while admitting that neither Mark nor Luke was written before the death of Paul in 62 CE or the fall of Jerusalem in 70 CE—and this in order to keep within the lifetime of a companion of Paul, which is who tradition says Luke was.

The Tübingen critics of the nineteenth century (F. C. Baur, Franz Overbeck, Edward Zeller) dated Luke-Acts to the second century. More recently, Walter Schmithals, Helmut Koester, and John C. O'Neill have maintained this second-century date. Baur placed Luke-Acts late on the historical time line because of its catholicizing tendency, which is to say he showed the conflict in early Christianity between the nationalist, Torah-observant Jewish Christians and the more open, Torah-free Hellenistic, gentile Christians. The first group was led by James, Peter, and the twelve, while the latter was led by Paul, Apollos, Priscilla, Aquila, and others. Baur showed how most of the New Testament documents could be placed on either side of this great divide. On the Jewish side were Matthew, James, and Revelation. On the gentile side were the authentic Pauline epistles to the Corinthians, Galatians, and Romans (1-14), along with Hebrews, the

b. See Plato's *Crito*, the *Testament of Abraham*, *Testament of Job*, *Testament of Moses*, and *Testaments of the Twelve Patriarchs*.

Gospel of John, the Johannine epistles, and the Gospel of Mark. Later there arose the catholicizing tendency to reconcile Jewish and gentile Christians. The pseudonymous 1 and 2 Peter are catholicizing works which give Peter's name to Pauline thought or have Peter speak favorably of Paul while also denigrating those who quote Paul against the memory of Peter. Catholicizing interpolations into the Pauline epistles, as well as pseudonymous epistles attributed to Paul, make him friendlier to Judaism and the Law. But the catholicizing writing *par excellance* is Luke-Acts, which attempts to bring together the Petrine and Pauline factions by a series of clever moves.

First of all, Peter and Paul are paralleled, each raising someone from the dead (Acts 9:36-40; 20:9-12), each healing a paralytic (3:1-8; 14:8-10), each healing by extraordinary, magical means (5:15; 19:11-12), each besting a sorcerer (8:18-23; 13:6-11), each miraculously escaping prison (12:6-10; 16:25-26). If one praises God for the work of Peter, then one can scarcely deny him to have been at work in Paul too, and vice versa. Second, Luke makes Peter a universalizing preacher to the gentiles. For instance, consider the Cornelius story and especially the speech of Peter in Acts 15, which echoes that of Paul in Galatians 2 aimed at Peter! At the same time, Luke makes Paul an observant Jew still claiming to be a Pharisee (23:6), piously taking vows and paying for those of others (21:20-24), attending Jerusalem worship on holy days. He makes it clear there is no truth to the prevalent rumors that Paul had abandoned legal observance (21:24), something not at all clear from the Pauline epistles.

Having vindicated Paul as a true and divinely chosen preacher of the gospel, and this conspicuously in the teeth of Jewish Christian opponents, Luke seems to deny him the dignity of the apostolate itself, redefining the office in an anachronistic fashion which would have excluded most of the twelve as well (Acts 1:21-22). Paul is subordinated to the twelve as their dutiful servant. He makes a beeline to them after his conversion, in direct contradiction to Galatians 1:15-19. He does nothing without their approval and preaches of their witness to the risen Christ (13:30-31), not his own. In short, Luke has Petrinized Paul and Paulinized Peter in order to bring their respective factions closer together. All this bespeaks a time well after Paul himself.

The historical perspective

Hans Conzelmann, who does not place Luke-Acts quite so late, argued in *The Theology of St. Luke*[c] for a date significantly after Paul, presupposing enough time for Luke to have become aware that history had not ended and that the world had entered a new era. Conzelmann argued that in Luke's day it became evident the apocalyptic enthusiasm of earlier Christians, still evident in Mark, had been premature, that the world would keep on going and a new era of salvation history had commenced that might continue on indefinitely. This is why we read in Acts that the story of salvation was not yet over. Jesus had been the decisive "center" rather than the culmination of history. Luke rewrote the story to de-eschatologize it and make it fit into an ongoing world in which the church had more of a role than merely awaiting the end.

Luke, according to Conzelmann, saw salvation history as consisting of three great eras. The first was that of Israel. It is represented in Luke by Zachariah, Elizabeth, Miriam (Mary), Simeon, and Anna as quintessential Old Testament characters. They are actually modeled on the stories of the infancy of Samuel, a connection Conzelmann did not make because he believed the first two chapters of the gospel were a later addition, but it seems to fit his theory pretty well. The second period was that of Jesus. It forms the middle of time, the strategic pivotal zone of history. It culminates the story of Israel and commences that of the church. John the Baptist is pivotal, marking the shift of the eons (Luke 16:16) from the time when the Law is preached to the time when the kingdom of God is preached.

Within this central period of time, there is a further division with the public ministry of Jesus occupying the middle zone when the full blaze of heavenly light dispelled all shadows; wherever Jesus goes, evil flees like the Canaanites before the advancing Israelites. This is what Conzelmann called the "Satan-free" period beginning with Jesus' warding off of Satan by successfully withstanding the temptations. At the end of this story, Luke 4:13 says Satan "departed from

c. Hans Conzelmann, *The Theology of St. Luke,* trans. Geoffrey Buswell (London: Faber and Faber, 1960); originally published as *Die Mitte der Zeit: Studien zur Theologie des Lukas* (Tübingen: Mohr, 1954).

him until an opportune time (*kairos*)." The time in question came in the betrayal story when, as in John, Luke says Satan entered into Judas Iscariot to engineer the death of Jesus. Between these two events, we see either an editorial elimination of Satan's activity or a continual banishing of his forces from the field. In the first case, notice that Luke has omitted the rebuke of Peter, "Get behind me Satan!" from the confession of Peter. Even Matthew, who does not want to make Peter look bad, evident in the "you are Peter" material, retains the rebuke. Why does Luke omit it? Notice that Luke has Jesus ride roughshod over all the forces of evil. He witnesses Satan fall precipitously from his position of power to one of the lower heavens (10:18-19) and sees "the powers of the heavens ... shaken" (21:26b); he frees those oppressed by the devil (Luke 13:16; Acts 10:38) without resistance. But once the Satan-free period is over at the conclusion of the Last Supper, Jesus warns the disciples that things will not be so easy from then on. Where previously they had been able to travel unmolested in preaching the gospel, now they would need to carry weapons to protect themselves (22:35-36). It is only now we learn of Satan's demand to thresh the twelve like wheat (22:31). Here we can detect for the first time the perspective that has continued today that Jesus lived in a pristine "once upon a time" era, one that, from the standpoint of both writer and reader, is long over.

Nascent Catholicism

Luke's intended readers lived in the third period of time when the gospel was to be preached and tribulation would have to be endured. The church was fast becoming an institution of salvation. This is probably why Luke systematically eliminates any reference to the death of Jesus as containing saving power in its own right. For Luke-Acts, it is the church that dispenses salvation through baptism, which requires faith in the name of Jesus and in the leadership of the apostles. This is not a work of the apostolic age.

Conzelmann's Luke tends to push the eschatological fulfillment off into the future. At first, this is not obvious since Luke retains the Markan apocalypse in which we are told this generation will not pass before all these things are fulfilled (Luke 21:32). But we dare not ignore the many subtle changes Luke makes in his sources elsewhere.

In the Olivet Discourse itself, the *false* prophets are those who not only announce "I am he" but now also that "The time is at hand!" (21:8; cf. 2 Thess. 2:1-3). Both are lies. The events Jesus predicts now lead only to the historical destruction of the Jerusalem temple by Roman troops (21:20), not to the very end of all things as Mark had expected. The fall of Jerusalem will usher in a new period, the times of the gentiles, which apparently means gentile dominion over Israel as in the visions of Daniel 7. Thus there is a distancing buffer between the events of 70 CE and the end, with Luke standing squarely in the middle.

In the confession of Peter story, Jesus predicts that some would see the kingdom of God, but not "coming in power" as Mark had it (9:1; cf. Luke 9:27); Luke wants to avoid the embarrassment over the fact that the twelve had died and there still had been no second coming (cf. 2 Pet. 3:4; John 21:23). At the trial scene, Jesus no longer tells his contemporaries that *they will see* the Son of Man seated at the right hand of power (Mark 14:62) but rather simply that the Son of Man will be seated there from now on (Luke 22:69). After all, the Sanhedrin, too, are long dead and the coming of the Son of Man and the kingdom of God has not materialized.

And then there are the *three impatient questions*. In Luke 17:20-21, Jesus is asked of signs whereby the arrival of the kingdom may be counted down—signs such as he himself presented in the Olivet Discourse but repudiated in Q. His answer is that there will be no such anticipation. The kingdom is not the kind of thing that could be predicted since it is an inner spiritual reality. Again in Luke 19:11ff, the writer has heavily redacted the parable of the talents, which survives in something more like its Q form in Matthew 25:14ff, to show that before the kingdom comes, the Son of Man will have to go very far away—even to heaven in Acts 1:10-11—and be absent a long time before he can return as king. Luke says explicitly that by this parable he meant to counter the notion of an imminent arrival of the kingdom (19:11). Finally in Acts 1:6-7f, after forty days of "inside teaching" from the risen Christ himself, the twelve are portrayed as being so dense they still expect an immediate theocratic denouement. The artificiality is plain, hence redactional. It is the reader, not the twelve,

who should not trouble himself about matters of eschatology but should get busy spreading the gospel.

It is also significant that Luke replaces *horizontal* eschatology with a *vertical* orientation. In other words, Luke is alone among the gospel writers in speaking of people going to heaven or hell as soon as they die. The parable of Lazarus and the rich man (17:19-31) and the thief on the cross story (23:43) have such a picture. In the latter, the eschatological enthronement of Jesus is replaced by "going to heaven." In Luke 20:38b, the gospel writer adds the idea of present immortality, "for all live unto him," just as in 4 Maccabees 7:19, where we read that "to God they do not die, as our patriarchs Abraham, Isaac, and Jacob died not, but live to God." Earlier Christians thought of attaining the future kingdom to be an earthly achievement. It is only when the prospect of an imminent end has faded that one thinks of going to heaven.[d]

Conzelmann argued that if Luke was not an early work representing a radical millenarian movement, then perhaps the ethic it implied was more bourgeois and intended to be lived by those who no longer imagined they had the option of remaining aloof from the world. Luke represents the rejection of the "interim ethic" of radical apocalyptic movements. The way Luke points up the innocence of Jesus and Paul at every opportunity surely leans in this direction. Luke wanted to find an accord between church and empire. All in all, we get a view very much like that of the late first- to early second-century Pastoral Epistles to Timothy and Titus. We will see there is reason to believe the similarity stems from more than just a common church-historical milieu, perhaps from actual common authorship.

Conzelmann pointed also to the expanded preaching of John the Baptist in Luke where the Baptist includes ethical teachings for the crowds. This is not present in Mark and Q. Why the difference? Because Luke understands John was ushering in a new historical era for which concrete guidelines would be necessary, not merely the end of an age for which one can do nothing but repent and wait with bated breath.

---

d. 1 Thess. 4:13-14; 2 Cor. 5:1-4; Phil. 1:23

Acts of the apologists

Charles H. Talbert (*Luke and the Gnostics*), though again without actually holding to a second-century date, showed that Luke shared the agenda and views of the second-century apologists Irenaeus, Justin Martyr, and Tertullian. These men responded to the "heresies" by claiming an exclusive copyright on the "apostolic tradition." The apologists relied heavily in their polemics against the Gnostics on the idea of the apostolic succession of bishops. That is, the twelve apostles had ostensibly been the apprentices of the Son of God. They alone saw the whole of his ministry and were thus in no danger of taking things out of context, as Irenaeus accused the Valentinians of doing. In the pseudo-Clementines, Peter takes Simon Magus to task precisely over this issue: how can the Magus hope to properly understand Christ and his teachings on the basis of occasional visions of him? If he really had been taught by Christ, he ought to agree with Peter, who saw and heard everything the Messiah did and said. Luke seems already to be setting up the twelve apostles as a college of guarantors of the orthodox tradition. As Talbert points out, Luke made explicit in Acts 1:21-22 that he considered an apostle one who saw and could verify all events in Jesus' life from his baptism on through the ascension. The artificiality of this is evident from the simple fact that the twelve themselves were not present at all these events since Jesus recruited most of them after the baptism of John. But Luke does make the effort, as Talbert shows, to have the disciples present at everything after their conversions. While they are away preaching, nothing is recorded of Jesus, otherwise the witnesses would not have been able to attest it.

Note that Luke has every step of the fledgling church carefully overseen by the vigilant eye of the twelve, who stay magically untouched in Jerusalem even when the whole church is otherwise scattered by persecution (Acts 8:1): The twelve authenticate the conversion of the Samaritans, the ordination of the Seven, the conversion of Cornelius, and the ministry of Paul. The apologists held that the bishops were appointed by the apostles to continue their work, teaching what the apostles themselves had been taught from the horse's mouth, as it were. Paul tells the Ephesian elders he taught them everything he

knew (Acts 20:20), implying he had not taught Gnostic concepts to the illuminati, which contradicts Paul's pointed statement in 1 Corinthians 2:6f. Luke calls the elders "bishops" in Acts 20:28, though many translations hide this fact (cf. 2 Tim. 2:2).

Tertullian denied the right of heretics even to quote scripture in their own defense, much as Justin did with Jews, claiming scripture was meaningless unless interpreted in accordance with the tradition of the apostles. And what was that? It was whatever the current Catholic interpretation happened to be. Even so, Luke was careful to have the twelve appear as recipients of the risen Christ's own scriptural exegesis (Luke 24:25, 43-44), which Luke nevertheless refrains from giving any detail about, thus writing a blank check.

Tertullian fought against the Gnostic idea of a spiritually resurrected Christ. Is it any accident that Luke has the same concern, as opposed to the presumably earlier view of 1 Corinthians 15:49-50 and 1 Peter 3:18? Gnostics claimed Jesus had remained on earth some eighteen months, perhaps even eleven years, teaching the apostles, from whom the Gnostics too claimed apostolic succession. According to the Gnostics, Paul trained Theodas, who in turn trained Valentinus. Peter trained Glaukias, who then trained Basilides. This was, of course, a way of saying they had the inside story without the veiled language intended for the general public. It is no wonder Luke appropriates the device of the post-Easter period of teaching, of forty days, claiming such warrant for whatever the bishops may teach—which is, again, why Luke does not tell you what Jesus taught them!

Talbert notes that Luke's decision to write an account of Jesus, then an account of his major authorized successors (Paul and Peter), reflected the practice of philosophical schools at the time: producing two-volume treatises, one devoted to the founder's life and teachings, the second to the duly appointed successors' lives, with the effect of legitimatizing the current leadership of the school. Sometimes they might append a collection of epistles, genuine or spurious. This fits well with the theory of Jerome D. Quinn that Luke wrote the Pastorals to follow Acts as volume 3 in a series.

J. C. O'Neill (*The Theology of Acts in Its Historical Setting*) argued that Acts belonged to the early second century because its theol-

ogy has most in common with the writings of that time, writings derived from apologists. That Jews had forfeited their claim on God and had been shunted to the side is surely impossible before the second century. Had it become clear earlier than this that Jews had uniformly rejected the message? Hardly! Yet in Acts, not only is this a *fait accompli,* but as Jack T. Sanders shows in *The Jews in Luke-Acts,* the evangelist seems to view the Jews of the Diaspora as devil-horned caricatures opposed to the gospel out of base envy—something retrojected from a later period when Christianity had begun to overwhelm Judaism in numbers, surely too late for the lifetime of Paul or one of his companions.

The theology of the supercession of the temple seen in Stephen's speech in Acts 7 is borrowed from post-70 CE Hellenistic Judaism where, as in Justin's *Dialogue with Trypho* and the *Sibylline Oracles,* Jews had begun to make virtue of necessity and spiritualized temple worship, denying the necessity for a temple of stone, which they, in any case, no longer had. The apostolic decree (Acts 15:19-29; 21:25) stipulating that Jewish Christians had every right to observe the ancestral Law of Moses and the stress on James securing Paul's public endorsement of this, seem also to reflect a period attested to by Justin when Jewish Christians were on the defensive against their gentile Christian brethren, who deemed them heretical for keeping the Law at all. Justin himself allowed their right to observe the Law if they did not try to coerce gentiles to keep it. This dispute seems to provide the *Sitz-im-Leben* for Acts 21, making Luke a contemporary of Justin. Similarly, the decree as set forth in Acts 15 seeks to provide, long after the fact, the apostolic legitimation for the cultic provisions attested to in second-century sources but not earlier, at least for the most part. Minucius Felix, the pseudo-Clementines, Biblis (in Eusebius), the Syriac *Apology of Aristides,* and Tertullian all mention that Christians do not eat the blood of animals or the meat of strangled animals. The Revelation of John and the late section of 1 Corinthians 8-10 ban eating meat that has been offered to idols. Matthew forbids consanguineous marriages (*porneia*) for gentile converts at about the same time (Matt. 19:9). The strange thing about this is that in none of these cases is the prohibition traced back to the apostolic decree of Jerusa-

lem which, if genuine, must have been treasured as the first ecumenical conciliar decision in the church. Conversely, when Paul's epistles deal with these issues, they never mention the decree, which would seemingly have been an authoritative way of dealing with the questions. Luke has simply collected these various second-century Christian mores and retrojected them into the golden age of the apostles to give them added weight. That should hardly surprise us since every early church order for centuries after (*Didache, Didascalia, Apostolic Constitutions*) did the same thing.

The titles of Jesus, particularly "servant of God" (Acts 3:13; 4:27), smack equally of second-century Christianity. Despite the desperate desire of Joachim Jeremias and others to trace this title to an imaginary "suffering servant of Yahweh" theology of the earliest church, there is no evidence that such a spectre ever existed. But the title does occur in later documents like the Didache, 1 Clement, and the Martyrdom of Polycarp. It is late Christology, not an early belief. The natural theology of Acts 17, the Areopagus speech, reflects the views of second-century apologists who sought to make common ground with their pagan audience through Justin's "Christians before Christ" theory.

Apostolic adventures

The Acts of the Apostles bear a number of similarities to the ancient Hellenistic novels, whose height of popularity was, again, the second century.[e] These were most often romances but also sometimes chronicled the travels and miracles of teachers like Apollonius of Tyana. Rosa Söder notes five features shared by the novels and the Apocryphal Acts of the second century, discussed below.[f] These features are also evident in the canonical Acts of the Apostles: travel (the apostolic journeys of Peter and Paul), aretalogy (miraculous oddities such as Peter's healing shadow, Paul's healing hankies, and Peter striking Ananias and Sapphira dead with a word), accounts of fabulous and exotic peoples (bull-sacrificing pagans of Lycaonia in Acts

e. See Richard I. Pervo, *Profit with Delight: The Literary Genre of the Acts of the Apostles* (Philadelphia: Fortress Press, 1987).

f. Rosa Söder, *Die apokryphen Apostelgeschichten und die romanhafte Literatur der Antike* (Stuttgart: Kohlhammer, 1932).

14:8-19, superstitious natives of Malta in 28:1-6, and philosophical Athenian dilettantes in chapter 17), religious propaganda illustrating the providence of favorite gods, and chaste eroticism between separated lovers who resist temptation during separation (Joanna and the female entourage of Jesus in Luke). Söder adds five more important traits less often found in the Apocryphal Acts but common to the novels and present in the canonical Acts: the sale of a hero into slavery (in this case the imprisonment of Paul, Peter, and Silas in Acts 12, 16, 21, 26), persecution, crowd scenes (in this case in Ephesus and Jerusalem), divine help in time of need, and reliance on oracles, dreams, and divine commands.

Luke fits best as a contemporary and kindred spirit of Papias, bishop of Hierapolis in Asia Minor about 140-50 CE. Papias collected traditions, many legendary, of the days of the apostles. His accounts and Luke's are strikingly similar at five points. Both mention extant written gospels—"many," according to Luke 1:1, while Papias says Mark transcribed Peter's preaching and Matthew recorded the oracles of Jesus. Both claim to prefer research derived from people who heard the accounts from the first apostles, although neither Papias (according to Eusebius) nor Luke claimed to have heard the original apostles for themselves.[g] Both mention the prophesying daughters of Philip (Acts 21:8-9; Eusebius, 3:39:8-9). Both know the grotesque legend of the ghastly death of Judas, who swelled up and exploded. Both wrote their own gospels, Papias's *An Exposition of the Oracles of Our Lord* containing what Eusebius called "certain strange parables" of an apocalyptic nature. Papias does not mention Luke's gospel alongside Mark and Matthew, presumably because he did not know of it. It had not been written yet.

Paul's companion?

Traditionally we have thought the author of Luke's gospel and the Book of Acts to be Luke, the "beloved physician" and companion of Paul mentioned in Colossians 4:14 and 2 Timothy 4:11. The text itself, like all the gospels, is anonymous. The traditional identification of Luke rests on the assumptions that the "we" narrative parts of Acts

g. Eusebius, *Ecclesiastical History,* 3.39.3-4.

go back to an actual eyewitness and that the letters in question are genuinely Pauline. If some companion of Paul wrote Acts, which one was it? Most names can be eliminated since the author mentions them in distinction from himself among the "we." Luke is one of the names occurring in the epistles that is not mentioned in Acts. Titus is another. Even though there is good reason to suspect the authenticity of both letters that mention Luke, they still attest, even as pseudepigraphs, the tradition that Paul had a companion named Luke.

This whole line of argument has been rendered superfluous by Vernon K. Robbins's observation that the "we" style of narration was a contemporary novelistic technique.[h] Virtually all of the "we" passages in Acts are associated with portions of the story set on ships and depicting sea travel. So much for all the efforts to identify a pre-Lukan "we" source or to argue for authorship of the Acts as a whole by a participant in some of its events.

Irenaeus claimed Luke wrote down the gospel as preached by Paul, but this is doubly hard to believe since Paul, in his letters, scarcely makes reference to the earthly Jesus and none at all to his miracles. Another major problem facing this ascription is the divergence between the authentic letters of Paul, provided there are any, and Acts. The differences are so great, it seems doubtful a companion of Paul could have so grossly misrepresented his master. For instance, there are chronological problems: as John Knox has shown *(Chapters in a Life of Paul)*, followed recently by Gerd Lüdemann, if we read the epistles on their own without trying to fit them into Acts, we come up with a rather different scenario than that of Acts; Acts schematizes the ministry of Paul into three missionary journeys. Any reading of Acts shows it to be at least quite selective, omitting most of the Pauline vicissitudes listed in 2 Corinthians 11:21-27. Acts is irreconcilable with Galatians on the matter of Paul's movements following his conversion. Acts 9:20-26 tells precisely the version that Paul (Gal. 1:15ff) expressly repudiates: he did *not* go to Jerusalem to consult those who were apostles before him. Again there is the problem of the Council of

h. Vernon K. Robbins, "By Land and by Sea: The We-Passages and Ancient Sea Voyages," in Charles H. Talbert, ed., *Perspectives on Luke-Acts* (Danville, VA: Association of Baptist Professors of Religion, 1978).

Jerusalem (Acts 15) and its decree. Paul never mentions it. Had he submitted to such a stipulation, why would he not mention it to settle such issues as the business about eating idol sacrifices in 1 Corinthians 8-10? It is even harder to see how he could have submitted to its imposition in the first place. Does Galatians 2:6 not rule it out?

There are also theological problems. As Philipp Vielhauer pointed out,[i] the author of Acts misunderstood Paul's thought at several key points. In light of this, how can he have been Paul's bosom companion? In Acts 17, Paul grants that pagans are on the right track in searching for God, their problem being that they have remained stalled, never making the connection that there must be one transcendent God. In Romans 1-3, Paul's estimate of pagans is more severe: none of them is righteous; paganism is nothing but a repudiation of the Almighty from the very start. Gentiles are not searching for God at all but rather running from him. Natural theology provides a bridge in Acts and a barrier in Romans. Acts portrays all humans as "his offspring," which is unthinkable for Paul. Nor is sin even hinted at in Acts 17.

What about the Jewish Torah? The book of Acts has Paul still a Pharisee (23:6; 26:5), while Philippians has him an ex-Pharisee. Acts has him obeying the Torah as a regular habit (21:18ff), while 1 Corinthians (9:19-23) allows it as an occasional, opportunistic exception. In Acts 13, Paul says the gospel supplements the Law, expunging offenses for which the Torah made no provision, while for Paul in Galatians, the Law has been superseded by the gospel as a new dispensation. In Acts, Paul preaches first in the synagogue of each city, turning only reluctantly to the gentiles after the Jews reject him, something never hinted at in the epistles, where Paul is "the apostle to the gentiles," not to the Jews.

The same author?

Jan Hendrik Scholten suggested in the nineteenth century that Luke and Acts may not come from the same author. Today there is near unanimity among scholars that they do, but such investigators as

---

i. Philipp Vielhauer, "The 'Paulinism' of Acts," in Leander E. Keck and J. Louis Martyn, eds., *Studies in Luke-Acts* (Nashville: Abingdon Press, 1966).

Albert C. Clark and A. W. Argyle have agreed with Scholten on the basis of striking differences in vocabulary.[j] On the other hand, many studies by Joseph A. Fitzmyer, Robert C. Tannehill, and others have demonstrated thematic consistency between the two works.

The solution to this dilemma lies with Marcion. We are told that his *Apostolicon* contained a shorter version of the Gospel of Luke. The Catholic fathers were quick to allege that Marcion had shortened our traditional Luke, trimming away portions that were doctrinally objectionable to him, especially parts that served to link Christianity with Judaism or the Old Testament. Albrecht Ritschl, in his period of adherence to Baur's Tübingen School, made the suggestion, later revived by John Knox and Joseph Hoffmann,[k] that it had been just the reverse: Marcion had instead possessed a shorter, earlier version of Luke which scholars call Ur-Lukas. The Catholic Church proceeded to expand Ur-Lukas by the addition of material that was anti-Marcionite. If we may borrow Rudolf Bultmann's term for the unknown figure who rehabilitated John's gospel for the Catholic canon, let us call the Catholic editor who produced our Gospel of Luke the Ecclesiastical Redactor. This redactor would have gone on to write Acts to supplement Marcion's exclusive focus on Paul at the expense of the twelve. In fact, this is clearly the most natural explanation for the Peter-Paul parallelism in Acts: the particular Paulinists and Petrinists the book of Acts wants to reconcile are the Marcionites and Catholics.

This approach to Luke and Acts is easily compatible with the work of Conzelmann and others. The only modification is this: where previous scholars spoke of Luke redacting Mark to introduce his distinctives, including the de-eschatologizing Conzelmann traced so convincingly, the Lukan Ecclesiastical Redactor edited Ur-Lukas, which in relevant passages was more like its Markan original. Thus the author of Acts was merely the redactor of Luke. This accounts for the thematic consistencies and vocabulary differences.

---

j. Albert C. Clark, *The Acts of the Apostles: A Critical Edition* (Oxford: Clarendon, 1933); A. W. Argyle, "The Greek of Luke and Acts," *New Testament Studies* 20 (1974).

k. John Knox, *Marcion and the New Testament* (Chicago: University of Chicago Press, 1942); R. Joseph Hoffmann, *Marcion: On the Restitution of Christianity* (Chico, CA: Scholars Press, 1984).

Luke-Acts-Pastorals

Some scholars[1] have argued that Luke wrote not only Acts but the Pastoral Epistles as well. There are striking similarities of ideas and vocabulary between Luke-Acts and the Pastorals beyond what one would expect even from books sharing the same milieu. Paul cannot have written them, as a surfeit of differences makes all too plain. As P. N. Harrison showed *(The Problem of the Pastoral Epistles)*, the vocabulary is rather that of the second-century Apostolic Fathers. In addition, Luke-Acts and the Pastorals share a large number of words which are found nowhere else in the New Testament. For instance, Acts uses Lukan particles and the preposition *sun* for "with." It is precisely such differences that Clark invoked in order to drive a wedge between Luke and Acts. If this proves anything, it proves too much for those who deny Luke authorship of the Pastorals yet retain Acts for him. However, it would fit quite nicely with the hypothesis that Acts and the Pastorals were written by the same author, who redacted but did not write Ur-Lukas.

The Pastorals and Luke-Acts are almost alone in their use of *euseb-* words for piety. So for *time* as meaning "payment," *zogrein* ("to catch alive"), and *zoogonein* ("to preserve alive"). So with the idea of being "lovers of money" (1 Tim. 6:10; 17:2; 2 Tim. 3:2; Luke 16:14). The notions of "laying up a foundation" for the future by means of charitable deeds rather than by hoarding money occurs in both Luke 12:21 and 1 Timothy 6:18-19. Both Luke 22:28 and 2 Timothy 2:12 have the idea of enduring trials in order to inherit the kingdom (see Acts 14:22). "The laborer is worthy of his hire": Matthew 10:10 has *tophes* ("keep") while Luke 10:7 and 1 Timothy 5:18 have *misthou* ("pay"). There are very similar passages in 2 Timothy 4:1, Acts 10:42, and Acts 17:31 about Christ being destined as the judge of all alike, of the whole world, the living and the dead. Both Acts 20:24 and 2 Timothy 4:7 have Paul declaring himself finished with the race he had to run for Christ. In Acts 13:25, the same thing is

1. C.F.D. Moule, "The Problem of the Pastoral Epistles: A Reappraisal," *Bulletin of the John Rylands Library* 47 (1964-65): 430-52; Stephen G. Wilson, *Luke and the Pastoral Epistles* (London: Society for Promoting Christian Knowledge, 1979); Jerome D. Quinn, "The Last Volume of Luke: The Relation of Luke-Acts to the Pastoral Epistles," in Talbert, ed., *Perspectives on Luke-Acts.*

said about John the Baptist ("when he was finishing his course"). The idea that serious sin can be mitigated by ignorance is found in Luke 12:47; 23:34; Acts 3:17; 7:60; and 1 Timothy 1:13.[m] The image of plowing a straight furrow in one's Christian work is found in Luke 9:62 and 2 Timothy 2:15.

As Talbert and Quinn have pointed out, there is precedent in classical biography, as in the biblical tradition for affixing letters to a book by the same author.[n] That Luke intended the Pastorals to be the third volume of a trilogy is hinted at in the prologue to Acts where he calls his gospel the "first," not the "former." This connection with the Pastorals provides us with a viable guess as to the actual identity of this major New Testament author. Hans von Campenhausen noticed the strong similarity between the Pastorals and the second-century epistle of Polycarp, thereby nominating Polycarp author of the Pastorals. From here, Stephan Hermann Huller (*Against Polycarp: In Defense of "Marcion"*) has connected the dots, suggesting there is no better candidate than Polycarp as redactor of Ur-Lukas and author of Acts. It would certainly fit our information that Polycarp had publicly denounced Marcion as the first-born of Satan. He was someone with opportunity and motive to undo Marcion's work by co-opting his scriptures for the benefit of Catholicism. With the identification of Polycarp as our pseudonymous author, we receive another bonus in the possible identification of the hitherto-mysterious Theophilus. Huller, following Alvin Boyd Kuhn, plausibly suggests Theophilus of Antioch, a contemporary of Polycarp, as the recipient of the work.

Sources of Ur-Lukas

We may easily describe in summary the source materials employed by the author of both the Gospel of Marcion and the Gospel according to Luke. We may say of Ur-Lukas what traditional source critics say of Luke. Ur-Lukas used Mark's gospel, though perhaps in an earlier version without the "great omission" (Mark 6:45-8:21). Ur-Lukas used over 60 percent of our Mark, making some changes in

m. Cf. also Acts 7:60; 2 Tim. 4:16.

n. Examples would be Syriac Baruch; 1 Enoch, a composite book of Enoch writings, the last of which is the Epistle of Enoch; and the trilogy of Jeremiah, Baruch, and the Epistle of Jeremy.

it, though none of the distinctive changes made by the Ecclesiastical Redactor such as Conzelmann catalogued as Luke's redactions of Mark. Ur-Lukas used the Q source, a collection of sayings attributed to Jesus with very little in the way of narrative. The Q source was also used by Matthew and is, in fact, defined as material Matthew and Luke have in common that didn't com from Mark. Often where the two expanded gospels overlap, they used Mark; where they overlap without Mark, they used Q. None of this changes by substituting Ur-Lukas for Luke.

There is a good bit of very striking Lukan material found nowhere else in the traditionally canonical gospels, though some of it has echoes in the Gospel of Thomas. This material includes the parables of the prodigal son, unjust steward, good Samaritan, and the rich man and Lazarus; stories of the Samaritan leper, bent woman, Mary and Martha, Zacchaeus, and widow of Nain; and sayings such as contained in "the woes" of the Sermon on the Plain. Where do these come from? Scholars speak of Luke's special source as "L." Most of the material would have been in Ur-Lukas. Some of it would have been added subsequently by the Lukan Ecclesiastical Redactor. Some may have been floating oral tradition, but most was probably free composition by the author of Ur-Lukas.

1

In view of the fact that many took in hand to draw up a narrative concerning the matters which have been carried to completion among us, [2]just as handed on to us by those who from the start became eyewitnesses and attendants of the message, [3]it seemed proper that I, too, who have traced all things accurately from their source, should write to you, most excellent Theophilus, [4]so you might know the reliability of those things in which you have been catechized.

[5]In the reign of Herod the Great, king of Judea, there was a certain priest named Zachariah of the Abijah shift, and his wife of the daughters of Aaron, and her name was Elisabeth. [6]And they were both righteous before God, living blamelessly by all the commandments and ordinances of the Lord. [7]And they were without children because Elisabeth was barren and both of them were of advanced days. [8]It came about that as he officiated before God in the course of his shift, [9]as was customary for the priesthood, it came up his lot to enter into the holy place of the Lord and

to burn incense. [10]And all the masses of the people were praying outside
at the hour of incense. [11]And an angel of Adonai appeared to him, standing to the right of the altar of incense. [12]And Zachariah shuddered and
was overcome with fear. [13]But the angel said to him, "Do not fear, Zachariah! I am here because your petition was heard, and Elisabeth your wife
will bear you a son and you shall call his name John.

> [14]And there shall be joy for you and gladness,
> and many will rejoice at his birth.
> [15]For he will be great in the eyes of Adonai
> and wine and strong drink he may by no means drink,
> and with Holy Spirit he will be filled from his mother's womb.
> [16]And many of the sons of Israel will he reconcile to Adonai their
> God;
> [17]and he will precede him in the spirit and power of Elijah
> to reconcile the hearts of the fathers to the children
> and the disobedient to the understanding of the righteous,
> to prepare a people ready for Adonai."

[18]And Zachariah said to the angel, "By what sign shall I know this for
sure? After all, I myself am old and my wife is advanced in her days!"
[19]And answering, the angel said to him, "I am Gabriel! I stand in attendance upon God. And I was sent to speak to you and to announce these
things to you. [20]Now behold, you shall be silent and incapable of speech
until that day these things transpire because you dared doubt my words,
which nonetheless will be fulfilled in due time. There's your sign!"

[21]And the people awaited Zachariah and they were amazed how long
he lingered in the holy place. [22]And emerging, he was not able to speak to
them, and they realized he had seen a vision in the holy place because he
was gesturing to them and remained mute. [23]And it came about when his
days of liturgy were completed, he went away to his dwelling; [24]and after
these days, Elisabeth his wife conceived and stayed out of sight for five
months, reflecting, [25]"Thus has Adonai done to me in the days when he
smiled upon me to take away my reproach in the eyes of others."[o]

[26]Now in Elisabeth's sixth month, the angel Gabriel was sent from
God to a city of the Galilee named Nazareth, [27]to a maiden betrothed to
a husband named Joseph of the lineage of David, and the maiden was

---

o. Nowhere does the narrative ever quite say that Zachariah fathered the child, leaving the possibility that it was meant to imply a miraculous, fatherless birth.

named Mariam. [28]And going in to her, he said, "Hail, favorite one! The Lord is with you." [29]And she trembled greatly at the thing, and she reasoned within herself what to make of such a greeting. [30]And the angel said to her, "Do not fear, Mariam! You have pleased God. [31]And behold, you will conceive in the womb and bear a son and you will call his name Jesus.[p]

> [32]This one will be great,
> and he will be called a son of Elyon,
> and the God Adonai will give him the throne of his father David,
> [33]and he will reign over the house of Jacob for the ages,
> and of his reign there will be no end."[q]

[34]*And Mariam said to the angel, "How will this happen, since I have no relations with a husband?"*[r] [35]*And answering, the angel said to her,*

> "Holy Spirit will hover over you
> and the power of Elyon will loom over you,
> which is also why your holy offspring
> will be called a son of God."[s]

[36]"And if you doubt, know this: behold, your relative Elisabeth, she too

---

p. Cf. Gen. 17:19; 18:9-15: "Sarah, your wife, shall bear you a son and you shall call his name ..."; Judg. 13:2-5: "you shall conceive and bear a son ... and he shall begin to deliver Israel."

q. A major source for Luke's nativity story is the nativity of Moses told in pseudo-Philo's *Biblical Antiquities*. Accordingly, during Pharaoh's assault on Hebrew babies, Amram defies Pharaoh by having a son. God makes known his will by sending an angel to the virgin Miriam. "And the Spirit of God came upon Miriam one night, and she saw a dream and told it to her parents in the morning, saying, 'I have seen this night, and behold a man in a linen garment stood and said to me, Go and say to your parents, behold, he who will be born from you will be cast forth into the water; likewise through him the water will be dried up. And I will work signs through him and save my people, and he will exercise leadership always'" (9:10).

r. The story borrows from the commissioning stories of Moses (Exod. 3:10-12) and Jeremiah (1:4-8), where God's servant objects to the divine summons but his objection is overruled.

s. One cannot quite exclude the possibility that Gabriel, himself an angelic "power," begets the child upon Mariam. The angel's predictions derive from an Aramaic version of Daniel: "[And when the Spirit] came to rest up[on] him, he fell before the throne. [Then Daniel rose and said,] 'O king, why are you angry; why do you [grind] your teeth? [The G]reat [God] has revealed to you [that which is to come].... [Peoples will make war,] and battles shall multiply among the nations, until [the king of the people of God arises].... [All the peoples will serve him] and

conceived a son in her old age, and this is the sixth month with her who
was called barren. 37You see, one can say nothing that shall prove impossible for God." 38And Mariam said, "Behold the slave of Adonai. Let it
happen to me as you have said." And the angel departed from her. 39And
waking up, Mariam journeyed during these days into the mountain country with haste to a city of Judah. 40And entering into the dwelling of
Zachariah, she greeted Elisabeth. 41And it happened, as Elisabeth heard
Mariam's greeting, that the baby leaped inside her womb[t] and was filled
with Holy Spirit. 42And she shouted with a great cry and said, "Blessed
are you of all women, and blessed the fruit of your womb! 43And how do
I deserve that the mother of my Lord should come to me? 44For behold, as
the sound of your greeting came to my ears, the baby leaped with joy inside my womb. 45And blessed be she who believed, for the things spoken
to her will reach completion." 46And Elisabeth said,[u]

> "My soul tells the greatness of the Lord
> 47and my spirit exulted in God my savior,
> 48because he smiled upon the humiliation of his slave!
> For behold, from now on all the generations will call me blessed
> 49because Shaddai did great things for me,
> and holy is his name.
> 50And his mercy extends to generations
> and generations of those who revere him.
> 51He acted mightily with his arm,
> he sent fleeing those who imagined themselves great.
> 52He pulled down dynasties from thrones
> and raised up the humble in their place.
> 53The hungry he satisfied with good food
> while sending the rich from the door empty-handed.

---

he shall become gre[at] upon the earth.... He will be called [son of the Gr]eat [God;] by his Name shall he be designated. He will be called the son of God. They will call him son of the Most High.... His kingdom will be an eternal kingdom, and he will be righteous in all his ways" (*The Son of God,* 4Q246).

t. Luke refers to Genesis 25:22 LXX, where Rebecca is in pain because her two rival sons strive within her as a sign of fraternal discord to come: "And the babes leaped within her." Luke seeks to reverse this by having the older cousin, John, defer in the womb to his younger cousin, the point being to conciliate and co-opt the rival John the Baptist sect.

u. Some few mss. read "Elisabeth," others have "she," implying Elisabeth, the last proper name mentioned. The content is certainly more appropriate to her than to Mary.

[54]He came to his servant Israel's aid, remembering
[55]his promises of mercy to our fathers,
to Abraham and to his posterity throughout the ages."[v]

[56]And Mariam stayed with her about three months, then returned to
her own dwelling. [57]Now the time arrived for her to bear, and she gave
birth to a son. [58]And her neighbors and relatives heard how Adonai magnified his mercy to her, and they rejoiced with her. [59]And it came about
that on the eighth day, they came to circumcise the child and were calling
it by its father's name, Zachariah. [60]And correcting them, his mother
said, "No! Instead, he shall be called John."[w] [61]And they said to her,
"There is no one among your relatives who is called by this name!" [62]And
they gestured to his father, to ask what he might wish him to be called.[x]
[63]And asking for a tablet, he wrote, saying, "John is his name."[y] And they
all marveled. [64]And his mouth was opened instantly and his tongue loosened and he spoke, eulogizing God.[z] [65]And awe came upon all their
neighbors, and in the whole mountain country of Judea all these things
were discussed; [66]and all who heard laid it away in their hearts, asking
themselves, "What then will this child grow up to be?" For the hand of
Adonai was plainly with him.

[67]And Zachariah, his father, was filled with Holy Spirit and prophesied, saying,

[68]"Blessed be Adonai, the God of Israel,
for he has intervened in our fortunes
and effected redemption for his people
[69]and lifted up a trumpet announcing salvation for us
in the royal house of David, his servant,
[70]as he promised through the mouths of his holy prophets an age ago:
[71]deliverance from our enemies
and out of the grasp of all those hating us
[72]to enact the mercy owed our fathers,
by no means to forget his holy covenant,

---

v. Based on 1 Sam. 1-10.

w. Because Zachariah was not the father?

x. This implies Zachariah had been rendered deaf as well as mute.

y. The name Yah-hannan, "gift of Yahve," implies John was begotten by the angel, not by his ostensible father Zachariah.

z. By acceding to the name assigned by the angel, Zachariah confesses faith in what he first doubted: the divine parentage of the child. Thus, his punishment is revoked.

[73]that oath he swore to Abraham, our father,
[74]to grant us fearless deliverance
from the grasp of our enemies,
to worship him [75]in holiness
and righteousness before him all our days;
[76]and like them, child, you will be called a prophet of Elyon,
for you will precede Adonai to prepare his ways,
[77]to impart to his people a knowledge of salvation
by forgiveness of their sins
[78]because of the reservoir of deep mercy of our God,
because of which a rising star from the apogee will visit us,[a]
[79]an epiphany to the ones sitting in darkness,
in the advancing shadow of death,
to guide our feet in a path that leads to peace."

[80]And the child grew and became strong in spirit,[b] and he was in the desert until the days he should show himself again to Israel.

2

[1]Now it came about that in those days, a decree was issued by Caesar
Augustus for the whole inhabited earth to be registered for taxation.
[2]Now this registration was the first, Quirinius ruling as governor of
Syria, [3]and all journeyed to be registered, each to his own city. [4]Accord-
ingly, Joseph went up from the Galilee out of a city, Nazareth, into Judea
to a city of David which is called Beth-Lehem, on account of his being
from the house and patrimony of David, [5]to be enrolled with Mariam,
the one betrothed to him, who was pregnant. [6]And it came about that
while they were there, her term was fulfilled [7]and she bore her firstborn
son, and she wrapped him in swaddling and laid him on the open ground
since there was no place for them in the hostel. [8]And there were shepherds living in the same country and keeping night-watch over their
flock. [9]And an angel of Adonai suddenly stood there before them, and the
radiance of Adonai dispelled the darkness around them and they shook
with terror. [10]And the angel said to them, "Do not fear! For behold, I announce to you great and joyful news which will come to all the people of
Israel, [11]because today a savior was born to you, who is the anointed of
Adonai, in David's city. [12]And this will be the sign for recognizing him:
you will find a baby swathed and lying on the open ground." [13]And suddenly the angel was joined by a horde of the heavenly army praising God

a. Suggested by Matt. 2:2?

b. 1 Sam. 2:26

and saying, [14]"Glory in the highest spheres to God, and on earth, peace
among the worthy of mankind!" [15]And it happened, when the angels
went away from them into the sky, the shepherds said to one another,
"So let us go into Beth-Lehem and see this thing that has taken place,
which the Lord announced to us." [16]And they came, wasting no time, and
found both Mariam and Joseph and the baby lying on the open ground.
[17]And seeing, they reported the message spoken to them concerning this
child. [18]And all who heard marveled concerning what was spoken to
them by the shepherds. [19]And Mariam kept all these words in her heart,
pondering; [20]and the shepherds returned, worshipping and praising God
for all they heard and saw, just as it was described to them.

[21]And with the eighth day the time to circumcise him arrived, and his
name was called Jesus, the one assigned by the angel before his conception in the womb. [22]And when the days till their purification according to
the Law of Moses arrived, they took him to Jerusalem to present him to
the Lord, [23]as it is prescribed in the Law of Adonai, "Every male opening
a womb shall be consecrated to Adonai," [24]and to offer a sacrifice according to that which is stipulated in the Law of Adonai, a pair of turtle
doves or two dove nestlings. [25]And behold, a man was in Jerusalem
whose name was Simeon, and this man was righteous and devout, looking forward to the comforting of Israel, and the Holy Spirit was upon
him; [26]and it had been related to him by the Holy Spirit that he was not to
see death before he should see the anointed of Adonai. [27]And he went, directed by the Spirit, into the temple just as the parents brought in the
child Jesus to perform for him what the custom of the Law prescribed,
[28]and he welcomed him in his arms and eulogized God and said,

[29]"Now give your slave leave to go in peace, Master, as you
promised,
[30]because my eyes saw your salvation,
[31]which you prepared in the face of all the peoples,
[32]a beacon of revelation for the gentiles
and a shining glory of your people Israel."

[33]And his father and mother were marveling at what was being spoken
about him. [34]And Simeon eulogized them and said to Mariam his mother,
"Behold, this one is set for the fall and rising again of many in Israel and
for a sign to be spoken against—[35]to say nothing of his being a sword that
will run your own soul through—in order that the deliberations of many
hearts may be exposed."

36 And there was Hanna, a prophetess, daughter of Phanuel of the tribe of Asher; this woman who had run a course of many days, having lived with a husband seven years from her virginity 37 and as a widow for eighty-four years, did not leave the temple, serving with fasts and petitionary prayers night and day. 38 And at the identical hour, coming upon the scene, she confessed to God and spoke about him to the underground of all those anticipating redemption in Jerusalem.

39 And when they completed all their obligations to the Law of Adonai, they returned into the Galilee to their city Nazareth. 40 And the child grew and became strong, filled with wisdom, and the divine charisma was upon him.[c]

41 And his parents journeyed annually to Jerusalem at the Feast of the Passover. 42 And when he reached twelve years, as they went up according to the custom of the feast 43 and completed the allotted days and were returning, Jesus the boy remained in Jerusalem and his parents did not know it. 44 But assuming he was somewhere in the caravan, they went a whole day's journey before starting to look for him among the relatives and acquaintances, 45 and failing to find him, they returned to Jerusalem searching for him. 46 And it came about after three days that they discovered him in the temple, sitting in the middle of the teachers, both hearing them and questioning them. 47 And all those hearing him were astonished at his intelligence and at his responses. 48 And seeing him, they were astonished, and his mother said to him, "Child, why did you treat us this way? Behold, your father, and I, too, have been frantic searching for you!" 49 And he said to them, "Didn't you know to come directly here? Where else would I be but seeing to my Father's business?" 50 And they did not understand what he said to them. 51 And he went down the mountain road with them and came to Nazareth and he was submissive to them. And his mother stored away all these matters in her heart. 52 And Jesus steadily advanced in wisdom as well as age and in the approval of God and of his contemporaries.[d]

3

1 Now in the fifteenth year of the hegemony of Tiberius Caesar, with Pontius Pilatus governor of Judea, Herod tetrarch of the Galilee, and Philip, his brother, tetrarch of the region of Iturea and Trachonitis, and Lysanias tetrarch of Abilene, 2 in the pontificate of Annas and Caiaphas, a revelation from God came upon John, the son of Zachariah, in the desert.

---

c. Ibid.

d. Ibid.

[3]And he came into all the vicinity of the Jordan, announcing a rite of baptism for forgiveness of sins. [4]Just as it is written in the scroll of the words
of Isaiah the prophet, "a voice of one crying out in the desert: Prepare the
way of Adonai, all of you; make his route straight; [5]every valley shall be
filled in and every mountain and hill shall be leveled and the crooked
roads shall be straightened and the rough roads repaved, [6]and all flesh
shall behold the salvation of God." [7]He said, therefore, to the crowds
making their way out to be baptized by him, "Spawn of snakes! Who
alerted you to flee the impending rage? [8]Therefore, produce fruits befitting repentance and don't start reassuring yourselves, 'For father, we
have Abraham!' For I tell you, God is fully capable of raising up sons to
Abraham from these stones. [9]Even now, the axe is poised at the root of
the tree; therefore, every tree failing to produce good fruit is being
chopped down and thrown into fire." [10]And the crowd asked him, saying, "Then do not keep us in suspense. What can we do?" [11]And answering, he said to them, "Anyone having two tunics, let him share one with
anyone who lacks. And anyone with food to share, let him do the same."
[12]Customs agents also came to be baptized and said to him, "Teacher,
what should we do?" [13]And he said to them, "Exact nothing more than
the stipulated amount." [14]Also those going off to war asked him, saying,
"And us, what shall we do?" And he replied, "Do not extort money by
false accusation and be content with your pay."

[15]Now with all the people of Israel anticipating the Christ and reasoning within their hearts whether John might perhaps be he, [16]John answered, saying to all, "As for me, I baptize you with water, but one
stronger than me comes, compared to whom I am not fit to untie the
thongs of his sandals; he shall baptize you in Holy Spirit and fire. [17]His
winnowing fan is in his hand to wipe clean his threshing floor and to
gather the wheat into his granary. But the chaff? He will incinerate it
with inextinguishable fire!" [18]Thus, with many and various preach-
ments, he evangelized the people of Israel. [19]But Herod, the tetrarch, being publicly denounced by him over Herodias, his brother's wife, and
over all the wicked things Herod did, [20]capped them all by shutting John
away in prison. [21]Now it came about that during the baptism of all the
people, Jesus, too, being baptized and praying, the sky was opened,
[22]and the Holy Spirit came down and rested upon him in bodily form as
a dove and a voice came out of the sky, saying, "You are my beloved son;
today I have begotten you!"[e]

---

e. Most manuscripts make the heavenly voice agree with Mark's version:

[23]And Jesus himself was embarking on his early thirties, the son, as was generally assumed, of Joseph, of Eli, [24]of Matthat, of Levi, of Melchi, of Jannaeus, of Joseph, [25]of Mattathiah, of Amos, of Nahum, of Esli, of Naggai, [26]of Mahath, of Matthiah, of Shemein, of Josech, of Jodah, [27]of John, of Rhesa, of Zerub-babel, of Salathiel, of Neri, [28]of Melchi, of Addai, of Kosam, of El-madam, of Er, [29]of Jesus, of Eli-ezer, of Jorim, of Matthat, of Levi, [30]of Simeon, of Judah, of Joseph, of Jonam, of Eliakim, [31]of Melea, of Menna, of Mattatha, of Nathan, of David, [32]of Jesse, of Obed, of Boaz, of Shela, of Naasson,[f] [33]of Amminadab, of Admin, of Arni, of Hezron, of Perez, of Judah, [34]of Jacob, of Isaac, of Abraham, of Terah, of Nahor, [35]of Serug, of Rehu, of Peleg, of Eber, of Shelah, [36]of Kenan, of Arphaxad, of Shem, of Noah, of Lamech, [37]of Methu-Shelah, of Enoch, of Jared, of Mahalaleel, of Cain, [38]of Enosh, of Seth, of Adam, of God.

4

[1]And Jesus, full of Holy Spirit, returned from the Jordan and was led by the Spirit in the desert [2]forty days being tested by the accuser, and he did not eat anything in those days; and when they were over, he hungered. [3]And the accuser said to him, "If you are God's son, tell this stone to become a roll." [4]And Jesus replied to him, "It is written, 'Mankind shall not live solely on bread, *but on everything that God has said*.'" [5]And leading him up, he displayed to him all the kingdoms of the inhabited earth in a point of time. [6]And the accuser said to him, "I will give you all this authority and their glory because it has been handed over to me, and I delegate it to whomever I wish. [7]So if you swear fealty to me, all will be yours!" [8]And answering, Jesus said to him, "It is written, 'You shall bow before Adonai your God and you shall serve him only.'" [9]He led him next to Jerusalem and stood him on the turret of the temple and said to him, "If you are God's son, throw yourself down from here; [10]for has it not been written, 'He will command his angels concerning you to keep you safe, [11]and they will catch you up lest you should so much as stub your toe on a stone?'" [12]And answering, Jesus said to him, "They say, 'You shall not presume on the good will of Adonai your God.'" [13]And having com-

"You are my son, in whom I was quite pleased." But with Adolph von Harnack, I take as authentic the reading of Codex Bezae and a few other manuscripts which have the voice quote the enthronement protocol of Pss. 2:7: "You are my son; today I have begotten you." Luke would have gotten this version from Q, while Matthew used, and tinkered with, Mark's version.

f. An old name surviving from the period of Israelite worship of Nehushtan, the serpent, or Babylonian Tiamat (2 Kings 18:4; 1 Sam. 11:1).

pleted his tests, the accuser left him alone until an opportune time.[g]

[14]And Jesus returned in the power of the Spirit to the Galilee, and a report of him circulated through the whole vicinity. [15]And he taught in their synagogues, lionized by all. [16]And he came into Nazareth where he had been brought up, and according to his usual practice, he went into the synagogue on the day of the Sabbath and he stood up to read. [17]And a scroll of the prophet Isaiah was handed to him, and having opened the roll, he located the passage where it is written,

> [18]"The Spirit of Adonai rests upon me
> because he anointed me to evangelize the poor;
> he has made me an apostle
> to herald release to the prisoners and sight to the blind,
> to liberate the oppressed,
> [19]to proclaim a year of amnesty decreed by Adonai."

[20]And having rolled up the scroll and handed it back to the attendant, he sat, and the eyes of all in the synagogue were riveted on him. [21]And he began his discourse to them. "Today this scripture has been fulfilled in your very ears!" [22]And all attested to him and marveled at the inspired words proceeding from his lips. And they said, "Isn't this man one of Joseph's sons?" [23]And he said to them, "No doubt, you will quote me this old saw, 'Physician, heal yourself!' meaning: 'What we heard happened in the village of Nahum, do here in your birthplace, too.'"[h] [24]And he said, "Amen: I tell you, no prophet is welcomed in his birthplace. [25]But to tell you the truth, many widows were in Israel in Elijah's days when the sky was locked tight for three years and six months, when a great famine covered all the earth, [26]and Elijah was sent to none of them but to Zarephath of Sidon, to a widow woman. [27]And many with skin disease were in Israel during Elisha's tenure, and not a single one of them was purified except for Naaman the Syrian." [28]And all in the synagogue were filled with anger at hearing these things, [29]and rising up, they swept him outside the city and led him captive to the precipice of the hill on which

---

g. Jesus resists the devil's blandishments by citing three texts from Deut. (8:3; 6:16; 6:13) referring to the trials in the wilderness (manna, Massa, idolatry), all of which the people of Israel failed, but which Jesus, embodying a new Israel, passes with flying colors.

h. Mark's likely source of Jesus' frosty reception by his own townsfolk is 1 Sam. 10:1-27. Luke has heavily rewritten it here.

their city was built, intending to push him over. [30]But he, passing through the thick of them, departed.[i]

[31]And he went down to the village of Nahum,[j] a city of the Galilee. And he was teaching them on the Sabbaths. [32]And they were astounded at his teaching, for his word carried authority. [33]And in the synagogue was a man having a spirit of an unclean demon, and he cried out with a loud voice, [34]saying, "What business is there between us and you, Jesus, Nazarene? Did you come to destroy us? I recognize you, who you are! The saint of God!"[k] [35]And Jesus rebuked him, saying, "Silence! And come out of him!" And casting him aside, the demon came out of him into their midst without injuring him. [36]And astonishment overcame all, and they spoke to one another, saying, "What does this portend? For he commands the unclean spirits with authority and power, and they come out!" [37]And a report of him went out into every place in the vicinity.

[38]And getting up from the synagogue, he came into the dwelling of Simon. Now the mother-in-law of Simon was being possessed by a great fever, and they ask him about her. [39]And standing over her, he rebuked the fever and it left her, and immediately, getting up, she fed them.[l] [40]When the sun was setting, everyone who had infirm relatives with various diseases brought them to him, and he cured each one with the laying on of hands. [41]And demons, too, came out from many, shouting and saying, "You are the Son of God!" And rebuking them, he forbade them to speak because they knew him to be the Christ.

[42]And with the day dawning, going forth, he journeyed into a desert place. And the crowds looked for him till they found him and detained him, begging him not to journey away from them. [43]And he said to them, "I must preach the news of the kingdom of God in the other cities, too, for this is what I was sent to do." [44]And he was preaching in the synagogues of Judea.[m]

---

i. A fossil of docetism in Luke's source material, the Ur-Lukas used by Marcion. Is it a fragment of an alternative Passion narrative?

j. The town's name is perhaps derived from Nah. 1:15a, the only passage outside of Isaiah to use the term ευαγγελιζομενου in a strictly religious sense: "Behold, upon the mountains, the feet of him that brings glad tidings and publishes peace!"

k. This cry comes directly from the defensive alarm of the Zarephath widow in 1 Kings 17:18: "What have you against me, O man of God? You have come to me to bring my sin to remembrance and to cause the death of my son!"

l. Here we see a reshuffling of elements from 1 Kings 17:8-16.

m. Already we see here Luke's tendency to shift the center of gravity from Galilee to Jerusalem, at least to Judea.

5

[1]Now it came about as the crowd mobbed him to hear the message of God, he was standing beside the Lake of Gennesaret [2]and spotted two boats standing by the lake, but the fishermen from them, having left, were washing their nets. [3]And embarking in one of the boats, which was Simon's, he asked him to put out a little from the shore. And sitting, he taught the crowds from the boat. [4]And when he stopped speaking, he said to Simon, "Put out into the deep and let down your net for a catch." [5]And answering, Simon said, "You're the boss, but we worked all night with nothing to show for it. But if you say so, I'll let down the nets." [6]And doing it, they enclosed a huge load of fish and their nets were splitting open. [7]And they gave their partners in the other ship the heads up to come and assist them. And they came and filled both ships so as to sink them. [8]Seeing this, Simon Peter fell down at Jesus' knees, saying, "Depart from me, for I am a sinful man, my Lord," [9]for amazement seized him and all those present with him at the catch of fish they took in—[10]likewise both Jacob and John, sons of Zebediah, who were partners with Simon. And Jesus said to Simon, "Do not fear. From now on you will be reeling in human beings." [11]And docking the ships on land, abandoning everything, they followed him.[n]

[12]And it came about that as he was in one of the cities, behold, there was a man covered with skin disease. And seeing Jesus, prostrating himself, he begged him, saying, "Lord, if only you will, you are able to purify me." [13]And stretching out his hand, he touched him, saying to him, "It is my wish: be purified!" And at once the skin disease left him.[o] [14]And he sternly warned him to tell no one, but "going away, show yourself to the priest and offer the things Moses commanded concerning your cleansing, for their certification." [15]But instead, the report of him circulated, and many crowds accompanied him to hear and to be cured of their infirmities. [16]But he was retreating into the desert and praying every chance he got.

[17]And it came about one day he was teaching—and Pharisees and canon lawyers had come from every village in the Galilee and Judea and Jerusalem—and a power from Adonai[p] was in him to cure. [18]And behold:

n. Luke has added to Mark's brief calling narrative, dramatic as it was, the Pythagorean story of the miraculous catch of fish. In John 21, it appears as a resurrection appearance anecdote.

o. This story is meant to recall the credential miracle vouchsafed by God to Moses whereby he could turn his hand leprous white (Exod. 4:6-7).

p. The healing archangel Raphael is the angelic "Power of Adonai."

men came carrying on a couch a man who was paralyzed, and they intended to carry him in and to lay him before him. [19]And not seeing how they might carry him in through the crowd, going up onto the roof, they lowered him with the couch through the tiles in the middle of the scene in front of Jesus. [20]And seeing their faith, he said, "Man, the sins you were being punished for are forgiven you." [21]And the scribes and the Pharisees began to dialogue, saying, "Who is this fellow who speaks blasphemies? Who can forgive sins except one, namely God?" [22]But aware of their dialogue, Jesus answered them, saying, "Why do you dialogue secretly? [23]What, after all, is easier to say, 'Your sins are forgiven you' or 'Get up and walk around'? Let's see, shall we? [24]To demonstrate to you that a man has authority to forgive sins on earth as God does in heaven"—here he spoke to the paralytic—"to you I say, get up, take your mat and go to your dwelling." [25]And getting up at once in the sight of all and taking the mat, he went away to his dwelling, worshipping God. [26]And ecstasy overtook them all, and they worshipped God and were filled with awe, saying, "We have beheld paradoxes today."[q]

[27]And after these events, he went out and spotted a customs agent named Levi sitting at the customs booth, and he said to him, "Follow me." [28]And dropping everything, getting up, he followed him.[r] [29]And Levi held a great feast in his honor at his house, and there was a large crowd of customs agents and their associates reclining. [30]And the Pharisees and their scribes murmured at his disciples, saying, "Why do you eat with the customs agents and the backsliders?" [31]And answering, Jesus said to them, "The healthy do not have need of a physician, but those who are in a bad way. [32]My mission was not to summon the righteous, but the sinful, to repentance."

[33]And they said to him, "The disciples of John fast frequently and offer prayers, and the same with those of the Pharisee sect, but yours eat and drink." [34]And Jesus explained to them, "Can you require the groomsmen to fast in the middle of the wedding feast? [35]But inevitably the days come when the feasting is over; to everything its proper season." [36]And he also told them a parable: "Look, no one is so stupid that he cuts a patch from a new garment to cover the hole in an old one. Otherwise, the new section will shrink with washing and tear away and the patch from the new will not agree with the old. [37]And no one fills old wine skins with

---

q. This seems to be based on an Elijah story in 2 Kings 1:2-17a, where King Ahaziah falls from his roof through the lattice and languishes in bed.

r. The story comes from Elijah's recruitment of Elisha in 1 Kings 19:19-21.

new wine; otherwise, when the new wine ferments, it will burst the taut skins; the wine will be spilled and the skins destroyed. [38]But one must put new wine into new skins. [39]And no one accustomed to vintage wine wants the new, for he thinks the old is good."[s]

6

[1]And it came about that on the Sabbath he was passing through the grainfields, and his disciples plucked and ate the ears of grain, rubbing with their hands. [2]And some of the Pharisees said, "Why do you do what is not legal on the Sabbaths?" [3]And replying to them, Jesus said, "Did you never read what David did when he hungered, and those with him? [4]How he entered into the house of God, and taking the loaves of show-bread, which is not legal for anyone but the priests to eat, he ate and gave to those who were with him?"

On the same day, noticing a man working on the Sabbath, he said to him, "Man, if you truly know what you are doing, blessed are you! But if you do not know, then cursed are you, and a Torah violator."[t] [5]And he said to them, "Man was given dominion over the Sabbath."

[6]And it came about on another Sabbath, he entered into the synagogue to teach and there was a man there and his right hand was withered. [7]And the scribes and the Pharisees watched him closely to see if he heals on the Sabbath, that they might find grounds to accuse him. [8]But he was aware of their designs, and he said to the man who had the dried-up hand, "Get up and stand where everyone can see you." And getting up, he stood there. [9]And Jesus said to them, "I ask you: is it legal on the Sabbath to do good deeds or to do evil? To save life or to kill it?" [10]And looking around on them, he said to him, "Extend your hand!" And he did, and his hand was restored to health. [11]But they were filled with mindless rage and exchanged ideas with one another as to what they might do to Jesus.[u]

[12]Now in these days he went out into the mountain to pray and he passed the night in prayer to God. [13]And when it became day, he summoned his disciples, selecting twelve of them,[v] whom he also named apostles: [14]Simon, whom he also named Peter, and Andreas, his brother; and Jacob and John; and Philip and Bar-Ptolemy; [15]and Matthew and

s. This last part has been tacked on by the Ecclesiastical Redactor to negate the Marcionite thrust of the preceding.

t. Codex Bezae adds this pericope. See Rom. 14:5-6.

u. The substance of this scene derives from the miracle of the Judean prophet of 1 Kings 13:1-7ff, LXX.

v. This is based on the choice of the twelve spies in Deut. 1:23.

Thomas; Jacob of Alphaeus and Simon, the one called the Zealot; and Judas of Jacob, 16and Judas the False One, who became a traitor. 17And coming down with them, he stood on a level place and faced a great crowd of his disciples and a huge mass of the people from all Judea and Jerusalem and the seaboard region of Tyre and Sidon, 18who came to hear him and to be cured of their diseases, and those in torment from unclean spirits were cured. 19And all the crowd tried to touch him, for a power[w] went forth from him and healed all.

20And raising his eyes to look at his disciples, he said,

"Blessed are the poor because the kingdom of God belongs to you.
21Blessed are those hungering now because you shall be filled.
Blessed are those weeping now because they will have the last laugh.
22Blessed are you when people hate you
and when they excommunicate you and insult you
and put your name on the public enemies list
on account of yours truly.
23Rejoice in that day and jump for joy, for don't you see your reward in heaven is great? Because their fathers treated the prophets according to the very same pattern.
24But woe to you plutocrats because you already enjoy your consolation.[x]
25Woe to you, those satiated now, because you will hunger[y]
Woe! Those laughing now will one day mourn and weep.
26Woe when everyone speaks admiringly of you, because their fathers treated the pseudo-prophets according to the very same pattern.

27But I tell you, my audience: love your enemies, treat them well who hate you, 28bless those who curse you, pray for those insulting you. 29To the one who slaps you on one side of the face, offer him the other, too; and as for the one taking your cloak, do not prevent him from taking your tunic, as well. 30To all who ask of you, give! And from the one taking your possessions? Do not demand them back. 31Just as you wish others would treat you, why, treat them the same way. 32And if you love those loving you, what thanks do you expect? For even the irreligious love those loving them. 33And if you do good for those who do good for you, what

w. Raphael, the archangel of healing.

x. Like the rich man in Luke 16.

y. Like Tantalus in Hades.

thanks do you expect? [34]Even the irreligious lend to their fellows to get
the same amount back again. [35]But love your enemies and do good and
lend expecting no return, and your reward will be great: you will be sons
of Elyon[z] because he is good to the ungrateful and wicked. [36]Be compassionate just as your Father is compassionate. [37]And do not judge, so you
may never be judged. And do not condemn, so you may never be condemned. Forgive others and they will forgive you. [38]Give, and others will
give to you; they will give you what you need as generously as the grain
merchant shakes the air out and compacts the gain before pouring it overflowing into your held-up shirt hem. This is how it works: others will use
the same scale of generosity you used for them in their time of need."

[39]And he told them a parable: "A blind man is not capable of guiding
a blind man. Won't the pair of them end up in the ditch? [40]In the nature of
the case, a disciple is not superior to the teacher so as to be able to correct
him. But once he finishes his study, every disciple will be the equal of his
teacher and then he might presume to offer a worthwhile dissenting opinion. [41]And why do you notice the sawdust speck in your brother's eye
while oblivious of the wooden beam in your own? [42]How dare you say to
your brother, 'Brother, here, let me just delicately remove that nasty
speck from your eye,' when you can't even see the board sticking out of
your own? Hypocrite! First remove the beam from your own eye and
then perhaps you will see well enough to remove the speck from your
brother's eye.

[43]"For there is no sound tree that produces bad fruit, nor again a bad
tree producing luscious fruit. [44]For each tree is recognized by its distinctive fruit; for no one gathers figs from thorns, nor does anyone pick a
grape from a thornbush. [45]The good person brings forth the good out of
the store of good in the heart and the wicked person brings forth the
wicked out of the deposit of wickedness. For he speaks out of what fills
the heart. [46]And why bother calling me 'Lord! Lord!' when you pay no
heed to what I say? [47]Everyone coming to me and hearing my words and
doing them, well, I will show you who he is like. [48]He is like a man building a house, who dug ever deeper and laid a foundation on bedrock. And
a flood coming, the river crashed against that house and was not able to
shake it because it was built well. [49]But the one hearing and not doing is
like a man having built a house on the ground without any foundation at
all, which a river crashed against and it promptly fell flat. And it was
completely demolished."

---

z. Like Elyon, the highest god, lesser deities being peevish.

7

[1]When he came to the end of all his sayings for the benefit of the people, he entered into the village of Nahum. [2]Now a certain slave belonging to a centurion and dear to him, being in a bad way, was near death. [3]And hearing about Jesus, he sent to him elders of the Jews, asking him to come and make his slave recover. [4]And approaching Jesus, they sought earnestly to persuade him, saying, "He deserves your granting him this favor, [5]for he loves our nation and even built our synagogue for us." [6]And Jesus agreed to go with them. And while he was not far from the house, the centurion sent friends with the message, "Lord, do not trouble yourself, for I do not deserve to have you come under the roof of my house. [7]Thus, I did not account myself worthy to come to you in person. Just pronounce an incantation and let my servant be cured. [8]For I, too, am myself a man set under authority and having soldiers under me, so I know how it works: I say to this one, 'Off with you!' and he is off at once, and to another, 'Come!' and he comes, and to my slave, 'Do this' and he does." [9]At hearing these words, Jesus marveled at him, and turning to face the crowd following him, he said, "I tell you, I found no such faith in Israel!" [10]And returning to the house, those sent found the slave in good health.

[11]And it came about on the next day he journeyed into a city called Nain, and his disciples journeyed with him, as well as a large crowd. [12]And as he neared the gate of the city, behold, there was being carried out a man who had died, the only-begotten son of his mother, a widow, and a large number of the city's populace crowded along behind. [13]And seeing her, the Lord felt compassion for her and said to her, "Do not cry." [14]And coming up to the bier, he touched it, the pallbearers having halted, and he said, "Young fellow, to you I say, get up!" [15]And the corpse sat up and began to speak. And Jesus gave him to his mother. [16]And all were overcome with awe and they worshipped God, saying, "A great prophet was raised among us!" and "God has intervened among his people Israel." [17]And word of this went out in all Judea and the whole vicinity concerning him.[a]

---

a. We seem to have in this story a cameo of gospel Christology, Jesus playing the role of God, the widow playing Mary, and the dead man representing Jesus himself, the only-begotten son raised from the dead. Notice that immediately after the young man is "raised," the crowd acclaim Jesus by saying "a great prophet has been raised" as if they were one and the same. The story as a whole is based on 1 Kings 17:8-24, esp. vv. 10, 23. In fact, Nain had no city gate and this embellishment comes from 1 Kings. The story belongs generally to a class of Hellenistic wonder tales in which a miracle-worker or expert physician stops a funeral to

[18]And John's disciples reported to him about all this. And summoning a certain pair of his disciples, John [19]sent word to the Lord saying,
"Are you the Coming One? Or must we look for another?" [20]And coming to him, the men said, "John the Baptist sent us to ask you, 'Are you
the Coming One? Or must we look for another?'" [21]In that very hour he
cured many of diseases and plagues and wicked spirits and to many blind
he gave sight. [22]And answering them, he said, "When you get back to
John, report what you saw and heard: blind folk see again, lame people
walk around, those with skin disease are purified, deaf ones hear, corpses
are raised, and poor people are evangelized. [23]And blessed is the one who
is not scandalized by me."[b]

[24]As John's messengers were departing, he began to speak to the
crowds about John: "What did you go out into the desert to look at? A
reed swept by the wind? [25]No? Then what did you go out to see? A man
dressed in effeminate clothing? Behold, those in rich clothing and appointed in luxury are in royal palaces. [26]So what did you go out to see? A
prophet? Yes, I tell you, and more than a prophet. [27]This is the one about
whom it is written, 'Behold, I send my angel right in front of you, who
will get the path ready in advance of you.' [28]I tell you, no mortal is greater
than John, but the least of the angels in the kingdom of God is greater

---

raise the dead or prevent premature burial. Such stories are told of Apollonius of Tyana, Asclepiades the physician, and others.

Thomas L. Brodie has analyzed other parallels in "Luke the Literary Interpreter: Luke-Acts as a Systematic Rewriting and Updating of the Elijah-Elisha Narrative in 1 and 2 Kings," Ph.D. diss., Pontifical University of Saint Thomas Aquinas, 1981. For instance, the prophetic word in 1 Kings 17 relieves the famine and the mere word of Jesus is enough to heal the centurion's servant/child at a distance in Luke 7. Elijah journeys to the Transjordan to meet a gentile in need, the widow of Zarephath, and Jesus travels to Capernaum, where he encounters a Roman centurion. Both gentiles are in dire need, the widow and her son near starvation, the centurion desperate to avert his son's/servant's imminent death. The miracle worker ascertains the facts and then utters a series of commands, upon which divine deliverance is secured. In one case we see the multiplication of food and in the other the return of health. Luke opens his second episode with "after this," the opening from 1 Kings, "And it happened afterward." When Elijah finds the widow's son dead, he cries out in anguish. This is unlike Jesus, who nevertheless tells the widow not to cry. Elijah prays for the boy's spirit to return, Jesus commands the boy to rise, and the dead rise, confirming their reanimation by crying out. It is recorded that the wonder-worker "gave him to his mother" (verbatim identical), upon which those present glorify the hero.

b. Poor John is left exactly where he started. He had already heard such reports.

than he."[c] [29]And all the people hearing this, including the customs agents, attested to it,[d] having been baptized with the baptism of John. [30]The Pharisees and the canon lawyers, on the other hand, spurned God's advice to them, not having been baptized by him. [31]"To what, then, may I compare the people of this race? And what are they like? [32]They are like children sitting idle in a marketplace taunting one another, the boys saying, 'We played the pipe for you, and you refused to dance!' And the girls reply, 'That's a boy's game! We mourned, and you would not weep with us because it's a girl's game.' [33]For John the Baptist's approach was not to eat bread or drink wine, and you say, 'He is a demoniac.' [34]But now a man has come eating and drinking, and you say, 'Nothing but a glutton and a lush, a crony of customs agents and backsliders.'" [35]And all her children attested wisdom.[e]

[36]And a certain member of the Pharisee sect asked him to eat with him, and entering in to the house of the Pharisee, he reclined at table. [37]And behold, a notorious woman of the city, aware of his dining in the house of the Pharisee, bringing an alabaster box of ointment [38]and standing behind by his feet and weeping, commenced to get his feet wet with her tears, and with the hair of her head she wiped them off and ardently kissed his feet and anointed them with the ointment. [39]But seeing this, the Pharisee who invited him reflected, "If this man were a genuine prophet, he would have known who and what sort of woman this is who is touching him because she is notorious." [40]And answering, Jesus said to him, "Simon, I have something to say to you." And he says, "Teacher, say on." [41]"Two people were in debt to a certain creditor. The one owed five hundred denarii and the other fifty. [42]Neither one of them having the wherewithal to repay, he forgave the debt of both. Which of them would you say will love him more?"[f] [43]Answering, Simon said, "I should think the one whom he forgave the greater sum." [44]He said to him, "You judged rightly." [44]And turning to the woman, he said to Simon, "Look at this woman. I entered your house; you did not pour water on my feet, but this woman wet my feet with her tears and dried them with her hair.

---

c. According to the Nasorean/Mandaean sect, John was the earthly proclaimer for Enosh-Uthra, Hibel-Ziwa, and Manda de'Haiye. This saying will have originated as a precaution against over-enthusiasm for John in that sect.

d. Literally "justified God," an idiom for confession or testimony. Cf. Pss. 51:4; Josh. 7:19; John 9:24.

e. Literally "wisdom is justified by all her children." Once again, the repentant and baptized testify to the wisdom of "God's advice" to be baptized (cf. v. 30).

f. Based on Matt. 19:23-35?

[45]You did not greet me with a kiss, but since I entered, this woman has not stopped ardently kissing my feet. [46]You did not anoint my head with oil, but she anointed my feet with oil. [47]For the sake of this, her sins, which are many, have been forgiven her because she loved much; but one who needs little forgiveness, as for your mere lapses of etiquette, loves little." [48]And he said to her, "The sins are forgiven you." [49]And those reclining with him began to whisper to one another, "Who does he think he is, presuming to forgive sins?" [50]But he said to the woman, "Your faith has saved you. Go in peace."[g]

8

[1]And afterward, it came about that he toured every city and village proclaiming and evangelizing the kingdom of God, and the twelve with him, [2]and certain women who were cured of wicked spirits and infirmities: Maria, called the hairdresser, from whom seven demons had exited, [3]and Joanna, wife of Chuza, Herod's steward, and Susanna, and many others, who provided for them out of their possessions.

[4]And when a great crowd had collected, people from each city traveling to hear him, he said by means of a parable: [5]"A sower went out to sow his seed. And it came about in the process of sowing, this seed fell beside the road and was trampled and the birds of the sky ate it up. [6]And other seed fell on the rock, and once grown, it withered on account of not having moisture. [7]And other seed fell into the thorns, and growing up with it, the thorns choked it. [8]And other seed fell into the good earth, and once grown, it gave fruit a hundredfold." Saying these things, he called out, "Whoever has ears to hear, let him hear!" [9]And his disciples questioned him as to what this parable might mean. [10]And he said, "It has been given you to know the mysteries of the kingdom of God, but to the rest it has

g. According to Brodie, "Luke the Literary Interpreter," the gospel writer created this rather cumbersome story from a pair of Elisha's miracles in 2 Kings 4, the never-failing cruse of oil and the raising of the Shunammite's son. The widow of Elisha's disciple is in financial debt, her creditors about to take her two children in payment. Adapted in Luke 7, her arrears have become a debt of sin. Where Elisha causes her oil to multiply, Jesus pronounces her forgiven. As for the oil, it has become the myrrh with which the woman anoints Jesus' feet. In Luke's version, Simon the Pharisee has invited the itinerant Jesus to dine, a reflection of the Shunammite's invitation to Elisha to eat with her whenever passing by. As a reward, Elisha grants her a son. Years later her son dies of sunstroke and she journeys to Elisha for help, falling at his feet just as the suppliant woman anoints the feet of Jesus. There is no need to posit Luke's creation of the whole anointing story, the core of which comes from Mark 14, but he substantially rewrote it in light of 2 Kings.

been given in parables so that seeing, they may not see and hearing, they may not understand." [11]And he says to them, "Now this is the parable. The seed is the message of God. [12]And the ones beside the road are those hearing, and then the accuser comes and takes the message from their heart, lest believing, they might be saved. [13]And those on the rock are those who, when they hear it, receive the message with joy, but these lack roots, believing for a while, and in time of trial they apostatize. [14]And the ones falling into the thorns, these are those hearing and going their way, then are choked by the worries and riches and pleasures of life and do not bear to maturity. [15]And the ones in the good earth, these are those who, hearing the message in a noble and good heart, hold onto it and bear fruit through patience.

[16]"Now no one, having lit a lamp, hides it in a vessel or puts it underneath the couch. But he puts it on a lamp stand so that those entering may see the light. [17]For a thing is not hidden unless it is later to be made manifest, nor is anything hidden away except in order for it to be known and to reappear. [18]So listen carefully! For the one who has, it will be given to him, and the one who has not, even what he seems to have will be taken from him."

[19]And his mother and his brothers came to see him, and they were unable to reach him because of the crowd. [20]And it was relayed to him: "Your mother and your brothers are standing outside wishing to see you." [21]And answering, he says to them, "My mother and my brothers! These are the ones hearing and obeying the commandment of God. By all means, show them in!"[h]

[22]And it came about one day that he and his disciples cast off in a boat, and he said to them, "Let us cross to the other side of the lake." And they put to sea. [23]And as they sailed, he fell asleep. And a storm of wind descended on the lake, and they were filling up and were in danger. [24]And approaching him, they got him up, saying, "Master! Master! We are perishing." And having been awakened, he rebuked the wind and the choppiness of the water and they ceased, and there was a calm. [25]Then he said to them, "Where is your faith?" Awestruck, they marveled, saying to one another: "Who, then, is this man, that he commands even the winds and the water and they obey him?"[i]

[26]And they sailed down to the region of the Gerasenes, which is opposite the Galilee. [27]And as he was stepping out onto the shore, a certain

h. Based on Exod. 18:1-22, rejecting Mark's ironic twist.

i. The basis for this story is Jon. 1:4-6; Pss. 107:23-29; *Odyssey* 10:1-69.

man from the city met him. He had demons and had not worn a garment
in a long time. He did not stay in a house, but among the tombs. [28]And
seeing Jesus, he cried out and fell prostrate in front of him and said in a
loud voice, "What business is there between me and you, Jesus, son of El
Elyon? I beg you, do not torture me!" [29]He said this because Jesus ordered the unclean spirit to come out of the man. For many were the times
it had fastened on him, and he was guarded, restrained with chains and
fetters, and ripping apart the restraints, he was driven by the demons
into the desert places. [30]And Jesus interrogated him: "What is your
name?" And he said to him, "Legion," for many demons entered into
him. [31]And they pleaded that he would not order them to depart into the
abyss. [32]Now there was a herd of many pigs feeding in the mountain.
And they pleaded with him to allow them to enter into those. And he allowed them. [33]And coming out from the man, the demons entered into
the pigs and stampeded the herd down the ledge into the lake where they
choked. [34]And those feeding them, seeing what happened, fled and reported in the city and in the fields. [35]And they came to see what had happened. And they came to Jesus and found the man from whom the demons had gone out sitting dressed and clear-headed at the feet of Jesus,
and they were afraid. [36]And those seeing how the demoniac was saved
recounted it to them. [37]And all the masses of the vicinity of the Gerasenes
asked him to depart from them, for they were stricken with terror. [38]So,
embarking in the boat, he returned. And the man from whom the demons had gone out pleaded with him that he might accompany him. But
he dismissed him, saying, [39]"Return to your home and recount what
God did to you." And he went out throughout the city proclaiming what
things Jesus did to him.[j]

[40]And when Jesus returned, the crowd welcomed him, for they were
all expecting him. [41]And behold, a man came whose name was Jairus,[k]
and this man was a ruler of the synagogue, and falling at the feet of Jesus,
he pled with him to enter his house, [42]because he had an only-begotten
daughter of about twelve years and she was dying. And as he went, the
crowd mobbed him. [43]And a woman, subject to a flow of blood for twelve
years and not able to be cured by anyone, [44]approaching behind, touched

j. The core of the story derives from *Odyssey* 9:101-565. The demoniac is based on Polyphemus the Cyclops; the pigs possessed by Legion come from Circe's transformation of Odysseus' soldiers into swine. See MacDonald, *Homeric Epics*; Pss. 107.

k. The name Jairus means "he will awaken," clearly a fictive character.

the fringe of his garment. And at once the flow of her blood stood still.
45 And Jesus said, "Who is it who touched me?" And all denying it, Peter
said, "Master, the crowds mob and jostle you." 46 But Jesus said, "Someone in particular touched me, for I sensed a power[l] going forth from me!"
47 And the woman, seeing she could not escape notice, came trembling and
fell down before him and declared before all the people why she had
touched him and how she was instantly cured. 48 And he told her,
"Daughter, your own faith has saved you. Go, relieved of your burden."

49 While he was still speaking, someone comes from the synagogue
ruler, saying, "Your daughter has died. Inconvenience the teacher no
more." 50 But Jesus, overhearing, answered him, "Do not fear. Just believe and she will be saved." 51 And coming into the house, he did not permit anyone to enter with him except Peter and John and Jacob and the father and mother of the girl. 52 And all were sobbing and lamenting her.
But he said, "Do not weep! She did not die but sleeps." 53 And they derided him, knowing full well that she died. 54 But he, grasping her hand,
called out, saying, "Girl, get up!" 55 And her spirit returned and she got
up at once. And he ordered that something should be given her to eat.[m]
56 And her parents were ecstatic, but he commanded them to tell no one
what really happened.[n]

9

1 And summoning the twelve, he gave them powers and authorities
over all the demons and to cure diseases, 2 and he sent them to proclaim
the kingdom of God and to cure. 3 And he said to them, "Take nothing on
the road, neither staff, nor pouch, nor bread, nor silver, nor two tunics
each.[o] 4 And whatever dwelling you enter, stay there and go out from
there. 5 And as many as may not welcome you, as you leave that city,
shake off the dust from under your feet as a reproach to them." 6 And going forth, they went throughout the villages evangelizing and healing everywhere. 7 And Herod, the tetrarch, heard all the things occurring and
was bemused because it was said by some that John was raised from the
dead 8 and by some that Elijah appeared, but by others that a certain
prophet of the ancients rose again. 9 But Herod said, "John I decapitated,

l. Raphael, the angel of healing.

m. This was to assure them she was no ghost.

n. The two anecdotes of Jairus's daughter and the bleeding woman are interdependent parts of a single story, a retelling of Elisha and the Shunammite woman (2 Kings 4).

o. 2 Kings 4:29; 5:22

but who is this about whom I hear such reports?" And he made efforts to see him.

[10]And once they returned, the apostles recounted to him what they did. And taking them along, he left privately for a city called Beth-Saida. [11]But the crowds knew it and followed him, and welcoming them, he spoke about the kingdom of God, and he cured those having need of healing. [12]But the day began to decline and the twelve came to him and said, "Dismiss the crowd, that they may go to the surrounding villages and fields to find lodging and provisions because here we are in a desert place." [13]And he said to them, "You give them something to eat!" And they said, "We have no more than five loaves and two fish unless we are to go and buy food for all these people."[p] [14]For there were about five thousand men. And he said to his disciples, "Have them recline in groups of about fifty each." [15]And they did so, and they had all recline. [16]And taking the five loaves and two fish, looking up to the sky, he blessed and broke them and gave them to the disciples to set before the crowd. [17]And they all ate and were satisfied, [43]and twelve baskets of fragments were taken to them.[q]

[18]And it came about that as he was praying silently, the disciples were with him and he questioned them, saying, "Who do people think me to be?" [19]And they answered and said, "John the Baptist, but others Elijah, and others that a certain prophet of the ancients rose up again." [20]And he said to them, "But what about you? Who do you think me to be?" And Peter, answering, said, "You are the Christ of God." [21]And he warned them that they must tell this to no one, [22]saying that a man has to suffer many indignities and be excommunicated by the elders and archpriests and scribes and be executed and be raised on the third day. [23]And he said to all, "If anyone wants to come after me, let him repudiate himself and pick up his cross daily and let him follow me. [24]For whoever tries to save his life will lose it, but whoever will sacrifice his life for my sake, he will save it. [25]For what profit would a person make if he managed to acquire the whole world, only to be fined his own life or to suffer loss? [26]I say this because whoever will not stand up for me and my words, neither will the one like a son of man stand with him when he comes in his radiance and that of the Father and of the holy angels. [27]And I tell you truly:

p. We catch an echo of Moses's weariness at the people's complaints in Num. 11:13-15.

q. The basis for the miraculous feeding stories is Elisha's multiplication of twenty barley loaves for a hundred men in 2 Kings 4:42-44.

there are some of those standing here who will certainly not taste of death
before they see the kingdom of God."
[28]And it happened that about eight days after saying these things,
taking along Peter and John and Jacob, he went up into the mountain to
pray. [29]And as he prayed, the appearance of his face became different and
his clothing sparkling white. [30]And behold, two men spoke with him,
who were Moses and Elijah, [31]who appearing in glory spoke of his exodus, which he was about to accomplish in Jerusalem. [32]But Peter and
those with him had been overcome with sleep, and coming awake with a
jolt, they saw his glory and the two men standing with him. [33]And it happened that when they left him, Peter said to Jesus, "Master, it is good for
us to be here! And let us make three tents: one for you and one for Moses
and one for Elijah," not knowing what he said. [34]As he said these things,
a cloud appeared, overshadowing them, and they feared as they ascended
into the cloud. [35]And a voice came out of the cloud, saying, "This one is
my son, the chosen. Hear him!" [36]And when the voice came, Jesus was
found alone. And they were silent and reported to no one in those days
any of the things they had seen.[r]
[37]And it came about that on the following day as they were descending the mountain, a great crowd met him. [38]And behold, a man from the
crowd called out, saying, "Teacher, I beg you to look at my son because
he is my only-begotten [39]and, as you can see, a spirit takes him and yells
out abruptly and throws him down foaming and leaves him only with difficulty, bruising him in the process. [40]And I begged your disciples that
they might cast it out, but they were not up to the task."[s] [41]And answering them he says, "O unbelieving and perverted race! How long till I am
free of you? How long must I endure you? Bring your son here." [42]And
while he was still approaching him, the demon ripped his flesh and hurled
him violently. And Jesus rebuked the unclean spirit and cured the boy
and restored him to his father. [43]And all were astonished at the greatness
of God. And even while they marveled at all that he did, he said to his disciples, [44]"Embed these words in your ears: for a man is about to be betrayed into the clutches of men." [45]But they did not understand this say-

r. See Exod. 24; 34:29. The glowing apparition of Jesus is obviously derived from that of Moses in Exod. 34:29.

s. Just as Elisha succeeded where Gehazi failed (2 Kings 4:32-35) simply because Gehazi was not Elisha, so here Jesus is irreplaceable because he is the divine hero of the story.

ing, and it had been veiled from them so they should not perceive it, and they were afraid to learn what it meant.

46And they entered into debate over which of them might rank highest. 47And Jesus, aware of their whispered debate, took a child and stood him beside him, 48and he said to them, "Whoever welcomes one of these children on account of my name welcomes me, and whoever welcomes me, welcomes not me but the one who commissioned me. For the lowliest one among you all, this one is great."

49And answering, John said, "Master, we caught someone casting out demons using your name, so we told him that since he was not one of our group, he must cease and desist." 50But Jesus said to him, "Why on earth did you forbid him? For anyone who is not actually opposing you is on your side."[t]

51And it came about that as the days to his assumption into the sky were counting down,[u] he set an unswerving course for Jerusalem, 52and he sent messengers in advance of him. And on their journey, they entered into a village of Samaritans to prepare for his arrival. 53And they withdrew their welcome once they heard his destination was Jerusalem. 54And the disciples Jacob and John, seeing this, said, "Lord, do you want us to call down fire from the sky to destroy them *just as Elijah dealt with Samaritans?*"[v] 55But turning, he rebuked them, *saying, "You don't realize which spirit you belong to! For a man's task is to save human lives, not to destroy them.*" 56And they journeyed into another village.

57And as he traveled along the road, one said to him, "I will follow you wherever you may go!"[w] 58And Jesus said to him, "Think twice! The foxes have holes and the birds of the sky nests, but a man has no permanent abode." 59And he said to another, "Follow me!" But he said, "Gladly, Lord! First just let me see to my father's burial." 60But he said to him, "Let the dead bury themselves! You go and announce the kingdom of God." 61And yet another said, "I will follow you, Lord, if you will just let me say good-bye to the ones back home." 62But Jesus said to him, "No one pressing his hand on the plow and looking at what is behind is fit for the kingdom of God."[x]

---

t. Written directly from Num. 11:24-30.

u. See 2 Kings 2:1.

v. 2 Kings 1:9-14

w. Ruth 1:16

x. 1 Kings 19:19-21; 2 Tim. 2:15

10

[1]Now after these things, the Lord appointed seventy-*two* others, and he sent them in pairs in advance into every city and place where he was about to come[y] [2]And he said to them, "Indeed, there is much to be harvested,[z] but so few workers are available. So prevail upon the harvest master to dispatch workers into his fields. [3]Go! Behold, I send you like lambs into a ravening wolf pack.[a] [4]Do not bring a change purse or a wallet or sandals [5]and do not stop to chat with anyone you meet on the road.[b] [5]And whatever dwelling you enter, first say, 'Peace to this house.' [6]And if a peaceful man is there, your blessing of peace shall protect it; otherwise, it shall cover you alone. [7]And remain in the same house, eating and drinking with them, for the worker deserves his pay. Do not flit from house to house. [8]And whatever city you may enter and they welcome you, eat the things set before you, [9]and cure the sick in it and tell them, 'The kingdom of God is closer than you might think.' [10]And whatever city you enter and they do not welcome you, go out into its streets and say, [11]'Even the dust of your city sticking to our feet we shake off at you.[c] Nevertheless, we warn you. The kingdom of God has drawn dangerously near.' [12]I tell you, It will go easier on that day for Sodom than for such a city. [13]Woe to you, Chorazin! Woe to you, Beth-Saida! Because if the powerful deeds performed in you had been performed in Tyre and Sidon, they would have repented long ago, sitting in sackcloth and ashes. [14]Even so, it will go easier for Tyre and Sidon in the Judgment than for you! [15]And you, village of Nahum! Will you be lifted as high as heaven, as you boasted? No, like the king of Babylon, you shall descend to Hades!

---

y. Cf. Matt. 10:23. The whole section is a missionary manifesto, symbolically referring to the mission to gentile nations. It was thought there were some seventy or seventy-two nations in the world, hence the two manuscript readings. The mission had to be carried out before Jesus could return. In the central section (10:1-18:14), Luke depicts Jesus as a prophet like Moses, promulgating a "second law" just as Moses offered in Deuteronomy. See C. F. Evans, "The Central Section of St. Luke's Gospel," in D. E. Nineham, ed., *Studies in the Gospels: Essays in Memory of R. H. Lightfoot* (Oxford: Blackwell, 1955), 37-53. Luke organized traditional material and created some of his own based on suggestions in the scripture he was emulating. The Lukan deutero-Deuteronomy covers 10:1-18:14.

z. Deut. 1:25

a. Deut. 1:22-23

b. 2 Kings 4:29

c. Deut. 2:5

16"Whoever hears you hears me, and whoever rejects you rejects me, and
whoever rejects me rejects him who sent me."[d]

17And the seventy-*two* returned with joy, saying, "Lord, even the demons acquiesce to us in your name!" 18And he said to them, "I watched
the adversary plunge like lightning from the sky. 19Behold, I have given
you the authority to walk over snakes and scorpions and over all the
powers of the enemy and nothing shall harm you at all.[e] 20Nevertheless,
do not rejoice in this, the fact that the spirits yield to you, but that your
names have been registered in the heavens."

21In that very hour, he felt rapture in the Holy Spirit and said, "I applaud you, Father, Lord of sky and earth, because you concealed these
things from the sages and the intellectuals, revealing them instead to infants. Yes, Father, because it seemed good sport to you.[f] 22All things were
bestowed on me by my Father, and no one knows *who the Son is except
for the Father, nor* who the Father is, except for the Son—and him to
whom the Son shall deign to reveal him."[g] 23And turning privately to the
disciples, he said, "Blessed the eyes that see what you see. 24For I tell you
that many prophets and kings wished to see what you see and did not see
and to hear what you hear and did not hear!"[h]

25And behold, a certain canon lawyer stood up with a question to
feel him out, saying, "Teacher, what should I do to inherit eternal life?"
26He said to him, "What is written in the Law? What is your reading of
it?" 27And answering, he said, "You shall love Adonai from your whole
heart and with your whole soul and with all your strength and with all
your mind and your neighbor as yourself." 28And he said to him, "You
answered correctly. Do this and you will live."[i]

29But wishing to make himself look good, he said to Jesus, "And who

---

d. Here we see an attempt to have the apostles and bishops ride on the coat-tails of Jesus; Luke 10:4-16 also corresponds to Deut. 2:1-3:22.

e. A reflection of Zoroastrianism. The "creeping things," as the Bible calls them, were considered the anti-creation of Ahriman and his demonic henchmen. Thus, they represent demonic Powers here.

f. Deut. 3:23-4:40

g. Cf. Akhenaten's *Hymn to the Sun*: "O Aten, no man knoweth thee, save for thy son Akhenaten." With Harnack and Julius Wellhausen, I take the italicized clause to be a later interpolation.

h. Deut. 4:3, 9, 34, 36

i. This is the gist of Deut. 5-6; Lev. 19:18. In rewriting Mark 12:28-34, which listed some of the ten commandments, albeit loosely, Luke's version closes with, "Do this and you will live," from Lev. 18:5.

exactly counts as my neighbor?" 30Taking him up on the question, Jesus
said to him, "This man was going down from Jerusalem to Jericho and
fell prey to thieves, who both stripping him naked and pummeling him
with blows, fled, abandoning him half-dead. 31It just so happened that a
certain priest was going down the same road and, seeing him, crossed the
street to avoid him. 32In the same way, a Levite, too, coming upon the
place, crossed the street to avoid him. 33And a certain Samaritan on a
journey came upon him and was filled with compassion as soon as he saw
him. 34Approaching him, he bandaged his wounds, treating them with oil
and wine. And hoisting him onto his own animal, he brought him to an
inn and took care of him. 35And in the morning, taking out two denarii,
he gave them to the innkeeper and said, 'Take care of him, and whatever
you may spend additionally, I will pay you when I return.' 36Which of
these three seems to you to have become a neighbor to the man who fell
prey to the robbers?" 37And he said, "The one showing mercy." And Jesus said to him, "You go and do likewise."[j]

38And as they journeyed, he entered into a certain village and a certain woman named Martha[k] welcomed him into the house. 39And this
woman had a sister named Mariam who, sitting beside the Lord at his
feet, was absorbed in his teaching. 40But Martha was preoccupied with
much serving and, standing over him, she said, "Lord, doesn't it make
any difference to you that my sister has left all the work to me? So tell her
to help me!" 41And answering, the Lord said to her, "Martha, Martha,
calm down! You are anxious and agitated over many things, 42but few
things are needed—really only one. Mariam chose the good portion for
herself, and I for one refuse to take it away from her."[l]

11

1And it came about as he was in a certain place praying, as he finished, a certain one of his disciples said to him, "Lord, teach us a prayer,
just as John also taught his disciples." 2And he said to them, "When you
pray, say this:

> Father,
> may your name[m] be revered;

---

j. Countering Deut. 7, which forbids mercy to foreigners.

k. The name *Martha* means "lady of the house," signifying a symbolic character.

l. Deut. 8:1-3

m. Yahve

may your kingdom come.
[3]Give us each day tomorrow's bread,
[4]and forgive us our sins,
for we ourselves also forgive everyone indebted to us,
and lead us not into temptation."

[5]And he said to them, "Suppose one of you has a friend who comes to him at midnight saying, 'Friend, lend me three loaves, [6]since a friend of mine arrived at my house from a long journey and I have nothing to set before him!' [7]Would you answer him from inside, 'Don't bother me now that the door has been shut and my children are around me in the bed and I can't get up to get you anything'? [8]I tell you, even if you won't get up and give him what he asks simply because he is your friend, still on account of his being such a nuisance you will get up and give him as many loaves as he needs just to get rid of him. [9]And I tell you, ask and it will be given you. Look for it and you will find it. Keep knocking and the door will be opened to you. [10]For it is only the one who asks who receives and only the seeker who finds, and it is only to the one who knocks that the door opens. [11]And which of you fathers, if his son asks him for a fish, will hand him a snake instead? [12]Or also what sort of a father, if his son asks for an egg, would hand him a scorpion? [13]And if you, being sinners, know to give good gifts to your children, how much more can you depend on your Father to give a Holy Spirit from heaven to those who ask him?"[n]

[14]And he was casting out a demon and it was mute. And it happened that as the demon was leaving, the mute man spoke. And the crowds marveled. [15]But some of them said, "It is plain magic! By enlisting Baal-Zebul, ruler of the demons, he casts out demons."[o] [16]And others challenged him, daring him to produce a sign from heaven. [17]But knowing what was going through their minds, he said to them, "Every kingdom divided against itself is laid waste and houses will collapse against one another. [18]And if the accuser is divided against himself, how will his kingdom remain standing? I say this because you say I cast out demons by means of Baal-Zebul. [19]But if I cast out demons with Baal-Zebul's aid, by what authority do your protégées cast them out? Ask them what they think of your logic. [20]But suppose it is by means of a finger of God that I

---

n. Deut. 8:4-20 deals with fatherly provision and tests of fortitude.

o. Beel-zebul denotes "lord of the house" (implying "of the world"), a powerful patron of exorcists, while Beel-zebub means "lord of the flies," in reference to an oracle (2 Kings 1:2) since priests heard a sound like buzzing when the voice of spirits told the desired fortune. Jesus' reply in v. 21 seems to come from Isa. 49:24.

cast out demons?[p] In that case, the kingdom of God has overtaken you!
[21]When the strong man, well armed, guards his palace, his possessions
are safe. [22]But when someone stronger overtakes him and prevails over
him, he relieves him of his armor, on which he had relied, and scatters his
weapons. [23]Whoever is not with me is against me, and whoever does not
join me in the harvest scatters seed instead. [24]When the unclean spirit departs from a man, he wanders through arid places seeking relief, and failing to find it, he says, "Why not return to my dwelling that I left?" [25]Once
he arrives, he finds it tidied up and renovated. [26]Then he goes and rounds
up seven other spirits even more wicked than himself, and entering, he
makes himself at home. And the last state of that man becomes worse
than the first!"[q]

[27]And it happened that as he said these things, a certain woman from
the crowd raised her voice and said to him, "Blessed the womb that bore
you and the breasts that nursed you!" [28]But he said, "Rather, blessed the
ones who hear the command of God and keep it."

[29]And as the crowds mobbed him, he began to speak. "This race is a
wicked race! It wants to see a sign, and a sign will not be given to it except
for the example of Jonah. [30]For in just the same way Jonah became a sign
to the Ninevites by preaching repentance, so will a man be to this race
also. [31]The Queen of Sheba will rise from the dust on Judgment Day
along with the men of this race and will be a living rebuke to them because she came from the farthest regions of the earth to hear the wisdom
of Solomon, and behold, something greater than Solomon is available
here. [32]Ninevite men will rise up in the Judgment alongside this race as a
living rebuke because they repented at the preaching of Jonah, and behold, something greater than Jonah is active here.

[33]"No one having lit a lamp hides it, nor places it under a bushel basket, but on the lamp stand so whoever enters may see the light. [34]Well, the
lamp of the body is your eye; when your eye is focused, your whole body
is seen clearly. When it is misbehaving, you can't see your hand in front of
your face. [35]So watch out that you do not imperceptibly lose your focus!

---

p. Compressed into these verses is an unmistakable midrash on the Exodus story of the contest between Moses and Pharaoh's magicians. Initially able to match Moses feat for feat, the magicians prove incapable of copying the miracle of the gnats. They therefore warn Pharaoh to give in, saying "this is the finger of God" and not mere sorcery like theirs (Exod. 8:19).

q. Verses 14-26 are parallel to Deut. 9:1-10:11. The Sons of Anak (Rephaim, Nephilim) were later associated with the fallen sons of God, thus linked here with demons. Note also the Deuteronomic reference to "the finger of God."

36Thus, when you are wholly transparent, with nothing to hide, you will
be a shining example like the lamp that shines its light on others."[r]

37Now as he was out speaking, a Pharisee asks him to dine with him.
And entering, he reclined at table. 38But the Pharisee was shocked to see
that he did not baptize his hands before the dinner. 39But the Lord said to
him, "Now you of the Pharisee sect purify the exterior of the cup and of
the dish, but your own interior is full of robbery and wickedness! 40Fools!
Didn't the one who made the outside make the inside, too? 41At any rate,
give away your possessions, the desire for which fills your hearts, and behold, the whole thing is purified for you, inside and out.

42"But woe to you, the Pharisees, because you meticulously tithe
mint and rue and every single herb and ignore the judgment and the love
of God. But you had the obligation to tend to these things and not to neglect those. 43Woe to you Pharisees! You love to be shown the chief seats
in the synagogues and the deferential greetings in the market places.
44Woe to you because you are like the unmarked graves which people
walk right over, never knowing." 45And one of the canon lawyers, answering, said to him, "Teacher, saying such things, you insult us, too!"
46And he said, "If the shoe fits, wear it! You burden people with unwieldy
loads which you yourselves make not the slightest effort to budge. 47Woe
to you because you construct monuments for the prophets, and it was
your fathers who killed them in the first place! 48You testify against yourselves. You are endorsing your fathers' deeds: they killed, you build!
49Therefore, divine Wisdom said, 'I will send to them prophets and apostles, and some of them they will kill and persecute, 50so that this race will
answer for the blood of all the prophets spilled ever since the world was
laid on its foundations:[s] 51from the blood of Abel to the blood of Zechariah, destroyed between the altar and the dwelling of God in the ark.'
Yes, I tell you, this race will answer for it. 52Woe to you, canon lawyers,
because you absconded with the key of knowledge; you did not enter
yourselves and you prevented those on their way in!"

53And as he got up and left, the scribes and the Pharisees became livid
with rage and began a campaign to bait him with all kinds of trick questions to embarrass him publicly.

12

1As a crowd of many thousands gathered to the point of trampling

r. Verses 27-36 parallel the themes of impartiality and clear vision in Deut. 10:12-11:32.

s. The vocabulary is similar to Deut. 12:16, though on a different subject.

one another, he began speaking to his disciples first. "Be on your guard against the insidious leaven of the Pharisees, in other words, hypocrisy. [2]And there is nothing covered up which will not be revealed, nor hidden that will not sooner or later be made known. [3]Therefore, whatever you said under cover of darkness will be heard in the light of day and whatever you whispered in someone's ear in the private rooms will be proclaimed from the roof tops. [4]And my friends, I tell you, you have nothing to fear from those who kill the body but can do nothing more than that. [5]No, I will warn you whom to fear. Fear the one who, after killing, has authority to throw you into the Valley of Hinnom. Yes, I tell you, fear this one!

[6]"Are not five sparrows sold for two assaria? And not one of them escapes God's attention. [7]But even each hair on your head has its number. Do not fear, for you outweigh many sparrows in importance!

[8]"But I tell you, whoever confesses allegiance to me in the presence of others, one like a son of man will acknowledge him in the presence of the angels of God. [9]And whoever repudiates me in the presence of others will himself be repudiated in the presence of the angels of God. [10]And everyone who shall say a thing against a human being, it will be forgiven him, but the one who blasphemes against the Divine Spirit will not be forgiven. [11]And when they haul you in before synagogues and rulers and authorities, do not worry about how or what you may speak by way of apologia or what you should say. [12]For the Holy Spirit will teach you in that very hour the things you ought to say."[t]

[13]And someone out of the crowd said to him, "Teacher, order my brother to divide the inheritance with me!" [14]But he said to him, "Man, who made me the executor?"[u] [15]And he said to him, "Watch out! Be on your guard against every kind of covetousness because no one's life is valued at the number of possessions he has."

[16]And he told them a parable, saying, "The land of a certain rich man bore well. [17]And he deliberated, reflecting, 'What am I to do? I lack sufficient space to store my harvest.' [18]And he concluded, 'I know! I will do this: I will pull down my barns and I will build bigger ones and there I will store all my wheat and my goods. [19]And then I will congratulate myself, My boy, you have many goods laid up for many years to come. So relax: eat, drink, be merry!' And he did so. [20]But God said to him, 'Fool! This

t. Cf. John 16:7, 13; Luke 11:27-12:12, corresponding to the discussion of clean and unclean food in Deut. 12:1-16.

u. Based on Exod. 2:14a, "Who made you a prince and a judge over us?"

very night they clamor for your soul.[v] Then all this which you so carefully
prepared—who will inherit it?' [21]You see here the fate of anyone who
sees to his own treasure but is not rich where God is concerned."[w]

[22]And he said to his disciples, "That is why I tell you, do not be preoccupied with the necessities of life: what you will find to eat, or about
your body, what you will find to wear. [23]For one's life is more than mere
survival and the body more than a mannequin. [24]Think of the ravens,
how they neither plant crops nor harvest them. They do not maintain
warehouses or barns and yet God sees to it they are fed. How far superior you are to birds! [25]And who here has the ability to add a cubit to his
height by worrying about it? [26]If you cannot do even that, why bother
worrying about the rest? [27]Think of the lilies, how they waste no time at
spindle or loom but, I assure you, not even Solomon in all his finery was
adorned like one of them. [28]And if this is the way God decks out the
common grass of the field, which is here today and tomorrow heats the
oven, how much more care will he take for you! Scant is your faith!
[29]And do not busy yourselves with obtaining food and drink—and do
not sweat over it. [30]For these are the matters all the heathen nations pursue; but your Father knows your situation, that you need these things.
[31]Instead, seek admittance to his kingdom and all these things will be
provided you. [32]Do not fear, little sheepfold, because your Father was
quite pleased to give you the kingdom. [33]Sell your possessions and give
alms. Furnish yourselves purses that do not wear out, an inexhaustible
treasure in the heavens where no burglar comes near it, nor do moths devour your heavenly robes. [34]For wherever your treasure is located, your
heart will be there, too.[x]

[35]"Be dressed and ready, lamps burning, [36]like men expecting their
lord when he returns from the wedding reception, so whenever he appears they may be ready to open immediately to his knock. [37]Good for
those slaves whom the lord will find waiting when he arrives.[y] Amen: I
say to you, he will don an apron, tell them to recline at table, and he will
wait on them one by one.[z] [38]And if he arrives in the second watch or the
third and finds them so, good for them!

[39]"But be sure of this. If the master of the house knew what hour to

---

v. This begs the question of *who* exactly clamors for his soul. See Thomas 88.

w. Ecclesiastes/Qoheleth 6:2

x. Verses 13-34 correspond to Deut. 12:17-32.

y. Is this based on Matt. 25:1-12?

z. Cf. John 13:4-5; Luke 22:27

expect the thief, he would have prevented his digging through the walls of his house. [40]You, too, be prepared because a man will come at some hour you do not expect." [41]And Peter said, "Lord, are you directing this parable just to us or to the reader, too?" [42]And the Lord said, "What do you think? Who fits the description of the faithful, prudent steward whom the lord will appoint over his household staff to give them their meals at the proper time?[a] [43]That slave will be very glad when his lord arrives and finds him carrying out his duties. [44]Truly I tell you, he will put him in charge of all his possessions. [45]But suppose that slave says to himself, 'My lord delays his arrival,' and starts to beat the servant boys and serving maids and starts to eat and drink and to get drunk? [46]The lord of that slave will appear unexpectedly one day, undetected while the slave is in a stupor, and he will have him drawn and quartered and will assign him his place among the irresponsible. [47]That slave who knew his lord's will and who failed to prepare for his return or to do his will, will receive many lashes. [48]But the one who didn't know but did things worthy of a flogging will be beaten with only a few lashes. But from everyone to whom much was given, much shall be expected. And whoever was entrusted with much, of him they will ask much more.

[49]"I came to hurl fire onto the earth, and how I wish it were already ignited! [50]And I have a baptism to be baptized with, and how I dread it till it is over![b] [51]Surely you don't think my mission was to give peace to the earth?[c] Ha! I tell you, division! [52]For from now on, there will be five at odds in the same house, three versus two and two versus three. [53]Father will be divided against son and son against father, mother versus daughter and daughter against the mother, mother-in-law against her daughter-in-law and daughter-in-law against the mother-in-law."[d]

[54]And he said also to the crowds, "When you see a cloud rising over the west, at once you say, 'A storm is coming,' and so it happens. [55]And when a south wind is blowing, you say, 'It will be hot,' and so it happens. [56]Hypocrites! You know well enough how to interpret the earth and the sky, but how is it you do not know what to make of this present time? [57]Why do you not even judge for yourselves the just verdict? [58]For as you go with your accuser to a ruler, while still on the road, take pains to settle with him lest he haul you before the judge and the judge will hand you

a. Cf. John 21:15-17

b. Based on Mark 10:38?

c. Cf. Luke 2:14

d. Micah 7:6; Luke 12:35-53, which corresponds to Deut. 13:1-11.

over to the bailiff and the bailiff will throw you into prison. [59]I tell you, you will never come out of there until you pay the very last lepton."

13

[1]On the same occasion, some were present reporting to him about the Galileans whose blood Pilatus mixed with that of their sacrifices. [2]And answering, he said to them, "Do you deem these Galileans worse sinners than the common run of Galileans because they have suffered these things? [3]No, I tell you, but unless you change your minds, all of you will be destroyed the same way![e] [4]Or those eighteen on whom the tower in Siloam collapsed, crushing them—do you consider them debtors worse than the rest of the Jerusalemites? [5]No, I tell you, but unless you change your way of thinking, you too will all be destroyed the same way!"[f]

[6]And to reinforce the point, he told this parable: "Once there was a man who had a fig tree planted in his vineyard, and he came to look for fruit on it and didn't find any. [7]And he said to the vine dresser, 'Look here, for three years now I have looked for fruit on this fig tree and I never find any. Chop it down! Why even let it take up the space?' [8]But answering, he says to him, 'Lord, leave it this year, too, until I can dig around it and fertilize it. [9]And if, indeed, it bears fruit in the future, well and good, but if not, then chop it down.'"[g]

[10]And he was teaching in one of the synagogues on the Sabbath. [11]And behold, a woman having a spirit of infirmity for eighteen long years was present, and she was bent double, unable to straighten up completely. [12]And seeing her, Jesus summoned her and said to her, "Woman, you have been released from your infirmity!" [13]And he laid his hands on her, and at once she was straightened out and worshipped God. [14]But the synagogue ruler, upset that Jesus healed on the Sabbath, retorted and said to the crowd, "There are six days on which one ought to work, so come then and be cured and not on the Sabbath day!" [15]But the Lord answered him and said, "Hypocrites! Doesn't every one of you untie his ox or his

---

e. This sounds like a garbled reference to Archelaeus's troops attacking pilgrims offering sacrifice in the temple in 4 BCE. One would expect the point to have been outrage at the Romans. Is he saying that if they blame the victims they will not be in a position to mobilize against Roman oppression?

f. This seems to reverse the point of the preceding verses which lampoon the "blame the victim" mentality. Luke has added v. 5 to serve his agenda of predicting the destruction of Jerusalem. Luke 12:54-13:5 correspond to Deut. 13:12-18 about apostate cities and their doom.

g. This is based on the cursing of the fig tree in Mark 11:12-14, 20-21; Matt. 21:18-20; corresponding to Deut. 14:28.

donkey from the manger on the Sabbath and lead it away to give it a
drink? 16And this woman, being a daughter of Abraham, whom, behold,
the adversary bound these ten years and eight, hadn't she every right to be
loosed from this bond on the Sabbath day?" 17And as he said these
things, all his critics were put to shame and all the crowd rejoiced at all
the glorious things happening through him.[h]

18So he said, "What is the kingdom of God like? And what can I
compare it to? 19I know! It is just like a grain of mustard which a man
took and planted in his garden and it grew and grew into a tree and the
birds of the sky found lodging in its branches."

20And again he said, "What may I compare the kingdom of God to?
21It is like yeast which a woman took and hid in three measures of meal
until finally the whole thing was leavened."[i]

22And he journeyed through cities and villages, making his way to Jerusalem. 23Someone said, "Lord, what if only a few are saved?" And he
said to them, 24"Do your best to squeeze through the door frame because
many, I assure you, will try to enter and will not be equal to it. 25For when
the householder gets up to shut the door and you begin to congregate outside and pound on the door, saying, 'Lord, open up! It's us!' he will say to
you, 'You are total strangers to me.' 26Then you will try another angle,
'Remember? We ate and drank across the table from you and you taught
in our streets.' 27And he will reply, telling you, 'You are total strangers to
me, I tell you! Get out of here, all workers of unrighteousness!' 28There
will be weeping and grinding of teeth when you Jews see Abraham and
Isaac and Jacob and all the prophets in the kingdom of God, you yourselves being ejected. 29And they will come from east and west, from north
and south, and they will feast in the kingdom of God. 30And behold, there
are those ranking last who will be first, and there are those ranked first
who will be last."

31In that very hour some Pharisees approached him, saying to him,
"Make yourself scarce and journey on from here because Herod wishes
to kill you."[j] 32And he said to them, "You can tell that fox this for me:
'Behold, I cast out demons and perform cures today and tomorrow, and
on the third day I am finished. 33Nevertheless, I am obliged to journey today and tomorrow and the day after, for no prophet can perish outside

h. Luke has composed vv. 10-17 to correspond to Deut. 15:1-18.

i. This is a secondary formation based on the distinctive rewording of the mustard seed simile before it, which is quite different in Mark 4:30-32.

j. Based on Matt. 2:13?

Jerusalem.' [34]Jerusalem! Jerusalem! Killer of the prophets, stoning those sent to you! How often I wished to gather your children as a bird gathers her nestlings under her wings and you refused. [35]Behold, your house is left desolate. I tell you, you will never see me until the moment comes when you say, 'Blessed in the name of Adonai be the Coming One!'"[k]

14

[1]And it came about, as he entered the dwelling of one of the leaders of the Pharisee sect on a Sabbath to eat bread, they were observing him closely. [2]And behold, a certain man with dropsy appeared before him. [3]And answering their expectant stares, Jesus spoke to the canon lawyers and Pharisees, saying, "Is it legal to heal on the Sabbath or not?" [4]And they were silent. And taking hold of him, he cured and dismissed him. [5]And to them he said, "Whose son or ox shall fall into a pit and you will not at once pull him out on the Sabbath?" [6]And there was nothing they could say to these things.[l]

[7]And he told a maxim to the other dinner guests, observing how they scrambled for the seats of honor, saying to them, [8]"Whenever you are invited by anyone to a wedding reception, do not recline in the seat of honor in case someone more prestigious than you has been invited by the host, [9]and the one who invited you both will come and say to you, 'Give up your seat to this man,' and you will slink down to the last seat. [10]Instead, when you are invited, go recline in the last seat so that when your host comes, he will say to you, 'Friend, what are you doing sitting all the way down here? Go up higher!' Then you will shine before all your fellow guests [11]because whoever exalts himself will be humiliated, and whoever humbles himself will be exalted."[m]

[12]And he said also to the one who had invited him, "When you plan a dinner or a supper, do not call your friends or your brothers or your kinsmen or rich neighbors for hope they will return the favor and it becomes payment to you. [13]But when you plan a party, invite the poor, the maimed, the blind. [14]Then you will be blessed because they have no

---

k. Verses 22-35 correspond to Deut. 16:1-17:7 regarding pilgrimage to Jerusalem.

l. This is based on the healing of the man with the withered hand (6:6ff.), the woman with the hemorrhage (8:43ff.), and the anointing in the house of Simon the Pharisee (7:36ff).

m. As clever advice for more ingenious social posturing, this is unworthy of Jesus.

means to repay you, and you will be repaid by inclusion in the resurrection of the just."[n]

[15]Hearing these things, one of those at the table said to him, "Amen! Blessed is he who eats bread in the kingdom of God." [16]And he said to him, "Too bad you won't be one of them! A certain man gave a great supper and invited many, [17]and he sent his slave at suppertime to say to the invited guests, 'Come because now it is ready.' [18]And as one man, they all began to beg off. The first said, 'I, uh, bought a farm and need to go out and look it over. Render my apologies, will you?' [19]And another said, 'I, er, bought five yoke of oxen and I need to go try them out. Render my apologies, will you?' [20]And another said, 'I, um, married a woman and she will not let me out of the house. You know how it is!' [21]And coming up to the house, the slave reported these things to his lord. Then, enraged, the master of the house ordered his slave, 'Go out quickly into the streets and lanes of the city and bring the poor, the maimed, the blind, and the lame in here." [22]Afterward, the slave said, 'Lord, what you ordered has been done and there is still room.' [23]And the lord said to the slave, 'Go out into the roads and hedges and round up the vagrants so my house may be filled! [24]For I tell you that not one of those I originally invited will get so much as a taste of my supper.'"[o]

---

n. A bizarre piece of advice for calculating the best investment of one's good works in order to maximize one's reward! Is this based on the equally calculating counsel of Matt. 25:31-46? Verses 1-14 loosely correspond to Deut. 16:18-20; 17:8-18, regarding people accepting oracular verdicts of priests and judges and about limiting the king's prerogatives. Luke sets the scene in a ruler's house and introduces the dropsical man to exalt Jesus' judgment over that of the scribes. The rest of the Lukan passage refers back to the preceding Deuteronomic text (16:14), the ranking of various guests being a piece of table etiquette borrowed from Prov. 25:6-7. The widow and sojourner from Deut. 16:14 inspired Luke's admonition to invite the poor, the maimed, the blind, and the lame instead of simply one's friends and relatives.

o. The story comes from the rabbinic parable (Jerusalem Talmud, *Hagigah* II, 77d) of the wealthy tax collector Bar-Majan, who sought to curry social favor by inviting aristocrats to a great party. Realizing how he intended to use them, all snubbed him. In disgust, Bar-Majan decided to call in the poor. For this grudging act of charity, he had a well-attended funeral but immediately went to hell. Note the similarity between the excuses offered by those invited to the great supper in Q (Matt. 22:1-10; Luke 14:16-24), which are implicitly sneered at by the narrator, and the circumstances exempting an Israelite from serving in holy war in Deut. 20: building a new house, planting a new vineyard, getting married. One suspects Q tightens up what were considered by an enthusiastic sect to be lax standards, just as the divorce rules were tightened by Christians. Those same strict standards were apparently considered appropriate to the spiritual crusade of evangelism.

[25]And great crowds gathered around him, and turning to them he said, [26]"If anyone comes to me and does not spurn his father and mother and his wife and children and brothers and sisters and, besides this, even his own life, he cannot be a disciple of mine. [27]Whoever does not carry his cross and come after me, he cannot be a disciple of mine. [28]For which of you, if he wants to build a tower, does not first sit down and estimate the cost to see if he has enough to complete the job? [29]Otherwise, if he has laid the foundation but is not able to finish, those who see it begin to mock him, [30]saying, 'This fool began to build and was not able to finish!' [31]Or what king would go forth to attack another king in war without first sitting down and deliberating whether he, with his ten thousand troops, is going to be able to meet the challenge of the one who fields twenty thousand against him? [32]If not, while his foe is still far off, he will send a delegation to ask terms of peace. [33]Even so, every one of you who does not say good-bye to all his possessions cannot be a disciple of mine. [34]Thus, salt tastes good, but suppose the salt were to become useless? What else could you possibly use to season salt? [35]It is suitable neither for the soil nor for the compost heap. They sprinkle it outside. Whoever has ears to hear, let him hear!"

15

[1]Now all the customs agents and backsliders were drawing near to hear him. [2]And both the Pharisees and the scribes murmured much against him, saying, "This fellow welcomes backsliders and eats with them!" [3]And he told them this parable, saying, [4]"Which of you men, if he had a hundred sheep and lost one of them, would not leave the ninety-nine in the desert to go look for the lost one until he finds it? [5]And finding it, he places it across his shoulders, rejoicing. [6]And coming into the house, he calls together his friends and the neighbors, saying to them, 'Rejoice with me because I found my lost sheep!' [7]I tell you, there will be the same joy in heaven over a single backslider repenting than over ninety-nine righteous individuals who require no repentance. [8]Or what wife, if she had ten drachmas and lost one, would not light a lamp and sweep the house and look carefully until she finds it? [9]And finding it, she calls together the friends and neighbors, saying, 'Rejoice with me because I found the drachma which I lost!' [10]Even so, I tell you, the angels witness the joy of God over one backslider repenting."[p]

[11]And he said, "A certain man had two sons. [12]The younger of the

p. A passage in Deut. 22:1-4 stipulates all manner of lost objects which must

two said to the father, 'Father, give me the share of the property that falls to me.' And he divided the living between them.[q] [13]And after not many days, the younger son, having packed his things, left for a distant country and there squandered his property with a life of excess. [14]When he had spent everything, a severe famine hit that country and he began to feel the pinch. [15]And he went looking for work and attached himself to one of the citizens of that country who sent him into his fields to feed the pigs. [16]And he longed to ease his hunger with the husks the pigs ate, and no one gave him food. [17]And one day he came to his senses, and he said, 'How many of my father's hirelings have plenty of loaves, but as for me, here I am dying of hunger. [18]I will get up and go my father and I will say to him, 'Father, I sinned against heaven and before you. [19]No longer am I worthy to be called a son of yours. Demote me to be one of your hirelings.' [20]And getting up, he began the journey to his father. But while he was still far away, his father saw him and was touched with pity and ran to his son, embracing him and kissing him tearfully. [21]And the son said to him, 'Father, I sinned against heaven and before you; no longer am I worthy to be called a son of yours.' [22]But the father said to his slaves, 'Quickly! Bring out the best robe and clothe him and put a ring on his hand and sandals on his feet, [23]and bring the fattened calf, kill it, and let us celebrate with a feast [24]because this son of mine was dead and lives again, was lost and is found.' And they began to celebrate. [25]But his older son was in a field,[r] and as he came near the house, he heard music and dancing. [26]And calling over one of the serving boys, he asked what was going on.[s] [27]And he said to him, 'Your brother has arrived, and your father killed the fattened calf because he got him back safe and sound.' [28]But he was furious and refused to enter, so his father came out and pleaded with him. [29]But answering, he said to the father, 'Behold, as many years as I served you, never in all that time disobeying a single order from you, you never allowed me a goat so that I might feast with my friends. [30]But when this son of yours arrived, after consuming your living with prostitutes, you killed the fattened calf in his honor!' [31]And he said to him, 'My child, you are always with me, and whatever I have is yours. [32]But it was only proper

---

be returned if found, just as Luke 15:3-7 and 8-10 provide examples of lost things zealously sought and found.

q. The parable is a Lukan construction suggested by Deut. 21:15-21, a discussion of the inheritance due loved and unloved sons.

r. This recalls Cain and Abel in the field, leading to the murder (Gen. 4:8).

s. Based on Exod. 32:17-19.

for us to rejoice because your brother was dead and came to life, and having been lost was also found.'"[t]

16

[1]And he said also to the disciples, "There was a certain rich man who had a steward, and he received a complaint that this man was wasting his possessions. [2]And calling him, he said to him, 'What is this I hear about you? Make a full report of your stewardship, for you can no longer represent me.' [3]And the steward said to himself, 'What am I to do now that my lord takes the stewardship away from me? I am not equal to digging. I am ashamed to beg. [4]I know what to do! This way, when I am fired from the stewardship, they will welcome me to be steward in their own houses.' [5]And summoning each one of his lord's debtors, he said to the first, 'How much do you owe my lord?' [6]And he said, 'A hundred baths of oil.' And he told him, 'Not any more! Take your invoice, sit down quickly, and write fifty.' [7]Then he said to another, 'And how much do you owe?' And he said, 'A hundred cors of wheat.' He tells him, 'Not any more! Take your invoice and write eighty.' [8]And his master exclaimed, 'Clever rogue! It's a shame to lose him!' Because the sons of this temporal world are more prudent among their own kind than the sons of the light. [9]And I tell you, make friends for yourselves by the mammon of unrighteousness so that when it runs out, they may welcome you into the everlasting mansions. [10]The one faithful in the least is faithful also in much, and the one who is unrighteous in the least is unrighteous also in much.[u] [11]Thus, if you were not faithful with unrighteous mammon, who will entrust the true riches to you? [12]And if you were not faithful in that which belongs to another, who will give you your own? [13]No domestic slave can be enslaved to two lords at the same time. Either he will hate the first and love the second or he will pledge loyalty to the first and despise the second. You are not able to be slaves to both God and Mammon."[v]

[14]Now the Pharisees, who were money lovers, heard all these things and they scoffed at him. [15]And he said to them, "You are those who put

t. The parable is perhaps based on Matt. 21:28-31 and the *Odyssey* episode of the return of Odysseus and Telemachus, the swineherd Eumaeus, and Penelope's suitors.

u. Verse 10 is an attempt to assure the reader that Jesus does not commend the steward's shady solution; it is just an analogy for decisive action.

v. Luke uses Deut. 23:15-16's provision for welcoming an escaped slave as the basis for his parable of the dishonest steward. By manipulating his master's accounts, the steward assures he will be welcomed into his grateful clients' midst after his dismissal.

on a good front for mortal men, but God knows your hearts. For whatever is highly exalted by mortal men is an abomination in the eyes of
God.[w]
[16]"The Law and the Prophets pointed to John; from then on, the
news of the kingdom of God is proclaimed and everyone forces his way
into it. [17]But it is easier for sky and earth to pass away than for one serif
of the Law to drop off. [18]Everyone dismissing his wife and marrying another commits adultery, and the one who marries a wife cast off by a previous husband commits adultery.[x]
[19]"Now a certain man was rich, and he used to dress in a purple robe
and a fine linen tunic and he feasted lavishly every day. [20]And a certain
poor man, Lazarus by name, had been dropped off by his gate, covered
with sores [21]and desiring to satisfy himself with what fell from the rich
man's table. But even the dogs came and licked his sores. [22]And it came
time for the poor man to die and to be carried away by the angels to Abraham's welcoming embrace. And the rich man also died and was buried.
[23]And looking up from Hades, writhing under torture, he glimpses Abraham at a great distance welcoming Lazarus.[y] [24]And calling, he said, 'Father Abraham! Pity me and send Lazarus to dip his finger in water and
cool my tongue, for I am suffering in this flame.' [25]But Abraham said,
'My child, remember how you received your good things in your lifetime?
Well, Lazarus likewise received the bad. Accordingly, now he is comforted here but you are suffering. [26]And part of the arrangement is that a
great chasm has been firmly installed so that any who wish to pass from
here to you on a mission of mercy cannot, nor may any escape from there
to us.' [27]And he said, 'I ask you, then, Father, to send him to my father's
house, [28]for I have five brothers, and let him warn them of what awaits
them lest they, too, end up in this pit of torture.' [29]But Abraham says,

w. What a radically world-negating, Gnostic saying!

x. The discussion in Deut. 23:19-20 about debts and usury inspires the condemnation of Pharisees for being "lovers of money" (16:14). Greed like theirs is an abomination (βδελυγμα) before God, a word borrowed from the same Deuteronomic passage about remarrying a divorced wife after a second man has divorced her (24:1-4). On the question of divorce, Luke oddly juxtaposes against the Deuteronomic provision the diametrically opposite Markan rejection of divorce, even while asserting that the Torah cannot change.

y. This parable is based on the Bar-Majan story (see above). The rich tax collector went to hell despite his well-attended funeral, while a poor scholar whose death went all but unnoticed rejoiced beside the sparkling river in heaven. The parable corresponds to Deut. 24:10-15.

'Why bother? They have Moses and the Prophets; let them heed the scriptures.' [30]But he said, 'No, Father Abraham, believe me, that will never work. I know these men. But if someone from the dead should go to them, they'd have to repent!' [31]But he said to him, 'Look, if they are deaf to Moses and the Prophets, they'd find a way to discount someone rising from the dead, too.'"

17

[1]He said to his disciples, "It is impossible for scandals not to come, but woe to him by whom they come! [2]He is better off if his head is put through the hole in a millstone and he is dumped overboard than if he should scandalize one of these new converts.[z] [3]Consider your situation! If your brother sins, rebuke him, and if he repents, forgive him. [4]And if he sins against you seven times a day and seven times turns back to you saying, 'I'm sorry!' forgive him."

[5]And the apostles said to the Lord, "Give us more faith!" [6]And the Lord said, "You either have it or you don't. If you had faith the size of a mustard grain, you would have said to this sycamine tree, 'You! Pull up your roots and transplant yourself in the sea,' and it would have obeyed you![a] [7]But which of you, having a slave out plowing or herding, when he comes in from the field, would say to him, 'Come at once, take a load off your feet'? [8]Instead, wouldn't you say to him, 'Prepare something for my dinner! Change your clothes and serve me until I finish eating and drinking, and after these tasks, you may eat and drink'? [9]Do you thank the slave because he did the things he was commanded? Hardly! [10]In the same way, when you do all the things commanded, you must say, 'We are unprofitable slaves, all we have done is the minimum required.'"

[11]And it came about that as he went to Jerusalem, he passed through the middle of Samaria and Galilee. [12]And as he entered into a certain village, ten men with skin disease met him, standing at a distance, [13]and they lifted their voices to say, "Jesus, master, pity us!" [14]And seeing them, he said to them, "Go and let the priests inspect you." And it happened that as they went, they were purified. [15]But one of them, realizing that he was cured, returned, worshipping God at the top of his voice, [16]and he fell on his face at his feet, thanking him. And he was a Samaritan. [17]And answering, Jesus said, "I could have sworn all ten were purified! But what happened to the other nine? [18]I found none returning to give thanks

z. Deut. 24:6

a. Based on Mark 11:23.

to God except for this foreigner." [19]And he said to him, "Rise up and go. Your own faith has cured you."[b]

[20]Being questioned by the Pharisees as to when the kingdom of God comes, he answered them and said, "The kingdom of God does not come visibly, [21]nor will they say, 'Behold here!' or 'There!' for behold, the kingdom of God is within you."

[22]And he said to the disciples, "The time will come when you will be desperate to see day one of the reign of one like a son of man, and you will not see it. [23]And they will say to you, 'Look there! Look here!' Do not go away or follow. [24]For just as the lightning flashes from one horizon and shines clear over to the other horizon, so will the one like a son of man appear in his day. [25]But first he is obliged to suffer many indignities and to be disowned by this race.

[26]"And as it was at the time of Noah, it will be the same in the time when one like a son of man comes. [27]They were eating, drinking, men marrying and giving women in marriage, business as usual, until that day when Noah entered the ark and the cataclysm came and destroyed everything. [28]Likewise, as it was at the time of Lot: they were eating, drinking, buying, selling, planting, building, [29]but on that day when Lot fled Sodom, it rained fire and brimstone from the sky and destroyed everything. [30]It will be the same thing on that day when one like a son of man is revealed. [31]In that day, whoever finds himself on the roof with his vessels in the house, let him not try to retrieve them but rather let him climb down the fire escape and flee. And the one working in the field when that hour strikes, let him not turn back to the things left behind. [32]Remember what happened to Lot's wife! [33]Whoever may try to save his skin, he will lose it, and whoever will let it go, he will preserve it. [34]I tell you, in this night there will be two on one couch; the one will be taken and the other will be left! [35]There will be two grinding grain together; the one will be taken but the other will be left! [36]*There will be two in the field; the one will be taken, and the other will be left!*" [37]And answering, they say to him, "Taken where, Lord?" And he said to them, "Where do you think? You'll find the body where the vultures are circling."

18

[1]And he told them a parable to show they were obliged always to pray and not give up, [2]saying, "There was a certain judge in a certain city,

b. The provision for a leper's cure and certification (Deut. 24:8-9) prompts Luke to create another pro-Samaritan story with Deut. 24:14's counsel to treat the sojourning foreigner fairly.

not fearing God and caring nothing for human rights. [3]And there was in that city a widow, and she came before him saying, "Exonerate me from the slanders of my accuser!" [4]And for a while, he would not. But after these constant appeals, he said to himself, 'Though indeed I do not fear God nor give a fig for justice, [5]if only because this widow annoys me I will exonerate her; otherwise, she will finally assault me.' [6]And the Lord said, 'Do you hear what the unrighteous judge says? [7]And will not God by all means render justice to his chosen people Israel who cry out to him day and night? Will he take his time over them? [8]I tell you, he will render them justice quickly! On the other hand, when one like a son of man comes, will they all have given up in despair?"[c]

[9]And he aimed this parable at people who congratulated themselves for their own righteousness, despising everyone else. [10]"Two men went up to the temple to pray, the one a Pharisee, the other a customs agent. [11]The Pharisee, standing there, prayed these things silently: 'God, I thank you that I am not like the rest of mankind, rapacious, unjust, adulterers, or even as this customs agent. [12]I fast twice a week, I tithe everything I get.' [13]But the customs agent, keeping his distance, dared not even look up toward heaven but beat his breast, saying, 'God, be merciful to me, a sinner!' [14]I tell you, this man descended the temple mount to his dwelling having been accepted by God rather than that one. Because every one who exalts himself will be humiliated and every one who humbles himself will be exalted."[d]

[15]And they brought babies to him, hoping he would touch them and utter some blessing, but seeing it, the disciples rebuffed them. [16]But Jesus called to them, "Let the children come to me. What's the matter with you? Don't you know them? These are the very angels of the kingdom of God. [17]Amen: I tell you, whoever does not welcome the kingdom of God when it comes to him in the form of a child will be forever excluded from it."[e]

[18]And a certain ruler questioned him, saying, "Good teacher, what may I do that I may inherit age-long life when I die?" [19]And Jesus said to him, "Just a moment, if you please. Why do you call me 'good'? No one is

c. The parable corresponds to Deut. 24:17-18; 25:1-3, with its concern for fair judgments rendered on behalf of the poor and fair treatment of widows.

d. In Deut. 26:12-15, someone offering the first fruits of his crops may confess his perfect obedience to the commandments. This must have struck Luke as pretentious, and he satirizes the section in this parable.

e. This is part of an infant baptism liturgy, as Oscar Cullmann demonstrated. It is suggested in part by 2 Kings 4:26-27.

good except one: God. [20]Surely you already know the ten commandments: Do not commit adultery, do not murder, do not steal, do not testify falsely, take care of your father and mother. Well?" [21]But he said to him, "I observed all these since I was young." [22]But hearing this, Jesus said to him, "You still lack one thing. Sell everything, whatever you own, and distribute the price to poor people and then you will have the treasure in heaven that you seek. And come follow me." [23]But hearing these words, he became very sad, for he was extremely rich. [24]And seeing his reaction, Jesus said, "You see with what difficulty those who have property enter into the kingdom of God? [25]For it is easier for a camel to squeeze through the hole of a needle than for a rich man to enter into the kingdom of God." [26]And his hearers said, "If even God's favorites cannot enter heaven, then who can save himself?" [27]And he said, "Human impossibilities are possible for God."

[28]And Peter said, "Behold, abandoning our own things, we followed you." [29]And he said to them, "Amen: I tell you, there is no one who has abandoned dwelling or wife or brothers or parents or children for the sake of the kingdom of God, [30]who does not by all means receive many times as much in this time and, in the coming age, age-long life."

[31]And taking the twelve aside, he said to them, "Behold, we are going up to Jerusalem and all things written by the Prophets about yours truly will be fulfilled. [32]For he will be delivered up to the gentiles and will be mocked and insulted and spat on, [33]and once they have flogged him, they will kill him, and on the third day he will stand up again." [34]And they understood none of these words, and this speech was hidden from them and they did not know what he was talking about.

[35]And it came about as he came close to Jericho, a certain blind man sat at the roadside begging. [36]And hearing the noise of the approaching crowd, he asked about the ruckus. [38]And he shouted, saying, "Jesus, son of David, pity me!" [39]And those in the vanguard rebuked him, telling him to be silent, but he only shouted all the more, "Son of David, pity me!" [40]And coming to a stop, Jesus ordered him to be brought to him. And as he approached, Jesus questioned him. [41]"What do you want me to do for you?" And he said, "Lord, I want to see again." [42]And Jesus said to him, "Then see again! Your own faith has healed you." [43]And at once he saw again, and he followed him, worshipping God. And all the people with sight gave praise to God.[f]

f. Isa. 35:6

19

[1]And having entered, he passed through Jericho. [2]And behold, a man
called by the name Zacchaeus[g] was a chief customs agent and he was rich.
[3]And he tried to see Jesus, who he was, and he was not able to on account
of the crowd because he was small in stature.[h] [4]And having run forward
to the front of the crowd, he climbed onto a sycamore tree so that he
might see him because he was about to pass that way. [5]And as he reached
the spot, Jesus, looking up, said to him, "Zacchaeus, hurry on down! For
today I must stay in your house." [6]And he hastened down and welcomed
him, rejoicing. [7]And seeing this, everyone murmured, saying, "Did you
see that? He went in to lodge with an impious man!" [8]And Zacchaeus
said to the Lord, "Not so! Behold, the half of my possessions I give to the
poor, Lord, and if I find I have accused anyone of anything falsely, I restore fourfold."[i] [9]And Jesus said to him, "Today salvation[j] came to this
house, because he, too, is a son of Abraham. [10]For a man ought to seek
and to save what was lost."

[11]And as they heard these things, he added a parable to his remarks
because of his nearness to Jerusalem and their thinking that the kingdom
of God was about to appear at once. [12]Therefore he said, "A certain nobleman made the journey to a distant country to receive kingship and
then return. [13]And having summoned ten of his slaves, he gave them ten
minas and said to them, 'See to business while I am away.' [14]But his citizens hated him and sent a party after him, saying, 'We do not want this
man as king over us.' [15]And it came about when he returned, having successfully received the kingship, he ordered his slaves to be summoned,
those to whom he had given the silver, so as to know what any of them
had gained in business. [16]And the first came and said, 'Lord, your mina
gained ten minas!' [17]And he said to him, 'Well done, good slave! Because
you were conscientious in a small matter, I grant you authority over ten
cities.' [18]And the second came and said, 'Your mina, Lord, has made five
minas.' [19]And he said to this one also, 'Thus, I place you over five cities.'
[20]And the other came and said, 'Lord, see your mina? I took the precaution of storing it away in a napkin. [21]You see, I feared you because you

---

g. Zacchaeus is a fictional, symbolic character since his name is derived from the Aramaic *zakki,* "to give alms," related to Islamic almsgiving, *zakat.*

h. Zacchaeus or Jesus?

i. Zacchaeus is here understood to be defending himself, protesting that he already follows these charitable practices.

j. The name "Jesus" means "salvation."

are an austere man: you pick up what others laid down on the gambling table and you harvest crops that others sowed, seizing the fields of your debtors.' [22]He says to him, 'Out of your own mouth I will judge you, wicked slave! You say you knew me for an austere man, picking up what others laid down and harvesting what others sowed? [23]Then why on earth did you not take my money to the banker's table? That way, on my return, I would have withdrawn my money with interest.' [24]And to those standing by, he said, 'Take the mina from him and give it to the one who has ten minas.' [25]And they said to him, 'Lord, he already has ten minas.' [26]'I tell you that to everyone who has the knack, more will be given, and from the one lacking it, even what little money he has will sooner or later be taken away. [27]But enough of that! Bring my enemies here, those who did not want me to be king over them, and execute them in front of me.'"[k]

[28]And when he had said these things, he went in front of the crowd going up the mountain path to Jerusalem. [29]And it came about, as he came close to Beth-Phage and Beth-Anu toward the mountain named for its olives, he assigned two of his disciples, saying, [30]"Go into the village over there and as soon as you enter into it you will discover a colt tethered, one on which no one has ever sat. Untie it and bring it back. [31]And should anyone ask, 'Why do you untie it?' you are to say this: 'Because the Lord requires it.'" [32]And the ones he sent found all as he told them. [33]And as they were freeing the colt, its owners said to them, "Why are you freeing the colt?" [34]And they said, "Because the Lord requires it."[l]

[35]And they led it to Jesus. And throwing their garments on the colt, they hoisted Jesus onto it. [36]And as he rode, they strewed their garments in the road. [37]And as he now drew near to the descent of the Mount of Olives, all the mass of the disciples began to rejoice and to praise God with a loud voice about all the powerful deeds they saw, [38]saying, "Blessed in the name of Adonai be the Coming One,[m] the king! Peace in heaven and glory in the highest spheres!" [39]And some of the Pharisees, emerging from the crowd, said to him, "Teacher, rebuke your disciples!" [40]And an-

---

k. To the original Q parable, preserved more accurately in Matt. 25:14-18, Luke has added the political element based on the Jewish embassy to Caesar, which had Archelaeus successfully deposed. The original point was, "What have you done with the life God entrusted you with?" In Luke, it has become a warning neither to oppose Jesus nor to become a fanatic expecting him to return soon.

l. This story derives from 1 Sam. 9.

m. Based on the entrance liturgy of Pss. 118:26-27, in which "he who comes in the name of the Lord" refers to any pilgrim.

swering, he said, "I tell you, if these fall silent, the stones will shout."[n]
[41]And as he came, seeing the city, he wept over it, [42]saying, "If you only
realized, even at this late date, what is needful for peace! But now it is hidden from your eyes. [43]Indeed, the days will overtake you when your enemies will erect a siege wall around you and will surround you and will
hem you in on all sides, [44]and will dash your brains out on the ground,
and your children's, and they will not leave stone standing upon stone in
you. And all because you did not recognize your hour of opportunity."
[45]And going into the temple, he started ejecting those selling sacrificial
animals,[o] [46]telling them, "It is written, 'And my house shall be a house of
prayer,[p] but you made it a robbers' cave.'"[q] [47]And he was teaching day by
day in the temple, but the archpriests and the scribes and the leading citizens looked for a way to eliminate him, [48]and they found nothing they
could do, for all the people hung upon his every word.

20

[1]And it came about, one day as he was teaching the people in the
temple and evangelizing, the archpriests and the scribes, with the elders,
came up to him [2]and spoke, saying to him, "Tell us, with what authorization do you do these things? Who gave you this authorization?" [3]And answering, he said to them, "First I will question you on one matter. You
tell me. [4]Remember the baptism of John? Was it authorized by God in
heaven or only by mortals?" [5]And they huddled, debating, whispering,
"It's a trap. If we say 'from heaven,' he will surely say, 'Then why didn't
you believe in him when you had the chance?' [6]But if we say, 'from mortal men,' the people will stone us, for they have been deluded that John is
a prophet." [7]So they answered that they did not know where John's mandate came from. [8]And Jesus said to them, "Why am I not surprised? Then
I'm afraid I cannot tell you the authority behind my actions either."
[9]And he began a parable, saying to the people, "A man planted a

n. Based on Matt. 21:15-16, by means of an implied Hebrew pun changing "sons" (*beni*) to "stones" (*ebeni*).

o. Though it is not unlikely the story preserves some faded memory of Simon bar-Gioras cleansing the temple of John of Gischala and his band of robbers on the eve of the temple's destruction, the story may simply conflate various scripture passages—which it seems to do in any case. The "cleansing" must have in view that of Malachi's messenger of the covenant who will purify the sons of Levi (3:1-30) and the oracle of Zech. 14:21b: "And there shall no longer be a trader in the house of the Lord of hosts on that day."

p. Isa. 56:7

q. Jer. 7:11

vineyard and leased it out to sharecroppers and went away for extended periods.[r] [10]And at harvest time, he sent a slave to the sharecroppers so that he might collect from the sharecroppers his due from the produce of the vineyard. But the sharecroppers beat him and sent him away empty-handed. [11]And again the following year he sent an additional slave. But that one, too, they beat, and they insulted him and sent him off empty-handed. [12]And he sent yet a third. But they wounded this one also and threw him out. [13]And the owner of the vineyard said, 'What shall I do? I know! I will send my beloved son. Likely enough, they will pay heed to this one.' [14]But seeing him, those sharecroppers conspired: 'The old man must be dead. This one is his heir. Come, let us kill him and the inheritance will pass to us!' [15]And throwing him out of the vineyard, they killed him. So what do you think the owner of the vineyard will do to them? I'll tell you. [16]He will come in person and will destroy those sharecroppers and he will give the vineyard to others." And hearing this, they said, "Never!" [17]And he looked at them and said, "Then why is it written, 'A stone which the house builders deemed unusable, this very one became the cornerstone.[s] [18]Everyone falling on that stone will be shattered, but whomever it falls on will be pulverized.'?"[t] [19]And the scribes and the archpriests tried to get their hands on him then and there, but they checked themselves, fearing the people, for they were well aware that he aimed the parable at them.

[20]And they kept a close eye on him, sending shills posing as sincere inquirers, hoping to seize on something he might say to use as grounds to hand him over to the rule and authority of the governor. [21]And they questioned him saying, "Teacher, we know you speak and teach frankly. You are not intimidated by anyone as you teach the way of God. [22]So then. Is it legal to pay tribute to Caesar or not?" [23]But aware of their duplicity, he said to them, [24]"Show me a denarius. Whose image and epigraph does it have?" And they said, "Caesar's, of course." [25]And he said to them, "So give Caesar's coins to Caesar in taxes and God's coins to God in the temple." [26]And they were unable to pounce on anything he said in the presence of the people and, flabbergasted at his answer, they were silent.

[27]Next some of the Syndics came to him, those who, in opposition to the Pharisee sect, say there is no resurrection, and they questioned him, [28]saying, "Teacher, Moses wrote us that if a brother of anyone should die

r. Isa. 5:1-7

s. Pss. 118:22-23

t. Isa. 8:14-15

leaving a wife behind him and without leaving a child, the brother should
take his wife and beget heirs for his brother. [29]Suppose there were seven
brothers and the oldest took a wife and died childless. [30]And the second
married her, and he died childless, [31]and the third married her, and similarly the seven did not leave children and died. [32]And last of all, the
woman died. [33]In this 'resurrection,' which one's wife will she become?
After all, all seven of them had her as their wife at one time or another."
[34]And Jesus said to them, "The sons of this temporal world marry and are
given in marriage, [35]but the ones deemed worthy to gain that world by
the resurrection from the dead neither marry nor are they given in marriage. [36]For neither can they die anymore, for they are the same as angels
and sons of God, being born of the resurrection. [37]But that the dead are
raised, even Moses indicated as much in the passage about the burning
bush, as he calls Adonai 'the God of Abraham and God of Isaac and God
of Jacob.' [38]He is not a God of corpses, but of living men. For to him, all
are alive." [39]And answering, some of the scribes said, "Teacher, well
said!" [40]For they no longer dared ask him about anything.

[41]So he turned the tables and said to them, "How can they say the
Christ is a son of David? [42]For David himself says in the scroll of Psalms,
'Adonai said to milord, Sit at my right [43]till I make the necks of your enemies a footstool for your feet.' [44]Therefore, David calls him 'lord.' So
how can he be his son?"

[45]And in the hearing of all the people, he said to the disciples, [46]"Be
on guard against the scribes, who delight in parading around in flowing
robes and basking in deferential greetings in the marketplaces and being
shown to the platform seats in the synagogues and the head tables at banquets, [47]who evict poor widows and make a performance of long prayer.
These will receive more severe judgment than common sinners!"

21

[1]And looking up, he watched the rich tossing their donations into the
treasury box. [2]And he saw a certain poor widow throwing in two lepta,
[3]and he said, "Truly, I tell you that this poor widow put in more than all
the rest combined, [4]for all these gave out of their abundance, but this
woman gave out of her privation everything she had, all her living."

[5]And as some spoke about the temple, that it has been decorated
with fine stones and gifts, he said, [6]"These things which you behold, days
will come in which no pair of stones will remain together amid the rubble." [7]And they questioned him, saying, "Teacher, so when will these
things happen? And what will be the signal that they are about to hap-

pen?" [8]And he said, "Watch out so that you are not deceived, for many
will appear trading on my name, saying, 'It is I!' and 'The time has come
near!' Do not go off after them. [9]But when you hear of wars and upheavals, do not panic, for these things are destined to happen first, but the end
is not imminent."[u]

[10]Then he said to them, "Nation will be pitted against nation and
kingdom against kingdom. [11]And there will be great earthquakes in scattered places and plagues and famines.[v] [12]But before all this, they will get
their hands on you and persecute you, delivering you up to synagogues
and thence to prisons, being hauled before governors and kings for the
sake of my name. [13]It will be an opportunity for you to bear witness. [14]So
resolve not to practice beforehand to defend yourselves, [15]for I will give
you a mouth[w] and wisdom which none of your opponents will be able to
resist or confute. [16]And you will be betrayed even by parents and brothers
and relatives and friends, and they will put some of you to death.[x] [17]And
you will be hated by all on account of my name. [18]But a hair of your head
will by no means perish; [19]by your endurance you will gain your lives.

[20]"But when you see Jerusalem being surrounded by armed camps,
then you will know that its desolation is near.[y] [21]Then let those in Judea
flee to the mountains, and let those in the midst of the city depart.[z] Let
those in the outlying quarters not enter the city, [22]because this is a time of
vengeance to fulfill all that has been written. [23]Woe to those with a child
in the womb and those nursing in those days, for there will be great tur-
moil on the earth and rage toward this people. [24]And they will be devoured by the sword, and they will be forcibly deported to all nations,
and Jerusalem will be trampled by the gentiles until the time allotted for
gentile hegemony is up. [25]And there will be signs in sun, moon, and stars;
and on earth nations will cower with dread and alarm at the roaring of
the sea and its waves, [26]while people will faint from fear and anticipation
of what is coming on the whole inhabited earth, for the Powers of the
heavens will be shaken from their thrones.[a] [27]And then those angels will

u. Dan. 2:28

v. Isa. 19:2; 2 Chron. 15:6

w. Cf. Exod. 4:10-12: "Who has made man's mouth? ... I will be with your mouth."

x. Mic. 7:6

y. Dan. 9:27; 12:11

z. Gen. 19:17

a. Isa. 34:4

see one like a son of man on a cloud chariot with power and great brilliance.[b] 28And when these things start to happen, stand up straight and raise your heads because your redemption is fast approaching."

29And he told them a parable: "Look at the fig tree and, for that matter, all the trees. 30As soon as they burst into leaf, you can see for yourselves that summer is near. 31So you also know when you see these things transpire that the kingdom of God is near. 32Amen: I tell you, this present generation will by no means go past until these things all happen. 33The sky and the earth will pass away but my predictions will not fail. 34Consider your position, that your hearts not become gross with wild feasting and drunken binges and the worries of life, lest that day suddenly overtake you 35like a hunter's trap. For it will overtake everyone sitting on the face of all the earth. 36But be ever vigilant, praying earnestly that you may be able to escape all these impending things and to stand unscathed before the one like a son of man."

37Now he was teaching daily in the temple, going out each night to lodge in the mountain named for its olives. 38And every morning all the people came to him in the temple to hear him.

22

1Now the feast of unleavened bread called Passover drew near. 2And the archpriests and the scribes looked for a way to destroy him, carefully, for they feared the reaction of the people. 3And the adversary entered into Judas, called the False One, who was included in the ranks of the twelve. 4And going off, he discussed with the archpriests and captains how he might deliver him up. 5And they rejoiced, readily agreeing to give him money. 6And he agreed and looked for a good opportunity to deliver him to them away from the crowd.

7And the day of unleavened bread came, when it is required to kill the Passover lamb. 8And he sent Peter and John, saying, "Go prepare the Passover seder for us that we may eat." 9And they said to him, "Where do you want us to prepare it?" 10And he told them, "Behold, as you go into the city, a man carrying a pitcher of water will meet you. Follow him into the house he enters, 11and you will tell the inn-keeper, 'The teacher says to you, Where is the guestroom where I may celebrate the Passover with my disciples?' 12And that man will show you a large second-story room, already furnished and ready. Prepare it there." 13And going, they found things just as he told them, and they prepared for Passover.[c]

---

b. Dan. 7:13

c. This story is based on 1 Sam. 9. The upper room of the Last Supper may

[14]When the hour arrived, he reclined, and the apostles with him. [15]And he said to them, "With eager expectation I anticipated eating this Passover with you before I suffer. [16]For I tell you, I will by no means eat it any more until its symbolism is fulfilled in the kingdom of God." [17]And taking a cup, having given thanks, he said, "Take this and divide it among yourselves. [18]For I tell you, I will by no means drink from the fruit of the vine from now until the kingdom of God comes." [19]And taking a loaf, having given thanks, he broke it and gave it to them, saying, "This is my body *which is being given for you. Do this for my memorial.* [20]*And similarly he took the cup after supper, saying, "This cup is the new covenant in my blood being shed for you.*[d] [21]And yet, just look and you will see the hand of my betrayer on the table with my own. [22]For one goes when his preordained time comes, but woe to that wretch through whose agency he is delivered up!"

[23]And they began to argue among themselves which one of them it might be who was about to do this. [24]And there was also contention among them over who should be in charge after Jesus was gone. [25]So he said to them, "The kings of the gentiles lord it over them, and the ones wielding authority over them are often called Euergetes.[e] [26]But not among you in Israel! Let the greater among you become like the younger and the governor like the servant. [27]After all, who is greater, the one reclining or the one serving? Isn't it the one reclining? And yet, here I am in your midst as the one serving.[f] [28]But you are those who have stuck with me throughout all my trials, [29]and as my Father conferred kingship on me, [30]so I confer on you the privilege of feasting at my table in my kingdom.[g] And you will sit on thrones governing the twelve tribes of Israel.

[31]"Simon, Simon, the adversary has insisted on his right to sift you twelve like the wheat. [32]I, however, requested that in your own case, your faith may not give out, or at least that when you have recovered yourself, you may support your brothers."[h] [33]And he said to him, "Lord, I am

---

hark back to the second-story rooms provided by benefactors for Elijah (1 Kings 17:19) and Elisha (2 Kings 4:10).

d. Exod. 24:8

e. A common epithet for Hellenistic kings meaning "benefactor."

f. Cf. John 13:4-5.

g. Cf. Mark 10:37-40.

h. It is the duty of the Satan or "adversary" to prove the ostensibly righteous favorites of God (Job 1:6-12; 1 Chron. 21:1; Zech. 3:1-5; Mark 1:13; Matt. 4:1-11; Luke 4:1-13), who often fail but are nevertheless affirmed by God, as an-

ready even to go to prison and to death with you!"[i] 34But he said, "I tell you, Peter, a rooster will not have time to sound today before you three times deny even knowing me."

35And he said to them, "When I sent you forth without purse and wallet and sandals, did you lack anything?" And they said, "Nothing." 36And he said to them, "But now let whoever has a purse take it, likewise a wallet, too, and let anyone who does not have one sell his garment and buy a sword. 37For I tell you that this, having been written of me, must be fulfilled: 'And he was counted as one of the outlaws,'[j] for indeed the prophecy about me has a death scene." 38And they said, "Lord, look, here are two swords!" And he said to them, "That ought to be enough."

39And leaving there, he went, as was his habit, to the Mountain of the Olives, and the disciples also followed him. 40And arriving at the place he sought, he said to them, "Pray that you may be spared the trial." 41And he distanced himself about a stone's throw from them and, kneeling, he prayed, 42saying, "Father, if you will, take this hemlock cup from me. Nevertheless, let your will be done, not mine." 43*And an angel from heaven appeared to him, strengthening him.*[k] 44*And entering into agony, he prayed all the more earnestly and his sweat became like drops of blood spilling onto the ground.* 45And getting up from prayer, he returned to the disciples only to discover them sleeping, depressed from grief. 46And he said to them, "How can you sleep? Get up and pray, otherwise you will find yourselves unprepared for temptation." 47And while he was still speaking, a mob arrived and the one called Judas, one of the twelve, advanced before them and approached Jesus to kiss him. 48But Jesus said to him, "Judas, would you betray a man with a kiss?" 49And those around him, seeing what was going to happen, said, "Lord, shall we strike with the sword?" 50And a certain one of them struck the slave of the archpriest but only managed to slice off his right ear. 51But answering, Jesus said, "Let it proceed thus far and no farther." And touching the ear, he healed

---

ticipated here. Note how Jesus is depicted as privy to what happens in heaven (cf. Luke 10:18; 15:7). His intercession on Peter's behalf is a historical retrojection of Rom. 8:34; Heb. 7:25.

i. 1 Sam. 15:21

j. Isa. 53:12

k. Luke adds the element of an angel appearing beside the tormented Jesus to "strengthen" him, a detail borrowed from 1 Kings 19:7-8 LXX: "And the angel of the Lord returned again and touched him and said to him, 'Arise, for the journey is far from thee.' And he arose, and ate and drank, and went in the *strength* of that meat forty days and forty nights to mount Horeb."

him.[l] [52]And Jesus said to the archpriests and captains of the temple police and elders who were surrounding him, "You came armed with swords and clubs as against some desperado? [53]Every day I was with you in the temple and you did not apprehend me, but then, this is your hour: darkness holds sway!"[m]

[54]And arresting him, they marched him to the house of the archpriest, and Peter followed him at a safe distance. [55]And once they had lit a fire in the center of the courtyard and seated themselves together around it, Peter sat among them. [56]And noticing him, a certain serving maid of the archpriest sitting near the light scrutinized him and said, "This man was with him too!" [57]But he denied it, saying, "I do not know him, woman!" [58]And after a short while, another noticed him and said, "You, too, are one of them." But Peter said, "Man, I am not!" [59]And after an hour's interval, a certain other one declared emphatically, "It's true: this man was with him, for he too is a Galilean!" [60]But Peter said, "Man, I don't know what you're talking about." And at once, while he was still speaking, a rooster crow sounded. [61]And turning, the Lord looked at Peter; and Peter recalled the Lord's prediction, how he told him, "Before a rooster sounds today, you will repudiate me three times." [62]And going outside, he cried bitterly.

---

l. Cf. Matt. 26:52; John 18:11. All the gospel writers after Mark knew of a version in which Jesus said, "Let it be restored to its place." Matthew and John took this to mean the sword, while Luke imagined the reference to be to the ear!

m. The basis of this whole scene can be found in 2 Sam. 15-16. There a weeping David, fleeing his usurping son Absalom, a Judas figure, heads up the Mount of Olives and sends three of his allies (15:27 LXX) back to Jerusalem. David finds himself mocked and harassed by one Shimei who curses the fallen king, and David's man Abishai offers to chop the mocker's head off, but David prevents him, musing that God must have bidden Shimei to curse David. As they slink along in silence, Shimei continues to pelt the refugees with rocks. Here we find more elements underlying the Passion story. Abishai is the prototype of the disciple who attempts to behead Malchus in the arresting party. Shimei, another form of Shimeon or Simon, is the prototype for Simon, who denies Jesus repeatedly, the stony missiles suggesting "Peter," as well. If God assigned Shimei to utter curses on David, so Jesus predicts the denials which will be uttered by Peter, who curses himself (or Jesus) in the high priest's courtyard (14:71). But what of Jesus' prayer? The disciples are absent from the scene so no one is there to listen in on it. The contents derive from a traditional Passover hymn (Pss. 116:10-15), which Jesus sings at the close of the supper: "My distress was bitter. In panic I cried, 'How faithless all men are!' ... I will take in my hand the cup of salvation and invoke the Lord by name.... A precious thing in the Lord's eyes is the death of those who die faithful to him." The betraying kiss of Judas (14:44-45) would seem to derive from 2 Sam. 20:7-10, where Joab, backed by armed men, greets Amasa as a brother, kisses him, then stabs him.

[63]And the men in charge of him mocked him as they beat him, [64]and blindfolding him, they taunted him, saying, "Prophesy! Which one hit you?" [65]And they said many other things against him, blaspheming. [66]And when day dawned, the presbytery of the people convened, both archpriests and scribes, and they led him away to their Sanhedrin, [67]saying, "If you are the Christ, tell us!" And he said to them, "Why bother? If I tell you, there is no way you will believe me. [68]And if I question you, there is no way you will answer.[n] [69]But from now on, one like a son of man will be seated at the right of the power of God."[o] [70]And they all said, "That means you are the son of God." And he said to them, "You say that I am." [71]And they said, "Is there any further need for witnesses? For we heard it for ourselves from his own mouth!"[p]

23

[1]And standing to their feet, the whole body of them led him before Pilatus. [2]And they started accusing him, saying, "We discovered this fellow corrupting our nation and forbidding payment of tribute to Caesar and making himself out to be Christ, a king." [3]And Pilatus interrogated him, saying: "So you are the king of the Jews." And answering him, he says, "If you say so." [4]And Pilatus said to the archpriests and to the crowds, "I find no crime in this man." [5]But they insisted, saying, "He incites the people, teaching throughout all Judea, beginning from all the way in the Galilee to here!" [6]And Pilatus, hearing this, inquired whether the man was in fact a Galilean; [7]and realizing that he fell under Herod's jurisdiction, he remanded him to Herod, who was also in Jerusalem for the feast. [8]And when he saw Jesus, Herod was delighted, for he had for some time wished to see him, having heard about him, and he hoped to see him perform some feat. [9]And he interrogated him with many questions, but he gave no answer.[q] [10]And the archpriests and the scribes stood there hurling accusations at him. [11]And Herod and his soldiers treated him with contempt and mocked him, draping him in royal purple, and packed him off back to Pilatus. [12]And both of them, Herod and Pilatus, became fast friends that day; previously they had been feuding.

---

n. Luke 20:3, 8

o. Dan. 7:13-14

p. Rewritten from 1 Kings 22:24: "Then Zedekiah, the son of Chenaanah, came near and *struck Micaiah on the cheek*, and said, 'How did the spirit of the Lord go from me to speak to you?' And Micaiah said, 'Behold, *you shall see* on that day when you go into an inner chamber to hide yourself.'"

q. Isa. 50:7; 53:7

[13]And Pilatus, calling together the archpriests and the rulers and the people, [14]said to them, "You brought this man to me as corrupting the people, and behold, examining him in your presence, I found this man guilty of none of the crimes you allege against him. [15]And neither did Herod, for he sent him back to us, and it is plain he has done nothing worthy of death. [16]Therefore, I will let him go with a flogging." [17]*For he was obliged to release one prisoner to them at the feast.* [18]But the whole mass shouted, saying, "Take this fellow away and release to us Bar-Abbas!" [19]He was thrown in prison on account of some insurrection in the city and for murder. [20]But again, Pilatus appealed to them, wanting to let Jesus go. [21]But they shouted, saying, "Crucify! Crucify him!" [22]But he said to them a third time, "But what evil did this fellow do? I found no reason to put him to death, so I will let him go with a flogging." [23]But they insisted with loud shouting, calling for him to be crucified, and their voices won out. [24]And Pilatus decided to carry out their request.[r] [25]And he released the one thrown into prison for insurrection and murder, whom they requested, but Jesus he delivered over to their will.

[26]And as they led him away, they commandeered Simon, a certain Cyrenian on his way in from the fields, and they placed the cross on him to carry behind Jesus. [27]And a great mass of the people followed him, including women who mourned and lamented him. [28]And turning to them, Jesus said, "Daughters of Jerusalem, do not waste your tears on me. Weep on your own account and that of your children! [29]Because look: a time is coming when they will say, 'Blessed the barren, the wombs that did not bear, and the breasts which never nursed.' [30]Then they will begin to say to the mountains, 'Crush us!' and to the hills, 'Hide us!' [31]Because if they do these things when a tree is running with sap, who knows what may happen when it is sere?"

[32]And other criminals, too, were led off with him to be killed. [33]And when they reached the place called "the Skull," there they crucified him[s] and the criminals, one to the right and one to the left. [34]*And Jesus said, "Father, forgive them, for they don't realize what they are doing!"* And dividing up his garments, they cast lots.[t] [35]And the people stood watching. And the rulers also scoffed, saying, "Some savior! If this fellow is the

---

r. Surely Hyam Maccoby is correct in suggesting this exchange would make better historical sense if we gave the crowd Pilatus's lines and vice versa. As we read it here, it is a perverse attempt to exonerate Pilatus and to vilify Jews.

s. Pss. 22:16b

t. Pss. 22:18

Christ of God, the Elect One, let him save himself." [36]And the soldiers joined in mocking him, approaching him to offer him vinegar[u] [37]and saying, "If you are the king of the Jews, save yourself!" [38]And there was also an epigraph above him: "This is the king of the Jews." [39]And one of the hanged criminals blasphemed him, saying, "Aren't you supposed to be the Christ? Save yourself—and us as well!" [40]But the other answered, rebuking him, "Don't you fear God? After all, you are under the same sentence. [41]And we indeed deserve it! All we're doing is receiving the just desserts for what we did, but this poor fellow has done nothing amiss." [42]And he said, "Jesus, remember me when you come to your throne, will you?" [43]And he said to him, "Amen: I tell you, today you will join me in the paradise of the saints." [44]And it was, by now, about the sixth hour,[v] and darkness appeared over the whole earth until the ninth hour, [45]the sun having gone out,[w] and the hanging veil of the holy place was torn down the middle. [46]And shouting with a loud voice, Jesus said, "Father, I entrust my spirit into your hands!" And saying this, he breathed his last. [47]And the centurion, seeing what happened, testified before God, saying: "This man really was righteous after all!" [48]And all the crowds gathering together at the spectacle, once they saw what happened, beat their breasts and went back home. [49]And all his acquaintances stood far away, particularly the women accompanying him from the Galilee, watching these things.

[50]And behold, a man named Joseph, a counsel member, a good and just man, [51]not having consented to the council and their action, and being from Arimathea, a city of the Jews, a man also looking forward to the kingdom of God, [52]approached Pilatus and requested custody of the body of Jesus.[x] [53]And taking it down, he wrapped it in linen and placed him in a tomb cut from living rock where no one was yet laid out. [54]And it was the day of preparation, and the Sabbath was coming on fast. [55]And the women who had accompanied him out of the Galilee followed behind him and saw the tomb and how the body was positioned. [56]And returning to the city, they prepared spices and myrrh. And they rested on the Sabbath.

---

u. Pss. 69:21

v. Noon.

w. Amos 8:9

x. Joseph is a combination of King Priam, who courageously comes to Achilles' camp to beg the body of his son Hector, and the patriarch Joseph, who asked Pharaoh's permission to bury the body of Jacob in a cave Jacob had hewn back beyond the Jordan (Gen. 50:4-5).

24

[1]And on the first of the week while it was still quite early, they arrived at the tomb carrying the spices which they had prepared.[y] [2]And they discovered the stone rolled away from the tomb, and [3]venturing inside, they did not find the body of the Lord Jesus.[z] [4]And it happened, as they were perplexed about this, behold, two men appeared beside them in shining clothing. [5]And as they were stricken with terror and bowed with faces to the ground, they said to them, "Why are you looking for a living man among the dead? [6]*He is not here, but was raised!* Think back to how he once told you when he was in the Galilee, [7]'A man must be delivered into the clutches of sinful men and be crucified and on the third day stand up again.'" [8]And they did remember what he had said. [9]And returning from the tomb, they reported all these things to the eleven and to all the rest. [10]Now those who told the apostles these things were Maria the hairdresser, Joanna, Maria of James, and the rest with them; [11]but these words seemed like nonsense when spoken aloud, and they gave the women no credence. [12]*Then Peter got up and ran to the tomb, and bending down, he saw the linen wrappings by themselves and left, speculating over what might have happened.*

[13]And behold, on the same day, two of them were journeying to a village situated sixty stadia from Jerusalem, called Emmaus, [14]and they discussed with each other all these things that had occurred. [15]And it happened that as they were walking and discussing, Jesus himself approached and journeyed with them, [16]but their eyes were prevented from recognizing him. [17]And he said to them, "What are you talking about as you walk?" And they halted, downcast. [18]And one, Simon bar-Cleopas by name, answered, saying to him, "You must be the only pilgrim in Jerusalem unaware of the events transpiring there these past days!" [19]And he said to them, "What events?" And they said to him, "The events surrounding Jesus the Nazarene, who was deemed a prophet powerful in deed and word by God and all the people, [20]how both our archpriests and rulers handed him over to the death sentence and crucified him. [21]And we were hoping that he is the one about to redeem Israel from oppression. [22]But it is now the third day since all this happened. But also some of our women astonished us—being at the tomb early [23]and not finding his body—saying they had seen a vision of angels who declare him to live!

---

y. The women's mourning vigil brings to mind the women's cult of the dying and rising god, long familiar in Israel (Ezek. 8:14; Zech. 12:11; Canticles 3:1-4 2).

z. Josh. 10:26-27, 18, 22

[24]And some of those with us went off to the tomb and found it as the women had described, but him they did not see." [25]And he said to them, "You fools! Too slow-witted to grasp all the things that the prophets predicted! [26]Was not the Christ obliged to suffer and only then to enter into his glory?" [27]And beginning from Moses and all the Prophets, he interpreted all the references to himself in the Writings. [28]And they drew near the village where they were journeying, and he made as if to journey farther. [29]And they urged him, saying, "Stay with us, for it is toward evening and the day has now declined." And he went in to stay with them. [30]And it came about as he reclined at table with them, taking the loaf, he blessed it and, having broken it, handed it to them. [31]And their eyes were opened up, and they recognized him—and at once he became invisible to them. [32]And they said to each other, "Did not hope begin to rekindle inside us as he spoke to us on the road, as he disclosed the hidden meaning of the scriptures to us?" [33]And getting up despite the lateness of the hour, they retraced their steps to Jerusalem, and they discovered the eleven and those with them already gathered [34]and said, "The Lord was really raised and appeared to Simon bar-Cleopas!" [35]And they recounted the events on the road and how he was recognized by them in the act of breaking the loaf.

[36]And as they were saying these things, he stood in their midst. [37]But frightened and terror-stricken, they thought they beheld a spirit. [38]And he said to them, "Why do you tremble and why do such thoughts arise in your hearts? [39]Look at my hands and my feet, that it is I myself! Take hold of me and see for yourselves: because a spirit has not flesh and bones as you can see I have." [40]*And when he had said this, he showed them both hands and feet.* [41]And with them stunned, still thinking it too good to be true, he said to them, "Do you have any food here?" [42]And they handed him part of a broiled fish, [43]and taking it, he ate it before their eyes.[a] [44]And he said to them, "Remember my words which I spoke to you when I was still with you on earth, that all the predictions of me in the Law of Moses and the Prophets and the Psalms must be fulfilled?" [45]Then he opened up their minds to understand the esoteric meaning of the scriptures. [46]And he said to them, "You see? It is written that the Christ must suffer and get up from the dead on the third day [47]and that repentance for forgiveness of sins must be proclaimed in his name among the nations beginning from Jerusalem. [48]You are witnesses of these things coming true. [49]And behold, I send to you what my Father prom-

---

a. This was to demonstrate his bodily reality since it was believed spirits, ghosts, and angels could not eat (Judges 6:19-23; 13:15-23; Tobit 12:19).

ised. But sit in the city until you are clothed with a power[b] from the zenith of heaven."

[50]And he led them out as far as the approach to Beth-Anu[c] and, lifting up his hands, he blessed them. [51]And it came about that while he was uttering the blessing, he was separated from them *and was carried up to heaven.* [52]And they returned to Jerusalem with great joy, [53]and they were constantly in the temple blessing God.[d]

---

b. The Holy Spirit, thought of here as an angel.

c. Literally "house of the sun," no coincidence because the ascension is like the rising noonday sun; cf. 2 Kings 2:11; Gen. 5:23-24.

d. Luke's ascension narrative is the only one in the gospels and is based on the account of Elijah's ascension in 2 Kings 2, though Luke also seems to include elements from Josephus about Moses's ascension: "And as soon as they were come to the mountain called Abarim, ... he was going to embrace Eleazar and Joshua, and was still discoursing with them, [when] a cloud stood over him on the sudden, and he disappeared in a certain valley" (*Antiquities* V.1.48, Whiston trans.). In 2 Kings 2:9, Elijah bequests Elisha a double share of his spirit or power. Likewise, before his own ascension, Jesus gives his disciples "the promise of my Father" (Luke 24:49), which will be a "clothing" of power—recalling how Elisha parted the Jordan with Elijah's mantle (1 Kings 2:12). Both Elijah and Jesus are assumed into heaven (1 Kings 2:11; Luke 24:50-53: Acts 1:1-1), the former with the aid of Apollo's chariot, but both are pointedly separated from their disciples (2 Kings 2:11; Luke 24:51). After this, the promised spirit comes, empowering the disciples (2 Kings 2:15; Acts 2:4). Elijah's ascent is confirmed by his disciples, whose search fails to turn up his body (2 Kings 2:16-18); Jesus' ascent is confirmed by the empty tomb (Luke 24:3; Acts 1:9-11).

23.

The Acts of All the Apostles

I HAVE DECIDED TO USE THE TITLE that appears in the Muratorian canon list as it grasps the point of this work quite well, namely, to accentuate Paul's rivals and place them on a par with him in the eyes of Marcionite and other Paulinist readers, whom it hopes to convert to the Catholic (Petrine) fold. The Book of Acts presents a major textual problem like that of Jeremiah in the Old Testament in that there are two rather different versions of the Greek text. The Western text, represented especially by the Greek and Latin Codex Bezae, is about 20 percent longer than the version usually employed in modern English translations. Text critics commonly accept a few readings here and there from the Western text, but I have thought it best to include just about all of the additional material in italics. I have put alternate readings, as opposed to expansions to the text, in footnotes. Where the Western text omits words appearing in the other, I have italicized the additional words and added a dagger (†) symbol. It may well be that Western Acts represents a subsequent re-editing of the work by the original author. It reads like the same author only more so, as one might say. For other introductory matters, see the introduction to Luke-Acts prefacing the Gospel according to Luke.

1

The first account I composed covering all the things, O Theophilus,
that Jesus started to do and to teach [2]up to that day on which he was
taken up, having issued instructions through the Holy Spirit to the apostles whom he had chosen *and ordered to proclaim the news,* [3]to whom

also he displayed himself alive after his suffering by means of many proofs that could not fail to convince, being seen by them over a period of forty days and speaking of the details of the kingdom of God; [4]and as he was eating with them, he ordered them not to leave Jerusalem but to wait for what the Father promised, what you all have heard of from me *from my mouth,* [5]because just as John baptized in water, you will be baptized in Holy Spirit, *which you are about to receive* not too many days from now *at Pentecost.*[a] [6]So then, once assembled, they questioned him, asking, "Lord, is this the moment you will restore sovereignty to Israel?" [7]He said to them, "It is no concern of yours what times and turning points the Father has scheduled by his sovereign will. [8]All you need to know is that you will receive power when the Holy Spirit overtakes you and you will be my witnesses both in Jerusalem and in the whole of Judea and Samaria and to the last reaches of the earth."[b]

[9]And when he had said these things, *with them looking on,* he was taken up, and a cloud concealed him from their view. [10]And as they were staring at him receding into the sky, behold, two men suddenly stood beside them in white garments, [11]who said, "Men! Galileans! Why do you stand gaping at the sky? You haven't seen the last of him. This Jesus, the one taken up from you *into the sky* in this way will return in the same way you saw him traveling into the sky."[c] [12]Then they returned to Jerusalem from the mountain named Olivet, which is close to Jerusalem, about the distance allowed for travel on a Sabbath. [13]And when they went into the second-storey room, they went up into the place they were waiting, both Peter and John, *and* Jacob and Andreas, Philip and the Twin, Bar-Ptolemy and Matthew, Jacob of Alphaeus, *and* Simon the Zealot and Judas of Jacob. [14]These all were persevering in prayer with dedication and single-mindedness with *the* women *and children* including Mariam the mother of Jesus and his brothers.

[15]And during those days of waiting, Peter stood to his feet in the midst of the brothers[d] to say to the crowd of about one hundred twenty

---

a. Unless Alvin Boyd Kuhn and Stephan Hermann Huller are correct that Theophilus is to be identified with Theophilus of Antioch, we might guess that Luke's Theophilus and his household were catechumens (Luke 1:4) preparing for baptism, for whom Luke prepared his work.

b. A Lukan parallel to John 21:20-23, similarly aimed at deflecting an earlier, disappointed expectation of the soon arrival of Jesus.

c. Mark 13:26-27; Matt. 24:26-27; Luke 17:22-24

d. The Western text has "disciples" instead of "brothers."

names, [16]"Men, brothers, the scripture had to be fulfilled, which the Holy Spirit predicted through David's mouth concerning Judas, he who acted as guide to those who arrested Jesus, [17]because he was counted as one of us and had gained a share in this ministry." [18]Therefore, to fulfill scripture, this fellow bought a field from the reward he got for his unrighteousness, and swelling up, he burst open in the middle and all his intestines poured out.[e] [19]And it became known to everyone living in Jerusalem, with the result that this field became known in their own language as *Akeldamach* or "field of blood."[f] [20]"For it is written in the scroll of Psalms, 'Let his estate be deserted with no one to dwell in it' and 'Let another take his bishopric.' [21]Therefore, it is required that one of these men who accompanied us the whole time the Lord Jesus *Christ* associated with us, [22]starting with John's baptism until the day he was taken up from us, must become a witness along with us of his resurrection." [23]And they[g] nominated two, Joseph born-on-the-Sabbath, who was surnamed Justin,[h] and Matthias.[i] [24]And they prayed, saying, "You, Lord, knower of the hearts of all, show which one of these two you chose [25]to take the place in this ministry and apostleship from which Judas fell to go to his proper place." [26]And they cast lots for them, and the lot fell on Matthias, and henceforth he was counted along with the eleven[j] as apostles.

2

[1]And *it came about that in those days* when the Day of Pentecost had finally arrived, they were all *in one place* together. [2]And *behold,* suddenly there was a sound from the sky like a violent, whipping wind. And it filled the whole house where they sat, [3]and tongues of flame appeared to them,

---

e. Luke has modeled his version of Judas's miserable death on that of Amasa, about whom we learn from 2 Sam. 20:10 LXX that his "bowels poured out (εξεχυθη) upon the ground."

f. This comes originally from the bloody field on which Anath discovered the death of Baal, then determined to raise him from the netherworld. It is a Christian replacement etiology. Verses 18-19 seem to be parenthetical, intended as an authorial aside to the reader, not part of Peter's speech, which continues naturally in v. 20 from v. 17.

g. The Western text has "he."

h. The Western text substitutes "Bar-Nabas." One also thinks of Justin Martyr, who claimed to have read the "memoirs of the apostles."

i. This may be the same as Matthaias (Matthew) with whom Matt. 9:9 has replaced Mark's Levi, the customs agent (2:14). In fact, his appearance here may have prompted the narrative retrojection into the gospel.

j. The Western text has "among the twelve."

dividing up among them, and one[k] rested on each one of them,[l] [4]and they were all filled with the Holy Spirit and started speaking in other tongues as the Spirit granted them to speak out.[m] [5]There were Jews living in Jerusalem, pious men from every nation under the sky. [6]When this sound occurred, the crowd came together and was confounded because[n] it seemed to each hearer that the whole group was speaking in his own language.[o] [7]And they were *all* amazed and marveled, saying, "Behold, aren't all these speakers Galileans? [8]Then how on earth can each one of us be hearing it as if they were all speaking each one's native language? [9]Parthians and Medes and Elamites, the inhabitants of Mesopotamia, of both Judea and Cappadocia, Pontus and Asia, [10]both Phrygia and Pamphylia, Egypt and the districts of Libya adjacent to Cyrene, and Roman pilgrims, [11]both Jews and proselytes, Cretans and Arabs. We hear them speaking in our tongues the great deeds of God!" [12]All were amazed and disturbed *over what had occurred,* saying to one another, "What is going on here?" [13]But others made fun of them, saying, "They are filled with sweet wine!"[p] [14]But Peter stood up with the eleven[q] and raised his voice *first,* saying to them, "Men! Jews and Jerusalemites all! Let this be known to you,[r] *and* listen to what I have to say. [15]For it is not as you imagine, that these men are drunk, since it is only the third hour of the day.[s] [16]Instead, this is the very thing spoken of through the prophet *Joel*:

> [17]'*And* it shall be in the last days, says God,
> I will pour out some of my Spirit on all flesh
> and your[t] sons and your[u] daughters shall prophesy
> and your[v] young men shall see visions

---

k. Western text: "they."

l. Euripides' *Bacchae* is the source here: "Flames flickered in their curls and did not burn them" (lines 757-58).

m. The whole scene comes, obviously, from the descent of the Mosaic spirit upon the seventy elders in Num. 11:16-17, 24-25.

n. The Western text has "and."

o. Western text: "tongue."

p. 1 Cor. 14:23

q. The Western text has "ten apostles."

r. Western text: "us."

s. 9:00 AM; cf. *Bacchae,* lines 686-87: "not, as you think, drunk with wine."

t. The Western text has "their."

u. Western text: "their."

v. Western text: "the."

and your[w] elders will dream dreams.
18And on my slaves and on my slave girls,
I will, in those days, pour of my Spirit
and they shall prophesy,
19and I will provide wonders in the sky above
and signs on the earth below:
blood and fire and drifting smoke,
20the sun will be transformed into darkness
and the moon into blood
before the great[x] day of Adonai shall dawn.
21And this is how it will be: everyone who may invoke
the name of Adonai shall be delivered.'

22"Men! Israelites! Hear these words! Jesus the Nazorean, a man having
been certified by God among you by means of powerful deeds and wonders and signs which God performed through him in your midst, as you
yourselves know, 23you *took and* killed this man, who was delivered up
by the providential wisdom and foreknowledge of God to be fastened to
a cross by the agency of gentiles, 24a man, however, whom God raised up,
loosening the painful chains of death,[y] because it was not possible for the
grim reaper to keep him captive. Why not? Scripture forbade it. 25For David speaks to his situation:

'I foresaw the[z] Lord ever in front of me
because he is at my right so I will not be shaken.
26That is why my heart rejoiced
and my tongue exulted in song,
and now, too, my flesh will live on in hope,
27because you will not abandon my soul to Hades,
nor will you allow your saint to rot away.
28You indicated to me the ways to life
and you will fill me with gladness at your presence.'

29"Men *and* Brothers! It is safe to say straight out that the patriarch David both died and was buried—his tomb is among us to this day.
30Therefore, being a prophet and knowing that God swore an oath to him

w. Western text: "the."

x. Western text: "momentous."

y. Western text: "Hades."

z. Western text: "my."

that a successor from the fruit of his loins[a] should sit on his throne, 31he
spoke clairvoyantly of the resurrection of the Christ, that neither should
he be abandoned to Hades, nor should his flesh suffer decomposition.
32God *therefore* raised up this Jesus, and we can all attest that. 33So then,
having been exalted to the right of God, and receiving the promise of the
Holy Spirit from the Father, he poured out *upon you* this which you both
see and hear. 34For David did not ascend into the skies, but he says,

> 'Adonai said to milord, Sit to my right
> 35until I make the necks of your foes
> a footstool to rest your feet.'

36"Therefore, let all the house of Israel know without doubt that God
made *him* both Lord and Christ, this Jesus whom you crucified."

37Hearing this, they[b] were stung in conscience and *some of them* said
to Peter and to the *rest of the* apostles, "*Therefore,* what are we to do,
men? Brothers? *Show us!*"[c] 38And Peter said to them, "Repent, and each
of you let yourselves be baptized in the name of *the Lord* Jesus Christ for
the forgiveness of *your* sins and you will receive the gift of the Holy Spirit.
39For the promise extends to you[d] and to your[e] children and to all far
away,[f] as many as Adonai our God may happen to call."

40And with many other words he solemnly testified and pleaded with
them, saying, "Save yourselves from this twisted race!" 41So those who
welcomed[g] his message were baptized, and that day about three thousand
souls were added, 42and they were persevering in the teaching of the apostles *in Jerusalem* and in the fellowship, in the breaking of the loaf and in
the prayers. 43And awe shook every soul, and many wonders and signs
occurred through the apostles. 44And all those who believed were together and shared all things in common, 45and they *who had them* sold
the properties and possessions and *daily* distributed the proceeds to all,
according to each one's needs. 46And daily, persevering with dedication
and unanimity in the temple, and breaking bread from house to house,

a. Western text: "of his heart according to the flesh."

b. Western text: "all who had come together."

c. 1 Cor. 14:24

d. The Western text has "us."

e. Western text: "our."

f. Theophilus and his family are in view here.

g. The Western text has "believed."

they *all* took meals in gladness and sincerity of heart, [47]praising God and enjoying favor with all the people.[h] And every day the Lord added together *in the congregation* those who were being saved.

3

[1]*In these days* Peter and John were going up to the temple *in the evening* at the hour of prayer, the ninth hour.[i] [2]And *behold,* a certain man, being lame from his mother's womb, was being carried, as they did every day, to the gate of the temple called the Beautiful Gate, where he would beg alms from those entering into the temple. [3]Once he saw[j] Peter and John on their way into the temple, he asked to receive alms *from them.* [4]And Peter, fixing his attention on him, along with John, said, "Look us in the eye." [5]And he looked at them expectantly, assuming he would receive something from them. [6]Peter said, "I have no silver or gold, but what I do have I'll be happy to give you! In the name of Jesus Christ the Nazorean—walk!" [7]And grasping his right hand, he pulled him to his feet. At once *he stood and* his feet and ankle bones were made firm, [8]and leaping up, he stood and walked around *rejoicing* and accompanied them into the temple, *walking and leaping and* praising God as he went. [9]And all the people observed him walking and praising God; [10]and they recognized him, that this was the one who sat at the Beautiful Gate of the temple soliciting alms, and they were filled with wonderment and confusion at what had happened to him.[k]

[11]And *as Peter and John went,* he clung to Peter and John,[l] and all the people, *standing* greatly amazed, ran together to them at the enclosure called Solomon's Portico. [12]And seeing this, Peter answered their unspoken question: "Men! Israelites! Why should you marvel at this fellow? Or why do you stare at us as if we had made him walk[m] by token of our own power or piety? [13]No, the God of Abraham and *the God of* Isaac and *the God of* Jacob, the God of our fathers has glorified his servant Jesus *Christ,*[n] whom you handed over *to judgment* and repudiated in front of Pilatus when he had decided *and desired* to set him free. [14]But you

h. Western text: "world."

i. 3:00 PM

j. The Western text has "staring at."

k. This appears to be a variant of John's story (chap. 9) of the man who was born blind.

l. The Western text has "them."

m. Western text: "done this thing."

n. Note the anti-Marcionite emphasis: Jesus was sent by the Hebrew God.

repudiated[o] the righteous saint and requested that a man who was a murderer be granted you instead. 15And you killed the prince of life, whom God raised from the dead, of which we are witnesses. 16And on the strength of the faith named for him, his name strengthened this man whom you see and recognize, and the faith that comes by him gave him this soundness before all of you. 17Rest assured, *men and* brothers, I[p] know you acted[q] by way of ignorance,[r] as your rulers did, too. 18But in this way, God fulfilled the things he had announced beforehand by the mouth of all the prophets, that his Christ was to suffer. 19So repent and turn back for your sins to be expunged, 20so the times of restoration[s] may arrive from the presence of the Lord and he may send the Christ already appointed for you, Jesus, 21whom heaven is required to keep until the times of restitution of all things,[t] which God spoke about through the mouth of all his holy prophets from antiquity. 22For example, Moses said *to our fathers,* 'The God Adonai will resurrect from your brothers a prophet like me. You must pay heed to him in whatever matters he may address. 23And this is how it shall be: every soul who does not take that prophet seriously will be utterly eradicated from the nation.' 24And all the prophets in succession from Samuel, as many as spoke, also announced these days; 25you are the heirs of the prophets and the covenant which God made with our fathers when he said to Abraham, 'And in your lineage all the families of the earth shall be blessed.' 26Having resurrected his servant,[u] God sent him to you Jews first,[v] blessing you by turning each one of you away from his evils."

4

1And as they spoke *these words* to the people, the priests *and the*

---

o. The Western text has "oppressed."

p. Western text: "we."

q. Western text: "did an evil thing."

r. Luke 23:34

s. This phrase, also in the next verse, refers to the era of resurrection and restoration of Jewish sovereignty. See Luke 2:25, 38; 17:22; 24:21; Mark 9:12; Matt. 19:28; Thomas 51.

t. See John A. T. Robinson, "The Most Primitive Christology of All?" in John A. T. Robinson, ed., *Twelve New Testament Studies* (London: SCM Press, 1962), 139-53. Jesus is pictured here like the Orthodox Emperor Constans, deposed by his heretic brother Constantius and waiting in heaven to return as Emperor of the Last Days, or Muhammad al-Mahdi, Shi'ite imam assumed into heaven, where he waits to return as the Qa'im, "He Who Shall Arise."

u. The use of the term "servant" for Jesus (3:26; 4:25, 27, 30) is modeled on

commander of the temple police and the Syndics arrived on the scene. [2]They were greatly agitated that they were teaching the people the doctrine of resurrection from the dead and pointing to Jesus as an instance of it. [3]So they grabbed them and placed them under guard till the next day, for by now it was evening. [4]But many in the audience believed the message, and the number of men grew to about five thousand. [5]It came about the next day that their rulers and elders and scribes [6]and Annas, the archpriest, and Caiaphas and John[w] and Alexander, and as many as belonged to the archpriestly house, gathered in Jerusalem. [7]And once they had stood them in the middle of the chamber, they asked, "By what angelic power or in what divine name did you do this?"

[8]Then Peter, full of Holy Spirit, said to them, "Rulers of the people and elders *of Israel,* [9]if today we are being examined *by you* for a good deed done an infirm man, asked by what means this man was cured, [10]let it be known to you and to all the people of Israel that by the name of Jesus Christ the Nazorean, whom you crucified, whom God raised from the dead—by this means, I say, this man stands before you whole. [11]This is the famous stone disdained by you builders, the one that has become the head of the corner. [12]Nor is there *salvation* available by any other means, for neither is there any other name that has been provided on earth by which we are required to be saved." [13]As they observed the boldness of Peter and John, in view of their being untutored *and ignorant* laymen, they marveled. And they recognized them as associates of Jesus. [14]And seeing the man who had been cured standing beside them, there was nothing for them to say.

[15]So they ordered them to step outside the council chamber, then exchanged ideas, [16]saying, "Well? What do we do with these men? For it is *more than* obvious to everyone in Jerusalem that a remarkable sign has been worked through them and we cannot deny it. [17]But to prevent it spreading any further among the people, let us threaten them not to speak

---

the Old Testament "my servant David" as a mark of some primitive tradition incorporated by Luke. Rather, the title is attested only in second-century sources such as the Coptic Didache (9:2; 10:7); *Martyrdom of Polycarp* (14:1, 3; 20:2); and 1 Clement (59:2ff). See J. C. O'Neill, *The Theology of Acts in Its Historical Setting* (London: Society for Promoting Christian Knowledge, 1961), 133-39.

v. This refers to apostolic preaching rather than to the ministry of Jesus himself; the gospel was only preached to the gentiles after Jews were given the first shot at it (Acts 13:46; 18:5-6; 28:28; Mark 7:27; Rom. 2:10).

w. The Western text has "Jonathan."

any more to anyone about this name."[x] [18]And *agreeing to this decision,* calling them back in, they ordered them never again to either preach or teach about the name of Jesus. [19]But Peter and John, answering, said to them, "Whether it is right in God's sight to listen to you rather than to God, you tell me! [20]As for us, we can hardly refrain from speaking about what we saw and heard." [21]And they reiterated their threats and released them, finding no way to punish them because of the people, since all praised God on account of what had happened. [22]For the man on whom this healing sign had been performed was over forty years old. [23]Once released, they went to their own compatriots and recounted what the archpriests and the elders said to them. [24]Having heard it *and recognized the working of God,* they raised their voice harmoniously to God and said, "O Despot, *the God* who made the sky and the earth and the sea and everything in them,[y] [25]who said through the Holy Spirit by the mouth of *our father* David, your servant,

> 'Why did nations rage
> and peoples devise futile plans?
> [26]The kings of the earth came together
> and the rulers made common cause
> against the Lord
> and against his Christ.'

[27]For in truth, both Herod and Pontius Pilatus did conspire with gentile 'nations' and 'peoples' of Israel against your holy servant Jesus, whom you anointed Christ, [28]to do what your guiding hand and wisdom foreordained to happen. [29]And now, Lord, consider how they threaten, and grant that your slaves may speak your message with complete boldness [30]by extending your hand to cure and perform signs and wonders through the name of your holy servant Jesus." [31]And even as they were petitioning God, the place where they were gathered was shaken and they were all filled with the Holy Spirit and spoke the message of God with boldness *to every one who wanted to believe.*[z]

[32]The community of those who believed shared one heart and soul

---

x. Notice the curious lack of connection with the Gospel Passion narrative. The Sanhedrin makes no mention of the recent events surrounding Jesus, and it is merely the heresy of resurrection belief per se, Jesus or no Jesus, which primarily rouses their ire.

y. Reference to the Christian God as the Creator is anti-Marcionite.

z. The answer does not really fit the prayer: they ask for bravery in the face of

and there was no distinction at all among them and not one of them claimed his possessions for his own, but all things were held in common.[a] [33]And with great effect the apostles of the Lord Jesus *Christ* bore witness to his resurrection, and great charisma radiated from them all. [34]For neither was anyone among them needy, for as many as owned properties or houses sold them and brought the proceeds of the sales [35]and placed it at the feet of the apostles, and the funds were distributed to each one as needed. [36]And Joseph, whom the apostles surnamed Bar-Nabas, which is translated "son of encouragement,"[b] a Levite, a Cypriot by race, [37]had a field and sold it and brought the proceeds to the apostles and laid it at their feet.[c]

5

[1]But a certain man named Ananias with his wife Sapphira sold a piece of land, [2]and he kept for himself, with his wife's knowledge, some of the money and then brought a certain portion of the price and laid it at the apostles' feet. [3]But Peter said, "Ananias, how did the adversary manage to fill your heart with the idea of deceiving the Holy Spirit and keeping part of the price of the land? [4]Before you sold it, wasn't it yours to do with as you pleased? Wasn't it sold with your free consent? What put this *wicked* scheme into your head? You did not lie to mortals, but to God." [5]Hearing these words, Ananias *at once* dropped dead. And terror seized everyone who heard. [6]And the young men got up and wrapped him up and carried him out to bury him. [7]And after an interval of about three hours, his wife came in looking for him, unaware of what had happened. [8]And Peter answered her, "Remind me, was this the price you got for the land you two sold?" And she said, "Yes, that was the amount." [9]And

---

persecution, but the result is an immediate self-contained spiritual ecstasy as if they had begun speaking in tongues (cf. 2:4; 10:44; 19:6).

a. This is an idealized portrait of an imagined "primitive communism" thought by the ancients to have existed at the dawn of history. It does not mean that some early Christians did not try to put it into practice just as their parent sect, the Essenes, did. Such liquidation of assets would readily explain the subsequent poverty of the Jerusalem church (Gal. 2:10).

b. Actually, it is an old name stemming from the Babylonian exile and means "son of Nebo (Nabu)," god of good luck and fate. Here he is an ideal figure, "Bar-Nabas" standing for "son of Naboth," as his association with a field recalls the story of Naboth's vineyard (1 Kings 21). Elements of the same story were used to construct the story of Stephen's stoning in Acts 6-7, as Thomas L. Brodie has demonstrated in "Luke the Literary Interpreter," Ph.D. diss., Pontifical University of Saint Thomas Aquinas, 1981.

c. Could Luke have imagined Bar-Nabas sold the field to Judas?

Peter said to her, "Why did you conspire to trick the Spirit of Adonai? Listen! The footsteps of those who buried your husband are at the door now and they will get rid of you, too." 10And at once, she dropped dead at his feet. And as they entered, the young men found her, and *having wrapped her up,* they carried her out and buried her beside her husband. 11And terror seized the whole assembly and everyone else who heard it.[d]

12And at the hands of the apostles, many signs and wonders were wrought among the people, and all gathered harmoniously *in the temple* in the Portico of Solomon.[e] 13And of the Levites,[f] no one dared associate with them, but the people spoke openly of their greatness. 14More and more believers were added to the Lord's flock, great numbers both of men and of women, 15so that they even brought the infirm into the streets on stretchers and mats, hoping that as Peter passed by his shadow might fall across this one or that. *For they were freed from every sickness that each one had.*[g] 16And *also* a great mass gathered from the cities surround-

---

d. As Alfred Loisy said, this cautionary tale warns readers not to even think of welching on a church pledge. According to Brodie, "Luke the Literary Interpreter," it is modeled upon the sticky-fingered Achan in Josh. 7 and the conspiracy of Ahab and Jezebel to cheat the pious Naboth out of his vineyard (1 Kings 20:1-21:21). Luke has punningly made Naboth into the righteous Barnabas and possession of a field into the sale of a field, both exciting a wicked couple's jealousy. Ananias plays Ahab, Sapphira plays Jezebel, only they do not conspire to murder anyone. That element is reserved for the martyrdom of Stephen. The crime of Ananias and Sapphira is borrowed instead from that of Achan, who appropriated for himself the treasure earmarked for God. Wanting to be admired like Barnabas, Ananias and Sapphira sell a field but only donate part of the revenue—something they have no business doing since it is "devoted to the Lord." Peter confronts them, as Joshua did Achan (Josh. 7:25) and as Elijah did Ahab (1 Kings 20:17-18). Luke transforms Ahab's disturbance in spirit (20:4) into a charge that the couple had lied to the Spirit of God (Acts 5:3b-4, 9b). Punishment is delayed for Ahab and Jezebel, but Elijah's and Peter's pronouncements of death are immediately effected (5:5a, 10a). Just as fear fell on all who heard of Ananias's and Sapphira's fate, poor indecisive Ahab was struck with the fear of God by Elijah's doom oracle (1 Kings 20:27-29). Not long after the Naboth incident in the Old Testament, we learn that the young men of Israel defeated the greedy Syrians (21:1-21), which likely made Luke think of having the young men, never in evidence elsewhere in Acts, carry out and bury the bodies of the greedy couple (5:6, 10b).

e. This location, otherwise a pointless detail, is perhaps meant to remind the ancient reader of the *stoa* ("porch") where the original Stoics, disciples of Xeno of Citium, used to meet. See Acts 17:18.

f. Extant texts read "and of the rest," which belies the context. Hilgenfeld suspected a copying error for "and of the Levites," which looks similar in Greek.

g. Cf. Acts 19:11-12. Peter and Paul are paralleled to symbolically reconcile Catholicism and Marcionism, of which the two served as figureheads.

ing Jerusalem, carrying the infirm and those haunted by unclean spirits, and all were healed.

[17]And the archpriest and all his associates in the party of the Syndics took action, being filled with jealousy, [18]and they grabbed the apostles and publicly took them into custody. *And each one returned to his own dwelling.* [19]But an angel of Adonai opened the doors of the prison during the night and led them out, saying, [20]"Go stand in the temple and speak to all the people the truth of this life!" [21]And having marked his words, they entered the temple about dawn and taught. And once they arrived, *having awakened early,* the archpriest and his associates called together the Sanhedrin and the whole counsel of elders of the sons of Israel and they sent word to the jail to bring them. [22]But once they got there *and opened the prison,* the attendants did not find them in the prison; and once they returned, they gave their report, [23]saying, "We found the jail securely locked and the guards posted at the doors, but when we opened the doors we found no one inside!"[h]

[24]Hearing this report, both the captain of the temple police and the archpriests began to wonder just what they had gotten into. [25]And someone rushed in to report, "Behold, the men you put into prison are standing in the temple, teaching the people!" [26]Then the captain with his lieutenants fetched them, not forcibly, for they feared the people, not wanting to be stoned. [27]Bringing them, they placed them in the middle of the council chamber. [28]And the archpriest interrogated them, saying, "I thought we gave you strict orders not to teach about this name, and here you have filled Jerusalem with your teaching and you are trying to pin this man's death on us!"[i] [29]In answer, Peter *and the apostles*[†] said *to them,* "We are obliged to obey God rather than mortals.[j] [30]The God of

h. This happens again to Peter alone (12:1-19) and to Paul and Silas (16:23-34). The point, again, is to harmonize Marcionism/Paulinism with Catholic Christianity represented by the figurehead of Peter. Though embodying a common motif in Hellenistic literature, these scenes seem directly borrowed from Euripides' *Bacchae,* trans. Gilbert Murray: "As for those women you clapped in chains and sent to the dungeon, they're gone, clean away, went skipping off to the fields crying on their God Bromius. The chains on their legs snapped apart by themselves. Untouched by any human hand, the doors swung wide, opening of their own accord" (lines 444-49).

i. No mention of their escape?

[†]Present in the Alexandrian, but not the Western (Roman), version of Acts.

j. This comes from Plato's *Apology,* 29d, where Socrates says to his judges: "I will obey God rather than you."

our fathers raised Jesus, whom you killed, hanging him on a tree. [31]This man God exalted *for his glory, to the right of him,* as a ruler and a savior, to provide repentance to Israel and forgiveness of sins.[k] [32]And we are witnesses to *all* these things, and so is the Holy Spirit which God gave to those who obey him."

[33]And his audience were stung and were moved to kill them. [34]But a certain Pharisee named Gamaliel, a sage of the Torah esteemed by all the people, stood up in the Sanhedrin and ordered that the men[l] step outside for a bit. [35]And he said to them,[m] "Men, Israelites, consider well what you intend to do with these men. [36]For before these days, Theudas appeared and claimed to be somebody *important,*[n] and about four hundred men joined him. He was killed *by himself,* and all who took orders from him scattered and it all came to nothing. [37]After this, Judas the Galilean appeared in the time of the Roman taxation census and drew away his share of people after him. That one perished, and all who took orders from him scattered, too.[o] [38]And now *brothers,* I say to you, stand down and leave these men alone, *not bloodying your hands,* because if this enterprise or this work is of mortal origin, it will collapse under its own weight. [39]But if it should come from God after all, you will not be able to destroy them no matter what you do, *neither you nor kings nor tyrants: so keep away from these men.* At worst, you might even turn out to be fighting against God."[p] And they yielded to him. [40]And summoning the apostles, they roughed them up and ordered them not to speak about the name of Jesus, then released them. [41]So they[q] left the presence of the Sanhedrin rejoicing because God had considered them worthy to be humili-

k. The Western text has "in him."

l. Western text: "apostles."

m. Western text: "the rulers and members of the Sanhedrin."

n. Theudas, who seemingly claimed to be Joshua returned to earth, promised to stop the Jordan River in its course to verify his messianic credentials.

o. This much of the speech is derived from Josephus, only Luke has confused the historical order. Josephus discusses the later Theudas first (*Antiquities of the Jews,* 20.5.1), followed by a flashback reference to the earlier Judas the Galilean (20:5:2). Luke confuses the order of events with their order of narration. In fact, Theudas appeared in 40 CE after the time of this very scene.

p. Luke has borrowed this half of the speech from Euripides' *Bacchae,* where the sages Cadmus and Teiresius, then Dionysus himself, warn King Pentheus not to persecute the new sect of Dionysus in case it turns out to be true and they would be found fighting God and earn his vengeance. "I warn you once again," reads line 789, "do not take arms against a god!"

q. The Western text has "the apostles."

ated on account of the name. [42]And every day in the temple and door to door they did not cease teaching and evangelizing *the Lord* Christ Jesus.

6

[1]In these days, as the number of disciples grew rapidly, there arose a murmuring from the Hellenists against the Hebrews because their widows were overlooked in the daily meals *distributed by the Hebrews.* [2]And the twelve, summoning the whole community of disciples, said, "It makes no sense for us to leave off preaching the message of God to waste our time waiting tables. *What to do, then, brothers?* [3]But brothers, look over your ranks and choose seven men known to be full of the Spirit and of wisdom and we will appoint them to this matter. [4]As for us, we have more important matters to see to: prayer and the ministry of preaching." [5]And the idea sounded good to the whole community *of disciples,* so they chose Stephen, a man full of faith and of Holy Spirit, and Philip, and Prochorus, and Nicanor,[r] and Timon, and Parmenas, and Nicolaus, a proselyte from Antioch, [6]whom they presented to the apostles, and having prayed, they laid hands on them.[s]

[7]And the influence of the message of God grew, and the number of disciples in Jerusalem multiplied greatly. A large number of priests submitted to the faith. [8]And Stephen, full of charisma and power, performed wonders and great signs among the people *through the name of the Lord Jesus Christ.*[t] [9]But some members of the Synagogue of the Freedmen, as it was called, and Cyrenians and Alexandrians and those from Cilicia *and Asia*[†] got together to mount a response to Stephen, [10]but they found themselves unable to deal with the wisdom *that was in him* and the *Holy* Spirit with which he spoke[u] *because they were continually rebuffed by him boldly.* [11]Finally,[v] they suborned men *against him,* coaching them, "We have heard him uttering blasphemies against Moses and God." [12]And they stirred up the people and the elders and scribes. And finding him, they grabbed him and hauled him before the Sanhedrin. [13]And false witnesses stood up, saying, "This man will not stop railing against this holy place and the Torah! [14]For we have heard him say-

r. Western text: "Nicor."

s. The story is modeled on that of the appointment of the seventy elders to assist Moses in Exod. 18:13-26.

t. Stephen ("crown") is named for winning the crown of martyrdom, thus signaling that he is a fictitious character.

u. Luke 21:12-15

v. The Western text has "So unable to admit the truth."

ing, 'Jesus the Nazorean will demolish this place and will tamper with the customs Moses delivered to us.'"[w] [15]And as all those sitting in the Sanhedrin stared at him, his face looked to them like the face of an angel *standing among them.*

7

[1]The archpriest said *to Stephen,* "Tell us if these things are so." [2]And he said, "Men, brothers, and fathers, listen to me. The God of glory appeared to our father Abraham in Mesopotamia before he lived in Harran, [3]and he said to him, 'Go forth from your land and your relatives and enter whatever land I may show you.' [4]Then, leaving the land of the Chaldeans, he[x] lived in Harran. And *he stayed there* after his father died; God took him away from there into the land you now dwell in, *like our fathers before us,* [5]and he did not give him an inheritance there, nor even sufficient space to set his foot down, but he promised to give it to him and his subsequent descendants to possess, and this while he still had no child. [6]And God spoke like this *to him,* to the effect that his posterity would sojourn in a land belonging to others who would enslave them and ill-treat them some four hundred years. [7]And God said, 'Whatever nation they serve, I will judge, and afterward they will emerge and will worship me in this place.' [8]And he gave him the covenant of circumcision; and accordingly, when he fathered Isaac, he circumcised him on the eighth day. And Isaac fathered Jacob, and Jacob fathered the twelve patriarchs.

[9]"And when the patriarchs grew jealous, they sold Joseph into Egypt, and God went with him [10]and extricated him from all his vicissitudes and imparted to him inspired wisdom for Pharaoh, king of Egypt, to see, so that he appointed him vizier over Egypt and steward over all his affairs. [11]But a famine devastated all Egypt and Canaan, and our fathers could find nothing to eat. [12]But Jacob, having heard there was grain in Egypt, *therefore* he dispatched our fathers there a first time. [13]And the second time they went, Joseph revealed his identity to his brothers, and Joseph's racial identity became known to Pharaoh. [14]And Joseph sent word, calling his father Jacob and all his relatives, seventy-five souls. [15]And Jacob went down into Egypt and he died, he and our ancestors. [16]And they were transferred to Shechem and were interred in the tomb that Abraham bought for an amount of silver from the sons of Hamor in Shechem.

---

w. These charges have been taken by Luke from Jesus' trial scene in Ur-Lukas (=Mark 14:58). He does not include them in his version of Jesus' trial before the Sanhedrin, preferring to use them here.

x. The Western text has "Abraham."

[17]"And as the time of the promise God declared to Abraham drew near, the people grew and multiplied in Egypt, [18]until another king took the throne *of Egypt,*[†] to whom Joseph meant nothing. [19]This fellow dealt treacherously with our race and mistreated the ancestors, making them expose the infants to prevent them being preserved alive. [20]Just then Moses was born. He was divinely beautiful. He was brought up three months in the house of his father, [21]and when he was exposed *from the riverbank,* Pharaoh's daughter retrieved him and brought him up as her own son. [22]Thus, Moses was trained in all the esoteric wisdom of the Egyptians and was formidable in both word and deed. [23]But when he had reached the age of forty years, it came into his head to visit his brothers, the sons of Israel. [24]And seeing one *of his race* being treated unjustly, he defended him, and he took vengeance for the one getting the worst of it, felling the Egyptian *and burying him in the sand.* [25]Now he assumed his brothers would understand that God would bring salvation to them through his hand, but they did not understand. [26]And *then,* on the following day, he appeared to two of them as they were fighting,[y] and he tried to make peace between them, saying, '*What are you doing?* Men, you are brothers! Why do you treat one another unjustly?' [27]But the one treating his neighbor unjustly shoved him away and said, 'Who appointed you ruler and judge over us? [28]Are you planning to kill me the same way you killed the Egyptian yesterday?' [29]Hearing this, Moses ran away and became a sojourner in the land of Midian, where he fathered two sons.

[30]"And after the span of forty years,[z] an angel *of the Lord* appeared to him in a flame of fire in a thorn bush on Mount Sinai in the desert. [31]And when he saw it, Moses marveled at the vision. As he approached to get a closer look, there came a voice from Adonai: [32]'I, the God of your ancestors, the God of Abraham and *the God* of Isaac and *the God* of Jacob!' But Moses shuddered and dared not look. [33]And the Lord[a] said to him, 'Unlace the sandals of your feet, for the place on which you stand is holy ground. [34]I looked and saw the evils that befell my people in Egypt, and I heard their groaning, and I came down here to rescue them. So now come, I will send you to Egypt.' [35]This Moses, whom they repudiated, saying, 'Who appointed you ruler and judge over us?' this man God sent as both ruler and redeemer by the hand of the angel who appeared to him in the bush, [36]this man led them out performing wonders and signs in the

y. Western text: "and saw them acting wickedly."

z. Western text: "after these events."

a. Western text: "a voice."

land of Egypt and at the Red Sea and in the desert over forty years. [37]This is the same Moses who says to the sons of Israel, 'God will resurrect a prophet like me for you from among your brothers. *Listen to him.*' [38]This is he who was in the congregation in the desert with the angel speaking to him on Mount Sinai and with our ancestors who received living oracles to bequeath to you.

[39]"To him, our ancestors did not want to become obedient, but shoved him away and directed their hearts' longings back to Egypt, [40]demanding of Aaron, 'Make us gods to ride at the head of the procession. As for this Moses fellow who led us out of the land of Egypt, who knows what may have happened to him?' [41]And they molded a calf in those days and led a sacrificial animal up to the idol, and they celebrated the work of their hands. [42]And God turned away and handed them over to worship the starry armies of the sky, as it is written in the scroll of the Prophets: 'Did you offer me those animals and sacrifices during the forty years in the desert, O house of Israel? [43]And you picked up the tabernacle of Moloch and the star of your god Rephan, whose likenesses you made to worship. Therefore, I will deport you to *the region of* Babylon.' [44]He meant the tabernacle of witness that our ancestors had in the desert, just as the one who spoke to Moses commanded him to make it according to the likeness he had seen.

[45]"When our ancestors, with Joshua, received it, they brought it in during the conquest of the nations whom God ejected from the sight of our ancestors until the time of David. [46]He pleased God and asked permission to find a structure for the house of Jacob. [47]But in fact, it was Solomon who built him a house. [48]But Elyon does not live in places built by hand, just as the prophet says: [49]'The sky is my throne and the earth a footstool for my feet; what sort of house could you build for me, says Adonai, or what *kind* is my resting place? [50]Did not my hand make all these things?' [51]Stubbornly obtuse, with rude heathen hearts and ears, you constantly oppose the Holy Spirit just like your ancestors did! [52]Name one prophet your ancestors did not persecute! And in order to silence them, they killed the ones who announced in advance the coming of the Just One, whose betrayers and murderers you have now become.[b]

b. This reference to "the Just" is a vestige of the original version of the story in which it was not "Stephen," but rather James the Just who was stoned by the Sanhedrin, as Hans-Joachim Schoeps and Robert Eisenman have shown. We still read of the stoning of James in Josephus, *Antiquities*, 20.9.1; Eusebius, *Ecclesiastical History,* 3:23; and 2 Apocalypse of James, 61-63. As Brodie shows, the story

[53]They received the Torah by the mediation of angels and disdained to keep it."[c]

[54]When they heard all this, they were deeply stung and ground their teeth in barely suppressed fury at him. [55]But being full of the Holy Spirit, he stared into the sky and saw the radiance of God and Jesus *the Lord* standing to the right of God. [56]And he said, "Look! I see the heavens standing open and one like a son of man standing to the right of God!" [57]And shouting loudly to drown him out, they pounced on him as one, [58]and driving him out of the city, they stoned him. And the witnesses who had lied at his trial stashed their cloaks at the feet of a *particular* youth named Saul, [59]and they stoned Stephen, who invoked Jesus, saying, "Lord Jesus, welcome my spirit." [60]And falling to his knees, he shouted loudly, "Lord, do not count this sin against them!" And saying this, he fell asleep.

8

[1]And Saul happily went along with his murder. And on that day, a great persecution *and affliction* against the assembly in Jerusalem commenced; all were scattered throughout the regions of Judea and Samaria except for the apostles, *who remained in Jerusalem.* [2]And devout men collected Stephen and chanted long dirges over him. [3]But as for Saul, he devastated the congregation with house-to-house searches, dragging out men and women and handing them over to prison. [4]So those scattered preached the message as they traveled. [5]But Philip went down to the city of Samaria and proclaimed to them the Christ. [6]And *once they heard it,* with one accord the crowds accepted what Philip said when they heard

---

was filled out with various details from the tale of the hapless Naboth in 1 Kings 20:1-21:21. Naboth was railroaded by Jezebel, who schemed to have the elders and *freemen* condemn Naboth on the basis of lying witnesses. Stephen suffers the same at the hands of the synagogue of *freedmen.* Like Naboth, Stephen is accused of double blasphemy—to have blasphemed God and Moses, where Naboth blasphemed God and king. Both are carried outside the city limits and stoned to death. When Ahab heard of the fruit of his desires, he tore his garments in remorse. Luke carries this over into a detail about the young Saul of Tarsus checking coats for those in the stoning mob.

c. Elsewhere (Gal. 3:19-20; Heb. 2:2), we read that the Torah was delivered by angels. This reflects the trend in Jewish thought to protect God's transcendence by saying it was really angels who performed the acts the Bible ascribes directly to God. Moses and the patriarchs saw angels, not God. The angels were God's agents in creation, providence, nature, and revelation. See Alan F. Segal, *Two Powers in Heaven: Early Rabbinic Reports about Christianity and Gnosticism* (Leiden: Brill, 1977). It is but a short step from this to Gnosticism, wherein one alienates the extensions of God and declares them fallen or evil.

and saw the signs he performed. [7]For the unclean spirits came out of many with a loud shout, and many paralytics and lame were cured, [8]and joy reigned in that city.

[9]And a certain man named Simon had previously practiced sorcery in the city and had the whole population of Samaria flummoxed, claiming to be someone great, [10]and all listened to him, from the small to the great, saying, "This one is the Power of God called The Great!" [11]They listened to him because for a long time he had bedazzled them with his tricks. [12]But when they believed Philip's proclamation of the kingdom of God and the name of Jesus Christ, they were baptized, both men and women. [13]Even Simon himself believed, and once baptized, he followed Philip closely, and he was amazed at the signs and great deeds of power that occurred.

[14]When the apostles in Jerusalem heard that Samaria had welcomed the message of God, they sent Peter and John to them, [15]who went down and prayed for them to receive the Holy Spirit. [16]For it had not yet fallen on any of them; they had gone no farther than being baptized in the name of the Lord Jesus *Christ*. [17]Then they laid hands on them, and they received the Holy Spirit.[d] [18]When Simon saw that the Spirit is imparted by the laying on of the apostles' hands,[e] he offered them money *and urged them,* saying, [19]"Give me, too, this authority so whomever I lay hands on may receive the Holy Spirit!" [20]But Peter said to him, "May your silver follow you into perdition for thinking you could buy the gift of God with money! [21]You have no share or role in this ministry, for your intentions are not honorable, and that is plain to God.[f] [22]Abandon this evil scheme of yours and petition the Lord in case he is willing to forgive you for your first thought.[g] [23]For I can see the future that awaits you, gagging on bitter

d. Oscar Cullmann, *The Johannine Circle,* trans. John Bowden (Philadelphia: Westminster Press, 1976), 46-49, sees in this co-optation of the Hellenists' mission by the Jerusalem apostles the referent of John 4:38.

e. Presumably those who received the Spirit manifested it by some discernible phenomenon like speaking in tongues.

f. On the surface level of the narrative, we are to see a half-repentant charlatan who cannot help seeing things in terms of his trade. He asks Peter to sell him a trick, some charm to recite; but in fact, Luke has only thinly veiled the original import of the story, which we still see on display in the Preaching of Peter: a confrontation between Peter and his rival, Paul, who presents his collection of relief funds to Jerusalem, a task imposed upon him, as he thought, as a condition of their recognizing his apostolic mission (Gal. 2:9-10). This is rebuffed (Rom. 15:25-31) as a cheap attempt to buy apostolic standing.

g. Gerd Lüdemann points out that Luke's use of this word *epinoia* is a pun-

fruit[h] and bound in the chains of unrighteousness."[i] 24And Simon replied,
saying *to them, "I beg* you, petition the Lord[j] for me so none of these
judgments you speak of may befall me!" *And he could not stop weeping
uncontrollably.*

25So having borne witness and spoken the message of the Lord, they
returned to Jerusalem, evangelizing many Samaritan villages along the
way. 26But an angel of Adonai spoke to Philip saying, "Get up and journey south along the road going down from Jerusalem to Gaza." This is a
desert. 27And he got up and went. And behold: an Ethiopian man, a eunuch and a powerful official serving Candace, queen of Ethiopia,[k] the
steward of all her treasury, had come to Jerusalem to worship 28and was
on his way home, sitting in his chariot and reading the prophet Isaiah.
29And the Spirit said to Philip, "Approach this chariot and jog alongside
it." 30As he ran up, he heard him reading aloud from Isaiah the prophet,[l]
and he said, "I assume you understand what you are reading?" 31And he
replied, "Indeed, how can I, unless someone guides me?" And he urged
Philip to come up and sit with him. 32Now the passage of scripture he was
reading was this: "He was led like a sheep to be slaughtered, and as a
lamb is mute before its shearer, neither does he open his mouth. 33In humiliation, his authority was taken away; no one will be able to recite a list
of his descendants because his life is erased from the earth." 34Com-
menting on it, the eunuch said to Philip, "I ask you, who is the prophet referring to? Himself or someone else?"[m] 35And Philip started to speak, and
beginning with this scripture, he preached to him the news of Jesus.
36And as they continued down the road, they came upon a body of water
and the eunuch says, "Look, water! Is there anything preventing me from
being baptized?" 37*And Philip says, "If you believe whole-heartedly, you*

---

ning reference to Simonian Gnostic doctrine whereby Simon's consort, Helen, was the incarnation of the *Epinoia,* or First Thought.

h. Koran 37:60: "It is a tree which sprouts up from the bottom of hell; its fruits are like the heads of Satans. And, lo! the damned shall surely eat of it and fill their bellies with it!" Cf. 44:43; 56:52.

i. Jude 6

j. The Western text has "God."

k. Like many ancient writers, Luke has mistaken the Ethiopian royal title *kandake* for a proper name, Candace.

l. Reading aloud even to oneself was the common practice in antiquity.

m. Originally this text formed part of the yearly ritual of humiliation and symbolic death of the king of Judah as he carried away the sins of the nation, guaranteeing the mandate of heavenly favor for his reign in the ensuing year.

may." And he answered and said, "I believe that Jesus Christ is the Son of
God." 38And he commanded the chariot be stopped, and both descended
into the water, both Philip and the eunuch, and he baptized him.[n] 39When
they came up out of the water, an ecstasy from Adonai seized Philip, and
the eunuch saw no more of him, for Philip went on his way rejoicing.
40And Philip was next seen in nearby Ashdod, and as he passed through,
he evangelized all the cities until he arrived in Caesarea.

9

1Meanwhile, with every breath, Saul was threatening the disciples of
the Lord with murder. Approaching the archpriest, 2he requested letters
from him to the synagogues of Damascus, authorizing him to manacle

---

n. This episode, as shown by Robert Eisenman, *James the Brother of Jesus: The Key to Unlocking the Secrets of Early Christianity and the Dead Sea Scrolls* (New York: Viking, 1997), is a combination of elements from a sequence in Josephus. The queen of Ethiopia (there were none at this time) is based on Queen Helena of Adiabene, a proselyte to Judaism who goes on pilgrimage to Jerusalem (*Antiquities*, 20.2.1, 4). Candace is a New Testament counterpart to the Queen of Sheba, just across from Ethiopia, who went to Jerusalem to meet Solomon, a trip ascribed here to her eunuch. The element of a proselyte puzzling over scripture until coached by a traveling teacher, who then initiates him, comes from the story of Helena's son, King Izates, who followed her into Judaism but hesitated at circumcision for fear his people would see him as a Judaizing traitor. But then one Eleazer, a Jewish missionary, came upon him reading the Torah and explained the necessity of circumcision, whereupon he hesitated no longer (20.2.4, 39f). The eunuch is baptized, not circumcised, but the original element of circumcision has suggested his being a eunuch in the first place (cf. Gal. 5:12).

The story recalls several key features of the story of Elisha and Naaman the Syrian (2 Kings 5:1-14), as documented by Brodie, "Luke the Literary Interpreter." The Elisha narrative depicts both healing from leprosy and conversion from Syrian Rimmon worship, while the Acts version tells of conversion from a God-fearer to a Christian. Luke was apparently reluctant to strain plausibility or good taste by having Philip physically restore a eunuch. Both Naaman and the Ethiopian are foreign officials of high status, both close to their monarchs (2 Kings 5:5; Acts 8:27c). Naaman came to Samaria to ask the king's help in contacting the prophet Elisha. The Ethiopian had journeyed to Jerusalem to seek God in temple worship, but the need of his heart remained unmet. This would be satisfied on his way home, just like those other Lukan travelers, the Emmaus disciples (Luke 24:13ff). The Israelite king fails to grasp the meaning of the letter Naaman presents to him, but a word from the prophet supplies the meaning, just as Luke has the Ethiopian fail to grasp the true import of the prophetic scroll till aided by the hitchhiking evangelist. In both cases, salvation is to be sought by immersion. Naaman balks, but his servant persuades him. Luke has this temporizing in mind when he has the Ethiopian ask rhetorically, "What prevents me from being baptized?" (Acts 8:36). Healing or conversion follow, though in both cases the official must return, alone in his faith, to a heathen court.

any he found there, men or women, who belonged to the Way and to
bring them to Jerusalem.[o] [3]As he was on his way, it happened that as he
neared Damascus, suddenly a light from heaven blazed around him, [4]and
falling to the ground, he heard a voice saying to him, "Saul, Saul, why do
you persecute me?" [5]And he said, "Who are you, Lord?" And he said,
"Why, I am Jesus, the one you are persecuting.[p] [6]But enough of that. Get
up and enter the city and there you will be instructed what to do next."
[7]The men traveling with him stood there dumbfounded because, though
they heard the sound of the voice, they saw no one. [8]They helped Saul to
his feet, and when he opened his eyes, he saw nothing. Leading him by the
hand, they brought him into Damascus, [9]and for three days he could not
see and neither ate nor drank.

[10]Now there was a certain disciple in Damascus named Ananias, and
in a vision the Lord said to him, "Ananias!" And he replied, "At your
service, Lord." [11]And the Lord said to him, "Get up and go to the street
called Straight and in the house of Judas look for a Tarsian named Saul.
Behold, he is praying [12]and has seen in a vision a man named Ananias entering and laying hands on him to restore his sight.[q] That's your assignment." [13]Ananias replied, "Lord, I heard from many about this man,
how many evils he inflicted on your saints in Jerusalem. [14]And he is here
with authorization from the archpriests to handcuff all who invoke your
name!" [15]But the Lord said to him, "Be on your way because this man is a
unique instrument for me to carry my name before both the nations and
kings and sons of Israel, [16]for I will show him how many things he is fated
to suffer on account of my name."

[17]So Ananias left and entered into the house. Laying his hands on
him, he said, "Saul, my brother, the Lord Jesus, the one who appeared to
you on the road you traveled, has sent me so you may see again and be

---

o. The archpriest had no such authority outside Judea. Paul's involvement with this persecution is a fiction, as implied in Gal. 1:22, in that Christians in Judea had never seen him.

p. The notion that in persecuting Jesus' followers Saul is actually persecuting Jesus himself may come from Euripides' *Bacchae* wherein Pentheus persecutes the Bacchic maenads, making sure he arrests and imprisons their chief evangelist, a man who turns out to be the earthly avatar of the god Dionysus himself.

q. The baptism of Paul is based on that of Jesus from Luke: Ananias (*Hanan-Yah,* "gift of Yahve") is equivalent to John (*Yah-annan,* "Yahve's gift"), both baptizers. Paul is praying when he sees and is baptized, recalling Jesus praying after his baptism, then seeing a vision (Luke 3:1-22). Ananias finds Saul on Straight Street, recalling John the Baptist's call to make the way of the Lord straight (Luke 3:4).

filled with the Holy Spirit." [18]And at once it seemed as if scales fell from
his eyes and he saw again, and he got up and was baptized.[r] [19]And taking
food, he regained his strength. He stayed with the disciples in Damascus
for some days.[s] [20]And he lost no time in proclaiming in the synagogues[t]

---

r. He was presumably baptized by pouring, as provided for in *Didache* 6:3.

s. The story of Paul's conversion not only has no real basis in the Pauline Epistles but seems largely based on that of Heliodorus in 2 Maccabees 3. In it, one Benjaminite named Simon (3:4) tells Apollonius of Tarsus, governor of Coele-Syria and Phoenicia (3:5), that the Jerusalem temple houses unimaginable wealth the Seleucid king might want to appropriate for himself. The king sends his agent, Heliodorus, to confiscate it. The prospect of such a sacrilege prompts universal wailing and praying among the Jews. But Heliodorus is miraculously turned back by a shining warrior angel on horseback. The stallion's hooves knock Heliodorus to the ground where two more angels lash him with whips (25-26). He is blinded and unable to help himself, carried to safety on a stretcher. When pious Jews pray for his recovery lest the people be held responsible for his condition, the angels reappear and announce God's grace: Heliodorus will live and must henceforth proclaim the majesty of the true God. Heliodorus offers sacrifice to his saviour (3:35) and departs again for Syria, where he reports all this to the king. In Acts, the plunder of the temple has become the persecution of the church by Saul, a Benjaminite from Tarsus. Heliodorus's appointed journey to Jerusalem from Syria has become Saul's journey from Jerusalem to Syria. Saul is stopped in his tracks by a heavenly visitant, goes blind, and must be taken into the city, where the prayers of his former enemies avail to raise him up. Just as Heliodorus offers sacrifice, Saul undergoes baptism. Then Saul is told henceforth to proclaim the risen Christ, which he does.

Luke has again added details from Euripides. In a sequence from *The Bacchae* which Luke elsewhere rewrote into the story of Paul in Philippi, as outlined by Lilian Portefaix, *Sisters Rejoice! Paul's Letter to the Philippians and Luke-Acts as Seen by First-Century Philippian Women* (Stockholm: Almqvist & Wiksell, 1988), Dionysus appears in Thebes as an apparently mortal missionary for his own sect. He runs afoul of his cousin, King Pentheus, who wants the licentious cult, as he views it, driven out of the country. He arrests and threatens Dionysus only to find him freed from prison by an earthquake. Dionysus takes revenge on the proud and foolish king by magically compelling him to undergo conversion to faith in him: "Though hostile formerly, he now declares a truce and goes with us. You see what you could not when you were blind" (922-24). The king is sent in a woman's guise to spy upon the maenads, Dionysus' female revelers. He does so, is discovered, and is torn limb from limb by the women under the leadership of his own mother. Some of Dionysus' comments include: "Punish this man. But first distract his wits; bewilder him with madness.... After those threats with which he was so fierce, I want him made the laughingstock of Thebes" (850-51, 854-55). "He shall come to know Dionysus, son of Zeus, consummate god, most terrible, and yet most gentle, to mankind" (859-61). Similarly, Paul must be made an example. His conversion is his punishment. Do we not detect a hint of ironic malice in Christ's words, "I will show him how much he must suffer for the sake of my name" (Acts 9:16)?

Jesus, that this one is the Son of God. [21]And all who heard him were amazed and said, "Isn't this man the one who destroyed those in Jerusalem who invoke this name? In fact, didn't he come here just to manacle them and bring them to the archpriests?"[u] [22]But Saul was filled yet more with power and confounded the Jews dwelling in Damascus, proving that this one is the Christ. [23]And after a great many days of this, the Jews conspired to kill him, but Saul discovered their plot. [24]And they kept close watch on the gates both day and night so as to apprehend him and destroy him. [25]But his disciples, taking him by night, let him down through the city wall, lowering him in a basket.

[26]Upon his arrival in Jerusalem, he tried to join the disciples, and all feared him, suspecting he was only pretending to be a disciple. [27]But Bar-Nabas took him to see the apostles and told them the story of how he saw the Lord on the road and that he spoke to him and how in Damascus he spoke boldly in the name of Jesus.[v] [28]And he accompanied them on their rounds in Jerusalem, speaking boldly in the name of the Lord. [29]And he both spoke and debated with his old compatriots the Hellenists; and they attempted to kill him as they had Stephen. [30]But discovering this, the brothers brought him down to Caesarea and sent him on to Tarsus.

[31]So the congregation throughout all Judea and the Galilee and Samaria enjoyed peace, being fortified by the comfort of the Holy Spirit and conducting themselves in the fear of the Lord, and their numbers multiplied.

[32]Now it came about that as Peter was passing through the various communities, he came down in turn to the saints at Lydda. [33]And there he found a certain man named Aeneas, a paralytic lying on a mat for eight years. [34]And Peter said to him, "Aeneas, Jesus Christ cures you![w] Get up and get ready to go." And at once he got up. [35]And everyone who lived in Lydda and Sharon saw him and turned to the Lord.

---

t. It is his letters from the archpriest, which give him access to the synagogues.

u. This whole episode is based on Jesus' rejection at Nazareth (Luke 4:16-30).

v. It is clear from Gal. 1:15-17 that no such initial visit took place. Luke has taken the visit described in Gal. 2:1ff and used it three times (9:27; 15:1ff; 21: 17-25).

w. An echo of Virgil's *Aeneid*: Aeneas survives the sack of Troy and founds Rome. Peter's cure of the hero's namesake anticipates the gospel coming to Rome, as well as the later tradition of Peter's role in it. In the same way, Paul will go from Troy (16:8-11) to Rome to found the church. Paul actually departs from Alexandria Troas (Trojan Alexandria), as opposed to a different Troas, the actual site of Homeric Troy. But Luke is interested in symbolic connections, not historical ones.

Now there was in Joppa a certain disciple named Tabitha, [36]which is translated Dorcas;[x] this woman abounded in good works and almsgiving which she had done. [37]And in those days, having been sick, she died. And they washed her and put her in an upstairs room. [38]Now as Lydda was near Joppa, the disciples, having heard that Peter was there, sent two men to him, pleading with him, "Do not delay to come to us!" [39]And Peter got up and went with them. As soon as he arrived, they led him to the upstairs room, and all the widows stood by him crying and showing tunics and garments Dorcas made while she was with them.[y] [40]And putting them all outside, Peter knelt down and prayed, then turned to the body and said, "Tabitha, get up!"[z] And she opened her eyes, and seeing Peter, she sat up. [41]And extending his hand, he helped her up. He called in the saints and widows and presented her alive. [42]And the news spread all throughout Joppa and many believed on the Lord. [43]And it came about that he remained several days in Joppa with one Simon, a tanner.[a]

10

[1]A certain man in Caesarea named Cornelius, a centurion of a cohort called the Italian Cohort, [2]pious and God-fearing like all his household, making many charitable contributions to the Jewish people and always petitioning God, [3]saw a clear vision of an angel about the ninth hour of the day.[b] An angel from God came in to him and said to him, "Cornelius!" [4]Staring at him in terror, he replied, "What is it, Lord?" And he said to him, "Your prayers and your alms have gone up to God and caused him to take note of you. [5]And now, send men to Joppa and send for one Simon who is surnamed Peter. [6]This man is staying with one Simon, a tanner, who has a house beside the sea." [7]And as the angel who spoke to him went away, he called two of the domestics and a pious soldier, one of several retainers, [8]and explaining the whole business to them, he sent them to Joppa. [9]And the next day, as they traveled and came near the city about the sixth hour,[c] Peter went up onto the roof to pray. [10]And he grew ravenous, wishing for something to eat. And while they were preparing

---

x. Both names mean "gazelle."

y. The widows are already an enrolled order on the church dole, a second-century development.

z. Borrowed from Mark 5:41: *Talitha cumi* ("Maiden, get up").

a. Another hint of the identification of Paul, who is a tent-maker (18:3), with Simon Magus. This Simon is a leather worker.

b. 3:00 PM

c. 12:00 noon

the noon meal, an ecstasy seized him, [11]and he beholds the sky standing open and a certain vessel like a giant sheet descending, being lowered by the four corners onto the earth. [12]In it were all the quadrupeds and reptiles of the ground and birds of the sky. [13]And a voice spoke to him, "Get up, Peter! Slaughter and eat!" [14]But Peter said, "Not a chance, Lord, because I never ate anything profane or unclean!" [15]And a voice spoke to him a second time, "If God has declared something pure, who are you to call it profane?" [16]And this happened three times, and at once the vessel was taken back up to the sky.[d]

[17]And as *he regained consciousness,* Peter mused what the vision he saw might mean, behold, the men sent by Cornelius stood at the gate asking if this were the house of Simon. [18]And calling out, they asked if Simon called Peter is staying here. [19]And as Peter pondered the vision, the Spirit said, "See, two men are looking for you. [20]Get up and go downstairs and go with them without qualms because I have sent them." [21]And going downstairs, Peter said to the men, "Over here. I am the one you seek. *What do you want?* What is the occasion of your visit?" [22]And they said *to him,* "*A certain* Cornelius, a centurion, a just and God-fearing man whom the whole Jewish nation vouches for, was urged by a holy angel to send for you to come to his house and to hear you speak." [23]So he invited them in and put them up. And getting up the next day, he went off with them, accompanied by some of the brothers from Joppa.

[24]And on the following day, he entered into Caesarea where Cornelius was waiting for them, having called together his relatives and close friends. [25]*And as Peter neared Caesarea, one of the slaves ran on ahead and announced his arrival.* Now it happened that when Peter entered, Cornelius *jumped to his feet and* came to meet him, then fell at his feet and prostrated himself before him. [26]But Peter helped him to his feet, saying, "*What are you doing?* Stand up! I, too, am but a mortal *like you.*"

d. As shown by Randel Helms, *Gospel Fictions* (Buffalo, NY: Prometheus, 1988), the vision is borrowed from Ezekiel. Peter beholds the heavens open (την ουρανον ανεωγμενον, Acts 10:11), just like Ezekiel did (ηνοιχθησαν οι ουρανοi, Ezek. 1:1 LXX). Peter sees a vast sheet of sail cloth containing every kind of animal, ritually clean and unclean, and the heavenly voice commands him to "Eat!" (Φαγη, 10:13), just as Ezekiel is shown a scroll and told to "Eat!" (Φαγη, 2:9). Reluctant to violate kosher laws, Peter balks, saying, "By no means, Lord!" (Μηδαμοξ, Κυριε, 10:14), echoing Ezekiel verbatim (Μηδαμωξ, Κυριε, Ezek. 4:14) when the latter is commanded to cook his food over a dung fire. Peter protests that he has never eaten anything unclean (ακαθαρτον) before (10:14), nor has Ezekiel (ακαθαρσια, 4:14).

27 And *talking with him,*[†] he entered. And he finds many already assembled. 28 And he said to them, "You understand *quite well* how illegal it is
for a man who is a Jew to join or even to approach a foreigner. Well, God
has shown me never to call any human being profane or unclean.
29 Accordingly, I came without objection when summoned *by you.* I ask,
then, why did you summon me?" 30 And Cornelius said, "Four days ago I
undertook a fast that continues even now. At the ninth hour, I was praying in my house and, behold, a man suddenly stood in front of me in shining clothing, 31 and he says, 'Cornelius, your prayer was heard, and the
angels reminded God of all your almsgiving. 32 So send word to Joppa and
send for Simon, who is called Peter; this man is staying in the house of Simon, a tanner, by the sea. *When he arrives, he will speak to you.*' 33 So I
sent word to you at once, *urging you to visit us,* and you did me great
honor by coming *so quickly*. So here we all are, gathered in the presence
of God[e] to hear everything the Lord[f] has commanded you to say."

34 And Peter commenced to speak, saying, "In truth, I perceive God
does not draw distinctions between people. 35 Instead, in every nation
whoever reveres him and does good deeds is equally acceptable to him.
36 You already know the message which he sent to the sons of Israel, a
proclamation of peace through Jesus Christ—the Lord of all alike[g]—
37 and what transpired throughout all Judea, starting in the Galilee after
the baptism which John offered, 38 how God anointed Jesus, the one from
Nazareth, with Holy Spirit, even a power, so that he went about doing
good deeds and curing all those who were oppressed by devils because
God was with him. 39 And we are *his* witnesses of everything he did both
in the country of the Jews and in Jerusalem where they killed him by sus-
pending him from a tree. 40 This man God raised on[h] the third day and
granted him to become visible, 41 not to all the people, to be sure, but to
witnesses previously appointed by God, to us who ate with him and
drank with him *and accompanied him for forty days* after he got up from
the dead. 42 And he commanded us to proclaim to the people and to bear
sober witness that this man is the divinely appointed judge of the living
and the dead. 43 To this man all the prophets attest, that everyone believing in him receives forgiveness through his name."

44 While Peter was still speaking, the Holy Spirit fell on all hearing the

---

e. The Western text has "before you."

f. Western text: "God."

g. Eph. 2:14-17; Rom. 3:29-30

h. The Western text has "after."

message. [45]And every one of the circumcised believers who accompanied Peter was amazed to see the gift of the Holy Spirit poured out even on the gentiles; [46]for they heard them speaking in tongues, telling of the greatness of God. Then Peter answered them, [47]"Does anyone dare deny water to these people, that they should not be baptized? The Holy Spirit welcomed them just like us!" [48]And he ordered them to be baptized in the name of *the Lord* Jesus Christ. Then they asked him to stay with them for some days.[i]

11

[1]Now the apostles and brothers throughout Judea heard that the gentiles, too, welcomed the message of God. [2]And *when*† Peter went[j] up to Jerusalem and *summoned the brothers and stengthened them, giving a lengthy speech, teaching his way through the villages, he went on to meet them, reporting to them of the favor of God. But* those *brothers* from the ranks of the circumcised[k] criticized him, [3]saying, "You went to associate with uncircumcised men and ate with them! Are you out of your mind?" [4]And Peter began to explain the matter to them in order. [5]"I found myself in the city of Joppa, praying. Then, swept into an ecstasy, I saw in a vision some sort of vessel like a giant sheet, having been lowered from the sky by the four corners. And it approached me. [6]Peering into it, I could see in it the quadrupeds of the earth and the wild beasts and the reptiles and the birds of the sky. [7]And I also heard a voice speaking to me, 'Get up, Peter! Slaughter and eat!' [8]And I replied, 'Not a chance, Lord, because no profane or unclean thing has ever crossed my lips!' [9]And a voice out of the sky answered *me / a second time,*† 'If God has declared something pure, who are you to call it profane?' [10]And this happened three times and ev-

---

i. The household of Cornelius are narrative counterparts to Theophilus and his family. They are not merely "God-fearers," semi-converts admiring Judaism from a distance, lacking only circumcision. Verses 36-37 imply they are well-acquainted with the gospel but lack full Christian initiation, much like the Samaritan converts in chapter 8. Like Theophilus, they have been "catechized" in the story of Jesus (Luke 1:4) and need only a refresher course by way of confirmation before baptism. As examined by Helms, *Gospel Fictions,* 20-21, the story seems to be composed from Septuagint Ezekiel 1:1; 2:9; 4:14. It also includes elements from Luke 7:1-5; John 18:3-8, where the falling soldiers suggest the ecstasy of the Spirit that overcomes Cornelius and his household.

j. The Western text has "wanted for some time to go."

k. Given the whole point of the story, wouldn't *all* of these people have been circumcised Jews? The point at issue is whether anyone *but* circumcised Jews can join the club. Luke has imported a scene such as occurred in mixed Antioch, as described in Gal. 2:12.

erything receded into the sky again. [11]And behold, all at once three men stood at the house where I was staying, having been sent to me from Caesarea. [12]And the Spirit told me to go with them *without objection.*† And these six brothers came with me, too, and we entered the house of the man. [13]And he related to us how he saw the angel standing in his house and saying *to them,* 'Send word to Joppa and send for Simon called Peter, [14]who will speak words to you by which you may be saved, you and your whole household.' [15]And as I started to speak, the Holy Spirit fell on them as on us at the beginning. [16]And I recalled the promise of the Lord, how he said, 'John baptized in water, but you will be baptized in Holy Spirit.' [17]So if *God*[l] gave them the same gift as he also gave to us, having believed on the Lord Jesus Christ, who was I to get in God's way, *that I should refuse to give them the Holy Spirit when they embraced faith in him?*"

[18]And hearing these things, they were speechless for a moment as it settled upon them, and then they worshipped God, saying, "Then even to the gentiles God granted the opportunity to repent and gain the life!"[m]

[19]So then, those scattered by the disturbance over Stephen reached as far as Phoenicia and Cyprus and Antioch, speaking the message to no one but Jews. [20]But some of these men, Cypriots and Cyrenians, once they reached Antioch, spoke to Greeks, too, preaching the Lord Jesus *Christ.* [21]And the hand of Adonai reinforced their efforts and a great number believed and turned to the Lord. [22]And the report about them came to the ears of the congregation in Jerusalem, and they dispatched Bar-Nabas *to go* to Antioch. [23]Arriving and seeing the grace of God, he *too* rejoiced, and he exhorted all to determine in their hearts to remain with the Lord, [24]because he was a good man, full of the Holy Spirit and of faith. And a remarkable number of people were added to the Lord's flock. [25]And he left for Tarsus to look for Saul, *having heard he was there,* [26]and finding him, he brought him[n] to Antioch. And it came about that they attached themselves to the congregation and taught a remarkable crowd. And it was in Antioch that the disciples were called "Christians" for the first time.

---

l. The Western text has "he."

m. How was this dispute possible if the parting words of the risen Son of God (Luke 24:47-49) were to evangelize the nations? Granted, Luke's account is itself fictitious, but it is an attempt to settle an even longer-standing disagreement on the same issue. Both the spurious resurrection sayings and the Cornelius stories are attempts to settle the issue in favor of the gentile mission.

n. The Western text has "urged him to come."

[27]In these days prophets came down from Jerusalem to Antioch *and everyone was excited; and when we had assembled,* [28]one of them, named Agabus, got up and pantomimed in a trance that a great famine was about to cover the inhabited earth, which happened during the reign of Claudius. [29]So as many of the disciples as were prosperous each volunteered to send relief to the brothers dwelling in Judea, [30]which indeed they did, sending it to the elders in the care of Bar-Nabas and Saul.[o]

12

[1]At that time, Herod[p] the king got his hands on some in the congregation *in Judea* to mistreat them. [2]He killed Jacob, the brother of John, with a sword. [3]And seeing how pleasing *his violence against the faithful* was to the Jews, he followed it up by arresting Peter—and it was during the days of unleavened bread—[4]whom he also grabbed and threw into prison, assigning four quaternions to guard him, intending after the Passover to bring him before the people for the crowd to denounce him. [5]So Peter was shut away behind bars, but the congregation was earnestly offering *much* prayer to God on his behalf. [6]And when Herod was about to bring him out, that night Peter was sleeping, bound with two chains between two soldiers, and guards were posted at the doors. [7]And behold: an angel of Adonai stood over him[q] and a light shone in the building. And poking Peter in the ribs, he awakened him, saying, "Quick, get up!" And his chains fell off his hands. [8]And the angel said to him, "Get ready and put on your sandals." And he did so. And he tells him, "Wrap yourself in your cloak and follow me." [9]So going out, he followed him, and he had no way of knowing whether what was happening with the angel was real, thinking he might be seeing a vision. [10]And passing through the first cell block and the second, they reached the iron gate that led to the city, which opened for them automatically. Going out *and descending the seven steps,* they went forward one block, and at once the angel left him. [11]And Peter, having now snapped out of it, said, "Now I know for sure

o. Luke again draws on Josephus's account of the converted Queen Helena of Adiabene who, on her pilgrimage to Jerusalem, saw the raging famine and paid for grain to be bought for famine relief. Agabus, as Eisenman shows, is based on Helena's husband, King Abgar, or Agbar of Edessa, whom legend made a Christian convert and correspondent with Jesus before the Passion. There was even another Antioch in Adiabene and Eisenman suggests it was the real source of the famine relief, as it came from Helena.

p. Herod Agrippa I

q. The Western text has "Peter."

that the Lord has sent out his angel to rescue me from Herod's clutches and from everything the Jewish people expected to befall me!" 12Just as he realized this, he found himself before the house of Maria, the mother of John, surnamed Mark, where many had gathered to pray. 13And when he knocked on the door of the courtyard gate, a serving maid named Rhoda came up to listen. 14And recognizing Peter's voice, she was so flustered with joy that she forgot to open the gate but ran in and announced that Peter was standing at the gate. 15But they said to her, "You're crazy!" She vehemently insisted it was so. So they said, "Then it must[r] be his guardian angel." 16But Peter kept knocking, and when they finally opened it, they were amazed. 17And gesturing with his hand for quiet, he *entered and* related to them how the Lord led him out of the prison. And he said, "Report these things to James and the brothers." And leaving again, he journeyed to some undisclosed location.[s]

18And when day dawned, there was *no little*[†] commotion among the soldiers: what had become of Peter? 19And Herod, having searched for him and failed to find him, interrogated the guards and ordered them to be led off to execution. And he left Jerusalem and stayed in Caesarea. 20Now the inhabitants of Tyre and Sidon had done something to offend Herod, who was furious with them, and they agreed to send a joint delegation *from both the cities to the king*. And having won over Blastus, the king's chamberlain, they sued for peace. Their country was fed from the royal treasury. 21And on the appointed day, Herod—dressed in royal finery and seated on the throne of judgment—*having made peace with the Tyrians,* made a public address to them. 22And the populace cried

---

r. Western text: "might."

s. The story of Peter's near-martyrdom shares with other "apocryphal" Acts of Apostles the tendency to make the apostle into another Christ, including the apostle's own Jesus-like Passion narrative. Note how Jacob's beheading echoes that of John the Baptist. Peter's death is postponed because of the Passover, just like Jesus. Peter's cell is analogous to Jesus' tomb, from which an angel delivers him. The door, like the stone at the tomb, is moved away by the presence of an angel. As in Matthew, the guards standing watch are futile. The chains can hold Peter no more than the "pangs of death" could hold Jesus (Acts 2:24). The "risen" Peter, like Jesus, appears suddenly where his despairing disciples are gathered behind locked doors. A woman is the first to discern his presence, recognizing his voice, as in John 20:16. She runs to report the news, as do Mary Magdalene and the others, but the hard-headed men dismiss it as nonsense until Peter forces himself upon their notice. He gives them parting directions, implicitly putting James the Just in charge, as Jesus did Peter. As Jesus went to heaven, Peter goes into hiding, much like the Shi'ite Imam. Peter will briefly reappear when needed to endorse the gentile mission, as Jesus himself does in Acts from time to time.

out, "A god's voice, not a man's!" [23]And at once an angel of Adonai struck him down because he did not give the glory to God.[t] And *pitching forward off the throne,* he was devoured by worms *while still living* and breathed his last.[u]

[24]But as for the message of the Lord, it only grew and increased in influence. [25]And Bar-Nabas and Saul returned from Jerusalem, having finished their mission of mercy and bringing with them John, surnamed Mark.

13

[1]There were in the congregation located in Antioch prophets and teachers, *among whom were* both Bar-Nabas and Simeon called Niger and Lucius the Cyrenian and Manaen, foster brother of Herod the tetrarch, and Saul. [2]As they conducted the divine worship and fasted, the Holy Spirit said, "So then, set apart for me Bar-Nabas and Saul for the work to which I have called them." [3]Then, having fasted and prayed, and laying hands on them, they dispatched them. [4]So they, being sent out by the Holy Spirit, went down to Seleucia,[v] and from there they sailed for

t. As Jesus did in Luke 18:18-19, Peter did in Acts 10:25-26, and Paul and Bar-Nabas will do in Acts 14:15.

u. Luke has borrowed the reason for Herod's death from Josephus's *Antiquities,* trans. William Whiston, 19.8.2: "Agrippa ... came to the city Caesarea.... At a festival a great multitude was gotten together of the principal persons.... On the second day ... he put on a garment made wholly of silver, and of a contexture truly wonderful, and came into the theatre early in the morning; at which time the silver of his garment being illuminated by the fresh reflection of the sun's rays upon it, shone out in a surprising manner, and was so resplendent as to spread a horror over those that looked intently upon him: and presently his flatterers cried out ... that he was a god; and they added, 'Be thou merciful to us; for although we have hitherto reverenced thee only as a man, yet shall we henceforth own thee as superior to mortal nature.' Upon this the king did never rebuke them, nor reject their impious flattery. But as he presently afterwards looked up, he saw an owl sitting on a certain rope over his head, and immediately understood that this bird was the messenger (Greek: *angelos*) of evil tidings.... A severe pain also arose in his belly, and began in a most violent manner. He therefore looked upon his friends, and said, 'I, whom you call a god, am commanded presently to depart this life; while Providence reproves the lying words you just now said to me.'" Luke has combined this with the grisly fate allotted the similarly self-divinizing Antiochus IV Epiphanes from 2 Maccabees 10:9 (New American Bible): "The body of this impious man swarmed with worms, and while he was still alive in hideous torments, his flesh rotted off, so that the entire army was sickened by the stench of his corruption."

v. Antiochus IV Epiphanes, whose death Herod Agrippa I has just emulated, had once been the Seleucid Emperor.

Cyprus. [5]And once in Salamis, they declared the message of God[w] in the synagogues of the Jews and John worked as their attendant.

[6]And passing through the whole of the island as far as Paphos, they encountered a certain man who was both a sorcerer and a Jewish pseudo-prophet whose name was Bar-Jesus,[x] [7]whose patron was the proconsul Sergius Paul, an intelligent man. This man summoned Bar-Nabas and Saul, wanting to hear their message. [8]But Elymas[y] the Mage, for that is his given name,[z] lobbied against them, hoping to turn the proconsul away from the faith *since his patron liked what he heard.* [9]But Saul, who was also Paul, filled with the Holy Spirit and glaring at him, said, [10]"O sewer of all fraud and subterfuge! Son of the slanderer! Foe of all righteousness! Won't you stop twisting the straight paths to the Lord off course? [11]Just watch this. The hand of Adonai has seized you and you will be blind, unable to see the sun for a while." And instantly a blanket of mist and darkness fell over him, and wandering about, he asked for someone to lead him by the hand. [12]When the proconsul saw what happened, he believed[a] *in God,* being astounded at the power that accompanied the teaching of the Lord.[b]

[13]And setting sail from Paphos, Paul and his associates came into Perga of Pamphylia and John left them to return to Jerusalem. [14]And leaving Perga, they passed on through to the Pisidian Antioch and entered the synagogue on the Sabbath day and sat down. [15]And following the readings from the Torah and the Prophets, the synagogue rulers passed word to them, saying, "Men, brothers, if any of you has a message of ex-

---

w. The Western text has "the Lord."

x. Bar-Jesus means "son of Joshua," possibly denoting a claim like Theudas's to be the returned Joshua and thus the prophet like Moses. Otherwise, Elymas "bar-Jesus" may be intended as one of the pseudo-prophets of Luke 21:8 who come trading on the name of "Jesus," but whose advent does not yet signal the end.

y. Different Western manuscripts substitute for "Elymas" that of "Etimas" or "Etoimas."

z. Luke erroneously imagines this is the Greek equivalent of Bar-Jesus.

a. The Western text has "marveled."

b. Luke has created this scene to match the contest of Peter with Simon Magus in 8:9ff. Originally, Peter opposed Paul, but Luke gives Paul the other name of Peter: Simon. Here Saul takes the role of Peter while Simon Magus becomes Elymas and takes Jesus' own name, as well, and Saul treats him as Jesus treated Saul in Acts 9:3-9, blinding him for his mischief. In the process, the proconsul Paul yields his name to Saul. As for Sergius, this is the name of a spy among the twelve who betrayed Jesus according to an old Islamic source, a role analogous to that of Elymas here.

hortation for the people, say it." [16]So Paul stood up and gestured with his hand, and he said, "Men, both Israelites and God-fearers, give ear. [17]The God of this people, Israel, chose our fathers and multiplied the people during the sojourn in the land of Egypt, and with mighty arm poised to strike, he led them out of it. [18]And he put up with them *about*[†] forty years' time in the desert, *caring for them like a nurse.* [19]And having destroyed seven nations in the land of Canaan, he gave them the land *of the Philistines* as an inheritance. [20]And for about four hundred fifty years after these things, he gave them judges until Samuel, a prophet. [21]And after that, they requested a king, and God gave them Saul, son of Kish, a man of the tribe of Benjamin, for forty years. [22]And removing him, he brought David to the fore as their king, of whom also he said by way of commendation, 'I discovered in David, the son of Jesse, a man I could cherish, who will carry out my every wish.' [23]From this one's lineage, *therefore,* God provided Israel with a savior, as he promised, namely Jesus.

[24]"John heralded him to all the people of Israel, just ahead of his coming on the scene, by means of a baptism of repentance. [25]Now as John neared the end of his task, he said, 'What[c] do you suppose I am? It is not I, but behold, after me he comes, the shoes of whose feet I am not worthy to untie.'[d] [26]Men! Brothers! Sons of Abraham's race and those gentiles among you[e] who fear God! To us the news of this salvation was sent out. [27]For the inhabitants of Jerusalem and their rulers, *not recognizing this man,*[†] condemned him, thus echoing the voices of the prophets that are read every Sabbath. [28]And finding him guilty of no capital offense, *once they had condemned him, they handed him over and* asked Pilatus to destroy him. [29]And when they finished all the things written of him, *they asked Pilatus to crucify him. And once they had won this, too,* taking him down from the tree, they laid him out in a tomb.[f] [30]But God raised him from the dead. [31]He appeared over many days to those who came up from the Galilee to Jerusalem, who now function as his witnesses to the people. [32]And we preach to you the news of what was promised to the fathers, [33]which God has fulfilled to us, their children, by rais-

---

c. The Western text has "Who."

d. As Darrell J. Doughty suggests, this saying may originally have referred to Simon Magus as the chosen successor of John. The Clementine Homilies make him the successor.

e The Western text has "us."

f. Here is an alternative to the gospels' tradition, which has Joseph of Arimathea obtaining permission to bury Jesus.

ing up *the Lord* Jesus *Christ,* just as it is written in the second Psalm: 'You
are my son, today I have begotten you. *You have only to ask and I will
present you with the nations as your inheritance and the far reaches of
earth as your own.*' [34]And that he raised him from the dead, no longer on
the brink of sinking into corruption, he has said this: 'I will give you the
sacred prerogatives of faithful David.' [35]Which is why in another place he
says, 'You will not abandon your saint to corruption.' [36]For while David,
having served his nation, fell asleep as God planned and went to join his
ancestors and experienced corruption, [37]the one God raised did not experience corruption. [38]Therefore, know this, men, brothers: through this
man forgiveness of sins is announced to you and *the opportunity to repent* from all the offenses from which you could not be justified by the
Torah of Moses, [39]by this man; *therefore,* everyone who believes is justified *in God's sight.*[g] [40]Watch out, lest you fall victim to what the prophets
warned of: [41]'Watch this, you scoffers, marvel and perish! Because I perform a deed in your days, *a deed*[†] you will never believe if anyone tells
you!'" *And they had nothing to say.*

[42]And as they were leaving, they asked them to tell them more about
these things during the next week. [43]And when the synagogue adjourned,
many of the Jews and of the pious proselytes followed Paul and Bar-
Nabas, who spoke to them, urging them to go on further in God's favor.
And it came about that the message of God penetrated the entire city.

[44]And when the new week began, practically the whole city had
gathered to hear the message of God.[h] [45]But getting a look at the size of
the crowd, the Jews were filled with jealousy and blasphemed, *harangu-
ing and* contradicting what Paul said. [46]And speaking boldly, Paul and
Bar-Nabas said *to them*: "We were obliged to speak the message of God
to you first. But since you cast it aside and apparently regard yourselves
as unworthy of age-long life, we are turning to the gentiles. [47]For the
Lord has commanded *us*[†] to do so: 'I have set you up as a beacon to the
nations, to project the news of salvation to the far reaches of the earth.'"[i]

---

g. There is a brief echo here of Pauline thought—among the few instances in Acts when such lines are put in Paul's mouth, and then merely cosmetically. Luke knows a bit of Pauline terminology but places it in a theological context wholly alien to the Pauline Epistles.

h. The Western text has "Paul saying a great deal about the Lord."

i. Traditionally Jews believed God had offered the Torah covenant to all nations, but that only Israel had accepted it. This piece of theology is reversed here: Jews had access to the gospel, and in rejecting it, they lost their chosen status. Such

[48]Hearing this, the gentiles rejoiced and testified to the message of the Lord, and as many as had been predestined to life believed. [49]And the message of the Lord was carried throughout the countryside. [50]But the Jews urged the pious aristocratic women and the leading men of the city and stirred up *great affliction and* persecution against Paul and Bar-Nabas and expelled them from their borders. [51]But shaking the dust off their feet as a witness against them, they came to Iconium, [52]and the disciples were full of joy and of the Holy Spirit.

14

[1]And it came about in Iconium that, *in the same way,* they[j] entered together into the synagogue of the Jews and spoke *to them* so that a great number both of Jews and of Greeks believed. [2]But *the rulers of the synagogue of* those Jews who did not believe *and the head men of the synagogue* incited *among them a persecution of the righteous* and poisoned the minds of the gentiles against the brothers. *But the Lord swiftly restored the peace.* [3]So they continued for quite some time, speaking boldly about the Lord, who authenticated the message of his favor, granting that signs and wonders should be wrought at their hands. [4]But the populace of the city was divided, some siding with the Jews, others with the apostles, *adhering to the latter because of the message of God.* [5]And when both the gentiles and the Jews and their rulers planned to ambush them, to insult and to stone them, [6]they discovered it and escaped to the cities of Lycaonia, *to* Lystra and Derbe and the *entire* vicinity. [7]And there they were evangelizing. *And the whole audience was moved at the teaching. Now Paul and Bar-Nabas spent a good while in Lystra.*

[8]And in Lystra, there sat a certain man who was disabled in the feet, lame from his mother's womb, never having walked. [9]This man, *full of fear,* heard Paul speaking, who watching him and judging that he has faith to be healed, [10]said loudly, "*I tell you in the name of the Lord Jesus-Christ*: Stand up straight on your feet *and walk!*" And *immediately*[k] he leaped to his feet and walked about.[l] [11]And when the crowd saw what Paul did, they raised their voices, shouting in Lycaonian, "The gods, made like men, came down to us!" [12]And they decided Bar-Nabas must

competition formed no part of the Marcionite agenda since Jews were considered to be in a special position of favor with their God, just not with the Christian God.

j. The Western text has "he."

k. Western text: "suddenly."

l. Here is the requisite parallel to Peter's healing of a lame man in 3:1-10.

be Zeus and Paul Hermes since he was the chief speaker. [13]And the
priest[m] of the temple of Zeus-Outside-the-City brought *them* bulls and
garlands of flowers to the gates and wanted to offer sacrifice with the
crowds. [14]Hearing this, *the apostles*† Bar-Nabas and Paul[n] ripped their
garments in horror and hurried down into the crowd, shouting [15]and saying, "Men! What are you doing? We, too, are mortals of like passions
with you. We are trying to tell you to turn aside from this mummery to a
living God who made the sky and the earth and the sea and everything in
them.[o] [16]In previous generations, he allowed the nations to go their own
ways, [17]not that he left himself unattested,[p] doing good, giving us rain
from the sky and seasons of fruit-bearing, filling us with food and our
hearts with joy." [18]Even saying these things, they were scarcely able to
dissuade the crowds from offering them sacrifice.

[19]*While they were spending some time there in teaching, certain* Jews
from Antioch and Iconium showed up to win over the crowds. They
stoned Paul and dragged him out of the city, assuming he was dead. [20]But
with his disciples gathered around him, he rose to his feet and re-entered
the city *of Lystra*. And on the next day, he left with Bar-Nabas for Derbe.
[21]And once they evangelized *the inhabitants of* that city and recruited a
good many disciples, they went back to Lystra and to Iconium and to
Antioch, [22]reinforcing the souls of the disciples *and* exhorting them to
stick with the faith and warning, "We are obliged to enter the kingdom of
God only through many afflictions." [23]And having designated elders for
every congregation, after prayer and fasting they committed them to the
Lord in whom they had believed. [24]And passing through Pisidia, they arrived in Pamphylia, [25]and once they told the message in Perga, they came
down to Attalia, *evangelizing them,* and sailed away from there to Ant-

---

m. The Western text has "priests."

n. It is striking that only in this chapter, unless the Western text preserves the original reading here, does Luke call Bar-Nabas and Paul "apostles," reserving the term otherwise for the Jerusalem twelve. It may be significant that in the Hellenistic world "apostle" often denoted a divine being or savior visiting the earth in human form, which is what Paul and Bar-Nabas are thought by the Lycaonians to be. The famous visit of Zeus and Hermes to the aged couple Baucis and Philemon (Ovid, *Metamorphoses,* Book 8) occurred in Lycaonia and forms the background for Luke's tale.

o. The Lycaonians already believed in what they considered a living God who gave rain and food. Their God was Zeus, and their offering of bulls was essentially nothing different from Israelite worship at that very time. Luke is able to sneer at it because, by his time, it is long defunct and seems alien.

p. It was the Marcionite deity who had left himself unattested.

ioch, [26]from whence they had been entrusted to the providential care of God for the task they had now accomplished. [27]And having arrived, assembling the congregation, they reported what God did with them *for their souls,* and how he opened up for the gentiles an opportunity for faith. [28]And they stayed on no little time with the disciples.

15

[1]And some going down from Jerusalem taught the brothers, "Unless you are circumcised *and live* according to the custom of Moses, you cannot be saved." [2]And no little strife and disputation arose between them and Paul and Bar-Nabas, *for Paul replied, strongly insisting that they should remain as they had been when they first believed. But those who had come from Jerusalem* assigned Paul and Bar-Nabas and some of the rest *of their number*† to go up to consult the apostles and elders in Jerusalem *for their judgment.*[q] [3]So being sent out by the congregation,[r] they passed through both Phoenicia and Samaria, relating in some detail the conversion of the gentiles, and brought great joy to all the brothers. [4]And once they arrived in Jerusalem, they were *given a royal* welcome by the congregation and the apostles and the elders, and they reported what God had accomplished with them. [5]But *those who had urged them to go up to the elders, namely* some members of the Pharisee sect who had believed, stood up and said, "We must require them to be circumcised and order them to keep the Torah of Moses."

[6]And the apostles and the elders convened to consider the matter. [7]And after much questioning had taken place, Peter stood up, *inspired by the Spirit,* and said to them, "Men, brothers, you understand that in the days of antiquity God chose among you[s] my own mouth, from which the gentiles might hear the message of the news and believe.[t] [8]And God, the knower of hearts, vouched for them by giving[u] them the Holy Spirit, just

q. Who are these elders? They must stand for church leaders in Luke's own day, the leaders actually in office when these issues were decided. The apostles, by contrast, are theological showpieces.

r. What congregation? Acts 8:2 had the apostles alone and in hiding in Jerusalem, as they were after the crucifixion. Perhaps in view of Acts 21:20, Luke supposes the apostles started over and created a new Jerusalem congregation which, lacking the Hellenist element, grew up as a consistently Torah-zealous sect like the Pharisees mentioned here.

s. The Western text has "us."

t. As in 2 Pet. 3:1-2ff, the author betrays his hand, admitting Peter is a figure of the more distant past.

u. The Western text has "putting upon."

as to us, [9]and distinguished them from us in no respect, cleansing their hearts by faith. [10]So why do you provoke God now by hanging a yoke on the neck of the disciples, which neither our ancestors nor we were able to carry? [11]But we understand ourselves to be saved in the same way as them: through the favor of the Lord Jesus *Christ*."[v]

[12]*And the elders agreed with what Peter said.* And the whole assembly listened in silence as Bar-Nabas and Paul explained what signs and wonders God performed among the gentiles through them. [13]And following the silence, James *stood to his feet and* answered, saying, [14]"Men, brothers, hear me. Simeon explained how God first acted to choose from the gentiles a people to carry his name. [15]And the words of the Prophets accord with this:

> [16]'After these things, I will turn back to you
> and I will rebuild the tent of David that lies in ruins,
> and its remains I will rebuild and I will raise it up again,
> [17]so the rest of humanity may seek the Lord,
> even all the nations over whom my name has been invoked,
> says Adonai, who does these things, [18]known *to the Lord* from ages past.'

[19]"This is why my decision is not to make it difficult for the gentiles who are turning to God, [20]but to send word to them to steer clear of the taint of idolatry, namely sacred prostitution, *meat from strangled animals,*[†] and eating blood. *And whatever they would prefer no one do to them, do not do to others.* [21]For Moses' partisans can be found in every city from ancient generations till now, preaching him in the synagogues every Sabbath day."[w] [22]Then it pleased the apostles and the elders and the whole congregation to send chosen delegates to Antioch along with Paul and Bar-Nabas, namely Judas-born-on-the-Sabbath[x] and Silas,[y] leading men

---

v. This speech echoes quite closely that of Paul in Gal. 2:15-21 and may well have been borrowed from it. The point again is to assimilate Peter to Paul, as also in 1 Peter. Note the gentile viewpoint: it is inconceivable for a Jew to see the Torah as a burden, while a gentile, facing the prospect of conversion to Judaism, had to adopt a whole raft of, to him, alien cultural mores.

w. Gal. 2:9-10 flatly contradicts this account. No such stipulations were imposed, though the Pauline epistles do occasionally inveigh against the same practices.

x. The Western text has "Judas Bar-Abbas," meaning "Judas, son of the Father."

y. Eisenman notes that Silas may derive from the Arabic for "the righteous." Thus, Silas may originally have been intended as James the Just.

among the brothers, [23]to carry their letter *they had written, as follows*:

> The apostles and the elder brothers, to the gentile brothers
> throughout Antioch and Syria and Cilicia, greeting!
> [24]Since we hear that some of our number, acting without our
> knowledge, said things that upset you and disturbed your peace of
> mind, [25]we have unanimously decided to choose men to send to you,[z]
> along with our[a] beloved Bar-Nabas and Paul, [26]men who have put
> their lives on the line for the sake of the name of our Lord, Jesus
> Christ *in trial after trial.* [27]So we have sent Judas and Silas, and they
> will confirm the same things orally. [28]For it seemed good to the Holy
> Spirit, and we concurred, to impose on you no heavier burden than
> these necessities: [29]to shun eating meat slaughtered as a sacrifice to
> idols and blood, *and the meat of strangled animals,*[†] and cult prosti-
> tution. *And that whatever you would prefer no one do to you, do not
> do to another.* You will be well-advised to steer clear of these things,
> *kept strong by the Holy Spirit.* Farewell.

[30]So being dismissed, *in a few days* they went down to Antioch, and calling the congregation together, they delivered the letter. [31]And once it was
read, they rejoiced at the exhortation. [32]Judas and Silas, themselves
prophets *full of the Holy Spirit,* added *much*[†] more exhortation orally,
confirming the letter's message.[b] [33]And after they had remained there for
a while to be sure they obeyed the letter, they were given an amicable
send-off by the brothers to return to the ones who sent them. [34]*But Silas
thought it would be a good idea to stay there, so Judas returned alone.*[c]
[35]But Paul and Bar-Nabas stayed in Antioch, teaching and evangelizing
the message of the Lord, along with many others.

[36]But after some days, Paul said to Bar-Nabas, "Let us go back and
visit the brothers in every city where we announced the news of the Lord
to see how they have fared." [37]And Bar-Nabas also wanted to take along
John, called Mark. [38]But Paul thought it best not to take him with them
since he had withdrawn from them at Pamphylia, not proceeding with
them to the work *they had been sent to do.* [39]And such a paroxysm
erupted that they severed their partnership. *Then* Bar-Nabas took Mark

---

z. 1 John 2:18-19; 2 John 10

a. The Western text has "your."

b. Judas and Silas appear in the Koran as Hûd (Yehudah) and Salih, as Eisenman has shown.

c. This reads like a harmonization in light of v. 40.

to embark for Cyprus.[d] [40]But Paul chose Silas as his new partner and went out, committed by the brothers to the Lord's providential care. [41]And he went through Syria and Cilicia, confirming the congregations and *promulgating among them the commandments of the elders.*

16

[1]And *after passing through these countries,* he also came down to Derbe and Lystra. And behold, a certain disciple named Timothy was there, the son of a faithful Jewish mother and a Greek father, [2]and the brothers in Lystra and Iconium vouched for him. [3]Paul wanted to take this man along with him, so he had him circumcised in deference to the Jews in those parts since they all knew his father was a Greek.[e] [4]As they made their way through the cities, they *very boldly preached and passed on the Lord, Jesus-Christ. They also* delivered the decrees the apostles and elders in Jerusalem had stipulated for them to keep. [5]As a result, the congregations were strengthened in faith and daily grew in membership.

[6]And they passed through the countryside of Phrygia and Galatia, being forbidden by the Holy Spirit to speak the message *of God to anyone* in Asia; [7]but when they came up to Mysia, they attempted go into Bithynia but the Spirit of Jesus did not allow them.[f] [8]So skipping[g] Mysia, they went down instead to Troy. [9]And in the course of the night, a vision appeared to Paul. *It was as if* a certain man, a Macedonian,[h] was standing there *in front of him,* pleading with him, saying, "Cross over to Macedonia and help us!" [10]So when he saw the vision *and got up and told us about it,* we got ready at once to go to Macedonia, concluding that God[i] has called us to evangelize them.[j]

d. What we are told in Gal. 2:13 is that the dispute between Paul and Bar-Nabas at Antioch was over the much more substantive issue of whether the gentiles should be forced by boycott to Judaize. Luke makes it a mere clash of personalities.

e. See 15:21. Would the Paul of the epistles have done this? Then again, see 1 Cor. 9:20.

f. Why? As Joseph Tyson has suggested, Luke seeks in this way to undermine the Pauline pedigree of Marcion who hailed from this very area. Like Tertullian and Ireneaus, Luke wants to co-opt Marcionite Paulinism for Catholic Christianity.

g. The Western text has "passing through."

h. The intended apparition is Philip of Macedon or his son Alexander the Great, Paul's counterpart to Peter's vision leading him to Cornelius.

i. The Western text has "the Lord."

j. This verse, unless 13:47 is accurately preserved in the Western text, begins the sporadic "We" passages, where the narrator shifts from third- to first-person.

[11]And *the next morning,* setting sail from Troy, we pursued a
straight course to Samothrace, and on the following day to Neapolis,
[12]and from there to Philippi, which is the chief city of that part of Macedonia and a Roman colony in its own right. And we were staying in this
city for several days. [13]And on the Sabbath day, we went out through the
gate to the riverside where we thought a place of prayer[k] would be, and
taking a seat, we spoke to the women who assembled. [14]And a certain
woman named Lydia, a dealer in purple dyed goods from the city of
Thyatira, a God-fearer, was listening and the Lord opened up her heart to
take seriously what Paul was saying. [15]When she was baptized along with
her *whole* household, she urged us, saying, "If you have decided I am
truly pledged to the Lord,[l] come into my house and stay there." And she
insisted. [16]And it came about as we went to the place of prayer, a certain
maiden having a spirit of a python intercepted us. She brought great
profit to her masters by *this,* her soothsaying practice.[m] [17]This girl followed after Paul and the rest of us, incessantly shouting, "These men are
slaves of El Elyon and they announce to you *the news of* a way of salvation!" [18]And she did this over many days. But Paul, becoming exasper-
ated, turned to the spirit and said,[n] "I order you in the name of Jesus
Christ to come out of her!" And it did come out that very moment.

[19]Once her[o] masters realized that their livelihood *derived from exploiting her* had disappeared, they grabbed Paul and Silas and hauled
them before the rulers who convened in the marketplace. [20]Bringing them
to the praetors, they said, "These men are stirring up our city, and being
Jews, [21]they are advocating customs that are not legal for us as Romans
to adopt or perform." [22]The *great* crowd rallied against them, *shouting,*

As Vernon K. Robbins has shown in "By Land and by Sea: The We-Passages and Ancient Sea-Voyages," in Charles H. Talbert, ed., *Perspectives on Luke-Acts* (Edinburgh: T&T Clark, 1978), 215-42, this is a widespread Hellenistic device, serving to make the action more immediate and vivid to the reader, like the present tense verbs in the gospels and occasionally in Acts. First-person narrative is associated with sea voyages from the *Odyssey* onward, always being confined to the parts of the story set at sea. Likewise, Acts has "we/us" only in parts set at or near the sea.

k. A synonym for a synagogue.

l. The Western text has "to God."

m. She is an inspired oracle like those of Pythian Apollo. Here she plays the same role as the Christian Sybilline Oracles, as if providing pagan witness to the truth of Christianity.

n. The Western text has "turned and, inspired by the Spirit, said."

o. Western text: "the girl's."

and the praetors stripped their clothes off their backs and ordered them to be flogged. [23]And after laying many stripes on them, they threw them into prison, ordering the jailer to keep them secure. [24]Having received such orders, he threw them into the inner cell block and fastened their feet in the stocks. [25]And about midnight, Paul and Silas were praying and lifted up a hymn of praise to God and the prisoners listened to them. [26]And suddenly there was a massive earthquake, sufficient to shake loose the foundations of the jail. And at once all the doors were sprung open and all the manacles were loosened from their settings in the walls. [27]The jailer was jolted awake, and when he saw the prison doors hanging askew, he drew his sword and was about to kill himself, assuming the prisoners had escaped.[p] [28]But Paul shouted loudly, "Do yourself no harm! We are all here!"[q] [29]And calling for lights, he hurried in and, trembling, fell before *the feet of* Paul and Silas, [30]and leading them forth outside *once he had secured the rest,* he said, "My lords, what must I do that I may be saved?" [31]And they replied, "Believe on the Lord Jesus *Christ* and you will be saved and your household with you." [32]And they told him and everyone in his house the message of God. [33]And despite the lateness of the hour, he took them and treated their wounds, and he was baptized, himself and his household all at the same time. [34]And bringing them up to his house, he spread a table for them and celebrated with all his household their new belief in God.

[35]When day dawned the praetors *gathered in the marketplace, afraid because of the earthquake; and they* sent the lictors with the message: "Release those men *you arrested yesterday.*" [36]And the jailer communicated this message to Paul, "The praetors have sent word that you may be released. You're free to go your way *in peace.*"[†] [37]But Paul said to the lictors, "Not so fast! Having beaten us publicly, men who are Romans and convicted of no crime, they threw us into prison—and now they want to slip us out quietly? No indeed! Instead, let them come in person and escort us out!" [38]And the lictors reported to the praetors *themselves* these words *intended for them.* Hearing that they were Roman citizens, they were afraid, [39]and coming *with many supporters to the jail,* they pleaded with them, *saying, "We didn't realize you were innocent men,"*

p. See Acts 12:19; Matt. 28:14.

q. Are we to believe that all the prisoners, like Socrates, refuse to escape when they have the chance? In the darkness and confusion, how does Paul even know they are still there? Then what happens to them? Their creator, Luke, soon tires of them—forgets them—since they have served their narrative purpose.

and escorting them out, they requested that they leave the city, "*otherwise they may form another mob threatening us and accusing you.*" [40]And leaving the prison, they entered the house of Lydia, and after seeing the brothers, they *reported everything the Lord had done for them,* exhorted them, and left.[r]

17

[1]Going through Amphipolis and *down to* Apollonia, *from there* they arrived at Thessalonica where there was a synagogue of the Jews. [2]And as he customarily did, Paul entered their congregation and on three Sabbaths reasoned with them from the scriptures, [3]opening up their hidden meaning and proposing, "The Christ had to suffer and rise again from the dead" and "This Jesus whom I announce to you is the Christ." [4]And some of them were persuaded to join Paul and Silas *in the teaching,* a great number of the devout gentiles and no small number of the leading women. [5]But the Jews, turning jealous, recruited some marketplace roustabouts and some male prostitutes, and having assembled a mob, they created a disturbance in the city. Massing at the home of Jason, they demanded he hand them over to the mob. [6]But when they couldn't find them, they hauled Jason and some of the brothers to the politarchs, shouting *and alleging,* "These men who have turned the whole inhabited earth on its head have now come here, too. [7]And Jason has welcomed them, and they all behave in contravention of Caesar's decrees, claiming there is another king, Jesus." [8]They succeeded in troubling the crowd and the politarchs by saying these things. [9]And *when they heard this,* taking bail from Jason and the rest, they released them. [10]And at once, in the middle of the night, the brothers sent both Paul and Silas to Beroea, and once they arrived, they headed straight for the synagogue of the Jews. [11]These turned out to be more noble than their counterparts in Thessalonica, welcoming the message with complete enthusiasm, daily examining the scriptures to verify these things. [12]Accordingly, many[s] of them believed, *though others did*

---

r. This chapter is based on Euripides' *Bacchae,* the story of the futile persecution of the imported cult of Dionysus, brought to Thebes from Lydia by an apostle who turns out to be Dionysus himself. King Pentheus has the preacher arrested and imprisoned, but Dionysus is freed by an earthquake, doors and shackles opening by themselves, following which the persecutor himself yields and converts. Paul plays the role of Pentheus in chap. 9 but takes the place of Dionysus here, while Pentheus' role has been assumed by the Philippian jailer. See Portefaix, *Sisters Rejoice,* 169-70.

s. The Western text has "some."

not, not to mention a few[t] of the aristocratic Greek women and men.
13But when the Jews from Thessalonica learned that the message of God
was announced *by Paul*† in Beroea, *too,*† *and that they believed,* they
came there also, *incessantly* agitating and disturbing the crowds. 14So
then *at once*† the brothers sent Paul away, to go *as far as*† to the sea, but
both Silas and Timothy remained there. 15And those escorting Paul
brought him as far as Athens. *But he skipped Thessaly for he was forbidden to preach the message to them.* And, obeying a command *from Paul*
for Silas and Timothy to come join him as soon as possible, they departed.

16And while Paul was waiting for them in Athens, his spirit went into
paroxysms of frustration as he saw how full of idols the city was. 17So he
addressed the Jews and the devout gentiles in the synagogue on the Sabbath and those who chanced to be in the marketplace each day. 18But also
some of the Epicureans and Stoic philosophers happened to notice him,
and some said, "What can this windbag be trying to say?" And others
said, "He would appear to be a preacher of foreign deities." *This, because he evangelized for Jesus and Anastasis.*†[u] 19And *a few days later,*
surrounding him, they led him to the Hill of Ares, *questioning him and*
saying, "May we know the nature of this new teaching which you propound? 20For our ears perk up at some of the startling things you say. So
we are determined to know what these things are intended to mean."
21You see, all Athenians as well as the foreigners who come to live there
waste time on nothing else than saying or hearing some new thing.[v]

22So Paul stood in the middle of the Hill of Ares and said, "Men!
Athenians! I notice how in all things you are quite superstitious. 23For
passing along and looking up at your objects of worship, I even found an
altar inscribed, 'To any unknown God.'[w] Well, what you worship in ig-

---

t. Western text: "many."

u. That is, his teaching reminded people of Isis, Cybele, Ishtar, Anath, and Aphrodite, goddesses who resurrected their divine consorts, Osiris, Attis, Tammuz, Baal, and Adonis. Anastasis means "resurrection," and it seems likely that in the original resurrection faith, Christians did believe in a resurrecting goddess, who has become Mary Magdalene (Maria the hairdresser) in the Gospels.

v. Note the travelogue tone. Such characterizations of the Athenians were quite common in ancient literature, as were scenes in which the audience listens for the reader's sake to propagandists for foreign gods. Luke, being a stolid churchman with no intellectual curiosity, has no patience for what he considers such dilettantism. See 2 Tim. 3:6-7.

w. Legend had it that Athens had long ago suffered a plague and resorted to the miracle-working sage Epimenides, whom Paul will momentarily quote, to help them. He decided they had inadvertently neglected to sacrifice to a god they

norance,[x] it is my privilege to make known to you! 24The God who made the world and all things in it, being Lord of sky and earth, does not dwell in handmade shrines, 25nor is he served food by human hands as if he required something to eat, himself being the one who provides life and breath and everything else for all beings. 26And he made from one *blood* every nation of mankind to dwell upon the broad face of the earth, ordaining beforehand both the period of their dominion[y] and the boundaries of their dwelling, 27prompting them to look for God as if they might grope after him[z] and chance to discover him,[a] though in reality he[b] is not far from each one of us.[c] 28'For in him we live and move and exist, *day after day,*' as some poets among you have said.[d] Also, 'For we are his offspring.'[e] 29So being the offspring of God, we have no business supposing the Godhead to be like gold or silver or stone, like an engraved work of artistic craft and human imagination. 30So then, having turned a blind eye to *these* times of ignorance, God now announces that all people everywhere must repent, 31because he has scheduled a day when he is about to judge the inhabited earth in righteousness by a man, *namely Jesus,* he ordained for the task, offering a guarantee of this to everyone by raising him from the dead." 32Upon hearing about the dead being raised, some burst out laughing, but others said, "We would like to hear you speak

---

did not know and that this god had become the squeaky wheel demanding attention. He advised them to erect an altar to the "unknown gods," which they did, and the slighted and still nameless deity relented. In another version, Epimenides actually journeys to the Hill of Mars where he lets loose black and white sheep and tells the Athenians to build altars wherever the sacrificial beasts stop. Diogenes Laertius, *Lives of Eminent Philosophers,* 1:110.

x. John 4:22

y. Luke 21:24

z. The Western text has "seek most of all what is divine."

a. Western text: "it."

b. Do.

c. It seems possible Luke is disguising Mandaean/Nasorean doctrine whereby the human race stems from the Primal Man, Enosh ("man," Gen. 5:6, 9-10), hidden here behind *enos,* Greek for "one." The original would have said that "any one of us is not far from Enosh," he being our progenitor (Heb. 7:9-10; Rom. 5:12-19; 1 Cor. 15:21-22), which is how "we live, move, and exist in him."

d. This is half of a couplet ascribed to Epimenides, the other half of which appears in Titus 1:12, the thrust of which is to condemn the Cretans for claiming to have custody of the tomb of Zeus, who cannot be dead.

e. A quote from either Aratus' *Phaenomena,* 5, or Cleanthes' *Hymn to Zeus,* vv. 3-4.

about this some other time." 33So Paul left the platform. 34Some men
joined him and believed, including both *a certain* Dionysius of the Hill of
Ares, a woman named Damaris, and others with them.

18

1And *after these events,*† he left Athens and came to Corinth. 2And he
met a certain Jew named Aquila from Pontus by nationality[f] and Priscilla,
his wife, having recently emigrated from Italy on account of Claudius's
edict that all Jews must leave Rome, *and these had settled in Greece*; 3and
because *Paul* practiced the same trade, he stayed with them and they
worked together, for they were tentmakers by profession. 4And he *entered and* lectured in the synagogue every Sabbath *and made known the
name of the Lord Jesus,* winning over both Jews and Greeks. 5And when
both Silas and Timothy came down from Macedonia, Paul concentrated
on preaching, emphatically testifying to the Jews that *the Lord* Jesus is
the Christ. *And after a long speech with much scripture interpretation, /*
6*once*† they began refusing him and blaspheming, he shook out his
garments[g] and said to them, "Your blood be on your own head! I am
clean of it![h] *From here on in,*† I will go to the gentiles!" 7And leaving
there,[i] he went into the house of a man named Justus,[j] a God-fearer
whose house was next door to the synagogue. 8As it happened, Crispus,
the ruler of the synagogue, believed the Lord, with all his household,[k] and
many of the Corinthians, hearing this, believed and were baptized, *believing in God through the name of the Lord Jesus Christ.* 9And during
the night in a vision, the Lord said to Paul, "Do not fear, but speak and
do not keep silent, 10because it is I with you and no one will get his hands

---

f. It is possible Aquila stands for Marcion, who was also from Pontus. Marcion was well known for having derived his wealth from his family ship-building business, and this may have become transformed into Aquila's livelihood as a laborer, especially if his activity as a tent maker overlaps with that of sail making. Like Marcion, Aquila journeys to Rome, then has to turn back east. It is worth noting that in the Clementine Homilies, Simon Magus, who teaches Marcionite doctrine and stands for Paul, has a disciple named Aquila. Yet again, Acts 10:32 mentions a "Simon the tanner," possibly a match for Paul, the leather worker.

g. Luke 10:10-11; 4 Ezra 15:13

h. The Western text has "I am clean from you" (cf. Matt. 27:24; Mark 6:11).

i. Western text: "leaving Aquila."

j. Western text: "Titius," perhaps the same character to whom one of the Pastoral Epistles is fictively addressed.

k. 1 Cor. 1:14

on you to mistreat you, for numerous people are loyal to me in this city."[l]
11And he stayed in that city[m] a year and six months with them, teaching
the truth of God.

12While Gallio[n] was proconsul of Achaia,[o] the Jews conspired to ambush Paul and haul him before the judgment seat, 13*and shouted,* saying, "This fellow urges people to worship God in a manner diverging from the Torah." 14And as Paul was just about to begin his defense, Gallio said to the Jews, "O Jews, if it were some injustice or evil hooliganism, I would have reason to bear with you; 15but if it is only questions about a word and names and your private law *in which you wish to indulge,* see to it yourselves.[p] I have no intention of acting as a judge in such matters."[q]
16And he had them dispersed from the judgment seat. 17But the crowd *of Greeks* grabbed Sosthenes, the synagogue ruler,[r] and beat him right in front of the judgment seat. *But none of it phased Gallio.*† *And he pretended he saw none of this.*

18But Paul, now having lingered many days, bade farewell to the brothers and sailed for Syria, taking with him Priscilla[s] and Aquila. In Cenchrea he shaved his head because of a Nazirite vow he had taken.[t]
19And they[u] came down to Ephesus, where he left them *on the next Sabbath* when he entered the synagogue and lectured to the Jews. 20They asked him to stay longer, but he did not agree to it, 21bidding them farewell and saying, "*I must by all means observe this next feast day in Jerusalem.* I will return to you again, God willing!" And he set forth from

l. This vision is based on the comfort offered Elijah by God in 1 Kings 19:18.

m. The Western text has "Corinth."

n. Gallio was the brother of the Stoic philosopher Seneca, with whom Paul supposedly corresponded. This may be the beginning of that apocryphal trajectory.

o. His term was somewhere between 51 and 53 CE.

p. Matt. 27:24

q. Luke 12:14

r. 1 Cor. 1:1

s. Is it possible this Priscilla stands for Priscilla the Montanist, prophetess of Phrygia? Verse 23 has Paul pointedly visit Phrygia without her, perhaps to undercut any apostolic succession claim she may have made or that others made for her. In the same way, one wonders if the Montanist prophetess Maximilla stands behind the encratite convert of that name in the Acts of Andrew.

t. According to Num. 6:1-21, one could not cut one's hair for the duration of the vow, so Paul cuts it just beforehand so it doesn't grow too long before he can have it trimmed again.

u. The Western text has "he."

Ephesus. [22]Coming down to Caesarea, he went up and greeted the congregation; he went down to Antioch, [23]and once he had spent some time there, he left, passing systematically through the Galatian countryside and Phrygia, confirming all the disciples in their faith.

[24]A certain Jew named Apollo,[v] an Alexandrian by nationality, an eloquent man, arrived in Ephesus, and he was expert in the scriptures. [25]This man had been catechized *in his own country* in the way[w] of the Lord and, afire with spirit, he spoke and taught accurately the facts about Jesus, though he had heard only of the baptism of John.[x] [26]And this man began to speak boldly in the synagogue. And when Priscilla and Aquila heard him, they took him aside and explained the way of God to him more accurately.[y] [27]*And when he decided to continue to Achaia, the brothers were encouraged and wrote to the disciples to welcome him.*[z] When he arrived, he proved to be of great help to those who had believed on account of his gifts,[a] [28]for he tied the Jews in knots in public debate, proving from the scriptures that Jesus is the Christ.[b]

19

[1]*And when Paul wanted to fulifil his desire to go to Jerusalem, the Spirit told him to return to Asia.* And it came about, *while Apollo was in Corinth,*[†] Paul, having come through the upper coasts, arrived at Ephesus, where he found some ascetics. [2]So he said to them, "Tell me if you received the Holy Spirit when you believed." But they said to him, "To tell you the truth, we have never heard of any *receiving the* Holy Spirit." [3]And he said, "What sort of baptism did you have?" And they said, "The baptism of John." [4]And Paul said, "John administered a penitential bap-

---

v. Western text: "Apollonius."

w. Western text: "message."

x. All these characterizations hint at his being a John the Baptist sectarian, especially references to "the way of the Lord," "fire," "spirit," and having only John's baptism. In such a context, "the facts concerning Jesus" may mean simply the Baptist's predictions of him, as in Acts 13:24-25; 19:4a.

y. Acts 13:33; 19:4b-5

z. The Western text has: "Now certain Corinthians were staying in Ephesus. Once they heard about him, they urged him to cross over with them into their native country. When he agreed, the Ephesians wrote to the disciples in Corinth, directing them to welcome him."

a. See 1 Cor. 1:12; 3:5-6, 21-23; 4:6

b. It is possible the New Testament character Apollos, short for Apollonius, and actually called Apollonius in the Western text, is a Christianizing co-opting of Apollonius of Tyana, a wandering first-century philosopher and miracle worker of neo-Pythagorean leanings. He also stopped in Corinth.

tism, telling the people they ought to believe in the one coming after him,[c] namely Jesus."[d] [5]And hearing this, they agreed to be baptized in the name of the Lord Jesus *Christ for the cancellation of sins*. [6]And when Paul laid hands on them, *at once* the Holy Spirit came[e] on them, and they spoke in tongues and prophesied. [7]There were twelve men in all.[f]

[8]And entering the synagogue, he[g] spoke boldly *with great effectiveness* for three months, lecturing and persuading those in attendance about the kingdom of God. [9]But when some grew stubborn and disobeyed the will of God, disparaging the Way before the *gentile* crowds, he split from the synagogue and took his disciples with him, lecturing daily in the school of *a certain* Tyrannus *from the fifth to the tenth hour*. [10]And this went on for over two years so that all the inhabitants of the province of Asia heard the message[h] of the Lord, both Jews and Greeks. [11]And God did extraordinary deeds of power through Paul's hands, [12]so that they even brought handkerchiefs and work aprons that had come in contact with his skin and put them on those who were sick and their diseases fled them and the evil spirits went out of them.[i]

[13]And some of the itinerant Jewish exorcists also tried their hand at uttering the name of Jesus over those having evil spirits, saying, "I command you by the Jesus whom Paul preaches!" [14]And *among them* were *seven*[j] men who billed themselves as sons of a certain Sceva, a *Jewish arch-*[†]priest, and they were doing this.[k] [15]And replying, the evil spirit said

c. As the rest of the verse is manifestly a gloss, Darrell J. Doughty has suggested that the statement originally referred to Simon Magus as John's designated successor.

d. The Western text has "Christ."

e. Western text: "fell."

f. "John" seems to imply John the apostle ("twelve disciples"), with whom earlier Catholic tradition sought to replace Paul as the patron saint of Ephesus since Paul's name had become synonymous with what the church considered heresy. Luke's strategy is to rehabilitate the name of Paul in order to win over his followers, the Marcionites and Gnostics.

g. The Western text has "Paul."

h. Western text: "words."

i. The Pauline parallel to Peter's feats in Acts 5:15.

j. This has to be a copying error; an early scribe's eye fell on the name Sceva and misread it as the Hebrew word for "seven" (*sheva*) and made it the number of sons. The number does not appear in the Western text. See Hugh J. Schonfield, *The Authentic New Testament: Edited and Translated from the Greek for the General Reader* (London: Dobson, 1956), on this verse.

k. The Western text has: "wanted to do the same thing, it being their practice

to them, "Jesus I know, and I have heard of Paul, but who the hell are you?" [16]And the man in whom the evil spirit lurked leaped on the men and overpowered both so that they barely managed to escape naked and wounded from that house.[l] [17]And this news spread to everyone in Ephesus, both Jews and Greeks, and fear went through all of them, and the name of the Lord Jesus was held in high regard. [18]And many of those who, because of this, believed came forward, confessing and recounting their former practices. [19]And a remarkable number of those practicing the occult arts brought together their grimoires and burnt them publicly. And they totaled up the value and it came to fifty thousand silver coins. [20]In this way the message[m] of the Lord increased mightily in prestige and was a force to be reckoned with.

[21]And when all this was over, Paul resolved in the Spirit to journey to Jerusalem, passing through Macedonia and Achaia on the way, saying, "After that, I must also see Rome." [22]And he sent two of his attendants, Timothy and Erastus, into Macedonia while he lingered for a bit in Asia. [23]It was about that time when no little commotion arose over the Way. [24]One Demetrius by name, a silversmith[n] who dealt in silver miniatures of the shrine of Artemis,[o] provided no little business for the artisans. [25]He called together the workers of related trades and said, "Men, you understand that we make a good living from this trade, [26]and you can see and hear for yourselves that not only in Ephesus, but practically throughout the whole of Asia this Paul character has won over and perverted a sizable crowd, saying that gods made by hand are not gods at all. [27]Not only does this threaten our livelihood, but also the temple of the great goddess Artemis is about to be considered nothing, and *her greatness*[†] will be diminished, she whom all Asia, indeed the whole inhabited earth, worships. Are we going to stand for that?" [28]Hearing this, and seething with

---

to exorcize such people. And they came to see a demonized man and commenced invoking the name, saying, 'We command you by Jesus whom Paul preaches, to come out!'"

l. The Ephesian wild man is Luke's pastiche of Mark's Gerasene demoniac (Mark 5:1-20; Luke 8:26-39), who in turn, as Dennis R. MacDonald has shown in *The Homeric Epics and the Gospel of Mark* (New Haven: Yale University Press, 2000), is based on Polyphemus the Cyclops from Homer's *Odyssey*.

m. The Western text has "faith."

n. In 2 Tim. 4:14, he is confused with the Jew named Alexander (below) and is made into a coppersmith.

o. Excavations show Luke has it slightly wrong because artisans made statuettes of the goddess herself rather than replicas of her shrine.

rage, they *spilled into the street and* shouted, saying, "Great is Artemis of
the Ephesians!" [29]And the city was filled with confusion and they stampeded like a herd into the theatre, with Gaius and Aristarchus, Macedonian traveling companions of Paul, in tow. [30]Paul intended to face the
mob if they would let his friends go, but the disciples did not allow him.
[31]And some of the Asiarchs, too, friends of his, sent word to him, begging
him not to surrender himself in the theatre. [32]Various people shouted
now one thing, now another, for the assembly was confused and the majority did not even know what they were doing there. [33]But some in the
crowd coached Alexander, whom the Jews put forward, and Alexander,
waving his hand for silence, attempted to defend himself before the mob.[p]
[34]But recognizing him as a Jew, they all spoke in unison for about two
hours, shouting him down with "Great is Artemis of the Ephesians!"
[35]And the scribe Alexander, at length succeeding in quieting down the
crowd, says, "Men! Ephesians! Is there anyone on earth who is ignorant
of the fact that the city of the Ephesians[q] is host to the temple of the great
Artemis and of her image that fell down from Zeus? [36]Since these things
are undeniable, it is imperative for you to remain calm and not to do anything rash. [37]For you have brought these men here, though they are neither temple robbers nor blasphemers of your goddess. [38]If in fact Demetrius and his artisans have a[r] complaint against anyone,[s] there are public
tribunals and proconsuls; let them bring formal charges against one another. [39]But if there is anything else you want, let it be settled in the lawful
assembly. [40]For we are in very real danger of being charged with rioting
because of today's events since there is no cause we can name to account
for this ruckus." [41]And with these words, he broke up the assembly.

20

[1]After the uproar died down, Paul summoned the disciples and exhorted them *at length*. Taking his leave, he embarked *on his journey*[†] to
Macedonia. [2]And having gone through those parts and having exhorted
them with much speech, he came into Greece [3]and spent three months
there. On account of a plot laid against him by the Jews, just as he was
about[t] to set sail for Syria, he thought it best[u] to return by way of Mace-

p. In addition to Paul and his colleagues, their Jewish rivals were also objects of the crowd's wrath since both were known to condemn idolatry.

q. The Western text has "our city."

r. Western text: "any."

s. Western text: "them."

t. Western text: "he wished."

donia. 4*So when he was ready to leave for Asia,* he was accompanied by Sopater of Pyrrho,[v] a Beroean, and the Thessalonians Aristarchus and Secundus, Gaius from Derbe, Timothy, and the Asians Tychicus[w] and Trophimus.[x] 5And these, going on ahead, waited for us[y] in Troy. 6And after the days of unleavened bread, we sailed away from Philippi, and in five days we came to them in Troas, where we stayed for seven days.[z] 7And on the first day of the week, when we assembled to break bread, Paul lectured to them; and planning to depart in the morning, he continued speaking until midnight. 8Quite a number of lamps were burning in the upstairs room where we were gathered. 9And a certain youth named Eutychus was sitting on the windowsill. Unable to fight off a deep sleep, with Paul lecturing on and on, he dozed off and fell down from the third floor and was picked up dead. 10But rushing downstairs, Paul fell on him and hugged him close,[a] saying, "Don't panic—his life is in him!" 11And he went back up, broke bread and ate a bit, and talked with them for some time until daylight, whereupon he departed. 12And *as they were bidding him farewell,* they brought the boy home alive and were more than moderately relieved. 13And we, having boarded the ship earlier,[b] shoved off for Assos, intending to take Paul aboard there, for that was the arrangement, he preferring to cover the distance on foot. 14When he joined us in Assos, we took him aboard and came to Mitylene; 15and sailing off from there the following day, we arrived off Chios; and on the next day we crossed over to Samos *and lingered at Trogyllium*; and on the next we came to Miletus. 16For Paul had decided to sail past Ephesus

---

u. Western text: "the Spirit told him."

v. This might be understood as denoting that Sopater "belonged to" Pyrrho, meaning he was a member, or former member, of the Skeptics, founded by Pyrrho.

w. The Western text has "of the Ephesians, Eutychus."

x. See 2 Cor. 8:18-23; these men, representing the churches that had contributed to Paul's collection for Jerusalem (Gal. 2:10; Rom. 15:26-28), were to be witnesses to the fund's proper use. Luke has scattered references to this episode throughout Acts (8:18-20; 11:29; 21:24; 24:17) but obscures the spectacle of the Jerusalem church rejecting Paul's charity as a cheap ploy for recognition and then clamoring for his blood. See note at 21:27.

y. The Western text has "him."

z. Here we see the resumption of the "we" passages, beginning with v. 5 in the Alexandrian text, continuing through v. 15 and then picking up again in chap. 21.

a. 1 Kings 17:21-23

b. The Western text has "went down to the ship and."

so as to avoid getting tied down in Asia because he wanted, if he could manage it, to be in Jerusalem for the Day of Pentecost.

17Sending word from Miletus to Ephesus, he summoned the elders of the congregation. 18And when they joined him *and were all assembled,* he said to them, "You know, *brothers,* how from the first day I set foot in Asia, I was with you the whole time,[c] 19serving the Lord with all humility, not to mention the tears and testings that came my way through the Jews, 20and how I did not hesitate to share with you any beneficial thing but have preached to you and taught you publicly and from house to house, 21urgently testifying to both Jews and Greeks of the need for repentance toward God and toward[d] our Lord, Jesus. 22And now, behold, I am compelled in spirit to travel to Jerusalem, not knowing what lies in store for me there, 23except that the Holy Spirit in every city gives me serious warnings through the local prophets, saying that chains and afflictions await me.[e] 24But I consider my life on no account precious if I may only finish my course and the mission *of preaching the message* I received from the Lord Jesus to bear urgent testimony *to Jews and Greeks* of the news of the favor of God.[f] 25And now, behold, I realize none of you will ever see my face again, all you among whom I made my rounds preaching the kingdom *of Jesus.* 26Accordingly, *I testify to you,*† *to* this day I am unstained from the blood of all. 27For I have not neglected to announce to you everything God wants of you. 28Watch out for yourselves and for all the flock in which the Holy Spirit posted you as bishops to shepherd God's[g] congregation, *which he acquired at the price of his own blood.*†[h] 29I know good and well that after I leave, bloodthirsty wolves will attack your flock, sparing no one, 30and men will emerge from your own ranks[i] speaking perverse things to siphon off disciples for themselves.[j] 31So stay

c. Western text: "for three years or more."

d. Western text: "through."

e. This is the equivalent of the Synoptic Passion predictions, reassuring readers that the hero's tragic fate is no mere happenstance, much less the triumph of evil.

f. Phil. 3:7-14

g. The Western text has "the Lord's."

h. A cluster of variant readings makes this look like an anti-docetic or Patripassian gloss. The original may have read, "which you must defend at the price of your own blood," which is a better fit with the metaphor and context (see John 10:11).

i. Meaning heretical bishops.

j. Paul's Jewish rivals would have seen his activities in precisely the same

vigilant, taking as your example how for three years, night and day, I never ceased tearfully admonishing each individual. [32]And now I place you in the hands of the Lord and leave you to the promise of his favor, as he is quite capable of building you up and providing you an inheritance as one of those who are holy. [33]I cast no greedy eye upon anyone's silver or gold or clothing. [34]You remember how these hands served my own needs as well as those of my colleagues. [35]I demonstrated all these things to you, that in our work we are obliged to give aid to the infirm and to keep in mind the words of the Lord Jesus, that he said, 'Blessed is it to give rather than to receive.'" [36]And when he concluded his remarks, he knelt down with them all and prayed. [37]And there was a considerable amount of weeping on everyone's part, and they came up and hugged him with great feeling. [38]What upset them most was his saying that they are no more to see his face. And they escorted him to his ship.

21

[1]Now when *the time came for us,*[†] *we* set sail; having torn ourselves away from them, we took a straight course and came to Cos, then the next day to Rhodes, and from there to Patara *and Myra.* [2]And locating a ship crossing over to Phoenicia, we embarked and set sail. [3]Sighting Cyprus and passing it on the left, we sailed for Syria and came down to Tyre, where the ship was to unload cargo. [4]We looked up the local disciples and stayed there seven days. Inspired by the Spirit, they told Paul not to go up to Jerusalem.[k] [5]And when we reached the end of our stay, we left and resumed our journey, with everyone escorting us, including women and children, as far as the city limits. Once we had knelt on the beach to pray, [6]we spoke parting words to one another and embarked on the ship and they returned home. [7]And finishing the voyage from Tyre, we arrived at Ptolemais, where we greeted the brothers and stayed with them for the day. [8]On the next morning, we left there and came to Caesarea and en-

---

terms (cf. 19:8-9). Nonetheless, Luke has in mind Marcion and Bardesanes, the first Christian leaders in the region. Marcion and some Gnostics claimed Pauline credentials, which Luke here seeks to undermine.

k. Was Paul, then, disobeying the express will of the Holy Spirit by proceeding to Jerusalem? Was the Spirit forbidding him to go there as he had forbidden him to go to Asia and Bithynia in 16:6-7? More likely what the author means is that local prophets announced, by revelation, what must happen to Paul in Jerusalem, providing he went, and then the prophets, speaking for themselves, echoed Peter in Matt. 16:22. Like Peter, they had been the vehicle for the prophecy of their friend's doom; but precisely as his friends, they hated the thought of his perishing, and said so.

tered the house of Philip, the evangelist, one of the Seven, and stayed with him. 9Now this man had four daughters, prophesying virgins.[l] 10And while we remained there many more days, a certain prophet named Agabus came down from Jerusalem. 11And coming to us, he borrowed Paul's belt and, having tied his own hands and feet, said, "Thus says the Holy Spirit: 'The man to whom this belt belongs, the Jews in Jerusalem will truss him up the same way and deliver him into the hands of the gentiles!'"[m] 12When we heard these words, both we and the locals begged *Paul* him*self* not to go up to Jerusalem but to send the others. 13Then Paul said, "What are you doing by weeping except undermining my resolve? As for me, I am quite ready[n] not only to be tied up but even to die in Jerusalem on behalf of the name of the Lord Jesus *Christ.*" 14Being unable to change his mind, we knew there was no more to say except *to each other,* "May the will of the Lord[o] be done!"

15And after these *two* days, we prepared ourselves[p] and headed up to Jerusalem *from Caesarea*; 16and some of the disciples from Caesarea also went with us, bringing us to one with whom we might lodge, Mnason, a certain Cypriot, a disciple from the very early days. 17And *leaving there,* we arrived in Jerusalem, where the brothers gave us a joyful welcome. 18And on the next day, Paul went in with us to James and all the elders joined *him.* 19And once he greeted them, he recounted one by one each of the successes God had granted among the gentiles through his ministry. 20Hearing it, they worshipped God[q] and said to him, "As for our work: you can see for yourself, brother, how many tens of thousands of the Jews[r] have believed,[s] and every one of them is a zealot for the Torah.

l. Papias interviewed these women in the mid-second century; they are an anachronism here.

m. Luke must be drawing on an earlier story or his own earlier draft in which the daughters of Philip delivered this oracle while wearing the sacred girdles of prophecy mentioned in the Testament of Job 46-50. But as with Anna the prophetess (Luke 2:36-38) and the Pythoness (Acts 16:18), Luke suppresses her prophecy (see 1 Tim. 2:12; 1 Cor. 14:34). Luke reintroduces the fictive prophet Agabus from 11:27-28 to give the prophecy, necessitating a reinterpretation of the girdle or belt. The prophecy itself is another Pauline Passion prediction.

n. The Western text has "I desire."

o. Western text: "God."

p. Western text: "wished them farewell and."

q. Western text: "the Lord."

r. Western text: "in Judea."

s. Gal. 2:9

[21]And they have been informed about you that you teach *all*† the Jews throughout the nations to commit apostasy from Moses, telling them not to circumcise their children, nor to live by the customs. [22]So what is to be done? *The mob will surely gather, for* they will certainly hear of your arrival. [23]So we suggest you follow this plan: There are four men among us who are under a vow. [24]You, too, are completing a vow, aren't you? Take these and be purified jointly with them and pay for having their heads shaved, and this will reassure everyone that there is nothing to the rumors they have heard about you, but that you yourself live scrupulously by the Torah. [25]And as for the believing gentiles, *they have no complaint against you since* we wrote them, ruling that they need *observe nothing of that sort except* to steer clear of both idol sacrifice and blood—*anything strangled*†—and prostitution."[t] [26]Then Paul took the men the next day and, undergoing purification along with them, went into the temple, setting the end of the purification period when the requisite offering should be made on behalf of each.

[27]Now when the seven days were nearly done, the Jews *who had come up* from Asia[u] spotted him in the temple and stirred up the crowd and got him in their clutches, [28]yelling out, "Men! Israelites! Help! This is the man—the one who teaches all men everywhere against the Jewish people and the Torah and against this holy place! And if that weren't enough, now he has even brought Greeks into the temple, profaning its sanctity." [29]They had earlier seen Trophimus the Ephesian in the city with Paul, and they assumed Paul had brought him into the temple. [30]The whole city was in an uproar, with masses of people rushing together, and they grabbed hold of Paul and dragged him out of the temple, immediately closing the doors.[v] [31]And while they were about to lynch him, the report came to the commander of the cohort that all Jerusalem was in

t. Note that Luke allows Paul no word of defense to say there is no truth to the rumors. One is left with the nagging possibility that it is all a crafty charade, a public relations trick to mislead the Torah zealots. Luke does, however, tell us beforehand (18:18) about Paul's voluntary Nazirite vow, which comes in handy here to suggest perhaps Paul was no scofflaw.

u. Surely F. C. Baur is correct in saying Luke has substituted the Ephesian holiday pilgrims for the original villains of the story, who must have been James's Jewish-Christian "zealots for the Torah." This is just the reaction James's scheme was intended to avoid. Luke's agenda is to paper over such rifts, making the early days of Christianity appear as a golden age of unity and a platform for ecumenical unity in his own day.

v. This temple disturbance matches Jesus' "cleansing of the temple." Paul's Christ-like Passion narrative proceeds.

chaos. [32]At once he took soldiers and centurions and burst in on them.
Once they saw the commander and the soldiers, they left off beating Paul.
[33]Then the commander came near and took Paul in hand, ordering that
he be bound with two chains. He asked who he might be and "what has
he done?" [34]And various voices in the crowd called out one thing or another, and being unable to determine anything for certain because of the
uproar, he ordered him to be brought into the fortress. [35]And once they
reached the steps, he had to be bodily carried by the soldiers on account
of the violence of the crowd, [36]for the mass *of the people*† followed
closely, shouting out, "Take him away!"

[37]And as they were about to bring him inside the fortress, Paul *answers and* says to the comander, "Tell me if it is legal for me to say something to you." And he said, "So you know Greek! [38]*Then*† aren't you that
Egyptian who some time ago caused trouble and led those four thousand
men of the Sicarii into the desert ?"[w] [39]Paul said, "I am in fact a Jew, a
man from[x] Tarsus in Cilicia, *a citizen of no average city.*† And I beg you,
let me speak to the people." [40]And when he[y] granted permission, Paul
stood on the steps and waved his hand at the people; when they had much
quieted down, he spoke to them in the Hebrew language, saying:

22

[1]"Men! Brothers and fathers! Hear now my defense before you!"
[2]Once they heard him speaking in the Hebrew language, they quieted
down still more. And he says, [3]"I am a Jew, a man born in Tarsus of
Cilicia and brought up in this city, having been trained at the feet of
Gamaliel according to the strictest standard of our ancestral Torah, being
a zealot for God just like all of you today. [4]Zealous to the point of persecuting this Way to the death, manacling and delivering to prison both
men and women. [5]Just ask the archpriest and all the council of elders.
From them I secured letters and journeyed to the brothers in Damascus,

---

w. The Sicarii were a band of Zealot assassins whose name was derived from the short sword (*sica,* like "sickle") they concealed in their sleeves. Their *modus operandi* was to approach a dignitary, stab him, and then pretend to share in the general alarm. Some think Judas's epithet "Iscariot" denotes association with the group. At any rate, Luke derives this reference to the Egyptian messiah from Josephus, *Antiquities,* 20.8.6; *Wars,* 2.13.5, where he is said to have commanded 30,000 men in his failed coup attempt. His goal was to make the walls of Jerusalem fall down as Joshua did Jericho's. He was thus another would-be "prophet like Joshua."

x. The Western text has "born in."

y. Western text: "the commander."

even leading those there up to Jerusalem in bonds to punish them. 6Now
it came about as I was journeying† and I approached Damascus, about
midday a powerful light from the sky encompassed me, 7and I fell to the
ground and heard a voice speaking to me, 'Saul, Saul! Why are you persecuting me?' 8And I replied, 'Who are you, Lord?' And he said to me, 'I? I
am Jesus the Nazorean whom you are persecuting!' 9Now while my companions did see the light *and were terrified,* they did not hear the voice of
the one speaking to me. 10And I said, 'What shall I do, Lord?' And the
Lord[z] said to me, 'Get up and proceed into Damascus, and there you will
be told about everything that has been assigned you to do.' 11And *when I
stood up,* on account of the brilliance of that light I could not see, so I entered Damascus led by the hands of my companions. 12And a certain
Ananias, a devout man, observant of the Torah, highly esteemed by all
the local Jews, 13came to me *and stood by me,*† saying, 'Saul, brother
Saul, look up.' So at once I looked up at him. 14And he said *to me,* 'The
God of our fathers preordained you to know his will and see the Just One
and hear a voice from his mouth,[a] 15because you will be his witness before all mankind of the things you have seen and heard. 16And now, what
are you waiting for? Get up! Be baptized and wash away your sins, invoking his name.' 17And it came about that when I returned to Jerusalem and
was praying in the temple, I passed into an ecstasy, 18and I saw him
speaking to me. 'Hurry! Get out of Jerusalem quickly because they will
not welcome your testimony about me.' 19And I said, 'Lord, they realize
that I used to raid the synagogues, imprisoning and beating those who believed on you. 20And when the blood of your witness Stephen was being
spilled, I myself stood there approving and watching over the coats of his
murderers. For someone like me to have turned…!' 21And he said to me,
'Be on your way because I will send you far from here to the gentiles.'"

22They listened up till this last word, then raised their voices, saying,
"Erase such a one from the earth! For he is an abomination against nature." 23And as they screamed and ripped their clothes and pitched dust
in the air, 24the commander ordered that he be brought into the fortress,
commanding that he be interrogated under the lash so as to find out for
sure just what he had done to account for their howling for his blood.
25But while they were spread-eagling him to tie him with thongs, Paul
said to the centurion on duty, "Tell me if it is legal for you to flog a man, a

z. Western text: "he."

a. As G. A. Wells points out, Luke does not quite sound like he is referring to a recent historical figure—rather some distant, invisible deity.

Roman, convicted of no crime." [26]Once he heard this, *that he made himself out to be a Roman,* the centurion approached the commander and reported to him, "*Consider carefully* what you are about to do. For this man is a Roman!" [27]So the commander approached and asked him, "Tell me, are you a Roman?" And he said, "Yes." [28]And the commander answered, "*I know* how much it cost me to obtain this citizenship!" And Paul said, "But I have been born *a Roman.*" [29]So at once the interrogators standing around him stepped discretely away.[b] Even the commander was afraid once he realized he was dealing with a Roman and that he was having him tied to the rack. [30]The next day, determined to know for sure exactly what the Jews had against him, he released him and ordered a meeting of the archpriests and the whole Sanhedrin, and he brought in Paul and had him stand among them.[c]

23

[1]Paul, his gaze sweeping the Sanhedrin, said, "Men, brothers, I have lived my whole life with a clear conscience before God." [2]And the archpriest Ananias directed those flanking him to strike him on the mouth. [3]Then Paul said to him, "God is about to strike you, you whitewashed wall! You sit here judging me according to the Law and you transgess the Law by commanding me to be struck?" [4]And those standing there said, "You dare revile the archpriest of God?" [5]And Paul said, "I did not know, brothers, that he is the archpriest. In that case, you're right—for it is written, 'You shall not speak evil of a ruler of your people.'"[d] [6]Paul, mindful that one faction of the Sanhedrin is composed of Syndics but the other of Pharisees, cried out in the Sanhedrin, "Men, brothers, I am a Pharisee from a long line of Pharisees. And it is essentially on account of the hope for the resurrection of the dead that I am on trial today." [7]And as he said this, static arose between the Pharisees and Syndics, and a schism opened up in the group. [8]For the Syndics say there is no resurrection nor afterlife as either angel or spirit,[e] but the Pharisees confess faith in both. [9]And there was a shouting match and some of the scribes who sided with the Pharisees jumped to their feet and argued ve-

---

b. John 18:6

c. Again, Paul's story mimics that of Jesus, this time with a trial before the archpriests and the Sanhedrin—not coincidentally.

d. Why did Ananias order him struck? Probably to provide another parallel to Jesus (John 18:22-23). There is a redactional motivation for the blow but not a narrative one.

e. Acts 12:15

hemently, saying: "We find this man guilty of nothing evil. What if a spirit or an angel did speak to him?" 10And as the discord was rising to a fever pitch, the commander feared that Paul might be torn limb from limb by them and commanded the troops to intervene and escort him out of their midst and into the fortress. 11And the next night the Lord came to him and said, "Brace up! For just as you earnestly testified to the facts about me in Jerusalem, so you must also bear witness in Rome."

12When dawn came, the Jews entered into a conspiracy, swearing an oath neither to eat nor to drink till they had killed Paul. 13And there were over forty who entered into this compact. 14They approached the archpriests and the elders and said, "We swore an oath to taste nothing until we succeed in killing Paul—or may God kill us! 15Now therefore, you, together with the Sanhedrin, request of the commander that he bring him down to you so you may examine his case more closely. And by the time he comes near, we will be ready to kill him." 16And the son of Paul's sister heard the treachery; then coming to the fortress and gaining entrance, he reported it to Paul. 17And Paul, calling one of the centurions over, said, "Bring this youth up to the commander, for he has something to report to him." 18So taking him, he brought him up to the commander and says, "The prisoner Paul called me over and asked me to bring this young man to you with something to tell you." 19And taking hold of his hand, the commander took him aside privately and asked, "What is it you have to report to me?" 20And he said, "The Jews agreed to request that you bring Paul down to the Sanhedrin, as if they wanted to make more specific inquiries about him. 21But do not be taken in by them, for more than forty men are there lying in wait for him, who have placed themselves under a curse neither to eat nor to drink until they kill him, and now they stand ready, just waiting for your promise." 22So the commander dismissed the young man, ordering him to "divulge to no one you reported these things to me." 23And summoning a certain pair of centurions, he told them, "Have your two hundred soldiers ready to journey as far as Caesarea, together with seventy horsemen and two hundred spearmen, as of the third hour of the night,[f] 24with mounts standing by for Paul so they may take him safely to Felix, the governor." 25And he wrote a letter to this effect:

26Claudias Lysias,
to the most excellent governor Felix.
Greetings.

---

f. 9:00 PM

> [27]This man was arrested by the Jews and about to be killed by them when I, coming on the scene with my troops, rescued him, learning that he is a Roman. [28]And determined to ascertain the exact nature of their accusation, I brought him down to their Sanhedrin, [29]where I found he was accused over questions of their Law, but charged with no crime worthy of death or even of chains. [30]And when it was revealed to me that there was a plot against the man, at once I sent word to you, also commanding his accusers to make their case before you.

[31]Therefore, the soldiers, according to their assigned duty, took Paul and brought him by night to Antipatris. [32]And the next day, allowing the horsemen to go on with him, the soldiers returned to the fortress. [33]When the horsemen entered Caesarea, they delivered the letter to the governor and also presented Paul to him. [34]Reading it, he asked Paul which province he belonged to and learned "from Cilicia." [35]"I will hear you," he said, "when your accusers get here, too." And he commanded that he be kept in the praetorium of Herod.

24

[1]After five days, the archpriest Ananias came down with some elders and an orator, one Tertullus, who set forth before the governor the case against Paul.[g] [2]And when he was called, Tertullus began to accuse Paul, saying, "Most excellent Felix, we welcome with utmost gratitude the great peace we have obtained through you and the reforms that have come to the nation [3]in all respects both here and everywhere, thanks to your foresight. [4]But let me not keep you longer than necessary; I beg you to hear us briefly in your forbearance. [5]For having found this man a pestilence, fomenting sedition among all the Jews throughout the inhabited earth, even a ringleader of the Nazorean heresy, [6]who even tried to profane the temple, we captured him [7]*until the commander Lysias appeared and most violently took him out of our custody.*[†] [8]Once you have interrogated him yourself concerning all these matters, you will be able to see the complete truth of all these accusations we make against him." [9]And the Jews joined in, too, alleging that these things are true.

[10]And when the governor gestured for Paul to speak, he answered,

---

g. In view of the tradition that Tertullian, the Carthaginian lawyer and orator who converted to Christianity around 190 CE, died a very old man, it is tempting to wonder if some tried to identify him with this Tertullus, speculating that like Paul he was subsequently converted to the faith he once persecuted.

"Understanding that for many years you have served as judge to this nation, I cheerfully defend myself on the charges aimed at me.
11Just to make you fully informed, twelve days ago I went up to Jerusalem to worship.
12And they found me neither discoursing with anyone in the temple nor gathering a crowd, neither in the synagogues nor anywhere in the city.
13Nor are they able to prove to you any of the things they now accuse me of.
14But this I will confess to you: I worship the ancestral God according to the Way, which they call a heresy; thus I believe all the doctrines of the Torah and the predictions of the Prophets,[h]
15placing my hopes on God for that which they too expect—an impending resurrection, both of the righteous and the unrighteous.
16Because of this, I try my best to cultivate a conscience ever blameless in the eyes of God and other people.
17And after many years, I arrived bringing alms and offerings to my nation.[i]
18With these, some Jews from Asia found me in the temple, having been purified, not with a crowd nor with an uproar.
19They should have been the ones to appear before you if they had any case to make against me.
20Or let these say for themselves what crime they found as I stood before the Sanhedrin.
21Or wasn't it just this one thing I cried out as I stood before them? 'It is essentially over the resurrection of the dead that I am on trial before you today'?"

22And Felix, being now more accurately informed about the Way, postponed the proceedings, saying, "When Lysias the commander arrives, I will decide your case."
23Putting him in the centurion's custody, he ordered that he be well treated and to forbid none of his own people to attend him.

24And after some days, Felix arrived with his own wife Drusilla, who was a Jewess,[j] and he sent for Paul and listened to him speak about the faith in Christ Jesus.
25And as he discoursed about righteousness and con-

h. To say that Christianity automatically entailed adherence to the Hebrew God and his scriptures was contrary to Marcion's position.

i. This must refer to the collection Paul had taken up among the gentiles. It is the money Paul, as Simon Magus, offered Peter for the gift of apostleship (Acts 8:18-20), or to pay for purification sacrifices for himself and the other four men after their vows (Acts 2:24), to legitimize Paul's ministry among skeptical Jewish-Christian Torah zealots, as in Gal. 2:9-10.

j. Josephus, *Antiquities,* 20.7.2, tells that Simon Magus helped Felix persuade Drusilla to leave her husband, King Azizus of Emesa, who had become circumcised in order to marry her, and take up with the uncircumcised Felix instead. Josephus makes this Simon a Cypriot, but this may represent the fluidity between "Kittim" (Phoenicians/Philistines, including Cypriots) and "Gittites" (Samaritans from the Philistine city of Gitta, or Gath, home to Goliath and Simon Magus).

tinence and the impending judgment, Felix began feeling uneasy and answered him, "For the time being, be on your way; when I have more time I will send for you later."[k] 26He was also hoping that Paul will offer him some of that money, which is why he sent for him more frequently and conversed with him. 27And after two whole years had passed, Felix was succeeded by Porcius Festus. And wanting to curry favor with the Jews, Festus left Paul in captivity.[l]

25

1So three days after his arrival in the province, Festus went up from Caesarea to Jerusalem, 2where the archpriests and the first rank of the Jews informed him against Paul, and they petitioned him, 3requesting a favor against him, that he might summon him to Jerusalem, hatching a plot to kill him along the road. 4Suspecting such a plan, Festus answered that Paul should be kept in Caesarea where he himself should soon return. 5"Therefore, let capable men among you go down with me, and if he is guilty of any crime, let them accuse him." 6And having remained among them no more than eight or ten days, he went down to Caesarea. On the next day, sitting on the throne of judgment, he ordered Paul to be brought. 7And when he arrived, the Jews who came down from Jerusalem surrounded him, bringing many grave charges against him, none of which they were able to prove. 8Paul defended himself: "I have sinned in no respect against the Torah of the Jews nor against the temple, nor against Caesar." 9But Festus, looking to curry favor with the Jews, answered Paul, saying, "Do you want to go up to Jerusalem to stand trial before me on these charges there?" 10And Paul said, "I am standing in front of Caesar's tribunal where I must be tried. I have done the Jews no wrong, as in fact you know very well. 11If I do wrong, and if I have done anything worthy of death, I do not seek to evade execution. But if there is nothing to the things they accuse me of, no one can hand me over to them. I appeal to Caesar!" 12Then Festus, once he discussed it with the council, answered, "To Caesar you have appealed—to Caesar you shall go!"

13When some days had passed, Agrippa the king and Bernice arrived at Caesarea and called on Festus.[m] 14And as their visit lasted longer and

---

k. Paul was given the same brush-off by the Athenian philosophers (Acts 17:32) as was Socrates by the uncomfortable Euthyphro.

l. Like Jesus before Pilate, Paul has a trial, actually two, before Roman governors.

m. This was Herod Agrippa II, whose namesake father put Jacob to death in chap. 12 and wanted to kill Peter too. Bernice was the sister of Drusilla and

longer, Festus explained the business with Paul, saying, "There is a certain man whom Felix left in prison, [15]about whom the archpriests and the elders of the Jews informed me when I was in Jerusalem, requesting sentence against him. [16]I answered them that it is not a custom with Romans to deliver a man to death before allowing him to meet his accusers face to face and to defend himself against the charges. [17]So when they came together, without delay the next day I sat on the judgment seat and commanded the man to be brought in. [18]The accusers stood up and made no charge of evil deeds such as I expected; [19]instead, they had a dispute with him over certain questions of their own religion and over one Jesus, who died, but whom Paul averred to be alive. [20]And finding myself puzzled at the debate about these things, I asked if he would be willing to journey to Jerusalem and to be tried there about these things. [21]But when Paul appealed to be remanded to the decision of the Augustus, I commanded him to be kept until I have the opportunity to send him to Caesar."

[22]And Agrippa said to Festus, "I should like to hear the man for myself." "Tomorrow," he says, "you shall." [23]So on the next day when Agrippa and Bernice arrived with great pomp and entered into the auditorium with both commanders and the chief men of the city, Festus gave the order and Paul was brought in. [24]And Festus says, "King Agrippa and all the men present, together with us, you see before you the man concerning whom the whole mass of Jews, both in Jerusalem and here, petitioned me, shouting that he must live no longer. [25]But I found him to have done nothing worthy of death. But when he himself appealed to the Augustus, I decided to send him. [26]But I have nothing definite to write to the lord concerning him, which is why I brought him before you all and especially before you, King Agrippa, so that once there has been an interrogation, I may have something to write. [27]For it seems unreasonable to send a prisoner without even indicating the charges against him."

26

[1]And Agrippa said to Paul, "It is permitted you to speak on your own behalf." Then Paul extended his hand and began his defense. [2]"As for all I am accused of by the Jews, King Agrippa, I consider myself fortunate indeed to defend myself before you today, [3]most of all because of your being an expert in all of both the customs and questions debated among

---

Agrippa II. It was widely supposed that Agrippa and Bernice lived in incest. Juvenal, *Satire* VI, trans. Peter Green, wrote of "a famous diamond ring, once worn by Queen Bernice.... She had it from her brother, that barbarous prince Agrippa, as a token of their incestuous love" (lines 155-59).

Jews; wherefore, I beg you to hear me patiently. [4]So then, my manner of life from youth on, which has been well known from the beginning to Jews both in my own country and in Jerusalem, [5]who had previously known me from the first, if they are willing to admit it, was that in accordance with the strictest sect of our religion, I lived as a Pharisee. [6]And now I find myself standing before the judgment seat on account of hope in the promise made by God to our fathers, [7]to which our twelve tribes, fervently worshipping day and night, hope to attain. It is concerning that hope that I am being tried—by Jews—O King! [8]Why do you all dismiss it as incredible that God should raise the dead?

[9]"Indeed, back then I thought myself obliged to do anything I could against the name of Jesus the Nazorean, [10]and indeed I did in Jerusalem, and having received authorization from the archpriests, I shut away many of the saints in prison, and I cast my vote for their execution, [11]and frequently punishing them wherever I found them among the synagogues, I forced them to denounce the pseudoprophet; and my rage against them surpassing all reason, I extended the range of my persecution even to the outlying cities. [12]It was while journeying to Damascus with judicial authority from the archpriests that, [13]at midday, treading the road, I saw, O King, a brightness from the sky outshining the sun,[n] shining around me and my companions. [14]And all of us having fallen to the ground, I heard a voice speaking to me in the Hebrew language, 'Saul, Saul! Why are you persecuting me? It must be hard for you, kicking against the ox goads!'[o] [15]And I replied, 'Who are you, Lord?' And the Lord said, 'I am Jesus, whom you persecute! [16]But get up and stand on your feet; the reason I appeared to you is to appoint you an attendant and a witness of both what you have seen of me and what you will see as I appear to you henceforth, [17]rescuing you from the Jewish people and from the gentiles, to whom I propose to send you, [18]to open their eyes, to turn them from darkness to light, and from the authority of the adversary to that of God so they may receive forgiveness of sins and a share with those sanctified by faith in me.'

[19]Needless to say, King Agrippa, I was not disobedient to the heav-

---

n. Cf. Euripides' *Bacchae,* line 918: "I seem to see two suns blazing in the heavens!"

o. A common Hellenistic maxim, but here probably derived from Euripides' *Bacchae,* lines 793-96, where Dionysus advises the soon-to-be-converted Pentheus who is persecuting Dionysus' followers, "I would offer him sacrifice, not rage, [nor] kick against necessity, a man defying god."

enly vision, [20]but I preached the need for repentance, turning to God, and doing good deeds worthy of repentance, first to those in Damascus, then Jerusalem, the whole country of Judea and to the gentiles. [21]It was on account of these things the Jews grabbed me in the temple and tried to kill me. [22]Having obtained God's help to the present day, I stand testifying to everyone, both small and great, about nothing other than what both the prophets and Moses said was about to happen, [23]that the Christ should be subjected to suffering, that as the first in a resurrection of the dead, he is about to announce a light both to the Jewish people and to the gentiles."

[24]And as he defended himself with these words, Festus exclaimed loudly, "Paul, you are crazy! Your great learning has driven you insane!" [25]But as for Paul, "I am no ranter, O Festus!" he says, "rather, I set forth words of truth and eminent sense. [26]The king knows all about these things, which is why I can speak frankly to him, for I am quite sure none of this can have escaped his notice. After all, none of it happened off in a remote corner somewhere. [27]King Agrippa, do you believe the prophets? I know that you believe. Well..."

[28]And Agrippa to Paul: "Not so fast! Are you trying to make me into a Christian?" [29]And Paul: "I would pray to God that, whether quickly or slowly, all who hear me today might become as I am—except for these chains!" [30]Both the king and the governor, with Bernice and those sitting with them, got up [31]and, having left, discussed what they had heard, saying, "This man is doing nothing that merits death or chains." [32]And Agrippa remarked to Festus, "Too bad he appealed to Caesar; otherwise he could have been released."[p]

27

[1]And when it was decided we should sail to Italy, they handed both Paul and some other prisoners over to a centurion named Julius of the Augustan Cohort.[q] [2]And embarking in a ship out of Adramyttium that was about to sail for ports along the coast of Asia, we set sail, accompanied by Aristarchus, a Macedonian of Thessalonica. [3]On the next day, we docked at Sidon, and Julius, treating him kindly, allowed Paul to go to his friends to get medical attention. [4]And putting to sea from there, we sailed close to Cyprus because of the opposing winds. [5]And sailing over the sea to Cilicia and Pamphylia, we came down to Myra of Lycia. [6]There the

p. This scene echoes Jesus' trial in Luke before another Herodian petty prince, Herod Antipas.

q. Notice the resumption of first-person narrative, which continues inconsistently through the end of Acts.

centurion found an Alexandrian ship bound for Italy and he put us aboard. [7]And sailing slowly for a number of days, hardly even coming against Cnidus, the wind prevented us and we sailed close to Crete against Salmone; [8]and barely sailing along it, we arrived at a certain place called Fair Havens, which was near a city called Lasaea. [9]And a long time had passed and the voyage had become dangerous on account of the fast now being over, so Paul advised them, [10]saying, "Men, I see that this voyage will end in injury and great loss, not only of the cargo and the ship, but even of our lives." [11]But the centurion found the shipmaster and the steersman more convincing than the things Paul said. [12]And as the port turned out to be unsuitable to winter in, the majority decided to sail from there on the chance they might be able to reach Phoenix and spend the winter there. This was a port of Crete facing southwest and northwest. [13]And a gently blowing south wind made them think their plan had succeeded, so they coasted close inshore by Crete.

[14]But shortly thereafter, a stormy wind called Euraquilo roared down the coast, [15]and the ship was seized, and not being able to withstand the force of the oncoming wind, we lost control of the ship and were carried away. [16]And running under the lee of a certain atoll called Clauda, we were just able to get hold of the lifeboat. [17]And when they had hoisted it up, they did what they could to undergird the ship. And fearing that they might be driven off course to Syrtis, they lowered the tackle and in this way they were carried along. [18]But the next day, being utterly helpless in the grip of the storm, they began to jettison what they could. [19]And on the third day, they threw the tackle overboard with their own hands. [20]And when neither sun nor stars appeared for many days, and with stormy weather still pressing hard, all hope of rescue now disappeared.

[21]And after a long abstenance to conserve food, Paul stood up among them and said, "You really should, O men, have taken my advice not to set sail from Crete and you would have avoided this injury and loss. [22]This time I advise you to cheer up, for no one here will lose his life, only the ship. [23]For during the night, an angel of the God to whom I belong and whom I serve stood beside me, [24]saying, 'Do not fear, Paul! You must still stand trial before Caesar, and God has given you all those sailing with you.' [25]So cheer up, men! For I believe God that it will happen just the way it has been spoken to me. [26]But we must be driven off course to a certain island."

[27]Now when the fourteenth night came and we were being tossed about in the Adriatic, the sailors surmised that they were approaching

some country. 28They took a sounding and found a depth of twenty fathoms, and once they moved a bit farther, another sounding disclosed fifteen fathoms. 29And fearing that we might be driven aground on the
rocks, they threw four anchors to stern and prayed for day to come.
30And the sailors were planning to abandon ship, lowering the lifeboat
into the sea, pretending to cast the anchors out of the prow. 31Paul said to
the centurion and to the soldiers, "Unless these men remain in the ship,
you cannot come out of this safely!" 32Then the soldiers severed the ropes
holding the boat and let it drift away. 33And with dawn coming, Paul
urged everyone to take some food, saying, "Today marks a fortnight that
you have continued waiting without food, eating nothing. 34So I urge
you, have some food. This will work out for your rescue—you will need
your strength. Not so much as a hair from any of your heads will perish."
35Having said this, he took bread and he gave thanks to God before all of
them, and breaking it, he began to eat. 36And recovering their good spirits, everyone else took food, too. 37Now all of us in the ship came to two
hundred and seventy six. 38And having had enough food, they lightened
the ship by throwing the wheat overboard.[r]

39When day came, they did not recognize the land, but they spotted a
certain bay with a shore, into which they decided to drive the ship if possible. 40And having cast off the anchors, they left them in the sea, simultaneously loosening the fastenings of the rudders. Raising the foresail to the
breeze, they held the ship on course to the shore. 41And coming upon a
place between two seas, they drove the vessel on, and when the prow ran
into the ground and was immovable, the stern was shattered by the force
of the waves.† 42Now the soldiers were of a mind to kill the prisoners so
none of them should swim away and escape. 43But the centurion, determined to save Paul, forbade them and commanded those who were able
to throw themselves overboard and swim ashore. 44And of the rest, some
made it in by clinging to planks, others to various items from the ship.
And in this way it came about that all arrived safely on land.

28

1Once we were safe, we discovered that the island was called Malta.
2And the barbarians showed us extraordinary kindness: having lit a fire,
they welcomed us all because of the oncoming rain and the cold. 3When
Paul collected a quantity of sticks and put them on the fire, a viper came

r. This is the Pauline Last Supper preceding Paul's execution. It is modeled upon the gospel stories of multiplying the loaves and fish, which also have a large group stranded far away from safety and food and who eat and are satisfied.

out fleeing the heat and fastened on his hand. 4And when the barbarians
saw the creature hanging from his hand, they said to one another, "Are
not these men criminals? This man is surely a murderer! He was saved
from the sea, but Lady Justice would not allow him to live!" 5Then he
shook off the creature into the fire and suffered no ill effect. 6They expected him momentarily to swell up or to drop dead.[s] For some time, they
expected this; but as they kept watching him and saw that nothing bad
befell him, they changed their minds and said he must be a god. 7Nearby
were the estates of the head man of the island, named Publio, who gave us
a friendly welcome and put us up for three days. 8As it happened, Publio's
father was sick in bed, suffering from fevers and dysentery. Paul went in
to see him; praying and laying on hands, he cured him. 9When this happened, the rest of the islanders who had ailments came up and were cured,
too. 10And they honored us with many tokens of appreciation, and when
we put out to sea, they piled our arms high with supplies for the trip.

11It was after three months that we embarked, having wintered on
the island. The ship was from Alexandria and bore the sign of the
Dioscuri.[t] 12And being brought to land at Syracuse, we remained three
days, 13and from there we made a circuit to Rhegium. And after one day,
when a south wind came on, on the second day we came to Puteoli,
14where we found some brothers who urged us to remain with them seven
days, and in this way we arrived at Rome.

15And from there, the brothers, having heard the reports about us,
came to intercept us as far out as the Appian Forum and Three Taverns.
Seeing them, Paul thanked God and was encouraged. 16And when we entered Rome proper, Julius the centurion permitted Paul to stay by himself, guarded by one soldier.

17And it happened that three days later, he summoned the first rank
of the Jews, and when they assembled, he said to them, "As for me, men,
brothers, though having done nothing against the people or the ancestral
customs, I was handed over as a prisoner in Jerusalem into the hands of
the Romans, 18who examined me and were of a mind to release me since
they could find me guilty of nothing deserving death. 19But when the Jews
urged against this, I was forced to appeal to Caesar, but not as if I had any

s. Swelling up and dropping dead brings to mind Judas or Ananias and Sapphira.

t. The *dioskouroi* ("sons of Zeus") were the twins Castor and Pollux, for whom the constellation was named. It was after these twins that Jacob and John were dubbed "Boanerges." The Hebrew name for the constellation was "Thomas."

intention of accusing my own nation. [20]And this is why I invited you, to meet you and to speak to you. For it is for the sake of the hope of Israel that I am bound with this chain."

[21]And they said to him, "Neither have we received letters about you from Judea, nor did any of the brothers arriving from abroad tell or speak anything evil about you personally. [22]But we think it worthwhile to hear from you your ideas. For indeed, all we know of this sect is that it is disparaged everywhere." [23]And setting a day with him, more came to him in his lodging, and to them he discoursed urgently, testifying about the kingdom of God and seeking to persuade them about Jesus from both the Torah of Moses and the Prophets, from morning till evening. [24]And some were won over by what he said, [25]but others disbelieved. And finding themselves in disagreement, they broke up after a parting word from Paul: "The Holy Spirit, speaking through Isaiah the prophet, put it beautifully when he predicted you to your fathers, saying, [26]'Go to the people and say that "hearing, you will hear but by no means understand, and looking, you will look but by no means see." [27]The mind of this people was dulled, and with their ears they barely heard, and their eyes they closed so as never to see with the eyes and hear with the ears and understand with the mind and turn back to me for me to cure them.' [28]Therefore, know this: this salvation from God was sent to the gentiles and they will listen!" [29]*When he had said these words, the Jews left and had great disputes among themselves.*[†]

[30]And he remained a whole two years in private rented rooms and welcomed anyone who came to him, [31]preaching the kingdom of God and teaching the facts about the Lord Jesus Christ with complete boldness and without hindrance.

....

Addendum

An additional textual curiosity, the following is a spurious twenty-ninth chapter of Acts. Published first in 1871, it cannot have been written much earlier. No Greek text exists, though those promoting it claimed their chapter was a translation of a Greek original and that it existed also in Syriac and Coptic versions. All these spurious claims were made by clever members of the British-Israel movement, an informal sect who believed that northern Europeans, especially Britons (and thence, Americans), were descended from the so-called Lost Tribes of Israel. Thus they saw the need for direct, personal apostolic preaching to these lost sheep of the house of Israel. In this modern apocryphon, they provided it. And

just like the Grail legends, this chapter secured a pre-Catholic foundation for the Celtic church. As the text was originally written in English, there is no need to modernize its language, as if translating an ancient text from another language. I have only modernized the punctuation, adding quotation marks, for instance. More information about this chapter and its publication history is available in Edgar J. Goodspeed's *Famous Biblical Hoaxes, or, Modern Apocrypha* (Grand Rapids: Baker Book House, 1956), 58-69.

29

[1]And Paul, full of the blessings of Christ and abounding in the spirit, departed out of Rome, determining to go into Spain,[u] for he had a long time purposed to journey thitherward and was minded also to go from thence into Britain. [2]For he had heard in Phoenicia that certain of the children of Israel, about the time of the Assyrian captivity, had escaped by sea to the "isles afar off," as spoken by the prophet[v] and called by the Romans Britain. [3]And the Lord commanded the gospel to be preached far hence to the gentiles and to the lost sheep of the house of Israel. [4]And no man hindered Paul,[w] for he testified boldly of Jesus before the tribunes and among the people; and he took with him certain of the brethren which abode with him at Rome and they took shipping at Ostium, and having the winds fair were brought safely into an haven of Spain.

[5]And much people were gathered together from the towns and villages and the hill country, for they had heard of the conversion of the apostle and the many miracles he had wrought.[x] [6]And Paul preached mightily in Spain, and great multitudes believed and were converted, for they perceived he was an apostle sent from God.

[7]And they departed out of Spain; and Paul and his company, finding a ship in Armorica sailing unto Britain, they went therein, and passing along the south coast they reached a port called Raphinus.[y] [8]Now when it was noised abroad that the apostle had landed on their coast, great multitudes of the inhabitants met him, and they treated Paul courteously, and

u. Rom. 15:24

v. Isa. 66:19

w. Acts 28:31

x. This ought to mean that someone had reached them with the Christian message. Who else but Christian missionaries would be spreading such reports about Paul? Yet in v. 6 we are given to think Paul is the first to bring the news of Christ to Spain.

y. Apparently Sandwich in Kent.

he entered in at the east gate of their city and lodged in the house of an Hebrew and one of his own nation. [9]And on the morrow, he came and stood upon Mount Lud,[z] and the people thronged at the gate and assembled in the Broadway; and he preached Christ unto them, and many believed the word and the testimony of Jesus.

[10]And at even, the Holy Ghost fell upon Paul, and he prophesied, saying, "Behold, in the last days, the God of peace shall dwell in the cities and the inhabitants shall be numbered; and in the seventh numbering of the people,[a] their eyes shall be opened and the glory of their inheritance shall shine forth before them. And nations shall come up to worship on the mount that testifieth of the patience and long suffering of a servant of the Lord. [11]And in the latter days new tidings of the gospel shall issue forth out of Jerusalem and the hearts of the people shall rejoice, and behold, fountains shall be opened and there shall be no more plague. [12]In those days there shall be wars and rumors of wars, and a king shall rise up and his sword shall be for the healing of the nations, and his peacemaking shall abide, the glory of his kingdom a wonder among princes."[b]

[13]And it came to pass that certain of the Druids came unto Paul privately and showed by their rites and ceremonies they were descended from the Jews which escaped from bondage in the land of Egypt, and the apostle believed these things, and he gave them the kiss of peace.[c] [14]And Paul abode in his lodgings three months, confirming in the faith and preaching Christ continually.

[15]And after these things, Paul and his brethren departed from Raphinus and sailed unto Atium in Gaul. [16]And Paul preached in the Roman garrisons and among the people, exhorting all men to repent and confess their sins. [17]And there came to him certain of the Belgae to inquire of him of the new doctrine and of the man Jesus, and Paul opened his heart unto them and told them all things that had befallen him, howbeit that Christ

---

z. This is where Saint Paul's Cathedral would later be built. Thus this episode functions exactly like Gen. 28:1-19, where Jacob has a dream at Luz and erects a memorial pillar there, marking the place as the future site of Jeroboam's temple at Bethel (1 Kings 12:26-30). In both cases, the story supplies a retrospective, artificial foundation narrative.

a. Paul is thus made to predict the seventh British census, 1861, which occurred just before the rise of the British-Israel movement.

b. British-Israel believers consider the modern British monarchy to be Davidic, its rulers descended from the daughter of Jewish King Zedekiah.

c. Here is the all-important, albeit imaginary, credential: Paul endorses the British-Israel doctrine.

came into the world to save sinners;[d] and they departed, pondering among themselves upon the things which they had heard.[e]

18And after much preaching and toil, Paul and his fellow labourers passed into Helvetia and came unto Mount Pontius Pilate where he who condemned the Lord Jesus dashed himself down headlong and so miserably perished.[f] 19And immediately a torrent gushed out of the mountain and washed his body broken in pieces into a lake.[g] 20And Paul stretched forth his hands upon the water and prayed unto the Lord, saying, "O Lord God, give a sign unto all nations that here Pontius Pilate, which condemned thine only-begotten Son, plunged down headlong into the pit."[h]
21And while Paul was yet speaking, behold, there came a great earthquake, and the face of the waters was changed and the form of the lake like unto the form of the Son of Man hanging in an agony upon the cross.[i]
22And a voice came out of heaven, saying, "Even Pilate hath escaped the wrath to come, for he washed his hands before the multitude at the blood-shedding of the Lord Jesus."[j] 23When therefore Paul and those that were with him saw the earthquake and heard the voice of the angel, they glorified God and were mightily strengthened in the spirit.

24And they journeyed and came to Mount Julius,[k] where stood two pillars, one on the right hand and one on the left hand, erected by Caesar Augustus. 25And Paul, filled with the Holy Ghost, stood up between the two pillars, saying, "Men and brethren, these stones which ye see this day shall testify of my journey hence; and verily I say,[l] they shall remain until the outpouring of the spirit upon all nations, neither shall the way be hindered throughout all generations."

---

d. 1 Tim. 1:15

e. Luke 2:19

f. Pilate's suicide in Vienna represents a late confusion with Archelaus's exile there.

g. This disgusting gore geyser recalls the fate of Judas in Acts 1:18 where he falls "headlong" and portions of his anatomy "gush out."

h. Here we think of the suicidal stampede of the (Roman) "legion" of demons into "the pit" by way of a lake in Luke 8:31-33.

i. This is what Hermann Gunkel called a "geological myth," offering a fanciful explanation of why Lake Lucerne is shaped somewhat like a crucifix.

j. The reference assumes the reader is familiar with Matt. 27:24 and implicitly with the New Testament canon. It is grossly anachronistic for Luke.

k. The Julian Alps are situated between Italy and Austria.

l. As Goodspeed points out, in the New Testament Jesus uses the phrase "truly/ verily I say," but never Paul.

[26]And they went forth and came to Illyricum, intending to go by Macedonia into Asia; and grace was found in all the churches, and they prospered and had peace. Amen.

24.

The Epistle to Titus

Jerome D. Quinn, Stephen G. Wilson, and others have argued that Titus and 1 and 2 Timothy appear to be the work of the Ecclesiastical Redactor—perhaps Polycarp, as Hans von Campenhausen and, more recently, Stephan Hermann Huller have suggested—who wrote canonical Luke and the Acts of the Apostles. As Charles L. Talbert has indicated, it was common in contemporary philosophical schools to provide a three-fold canon featuring an account of the founder's life, a narrative of his disciples that zeroed in on the approved successor, and then an appended set of letters. That is what we seem to have in the sequence Luke-Acts-Pastorals.

Virtually all critical scholars agree that the Pastoral Epistles belong together, separated from the Pauline Epistles by a variety of factors. The most important of these is that of vocabulary and theological conceptuality, an overwhelming amount of which is starkly different from that of the earlier epistles but in harmony with the later writings of the Apostolic Fathers. The same vocabulary and other idiosyncracies are shared to a remarkable degree among Luke, Acts, and the Pastorals. Of about equal weight is the stage of ecclesiastical institutionalism we meet in these letters, which is much more formal than either the charismatic sectarianism of the earliest church or the second-generation bourgeois retrenchment characteristic of the catholicizing portions of Romans and 1 Corinthians, as two examples. In the Pastorals we run across paid clergy, a stipendiary Order of Widows (nunnish virgins betrothed to Christ), ranks of bishops and deacons, and other aspects of the institutional church.

The epistle opens with a long prologue parallel to how Luke's

gospel and Acts commence, indicating that Titus was supposed to precede 2 Timothy. As we shall see, 1 Timothy belongs last as it is not even by the same author, being rather a pastiche intended to replace the other two Pastorals. Titus is easily recognizable as a letter in form only and is actually a church order with longer and more detailed examples of what we find throughout the next centuries in the *Didache,* the *Didascalia,* and the *Apostolic Constitutions,* stipulating rules of conduct for congregations newly drawn into the Catholic orbit from heretical Paulinism. This co-optation was facilitated by the circulation of an ecclesiastically redacted edition of the Pauline corpus, the old letters now riddled with Pastoral interpolations,[a] and with the addition of Titus and 2 Timothy as a lens through which to read the newly domesticated Marcionite scriptures. It is no accident Marcion's canon did not include the Pastorals. They had not been written yet! And it is Marcionism, along with its sister "heresies," at which the Pastor aims his guns. Hence, the jibe at vegetarianism (1:14-15) and the otherwise pointless urging to train young wives to love their husbands and be satisfied with domestic duties (2:4-5), opposed to embracing charismatic celibacy and ministerial privileges such as Marcionite and encratite women notoriously did. Of special interest is also the use of catechetical formulae, called here (3:4-7) and in the other Pastorals the "trustworthy sayings," another mark of a post-apostolic setting.

1

Paul, a slave of God and an apostle of Jesus-Christ, as the elect of
God believe him to be, and according to the full knowledge of religious
truth, 2in hopes of age-long life which God, who cannot lie, promised before the ages of time, 3but in his own time he made manifest his message
in a proclamation with which I was entrusted by the command of our
Savior, God, 4to Titus, a true child by virtue of a common faith. May the
favor and protection of God the Father and Christ-Jesus our Savior be
with you.
5You may be wondering why I left you in Crete.[b] It was so you might

a. See Winsome Munro, *Authority in Paul and Peter: The Identification of a Pastoral Stratum in the Pauline Corpus and I Peter,* Society for New Testament Studies Monograph Series 45 (Cambridge: Cambridge University Press, 1983).

b. Actually, we must wonder why, if the author had given Titus instructions

organize what was still undone and appoint elders in each city as per my instructions: [6]whoever is irreproachable, not remarried if a widower, has believing children, and not liable to accusations of promiscuity or wild conduct. [7]For a bishop is obliged to be irreproachable, as befits an administrator put in charge by God, not self-centered, not irritable, no drunken brawler, not looking to enrich himself, [8]but hospitable, a lover of the good, prudent, just, pious, celibate, [9]holding fast the reliable message according to the standard teaching in order that he may be able both to exhort on the basis of wholesome teaching and to convince the objectors.

[10]For there are many non-conformists, empty talkers and deceivers, especially those of the circumcision faction, [11]whose mouths must be shut, who throw whole households into confusion, teaching things they should never say, and all for crass profit. [12]A certain one of them, a prophet of their own, said it well: "Cretans are always liars, vicious beasts, idle gluttons."[c] [13]This witness is true, which is why you will need to rebuke them harshly if they are ever to be healthy in the faith, [14]ignoring Jewish myths and man-made commandments that twist the truth.[d] [15]On the contrary, to the pure in heart, all things are pure, but to those who are defiled and unbelieving, nothing can be pure since both their minds and their consciences have been permanently defiled. [16]Oh, they claim they know God, but by their actions they repudiate him, being abominations unto the Lord, disobedient to his commandments, and hypocrites when it comes to good deeds.

2

[1]But, as for you, speak the things conducive to wholesome teaching. [2]Older men ought to be sober, sombre, prudent, sound in faith, in love, in endurance. [3]Elderly women, similarly, ought to behave reverently—not

---

about what to do in Crete before he left him, he reviews such basic matters at all? Of course, the circumstances referred to are fictive, as are the narrator, "Paul," and the narratee, "Titus."

c. The reference is to the legendary Cretan hero Epimenides, to whom this poem was attributed: "They carve a tomb for thee, O high and holy one, / The Cretans, always liars, vicious beasts, idle gluttons; / For thou art not dead forever but alive and risen, / For from thee we live and move and have our being." His fellow Cretans claimed to have custody of the tomb of Zeus/Dionysus, mauled by a boar like Adonis. But Epimenides countered that the God had arisen and yet lived. Luke quotes more of the poem in Acts 17:28.

d. The author seems to oppose Marcionism but still shares a gentile antipathy toward Jewish beliefs and customs.

slanderers, nor addicted to a lot of wine, teachers of what is good, [4]that
is, instructing the younger women to love their husbands and their children, [5]prudent, pure, doing their housework, good, obedient to their husbands; otherwise the message of God may be libeled because of their bad
examples.[e] [6]In the same way, urge the younger fellows to be prudent
[7]about everything, providing in your own case a good example of behavior, demonstrating in your teaching the qualities of being incorruptible,
of gravity, [8]of healthy, admirable speech, in order that anyone opposed
to us may be embarrassed, at a loss to say anything bad about us. [9]Slaves
are to be obedient to their various masters in every matter,[f] to be courte-
ous and never to talk back, [10]not pilfering, but examples of complete reliability, all in order to make the teaching of our Savior, God, more attractive in every way.

[11]For the saving favor of God was shown to all humanity, [12] instructing us that, repudiating impiety and worldly passions, we might live prudently, righteously, and piously in this present age, [13]anticipating the
blissful prospect of the epiphany of the splendor of our great God and
Savior Christ-Jesus,[g] [14]who gave himself on our behalf that he might ransom us from all lawlessness and purify a people for himself to possess,[h]
one eager for good deeds. [15]Speak this sort of thing and exhort and rebuke with all due authority; leave no room through indecisiveness for
anyone to have contempt for you.

3

[1]Remind them to be law-abiding citizens, obedient to rulers and authorities, prepared for every good deed, [2]blaspheming no one,[i] avoiding

---

e. To us, these instructions seem so tame, it is hard to understand their inclusion. But as Dennis R. MacDonald, *The Legend and the Apostle: The Battle for Paul in Story and Canon* (Philadelphia: Fortress Press, 1982), has shown, the author means to invoke Paul's name against radical Paulinists who advocated apocalyptic, egalitarian, anti-family, celibate, vegetarian doctrines such as Gnosticism, Encratism, Montanism, and Marcionism.

f. Presumably this blank check would imply sexual favors demanded by one's master, for which the Christian would be absolved of guilt.

g. Such direct identification of Christ and God, reminiscent of Ignatius, shows the lateness of the epistle.

h. This is analogous to God choosing Israel.

i. Did the author really have to worry about Christian hooliganism or is this not rather a misunderstanding of Gnostics gloating over the defeated *archons* ("rulers") and *exousioi* ("authorities"), hence "blaspheming" them as in Jude 8-10? In precisely the same way, the death of Christ at the hands of the supramundane archons (1 Cor. 2:8; Col. 2:14-15) has been historicized, perhaps by later

brawls, being patient with others, demonstrating unobtrusiveness to everyone. [3]For once, we too were unthinking, disobedient, completely deceived by and enslaved to various lusts and pleasures, living in evil and envy, hateful and hating each other.[j] [4]But "when the kindness and philanthropy of our Savior God appeared, [5]he saved us, not by any righteousness of ours, but by token of his mercy through the regenerating bath and the renewal of the Holy Spirit[k] [6]which he richly lavished upon us through Jesus-Christ our Savior, [7]in order that, having been accepted by his favor, we might become heirs awaiting the prospect of age-long life." [8]The saying is trustworthy, and I want you to make confident affirmation of these things so those who have believed in God may not leave it at that but keep on doing good deeds. These words are good and beneficial. [9]But waste no time on carping objections and genealogical credentials,[l] discord and arguments over the Jewish law, for these do no one any good, being entirely moot. [10]Mark a quarrelsome man and avoid him after you have rebuked him once, then twice, [11]at which point you can be sure he is just being stubborn and doing what he himself knows is wrong.[m]

[12]Whenever I get around to sending Artemas or Tychicus to relieve you, hurry and come join me in Nicopolis, where I have decided to pass the winter. [13]Outfit Zenas the lawyer and Apollo[n] for the next stage of their journey so they may be fully provisioned, [14]and see to it that our people also learn to keep up their contributions for such needs so the work may bear fruit.

---

misunderstanding, into an execution at the hands of earthly, civil powers, Herod and Pilate.

j. Our author has entirely lost sight of the Pauline biography, betraying his gentile origins. On the other hand, the passage recalls the Ebionite claim that Paul was first a convert from paganism to Judaism.

k. John 3:5

l. In view here are the impressive sounding claims made by Jewish charlatans, fortune-tellers, and magicians of the Diaspora, as if priestly descent gave them supernatural power, as in Acts 19:14. To condemn them is ironic in view of our writer's own claim of authority stemming from Paul and his successor, Titus. See 2 Tim. 2:2 for such a genealogy.

m. Note the impatience with intellectual debate: if some doubter still does not accept the party line after a few attempts to convince him, the fault must be his, not that of a church authority, and we may write off his failure to see it our way to sheer contrariness.

n. It seems somehow strange that the author should endorse the mission of a Jew and a lawyer, given the sneering at "those of the circumcision" and "arguments over the Jewish law."

[15]All those with me greet you. Greet the ones who love us in a common faith.[o] May God's favor be with you all.

o. The greeting specifically excludes heretics and dissenters in Crete.

25.

The Second Epistle to Timothy

If Titus is a church order manual, 2 Timothy belongs to another common genre, the testament, of which there are many biblical and quasi-biblical examples.[a] These writings purport to provide what we would call the famous last words of a wise man as he looks into eternity and imparts some of its secrets to those he is about to leave behind. What is envisioned in 2 Timothy is Paul's view while awaiting trial and execution in Rome and his passing the torch to a successor, Timothy, representing the bishops as the apostles' successors according to the Catholic myth of pedigree (2:2). On analogy with other testament books which bless or censure this or that tribe, we must assume references to former Pauline colleagues, some quite severe and others damnatory with faint praise, are intended to rank various lines of episcopal succession or theological legacies descending through those names.

We can witness in this epistle the rivalry developing in the "nascent catholic" church between the fading clout of charismatic itinerant apostles, prophets, and the settled office holders of local congregations. The same tension is on display in the Epistle to Gaius (3 John) and the *Didache* where wandering apostles are portrayed as likely freeloaders and bums. Ironically, though a number of stories and sayings came into Luke's gospel (actually to its predecessor, Ur-Lukas) from the communities of charismatic widows, patrons to the itinerant

---

a. Gen. 49; Deut. 33; John 13-16; Acts 20:17-35; 2 Peter; Testament of Abraham; Testaments of the Twelve Patriarchs; Testament of Job; Testament of Solomon

apostles,[b] 2 Timothy caricatures both groups in 3:6. For the author, masquerading as Paul, it is the settled authority of bishops, not the loose-cannon prophets, who are the true successors of Paul. Of course, this is inevitable as the lone-wolf itinerants and hermits who renounced home, family, and employment would have had little useful to say to settled Christian communities. Note again the use of the catechetical formula (1:13) or "trustworthy saying" at 2:11-13.

1

Paul, an apostle of Christ-Jesus by the decision of God, to make known the promise of life available in Christ-Jesus, [2]to Timothy, beloved child. May you enjoy favor, mercy, and protection from God our Father and Christ-Jesus our Lord.

[3]I give thanks to God, whom I worship as my forefathers did,[c] with a clear conscience, as I remember you without fail in my prayers night and day, [4]longing to see you, reminded of your tears at our parting, so that I may be filled with joy. [5]I recall your sincere faith, which dwelt first in your grandmother Lois and in your mother Eunice, and now, I am convinced, in you as well.

[6]And this is why I remind you to fan into flame that gift of God that is in you through the imposition of my hands.[d] [7]For God did not give us a spirit of cowardice, but rather of power, of love, and of temperance. [8]So do not be ashamed of our testimony to the Lord or of me, his prisoner, but be ready to suffer adversity for the news, drawing upon the power of God, [9]the one who has saved us and called us to a holy vocation—not as our deeds deserved, but on the sole basis of his plan and the favor shown us in Christ-Jesus long ages ago [10]but made manifest now through the epiphany of our Savior Christ-Jesus, on the one hand canceling death, on the other bringing into view life and freedom from decay through the news, [11]for which I was appointed herald and apostle and teacher, [12]and for which cause, too, I am suffering all these things. Nonetheless, I am not ashamed, as if I had made some terrible mistake, for I know who it is I have believed and I am fully convinced he is able to safeguard the deposit

b. See Stevan L. Davies, *The Revolt of the Widows: The Social World of the Apocryphal Acts* (London: Feffer and Simons, 1980); Robert M. Price, *The Widow Traditions in Luke-Acts* (Atlanta: Scholars Press, 1997).

c. Acts 22:3; 23:1, 6; 26:22

d. Acts 6:6, 8; 8:17; 19:6

I have left with him against that day when full payment will be mine.
[13]Use a model of wholesome words which you heard from me that bespeaks faith and love shared in Christ-Jesus. [14]Guard the good deposit by
means of the Holy Spirit dwelling inside us.

[15]You know how all those in Asia broke with me,[e] including Phygelus and Hermogenes.[f] [16]May the Lord show mercy on the household of
Onesiphorus because he frequently refreshed me[g] and was not ashamed
to be associated with a prisoner, [17]but coming to Rome, he tirelessly
searched for me till he found me. [18]May the Lord grant that he find
mercy on that day! And the service he rendered me in Ephesus, you know
very well.

2

[1]You, therefore, my child, be empowered by the charisma that is to
be had in Christ-Jesus, [2]and whatever you heard from me through many
witnesses,[h] entrust these words to faithful persons who will be competent
to teach others, as well. [3]Shoulder your share of suffering as a good soldier of Christ-Jesus: [4]No soldier on active duty involves himself with concerns of civilian life because he wants to win the approval of his recruiter.
[5]And no wrestler wins the championship unless he follows the rules. [6]It is
only right that the hard-working farmer be the first to enjoy the fruits.
[7]Consider what I am saying, for the Lord will make everything clear to
you. [8]Always have in mind Jesus-Christ, raised from the dead, sprung
from David's line, as in the news I proclaim, [9]in the service of which I endure adversity to the point of being chained up like a criminal—not that
the message of God has been confined.

---

e. See Acts 20:29-30. Asia swarmed with Paulinist "heretics": Encratites, Gnostics, Marcionites, and others. A Catholic reaction was to write off Paul, along with the sectarians who claimed descent from him, in favor of the legend of John, son of Zebedee, as a substitute apostle to Ephesus. In Acts 19:1-7, Luke rejects this and follows the same strategy as his successors Irenaeus and Tertullian in co-opting Paul as a figurehead of Catholic orthodoxy, accepting him as the apostle to Asia/Ephesus, but disassociating him from the Paulinist heretics.

f. Hermogenes, "Son of Hermes," is a character in Acts of Paul and Thecla, chaps. 1-3, where he is paired not with Phygelus but with the worldly Demas from 2 Tim. 4:10.

g. The idea is the same as in Josh. 2:12-14ff: because of her aid and comfort rendered to Joshua's spies, Rahab and her household are spared the general destruction of Jericho. In the same way, "Paul" expects imminent judgment on his fair-weather friends in the province of Asia but prays for an exception for Onesiphorus's household because of past kindness shown.

h. Cf. Luke 1:2. For a moment the mask slips and our author acknowledges he is summing up traditional teachings of Paul that have come down in his circle.

[10]This is why I endure everything, on account of the chosen ones, in order that they, too, may attain to salvation in union with Christ-Jesus, with age-enduring splendor. [11]The saying is trustworthy: "If we died with him, we shall live with him, too. [12]If we persevere, we shall reign with him, too. If we deny him, he will deny us, too.[i] [13]Our faith may fail, but his faithfulness endures,[j] for he cannot contradict himself." [14]You remind them of these things, soberly testifying before God, urging them to avoid verbal battles which do no one any good but undermine the faith of those who listen. [15]Be anxious to present yourself for approval before God as a workman proud of his labor, plowing a straight furrow with the message of truth.[k] [16]But steer clear of profane and empty jabbering, for these lead to ever greater impiety. [17]And such words will eat away like a cancer. Hymenaeus and Philetus are a case in point. [18]They shot wide of the truth by teaching that the resurrection has already come, overturning some people's faith. [19]However, the firm foundation of God stands and will not be overturned. It bears this seal: "The Lord knows which ones are his"[l] and "Let every one who invokes the name of the Lord repudiate unrighteousness."

[20]Now in a large house you will find not only vessels of gold and silver but wooden and ceramic ones, too. There is the best dinnerware as well as the chamber pot. [21]If anyone purifies himself out of the latter category, he will become one of the former, having been sanctified, suitable for the master's table, prepared for every noble use. [22]Even so, run away from the lusts of youth, but run after righteousness, faith, love, and peace, along with all who invoke the Lord from a pure heart. [23]But refuse to waste time with moronic and uninformed questions, knowing that they lead only to arguments, [24]and it is unbecoming for the Lord's slave to be argumentative, but he ought rather to be gentle toward everyone, able to teach, tolerant, [25]instructing without defensiveness those who oppose you on the chance God may grant them a change of mind, to know the full truth, [26]that they may snap out of it and extricate themselves from the accuser's net, having been snared by him according to his scheme.

3

[1]And you know this: how in the last days, dangerous crises will be at

i. This sentiment will wind up ascribed to Jesus in first person in Mark 8:38; Luke 12:8-9.

j. See Rom. 3:4: "Let God be true, though every man prove a liar."

k. Luke 9:62

l. Num. 16:5

hand; [2]for people will be self-absorbed, lovers of money, braggarts, conceited, blasphemers, disobedient to parents, ingrates, unholy, [3]sociopaths, pitiless, slanderers, promiscuous, wild, haters of the good, [4]traducers, impetuous, ego-inflated, lovers of pleasure rather than lovers of God, [5]having the veneer of godliness but denying its power. Avoid people like this![m] [6]For it is people of this ilk who sneak into houses and captivate frivolous women who are burdened with sins and led by various lusts, [7]always disciples, yet never arriving at any definite conclusions about the truth.[n] [8]Now in just the same way that Jannes and Jambres opposed Moses,[o] so too, these oppose the truth, people with corrupt minds, disquali-

---

m. The envisioned time frame is confused on a literal reading in that "Paul" starts out predicting the perversions of the future and ends up assuming Timothy lives amid just such outrages. Of course, the writer means to say the crimes of his own day are those which lay in the future as distinct from those which existed at the time of the historical Paul.

n. This is the typical smear aimed at intellectual women by Hellenistic chauvinists such as Juvenal in his *Sixth Satire.* Women were typically represented as dilettantes—easy prey for mystagogues who would seduce them into dependency with the promise of spiritual enlightenment. Not surprisingly, the same charges were leveled by Catholic bishops against consecrated Christian women and itinerant apostles in the early second century, not to mention the Gnostics and women among their disciples. Irenaeus, *Against Heresies,* 1.13.3, describes the wiles of Marcus the Magician:

> He devotes himself especially to women, ... addressing them in such seductive words as these: "I am eager to make thee a partaker of my Charis.... Adorn thyself as a bride who is expecting her bridegroom.... Behold Charis has descended upon thee; open thy mouth and prophesy." On the woman replying, "I have never at any time prophesied, nor do I know how to prophesy;"... he says to her, "Open thy mouth, speak whatsoever occurs to thee, and thou shalt prophesy." She then ... impudently utters some nonsense as it happens to occur to her.... Henceforth she reckons herself a prophetess, and expresses her thanks to Marcus ... not only by the gift of her possessions ... but also by yielding up to him her person, desiring in every way to be united to him. (*Ante-Nicene Fathers*)

The church fathers supposed women unable to grasp more than simple, pat answers spoon-fed them by ecclesiastical shepherds.

o. Jannes and Jambres, widely mentioned in old Jewish traditions, are supposedly two of the Egyptian sorcerer priests in Pharaoh's court. The meaning of the names, and thus the reason for their choice, is not clear, though various plausible conjectures have been made. Jannes, like "Jannaeus," appears to be a version of Jonathan, or "Yohannon." But we must suspect it derives from "Ioannes," equivalent to fishy Dagon, the father of the Old Testament deity-cum-hero Joshua. Ioannes emerged from the sea and taught wisdom to men. Jambres sometimes occurs in the texts as "Mambres," apparently another form of the Old Testament *mamre,* which means "apostate." Robert Eisler held out the possibility

fied for the faith. [9]But they will advance no farther, for their nonsense will be too obvious to everyone, just as the old magicians' hokum was publicly refuted. [10]But you have closely followed[p] my teaching, behavior, determination, faith, long-suffering, love, endurance, [11]and the persecutions and sufferings that befell me at Antioch, at Iconium, and at Lystra, what persecutions I endured, and out of all of them the Lord delivered me.[q] [12]And indeed, all those who want to live piously in the faith of Christ-Jesus will be persecuted. [13]But evil-doers and charlatan magicians[r] will only get worse in the last days, deceiving others and finally believing their own lies. [14]But you make sure you continue in the teachings you learned and have been assured of, remembering those from whom you learned them,[s] [15]and that from infancy you have known the holy scriptures, which are able to educate you about salvation through belief in Christ-Jesus. [16]Every passage of scripture is the very exhalation of God, advantageous for teaching, for reproving, for correcting, for schooling in righteousness, [17]in order that the servant of God may be equipped for every good deed that may be required of him.[t]

4

[1]I bear sober witness before God and Christ-Jesus, who is ready to judge the living and the dead, by his epiphany and his kingship: [2]you are

---

that John the Baptist, who emerged on the shore to preach, was a historicized version of Ioannes. Similarly, Levy, in his *Chaldean Dictionary,* suggested that by singling out two magicians and opposing them to Moses, the ancient rabbis intended John the Baptist and Jesus!

p. Same word as Luke 1:3, where the writer has "followed all things closely" and thus reconstructs the history of his subject.

q. Acts 13:13-14:23, a cross reference to the same author's work.

r. He is thinking of people like Apollonius of Tyana, Proteus Peregrinus, and especially Marcus the Magician. Significantly, both Proteus and Marcus have been conjecturally identified as caricatures of Marcion—the former by Hermann Detering, the latter by Stephen Hermann Huller—while Margaret Morris argues in her *Jesus Augustus* that Apollonius of Tyana was originally none other than Paul himself.

s. He was taught by his mother and grandmother. Insofar as the historical Timothy is in view, we may imagine his mother and grandmother were converted to Christ on the same occasion. But the mention of two previous generations hints at the intended reader: third-generation Christians raised in the faith, not original converts.

t. The author repudiates the Marcionite/Gnostic view of the Old Testament as a non-Christian book. The specification of "every scripture" implies awareness of Valentinian theories that various texts had been inspired by the Demiurge, Moses himself, and his elders, and thus had different levels of authority.

to preach the message, attending to it when convenient as well as when inconvenient. Reprove, upbraid, encourage, all the while showing great patience and teaching the better way. [3]For there will come a time when one's hearers will not put up with the wholesome teaching but, moved by their own lusts, will collect innumerable teachers of various doctrines who will entice their ears. [4]On the one hand, their ear will recoil from the truth, and on the other, they will gravitate to myths. [5]But you remain clear-headed amid all this confusion, endure adversity, do the work of the evangelist, fulfill your obligation to the ministry. [6]For I am already spent and the time of my departure has overtaken me. [7]In retrospect, I have fought a good battle, I have reached the finish line, I have held onto the faith. [8]What now remains for me is the crown of salvation which the Lord, the righteous judge, will bestow on me on that day and not only on me but also on all those who cherished the prospect of his epiphany.

[9]Make every effort to come and join me as soon as you can. [10]For Demas abandoned me, preferring this present age, and went to Thessalonica,[u] Crescens to Galatia, Titus to Dalmatia.[v] [11]Luke is the only one left with me. Find Mark and bring him with you. [12]I sent Tychicus to Ephesus. [13]When you come, be sure to bring the cloak I loaned to Carpus in Troas and the scrolls, too, especially the parchments.[w]

[14]Alexander, the coppersmith, sent much trouble my way. The Lord will see he gets his due reward. [15]But watch out for him, for he powerfully opposed our message.[x] [16]At my first defense, no one stood beside me, but

u. The legend of Paul overlaps that of Apollonius of Tyana at various points. This is one of them. Apollonius was in prison awaiting trial before Domitian and sent his disciple Damis back east; here Demas retreats eastward. Paul's faithless companion appears paired with Hermogenes from 2 Tim. 1:15 in the Acts of Paul and Thecla.

v. The picture is the same as that of Jesus' arrest at Gethsemane: the disciples flee and are scattered. One wonders if we are to catch here a parallel to the division of Alexander's empire after his death. Are Paul's lieutenants scrambling to divide up his sphere of influence, promoting themselves as his successors in various areas of his activity? It is surprising to see Paul's colleagues, who are mentioned favorably in the other epistles, bad-mouthed here. It must reflect a later schism or schisms within the Paulinist movement.

w. Though the association is not explicitly intended, we must suspect the "cloak" is an allusion to the letter's pseudonymous authorship, while the "scrolls" hint at further "unknown," spurious epistles of Paul which may come to light as needed. Could "Carpus" be none other than Polycarp?

x. Our author, also the author of Luke-Acts, has confused two of his characters: Demetrius the silversmith (Acts 19:23ff) and Alexander, the Jewish apolo-

everyone abandoned me. May it not be counted against them.[y] [17]But the Lord stood with me and empowered me in order that through me the destined proclamation might be fulfilled and all the nations might hear the news,[z] and I was delivered out of the very mouth of the lion. [18]The Lord will deliver me from every evil deed plotted against me and will see me safely to his heavenly realm. To him be all worship throughout ages multiplied by ages! Amen.

[19]Greet Prisca and Aquila[a] and the household of Onesiphorus.[b] [20]Erastus stayed behind in Corinth, but I left Trophimus sick in Miletus. [21]Make every effort to come to me before winter makes travel so difficult.[c] Greetings from Eubulus and Pudens and Linus and Claudia and all the brothers.

[22]May the Lord fortify your spirit. May his favor accompany you.

---

gist (Acts 19:33-34) who sought to turn away the Ephesian hostility toward Jews for their antipathy toward idols, which Demetrius manufactured.

y. Luke 23:34; Acts 7:60

z. This would fulfill the prophecy of the risen Christ in Luke 24:47; Acts 1:8.

a. Acts 18:1-3, 18, 26

b. As to Onesiphorus and company, see 1:16-18; The Acts of Paul and Thecla 1:4-11; 6:1-7:1; 10:6.

c. Cf. Acts 27:12.

26.

The First Epistle to Timothy

FRIEDRICH SCHLEIERMACHER demonstrated that 2 Timothy was written before 1 Timothy, and that 1 Timothy is based on 2 Timothy and Titus in roughly the same manner as 2 Peter depends on 1 Peter and Jude. Schleiermacher employed much the same argument as is employed today to show the three Pastorals collectively stem from a post-Pauline period. For instance, 1 Timothy repeats but misuses words and phrases found verbatim in the other two Pastorals. Where 1 Timothy picks out of Titus (1:14; 3:9) references to controversial "myths" and "genealogies" (1 Tim. 1:4), the author fails to grasp that for Titus the terms denoted false doctrines spread by errant teachers of "the circumcision party," who appealed to priestly genealogies to authenticate their credentials. 1 Timothy no longer understands the connection and makes it sound like the myths and genealogies are some sort of esoteric riddles forming the stock-in-trade of false teachers.

Some additions and alterations seem to reflect ecclesiastical developments subsequent to 2 Timothy and Titus. First, it is obvious the hierarchy has become more elaborate. A passage in Titus 1:5-9 deals only with bishops, but by the time of 1 Timothy we are reckoning with a separate order of deacons and an order of enrolled widows (5:4-16). Second, the author of 2 Timothy refers to his ordination at the hands of Paul himself (1:6), while in 1 Timothy it is credited to the presbyters (4:14). Why the change? The later author wants to distribute the authority of Paul among certain successors (cf. Matt. 18:18; 16:17-19).

A third hint as to the later composition of 1 Timothy is that personal references (2 Tim. 4:9ff) are dropped for the same reason Matthew omitted most of Mark's unflattering references to the disciples of Jesus. In 2 Timothy, we see the companions of Paul in a light not unlike that of the disciples fleeing their master in Gethsemane. All of Paul's followers abandoned him at an earlier trial (4:16), and only Luke remains with him on the eve of the present one. Apparently everyone else had something more important to do, including Crescens, Demas, Erastus, and Titus (4:10, 20). The derivative epistle tries to efface this slur against Paul's circle of disciples. In fact, since Titus is among the unfaithful disciples, this may be why the later author chose Timothy, who was supposed to be soon on his way to Paul's side, rather than Titus, as his fictive narrate.

Fourth, in 2 Timothy (3:8) we find reference to Jannes and Jambres, Egyptian rivals of Moses. Why are these names absent from 1 Timothy? It is because of a tendency to clean up non-canonical references from earlier sources. Likewise, 2 Peter borrows much verbatim from Jude but takes the trouble to omit Jude's references to 1 Enoch and the *Assumption of Moses*. Anxiety over canon is a sign of a late date of composition.

Of all the epistles, only 1 Timothy mentions Pilate as the interrogator of Jesus: "Christ Jesus who in his testimony before Pontius Pilate made the good confession" (6:13). Of all the Passion narratives, only in John's do we find the clear language of testimony and bearing witness: "You say I am a king. For this I was born, and for this I have come into the world, *to bear witness to the truth*" (John 18:37). It is evident the author of 1 Timothy knows the Gospel of John, which marks 1 Timothy as very late indeed. Such anachronisms constitute a fifth level of evidence for the distinct authorship of the epistle.

Similarly, it is significant that 1 Timothy mentions by name Marcion's tract *Antitheses,* which invidiously contrasted Jewish and Pauline scriptures. True, the author confuses Marcionism with Gnosticism ("the *Antitheses* of the falsely dubbed gnosis"), but this is not uncommon even today. The Jewish scriptures are upheld in 1 Timothy as inspired and beneficial for Christian ministry (3:16-17), something obvious to anyone but a Marcionite. That affirmation here

again betrays Marcionism as the writer's target and confirms the late date of composition.

1

Paul, an apostle of Christ-Jesus by the command of God our Savior
and of Christ-Jesus, our hope. 2 To Timothy, a true child by virtue of a
common faith.[a] May you enjoy favor, mercy, and protection from God
the Father and Christ-Jesus our Lord.

3 As you recall, I urged you to stay behind in Ephesus as I left for
Macedonia so you might command certain individuals to stop teaching
heterodoxy,[b] 4 nor to give attention to myths and to endless genealogies[c]
which only lead to speculations rather than facilitating the faithful administration of God's favor. 5 The goal of such commands is love from a
pure heart, a good conscience, and nonhypocritical faith, 6 goals which
some, misjudging their aim, have failed to reach, veering off course toward empty talk, 7 desiring to be teachers of the law but neither realizing
what they are saying nor understanding the matters they pontificate
about. 8 Of course, we know that law is good as long as one uses it lawfully, 9 remembering that laws are not laid down to govern righteous people but the lawless and hellions, the impious and sinners, the unholy and
the profane, murderers of fathers, of mothers, of husbands, 10 prostitutes,
men who lie with men,[d] child prostitute recruiters, liars and perjurers,
and those who practice anything else opposed to wholesome teaching,[e]
11 stemming from the news of the splendor of the God who ever abides in
bliss, with which I was entrusted.

12 I give thanks to the one who empowers me, Christ-Jesus our Lord,
because he decided I was trustworthy and placed me in his service,
13 despite my previously having been a blasphemer, a persecutor, and

---

a. Titus 1:4

b. Titus 1:5

c. As Schleiermacher noted, the author has misunderstood the point of Titus 3:9 referring to genealogies as credentials. Who knows what the author of 1 Timothy intends?

d. For this translation of αρσενοκοιται , see Robin Scroggs, *New Testament and Homosexuality* (Philadelphia: Fortress Press, 1983). It is equally possible this rare word denotes "male prostitutes," for which see John Boswell, *Christianity, Homosexuality, and Social Tolerance* (Chicago: University of Chicago Press, 1980), 107.

e. Our writer lifts the business about "teaching the law" from Titus 1:14-15 but he no longer understands the reference to regulations of the Torah.

filled with overweening pride. But I managed to get mercy because, being ignorant, I acted in unbelief.[f] [14]And our Lord's favor overflowed in the form of faith in Christ-Jesus and love for him. [15]The saying is trustworthy and deserves universal acceptance: "Christ-Jesus entered the world to save sinners," of whom I am number one; [16]but it was just because of this that I obtained mercy in order that in my case, as the worst, Jesus-Christ might demonstrate the full extent of his long-suffering, to serve as an example for those coming to believe in him for age-long life. [17]Now to the King of the eons,[g] unchanging, invisible, solely God, be honor and worship unto ages multiplied by ages! Amen.

[18]I command you this, child Timothy, according to the prophecies once uttered about you, that encouraged by them you may wage a good war,[h] [19]armed with faith and a good conscience, which some have thrown aside and made of their faith a shipwreck. [20]I am thinking of Hymenaeus and Alexander, whom I had to consign to the adversary so they may learn the hard way not to blaspheme.

2

[1]Therefore, I urge, first of all, that petitions be made, prayers, intercessions, thanksgivings, [2]on behalf of all people, on behalf of kings and all those in positions of prominence, in order that we may lead a tranquil and quiet life in all piety and gravity. [3]This is a fine and approved thing in the sight of our Savior, God, [4]who only wants all humanity to be saved and to arrive at a full realization of the truth. [5]For there is one God[i] and also one mediator between God and humankind, a man, Christ-Jesus, [6]the one who has given himself as a ransom on behalf of all, the martyrdom at just the proper moment. [7]Of all this I was appointed herald and apostle—I speak the truth and do not lie![j]—a teacher of the nations about faith and truth.[k] [8]Therefore, I want the husbands in every place to pray, lifting up

f. Luke 24:47; Acts 3:17; 13:27. Note how the author wants to make Paul the greatest sinner of all and yet mitigates his sin on account of naïve ignorance!

g. One suspects the author has appropriated the Gnostic designation of God as chief among his own emanated hypostases, or aions, and mistakenly interpreted the term to mean temporal "ages."

h. 2 Tim. 4:7

i. A shot, not at pagan polytheism, but at Marcionism with its two deities, Hebrew and Christian.

j. As Schleiermacher observed, this protest seems out of place here, most likely copied without understanding from Gal. 1:20 where, unlike here, Paul's apostolate is at issue.

k. 2 Tim. 1:11

pious hands without anger or second thoughts. [9]In the same way, I want
wives to pray dressed with modesty and sobriety, not with gold or pearls
plaited into their hair or wearing expensive clothing, [10]but with such
adornment as befits women claiming to be reverent, that is, good deeds.
[11]Let a wife learn in silence and complete submission. [12]But I do not permit woman to claim to have created man,[l] but to keep silent. [13]For Adam
was not the one deceived,[m] [14]but it is the woman who, having been deceived, has fallen into transgression. [15]But "she will yet be saved through
child-bearing[n] as long as they remain steadfast in faith and love and sanctification with proper sobriety." [3:1a]This saying is trustworthy.

3

[1b]If anyone aspires to the office of bishop, it is a worthy task he seeks.
[2]Thus it is incumbent on a bishop to be irreproachable, not remarried if a
widower, temperate, prudent, well-organized, hospitable, a good teacher, [3]not a wine-lover, not violent, but patient, given neither to arguments
nor to greed, [4]governing his own household well, having his children in
subjection with proper seriousness.[o] [5]If someone does not know how to
govern his own household, how will he take care of a congregation of
God?[p] [6]Let him not be a neophyte or he may become swell-headed and
repeat the accuser's error.[q] [7]And it is needful that he have a good reputation among those outside, [7]or he may become embroiled in some scandal
and be snared by the accuser.

---

l. The author silences women, according to Catherine Clark Kroeger, "1 Timothy 2:12 - A Classicist's View," in Alvera Mickelsen, ed., *Women, Authority, and the Bible* (Downers Grove, IL: InterVarsity Press, 1986), 225-44, because Ephesian women are said to be teaching the Gnostic version of creation preserved in the Nag Hammadi text, *On the Origin of the World* (115:31-116:8). Accordingly, Adam was an inert body until the spiritual entity Eve appeared and gave him a conscious soul, saying: "Adam, live! Rise up upon the earth!" Awaking, he exclaimed, "You will be called 'the mother of the living' because you are the one who gave me life."

m. The Gnostics taught that Adam was the one deceived, since he believed the Demiurge's lie that the Demiurge had created him.

n. The curse of Yahve Elohim on the woman in Eden (Gen. 3:16) was that, having wrested the secret of procreation, she was henceforth to pay the price of agonizing labor pains. Our author supposes Christ has mitigated this curse for Christian women.

o. Titus 1:5-9

p. Luke 16:10

q. This is a reference to the myth, never actually outlined in the Bible, of Lucifer's pride and rebellion against God that resulted in his fall from heavenly dignity. The myth was based on an out-of-context reading of both Isa. 14 and Ezek. 28.

8 In the same way, it behooves deacons to be dour, not fork-tongued, not addicted to too much wine, not preoccupied with crass profit, 9 holding to the mystery of the faith without reservations. 10 And make sure these are given an initial probationary period; then if they turn out to be irreproachable, let them serve. 11 Their wives, too, need to be dour, not slanderers, sober, and altogether reliable. 12 Let deacons not remarry if widowers, aptly governing their children and their own households. 13 For those who have served well acquire a good position for themselves, as well as great authority in the religion of Christ-Jesus. 14 I write you these things because, though I hope to come to you shortly, 15 in case I am delayed, I want you to know what behavior is appropriate in the household of God. It is the congregation of the true God, pillar and bulwark of the truth. 16 And admittedly, the mystery of piety is great:

Whose epiphany was in flesh,
Vindicated by the Spirit,
Seen by angels,
Proclaimed among nations,
Believed in the world,
Assumed in glory.

4

1 Now the Spirit says verbatim, "In the last times, some will apostatize from the faith, heeding misleading prophecies and demonic teachings 2 from lying hypocrites whose crimes are branded on their consciences to the point of moral insensitivity."[r] 3 For example, they forbid marriage, command abstinence from foods that God created for believers and those who know the truth to share in with thankful hearts.[s] 4 For every creation of God is good and nothing is to be placed off limits if it is welcomed with thanksgiving, 5 for it has been rendered holy by means of the command of God[t] and prayer. 6 By assuring the brothers of these things, you will be a good servant of Christ-Jesus, nourished by the trustworthy sayings[u] and the fine teaching which you have followed. 7 But pay no mind to pagan myths or old wives' tales. Train yourself in piety. 8 For though bodily

r. 2 Tim. 3:1-5

s. The author takes aim at Encratite, Gnostic, and Marcionite asceticism, rampant in Asia Minor.

t. Acts 10:13-15

u. That is, the "trustworthy sayings" in 1 Tim. 1:15; 2:15; 4:10; 2 Tim. 2:11-13; and Titus 3:8.

training is worthwhile, its value in the scheme of things is small. But piety is advantageous in every area of life, being full of promise for the present life as well as the coming one. [9]The saying is trustworthy and deserves everyone's acceptance: [10]for this we labor and strive because "we have set our hope on a living God who is the savior of all humanity, mostly of believers." [11]Command and teach these things. [12]Give no one room to disregard you for your youth, but become a model for believers in speech, in conduct, in love, in faith, in purity.[v] [13]Until I arrive, see to the public reading of scripture, to exhortation, to teaching. [14]Do not take for granted the charisma within you, which was imparted to you by means of prophecy with the imposition of hands by the council of elders.[w] [15]Give attention to these matters; immerse yourself in them and your progress will be plain to all. [16]Pay close attention to your own sanctification and the teaching: persevere in them. By so doing, you will save yourself and your hearers.

5

[1]Do not presume to reprimand one of the elders, but exhort him as you would a father, younger men as brothers, [2]older women as mothers, younger women as sisters, in strict purity. [3]Support the genuine widows. [4]But if any widow has children or grandchildren, let them learn to show piety first of all toward their own household and to return the favor of their parents' care: this is what God approves.[x] [5]By a "genuine widow," I mean one who has been left alone, who has cast her hope on God and perseveres in the assigned petitions and prayers night and day. [6]But the "widow" who is promiscuous is one of the living dead. [7]And you must speak out on this so they may be free from scandal. [8]But if anyone does not provide for his own relatives, and especially his immediate family, he has in effect denied the faith and is worse than an outright unbeliever. [9]Let a woman be enrolled among the widows only if she is no younger than sixty years of age, having never remarried, [10]with a reputation for good deeds such as bringing up children, giving hospitality to strangers, washing the feet of the itinerant holy men, relieving the afflicted, actively following up every opportunity to do good. [11]But refuse to enroll younger women as widows, for sooner or later they will grow restive, unfaithful to Christ, and they will want to get married, [12]incurring judgment because they violated their original pledge.[y] [13]And in the meantime they

v. Titus 2:7, 15

w. 2 Tim. 1:6

x. Exod. 20:12; Mark 7:10-13

y. The precursors of nuns, they had been betrothed to Christ, pledged them-

learn the ways of idleness, making the rounds of the houses, and become not only idle but also gossips, attending to others' business, speaking of things that are not their responsibility.[z] [14]I would rather have these younger women marry,[a] bear children, take charge of a household so they will avoid giving any excuse for our critics to reproach us. [15]It is too late for some, who have already turned off the path to follow the adversary.

[16]If any consecrated woman has celibate women living with her,[b] let her provide for them rather than letting the congregation bear the financial burden, in order that it may provide for the literal widows.

[17]Let the elders who govern well be considered worthy of double compensation, especially those engaged in speech and teaching. [18]For the scripture says: "You shall not muzzle the ox while he is treading out the grain"[c] and "The workman is worthy of his wage."[d] [19]Do not credit any accusation against an elder unless two or three witnesses confirm it. [20]Those who are found to be guilty, you must publicly rebuke so as to instill fear in the others. [21]I solemnly command you in the sight of God and Christ-Jesus and the chosen angels[e] that you follow this procedure without partiality, doing nothing out of favoritism. [22]Do not ordain anyone prematurely or you will be liable for his mistakes.

Keep yourself pure. [23]No longer drink only water, but have a little wine for the sake of your nervous stomach. [24]The sins of some people are evident early on, leading them to judgment, but some indeed come to light only later. [25]In the same way, good deeds are evident right up front, but those that are not cannot remain hidden forever.[f]

6

[1]Let all those who bear the yoke of slavery consider their masters

selves to celibacy. 1 Cor. 7:28 advises just the opposite strategy: to avoid sexual sin, let younger women leave the celibate order to marry after all.

z. The writer associates the younger consecrated women ("virgins," "widows") with heresies (2:12-14). He caricatures their house-to-house ministry as coffee-klatch gossip sessions, a misuse of the leisure made possible by their church stipend. They presume to teach, but this should be left to others, in his view.

a. Our writer thinks widows and widowers should not remarry in the literal sense. Here he refers to younger women like Thecla, initially attracted to the celibate life, who he thinks cannot persevere in their commitment.

b. Acts of Paul and Thecla 10:15

c. Deut. 19:15

d. Luke 10:7

e. Presumably the archangels Gabriel, Jeremiel, Michael, Raphael, Raziel, Sarakiel, and Uriel.

f. Mark 4:21-22

worthy of all honor; otherwise the name of God and the teaching may be
blasphemed. [2]And those who have believers for masters, let them not despise them because they are brothers, but rather let them slave for them
precisely because the ones receiving their good service are believers and
thus should be beloved.[g]

Teach and exhort all this. [3]If anyone teaches heterodoxy and does
not agree to the wholesome sayings of our Lord, Jesus-Christ, and to the
edifying teaching, [4]he is a windbag who understands nothing but is obsessed with questions and verbal battles which yield only envy, discord,
blasphemies, suspicions, evil, [5]in short, the pointless disputes of people
with corrupt minds, bereft of the truth,[h] viewing piety as one more
money-making gimmick.[i] [6]In fact, piety with self-sufficiency is a great
profit, [7]for we have brought nothing into the world and we will be carrying nothing out of it.[j] [8]As long as we have food and clothing, we will be
satisfied. [9]But those who make it their goal to be rich fall into temptation
and snares and many foolish and harmful lusts which cause people to
sink into the quicksand of ruin and destruction. [10]For the love of money
is a root of all manner of evils, and some who have yearned for it have
drifted away from the faith and been feathered with the shafts of many
sorrows. [11]But you, O man of God, flee from these things; pursue righteousness, piety, faith, love, perseverance, a slow temper. [12]Fight the noble fight of the faith, grab hold of the prize of age-long life to which you
were summoned and concerning which you affirmed the noble confession before many witnesses. [13]I command you in the sight of God, the one
who gives life to all creatures, and Christ-Jesus, the one who witnessed to
the noble confession in the presence of Pontius Pilatus,[k] [14]to keep this
command without reproach until the epiphany of our Lord, Jesus-Christ,
[15]which the blessed and sole potentate, the king of kings and lord of
lords, will signal at its own appointed time, [16]the only possessor of immortality, dwelling at the center of unapproachable light, whom no mortal has beheld or ever may behold, to whom be honor and sovereignty
throughout the ages! Amen.

[17]Command those who have worldly wealth not to be snobbish, nor
to set their hopes for the future on uncertain riches but on that God who

g. Mark 10:43-45

h. Titus 3:9-11; 2 Tim. 2:14

i. Titus 1:11

j. Job 1:21; Mark 8:36

k. John 18:37

lavishly offers us all creation to enjoy. 18Command them to practice benevolence, to be rich in good deeds, to be ready to donate, willing to
share, 19amassing for themselves a good foundation for the future in order that they may grab hold of age-long life.[l]

20O Timothy, guard the precious deposit,[m] recoiling from profane
and empty jabbering and the *Antitheses* of the falsely labeled "gnosis,"[n]
21for some who profess it have shot wide of the faith.[o] May God's favor
be with you.

---

l. Matt. 6:19-21; Luke 12:33

m. 2 Tim. 1:12, 14

n. The reference is to Marcion's work, the *Antitheses,* which contrasts Jewish scripture with the gospel of Jesus.

o. 2 Tim. 2:17-18

V.
The Testament of John

27.

The Gospel according to John

Dates, sources, and editions

THE GOSPEL OF JOHN APPEARS TO be the latest of the traditional four gospels, most likely from the late second century because of its dependence upon Luke and Mark. Some seek to clamp a lid of CE 100 on the gospel because of the conventional paleographic dating of the earliest known fragment of some version of the gospel, Papyrus 46, at about CE 125-175. But as Alvin Padilla has shown, such a dating is arbitrary because too few specimens of relevant penmanship from the period survive to compare it with. Internal evidence, as always, must tell the tale. And the tale it tells is a confusing one.

First, there is the problem of the climate of thought that pervades John's writing. As C. H. Dodd (*The Interpretation of the Fourth Gospel*) has shown, the book has affinities with the Hermetic literature, a kind of pagan Gnosticism. Rudolf Bultmann (*The Gospel of John: A Commentary*) has demonstrated how strikingly and consistently the gospel parallels the revelation discourses of Gnostic literature, notably Mandaean scriptures, but others as well. As Raymond E. Brown liked to emphasize, John has similarities to the Judaism of the Dead Sea Scrolls; but this is not an alternative to Bultmann as Brown thought since Bultmann was surely right in seeing in the Scrolls a kind of Gnosticizing Judaism. As we will see, there is a heavy dose of Marcionite doctrine in the gospel. Does all this require us to picture a single author who was influenced by all these currents of thought? While that would not be implausible, there are also internal contradictions in the text indicating that it is a composite text, bearing the

marks of editing and adaptation by the various sects which cherished and used it, as well as by whichever group may have originated it.

Second, we must reckon with the question of sources used by the writer or compiler. Bultmann's answer still seems the best to me: the evangelist combined a Synoptic-type narrative containing a numbered list of Jesus' miracles that scholars have come to dub the Signs Source or Signs Gospel. He also used a Gnostic-Mandaean revelation source for speeches by the heavenly revealer, originally perhaps ascribed to John the Baptist but here put into the mouth of Jesus. Finally, he used a Passion narrative. However, it seems the Passion account may be that of Mark or Luke or both. At various points, John seems to be correcting previous evangelists, not just drawing on a common tradition and handling scenes in different ways, which is what Dodd argued in *Historical Tradition in the Fourth Gospel.*

Third, there is the problem of narrative discontinuity in the book, which has led many to suggest that early on the text suffered reshuffling and clumsy restoration. There have been several attempts to smooth out the discontinuity and restore the original order of incidents and sayings. I have adopted the approach of Thomas Cottam (*The Fourth Gospel Rearranged*), which is to some degree an alternative to Brown and others who posited stages of enlargement as a way to account for narrative inconsistency. But then one has to ask why so little care was taken to smooth out the result, placing Jesus in a location he has just left or putting him somewhere with no notice of having gone there. Again, it makes most sense to me to adopt Bultmann's twin solutions: the pages were accidentally juggled and there was one major redactional stage of enlargement on the part of the anonymous Ecclesiastical Redactor. Stephan Hermann Huller nominates Polycarp, bishop of Smyrna, as the most plausible candidate—a redactor we know had little compunction against adding sizable chunks of prose to an original he found heretical and Gnostic sounding. The suspected additions are rendered here in italics. Even the book as we now have it still reeks rather strongly of Gnosticism, and there were those early on who sought to prevent its canonization on the assumption it was the work of Cerinthus. In any case, the Ecclesiastical Redactor found a gospel lacking any mention of a future final judgment

or second coming, a gospel with no sacramentalism of table or baptism. He felt compelled to "restore" these. As anticipated, the community which produced the gospel followed a path of fragmentation and schism (1 John 2:18-18) along Christological lines. As they disputed whether Jesus Christ was incarnated in a genuinely physical body or only in the likeness of sinful flesh, each copyist began to "correct" his heretical predecessor, the result being that our gospel points in various directions, sometimes in the space of a sentence or two. Finally, someone has added chapter 21 onto the end of the book, which otherwise seemed to conclude with 20:30-31. So the gospel is a bit of a mess, without one consistent theology or doctrine of Christ that can be derived from it without twisting the passages one happens not to favor—gerrymandering the text, as Walter Kaufman called it.

Author, apostle, Paraclete

As for the vexing question of gospel authorship, we may immediately dismiss the claim that it was one of the twelve disciples of Jesus. There is some confusion because John 19:34-35 introduces the testimony of a supposed eyewitness to the crucifixion in a way that seems to protest rather too much. Again, 21:24 pointedly makes one of the disciples, the longest lived and apparently recently deceased, the writer of the previous chapters. However, this is in the appendix, not the main body of the work, and may be by a different author. Even if not, it would be wrong to assume the author is the same as the book's ostensible narrator in any case. The author may have decided to create a fictive narrator, a device that was already classic at the time, not least among the gospel writers who did not hesitate to ascribe their works to Matthias, Peter, Thomas, or others, though these cannot have been the authors. In this instance, it means that even though the narrator is close to the events, like Ishmael in Melville's *Moby Dick,* this does not mean we are dealing with the author himself.

It is interesting to speculate whether the traditional ascription of authorship might be part of a larger observable tendency to make John the patron saint of Ephesus and Asia Minor, replacing Paul for reasons other than historical fact. As Walter Bauer (*Orthodoxy and Heresy in Earliest Christianity*) suggested, the speech of Paul to the el-

ders in Acts 20 is at pains to absolve Paul, fictively and retroactively, of the responsibility for the various "heresies" that flourished in Ephesus in the first and second centuries and traced themselves to him (20:29-30), including Encratism and Gnosticism. Other Catholic Christians did blame Paul, no doubt correctly, for the theological black sheep. Just as later tradition imported Mark into heretical Alexandria as the fictive first bishop, others placed the apostolic labors of John, son of Zebedee, in Ephesus. The Acts of John are full of adventures in the region and never a word about Paul. As for John ben Zebedee, he seems to have been an independent character, a famous Jewish physician mentioned in the Qumran-style *Sepher Refu'ot* ("Book of Medicines"), later pulled fictively into the Christian orbit.

What this means is that the so-called Gospel of John may originally have been attributed to Paul. Even if honorific, such an ascription would make sense of two striking data. First, the book is heavily Marcionite in outlook, denying that anyone before Jesus had seen or known God, as well as calling the Jewish Bible "your Law." Of course, the Marcionites were the great Paulinists of the early church, so it would be natural for them to ascribe a gospel to Paul. Second, one ancient tradition has it that Marcion served as the amanuensis for John, who dictated the book to him, and that John let him go after observing how badly he had corrupted the text. This at least indicates an early recognition of Marcionite elements in the Gospel of John.

It is also striking that Origen mentions a party of apparent Marcionites who claimed Paul was intended in the Gospel of John's predictions of the Paraclete (14:16-17; 15:26; 16:7-15). It does, as Bultmann saw, seem the Paraclete is not merely a superfluous term for the Holy Spirit, but rather the title of a second revealer who elucidates the message of Jesus exactly in the *syzygy* ("yoke fellow") fashion of Gnostic, Ismail'i, and Druze doctrine whereby new revealers come into the world in pairs, the second on the heels of the first to give an esoteric reading of his public pronouncements. In the mid-second century, Montanus, herald of the New Prophecy movement sweeping out of Phrygia, would claim to be the vessel of the Paraclete, as would the Apostle Mani and the Prophet Muhammad centuries afterward. It would appear that the Paraclete doctrine was understood to imply a

succession of new imams or manifestations of the Christ, parallel to the True Prophet doctrine of the Ebionites (Preaching of Peter). The gospel writer seems to seek to enhance his own authority as the implied Paraclete, the one who will bring to light the "forgotten" and not-yet-revealed advanced teaching which Jesus did not provide during his earthly lifetime (18:20). Who would this have been? Given the lateness of the book, we certainly cannot rule out Montanus himself. But then, in view of the blatant Marcionism of the gospel, Paul may be intended. Huller makes Paul the author of the gospel in its original form, and it might have been Marcion or some anonymous Marcionite who wanted to make Paul the predicted Paraclete, just as Matthew 5:19 makes Paul the least in the kingdom of heaven and Acts makes him Simon the Magician.

1

1In the beginning
there was the Word,
and the Word stood before God,
and the Word was a God.
2This one was there in the beginning with God.
3All came about through him,
and apart from him, not one thing came about.
What came about 4in him was life,
and the life was the light of mankind;
5and the light shines in the darkness,
and the darkness did not understand it.

6There appeared a man, sent from God, named John. 7This one came for a witness, to witness concerning the light so all might believe through him. 8Not that he was that light, but that he might witness concerning the light.

9It was the light of truth,
which illuminates every human being,
coming into the world.
10He was in the world,
and the world came about through him,
and the world did not recognize him.
11To his own creations he came,

but his own creatures did not welcome him.
[12]But whoever did welcome him,
he gave them authority to become children of God,
to those who believed in his name,
[13]who were born not of bloodlines nor of the desire of the flesh,
nor of the will of a husband, but of God.
[14]And the Word became flesh,
and pitched his tent among us,
and we witnessed his glory,
the glory of an only-begotten of a father,
full of grace and truth.

[15]John witnesses concerning him and has cried out, saying, "This was he of whom I said, 'The one coming after me has come before me, for he was first before me.'"

[16]Because we all received from his fullness,[a]
one gift replaced another,
[17]because the Law was given through Moses,
the grace and the truth came about through Jesus Christ.
[18]God, no mortal has ever seen;
the only-begotten God who embraces the Father,
that one revealed him.[b]

[19]And this was the witness of John when the Jews sent to him from Jerusalem priests and Levites to ask him, "You are who?" [20]And he confessed and did not deny, and he acknowledged, "It is not I who am the Christ." [21]And they asked, "Then what? Are you Elijah returned?" And he says, "I am not." "Are you the Prophet like Moses?" And he answered, "No." [22]Therefore, they said to him, "Who are you? That we may give some answer to those who sent us. What do you say about yourself?" [23]He said, "I am 'a voice of one crying out in the desert: Straighten out the road of Adonai,' as Isaiah, the prophet, said." [24]And some of those sent belonged to the Pharisee sect. [25]And they asked him and said to him, "Then what is the point of your baptism if you are neither the Christ nor Elijah nor the Prophet?" [26]John answered them, saying, "I baptize in water; one stands in your midst whom you do not recognize, [27]the one

a. Literally "pleroma," a Gnostic term for the Godhead.

b. This sounds Marcionite or Valentinian. Did Moses, Isaiah, and others not see God?

coming after me, the one of whom I am not worthy that I should loosen
the thong of his sandal." 28These things transpired in Beth-Anu across the
Jordan where John was baptizing.
29On the following day, he sees Jesus coming toward him and he
says, "Look! The lamb of God, who takes the sin of the world. 30This is
he of whom I said, 'After me comes a man who has come into being before me because he was first, ahead of me.' 31And I did not know who he
was, but in order that he might become manifest to Israel, therefore I
came baptizing in water." 32And John testified, saying, "I have beheld the
Spirit descending out of the sky, and he remained on him. 33Until then I
did not know who he was, but the one who sent me to baptize in water,
that one said to me, 'Whomever you see the Spirit descending and remaining on, this is the one who baptizes in the Holy Spirit.' 34Now I have
seen and have testified that this one is the son of God."
35The following day, John stood again with two of his disciples,
36and looking at Jesus walking, he says, "There! The lamb of God!"
37And the two disciples heard what he said and they followed Jesus.
38Jesus, turning and seeing them following him, says to them, "What do
you want?" And they said, "Rabbi," which is translated as "my teacher,"
"where are you staying?" 39He says to them, "Come and see for yourselves." So they went and saw where he was staying, and they stayed with
him that day. It was about the tenth hour.[c] 40One of the two who heard
John and was following him was Andreas, the brother of Simon Peter.
41This one first finds his own brother, Simon, and tells him, "We have
found the Messiah"—which is translated as "Christ." 42He led him to Jesus. Looking at him, Jesus said, "You are Simon, the son of John, but you
shall be called Cephas"—which is translated as "Peter."
43On the following day, he wished to leave for the Galilee and he
finds Philip, and Jesus says to him, "Follow me." 44Now Philip was from
Beth-Saida, from the city of Andreas and of Peter. 45Philip finds Nathaniel and tells him, "He of whom Moses wrote in the Law, and of whom the
prophets also wrote—we have found him! Jesus, son of Joseph, from
Nazareth." 46And Nathaniel said to him, "Nazareth! Can anything good
be from there?" Philip says to him, "Come and see for yourself!" 47Jesus
saw Nathaniel coming toward him and says of him, "Look! Truly an Israelite who lacks all duplicity!" 48Nathaniel says to him, "Where do you
know me from?" Jesus answered and said to him, "Before Philip called
you, I saw you in the shade of the fig tree." 49Nathaniel answered him,

c. 4:00 PM. Are vv. 35-42 a variant of Luke 24:13-35?

"You are the son of God! You are the king of Israel!" [50]Jesus answered and said to him, "It doesn't take much to convince you, does it? Just because I told you I saw you in the fig tree's shadow? You have not seen anything yet." [51]And he says to him, "Amen, amen: I tell you, you shall see the sky gaping open and the angels of God ascending and descending upon one like a son of man."[d]

2

[1]And the third day, there was a wedding in Cana in the Galilee and the mother of Jesus was there. [2]And both Jesus and his disciples were invited to the wedding. [3]And when they ran short of wine, Jesus' mother says to him, "They have run out of wine." [4]And Jesus says to her, "Why do you involve me, woman? My hour has not yet arrived." [5]Ignoring what he said, his mother says to the servants, "Whatever he tells you, do it." [6]Now six stone water jars for Jewish rites of purification lay stacked there, each with a capacity of two or three measures. [7]Jesus tells them, "All right. Fill those jars with water." And they filled them to the brim. [8]And he tells them, "Now ladle some out and take it to the master of ceremonies." And they took it. [9]But when the master of ceremonies tasted the water, now turned to wine—not knowing where it came from, though the servants knew, having ladled out the water—the master of ceremonies calls over the bridegroom [10]and says to him, "Everyone sets out the good wine first, and when the guests have gotten drunk, he opens the cheap stuff, but you have saved the good wine till now!" [11]This initial sign Jesus performed in Cana of Galilee, disclosing his glory, and his disciples believed in him. [12]After this, he and his mother and brothers and his disciples went down to the village of Nahum and stayed there no long time.[e] [13a]And the Jewish Passover was near.

---

d. The whole episode is based on the vision of Jacob's ladder in Gen. 28:10-17, combined with Dan. 7:13.

e. As Raymond E. Brown suggested, this story, originally absent Jesus' disciples, must have been a piece of apocryphal gospel tradition featuring the child Jesus, already known to his mother as a worker of convenient miracles to bail out the dull-witted adult mortals around him. She plainly expects him to save her from social embarrassment, and she knows he will do so despite his initial petulant refusal. How can she know this if it is his first miracle, as the redaction in v. 11 has it? Though the central feature of this miracle story is turning water to wine, no doubt derived from the lore of Dionysus, the basic story outline owes much to Elijah (1 Kings 17:8-24 LXX), as shown by Randel Helms, *Gospel Fictions* (Buffalo, NY: Prometheus Books, 1988), where he is scolded by the widow of Zarephath: "What have I to do with you, O man of God?" (τι εμοι κοι σοι, 17:18). John transfers this brusque address to the mouth of Jesus in his rebuke of his

5

1After this, there was a Jewish feast and Jesus went up to Jerusalem. 2Now in Jerusalem, at the Sheep Gate, there is a pool called in Hebrew Beth-Zatha, having five porches. 3In these there lay a great number of the infirm: blind, lame, withered, *waiting for the water to bubble up.* 4*For an angel used to descend into the pool at certain intervals and made ripples in the water. The first one in after the bubbling of the water would be cured of whatever disease afflicted him.* 5And there was a certain man there who had had an ailment for thirty-eight years. 6Jesus, seeing this man lying there and aware that he had been there already quite some time, said to him, "Do you even want to become well?" 7The sick man answered him, "Lord, I have no man to put me into the pool when the water bubbles up. While I am on my way, someone else always goes in ahead of me." 8Jesus says to him, "Get up! Pick up your mat and walk!" 9And at once the man became well, and he did pick up his mat and walked. And that day happened to be a Sabbath. 10Therefore, the Jews said to the man who had been cured, "It is a Sabbath! It is not legal for you to carry that mat." 11But he answered them, "The one who made me well, that one told me, 'Pick up your mat and walk.' What was I supposed to do, disobey him?" 12So they asked him, "So it's his fault. Who is the man who told you, 'Pick it up and walk'?" 13But the man who was cured could not point him out because Jesus had slipped away among the crowd that filled the place. 14Afterward, Jesus finds him in the temple and said to him, "See here: You have become well; leave off sinning before something worse happens to you." 15But the man left and told the Jews that Jesus was the one who made him well. 16Because of this, the Jews persecuted Jesus and tried to kill him because he did these things on the Sabbath. 17But he answered them, "My Father has not stopped working even now, so I too work." 18Because of this, the Jews only sought more eagerly to kill him, not only for Sabbath breaking but also for calling God his own father, in effect placing himself on a par with God.

19So Jesus answered and said to them, "Amen, amen: I say to you, a son can do nothing on his own unless he first sees his father doing it, for whatever that one does, the son will also do. 20For a father loves a son

---

mother (τι εμοι κοι σοι, γυναοι, 2:4). Jesus and Elijah both tell the women to take up empty pitchers (υδρι α, 1 Kings 17:12; υδρι οι , John 2:6-7), from which sustenance miraculously emerges. Just as this feat causes the woman to declare her faith in Elijah ("I know that you are a man of God," v. 24), so does Jesus' wine miracle cause his disciples to put their faith in him (v. 11).

and teaches him everything he does.[f] And he will teach him greater feats than these to your astonishment! [21]For just as the Father raises the dead and vivifies them, so also does the Son vivify whomever he wishes. [22]For the Father judges no one, but he has delegated all judgment to the Son, [23]so that all should accord the Son the same honor as the Father. The one who does not honor the Son does not honor the Father who sent him. [24]Amen, amen: I say to you, 'The one hearing my word and believing him who sent me has age-long life and does not come under judgment but has already crossed over from death into life.'[g] [25]Amen, amen: I say to you, 'A time is coming—in fact, it is here already—when the dead will hear the voice of the Son of God and those who heed it will live.' [26]For as the Father has life inherently, so also he decreed that the Son should have life inherently.[h] [27]And he gave him authority to render judgment because he is a mortal man. [28]*If that surprises you, know this: an hour is coming in which all those in the tombs will hear his voice* [29]*and will come forth, the ones who did good deeds to a resurrection of life, the ones who did wicked deeds to a resurrection of damnation.*[i] [30]I cannot do anything by myself. I judge based on what I hear, and my judgment is righteous because I have no vested interest but seek only to advance the will of the one who sent me. [31]If I were to testify about myself, my testimony would carry no weight. [32]There is someone else who testifies about me, and I know that the witness he bears about me is true.[j] [33]You have consulted John and he has attested the truth. I do not adduce testimony from mortal men; [34]I mention it only if it helps you to believe and be saved. [35]That man was the burning and shining lamp, and for a while you were happy to bask in his light. [36]But I have weightier testimony than John's, for the tasks my Father has given me to complete themselves attest that the Father has sent me.[k] [37]And the Father who sent me, he has testified about me. You have neither heard his voice nor seen his bodily form, [38]and his word has not taken root in you because he whom that one sent, this one you do not believe. [39]You pore over the scriptures, for in them you think you will find the secret of age-long life. [40]The irony is, they point to me,

f. C. H. Dodd calls this the Parable of the Apprenticed Son.

g. 1 John 3:14

h. John 1:3b-4a

i. An addition by the Ecclesiastical Redactor to supply traditional futuristic eschatology, absent from the Gnostic original.

j. John 21:24

k. John 3:2

yet you refuse to come to me to get that life. [41]I do not curry the esteem of mortal men, [42]but I have come to know you well enough to know that you are bereft of the love of God.[l] [43]I have come representing my Father, and you do not welcome me; but if someone else comes representing only himself, you will welcome him readily enough.[m] [44]How can you believe when you bask in the esteem of your colleagues,[n] indifferent to the approval that comes from the only God?[o] [45]It is not that I will accuse you to the Father; there is already someone accusing you—Moses, the very one on whom you pinned your hopes. [46]For if you believed Moses, it would have been a simple matter to believe me, for it was about me that he wrote. [47]But if you do not believe what he wrote, how will you ever believe what I say?"

7

[15]At this, the Jews marveled, saying, "How is this fellow so literate when he has never formally studied?" [16]Therefore, Jesus answered them and said, "What I teach is not my idea but comes from the one who sent me. [17]If anyone desires to do his will, he will have no difficulty determining whether the teaching is from God or whether I am offering my own opinions. [18]Whoever spouts his own ideas seeks fame for himself, but whoever seeks honor for the one who sent him, such a one is faithful and free from unrighteousness. [19]Did not Moses give you the Law? And not one of you practices the Law! Why do you seek to kill me?"

[20]The crowd answered, "You are a demoniac! Who's trying to kill you?" [21]Jesus replied and said to them, "I worked one miracle, and you all marvel. [22]Because Moses has given you circumcision, not that it comes from Moses originally, but rather from the patriarchs, on a Sabbath you circumcise a man. [23]If a man's member receives circumcision on the Sabbath so as not to violate the law of Moses, why are you angry with me because I made a whole man well on the Sabbath? [24]If you are to judge righteously, you must learn to look beneath the surface of things."

3

[22]After all this, Jesus and his disciples went into Judean territory, and he remained there with them and baptized. [23]John, too, was baptizing in

l. 1 John 2:15

m. Simon bar-Kochba, a messianic king whom Rabbi Akiba endorsed in 132 CE.

n. Matt. 6:2

o. Luke 16:13-14

Ainon near Salim because there was ample water there, and people came and were baptized. [24]You see, John had not yet been incarcerated. [25]There arose a dispute between some disciples of John and a Jew[p] about purification rites. [26]And they came to John and said to him, "Rabbi, the one who was with you beyond the Jordan, to whom you have born witness, behold, this fellow baptizes, and all are coming to him!" [27]John answered and said, "A man is not able to receive anything unless it has been vouchsafed him from heaven. [28]You yourselves heard me say, 'I am not the Christ, but I have been sent before that one.' [29]The only one entitled to the bride is the bridegroom, but the bridegroom's friend, waiting to hear his voice, rejoices greatly at the sound of the bridegroom's voice. Therefore this, my joy, has been fulfilled. [30]He must increase, but I must decrease."

4

[1]Therefore, once the Lord learned the Pharisees knew he makes and baptizes more disciples than John, [2]though strictly speaking it was not Jesus himself who baptized but his disciples,[q] [3]he left Judea and departed again for the Galilee. [4]And he had to pass through Samaria. [5]So he comes to a city of Samaria called Sychar, near the plot of land Jacob gave to his son Joseph. [6]And Jacob's fountain was located there. So Jesus, wearied from his journey, sat exhausted at the fountain. It was about the sixth hour. [7]A woman of Samaria comes to draw water. Jesus says to her, "Give me to drink."[r] [8]He asked her because his disciples had gone off into the city to buy food. [9]So the Samaritan woman says to him, "How dare you, being a Jew, ask a drink of me, being a Samaritan woman?" *For Jews do not use dishes in common with Samaritans.* [10]Jesus answered and said to her, "If you recognized the gift of God,[s] and who it is who is saying to you, 'Give me to drink,' you would have asked him, and he would have given you living water." [11]She says to him, "Lord, you have no pail and the well is deep. So where do you get the running water?" [12]Surely you are not greater than our common father Jacob, who bequeathed us the fountain, and drank of it himself, as did his sons and his cattle?" [13]Jesus answered and said to her, "Whoever drinks of this water will thirst again, but whoever drinks of the water that I will give him will

p. From the context, the Jew referred to here is apparently intended to be one of the Pharisees.

q. See 1 Cor. 1:13-17.

r. Some see here an anti-docetic portrayal, but see note to v. 34 below.

s. "Dositheus" means "gift of God." Was he the original messiah of this story?

never thirst till the end of the age. 14But the water I will give him will become in him a fountain of water springing up to age-long life." 15The woman says to him, "Lord, give me this water, so I will neither thirst nor have to come here to draw water!" 16He says to her, "You're not getting it. Go call your husband and come back."[t] 17The woman answered and said, "I have no husband." Jesus says to her, "I have no husband—well said! 18For I happen to know you have had five husbands, and the one you sleep with now is not even your husband.[u] You spoke the truth, all right!" 19The woman said to him, "Lord, I can see you are a prophet. 20Maybe you can answer a question for me. Our ancestors worshipped in this mountain[v] and you Jews say the place one is obliged to worship is Jerusalem. Which are the true worshippers?" 21Jesus says to her, "Believe me, woman, a time is coming when you will worship the Father neither in this mountain nor in Jerusalem since both alike will lie in ruins. 22You Samaritans worship in ignorance; we Jews worship what we know because salvation comes to the world from the Jews.[w] 23But a time is coming—in fact, it is here already—when the true worshippers will be the ones who worship the Father spiritually and truly, for it is such worshippers that the Father seeks for himself. 24God is a spirit, having no bodily needs to be served, and his worshippers ought to worship him spiritually and truly, not with vain sacrifices." 25The woman says to him, "How interesting! Well, I know that Messiah is supposed to come, the one they call Christ.[x] When that man comes, he will straighten all these things out." 26Jesus says to her, "Be that as it may, I am the one speaking to you now."[y] 27And at this point, his disciples arrived, and they marveled that he was speaking with a woman. However, no one dared ask, "What do you want with him?" or "Why are you speaking to her?" 28So the woman left her water jar and went off into the city, and she says to the people,

t. 1 Cor. 14:35

u. The Samaritan woman stands for Helen, consort of Simon Magus, herself a Samaritan mystagogue who claimed she incarnated the Epinoia (First Thought) of God, as the fallen Sophia of Gnosticism. She had had many lovers in many incarnations including her life as Helen of Troy and the prostitute Simon rescued from a brothel.

v. Mount Gerizim would be in plain view in this setting.

w. Rom. 11:11-12

x. This is an error. The Samaritans expected the Taheb ("restorer") to be a prophet like Moses, definitely not the Davidic Jewish messiah (1 Kings 12:16) or "Christ."

y. Thomas, saying 52

[29]"Come see a man who told me everything I ever did. Is this not the Christ?" [30]They went forth out of the city and came to him.[z]

[31]Meanwhile, the disciples urged him, saying, "Rabbi, eat! Eat!" [32]But he said to them, "I have food to eat that you are unaware of." [33]Therefore, the disciples said to one another, "Surely no one brought him food while we were gone?"[a] [34]Jesus says to them, "My food is doing the will of the one who sent me and finishing his work.[b] [35]Don't you people say, 'It is still three months till the harvest comes'? Just look, I tell you, look up at that crowd headed this way and you will see the fields because they are already white for harvest! [36]The reaper receives wages and garners fruit for age-long life so the sower and the reaper may rejoice together. [37]For in this case the saying is true that two different people sow and reap. [38]I sent you to reap where you did not do the work sowing; others did that work and you have entered the field they prepared."[c]

[39]And many from that city of Samaritans believed in him because of the testimony of the woman, "He told me everything I ever did." [40]So when the Samaritans came to him, they asked him to stay with them, and he stayed there two days. [41]And many more believed because of his teaching, [42]and they said to the woman, "We believe no longer because of

z. As noted by Robert Alter, *The Art of Biblical Narrative* (New York: Basic Books, 1981), this is a variant of a biblical "type scene" whereby a young man leaves home and happens upon young women at a well and marries one. Other instances include Abraham's servant meeting Rebecca (Gen. 24), Jacob meeting Rachel (Gen. 29), Moses meeting Zipporah (Exod. 2), Ruth meeting Boaz (Ruth 2); and Saul meeting the maidens at Zuph (1 Sam. 9). Helms, *Gospel Fictions,* adds Elijah's encounter with the widow of Zarephath (1 Kings 17) as a variant which seems to have supplied the immediate model for John 4. Elijah and Jesus alike leave their home turf for foreign territory. Each is thirsty and meets a woman, of whom he asks a drink. In both stories the woman deviates from the type scene pattern because, though unmarried as usual, these two women are mature and both previously married. The woman of Zarephath is a widow, while the Samaritan woman has had five previous husbands, dead or divorced, and is presently cohabiting. In both stories it is the woman, more than the prophet, who stands in need, and the latter offers the boon of a self-renewing supply of nourishment, physical food in one case and in the other the water of everlasting life. Just as the widow exclaims that Elijah must have come to disclose her past sins ("You have come to me to bring my sin to remembrance," 1 Kings 17:18), the Samaritan also admits Jesus has the goods on her ("He told me all that I ever did," John 4:39).

a. Mark 8:15-16

b. A piece of docetism: Jesus does not require earthly food.

c. As Oscar Cullmann suggested (*The Johannine Circle*), this must refer to a Samaritan mission undertaken by one faction of Christians and co-opted by another (Acts 8:5-17; cf. Matt. 25:24; 1 Cor. 3:6-8).

what you said. Now we have heard for ourselves and we know that this man is truly the savior of the world."

[43]After the two days, he departed from there into the Galilee. [44]For Jesus himself testified that a prophet gets no respect in his own birthplace.[d] [45]So when he arrived in the Galilee, the Galileans welcomed him, having seen all the things he did in Jerusalem at the feast, for they also went to the feast. [46]So he came again to Cana of the Galilee, where he made the water wine. And there was a certain royal official whose son was sick in the village of Nahum. [47]This man, hearing that Jesus comes out of Judea into the Galilee, went to him and asked him to come down and cure his son, for he was on the point of death. [48]Therefore, Jesus said to him, "Unless you people see signs and prodigies, you never believe!"[e] [49]The royal official says to him, "Lord, come down before my child dies." [50]Jesus says to him, "Your son lives!" The man believed what Jesus said to him, and he left. [51]And already while he was going down, the slaves met him, reporting that his boy lives. [52]So he asked them what time it was when he got better, and they said to him, "Yesterday at the seventh hour[f] the fever left him." [53]The father recognized it as the time when Jesus told him, "Your son lives," and he believed, and his whole household. [54]And this, again a second sign, Jesus did, having come out of Judea into the Galilee.

6

[1]Afterward, Jesus departed across the Sea of Galilee, or Tiberias. [2]And a large crowd followed him because they saw the signs he performed on the sick. [3]And Jesus went up into the mountain and there sat with his disciples. [4]And the Jewish feast of the Passover was near. [5]So looking up and seeing that a great crowd was approaching him, Jesus says to Philip, "Where may we buy loaves so these people may eat?" [6]And he said this to test him, for he knew what he was about to do. [7]Philip answered him, "Two hundred denarii worth of loaves would not be sufficient for them, even if each took only a little." [8]One of his disciples, Andreas, the brother of Simon Peter, says to him, [9]"There is a lad

---

d. That is, in Judea, implying he was born in Beth-Lehem.

e. Why does Jesus upbraid this poor man who plainly already believes? It is a common element of miracles stories for the miracle worker to raise the bar, placing an obstacle in the suppliant's path in order to gauge the strength and determination of his faith. In other words, it may be a Socratic pose. See also Mark 7:27-29; 9:23; John 2:4; 6:6.

f. 1:00 PM.

here who has five barley rolls and two dried fish, but what are these among so many?" 10But Jesus said, "Have the people recline." Now the place was carpeted with grass. So the men, about five thousand in number, reclined. 11So Jesus took the loaves and, once he had given thanks, distributed as much as they wished to those reclining and also with the fish. 12Now when they were satisfied, he tells his disciples, "Collect the leftover pieces so nothing gets wasted." 13So they collected them and filled twelve baskets with the pieces of the five barley loaves which the ones who had eaten left over.[g]

14Therefore, the people, seeing the sign he performed, said, "This is truly the Prophet like Moses who is to come into the world!" 15Once Jesus realized they were about to rally and seize him to proclaim him king, he slipped away back into the mountain by himself. 16And when evening came, his disciples went down to the sea 17and, shoving off in a boat, made for the village of Nahum across the sea. And darkness had descended without Jesus having yet rejoined them. 18And with a strong wind blowing, the sea was roused up against them. 19Having rowed about twenty-five or thirty stadia, they caught sight of Jesus walking around beside the sea and nearing the boat through the surf, and they were seized with fear. 20But he says to them, "It's only me! Do not be afraid!" 21So they were willing to help him into the boat, but the boat was already at the land they were headed for.[h]

22The next day, the crowd, standing back on the far side of the sea, saw there was no other boat and that Jesus had not gone with his disciples but that his disciples left without him. 23Other boats from Tiberias came near the place where they ate the bread once the Lord had given thanks. 24So when the crowd saw that Jesus is not there, nor his disciples, they embarked in the boats and came to the village of Nahum looking for Jesus. 25And finding him across the sea teaching in the synagogue, they said to him, "Rabbi, when did you arrive?" 26Jesus answered them and said, "Amen, amen: I say to you, you are looking for me not because you saw signs, but because you ate of the loaves and were satisfied! 27Do not work for the food that perishes but for the food that endures into age-long life which a man will give you, whom the Father authenticated as God." 28So they said to him, "What sort of works does God require?"

---

g. The basis for the miraculous feeding stories is that of Elisha multiplying the twenty barley loaves for a hundred men in 2 Kings 4:42-44.

h. Pss. 107 (LXX 106): 23-30; Job 9:8b, *Iliad* 24:332, 340-41, 345-46, 351-52.

29 Jesus answered and said to them, "This is the work that God requires:
that you believe in him whom he sent." 30 So they said to him, "Then what
sign will you perform for us to see and believe you? What miracle will
you work? 31 Our ancestors ate the manna in the desert, as it is written,
'He gave them bread out of heaven to eat.'" 32 So Jesus said to them,
"Amen, amen: I say to you, the text does not mean 'Moses' has given you
bread out of heaven, but that 'my Father' gives you the true bread out of
heaven. 33 For the bread of God is whatever comes down from heaven and
gives life to the world." 34 So they said to him, "Lord, always give us this
bread!" 35 Jesus said to them, "I am the bread of life; whoever comes to
me never hungers, and whoever believes in me will never thirst. 36 But I
told you, you have both seen me and not believed. 37 All that the Father
gives me will come to me, and whoever comes to me I will never expel,
38 because I have descended from heaven not to do my own will but rather
the will of the one who sent me. 39 And this is the will of the one who sent
me, that I shall not lose any of what he has given me but shall make it
stand again at the last day. 40 *For this is the will of my Father, that every-*
one who looks upon the Son and believes in him may have age-long life,
and I will make him stand up again in the last day."

41 *Therefore, the Jews murmured*[i] *at him because he said, "I am the*
bread that descended out of heaven." 42 *And they said, "Is not this fellow*
Jesus, the son of Joseph, whose father and mother we know? How is it
that now he says, 'Out of heaven I have descended?'" 43 *Jesus answered*
and said to them, "Do not murmur with one another! 44 *No one is able to*
come to me unless the Father who sent me shall draw him, and I will
make him stand again in the last day. 45 *It is written in the Prophets, 'And*
they shall all be taught directly by God.' Everyone who hears and learns
from the Father comes to me. 46 *Not that anyone has seen the Father ex-*
cept for the one who is with God, and this one has seen the Father.[j]
47 *Amen, amen: I say to you, whoever believes has age-long life!* 48 *I am the*
bread of life. 49 *Your ancestors ate the manna in the desert and still they*
died. 50 *This is the bread descending from heaven such that anyone may*
eat of it and not die. 51 *I am the living bread descended from heaven. If*

---

i. The "murmuring" motif means to compare these gainsayers with the carping people of Israel on the exodus who "murmured" at Moses no matter what miracles they saw.

j. Did Aaron, Moses, Nadab, Abihu, and others not see God (Exod. 24:9-11; Deut. 34:10)? This is either a Marcionite (different God) or rabbinical (an angel; God is too transcendent to be seen) element.

anyone eats of this bread, he will live unto the age. And indeed, the bread
which I will give for the life of the world is my flesh."
52*Therefore, the Jews argued with one another, saying, "How can*
this fellow give us his flesh to eat?" 53*Therefore Jesus said to them,*
"Amen, amen: I say to you, unless you eat the flesh of the man and drink
his blood, you do not have life in yourselves. 54*Whoever eats my flesh and*
drinks my blood has age-long life, and I will make him to stand again in
the last day! 55*For my flesh is real food and my blood is real drink.*
56*Whoever eats my flesh and drinks my blood remains in me and I remain*
likewise in him. 57*Just as the living Father sent me, and I live because of*
the Father, so also the one who eats of me, even that one will live because
of me. 58*This is the bread that descended from heaven, not such as the an-*
cestors ate, and died; whoever eats this bread will live unto the age."[k]
59These things he said teaching in a synagogue in the village of
Nahum. 60Many of his would-be disciples, hearing this, said, "This is a
difficult teaching! Who can accept it?" 61But Jesus, well aware that his
disciples are murmuring about this, said to them, "This offends you?
62What if you were to behold the man ascending to where he was at first?
63The spirit of the teaching is what imparts life: the literal flesh accomplishes nothing.[l] The discourse I have just spoken to you is spirit and it
gives life. 64But there are some of you who do not understand." For from
the very beginning, Jesus knew who the ones are who do not believe and
even the one who would betray him. 65Accordingly, he said, "This is the
reason I have told you, 'No one comes to me unless it is given him to do so
by the Father."
66At this point, many of his disciples left and returned home and no
longer walked about with him. 67Therefore, Jesus said to the twelve,
"You don't want to go, too?" 68Simon Peter answered him, "Lord,
whom should we seek out instead? You are the one with the words of
age-long life. 69Besides, we have come to believe, even to know, you are
the saint of God." 70Jesus answered them, "Was it not I who chose you
twelve? And of you, one is a devil." 71He was referring to Judas of Simon,
the False One. For this one was about to betray him—one of the twelve.

7

1And after these events, Jesus toured the Galilee, for he did not want

---

k. This is a sacramental and eschatological correction by the Ecclesiastical Redactor in order to tone down the originally Gnostic character of the gospel.

l. An anti-sacramental counter-gloss.

to move about in Judea because the men of Judea were trying to kill him.
[2]Now the Jewish Feast of Tabernacles was near. [3]Therefore, his brothers
said to him, "Leave here and go into Judea so that your disciples, too,
may behold the powerful works you do. [4]For no one acts in secret if he
hopes to become known in public. If you do these miracles, let the world
see you!" [5]For his brothers did not understand him. [6]Therefore, Jesus
says to them, "My time has not yet arrived, but for you there is no special
time. [7]The world has no reason to hate you, but it does hate me because I
remind it that its deeds are wicked. [8]You go on up to the feast. I am not
going to this feast because my appointed time has not yet arrived." [9]And
saying these things to them, he remained in the Galilee. [10]But when his
brothers went up to the feast, then he too went up, not openly, but in secret. [11]So the people of Judea looked for him at the feast and said,
"Where is that fellow?" [12]And there was a lot of murmuring about him
among the crowds. Some said, "He is a good man." Others said, "No,
but he deludes the crowd." [13]However, no one spoke openly about him
for fear of the rulers of the Jews.

[14]But the feast now having reached the midpoint, Jesus went into the
temple and taught. [25]Therefore, some of the Jerusalemites said, "Isn't this
the fellow they are looking to kill? [26]Look! He speaks openly and they
make no move to silence him. Surely the rulers have not actually decided
that this is the Christ?" [27]"But we know where this fellow hails from;
when the Christ comes, he will mysteriously appear out of nowhere."
[28]Therefore, Jesus, teaching in the temple, cried out, saying, "You know
me and where I hail from, but I have not come on my own initiative; he
who sent me is faithful, and he is the one you do not know. [29]I know him
because I am from him, and he sent me."

[40]So some in the crowd, hearing these words, said, "This is truly the
Prophet like Moses!" [41]Others said, "This is the Christ!" But others said,
"So the Prophet comes out of the Galilee, does he? [42]Did not the scripture
say that the Christ comes from the line of David and from Beth-Lehem,
the village where David lived?" [43]Therefore, a schism emerged in the
crowd on account of him.

[30]Therefore, they tried to arrest him, and no one got their hands on
him because his appointed hour had not yet arrived. [31]But many in the
crowd believed in him and said, "When the Christ comes, is he likely to
perform more signs than this fellow did?" [32]The Pharisees heard the
crowd whispering these things about him and the archpriests and the
Pharisees sent their henchmen to arrest him.

[44]And some of them tried to arrest him, but no one got their hands on him. [45]So the henchmen reported to the archpriests and Pharisees, who said to them, "Why did you not bring him?" [46]The henchmen answered the Pharisees, "No one ever spoke as this man speaks!" [47]Therefore, the Pharisees replied to them, "What, has he deceived you, too? [48]Has any of the rulers, or any of the Pharisees, believed in him? [49]But this mob that is ignorant of the Torah is cursed!" [50]Nicodemus, one who had just gone to him, and being one of them, says to them, [51]"But does our Law judge a man before hearing him out and establishing what he has done?" [52]They answered and said to him, "You aren't from the Galilee,[m] too, are you? Search the scripture and you will find that no prophet ever arises out of the Galilee."

[37]Now on the last day, the climax of the feast, Jesus stood and cried out, saying, "If anyone thirsts, let him come to me, and let him drink [38]who believes in me!" As scripture said, "Out of his belly will flow rivers of living water." [39]But this it said concerning the Spirit whom those who believed in him were about to receive. For the Spirit did not yet exist[n] because Jesus was not yet glorified.[o]

9

[1]And passing by, he noticed a man blind from birth. [2]And his disciples asked him, saying, "Rabbi, who sinned, this poor wretch or his parents, that he was born blind?"[p] [3]Jesus answered, "Neither this man nor his parents sinned; he was born blind so that the mighty works of God might be displayed through him. [4]We are obliged to do the tasks of him who sent me while there is still daylight left, for night is closing in when no one can work. [5]While I linger in the world, I am the light of the world." [6]Having said these things, he spat on the ground and made mud with the saliva, and he smeared the mud on his eyes, [7]and said to him, "Go, wash it off in the Pool of Siloam," which is translated as "the one sent." So he went and washed and came back seeing. [8]Therefore, his neighbors and those who used to see him begging said, "Surely this isn't the one who

m. This might denote either that Nicodemus is supposed to be associated with Jesus and Christians as Galileans (cf. John 9:28) or that he, like the Galileans, is ignorant of and indifferent to the Torah: "O Galilee that hatest the Torah!"

n. Acts 19:2

o. 1 Cor. 15:45

p. The text clearly presupposes a belief in reincarnation, familiar to Pythagoreans and Gnostics and attested in later Judaism, or possibly *pre*incarnation: the man would have sinned in his previous disincarnate life, perhaps as a fallen angel.

used to sit and beg?" [9]Some said, "It's him, all right!" Others said, "No, it can't be! He just looks like him!" The man confirmed, "It is I!" [10]So they said to him, "Then how were your eyes opened?" [11]He answered, "The man named Jesus made mud and anointed my eyes with it and told me, 'Go to Siloam and wash.' So I went, and when I washed, I could see!" [12]And they said, "Where is that man?" He says, "I do not know what he looks like." [13]They take him, the once-blind man, to the Pharisees. [14]Now the day Jesus made the mud and opened his eyes was a sabbath.

[15]So once again the Pharisees asked him how he saw again. And he said to them, "He smeared mud on my eyes and I washed it off, and now I see." [16]So some of the Pharisees said, "This man is not from God because he does not observe the Sabbath!" But others said, "How can a sinful man perform such signs?" And there was a division among them. [17]Therefore, they turned to the blind man again, saying, "Well, what do you have to say about him? It was your eyes that he opened!" And he said, "He is a prophet!" [18]Therefore, the Jewish authorities did not believe he was blind and then saw until they sent for his parents [19]and asked them, "Is this your son, whom you say was born blind? If so, how does he see now?" [20]So his parents answered and said, "We know this is our son and that he was born blind, [21]but how it is he now sees, we do not know, or for that matter who opened his eyes, we do not know. Ask him. He is of age and can speak for himself." [22]His parents said these things because they feared the rulers of the Jews, for the rulers of the Jews had already agreed that if anyone would confess him as Christ, they would be ejected from the synagogue.[q] [23]That is why his parents said, "He is of age, ask him."

[24]So a second time they summoned the man who was blind and enjoined him, "Give glory to God, now![r] We know this man is a sinner." [25]So that one answered, "He may be a sinner, for all I know. But one thing I know: having been blind, I now see!" [26]So they said to him, "What exactly did he do to you? How did he open your eyes?" [27]He answered them, "I told you already, but I guess you didn't hear me. Why do you want to hear it again? Do you want to become his disciples, as well?" [28]And they reviled him and said, "You are a disciple of that fellow! We are disciples of Moses! [29]We know that God has spoken by Moses, but as for this fellow? We do not even know who he represents."[s] [30]The man answered and said to them, "Here's the miracle. You don't know whether

---

q. John 7:49

r. They are putting him on oath before God as in Josh. 7:19.

s. Mark 11:30-33

he comes from God despite the fact that he opened my eyes. [31]We know
that God does not hear the prayers of hypocrites, but if anyone is pious
toward God and obeys his will, he will be heard. [32]From ages past, no one
ever heard of anyone opening the eyes of the congenitally blind. [33]So if
this fellow were not from God, he could never do such a thing." [34]They
retorted and said to him, "You son of a whore! You think you can lecture
us?" And they threw him into the street.

[35]Jesus heard that they threw him out, and finding him, he said, "Do
you believe in this man?" [36]That one answered and said, "Point him out
to me, Lord, that I may know which one to believe in." [37]Jesus said to
him, "You're looking at him right now, and he is the one talking with
you." [38]And he said, "Lord, I believe!" And he bowed before him. [39]And
Jesus said, "I came into this world to render judgment so that those who
do not see may see and the sighted may go blind." [40]Some of the Pharisees
who were with him heard this and said to him, "Oh, so we're blind, too?"
[41]Jesus said to them, "If you were blind, you wouldn't be responsible; but
now that you say, 'We can see just fine,' your guilt remains."

8

[12]Therefore, Jesus spoke to them again, saying, "I am the light of the
world. Whoever follows me will never grope about in darkness but will
have the light of life." [13]So the Pharisees said to him, "Aha! You bear witness on your own behalf. Your witness is worthless!" [14]Jesus answered
and said to them, "Even if I do testify on my own behalf, my witness is
true. I know where I came from and where I am going; but you do not
know where I come from or where I am going. [15]You judge by worldly
standards; I judge no one. [16]But even if I were to judge, my judgment
would be true because I am not alone on the judgment seat, but I confer
with the one who sent me. [17] Even in your Torah, it is written, 'the testimony of two men is true.'[t] [18]Well, I am one testifying about myself and
the Father who sent me testifying for me is the second." [19]So they said,
"Where is your father?" Jesus answered, "You do not recognize either
me or my Father; if you recognized me, you would know my Father."[u]
[20]He said these things teaching in the treasury of the temple and no one
seized him because his appointed time had not yet arrived.

10

[19]Again a schism arose among the Jews over these words. [20]And

t. Note the Gnostic/Marcionite repudiation of the Jewish scripture.

u. Matt. 11:27; Luke 10:22

many of them said, "He is a raving demoniac! Why do you listen to
him?" [21]Others replied, "These are not the words of a demonized man!
Can a demon open the eyes of the blind?"

[22]There was at that time in Jerusalem the Feast of Dedication. It was
winter. [23]And Jesus was walking about in the Porch of Solomon. [24]So the
Jews surrounded him and said to him, "How long do we have to hold our
breath? If you are the Christ, tell us straight out!" [25]Jesus answered them,
"I told you, you just don't believe it. The answer is implied in the works I
perform in the name of the Father, but you don't believe [26]because you do
not belong to my flock. [27]My sheep have no difficulty hearing my voice,
and I can identify them as distinct from others' sheep, and they follow
me; [28]and I give them age-long life, and they will by no means perish to
the end of the age. And no thief shall snatch them away from my protection. [29]My Father, who gave them to me, is greater than all and no one
can steal from the Father.[v]

[1]"Amen, amen: I say to you, the one who does not enter through the
door into the sheepfold but climbs up some other way, that one is a thief
and a robber. [2]But he who enters through the door is the shepherd of the
sheep. [3]The doorkeeper opens to him and the sheep recognize his voice,
and he calls his own sheep by name and leads them out. [4]And when he
leads them all out, he goes before them and the sheep follow him because
they know his voice. [5]They never follow a stranger, but will run away
from him because they do not know the voice of strangers." [6]Jesus told
them this analogy, but they did not grasp the meaning of what he said to
them. [7]Therefore, Jesus tried again: "Amen, amen: I say to you, I am the
door of the sheep. [8]All who came before me are the thieves and robbers,
but the sheep did not listen to them.[w] [9]I am the door. If anyone enters
through me, he will be safe and will freely go in and out and will find pasture. [10]The thief comes for one purpose: to steal and kill and destroy.[x] I,
on the other hand, came that the sheep might have life and plenty of it. [11]I
am the good shepherd. The good shepherd lays down his life for the
sheep. [12]The mere hireling, who is not a shepherd and does not own the

---

v. Matt. 6:20

w. The reference is to failed messiahs: Athronges, the shepherd king; Judas, son of Hezekiah; Simon, the servant king—all of whom flourished after the death of Herod the Great. Possibly in view are also the messiahs who appeared after Jesus but before this gospel such as Theudas the Magician, the unnamed Jeroboam redivivus out of Egypt, Simon bar-Gioras, Menahem, and Simon bar-Kochba.

x. Thomas, saying 60

sheep, no sooner spots the wolf coming than he runs away, leaving the sheep to their fate. And the wolf seizes some and the rest scatter. [13]After all, he is only a hireling; what does he care about the sheep? [14]I am the good shepherd and I recognize my flock, and my flock know me. [15]Just as the Father knows me and I know the Father and I lay down my life for the sheep. [16]I have other sheep, too, not belonging to this fold: those, too, I must bring, and they will hear my voice and they will become one single flock with a single shepherd. [17]This is why the Father loves me: because I lay down my life in order to pick it back up. [18]No one took[y] it from me against my will; no, I lay it down of my own free will.[z] I am authorized to lay it down and I am authorized to pick it up again because my Father commanded me to do so. [30]I and the Father, we are one!" [31]The Jews again reached for stones to stone him.

[32]Jesus answered them, "I showed you many good deeds from the Father—which one of them do you propose to stone me for?" [33]The Jews answered him, "We're not stoning you for any good deed but for blasphemy! Because you, a mortal man, make yourself a God!" [34]Jesus answered them, "Is it not written in your Torah,[a] 'I said, You are gods'?[b] [35]Now if he called those people 'gods' to whom the decree of God was directed, and scripture cannot be flouted, right? [36]why do you say to him whom God set apart[c] and sent into the world, 'You blaspheme,' because I merely said, 'I am God's son'? [37]If I do not perform the works of my Father, do not believe me. [38]But if I do, even if you won't take my word for it, believe your own eyes so you may realize and be convinced that the Father is in me and I am in the Father."[d] [39]At this, they made another attempt to arrest him, but he passed right through their hands.[e]

---

y. Notice the past tense, implying it was really written long after the fact.

z. This is the equivalent of the Synoptic Passion predictions, reassuring the reader that Jesus was not overtaken by events; he was in perfect control from the first, no matter how bad things might seem to the reader.

a. Here and in v. 35, Jesus speaks *ad hominem* of the scripture belonging to "you" Jews, not to him. This is Marcionite/Gnostic.

b. Pss. 82:6, where Yahve condemns the sons of God for their misrule. These are lesser gods who rule the nations as his deputies. In Jesus' day, monotheistic Judaism interpreted the words as referring somehow to human judges.

c. This may refer to those like Jeremiah, set apart at birth (1:5), or heavenly sons of God, as in Catharist belief.

d. This paragraph sounds like a cautious Christian "correction" to the Patripassian modalism of v. 30, trying to take the high Christology down a notch or two.

e. Docetism again.

[40]And he went away, back across the Jordan where John was baptizing at the first, and he remained there. [41]And many of John's followers
came to him and said, "True, John performed no sign, but all he said
about this man was true." [42]And many believed in him there.

11

[1]Now there was a certain man ailing, Lazarus of Beth-Anu,[f] the village of Mariam and Martha, her sister. [2]And it was Mariam who
anointed the Lord with myrrh and wiped off his feet with her hair, whose
brother Lazarus ailed. [3]Therefore the sisters sent word to him, saying,
"Lord, behold, the one you love is ill." [4]And hearing it, Jesus said, "This
ailment is not fatal, but for the glory of God so that the Son of God may
be glorified by means of it." [5]Now Jesus loved Martha and her sister and
Lazarus. [6]So when he heard that he was ill, he then remained two days in
the place he was. [7]Then, after this, he says to the disciples, "Let us go
back into Judea." [8]The disciples say to him, "Rabbi, the Jews were just
now looking to stone you and you want to go back there?" [9]Jesus answered, "Are there not twelve hours of daylight? If anyone walks in the
daytime, he does not stumble because he sees the daylight of this world.
[10]But if anyone walks in the night, he is liable to stumble because he cannot see the light." [11]He said these things, and after this he says to them,
"Our friend Lazarus has fallen asleep, but I am going there to wake him
up." [12]Therefore, the disciples said to him, "Lord, if he has fallen asleep,
the fever has broken and he will recover." [13]Now Jesus had been referring
to his death, but they thought he had reference to the literal sleep of slumber. [14]Therefore, Jesus then told them plainly, "Lazarus died. [15]And for
your sake, I am glad I was not there to stop it so you may believe. But let
us go to him." [16]Therefore, Thomas, which means the Twin, said to the
fellow disciples, "Let us go, too, so we may die with Lazarus!"

[17]When Jesus arrived, he found him already having been entombed
four days. [18]Now Beth-Anu was near Jerusalem, about fifteen stadia
away. [19]And many of the Jews had come to Martha and Mariam to console them over their brother. [20]So when Martha heard that Jesus is coming, she met him, but Mariam sat in the house. [21]So Martha said to Jesus,
"Lord, where have you been? If you had been here, my brother would not
have died! [22]I know that even now, whatever you may ask of God, God

f. I.e., El-Osiris, whose worship was centered in Egyptian Heliopolis, "City of the Sun," equivalent to the Hebrew Beth-Shemesh ("House of the Sun") or Beth-Anu ("House of On"). "On" is a short form of Osiris, the dying and rising God of Egypt.

will give you." 23Jesus says to her, "Your brother will rise again."
24Martha says to him, "Oh, I know that he will rise again in the resurrection in the last day." 25Jesus said to her, "I am the resurrection and the
life. 26The one who believes in me, even if he dies, he will live; and whoever among the living believes in me will by no means die till the end of
the age. Do you believe this?" 27"Yes, Lord, I have believed that you are
the Christ, the Son of God coming into the world."

28And saying this, she went away and called her sister secretly, saying, "The teacher is here and calls for you!" 29And when she heard, she
got up quickly and came to him. 30Jesus had not yet come into the village
but was still in the place where Martha met him. 31Therefore, the Jews
who were with her in the house consoling her, seeing that Mariam quickly
got up and went out, followed her, thinking, "She must be going to the
tomb to cry there." 32So Mariam, when she arrived where Jesus was waiting, seeing him, fell at his feet, saying to him, "Lord, if you were here, my
brother would not have died!" 33So when Jesus saw her crying and the
Jews accompanying her crying too, he was deeply moved and troubled.
34And he said, "Where have you laid him out?" They say to him, "Lord,
come and see." 35Jesus shed tears. 36Therefore, the Jews said, "See how he
loved him!" 37But some of them said, "Could not a man who opened the
blind man's eyes have prevented this poor man from dying?" 38Therefore,
Jesus, deeply moved, approaches the tomb. It was a cave and a stone was
lying against it. 39Jesus says, "Lift the stone!" Martha, the sister of the
dead man, says to him, "Lord, he reeks now, for it is the fourth day."
40Jesus says to her, "Didn't I tell you that if you only believe, you will see a
divine spectacle?" 41So they lifted the stone. And Jesus gazed skyward and
said, "Father, I thank you that you heard me! 42Of course, I knew that
you always hear me; I only said it because of the crowd standing around
me, that they may understand that you sent me and that I didn't do this on
my own." 43And having said this, he cried out with a loud voice, "Lazarus! Come out!" 44The dead man came out, bound hand and foot with
wrappings, and his face had been masked with a napkin. Jesus says to
them, "Free him and let him go."

45Therefore, many of the Jews who had visited Mariam and witnessed what he did believed in him on the spot. 46But some of them went
off to the Pharisees and told them the things Jesus did. 47Therefore, the
archpriests and the Pharisees assembled in council and said, "What are
we to do? Because this man performs many signs. 48If we let him keep it
up, everyone will believe in him and the Romans will come and seize both

our holy place and our nation!"[g] [49]But a certain one of them, Caiaphas, serving as archpriest for that year,[h] said to them, "You fail to grasp the situation. [50]Nor do you see that it is best for us if one man should die for the people and the entire nation not perish." [51]But he did not say this from himself, but being archpriest for that year, he prophesied that Jesus was about to die for the nation, [52]and not for the nation only, but also that he might gather the scattered children of God into one flock. [53]Therefore, from that day on, they conferred on how to kill him. [54]Therefore, Jesus no longer openly circulated among the Jews but went away from there into the region near the desert to a city called Ephraim and remained there with the disciples.[i]

[55]And the Jewish Passover was near, and many went up to Jerusalem from the countryside before the Passover in order to purify themselves. [56]So they looked for Jesus and said to one another as they stood in the temple, "What do you think? That he will not dare to attend the feast?" [57]The archpriests and the Pharisees had issued orders that anyone knowing his whereabouts should supply the information for them to arrest him.

12

[1]Therefore, Jesus came to Beth-Anu six days before the Passover, where Lazarus lived, whom he raised from the dead. [2]So they hosted a supper for him there and Martha served,[j] [3]and Lazarus was among the guests reclining at table with him. So Mariam took a pound of ointment, pure muskroot and quite expensive and anointed Jesus' feet[k] and wiped off his feet with her hair, and the house was permeated by the scent of the ointment.[l] [4]And Judas the False One, one of his disciples who was shortly

---

g. They assume Jesus would ride the envisioned wave of popular support all the way to a violent revolution.

h. The author falsely imagines the office of the archpriesthood as an annually rotating position when, in fact, an archpriest served for life.

i. The Genesis patriarch Joseph, too, is a Hebrew version of Osiris, and that theme continues here since Ephraim is named for one of Joseph's two sons.

j. Luke 10:38, 40

k. Luke 10:39

l. In Mark 14:9; Matt. 26:13, Jesus says the anointing woman's deed will be recounted as part of the gospel preached throughout the world. And yet her name is omitted! The story is a Christian version of Isis anointing the slain Osiris to raise him from the dead. In the initial Christian version, which must have been set on Easter morning, Isis becomes Mary Magdalene ("the hairdresser"). John probably did not identify these two Marys; he wants to suppress the role of Mary Mag-

to betray him, says, [5]"Why was this ointment not sold for three hundred denarii and the proceeds given to the poor?" [6]But he said this, not because the poor mattered to him, but because he was a thief, having charge of the money bag and carrying on his person the donations put into it.[m] [7]So Jesus said, "Let her keep it till the day of my burial. [8]There will always be poor on hand for you to assist, but this is a special occasion in my honor."

[9]The great crowd of the Jews knew of his presence there, and they showed up not only because of Jesus but also to get a look at Lazarus, whom he had raised from the dead. [10]But the archpriests conspired to kill Lazarus, too, [11]because on his account many of the Jews went over to believing in Jesus. [12]The next day, the great crowd approaching Jerusalem for the feast heard that Jesus was coming to Jerusalem, [13]and they took palm branches and went out to intercept him, crying out, "Hosanna! Blessed in the name of Adonai is the Coming One,[n] the king of Israel!" [14]And finding a young donkey, Jesus mounted it, as it is written: [15]"Fear not, daughter of Zion! Behold: your king approaches riding a donkey's foal."[o] [16]His disciples did not at first see the significance of these events. Only once Jesus was glorified did they realize these things had been written about him and that they had carried them out.[p] [17]The crowd who were with him when he called Lazarus out of the tomb and raised him from the dead bore witness to everyone else about what they had seen. [18]This is also why the crowd of pilgrims rallied to meet him, because they heard he had performed this sign. [19]Accordingly, the Pharisees said to one another, "You can see your efforts are useless—look! The whole world has gone after him!"[q]

---

dalene, so he has chosen a "safe" substitute, as well as omitting Jesus' blessing. Now it is only the scent of the perfume, not the woman's renown, that "fills the house," a pun on the *oecumene,* or inhabited world, as also in the name Baal-Zebul, "Lord of the House," meaning "Lord of the Inhabited World."

m. Judas is a fictive character representing Christ-betraying Jews. This verse in particular sounds like an anti-Semitic slur, making Jews crooked financiers and greedy cheats.

n. This is based on the entrance liturgy of Pss. 118:26-27, in which "he who comes in the name of the Lord" refers to any pilgrim.

o. Zech. 9:9

p. Here we have an astonishing admission that if any historical event underlies the story at all, it was not construed as a messianic event at the time, only the entrance of a crowd of pilgrims including Jesus, using the entrance liturgy of Pss. 118.

q. This is not mere hyperbole. It is a comment long after the fact that the as-

7

[53]*And each one retired to his dwelling.*

8

[1]*But Jesus went to the Mount of Olives.* [2]*And at dawn, he arrived again at the temple, and all the people came to him, and sitting, he taught them.* [3]*And the scribes and the Pharisees bring in a woman caught committing adultery, and standing her in the midst,* [4]*they say to him, "Teacher, this woman has been caught in the act of committing adultery.* [5]*Now in the Torah, Moses commanded us to stone such transgressors. So what do you say?"* [6]*But they said this to test him, that they might have grounds to accuse him.*[r] *But Jesus stooped down and wrote on the ground with his finger.* [7]*But as they persisted in questioning him, he stood up and said to them, "Let the one of you who is sinless aim the first stone at her."* [8]*And stooping down again, he wrote in the dirt.* [9]*And once they heard this, they left, one by one, beginning with the older men, and he was left alone with the woman standing in front of him.* [10]*And standing up, Jesus said to her, "Woman, where are they? You mean, no one condemned you?"* [11]*And she said to him, "No one, Lord." So Jesus said, "Then I can hardly condemn you, can I? Go your way, and from now on, leave off sinning, all right?"*[s]

2

[13b]And Jesus went up to Jerusalem. [14]And in the temple he discovered those selling oxen and sheep and doves and the moneychangers sitting at their tables. [15]And having braided a whip from ropes, he ejected all from the temple, both the sheep and the oxen, and he poured out the coins of the moneychangers and overturned the tables. [16]And to the ones selling doves, he said, "Get these things out of here! Do not make my Father's house an emporium."[t] [17]His disciples would remember how it is

---

sumed Jewish intent to strangle Christianity in its cradle failed to stop the religion's destined rise to prominence in the empire.

r. Presumably they think he will set aside the Torah and let her go or that he will insist the commandment be carried out despite the lack of Roman authorization. In either case, he circumvents them by getting them to drop the charges.

s. The motif of writing in the dirt recalls Plato's *Meno* dialogue where by drawing geometric figures in the dirt, Socrates demonstrated that an uneducated slave boy already had the knowledge of mathematics within him, waiting to be awakened through the right questions. Here, too, Jesus elicits the answer from his opponents by means of a Socratic pose. This passage does not appear in early copies of the Gospel of John and is almost certainly a later addition.

t. Though it is not unlikely the story preserves some faded memory of the en-

written, "Zeal for your house will consume me."[u] [18]The rulers of the Jews answered and said to him, "What sign can you show to demonstrate your right to do these things?" [19]Jesus answered and said to them, "Destroy this shrine, and in three days I will raise it!" [20]Therefore, the Jewish authorities said, "In forty-six years this shrine was built, and you will raise it up in three days?" [21]But he was referring to the "shrine" of his body. [22]Thus, when he was raised from the dead, his disciples remembered that he said this and they believed both the scripture and the saying of Jesus. [23]And while he was in Jerusalem at the Passover, at the feast, many believed in his name, seeing the signs he was performing. [24]But as for Jesus, he did not trust them because he knew people, [25]nor had he any need for anyone to warn him about people. For he was under no illusions about human nature.

8

[31]Therefore, Jesus said to the Jews who believed in him, "If you persist in my teaching, you will be genuine disciples of mine.[v] [32]And you will learn the truth and the truth will set you free."[w] [33]They replied to him, "We are Abraham's descendants and we have never been enslaved to anyone.[x] What do you mean, we will become free?" [34]Jesus answered them, "Amen, amen: I say to you, 'Everyone committing sin is a slave to sin.'[y] [35]Like Eliezer of Damascus, a slave does not inherit the estate; like Isaac, a son inherits it in perpetuity.[z] [36]Thus, if the son sets you free, you will be really free. [37]Of course you are descendants of Abraham, but you are looking to kill me because my words strike no echo in you. [38]I only speak of what I have seen for myself in the Father's presence; and you, in the same way, do what you have learned from observing your father."

---

try of Simon bar-Gioras into the temple to clean out the "robbers" of John of Gischala on the eve of the temple's destruction, the story may simply conflate various scripture passages, which it seems to do in any case. The "cleansing" must have had in view that of Malachi's messenger of the covenant who will purify the sons of Levi (3:1-30), as well as the oracle of Zech. 14:21b, "And there shall no longer be a trader in the house of the Lord of hosts on that day."

u. Pss. 69:9

v. Luke 14:27; Mark 4:16-20

w. Thomas, saying 2; also a Stoic maxim.

x. This is reminiscent of the self-designation of the Jewish Sethian Gnostics, "the kingless race."

y. Rom. 6:15-19; also a well-known Stoic maxim.

z. Gen. 15:1-4

39They answered and said to him, "Remember, our father is Abraham!"
Jesus says to them, "If you are Abraham's children, act like Abraham!
40But as it is, you want to kill me, a man who has told you the truth which
I heard directly from God. That doesn't sound like Abraham. 41You do
imitate the deeds of your father, though." They said to him, "We are not
bastards of a prostitute. We have one father, God!" 42Jesus said to them,
"If God were your father, you would have loved me. For I came forth
from the Godhead and have appeared. Nor was it my own idea to come,
but he sent me. 43Why is my speech utter gibberish to you? Because you
are deaf to my message. 44You are born of your father, the slanderer, and
you naturally want to do what your father desires. That one was a homi-
cide from the start, and he fell from the truth because the truth is alien to
him. When he lies, he but speaks his own language because he is a liar and
the inventor of lying. 45It is precisely because I speak the truth that you
don't believe me. 46Which of you can point to any sin of mine? Well? If I
speak the truth, why do you not believe me? 47The one born of God hears
God's words clearly enough; that is the reason you cannot hear them: you
are not born of God."[a]

48The Jews answered and said to him, "Don't we have it exactly
right when we say that you are a Samaritan and command a demon?"[b]
49Jesus answered, "I have no demon; rather, in my signs I honor the Father and you dishonor me.[c] 50Not that I seek my own glory, but there is
one who seeks it—and judges! 51Amen, amen: I say to you, if anyone
keeps my commandment, he will by no means see death, age after age."
52The Jews said to him, "Now we know you are a raving demoniac!
Abraham died! And the prophets! And you say, 'If anyone keeps my
commandment, he will by no means taste death, age after age'? 53Surely
you are not greater than Abraham, our father, who died and the prophets
who died? Just who are you making yourself out to be?" 54Jesus said, "If
I glorify myself, my glory is empty. The one who glorifies me is my Fa-

a. 1 Cor. 2:13-14. This is pure Gnosticism, similar to Sethianism whereby humans spring from either the heavenly Sethite line or the infernal Cainite line. Salvation is the natural heritage of the first, impossible for the second. Bultmann claims John's is an existential "dualism of decision," but so was Gnosticism, and even Calvinism: it was up to the hearer to decide which category he belonged in.

b. They suspect he is Simon Magus, who claimed to have appeared previously among the Jews. It may have been a Jewish polemic against Jesus to say he was really Simon and used the demons and ghosts of the slain to work miracles.

c. Mark 3:22, 28-30

ther, of whom you say, 'He is our God.' [55]And you have never known him, but I know him.[d] And if I said I did not know him, I would be a liar like you. But in fact, I do know him and I keep his commandment. [56]Your father Abraham was glad to see my day, and he glimpsed it and rejoiced." [57]Therefore, the Jews said to him, "You have not even fifty years on you and you have seen Abraham?" [58]Jesus said to them, "Amen, amen: I say to you, before Abraham came into being, I am!" [59]At this, they picked up stones to throw at him, but Jesus vanished before their eyes and left the temple.[e]

3

[1]Now there was a man belonging to the Pharisee sect, Nicodemus by name, a ruler of the Jews.[f] [2]This man came to him one night and said to him, "Rabbi, we know you are a teacher sent from God, for no one can perform these signs that you perform unless God is with him. Tell me, then, what must I do to inherit age-long life?" [3]Jesus answered and said to him, "Amen, amen: I tell you, unless one is born from above, he is not able to see the kingdom of God." [4]Nicodemus says to him, "How can an old man be born? Can he enter his mother's womb to be born a second time?" [5]Jesus answered, "Amen, amen: I tell you, unless one is born from the union of water and spirit, he is not able to enter into the kingdom of God. [6]The offspring of the flesh is flesh, the offspring of the spirit is spirit. [7]Do not be so surprised that I told you, you are required to be born from above. [8]After all, the wind of the Spirit blows where it wishes, and you hear its sound, but you do not know where it has come from or where it is off to next. Everyone born from the Spirit is the same way." [9]Nicodemus said to him, "How can these things happen?" [10]Jesus answered and said to him, "Here you are a teacher of Israel and you do not grasp these things? [11]Amen, amen: I tell you, we speak of what we know and witness to what we have seen[g] and you do not accept our testimony. [12]If I told you the earthly mysteries and you do not believe, how will you ever believe if I disclose to you the heavenly mysteries? [13]And no one has gone up

d. This is outright Marcionism: Jesus' Father was hitherto unknown and had been wrongly identified with the Hebrew God.

e. A vestige of docetism (see Luke 4:29-30).

f. Nicodemus means "victor over the people." It was a real name, but here it marks the character as a "narrative-man" (Tzvetan Todorov), a simple embodiment of his function in the story and thus as a fictive character.

g. 1 John 1:1-3

into the heaven except the one who descended from the heaven, the one like a son of man.[h]

[31]The one coming from above ranks above all, the one who is a creature of the earth is earthly and speaks of the earthly mysteries. The one coming from heaven is above all.[i] [32]What he has seen and heard, he testifies to this and no one accepts his testimony. [33]Whoever does accept his testimony has attested that God is true. [34]For he whom God sent speaks God's oracles, for he does not give out the Spirit sparingly. [35]The Father loves the Son and has delegated everything to him. [36]The one who believes in the Son has age-long life. But the one disobeying the Son will not see the life, for he remains the object of the wrath of God."

12

[20]Some Greeks were going up to Jerusalem to worship at the feast. [21]So these men approached Philip, the one from Beth-Saida in the Galilee,[j] and asked him, saying, "Lord, we wish to see Jesus." [22]Philip comes and tells Andreas, and Andreas and Philip come and tell Jesus. [23]And Jesus says to them, "The time has come for man to be glorified. [24]Amen, amen: I say to you, unless the grain of wheat falls into the ground and dies, it remains alone. But if it dies, it bears much fruit. [25]The one clutching his life will lose it, while the one ready to renounce his life in this world will trade it for age-long life.[k] [26]If anyone serves me, let him follow me;[l] and where I am, my servant too will be. If anyone serves me, the Father will honor him.

[27]"Just now I find myself deeply disturbed. And what am I to say—Father, rescue me from this fateful hour? This is why I came—to meet this hour![m] [28]Father! Glorify your name!" In answer, a voice sounded from the sky, "I both glorified it and will glorify it once more!" [29]The crowd standing there heard it and said it had thundered.[n] Others

---

h. Not even Elijah? Enoch? This sounds like a Gnostic/Marcionite denial of the Old Testament.

i. Thomas, saying 77; 1 Cor. 15:44-49

j. Is this an attempt to differentiate him from Philip, one of the seven in Acts?

k. Phil. 2:6-11

l. Verses 24-25 are John's version of Mark 8:34-35.

m. Notice how disdainfully John repudiates the Synoptic Gethsemane scene (cf. Mark 14:34-36).

n. Rev. 10:3-4

said, "An angel has spoken to him."[o] [30]Jesus answered and said, "This voice came not for my sake but for yours."[p]

[31]"Now is the judgment of this world. Now shall the archon of this world be cast outside it.[q] [32]And as for me, once I am lifted up, I will rally all to myself as a battle standard."[r] [33]He said this to signal what mode of execution he was about to undergo.

7

[33]Therefore, Jesus said, "I am with you for such a short time before I go to the one who sent me.[s] [34]You will seek me and not find me,[t] and where I am, you cannot come."[u] [35]Therefore, the Jews said to each other, "Where is this fellow about to go that we will not find him? Surely he is not about to journey to the Diaspora among the Greeks, to teach the Greeks? [36]What is the meaning of this thing he said, 'You will seek me and will not find, and where I am, you cannot come'?"

8

[21]So he said to them again, "I go and you will look for me too late, and you will die in your sin because where I go you cannot come."[v] [22]So the Jews said, "Surely he does not intend to kill himself when he says, 'Where I go you cannot come'?" [23]And he said to them, "You belong below, I belong above. You are of this world, I am not of this world.[w] [24]That is why I said to you that you will die in your sins. For if you do not believe that I am ____, you must die in your sins!" [25]Therefore, they said to him, "You are who?" Jesus said to them, "Why do I waste my time talking to you? [26]I have many things to say about you—and to judge. But the one who sent me is true, and what I heard from him I speak in the world." [27]They did not realize he was referring to the Father. [28]There-

---

o. Acts 23:9

p. By the time this gospel was written, Luke's text already contained the insertion (22:43) of a strengthening angel, and John repudiates the whole idea as unworthy of Christ.

q. According to Gnostics and Marcionites, the ruler (archon) of the world was the Demiurge, the Creator God of Judaism, but not the Father of Jesus.

r. This, if anything, must be Jesus' response to the request of the Greeks to see him, just as the comment of the Pharisees in v. 35 alludes to it.

s. John 1:14

t. Luke 17:22

u. Matt. 6:20b

v. Luke 13:24-27; Matt. 25:10-12

w. Hear the voice of the Gnostic revealer!

fore, Jesus said to them, "When you lift up the man, then you will know that I am _____ and that I do nothing on my own initiative, but I speak the things the Father taught me. [29]You ask, 'Where is your Father?' Why, the one who sent me is with me; he has not abandoned me because I always do the things that please him."[x] [30]As he said these things, many believed in him.

12

[34]Therefore, the crowd answered him, "We always heard from the Torah that the Christ remains till the end of the age, so how can you say 'the man is obliged to be lifted up'? Who is this man?" [35]So Jesus said to them, "You have the light among you for only a little time now. Walk in the light while you still can so that darkness does not take you by surprise. The one walking around in the dark has no idea where he is going.
[36]While you have the light, believe in the light."

3

[14]"And as Moses held aloft the serpent in the desert, so is a human being obliged to be held aloft, [15]so everyone who believes in him may have age-long life. [16]For God loved the world so much that he gave the Son, the only-begotten, so everyone who believes in him may not perish but may instead have age-long life. [17]For God did not send the Son into the world so he might judge the world, but that the world might be saved through him. [18]The one who believes in him is not judged; the unbelieving one has been judged already because he has not believed in the name of the only-begotten Son of God. [19]And this is the verdict: The light has come into the world and mankind loved the darkness rather than the light, for their actions were wicked. [20]Everyone doing evil hates the light and shuns the light for fear that his actions, once exposed, will be rebuked. [21]On the other hand, the one who lives by the truth emerges into the light without hesitation so it may become evident to all that his deeds have been done in accordance with the will of God."[y]

12

[44]But Jesus cried out and said, "The one who believes in me does not believe in me, but in the one who sent me,[z] [45]and whoever beholds me be-

x. Here is a critique of the crucifixion scene in Mark 15:34: even though Jesus is lifted up on the cross, his Father has by no means forsaken him.

y. Nicodemus, for example, showed himself unwilling to step fully into the light, visiting Jesus under cover of darkness.

z. This sounds like a subordinationist gloss to stifle the growing Christ cult

holds the one who has sent me.[a] 46My mission was to illuminate the
world so that everyone who believes in me may not remain in darkness.
47And if anyone hears my words and fails to keep them in practice, I do
not judge him; for my mission was not to judge the world, but to save the
world.[b] 48However, anyone who rejects me and dismisses my words does
have a judge: the very words which I spoke will judge him on the last day!
49Because what I said was not my own idea, but that of the Father who
sent me—he commanded me what to say and what to teach. 50And I
know full well that to obey his commandment is rewarded with age-long
life. Whatever I speak is what the Father has told me to speak. Thus I
speak, 36bso that you may become sons of light."

Jesus said these things, left, and went into hiding. 37But though he
performed so many signs in their presence, they did not believe in him,
38so the prediction of Isaiah the prophet might be fulfilled when he said:
"Adonai, who has believed our report? And the mighty arm of Adonai—
to whom was it revealed?" 39For this reason, it was never possible for
them to believe because, again, Isaiah said, 40"He has blinded their eyes
and made their heart stubborn to prevent them from using their eyes to
see and their heart to understand; otherwise they might turn back to me
and I must cure them." 41Isaiah said these things because he glimpsed his
glory and spoke about him.[c] 42Despite this, even many of the rulers believed in him; but because of the Pharisees, they did not confess their faith
to avoid being banned from the synagogue, 43for the esteem of their colleagues meant more to them than the glory they might receive from God.

13

1Now before the feast of the Passover, Jesus, mindful that his time
was short till he must return from this world to the Father, loved his own
while he was in the world and he loved them to the very end. 2And when
supper was underway, despite the accuser having by now planted in the
heart of Judas of Simon, the False One, the idea of betraying him, 3and
knowing equally that the Father had put everything under his control and
that he had come forth from the Godhead and goes to God, 4he gets up
from the supper, he rises from the table, and puts aside his garments, and

---

and refocus Christian devotion on God the Father, as in 1 Cor. 11:3; Mark 10:18; John 14:28b.

a. A counter-correction in favor of Patripassianism: Jesus is the Father.

b. Luke 9:55c

c. 1 Pet. 1:10-12

taking a towel, he tied it around his waist. [5]Then he pours water into a basin and started washing the feet of the disciples and to wipe them off with the towel he was wearing.[d] [6]So he comes to Simon Peter. He says to him, "Lord, you are going to wash my feet? Rather, I should be washing yours!"[e] [7]Jesus answered and said to them, "Let it be so now. You don't yet understand what I am doing, but eventually you will understand." [8]Peter says to him, "Lord, there is no way you are ever going to wash my feet as long as the world lasts!" Jesus answered him, "Unless I wash you, you have no place with me." [9]Simon Peter says to him, "Well, in that case, Lord, not only the feet, but the hands and head as well!" [10]Jesus says to him, "One who has just bathed does not need to wash *except for washing the dust of travel from his feet*, but is clean all over. And you are clean, though not all of you." [11]For he was aware of the one betraying him; that is why he said, "Not all of you are clean."

[12]So when he had washed their feet, donned his garments, and reclined again, he said to them, "Do you understand what I have done for you? [13]You call me the teacher and the Lord, and rightly so, for I am. [14]Therefore, if I, the Lord and the teacher, washed your feet, you too ought to be willing to wash one another's feet. [15]The reason I gave you an example was so you may do what I did for you.[f] [16]Amen, amen: I say to you, a slave is not greater than his lord, nor an apostle greater than the one sending him. [17]If you know these things, blessed are you as you do them. [18]I am not referring to all of you; I know the men I chose, but I picked one of you to fill the role assigned in scripture: 'My own dinner companion kicked me when I fell.'[g] [19]From now on I am going to tell you what to expect before it happens so that when it does, you may believe that I am_____. [20]Amen, amen: I say to you, anyone who welcomes whomever I may send welcomes me, and anyone who welcomes me welcomes him who sent me."[h]

[21]Having said these things, Jesus was deeply agitated and testified,[i]

---

d. Jesus acts as both host and household slave, doing what the slave would do to welcome his guests (Luke 7:44).

e. Cf. Matt. 3:14; note also the similarity with the anointing of Jesus (12:3).

f. The whole scene seems to have originated as a dramatization of the metaphor in Luke 22:24-27.

g. Pss. 41:9

h. 3 John 5-8

i. This is implied every time he says "Amen, amen," which is a solemn affirmation formula. It is exactly equivalent to the formula in the Pastoral Epistles,

saying, "Amen, amen: I say to you, 'One of you will betray me!'" [22]The disciples looked at each other in confusion, wondering who he means. [23]One of his disciples was reclining next to Jesus, and he was Jesus' favorite. [24]Simon Peter nods to this one, gesturing, "Tell us who he is referring to." [25]So leaning back, the one reclining next to Jesus whispers to him, "Lord, who is it?" [26]So Jesus answers, "It is the one whom I will give the bread after I dip it in the herb sauce. So dipping the bread, he takes it and gives it to Judas of Simon, the False One. [27]Then, along with the bread, the Satan entered into him. Therefore, Jesus says to him, "What you are going to do, do it quickly!" [28]But none of those reclining at table were aware of any of this, [29]some assuming that since Judas had charge of the money bag, Jesus meant "Buy what we need for the feast" or that he should go make a donation to the poor. [30]As soon as he took the bread, that one left at once and night had fallen.

[31]So when he had gone out, Jesus says, "Just now the man was glorified, and God was glorified in him. [32]If God was glorified in him, God will both welcome him into his own glory and will glorify him at once. [33]Children, I am with you only a little longer now. You will look for me, and as I told the Jews that where I am headed you cannot follow, so I say to you now. [34]A new commandment I give you, that you love one another as I have loved you. [35]By this token, all will be able to distinguish you as my disciples, if you keep love kindled among you.

15

[9]"Just as the Father loved me, I also loved you; dwell in my love. [10]If you keep my commandments, you will dwell in my love as I have kept the commandments of the Father and dwell in his love. [11]I have told you these things so I may have cause to rejoice over you and that you may be filled with joy. [12]This is my commandment: that you love one another as I loved you. [13]No one has greater love than this: that anyone should lay down his life for his friends.[j] [14]You are my friends if you do what I command you.[k] [15]I no longer call you slaves because a slave is not privy to his lord's affairs; but you I have called friends because everything I have heard from the Father I communicated to you.[l] [16]It was not you who

"The saying is trustworthy and deserving of full acceptance" (1 Tim. 1:15; 3:1; 4:9; 2 Tim. 2:11; Titus 3:8).

j. Rom. 5:6-8

k. The conditionality of God's love is clear in John: 14:21, 23; 15:10, 14.

l. Judging by this gospel, precious little has been communicated to the disci-

chose to follow me, but I who chose you and appointed you to go forth and bear fruit and for that fruit to remain till harvest so that whatever you may ask the Father in my name he may give you. [17]These things I command you so that you will love one another."

14

[15]"If you love me, you will observe my commandments. [16]I will petition the Father, and he will give you another Paraclete[m] to be with you throughout the age, [17]the Spirit of Truth, which the world cannot receive because it does not see it[n] and does not recognize it. You recognize it, though, because he remains with you for now and soon will be inside you. [18]I will not abandon you like orphans. I am coming back to you. [19]Just a little while now and the world will have seen the last of me, but you will behold me because I live and you will live. [20]In that day, you will realize that I am in my Father, and you are in me, and I am in you. [21]The one who has my commandments and keeps them, he is the one who loves me. And the one who loves me will be loved by my Father, and I will love him and I will manifest myself to him."

[22]Judas, not the False One, says to him, "Lord, what can have happened that you are about to manifest yourself to us and not to the world at large?"[o] [23]Jesus answered and said to him, "If anyone loves me, he will keep my commandments and my Father will love him, and we will come to him and we will make our dwelling with him. [24]The one who does not love me does not keep my commandments, and the statement you are hearing is not mine but comes from the Father who sent me."

15

[1]"I am the true vine and my Father is the vine-dresser. [2]Every branch in me not bearing fruit, he removes it, and every one bearing fruit, he purifies it so it may bear more fruit. [3]Now you are pure via the teaching I have imparted to you; dwell in me and I will dwell in you. [4]Just as the branch is not able to bear fruit by itself apart from the vine, neither can

---

ples. John provides a blank check for future Christian teachers, whether the Paraclete or, as in Acts, the bishops, to add subsequent Christian teachings.

m. Paraclete may also be translated as "advocate"—the ascended Jesus himself, as envisioned earlier in this verse, representing mortals before the throne of God like the angel of Yahve in Zech. 3. Insofar as the Paraclete is supposed to be the Holy Spirit, the "court advocate" image will have come from sayings like Mark 13:11; Matt. 10:19-20.

n. Worldly empiricism: John 3:8-12.

o. Luke 17:20-21; 19:11 ff.; Acts 1:6 ff. A rejection of futuristic eschatology.

you unless you dwell in me. [5]I am the vine, you are the branches. The one dwelling in me, with me in him, this one bears much fruit because apart from me you are able to do nothing. [6]Unless one dwells in me, he is cast away like the branch and dried up, and they collect them and toss them into the fire and they are consumed. [7]If you dwell in me and my words dwell in you, ask whatever you wish and it shall happen for you.[p] [8]My Father is glorified in this, that you bear much fruit, and in this way you will be my disciples.

[18]If the world hates you, remember: before you, it has hated me. [19]If you belonged to the world, the world would have loved its own kind; but because you do not belong to the world, but I selected you out of the world, for this reason the world hates you.[q] [20]Remember what I said to you: a slave is not greater than his lord. Whoever persecuted me will persecute you, too. Whoever kept my teaching will keep yours, too. [21]But they will do all these things to you because of my name, because they do not know the one who sent me.[r] [22]Had I not come and spoken to them, they would not have had sin counted against them, but now they have nothing to hide behind. [23]Whoever hates me also hates my Father. [24]If I had not performed deeds among them that no one else ever performed, they would not have sin counted against them. But as it is, they have both seen and hated both me and my Father [25]But it happened so that the oracle written in their Torah may be fulfilled: 'They hated me gratuitously.'[s] [26]When the Paraclete comes, whom I will send you from the Father, the Spirit of Truth which proceeds from the Father, that one will testify about me;[t] [27]you, too, will testify because you are with me since the beginning."[u]

16

[1]"These things I have spoken to you to prevent your being scandalized. [2]They will ban you from the synagogue,[v] but it will get worse: peo-

p. Mark 11:23-24. The fig tree there has become a vine here.

q. This is pure Gnostic/Marcionite soteriology.

r. This rings of Marcionism, with Jesus' Father a deity unknown to Jews.

s. Pss. 35:19; 69:4

t. An example would be this very gospel, "channeled," so to speak, to the amanuensis.

u. Acts 1:21-22

v. Thus the threats of excommunication in Jesus' own day (John 9:22; 12:42) are anachronisms. The story is set in the evangelist's time, including the whole notion of "believing in" Jesus, something befitting Jesus as a sect figurehead or cause, not a living contemporary.

ple will eventually come to regard killing you as an act of religious devotion. 3And they will do these things because they knew neither the Father nor me. 4But I have told you all this so that when the time for these events arrives, you may remember that I told you about them and not think something has gone horribly wrong. I did not tell you these things at first because I was with you.[w] 5Now I am going back to the one who sent me, and not one of you so much as asks me, 'Where are you going?' 6But because I have said these things to you, grief has overcome you. 7But to tell you the truth, it is good for you that I go. Because if I do not go away, the Paraclete can never come. Only if I go can I send him to you.[x] 8And, once he comes, he will rebuke the world about sin, about righteousness, and about judgment:[y] 9about sin because they do not believe in me; 10about righteousness because I am going to the Father and you no longer see me and someone must take up the task; 11about judgment because the archon of this world has been judged.

12I have many more things to tell you, but they would be too much for you to deal with now. 13But when that one comes, the Spirit of Truth, he will guide you into all the rest of the truth. For he will not speak his own opinions, but he will relay what he hears and he will announce future events to you.[z] 14He will glorify me because he will receive revelation from my treasury and announce it to you. 15All that the Father has is mine, which is why I said he will receive from what is mine and will announce it to you.[a] 16Just a little while now and you will no longer see me, and again after a little while you will see me."

17Therefore, some among his disciples said to one another, "What does he mean, 'A little while and you do not see me, and again a little while and you will see me again' and 'because I am going to the Father'?" 18The others answered, "What does he mean by 'a little while'? What on earth is he talking about?" 19Jesus knew they wanted to question him and

---

w. Where, then, is Jesus when he says these words? Not "with them"? He is apparently in heaven, speaking through the Paraclete—the evangelist or his source (Luke 24:44).

x. It seems quite likely the resurrection of Jesus and the coming of the Paraclete are really the same thing in the evangelist's mind.

y. Acts 24:25

z. The synagogue ban would be one such example. Of course, the Paraclete is the evangelist, ideally represented in the narrative as the beloved or "favorite" disciple.

a. This is a pedantic gloss attempting to keep Jesus' own godlike prerogatives in perspective vis-à-vis his Father's.

he said to them, "Are you asking one another about my having said, 'A
little while and you do not see me, and again a little while you will see
me?' [20]Amen, amen: I say to you, you will sob and lament and the world
will celebrate; you will be grieved, but your grief will be transformed into
joy. [21]The woman giving birth is in pain because her time has come, but
when she bears the child, she no longer remembers the distress because of
her joy that a human being was born into the world. [22]So you now indeed
ache with grief, but I will see you again and your heart will rejoice and
that joy will be inextinguishable. [23]And in that day, it will all have become plain to you."

14

[1]"Do not let your hearts be troubled! Believe in God. Believe in me,
too. [2]Where my Father dwells, there are many abodes. If there were not, I
should have told you that I go to prepare a place for you. [3]And in any
case, I will come back to you and welcome you to join me so that you,
too, may be where I am. [4]As for my destination, you know the way."
[5]The twin says to him, "Lord, we do not even know your destination!
How can we possibly know the way?" [6]Jesus says to him, "I am the way!
And the truth and the life. No one comes to the Father except by me. [7]If
you had recognized me, you would have recognized my Father, too. So
now, you know him and have seen him." [8]Philip says to him, "Yes, Lord,
show us the Father! That will satisfy us!" [9]Jesus says to him, "I am with
you such a long time and you have not recognized me, Philip! Anyone
who sees me has seen the Father.[b] How can you still ask, 'Show us the Father'? [10]Don't you believe that I am in the Father and that the Father is in
me? The things I say to you are not my own invention; rather, my Father
who remains in me does his own deeds. [11]Believe that I am in the Father
and the Father is in me. At least, believe the deeds that I do that bespeak
his presence.[c]

[12]"Amen, amen: I tell you, whoever believes in me, the deeds I do, he
too shall perform; even greater than these will he do, for I am going to the
Father and someone must do them.[d] [13]And whatever you ask in my name,
this I will do, that the Father may be glorified in the Son. [14]If you ask me
anything in my name, I will do it."

---

b. Both barrels of Patripassianism!

c. Verses 10-11 sound like clumsy and pedantic Christological backpedaling by a glossator who blanches at the too-high estimate of Christ in v. 9.

d. Mark 16:17-19

16

23b“Amen, amen: I tell you, whatever you request of the Father in my
name, he will give you.[e] 24Up to now, you requested nothing in my name;
go ahead: ask and you will receive[f] so that your joy may be undiluted by
any sense of lack. 25I have spoken these things by way of analogy; a time
is coming when I will no longer speak to you in figures, but I will inform
you plainly about the Father. 26At that time, you will ask in my name and
I tell you not that I will petition the Father on your behalf, 27for the Father himself loves you because you have loved me and have believed that I
emerged from the Godhead. 28I emerged out of the Father and have come
into the world; I abandon the world again and head back to the Father.”

29His disciples say, “All right! Now you are speaking clearly without
retreating into figures of speech. 30Now it is plain that you know all
things and your words do not need elucidation. Now we’re clear on it:
you emerged from the Godhead.” 31Jesus answered them, “You finally
believe that, do you? 32Behold! A time is coming—in fact, it has arrived—when you scatter, each to his own hiding place, abandoning me.
But I am not alone because the Father is with me. 33I have said these
things to reassure you. In the world, you have only distress, but cheer up!
I have defeated the world!”

14

25“These things I have said to you while remaining with you. 26But
the Paraclete, the Spirit, the saint the Father will send in my name, he will
teach you all things and remind you of all things that I told you.[g]

27“I bequeath you peace; I give you my peace. Not as the world gives
do I give you, but without stint. Do not let your heart be agitated, nor let
it be fearful. 28You heard me tell you, ‘I go and come back to you.’ If you
loved me, you would rejoice that I am going to the Father because the Father is greater than I. 29And now I have told you before it happens so that

---

e. Matt. 18:19-20

f. Matt. 7:7-8

g. A Gnostic/Ismail’i/Druze doctrine: divine revelators emanate from the Godhead in “yoked” pairs (*syzygies*) and appear in the world as “the Proclaimer” (Adam, Noah, Abraham, Moses, Jesus, Muhammad, al-Hakim), immediately followed by “the Foundation” (Seth, Shem, Ismail, Aaron, Peter, Ali, al-Hamsa), who explains the esoteric meaning of the revelation propounded exoterically by his predecessor. In the Gospel of John, the beloved disciple is intended as the Paraclete, who amplifies and clarifies the teaching of Jesus. Cf. John 1:18; 13:23-25. The author’s contemporary Montanus, if the two are not in fact the same person, made the same claim.

when it does happen, you may believe. 30I will no longer speak much with you, for the archon of the world is on his way and he has no claim on me;[h] 31but so the world may know I love the Father, and as the Father commanded me, so I do. Get up. Let us leave here."

13

36Simon Peter says to him, "Lord, just where are you going?" Jesus answered him, "Where I am headed, you are not at present able to follow; but rest assured, you will follow me in due time." 37Peter says to him, "Lord, why can I not follow you yet? I will gladly lay down my life for you!" 38Jesus answers, "Oh, will you, now? Amen, amen: I say to you, cock-crow will not roll around till you have repudiated me three times!"

17

1Jesus said all this, then looked up to the sky and said, "Father, the time has arrived. Glorify your Son so your Son may glorify you, 2as you gave him authority over all flesh so that he may give age-long life to all you have given him. 3And this is the secret of age-long life: to know you for the only true God and to know him whom you sent, Jesus Christ.[i] 4I glorified you on earth, finishing the task you assigned me. 5And now, Father, glorify me alongside yourself with the splendor I shared with you before the world existed. 6I revealed your name to the mortals you gave me out of the world. They were yours and you gave them to me, and they have kept your command.[j] 7Now they have understood that all the words you gave me to speak are really from you, 8because I gave them the words you gave me and they welcomed them and knew for certain that I emerged from you, and they believed that you did send me. 9I petition you on their behalf. I do not petition you on behalf of the world, but on behalf of those you have given me because they are yours. 10And all that are mine are yours, and yours are mine, and I have been glorified in them. 11And I am no longer in the world and they are in the world, and I come to you. Holy Father, keep them faithful to your name you have given me

h. This is why the docetic Christ did not take human flesh, because he would then have been beholden to the Creator. See Thomas, saying 21a.

i. This is overt theological anachronism on the lips of Jesus. Rather, the whole prayer must be based on the testamentary farewell prayer of the Paraclete, the beloved disciple, who we are to understand died just before the compilation of the gospel (21:23).

j. They already shared the divine essence, though it was lost in the cosmos of matter. The Father sent the redeemer into the material world to rescue the elect by means of revealing the true Godhead to them, unknown to Judaism.

so they may be one as we are. [12]When I was with them, I kept them faithful to your name, which you gave me, and I guarded them and none of them perished except for the Son of Perdition so the scripture might be fulfilled. [13]But now I come to you and I speak these things in the world so they may experience the joy I feel. [14]I have given them your revelation, and the world immediately hated them because they belong to the world no more than I do.[k] [15]I do not ask you to remove them from the world, but that you should keep them from the clutches of the wicked. [16]They do not belong to the world, just I do not belong to the world. [17]Consecrate them by the truth. Your promise is truth. [18]As you sent me into the world, I also sent them into the world; [19]and on their behalf I consecrate myself to the end that they, too, may be consecrated by the truth. [20]I petition you not only on their behalf but also on behalf of those who believe in me through their witness, [21]so that all may be one, as you, Father, are in me and I am in you, that they, too, may be in us so the world may believe that you sent me. [22]And I have given to them the glory you gave me, the glory of being one as we are one—[23]I in them and you in me—so they may be perfectly one, so the world may know that you sent me and loved them as you loved me. [24]Father, as for those you have given me, I ask that those may join me where I am, to behold my glory, which you gave me before the founding of the world because you loved me. [25]Righteous Father, truly the world did not know you, but I knew you and these knew that you sent me. [26]And I communicated your name[l] to them and will communicate it so that the love with which you loved me may be in them and that I may be in them."

18

[1]Having said these things, Jesus went forth with his disciples across the Brook Kidron where there was a garden, into which he and his disciples entered. [2]Judas, too, the one betraying him, knew the place because Jesus often met with his disciples there. [3]So Judas, taking the band of henchmen from the archpriests and from the Pharisees, arrives there with lanterns, lamps, and weapons. [4]Jesus, fully aware of all that was about to happen to him, stepped forth and says to them, "Who are you looking

---

k. The Gnostic redeemer vouchsafes the essential divinity of select mortals. Once exposed, they are marked as enemies of the archon and his angelic henchmen.

l. The familiar divine name Yahve cannot be intended here, so he must mean simply "Father," which makes sense only as the name of the hitherto-unknown Marcionite deity.

for?" [5]They answered, "Jesus the Nazorean." He tells them, "I am!" Now Judas, the one betraying him, also stood with them. [6]And when he told them, "I am," they were knocked back and fell to the ground.[m] [7]So he asked them again, "Who are you looking for?" And they said, "Jesus the Nazorean." [8]Jesus answered, "I told you that I am he, so if it is I you seek, let these men go," [9]so his prediction might come true that "those you have given me, I lost none of them." [10]Simon Peter, having a sword, unsheathed it and struck a clumsy blow at the slave of the archpriest, hacking off his right ear. The slave's name was Malchus. [11]Therefore, Jesus said to Peter, "Plunge the sword into the sheathe! The cup which the Father has given me—shall I not drink it?"[n]

[12]So the band and the commander and the henchmen of the Jews apprehended Jesus and tied him up, [13]and led him first to Annas, for he was the father-in-law of Caiaphas. [19]So the archpriest questioned Jesus about his disciples and about his teaching. [20]Jesus answered him, "I have spoken plainly to the world. I always taught in a synagogue and in the temple where all the Jews assemble, and I spoke nothing secretly.[o] [21]Why interrogate me? Question the ones who heard what I spoke to them. Behold, these know what I said." [22]When he said this, one of the attendants standing by cuffed Jesus, saying, "You dare address the archpriest that way?" [23]Jesus retorted, "If I said something amiss, what was it? But if I said nothing wrong, why hit me?"[p] [24]Therefore Annas sent him tied up to Caiaphas the archpriest.

[13b]It was Caiaphas, serving as archpriest for that year, [14]who advised the Jews that it was better for one man to die on behalf of the people.

[15]And Simon Peter and another disciple followed Jesus. And that disciple was an acquaintance of the archpriest and accompanied Jesus into the court of the archpriest. [16]But Peter waited at the door outside. And

m. The artificiality of this "sword of his mouth" miracle is evident in that it leaves no impact on the scene. No one says anything about it, contrary to the analogous situation of 2 Kings 1:13-14. It is the narrative equivalent to Matt. 26:53.

n. The author again repudiates the Synoptic Gethsemane.

o. This must be a lie unless, as is otherwise evident, the esoteric teachings in this gospel represent later elucidations by the evangelist, the Paraclete, for the benefit of the readers, not anything the original disciples ever heard. At any rate, John has most likely borrowed it from Plato's *Apology* 33b, where Socrates says to his judges, "If anyone says that he has learned anything from me, or that he heard anything privately that the others did not hear, be assured that he is not telling the truth."

p. Acts 23:2-5. This is a repudiation of the unbecoming meekness of Jesus before his accusers in the Synoptics and 1 Pet. 2:23.

the other disciple, the one acquainted with the archpriest, went to the woman keeping the door and she admitted Peter. [17]Therefore, the serving girl at the door said to Peter, "Aren't you one of this man's disciples, too?" He says, "I am not!" [18]And the slaves and the attendants stood by a fire they had made since it was cold, and they were warming themselves. Peter, too, was standing with them and warming himself.

[25]So they said to him, "Aren't you also one of his disciples?" He denied and said, "I am not." [26]One of the archpriest's slaves, a relative of the one whose ear Peter had severed, says, "Didn't I see you in the garden with him?" [27]So Peter denied it again, and at once a rooster crowed.

[28]So they led Jesus from Caiaphas to the praetorium. It was early and they did not actually set foot in the praetorium so as to avoid defilement and to be able to eat the Passover. [29]So Pilatus went outside to them and says, "What accusation do you bring against this man?" [30]They answered and said, "Rest assured, if he weren't an evil doer, we wouldn't be bringing him to you. Can we leave it at that?" [31]So Pilatus said to them, "Then you take him and judge him by your own law." The Jews said to him, "There's one small problem. It is not legal for us to execute anyone." [32]They sought Roman execution so Jesus' prediction might come true as to the manner of his death. [33]So Pilatus went back into the praetorium and called for Jesus and said to him, "So you are the king of the Jews." [34]Jesus answered, "Is this your own opinion or did others prompt you?" [35]Pilatus answered, "Am I a Jew? It was your nation and the archpriests who handed you over to me. What did you do?" [36]Jesus answered, "My kingdom is not in this world. If my kingdom was in this world, my retainers would have fought to avoid handing me over to the Jews. For now, my kingdom is not an earthly one." [37]So Pilatus said, "But you are a king?" Jesus answered, "You say that I am a king. For this I have been born and for this I have come into the world, to witness of the truth. Everyone who belongs to the truth recognizes my voice." [38]Pilatus says to him, "What is truth?"

And having said this, he went back out to the Jews and tells them, "I can find no crime in him. [39]And there is that custom of yours that I should release one prisoner to you at the Passover. So do you want me to release to you the king of the Jews?" [40]So they shouted again, saying, "Not this fellow, but Bar-Abbas!" Bar-Abbas was a brigand.

19

[1]So then Pilatus sent Jesus to be flogged. [2]And the soldiers made a wreath of acanthus leaves and placed it on his head and draped a purple

garment about him, [3]and they approached him and said, "Hail, king of the Jews!" And they dealt him blows. [4]And Pilatus went outside again and says to them, "Behold, I am bringing him out to you to show you I find no crime in him." [5]So Jesus came forth wearing the wreath of acanthus leaves and the purple garment. And he says to them, "Behold the man!" [6]So when the archpriests and the attendants saw him, they shouted, "Crucify! Crucify!" Pilatus says to them, "You take him and crucify, for I find no crime in him!" [7]The Jews answered him, "We have a law, and according to that law he must die because he styled himself a son of God!" [8]So when Pilatus heard this news, he felt a chill.

[9]And he went back into the praetorium and says to Jesus, "Where are you from? Heaven or this world?" But Jesus did not deign to respond. [10]So Pilatus says to him, "You will not speak to me? Don't you realize I have the authority to release you and I have the authority to crucify you?" [11]Jesus answered, "You should have no authority over me at all had it not been delegated to you from above; therefore, the one who handed me over to you has a greater sin." [12]Based on this, Pilatus redoubled his efforts to release him. But the Jews shouted, saying, "If you release this fellow, you are no friend of Caesar! Anyone who calls himself a king is automatically speaking against Caesar." [13]So when he heard these words, Pilatus brought Jesus outside and sat on the judgment seat in a place called the Pavement, or in Hebrew, Gabbatha. [14]It was now the day of preparation for Passover, about the sixth hour.[q] And he says to the Jews, "Look! Your king!" [15]Therefore, they shouted, "Take him! Take him! Crucify him!" Pilatus taunts them, "What? Crucify your king?" The archpriests answered, "We have no king but Caesar!" [16]Then he handed him over to be crucified.

Therefore they took Jesus, [17]and carrying his cross by himself,[r] he went out to the site called "Place of a Skull," which in Hebrew is called Golgotha, [18]where they crucified him[s]—and with him two others on this side and that, with Jesus in the middle. [19]And Pilatus also wrote a title and attached it to the cross, and it was written "Jesus the Nazorean, the King of the Jews." [20]Thus many of the pilgrims read the title because the place Jesus was crucified was near the city and it had been written in Hebrew, in Latin, and in Greek. [21]Therefore, the archpriests of the Jews ob-

---

q. 12:00 noon.

r. A repudiation of the Synoptic version where Jesus appears unable to bear his cross.

s. Pss. 22:16b

jected to Pilatus, saying, "It should not say, 'The King of the Jews,' but rather, 'This man said, I am King of the Jews.'" 22Pilatus replied, "What I have written, I have written."

23So when the soldiers crucified Jesus, they took his garments and divided them into four portions, one for each of them, and the tunic. As for the tunic, it was seamless, woven in one piece from the top. 24Therefore, they said to one another, "Let's not tear it, but let us cast lots to decide who will get it," so the scripture might be fulfilled: "They divided my garments among themselves and they cast the lot over my clothing."[t] That is why the soldiers did these things.[u]

25His mother and his mother's sister, Maria of Clopas and Maria the hairdresser, stood there by the cross of Jesus. 26When Jesus saw his mother and his favorite disciple, he says to his mother, "Woman, look! Your son!" 27Then he says to the disciple, "Look! Your mother!" And from that very hour, that disciple took her into his own home.[v] 28After this, Jesus, confident that now all the prophecies were fulfilled, says, so that the scripture might be fulfilled, "I thirst." 29A vessel filled with vinegar was set there; therefore, impaling a sponge full of the vinegar on a pike,[w] they brought it to his mouth.[x] 30Therefore, when Jesus accepted the vinegar, he said, "It is done." And letting his head hang limp, he released the spirit.[y] 31Therefore, since it was the Day of Preparation, the Jewish authorities asked Pilatus to have their legs broken to hasten death and their bodies taken down so they might not remain hanging on the

---

t. Pss. 22:18

u. More precisely, this is why the gospel writers *say* the soldiers did these things. The passage draws from Pss. 22:18, an ancient lamentation envisioning someone's enemies prematurely gloating over his death and dividing up his possessions including his whole wardrobe. By contrast, how much clothing could Jesus have worn to Golgotha? Four piles worth? Not likely. The very idea of ripping the tunic for rags is absurd. The evangelist has the soldiers discard the initial idea only to provide narrative motivation for casting lots, as if this were different from "dividing my garments among them" and now only one piece is left over. The psalm does not intend a single piece of clothing, but "garments" generally. Note that, unlike Mark, John makes the crucifixion events into fulfillment of scriptural prophecies, whereas Mark silently appropriates Psalm 22 as the skeleton for his crucifixion account, being not at all eager to point out the source for his story.

v. This implies the twelve were not homeless itinerants.

w. Correcting υσσωπω (hyssop) as a copyist error for υσσω (pike), which makes much more sense.

x. Pss. 69:21

y. John 7:38-39

cross during the Sabbath, for the day of that Sabbath was particularly sacrosanct. [32]So the soldiers came and they broke the legs of the first and of the other crucified with him, [33]but when they came to Jesus, they saw he was already dead, hence they did not break his legs. [34]But one of the soldiers nicked him in the side, and at once there came out blood and water.[z] [35]And the one who saw it has testified, and his testimony is true; and that man knows that he speaks truly, so you, too, may believe.[a] [36]For these things happened for scripture to be fulfilled: "A bone of him shall not be broken."[b] [37]And again, another scripture says, "They shall look at the one they pierced."[c]

[38]After these events, Joseph from Arimathea, a disciple of Jesus, albeit secretly for fear of Jewish reprisals, petitioned Pilatus that he might take charge of the body of Jesus, and Pilatus allowed him.[d] [39]And Nicodemus came, too, the one who had earlier come to him by night, the two of them lugging a mixture of myrrh and aloes, about a hundred pounds worth. [40]Therefore, they took the body of Jesus and wrapped it in linen sheets with the spices smeared on it as is the Jewish burial custom. [41]There was a garden in the place he was crucified, and in the garden a new tomb into which no one had yet been deposited. [42]In view of the preparation for the Jewish Passover, since the tomb was ready to hand, they put Jesus there.

20

[1]On the first day of the week, Maria the hairdresser comes to the tomb while it is still dark,[e] and she sees the stone having been removed from the tomb. [2]So she runs and comes to Simon Peter and to the other disciple, Jesus' favorite, and says to them, "They removed the Lord from

---

z. John 7:38-39

a. Verses 34-35 appear to be an anti-docetic gloss to rule out the possibility that Jesus did not die on the cross but passed out and was taken down prematurely, surviving and leaving Palestine to teach elsewhere. On the other hand, if the body bled, it might seem not to be dead.

b. Exod. 12:46; Num. 9:12; Pss. 34:20

c. Zech. 12:10

d. Joseph is surely a combination of King Priam, who courageously came to Achilles' camp to beg the body of his son Hector, and the patriarch Joseph who asked Pharaoh's permission to bury Jacob in the cave Jacob had hewn beyond the Jordan (Gen. 50:4-5).

e. The vigil of mourning women reflects the women's mourning cult of the dying and rising god, long familiar in Israel (Ezek. 8:14; Zech. 12:11; Canticles 3:1-4 2).

the tomb and we do not know where they put him!" [3]So Peter and the other disciple went forth and came to the tomb. [4]And the two ran together; and the other disciple outdistanced Peter, running more swiftly, and reached the tomb first, [5]and stooping, he sees the sheets lying there—however, he did not venture to enter. [6]So Simon Peter also comes, following him, and he entered into the tomb; and he beholds the sheets lying there, [7]and the kerchief which was binding his jaw not lying with the sheets but wrapped up separately in one place. [8]Therefore, the other disciple who reached the tomb first also entered, and he saw and understood, [9]for as yet they did not grasp the scripture that he was obliged to rise again from the dead. [10]So the disciples left for their own lodgings. [11]But Maria stood outside at the tomb crying. So as she was crying, she stooped into the tomb [12]and sees two angels in white, sitting one at the head and one at the feet where the body of Jesus lay. [13]And they say to her, "Woman, why are you crying?" And she says to them, "They took my Lord and I do not know where they put him!" [14]Once she said these things, she turned around to see Jesus standing, but she did not recognize him as Jesus.[f] [15]Jesus says to her, "Woman, why are you crying? Who are you looking for?" She, thinking it is the gardener, says to him, "Lord, if you carried him off, tell me where you put him and I will take him." [16]Jesus says to her, "Maria!" Turning, she says to him in Hebrew, "Rabboni!" which means "my teacher." [17]Jesus says to her, "Do not touch me, for I have not yet ascended to the Father. But go to my brothers and tell them, "I ascend to my Father and your Father and my God and your God."[g] [18]Maria the hairdresser comes announcing to the disciples, "I have seen the Lord," and that he said these things to her.

---

f. It is possible, if one reads this verse in connection with 19:26, that we see a recognition that Jesus has returned in the form of the beloved disciple, the Paraclete, and is henceforth to be recognized as such.

g. This story owes much to the climax of the Book of Tobit, as Helms, *Gospel Fictions,* shows. When Tobias first saw Raphael, he "did not know" he was an angel (Tobit 5:5), just as Mary, weeping outside the tomb, "did not know" who Jesus really was (20:14). Having delivered Sarah from her curse, Raphael reveals himself to Tobit and son Tobias and announces, his work done, "I am ascending to him who sent me" (Tobit 12:20), just as Jesus tells Mary, "I am ascending to my father and your father, to my God and your God" (John 20:17). Why does the risen Jesus warn Mary "touch me not, for I have not yet ascended to the father" (20:17a)? This is probably docetic—Jesus, at least the risen Jesus, cannot be touched because he lacks a fleshly body. This completes the parallel between John 20 and Raphael's ascension where the angel explains he is a semblance of a physical being: "All these days I merely appeared to you and did not eat or drink, but you were seeing a vision" (Tobit 12:19).

[19]When it was early evening on that day, the first of the week, with
the doors having been shut where the disciples were for fear of the Jewish
authorities, Jesus came and stood in their midst, and he says to them,
"Peace to you!" [20]And saying this, he showed them both hands and side.[h]
So the disciples rejoiced seeing the Lord. [21]So Jesus repeated, "Peace to
you! As the Father has sent me, I send you, too." [22]And so saying, he
breathed into their nostrils and says to them, "Receive Holy Spirit.[i] [23]If
you forgive the sins of anyone, they have been forgiven them; if you retain
anyone's guilt, they remain guilty."

[24]But Thomas, one of the twelve, which means the twin, happened
not to be present when Jesus came.[j] [25]Therefore, the other disciples said
to him, "We have seen the Lord!" But he said to them, "Sorry, but unless
I see in his hands the mark of the nails[k] and thrust my hand into his side,
there is no way I will believe." [26]And after eight days, his disciples were
again inside and this time Thomas was with them. Jesus comes, the doors
having been shut, and stood in their midst[l] and said, "Peace to you!"
[27]Then he says to Thomas, "Bring your finger here and see my hands and
bring your hand and thrust it into my side and be no more an unbeliever,
but a believer."[m] [28]Thomas answered and said to him, "My Lord and my
God!" [29]Jesus says to him, "Because you have seen me, you have believed. Blessed are those who do not see and yet believe."[n]

[30]Jesus also performed many other signs before the disciples that are
not recorded in this scroll, [31]but these have been recorded so you may believe that Jesus is the Christ, the Son of God, and that so believing, you
may have the life in his name.

---

h. The evangelist has altered Luke 24:39-40 where Jesus showed his hands and feet. Here the point is to accommodate the pierced side, which is unique to John.

i. If taken literally, this scene is grotesque, Jesus giving eleven men artificial respiration. Its point is simply to recall Gen. 2:7; cf., 1 Cor. 15:45 for exactly the same idea.

j. This episodic afterthought is to buttress the faith of the reader, for whom Thomas stands. In the previous episode, it is clearly supposed that all but Judas are present.

k. Here is the sole place in the New Testament where Jesus is said to have been nailed onto the cross.

l. This scene is hardly anti-docetic, at least not consistently so, as Jesus passes through closed doors like Jacob Marley and still presents physical wounds to identify himself. The latter was nevertheless common in ancient ghost stories.

m. Note that Thomas actually does not touch Jesus!

n. This is an artificial aside addressed to the reader just as much as v. 31.

21

[1]After these things, Jesus manifested himself again by the Sea of Tiberias. And this is how he manifested himself. [2]There were together Simon Peter and Thomas, called the twin, and Nathaniel, from Cana in the Galilee, and the sons of Zebediah and two others of his disciples. [3]Simon Peter says to them, "I am going to fish." They say to him, "Wait up, we are coming along with you!" They went out and embarked in the boat and in that night they caught nothing. [4]It was now becoming early morning, and Jesus himself stood in the surf. The disciples, however, did not realize it is Jesus. [5]Therefore, Jesus says to them, "Lads, do you have any fish at all? They answered him, "No." [6]He said to them, "Throw the net over the right side of the boat and you will find some." So they threw it and they were no longer able to drag it on account of the sheer number of fish. [7]So Jesus' favorite disciple says to Peter, "You know who that is, don't you? It is the Lord!" Therefore, Simon Peter, hearing it is the Lord, tied his coat around himself, for he had stripped, and launched himself into the sea. [8]But the other disciples came in the little boat, for they were not far from land, only about two hundred cubits,[o] dragging the net full of fish. [9]When they stepped out on land, they see a coal fire spread there and a fish lying on it, as well as bread. [10]Jesus says to them, "Bring some of the fish you have now caught." [11]Simon Peter went up and dragged the net to land, full of large fish—one hundred and fifty-three; and despite the vast number, the net was not torn.[p] [12]Jesus says to them, "Come, have breakfast!" None of the disciples dared ask him "Who are you?" knowing it is the Lord.[q] [13]Jesus comes and takes the bread and gives it to them, and the fish likewise.[r] [14]This makes the third time now that Jesus was manifested to the disciples, raised from the dead.

[15]So when they had broken their fast, Jesus says to Simon Peter, "Simon of John, do you love me more than these others?" He says to him, "Yes, Lord, you know that I love you." He says to him, "Feed my

o. Two hundred cubits is about 100 yards. This is another version of John 6:16-21.

p. The episode is borrowed from a story about the vegetarian sage Pythagoras, son of Apollo, who made a bet with some fishermen that he could correctly guess the exact number of fish they had caught. He did and they had to let the fish go. This is the origin of the mention, vestigial here, of the number of fish, especially since 153 is one of the sacred Pythagorean "triangular" numbers.

q. Obviously, this is intended as the first resurrection appearance despite its inclusion at this point.

r. John 6:11

lambs." 16Again, he says to him a second time, "Simon of John, do you
love me?" He says to him, "Yes, Lord, you know that I love you." He
says to him, "Shepherd my little lambs." 17He says to him the third time,
"Simon of John, do you love me?" Peter was grieved that he said to him a
third time, "Do you love me?" and he said to him, "Lord, you know all
things: you know good and well that I love you!" Jesus says to him, "Feed
my little sheep. 18Amen, amen: I say to you, when you were younger, you
strapped your belt on and walked where you wished, but when you grow
old, you will stretch out your hands and another will strap you up and
carry you where you do not wish." 19And he spoke this riddle to signal in
what manner of death he will glorify God. And saying this, he tells him,
"Follow me." 20Turning, Peter notices Jesus' favorite disciple following
them, the one who also leaned back during supper next to him and asked,
"Lord, who is the one betraying you?" 21So when Peter noticed this man,
he says to Jesus, "Lord, and what of this one?" 22Jesus says to him, "If I
wish him to linger till I come, what is it to you?[s] You follow me!" 23This is
how it came about that the saying circulated among the brothers, "That
disciple is immortal." But in fact, Jesus did not say to him, "he is immortal,"
but rather, "if I wish him to linger till I come, what is that to you?"

24This is the disciple who testifies to these things and recorded these
things, and we know that his testimony is reliable.[t] 25And there are also
many other things which Jesus did, and if they were each recorded, I
think the world itself could not contain the scrolls that must be written.[u]

s. Mark 9:1

t. 3 John 12; Rev. 22:8

u. The final chapter is an appendix. Plainly, 20:31 was the intended ending, and the paraphrase, a classic redactional seam, repeats the tag where the redactor hung his addition. It allows him to resume the original flow of thought. However, this does not imply the appendix necessarily was composed much later than the rest of the gospel.

28.
The Preaching of John

Echoes of John

THIS INTRIGUING DOCUMENT IS PART of a larger work, the Acts of John, which recounts the exploits of John, the son of Zebedee. The portion excerpted here is different in that it is completely devoted to the apostle's alleged recollections of Jesus. The uniqueness of the material indicates that it was no doubt originally a separate work, implicitly a rival or counterpart to John's gospel. As we have seen, the Gospel of John bears the theological fingerprints of the sects that used and copied it, including the opposing views on whether Jesus had a physical body and suffered physically. It seems the Preaching of John arose out of the same sectarian milieu and attempted to set forth a consistently docetic version of the story of Jesus. It embodies the docetism scorned in 1 John, where we are told that anyone denying that "Jesus Christ has come in the flesh" has been sent by the devil. Indeed, the Preaching of John contains the clearest possible statement of docetism. For that reason, it would be well to consider more fully this theological concept before proceeding to the document itself.

Docetic doctrine

Docetism comes from the Greek word δοκεω, "to seem, to appear," the idea being that something about Jesus Christ was more apparent than real. Some aspect of his human presentation to his contemporaries was thought to be a divine accommodation to human senses, that he did not quite fully share the human lot, as if this would have been beneath the divine dignity. Of course, the point of the in-

carnation, according to the Council of Nicea, was that God gladly undertook to share a condition that was precisely beneath his dignity. But the docetists believed it was unbecoming the divine Christ that he should have suffered or died. There are various forms or degrees of docetism. The mildest, on display in the Gospel of Peter, is that Christ, for whatever reason, did not really suffer on the cross, though he was otherwise human enough. In fact, Peter's gospel says he *seemed not* to suffer! A second docetism, embraced by Basilides and by a billion Muslims today, is that Jesus was not even crucified but that someone else was or possibly that no one was on the cross—only a phantom projection, as implied in the dream sequence of *The Last Temptation of Christ*. Closely related to these views was a Gnostic understanding called separationism, that Jesus, having functioned as the human host (or "channeler") for Christ ever since his baptism, was bereft of the Spirit at his crucifixion or that his physical form was not the real Jesus any more than anyone's bodily shell is the true self, as espoused in the Nag Hammadi Gospel of Peter. But surely the most radical and thoroughgoing version of docetism is that presented in the Preaching of John, whereby the physical presence of Jesus on earth was entirely a shadow play. His divine presence might assume any chosen form from insubstantiality to steely invulnerability. He might take on various bodily shapes, even appearing differently to different observers simultaneously.

This kind of docetism is not restricted to Christianity. It prevailed as the normative understanding of Buddhism in the form of the *Trikaya* doctrine of the three bodies of the Buddha. All Buddhas are cosmic entities, ultimately sharing the ultimate reality of the *Dharmakaya* (truth body) but differentiated as distinct celestial personae (Amitabha, Dipankara, Gotama, Maitreya, Manjushri) in a heavenly dimension, the *Samboghkaya* (glory body, like the Son enthroned at the right hand of the Father). In addition, the *Nirmankaya* (transformation body) is the visible form circulating among mortals on earth. The average person looks at the Buddha and sees but a fellow human being, but the spiritual adept beholds the marks of the superman including towering height, glowing skin, long earlobes, a tuft of hair between the eyes marking the open third eye, and a topknot of hair

marking the active crown chakra. The point is the same in the gospel Transfiguration narratives when the elite three disciples see Jesus in his true heavenly form. Ultra-Shi'ite Islam developed its own form of the belief, making Ali, the successor of the Prophet Muhammad, an earthly manifestation of Allah, only apparently flesh and blood. One may wonder if docetism has not, after all, prevailed as well in popular Christianity where people find it hard to imagine Jesus needing to eat, defecate, have sex, or learn anything he did not already know.

The church behind the book

The Preaching of John was no abstract treatise written by a speculative theologian off in an ivory tower somewhere. It was scripture used to guide the life of a pious sect—something we can be sure of because of the liturgy for the Round Dance of the Savior, a ritual celebration analogous to the eucharist or to the ritual washing of the feet. It would no doubt be most impressive to see the rite performed today. What sort of a community stood behind this text? Were they full-fledged Gnostics? One must remember there were various currents drifting through early Christianity, various collections of logically connected themes, and that different churches and individuals partook of each by different degrees. Reality does not often precisely match textbook categories or ideal types. Accordingly, this or that early Christian group may have been closer to Gnosticism or Catholicism or Ebionism, but any group may have combined elements of all of them. The hallmark of Gnosticism was an elite grasp of saving truths not to be shared with the rank and file. Whether Jesus as the Gnostic revealer had worn a body of genuine flesh was secondary. As in the Preaching of John, he may not have. As in the Hymn of the Pearl contained in the Acts of Thomas, he may have, though if he did he stripped off the cramping scuba suit of human hide as soon as he got the chance and ascended incorporeally to heaven.

Having said that, the Preaching of John does have something of a Gnostic as well as merely a docetic tinge. Note how John says he laughed to scorn the poor chumps who imagined they were crucifying the real Christ. That rings of contemptuous elitism, as bemoaned in 1 John 2:9-11 and suspected of being the view of the Gnostic vis-à-vis

his unenlightened Catholic brethren. Besides, the lyrics to the Round Dance of the Savior picture the angels and Powers of the Ogdoad, or eighth heaven, participating invisibly in the rite, implying a Gnostic world-picture.

Docetic praxis

The Round Dance appears to take the place of the eucharist, the eating of the body and blood of Christ. Why is this? It is no accident. Though the eucharist could be practiced with a Gnostic understanding, as in the Acts of Thomas, more often Gnostics shunned the meal for the simple reason that they despised the flesh as an inadequate, even unclean vehicle for the presence of Christ. If the Lord deigned not to enter into a true body of gross flesh, what more sense would it make for his spiritual essence to be present in bits of physical food and drink? Again, an emphasis on docetism was often accompanied by asceticism, the denial of the flesh and its desires by means of fasting, isolation, sleep deprivation, celibacy, vegetarianism, and shunning the bath. One would only take such extreme measures to mortify the flesh if one viewed it as inherently sinful, the same reason one would find it impossible to countenance Jesus ever having taken on a fleshly body. For what it is worth, the Acts of John, into which the Preaching of John was finally incorporated, preaches celibacy and asceticism.

Name and form

A final note on literary form and authorship. Ancient writers grouped together five works: the Acts of Andrew, Acts of John, Acts of Paul, Acts of Peter, and Acts of Thomas, and ascribed them all to "Leucius," a form of the common name Luke. This Leucius was said to be a Gnostic teacher. While these works do in fact share certain important features (see the introduction to the Acts of Paul and Thecla), they were certainly not the products of a single author. The strategy behind this disingenuous claim to Leucian authorship was to make it appear they represented the wild imaginings of a single mischievous individual rather than repositories of widespread early Christian belief. We thus have no idea who really wrote any of them. But it is well worth noting that, at least here in the Preaching of John, we have a sample, albeit fictive, of what "memoirs of the apostles" (Justin Mar-

tyr) would have looked like. We read in Eusebius that Mark reports the recollections of Peter, that Luke represents the memories of Paul, but these gospels do not at all read like table talk. By contrast, the Preaching of John does sound, at least in literary form, like an eyewitness's reminiscences, though of course it is fiction. The Gospel of Mark, by contrast, does not even make the effort to appear to be based on actual eyewitness reports.

In what follows, I preserve the standard paragraph numbering from the larger Acts of John. I have also included the individual line numbering for the round dance section.

88.

Men and brothers, you have experienced nothing untoward or unbelievable in the manner of your seeing the Lord, since we, too, whom he chose to be his apostles, were tested in many ways. Truly, I am unable either fully to recount or to record everything I both saw and heard. But now it has become necessary for me to accommodate them to your understanding, and so I will relate as much to you as you can grasp so you may behold the glory that surrounds him, which was and is, both now and forever.

For once he had called Peter and Andreas, who were brothers, he comes next to me and my brother Jacob, saying, "I need you! Come to me!" And my brother, on hearing it, said, "John—this child standing on shore and calling us. What can he want?" And I said, "What child?" And he replied, "That one, motioning to us." And I answered, "We have kept watch at sea too long, my brother. You are not seeing straight! Can't you see it is a man standing there? Handsome, light-skinned, and smiling?" But he said to me, "Him I do not see, my brother. But let us go to shore and we will learn what it is he wants of us."

89.

And so, when we had docked the boat, we saw him helping us secure the boat. And when we left there, inclined to follow him, I saw him this time as largely bald but with a thick and curling beard, while Jacob saw him as a youth with only fuzz on his cheeks. So we were both uneasy and confused. What we saw: what could it mean? Subsequently, as we followed him, we gradually became only more confused as we pondered the thing. But next, something even more amazing appeared to me, for I would try to catch him off guard and never once did I see his eyes blinking; they were constantly open. And often he would appear to me as short

and ugly and then again as a man as tall as the sky. Also, another marvel about him: when I reclined next to him at meal time and leaned back against him to ask him something, sometimes I felt his breast as smooth and soft, but other times hard as stone. Thus I was inwardly troubled and reflected, "How can I be experiencing this?" And as I thought about this, he turned and said to me, "John, you see yourself in me: if your own heart is tender, then I am tender to your touch; but if your heart is stony, then thus also will you find me."

90.
And another time he takes me, along with Jacob and Peter, into the mountain where he was accustomed to pray, and we saw shining forth from within him a light no mortal words can begin to describe. A second time he brought us three up into the mountain, and he said, "Come with me." And we went again. And we watched him pray at some distance. So I, being his favorite, approached him quietly, supposing he could not hear me. I stood gazing at his back,[a] and I could see that he was completely undressed; rather, we saw him naked and not at all like any mere mortal, for his feet were whiter than mountain snow so that the surrounding ground was lit up by his feet. And as for his head, it reached the very sky! I was afraid and cried out. He turned around, now appearing as a man of short stature. He caught hold of my beard, yanked it, and said to me, "John, be no longer without faith, but a believer!" And I said, "But what have I done wrong, Lord?" And I tell you, brothers, I felt such pain for thirty days where he had yanked my beard that I remarked to him, "Lord, if your mere tug made in sport has hurt me so much, what if you had actually struck me?" And he said to me, "Let it be your lesson from now on not to tempt one who cannot be tempted."

91.
But Peter and Jacob were angry because I spoke with the Lord, and they motioned to me to rejoin them and leave the Lord alone. So I went, and both of them asked me, "The old man who was speaking with the Lord on the summit—who was he? We heard both of them speaking." And I, recalling his great condescension, and his unity behind many faces, as well as his omniscient vigilance over us, replied, "If you want to know that, you will have to ask him."

92.
Again, one time when all of us, his disciples, were lodging in one

a. Exod. 33:17-23

house in Gennesaret, I alone spied from beneath my blanket to see what he would do. First I heard him say, "John, go to sleep!" So I pretended to sleep and I saw another like him, and I heard him say to my Lord, "Jesus, those whom you have chosen do not yet believe in you." And my Lord said to him, "You speak truly, for they are but mortal men."

93.
I will recount another glory, brothers. Sometimes when I would take hold of him, I encountered a solid, material body, while other times when I touched him the substance was immaterial, as if it did not even exist. And on any occasion he was invited by one of the Pharisees and attended the dinner, we went with him, and our hosts set a roll before each one of us and he received one as well, and he would bless his own and divide it between us, and everyone was satisfied with so small a morsel and our own rolls were left over untouched, which amazed our hosts.

And often, as I walked beside him, I wanted to see the impression of his foot, whether his foot left any print on the ground, for it appeared to me that he walked just above the ground and I never saw a footprint. And I tell you these things, brothers, to encourage your faith in him; but at present it is not permitted for us to speak of his powerful deeds and wonders, for these surpass mortal speech and, perhaps literally, cannot be put into words or heard with the ear.

94.
Now before he was apprehended by the renegade Jews who received their Torah from the outlaw serpent, he called us all together and said, "Before I am handed over to them, let us raise a hymn to the Father and fortify ourselves to face what awaits us." So he told us to form a circle, holding one another's hands, himself standing at the center. He said, "Answer 'amen' to what I say." He began then to sing a hymn, saying,

1"Glory to you, Father!"
And we, going round in a circle, answered him, "Amen!"
Glory to you, Word!
Glory to you, Grace! —Amen!
2Glory to you, Spirit!
Glory to you, Saint!
Glory to your glory! —Amen!
3We praise you, O Father!
We render thanks to you, O Light, where no darkness hides!
—Amen!

95.
And as to that for which we render thanks, I say,

4I would be saved, and I would save. —Amen!
5I would be freed, and I would free! —Amen!
6I would be wounded, and I would wound! —Amen!
7I would be born, and I would bear! —Amen!
8I would eat, and I would be eaten! —Amen!
9I would hear, and I would be heard! —Amen!
10I would be thought, being essentially thought! —Amen!
11I would be washed, and I would wash! —Amen!

Grace dances!

12I would sing! All of you, dance! —Amen!
13I would mourn! All of you, lament! —Amen!
14The eighth heaven sings praise with us! —Amen!
15There are Twelve who dance on high! —Amen!
16The Whole on high shares in our dancing! —Amen!
17Whoever does not dance, does not know what is coming to pass! —Amen!
18I would flee, and I would remain! —Amen!
19I would adorn, and I would be adorned! —Amen!
20I would be united, and I would unite! —Amen!
21A house I have not, and I have houses! —Amen!
22A place I have not, and I have places! —Amen!
23A temple I have not, and I have temples! —Amen!
24A lamp am I to you who see me! —Amen!
25A mirror am I to you who recognize me! —Amen!
26A door am I to you who knock at me! —Amen!
27A way am I to you, a pilgrim! —Amen!

96.
28"Now answer to my dancing! 29Behold yourself in me as I speak,
30and seeing what I do, keep my mysteries in silence. 31aYou who dance,
understand what I do, 32for this passion of human nature, which I am
about to suffer, 31bis yours. 33For you could never have understood what
you will experience 34had I not been sent as the Word of the Father.
35You who saw what I endure saw me as if suffering, 36and once you saw
it, you did not stand firm but panicked and fled.

37"You have me as a bed; rest upon me! 38Who I am, you shall know
when I leave you. 39I am not what I appear to be now. 40You shall see

when you come.[b] [41]If you had known how to suffer, you would have been able not to suffer. [42]Learn how to suffer and you shall be immune from suffering. [43]What you do not know, I will teach you myself. [44]I am your God and not the God of the traitor. [45]I would stay in tune with holy souls. [46]In me you recognize the Word of Wisdom. [47]And as for me, if you would know what I was, [48]I deceived all things with a single saying[c] but I was not at all deceived. [49]I have leaped up from the earth, but in my absence you shall understand the Whole; [50]and once you have understood it, say 'Glory to you, Father! Amen.' Again, say with me, [51]'Glory to you, Father! Glory to you, Word! Glory to you, Holy Spirit!'"

97.
Thus, my beloved ones, when he had danced with us, the Lord went forth. And we fled in every direction like lost travelers or men startled awake from sleep. When I saw him suffering, even then I did not stand by him in his suffering. Instead, I fled to the Mount of Olives, weeping at what had come about. And when he was crucified, Friday at the sixth hour of the day,[d] darkness enveloped the whole earth. And at once my Lord stood in the midst of the cave, shining with radiance that lit up the whole interior, and he said, "John! To the masses of people below, I am being crucified and pierced with lances and reeds and I am being offered gall and vinegar to drink. But to you I am speaking and you must listen to what I say. It was I who placed in your mind the notion to come up into this mountain so you might hear those things which a disciple ought to learn from his teacher, and a mortal from his God."

98.
And having said this, he showed me a cross of light standing erect, with a crowd gathered round the cross, having no one appearance. But in the cross there was a lone form, a single likeness. And the Lord himself I saw above the cross, having no shape at all but only a voice; nor was it the voice familiar to us but one winsome and gentle and truly divine, saying to me, "John it is necessary for someone to hear these things from me, for I will need one who will understand. I sometimes, for your sake, call this cross of light the Word, sometimes Mind, sometimes Jesus, sometimes Christ, sometimes Door, sometimes a Way, sometimes Bread, sometimes Seed, sometimes Resurrection, sometimes Son, sometimes Father, some-

b. He means when John arrives at the cave during the crucifixion, as below.

c. "My God, my God, why did you forsake me?"

d. 12:00 noon.

times Spirit, sometimes Life, sometimes Truth, sometimes Faith, sometimes Grace.[e] It is called these various names for the sake of mortal men. But as for what it is in truth, as conceived of in itself and as explained to us, it is the delimitation of all things, and that which supports immovably all things in the shifting world of matter, as well as the harmony of wisdom and indeed the wisdom in harmony. There are places of the right hand and of the left where the Powers, Authorities, Principalities, and demons, machinations, threats, wrath, devils, and the adversary are held at bay—that subterranean root from which the nature of all created things stemmed forth.

99.
"So this cross is that which established all things in their due places by a word and separated the living from those below and then, being a singularity, streamed forth into all things. But this is not the cross of wood which you will see when you descend from here. Nor am I the one on the cross, I whom you do not see now but whose voice you hear. I was considered to be that which I am not, not being what I seemed to many others. But they will say of me something vile and unworthy. Then, just as the place of rest is both invisible and ineffable, much more shall I, the Lord of it, be invisible and ineffable.

100.
"As for the mass of people with many aspects around the cross, they are of the base nature. And those whom you see in the cross, if they do not all share a single form, it is because not every destined member of the one who descended into the world has yet been gathered. But when the higher nature is taken up, even the race which draws near to me and obeys my voice, the one who now hears me, shall be united with it, no more to be what he is now but superhuman as I also am now. For as long as you do not call yourself mine, I am not that which I was.[f] But if you hear me, you shall, as you hear, become as I am and I shall be what I once was when I have you as I am in myself. For you are originally from me. Give no heed to the many; despise them who are outside the mystery and know this: I am wholly with the Father and the Father is with me.

101.
"So I have suffered none of the things they will say I suffered. No, even that suffering I showed to you and the rest in the dance, let it be

e. Of course, these all refer to predicates of Jesus in the Gospel of John.

f. That is, until every true spirit rejoins its Redeemer, his primordial light-body will remain incomplete.

called a mystery rite. For what you are, you can see for yourself, for I showed it to you. But what I am, I alone know and no one else. Let me then keep what is mine, and as for what is yours, behold it through me and behold me in truth, that I am not what I said but what you are able to know because you are akin. You hear that I suffered, yet I did not suffer; that I did not suffer, yet I did suffer; that I was pierced, yet I was not struck; hanged, yet I was not hanged; that blood issued from me, and it did not issue forth. In sum, what they say about me did not happen to me, but what they do not say, that I did suffer![g] As to what those things are, I will relate to you, for I know that you will understand. So now perceive in me the slaying of the Word, the piercing of the Word, the blood of the Word, the wound of the Word, the hanging up of the Word, the suffering of the Word, the nailing of the Word, the death of the Word. And so I say, sloughing off the humanity. First of all, then, perceive the Word, then you shall perceive the Lord; and thirdly, the man and what he has suffered."

102. When he had spoken these things to me, as well as others which I do not know how to express as he would wish, he was taken up, without anyone among the masses having beheld him. And when I descended the mountain, I laughed them all to scorn in view of what he had told me they have said about him. And I kept one thing clearly in mind: that the Lord had arranged everything symbolically as part of a plan for the conversion and salvation of human beings.

103. Since we have beheld the grace of the Lord and his gentle affection for us, let us worship him gratefully as those who have been shown mercy and, not merely with our fingers or our mouth or tongue or with any of our members, but with the attitude of our soul, worshipping him who became a man except for this body. And let us keep prayerful vigil because now he watches over prisons for our sake and over tombs, in chains and dungeons, in rebuffs and insults by sea and on dry land, in floggings, sentencings, collusions, frauds, punishments—and in sum, he is with all of us when we suffer, brothers. When each of us invokes him, he cannot bear to turn a deaf ear to us, but as he is omnipresent, he listens to all of us, bringing us help out of his compassion.

104. Be convinced, then, beloved, that it is no mere man I preach to you to

g. The reference is to the sufferings of his elect, below.

worship, but the immutable God, the invincible God, the God superior to all Authorities and Powers, older and mightier than all angels and creatures that can be named and all aions. So if you remain in him, you shall win through to immortality.

29.

The Letter to Gaius

Scholars since Ernst Käsemann have posited as the occasion for this epistle the increasing late-first-century isolation of local churches and their suspicion of traveling charismatic preachers and prophets. We read of such tensions in the *Didache,* chapters 11-13, where the dangers of charlatan itinerants are discussed, both wisely and a bit amusingly. No ostensible prophet is to be honored if, rapt by the Spirit, he commands to be given money. He is not to be allowed to freeload off the congregation. He should be allowed to consecrate the eucharist in any way he prefers. Even ordinarily immoral behavior may be tolerated as a sign of his Spirit-induced superhumanity, but not imitated by the ungifted. Eventually such prophets, whether sincere or insincere, proved to be too inconvenient for the consolidating authority of local bishops, who warned their people no longer to give the prophets either hospitality or attention. No doubt, this is what we see going on in the background of the Epistle to Gaius, otherwise known as 3 John. However, I think we can fill in even more of that background.

We have seen how Johannine Christianity was increasingly split between docetic proto-Gnostics and others who rejected such new insights as blasphemous innovations. The Preaching of John represents the docetic version of Johannine faith, while we can see both versions competing in the text of the Gospel of John, which passed through the hands of redactors belonging to both factions. It is this theological factionalism that gave rise to the three Johannine Epistles.

First, we must picture a Johannine cluster of congregations, perhaps those listed in Revelation 1:11, overseen by the Elder and his cir-

cuit-riding brothers, prophets, and teachers. Two are sent out at a time, teaching the faithful in the name of the Elder. Some of the advanced, newly Gnostic, Johannine teachers, previously having kept such beliefs to themselves, set out on their scheduled preaching circuit and decide to start spreading their new version of the Johannine message. Presumably they receive mixed reactions from their audiences, and word is spreading among the Johannine communities that the itinerant brothers can no longer be trusted for sound doctrine. No complaint is addressed to the Elder, though, because it is taken for granted the heresy stems from him: the itinerants do after all present themselves as his delegates.

How does the Elder finally discover that something is amiss? He hears it first from a couple of non-docetic missioners who return home early with bad news: they have been refused hospitality and a hearing by Diotrephes, local head of one of the congregations. They do not know why. Only a single church member named Gaius received them. It is possible that Gaius was absent during the trouble and did not himself know why everyone else was shunning the itinerants. The Elder assumes Diotrephes must be full of conceit and wanting absolute control over his little fief. The Elder writes him but receives no reply, so he sends some more brothers on their rounds, directing them specifically to Gaius. One of them is Demetrius, who carries the present letter. Why are they even stopping there? The Elder knows his men will not receive a hearing in the general assembly at Diotrephes's church, but his missioners will nevertheless need lodging at this traditional stop on their rounds. As for the congregation, the Elder himself plans to appear in full thunder to get to the root of the matter. Once he finally does, he learns what has been going on behind his back and promptly excommunicates the Gnostic subversives and adopts Diotrephes's own policy, as we see in 2 John, the Letter to Kuria.

The Elder, to the beloved Gaius, whom I love in the truth that binds us together.

[2]Dear friend, I pray that in every regard you may flourish and enjoy good health, just as your soul flourishes. [3]For I rejoiced greatly when some of the brothers returned from their rounds and vouched for your commitment to the truth, since you do in fact live by the truth. [4]I can have

no greater joy than this: to hear that my children are living by the truth! [5]My friend, you act faithfully whatever service you render to the brothers, especially those with whom you had not previously been personally acquainted, [6]both those who have lovingly commended you in the hearing of the whole community here and these now whom you do well to speed on their way with provisions in a manner befitting the servants of God. [7]For it was on behalf of the Name that they went out, accepting no contribution from the gentiles. [8]This is why it is incumbent on us to provide hospitality for such men, so we may count as their colleagues in spreading the truth.

[9]Previously I wrote something to the congregation, but that fellow who thirsts for preeminence, Diotrephes, does not welcome our people. [10]Rest assured, if I visit, I will not forget the deeds he does, condemning us with empty blather. As if this did not satisfy him, he refuses to welcome the brothers and he stops those who would entertain them, excommunicating them.

[11]My friend, imitate the good example, not the bad one. Whoever does good deeds belongs to God. Whoever does evil deeds would not recognize God if he saw him.

[12]Everyone vouches for Demetrius, as does the truth itself. And we, too, vouch for him, and you know our witness is true.[a]

[13]I had many things to write you, but I would rather forgo the use of ink and pen to write you. [14]Instead I am hoping to see you soon, and we will speak face to face. [15]May you enjoy peace! The friends[b] here greet you. Be sure to greet our friends by name.

---

a. John 21:24

b. John 15:14-15

30.

The Letter to Kuria

THE JOHANNINE MISSIONARY fellowship has become divided over the issue of docetism, which some of the brothers have been preaching without authorization from their venerable master, the Elder. The individuals involved have not come forward to admit their real beliefs, hoping to trade a bit longer on the Elder's credentials, and their hearers perhaps cannot remember precisely who among their frequent visitors has said what. Therefore, the Elder adopts the method of Diotrephes, who had recognized the danger before anyone else. He excommunicates every docetist he finds out about; but as for the rest, all he can hope is that they will be caught and will be reported to him. To that end, he inaugurates a short-lived letter-writing campaign, warning the leaders of his affiliated congregations to shun anyone who, in the Elder's name, teaches that Jesus' coming was not in real, solid flesh. The present note, also known as 2 John, is addressed to Kuria and her house church. Though Kuria means "lady," it is widely attested as a proper name, and there is no reason to doubt it is intended as such here, not as some abstract allegory for the church in general, as one usually hears.

The Elder, to the elect Kuria and her children, whom I truly love, and
not I only but also all who have learned the truth, 2and for the sake of the
truth which remains among us and will be with us to the end of the age.
3We will enjoy favor, mercy, and protection from God the Father and
from Jesus-Christ, the Son of the Father, as long as we remain in truth and
love.

4I rejoiced greatly because I ascertained that at least some of your
children are continuing in the truth as we were commanded by the Fa-

ther. 5And now I ask you, Kuria, not as if I were issuing you some new commandment but only the same one we had from the beginning, namely, that we should love each other. 6And love consists in this: that we should live by his commandments. This is the same commandment you heard from the start. You should persevere in it. 7I reiterate this because many deceivers have fanned out into the world, those not confessing Jesus-Christ as coming in the flesh. This is the deceiver and the antichrist. 8Look to yourselves so that you do not forfeit credit for the good deeds we performed together, but that instead you may receive a full reward. 9Everyone who goes on to something new instead of remaining under the doctrine of Christ is bereft of God. Anyone remaining under the doctrine has both the Father and the Son on his side. 10Should anyone arrive there not bringing this doctrine, do not welcome him into your home, neither give him a polite greeting; 11anyone who so much as says hello to him is an accomplice to his evil deeds.

12Though I have much to write to you, I believe I will forgo paper and ink, hoping instead to be with you and speak face to face so our joy may be full. 13The children of your elect sister send their greeting.

31.
Concerning the Word of Life

The Johannine community suffered schism over the issue of docetic Christology. Had Jesus Christ really become a fleshly human being or had he only appeared to be human for the sake of facilitating communication with humans? Had he actually been, in the phrase of Robert W. Chambers, the Phantom of Truth? Not everyone holding to the latter belief had declared himself; the Elder, venerable head of the community and the missionary fellowship serving it, began writing the leaders of the various congregations to determine how widespread the belief was. The Letter to Kuria, traditionally called 2 John, was one of these letters. Apparently our author, ever reluctant to put pen to paper, must have finally decided to compose an encyclical—a circular letter to all his congregations. This is it, and following Hugh J. Schonfield, we find the title in the first verse: "Concerning the Word of Life." It sets forth the definitive statement of the faith of the Johannine community, minus the docetists! And it stipulates doctrinal shibboleths that must be employed to test wandering prophets: do they confess faith in the incarnation? Do they draw any distinction between the Christ Spirit and the human Jesus as a temporary channeler? The latter was another frequent Gnostic mytheme.

The epistle tells us more about the docetic schismatics. They appear to have claimed the classic Gnostic prerogatives of sinless perfection by virtue of placing themselves above the laws of the Demiurge/Creator and claiming advanced, elite *gnosis* ("knowledge"). Perhaps they had an ugly attitude of aloof arrogance toward those they considered unenlightened, but this is an inference drawn by outsiders

who assume Gnostics *must* regard outsiders in this way, whether or not they actually did.

Comparing the anti-Gnostic basis of the document with the Gospel of John, it becomes clear that Concerning the Word of Life comes from the same side of the controversy as the Johannine Ecclesiastical Redactor. There is a definite future eschatology despite a certain residual tendency to realize eschatology. For example, the Elder says the predictions of the Antichrist had already come true in his own day, reminiscent of gospel passages like John 5:25. Yet he lays heavy emphasis on a future Parousia of Christ, though it must be in the very near future: "This is the last hour!"

It appears that the encyclical suffered the same fate as the Gospel of John. It was appreciated and edited by both sides in the controversy, the result being that what we have is a contradictory, composite document. Probably some scribe, finding two different versions and not wanting to risk losing any possibly sacred text, copied everything, whether or not the result made much sense. I have accordingly sought to bring the reader's attention to the portions that reflect the views of the Gnostics by placing them within fancy brackets {like this}, allowing each message to make its point clearly. It should be no surprise that both voices sound much alike as to style and vocabulary, both stemming from the same hot-house atmosphere of piety and doctrine. It will be some time before new distinctives of expression begin to evolve. Specifically, both stress the error of hating one's sect brothers. The Elder speaks of the contempt he assumes the Gnostics must feel for their unenlightened former compatriots. The Gnostics themselves refer to the vilification they receive at the hands of the Elder and his followers.

1

Concerning the Word of Life: what was from the beginning, what we
have heard, what we have seen with our own eyes, what we beheld and
our hands touched.[a] 2And the life was revealed, and we have seen and tes-

a. When it speaks of that which "our hands touched," can the intended reference be to Christians receiving the eucharist? The wording seems too broad to refer to the eleven disciples touching the historical Jesus himself.

tify and announce to you the life of ages, which was with the Father and
was revealed to us; [3]what we have seen and heard we announce to you in
order that you, too, may share in common with us. And indeed, our communion is with the Father and with his Son, Jesus-Christ. [4]And we write
these things in order that our joy may be made full.[b] [5]And here is the message we heard from him and announce to you: "God is light and there is
no darkness in him at all." [6]If we claim to have communion with him
while we walk in darkness, we are lying, not practicing the truth. [7]But if
we walk in the light, where he is in the light, we share communion between each other, and the blood of Jesus, his Son, purifies us from all sin.
[8]If we say we are without sin, we are deceiving ourselves and are bereft of
the truth. [9]If we acknowledge our sins, he is righteous and may be relied
upon to forgive us those sins and to purify us from all unrighteousness.
[10]To maintain that we have not sinned is to call him a liar and to be bereft
of his truth.[c]

2

[1]My children, I write you these words so you will not sin. And if anyone should sin, we have an advocate with the Father, Jesus-Christ, the
righteous one. [2]And he is a propitiation for our sins, and not only for ours
but for the whole world.[d] [3]And this is how to tell if we have truly known
him: do we keep his commandments?[e] [4]Whoever claims "I have come to
know him" but does not keep his commandments is a liar, and this one is
bereft of the truth. [5]But whoever keeps his command, truly in such a one
the love of God has been perfected. This is how we can tell that we are in
communion with him. [6]Anyone claiming to remain in communion with
him ought to comport himself as he did.

[7]Loved ones, I am not writing you a new commandment, but an old
one you have known from the start. This old commandment is the message you heard. [8]Yet, on the other hand, it is a new commandment I am
writing for you,[f] the truth of which is evident both in his case and in yours
because the old darkness is fading and the light of truth is already beginning to shine. [9]Anyone claiming to bask in the light while despising his

---

b. John 15:11

c. Here the Elder condemns Gnostic perfectionism.

d. The Elder may be countering a belief that the Christ aion had appeared in the world to rescue none but his elite, only the minority possessing the divine spark, as in John 10:26-27.

e. John 15:10

f. John 13:34

brother flounders in the darkness even now.[g] 10The one who loves his brother remains securely in the light and he is free of offense.[h] 11But the one who despises his brother is lost in the dark and gropes in the darkness without a clue as to where he is headed since the darkness has rendered his eyes useless.

{12I write to you, little children, because your sins have been forgiven you for his sake. 13Fathers, I write to you because you have known him from the beginning. 14I wrote you, youngsters, because you are acquainted with the Father. I wrote to you, fathers, because you have known him from the beginning.[i] I wrote you, young men, because you are strong and the seed of God[j] has taken root in you and you have defeated the evil one. 15See that you do not love the world, nor the goods of the world. If anyone does love the world, he is bereft of the Father's love. 16Why? Because all that the world offers, the lust of the flesh, the lust of the eyes, and all the vanity of life, comes not from the Father, but from the world. 17And the world is fading away along with its lust. But the one who follows the will of God remains to the end of the age.}

18Youngsters, it is the last hour! You have heard, "Antichrist is coming!" Even so, numerous antichrists have now arisen.[k] From this we can tell it is the last hour. 19They set out from us, but they were not our true representatives; had they truly belonged to our fellowship they would have stuck with us, but this has happened in order to make clear that they do not represent us. 20You, too, have an anointing from the Holy One, and all of you "know."[l] 21I wrote you, not because you are ignorant of the truth,[m] but precisely because you do know it and because every lie does not come from the truth. 22Who is the liar but the one who denies, saying, "Jesus is not the same as the Christ"? Such a one is the antichrist, denying the Father and the Son. 23Everyone denying the Son does not have the Father either.[n] The one who confesses faith in the Son has the Fa-

g. He condemns Gnostic elitism, real or imagined.

h. John 8:12

i. This refers to the Gnostic pre-existence of elect souls.

j. The spark of pleromatic light.

k. Mark 13:21-22

l. The schismatics are self-styled Gnostics, but in the fashion of anti-charismatics through the ages, the Elder denies these supposed adepts have anything special that your average pew-potato lacks.

m. His detractors would suggest otherwise.

n. John 5:23

ther as well. 24What you heard back at the beginning, stay with it. If what you heard at the start remains firmly rooted in you, you will remain in communion with the Son and with the Father. 25And this is the promise he made to us: age-long life.

26I wrote you these things about those who are leading you off the track. 27And the anointing you received from him is still inside you, so any novel teaching would be superfluous. And since his anointing teaches you about everything[o] and is true, not a lie, then as it taught you, stay in fellowship with him. 28And now, little children, remain in communion with him in order that, should he be revealed, we may be confident, not cringing from his gaze. 29If you know him as the Righteous One, then surely you know that it is only the ones behaving righteously that are born of him.

3

1Consider what kind of love the Father has given to us for us to be called children of God. And we are! That is why the world rejects us, just as it rejected him.[p] 2Loved ones, now we are children of God, but as to what we shall one day be, that has not yet been made clear. But we can at least be sure that if it is made clear, we shall resemble him, because we shall see him in his true form. 3And anyone with this prospect before him purifies himself to attain his degree of purity. 4Everyone committing sin is a law breaker since sin is by its very nature law breaking. 5And you know that That One was revealed so he could bear away sins,[q] and there is no sin in him.[r]

{6Everyone who remains in communion with him does not sin. Anyone who continues to sin has never either seen him or met him. 7Little children, do not let anyone lead you astray about this: no one can be called righteous unless he is practicing righteousness just as That One is. 8The one who practices sin belongs to the accuser, for the accuser sins from the beginning. It was for this very purpose that the Son of God was revealed: to nullify the handiwork of the accuser. 9Every one who has been fathered by God does not sin, because he has inherited his traits; nor is he even capable of sinning, having been fathered by God. 10This is how one distinguishes the children of God from the children of the accuser:

---

o. John 16:13-15

p. John 17:14-16

q. John 1:29

r. John 1:47

anyone who is not practicing righteousness is not a child of God, namely anyone who does not love his brother.[s] 11Because this is the message you heard from the start: We must love one another.[t] 12Not like Cain, who was the son of the evil one[u] and killed his brother. And why did he kill him? Because his deeds were evil and those of his brother were righteous. 13No wonder, brothers, that the world hates you.}

14We know we have moved out of death's domain into life's[v] because we love the brothers; anyone not loving remains in the realm of death. 15Everyone who hates his brother is a murderer.[w] And you know that every murderer is bereft of age-long life. 16This is how we know what love is: That One surrendered his life on our behalf. 17Whoever has a worldly livelihood and notices his brother in need and closes his heart to him: how can a drop of God's love be left in him? 18Little children, let us not speak glibly of love, but truly in actions.[x]

19This is how we can tell if we belong to the truth and how we shall reassure our heart when we stand before him. 20If the heart blames us, we are in trouble, for God is greater than our hearts and nothing can be hid from him. 21So loved ones, if the heart does not blame us, we can stand unflinching before God. 22And whatever we request, we can expect to receive from him as long as we keep his commandments and do those things that are pleasing to his eyes. 23And this is the commandment I have in mind: we must believe in the name of his Son, Jesus-Christ, and love each other in accord with the command he left us.[y] 24Whoever keeps his commandments remains in communion with Jesus-Christ, and Jesus-Christ remains likewise in communion with him. And this is how we can tell he is lingering within us: by the Spirit he gave us.

---

s. John 8:44

t. John 13:34-35

u. Cain was believed to be the literal offspring of Satan and Eve: Satan, in the form of a snake, had sexually seduced Eve, and Cain was the result. Some scribes thought the extant text of Gen. 4:1 ("I have gotten a man-child with the help of Yahve") was blasphemous, implying God had physically begotten Cain. They concluded that the text had been altered from "I have gotten a man-child with the help of Satan," influenced no doubt by Gen. 6:1-4. In the context of Johannine Gnosticism, such a mytheme signaled a dualistic division of the human race akin to that of Sethianism.

v. John 5:24

w. This becomes a saying of Jesus in Matt. 5:21-22.

x. James 2:14-17

y. John 13:34

4

[1]Loved ones, do not believe every spirit-utterance, but examine the spirits of the prophets to determine whether they come from God because the world is now infested with false prophets. [2]This is how you can tell the Spirit of God: any prophet who acknowledges Jesus-Christ as having come in the flesh[z] belongs to God, [3]while any prophet who does not so acknowledge Jesus does not belong to God.[a] Such a one is possessed of the spirit of the antichrist, of which you heard, "It is coming!" and is now at work in the world already.[b]

{[4]You belong to God, little children,[c] and have beaten them because the Spirit in you is mightier than the one in the world. [5]They belong to the world; accordingly, they speak in terms of the world and naturally the world listens to them.[d] [6]We belong to God. Whoever knows God listens to us; whoever does not belong to God does not listen to us.}[e]

[7]Loved ones, let us love each other, for love belongs to God and every one who loves has been fathered by God and consequently knows God. [8]Anyone who does not love can never have met God because God is love. [9]This is how God revealed his love to us: God has sent his only-begotten Son into the world in order that we might gain life through him.[f] [10]Love consists in this: not that we had any particular love for God, but that he loved us and sent his Son, a propitiation for our sins.[g] [11]Loved ones, if God loved us that much, surely we are obliged to love each other! [12]No one has ever beheld God,[h] but if we love each other, God remains among us and his love comes to perfection in us. [13]This is how we know

z. John 1:14

a. The intended heresy is plainly docetism.

b. 2 Thess. 2:7

c. The author's device, addressing readers (here and in 2:12-14) alternately as "little children," "youngsters," "young men," and "fathers," reflects the manner in which John and his brother beheld Jesus in rapid succession as a youth, a middle-aged man, and an old man in the Preaching of John.

d. 1 Cor. 2:13-14; John 7:7

e. John 10:26-27; 18:37

f. John 3:16-17

g. Rom. 5:8

h. What about Moses, whom Deut. 34:10 and Num. 12:6-8 say regularly conversed with God face-to-face as a familiar friend? Perhaps our author believed, as did many Jews, that Moses beheld an angel of God, not God himself. See Alan F. Segal, *Two Powers in Heaven: Early Rabbinic Reports about Christianity and Gnosticism.* Studies in Judaism in Late Antiquity XXV (Leiden: E.J. Brill, 1977). In any case, see John 1:18.

we remain in communion with him: because he has given some of his Spirit to us.[i] 14And we have beheld and now testify: The Father has sent the Son as the Savior of the world. 15Thus, whoever confesses "Jesus is the Son of God," God remains in communion with him and he remains in communion with God. 16Thus do we know and rely upon the love God feels for us. God is the same as love, with the result that whoever remains within love's bounds by the same token remains within God, and God dwells inside him.

17In this way love has matured with us in order that we may face the Day of Judgment with confidence because we live our lives in this world just as That One did. 18Fear has no place in love; rather, mature love expels the fear because fear has to do with punishment and anyone who fears has not yet grown mature in love. 19The reason we love is that he loved us first. 20If anyone says "I love God!" and yet despises his brother, he is a liar; how can he love God, whom he cannot even see, when he cannot bring himself to love his brother who is right in front of him? 21And this is the commandment we have received from him, that anyone who loves God shall love his brother too.

5

1Everyone who believes Jesus is the Christ has been fathered by God, and everyone who loves the parent loves his offspring. 2This is how we can tell if we really love God and keep his commandments: do we love his children?[j] 3For what is it to love God but to keep his commandments? Nor are his commandments onerous 4because everyone God has fathered triumphs over the world. And what is it that triumphs over the world but our faith? 5Who is it who defeats the world but the one who believes Jesus is the Son of God? 6This is the one who appears with water and blood, Jesus-Christ. Not merely with water, but with water and blood.[k] And we know this from the Spirit because the Spirit is the truth.[l] 7Because there are three witnesses *in heaven: the Father, the Word, and the Holy Spirit,*

i. Rom. 5:5

j. This seems to make more sense by itself and in context than the extant word order.

k. John 19:34. This is a refutation of docetism even though one who "bled" water might seem to be a god masquerading in human form. Our author insists Jesus was really human flesh.

l. John 15:26, 12-14. Here we learn that the piercing of the heart of Jesus in John 19:34 is not an item of historical memory but a revelation after the fact like those made to Anna Katherina Emmerich. Hence the appeal here to the Spirit's ve-

and these three are one, and there are three who testify on earth:[m] 8the Spirit, the water, and the blood, and their testimony is unanimous. 9If we are accustomed to accepting the testimony of two or three human beings, the testimony of God is weightier because he has testified about his Son.[n] 10Anyone who believes in the Son of God has the witness inside. Anyone who does not believe God is calling him a liar because he has rejected the testimony God has offered about his Son.[o] 11And here is that testimony: God gave us age-long life, and this life is in his Son. 12Whoever has the Son has that life; whoever lacks the Son of God lacks that life.

13I wrote these words to you who believe in the name of the Son of God to assure you that you have age-long life. 14And we have this confidence before him: If we request anything *that accords with his plan*,[p] he heeds us. 15And if we know he heeds whatever request we make, we can expect to receive whatever we have requested from him.[q] 16For instance, if anyone spots his brother committing a sin that is not mortal, let him ask forgiveness for him and God will grant him life as long as they are not committing mortal sins. There is such a thing as a mortal sin and I am not suggesting one intercede in that case. 17All iniquity is sin, that is true, but some sins are not fatal.

{18Remember, everyone fathered by God does not sin; instead, the One fathered by God protects him so that the evil one cannot touch him. 19We know that we belong to God and that the whole world lies in the grasp of the evil one. 20And we know that the Son of God has arrived and has imparted understanding to us,[r] enabling us to recognize the true God from the false, and we are in communion with him who is true and with his Son, Jesus-Christ. This is the true God[s] and the secret of age-long life. 21Little children, guard yourselves against idols.}

---

racious character as corroboration. This should make us think twice before taking 1 John 1:1-3 as eyewitness memory.

m. This is a medieval interpolation intended to provide a foothold for the doctrine of the Trinity.

n. John 8:17-18; Mark 9:7; John 12:28

o. 1 Cor. 15:15

p. The clause sounds like a more realistic corrective to the easily disappointed "blank check" view of prayer advocated in the original text.

q. This becomes a saying of Jesus in Mark 11:24.

r. Jesus the Gnostic revealer!

s. That is, not the Demiurge, who was the god of the Jews and of Catholic Christians.

32.

The Revelation of John

THE GREEK TITLE OF THIS BOOK, *Apocalypse* ("apo-calypso"), means to lift away or peel back, as in lifting a veil to reveal what lies underneath. There are many such ancient and medieval books, mostly in the Jewish, Christian, and Islamic traditions, though they are not altogether absent from other religions. John's book lent its name to the collective genre; hence, all are called "apocalypses" even though John's was by no means the first.

What are the characteristics of this type of literature? As Jacques Derrida pointed out in his "paradox of iteration," when we multiply instances of a thing, we rob the original of its distinctiveness, though thereby making possible the general definition: now the original is understood against the background of others of its kind. With that in mind, let us try to understand the Apocalypse of John by reviewing it in the context of apocalypses in general. What rules of interpretation can we derive from the general classification?

First, apocalypses, including this one, are in some measure pious frauds, and this in three senses. First, they are written under the name of an ancient figure or at least of a venerated saint of the past. Why do their writers not speak in their own names? This is a function of the evolutionary stage of a religion in which these works are written. Apocalypses are by nature latecomers and their authors set pen to paper at a time subsequent to the original period of revelation. New prophets are no longer welcome in their day because a canon of scripture is in the process of forming, along with a definitive creed to provide a template for orthodox reading of the scripture, and the religious establishment is claiming the scriptures as its revealed guar-

antee. The establishment does not want new prophets rocking the boat just when all the holes have been plugged and the course has been set. Oh, new prophets may very well show up, but their prophecies will be marginalized, and at their most successful they may spin off into a new religion. If one has a message one wants heard in the context of the parent tradition, one must sneak it in under the wire by pretending it comes from one of the canonical authors. The new author claims someone else's clout in order to gain a hearing. Again, the name may be that of an ancient patriarch or of the recent founder of the sect. Even in a new religion, the open window for new prophecy is usually short.

Second, apocalypses pretend to be predictive prophecies, but they are not. This is implied in the choice of a pseudonym from the past. The real author assumes the supposed historical vantage point to predict the future from that time on. This is easy to do since such a writer is in reality post-dicting, narrating events he knows in retrospect. It is amazing how accurate one can be with 20/20 hindsight. When an apocalypse seeks to encourage its readers in a time of persecution, the fictive stance is assumed in order to assure the readers God long ago foresaw these events, that things in the current time have not gone out of God's providential control. The apocalyptic writers wanted to forestall their readers giving up on the traditional belief in God's care, as we find Richard L. Rubenstein doing in *After Auschwitz*. The reader of such books as Daniel will be encouraged upon encountering what sounds like an accurate portrayal of history between the Babylonian Exile and the oppression of Antiochus IV Epiphanes, followed by a promise of soon-to-come divine deliverance—which may or may not come! In Daniel's case, at least the Hasmoneans overthrew the Seleucid tyrant; but that empire was not, in fact, supplanted by the supernatural kingdom of God. The false-future standpoint sometimes helps us date an apocalypse since their authors lacked genuine clairvoyant gifts. All we need to do is look for where the future history suddenly goes off the track; this is the spot where history writing left off and genuine predictive speculation began, swiftly ending in embarrassment. Such embarrassments eventually necessitate interpreters updating these writings, reinterpreting the symbols of any given

apocalypse to refer to later and later historical entities in order to make the predictions of an imminent end apply to each new generation's headlines. As an example, Hal Lindsay's *The Late Great Planet Earth* replaced the Roman Empire with the Common Market, Gog and Magog with the Soviet Union.

Third, apocalypses are piously fraudulent in that they pose as overwhelming visions but are actually pastiches of their genre predecessors. Granted, it is not absolutely impossible that a visionary might have primed himself by meditating on visionary passages of scripture, subsequently to have his subconscious mix these elements up and spew them out in visions of his own. In fact, this is what Jewish Merkabah mystics counted on as they meditated on the first chapter of Ezekiel and its vision of God in the heavenly throne chariot (*merkavah*). No wonder their visions were patterned upon it.[a] But a close reading of our apocalypses leaves little that cannot be accounted for as scriptural rewrite, much as the Book of Mormon draws from the Bible.

Now, how do these considerations weigh upon the Revelation of John? First, we must suppose it to be pseudonymous, though we cannot identify either the actual author or the fictive narrator. As Benjamin W. Bacon pointed out, if the Revelation of John is not pseudonymous, it has the improbable distinction of being the only apocalypse that isn't.[b] We have no reason to assume it is an exception to the rule. The fictive seer of Patmos, then, is someone named John, presumably someone of such prominence, at least in the circle of the seven churches of Asia Minor, that he needed no further identification. Traditionally, he was identified as John, son of Zebedee, but Eusebius, thinking Constantine's empire embodied the kingdom of Christ, found he could not abide Revelation's millenarianism and therefore posited a distinct character, a "John the Elder," separate from the apostle John. He got the idea from a passage in Papias's *Oracles of the Lord* referring to "John" the apostle and "the elder John." Euse-

---

a. Gershom G. Scholem, *Major Trends in Jewish Mysticism* (NY: Schocken Books, 1973), esp. "Merkabah Mysticism and Jewish Gnosticism," 40-79.

b. Benjamin W. Bacon, "The Authoress of Revelation: A Conjecture," *Harvard Theological Review* 23 (July 1930), 235-50.

bius assumed these must be two different people. But his denial of apostolic authorship was not based on historical judgments but simply on a distaste for the book's content. John was a common enough name, so we may guess that whoever attached particular importance to it in this case thought it needed no epithets or patronymics to distinguish it. The attitude seemed to be to let others be known as "John the lesser"!

Readers will unavoidably wonder about a possible connection between the Revelation and other works ascribed to "John" even though the New Testament gospel and epistles are works of anonymity rather than pseudonymity. Tradition alone dubs their authors "John." Revelation cannot be the work of the author of the gospel because the two Greek styles are drastically different. The Revelation may come from the same sect community as the others, but in that case it represents the extreme retrenchment wing of the Ecclesiastical Redactor, restoring futuristic eschatology with a vengence.[c]

Once we get past the red herring of John the Elder versus John the Apostle, and few commentators have, we find a small, scattered list of suggested candidates for authorship of Revelation: the prophesying daughter of Philip, who married and settled in Hierapolis (B.W. Bacon); Jesus (taking literally the ascription to Jesus of the seven letters to the churches); John the Baptist;[d] and what might be called a collaborative effort by John and James bar Zebedee, Tychicus, and Deutero-John.[e] Who knows?

What we can determine is what the writer's theological stance was, and that is more important in any case. It appears, as F. C. Baur suggested, that Revelation stemmed from non- or anti-Pauline Jewish Christians. For instance, one cannot help but notice the conspicuous absence of Paul's name from the list of apostles carved into the foundation stones of the New Jerusalem (21:14). The book seems to be

---

c. See Robert T. Fortna, *The Fourth Gospel and Its Predecessor: From Narrative Source to Present Gospel* (Philadelphia: Fortress Press, 1988), esp. section 2E., "Eschatology and Community," 284-93.

d. Josephine Massyngbaerde Ford, *Revelation*, Anchor Bible 38 (Garden City: Doubleday Anchor, 1975).

e. Barbara Thiering, *Jesus of the Apocalypse: The Life of Jesus after the Crucifixion* (NY: Doubleday, 1995).

plainly encratite in its sympathies, envisioning the salvation of a celibate elite (14:4). The celibacy gospel was rife in the very area of Asia Minor to which the work is addressed. The Revelator vilifies a prophetess as "Jezebel," no doubt a spite-name for a former colleague. She is said to entice the servants of Christ to prostitution or fornication. This may be nothing. Remember, we are hearing the fulminations of the Anti-Sex League here. As in the Dead Sea Scrolls, "fornication" probably meant some nit-picking sexual infraction, perhaps even having sex with one's own spouse.

When was the book written? Depending upon how we identify the eight emperors in chapter 17, the narrator seems to be positioning himself during the reign of Vespasian, fictively predicting the reigns of Titus and Domitian. Since he veers off the historical track after Domitian, predicting Rome's overthrow by the Parthians and has the emperor as the immediate precursor to the second advent of Jesus Christ, we should accept Irenaeus's placement of the book during Domitian's reign (81-96). It works out pretty well. Where we traditionally have spoken of widespread persecution engineered by Domitian, a second look reveals the evidence for this is pretty slim. Nonetheless, the writer of Revelation seems to have expected persecution due to the emperor's brazen claim to divinity, something made on behalf of all Caesars but not taken seriously by most of Domitian's predecessors.

Is the Revelation based upon visions actually experienced by some unknown author? There is no reason to think so. Close scrutiny reveals the astonishing degree to which the book was knit together from phrases and paraphrases of Old Testament prophetic books, especially from Daniel, Ezekiel, Isaiah, and Zechariah. This is no criticism; what it borrows, it uses to considerable effect.

As a genre, the roots of apocalypticism run deep, extending back to ancient Babylon, which means it was blessed with the authority of antiquity already in biblical times. In Babylon, apocalyptic was the handmaiden of government propaganda. As part of the royal ideology, it reinforced the divinity of the king's position. Each year, so the story went, the king entered the temple of Marduk and ascended into heaven to glimpse the Tablets of Destiny which informed him what lay in store for the coming year. This privilege made it superfluous

and blasphemous for anyone to second-guess the king and his policies. He knew what was coming; you didn't. Gradually the prerogative of kings was shared with sages, priests, and royal scribes, who took pen in hand to write in the names of Baruch, Enoch, Levi, and Moses. Apocalypses purport to describe the secrets these holy men brought back with them. However, history was only part of the concern of the scribes. Apocalyptic seers sought not only to project history horizontally into the future but to expand their grasp vertically into the heavens and map out the universe. The tendency stems from Babylon where astrology/astronomy was born. It was a Jewish priest in the Babylonian exile who bequeathed the priestly creation account (Gen. 1:1-2:2a) with its sketch of cosmogony and cosmology, even as later Jewish priests and sages would speculate on the furniture and layout of the heavens and hells, where the snow, rain, and lightning were stored, and where the damned and saved were stashed away till Judgment Day. Thus, it should come as no surprise that the Revelation makes extensive use of ancient astronomy and astrology.[f]

If it was the scribes who had the leisure and scholarly interest to map the universe and chart the future from their erudite imaginations, it was similarly their influence that led to the most vexing feature of apocalypses, whether Daniel, 4 Ezra, or Revelation—namely their puzzling cipher language. It used to be thought that the baffling symbolism was a code language made needful because of the persecution setting of the genre: Suppose a clear and gloating prediction of the doom of Rome were to fall into the wrong hands? The faithful are in enough trouble already! Therefore, best to write in code. But in fact, no persecution seems in view in most apocalypses, which must make us guess again. Most prevalent today is the assumption that the puzzle element was part of the scribal language. They wanted to make their readers work for it: He who has ears to hear, let him hear. Everyone else? Work on getting ears!

We probably also have scribalism, with its love of antiquity and antique lore, to thank for the appearance of archaic mythemes in Revelation such as that of Leviathan, the seven-headed dragon, as well as

---

f. Bruce J. Malina, *On the Genre and Message of Revelation: Star Visions and Sky Journeys* (Peabody: Hendrickson, 1995).

stray bits of unassimilated Greek myth surrounding Argus, Baucis and Philemon, Gaia, and Hades. How striking the Revelator vilifies Pergamum as the place "where Satan has his throne" (2:13), presumably in reference to the great shrine of Zeus there, yet still applies the old myth of Zeus and his father Kronos to the infant messiah in 12:4b-6, 13-14!

What is the abiding value of the Revelation? Why was it not simply discarded as a false alarm once Domitian's reign ended peacefully? For the same reason horoscope readers do not stop reading them after it ought to have become apparent that they do not really predict the future (any more than Revelation does!). Astrology believers always get the boon they really want from reading their horoscope: permission to sleep soundly in the belief that they are both forewarned and forearmed for the morrow. When the day dawns with unanticipated troubles, they are competent to deal with them spontaneously, so it matters not that they gained no real information from the horoscope. What counted was the permission they gave themselves not to worry the night before. In precisely the same way, as John G. Gager observed,[g] the hearing of Revelation read in church, or seeing an actual dramatic performance of it as a play, as John Wick Bowman suggests,[h] relieved the tension and boredom of the mundane world, temporarily propelling the hearer into eschatological bliss. For the moment, the blessed end had come and believers, disappointed through the rest of the week, basked in it: the kingdom of this world was transformed into the kingdom of our Lord and of his Christ, at least for a while. Such psychodrama was the only answer to the ever-longer delay of the Parousia. It probably still is, though Revelation's place in such a scenario has been supplanted to a large extent by novels and movies based on it. One need only think of *Left Behind, Distant Thunder,* and *Image of the Beast.*[i]

g. John G. Gager, *Kingdom and Community: The Social World of Early Christianity* (Englewood Cliffs: Prentice-Hall, 1975), 54-55.

h. John Wick Bowman, *The Drama of the Book of Revelation* (Philadelphia: Westminster Press, 1955).

i. Tim LaHaye and Jerry B. Jenkins, *Left Behind: A Novel of the Earth's Last Days* (Wheaton, IL: Tyndale House Publishers, 1995), the first in a series of Christian apocalyptic novels by LaHaye and Jenkins; *Distant Thunder* and *Image*

1

[1]A revelation of Jesus-Christ, which God vouchsafed him to show his slaves what must occur speedily now, and he communicated this by sending his angel to his slave John, [2]who testified to the message of Jesus-Christ and to the testimony Jesus-Christ offered to everything he saw.[j] [3]Blessed be the reader and the hearers of the words of the prophecy and those who take to heart the things written in it, for the time is upon us.

[4]John, to the seven congregations in Asia: Favor and protection to you from the One Who Is, the One Who Was, and the Coming One, and from the seven spirits who stand in readiness at his throne[k] [5]and from Jesus-Christ, the faithful martyr, the firstborn from the dead and the archon of the kings of the earth. To him who loved us and freed us from our sins by means of his own blood, [6]making us a kingdom, priests serving his God and Father, to him be the worship and the rule for ages multiplied by ages! Amen.

[7]Behold! He comes riding on the clouds[l] and every eye will see him, not least those who pierced his flesh,[m] and all the tribes of earth shall wail at the sight of him.[n] Yes, amen!

[8]"I am the alpha and the omega!" says the God Adonai, the One Who Is, and the One Who Was, and the Coming One, the Almighty.

[9]I, John, your brother and comrade in the affliction we must suffer if we are to enter the kingdom and the necessary endurance that are our lot in following Jesus, happened to be on the island called Patmos for the sake of preaching the message of God, namely the testimony to Jesus. [10]I happened to be in the ecstasy of the Spirit on the Lord's day when I heard behind me a voice as loud as a trumpet, [11]saying, "What you see, write in a scroll and send it to the seven congregations, to Ephesus and Smyrna and Pergamum and Thyatira and Sardis and Philadelphia and Laodicea."

[12]So I wheeled about to see the source of the voice that was address-

---

of the Beast, one of a four-part series of apocalyptic films (*Thief in the Night* series, 1972-83) produced by Russell S. Doughten of Mark IV Pictures, Des Moines, Iowa.

j. Rev. 22:16, 20

k. These are the archangels or angel princes: Gabriel, Jeremiel, Michael, Raguel, Raphael, Sauriel, and Uriel.

l. This is the ancient imagery common to Yahve and his cognate rival Baal Hadad in Syria: both were gods of storm and war. See Pss. 18:10-14; 104:3b; Dan. 7:13; 2 Samuel 22:10-15.

m. Zech. 12:10

n. This becomes a saying of the earthly Jesus in Matt. 24:30.

ing me. And once I had turned, I saw a circle of seven golden lamp stands
[13]and at the center of the lamp stands there stood one like a son of man,
robed to the feet, with a golden sash about his breasts.[o] [14]The hair on his
head was white like wool, white as snow, and his eyes blazed like coals of
fire. [15]His feet glowed like polished brass red hot in a furnace and his
voice thundered like the crashing of a cataract. [16]And he held in his right
hand seven stars, and from his open mouth emerged a double-edged
sword. And his face beamed like the sun shining at its height.[p] [17]And
when I saw him, I fell prostrate at his feet like a fallen corpse, and he
placed his right hand on me and said, "Do not be afraid. I am the first and
the last [18]and the living one. I became dead, but as you see, I am alive now
for ages multiplied by ages. And I wield the keys of Death and Hades.
[19]So write what you see, the things that are now as well as the events that
are about to occur after these things.[q] [20]The significance of the seven stars
which you saw in my right hand and of the golden lamp stands is this: the
seven stars are the delegates of the seven congregations, while the seven
golden lamp stands you saw are the seven congregations themselves.

2

[1]"To the delegate from the Ephesian congregation, write as follows:
Thus says the one who holds in his right hand the hebdomad of stars, the
one who paces among the seven golden lamp stands. [2]I am familiar with
your record, your labor and your endurance and the fact that you cannot
tolerate the wicked: you tested those fraudulently passing themselves off
as apostles and discovered their deceit. [3]And in your favor, you have endurance, bearing your share of affliction because of my name, and you
did not waver. [4]But I hold it against you that you forsook this initial love.
[5]So remember the height you once occupied. Repent and act as you did at

---

o. The reference to breasts reminds us of the many hermaphrodite angels of the Nag Hammadi Gnostic texts.

p. The heavenly visitant combines features of four divine figures from Daniel. The epithet "one like a son of man" derives from the triumphant dragon slayer Yahve, about to assume the throne of creation (Dan. 7:13a). The snow white, wool-white hair is that of El Elyon, the "ancient in days" (Dan. 7:9), while the rest of the description recalls that of Gabriel (Dan. 10:2-10). The seemingly redundant, contradictory detail of feet shining so brightly they look not only like polished bronze but bronze in the furnace recalls the "fourth man" in the furnace of Nebuchadnezzar, the "one like a son of Elohim" who protected Shadrach, Meschach, and Abed-Nego (Dan. 3:25). The speaker is an angel; just as the seven spirits of 1:4 are angels, so this one is called "the spirit" in each of the seven letters to follow.

q. Dan. 8:15-19

first! If you do not, then I am coming to you to remove your lamp stand from the circle—unless you repent! [6]But I admit, you do have this going for you: you detest the deeds of the Nicolaitan sect, which I hate too. [7]He who has an ear, let him hear[r] what the spirit says to the congregations. To the one who wins the victory I will give to eat of the Tree of Life which is in the paradise of God.[s]

[8]"And to the delegate from the Smyrnaean congregation, write as follows: Thus says the First and the Last, who became dead and yet lives. [9]I am well aware of your affliction and your destitution, though in fact you are rich, and of the blaspheming of those who say they are Jews but are not, being instead a synagogue of the adversary. [10]Do not be afraid of the fate that is about to befall you. Behold: the accuser is about to throw some of you into prison to test you,[t] and to this end you will have affliction for ten days. Be faithful till death and I will reward you with the crown of life. [11]He who has an ear, let him hear what the spirit says to the congregations. The victor need fear no harm from the second death.[u]

[12]"And to the delegate from the Pergamine congregation, write as follows: Thus says the one who wields the sharp and two-edged sword. [13]I realize where you live, where the adversary has his throne.[v] And you hold fast to my name, nor did you deny my religion even in the dark days of Antipas, my martyr, my confessor, who was killed in your very midst where the adversary makes his home. [14]Nevertheless, I hold a few things against you because you tolerate the presence there of some who follow

r. This exhortation to crack the code ("he who has an ear, let him hear") will be attributed to a historical Jesus of Nazareth in Mark 4:9, 23; Matt. 13:43. In the gospel context, Jesus is the one telling the parables. There was a natural transition from the apocalyptic genre to the parabolic since the former is also basically a matter of unraveling puzzles and riddles. Cf. Mark 13:14; Rev. 13:18.

s. Rev. 22:1-2. According to *The Life of Adam and Eve* 41:1-2; 42:1; *Apocalypse of Moses* 13:1-5, Seth and Eve left Adam on his deathbed and journeyed to Eden to ask for healing oil from the Tree of Life. Their petition was refused, but Michael promised the Tree of Life would again become available to mankind in the last days at the resurrection of the dead. Thus, the promise in Rev. 2:7.

t. The role of the accuser here is exactly as in Job 1:9-12; 2:4-7; 1 Chron. 21:1-7; Zech. 3:1-5; Mark 1:13; 8:33; Luke 22:31, namely, to put the ostensibly righteous to the test in case a gracious God proves too lenient. There is nothing evil about it. The adversary or accuser becomes an evil being only where he has been conflated with originally independent mythical villains such as Ahriman, Beel-Zebub, and Leviathan.

u. Rev. 20:14

v. The great statue of Zeus on his throne was located in Pergamum.

the advice of Balaam, who counseled Balak to trip up the sons of Israel, encouraging them to eat foods dedicated to idols and to visit prostitutes.[w] 15 In the same way, you also have people who have embraced the loathsome teaching of the Nicolaitan sect. 16 So it is time you repented of this. Otherwise, I am coming to you quickly and will attack them with the blade of my mouth![x] 17 He who has an ear to hear, let him hear what the spirit says to the congregations. To the victor I will give some of the hidden manna[y] and I will bestow upon him a white stone,[z] and on that stone is inscribed a new name,[a] secret to all but the one who receives it.

18 "And to the delegate from the Thyatiran congregation, write as follows: Thus says the Son of God, he who has eyes like blazing coals and feet like polished bronze. 19 I am acquainted with your record of good deeds, of love, of faithfulness, of service, of endurance, and that your deeds of late exceed even those at the first. 20 But it rankles me that you tolerate that woman Jezebel who passes herself off as a prophetess and teaches my slaves, deceiving them into prostitution and eating meat dedicated to idols. 21 I myself tolerated her for a while, hoping she might still repent, but she has no inclination to stop her prostitution! 22 Just watch: I am dumping her into a sickbed and her paramours along with her into great affliction—unless they repudiate her evil deeds. 23 And I will snuff out her bastard whelps with the hand of death. Then all the congregations will know that I am the one who scrutinizes emotions and thoughts, and so will I repay each one of you as your deeds deserve. 24 But my message to the rest of you in Thyatira is this, all who have not imbibed this teaching, who were not initiated into the so-called 'depths'—of the adversary. I am not loading on your shoulders any additional burden;[b]

---

w. Num. 22:5-31; 23:5; Josh. 13:22; Jude 11

x. 2 Thess. 2:8

y. The manna has been stored away in the Ark of the Covenant (Exod. 16:32-34). In Rev. 11:19, the Ark of the Covenant is opened to view and these objects revealed.

z. The Revelator seems to refer to the Urim and Thummim (Exod. 28:30; Lev. 8:8; Num. 27:21), divination stones—presumably black on one side and white on the other. The Deuteronomist (Deut. 10:5) substituted the inscribed tables of the Law as orthodox sancta in place of the original sacred tokens, the latter having long since fallen under theological suspicion. In more recent times, Joseph Smith claimed to use the Urim and Thummim in deciphering the engraved plates of Mormon.

a. Isa. 62:2

b. Luke 11:46; Gal. 2:6, 10

[25]just hold on to what you have until I come. [26]And the victor, namely the one who continues to do the deeds I require until the end, I will grant him authority over the pagans [27]and he will shepherd that flock with an iron rod; and like clay pots, they shall be smashed, [28]just as I have received authority from my Father.[c] And I will give him the morning star. [29]He who has an ear, let him hear what the spirit says to the congregations."

3

[1]"And to the delegate from the Sardian congregation, write as follows: Thus says he who has the seven spirits of God and the seven stars. I am acquainted with your deeds, that you have a reputation for living faith, though in fact you are quite dead. [2]Pay attention and strengthen what you have left that has not yet crossed over the line to death, for I have found your record of obedience lacking in the sight of my God. [3]So think back to when you first heard and welcomed the news; grasp hold of it again and make a new start. Because if you are not vigilant, you will not be able to prevent me from sneaking up on you and taking away your lamp stand, as I will surely otherwise do! [4]I see a few names on the list in Sardis,[d] individuals who have not unspeakably stained their clothing; and they shall walk with me in white robes, for they are worthy. [5]The victor shall accompany me dressed in white and I shall never mark through their names on the scroll of the living.[e] No, I shall proudly announce his name before my Father and before his angels. [6]He who has an ear, let him hear what the spirit says to the congregations.

[7]"And to the delegate from the Philadelphian congregation, write as follows: Thus says the holy one, the true one, he who holds the key of David, who opens and none shall close, who closes and none shall open.[f] [8]I know all about your deeds. Behold: I have given you a door standing wide open in front of you[g] because, having but little power, you kept my command and never repudiated my name. [9]Behold the humiliation of some in the synagogue of the adversary, those who present themselves as Jews though they are not, but are lying:[h] I will force them to come before

c. Rev. 12:5; 20:4; Pss. 2:8-9; Luke 22:28-30; Matt. 19:28; 2 Tim. 2:12a; 1 Cor. 6:2-3. Note how this saying, coined in various epistles and repeated in Revelation, becomes a saying of Jesus in Q, reflected in Matthew and Luke.

d. Rev. 20:12

e. Rev. 20:15

f. Isa. 22:22

g. That is, certain access to heaven: see 4:1.

h. Apparently, these are non-Christian Jews, sectarian rivals of the Revelator

you and fall prostrate at your feet, and they shall realize all too late that it was you God loved. [10]Because you kept my command to persevere, I will in return keep you safe from the hour of testing that is ready to befall the whole inhabited earth. [11]I am coming quickly now; keep hold of what you have so no one disqualifies you from receiving your crown. [12]I will make the victor a pillar in the temple of my God, and he will never have to leave it again,[i] and I will write upon him the name of my God and the name of the city of my God, the New Jerusalem descending out of the sky from my God, and my own new name as well.[j] [13]He who has an ear, let him hear what the spirit says to the congregations.

[14]"And to the delegate from the Laodicean congregation, write as follows: Thus says the Amun,[k] the martyr faithful and true, the beginning of the creation of God. [15]I am well aware of your deeds, that you are neither cold nor hot. Oh, would that you were either cold or hot! [16]Because you are merely tepid, neither hot nor cold, I am about to vomit you out of my mouth! [17]Because you boast, 'I am rich! I have struck it rich and want for nothing!' completely oblivious of the fact that you are wretched, pitiful, poor, blind, and naked,[l] [18]my advice to you is to buy from me gold refined by fire in order that you may be truly rich, so you may afford to be clad in white robes so your shameful nakedness will not be exposed. And then you will be able to afford eye-cream to apply to your eyes and recover your vision. [19]Every one I love, I reprimand and correct. Therefore, become hot again and repent! [20]Behold! I stand just outside the door and knock. Whoever acknowledges my voice and opens the door, I will come in to greet him and will dine with him, and we will dine together.[m] [21]I will invite the victor to sit beside my throne, just as I won the victory and sat beside my Father's throne. [22]He who has an ear, let him hear what the spirit says to the congregations."

---

and his Jewish Christian congregations whom the writer regards as the "real" Jews.

i. This is the boon granted to faithful Baucis and Philemon by Zeus (Ovid, *Metamorphoses,* book 8). See also Luke 2:36-37; Pss. 84:1-4, 10; 1 Kings 7:15.

j. Rev. 19:16; Phil. 2:9

k. The attestation "Amen!" appears to be derived from the name of the Egyptian deity Amun, who is invoked as a witness to the truth of what one is affirming. Thus the personified oath is naturally named "Amun."

l. Rev. 16:15

m. Luke 24:28-31; John 5:25. Wherein lies the victory in hearing his voice and opening the door? Perhaps the point is similar to that of John 10:3-5; Mark 13:5-6: discerning the true voice of the returning Christ and not being deceived by impostors.

4

[1]After these words, I looked, and behold, a door stood open in the sky! And the voice I heard initially addressing me, the one like a trumpet, was saying to me: "Come up here and I will show you events which must transpire after this." At once I passed into a trance. [2]Behold! A throne was set up in the sky and on the throne one sat in state. [3]And the one enthroned there appeared somewhat like a jasper stone and a sardius, and a nimbus radiated about the throne like a great emerald.[n] [4]And around the throne was a semicircle of twenty-four thrones, and on these thrones sat twenty-four elders clad in white robes, with golden crowns on their heads. [5]And from out of the throne resound lightnings and reverberations and thunders, and seven lamps of fire blaze before the throne, which are the seven spirits of God. [6]And in front of the throne was a glassy sea as if made of crystal.[o] And in the middle of the throne room and circling the throne were four life forms[p] covered with eyes in front and in back.[q] [7]And the first life form was like a lion. The second life form was like a calf. The third life form had a human face. The fourth life form was like a flying eagle.[r] [8]And the four life forms, considered one by one, each had six wings and each is circled with many eyes, inside and out. And they cry out unceasingly, day and night, "Holy! Holy! Holy is the God Adonai, the Almighty! The One Who Was, and the One Who Is, and the Coming One!"[s]

[9]And whenever those life forms may render worship and honor and thanks to the one seated upon the throne, to the one who lives for ages multiplied by ages, [10]the twenty-four elders drop to the ground before the one seated upon the throne and prostrate themselves before him who lives for ages multiplied by ages and toss their crowns at the foot of the throne, singing:

> [11]"Worthy are you, our Lord and God,
> to receive the worship and the honor and the power
> because you created the All!
> By your fiat they existed and were created!"

---

n. Ezek. 1:26-28

o. 1 Kings 7:23-26

p. Dan. 7:2-7

q. Argus-like, these life forms are intended here as constellations.

r. These are the four faces of each cherub in Ezek. 1:10.

s. The six wings are those of the seraphs of Isa. 6:2-3. The Trishagion is similarly derived from their celestial worship.

5

[1]And I saw, held in the right hand of him who sat upon the throne, a
scroll written on both sides[t] and sealed up with seven seals. [2]And I saw a
mighty angel proclaiming in a loud voice: "Is anyone here worthy to open
the scroll and to break its seals?" [3]And in all the heaven and on the earth
and underneath the earth there was no one equal to the task of opening
the scroll or even of peeking into it.[u] [4]As for me, I cried bitterly that no
one was found who could open the scroll or look into it. [5]But one of the
elders says to me: "Do not cry! See? The lion of the tribe of Judah, the
root of David, has won the contest to open the scroll and its seven seals."
[6]And I saw, standing in the middle of the throne room amid the four life
forms, among the twenty-four elders, a lamb looking as if it had been
slain,[v] possessing seven horns and seven eyes, which are the seven spirits
of God sent out into all the earth.[w] [7]And he entered. Now he has taken
the scroll from the right hand of the one seated upon the throne. [8]And
when he took the scroll, the four life forms and the twenty-four elders fell
prostrate before the Lamb, each one having a harp and golden bowls full
of incense, namely the prayers of the saints. [9]And they sing a new song
which goes like this:

> "Worthy are you to receive the scroll
> and to open its seals
> because you were slain,
> and with your blood, you purchased for God
> those belonging to every tribe and language group
> and people and nation,[x]
> [10]and made them into a kingdom

---

t. Ezek. 2:10

u. This need not mean that no one tried. The scene may be like the Arthurian legend whereby no one, no matter how hard he tried, was able to disengage Excalibur from the stone. A medieval Catharist gospel opens with the Father challenging the angels: any of them who wants to become God's Son will have to endure the humiliations and torments recorded in a heavenly book. Many of the angels try to glimpse what is written there, only to faint dead away, until the angel Jesus reads, loses consciousness for three days, then awakens and undertakes his mission.

v. Could the qualifier "as if" be a bit of docetism?

w. Zech. 4:10b. They are called seven lamps and seven eyes, hence they represent the seven planets known to ancient astronomy: Sun, Moon, Mercury, Venus, Mars, Jupiter, and Saturn. They are also the seven angel princes.

x. Dan. 7:13-14

and priesthood to serve our God,
and they will rule the earth!"[y]

[11]And I saw and heard a voice of many angels circling the throne
with the life forms and the elders, and in number they were myriads of
myriads and thousands of thousands, [12]exclaiming with a loud voice,
"Worthy is the slain Lamb to receive the power and riches and wisdom
and strength and honor and worship and blessing!" [13]And every creature
in the sky and on the earth and underneath the earth and on the sea, yes,
all that people them, I heard exclaiming: "To the one seated on the throne
and to the Lamb be all bliss and honor and worship and rule through ages
multiplied by ages!" [14]And the four life forms said "Amen!" And the elders fell and prostrated themselves.

6

[1]And I saw it when the Lamb opened the first of the seven seals, and I
heard one of the four life forms saying like a thunderclap: "Come!" [2]And
I saw, and behold! A white horse! And the one mounted upon it held a
bow, and a crown was set on his brow, and he rode out conquering and
meaning to conquer ever more.

[3]And when he broke open the second seal, I heard the second life
form exclaiming: "Come!" [4]At this, another steed sprang forth, fiery red,
and to its rider was assigned the task of depriving the earth of peace, that
its inhabitants should slay one another, and he was given a huge battle
sword.

[5]And when he broke the third seal, I heard the third life form cry out,
"Come!" And I saw, and behold! A black horse and one mounted upon it
holding a balance scale in his hand! [6]And I heard a sound like a voice
from among the four life forms saying, "A measure of wheat shall cost a
denarius! Let three measures of barley command a denarius! But do not
blight the oil and the wine!"[z]

[7]And when he opened up the fourth seal, I heard the voice of the
fourth life form cry out, "Come!" [8]And I saw, and behold! A nag of leprous green! And the one who sat upon it was named Death, and Hades
followed with him, and authority was given them over a quarter of the
earth, to kill with sword and with famine and with death and by the wild
animals of the earth.

---

y. Dan. 7:18; Rev. 1:5b-6

z. The Beast 666 will take advantage of this famine to secure loyalty by rationing grain. See 13:16-17.

[9]And when he broke the fifth seal, I saw beneath the altar the souls of
those who had been slain for the sake of the message of God and for the
sake of the witness they bore. [10]And they moaned with a loud voice, saying: "When, O Despot holy and true, will you finally judge and avenge
our blood on those who live on the earth?" [11]And each of them was given
a white robe, and they were told they must needs wait but a little longer
until the allotted quota of their fellow slaves and brothers should be
killed, as they had been.

[12]And I saw, when he opened the sixth seal, that a mammoth earthquake shook the world and the sun turned black as sackcloth, and the full
moon became like blood, [13]and the stars of the sky crashed to the ground
like a fig tree scattering its unripe figs onto the earth when a strong wind
shakes it, [14]and the sky retracted like a scroll rolling up,[a] and every mountain sank and each island was thrust up from the sea floor. [15]And the
kings of the earth and the grandees and the commanders and the wealthy
and the strong and every slave and free citizen took refuge in the caves
and in the rocky mountain crags, [16]and they wail to the mountains and to
the rocks, "Fall upon us! Conceal us from the scrutiny of the one who sits
on the throne and from the fury of the Lamb [17]because the great day of
their wrath has arrived, and who can stand against it?"

7

[1]After this I saw four angels posted at the four corners of the earth
holding in check the four winds of the earth to prevent the wind from
blowing on the earth or the sea or any tree. [2]And I saw another angel
coming up from the sunrise carrying the seal of the true God, and he
shouted with a loud voice to the four angels to whom it had been assigned
to damage the earth and the sea, [3]saying, "Do no damage to the earth or
the sea or the trees until we finish sealing the slaves of our God on their
foreheads!"[b] [4]And I heard the total of the ones receiving the seal, one
hundred and forty-four thousand sealed from all the tribes of the sons of
Israel: [5]from the tribe of Judah, twelve thousand sealed; of the tribe of
Reuben, twelve thousand; of the tribe of Gad, twelve thousand; [6]from the
tribe of Asher, twelve thousand; from the tribe of Naphtali, twelve thousand; from the tribe of Manasseh, twelve thousand; [7]from the tribe of
Simeon, twelve thousand; from the tribe of Levi, twelve thousand; from
the tribe of Issachar, twelve thousand; [8]from the tribe of Zebulon, twelve

a. Isa. 34:4; Thomas, saying 11

b. Ezek. 9:4

thousand; from the tribe of Joseph, twelve thousand; from the tribe of Benjamin, twelve thousand sealed.[c]

9 After these things, I saw and beheld a vast crowd which no one would be able to count—from all nations and tribes and peoples and language groups[d]—standing before the throne and before the Lamb, clothed with white robes, holding palm branches in their hands. 10 And they shout with a loud voice, saying "Hosanna to our God seated on the throne and to the Lamb!" 11 And all the angels stood in a circle around the throne, with the elders and the four life forms, and they fell on their faces before the throne, prostrating themselves before God, 12 saying, "Amen! Bliss and worship and wisdom and thanks and honor and power and strength be ascribed to our God for ages multiplied by ages! Amen."

13 And one of the elders remarked upon it, asking me, "These people dressed in white robes: who are they? Where do they come from?" 14 And I replied, "My lord, you know."[e] So he told me: "These are the ones emerging from the great tribulation. They washed their robes pure white in the blood of the Lamb. 15 That is what entitles them to appear before the throne of God and to minister to him day and night in his temple.[f] And the one seated on the throne will spread his canopy over them. 16 They will no longer hunger or thirst, nor will the sun or any heat oppress them 17 because the Lamb in the middle of the throne room will shepherd them and will lead them in the way to the fountain of the living waters, and God will wipe every tear from their eyes."

8

1 And when at last he opened the seventh seal, there ensued a silence in heaven of about half an hour. 2 And I saw the seven angels[g] who stood at the ready before God, and they were given seven trumpets. 3 And another angel appeared and stood atop the altar holding a golden censer, and he was given many scents of incense for him to send aloft carrying the prayers of all the saints on the golden altar before the throne. 4 And the smoke of the incenses wafted upwards, with the prayers of the saints,

---

c. Joseph has replaced Ephraim in this list—Ephraim and Manasseh being half tribes, both hailing from Joseph. In addition, Levi, who is not listed in Old Testament territorial allotments, appears in place of Dan. This may be due to the belief that the Antichrist would be born from Dan.

d. Dan. 7:14

e. Ezek. 37:3

f. Rev. 3:12

g. The seven archangels or angel princes.

from the angel's hand as he swung the censor back and forth. [5]And now the angel has taken the censer and filled it with fire from the altar and flung it to the earth, and there ensued thunder claps and reverberations and lightning blasts and an earthquake.

[6]And the seven angels holding the seven trumpets puckered up so each would be ready when his turn came. [7]And the first let go a ringing blast and the sky was filled with hail and sparks and a bloody mist and it all rained on the earth. Fully a third of the earth burned down, while a third of the trees were consumed and all green grass was turned to ash.

[8]And the second angel blew his trumpet and a flaming meteor the size of a mountain crashed into the sea so that a third of it was permeated with blood. [9]And a third of the creatures at home in the sea perished.

[10]Then the third angel sounded his trumpet and a massive star, blazing like a torch, plummeted out of the sky, and it affected a third of all rivers as it fell into the sources of the rivers. [11]And the name of the star is Absinthe. And a third of all water became poisonous, and much of the human race died because the waters had been rendered toxic.

[12]And the fourth angel sounded his note and a third of the sunlight was affected, and the same with a third of the moonlight and of the starlight, so that the world might be darkened by a third both day and night. [13]And I saw and heard one eagle flying in mid-heaven crying aloud, "Woe! Woe! Woe to those who live on earth in view of what the last three angels are about to summon forth!"

9

[1]And the fifth angel sounded forth and I saw a star[h] from the sky having descended to the earth where it received the key to unlock the shaft of the abyss. [2]And he proceeded to throw wide the lid of the abyss, and from the shaft poured a vast cloud like the smoke of a colossal furnace. The sun, and thus the air, was darkened by the exhalation of the shaft. [3]And from the sooty mist emerged locusts to land upon the earth, and they were given the same power as earthly scorpions have. [4]And they were cautioned not to harm the grass of the earth, nor any green plant nor any tree: nothing but those individuals lacking the ownership seal of God on their foreheads. [5]And even these they were warned not to kill, but rather to torture for five months. And the torture they inflict is like that of a scorpion when it stings its victim. [6]And in those days their victims will desperately seek death, but not find it. They will covet death, only to have

h. Stars were standard symbols for angels, as here.

it elude their grasp. 7And these locusts might be compared to horses caparisoned for battle, on their heads something like crowns made of gold and their faces resembling human faces. 8And they had hair like the hair of women and their teeth were like the fangs of lions 9and their thoraxes looked as if armored in iron breastplates and the sound of their wings was like the sound of many horse-drawn chariots clattering to war.[i] 10They wear tails like those of scorpions, with stings mounted in the tips, and it is these that give them the ability to make people writhe in pain for five months. 11And they have a king over them, the angel of the abyss, named in Hebrew, Abaddon,[j] and in Greek he bears the name Apollyon.[k] 12With this, the first woe is over; behold, still two more woes must come after these things.

13And the sixth angel blew his trumpet and I heard one voice originating from between the four horns of the golden altar that stands before God, 14telling the sixth angel, still holding his trumpet: "Release the four angels bound at the great River Euphrates!" 15And the four angels, long since prepared for this specific hour and day and month and year, were let loose to exterminate a third of humankind. 16And the count of the cavalry soldiers was two hundred million strong: I heard them count off. 17This is how I saw the horses in the vision, as well as those mounted upon them wearing breastplates of fiery bronze, of jacinth, and brimstone, with the heads of the horses like lions' heads, and out of their mouths stream fire and smoke and sulfur. 18And from these three plagues, a third of humankind was killed by the fire and the smoke and the sulfur streaming from their mouths. 19For the power of the horses lies in their mouths and in their tails. For their tails are like snakes, each having multiple heads, and with these they wreak havoc. 20And the rest of humanity who survived these plagues still refused to renounce their idolatry or to leave off prostrating themselves before demons and images of gold, silver, bronze, stone, and wood, which can neither hear nor see nor walk. 21Nor did they repent of their murders or drug use or whore mongering or theft.

10

1And I saw another mighty angel descending from the sky, clothed in

---

i. Lying thinly veiled beneath this description is a portrayal of the Parthian cavalry and chariots, feared enemies who it was believed would one day sweep across the Euphrates to conquer Rome.

j. Abaddon means "destroyer."

k. Apollyon means "ruination." For this creature's exploits, see 1 Cor. 10:10; Num. 16:41-50; cf. Exod. 12:23.

a cloud, and the halo of his head was a rainbow[l] and his face shone like the sun and his legs were like pillars of fire! [2]And in his hand he held a little scroll, already opened. And he planted his right foot on the surface of the sea and his left upon the land, [3]and he shouted loudly like a lion roaring. And when he shouted, the seven thunders spoke with their own voices. [4]And when the seven thunders spoke, I was ready to write, but I heard a voice speaking from out of the sky, saying: "Seal up what the seven thunders have spoken, nor may you transcribe them!"[m]

[5]And the angel whom I saw standing on the sea and the land raised his right hand to heaven [6]and swore by the one who lives for ages multiplied by ages, who created the sky and everything in it, and the earth and all things in it, and the sea and all things in it, that there should be no delay, [7]but that in the days when the sound of the seventh angel is heard, whenever he blows his trumpet, the secret providence of God will have been brought to completion, as he announced to his slaves, the prophets. [8]And the voice which I heard from the sky addressed me again, saying, "Go take the scroll that lies open in the hand of the angel standing astride the sea and the land." [9]So I made my way to the angel, asking him to hand me the little scroll. And he replies to me, "Take and eat it and it will make your stomach sour, though while in your mouth it will taste as sweet as honey." [10]So I took the little scroll from the angel's hand and gobbled it down,[n] and sure enough, it was sweet like honey in my mouth; but when I swallowed it, it turned my stomach sour.[o] [11]And they say to me, "You must once again prophesy in the hearing of peoples and nations and language groups and kings!"[p]

11

[1]And they handed me a reed straight as a staff, saying, "Get up and measure the temple of God, the altar, and those worshipping there.[q] [2]But

---

l. Ezek. 1:27-28

m. In view is brontology, the technique of telling the future by interpreting thunderclaps. This art was practiced by the Dead Sea Scrolls community. What did the seven thunders reveal? See the next chapter in this anthology (Thunder: Perfect Mind).

n. It may be the Revelator is signaling his incorporation of an earlier "little apocalypse," perhaps the basis of 11:1-12. In just the same way, Timothee Colani argued that Mark 13:5-31 was a separate apocalyptic tract subsequently interpolated into Mark.

o. Ezek. 2:9-3:3

p. Dan. 7:14

q. Ezek. chaps. 40-42

exclude the courtyard outside the temple. You may not measure it because it had always been assigned to the gentiles, but now they will trample the holy city for forty-two months.[r]

3“And I will assign my two martyrs to prophesy for one thousand two hundred sixty days, clothed in sackcloth. 4These are represented by the two olive trees and the two lamp stands which stand before the Lord of the earth.[s] 5And if anyone makes a move to injure them, a jet of flame pours from their mouths and consumes their enemies.[t] And if anyone should want to harm them, this is how he must be destroyed. 6These have authority to close the windows of heaven, to stop the rain falling for the duration of their prophesying.[u] Moreover, they possess power over all water to turn it into blood[v] and to thrash the earth with every plague whenever the mood strikes them. 7And whenever they complete their testimony, the Beast rising up out of the abyss[w] will wage war against them and will vanquish them and kill them. 8And their corpses will lie unburied on the open street of the great city,[x] which is esoterically called Sodom and Egypt, the same place their Lord was crucified. 9And from all the peoples and tribes and language groups and nations, people come to gloat over the corpses over three and a half days, refusing to allow their corpses decent burial in a tomb. 10And the inhabitants of the earth celebrate over them and make merry and send each other gifts because these two prophets tormented everyone on earth.

11But after the three and a half days, a spirit of life from God entered into them, and they stirred and stood to their feet[y] and all who saw it were terror-stricken. 12And they heard a loud voice from heaven addressing them, “Come up here!” And they rose up into the sky in the cloud chariot while their enemies looked on agape.[z] 13And just then a massive earthquake erupted, and a tenth of the city collapsed, and seven thousand

r. Luke 21:24

s. Zech. 4:3, 11-14, thus originally Zerub-Babel and Joshua.

t. 2 Kings 1:10

u. 1 Kings 17:1

v. Exod. 7:17, 19

w. Dan. 7:3. The Beast is not introduced until 13:1, to which this present verse seems to refer *back*, again implying that the “little scroll” was an originally independent patch sewn in here by our author who had already composed chap. 13.

x. Isa. 14:18-19

y. Ezek. 37:5, 10

z. 2 Kings 2:11

names of men were erased from the roll of the living in the earthquake, while the rest were terrified and ascribed glory to the God of the sky.
14Lo, the second woe is now over! Behold! The third woe follows upon its heels.

15And the seventh angel let loose his blast and there were loud voices echoing across the sky, saying: "The rule of the cosmos has passed to our Lord and his Christ, and he shall rule through ages multiplied by ages!"
16And the twenty-four elders who ever sit before God upon their thrones fell on their faces, prostrating themselves before God, 17singing, "All thanks to you, O Lord God, the Almighty, the One Who Is and the One Who Was, because you have taken the reins of power and begun to rule.
18Yes, the nations raged,[a] but your wrath came and, with it, the appointed time for the dead to be judged and to give the reward due your slaves the prophets, and the saints, and the ones who fear your name—to reward the insignificant and the great and to destroy those who destroy the
earth." 19And the temple in the sky was opened up and the ark of his covenant could be seen in his temple[b] and there erupted lightning blasts and reverberations and thunderclaps, an earthquake and a terrific hailstorm.

12

1And a great portent became visible in the sky, a woman swathed in the sun, the moon beneath her feet, with a crown of twelve stars resting
on her brow. 2And having a child in the womb, she cries out in labor and
in the pain of birthing. 3And another portent appeared in the sky, and behold, a vast, red Dragon, having seven heads, each head wearing a dia-
dem of ten horns, 4and his tail sweeps up a third of the stars of the night sky and flings them to the earth. And the Dragon stood poised in front of the woman who was about to give birth, to be ready to devour the baby
as soon as she might deliver it. 5And she bore a son, a male, who is destined to shepherd all the nations with an iron crook. And her child was
snatched up to God and to his throne.[c] 6As for the woman, she took flight into the desert where she is to find a place of refuge prepared by

a. Pss. 2:1

b. Mark 15:38

c. The virgin is the constellation Virgo, while the dragon is Draco, which appears after Virgo in the night sky, hence the myth of a dragon pursuing a virgin. We also see the old myth of baby Zeus' deliverance from the cannibalistic appetite of Kronos, the Titan king who stood ready to scoop up and eat each of Rhea's newborns to forestall any usurpation. Rhea gave Kronos a stone to swallow instead, while her mother Gaia took the baby away to be raised on the island of

God, where she will be taken care of for one thousand two hundred and sixty days.

7And a war erupted in the sky, Michael[d] and his angel legions battling the Dragon. The Dragon fought hard, and his own angels alongside him, 8yet they did not win out and it was clear there was no longer any place for them in heaven. 9And the Great Dragon was expelled, the archaic serpent,[e] the one called the accuser and the adversary, the deceiver of the whole inhabited earth; he was hurled down onto the ground[f] and his angels were thrown down with him. 10And I heard a loud voice resounding in the sky, saying, "Now it has come! The salvation and the power and the kingship of our God and the authority of his Christ! Because the accuser of our brothers has been toppled, he who used to accuse us before God day and night.[g] 11And our brothers vanquished him by the blood of the Lamb, their confession of faith at their martyrdom, and the fact they did not insist on holding onto their lives till the last.[h] 12Therefore, rejoice, you heavens and those sojourning there! But woe to you, O earth and sea, because the accuser came down to you livid with rage, knowing that little time is left to him."

Crete (Hesiod, *Theogony,* 459-91). This is also reflected in *The Apocalypse of Adam* 78:9-13, 19-23, and in the *Liqqute Midrashim,* 156: "In those days [before the Flood] only one virgin, Istahar by name, remained chaste. When the Sons of God made lecherous demands upon her, she cried: 'First lend me your wings!' They assented and she, flying up to heaven, took sanctuary at the Throne of God, who transformed her into the constellation Virgo" (Robert Graves and Raphael Patai, *Hebrew Myths: The Book of Genesis* [NY: Greenwich House, 1983], 101). See also Mark 1:9-13; Matt. 2:13-16, where the pursuing dragon has been split between the persecuting Herod and the place of refuge, Old Testament "Rahab" referring both to Egypt and to the chaos dragon.

d. Michael was the angel prince assigned to defend Israel against the angels/gods of other nations (Dan. 10:13, 21).

e. The reference is to the seven-headed dragon Lotan ("Baal will run through with his spear, even as he did Lotan, the crooked serpent with seven heads") or Leviathan (Job 41; Pss. 74:12-14; 104:26; Isa. 27:1), also called Rahab (Pss. 89:10; Isa. 51:9), Behemoth (Job 40:15-24; implied in Gen. 1:2 in *bohu,* "void"), and Tiamat (implied in Genesis 1:2 in *tehom,* "deep," and *tohu,* "amorphous").

f. Ezek. 32:4

g. Job 1:8-11; Zech. 3:1; Luke 22:31; Jude 9

h. How did the overthrow of the accuser/adversary save them? It seemed sufficient to rely on the blood of the Lamb and their own suffering to save them from the sentencing the adversary might press before God, but there is also the implication that they are safe because their accuser is no longer around to draw attention to their faults.

[13]And when the Dragon realized he had been exiled to the earth, he went after the woman who bore the male. [14]And they gave the woman the two wings of the great eagle for her to fly to the desert to her retreat where she is cared for and hidden from the questing snout of the serpent for a time, times, and half a time. [15]And the serpent, pursuing the woman, spewed out of his mouth a river of water to sweep her away.[i] [16]And Gaia came to the woman's rescue, opening her mouth to swallow the river that the Dragon has released from his own mouth. [17]And the Dragon was infuriated over the woman and stalked off to renew the battle against the rest of her sons, those who keep the commandments of God and bear witness to Jesus.

13

[1]And he stood on the seashore, waiting. And I saw a Beast rising up out of the sea[j] with ten horns[k] and seven heads, and for its ten horns, diadems, and upon its heads were written ten blasphemous names. [2]And this Beast I saw was like a leopard, having feet like the paws of a bear and its mouth like the maw of a lion.[l] And the Dragon gave it his power and throne and great authority. [3]And one of its heads looked to have been mortally wounded, but its death wound was healed. And everyone on earth marveled as they followed the progress of the Beast, [4]and they prostrated themselves before the Dragon since he was the source of the Beast's authority, and they prostrated themselves before the Beast whenever he might pass by, exclaiming, "Is there anyone like Therion?[m] Who would dare fight against him?" [5]And he was given the power of speech to make great boasts[n] and blasphemous claims, and he was granted authority to act as he wished for forty-two months. [6]And he opened his mouth to defame God, to blaspheme his name as well as his tabernacle, namely those sojourning in heaven. [7]And it was granted him to wage war on the saints and to vanquish them.[o] And he was granted authority over every tribe and

i. The river is the origin of Leviathan (Lotan, Litan) as the personification of the winding river Litani and its seven or more tributaries in Syria (Michael D. Goulder, *The Psalms of Asaph and the Pentateuch,* vol. 3, Studies in the Psalter (Sheffield, Eng.: Sheffield Academic Press, 1996), 69.

j. Dan. 7:2-3

k. Dan. 7:7

l. Dan. 7:3-6

m. Therion means "beast."

n. Dan. 7:8

o. Dan. 7:21

people and language group and nation.[p] [8]And all who live on earth shall prostrate themselves before him, at least those whose names had not been registered since the creation of the world in the slain Lamb's scroll of life.[q]

[9]He who has an ear—let him hear! [10]Anyone destined for captivity, to captivity he goes. If anyone kills by the sword, he must himself be killed by a sword.[r] This is why endurance and faithfulness are required of the saints.

[11]And I saw another Beast rising up from the caverns below. It had two horns like a ram and spoke like a Dragon. [12]And it wields all the authority of the first Beast as its representative. And it decrees that the earth and all who live on it should worship the first Beast, whose death stroke was healed. [13]And it performs great signs, calling down fire out of the sky onto the earth before mortal eyes.[s] [14]And it deceives all who live on earth by means of the signs it was enabled to do representing the beast, commanding the people of the earth to erect a statue of the beast who took the sword stroke and lived. [15]And he was given the power to animate the statue of the Beast so that the statue could even speak,[t] ordering that all who did not prostrate themselves before it should be executed.[u] [16]And he requires everyone, both peasants and nobles, both rich and poor, both free citizens and slaves, to receive a mark imprinted on their right hand or on their forehead [17]to make it impossible for anyone to buy or sell except for those who bore the mark, the name of the Beast or the number of its name.[v] [18]This requires wisdom: whoever has sufficient skill, let him

---

p. Gal. 2:7-9

q. Presumably the same scroll he received in Rev. 5:7. As a map of the future, it would naturally include the roll call of the saved.

r. This common maxim becomes a saying of Jesus in Matt. 26:52.

s. See 1 Kings 18:24, indicating the sign would be to prove the Beast is the true god.

t. This was a familiar ventriloquist stunt in the ancient world. Here it may be intended as genuine magic along the lines of the Golem legends. We read in *The Chronicles of Jerahmeel* 23:7 (trans. Moses Gaster) how "Enosh then took six clods of earth, mixed them, and moulded them and formed an image of dust and clay. 'But,' said they, 'this image does not walk, nor does it possess any breath of life.' He then showed them how God breathed into his nostrils the breath of life. But when he began to breathe into it, Satan entered the image so that it walked, and they went away after it, saying, 'What is the difference between bowing down before this image and before man?'"

u. Dan. 6:6-7

v. This tactic presupposes the famine anticipated in 6:5-6. The Beast is rationing precious grain, much as Joseph did in Egypt. On another level, given the

reckon up the number of the Beast, for it works out to the number of a particular man. And the number of it is six hundred and sixty-six.[w]

14

[1]And I saw, and behold, the Lamb standing upon the peak of Mount Zion! And with him were one hundred forty-four thousand who had his name and the name of his Father imprinted on their foreheads. [2]And I heard a sound from the sky like the sound of a crashing cataract and like deafening thunder. And the sound I heard was like harpists strumming their harps. [3]And they sing a new song before the throne and before the four life forms and the elders. No one could learn the song except for the hundred forty-four thousand who had been ransomed from the earth. [4]These are the ones who did not degrade themselves with women, for they are virgins. It is these who follow the Lamb wherever he may lead. These were purchased from among mankind to be dedicated as first fruits[x] to God and to the Lamb. [5]No lie was ever found on their lips. They are impeccable.

[6]And I saw another angel soaring in mid-heaven who had epoch-making news with which to evangelize all who sat on the ground below as he flew over every nation and tribe and language group and people, [7]saying in a loud voice, "Fear God and worship him while you can, for the hour of his judgment has struck! Prostrate yourselves before the one who made the sky and the earth and the sea and the subterranean fountains."

Jewish-Christian character of this book, we might wonder whether the Beast is intended as Paul, who was certainly regarded by Jewish Christians as the deceiver of the nations. The famine in question might then be identified with that under Claudius in Acts 11:27-30. Since F. C. Baur, we have become used to reading Acts 8:18-24 as preserving an invidious interpretation of Paul's collection among the gentiles on behalf of Jerusalem. In Gal. 2:10, the implication is that the collection was a condition of recognition of Paul's mission by the Pillars. Acts 8 makes it an attempt by Paul to buy the apostleship, which is not all that different. It may be that Rev. 13 sees Paul extorting apostolic recognition as the price of relief aid for Jerusalem. In view of this, note the perhaps satirical analogy between Rev. 13:16 and Gal. 3:27-28.

w. In ancient Greek, Hebrew, and Latin, the characters of the alphabet doubled as numbers and people found it amusing to convert their names into number totals, much as we might convert a name to its initials. Our author's choice of 666 was probably familiar to the original audience as Nero Caesar, who died in 68 CE, or Nero Redivivus (Domitian), who died in 96 CE. Roman folk belief expected Nero to return to exact revenge upon Rome. They thought he had probably staged his murder, having a stand-in killed, and escaped or had even risen from the dead. Hence, the beast in Rev. 13:3 bounces back from a mortal wound.

x. Exod. 34:26

8And another angel, a second one, followed, shouting, "Collapsed! Collapsed! Babylon the Great who made all the nations drink the wine of her lusty prostitution!"

9And another angel, a third one, followed, shouting at the top of his voice: "Whoever worships the Beast and his statue and allows a mark to be imprinted on his forehead or his hand, 10he shall choke on the wine of the fury of God, mixed full strength in the cup of his rage![y] He will be tortured by fire and sulfur to amuse the holy angels and the Lamb.[z] 11And the smoke from their torture rises up age after age,[a] nor have they any respite day or night, those who worship the Beast and his statue and if anyone accepts the mark of his name." 12Hence the need for endurance on the part of the saints, those who keep the commandments of God and the religion of Jesus. 13And I heard a voice from the sky saying, "Write this: 'Blessed are the dead who die for Adonai from now on! Yes,' said the spirit, 'for they rest from their labors. For their deeds accompany them into heaven.'"

14And I saw, and behold, a white cloud and one like a son of man seated upon the cloud. He wore a golden crown upon his head and grasped a keen-edged sickle in his hand. 15And another angel appeared from out of the temple, shouting in a loud voice to the one who sat upon the cloud, "Sweep with your sickle and reap! For the hour of reaping has struck. Because the harvest of the earth was desiccated." 16And the one seated on the cloud swung the sickle across the earth, and so the earth was harvested. 17And another angel emerged from the temple in heaven, and he, too, was armed with a sharp sickle. 18Yet another angel left the altar, whose task it was to tend the sacrificial flame, and he spoke loudly to his comrade with the sharp sickle: "Plunge in your sharp sickle to gather the clusters from the vines of earth because its grapes are ripe!" 19So the angel plunged his blade into the earth and gathered the fruit of the vine of the earth and threw it into the great winepress of the anger of God. 20And the place of pressing was outside the city, and the blood gushed out from the winepress to a depth even with the bridles of horses a thousand six hundred stadia away!

15

1And I saw another great portent in heaven, great and wondrous:

---

y. Isa. 51:17; Jer. 25:15-16; 49:12; 51:7

z. Luke 19:27

a. Isa. 34:10

seven angels[b] carrying the final seven plagues because with them the anger of God was exhausted. [2]And I saw something resembling a crystalline sea[c] with flashes of fire inside it. And those who emerged from the ordeal of the Beast and its statue and the number of its name, they were standing on the surface of the crystal sea, strumming harps given them by God.
[3]And they sing the song of Moses, the slave of God,[d] as well as the new song of the Lamb, saying:

"Great and wondrous are your deeds,
O Lord God, the Almighty!
Righteous and true are your ways,
O king of nations!
[4]Who will not fear your name, O Lord,
or fail to worship it?
For you alone are holy!
For all the nations will come
and prostrate themselves before you!
For your commandments were vindicated for all to see!"

[5]And after these things, I looked, and the holy place containing the
tent of witness in heaven was opened. [6]And the seven angels emerged
from the temple carrying the seven plagues. They were dressed in clean
white linen, with golden sashes around their breasts. [7]And one of the four
life forms passed out to the seven angels seven golden bowls filled with
the anger of God, who lives on through ages multiplied by ages. [8]And the
temple was filled with the smoke of the divine Shekinah and his power, so that none dared enter the temple until the seven plagues of the seven angels were over.[e]

16

[1]And I heard a loud voice echoing from the temple, telling the seven
angels, "Go and empty the seven bowls of the anger of God onto the
earth!" [2]And the first departed and spilled out his bowl onto the earth,
and painful, running sores erupted on all those bearing the mark of the
Beast and worshipping his statue. [3]And the second poured his bowl into
the sea, where it turned to blood, like the turgid blood of the dead, and

b. Again, the archangels.

c. 1 Kings 7:23-26

d. Exod. 15:1-18

e. 1Kings 8:10; Isa. 6:4

every entity dwelling in the sea was poisoned. [4]And the fourth emptied his bowl into the rivers and the fountains of the deep, and this water, too, became blood. [5]And I heard the angel in charge of the waters[f] saying, "Righteous are you in this judgment, the One Who Is and the One Who Was, the Holy One. [6]For they shed the blood of saints and prophets, and you have given them blood to drink just as they deserved!" [7]And I heard the altar exclaiming, "Yes, O Lord God, the Almighty, your judgments are true and right!"

[8]And the fourth flung the contents of his bowl into the sun, for it was his task to burn the human race with fire. [9]And people were burned with a terrific heat and they reviled the name of God, the master of the plagues, and they failed to think better of it and worship him instead.

[10]And the fifth dumped the contents of his bowl onto the throne of the Beast, and his kingdom sank deep into shadow and his subjects bit their tongues from the agony, [11]and they reviled the God of the sky in their agony and because of their sores and they did not abandon their sinful deeds.

[12]And the sixth emptied his bowl into the great river Euphrates, and suddenly the water dried up. This was to prepare the way for the kings from the sunrise.[g] [13]And I saw three unclean spirits hopping loathsomely like frogs from the open maw of the Dragon, from the dripping jaws of the Beast, and from the honeyed lips of the Pseudoprophet. [14]These are demoniacal spirits who perform signs; they fly forth to the kings of all the inhabited world to summon them to battle on the Great Day of God the Almighty. [15]"Behold: I am coming like a thief! Blessed is the one who stays dressed and ready so that disaster does not send him naked into the street where others will see him!" [16]And they were gathered in that place called, in Hebrew, Hill of Megiddo.

[17]And the seventh scattered the contents of his bowl into the atmosphere. And a loud voice resounded from the temple, from the throne, saying, "Thus it ends!" [18]And there were lightning blasts and reverberations and thunderclaps, and a massive earthquake erupted, such as never occurred since before human beings inhabited the earth, an earthquake of such magnitude it was! [19]And the great city was riven into three fragments and the cities of the nations collapsed. And thus God remembered to give Babylon the Great the cup of the fury of his rage. [20]From it every

f. The angel is one of the elemental spirits of Gal. 4:3, 9.

g. The reference is to the much-feared Parthian Empire.

island fled beneath the water and mountains were submerged. [21]And huge hailstones, each weighing about a talent, descend from the sky to crush people, and they reviled God for the plague of hail because the damage it wrought was extremely severe.

17

[1]And one of the seven pestiferous angels came and spoke with me, saying, "Come, let me show you the judgment of the great prostitute enthroned on many waters, [2]with whom the kings of the earth used to fornicate while all the people of the earth became drunk from the wine of her revels!" [3]With that, he carried me in a vision into a desert. And I saw a woman sitting astride a Scarlet Beast that was branded all over with blasphemous names,[h] with seven heads and ten horns on each. [4]And the woman was decked out in purple and scarlet and adorned with gold and precious stones and pearls, holding a golden goblet filled with menstrual blood from her unlawful fornications.[i] [5]And across her forehead a name had been tattooed, a riddle: "Babylon the Great, the Mother of All Prostitutes and of All Abominations on Earth." [6]And I saw the woman drunk from so much blood from the saints and from the martyrs of Jesus. And when I saw her, I was utterly amazed.

[7]And the angel said to me, "What is so amazing? Let me tell you the answer to the riddle of the woman and of the Beast with seven heads and ten horns that she rides. [8]The Beast that you saw, it was and is not and is about to rise up out of the abyss. It is destined for destruction. And all the people of the earth will marvel when they see the Beast that was, and is not, and is present,[j] at least those whose names are not to be found in the scroll of the living since the creation of the world. [9]This calls for a mind adept in wisdom! The seven heads are really seven mountains[k] where the woman sits and where seven kings reign. [10]Of these, five fell,[l] one rules now,[m] and the other has not yet arisen, but whenever he does, he must remain a little while.[n] [11]As for the beast which was and is not, he is an

h. The author is probably referring to the divine titles and epithets assumed by the Roman emperors, for instance "Jupiter, Our Lord and God."

i. Several Church Fathers report, correctly or not, that various Gnostics drank menses as a sacrament.

j. That is, he appeared as Nero, disappeared, and returned as Domitian.

k. Rome was built on seven hills.

l. The kings are the Caesars Augustus, Tiberius, Caligula, Claudius, and Nero.

m. Vespasian.

n. Titus.

eighth[o] and is yet one of the previous seven,[p] and then he goes to perdition.[q] 12And the ten horns you saw are ten kings who have not yet come to power but will receive authority to reign as kings alongside the Beast for a single hour. 13These are all of one mind and they rule in full accord with the will of the Beast. 14Those kings will wage war on the Lamb, but the Lamb will vanquish them because he is lord of lords and king of kings[r] and his companions are the called the chosen, the faithful."

15And he says to me, "The waters you saw where the prostitute sits enthroned represent populations and crowds and nations and language groups. 16And the ten horns you saw, together with the Beast, will turn on the prostitute and will leave her naked and bereft of her riches. They will eat bits of her flesh and will incinerate what remains. 17For God has prompted them to do as they wish, to act as one and to turn their authority over to the Beast until that time when the promises of God are made good. 18As for the woman you saw, she is that great city that rules over the kings of the earth."

18

1And after these things, I saw another angel descending from the sky, a high-ranking angel, and the earth became as noonday by means of his radiance. 2And he cried out very loudly, "Collapsed! Collapsed! Babylon the Great!"[s] And it became a haunt of demons, a prison for every profane spirit, a cage for every foul and loathsome bird[t] 3because all the nations have imbibed the wine of her lusty fornication and the kings of the earth have continually fornicated with her and the merchants of the earth grew rich off the abundance of her luxuries.

4And I heard another voice echoing from the sky, saying, "Get out of her, my people! Or you will be implicated in her sins and will suffer her plagues. 5For joined together end to end, her sins reach up to heaven and God has marked her misbehavior. 6Repay her in kind and double what is due her for her deeds! Take her poison cup and mix it double strength for her. 7As much as she glorified herself and lived in decadence, assign her

---

o. Domitian.

p. Nero returned.

q. Thus the Antichrist is also called the "Son of Perdition," as in 2 Thess. 2:3 and John 17:12. It means "the one who comes from, or rightly belongs in, hell."

r. A title of the Persian emperor.

s. Isa. 21:9

t. Jer. 50:39

the same weight of torture and sorrow. Because she says to herself, 'I
reign as queen and not in place of a dead husband! I need not mourn!'
8For this arrogance, plagues will befall her in a single day: she will be devoured by death, sorrow, famine, and flames. For the God Adonai is
strong and it is he who judges her!"

9And the kings of the earth who used to fornicate and revel with her
will sob and lament over her every time they look toward the column of
smoke from her burning. 10They keep their distance because they fear
they might share her torment. Listen to them: "Woe! Woe to the great
city! Babylon the strong city! For your judgment fell in a single hour!"
11And merchants all over the earth cry and mourn over her because there
remains no market for their cargo, 12shipments of gold and silver and precious stones and pearls, fine linen, purple and silk and scarlet, all thyine
wood, and every kind of ivory vessel, and all sorts of precious wooden
vessels and those of bronze and iron and marble, 13and cinnamon and
spice and incenses and myrrh and frankincense, wine, oil, fine meal, corn,
beasts of burden, sheep, horses, carriages, plus human bodies and souls.
14The fruit of your soul's lust have abandoned you and all your luxuries
and fine lamps have vanished away, never to be recovered.

15The dealers in these things, having made a fortune off her, will
stand at a safe distance for fear of sharing the torment of her weeping and
grief, 16lamenting: "Woe! Woe to the great metropolis, once regaled in
fine linen and purple and scarlet, gilded with gold and gems and pearls,
17for such great wealth was decimated in a single hour!" And every ship's
pilot, all the passengers and sailors and all engaged in the maritime trade
stood at a distance 18and exclaimed their anguish at the sight of her rising
smoke, saying, "There will never be another like her!" 19And they sprinkled the dust of mourning on their heads and sobbed and grieved aloud,
saying, "Woe! Woe to the great city by which all those maritime traders
were made wealthy from her economy because in one hour she was laid
waste!"[u]

20Gloat over her, heaven! You saints and apostles and prophets. Because God has avenged you upon her! 21And one mighty angel lifted a
huge millstone and hurled it into the sea, saying, "Thus shall the great
metropolis Babylon be thrown down all in a moment, never to be found
again! 22Nor shall the sound of harpists and musicians and trumpeters
ever be heard in your halls again! No artisan of any sort shall ply his trade

u. See the similar laments over fallen Tyre in Ezek. 27-28.

in your streets again! No mill shall henceforth grind your grain, [23]no lamp shall relieve the darkness of your doom, and none shall hear the bride and groom exchange sweet vows. And all because your merchants became the grandees of the earth, and by the witchery of your advertisements all the nations were mesmerized! [24]And in her were found bloodstains from prophets and saints and all those killed on earth."

19

[1]Afterwards, I heard what seemed perhaps to be a loud clamor of voices in the sky, saying, "Praise Yahve for the salvation and glory and power of our God! [2]For his verdicts are fair and righteous. For he judged the great prostitute who befouled the earth with her prostitution, and he exacted from her the vengeance due his saints!" [3]And second they said, "Praise Yahve! Her smoke mounts up for ages multiplied by ages!" [4]And the twenty-four elders and the four life forms fell and prostrated themselves before God as he sat on the throne, saying, "Amen! Praise Yahve!" [5]And a voice echoed from the throne, saying, "Praise our God, all you his slaves, those who fear him, the small and the great!" [6]And I heard a sound like that of a vast crowd and like a crashing cataract and like mighty thunderclaps, and it said, "Praise Yahve! For Adonai, our God, the Almighty, has begun to rule! [7]Let us rejoice, and let us exult! And we will give all credit to him because the wedding of the Lamb has arrived and his wife has prepared her finery." [8]And she was given fine linen, bright and clean, for the fine linen signifies the righteous deeds of the saints.

[9]And he tells me: "Write this: 'Blessed are those invited to the wedding feast of the Lamb!'" And he says to me, "This is a promise of God you may rely upon!" [10]And I fell to my feet before him to worship him. And he says to me, "Don't you see? I am only a fellow slave with you and your brothers who are martyrs for Jesus! Worship God! For martyrdom to Jesus is the theme of prophecy!"

[11]Next I saw the sky opened, and behold, a white stallion! And its rider was called the Faithful One and the True One, and he both judges and wages war righteously. [12]And his eyes glow like coals of fire and on his head are many concentric diadems with a name inscribed there unknown to any but himself. [13]And he was wearing a garment soaked in blood, and his name has been called the Word of God. [14]And the celestial armies followed him on white chargers, dressed in fine linen, white and clean. [15]And a sharp sword emerges from his mouth to cut down the armies of the nations. These he will shepherd with a crook of iron! And he tramples the grapes in the winepress of the raging fury of God the Om-

nipotent. [16]And he has, embroidered on his robe and branded on his thigh,[v] a name: “King of Kings and Lord of Lords.”

[17]And I saw one angel eclipsing the sun and shouting with a loud voice to all the birds flying in the middle of the sky, “Come! Gather for the great supper of God, [18]where you may feast upon the flesh of kings and of commanders and of heroes, horseflesh and rider flesh, the carcasses of free and slave alike, both peasant and noble!”[w] [19]And I saw the Beast and the kings of the earth with their armies gathered to wage war on the rider of the stallion with his army. [20]And he seized the Beast and the Pseudoprophet who performed signs before the Beast, deceiving those who had taken the mark of the Beast and prostrated themselves before his image. And he hurled them, still alive, into the lake of molten sulfur. [21]As for the rest, they were cut down with the sword emerging from the mouth of the horseback rider. And all the birds ate their fill of carrion that day.

20

[1]And I saw an angel descending from heaven carrying the key to the abyss and with a gigantic chain looped over his shoulder. [2]And he captured the Dragon, the archaic serpent who is an accuser and the adversary, and he chained him up for a thousand years [3]and he dropped him into the abyss. He replaced the lid and sealed it over him to prevent him from deceiving the nations any longer—until the thousand years are up. After that, he has to be released for a brief period.

[4]Next I saw thrones and those who sat upon them, those to whom jurisdiction was assigned: the souls of those whose heads were chopped off because they had confessed faith in Jesus and the promise of God and who had refused to bow the knee to the Beast or to worship his statue or to receive the mark on the forehead and on the palm. They returned to life and ruled alongside the Christ for a thousand years. [5]As for the remaining dead, they did not live until the thousand years were up. But this is the first resurrection. [6]Blessed and holy is the one who finds a place in the first resurrection![x] The second death has no claim upon them; rather, they will serve as priests of God and of Christ and will share power with him for a thousand years.

v. This is often a biblical euphemism for the penis.

w. Matt. 6:26

x. Only the martyrs, the elite, rise at this time. The rest of the righteous must wait a thousand years to rise, just like the wicked.

[7]But when the thousand years are finished, the adversary will be released from his prison [8]and he will go out to deceive the nations as far as the four corners of the earth, even Gog and Magog,[y] calling them to battle, and the number of their troops is like the sand on the seashore. [9]And they swept over the plains of the earth to besiege the camp of the saints and the beloved city. And fire descended from the sky and consumed them all.[z] [10]And the accuser who tricked them was hurled into the lake of molten sulfur where the Beast and the Pseudoprophet had long been awaiting him. And the three of them will be tortured day and night throughout ages multiplied by ages.

[11]Then I saw a huge white throne with one seated upon it, from whose gaze the earth and the sky fled away though they found no refuge. [12]And I saw the dead, the great and the small, standing in a vast multitude before the throne. And scrolls were opened. And a separate scroll was opened, the roll of the living. And the dead were judged by the records in the scrolls of what they had done. [13]And the sea surrendered the bloated dead from her depths and Death and Hades surrendered their ghostly subjects, and each one was judged by the things he had done. [14]Then Death and Hades themselves were pitched into the magma pit. This is the second death, the molten lake. [15]And if anyone's name could not be found listed on the scroll of the living, he was hurled into the molten lake.

21

[1]And I saw a new sky and a new earth to replace the original sky and earth which had been destroyed. And in the new earth there is no longer any sea.[a] [2]And I saw the holy city, New Jerusalem, descending out of the sky from God, prepared like a bride for her husband. [3]And I heard a loud voice from the throne saying, "Behold! The tabernacle of God is henceforth with mortals. And he will pitch his tent with them and they will be his peoples, and God himself will be with them[b] [4]and he will wipe

---

y. Ezek. 38-39. Originally Gog, "Gyges," was one of the fifty-headed, hundred-handed giants who were the children of Uranos and Gaia (Hesiod, *Theogony,* 147-53). In Ezek. 38:4, he is depicted much as Behemoth and Leviathan in Job 40:24; 41:1-2. "Magog" means "land of Gog."

z. 2 Kings 1:10-12

a. God's ancient enemy (Pss. 74:13; 89:9), and Baal's, Yamm, the sea personified, has been defeated along with Gog, Leviathan, and the rest.

b. This arrangement sounds like the ideal of Elijah, Jeremiah (7:8-26ff), and the Rechabites (Jer. 35), who wanted Israel to return to primitive purity without the contamination of Israelite society or Yahvist worship by Canaanites. In that

away every tear from their eyes, and there shall be no more death nor
sorrow, nor wailing nor pain, for the old order has faded away."[c] 5And
the one seated on the throne said, "Watch me make everything new!"
And he says, "Write it! For these words are reliable and true!" 6And he
said to me, "Thus it ends! I am the alpha and the omega, the beginning
and the end. To the thirsty, I will give freely from the fountain of living
water. 7The victor shall inherit these things and I will be his God and he
shall be a son to me. 8But as for the coward, the unbeliever, the degraded, murderers, whoremongers, drug dealers, idolaters, and all the
false ones, their place is in the molten lake of burning sulfur, which is the
second death."

9And I was approached by one of the seven angels who had carried
the bowls full of the final seven plagues. He spoke with me, saying,
"Come, let me show you the bride, the Lamb's wife!" 10And he carried
me off in a vision onto a vast high mountain and showed me the holy city,
New Jerusalem, descending out of the sky from God, 11ablaze with the
glory of God. Its brilliance was like that of a supremely precious jewel,
like a jasper stone clear as crystal. 12It had a high and massive wall with
twelve angels posted at the gates and with names chiseled there, the
names of the twelve tribes of Israel's sons. 13On the east were three gates,
three on the north, three on the south, and three on the west. 14And the
city wall had twelve foundation stones with twelve names chiseled upon
them: the twelve apostles of the Lamb. 15And the one who spoke with me
held a golden measuring reed to measure the gates and wall of the city.
16The city is a square, as long as it is wide. And he measured the city with
the reed at twelve thousand stadia. The length, width, and height are
equal. 17And he measured its wall at one hundred forty-four cubits, a cubit equaling the same distance on an angel as a man, measured from el-
bow to middle finger tip. 18And the coping of the wall was made of jasper, while the city was made of pure gold as unspotted as clear glass.
19The foundations of the city wall were inlaid with precious stones: the
first foundation stone with jasper, the second with sapphire, the third
with chalcedony, the fourth with emerald, 20the fifth with sardonyx, the
sixth with sardius, the seventh with chrysolite, the eighth with beryl, the
ninth with topaz, the tenth with chrysoprasus, the eleventh with hya-
cinth, and the twelfth with amethyst. 21And the twelve gates were made

---

golden era, God dwelt among his people in the ark of the covenant or the mobile tabernacle.

c. 2 Cor. 5:17

from twelve pearls, each gate carved from a single, massive pearl! As for the city street, it was pure gold and as transparent as glass.

[22]And I saw no temple in it, for the Lord God Almighty is himself its temple, as is the Lamb. [23]And the city has no need of either sun or moon to illuminate it, since the radiance of God provides its light, and its only lamp is the Lamb. [24]And the nations shall live in its light, and the kings of the earth are bringing their pomp into it. [25]And the gates of it shall not be closed each day, for there will be no night.[d] [26]And they will bring the pomp and the nobility of the nations into it as tribute. [27]But never shall anything profane enter it, nor anyone committing abominations or lies, only those recorded in the scroll of the living kept by the Lamb.

22

[1]And he showed me a river of the water of life, sparkling like crystal as it poured forth from the throne of God and of the Lamb [2]down the middle of the city street. And on either side of the river was a Tree of Life[e] putting forth twelve varieties of fruit, producing a different fruit every month, and the leaves of the tree will be used as a medicine for the nations.[f] [3]And the ground shall be cursed no more.[g] But the throne of God and of the Lamb will be in that city, and his slaves shall worship him [4]and they shall behold his face and his name will be imprinted on their foreheads. [5]And night will be a thing of the past, and they will have no need of either lamplight or sunlight because the God Adonai will shine upon them as they rule throughout ages multiplied by ages.

[6]And he said to me, "These things are reliable and true. The Lord, the God of the spirits of the prophets,[h] has dispatched his angel to show his slaves what must transpire quickly now. [7]And behold! I am coming quickly! Blessed is the one who takes to heart the prophetic oracles of this scroll."

[8]And I, John, am the one hearing and seeing these things.[i] And when I heard and saw all this, I fell to prostrate myself at the feet of the angel who showed me these things.[j] [9]But he tells me, "Don't you see? I am only

---

d. Isa. 60:11

e. Gen. 2:9

f. Ezek. 47:1-12

g. Gen. 3:17; 4:11; Rom. 8:19-22

h. 1 Cor. 14:32

i. John 19:35; 21:24; 3 John 12; Rev. 22:20

j. The angel is apparently Gabriel, as in 1:13-16. John takes him for Christ because he speaks Christ's words in the first person (v. 6 above; 22:12, 16).

a fellow slave with you and your brothers, the prophets, and the ones who cherish the oracles of this scroll. Worship God!" [10]And he tells me, "Do not seal up the prophetic oracles of this scroll, for the time it predicts is near! [11]It is too late to change. The one who acts unjustly, let him keep it up! The depraved one, let him stay that way. Let the righteous continue to act righteously and let the saint stay sacrosanct![k] [12]Behold! I am coming quickly! And I bring my reward with me to dispense to each individual in accordance with what he has done. [13]I am the alpha and the omega. The first and the last. The beginning and the end. [14]Blessed are those who wash their robes[l] and so gain the right to eat of the Tree of Life and to enter the city by the gates. [15]Barred from entry are male prostitutes, drug dealers, whoremongers, murderers, idolaters, and everyone who loves lies and invents them.

[16]"I, Jesus, dispatched my angel to you in the congregations to predict these things and to testify to you that they are going to happen. I am both the root and the offspring of David,[m] the glowing morning star!"

[17]And the spirit and the bride urge, "Come!" So let the one who hears say, "Come!" And whoever thirsts, let him come. Whoever wants to, let him drink freely of the water of life!"

[18]I solemnly warn every hearer of the prophetic words of this scroll: If anyone adds anything to them, God will add to his destiny the plagues described in this scroll. [19]And if anyone presumes to omit any of the words of the scroll of this prophecy, God will omit his name from the scroll of life and will deprive him of any place in the holy city and of the blessings described in this scroll.[n]

[20]The one who attests these things says: "Yes, it is so: I am coming quickly!" Amen! Come, Lord Jesus!

[21]May the favor of the Lord Jesus be with all.

---

k. God will not be mocked by deathbed repentance.

l. Rev. 7:14

m. Perhaps this is a proposed answer to the riddle of Mark 12:35. In Pss. 110:1, David, the assumed writer, could still call his son his lord if his son were also somehow his progenitor.

n. The Revelator seeks to forestall the sort of redaction that Matthew and Luke performed on the Markan apocalypse. Cf. Mark 13; Matt. 24-25; Luke 17:22-37; 21:5-36.

33.
Thunder: Perfect Mind

The fourth-century cataloguer of heresies, Epiphanius of Salamis, is not always either clear or reliable, but he supplies many hints for us to take up and use as best we can in reconstructing early Christian history and belief. He tells us at least a bit more about the intriguing sect of the Nicolaitans who so upset the writer of the Revelation that he called their doctrines hateful. They encouraged a faithful defiance of cultic superstition, claiming the right to eat meat dedicated to idols. Since pagan gods are zeroes, they reasoned, why consider their leftover sacrifices any more than a treat? The same reasoning is examined in 1 Corinthians 8:1-6ff. But it smacks of Gnosticism, and Epiphanius treats Nicolaitanism as such. There was also some type of unchasity involved (Rev. 3:20), which Epiphanius chalked up to Gnostic libertinism. But since the writer of Revelation guarantees salvation only to the celibate, and only to males at that (14:4), it clearly did not take much to start him fulminating about fornication. It never took much to get the Dead Sea Scroll ascetics going on that topic either. It is interesting the Revelator says he had for some time tolerated Jezebel (3:21), apparently as a colleague, though finally he decided she had no intention of coming around to his point of view. This fact mitigates the impression of some absolute gulf between the two positions. This may prove to be a fact of some importance.

Epiphanius tells us, if I read him right, that the Nicolaitans treasured two kindred scriptures, a *Gospel of Eve* and a *Gospel of Perfection*. He gives us a glimpse of the former with this quote: "I stood upon a high mountain and saw a tall man and another one short and I

heard something like the sound of thunder. And I approached to hear. And he spoke to me, saying: 'I am you, and you are I, and wherever you are, there am I, and I am scattered about in everything. And from wherever you wish, you gather me, but in gathering me, you but gather yourself'" (*Panarion,* 26.2.5-3.3). I believe the other text, the Nicolaitan *Gospel of Perfection,* was rediscovered in 1945 among the Nag Hammadi collection as "Thunder: Perfect Mind." It fits Epiphanius's description of a "seductive poem." Bentley Layton pointed out that Thunder: Perfect Mind has in common with Epiphanius' note on the *Gospel of Perfection* the implication that the text came by way of revelation conveyed by a voice of thunder. Like the *Gospel of Eve,* Thunder: Perfect Mind seems to present itself as a self-declaration from the lips of Eve, who reflects on the paradoxes of her twin existence as the heavenly Power who animated the inert Adam and the earthly substitute she created to throw the lustful archons off her trail when they wanted to rape her—and did rape her counterpart. In this, we see the double Eve was another version of the heavenly wisdom Sophia and her fallen counterpart Achamoth. She is also one with Isis, to whose votive stelae in Egypt, engraved with her self-praising aretalogies, Thunder: Perfect Mind makes explicit reference. Here we have the key to solving the riddle of how the speaker can be honored (heavenly Eve) and despised (fallen Eve), virgin (heavenly Eve) and wife (earthly Eve), harlot (fallen Eve) and consecrated virgin (heavenly Eve), childless (divine Eve) and mother of many (earthly Eve).

My proposal is that we have another reference to Thunder: Perfect Mind (or the *Gospel of Perfection*) in Revelation 10:1-4. A giant angel stands like the Colossus of Rhodes astride land and sea. He roars like a lion, and seven thunderous voices answer him with a revelation the narrator transcribes. When he is finished, the angel directs him not to destroy it, but to seal it up just as Daniel (12:9-10) had once been instructed by an angel to seal up his prophecy till the generation appeared for whose sake it was written. It would not make sense to anyone till then, and then only to the wise. In light of this, we must assume there was some sort of apocalypse of the seven thunders in circulation and that the writer of Revelation was concerned that readers, especially the Nicolaitans, were drawing dangerous inferences from it

à la 2 Peter 3:15-16. Thus he wants the book shut and withdrawn from circulation! That book was Thunder: Perfect Mind.

The "perfection" element is reflected in the number seven assigned to the thunders. We might picture Jezebel (whose secret identity has been guessed alternately as Simon Magus's partner, Helena; Lydia of Thyatira from Acts 16; or Mary Magdalene) assuming the persona of Wisdom Eve when reading from the text in worship, the devotees chanting strange words about being a virgin and a whore, none of which would have sounded very good to the writer of Revelation. If not blasphemous, then the book was at least not for the ears of the weaker brethren, and the author of the Revelation tries to "seal" it up, though without blasting it as false prophecy. The brethren of the Monastery of Saint Pachomius, the ones who buried the Nag Hammadi codices, knew they had to seal up the seven thunders, too, lest the revelation be lost forever to the pyres of ecclesiastical inquisitors. And in fact, that is exactly what the monks did. Now it is time, at last, to unseal Thunder: Perfect Mind and restore it to the place it might have had long ago in the New Testament canon. As always, the standard scholarly plug-ins for brief holes in the text are reproduced in italics and my own hypothetical restorations are placed in brackets.

1

1I was sent out from *the* Power
and I have come to the aid of those who meditate upon me,
and I can be found in the company of those who search earnestly for me.
2Look upon me, all you who meditate upon me!
And you who hear, listen to me!
You who await me, embrace me now!
3Do not put me away from before your eyes,
nor make your speech my enemy or foreign to your hearing.
4Never and nowhere let yourselves be ignorant of me.
Be vigilant so you do not lapse into ignorance!

2

1For I am the First and the Last.
I am the one who is both honored and despised.
2I am the harlot and the consecrated.

I am the wife and the virgin.
3 I am the mother and the daughter.
I am the body of my mother.
4 I am the barren one,
yet many are my sons.
5 I am she whose wedding is grand,
yet I have taken no husband to me.
6 I am the midwife and she who bears no young.
I comfort myself in my labor pains.
7 I am both bride and bridegroom.
My husband has fathered me.
8 I am the mother of my father
and the sister of my husband, who is my son.
9 I am the slave of him who trained me.
I am the ruler of my children.
10 But he is the one who *fathered me,*
before the due-date, on a birthday.
11 And he is my own offspring *at* the proper time,
and my power comes from him.
12 I am the sceptre of his power in his youth,
and he is the cane of my old age.
And everything befalls me according as he wills it.
13 I am the silence that is impenetrable
and the Epinoia, the idea to which the mind is drawn ever and again.
14 I am the voice of clashing echoes
and the word appearing under many forms.
I am the simple utterance of my name.

3

1 You who hate me, why do you love me,
yet hate those who love me?
2 You who deny me actually confess me,
while you who think to confess me deny.
3 You who tell the truth of me are lying concerning me.
And you who speak lies have told the truth of me.
4 You who know me—forget me!
And those who are ignorant of me, come learn of me!

5 For I am knowledge and unknowing.
I am cringing and boldness.

6I am shameless and ashamed.
I am strength and I am fear.
7I am both war and peace.
Heed my words!
8I who am both disgraced and esteemed most highly.

9Take note of my poverty and my wealth.
Be not haughty to me when I am fallen in the gutter
and you will find me among *those whose* turn is coming.
10Nor despise me *on* the dung-heap
or walk away without lifting me up
and you will see me again sitting enthroned.
11Let your gaze not linger upon me, expelled with the disgraced
to the lowest places, nor make sport of me there.
And do not fling me forth on the heap of murdered corpses.
12But as for me, I am compassionate and I am cruel.

13Beware!
Do not resent my service,
but cherish the temperance I require.
14When I am weak, abandon me not,
nor neglect to fear my power.
15For why will you hate the fear of me
and curse my boastful pride?
16But I am she who lies concealed in every fear,
the strength that fortifies him who trembles.
17I am she who is weak,
and I am sleek and favorably situated.
18I am oblivious and I am wise.

4

1Why do your reasonings shun me?
For I shall say nothing to those who care not to invoke me,
and I shall appear and have my say.
2So why have you hated me, you Greeks?
Because I am as a barbarian when with *the* barbarians?
3Verily, I am the wisdom *of the* Greeks
and equally the knowledge of *the* barbarians.
4I am the wise judgment of both Greeks and barbarians.
I am the one whose image is ubiquitous among the Egyptians

and who has no image among the ignorant barbarians.
[5]I am the one who is everywhere despised
and who has been beloved everywhere.
[6]I am the one whom they call life,
but whom you have called death.
[7]I am the one whom they call law,
but you call lawlessness!
[8]I am the one you have pursued,
the very one you seized and held.
[9]I am the seed you scattered,
and you have gathered my fruit together.
[10]I am the one before whose gaze you shrank,
yet you have been brazen to me.
[11]I am she who does not keep festival,
yet I am always the belle of the ball.
[12]I, even I, am godless,
and I am the one whose God is great.
[13]I am the one who mirrors your reflection,
and you have shunned me.
[14]I am untrained,
yet they apply to me for wisdom.
[15]I am the one you always hated,
and yet you are obsessed with me.
[16]I am the one from whom you have concealed yourself,
yet I see you plain as day.
[17]But whenever you may hide yourselves,
I myself come into view.
[18]But *whenever* you *appear,*
I am *no longer visible.*
[19]Those who have [sworn fealty] to it
senselessly [fail to heed it at all].

5

[1]Take me [as salvaging] *understanding* from sorrow
and embrace my lesson from understanding *and* grief.
[2]Learn from me in places desolate and grim
and take freely what they know, who are good, while mired in ugliness.
[3]In a shameless plight, shamelessly take me for your own
and, freed from shamelessness and shame alike,

reproach my limbs as you recognize them in yourselves.
4Do not hold back, but come to me, you who know me
and you who know me intimately.
5And plant the great ones among the young, small creatures.
Come, advance to childhood,
and do not disdain it because it is small and diminutive.
6And do not turn away unwittingly from the greatness
concealed here and there in insignificant things,
for the tiny things are known in comparison to the great.

7Why do you both curse me and honor me?
You have injured and have shown mercy.
8Do not separate me from those you *knew* most anciently.
And do not expel anyone *or* refuse anyone shelter,
[so that others will not] refuse you and [say, "I] don't *know* him."
9[For when you cast them out, you cast me out.]
What is mine [is theirs and theirs is mine.]
10I was with the *first intelligences,*
and all from that time on *knew* me.
11But I am the mind of [the perfect] and the repose of [the soul].
I am the very knowledge after which I inquire
12and the success of those who search me out
and the mandate of those who ask about me,
13and knowledge of me is the power of the Powers,
of the angels who have been dispatched at my command,
14and of gods, each in his time, as I deem best,
and of the spirit of every man who abides with me
and of each woman who dwells in my house.
15I am the one who is esteemed and praised,
and I am most scornfully despised.
16I am peace,
and war has come in my wake.
17And I am a foreigner and a citizen.
I am wealth itself and the destitute urchin.

18Those not keeping company with me are ignorant of me.
Those who share my substance, they [are the ones] who know me.
19Those close beside me are, in fact, ignorant of me,

and those now far removed from me are they who once knew
me.
[20]Whenever I am close to *you,*
you are far distant *from me,*
[21]and whenever I *am far* from you,
I am by your side.

6

[1]*I am* [your nature] within.
I am [the nature] of the natures.
[2]I am [the beginning] of the creation of the *spirits,*
[the reply to the] request of the souls.
[3]I am the hand that controls and the uncontrollable.
I am both uniting and dividing.
[4]I am the enduring as well as the dissolving.
I am that below, to which they rise up.
[5]I am both condemnation and justification.
I, even I, am without sin,
and the very root of sin stems from me.
[6]I am by appearance raging lust,
but the eye of my storm is self-control.
[7]I am the ear by which all hear
and that utterance which none can grasp.
[8]I am a mute who never speaks,
and endless is the flood of my words!
[9]Hear me in serenity,
but learn my truth only amid trouble.
[10]I am she who shouts aloud her invitation,
and I am hurled ignominiously to the ground.
[11]I make ready the feast, even my mind within.
I am the very knowledge of my name.
[12]I am the one who calls out,
and I listen quietly.
[13]I appear and [then I] walk in [your streets bearing the] seal
of my [God].
I am [the refuge and] the defense [of the humble].
[14]I am the one called truth,
and iniquity [is a stranger to me].

[15]You honor me [openly]
and you whisper against me.

16You who are defeated, judge them who defeated you
before they pronounce sentence upon you!
17For judgment and partiality are found within you.
18If you are condemned by this one,
who is left to acquit you?
19Or if you are acquitted by him,
who is left to condemn you?[a]
20For what is inside you is what is outside you,
and he who fashions you on the outside is the same as
the one who shaped the inside of you.[b]
21So whatever you see outside you,
you see inside you.
22It is visible to all
and clothes you like a garment.

7

1Hear me well, you listeners!
Learn my words, you who know me!
2I am the common hearing of the ear
and I am the impenetrable riddle.
3I am the name of the sound
and the sound of the name.[c]
4I am the shape of the letter
and the name assigned to the category.
5And I [am the sacred text
as well as the] light [shining upon the page].
6[Heed me, my] hearers, [for I speak] to you [of] the great
Power.
And [my tongue] will not move the name.
7[I give glory] to the one who created me
and I will utter his name.
8Then study his words
and every scripture that has been completed.
9Listen closely, then, you who hear me,
and you, too, all angels and apostles,
and you spirits who have risen from the dead!

---

a. Rom. 8:33-34; 1 John 3:19-21; 2 Cor. 2:2

b. Luke 11:40

c. A more contemporary translation: "I am onomatopoeia and I am Om."

[10]For I am the One who alone exists
and there is no one else to judge me!

[11]For sin lies in wait in many pleasing forms,
along with profligacies
and degrading lusts
and ephemeral delights,
which people embrace in their drunkenness
until they slink off to sober up.
[12]And in that hour they will find me, and they will live,
never to die again.[d]

d. Thomas, saying 28

VI.
The Petrine Corpus

34.
The Gospel according to Peter

TOWARD THE CLOSE OF THE SECOND century (ca. 190-200), the congregation at Rhossus, about thirty miles from Antioch in Syria, was found to be using a gospel ascribed to Peter. Someone thought this untoward and complained to Bishop Serapion, who at first thought it no serious aberration. But a second complaint caused him to take a closer look. Suspecting Marcionite influence, he sought out local docetists of some type, perhaps Gnostics, with whom he was on cordial terms and borrowed some of their writings, which may have included commentaries on the Gospel of Peter itself. Doing his homework, he finally decided the text in question was heretical. He wrote the congregation as follows: "For our part, brothers, we welcome both Peter and the rest of the apostles as we would Christ himself, but as seasoned men, we reject the writings that spuriously carry their names, knowing that we never accepted such writings. As for me, when I visited you, I assumed you all held fast to the true faith, so I saw no particular need to examine the gospel some circulate under the name of Peter. I said, 'If this is all that is troubling you, let it be read.' Since that time, however, I have been told more: that its partisans' minds were sunk in some snake-hole of heresy. Now I shall make sure to pay you another visit, so brothers, expect me soon. But we, brothers, mindful of what sort of heresy Marcion belonged to, ... were enabled by students of this very gospel, that is, successors of those who first circulated it, those we call Docetists, for most of the ideas are their doctrines, [I say,], using [works we borrowed] by them, [we] were enabled to go through [the gospel] and discover that, while

most of it was in fact quite compatible with the genuine teaching of the Savior, some things had been added." (Eusebius, *Ecclesiastical History,* 6:12:2-6)

A fragment of the Gospel of Peter was discovered in 1884 in a tomb in Akhmim, Egypt, bound as a small book along with part of 1 Enoch in Greek, as well as a fragment of the Apocalypse of Peter. Though there may have been some incriminating evidence in portions still lost to us, we can see from the little that remains how Serapion thought he spotted docetism. The mildest form of this teaching was the belief that, though Christ had a body of flesh, he suffered no pain on the cross, just as his mother had suffered no labor pains. The Gospel of Peter says it appeared as if the crucified Jesus felt no pain, but the point of the observation may have been simply to point out Jesus' stoical courage.

M. R. James dated the Gospel of Peter at about 150 CE, and most, even today, follow this dating. His judgment depended upon an earlier date for the traditional four gospels than I accept. Peter uses all four of the other gospels, drawing upon each for various details, as many think John did with the Synoptics. But John Dominic Crossan *(The Cross That Spoke: The Origins of the Passion Narrative*) has given strong reasons for thinking that Peter used a fifth gospel source, one older than Matthew, Mark, Luke, and John, which the canonized texts also seem to have used. It would have been a Passion gospel, pure and simple, unlike Peter's, of which only the Passion section remains, and Crossan calls it the Cross Gospel. The heart of the argument, it seems, is that the Gospel of Peter contains, besides obvious borrowings from the traditional four gospels, a good amount of material, especially so-called *testimonia,* that appears here in a more primitive, less derivative form than in the four gospels. *Testimonia* were Old Testament passages believed to predict or foreshadow events in the career of Jesus, often indirectly via symbolism. For instance, some details of the persecution of Jesus in Peter seem to come from more direct citations of the scapegoat passage (Lev. 16:7-10, 15-22) and to evidence fuller knowledge of the details of the ceremony as then practiced. By the time of the four gospels, all this had grown dimmer, the midrashic roots of the gospel episodes largely for-

gotten. Crossan demonstrates how certain story elements in Peter lack signs of secondary embellishment that we detect in the counterparts in Matthew, Mark, Luke, and John. These factors led him to divide the Peter fragment into three distinct strata. To make the present edition of Peter more useful to scholars, I present the text in three different typefaces. The text of the underlying Cross Gospel appears in roman type. Material borrowed from Matthew, Mark, Luke, and John for the Gospel according to Peter appears in san-serif type. Material added by the redactor to harmonize this borrowed gospel material with the Cross Gospel appears in **boldface**. But that is not all. As this book is intended as no mere anthology of bits and pieces surviving from early Christianity, but rather as a collection of New Testament books, it behooved me to try to round out the text more fully. I have therefore engaged in speculation to infer what must have immediately preceded and followed what remains of the text. There are plenty of clues, and I offer my reconstruction here in *italics*.

1

[1]*And the elders and scribes and Pharisees brought him to the procurator Pontius Pilatus and before Herod, King of Galilee and Perea, who was in the city for the Feast of Unleavened Bread and was the guest of Pilatus.* [2]*And they charged him with many offenses, saying, "This fellow styles himself the king of Israel, and he advocates customs that are illegal for us. And furthermore, he says he will burn down the temple that took forty-six years to build."* [3]*But the Lord made no rejoinder, and Pilatus was greatly surprised and said to him, "Have you no defense to make for yourself? Behold what they say of you!"* [4]*And Herod said to Pilatus, "Brother Pilatus, am I not king of the Jews? How then can this fellow be king?"* [5]*And they mocked him. Now there were many judges assembled there at the pavement called Gabbatha. And they all asked him questions, but he said nothing in reply.* [6]*Finally, Pilatus said to all who were present, "I find no guilt in this mad fellow. I will have him scourged and released."* [7]*But at this a clamor arose from the people, who said, "No! Release for us instead Bar-Abbas," which is Hebrew for "son of the father."* [8]*Now this Bar-Abbas was a brigand and much loved by the people. And Pilatus, wishing to avert a tumult among the people, yielded to their pleasure.* [9]*But his wife, Procula, motioned to him and told him, "Have no*

part in this man's blood, O my husband, for I have had a dream where I suffered persecution for the sake of his name." [10]*Therefore, Pilatus said to Herod, "Brother Herod, the man is a Galilean, is he not? Therefore, let it be your decision."* [11]*And Herod said, "I have long sought his death, so let him be crucified!"* [12]*So Pilatus called for a basin and water. He washed his hands in front of the people saying, "As for me, I am innocent of this man's blood!"*

2

[1]But none of the Jews washed their hands, nor Herod, nor any of his judges. They would have washed them, but just then Pilatus stood up, [2]whereupon Herod, the king, orders the Lord to be taken away, saying, "Do with him as I have commanded." [3]**And Joseph arrived, a friend of both Pilatus and the Lord, and aware that they are going to crucify him, he approached Pilatus and requested the body of Jesus for burial.** [4]**And Pilatus sent word to Herod, requesting his body,** [5]**and Herod replied, "Brother Pilatus, even had no one requested him, we would have to bury him, for the Sabbath already hastens. For it is written in the Torah that sunset must not find a slain person,** least of all on the day before their feast, the Feast of Unleavened Bread."

[6]But those who had taken charge of the Lord were prodding him on at a run, saying, "Let us salute the son of God, now that we have him in our clutches!" [7]And they adorned him in royal purple, and they seated him on a makeshift judgment seat, saying, "Judge fairly, O King of Israel!" [8]And one of them fetched a crown of thorns and set it on the Lord's head.

[9]And others standing around spat in his face, and still others slapped him on the cheeks. Others jabbed him with a reed and some were whipping him and saying, "This is honor befitting the dignity of the son of God!"

[10]And they brought two criminals and crucified the Lord between them. But he remained silent, as if he felt no pain at all. [11]And when they set up the cross, they inscribed the words, "This is the King of Israel." [12]And having piled up his garments in front of him, they divided them and cast lots for them.

[13]But one of the criminals rebuked them, saying, "Granted, we have suffered this way because of the evil acts we committed, but this man, who has now become the savior of humanity, what crime has he committed?" [14]And the Jews, provoked at him, ordered that his legs not be broken to assure he would die in torment.

15 And it was now mid-day, but darkness covered the whole land of Judea and they were perplexed and worried that the sun should already be setting since he was still alive. For it is written for them that the sunset must not overtake a slain man.

16 And one of them said, "Let us give him a drink of vinegar laced with gall." And when they had prepared it, they gave it to him to drink. 17 And in this way they brought all the prophecies to fulfillment, as well as completing the tally of sins they should have to answer for.

18 And many walked about with lanterns, thinking night had fallen, and they stumbled.

19 And the Lord shouted, "My power! My power! Have you abandoned me?" And when he said this, he was taken up. 20 And at the same time, the hanging veil of the Jerusalem temple was torn in two.

21 And then they withdrew the nails from the Lord's hands and laid him out upon the ground, and the whole earth was shaken, and great fear seized them. 22 Then the sun shone forth, and it was seen to be the ninth hour.[a] 23 **But the Jews rejoiced greatly, and they gave the body to Joseph to bury, for he had witnessed all the good deeds Jesus performed.**[b] 24 **And he took the Lord and washed him and wrapped him in a linen sheet, and interred him in his own tomb, which was called Joseph's Garden.**

3

1 Then the Jews and the elders and the priests, when they realized what a heinous crime they had committed against themselves, started to beat their breasts and to exclaim, "Woe to us on account of our sins! For the judgment and the end of Jerusalem are at hand!"

2 **And I was grieving with my companions, and wounded at heart, we went into hiding, for they were looking for us as seditionists and as plotters to set the temple on fire.** 3 **And we were fasting over all these things and sitting down to mourn and weep night and day until the Sabbath.**

4 And the scribes and Pharisees and elders were assembled, for they had heard reports that all the people were murmuring and beating their breasts, saying, "If such powerful signs are performed at his death, what a righteous man he is!" 5 The elders were afraid and came to Pilatus, pleading with him, saying, 6 "Assign us soldiers to guard his tomb for three days to prevent his disciples coming to make off with him and the

a. 3:00 p.m.

b. Is this from a different source? This is a slightly different explanation for Joseph's charity, offered as if we had not heard the earlier one.

people, supposing he is risen from the dead, doing us harm!" [7]So Pilatus assigned them Petronius, the centurion, with soldiers to guard the sepulchre. [8]And certain elders and scribes came along with them to the sepulchre. And they joined with the centurion and the posted soldiers to roll a massive stone and lay it at the door of the tomb, [9]and on it they plastered seven seals.[c] And they pitched a tent there and posted guards. [10]And early in the morning as the Sabbath was coming on, a crowd arrived from Jerusalem and from the surrounding region to see the sealed tomb.

[11]And during the night when the Lord's Day was coming on, the soldiers standing guard two by two in each watch, a loud voice sounded in the sky. [12]And they saw the skies standing open and two men descending from there, shining with bright light, and they came to a stop over the tomb. [13]But that stone which had been pushed against the door rolled away by itself and stopped to one side, and the tomb stood open and both young men entered.

[14]Now when those soldiers saw this, they awakened the centurion and the elders, for they, too, were [camped at] the vigil; [15]and as they were reporting what they had seen, this time they beheld three men coming out of the tomb, two of them bearing up the third between them—and a cross followed them. [16]And the heads of the two men touched the sky, but the head of him whom they led along reached higher than the skies. [17]And they heard a voice from the sky which said, "Have you made proclamation to them who sleep?" [18]A reply was heard from the cross, "Yes!"

[19]The ones keeping watch then deliberated among themselves whether to go and inform Pilatus of the events. [20]And while they still discussed the matter, the heavens appeared to open again and a man descended and entered into the tomb. [21]When those Jews who accompanied the centurion by night saw all this, they hastened to Pilatus, abandoning the sepulchre they were guarding, and they reported everything they had seen, being in a state of great agitation and saying "Truly this was the son of God!" [22]And Pilatus answered and said to them, "Well, I am innocent of the blood of the son of God; this deed was your idea." [23]Then they all surrounded him and pleaded with him to order the soldiers to say nothing of what they had witnessed. [24]"For it is better for us," they reasoned, "to be guilty of the most heinous sin in the sight of God than to fall into the clutches of the Jewish people and be stoned!" [25]So Pilatus ordered the centurion and the soldiers to say nothing.

c. Dan. 6:17

4

[1]Mary the hairdresser, a disciple of the Lord, for fear of the Jews, aflame as they were with rage, had not carried out the funerary rites at the sepulchre customary among women. [2]So at dawn on the Lord's Day, she gathered her friends and went to the tomb where he had been interred. [3]And they were afraid the Jews might see them, and they said, "Though it was not possible for us to perform the mourning and lamenting for him the day he was crucified, let us at least do it now at the tomb. [4]But on second thought, who will roll away the stone laid at the door of the tomb for us so we may go in and sit beside him and give him his due honor?" [5]For the stone was a massive one. "And we are afraid that someone may see us. If we are not able, let us set down at the door what we are carrying as a memorial to him, and let us then weep and lament till we reach our own homes again."

[6]And they arrived there only to discover the sepulchre already open; and approaching it, they stooped down and they see a young man, sitting in the middle of the sepulchre, beautiful and dressed in a most resplendent robe, who said to them, [7]"Why have you come? Who are you looking for? Is it the one who was crucified? He is risen and gone! If you don't believe it, stoop down and observe the place where he was laid out, for he is not there. For he is risen and has returned to the place from which he was sent." [8]Then the women fled away in fear.[d]

[9]**And it was the last day of the Feast of Unleavened Bread and many pilgrims were returning home, the feast being over.** [10]**But we, the twelve disciples of the Lord,**[e] **wept and mourned, and each of us, sunk in grief over what had happened, retreated to his dwelling.** [11]But I, Simon Peter, and my brother Andreas took our nets and left for the sea, and accompanying us also was Levi, son of Alphaeus, whom the Lord *had called from his customs booth, and Nathaniel of Cana and the two sons of Zebediah and the Twin and Philip.*[f] [12]*And we stayed out all night without catching anything. And as the sun was rising, we beheld a man standing with one foot on the shore and the other on the sea, his head in the clouds, his face shining like the sun, and he said, "Have you caught nothing this night?"* [13]*And we an-*

d. This gospel does not negate Mark's ending, as Matthew, Luke, and John do by having the women report to the disciples after all. This may be a sign of an early date.

e. There has been no drop-out of Judas from the group. This may represent an early stage of the tradition when there was not yet a Judas scapegoat figure to concretize the imagined guilt of Jews.

f. As reported in the Gospel of John, this episode is the third time the disciples see Jesus, although even in John it sounds out of place. Here in Peter, it appears in its natural sequence: the women did not relay the news and the twelve do not expect to see Jesus. Resuming their old livelihood, they are surprised to see the risen Lord.

swered, "Nothing, Lord!" And he said, cast your net over the right side
and you will make a catch." So we threw the net in, and at once it was
filled with a huge shoal of fish, such as I had never before seen. [14]*And I,*
Simon, leaving my brothers to deal with the nets, plunged into the sea and
swam for shore, for I knew it must be the Lord. [15]*And when I saw him, he*
was once more of the stature of a man, and I fell on my face before him,
saying, "Depart from me, O Lord, for I am a sinner." [16]*And he placed his*
hand on me and said, "Simon, the adversary demanded to sift you twelve
like wheat. But I prayed for you that, turning back, you would strengthen
your brothers."

[17]*And here did my brothers haul in the net full of fish, and my Lord*
instructed me to take some of the fish we had caught and prepare them to
eat. [18]*And I found the net filled with small fish. But I found one large fish*
and threw the others back at once. [19]*And seeing it, the Lord said to me,*
"Blessed are you, Simon son of John, for you have chosen wisely. And so
in like manner have I chosen you. [20]*Behold, I give you the keys of the*
kingdom, and whatever you decide upon the earth, so shall it be before
the face of God. [21]*You are the rock on which I am building my church.*
Do you believe this?" [22]*And I said to him, "Yes, Lord, I believe you are*
the king of Israel, even the Son of the true God." Amen.

35.

The Preaching of Peter

THE PREACHING OF PETER IS A SECOND-century Ebionite document that survives broken up and spliced into a larger fourth-century work called the Clementine *Homilies*. While *Homilies* credits Clement of Rome with transcribing the speeches of Peter, the Preaching of Peter does not, and we might wonder if it is the latter referred to by Papias when he said "Mark, having acted as Peter's interpreter, wrote down accurately, albeit not in any particular order, everything he remembered of what was either said or done by the Lord."[a] The book is valuable because it restores the voice of a silenced faction of early Christians. The Ebionites ("the poor")[b] were Jewish Christians springing directly from the same milieu that gave birth to the Essenes, the Mandaeans or Nazoreans, the John the Baptist sect, the Dositheans, and the Simonians. Their Christianity was a baptizing Jewish gnosis that revered the Genesis patriarchs as fountainheads of revelation at the dawn of time. Thus they venerated Adam, Seth, Abel, Shem, and Melchizedek as heavenly redeemers and revealers.[c] The Preaching of Peter understands Jesus to be the latest incarnation of Adam, something perhaps implicit in the more familiar "Son of Man" passages in Matthew, Mark, Luke, and John. This True Prophet Christology occurs also in the Gospel according to the Hebrews, where Jesus recalls his Mother, the Holy Spirit, telling him, "My son, in all the prophets I

a. Eusebius, *Ecclesiastical History,* 3.39.15.

b. Cf. Gal. 2:10; Dead Sea Scrolls.

c. In the present collection, see also the Book of John the Baptizer, Melchizedek, and Revelation of Dositheus.

was waiting for you to come so I might rest in you. For you are my rest. You are my first-begotten son who reigns forever." The same prophetology underlies the Islamic belief in Muhammad as the Seal of the Prophets, as well as Mani's belief that he was the reincarnation of the Buddha, Zoroaster, and Jesus.[d] Simon Magus, too, may have believed himself to be Jesus reincarnated.

Jesus' revelatory task, said the Ebionites, was to separate true from false passages in the Jewish scriptures. Peter gives us an almost satirical list of absurd and objectionable points in the scriptures, bringing to mind the Marcionite and Gnostic criticisms of the same writings. Some Gnostics, like the Valentinians represented by Ptolemaeus, classified the contents of the Old Testament similarly as human, angelic, and divine. This is much like where the Koran speaks notoriously of the "satanic verses" whispered by the devil but corrected by Gabriel: "Never have we sent a prophet or apostle with whose wishes Satan did not tamper. But Allah abrogates the introjections of Satan and confirms his own revelations" (22:51).[e] Marcion took a different tack and simply wrote off the whole Old Testament as scripture inspired by a different God. Ebionites believed the true readings had been preserved in a manner that bypassed the vicissitudes of the written text (4 Ezra 14:21) by means of oral memorization and transmission. Nonetheless, Peter speaks of the need for the True Prophet, Adam-Jesus, to come and set things right. It was he, according to the Ebionites, who warned, "I have come to abolish sacrifices, and if you cease not from sacrificing, the wrath of God shall not cease from you!"[f] This he did by reiterating Jeremiah's claim that God had never commanded sacrifices and that scribes had forged the passages requiring them (Jer. 7:21-23; 8:8). These Jewish Christians were zealous for the Torah but only once they had subjected it to inspired textual criticism.

Though Peter preaches about various issues, including the need for water baptism and for the regulation of sexual purity, he deals in

---

d. See Tor Andrae, *Mohammed: The Man and His Faith* (NY: Harper & Row, 1960), esp. "Mohammed's Doctrine of Revelation," 94-113.

e. Cf. Koran 2:106: "If we abrogate any verse or cause it to be forgotten, we will replace it with a better one, or one like it."

f. Gospel according to the Ebionites, cited in Epiphanius, *Panarion,* 30.13.5.

sectarian polemics on two fronts. First, he attacks the sect of John the Baptist, making John the mouthpiece of female, false prophecy. Peter propounds an apologetical schema by which the false prophet always precedes the true. This reverses the Baptist polemic which insisted that because Jesus was secondary, he was therefore derivative—a charge the Gospel of John had sought to fend off in a different manner by claiming Jesus was prior to John because of his cosmic pre-existence (John 1:15, 30). Second, using the same principle, Peter attacks Paul as the false apostle to the gentiles—false, again, because first! Acts 15:7 deals with this problem like John, equating chronological priority with rank and making Peter the initial missionary to the gentiles, not Paul. So we are witnessing the evolution of early Jewish-Christian polemic. What is especially interesting is that the Preaching of Peter mounts a head-on refutation of Paul's rebuke of Peter in Galatians (2:11-21). Paul meets us here, as F. C. Baur saw, under the guise of Simon Magus, just as he does in Acts 8:18-24. It is Paul's visionary calling by the risen Christ (Simon had none such) that followers of the twelve dismissed as diabolical delusion. The Ebionites regarded Paul as the Antichrist.

Finally, the frequent reference to the Gospel of Matthew is striking and important both as confirming the Jewish provenance of that gospel and as illustrative of the sort of readers it attracted. This is interesting, not least because early reader response may signal something about the text that modern readers, who bring different assumptions to the text, do not see. Remember the words of Lessing: "The Ebionites, I say, [who] according to Origen's testimony held a very poor opinion of Christ ... acknowledged no other Gospel than the Hebrew original of Matthew.... So also Cerinthus ... believed Christ to be simply the natural son of Joseph and Mary in the normal course of nature because he accepted either the Hebrew original of Matthew or the Greek Matthew for the only Gospel (though he may have accepted it as such because he held this view). The same is true of Carpocrates who similarly either could not hold any higher idea of Christ because he only accepted Matthew or could only accept Matthew because he believed he should hold no higher idea of Christ."[g]

g. Gotthold Lessing, "New Hypothesis concerning the Evangelists Regarded

My version is based on the selection of fragments from the Clementine *Homilies* made by Johannes Irmscher and Georg Strecker in volume 2 of the *New Testament Apocrypha*, edited by Edgar Schneemelcher and published by John Knox Press.

III

17.

[1]Anyone who denies that the man who sprang from the hand of the Creator of all things possessed the great and holy spirit of divine foreknowledge, while admitting that others did so who were fathered from impure seed—is he not culpable for a most serious sin? [2]I cannot imagine any such person will be pardoned even if he has been unwittingly misled toward such blasphemy against the All-Father by a spurious passage of scripture.

20.

[2]By contrast, anyone performs a pious deed by confessing that no one possesses that spirit except for him who, from the beginning of the world, changing his forms and his names, proceeds through cosmic time till, anointed for his labors by the mercy of God, he arrives in his own time period to enjoy rest forever.

21.

[1]He who alone is the True Prophet has, as vicar of the Creator, assigned an appropriate name to every living creature as befits its exact nature; for whatever name he might assign anything, that was the name adopted for it by its Creator. [2]If he could do this already, how could it be needful for him to eat from a tree in order to discern good or evil? To be sure, it is written: "He commanded the man, saying: 'You are allowed to eat your fill of any tree in the garden except for the Tree of the Knowledge of Good and Evil, for if you eat from it, you will die that very day.'"[h] But this will be credited only by the undiscerning, who seem to think that a speechless animal[i] is more generous than God who created them and everything else!

---

as Merely Human Historians," in *Lessing's Theological Writings*, ed. and trans. Henry Chadwick (Stanford: Stanford University Press, 1957), 80.

h. Gen. 2:16-17

i. It is the Edenic serpent Peter scoffs at. Unlike God, this "speechless animal" wanted to share knowledge with Adam and Eve. It is such absurdities that led the Ebionites, like their predecessor Jeremiah (Jer. 7:21-23; 8:8), to reject many passages as forged interpolations.

26.
[1]Anyone belonging to the human race has the innate capacity for prophesying, and as a male, [the Son of Man] proclaims in no uncertain terms the prospect of the world to come. That is why he named his son "Abel," which, without any ambiguity, one translates as "grief." [2]In this way he shows his sons that they ought to grieve over their deluded brothers. Without deceit, he assures them of consolation in the next world. [3]He urges them to pray to one God only. He does not speak of other gods, nor does he credit anyone else who speaks of them. He guards and multiplies the good that he has. Sacrifices, bloodletting, and sprinklings he hates, but he loves godly, pure, and holy ones. He extinguishes the fire from the altar, [4]brings an end to warring, proclaims peace, endorses self-control, does away with sinning, commands marriage, permits abstinence, and brings everyone to purity. [5]He makes people compassionate, endorses justice, places his seal on the perfect, promulgates the law of peace. His prophecy is understandable and his speech clear in meaning. [6]Oftimes does he remind of the age-long fires of punishment and preaches without ceasing the kingdom of God. He speaks of heavenly treasure, promises unending splendor, and manifests the forgiveness of sins by his deeds.

XI

19.
[1]Knowing that the world had sunk into error and allied itself with wickedness, the Prophet of Truth refused to continue in peace with it as long as it persevered in error. Instead, he unleashes unceasing wrath upon all who agree to wickedness. [2]In this way he supplies knowledge in place of error, and among those who are clear-headed he strikes fire like a torch against the insidious serpent. He bares the truth like a sword and by knowledge puts down ignorance, cleaving and dividing the living from the dead. [3]As long as wickedness is defeated by lawful knowledge, the universe is filled with war. In order to attain salvation, an obedient son is cut off from his stubborn father, a father from a son, a mother from a daughter, a daughter from a mother, relatives from their kinsmen, and friends from their associates.

III

22.
[1]Beside the True Prophet, a female being has been created as his counterpart, as much inferior to him as essence is to communion, as the moon is to the sun, as fire is to light. As a female, her reign is over the present world which is like her, and she counts as the first prophetess. She

proclaims her prophecy with all who are "among those born of woman, of whom John the Baptist is the greatest."[j]

23.
[1]There are two varieties of prophecy. One is male, [2]the other is to be found "among those who are born of woman." Preaching only that which applies to this present world, female prophecy wants to be taken for male. [3]For this reason she steals the male's seed, contains it within her own fleshly seed and permits her words to appear as if her own creation. [4]She pledges to give worldly wealth freely in this world and wants to trade the slow for the fleet, the small for the larger.

24.
[1]Not satisfied with speaking and hearing of multiple gods, she even believes that she herself will be deified! And because she dreams of becoming something that goes against her nature, she destroys what she does have. Pretending to offer sacrifice, she stains herself with blood during her menstrual period and thus defiles all who touch her. [2]When she conceives, she bears but short-lived kings and foments wars with great bloodshed. [3]Those who approach her to find the truth are led to seek it perpetually amid clashing and diverse theses and guesses, doomed never to find it before death intervenes. [4]For ever since the beginning, there is an inevitable death trap laid for the blind: she prophesies errors, things vague and obscure, deceiving all who believe in her.

25.
[1]Accordingly, she has also named her first-born son ambiguously: she called him "Cain," which has a double sense. It is translated both "possession" and "envy," denoting that he was at length to covet a woman, some possession, or his parents' love. [2]But if, in fact, he coveted none of these, then it was fitting he should be called "possession" since he was her first possession. This was good for her, given her nature, for he was both murderer and liar and had no wish to leave off sinning once he had the taste for it. [3]Besides, his descendants were the first to commit adultery. They fashioned harps and lyres and crafted weapons of war.[k] [4]This is why the prophecy about his descendants was full of adultery and harps,[l] secretly and sensually enticing for war.

---

j. Matt. 11:11

k. Gen. 4:21-22

l. Gen. 4:23-24

47.

[1]By word of mouth did Moses deliver the Torah of God to seventy sages so it might be handed on and implemented without interruption. Once Moses died, it was written down, not by Moses himself, however, but by persons unknown; [2]for the Torah itself says, "And Moses died and was buried near the house of Phogor, and no one knows the site of his tomb even today."[m] Pray tell, how could Moses write "And Moses died"? And just as in the period after Moses, some five centuries or so later [the Torah] was discovered in the temple, which had only recently been built, and after another five hundred years it was carried off so that during the reign of Nebuchadnezzar it was destroyed by fire. [4]Given that it was only set down subsequent to Moses and then repeatedly destroyed, Moses's wisdom was shown precisely in his refusal to write it down, knowing a written text would sooner or later vanish. But those who wrote down the Torah, oblivious of the prospect of its eventual destruction, are thereby exposed as ignorant and certainly as no prophets.

II

38.

[1]Once the prophet Moses had, at God's command, passed on the Torah, together with its commentary, to seventy picked men for them to prepare those who volunteered from the ranks of the people, the Torah was shortly fixed in writing. At that very time some spurious passages crept into it. These belittled the only God, who created sky and earth and all that they contain. The scheme of the wicked one was turned to good purpose: [2]in this way it might become evident which individuals are sufficiently shameless to countenance what is written against God and which ones, from their love for him, not only refuse to credit what may be said against him but will not stand hearing a word of it even should it chance to be true, since they reckon it safer to endanger oneself because of sincere belief than to cope with a bad conscience from hearing blasphemy.

III

48.

[2]Thanks to God's providence, one passage came down intact in the written Torah in order that it might serve as a touchstone for which written passages are true and which false.

49.

[1]At the close of the first book of the Torah, one finds it written: "A

m. Deut. 34:6

ruler from Judah shall not go wanting, nor a leader from his seed, until he comes to his rightful position, and the nations will expect him."[n] [2]Now anyone who sees that the leaders from Judah are a thing of the past and that a leader and ruler has in fact appeared and is expected by the nations to appear again can see from this fulfillment that this passage of scripture is true and that the one there promised has appeared. And anyone who accepts this teaching will come to see which parts of scripture ring true and which are spurious.

50.

[1]That the true is mingled with the spurious follows from this, too: that when, as I recall, he was once assailed by the Syndics, he replied, "Wherein lies your mistake? You do not know the true things in scripture and this is why you ignore the power of God."[o] His assumption that they failed to discern the true elements in scripture plainly means there are spurious elements as well. [2]Also his saying, "Be shrewd money changers," refers to the genuine and the counterfeit words of scripture. And when he says, "Why do you not grasp what is reasonable in the Scriptures?" he reinforces the discernment of the one who already judges prudently by his own reflection.

51.

[1]It is well known that he was referring to the scribes and the teachers of the extant scriptures because they knew about the true and authentic Torah but did not let on. [2]And when he said, "I have not come to destroy the Torah,"[p] though he surely destroyed something, he showed that what he did destroy had never truly belonged in the Torah. [3]His pronouncement, "The sky and the earth will come to an end, but no single vowel point or bit of calligraphy will fall out of the Torah,"[q] shows that anything that does pass away before the sky and the earth cannot have formed part of the true Torah.

52.

[1]For though sky and earth still exist, sacrifices, kingdoms, and the prophecies of those "among them who are born of women" have passed away, not having originated in the command of God.

---

n. Gen. 49:10

o. Mark 12:24; Matt. 22:29

p. Matt. 5:17

q. Matt. 5:18; 24:35

II

43.
[1]For this reason, far be it from us to believe the universal Lord, who created sky and earth and all they contain, shares his authority with others[r] or that he lies.[s] For if even he lies, who is truthful? Nor shall we admit that he tests anyone,[t] as if he were ignorant, for then who does have foreknowledge? [2]If even he sorrows or repents,[u] who then is perfect and unchanging in mind? If even he is jealous, then who can be satisfied with oneself? If it is he who makes hearts stubborn,[v] who is left to make hearts wise? [3]If it is he who blinds and deafens,[w] who then supplies sight and hearing? If he plans thefts,[x] who is it who demands justice? If he ridicules,[y] who is without guile? If he is powerless,[z] then who is all-powerful? If he acts with injustice, then who is just? If he "makes that which is wicked," then who is to effect what is good?

44.
[1]If he yet desires a "fertile hill" to dwell in,[a] to whom, pray tell, belong all things? If he is a liar, then who is veracious? If he lives inside a tent,[b] who then is incomprehensible? [2]If his mouth waters at the steam from burning fat, sacrifices, offerings, sprinklings,[c] who can it be who is above need, holy, pure, perfect? If he dotes on the details of lamps and candelabra,[d] who can have installed the lights of the firmament? [3]If in fact he hides in "shadows, darkness, storm clouds and smoke,"[e] who is it, then, who is light and who lights up the endless leagues of space? If he truly approaches with the "flurry of trumpets, shouts of war, projectiles and arrows,"[f] who embodies the peaceful repose for which everyone

---

r. Pss. 82:6; Deut. 32:8-9

s. 1 Kings 22:21-23; Gen. 2:17; 3:4-5, 7, 22

t. Gen. 22:1; Exod. 20:5; Job 2-3

u. Gen. 6:6-7; 1 Sam. 15:35

v. Exod. 4:21; 7:3

w. Exod. 4:11; 2 Kings 6:18

x. Exod. 3:21-22

y. Pss. 2:4

z. Gen. 3:22-23; 11:6-7

a. Pss. 68:15-16

b. Exod. 40:34

c. Gen. 4:3; Exod. 9:28; 24:6

d. Exod. 25:31-40

e. Deut. 4:11; Exod. 10:22; 19:18; 20:21

f. Exod. 19:13, 16; Num. 24:8; Deut. 32:23, 42

yearns? [4]If he is a warmonger,[g] who then wants peace? If he makes what is wicked,[h] who is it that produces the good? If he is cruel,[i] then who is kind? If he reneges on his promises,[j] who then can be trusted? [5]If it is the unrighteous that he prefers, the adulterers and murderers,[k] who then is a fair judge?

16.
[1]Just as in the beginning God, with right hand and left, so to speak, created the sky first, then the earth, in the same way he has put together in pairs everything subsequent. But in the case of mankind, he has adopted a different procedure, reversing the order. [2]For, having hitherto created the stronger first and the weaker second, in the case of human beings we see just the reverse: the smaller first, the stronger second. [3]Thus there came from Adam, created in the image of God, first the unrighteous Cain and second the righteous Abel. [4]Likewise, the one you gentiles call Deucalion sent out two tokens of spirits, clean and unclean, first the black raven, second the white dove. [5]And Abraham, forefather of our nation, fathered two firstborns, first Ishmael, then Isaac, the blessed of God. [6]Isaac likewise fathered a pair, the profane Esau and the pious Jacob. [7]Conforming to this pattern, the archpriest Aaron preceded the legislator Moses as the firstborn into the world.

17.
[1]In the same way, leaving for another time the question of Elijah and Elisha, which would seem to be an exception, [2]there appeared in the first place that one who was "among those born of women" and subsequently the one numbered among the sons of men. [3]Anyone who continues in this way can tell who it was who sent out Simon[l], who preceded me as first to reach the nations, and to whom I belong, having appeared on the scene after him and overtaken him as light does darkness, as knowledge dispels ignorance, as healing dispatches sickness.

XVII

13.
[1]When Simon heard this, he interrupted, saying, "You say you

---

g. Exod. 15:3; Deut. 21:10

h. Isa. 45:7

i. Job 20:31; Isa. 13:9

j. Gen. 18:13-15

k. 2 Sam. 12:13; Gen. 4:15; Exod. 2:12-15

l. That is, Paul.

learned accurately your master's teaching by hearing and seeing him immediately, face to face, and that it is impossible for anyone else to experience the same thing by means of dreams or visions. [2]Let me show you the fallacy of this: When one hears something directly, he is far from sure of what was said. He must ask himself if, given his human frailties, he has not been mistaken in what he thinks he heard. By contrast, a vision carries with it its own intuitive certainty that one is seeing the divine. Answer me that, if you can."

16.

[1]And Peter said, [2]"Everyone knows that any number of idol worshippers, adulterers, and other sinners have seen visions and dreams that predicted the future accurately and also that some have had visions conjured by demons. For my position is that mortal eyes can never behold the disembodied existence of the Father or of the Son because it is veiled in unbearable light. [3]Thus it is a sign of God's mercy, not of peevishness, that he remains invisible to fleshly humans. For if anyone sees him, he must die. [6]No one is capable of seeing the disembodied might of the Son or even of an angel. No, whoever has a vision ought to recognize he is the dupe of an evil demon.

17.

[5]"For the truth dawns of itself to any pious, natural, and pure mind. It is not gained through dreams. No, it is granted to the righteous through simple discernment.

18.

[1]For it was in this way that the Son was revealed even to me by the Father. Hence, I know the power of revelation; I myself learned it from him. For on that occasion when the Lord asked us what people called him, although I was aware that others called him something different, it arose in my heart to reply, nor do I know how I got it out, 'You are the Son of the true God.'[m] [6]From this you can see that it is only announcements of divine wrath that are mediated by visions and dreams, while conversation between friends happens by word of mouth, plainly and without riddles, visions and dreams, which are appropriate to converse with an enemy.

19.

[1]"And if our Jesus did appear to you as well, becoming known in a

m. Matt. 16:13-16

vision, intercepting you with anger as an enemy,[n] even so he has addressed you only with visions and dreams and superficial revelations. But who is rendered competent to teach through a mere vision? [2]And if you think it is quite possible, then why did our teacher bother to spend a whole year with us, who were awake and not airily dreaming? [3]How are we to believe you even if he did appear to you? And how can he have appeared to you if your goals are the opposite of what you must have learned from him? [4]No, if you really were visited by him for a single hour so he might teach you and you have thus become an apostle, then preach his words! Expound his teachings! Befriend his apostles and stop arguing with me, who am his closest advisor. In fact, you have hostilely opposed me,[o] a steadfast rock, the foundation stone of the church.[p] [5]If you were other than an enemy,[q] why would you slander me and insult my preaching, undermining the acceptance of my message when I preach what I heard with my own ears from the Lord? As if I were decidedly condemned and you were approved! [6]And when you say I am condemned, it is God you are accusing, since it is he who revealed Christ to me.[r] You are belittling him who pronounced me blessed because of the revelation vouchsafed me.[s] [7]Look, if you really want to further the truth, then start by learning from us what we learned from him, and as a student of the truth, join us as a colleague."[t]

XI

25.

[1]Come eagerly as a son to a father so God may consider your ignorance the root cause of your transgressions. But if, after having been invited, you refuse or delay to do so, then you will, according to the righteous judgment of God, be destroyed because of your unwillingness.

---

n. In Acts 9:4-5, 16, Jesus bears a surprising resemblance to Dionysus in Euripides' *Bacchae,* where Dionysus converts the persecutor Pentheus, only to take revenge on him by subjecting him to persecution in turn.

o. A rebuttal to Gal. 2:11-21: "But when Cephas arrived in Antioch, I *opposed* him to his face because he stood *condemned.*"

p. Matt. 16:18; cf. 1 Cor. 3:11.

q. Gal. 4:16

r. Matt. 16:17b

s. Matt. 16:17a

t. Gal. 2:6-9. The polemical, apologetical style is highly reminiscent of Galatians and 2 Corinthians, abundantly illustrating how the colorful manner of expression is just as likely pseudepigraphical there as it is here.

[2]And do not imagine any hope remains for you as long as you remain unbaptized, even if you are the most godly individual in history. No, your penalty would be all the more severe because you have done good deeds but not in a good way. [3]For good deeds are only good when performed according to the command of God. But if you defy his will in refusing to undergo baptism, then it is your own will you are serving. As for his command, you despise it!

26.

[1]But someone might object, "What does it add to piety for one to be immersed in water?" First, you are obeying God. Second, when you are born again in the water unto God, then by means of fear you negate your first birth which resulted from lust, and thus you are enabled to obtain salvation. And that is not possible by any other means. [2]This is why the prophet has appealed to us with an oath: "Amen, I say to you: if you are not born again from running water, you cannot enter the kingdom of heaven."[u] [3]So come! Ever since the beginning, there has been something about water that betokens mercy. It is a friend of those who receive baptism in the thrice-holy name[v] and rescues them from future punishment, offering as gifts to God all good deeds performed by the baptized after their baptism. [4]So hasten to the water, which alone can dowse the violence of fire. Anyone who has not yet decided to come still harbors the spirit of passion, and that is why he is reluctant to approach the running water to secure his own salvation.

27.

[1]So come now, whether you are one of the righteous or one of the unrighteous. If you are already righteous, all you need for salvation is baptism. But the unrighteous needs more than submission to baptism to be forgiven for sins committed ignorantly. He must also do as much good as he formerly did evil, which baptism requires. [2]Therefore, make haste, whether you are at present righteous or unrighteous, so you may soon be born to a life with God the Father, who fathers you through the water. To postpone it is dangerous because no one knows the hour he is to die. Demonstrate your likeness to God by doing good deeds, loving the truth, and honoring the true God as a father. Honoring him means to live the way he who is himself righteous wishes you to live. [3]The righteous individual focuses every effort on avoiding all wrongdoing. Wrongdoing includes mur-

---

u. John 3:5

v. Matt. 28:19

der, adultery, hatred, greed, and so forth, for there are numerous sorts of wrongdoing.

28.

[1]Besides these instructions, one must observe what is not binding on everyone but specifically on the worshippers of God. I mean maintaining one's own purity, a husband refraining from intercourse with his wife during her menstrual period, as the divine Torah stipulates.[w] [2]But suppose the guarding of one's purity were not in fact entailed by the worship of God, would you be happy to roll in defilement like a dung beetle? So purify your very thoughts from wickedness by preoccupation with heavenly thoughts as befits human beings who, as rationally endowed, rank above dumb beasts, and wash your bodies in water. [3]Keeping oneself pure is a goal worth pursuing, not because bodily cleanliness is more important than purity of the heart, but because purity follows goodness. [4]This is why our teacher rebuked some of the Pharisees and scribes among us, who separate themselves and, as scribes, certainly know the Torah better than anyone else, and called them hypocrites because they were concerned to purify only what others can see, neglecting purity of heart, which only God can see.

29.

[1]He aptly used this expression when referring to the hypocrites in their ranks, though not referring to all of them. He said that some ought to be obeyed because the cathedra of Moses had been assigned them.[x] [2]But to the hypocrites, he said, "Woe to you, scribes and Pharisees, hypocrites! For you purify but the exterior of the cup and the dish, but the interior is encrusted with filth. Blind Pharisee! First purify the interior of the cup and dish so their exterior may be clean, too."[y] [3]And he spoke the truth, for once the mind has been enlightened by means of knowledge, the one instructed can be good and purity will follow as a matter of course. For from the inner mental attitude proceeds the outward care due the body, just as it is impossible for the proper attitude to follow neglect of the body. [4]Thus the individual who is pure is in the position to cleanse both what is inside and what is outside. But whoever cleanses only the outside does so merely to curry the favor of others. And though onlookers may heap praise on him, he can expect no reward from God.[z]

---

w. Lev. 15:24; 18:19

x. Matt. 23:2-3

y. Matt. 23:27-28

z. Matt. 6:1

30.

[1]Who does not think it better to avoid intercourse with a woman during her monthly period, but only following purification and washing? And the man should also wash himself after intercourse. [2]If you have any hesitation about this, just remember how you kept some of the same purification rules when you worshipped lifeless idols. Be ashamed if you hesitate when you should commit yourself not just to more holiness but to complete purity. Remember him who created you, and you will at once realize who it is who now leads you to hesitate on the path to purity.

31.

[1]But someone might object: "You mean we must now do everything we used to do as part of the worship of idols?" My answer is, not everything, but what you did that was good, you now should do even better. For whatever one does well while captive to error still comes from the truth, just as anything done poorly while living in the truth proceeds from error. [2]So take from whatever source what is rightly yours, not what is foreign to you; and do not say, "If the errorists do something good, then we are released from any obligation of doing it." For by this logic, if any idolater does not kill, then we should kill? Just because one sunk in error happens not to be a murderer?

32.

[1]No, instead, we ought to do more: if the errorists do not kill, let us never even be angry.[a] If the errorist shuns adultery, let us nip it in the bud and refuse even to lust.[b] If he who lives in error loves his friends, let us love even the ones who hate us.[c] If one who is mistaken lends to those who have possessions, let us be generous with those who own nothing.[d] [2]To sum up: we who look toward the prospect of entering the endless age when we die are obliged to perform better deeds than those who know only this present world. [3]For we know that on the Day of Judgment when their deeds are compared with ours, if they are found to match our good deeds, we shall be heartily ashamed, though they shall be damned because, on account of their error, their good deeds are of no benefit to themselves. But our shame shall arise from the fact that we did no better than they did even though we knew better. [4]And if we are ashamed for

---

a. Matt. 5:21-22

b. Matt. 5:27-28

c. Matt. 5:43-44

d. Matt. 5:42

failing to exceed them in righteousness, how much more shame shall we bear if we turn out to have fewer good deeds to show than they!

33.

[1]That it is true the Day of Judgment will reveal the deeds of those who knew the truth on a par with the good deeds of the unenlightened, the Infallible One has taught us, when he told those who refused to come to him and hear him, "The queen of the south shall rise up with this race and shall condemn it because she came from the far reaches of the earth to listen to Solomon's wisdom. And behold, more than Solomon is here, but you do not believe."[e] [2]And to those of the people who would not repent in the face of his preaching, he said, "The Ninevites will rise up with this race and will condemn it because they repented at Jonah's preaching. And behold, more than Jonah is here and no one believes."[f] [3]And in this way, he juxtaposed with their impiety the gentiles who have done good, condemning all who possess the true religion and have fewer good deeds to show than do their unenlightened counterparts. And he urged the prudent to perform good works, not only to match the gentiles, but to do even better.[g]

[4]I have raised this for the sake of the need to keep the monthly courses and to wash following sexual intercourse and to raise no objection to such purity even though it also be practiced by the errorists. For those who perform good deeds even while captive to error will judge the possessors of the true religion, though that will not save them. [5]For they keep pure because of erroneous belief and not as a service offered to the true Father and God of the universe.

e. Matt. 12:42; Luke 11:32

f. Matt. 12:41; Luke 11:3

g. Matt. 5:47

36.

The First Epistle of Peter

F. C. Baur zeroed in on 1 Peter's defining characteristic: it is an attempt to make Peter over to look like Paul. Two major considerations rule against the genuineness of the epistle. First, it is chiefly taken up with encouragement to help its readers survive some pending persecution with their faith intact. This is especially clear once one removes the secondary Pastoral layer delineated by Winsome Munro, which adds later paraenetic and domesticating material to bring 1 Peter into line with the Pastorals. The persecution question is serious because we know of no empire-wide persecution until well after Peter's time. The second factor has to do with the Greek in which the epistle is written. The uneducated fisherman, as tradition made him (Acts 4:13), might have known enough Greek to get by in Galilean trade negotiations but would probably not have been able to write the highly educated prose of 1 Peter.

We may observe something probably closer to the historical Peter's attitude toward Paul in 3 Peter, but the ecumenical tenor of the present epistle tries to smooth over any split and deny even the possibility of it. By making Peter sound like Paul, the intent is to win acceptance for the Petrine legacy and authority in such strategic areas as Galatia, 1 Peter being almost a revisionist, whitewashing version of Paul's Epistle to the Galatians. Neighboring Pontus was within Galatia, the home province of the Paulinist apostle Marcion. Indeed, even without the Pastoral layer, 1 Peter sounds a lot like Paul's letter to the Ephesians—and that is the whole point. The persecution motif may

be secondary and is probably entirely artificial. Along with Acts, 1 Peter is a prime example of a New Testament book written as part of the Catholicizing tendency to co-opt Marcionism and Paulinism within the emerging Catholic Church. We may thus place it after Marcion (ca. 150 CE) and before Irenaeus (ca. 180 CE), who quotes it and ascribes it to Peter.

1

[1]Peter, apostle of Jesus-Christ, to the sojourners of the Diaspora in Pontus, Galatia, Cappadocia, Asia, and Bithynia, chosen [2]on the basis of the foreknowledge of God the Father by means of spiritual sanctification, and called to obedience and to the sprinkling of the blood of Jesus-Christ. May divine favor and protection be multiplied toward you.

[3]Let us bless the God and Father of our Lord, Jesus-Christ, who because of his great mercy has regenerated us to a thrilling prospect based on the resurrection of our Lord from the dead, [4]an inheritance that is immutable, above defilement, and unfading, preserved in the skies for you [5]who are guarded by the power of God through faith for a salvation about to be revealed in the last days. [6]You properly delight in the prospect, even if for a short while you have to grieve over various trials [7]in order that the proof of your faith, which is more valuable than gold, which though perishable is purified by fire, might be disclosed as redounding to the praise and glorification and honor of Jesus-Christ at his final revelation, [8]whom you love even though you have never seen him, in whom you believe even though you have not seen him even now,[a] and you thrill with inexpressible joy, imbued already with the divine splendor, [9]gaining the goal of your faith, the salvation of your souls. [10]The prophets who predicted this favor toward you looked for some clue and sought an answer from God to determine [11]what time or circumstance the Spirit of Christ inside them, clearly witnessing in advance your sufferings for Christ and the subsequent glories, was pointing to. [12]To them it was revealed that they were not serving themselves but you via these things that have now been announced to you by those who evangelized you by the Holy Spirit dispatched from heaven. Into these matters even the angels wish they could look![b]

---

a. John 20:29

b. Many scholars think 1 Pet. 1:3-12 is based on Eph. 1. Baur saw the significance of this: a "Pauline" epistle written in Peter's name, which tends to harmo-

[13]Therefore, readying your minds, staying clear-headed, set your hope undividedly on the favor to be brought to you when Jesus-Christ is revealed to all. [14]*Like obedient children, not conforming to the patterns shaped by the desires that used to motivate you during your time of ignorance* [15]*but according to the pattern of the holy one who called you, become holy yourselves in all manner of behavior* [16]*because it is written, "You shall be holy, for I am holy!"* [17]*And if you invoke as "our Father" the one who judges each individual without favoritism according to his deeds, you had best spend the time allotted your sojourn in fear,* [18]*mindful that you were not bought free of the futile ways bequeathed by your ancestors with perishable commodities like silver or gold* [19]*but rather with priceless blood as of a perfect and undefiled sacrificial lamb, that is, of Christ,*[c] [20]he who was on the one hand foreknown from the day the world was set on its foundation and on the other revealed in these latter times for your benefit, [21]you who, through him, believe in God who has raised him from the dead and bestowed divinity upon him *so your faith and hope might rest in God.* [22]*Having cleansed your souls by obeying the truth to the point where you feel non-hypocritical brotherly love, love one another fervently from deep inside* [23]*since it is not by mortal sperm that you have been regenerated but by immortal: the living and eternal promise of God.*[d] [24]For "all flesh is grass and the glory of it like the wildflower; the grass has withered and the flower dried up, [25]but the promise of Adonai stands inviolable."[e] And the reference to "the promise" is to that promise with which you were evangelized.

2

[1]*Repudiating, then, all ill will, all deceit, all hypocritical pretense, envies, all detraction,* [2]*hunger for the pure, rational milk so, being nourished by it, you may grow up to salvation.* [3]*If you "tasted to see that the Lord is good,"* [f] [4]then approach him as a monument of living rock, rejected by mortals on the one hand but hand-picked by God as precious on

---

nize the two figureheads of formerly hostile sects. This is precisely what we find in Acts, as Peter and Paul give each other's speeches.

c. Winsome Munro, *Authority in Paul and Peter: The Identification of a Pastoral Stratum in the Pauline Corpus and I Peter* (NY: Cambridge University Press, 1983), 37ff, makes vv. 14-19 part of the Pastoral Stratum, an added layer of conventional morality and dampening of earlier sect egalitarianism.

d. Munro makes 21c-23 part of the Pastoral Stratum.

e. Isa. 40:6-9

f. Pss. 34:8; Winsome Munro makes vv. 1-3 part of the Pastoral Stratum.

the other,[g] [5]while you yourselves are as fieldstones,[h] being built into a spiritual house for a holy priesthood to offer spiritual sacrifices acceptable to God through Jesus-Christ. [6]For it may be found in scripture: "Behold, I lay in Zion a hand-picked corner foundation stone, precious, and whoever declares for him will by no means be sorry he did."[i] [7]This honor goes to you who believe. To the unbelievers, "a stone which the builders cast aside turned out to serve as the head of the corner"[j] [8]and "a stone barrier and a rock to trip over."[k] *These stumble over the message, disobeying it, a fate to which, in fact, they were destined.*[l] [9]You, on the other hand, are a chosen race of priest-kings,[m] a consecrated nation, a people for him to claim as his own, consecrated to proclaim the virtues of him who summoned you out of pagan darkness into his wondrous light. [10]Back then, you were not a people, but now here you are a people of God! You had received no mercy, but now you have!

[11]*Brothers, I urge you, as sojourners and resident aliens, to avoid entanglement with the desires of the flesh which are no longer rightly your concern because they wage war against the soul.* [12]*Make sure your conduct among the nations is good, so that even if they slander you as evil-doers, once they see for themselves your good deeds, they may after all worship God on the day of divine visitation.*

[13]*Be subject to every mortal law for the sake of the Lord, whether to the king as the supreme power* [14]*or to governors as his agents to punish evil-doers and praise those who do good*[n] [15]*because this is the will of God: that you do good to silence the ignorant prattle of fools.* [16]*Live as free citizens, not using your freedom as a pretext for doing evil, but living as slaves to God.* [17]*Honor all, love the brotherhood, fear God, honor the king.* [18]*Domestics, submit yourselves in all due fear to your masters, not just to those who are good and patient, but also to the perverted.* [19]*For it is a work of supererogation to put up, for the sake of God and con-*

g. Pss. 118:22

h. Exod. 20:25

i. Isa. 28:16

j. Pss. 118:22

k. Isa. 8:14-15

l. Winsome Munro makes v. 8b part of the Pastoral Stratum.

m. Pss. 110:4

n. G. A. Wells, *The Jesus Myth* (Chicago, IL: Open Court, 1999), observes a problem here if the author believed a historical Jesus was executed by a Roman governor and yet asserts the Roman governors punish the wicked only.

science, with adversity suffered undeserved. [20]*After all, what glory accrues to you if you sin and get pummeled for it? But if you do good and have to put up with suffering, this brings merit with God.*[o] [21]For you were summoned to this role, *because Christ surely suffered for you, bequeathing you an example for you to follow in his bloody tracks.* [22]*He did not sin, nor was he proven to have lied to anyone.*[p] [23]*When he was insulted, he did not talk back; when put to suffering, he did not try to threaten his way out of it but consigned his tormentors to the one who judges righteously.* [24]*He himself shouldered our sins bodily onto the tree*[q] *in order that, dying vis-à-vis sin, we might awaken to righteousness. By his bruises you were healed.* [25]*For you were like straying sheep, but now you have turned to follow the shepherd who watches over your souls.*[r]

3

[1]*You, too, wives, submit to your own husbands in order that, even if any of them remain indifferent to the message, they may yet, through the behavior of their wives, be won over without you actually saying anything,* [2]*observing your pure behavior with amazement.* [3]*Let them not beautify themselves externally with styled hair and gold necklaces or expensive clothing* [4]*but beautify the hidden self in the heart by the unfading adornment of a meek and quiet disposition, on which God places great value.* [5]*For that is the manner in which the sainted women of old who trusted in God beautified themselves: submitting themselves to their own husbands,* [6]*just as Sarah obeyed Abraham, calling him "my lord." You will be her daughters as long as you do good and do not fear any abuse.* [7]*Husbands, similarly, live with them having a grasp of the situation: as with a weaker vessel, showing deference to her since you are co-heirs of the gift of Life; otherwise your prayers will be ineffective.* [8]*Now the goal is for all of you to be of one mind, sympathetic, loving the brothers, compassionate—in humble-mindedness,* [9]*not giving back evil in exchange for evil but rather eulogizing because this is the role you*

---

o. Winsome Munro makes vv. 11-20 part of the Pastoral Stratum.

p. There is an implied parallel here with anticipated slave offenses.

q. A tree is a natural metaphor for the cross (Josh. 10:26-27), but this epistle was additionally addressed to a region where the savior Attis was pictured as affixed to a tree in death, anticipating his rising three days later.

r. Here we have the ostensible recollections of an eye-witness of the sufferings of Jesus (5:1). Why then are all the details drawn from Isa. 53? It is because there was no historical memory of such events: all of it was derived via esoteric exegesis of scripture as implied in 1:10-12.

were summoned to in order that you might be well spoken of when you die.[s] [10]For the one who loves life and wants to see good days, let him stop his tongue from speaking evil and not let his lips deceive. [11]And let him do an about-face from evil and instead do good. Let him look for peace and chase after it [12]because the eyes of Adonai follow the righteous and his ears are open for their requests. But Adonai has determined to oppose those who do evil.

[13]And who, pray tell, is likely to mistreat you if you become eager to do good? [14]But if perchance you do suffer because of righteousness, blessed are you! Do not be afraid of them or be anxious, [15]but consecrate your hearts as a chapel for Adonai, Christ, being prepared always to mount an apologia to every one who may ask you about the prospect of salvation that keeps you going. [16]But be sure you answer with meekness and reverence, having a clean conscience, in order that while you are denigrated, those who abuse your good Christ-like conduct may be made to feel ashamed of themselves. [17]*For it is better, if the will of God so wills it, to suffer for doing good than to suffer for doing evil.*[t] [18]For Christ once died on account of sins, a righteous man in the place of the unrighteous, so he could lead you to God on the one hand through death physically but on the other by being vivified spiritually, [19]*in which form Enoch went to the angels in prison*[u] *to proclaim* [20]*to those who disobeyed in those days before the Flood when God's long-suffering waited while an ark was being readied, in which a few, actually eight, souls were kept safe through the inundation.* [21]*Baptism, the counterpart to this, now saves you, not the*

---

s. Winsome Munro makes vv. 2:21b-3:9 part of the Pastoral Stratum.

t. Munro makes v. 17 part of the Pastoral Stratum.

u. 1 Enoch 6-8; 18:12-21:10; the reference is to the sons of God, who mated with mortal women in Gen. 6:1-4. Originally a myth to account for the great height (six feet tall) of the Canaanite and Philistine groups called the Anakim and Rephaim (Num. 13:32; 2 Sam. 21:15-22), making them demigods. Later the story was reinterpreted, accounting for the rampant wickedness that led God to unleash the Flood. The sons of God were first said to be lesser gods, brothers of Yahve and sons of El Elyon, but were demoted to angels as Judaism crept toward monotheism, their mating with women deemed blasphemous. It was later posited that they had been imprisoned either under the earth (1 Enoch 14:5) or in the lower heavens. This is a Hebrew version of Hesiod's myth of Uranos consigning his monstrous sons to underground caverns. The Flood connection survived in the belief that the shades of the Rephaim float in the Tehom ("the deep," or chaos ocean) under the earth (Job 26:5-6). Rendel Harris suggested that a scribe accidentally dropped "Enoch" out of the text after the similar-looking Greek phrase *en o kai*, "in which also"; see 1 Enoch 12:3-13:10.

cleansing of the flesh from dirt, of course, but the response of a good conscience toward God, made effective by the resurrection of Jesus-Christ, [22]*who may be found to the right of God, having gone into heaven,*[v] angels and authorities and Powers all submitting to him.

4

[1]Since Christ has suffered in the flesh, arm yourselves with the same determination, *for whoever has suffered in the flesh is done with sin,* [2]*so he should live no more of his remaining years in the flesh in the grip of human lusts, but in the will of God.* [3]*Haven't you wasted enough time living by the plan of the nations, walking the road of profligacy, lusts, drunken binges, orgies, drinking contests, and forbidden idolatries?* [4]*While they are surprised at your refusal to run along to the same excesses of abandon and they slander you for it,* [5]*it is they who will answer for it to the one getting ready to judge the living and the dead.* [6]*For this is the reason the news was preached to certain of the dead, in order that, though having on the one hand been condemned in the flesh by human reckoning, they might on the other live in the spirit as far as God is concerned.*[w]

[7]Now the end of everything has come near! *So be clear-headed and be attentive to prayer.* [8]*Above all, have fervent love for each other because love hides a great number of sins.* [9]*Offer each other hospitality without grumbling about it.*[x] [10]Whatever charisma any of you may have received, use it to serve one another as delegated managers of the variegated blessing of God. [11]If anyone speaks, do so as if speaking the very oracles of God. If anyone ministers as a deacon, do so as by the strength that God provides *in order that in everything God may be worshipped through Jesus-Christ, to whom, as the visible vicar of God, all worship and rule belong throughout ages multiplied by ages.*

[12]*Beloved ones, do not be surprised at the fiery trial erupting among you, as though something untoward had befallen you.* [13]*But rejoice as*

v. Winsome Munro makes vv. 3:19-22a part of the Pastoral Stratum.

w. Munro makes vv. 4:1b-6 part of the Pastoral Stratum. Presumably, Christ preached salvation to them, too, during his descent to the netherworld. Enoch had not had such luck in his attempt to win salvation for the imprisoned angels. J. D. M. Derrett, *The Bible and the Buddhists* (Bornato in Franciacorta: Editrice Sardini, 2000), says the motif of a savior easing the torments of the damned in hell is a Buddhist theme, borrowed or developed independently over time but not originally Christian.

x. Winsome Munro makes vv. 4:7b-9 part of the Pastoral Stratum.

you share the sufferings of Christ so you may rejoice and exult also when his divine splendor is revealed to the world. [14]*If you are jeered at for bearing the name of Christ, then blessed are you! For the spirit and glory of God rest upon you.* [15]*Be sure none of you suffers as a murderer or a thief or an evil-doer or as an interloper into the affairs of others.* [16]*But if one suffers as a Christian,*[y] *far from being ashamed, let him rather praise God in this name.*[z] [17]Because the hour of judgment has sounded first among the household of God, and if it starts with us, one can only imagine the fate of those who refuse to bow to the news of God! [18]And if the righteous barely makes it out alive, what refuge is left for the impious and the sinner? [19]*So let those who are suffering by the will of God entrust their souls for safe keeping to a merciful creator as they continue to do good.*

5

[1]*I exhort you elders, being myself a co-elder and witness of the sufferings of Christ, as well as a sharer with you in the splendor about to be revealed:* [2]*between you, see that you tend the flock of God, not merely from a sense of obligation, nor because you hope to make a profit through it, but eagerly.* [3]*Don't take advantage of your office to lord it over your charges,*[a] *but become examples to the flock.* [4]*This way, when the chief shepherd appears, you will have earned the unfading crown of light.*

[5]*Likewise, you younger men, defer to the older,*[b] and all alike must arm themselves with humility because "God opposes the arrogant, but he shows favor to the humble."[c] [6]So humble yourselves under the hand of God's providence so he may lift you up when the time comes; [7]pile your anxieties on him, for you matter to him.[d] [8]Be clear-headed, be vigilant. Your adversary and accuser paces back and forth like a fearsome lion, looking for game to devour. [9]Oppose him, strong in your faith, mindful that the same sort of sufferings are the lot of your brotherhood throughout the world.[e] [10]Now the all-beneficent God, the one who summoned you to his age-abiding splendor manifest in Christ, will work on

---

y. This is one of only three times the word "Christian" appears in the conventional New Testament canon, the others being in Acts 11:26; 26:28.

z. Winsome Munro makes vv. 4:11b-16 part of the Pastoral Stratum.

a. In Matt. 24:48-49 this becomes a saying of Jesus.

b. Winsome Munro makes vv. 4:19-5:5a part of the Pastoral Stratum.

c. Prov. 3:34

d. Pss. 55:22a

e. Is it remotely possible there could have been empire-wide persecution in Peter's day or soon thereafter?

you once you have suffered a bit, will fortify you, strengthen you, and put you on a solid foundation. 11All rule is his throughout ages multiplied by ages! Amen.

12By way of Silvanus,[f] whom I consider a faithful brother, I have written to exhort you with a few words and to testify that you find yourselves in the true favor of God. 13Your fellow elect in Babylon[g] send their greetings, as does my son Mark.[h] 14Greet each other with a kiss of love. Peace to all of you, safe in Christ.

---

f. Some have seized on this note to suggest that Peter, an uneducated Galilean fisherman, asked his colleague, likely more fluent in Greek, to write the letter for his signature. And this is not entirely out of the question. But the fact that Silvanus is elsewhere depicted as a colleague of Paul (2 Cor. 1:19; 1 Thess. 1:1; 2 Thess. 1:1) implies his inclusion here is another Catholocizing attempt to make Peter sound Pauline, even to place him within the Pauline circle. Otherwise we might guess he was the pseudonymous author writing as Peter, here winking at the reader. In any case, the most natural reading would be a simple note that Silvanus carried the letter to its recipients.

g. This was an early Christian nickname for Rome.

h. As Mark is also associated with Paul, his mention here seems to be part of the Catholicizing agenda to make Peter appear to have been more like Paul.

37.

The Second Epistle of Peter

We are invited (2 Pet. 3:1) to understand the present epistle as a sequel to 1 Peter, but in fact, it cannot have been from the same writer. The Greek is much different, with an almost Byzantine complexity. Even without a supposed predecessor, we would have to make 2 Peter one of the last books of the New Testament because the writer knows the Gospel of John, including the later addition (John 21); the Marcionite Pauline collection, which he regards as scripture; and the late Epistle of Jude, which he borrows almost verbatim. One might almost consider 2 Peter a bowdlerized and expanded edition of Jude, as if someone wanted to trim away some slightly objectionable elements and then up the ante of apostolic authorship, changing the authorial ascription from the obscure Jude, ostensibly the brother of Jesus (Mark 6:3), to the famous Simon Peter—referring to him as "Symeon" in an attempt to archaize the name as in Acts 15:14 for authenticity's sake. I have italicized the material taken from Jude to illustrate 2 Peter's dependence on it.

It is remarkable that Origen and Jerome, both of whom accepted it, recorded that others doubted the epistle's authenticity. Jerome said it was doubted for stylistic reasons. Eusebius doubted the Petrine authorship, partly for a lack of earlier patristic citations and partly because writers whose opinion he regarded highly did not accept it. The Muratorian Canon, which seems to reflect the canon used in Rome in the second century, mentions neither 1 nor 2 Peter. So doubts about 2 Peter's authorship are nothing new.

The writer gets into trouble when he takes on the task of rational-

izing the delay of the Parousia. His first strategy is to imply that the Transfiguration fulfilled the promise of Jesus' coming, a step also ventured by Mark, who juxtaposed it immediately following the prediction that some "standing here will not taste death" (Mark 9:1). But to do this, our Petrine author implicated himself in blatant pretense, posing as a witness of the Transfiguration, which he certainly did not see any more than he saw the second coming. Then he tries to suggest the delay should not be a cause of concern since the apostles already predicted it long ago. That he is posing as one of the apostles seems to escape his notice for the moment! At any rate, that strategy suffers from the same fatal flaw as the predictions of delay in Matthew (24:48; 25:5): the *original* plan includes a *change* in plans. The only possible solution, which the writer finally tries, is to say God has all the time in the world and has decided to grant the human race a reprieve.

The surprising mention of Paul and his letters (3:15-16) tells us we are visiting a time late in the second century when Catholic Christians are co-opting Paulinists by claiming Paul, whom Tertullian dubbed "the apostle of Marcion and the apostle of the heretics," as one of their own. They claim Paul has been misunderstood and his writings distorted by Gnostics and Marcionites. Language like "our beloved brother Paul" is obviously diplomatic. It was the same strategy manifest in the decision to follow Marcion's lead in forming a Christian scriptural canon that would include Paul, but in this case a domesticated, sanitized Paul.

1

[1]Symeon Peter, a slave and an apostle of Jesus-Christ, to those who have obtained a faith equally precious with ours in the salvation of our God and Savior Jesus-Christ. [2]May God's favor and protection be multiplied to you by knowing fully God and Jesus-Christ, our Lord.

[3]Everything needful for salvation and piety has been provided us by his divine power through the full knowledge of the one who summoned us to share his own splendor and virtue, [4]through which he has given us the precious and very great promises in order that through them you might come to share divine nature,[a] fleeing away from the putrefaction of

a. These are the very words used in the creeds for the divine nature of Christ.

the world due to lust. [5]But for just this reason, provide yourselves with full diligence, supplement your faith with virtue, and virtue with knowledge, [6]and knowledge with self-mastery, and self-mastery with endurance, and endurance with piety, [7]and piety with fraternal friendship, and fraternal friendship with love. [8]For if these qualities are in you and increasing, it makes you neither barren nor unfruitful in your full knowledge of our Lord Jesus-Christ. [9]For whoever is lacking in these qualities is blind, myopic, and drinks from the Lethe[b] when it comes to that time in the past when his sins were cleansed. [10]For this reason, brothers, be diligent and confirm your calling and election; for by doing these things, you will never fall. [11]For this way the red carpet into the endless kingdom of our Lord and Savior Jesus-Christ will be rolled out for you.

[12]For this reason, I plan always to remind you about these things, though they are hardly unknown to you, merely receiving confirmation by the truth I now present. [13]And I think it good, as long as I reside in this tent of flesh, to stimulate you by way of reminder, [14]fully cognizant that I must soon cast off this tent, just as our Lord Jesus-Christ made clear to me.[c] [15]So I will be diligent to make sure that after my exodus you remember these things. [16]For we were not following out ingenious myths when we informed you about the coming in power of our Lord, Jesus-Christ, but spoke as eyewitnesses of that man's majesty![d] [17]For as he received recognition and radiant splendor from God the Father, a voice like this wafted to him from the Shekinah: "This is my beloved son, in whom I am quite pleased!" [18]And we ourselves heard this voice being wafted from the sky as we were right there on the holy mountain with him![e] [19]And thus, we have the prophetic prediction confirmed, something you will do well to pay attention to, as to a lamp shining in a gloomy place, waiting for the truth of it to dawn on you, for the morning star to begin to illumi-

---

b. Lethe is the River of Forgetfulness, from which souls entering Hades drink to forget their earthly lives.

c. The reference is to John 21:18-19, not to the events underlying it, since there are none.

d. The author is trying to fend off accusations that the Jesus story was mythical. Anticipating the discussion in 3:3-4ff regarding the delay of the apocalyptic second coming, the author uses the word *parousia*, trying to identify the event with the Transfiguration—something that had already transpired. Mark had adopted the same desperate strategy when he placed the Transfiguration immediately following the failed promise, "There are some standing here who will not taste death before they see the kingdom of God having come in power" (Mark 9:1).

e. This must be recognized as a blatant case of pious fraud.

nate your understanding. [20]But get this straight before you study prophecy: not every prophecy in scripture comes with its own solution, [21]for prophecy was never brought by human initiative, but mortals spoke from God as the Holy Spirit carried them along in a passive state.

2

[1]But there were also pseudoprophets among the people of Israel, just as there will be[f] teachers of falsehood among you *who will smuggle in soul-blasting heresies and repudiate the divine Despot who manumitted them, inviting sudden destruction.*[g] [2]And many will follow after their licentiousness, and because of them the way of truth will be blasphemed.[h] [3]And coveting your allegiance, they will buy you like a piece of merchandise, using fabricated teachings.[i] For them, the judgment will not wait, and their destruction does not sleep. [4]*For if God refused to show mercy*[j] *to the angels who sinned, but consigning them to the smoky pits, delivered them to Tartarus,*[k] *where they are kept pending judgment;*[l] [5]and if he had no mercy on the archaic cosmos,[m] but guarded, with seven others, his herald Noah,[n] bringing the cataclysm on a world full of impious men; [6]*and he condemned the cities of Sodom and Gomorrah, overthrowing them and burying them in ashes, an example was set for those who want to live impiously.*[o] [7]And he delivered righteous Lot, oppressed by the brutal behav-

---

f. The future tense is fictive, as in all apocalyptic prediction; the author is really editorializing about conditions existing in his own day.

g. Jude 4. Did not Peter himself famously deny his master? We can infer that Peter's denial was unknown to this writer or recognized as smear propaganda and therefore ignored.

h. Because of the supposed libertinism of a minority of Gnostics like the Phibionites, some pagans generalized that Christianity as a whole was a cult of immorality.

i. Irenaeus similarly accuses the Gnostics of spinning innovations purely out of their imaginations.

j. This may be a reference to Enoch's unsuccessful plea on their behalf (1 Enoch 18-21).

k. Tartarus is the netherworld of the damned in Greek myth; see 1 Pet. 3:19.

l. Jude 6

m. The author reflects the priestly version of the Flood whereby, as in the Gilgamesh Epic, the firmament and the earth disk are smashed like a cup and saucer under a mallet.

n. This recalls Shulat and Hanish, heralds of the storm in the Gilgamesh flood story.

o. Jude 7

ior of the lynchmob.[p] 8Imagine that righteous man living among them, seeing and hearing what they did, day after day! His saintly soul was mortified at their outlaw deeds.[q] 9Adonai remembers the pious, to deliver them from trial, but keeps the unjust under punishment pending a day of judgment, 10and especially *those who chase after flesh in the grip of degrading lust and who disdain Dominions.*[r] *Conceited and brazen, they do not tremble at blaspheming the Glorious Ones,* 11*whereas angels far superior in strength and power do not dare blaspheme them even when pleading against them before Adonai.*[s] 12*But these, like beasts by nature, bereft of reason, born for capture and death, are blaspheming in matters of which they are ignorant.*[t] The corruption infesting them will not stop short of its deadly goal, you may be sure, 13as they suffer wrong as the reward of their own wrongdoing. Taking their pleasure in daylight orgies, *they are disease spots and blemishes as they revel in their deceptions, feasting with you,*[u] 14with eyes sharp to spot an adulteress and indefatigable in sinning, tempting unstable souls, having a heart well trained in coveting. Spawn of damnation, 15*abandoning the straight path, they veered off down the road of Balaam, son of Beor,*[v] who loved the wages of wickedness 16until he received a rebuke for his transgression; a mute donkey speaking with a human voice reined in the madness of the prophet.[w] 17*These are dried-up springs and storm-tossed mists, for whom there is a place reserved in the*

---

p. A reference specifically to the mob's "pressing hard against" Lot to capture him in Gen. 19:9.

q. How had Lot maintained the reputation of a righteous man after offering his virgin daughters to the ravages of a howling mob? The ancients rated hospitality so highly among the virtues, they understood Lot to have gallantly protected the strangers to whom he had promised asylum. He was willing to make the ultimate sacrifice.

r. Jude 8. The reference is certainly to Gnostics, who were thought to practice libertinism and gloat over their freedom from archons and angels. "Dominion" was a rank of archons.

s. In Jude's original, the reference is to a scene in the Assumption of Moses, according to Origen, in which Satan challenged Michael for possession of Moses's corpse, a scene derived from Zech. 3:1-5. In 2 Peter, the author has avoided mentioning a non-canonical work. For the same reason, he omits Jude's quotation of 1 Enoch and substitutes Flood material from Genesis. This reluctance to quote heretical books marks 2 Peter as quite late.

t. Jude 8-10

u. Jude 12

v. Jude 11

w. Num. 22:5, 7

gloomy darkness.[x] [18]For *with grand and empty phrases, they* use the lusts of the flesh in excessive behavior to *entice*[y] those who had almost escaped from a life of error.[z] [19]While they promise them liberation, they themselves are found to be slaves of vice; for if anything has dominated you, you are enslaved to it. [20]For if, once one has escaped the defilement of the world through the enlightenment of the Lord and Savior Jesus-Christ, one then becomes entangled in it again, one is defeated, the last state being worse than the first. [21]For it was better for such people never to have come to full knowledge of the path of righteousness than, having come to know it well, to shrug off the holy commandment delivered to them. [22]In their fate, the old proverb has come true: "The dog turns back to eat its own vomit and the new-washed sow to rolling in the mud."[a]

3

[1]This is the second epistle, beloved ones, I have written you;[b] in both I hope to stimulate your sincere minds by way of reminder, [2]to *recall the words once spoken* by the holy prophets and the commandment of the Lord and Savior through *your apostles.*[c] [3]First of all, be sure of this: *in the last of the days, mockers will appear, following their own lusts,*[d] making wisecracks, [4]saying things like, "What happened to the promise of his coming?[e] After all, from the day the church fathers fell asleep, all remains as it was since the dawn of creation!" [5]But this is hidden from them, as they wish it: how in ancient times a firmament and an earth emerged from water and through water, held together by the command of God, [6]through which also that former world perished in a watery cataclysm.[f]

---

x. Jude 12-13

y. Jude 16

z. The implication is that people were choosing among the various Christian sects and because of their antinomian orientation, the Gnostics were enjoying some success. The same charge of libertinism was leveled at Cynic philosophers and Christians in general.

a. Prov. 26:11a

b. This epistle, then, is intended as a sequel to 1 Peter, though it is the work of a subsequent writer.

c. Jude 17. The author unwittingly lets his mask slip. He recalls the words spoken by the apostles as figures of the past, predicting events in his readers' time, therefore his own time as a pseudonymous writer.

d. Jude 18

e. Mark 9:1; John 21:22, which is similarly rationalized away by v. 23.

f. As in 2:5, the writer is thinking of the Priestly Code's Flood story in which the whole universe structure is smashed asunder.

[7]But the present heavens and earth, by the same command of God, have
been slated for destruction by fire in the day of judgment and destruction
for the impious. [8]But brothers, don't you let the fact be concealed from
you that "one day for Adonai is the same as a millennium, and a millennium as a single day."[g] [9]It is not so much that Adonai is tardy fulfilling his
promise, as some define tardiness. No, it is that he is long-suffering toward you, unwilling for any to perish and hoping everyone will come to
their senses. [10]Even so, the Day of Adonai will come as unexpectedly as a
burglar,[h] and in that day the heavens will pass away with a great roaring
while the elements burn and dissolve,[i] and the earth, as well as all the
deeds done in it, will be laid bare. [11]In the meantime, with everything
about to dissolve, what sort of people is it incumbent on you to be? Those
who conduct themselves with holiness and piety [12]as you wait for, and by
your good deeds even hasten, the arrival of the Day of God, on account of
which the skies will ignite and be dissolved and the very elements will
blaze and melt. [13]But we look forward to new skies and a new earth as he
promised, one in which only righteousness dwells. [14]Thus, beloved ones,
as you wait for these things, try your best to be found by him in peace, unstained and without blemish, [15]and think of the delay of our Lord as
long-suffering and a chance for salvation, just as our beloved brother Paul
wrote to you with the wisdom given him,[j] [16]just like he says in all his
epistles[k] when he discusses these things. Granted, there are some difficult
passages in them, which the uneducated and unstable twist, as they do the
rest of the scriptures, to their own ruin.[l] [17]But you, beloved ones, being
forewarned, watch out that you not become similarly unstable, led astray
by the error of those who reject the Law.[m] [18]Just see that you advance in
the favor and knowledge of our Lord and Savior Jesus-Christ. To him be
all worship, both now and throughout a day that is as a millennium.

---

g. Pss. 90:4

h. 1 Thess. 5:2. This becomes a saying of Jesus in Matt. 24:43-44.

i. Reflecting Stoic eschatology.

j. 2 Thess. 2:1-12

k. The writer has a collection of Pauline epistles! This means he is no contemporary of Paul.

l. By including the Pauline epistles as part of scripture, the author has placed himself in a post-Marcion period. He attempts to co-opt the epistles, or more importantly their readers, by embracing the texts, while also writing off the interpretations of the original Marcionite and Gnostic readers as eccentric misinterpretations.

m. Again, the implied referents are Marcionites and Gnostics.

38.

The Third Epistle of Peter

THE THIRD EPISTLE OF PETER IS FOUND in the Syriac Clemetine *Homilies,* a document compiled sometime in the fourth century from earlier, valuable sources stemming from Ebionite Christianity. The epistle itself would date from the third century if we agreed with some scholars who feel it must have been a preface to the Preaching of Peter; the latter uses a third-century work by the Syrian Gnostic teacher Bardesanes. But there is no certain link between the Preaching of Peter and 3 Peter except that both are Ebionite documents. As such, the epistle may be an earlier work.

It seems to function much as the Pastoral Epistles in presupposing an already well-known canon of epistles and seeking to fend off or disqualify a popular way of reading them. The Pastorals reject Marcionite, Gnostic, and encratite readings of Paul's letters, whereas this epistle apparently rejects a Paulinist reading of texts attributed to Peter. We do not know which writings are intended here, but one thinks of the catholicizing 1 Peter, which makes Peter sound like the Paul of Ephesians. We also think of Acts 15:7-11, where the catholicizing harmonist pretty much puts Paul's speech from Galatians 2:14-21 into Peter's mouth, making Peter the advocate for relieving gentiles of the Torah's yoke.

"Peter" pays lip service here to James the Just as bishop of Jerusalem, but the Moses-Peter parallel shows how much more important Peter was to the author and his community. We hear in this epistle another voice in the Syrian debate over Petrine versus Pauline authority

and succession, witnessed in Galatians and Matthew's gospel, perhaps also in Thomas, saying 13.

1

[1]Peter, to James, lord and bishop of the holy congregation: Peace be with you always from the All-Father through Jesus-Christ.

[2]Fully cognizant that you, my brother, are zealous for the common good of us all, I plead with you fervently never to entrust the transcripts of my preaching, herewith forwarded to you, to any gentile, nor to any belonging to our own tribe before he has successfully completed a period of testing. But once one of them has been examined and certified worthy, then you may place them in his care in the same way that Moses passed his own teaching office down to the Seventy.[a] [3]The fruits of his caution blossom even today. For no matter where they live, those of his nation preserve the identical rule of faith in a single God and in their pattern of behavior, refusing to change their minds despite the ambiguities of scripture. [4]Instead, they try to harmonize the contradictions in scripture according to the traditional rule of faith in case someone ignorant of the traditions should be thrown into confusion at the equivocal words of the Prophets. [5]For this reason, they forbid anyone to teach until he learns how one ought to use the scriptures. And this way, they maintain a unity of belief in one God, one Torah, and one hope of salvation.

2

[1]We, of course, would like to obtain the same result, and to this end be sure to entrust the transcripts of my preaching by the same manner of initiation to our own seventy[b] brothers so they may be equipped to prepare candidates for the position of catechist. [2]For if we go about it in any other fashion, our message of truth will fragment into a plethora of opinions. I do not need to be a prophet to predict this; on the contrary, I have already witnessed the start of this evil. [3]For some of the gentile converts have rejected my preaching that is according to the Torah in favor of the lawless and nonsensical teaching of the man who is my enemy.[c] [4]Besides this, some have even tried, while I am still on the scene, to distort my own teaching by interpreting it in various ways, to make it sound as if I, too, taught the dissolving of the Torah and that, though I thought so, I dared

a. Num. 11:25

b. Luke 10:1?

c. The reference is to either Paul or Simon Magus.

not say so publicly.[d] Never! Doing anything of the kind means to transgress the divine Torah which was disclosed by Moses and was reaffirmed as permanent by our Lord when he said, "Sky and earth will come to an end, but neither a vowel point or a dot of calligraphy will drop out of the Torah." [6]He said this to ensure that everything in scripture would come true. But those individuals who inexplicably claim they are well versed in my views want to explain my views, which they have heard, better than I myself who spoke them![e] They assure those they teach that something is my opinion when in fact it never entered my mind. [7]And if they make such false claims already during my lifetime, how much farther will their successors have the impudence to go after I am dead?

3

[1]So to forestall such a thing happening, I am begging you not to release the transcripts of my preachings, enclosed here, either to anyone of our tribe or to any gentile before their novitiate is completed. But if someone passes the test of worthiness, then let them be handed on [2]the same way Moses passed on his teaching office to the Seventy, in order for them to preserve the official doctrines and to expand the kingdom of the truth, interpreting every passage in agreement with our tradition. This way they may avoid being abducted into error through ignorance and mental uncertainty, much less becoming agents leading others into the same pit of destruction with them.

[3]I have now outlined to you what I consider the necessary measures. But whatever you, my lord, consider fitting, by all means implement. Farewell.

---

d. Gal. 2:11-20

e. We see a parallel claim in 2 Pet. 3:15-17, where the complaint is that some have twisted Paul's writings in ways he would never countenance.

39.

The Fourth Epistle of Peter

THERE IS NO SURE WAY TO DATE THIS epistle, written in Greek but transmitted to us in the Coptic translation as part of the Nag Hammadi library. It contains a somewhat complex Gnostic salvation myth, which might imply a mid-to-late second century composition. It employs two devices we have seen in John and Acts, where John removes Thomas from the first appearance of Jesus to the eleven disciples (John 20:24) so that in the sequel (vv. 24-29) Thomas can embody the anticipated skepticism of the reader. In this way, 4 Peter has Philip miss an important meeting so he, too, can be told about it later, with Philip standing in for the reader. In Acts 1:7, the disciples remain as ignorant as ever after a full forty days of instruction about the kingdom of God. For the same reason, the disciples in 4 Peter require a refresher course in soteriology—all, of course, for the sake of the reader.

The authors of the other Peter epistles would certainly not approve of the doctrine contained in this document, and no doubt this writer would be equally puzzled or outraged over their theology. It just goes to show once again that radically diverse factions may claim Peter or Jesus with equal fervor and yet ascribe the most radically divergent opinions to them.

It appears to me that the original redactor of 4 Peter must have found a revelation dialogue between Jesus and the apostles, in which Peter was the star, and only subsequently decided to encase this material in letter form. He carried his task through ineptly and incompletely. Although I have dared to try to complete the job, it is plain

enough that not quite all of the text was intended as an epistle. Therefore, I have left a narrative section at the end. In the main section, the epistle proper, I have changed the incongruous third-person references to the first-person. Italics indicate conventional scholarly attempts to supply missing content, and my own, sometimes more venturesome, guesses appear within brackets. Finally, I have provided more familiar chapter and verse divisions, replacing the codex, page, and line divisions of most versions of Nag Hammadi texts.

1

[1]Peter, the apostle of Jesus-Christ, to Philip, our beloved brother and fellow apostle, and to the brothers who are with you: Greetings!

[2]Now I want you to know, our brother, *that* we received commandment from our Lord and the Savior of the entire world to *assemble and* provide teaching and proclaim the salvation which our Lord, Jesus-Christ, promised us. [3]But in your case, you were not present when he issued this command and you did not favor the idea of coming together and organizing ourselves in order to preach the news. You would have been agreeable to the idea, our brother, to come in obedience to the commandment of our God, Jesus.

[4]We went to meet atop the Mount of Olives, the same place we used to meet with the blessed Christ when he was still in bodily form. [5]Then, the apostles having assembled, we threw ourselves to our knees and prayed, saying, "Father, Father, Father of the Light, possessor of immortality, give heed to us, even as *you did* your child Jesus-Christ, *in whom you were pleased*. [6]For he became for us an illuminator of the darkness. Yes, hear us!" [7]Again we prayed, saying, "Living Son of Life, Immortal Son who dwells in light, Son, Immortal Christ, our redeemer, empower us, for they mean to kill us!"

[8]Then a great Light appeared and the very mountain shone with the radiance of the one who appeared. [9]And a voice sounded forth, and it said, "Listen to my words, and I will speak to you. Why do you ask me for what you have already? For am I not Jesus-Christ, who is with you to the end of the ages?"

[10]Then we apostles answered, saying, "Lord, let us know of the weakness of the aeons and their Pleroma!" [11]And "How did we come to be imprisoned in his abode?" And furthermore: "How may we depart out of it again?" Yet again, "Whence may we gain authority and boldness to withstand the powers who contend against us?"

12Next a voice came forth from the light, saying, "You yourselves can attest that I told you all these things! But because of your little faith, I shall tell them again. 13First of all, as to *the weakness* of the aeons, that weakness became apparent with the foolish disobedience of the Mother, disdaining the kingly commandment of the Father. 14She desired to bear aeons of her own. And when she spoke offspring into being, the arrogant one resulted. 15And when she left a portion behind,[a] the arrogant one grabbed it up and it became a weakness. Herewith, the weak link of the aeons. 16Now, having seized it, the arrogant one sowed it as seed. And he stationed powers over it, along with authorities. And *he* swathed it in the aeons that are dead.[b] 17And all the powers of this cosmos rejoiced in their begetting. But they remain ignorant of the Pre-existent *Father* and are strangers to him. 18But this is the One to whom they unwittingly ascribed power and whom they worshipped by praising their creator. 19But the arrogant one, not realizing this, grew conceited through the adulation of the powers. He became one who envies and desired to fabricate a copy *of the heavenly image* of God, a form in place of a form of God. 20So he assigned the Powers who served him to craft mortal bodies. And they bore the distorted image of the likeness which resulted.

21"Now as to the pleroma: I am he who was sent down in the body for the sake of the seed that had been lost. And I descended into their mortal shape. 22But they failed to recognize me.[c] They assumed I was a mortal man. And I spoke to whomever belonged to me,[d] and he listened to me, even as you, too, listen today. 23And upon such I conferred the authority to enter upon the inheritance of his paternity. And I stripped [away the veil of ignorance and] they were filled [with knowledge and rejoiced] in his salvation. 24And since they were of the aeons, albeit a weakness, they became one with the Pleroma.

25"And this is why you are stuck here, because you are mine. When you strip off yourselves the tainted part, you too will become illuminators among mortal humanity. 26And this is why you must contend with the powers: since *they* can never enjoy repose like you, they begrudge you your salvation."

---

a. This might imply the placenta or perhaps simply her reflection.

b. That is, legions of counterfeit aeons: the archons, principalities, and powers created by the arrogant Demiurge to mimic the pleromatic pantheon above.

c. 1 Cor. 2:8

d. He communicated through the divine spark of light buried within the elect.

[27]Then we apostles worshipped again, saying, "Lord, tell us: how may we combat the archons, since *the* archons are our superiors?"

[28]In response, *a* voice addressed us out of the manifestation, saying: "This is how you will beat them. The archons attack the inner self, so you are to fight them this way. [29]Come together and teach the promise of salvation throughout the world. And armor yourselves with the power of my Father and make your prayers known to him. [30]And he, the Father, will help you as he helped you by sending me. Do not fear: *I am with you forever,* as I *told* you before when I was in bodily form." [31]Next came lightning and thunder from the sky, and that which appeared to us was withdrawn into the sky.

[32]Then we apostles rendered thanks to the Lord with every blessing we could think of, and we returned to Jerusalem. And coming up to the city, as we walked the road, we conversed with each other about the light which had appeared. [33]And one remarked concerning the Lord, saying, "If he, our Lord, suffered, how much can we expect to suffer?"

[34]I, Peter, replied, saying, "He suffered on *our* behalf, but it is necessary that we, too, suffer on account of our smallness." [35]Then a voice came, saying, "I have told you many times: it is necessary that you suffer. They must bring you before synagogues and governors so you will suffer. [36]But he who does not suffer and does not [confess the faith will not stand before] the Father [in heaven] in order that he may [receive his reward]."

[37]And we apostles rejoiced *greatly* as we approached Jerusalem. And we went into the temple and taught concerning salvation in the name of the Lord Jesus-Christ. And we healed a great number.

[38]And I, Peter, began to speak to my fellow disciples: "*Did* our Lord Jesus, when he was in the body, reveal to us everything? For he came down to our level. My brothers, give heed to my voice." [39]And I was filled with a Holy Spirit and spoke this way: "Our illuminator, Jesus, descended and was crucified. He wore a crown of thorns. He donned purple vesture. And he was *crucified* on a tree and he was interred in a tomb. [40]And he rose from the dead. My brothers, Jesus has no natural acquaintance with such suffering. But we do since we are sprung from the sin of the Mother. It was because of this that he underwent all of our trials. [41]For the Lord Jesus, Son of the incomprehensible splendor of the Father, is the author of our life. My brothers, let us refuse to obey these lawless ones and walk in [their way]." [42]Then I, Peter, *summoned the rest also* and said, "*O Lord Jesus*-Christ, author *of our* repose, grant us an understanding spirit so we too may work wonders."

2

1 [When Philip received this message and read it, he gladly went to see
Peter.] Then Peter summoned the rest, too. 2 Then Peter and the rest of the
apostles saw *him* and were filled with a Holy Spirit. And each of them
performed healings. 3 And they took leave of each other to go and proclaim the Lord Jesus. And periodically they gathered together and greeted
one another with reports of their deeds, responding with, "amen."

4 Then Jesus appeared to them, saying, "Peace to all of you and to all
who believe in my name. And when you depart again, go with joy and favor and power. And do not fear, for behold, I am with you forever."

5 Then the apostles took leave of each other for the last time and journeyed into the four quarters of the earth to preach. And by the power of
Jesus, they went in peace.

40.

The Apocalypse of Peter

PETER'S REVELATION OF HEAVEN AND its wonders and the horrors of hell was widely known and cited in the early church. Many reckoned it as canonical scripture; it appears in the "disputed writings" category in the Muratorian Canon and historical commentary by Eusebius, but it is listed simply as scripture in Codex Claromontanus alongside the Shepherd of Hermas and Acts of Paul. The fifth-century church historian Sozomen tells us that in his day the Apocalypse of Peter was publicly read every Good Friday in congregations throughout Palestine. A Greek-language fragment of about half the text was discovered in 1884 in a tomb in Akhmim, Egypt, in a little book also containing portions of 1 Enoch and the Gospel according to Peter. In fact, as M. R. James has suggested, the Petrine gospel probably had an edited version of the Petrine apocalypse as one of its chapters. The version presented here is based on the more complete and seemingly more faithful Ethiopic translation of the original Greek.

The Apocalypse seems to have incorporated material from 4 Ezra 8:44-47, which would mean it could not have been written earlier than about 100 CE. It is also based on both the Transfiguration scene and the Olivet discourse and is aware of Luke's parable of the barren fig tree (Luke 13:6-9). Clement of Alexandria cites it as scripture, and this implies it must have been extant by 150 CE.

The interest of Peter's apocalypse is obvious: unlike the Revelation of John, it gives many specifics of the judgment process and the blessings of heaven and punishments of hell. As the Akhmim fragment appears to have been copied in the ninth century, the Apocalypse

must have been in circulation for at least that long. As far as we know, it is the greatest single source of early and medieval Christian beliefs about the torments of hell. It is obviously an important precursor to Dante's *Inferno*. There is at least one other ancient text called the Apocalypse of Peter, discovered at Nag Hammadi, but it does not seem to have attained the circulation or esteem garnered by the present book, which is why only the latter is included here.

1

[1]And as he sat on the Mount of Olives, his own came to him, and several of us begged and pleaded with him and urged him, [2]"Reveal to us the tokens of your appearing and of the end of the world so we may recognize and mark the time of your appearing and teach our successors, [3]to whom we preach your news and whom we install in your church in order that they, hearing it, may be careful to mark the time of your arrival." [4]And our Lord answered us, saying, "Watch that no one deceives you and that you do not waver in faith and revert to idolatry. [5]Many will come in my name, saying, 'I am Christ!' Do not believe them and do not approach them. [6]For the coming of the Son of God will not be evident, but like the lightning which erupts from the east unto the west, so I shall come in my splendor on the clouds of the sky with a huge army. [7]I will come in my splendor with my cross carried in front of me. I will come with all my holy angels in my splendor, shining seven times as bright as the sun, [8]when my Father shall place the crown upon my head for me to judge the living and the dead and repay everyone as his work deserves.

2

[1]"And as for you, hear the parable of the fig tree on the subject: as soon as its shoots have appeared and its branches have sprouted, the end of the world will arrive." [2]And I, Peter, answered, saying to him, "Explain to me about the fig tree, and how to discern its import, for the fig tree sprouts each year throughout its life, bearing fruit for its owner. What does the parable of the fig tree signify? We do not know." [3]And the Master answered, saying to me, "Do you not comprehend that the fig tree is the house of Israel? [4]When a man planted a fig tree in his garden and it bore no fruit, and he looked for fruit from it year after year, he finally told his gardener, 'Uproot the fig tree so our land will no more be unfruitful for us.' [5]And the gardener said to God, 'We, your slaves, want to weed it and to break up the surrounding soil and water it. If, after that, it fails

to bear fruit, we will at once dig it up by the roots and replace it with another.'[a] [6]Have you not grasped that the fig tree is the house of Israel?
Amen, I tell you: when, at the end, its branches sprout, then it is that deceiving Christs shall appear and awaken the hope of many: 'I am the
Christ who has now arrived in the world.'[b] [7]And they shall go off to follow them and to deny the One our fathers praised, those who crucified
the first Christ, sinning terribly by doing so. [8]But this deceiver is not the
Christ. And when the people see the wickedness of his deeds[c] and reject
him, he will slay them with the dagger and the martyrs shall be many.
[9]That is when the branches of the fig tree, the house of Israel, shall
sprout,[d] and there shall be many martyrs by his hand. They shall be executed and so bear witness. [10]Enoch and Elijah will be sent to teach them
that this is the deceiver who had to appear in the world, performing signs
and wonders in order to lead astray. [11]And therefore, those killed by his
hand shall be martyrs, counted among the good and righteous witnesses
who pleased God with their lives."

3

[1]And he showed me, held in his right hand, the souls of all the martyrs, and on the palm of the right hand the image of what is to be fulfilled
on the last day: [2]how the righteous and the sinners must be separated and
what will become of the righteous in heart, as well as how the evil-doers
will be eradicated for all the ages. [3]We beheld how the sinners sobbed in
dire distress and grief until all who beheld it joined in their sobbing,
whether the righteous, the angels, or even the Lord himself. [4]And I inquired of him, saying, "Lord, rightly did you say concerning these sinners, 'It would have been better for them never to have been born in the
first place.'"[e] [5]And the Savior answered, saying, "O Peter, why do you
say such a thing, 'never to have been born at all'? You oppose God.
[6]Would you have more compassion than he does for his image, he who
created them and brought them forth when they did not yet exist? [7]You
are made sad by seeing the lamentations of the sinners in the last days, but
let me show you the deeds by which they sinned against Elyon.

---

a. Luke 13:6-9

b. Mark 13:6

c. I have moved this part of the sentence from the previous one, where it made less sense.

d. Mark 13:28-29

e. Mark 14:21

4

1“Now look upon what they shall undergo in the last days when the Day of God comes. 2On the day of the verdict of God’s judgment, all the human race shall be collected from east to west before my Father who lives forever, and he will order hell to slide open its steely bars and to disgorge all who are held therein. 3Likewise, he shall order the beasts and the birds to yield up all the human flesh they have eaten, for he desires that all people should appear again as they were; 4for nothing perishes as far as God is concerned, nor is anything impossible for him since he is in complete control of all things. 5For all the events of the day of the verdict, the Day of Judgment, occur at the command of God, and just as everything happened in the time of creation as he spoke and it was accomplished, so shall it transpire in the last days. 6For all things are possible for God, and he says in scripture, ‘Son of man, prophesy over the scattered bones and address the bones thusly: Join bone to bone! Add sinews, nerves, flesh, skin, and hair thereto!’[f] 7And at the command of God, the great Uriel shall supply soul and spirit, for God has placed him in charge of the resurrection of the dead on the Day of Judgment. 8See and consider the grains of wheat sown in the field. One plants them in the soil as if dry and lifeless,[g] but they live again, produce fruit, and the ground returns them to us as if a loan made to it. 9And what is this thing which is sown like seed in the ground to become alive and restored to life but the human being? 10How much more likely is it that God will raise up on the day of the verdict those who believe in him, who are his chosen, for whom he made the earth to dwell on? 11And on the day of the verdict, the earth shall give all this back since it shall face judgment along with them, and the sky, too.

5

1“And these things shall come about on the day when those who have fallen from the faith of God to commit sin are judged: torrents of flame shall be unleashed. 2Shadows and darkness shall overwhelm and cover the whole earth. The oceans shall be changed and turned into magma and all therein shall burn and the seas shall become flame. 3Everywhere beneath the firmament there shall blaze fierce and unquenchable fire that advances unto the judgment of wrath. 4Even the stars shall melt from the tongues of fire, as if they had never been made, and the locked chambers of heaven shall collapse for the want of water

f. Ezek. 37:4-6

g. John 12:24; 1 Cor. 15:36

and become as if they had never been. [5]And the thunderbolts of heaven shall exhaust themselves and, by their spectacle, shall terrify the world. [6]And the spirits of the corpses shall in like manner burst into flame at God's command. [7]And when the whole of creation has dissolved, those in the east shall flee westward and those in the west to the east, [8]those in the south shall make for the north while the people of the north shall seek refuge in the south, but everywhere they shall be overtaken by the wrath of the fearful fire. [9]And an unquenchable fire shall drive them on till they come to the judgment of wrath amid the stream of inextinguishable lava which flows, blazing with flames, [10]and when its waves seethe and rise, there shall be great grinding of teeth among the children of earth.

6

[1]"Then shall all behold in what manner I shall come upon a celestial glowing cloud with the angels of God flanking me as I sit on my shining throne to the right of my heavenly Father.[h] [2]He will place a crown on my brow. And when the nations see this, they shall weep, each nation for what it has done. [3]And he shall order them away into the Phlegethon, while the deeds of each individual in each nation will stand by in bodily form, [4]due return being meted to each as his deeds deserve, accusing them, saying: "Nay, but am I not a more heinous sin? Let the greater judgment be on my account." [5]And as for the elect, those who have done good, they will take refuge with me from the death by the devouring flame. [6]But all the spawn of evil, the sinners and the hypocrites, will stand in the depth of the endless darkness, their doom being the fire, [7]and angels will lay bare their sins and make ready for each a place where they shall be punished forever, each one as his sins dictate. [8]The angel of God Uriel drives forth the souls of those sinners who drowned in the Flood and of all the spirits, the so-called gods, who inhabit all idols, who lurk in every molded image, incubi and succubi, [9]in paintings, on all hilltop shrines and sacred stones and roadside chapels, and these shall be incinerated along with their shelters in never-ending fire. [10]After all of them, with the places they haunt, have been destroyed physically, they will be punished throughout the ages.

7

[1]"Then mortal men and women shall arrive at the place prepared for them. They shall be suspended by the very tongues they once used to blas-

h. Mark 8:38

pheme the way of the righteous. [2]There will be spread out beneath them a blanket of unquenchable fire to torture them.

[3]"And now, behold another place! This one is a vast pit filled with those who have repudiated righteousness, and angels of punishment visit them to light them afire with their punishment. [4]Here are a pair of women hung up by the neck and by the hair and cast thus into the pit. These represent the ones who fashioned their hair not simply to appear beautiful but to engage in prostitution, aiming to entrap men's souls to damnation. [5]And the men who lay with them in prostitution are suspended by their thighs[i] in that burning zone, lamenting to one another, 'If only we had known we were headed for never-ending torture!'

[6]"And the murderers, with their accomplices, are pitched into the inferno, into a place of poison-spitting beasts, and they are tormented without surcease, ever feeling their pangs and their feasting maggots clustered as a heavy cloud. [7]And the angel Ezrael[j] will bring out the souls of their victims and these shall look upon the torment of their killers and shall exclaim one to the other, 'Righteous and just is the verdict of God!' [8]And the damned shall cry out, 'Indeed, we heard of it, but we never believed we would actually come to such a place of eternal judgment!'

8

[1]"And nigh unto this geyser of flame lies a great and very deep pit into which there ever flow all manner of foulnesses from all quarters, even noisome excretions. [2]And the women are sunk into it to the neck and wracked with terrible pain. They are those who had abortions and destroyed the handiwork of God. [3]Just opposite them is another place where their aborted children sit, but alive and crying unto God. And from them, levin bolts go forth and lance the eyes of the prostitutes who engineered their destruction. [4]Yet other men and women stand above these, naked. Their children stand across from them in a place of delight. [5]And these last sigh and cry out to God on account of their parents, saying: 'These are the ones who ignored and disdained and transgressed your commandment. [6]They killed us and cursed the angel who created us and hung us up to die. And they deprived us of the light you meant for all to see.' [7]And the milk of those mothers flowing from their breasts congeals and stinks and gives birth to tiny flesh-ravening creatures, [8]which turn upon them to torture them and their husbands forever because they aban-

i. A biblical euphemism for penises.

j. Spelled "Sauriel" in the Book of John the Baptizer.

doned the commandment of God and killed their children. [9]And the children shall be entrusted to the angel Temlakos.[k] And their slayers shall undergo torment forever, as God has decided.

9

[1]"Ezrael, the angel of wrath, brings men and women, each with half the body on fire, and throws them into a gulf of darkness, the hell of mankind, where a wrathful spirit punishes them with every variety of punishment. [2]The sleepless maggot gnaws their entrails. Such is the destiny of all who persecute and inform on my righteous ones!

[3]"Nigh unto those enduring such were other men and women who chew their tongues as they are vexed by red hot irons, which also brand their eyes. Such are the slanderers and those who doubt my salvation.

[4]"Others, whose crime was deception, have their lips sliced away so they can no more prevent flames from entering their mouths and into their entrails. They are the ones whose lying caused the martyrs' deaths.

[5]"Placed near these, men and women dressed in filthy tatters are thrown onto a geyser of flame that erupts atop a stone, and they must suffer unending torture. [6]They put their faith in wealth, despising the widow, the mother with orphans who is blessed in the sight of God.

[7]"Close by in a pit of dung, they throw men and women in knee-deep. Such are the usurers and the loan sharks.

[8]"Still others, driven headlong by demons, jump from a precipice only to return again and again. [9]These are the hapless idolaters whose patrons drive them to the ledge, wherefrom they plunge headlong. Forced to do this continually, they are tormented forever. [10]They include those who ritually scar the flesh, as apostles of one who is a mere man, and the women they misled. [11]And thus also do they suffer who as men degraded themselves with each other in the manner of women. [12]And underneath them the angel Ezrael stokes a great furnace of fire for all the gold and silver idols, all idols made by human hands and representing the like of cats and lions, reptiles and wild animals, as well as the people who produced the images. [13]These shall be chained with fire, chastised for their error, ever reminded by their handiwork set up before their faces. [14]This is their sentence forever. Near them burn others in the flames of judgment, tortured forever, and they are those who have abandoned the commandment of God and followed the seductions of the devils.

k. Temlakos means "the protector."

11

[1]"And another exceedingly high peak [rises up from the floor of hell], where the men and women who stumble fall, rolling down to where fear lurks. [2]And upon them the fire flows which was readied for this purpose and, fleeing, they scale the mountain again only to fall once more, rolling down. [3]This is their sentence forever, these who neglected to provide for father and mother, thinking it better to cut them off. Therefore, they are punished without end. [4]Moreover does the angel Ezrael bring boys and girls to show them the victims of this punishment to learn their lesson: [5]they will be punished with pain, being hung up for carrion birds to come and gouge many wounds. [6]These are the ones who, bold in their sins, do not obey their parents, do not heed their fathers' instruction, and pay no respect to their elders. [7]Alongside them are displayed young women dressed in shadows for vesture; theirs is a sore punishment, to have their flesh ripped to shreds. [8]They are the women who cared not to safeguard their virginity before marriage. They shall be punished with these torments as long as they can feel them.

[9]"Yet others never stop gnawing their tongues in agony on account of age-enduring fire. They are slaves who disobeyed their masters. This is their sentence forever.

12

[1]"Close by this torment are the blind and deaf dressed in white, huddled in great masses, who nonetheless fall upon coals of unquenchable fire. [2]These are the people who give alms and assure themselves, 'We are now righteous in God's sight,' when in fact they have not tried to become righteous.

[3]"The angel of God Ezrael permits them all at last to emerge from this fire and announces a judicial verdict. [4]This, then, is their sentence: a stream of fire will flow and all the damned are sucked into the middle of the stream. And it is Uriel who places them there.[1] [5]And there shall be wheels of fire with men and women trapped upon them by the speed of their whirling. [6]Those in the deepest pit are the sorcerers and sorceresses. There are innumerable such wheels set up for judgment.

13

[1]"Then the angels brought my chosen and righteous, perfect in all

1. Remember, Uriel is in charge of the resurrection. Here both he and Ezrael are raising the wicked from temporary holding cells under the earth's surface, where they have passed years and centuries in torment while awaiting the final judgment of the Last Day.

righteousness, carrying them in their hands, dressed in the robes of age-long life. [2]They shall obtain satisfaction when they see how those who hated them are made to perish. [3]Every one is to be forever tormented as befits his deeds. [4]And all the damned will cry out as in chorus, 'Show mercy to us, who now know too well God's justice, which he warned us of before though we heeded him not!' [5]And the angel Tatirokos[m] will come and make them suffer greater torture, saying to them, 'Only now do you repent, when the time for repentance has run out and no more of life remains!' [6]And everyone shall say, 'The verdict of God is righteous, for we have both heard and seen for ourselves that his rulings are fair[n] since we are only being punished as our deeds deserve.'

14

[1]"Then I will bestow upon my chosen, my righteous, the precious baptism of salvation they sought from me in the Acherusian Lake, which is situated in what they call the Elysian Field. [2]And the portion of the righteous shall be adorned with flowers, and I will go with my rejoicing chosen, with the patriarchs, into my never-ending kingdom and there show them that which I have promised them, I together with my heavenly Father. [3]I have told you, Peter, and now I am showing you. [4]Go out, then, and travel to the city in the west where you will drink the cup I told you about at the hand of the son of him who dwells in Hades, that the destruction of his work may be achieved. [5]But you are chosen to receive the hoped-for salvation I have given you. [6]Spread my news through the entire world under my protection. [7]And there shall follow rejoicing in that place where my news originated, the news of the hope of life, and then all at once the world will be carried off to judgment."

15

[1]And my Lord Jesus-Christ, our king, told me, "Let us go up into the holy mountain." And his disciples accompanied him, praying as they climbed. [2]And behold, two men were there whose faces we could not stand to look upon, for a light shone from them brighter than the sun [3]and their clothing also glistened indescribably, and nothing in the world bears fit comparison to them. [4]And yet, they appeared to be as gentle as soft down so that no words may describe the beauty of their appearance, their aspect being amazing and overwhelming. [5]And a third great being, I say, shines in his appearance more brightly than crystal. The likeness of

m. The angel of Tartaros: angel of hell.

n. Pss. 19:9

both head and body was of the redness of roses. [6]His shoulders, like their foreheads, were adorned with a wreath of nard, woven of beautiful flowers. [7]His hair was like the rainbow reflected in water. Such was the beauty of his countenance, and he was arrayed with every variety of ornament. [8]And when, of a sudden, we beheld them, we gaped in amazement.

16

[1]And I stepped closer to the Lord and asked, "Who are these?" And he told me, "Know you not Moses and Elijah?" [2]And I replied, "Whence have they now come, from where Abraham, Isaac, Jacob, and the rest of the righteous patriarchs abide?" [3]And he showed us a vast, open garden full of beautiful trees and luscious fruits, redolent of fragrant perfume. [4]Its scent was beautiful and surrounded us. And I counted many wondrous fruits. [5]Those who lived in that place were dressed with the radiant raiment of angels, appropriate to their habitation. [6]Angels mixed freely among them, all who dwelt there sharing equal glory. [7]And every voice extolled God, rejoicing to be in that place. [8]The Lord said to us, "Here is the place of those who intercede for you, the righteous." [9]And my Lord said to me, "Have you seen the companies of the patriarchs? As splendid as their rest, so too is the honor and glory awaiting those persecuted for the sake of my salvation."

[10]I rejoiced and believed and understood what was written in the book of my Lord Jesus-Christ, and I said to him, "Lord, do you want me to build three tabernacles here? One for you, one for Moses, and one for Elijah?"[o] [11]And growing angry, he answered me, "The accuser wages war against you and has blindfolded your reason! Worldly goods defeat you! [12]Your eyes must needs be opened and your ears unclogged, that you may behold a tabernacle which no human hand has built, but which my heavenly Father has built for the chosen." [13]And we did see it, rejoicing greatly.

17

1 And behold, at once a voice sounded from the sky, saying, "This is my Son, whom I love and with whom I am pleased and who keeps my commandments." [2]And a huge and pure white cloud appeared above our heads and carried away our Lord and Moses and Elijah. [3]I shuddered

o. Mark 9:5. According to Alfred Loisy, *The Birth of the Christian Religion and the Origins of the New Testament,* trans. L. P. Jacks (1948; New Hyde Park, NY: University Books, 1962), it is to this passage that 2 Peter1:16-18 refers, not to Mark's version.

with fright and we looked up to see the heavens opening. [4]And we saw fleshly men coming and greeting our Lord and Moses and Elijah, and they entered the second heaven. [5]And the passage of scripture was fulfilled which said, "This generation seeks him and seeks the face of Jacob's God."[p] [6]And great fear, as well as great amazement, swept through heaven; the angels flocked together, fulfilling the passage, "Open the gates, you chiefs!"[q] [7]After this, the opened skies were closed, and we prayed and descended the mountain, praising God, who has inscribed the names of the righteous in heaven in the Book of Life.

p. Pss. 24:6
q. Pss. 24:7-9

VII.
Heirs of Jesus

41.

An Epistle on Works Righteousness

ROBERT EISENMAN (*James the Brother of Jesus: The Key to Unlocking the Secrets of Early Christianity and the Dead Sea Scrolls*) has drawn attention to the striking parallels, thus possible linkages, between two more or less contemporary reports or legends of royal conversions. Just as Eusebius (*Ecclesiastical History,* 1:13) tells of the supposed conversion of King Abgar of Edessa to Christianity at the preaching of Jesus' disciple Thaddaeus (Addai), Josephus reports the famous conversion of Helena, queen of Adiabene, and her sons, the princes Monobazus and Izates, to a form of Jewish baptismal sectarianism (*Antiquities of the Jews*, 20.2.3). They heeded the appeal of a pair of Jewish lay missionaries, Ananias and an unnamed companion. The missionaries at first told Izates he might skip circumcision since his people might think this too great a concession to foreign ways. It should be noted that Judaizing was common enough in certain circles in those days, as witness the reported secret conversion of Nero's wife, Poppea. Eisenman observes that some ancient sources make Helena the wife of Abgarus and Adiabene either adjacent to or part of Edessa. He suggests that since Christianity and baptizing sectarian Judaism would not yet have been strictly differentiated, the reports of Eusebius and Josephus may overlap and concern the conversion of the same royal house. This causes him to take a second look at several New Testament passages, especially in Galatians and Acts. Noting that several cities named for Alexander's general and Seleucid successor Antiochus were called Antioch, and that one of these was none other than Edessa, the Antioch dispute (Gal. 2) over Judaizing might

in fact be about the conversion of Izates. After the prince was assured he could dispense with circumcision, along came Eliezer, who convinced him to go through with it after all. Might the unnamed missionary in this story be Paul, who let circumcision slide and was working in Edessan Antioch rather than the one we usually think of, Syrian Antioch? In fact, the debate with Peter/Cephas may have occurred *there*, after the interference of Eliezer, whom Eisenman identifies as one of the "men from James" (Gal. 2:12). It may have been the dispute that led the Jerusalem Council to issue its decree (Acts 15).

That dispute, Luke tells us, was settled by James the Just, whose decree was circulated throughout "Antioch" and related congregations (Acts 15:23; 29). In Luke's version, the decree stops short of requiring full Torah observance for gentile converts and requires only the handful of so-called Noachian commandments. But Eisenman, again discerning strange and remarkable parallels between yet another set of documents and traditions, posits that what we read in Acts was not the original version of the decree. It would make more sense as a later, compromising, catholicizing substitute for a letter much more likely to have been sent in the circumstances: the letter contained in the Dead Sea scroll known as "An Epistle on Works Righteousness" ("Miqsat Ma'ase haTorah": MMT). It appears to be an epistle written by the Teacher of Righteousness to a ruler wanting to observe the Torah. Eisenman very plausibly identifies the Teacher of Righteous with James the Just, the so-called brother of the Lord and bishop of the Jerusalem church. His "Christianity" would have appeared to be simply another radical sectarian form of Judaism at a time when adherence to Jesus would have been a minor point of distinction in the sectarian milieu. Eisenman thinks the epistle was sent by James to Izates, inculcating strict Torah observance among the people of Edessa/Adiabene.

Nor was the Apostolic Decree of Acts 15 the only alternate version of the letter. The Epistle of James is a Hellenized version aimed at Diaspora Jews, in which faith in Jesus is portrayed as being secondary to a commitment to the Torah. The author wants his readers to keep the whole Law, making none of the distinctions between "moral" and "ceremonial" statutes that many assimilating Jews wanted to make.

However, instead of setting forth the minutiae of proper observance, the letter turns its guns on Paul, whose Torah-free doctrine was a dangerous temptation for assimilating Jews and Jewish Christians. On Eisenman's reading, Paul was already an object of scorn among the Essenes, where he was called the "Spouter of Lies," a betrayer of the covenant from within the community, an apostate from the Torah.

Yet another version of the letter, the one farthest removed from the original, was the Letter of Jesus to Abgarus blessing the foreign king for his faith and arranging for Addai to convert and baptize Abgarus's people. Like the original, it is a letter about the conversion of a king, only the sender is no longer the Teacher of Righteousness or James the Just but rather Jesus himself! And the whole business has been simplified, since in the Abgar letter, Judaizing is no longer the concern, only conversion. Nevertheless, one stills senses the tension over correct faith, whether adherence to the Torah without circumcision or Marcionism versus Catholic orthodoxy. Other links between the Abgarus letter and the Apostolic Decree include a possible equivalence between the names of senders and bearers. Addai is Thaddaeus. Thaddaeus is Theudas, which in turn is a contraction of Judas Thomas, another brother of Jesus and James. Jesus sends Thomas to King Gundaphorus of India in the Acts of Thomas, likely yet another variation of the same original scenario. In Acts 15, a pair of bearers, "Judas and Silas," stand for Judas Thomas and James since "Salih" is Arabic for "righteous." The courier said to have carried the letters between Jesus and Abgarus is named Ananias, just like one of the missionaries in the Izates conversion story of Josephus.

1

1 Of the first month, the fourth day shall be a Sabbath. The eleventh day shall be a Sabbath. The fourteenth day shall be the Passover. The eighteenth day shall be a Sabbath. The twenty-fifth day shall be a Sabbath. Afterward, the twenty-sixth day marks the wave offering of the Omer.

2 The second day of the second month: it shall be a Sabbath. The ninth day shall be a Sabbath. The fourteenth day shall be the Second Passover. The sixteenth day shall be a Sabbath. The twenty-third day shall be a Sabbath. The thirtieth day shall be a Sabbath.

[3]Of the third month, the seventh day shall be a Sabbath. The fourteenth day shall be a Sabbath. Afterward, the fifteenth day marks the Feast of Weeks. The twenty-first day shall be a Sabbath. The twenty-eighth day shall be a Sabbath. After Sunday and Monday, an extra Tuesday shall be added.

[4]Of the fourth month, the fifth day shall be a Sabbath. The eleventh day shall be a Sabbath. The eighteenth day shall be a Sabbath. The twenty-fifth day shall be a Sabbath.

[5]The second day of the fifth month is a Sabbath. Afterward, the third day marks the Feast of New Wine. The ninth day shall be a Sabbath. The sixteenth day shall be a Sabbath. The twenty-third day shall be a Sabbath. The thirtieth day shall be a Sabbath.

[6]Of the sixth month, the seventh day shall be a Sabbath. The fourteenth day shall be a Sabbath. The twenty-first day shall be a Sabbath. The twenty-second day marks the Feast of the New Oil. Afterward, the twenty-third day marks the Offering of Wood. The twenty-eighth day shall be a Sabbath. After Sunday and Monday, a Tuesday shall be added.

[7]The first day of the seventh month marks the Day of Remembrance. The fourth day shall be a Sabbath. The tenth day marks the Day of Atonement. The eleventh day shall be a Sabbath. The fifteenth day marks the Feast of Tabernacles. The eighteenth day shall be a Sabbath. The twenty-second day marks the Feast of Gathering. The twenty-fifth day shall be a Sabbath.

[8]The second day of the eighth month shall be a Sabbath. The ninth day shall be a Sabbath. The sixteenth day shall be a Sabbath. The twenty-third day shall be a Sabbath. The thirtieth day shall be a Sabbath.

[9]Of the ninth month, the seventh day shall be a Sabbath. The fourteenth day shall be a Sabbath. The twenty-first day shall be a Sabbath. The twenty-eighth day shall be a Sabbath. After Sunday and Monday, a Tuesday shall be added.

[10]Of the tenth month, the fourth day shall be a Sabbath. The eleventh day shall be a Sabbath. The eighteenth day shall be a Sabbath. The twenty-fifth day shall be a Sabbath.

[11]The second day of the eleventh month shall be a Sabbath. The ninth day shall be a Sabbath. The sixteenth day shall be a Sabbath. The twenty-third day shall be a Sabbath. The thirteenth day shall be a Sabbath.

[12]Of the twelfth month, the seventh day shall be a Sabbath. The fourteenth day shall be a Sabbath. The twenty-first day shall be a Sabbath.

The twenty-eighth day shall be a Sabbath. After Sunday and Monday, a Tuesday is added. Thus the year finishes with three hundred and sixty-four days.

2

[1]These are some of our teachings on the Torah of God, namely, some of the deeds that we consider as achieving your justification. All of them pertain to sacred offerings and questions of purity. Now as to the offering of grain by *gentiles who* [may wish to do so], and they touch it [in the process] and make it un*clean*, [we say:] *Let no one eat* any grain of the gentiles, nor let it be brought to the temple.

[2]*As to the offering for sin*, which is boiled in pans *of copper from the gentiles*, by this means the flesh that is offered *becomes unclean*. And they boil in the temple courtyard, defiling it with their soup.

[3]As to whether gentiles may offer sacrifice, *in our view they* are really sacrificing to an *idol, and* that is *like* a woman fornicating with him.

[4]*And as to the thanksgiving* sacrifice coincident with the peace offer*ings*, which they reserve one day unto the morrow, we *consider* that the *offered grain must be con*sumed along with fat and meat on the same day they are sacrificed.[a] *The priests are strictly obliged* to see to it that this is all done in order; otherwise they are liable to implicate the people in sin.

[5]And as to the heifer that cleanses one from sin,[b] whoever butchers it, whoever burns it up, whoever collects the ashes of it, whoever sprinkles *the water of absolution*, all shall be deemed purified as soon as the sun goes down. In this way, it will be none but the clean who sprinkles upon the unclean. Let Aaron's sons provide a warning of these things [lest the people sin inadvertently].

[6]As to the hides of cows and sheep, [one may make of] their hides vessels [for mundane use], but *they may not be brought* into the temple [for sacred use]. And as to the skin *and bones of impure animals, some using the bones* and skin to make handles for ves*sels, these may not be carried into the temple precincts.*

[7]*As to the skin* off a clean animal's carcass, whoever carries it must avoid contact with sacred objects vulnerable to defilement.[c] *And as to the* [skin, meat, and dung of it], *let them see to it that* [it is burned with fire].[d]

---

a. Lev. 7:11-18

b. Num. 19:2-10

c. Lev. 11:25-29

d. Lev. 16:27

[8]*Those who serve in* the priesthood must exercise great care in all these things *so that they avoid* implicating the people in sin. Scripture[e] says, "*And he must butcher it to the side of the altar,*" *but the priests* are butchering bulls, lambs, and female goats outside the camp. We consider that the place for butchering is to the north and within the camp. We judge that the temple *corresponds to the Tent of the Testimony and* Jerusalem counts as the camp. "Outside the camp," then, denotes "outside of Jerusalem," the "camp of their cities," that is, "outside the camp" of Jerusalem.

[9]As to the offering for sin, they must remove the filth from the altar and burn *it outside of Jerusalem, since* that is the place he singled out from among all the tribes of Israel to cause his name to dwell there [for all time. Again, scripture says, "If any man of the house of Israel kills an ox or a goat or a lamb outside the camp, or inside it, and does not carry it to the Tent of Meeting to offer it as a gift before the tabernacle of Adonai, blood guilt shall be ascribed to him,"[f] and yet] they do not butcher in the temple.

[10]*As to animals about to give birth,*[g] *we judge that* the mother and the fetus *shall not be butchered* the same day. *And as to him who may eat the fetus that was inside the womb when the mother was butchered, we judge* that he may eat it *only after it has been butchered separately. That this is the requisite practice is evident* since scripture addresses the matter thusly: "An animal about to give birth..."

[11]*As for the Ammonite* and the Moabite[h] and the illegitimate and whoever has *crushed testicles and him with an injured* member who are entering the congregation [of Adonai] and marrying wives to make themselves "one bone [and one flesh], they remain defiled. We also judge that *one may not* [marry] *them, nor have sexual relations* with them. *And they mus*t never be allowed to be included and made "one bone [and one flesh with the community], and they are not to be introduced [into the congregation]. *And as you know, so*me of the people [are falling into sin by] mixing [with them]. *For the sons of Israel must shun* all forbidden marriage and so treat the temple with due veneration.

[12]*And as to* the blind,[i] whose lack of sight prevents them from being

---

e. Lev. 17:3

f. Lev. 17:3a

g. Lev. 22:27-28

h. Deut. 23:1-4

i. Lev. 21:17-23

able to avoid impure mixing, to whom sinful mixing is invisible, and as to the deaf, who do not hear the reading of either law, statute, or purity rule and do not hear the statutes of Israel, for it says, "Whoever cannot see and cannot hear knows not how to observe," such persons transgress the purity of the temple.

13 As to poured liquids,[j] we judge that they do not have inherent purity. Poured liquids cannot feasibly be distinguished according to clean and unclean containers because the liquid that is poured and that remaining in any container into which they are poured are the same upon contact.

14 It is forbidden to introduce dogs into the holy camp since they are liable to eat bones in the temple while the sacrificial meat remains on them. Because Jerusalem is the holy camp, that place he picked from all the territory of Israel, this makes Jerusalem preeminent among "the camps of Israel."

15 As to trees cultivated for food in the land of Israel, the fourth year's fruit is comparable to an offering of first fruits; thus it goes to the priests. In the same way, the tithe of cattle and of sheep goes to the priests.[k]

16 As for those afflicted with skin disease,[l] we judge that they must not approach holy objects liable to defilement. Instead, they must remain by themselves *outside the camp*. 17 It is accordingly written: "Counting from when he shaves and takes a bath, he must remain in *his tent* for seven days." 18 But these days, while yet unclean, people afflicted *with skin disease are coming* home with holy objects liable to defilement! 19 As you know, *any individual unwittingly committing a sin, who violates a commandment* and is forgiven for it, is obliged to bring an offering for sin. *As for those who willfully disobey, it is written*, "He is a scoffer and a blasphemer."[m] 20 *During the period* of their uncleanness due to skin disease, no one is to serve them holy food till sunrise on the eighth day after they are pronounced cured.

21 As to *uncleanness occasioned by contact with the dead*, we judge that each bone, whether *skeletal* or still enfleshed, falls under the regulation for the corpse or the battlefield dead.

22 As to the fornication occurring among the people, the offspring are holy, as it is written: "Israel is holy."

---

j. Lev. 11:34-38

k. Lev. 19:23-24

l. Lev. 14:2-9

m. Num. 15:30

[23]As to *clean* animals *owned by an Israelite*, it is written that it is illegal to hybridize it.[n]

[24]As to one's clothes, *it is written: "They must not* be made of mixed fabric; nor should one plant his farm or *his vineyard with mixed crops."*[o] For Israel is holy, and the sons of Aaron are the most holy of all. [25]*Despite this, as* you are aware, some priests and *people are mixing.*[p] *They* intermarry and pollute the holy seed, *as well as* their own seed, by fornication.

3

[1][Judgment will befall the people of Israel in the latter days] because they visit [the temple in an impure state. For this they will be condemned;] and as to women, [they are heedless of the laws of blood]. [2]And the rebellion [against the covenant will be avenged]. *For because of such* [outrages], *because of* violence and fornication, *some* places have already been destroyed. [3]*Besides*, it is written *in the Scroll of Moses*: "You *shall not bring the abomination into your house for* the abomination is hateful."[q] [4]*As you know*, we separated from the multitude of the people, *refusing* to mix or to follow *them* in these things. [5]You are also aware *that* no apostasy or deceit or evil *should be* found in his temple. [6]*This is why* we offer *these teachings and wro*te you previously, so you can understand the Scroll of Moses *and the oracles of the* Prophets and of David, *as well as the records of all* generations. [7]In the Torah it is written: ["I declare to you today that you shall perish so that you shall not live long in the land."[r]] [8]It also says: *"If you stray* from the way, evil will meet you."[s] [9]Again it says: "It shall happen that when all these things overtake you at the end of days, the blessing *and* the curse *that I have placed in front of you, and when you remember* them and come back to me with your whole heart and with your whole soul, [Adonai will restore your fortunes] *at the end time*, and then you will live [in peace]."[t] [10]*Yet again, it says in the Scroll* of Moses and *the oracles of the Prophets* that *blessings and curses* will overtake *you*, [namely] *the* blessings *that* came upon Is-

---

n. Lev. 19:19a

o. Lev. 19:19b-c

p. Lev. 21:7

q. Deut. 7:26

r. Deut. 30:18

s. Deut. 31:29

t. Deut. 30:1-2

rael in *his* days *and* in the days of Solomon, the son of David, and also the curses *that* overtook Israel from the days *of Jer*oboam the son of Nebat, till the exile of Jerusalem and Zedekiah, the king of Judah. [11]*For* he may send them upon [a disobedient house]. And we can see that some of the blessings and the curses have already arrived, those described in the Scroll of Moses, [12]whereby we know this is the end of days when all in Israel must come back to the Torah *of God with their whole heart* and never turn back. [13]At the same time, the wicked will only grow more wicked and [serve Belial].

[14]Remember the kings of Israel and understand their deeds. All of them who had regard for the Torah were rescued from perils. [15]As soon as they sought the Torah, then their sins *were forgiven* them. [16]Remember David. He was a doer of pious deeds, and he too was delivered from many perils and forgiven.

[17]And in conclusion, we have written you about some of the deeds of Torah which we reckoned as being for your own good and that of your citizens, for we can see that you already possess discernment and knowledge of Torah. [18]Ruminate on all this and petition him to grant you proper advice and to separate you far away from evil thoughts and from the advice of Belial. [19]Then when the end times arrive, you will rejoice to discover that at least some of the things we said were true. [20]Thus it will be considered as justifying you since you will have done what is upstanding and good before him for your own good and the good of Israel.

42.

The Epistle of James

THIS GREAT CHARTER OF PRACTICAL Christianity is sometimes called the New Testament Book of Proverbs, not a bad way to describe it. Nor is it an accident because the epistle is of a piece with the anti-Pauline polemic regarding true faith being either incarnated in deeds or insubstantial and meaningless. James repudiates the docetic version of Christian life, although his own view of righteousness is not especially Christian. Most of the document is informed by familiar motifs from the Hebrew wisdom and prophetic books, as well as by popular Stoic ideas about righteousness being either 100 per cent perfect or non-existent. James is a Torah partisan, yet little of the Jewish character of the Mosaic law is mentioned. If the point were really to press the need to keep all Torah mandates equally, we might expect some attention to dietary laws and Sabbath observance.

And yet, one cannot miss the plain attempt of the writer to carry forward the legacy of James the Just, bishop of the Jerusalem church. In this sense, James 2:10-11 is the equivalent of Matthew 5:17-19: both seek to fend off what they consider the false gospel of the apostate Paul. Matthew has gentile converts in mind, while James speaks to Diaspora Jews, identifying the same danger of being tempted to accept Paul's easier gospel which did not require adherence to the mores of an alien (to gentiles) or increasingly alien (to assimilating Jews) Jewish culture. As befits a letter to the Greek-speaking Diaspora, James was written in Greek and is seasoned in Hellenistic wisdom, not that there was any longer much of a divide between Hellenism and Judaism. Many of the so-called distinctives of rabbinic Judaism had been borrowed from Stoicism and other Greek philosophical

schools, including the idea of a circle of disciples and use of allegorical and other exegetical methods.

The author tries to say, from his perspective, what the historical James might have said; but as Jerome already saw, the author is not James. For one thing, the Greek is too good for a xenophobic zealot, as Jesus is pictured in all of our traditions. For another, the writer is acquainted not with Paulinism in general, as a contemporary might have been (Acts 21:20-21), but with the Epistle to the Romans in particular, which he has open in front of him as he writes, offering specific rejoinders to specific points made in it (2:14-26). This means he is the reader of a published epistle. Too late for James.

It seems idle to deny that James is at odds with Pauline thinking: he means to reject Paul's own terminology of "faith apart from works" because he believes the formula offers a false promise of salvation. The author of James thinks salvation and justification are based on a faith that is firmly embodied in deeds. And it is safe to say that the modern figment that Paul intended, not "faith in Christ," but rather "faithfulness like that displayed by Jesus Christ," never occurred to James, much less to Paul.

As anticipated, there is precious little about this document that marks it as specifically Christian. This is not to say it is pre-Christian, for it is not primitive. However, it attests something equally important in that it implies Qumran's Essene ("Jessean," as Epiphanius called it) Christianity arose from the milieu of Jewish baptismal sectarianism and that this branch further diverged quickly enough from Nazoreanism to have little in the way of Jesus belief to carry with it. Mentions of Jesus were largely dropped out of the tradition by the time of the split between Jesus loyalists and partisans of his caliph, James the Just. And though the Epistle of James comes from after the early split, it comes from the same stream which continued to flow for some time along its own channel.

Many argue that, despite initial appearances, James is one of the most Jesus-flavored of the New Testament documents, for do not its memorable maxims everywhere remind one of similar sentiments in the Sermon on the Mount? Indeed they do, but as George A. Wells has suggested, the borrowing is more likely in the other direction: the

gospels are later products and their authors pillaged early Christian epistles for nuggets that would sound good in the mouth of Jesus.

Finally, as to the early reception of the Epistle of James, Origen quotes it as scripture written by James. Jerome detected that some unknown person had penned it under James's name, but he still cited it as scripture. It is absent from the Muratorian, the African, and the Syriac Canons. Eusebius ranks it as "disputed," admitting some early Christians branded it as "spurious." Martin Luther saw quite clearly the contradiction between this epistle and those of Paul and relegated it to an appendix to the canon, denigrating it as "an epistle made of straw" (cf. 1 Cor. 3:12-13).

1

1 James, slave of God and the Lord, Jesus-Christ, to the twelve tribes in the Diaspora, Greetings!

2 Consider it pure joy, my brothers, whenever you find yourselves amid various testings, 3 mindful that the probing of your faith effects endurance. 4 And let endurance come to full flower in order for you to become perfect and complete, in no respect inadequate. 5 But if any one of you should fall short in wisdom, he need only petition God, the one who gives to everyone unstintingly and without challenge, and it will be given him. 6 Only let him be sure to ask in faith, without ambivalence; for the doubter wavers like the tossing of the sea, driven and tossed by the wind. 7 Such a one need not imagine he is likely to receive anything at all from the Lord, 8 for he is of two minds, habitually indecisive.

9 May the humble brother brag on his exaltation! 10 May the rich acknowledge with equanimity his eventual humiliation since he must disappear like a wildflower. 11 For the sun rises with the hot wind and parches the desert grass, and its flower droops and the beauty of its appearance perishes: in just this way the rich man will one day perish while engaged in his business trips.[a] 12 Blessed is the one who endures testing because, having earned approval, he will receive the award of life after death, which God promised to those who love him. 13 May no one who is tested say, "I am being tempted by God!" For God neither is amenable to temptation by evil, nor does he tempt anyone else. 14 Each one is tempted by his own desires being coaxed forth, seducing him. 15 Then desire, hav-

a. Isa. 40:6-8

ing been impregnated, gives birth to sin, and sin, when grown to maturity, brings forth a child named death. [16]Do not imagine otherwise, my beloved brothers!

[17]Every good donation and every perfect gift is from above, descending from the Father of the stars, of whom one can predicate no change or shifting shadow. [18]Having made up his mind, he caused us to be born by speaking a true message so we might become, so to speak, the first of his creations to come ripe.

[19]Know this, my beloved brothers: let each one be eager to listen, slow to speak or to get angry, [20]for our anger does not perform the righteousness God requires. [21]This is why you must repudiate everything sordid, all abundant wickedness, in favor of gentleness and accept instead the implantation of the truth that has the power to save your souls. [22]And become those who implement that truth—not merely those who hear it, which is to deceive yourselves. [23]You see, if anyone merely hears the truth preached and fails to do anything about it, such a one is like a man who looks in the mirror at the face he was born with. [24]Imagine this: he took care to examine himself, then walked away and promptly forgot what he looks like! [25]But the one who has lingered long gazing into the flawless mirror of the law of liberty, not becoming a forgetful hearer, but rather one who performs the deeds required of him there, this one will have the blessing on what he does.[b]

[26]If anyone considers himself religious but makes no effort to keep his mouth under control and rationalizes what he says, this fellow's religion is a sham. [27]Religion that the God and Father deems pure and untainted is simply this: to see to the needs of destitute widows and orphans and to keep oneself unspattered from the world.[c]

2

[1]My brothers, do not think you can embrace the religion of the Lord whom we adore, Jesus-Christ, while showing partiality. [2]Suppose a gold-fingered man in splendid clothing should enter your synagogue and a beggar in reeking tatters enters, too, [3]and you pay attention to the man in the fine clothing, saying, "Have a choice seat right here," while you say to the beggar, "Are you still here? Uh, stand over there, out of sight," or "Sit below my footstool." [4]Wouldn't you be playing favorites among yourselves? Wouldn't you be like judges who take bribes? [5]Listen, my be-

b. Pss. 1:1-3

c. Mic. 6:8

loved brothers. Didn't God choose the poor[d] in this world to be rich in faith and heirs to the kingdom he promised to those who love him? 6But here you have disgraced the poor man. Isn't it the rich who oppress you and drag you into court for nonpayment of debts? 7Aren't they the ones who blaspheme the noble name invoked over you? 8If indeed you carry out a royal decree as scripture says, "You shall love your neighbor as yourself,"[e] you are doing fine. 9But if you show partiality, you are working at sin and you are denounced as transgressors by the Torah.

10For whoever manages to keep the whole Torah but trips up in one commandment has become guilty of breaking all of them. 11For the same one who said, "You shall not commit adultery," also said, "You shall not commit murder." So if you manage to abstain from adultery but do commit murder, you have still become a transgressor of the Torah.[f] 12Therefore speak and behave mindful of the fact that you are soon to be judged on the basis of a law of freedom. 13For the one who never showed mercy will find himself judged without mercy; in such a case, mercy rejoices at the verdict.[g]

14For what reward can be expected, my brothers, when someone claims to have faith but has no deeds to show for it? Can his faith save him? 15If a brother or a sister is found naked and not knowing where the next meal is coming from 16and one of you should say to him, "Good luck to you, finding clothes and food," but you don't actually give them the material necessities, where is your reward?[h] 17So indeed, faith, unless it has deeds, is dead by itself. 18*But someone might object, saying,*[i] You have faith and I have deeds. Show me your faith that has no deeds. I will show you my faith by means of my deeds. 19So you believe that there is one God, do you? Fine! The demons believe it, too—and shudder! 20Are you willing to be shown, O empty-head, that "faith apart from deeds" is sterile? 21Wasn't Abraham, our father, vindicated by means of deeds

d. This was the self-designation of the Jerusalem Christians under the leadership of James the Just.

e. Lev. 19:18

f. 1 John 3:4

g. Prov. 1:20-27

h. 1 John 3:17-18

i. The interposing of a heckler's presumed objections is a Stoic rhetorical device, added here erroneously unless our author has lost track of his own argument or, in trying to imitate Paul while simultaneously refuting him, he does not quite understand the function of the device.

when he offered up his son Isaac on the altar? [22]You can see for yourself the synergy between his faith and his deeds, that his faith was brought to perfection by his deeds [23]and the passage of scripture was fulfilled, namely, "Abraham believed God and it was reckoned to him for merit, and he was henceforth called a friend of God."[j] [24]So you see an individual is saved by deeds, not by faith alone.[k] [25]And in the same way, wasn't Rahab, the prostitute, delivered by token of her deeds, harboring the agents and smuggling them out? [26]For just as the body without a spirit is dead, so too is faith moribund without deeds.

3

[1]My brothers, few of you ought to aspire to become teachers; remember: we shall receive the more severe judgment. [2]For we all trip up in many ways; if anyone does not trip up in what he says, here you have a perfect man, able in fact to keep his whole life under control. [3]Now we put bits into the mouths of horses to make them obey us and so we direct their whole bodies. [4]Think of ships, so massive in size and driven along by mighty winds, but a small rudder directs them wherever the pilot's whim decides they should go. [5]So, too, the tongue is a little member and brags of great feats. Think of how little a flame it takes to kindle a huge forest fire! [6]Well, the tongue, too, is a fire, the very microcosm of iniquity. The tongue has been placed among our members to pollute our whole body and to set ablaze the whole wheel of birth.[l] In turn, it is set ablaze by hell. [7]For every species, both of beasts and birds, reptiles and sea-creatures, is now domesticated or has in the past been domesticated by the human species, [8]and yet no one has been able to domesticate the human tongue. It is a wild evil, full of deadly venom. [9]With it we eulogize our God and Father, and with it we curse human beings made in the image of God. [10]From the same mouth emerge blessing and cursing! It is not fitting, my brothers, for things to be so. [11]No fountain sends forth from the same opening both sweet and acrid water, surely? [12]Nor, my brothers, can a fig tree produce olives or a grapevine figs.[m] Nor can salt water yield sweet.

---

j. How was it "fulfilled," as if a prophecy? The quoted passage occurs earlier in the Abraham story when Isaac's birth is predicted (Gen. 15:6). He exercised faith at that time, but it was brought to perfection only later when he was called on to sacrifice the very child of promise (Gen. 22:1-19). The logic is much the same as in Heb. 11:17-19.

k. Verses 14-26 are a point-by-point rejoinder to Rom. 3:27-4:6ff, which our author has open in front of him.

l. This is an astonishing piece of apparent Buddhism!

m. This has become a saying of Jesus in Matt. 7:16-18; Luke 6:43-44.

[13]Who among you is wise and understanding? Let him demonstrate his good behavior through his deeds of wise gentility. [14]But if you harbor bitter jealousy and rivalry in your heart, do not brag about your supposed wisdom and falsify the truth! [15]Such "wisdom" is not that which rains down from above, but is rather worldly, cunning, demonic; [16]for wherever jealousy and rivalry thrive, there will be unrest and every base practice. [17]But the wisdom from above is first of all pure, then irenic, patient, easily prevailed upon, full of mercy and good manifestations, without indecisiveness and not hypocritical. [18]And those who make peace are sowing the seeds for a harvest of salvation.[n]

4

[1]Where do wars and battles among you come from? Are they not the result of your pleasures struggling against one another in your various bodily members? [2]You desire and are frustrated, you murder out of jealousy, and still you are unable to find satisfaction—so you fight and you battle. But the reason you are frustrated is your failure to ask. [3]Or perhaps you do ask but you receive nothing because you ask wrongly, merely wanting to spend money on your pleasures. [4]Adulteresses! Don't you realize that friendship with this world is enmity with God? Thus whoever decides to be friends with the world becomes *ipso facto* the enemy of God.[o] [5]Or perhaps you think scripture is joking when it says, "The spirit which came to dwell inside you ever tends toward envy"?[p] [6]But God provides even more spiritual help,[q] which is why it says, "God takes a stand against the arrogant but shows favor to the humble."[r] [7]Therefore submit to God and determine to resist the accuser, who will run away in fear. [8]Approach God and he will meet you halfway. Purify your hands, sinners, and cleanse your hearts, vacillators. [9]Panic, mourn,

---

n. There is some possible Gnostic coloring, both here and in v. 6, with apparent references to rebirth. Verses 13-16 might be understood as a contrast between the fallen Achamoth and the unfallen Sophia, both versions of so-called Dame Wisdom. And v. 6 suggests that since humans have tongues—a dangerous sin machine—who would have created them so but the Demiurge, misbegotten son of fallen Wisdom?

o. 1 John 2:15b

p. Gen. 6:3, 5?

q. This sounds like the rabbinical doctrine about evil and good imaginations, both having been planted by God in the human heart. The former, despite the tendency to sin, is necessary to supply lust for procreation and cruelty to punish criminals and fight enemies, and so on.

r. Prov. 3:34

weep! Let your laughter turn to mourning, your joy to depression. [10]Humble yourselves before Adonai and he will lift you up. [11]Do not talk behind one another's backs, brothers. Whoever slanders another or assumes the worst of his brother speaks in violation of the Torah and thinks himself superior to it; and if you have placed yourself above the Torah, you are no keeper of the Torah, but its critic. [12]There is but one legislator and judge, the one capable of both delivering and destroying. So who are you to judge your neighbor?[s]

[13]Come now, you who boast that "today or tomorrow we will take a trip to some city and we will trade there a year and make a profit." [14]You do not even know what will become of your life tomorrow. For you are a morning mist, visible for a short time, then as suddenly vanishing.[t] [15]This is how you ought to hedge your speech: "If the Lord wishes it so, we shall have another day to do this or that." [16]As it is, you wallow in your blusterings. All such bragging is evil. [17]Therefore, the one who knows the good thing and chooses not to do it, it is chalked up as sin for him.

5

[1]Come now, you rich! Weep and sob for the terrible fate about to overtake you. [2]You will awake to discover your riches have tarnished and your wardrobe is full of moth holes, [3]your gold and silver have rusted through[u] and their corruption will witness against you and will consume your flesh like fire![v] You made the mistake of amassing treasure in the Last Days. [4]Just listen! The tell-tale cry of the wages due the laborers who harvested your acreage but were cheated[w] and the cries of the laborers have reached the ears of the Lord of the harvest.[x] [5]On earth you lived as both connoisseur and orgiast, but all you did was to fatten up your hearts for the day of slaughter. [6]You condemned and murdered the Just One, who put up no resistance.[y]

[7]Be long-suffering, brothers, till the arrival of the Lord. Look, the

---

s. This has become a saying of Jesus in Matt. 7:1-2; Luke 6:37.

t. Luke 12:16-21

u. Matt. 6:19

v. 1 Cor. 3:12-15

w. Jer. 22:13-17

x. Exod. 3:7

y. This is an only slightly veiled reference to the martyrdom of James the Just, the ostensible writer of this epistle. His enemies of the high priesthood were scorned by the Qumran pietists as voluptuaries and apostates. The martyrdom is similarly disguised in Acts 7:52ff. in the story of fictional Stephen.

farmer anticipates the precious harvest of the earth, marking time over it as it soaks up first the early, then the latter rains. [8]You, like him, should be long-suffering and fortify your hearts since the arrival of the Lord has drawn near.[z] [9]Do not grumble against one another so you may avoid being judged. Just look! The judge is standing at the doors.[a] [10]Brothers, take the prophets who spoke in the name of Adonai as examples of enduring adversity and of long-suffering. [11]For we beatify those who endure. You are acquainted with Job's endurance and you saw the plan Adonai revealed in the end, that the Lord is very compassionate and merciful.

[12]But above everything else, my brothers, swear no oaths, whether by the heaven or by the earth or any other oath. No, just let your "yes" mean "yes" and your "no" mean "no" so you will avoid incurring judgment.[b]

[13]Is there anyone sick among you? Let him pray. Is anyone happy? Let him sing one of the psalms. [14]Is anyone among you enervated? Let him call the elders of the congregation to his bedside and let them pray for him once they have anointed him with oil in the name of the Lord. [15]And if they pray with faith, the sick will recover and the Lord will raise him up, and if some sin was at the root of the illness, it will be forgiven. [16]Therefore, confess your sins to one another and pray for forgiveness for one another so you may be cured. The supplication of a *zaddik*,[c] once set in motion, is very strong. [17]Elijah was a mortal, cut from the same cloth as us, and in prayer he asked that it might not rain and it did not rain on the earth for three years and six months. [18]Again he prayed and the sky gave rain and the earth produced its fruit.

[19]My brothers, if anyone of your number strays from the truth and someone steers him back in the right path, remember that whoever guides a sinner out of his false path will rescue his soul from death and will veil from sight a great number of sins.[d]

---

z. This has become a parable of Jesus in Mark 4:26-29.

a. This has become a saying of Jesus in Mark 13:29; Matt. 24:33; Rev. 3:20.

b. This has become a saying of Jesus in Matt. 5:34-37.

c. A special type of holy man whose extraordinary piety wins him the ear of God.

d. Gal. 6:1; Jude 23

43.

The Letter of Jesus to Abgarus

EUSEBIUS, THE CHURCH HISTORIAN and apologist for Constantinian orthodoxy, preserved for us what, if genuine, would be the matchless treasure of a document written by Jesus. He said (*Ecclesiastical History,* 1:13) he was shown the letter by the bishops of the church in Edessa, who cherished it as a pedigree of their orthodoxy and apostolic foundation: in it Jesus had declined an invitation to take up residence at Edessa but had promised to send a disciple to heal the king's malady and preach the gospel. When he did, he sent Thaddaeus (Addai). Ostensibly, Jesus had written in response to a letter from the king, a copy of which was also extant:

> Abgarus the Black, Toparch, to Jesus, the good Savior, who has appeared in the environs of Jerusalem, Greeting!
>
> I have heard about you and your cures, that you perform them without aid of drugs or herbs, for it is reported you make the blind to see again, the lame to walk, that you purify lepers and drive out unclean spirits and devils and that you heal those long afflicted with chronic illness and raise the dead. And once I heard all this about you, I had arrived at two possible conclusions: either you are God descended from heaven and this is how you are able to perform these feats or you are a son of God to be able to do these things. This is why I have now written to plead with you to take the trouble to visit me and heal my own affliction. In fact, I have heard that the Jews even whisper about you and wish to harm you. I have a very small city but it is attractive and large enough for both of us.

To have Jesus himself communicate with the king and arrange for the founding of a church was better even than having an apostle found the church on his own initiative. The possession of a letter from Jesus was equivalent to the legend of Joseph of Arimathea bringing the Grail to Britain: a claim of a direct, dominical foundation of the church. In fact, it sounds rather too good to be true, and is. As Walter Bauer *(Orthodoxy and Heresy in Earliest Christianity)* showed, the Abgar-Jesus correspondence is no more genuine than the Donation of Constantine or the letters between Paul and Seneca. The letters are pseudepigraphical substitutes for the inconvenient fact that the church in Edessa had actually been founded by Marcion and Bardesanes. That is, their varieties of Christian faith, deemed heretical by Eusebius and his contemporaries, had to be supplanted by the aid of a false claim for orthodoxy that pre-dated heresy. And a good letter from Jesus was just the thing to do the trick! It may even have been Eusebius's idea: perhaps he wrote the two letters.

The legend would continue to grow, with cross-fertilization from the legend of Veronica's Veil, so Jesus would be said to have sent King Abgar a miraculous image of the Savior's face imprinted on cloth. The Holy Image of Edessa was a long-lived relic that recent apologists for the authenticity of the Turin Shroud have implausibly sought to identify with that similarly fraudulent relic.

Blessed are you, having believed in me without seeing me! For it is written about me that the ones who have seen me shall not believe in me, while those who have not seen me shall believe and live. But concerning the matter on which you wrote me, to visit you: it is necessary for me to complete all the things I was sent here to do and, once I have completed them, to be taken up to him who sent me. But once I am taken up, I will dispatch one of my disciples to you to cure what ails you and to give Life to you and those who surround you.

44.

The Hymns of the Just

THESE HYMNS WERE DISCOVERED among the Dead Sea Scrolls. In form and subject matter, they have much in common with the Old Testament Psalms, corresponding rather neatly to the "psalm of thanksgiving," a form of song that was written to accompany a thank-offering made in gratitude for God's providential deliverance from some dismal predicament. Such a psalm typically rehearsed the peril of the singer and God's last-minute vindication or deliverance. Jewish spirituality, especially when cut off from the temple (whether by its destruction or by the excommunication of the psalmists, as here), began to view this kind of soulful singing as itself sufficient to glorify God. The Qumran sect appears either to have been excommunicated from Jerusalem temple worship or to have boycotted it for its unorthodoxy compared to the meticulous purity stipulations of this most strict of all Jewish sects. These hymns, therefore, even though they were corporate or cultic in nature and sung in the congregation, would not have found place in the temple even while it stood.

Many first-person psalms of lament and thanksgiving in the Old Testament were written for the king of Judah to sing or for Levitical choirs to sing on his behalf. They denote conditions of national emergency, the eve of battle, imminent defeat, crop failure, famine, and other disasters. The plight of the first-person lyricist of the Hymns of the Just presupposes sectarian rivalry and strife. He envisions pious Jews who, in the hymnist's judgment, have compromised the true meaning of the Torah to satisfy wealthy and lazy patrons. Terrible hatred had erupted between the factions, perhaps leading even to physical persecutions. The fears and boasts of the community that

sang these hymns focused on the figurehead of the Teacher of Righteousness, portrayed in the songs as speaking in the first person. The conflicts described in the lyrics are like those in the Old Testament psalms, often vague in detail but no doubt reflecting real conflicts, in this case between the Teacher of Righteousness and his rivals, the temple priests. This does not mean the Teacher of Righteousness is necessarily the author because the hymns may have been composed after his death, in his name, to cherish his memory.

On the other hand, it is not impossible to imagine the Teacher of Righteousness himself as the author of the hymns, which only raises anew the old question of his identity. Robert Eisenman argues that he was none other than James the Just—which is why I have placed the hymns in this section. If so, the conflict rehearsed here would have been between James the Just and Ananus, the archpriest, and between James and Paul. An equally intriguing possibility suggested by Robert Eisler and, more recently, Barbara Thiering posits that the Teacher of Righteousness was in fact John the Baptist and the community referred to was that of the baptized we see flocking to him in the gospels. In this scenario, the conflict would have been between John and Jesus, the latter having broken with John's apocalyptic asceticism to celebrate the coming of the kingdom of God among sinners. It is thrilling to think we may be reading here the inner thoughts of either of these great figures. The picture may be still more complicated if we take into account the possibility that the Dead Sea Scrolls may have emerged at various points along the time-line of the Jordan River fringe of baptizing sectarianism from which Jesus, John, James, Simon, and Dositheus all emerged. This means the Teacher of Righteousness may have been the title of several sect leaders in succession. This makes it all the more difficult to pinpoint a single author.

My version of the hymns paraphrases the English translation of Wilfred Watson.[a] It is necessarily loose because I feel it best to try to convey a sense of the poetry of the original, rendering it in iambic tetrameter and pentameter. Again, my goal is not merely to provide an autopsy of extinct religious fossils, as important as that admittedly is,

---

a. Florentino García Martínez, ed., *The Dead Sea Scrolls Translated: The Qumran Texts in English,* trans. Wilfred G. E. Watson (Leiden: E. J. Brill, 1994).

but to offer something reminiscent of the original embodiments of vital religious devotion. To the same end, I have skipped excessively fragmentary material.

1

1 I thank you, Lord, with all my soul
for secrets you vouchsafed to me
beyond the reach of common men,
well past the judgment of the mob
2 who cultivate but wickedness
and only make themselves more ripe
for Judgment Day when it may strike.
4 Your servant you have purified
from sins and failures manifold.
Compassion falls down from your skies
as in a cleansing avalanche.
5 It is as Moses once did say:
you pardon rebels, sinners, fools,
atoning for disloyalties.
6 For though you are a raging fire
that sets volcanoes to explode,
who fires the pits of Moloch's realm,
7 you show great tenderness to those
who shun their sins and seek your face.
8 Each one who loves your cause may know
your mighty hand protecting him.
His whole life span and progeny
you will not leave without defense.
9 Their names shall be remembered long,
as long as seas and sun endure.
For you yourself remember them,
except their sins which slip your mind.
10 You make them pure as Adam was
the day you formed him from the earth,
and they shall form his legacy
long decades from their father's birth.

2

1 I thank you fulsomely, O Lord,
for living spirits you assigned

2to fill my soul, renew my mind,
supply the word of knowledge choice,
and give immortal wisdom voice.
3The deeds of glory you have wrought
I sing to teach those hearing me.
4No less do I confess my sins
and grovel in humility.
5For I am heir, just like the rest,
of doom that one day catches up.
6I once walked in impurity,
abandoning the roots of truth,
foundations deep and solid, too.
7Of truth, I was no friend at all,
allied with Beliar, his son.
8But justice ever is your throne,
and from it you reached down to me,
9preserving me when all I earned
was your decree of judgment grim.
10But I have come to understand
how you make straight the path of him
11who bears your name by your command
and turn him round to heed your call.
12You keep his foot from damning sin
by clever providential means.
13Your punishments are chidings that
he learns to welcome as he grows.

14Thus this is my request to you:
prevent my straying feet to fall.
15Your servant keep from trespassing
your glorious commandment fair.
16Take pen in hand and write them down
in bloody furrows 'cross my heart,
17and then I will be strong to fight
each tempting demon's whisperings.
18I want a boon no less than this:
that perfectly I'll walk your path,
19loathe everything that you do hate,
and always live as pleases you.
20Plant now your word within my flesh,

I'm no pure spirit such as you.

21 I render thanks, my Lord and God,
for you have heard my meek request
22 and poured your spirit over me
to fill this heart, transform this will.
23 Henceforth, I count all documents
of man as merest noise and cant.
24 Your law alone commands my oath,
and those who swear their loyalty
will have your love for endless years.

3

1 Sing now with me a grateful song
to celebrate the Teacher wise,
whom God has sent to bring us light
and make the simple understand,
2 he who partakes in God's vast fund
of knowledge rare and wisdom choice
and stores it in an earthen jar,
the human breast of him whom God
made known, his servant from the first.
3 The council of the spirits blessed
the choice God made among mankind.
Through this one's teaching, he set forth
forgiveness wide and strength of pow'r
residing in abundant grace.
4 His wrath is slow to act but waits
in hope the sinner will repent.
But when unsheathed, his zeal is great
and there is no retreat therefrom.
5 All those with cultivated sense
will know the mysteries you share,
the providence that slowly rolls
like rivers to the distant sea.
6 Before the first command you gave,
your holiness illumined all
the centuries that were to come.
7 You knew them ere they knew themselves
or that your will they must needs serve.
Among the angels you are praised,

by fiery tongues your hymn is raised.

8Your mysteries lie all unveiled
before my dazzled, gazing eye!
I say it for your glory, Lord.
9The depth of oceanic dark
can never plumb profundity
like that which you have shown to me.
10No secret, now, the splitting paths
of righteousness, iniquity,
nor is their destination hid:
11the walkers on the way divine
may for a time regret their choice
for which they pass through thorns and mire.
12But sinners fare far worse than them:
they slide all heedless into fire!

13These men, this sect, are your own work:
you told your plan to angels strong,
the sons of God in Zaphon's throng
beneath the purple firmament,
14and those who find their home within
the earth, her crops, and beasts bovine.
Your word did echo through the deep:
15"Here is the human race in one;
you do well to rejoice in him,
for sure it is I mean to place
him at the helm of this new world!"
16A thing like this they never saw
and would not have it so, so they
rebelled against their sovran Lord,
17but victory was his! His might
descended with great force upon
the fleeing serpent who had dared
gainsay the will of Adonai.
18And thus he wiped away a world
as old as he except a day
and did make all things new, a world
for man. And it will last until
you give the word to uncreate.
19And so it stands: a mystery

now told and for his glory said.
What mind do you suppose could guess
it happened thus so long ago?
[20]Among the things that you have made,
a human mind is but a cup
too small for it to bear such truth.
[21]He is a pit of noisome filth,
impure, unworthy in your sight,
degenerate, perverse, unclean.

[22]Whatever evil he may do,
his acts are interchangeable;
it shall forever stand to mark
his infamy for years to come,
for generations of his sons.
[23]It is by no means but your grace
by which man is reclaimed from sin,
acquitted by your righteousness,
baptized in your compassion's flood.
[24]Your greatness rehabilitates
this sinful, misbegotten son.
[25]You take him from his ruined place
and give him paradise to rule,
with long-lived health, no end of days.
[26]As you are very truth itself,
you cannot now rescind your word.

[27]And I above all men do know,
thanks to the Spirit you imbued
me with, how all your deeds are pure
and just, without a second thought.
[28]You have ordained that day when souls
shall see what they have done in life
and then rejoice in recompense
unless they turn up reprobate
and face a future filled with hate.

4

[1]I give you thanks, O Adonai,
for placing wisdom in my heart,
your servant whom you chose to know

these secrets and to understand
your providential master plan.
2By this I'm strengthened in the face
of those who breathe their threats at me.
In justice I may bless your sons
who rally to your covenant.
3I teach them, every one, to love
those whom you love and imitate
the stubborn fury of your hate.
4You've taught your servant well the kinds
of men there are and spirits who
impel their acts to good or ill.
5But I, no stranger to your truth,
am well aware what kindly deed
you did for man, imparting to
him of your Spirit, strengthening
his feeble acts of righteousness.
6By this means nearer am I brought
to your intelligence sublime.
The nearer that I come to it,
the stronger blazes out my hate
to those who sin against your will.
7For anyone who draws near you
will feel no more desire for sin,
nor shall he dare to change your words,
which only sinners try to do.
8For you yourself are always just
and all your chosen ones you trust;
in them you have corrected sin.
9They stand as testimonials
to sanctifying grace and love.

10But unto me, above all men,
the secret things of God are known!
Your treasury of truth I sought
and plundered amply all therein.
11I issued to my soul commands
to shun all things that you forbade.
12And in this way, I recommend
to each man of the covenant

to make his progress manifest
among his fellow penitents.
13 If one shows promise, him I raise
and high regard him, give him praise.
I favor no one otherwise
and least of all consider gifts.
14 Far be it from me to take bribes
or favor such a one in court
or bend the Law to his desire
who thinks to make it worth my while.
15 Not so! I love but those you bless
with righteous acts and holiness.
The stranger to your way of light
will I evict from out my sight.

5

1 I give you thanks, O Lord of life,
as your great world-supporting pow'r
deserves, though my mute stammerings
can scarcely say the tenth of it.
2 From one end of eternity
to that far shore, infinity,
you span them both, yet do not move,
encompassing the heavens, vast!

3 You welcome him who turns about,
abandoning a sinful past.
Forgiveness flows where once wrath grew.
4 The wicked nonetheless must fear,
for your great anger follows them
the length of their depravity.
5 The truth you love with wide-thrown heart,
depravity you can't abide.

6 And as for me, your servant true,
you blessed me more than could be known
to fill my spirit with your own.
7 You made me love the truth, the right,
and to despise what flees your sight.
My heart's aflame with love for you,
my thirst for wisdom will not wait.

8For I would understand your deeds
since all that happens is your work.

6

1Of all men, I alone have known,
thanks to your perfect intellect,
that no one's path is straightened out
by fleshly effort gravely vowed.
2No human can be sure he walks
upon the track that you lay out.
3I know you fashioned ev'ry soul
and scheduled every day's ordeal
before you sent him to the womb.
4Decrees of yours no one can change.
You made the man of righteousness
the man he is, and not himself.
5Since first he saw the light of day,
you chose him for the upright walk,
gave him your Spirit to make sure
6he would embrace the destiny
you picked for him, your covenant,
to which he pledges solemn vows.
7Your hand it is that opens up
a tight-locked heart and makes it see
the vision of eternity.
8There everlasting peace shall reign.
Among the flesh, you blessed his brain.

9The wicked, though, were made for doom.
Straight from the womb, their fate was sealed!
They take the path to ruin's end,
they deem your covenant a bore.
10When told your laws, they sin the more;
all that you love, they fiercely hate.
Recoiling from your words with fear,
they also do your will, O God,
11for so you made them at the start
to make them targets of your wrath
so all the earth might see and mark
the fate of those who spurn your Law.
12For generations yet unborn,

they stand forever to exhort;
in this way will the future know
your power, glory, majesty!

13But how can flesh begin to grasp
such puzzles of your wisdom's depths?
How shall mere dust and grimy clay
discern the way ordained for it?
14The human spirit you designed
and plotted out its many steps;
you trace the course of each life form.

15But as for me, the truth is plain:
no fortune can compare with this
unearthly truth and holiness,
and I have chosen this instead.
16I know you chose my followers
and they will never stray from you.
Mere mortal man cannot expect
to buy his way to mercy's halls.
17For you, the God of simple truth,
whose wont it is to nullify
all sinners with their filthy deeds
till none pollutes your courts above;
18I realize the verdict comes
from you, the judgment yours alone,
and you will vindicate your name
and holiness through judgment swift
when that day dawns for all to see!

7

1I praise you, Lord, for keeping me
safe in the womb and afterward
when vicious fiends pursue my life.
2They ambush me and lay their traps
because I love your covenant.
3A council full of futile fools,
a parliament of demon dupes,
they cannot guess that I endure
4by your supernal energy,
that your compassion saves my life.

5Who else but you could guide my steps?
They seek my life because of you
6but don't imagine their true role
as lightning rods to draw your wrath
and glorify you by their doom.
7My own success will magnify
your glory in the sight of men
8who understand that I prevail
by drawing on your grace alone.
9Yes, once I said, "Their mighty men
have pressed me hard, surrounded me.
They bristle full of weaponry.
10Their arrow hails go on and on,
their lances, spears, like falling rain!
As waves surge forth to crash against
the shore, so are their cries of war.
11Their threats are like a hurricane
that whips the stars about like leaves."
12And yet, in fact, they're only wind,
for all the shivering I did!
13But you upheld me, gave me strength,
confirming me in covenant.
14They spread a hunting net for me,
but you saw to it, they fell in,
15my progress goes on straight ahead.
So in the congregation, I
shall praise your name forevermore.

8

1My praise ascends to you, my Lord,
I'm grateful for your watchful eye
that warned me of the treachery
of those who would corrupt your Law
by catering to backsliders
and lightening your Torah's yoke.
2They circled me like hungry dogs,
a poor man with no means to fight,
to lick the precious blood of one
whom you have made your servant true.
3But little did those sinners guess
you steered my steps in my distress.

They make their mockery of me
as laughingstock for those who wish
to undermine your truth with tricks.

4 But as for you, my God, you saved
this poor, defenseless vagabond
from forces far superior
to any I appeared to wield.
5 My life you snatched from cruel hands
and cheered me up when I allowed
their jests and jibes to sadden me.
6 You steeled my soul with faithfulness
so never did I think to flee.
7 No fear of foemen frightens me,
nor makes me question my resolve,
else I betray posterity,
abandoning your heritage.

9

1 I sat in darkness grim and deep
until you broke like morning light
and shone upon my weary face
your splendor brighter than the sun.
2 Your words of truth, they summoned me,
commanding me to stand against
betrayers of your holy Law.
3 But now, my soul, my enemies
have deemed me like a man adrift,
a sinking boat, a city sieged.
4 I felt the way a woman feels
when labor pangs oppress her sore.
5 It seems to her that beck'ning death
will claim her life in trade for that
she seeks to bear, and so she sinks
6 to Sheol's depth—then rises up
to heights of joy. She bears a son
who may grow up a king or sage!
7 Just like her ancient mother Eve,
with child by lustful serpent's seed,
8 who writhed in agonies supplied
by God's condemning verdict dire,

she trembles with the pain of it.
[9]When tempests rise, foundations shake,
the walls collapse and crush the men
inside them, while the ship at sea
veers crazily this way and that
and threatens to capsize and sink.
[10]These are my foes, confused with fear,
aghast at swelling waves and crests.
[11]And when the winds are wild enough,
the deep gates of the netherworld,
of Sheol and of Abaddon,
[12]creak open to receive their souls,
this brood of vipers going home.
[13]The heavy portals slam again
upon the progeny of Eve.
[14]Once bolted, they will never budge,
the serpent's spawn forever trapped.

10

[1]Receive my song of thanks, O Lord,
for rescuing me from the pit;
from Sheol and from Abaddon,
[2]you took me out and placed me on
a mountain top, bestowed on me
the freedom of an endless plain.
[3]Now I can entertain the hope
that even such a clod as I
may join your holy covenant,
[4]a sinful spirit purified
from long years' sin, to take a seat
amid the council of the saints,
the congregation of the just.
[5]You pre-arrange the destiny
of those you choose to worship you,
in company with angel choirs
who of their knowledge sing for you.
[6]Like them, I manifest your deeds
before the list'ning sons of men.
Behold a clay homunculus,
an earthenware, ceramic saint!
[7]How far removed am I from those

you destined for the pit of hell?
This poor man lived amid the strife
of hardship, peril dogged my steps.
8Hid trap doors lead me down to hell,
the devils spread their nets for me.
They fish and troll for human souls
and fire their shafts with poison barbs.
9When God's long patience peters out,
his wrath long building like a storm,
he readies cloudbursts for the fray,
for vengeance on the hypocrites!
10His ire at Lucifer erupts,
he ties the noose with no escape.
The flood tides strike Belial's dams
and sweep away his battlements.
11His levin bolts unleash a fire
which nothing wet extinguishes.
The greenery along the banks
of Satan's planting conflagrate.
12A fiery sword turns every way,
a cyclone flaming like the sun;
the wrath of God exterminates
the dust-parched damned who beg relief.
13The clay foundation, dusty road,
the mountain side all burn like wood.
The flinty roots of mountains firm
spew magma through the seething air;
14it burns down all to Sheol's lid,
Belial's tidal wave consumes
the kingdom grim of Abaddon.
15Those wicked shades who floated there
like sharks preparing evil schemes
against the living far above
now howl and scream in agony
as boiling heat evaporates.
16The earth protests its horrid fate,
its sinful dwellers scream as one
as madness overtakes them all.
17The earth itself melts in the flame
of God's own wrath, revealed at last.

18He shakes the skies with thund'rous blows,
his holy halls reverberate
with praises loud and paens long,
poured forth from angels' perfect throats.
19The firmament on pillars shakes
as God's great army sallies forth,
crusaders who will not return
until they take their destined toll:
20destruction of the universe.
No human eye has seen the like.

11

1Forever like a sheep I strayed,
my feet beneath me slipping fast,
but looking down, you pitied me
and set my feet on firm terrain.
2With all direction lost to me,
you placed me on the path of life
that leads off to eternity!
3My eager thanks I offer you,
O Adonai, who shines the light
upon my face—your covenant—
4so in the dark I look to you
till brightly dawns the radiance,
your countenance sublime.

5Alas! Your children led astray
by clever scribes who twist your law
to capture poor unwary souls.
6They trip them up with lying words
and plunge them blindly into sin.
In utter foolishness they scheme,
their vaunted wise futility.
7Myself they mock and ridicule
and render no regard for him
whom you have made the vessel of
your greatness over all the earth.
8See, they have cast me out, away
from friends and kin and land. They push
me from the nest and crush me like
a jar of clay that leaks its oil.

9They plant the seeds of lies and reap
a harvest of false prophecy.
Against me they lay wicked schemes.
10They aim to falsify your Law,
whose true text lies within my heart.
They customize commandments as
their customers request them to.
11The thirsty they have turned away
and given vinegar to drink
to those who wanted truth's clear draft;
they stagger now from sour wine.
12Like fools, they celebrate the feasts
a day before, a week too late,
birds twisting in a net in vain
while madly trying to escape.

13You, on the other hand, O God,
know well the plots of Beliar;
you hate them with a vengeance hot!
14Your truth has never changed a jot,
your ancient plan unvarying.
15Lo, hypocrites, Belial's tools,
they seek you out with scant concern
for finding you, for finding truth,
for all their hearts are poison-filled;
16with bitter gall they stupefy
the heart and dull the eye until
it cannot tell the living God
from images of wood and stone.
17Their false commands they consecrate
as idols dumb, pretending to
speak oracles for those who seek
some glimmer of the light of truth.
18Imposture is their only word;
with accents grave and echoing,
they gull the simple with their tricks.
19Their feet have never trod your path,
nor have their ears rung with the sound
of Sinai's thunderclaps of old.
20Your vision came, but they deny:

"Mere echoes from the mountain storms!
The track of Moses leads nowhere,
let's build ourselves a burnished calf!"
21 The last word shall be yours, my God,
Your judgment swift they soon shall hear,
no more made deaf by willful sin.
22 The hammer of your word shall smash
their idols into ashen dust!
Your sizzling bolts shall skewer them,
apostates from your covenant.
23 Your Judgment Day will spell the doom
of all deception's progeny.
No room left, then, for lying seers
since truth alone withstands your gaze!
24 Your mind, your mouth, know only fact.
And thus those who delight in truth
shall ever share your company.
25 Each soul that loves the path that leads
into your all-capacious heart
will never have to seek elsewhere.

26 And as for me, I always rise,
my strength renewed unto the task,
prevailing over all who sneer.
27 Yes, I am nothing in their sight,
though in me your great strength is shown,
your guiding rays shine forth from me.
28 You will not hide their face in shame,
the wise ones who believe in me,
who seek your testament divine.
29 All those who walk your way in love
have rallied to my side to hear
your voice resounding clear amid
the council of the sons of God.
30 "Oh vindicate him!" so they plead.
"Let truth prevail and lift him up!"
31 You will not give them up unto
the liars who would them destroy.
No, you will sober them with fear.
32 You'll banish every pagan foe,

set them at naught on Judgment Day,
with every traitor to your Law!

33I am your instrument, my God,
illuminating every heart
among the multitude of faith.
34Their number you have multiplied
as seashore sand, as nightly stars,
as many as the mysteries
you have unveiled before my eyes!
35The deepest counsel of the Lord
has fortified my standing in
the congregation's upturned eyes;
36for that they see the miracles
that vindicate your holiness
and manifest your might to all.
37How feeble, next to this, is flesh!
The hand of man can do none such—
sin's captive from the day of birth
until the day death comes for him.
38But well I know that righteousness
is not of humankind's device.
The son of man knows not that path.
39All righteous acts are El Elyon's.
The way of men is perilous
save for that spirit God renews
to guide our steps aright to him.
40Thus every creature comes to know
your power and your mercy great
toward every one who pleases you.

41But dread and doom, they hold me fast.
Doubts smash like hammers on my bones.
My heart, once as a candle flame,
now runs like melted rivulets.
42My knees give way like pylons in
the flood that carries homes away.
My sins are hid from me no more.
43The crime of cursed ancestry!
They rose up with the wicked at
your word of promise and of Law.

44Rebellion was its own revenge
that day, a heritage of shame
that cast me from your covenant.
45But then did I recall your strength,
shown in compassion as in blows;
46I rose upright to face my foes,
my spirit fortified by love,
and claimed your nature as my right,
to enter in your courts once more.
47For you alone make right man's sin,
your righteousness will make him pure.
48It does not lie with mortal flesh
the soul to save, the heart to cleanse;
you made him so if so he be.
49For saints and sinners both obey
your mighty dictate: "Let it be!"
50But insofar as I may speak,
I bear your bond, our pact, in joy.
51For you are truth personified,
whose every act works righteousness.

12.

1To you I render thanks, O Lord, my God,
for when among the foreigners I dwelt,
you never wrote my name out of your book,
2refrained from paying me my due reward,
or gave me to the spider's web I spun,
but rescued my poor life from out the pit.
3In truth, you placed my flesh among the beasts
who snap and raven, seeking to devour
the hapless carcasses of sinful men
and suck the marrow from their clean-picked bones.
4For them, the strong are as the weak, alike
a morsel, champion or challenger.
5You had me live among the fishermen
who cast their nets into the teeming sea
and those who fish for men's iniquity.
6Among their like, you taught me wisdom's way
so that I might teach justice from the heart.
Your covenant I guarded as a wall
and gave it free to all who sought me out.

7 The gaping jaws of lions you locked tight,
their fearsome dagger teeth securely sheathed.
Their fangs are spears adrip with adder's bane;
they close like prison bars upon their foe.
8 They sought me for repast but without luck,
for, Lord, you sheltered me against their fangs.
9 Safe from the sons of men, I hid your Law
within my secret soul till I became
the revelation of your saving will.
10 For in my hour of hopelessness, you heard,
despising not your servant's low estate.
11 You understood the message of my cry
and rescued me from lawless predators
who thrust their blades against the stone in vain.
12 My tender flesh you saved from bloody claws;
this poor man triumphed over vicious beasts.
Their tongues, like razors, sought my blood,
to ruin me with many lying words.
13 But you have silenced all their deadly plots
and shown yourself the innocent's true friend.
15 The sons of men all gasp in wonder at
the miracles you work for this poor slave:
16 you placed me living in the smelting fire
whence I emerged unscathed, thanks to your grace,
pure sevenfold, a vessel free of every flaw.
17 The wicked rulers of the people aim
to crush me yet into the earth below,
but you, my God, have stilled their tempest winds
and placed my barque in calmer waters far.
18 This soul, so fragile, you have strengthened well
and made me lion's match and viper's doom.

13

1 Be blessed, Lord, receive my thanks!
The wretched you will not forget,
nor put the orphan out of mind.
2 Incomprehensible your pow'r,
your splendor filling all the worlds.
3 The Mighty Ones await your word
to trample down a foolish folk,
their spines emerging from the mud

like cypress roots above a lake.
4 With thrilling strength, you deal with all
who rightly fear their recompense.
5 With mighty deeds, you did exalt
the meek among the brotherhood.
6 Remember me, I pray, who am
the target for my rivals' shafts
of lying slander, poison words
that set at odds old friends and true
and rend asunder covenant.
7 They murmur like the men of old
at Meribah who doubted you
and would not follow Amram's son.
8 My old companions at the board
have learned to kick me when I'm down.
9 With evil jokes, they mock at me,
those very ones who once did sit
surrounding me in council wise.
10 I rule among stiff-necked old men!
Each place I look, I see them slink
and glance, and whispering, they plot.
11 They know full well the secret truth
you hid in me, but this they use
to slander me before my foes;
12 but you have shown your holiness
in me, and this they cannot stand.
You hid in me the springs of truth
and understanding of the way.
13 They frame their evil stealthy schemes
against me, these of Satan's horde,
who lie with viper's tongue and bite
with adder's fangs my tender flesh.
14 Their maledictions cripple me;
with pain I double up and drop,
my spirit perishes away,
my strength is gone like last night's dream.
15 My soul is poised to jump the nest.
They ambush me in alleyways,
with no escape that I can see.
16 They take up harp and timbrel song

while sweetly chanting of my doom,
accusing me of heresy,
pronouncing me a casualty.
17My anger blazes at the thought
of traitors and inquisitors;
I writhe like women giving birth,
my heart is churning, pounding, mad.
18I drape my soul in black to mourn
my own impending urgent doom.
I cannot speak, dry as a corpse.
19Their shameful gazes skewer me.
Eyes filled with death, they aim at me.
My countenance, once bright with faith,
now darkens with the shroud of death.

20Though you, O God, have opened up
a boundless freedom zone within,
I find myself close-pressed without
by those who love oblivion.
21My bread is salty with my tears,
my weeping fills my drinking cup.
I move among sore agonies,
my countenance is masked in shame.
22My every meal time sees dispute,
each drink, the taste of argument.
I feel my agonies bone-deep;
23they make my inner spirit faint,
despoiling all my former strength
and working unsuspected plots
of evil pow'rs who undermine
the very saving deeds of God.
24My members strain against firm knots
no mortal shrewdness can untie;
with adamantine chains I'm bound.
25Imprisoned in a tower of might,
I'm captive to iron bars, bronze doors.
I languish in the belly of
Leviathan as Jonah did,
26no reason to torment myself
with freedom dreams that can't come true.

Belial's legions siege my soul.
27 They scoff at me and scorn my heart,
they twist the handle on the rack:
no end of pain in sight for me!

28 But you, O God, have long ago
enabled me to hear your word,
to rule my sect with just decrees
unknown to these who torment me,
co-plotters with the foolish ones.
29 You ushered me into the halls
of those whose counsel you esteem,
among whom never lingers blame.
30 For hope dies not for him who has
forsaken sin, sought refuge from
its ravages to trace your ways.
31 Hence, in the roar of sinners I'll
rejoice and at the rising of
the kings of wicked nations strong
in their united front of hate.
32 It only means the sooner you
will save the remnant of your heart,
survivors that you love, your heirs.
33 They shall arise, fire-purified,
no stain of guilt defiling them.
34 For all you do is wrought in truth,
your judgments writ with mercy's milk;
compassion's blood prevails for them.
35 You teach them word by blessed word,
a standard no less than your truth,
to make them worthy members of
your council of the wise on earth.
36 And this you did for your name's sake,
that mortals, seeing such wise saints,
might render glory to the one
who makes the simple man a sage.
37 You charged the men of counsel with
the duty to make known your acts
of liberation wide among
new generations who will think

upon your wonders without pause.
38Thus all the peoples soon will know
your truth, your glory, as of old.
39The men of your community
have bathed unveiled before the light
of angel princes met on high.
40They need no go-between for this,
for they themselves partake of heav'n.
You send them forth like dew at dawn
and they return as you command.
41The angel princes you have set
amid the number of your tribe,
they shall all blossom like a flower
but never shall they fade away.
42Its fragrant blossoms shield the world,
its stalk climbs high unto the vault,
cerulean like Babel's tip;
43its knotted roots descend to the
abyss where dead shades swim and float.
Well watered by Edenic streams,
its boughs spread out a second sky.
44Its glory covers all the world
to exile ev'ry shadow far
below to Sheol's well of night.
45In that long day, there shall be seen
volcanic bursts of blinding light;
the sons of sin shall roast therein.
46No guilty one shall stand against
Abaddon's fury emptied out.
I bore your testimony true,
47but those who heeded once have strayed,
bedazzled by the liars' words
and leaving off the service that
they used to render for the right.
48And this, though, Lord, you plainly said
all must avoid who wish to share
eternity with you on high,
far from the foreskins of the damned!
49As drunken, hypnotized buffoons,
they stumbled off the highway to

your heart and fell headlong into
the gutter of the godless ones.
50Old Beliar supplies the plans
that pop into their fevered brains,
suggestions they are quick to heed,
to delve the deeper into guilt.

51I'm like a sailor trapped aboard
a ship that's pitched about the sea
by roiling waves and batting gusts.
52The pounding surf descends on me,
a booted heel upon a bug!
I catch my breath to have it caught
away by whirlwind, maelstrom tides.
53I seem to hear Behemoth's tread,
to glimpse the gates of Yamm's deep realm.
54A refugee who flees the foe
to seek refuge within the walls
of some secure metropolis,
I have no hope of safe return
unless your truth support my frame.
55A deep foundation you have laid
in bedrock, building well and firm
with well-cut rafters, solid stone,
unshakable, a mason's pride.
56No one who enters there will find
the flagstones lurching 'neath his feet.
No foreign foeman gains access
through portals thick and barred with brass.
57None enters there without the key
for locks placed on the gates by God.
No armored troop, no soldiers strong,
shall penetrate its lofty walls
to carry fire and sword inside.
58But naught can stay the sword of God
from its resistless downward arc
in time of judgment when it comes,
at last, to summon warriors,
59the sons of truth who will destroy
the evil sons of wretched shame.

Each valiant bowman looses shafts
to break the evil-doers' lines,
60 to make a broad expanse amid
their crumbling ranks to end the siege.
The victor shall with all his might
crank open gates of solid iron.
61 And in that day, with battle done,
all weapons shall be cast aside,
the righteous ruling unopposed.
62 Those men who heed temptation's voice
shall find no place, shall have no choice,
but death, without remainder.
63 Their sharpened weapons count for naught,
their mighty men like slaughtered sheep,
for God alone prevails that day,
his sword blood-soaked, his arm untired.
64 Then let the corpses raise their flag,
their maggot allies lift the cry.
Against Sabaoth none can stand!
The campaigns of the blasphemers
must ever end in just this way.

14

1 I always give you thanks, O Lord;
your strength preserves me in my plight.
2 I should have stumbled but for you
assigning me your Spirit guide
and making me secure when foes
assail your righteous camp in vain,
3 creating trials, and still they fail
to shake my loyalty unto
your covenant community.
4 Your mason's trowel built me up
till I am like a fortress tall,
a castle built upon a rock
that never shall erode or crack.
5 The walls surrounding me are firm,
surviving tempests in the past.

6 Just so, my God, you made of me
a fount of wisdom for the ones

who thirsted sore but found it not.
7I am your covenant ally,
my mortal tongue receives your word;
8but of perdition's ghost I will
not speak, nor have the wicked aught
to say to me. I swear they speak
no language I can understand.
9At Judgment Day you will condemn
each one who now speaks ill of me,
and I shall be the shibboleth
by which the sons of men are judged!
10For you know every motive, you
examine every spoken word.
11Among your faithful pupils, I
am blessed with stature and with strength.
12You guide my steps along truth's way:
I make straight tracks for righteousness.
13Your holy presence points the way;
a fiery cloud, an angel voice
directs me to unending life.
14Indeed, you know my inner thoughts,
that I am far from being proud
or thinking I have self to thank
for all that you have blessed me with.
15Of worldly glory, I have none,
nor anyone to lean upon.
16For me there is no righteousness
unless you will forgive my sin.
17And thus I lean upon your grace,
your kindness all my confidence.
18For you will make salvation bloom,
its tender shoot and leaf to grow.
19And so I will my refuge seek
beneath your wings of righteousness.
20The statutes of your covenant
have propped me up and made me firm,
and I have held fast to your truth
so I may not forget a line.

21A father you have made of me

to all those men whom you approve,
a nurse to feed them purest milk,
for which they crave, although they lack
the teeth for revelation's meat.
22 My battle blast rings in the wake
of enemies who flee from me.
23 Those who accuse me are like chaff,
yes, ev'ryone who sneers at me.
24 For you, O Lord, redeemed my life,
wherefore I raise my shofar high.
25 I blaze with brilliance, seven times
the dazzling whiteness of the sun,
a candle lit from off your flame.
26 You are the source of all my light,
you showed to me the path of life.

15

1 I thank you, Lord, my God, for that
you deigned to teach me all your truth.
2 Your mysteries, unknown to men,
you wrote in fire upon my heart!
3 You condescend to sinful men,
dispensing kindness to their kind,
far be they still from wanting it.
4 What other god compares with you?
Whose priests can utter truth like yours?
5 Who could survive your scrutiny
the day you search their hearts, their books?
6 If you accuse the angels, they
are mute with guilt: what can they say?
7 Your anger no one can withstand;
but all those born of truth's strong seed
you take unto yourself with love.
8 Your goodness is so limitless,
your graciousness extends so wide,
you purify them of their sins
9 and make them qualify to stand
before your presence without shame.

10 Your Godhead is forever firm,
your circuits through the universe

unchanging routes where angels pass.
11No god exists besides yourself!
And how can man, mere owner of
his grave clothes, ever plumb your depths,
recite your deeds, which pass his mind?

16

1I magnify you, ancient Lord, for though
I stand in deserts dry, a wilderness,
you planted me beside abundant springs.
2I find myself amid oasis palms
and satisfy myself with sweetest dates
that flourish by canals of crystal flow.
3Edenic cypresses and elms grow thick,
your living glory for their nourishment.
4These are the famous Trees of Life which sprout
between the secret waters of your heart;
5your angels make a precious shoot to grow
among your everlasting forest wide,
6the roots of which will penetrate the stream
and slake its thirst on living wells of grace.
7Its buds will feed the creatures of the wood,
its mighty trunk will shade the weary soul.
8The birds take refuge 'neath its wide green leaves.
It will not be the tallest in the day
that river-watered trunks surpass its crest.
9They grow together side by side with roots
that farther wind until they sink into
the rivers cutting Eden's quadrant banks.
10The one who tends that hidden forest zone
alone protects the secret of its fruit,
so none shall lay upon it hungry hands,
nor interloper gain eternal youth.
11For long ago you posted cherubim
with molten swords to bar the way to it,
fierce spirits dealing death to those who would
steal life. I am, my Lord, that secret tree
which you have hid in their capacious shade.
12Can I then, cut off from the juicy clouds,
receive their sustenance? My roots are short
and cannot find your rushing torrent flood.

13Yet all the while the echoes of their scorn
have overwhelmed me like a rushing tide.
14I perish in the mess of poison silt.

15But still my eyes look up to you, my God,
and then I realize how you have made
my mouth a conduit of words that give
refreshment to the parched of soul and heart.
16These words of life will only rain more hard
till riverbed and gully overflow.
17Your skies will pour their deluge down to earth,
while those you love stand ready with their jars
and barrels, pots and vessels ready to
be filled to overflowing with your word.
18The rivers and the seas shall run with red,
the lifeblood of the Spirit of the Lord,
till earth itself be covered over thick
with saving knowledge of the living God.
19That swelling flood shall nourish every tree
that God has sown, but drown like heavy stones
the poison growths of Satan's secret seeds
20else like the tinder, they shall burn to ash.
But none shall find a harvest sparse or spare
within the vineyard garden God does tend.
21I am the tiller of your garden, he
whom you formed living from the muddy ground.
22And you appointed me to give to all
the men of the community your word,
life-giving ration for the rational.
23I irrigate your fields, plow straight your land.
If I should play my role as you command,
your garden of the godly, it shall thrive
like waving palms. But if I fail and hold
back their supply, your chosen ones shall, by
my failure, shrivel up and shortly die.

17

1I languish here among the sick;
my heart can't count the illnesses
that menace it relentlessly.
2In pain my friends abandon me,

Job's comforters, they play their role.
3My malady just grows the worse,
the pain increases day by day.
4The reaper's scythe sweeps viciously,
assigned my soul to gather up.
5But I am in Sheol's dim bog
already crowding with the shades
like rotting fruit too long unsold.
6My soul flits like the moth who's trapped
in window panes he cannot see,
all battered, bruising, desperate,
more frantic for his dull fatigue.
7And yet it rises like a fire,
a blasting furnace-fever heat
that enervates, consumes my strength
like kindling wood, like charring coal,
like Satan's fiery vitals deep.
8My life force flags, my heart dissolves!
My flesh rots even as I wear
it, manhood hanging sadly limp.
9My once-strong hand droops nervelessly,
my foot immobile in a trap,
my knees all liquid, boneless sway.
10I'm paralyzed. I pause, I stop,
my footsteps cease, their echo stilled;
11in chains of heaviness I crawl.

12One time, my Lord, you made me speak
your wisdom to the sons of men,
but now my mouth hangs silent, slack.
13I can no longer lift my voice,
no Torah teach, no wisdom tell.
14The halt and faltering I helped—
no more! These days they pity me.
15Wrapped round with adamantine chains,
I sink into Sheol's embrace.
16In bitterness, I rue my birth.
I'm like the rain returning to
the sea too soon, lost in its waves.
17I rise like mist to fall again,

and thus around the world I go
like water scattered far and wide.

18At night my red eyes seek the dawn,
all sleep long fled away from me.
19Compassion from the Lord is gone,
a memory that swiftly fades.
20Among his foes he counts me now
and writes my name upon his list.
21It's clear I'm marked down for his doom.
The waves assail me, drink me down.
22He tucks me into Sheol's bed.
My sickbed chants my passing grim,
my bed heaves sighs of mourning dim.
23My eyes are red as if from smoke,
my tears cascade to soothe them like
a river, but they lay too long
asleep, and now they will not wake.
24My strength, my life, have left me here
to journey where I cannot guess.
25I stagger from one ruin to
the next, annihilated by
my maladies, their torment, pain.
26Amid my tortures, I think back
to wonders that you used to work.
27I see you never cast me off!
Each minute of the day, your love
abounds toward man, forgetful though
he be, by grace sustaining him.
28Now know I what to say to him
who cuts me down, who slanders me,
who says, "God has rejected him!"
29His verdict is a lying screed,
yours on the other hand is just.
30For have I not confessed your truth?
Have I not welcomed your ordeal
to try my faith, to purify?
31I counted on your blessing me,
and so you have. But first you made
your servant cry aloud and plead.

32But never did you mean to do
me harm or wound me without balm.
33I never rued my trusting you!
But in the depths of my ordeal,
you stirred me up, my spirit's fire.
34You kept in mind that I meant well;
you sponged away my hapless sins.
35Your amnesty is my delight;
it soothes the pain of former sin.
36Your kindness in the past gives me
the hope you'll once again forgive;
despite my sins, I hope I'll live.
37No one survives your scrutiny
unscathed, emerges innocent,
though in the eyes of fellow men
one may appear superior
to others of his dwarfish kind.
38Before the looming wall of might
that is your glory, who will dare
to raise his head, to lift his eyes?

39It is on you I take my stand,
on you I built my bishopric
and not upon the shifting sands
of mortal men's professed esteem.
40For when they turn against my name,
rebel against your covenant,
you hasten, vindicating me,
and heap upon my enemies
the shame and blame they aimed at me.
41Pray, how can it be otherwise
when you are he who pleads my case?
42True, once you put me in my place,
obscured your truth behind a cloud,
but now the rainbow has emerged:
43I see your wisdom clear once more.
As once I shrank at your rebuke,
44now that your favor has returned,
my wounds all healed, I glow with joy!
45Where once my rival ridiculed,

he bears disgrace instead of me.
46My crown's a candelabrum lit,
by tine and tine, until it blaze
with purest radiance from your face.
47I wasted weak as mortal flesh
until you energized my limbs.
48The holy name of Adonai
has made me shine out in the dark,
a beacon for the blind of heart;
49the straw of mortal weakness he
has lit and turned into a torch.
50My soul, once bound in narrow scope,
extends, expands, like speeding light.
51Yes, you, Lord God, are my refuge,
protector, savior, rock of strength!
52You turn away their shafts like motes
that bounce within the sunny void.
53I know I may rely on you
as long as I shall live this life.
54For since that day I was conceived,
you watched me close, compassionate.
55Emerging from my mother's womb,
I met your friendly gaze and laughed.
56When I was weaned by nursemaids, you
were there and watched my falt'ring steps.
57From early on the wisdom of
your will was manifest to me,
your truth unchanging ever was
my guide, your Spirit my delight.
58You led my steps this far today,
correcting me if e'er my foot
should stray. At peace, your eyes attend
my path, forgiving each misstep,
reproving with compassionate
reminder of a better goal.
59This way I tread till old age ends
my progress on this earthly plane.
60I started out bereft of kin:
so father, mother, you were both.
61And so you are to all who vow

to make themselves the sons of truth.
62You endlessly rejoice in them,
in ev'ry step, in each new word.
63You gather them in fond embrace
who fly to you for bonds of love.

18

1The wisdom of your heart includes our plans;
without your willing them, they cannot be.
Your wisdom's depths, what mortal understands?
The wonders that you work surpass our thought.
2So tell me, Lord, what use to you is man?
Poor puppet, he is carven from the earth
and scarcely grows beyond this simple source.
3A refugee from Eden's humble mud,
he shall return to pay his debt in full.
And yet you deign and condescend to teach
him secrets even angels love to know.
4You let him gaze upon the roots of truth.
Behold me, man of dust and helpless clay!
What diff'rence makes it what I will to do
when all tomorrows are your yesterdays?
5Can I devise but what you have decreed?
What makes me stand erect against the wind
if you do not instill your strength within?
6Is there a thing to learn unless you teach?
Have I a thing to say you did not write?
What answer can I give I did not get?
7You are the Lord of gods, of angels chief,
the sovran of all spirits—they are yours.
Of all effects, you are the hidden cause.
No secret is discovered, just revealed.
8To left and right, you find no one beside,
for there is none among the gods of old
to match your strength, contest your throne.
9Your matchless might exceeds all estimates.
Is there a single one that you have made
who will presume to stand before your face?
10For surely, on the spot, the dust reclaims
those molecules that briefly bore a name.

For in your sight no mortal flesh may boast,
but only glorify you and expire.

19

1I bless you from the depths, O Adonai,
for your compassion fresh and ill-deserved,
2for by your gracious will you did vouchsafe
your ageless secrets deep, your myst'ries dark.
3Nor do I hoard them for myself, but speak
aloud your revelations true to those
with ears to hear the things till now unknown.
4Day after day, I will extol your love.
In your forgiving heart I will delight
and will exhort your fretting sons to trust
your mercies truly inexhaustible.
5You always warn before a danger comes,
there is no sickness past your curing balm.
6And mindful of these blessed truths, I sing
your glory and your name before the throng.
7They sit and listen, rapt in wonderment
at miracles of yours that I recount.
8Together do we take a vow to trust
your tender and forgiving countenance.
9For this, you fashioned me long years ago,
to tell the congregation of your truth.
10No robber's den for me, no palace grand,
but revelations for the son of man.
11I call upon no fleshly arm to save,
no sword or mace to fight my fearsome foe,
but you alone, the savior of the meek,
who ev'ry wicked host will overthrow.
12The mighty ones of this world love to boast
of castles strong and closely guarded coasts.
13Their beefy platters, jugs of wine, are full,
as are their treasures, vineyards, barns, and stalls;
14they bloom and sprout luxuriant and lush.
But for the men of truth, you save the best;
15your secrets, laws, and statutes do they hoard.
Their reverence goes to him who studies much,
to those whose hearts contain the living text
of your eternal word, which shall endure

when worldly glories to the dust devolve.
16The wealthy soul is he who worldly gold
and riches does despise but has a good
much greater in his eyes: the word of truth.

17So as for me, your covenant sublime
is all the fortune I could ever want.
18To me, it is the finest of the fine,
no connoisseur a better can discern.
19I flourish as the purple iris blooms—
no emperor was clad in robes so grand—
20and this because your word I most desire.
The garden of your Law knows only spring,
but those without, they suffer famine sore.
21For them I weep and gasp in pallid fright!
My gladness vanishes like dew to see
the desert wind of death that desiccates
their land, their crops, their flesh, as leather, dry.
22My anguish at your verdict on the great
among the sons of foolishness will ring
through Sheol's baleful halls and dusty streets.
23Your verdict on the sinners is severe,
enough to make the righteous shake with fear!
24For but a camel's hair shall separate
them from their unforgiven fellows' fate!

20

1I fill my mouth with thanks, O God,
acknowledging your miracle
of taking dust and making it
a being who can know your will.
2On its behalf, you act with might,
and all for such a clod of dirt!
For what am I, a mannikin,
for you to teach me of your Law?
3The rudiments of sacred truth,
the glories of your mighty deeds,
they prompt my tripping tongue to shout!
4I praise you, scarce as you deserve,
for can the worm describe the oak?
My lips are heathen, though my soul

delights your Torah to uphold.
5Your kindness forms my daily chant,
the subject of my constant thought.
I bless your name throughout the day
and boast your fame among the saints.
6What joy could make me happier
than your abundant fund of grace?
I know that naught but truth proceeds
from out your mouth, and firm decrees.
7All learning is but trickle-down
from God's high-surging fount of truth,
of wisdom vast and knowledge great,
beyond the creature's feeble grasp.
8All honor goes to you alone,
the justice of your verdicts none
denies. And none gainsays your great
compassion which you showered on
9the sons of your new covenant,
the beneficiaries of
your truth, of your deep mysteries.
10For your own sake, you undertake
to purify the sons of men,
else who will sanctify himself
that you may have a fitting choir
of adoration richly won?
11From every clinging shred of sin,
abomination's vice-like grip,
we pray you, set us free from it!
12Unite us with the sons of truth,
consider us among their ranks:
lift up from dust these maggot men,
expose them to your knowledge sweet,
13place them in fellowship divine,
strip off depravity and sin
and make them fit, eternity
to spend in your bright company.
14Let heaven's splendid host renew
their spirits with the fading world
so all together may partake
in everlasting songs of joy!

21

1 Receive my thanks, eternal Rock,
in whom my spirit refuge finds,
who works his wonders in my soul,
conveys to me the depths of truth
for me to try to contemplate.
2 Truth's rudiments are too advanced:
I am a baby sucking milk,
no sage to master mysteries.
3 At least I know that perfect right
still lives with you and fierce judgment,
yet straining at his splitting leash!
4 He bothers not to judge the man
on whom compassion makes no claim.
My own heart broods with bitterness,
the end of which I do not see.
5 Grief haunted me the day I looked
unflinchingly at man's true heart,
and equally his dismal fate,
inclined to sin, no less to guilt.
6 My heart is poisoned with these facts,
my bones diseased to think on them.
Remembrance is enough to plunge
me into meditation grim.
7 I pluck the harp in minor key,
my sighing takes the place of song.
8 I moan the dirge for sinful man
so long as sin shall reign in him,
till crime shall cease and illness stay
its punitive, corrective hand.
9 On that day I shall trade my sighs
for gladsome paens to your grace
on zesty zither, tambourine,
and tuneful flutes not winded soon.
10 Does any mortal live so long
to have sufficient time to tell
the sagas of your mighty acts?
11 Your name is praised by everything
as each one breathes or barks or sings,
both man and beast with every breath

they cannot help but glorify!
12Amid such symphony of praise,
iniquity and crime shall fade
till they are no more to be seen.
13Instead, your truth is on display
with endless glory, shouts of praise!
The peace shall no more be destroyed.

14May bliss be yours, O Adonai!
For you have blessed your servant thus,
that he can penetrate the veil
that drapes the future from the past.
15Your grace has done this, turned the latch,
let heav'nly truth come pouring out.
16Blest be, I say, compassion's Lord,
so generous with that which man
can never otherwise discern.
What kindness you bestow on him!
17Refresh your servant's soul with truth
and let your justice make me pure,
for ever have I trusted you,
your goodness and deliverance.
18Forgiving love dispels despair,
compassion speeds the dawning light.

19Accept my blessings, Adonai,
as small return for all your deeds
on my behalf, for which I praise,
composing songs to share my joy
with those men you have given me.

22

1In blessedness you lift my heart,
for happiness and ecstasy
become my habitation place!
2For in your holy presence now,
I bask in rays of rest and peace.
3Your blessings pitch a tent in which
the soul may stretch and take its ease.
4It's there I live, along with those
who fear and love your holy name.

[5]You are the one who teaches us
both praise and prayer, the rituals:
when to bow down and so entreat,
assigning periods to pray.
[6]When Samson from his tent comes out,
his progress 'cross the sky we chart
and pray at each bright junctioning.
[7]So we obey the sun's great laws.
Again when day departs, we bend,
as if to greet gray Shalman's shade,
[8]and on throughout the night we keep
the vigil till Shahar's proud wings
arise. And then she's gone in time
and day returns once more, acclaimed.
[9]Continual observance through
repeated births of time's long life.
[10]This God commanded when he made
the stars and sun and moon with their
commands, positions, duties, zones.
[11]The whole bright firmament he planned
to witness to his making word.
[12]This charge we keep with sleepless zeal,
to honor him, one greater far
than galaxies of flaming stars.
[13]His pattern for the heavens vast,
he has vouchsafed to us alone.
And me you made the teacher, Lord,
[14]you gave me of your Spirit, and
your knowledge floods my mortal brain,
the cosmic secrets you alone
once knew until you gave to me
a share in knowledge, power!

45.

The Epistle to the Hebrews

THE 1947 DISCOVERY OF THE DEAD Sea Scrolls initiated an epidemic of what someone called "Qumran fever." Everyone began to use the fascinating data of the sectarian library as a lens through which to take a second look at the New Testament since on any reading there seemed to be a good deal in common between the early Christians and the sect that produced the scrolls. At least, they moved in a similar atmosphere of sectarian, apocalyptic Judaism. But some thought it possible to go further and make specific identifications. Was the sect that produced the scrolls the Essenes described by Philo, Pliny the Elder, and Josephus? Might John the Baptist have been a member or even the leader of this sect—the enigmatic Teacher of Righteousness? Did Christianity begin, as Ernest Renan and various Protestant liberals and rationalists had long ago suggested, as "an Essenism"? Almost threatened with being lost in this flood of fascinating speculation was the theory of Hans Kosmala, Ceslas Spicq, and others that the Epistle to the Hebrews had striking Qumran affinities and might perhaps have been addressed to Christian converts from that quarter. If this seems like some exotic notion, it should not, for the theory gives much greater plausibility to the conventional hypothesis that the work was addressed to some sort of Hebrew Christians as the familiar title implies. Of course, the title is an ancient scribal stop-gap because the epistle bears no heading, nor is there any author designation or recipient. Constant references to the Old Testament need not imply a Jewish readership since presumably very many gentile converts to Christianity had already been attracted to the margins of Diaspora syna-

gogue life as "God-fearers" or "pious gentiles" and would therefore have been conversant with scripture. But if Spicq was right, the traditional theory was reinforced.

J. C. O'Neill[a] has put a whole new face on the Essene theory. He noticed how Jesus does not quite seem to belong in the epistle, and that in two ways. First, it is startling to discover that at virtually every occurrence of the name Jesus, there are textual variants and uncertainties suggesting the name has been added to an original text that lacked it. When read without the name, the text reads more naturally. Second, O'Neill notes various historico-theological incongruities between the usual account of Jesus' Passion and the sacrificial death of the Son of God described in Hebrews. For instance, as G. W. Buchanan pointed out, the epistle seems to suppose the Son was martyred on the Day of Atonement (5:3; 9:7, 11-12; 10:20; 13:11), which renders his death itself an atonement. Jesus, of course, is said to have died at Passover. There is no reference to the resurrection of Jesus until 13:20, part of a secondary ending suffixed to turn the original treatise into a Paulinist epistle. O'Neill argues that the basic document is about the suffering and exaltation of the Son of God and the new covenant wrought by him, but that this Son of God was none other than the Qumran/Essene Teacher of Righteousness. The text was subsequently lightly revised by Christians by sprinkling the name Jesus here and there. In the annotation, I will consider Robert Eisenman's theory that the Teacher of Righteousness was James the Just, in which case O'Neill's suggestion would become even more striking.

Hebrews is often said to employ Platonic allegory, a la Philo of Alexandria, with its talk of earthly copies of heavenly realities. But this is unnecessary. Nothing in the text goes beyond what Exodus itself says about Moses making sure the earthly tabernacle exactly conforms to its heavenly prototype, which God showed Moses atop Sinai (Exod. 25:9). References to Jewish sacrificial ritual are often said to imply a date before the destruction of the Jerusalem temple in CE 70, but that is to misread the text, which refers in ideal terms not to the Jerusalem temple but to the desert tabernacle, as if it were still in op-

a. J. C. O'Neill, "Jesus in Hebrews," *Journal of Higher Criticism* 6 (Spring 1999).

eration. The point is simply to compare and contrast the terms of two covenants on paper, as it were.

Finally, modern attempts to identify the author as someone in the Pauline circle (Apollos, Bar-Nabas, Clement, Priscilla, Luke) all run aground on the secondary character of the epistolary material in chapter 13 since the identifications all stem from references to Timothy and others in that section.

1

[1]By dribs and drabs, in various ways, God has anciently spoken to
the fathers by the prophets, [2]but in these last days he spoke to us by a son,
whom he appointed heir of all things, through whom, in fact, he fashioned the aions; [3]who is the radiance of his splendor and the representation of his person and upholds the All by his powerful word of command.[b] Having effected a purification of sins, he took his seat to the right
of the Greatness in the heights, [4]having become so much better than the
angels that he has inherited a more excellent name than them.[c] [5]After all,
to which of the angels did he ever say, "You are my son. Today I have
begotten you!"[d] And again, "I will be a father to him, and he shall be like
a son to me."[e] [6]And again, whenever he brings the firstborn into the
world of men,[f] he says, "And let all the angels of God worship him!"[g]
[7]And concerning the angels, it says, "The one who makes his agents into
spirits[h] and his worshippers into a jet of fire."[i] [8]But concerning the son,

b. Wisd. of Sol. 7:24-26

c. 3 Enoch 4:1

d. Pss. 2:7

e. 2 Sam. 7:14

f. Can this be a reference to the Ebionite doctrine of the True Prophet, the oft-reincarnated "firstborn" Adam? See the Preaching of Peter in this collection.

g. Deut. 32:43b LXX, where the angels are nevertheless bidden to worship God. Also see *Life of Adam and Eve* 14:1-2; 15:2; 3 Enoch 4:9. This verse must have once formed part of the myth of the fall of Satan, as in *Life of Adam and Eve* 12-16; Koran 38:72-83. God displayed the newly created Adam before the angels and commanded them all to prostrate themselves before him. Lucifer and his confederates deemed this idolatry and refused to do so. His harassment of Adam was to prove he had been right: Adam was his inferior and unworthy of God's preference.

h. 1 Cor. 15:45

i. Pss. 104:4; 2 Enoch 9:15-19; 3 Enoch 15:1-2. All these motifs have to do with the exaltation of Elijah, Enoch, and other saints who ascended into heaven in

he says, "Your throne, O God, lasts through ages multiplied by ages and the sceptre of righteousness is his royal sceptre.[j] [9]You loved righteousness and hated lawlessness; therefore, God, your God, anointed you with the festal oil above your fellows."[k] [10]Again: "At the beginning, Lord, you founded the earth, and the skies are the works of your hands; [11]they will one day perish, but you remain, and everything will wear out like a garment. [12]And like a cloak, you will roll it all up; like a garment, too, they shall be changed for something new. But you are the same and your years will not run out."[l] [13]But to which of the angels has he ever said, "Sit at my right till I make your enemies' necks a footstool for your feet"?[m] [14]Are not they all worshipping spirits, sent out on missions for the sake of those who are about to inherit salvation?

2

[1]Therefore, we are obliged to pay much closer attention to the things we have heard so that we do not drift away. [2]For if the law promulgated through angels[n] was inflexible and every transgression and act of disobedience called forth due recompense, [3]how could we hope to escape the consequences of neglecting such a great salvation, which having first been announced by the Lord was corroborated for us by his hearers,[o] [4]with God testifying by means of both signs and wonders and by various powerful deeds[p] and the apportioning of the Holy Spirit according to his will?[q]

[5]For it was not to angels that he subjected the inhabitants of the world to come, concerning which we speak. [6]But somewhere someone has given sworn testimony: "What is man that you remember him or a son of man for you to notice him? [7]You made him become scarcely less

---

fiery chariots and became fiery angels. The Son and Lord discussed here has been similarly transfigured to divine status, enthroned beside God. Just as certain angels refused to bow to Adam, so the angels protested the honoring of Enoch in heavenly glory, but God insisted he deserved it as having been the only righteous human being.

j. 3 Enoch 10:1, where Enoch is given a glorious throne like God's.

k. Pss. 45:6-7; 2 Enoch 9:17-18: the oil is what transfigures Enoch.

l. Pss. 102:25-27

m. Pss. 110:1

n. Gal. 3:19; Acts 7:53

o. Luke 1:1-2

p. Mark 16:20

q. Acts 2:3

than angels and you crowned him with honor. [8]You put all creation at his feet."[r] For subordinating everything to him, he left nothing outside his sway. To be sure, at present we do not yet see everything in subjection, [9]but we do see *Jesus*,[s] the one having been made for a little while lower than angels, having now been crowned with splendor and honor because of his suffering and death so that by the favor of God he might sample death for every human being. [10]For it was appropriate for him, because of whom all things exist and by whom all things exist, to perfect through sufferings the vanguard of their salvation as one who leads many sons home to divine splendor. [11]For both the sanctifier and those sanctified are all of one blood, which is why he is by no means embarrassed to acknowledge them as brothers, [12]since he says: "I will announce your name to my brothers, in the midst of the congregation I will sing your praise."[t] [13]And again: "I will commit my trust to him."[u] And again: "Here we are! I and the children whom God gave me."[v] [14]Since therefore the children have shared in blood and flesh, in like manner he too shared in the same in order that, through death, he might destroy the ruler of death, namely the accuser, [15]and release these, all who were enslaved their whole lives to the fear of death. [16]For, of course, he does not take on the form of angels, but he takes on the form of the progeny of Abraham. [17]This is why he was obliged to become like his brothers in every way, in order that he might become a merciful and faithful archpriest dealing with God, to make propitiation for the sins of the people. [18]Insofar as he has endured testing, he is able to help those who are tested.

3

[1]In view of this, holy brothers, partners in the heavenward vocation, consider the apostle and archpriest of our religion, *Jesus*,[w] [2]being faithful to the one who made him like Moses in all his household. [3]For this one has been judged worthy of greater splendor than Moses,[x] just as a con-

---

r. Pss. 8:4-6

s. There is not any room here for an appositional proper noun in a clause crowded with participles, nor does the sense require it. It sounds like a clarifying gloss.

t. Pss. 22:22

u. Isa. 8:17b

v. Isa. 8:18a

w. Origen and Cyril of Alexandria have "Christ" instead of "Jesus," implying both are alternative attempts to gloss the original, which would have lacked either one.

x. Exod. 34:29-35; 2 Cor. 3:7-8, 12-13

tractor has more honor than the house he builds. [4]For every house is built
by someone, but the one who built everything is God. [5]And Moses, on the
one hand, was faithful in all the business of his household to serve as a
testimony of the realities being foretold; [6]the anointed, on the other hand,
was faithful as a son over his household and we are that household as
long as we hold tightly to our confidence and our boast in the sure prospect of salvation to the end. [7]As the Holy Spirit says, "Today, if you
should hear his voice, [8]do not be stubborn as in the fateful provocation
during the testing in the Sinai desert [9]when your fathers tested my patience to see what I would do, and they beheld my deeds [10]over forty
years, which is why I was angry at this generation and I said, 'Their hearts
always go astray, and they never learned my ways,' [11]so I swore in my
rage, 'If they ever enter my rest ...!'"[y]

[12]Watch out, brothers, in case any one of you may harbor an evil
heart of unbelief alienated from the true God. [13]But exhort one another
each day, as long as you have another day, so none of you may grow re-
calcitrant through sin's deceit. [14]For we have become partners of the
anointed, if indeed we hold tight the assurance we had at the first until
the end. [15]Meanwhile, it is said, "Today, if you should hear his voice, do
not be stubborn as in the provocation,"[z] [16]for some, when they heard, did
provoke him, though by no means all of those who emigrated from Egypt
with Moses. [17]But with whom was he angry for forty years if not with the
ones who sinned and who dropped dead in the desert? [18]To whom did he
swear they would not enter his rest if not those who disobeyed? [19]Thus it
is evident that disbelief disqualified them from entry.[a]

4

[1]Let us fear, then, that since there remains a promise of entry into his
rest, any one of you might seem to have fallen short. [2]For after all, we too
have been evangelized just as they were, but the good promise did not
profit those who heard it because they failed to combine it with faith.

---

y. Pss. 95:7-11

z. Pss. 95:7-8

a. This whole discussion, drawing a parallel with the trials of a desert community, would fit ideally a conventicle like the monastic order of the Dead Sea Scrolls, nominated by J. C. O'Neill as the recipients of the epistle. Notice the layers of meaning behind the term "enter[ing] his rest." The author points to Israel's entry into the promised land of milk and honey after their travails in the desert and alludes to the reward of eternal repose in heaven after a life of pious striving—entering the eternal Sabbath rest of God, who was said to be at sublime ease, much like the Epicurean or Deist deity, ever since the sixth day of creation.

[3]For we who do believe enter into the rest, just as he said, "As I swore in my rage, 'If they ever enter my rest ...!'"[b] though in fact he finished his works long ago when he was done creating all things. [4]For somewhere he has spoken this way about the Sabbath: "And God rested the seventh day from all his labors,"[c] [5]and in this passage, too: "If they ever enter my rest ...!"[d] [6]Since therefore that rest remains for some to enter it and those formerly evangelized failed to enter due to disobedience, [7]again he specifies a certain day, "today," after so long a time, saying through David, "Today if you should hear his voice, do not be stubborn."[e] [8]For if Joshua had given them respite, David would not have mentioned another day after those events. [9]So a Sabbath rest remains for the people of God. [10]For the one who did enter his rest also rested from his labors as God rested from his. [11]Let us be eager, therefore, to press on into that rest so that no one may repeat that example of disobedience. [12]For the promise of God is still alive and effective and sharper than any double-edged sword and penetrates even between soul and spirit, severing joints and piercing marrow, and it exposes secret thoughts and schemes, [13]and there is no creature hidden from his sight, but all things are naked and exposed to the gaze of him who holds the record of our deeds.

[14]Therefore, having a great archpriest who has passed through the heavens, *Jesus,*[f] the son of God, let us hold onto our belief. [15]For it is not as if we have an archpriest unable to sympathize with our frailties, but rather having one who has been tested in every respect entailed in our semblance except for sin.[g] [16]Let us, then, approach the throne of mercy[h] confidently to receive mercy and find favor for timely help.[i]

5

[1]For every archpriest recruited from humanity is appointed on behalf of humans to deal with divine matters, to offer both gifts and sacrifices

---

b. Pss. 95:11

c. Gen. 2:2

d. Pss. 95:11

e. Pss. 95:7-8

f. "Jesus" added to "the Son of God" makes the confession here two-headed. Elsewhere Hebrews often uses simply "the Son of God" (6:6; 7:3; 10:29) or just "the Son" (1:2, 5, 8; 2:6; 3:6; 5:5, 8; 7:28).

g. Does this perhaps mean, after all, that he was incapable of being tempted to sin since he bore but the outward likeness of humanity?

h. The throne of mercy is the Ark of the Covenant.

i. This is a description of the function of the archpriest (high priest) on Yom Kippur, the Day of Atonement.

for sins, [2]being able to feel appropriate compassion for the ignorant and the deceived since he, too, is beset with weakness, [3]and because of this, he is obliged, both concerning the people and concerning himself, to make offerings for sins. [4]And no one appropriates the honor for himself, but he has to be called by God just like Aaron. [5]Accordingly, it was not the anointed who gave himself the glory of the archpriesthood, but rather the one who said to him, "You are my son. I have fathered you today!"[j] [6]Just as he also says in another passage: "You are a priest in perpetuity according to the Order of Melchizedek."[k] [7]While alive in the flesh, he offered both petitions and requests with loud cries and tears to the one able to save him from death, and he was heard as a reward for his piety.[l] [8]Though he was a son, he learned obedience from the things he suffered, [9]and once perfected,[m] he became the source of age-long salvation for all those who obey him,[n] [10]being designated by God an archpriest according to the Order of Melchizedek.

[11]Of him we have much to say, but it is difficult to explain because you have become hard of hearing. [12]Indeed, by this time you ought to be teachers, but you require again someone to teach you the elements of the early portions of the oracles of God[o] and you have come to require milk rather than solid food.[p] [13]For whoever partakes of milk is a novice in the teaching of righteousness, indeed he is a newborn. [14]But solid food is for mature adults, those who have had occasion to hone their faculties to distinguish between the good and the bad.

6

[1]Therefore, taking the fundamental teaching of the anointed as read, let us carry on to maturity, not backtracking to establish the foundation

---

j. Pss. 2:7

k. Pss. 110:4

l. If this is a reference to the Garden of Gethsemane scene, it assumes a docetic view that Jesus' request was granted and he did not have to drink the cup of martyrdom. Otherwise, it need denote only frequent rescue.

m. We must be careful not to read too much Christology in here. See 12:7-11.

n. This was the basis for the creed of Asterius, Arius, and Eusebius of Caesarea: the Savior was a mutable being who blazed the trail of salvation by first undertaking the quest himself.

o. The Gnostics, too, were much preoccuppied with Genesis as it seemed to provide the key to so much else. See the several Nag Hammadi retellings of the Eden myth in the *Apocryphon of John*, *Hypostasis of the Archons*, *Testimony of Truth*, and others.

p. 1 Pet. 2:2-3

of repentance from moribund deeds and of faith toward God, [2]of teaching about baptisms[q] and about the imposition of hands, of resurrection of the dead, and about age-long punishment. [3]And so we will, God willing. [4]And what would be the use of reiterating all that? It is impossible for any who have once been enlightened, sampling the heavenly gift and becoming sharers of the Holy Spirit [5]and the vintage promise of God and the miracles of a coming age, [6]but then fall away, ever to renew their repentance again since this would require re-crucifying[r] the son of God for their private benefit, exposing him to public disgrace. [7]For the earth, drinking the rain that often falls upon it and bearing vegetation for the good of those for whose sake it is cultivated, receives the blessing of God. [8]But should it bear thorns and thistles, it incurs disapproval and is inviting a curse, and its inevitable fate is to be burnt off.[s]

[9]But you need not worry, brothers: even though we speak this way, we are convinced of better things, things betokening salvation, in your case. [10]For God is not so unjust as to forget all your toil and the love for his name you have demonstrated, having ministered to the saints as you still do. [11]All we desire is that each of you show the same eagerness to gain complete confidence in our prospect of salvation till the end. [12]Otherwise you run the risk of becoming complacent. Rather, emulate those who, thanks to their faithfulness and long-suffering, are inheriting the promises. [13]For when God was making promises to Abraham, since he had no one greater by which to swear, he swore by himself: [14]"Surely, if blessing, I will bless you, and multiplying, I will multiply you!"[t] [15]And so being long-suffering, he obtained what was promised. [16]For mortals swear oaths by someone greater and the oath settles any further contradiction in order to confirm the pledge. [17]When God decided to make infinitely more clear to the heirs of his promise the immutability of his resolve, he added an oath [18]in order that, through two immutable things in which it is impossible for God to lie, we might have a strong consolation, those of us who have been swift to grab hold of the prospect set before us,

---

q. Implying daily baptism, typical of Judean baptizing sects.

r. O'Neill suggests that the anointed was the Teacher of Righteousness of the Dead Sea Scrolls and that he was crucified at the hand of Alexander Jannaeus, who also crucified hundreds of Pharisees. Crucifixion would not fit Eisenman's theory so well where, though the anointed is the Teacher of Righteousness, the Teacher is in turn James the Just.

s. Matt. 3:10; Luke 13:6-9; John 15:6

t. Gen. 22:16-17

[19]which we have as an anchor of the soul, both secure and firm, and entering into the esoterica behind the veil [20]where a precursor entered on our behalf, *Jesus,*[u] becoming a permanent archpriest according to the Order of Melchizedek.

7

[1]For this Melchizedek, king of Salem, priest of the Elyon, the one who intercepted Abraham as he returned from the slaughter of the kings and blessed him[v]—[2]to whom Abraham, in fact, apportioned a tenth of all the spoils—on the one hand, his name being interpreted "King of Righteousness,"[w] then on the other, "King of Salem," which is to say "King of Peace," [3]without father, without mother, without genealogy, having neither beginning of days nor end of life, but having been made like the son of God, he remains a priest in perpetuity.[x] [4]Now consider the greatness of this man, to whom even the patriarch Abraham gave a tenth of the spoils! [5]And on the one hand, those of the sons of Levi receiving the priesthood have a commandment to receive tithes from the people according to the Torah, that is, from their brothers, though they come out of the loins of Abraham; [6]on the other hand, the one not tracing his lineage from them has tithed Abraham and has blessed the one to whom the promises were made. [7]And no one will deny it is the lesser who is blessed by the greater.[y] [8]And here, on the one hand, mortals doomed to die receive tithes; there, on the other, it is attested that he lives. [9]And one might even say that through Abraham, Levi, the receiver of tithes, has in fact paid tithes, [10]for he was implicit in the loins of his father when Mechizedek encountered him.

[11]If, therefore, perfection was to be had through the Levitical priesthood, for under its auspices the people received the Torah, why was there the need for another priest belonging to the Order of Melchizedek to arise and not one belonging to the Order of Aaron? [12]For when the

---

u. Latin Mss. Ardmachanus (D) and Langobardus (L*) show that there was originally no name here, though sometimes "Christ" has been added, "Jesus" more often.

v. Gen. 14:17-20

w. Originally, "Melchi-Zedek" would have meant "Zedek is my king." Zedek ("righteousness") was a Jerusalemite god who continued on in the Yahvistic pantheon (Pss. 85:10b).

x. Melchizedek is yet another exalted angelic figure appearing as a patriarchal superman, along with Abel, Enoch, and Enosh.

y. This argument was also used by the John the Baptist sect to show John was greater than Jesus, the former having baptized the latter.

priestly office is changed, there also perforce occurs a change in the Torah. [13]For he about whom these things are said belongs to a different tribe, from which no one has devoted himself to the altar; [14]for it is obvious that our Lord has arisen from Judah, about which Moses never said anything concerning priests.[z] [15]And it is even more obvious, should another priest arise like Melchizedek, [16]he qualifies for his office, not by the law of a mortal commandment, but based on the power of an indestructible life. [17]After all, it is attested, "You are a priest *forever* in the Order of Melchizedek."[a]

[18]For on the one hand, an annulment of a previous commandment comes about because of the weakness and uselessness of it, [19]for the Torah perfected nothing; but on the other hand, we rejoice in the introduction of a better hope, through which we are enabled to draw near to God. [20]And appropriately, not without swearing oaths, for on the one hand, they have become priests without the swearing of an oath, [21]but he became a priest through one saying to him, "Adonai swore and will not change his mind, 'You are a priest in perpetuity.'"[b] [22]Indeed, it was by such a wide margin that he *Jesus*[c] has become the guarantee of a superior covenant. [23]And in the one case, many served as priests because death prevented any one of them continuing in office, [24]while in the other because he remains on duty through the ages, the priestly office has become intransmissable, [25]which is why indeed he is able to save completely those who approach God through him, ever living to make intercession on their behalf.[d] [26]For such an archpriest was just what we needed: pious, inno-

---

z. O'Neill admits the Teacher of Righteousness, as a sectarian priest, must have been of Levitical descent. He therefore tries to harmonize this supposition with the present passage by positing that the teacher might have been from Judah on his mother's side and Levi on his father's side ("Jesus in Hebrews," *Journal of Higher Criticism* 6 [Spring 1999]: 78). This seems unnecessary. As Eisenman reminds us, a radical sectarian priest might well have claimed authenticity based only on Phineas-like zeal (Num. 25:1-13), the Levites having "ordained (them)- selves" on the day they cut down the apostates of the Golden Calf (Exod. 32:25-29). This might well have been the case with the Teacher of Righteousness, whoever he was.

a. Pss. 110:4

b. Ibid.

c. There is a similar statement in 8:6 that leaves the mediator unnamed, and it seems to be an extraneous gloss in this sentence.

d. Jeremiah and the martyred archpriest Onias III were similarly believed to stand before the throne of God to intercede on Israel's behalf (2 Macc. 15:12-16). But this is strange logic: far from making the death of the anointed a complete and sufficient sacrificial work, as Paul says of Jesus, we are told that "complete salva-

cent of evil, undefiled, strictly separated from sinners,[e] and becoming taller than the heavens,[f] [27]without the need, as the Levitical archpriests have, to daily offer up sacrifices first for their own sins, then for those of the people; for this he did once and for all when he offered up himself. [28]For the Torah appoints as archpriests human beings beset by weakness, but the command of the oath swearing,[g] after the Torah, appoints a son who has been forever perfected.

8

[1]To place what has been said under a heading, we have such an archpriest who sat down to the right of the throne of the Greatness in the skies, [2]a minister of the holy things and of the true tabernacle which the Lord erected, not mortal man. [3]For every archpriest is appointed to offer both gifts and sacrifices, which is why it is necessary for this priest, too, to have something to offer. [4]If, therefore, he were on earth, he would not even be a priest since on earth you find the ones offering gifts in accordance with the Torah.[h] [5]They serve a token and a shadow of the heavenly realities, as Moses was warned as he was about to complete the tabernacle. For he says, "See that you make everything on the pattern shown you in the mountain."[i] [6]But now he has obtained a more excellent ministry as indeed the mediator of a better covenant which has been put into effect on the basis of better promises.[j] [7]For if that first covenant had been faultless, no one would have looked for an opportunity to replace it. [8]But finding fault with them, he says, "'Behold, the days are coming,' says Adonai, 'when I will promulgate a new covenant with the household of Israel and with the household of Judah, [9]not like the covenant I made with their fa-

---

tion" is carried on into the indefinite future by virtue of the fact that it will be forever mediated on our behalf by an undying mediator, as if the mortal Levites could only have begun their work when time came for them to die and their replacements started over.

e. This does not sound much like the Jesus of the gospels, who relished the company of tax collectors and sinners.

f. In the Gospel of Peter, the resurrected Christ, like the angels bearing him up, is a giant taller than the heavens. In 3 Enoch, the glorified Enoch assumes the vast proportions of world-dwarfing angels; cf. Preaching of John 90.

g. Pss. 110:4

h. As per Earl Doherty, *The Jesus Puzzle* (Ottawa: Canadian Humanist Press, 1999), 310-12, mustn't this mean the Savior did his saving work in heaven, not on earth?

i. Exod. 25:40

j. 2 Cor. 3

thers on the day I took their hand to lead them out of the land of Egypt,
because they did not persevere in my covenant and I lost interest in them,'
says Adonai. 10'Because this is the covenant which I will negotiate with Israel after those days,' says Adonai, 'implanting my laws directly into their
mind, and I will engrave them on their hearts, and I will be a God to them
and they shall be a people to me. 11And never again will each man teach
his fellow citizen, nor each man his brother, saying, "Know the Lord!"
because all will know me, from their little ones to their great ones.
12Because I will be merciful to their unrighteousness and I will never
again remember their sins.'"[k] 13In saying "new," he has rendered the first
obsolete, and that which is obsolete and superannuated is on the point of
vanishing altogether.

9

1So then, the first had ordinances stipulating the details of worship
and the earthly holy place. 2For a tabernacle was set up, the first, which
contained both the lamp stand and table and the display of the loaves, all
this being denominated the Holy Place, 3and beyond the veil a second tabernacle called the Holy of Holies 4containing a golden altar and the Ark
of the Covenant, plated all over with gold. In it were a golden pot containing the manna and the budded rod of Aaron and the tablets of the
covenant. 5And atop it mirror-bright Cherubim enveloped the mercy
seat. Concerning these things, we have not the time to treat in any detail.
6Once these items were prepared thusly, on the one hand the priests at all
times go into the first tabernacle, carrying out their duties, 7while on the
other, into the second the archpriest goes alone, once a year, and not
without blood, which he offers for himself and for the inadvertent lapses
of the people, 8the Holy Spirit thus showing the way into the Holy of
Holies had not yet been manifested while the first tabernacle was still
standing. 9This was a parable for the present time, according to which
both gifts and sacrifices are being offered that are not able to perfect the
one serving in respect to conscience 10since they pertained merely to
foods and drinks and various baptisms, all fleshly ordinances imposed
until a time of amendment.

11But once the anointed appeared, an archpriest of the good things
that have dawned, he came through the greater and more perfect tabernacle not made by hand, that is, not of this creation, 12nor by means of the
blood of goats and calves; but by means of his own blood, he entered

k. Jer. 31:31-34

once and for all into the Holy of Holies, having found permanent redemption. [13]For if the blood of bulls and of goats and the sprinkling of a heifer's ashes sanctify and purify the flesh of those who have been polluted, [14]by how much more will the sacrifice of the anointed, who through the spirit of the aions offered himself unblemished to God, cleanse our conscience from moribund deeds for the service of the true God![l] [15]And therefore, he is the mediator of a new covenant, so that his death having occurred for the redemption of transgressions during the first covenant, the ones having been called may receive the promise of the inheritance of the ages. [16]For a testament to be executed, the one who drew up the testament must perforce already have died. [17]For a testament is secure only once the death has occurred; it can never be binding as long as the testator lives since he can still change it if he so chooses. [18]This is why not even the first testament was ratified without blood. [19]For once Moses had finished reciting all the commandments from the Torah to all the people, dipping scarlet wool and hyssop in the blood of the calves and of the goats and in water, he sprinkled both the scroll and all the people, [20]declaring, "This is the blood of the covenant which God has imposed on you!" [21]He likewise sprinkled both the tabernacle and all the liturgical vessels. [22]And according to the Torah, virtually everything is purified by blood, and without bloodshed, remission is impossible. [23]Therefore, it was necessary on the one hand for the tokens of the heavenly realities to be purified by these sacrifices, while the heavenly realities themselves had to be purified by better sacrifices than these. [24]For the anointed did not enter the Holy of Holies made by hands, the counterpart of the real one, but into the very heaven in order to appear now on our behalf in the presence of God;[m] [25]not, however, in order that he might offer himself repeatedly, just as the archpriest enters the Holy of Holies annually with the blood of others, [26]since that would require him to have suffered regularly

---

l. Eisenman identifies the Teacher of Righteousness as James the Just and the Wicked Priest as Ananus who led the attack upon him. James would have been apprehended entering the Holy of Holies, acting as archpriest on behalf of his sect on the Day of Atonement, celebrated according to a heterodox calendar. The establishment priesthood would have considered James a blasphemer, hence his execution. Suppose O'Neill is correct in seeing the Teacher of Righteousness as the anointed one in Hebrews but Eisenman is right in making James the Teacher of Righteousness: this would make striking new sense of the apparent death of the anointed *offering his own blood* in the temple on the Day of Atonement.

m. If the anointed was James, is there any evidence anyone believed James had ascended to heaven? In fact, we know there was some sort of Jewish-Christian text, now lost, called *The Ascents of James*.

since the earth was set on its foundation stone. But now he has been manifested a single time at the consummation of the ages to abolish sin through his sacrifice. 27And since it is assigned to mortals to die once and then to face the judgment, 28so also the anointed, once having been offered to carry away the sins of many, will appear a second time without sin to those awaiting him for salvation.

10

1For the Torah, merely adumbrating the good things that were on the way, not itself being the image of those realities, could never perfect the suppliants by means of the same sacrifices monotonously offered year after year. 2After all, would they not have been suspended if the worshippers, once purified, had no lingering conscience of sin? 3All they are is an annual reminder of sins. 4And no wonder! It is absurd to suppose bull and goat blood could take away sins. 5Which is why, on the point of entering the cosmos, he says, "'Sacrifice and offering you did not desire, but you prepared a body for me. 6Holocausts and sin offerings never pleased you.' 7Then I said, 'Behold, my mission is to do your will, O God, as is written for me in the colophon of the scroll.'"[n] 8Beyond saying that "sacrifices and offerings and holocausts and sin offerings you did not want, nor did they please you," all of which however are offered in accordance with the Torah, 9he goes on to say, "Behold, my mission is to do your will." He removes the first to make room for the second. 10By that "will," we have been sanctified once and for all by the offering of the body *of Jesus Christ.*[o] 11And while, on the one hand, every priest goes through his daily routine ministering and repeatedly offering the same old sacrifices which can never take away sins, 12on the other hand, this priest, having offered one sacrifice for sins in perpetuity, sat down to the right of God, 13henceforth awaiting the day his enemies shall be placed under his heel. 14For by one offering, he has permanently perfected those who are being sanctified. 15And indeed, the Holy Spirit testifies to us; for after the aforesaid, 16"This is the covenant I will sign with them after those days," Adonai says: "Putting my laws in their hearts, I will also engrave them on their mind, 17and their sins and their iniquities I will by no means continue to recall."[p] 18Now where there is forgiveness of these, any offering for sins is superfluous.

---

n. Pss. 40:6-8, LXX.

o. One papyrus fragment (p^{46}) has "Jesus Christ" incorrectly in the nominative case, a typical glossing error, implying the name has been added to the text.

p. Jer. 31:33-34

[19]Having therefore confidence, brothers, to enter the Holy of Holies by the blood *of Jesus*[q] [20]which he dedicated for us as a fresh and living way through the veil, namely the veil of his flesh, [21]and having a great priest set over the household of God, [22]let us come near with a sincere heart in the complete assurance which faith provides; and having had our hearts sprinkled from a guilty conscience and having the body bathed in clean water,[r] [23]let us hold tight our profession of hope without budging an inch because the one who made the promise is faithful. [24]And let us think of ways to challenge each other to love and good deeds, [25]not absenting ourselves from the common assemblies, as some seem to have made a habit of doing, but publicly exhorting—and all the more as you see the day coming ever closer. [26]For should we sin deliberately after we have received full knowledge of the truth, there is no remaining sacrifice for sins, [27]nothing but a frightful prospect of judgment and raging fire about to devour the adversaries of God. [28]Anyone who defied the Torah of Moses died without mercy on the testimony of two or three witnesses;[s] [29]of how much worse punishment do you think one will be judged worthy who has trampled underfoot the garment of the likeness of the son of God[t] and spurned as profane the very blood of the covenant by which he was sanctified and brazenly insulted the Spirit of mercy? [30]For we are dealing with him who once said, "Vengeance is mine; I will repay!"[u] and again, "Adonai will judge his people."[v] [31]What a frightful thing to fall into the clutches of the true God!

[32]But think back to the early days in which, newly enlightened, you endured a great contest of sufferings, [33]on the one hand reduced to a laughingstock inviting both insults and afflictions, on the other becoming partners with those so treated. [34]For indeed, you suffered imprisonment

q. The Latin Vulgate and various minuscule manuscripts (294, 1827, 2400) read "of the Christ," probably original since Christian scribes would be less likely to have omitted the holy name of Jesus.

r. This reference to repeated ablutions again brings to mind the Dead Sea Scrolls.

s. Deut. 17:2-6

t. The picture is that of a reversal of the baptismal rite, in which one literally stripped off an old garment symbolizing the unregenerate life and donned a new linen robe symbolizing the new self and the implicit resurrection body. See Jonathan Z. Smith, "The Garments of Shame," in his *Map Is Not Territory: Studies in the History of Religions* (1978; Chicago: University of Chicago Press, 1993), 1-23.

u. Deut. 32:35a

v. Deut. 32:36a, where, however, it says, "Yahve will *vindicate* his people."

together and you cheerfully accepted the seizure of your possessions, knowing you have a better possession remaining to you. 35So do not throw away your confidence now. It has considerable recompense! 36For you just need endurance in order that, having fulfilled the will of God, you may obtain what is promised. 37For it will be only a little while before the Coming One will arrive and delay no more. 38"But my righteous one shall live off his faith, and if he flinches, I am seriously dissatisfied with him."[w] 39But we do not belong to those who shrink back and are destroyed, but to those with faith to win their souls.

11

1Faith is the underlying reality of things hoped for, the proof of things unseen. 2For by it the ancients earned their fame. 3It is by faith that we understand the planets were arranged by the command of God, with the result that what is seen is not derived from what we see now.[x] 4By virtue of his faith, Abel offered a sacrifice much superior to Cain's, through which he won the reputation of righteousness as God approved his offerings. And by faith, being dead, he still speaks.[y] 5By faith, Enoch was taken up so as not to experience death, and he was never found because God took him up.[z] 6For before he was taken up, he won the reputation of being well pleasing to God, and without faith it is impossible to be well pleasing to God. For anyone who seeks God is obliged to believe first that he exists and second that he always rewards those who seek him diligently. 7By faith, having been warned by God about things no one had yet seen, Noah, a devout man, prepared an ark for the rescue of his household, and through it he condemned the world and became heir to the salvation that comes by faith.[a]

8By faith, Abraham, when summoned to go forth to a place which he would receive as an inheritance, obeyed and set out, unaware of his eventual destination.[b] 9By faith, he resided as a foreigner in a land promised him, living in a succession of tents with Isaac and Jacob, co-heirs of the same promise; 10for he anticipated the city with foundations,[c] whose ar-

w. Hab. 2:3-4

x. 2 Macc. 7:28

y. Gen. 4:3-10

z. Gen. 5:21-24

a. Gen. 6-9

b. Gen. 12:1-8

c. A "city with foundations" is meant to contrast with the foundationless bedouin tents mentioned in the previous verse.

chitect and builder is God. [11]By faith also, Sarah herself received the ability to conceive from sperm long after menopause since she considered the one who promised to be faithful.[d] [12]For this reason, there stemmed from one man, and him practically dead, offspring as numerous as the stars in the sky and as innumerable as the sand on the seashore.[e] [13]All of these died walking the path of faith, not having won what was promised, though seeing and greeting it from a great distance and considering themselves strangers and resident aliens in the land. [14]For those who speak of themselves that way make it obvious that they are still seeking a homeland. [15]Had they longed for the place they came from, they certainly had the opportunity to return there, [16]but now they aspire to a better place, a heavenly one. For this reason, God is not ashamed to be called their God. He prepared a city for them.

[17]By faith, Abraham, being tested, offered up Isaac,[f] and the one who accepted the promises was offering up his only-begotten. [18]To him it had been said, "Your line shall descend through Isaac."[g] [19]So he reasoned that God was capable even of raising the dead if it came to that, which is, so to speak, exactly what happened.[h] [20]It was also by faith that Isaac blessed Jacob and Esau concerning future matters.[i] [21]By faith, the dying Jacob blessed each of the sons of Joseph and worshipped, propped on the head of his staff.[j] [22]By faith, the dying Joseph contemplated the exodus of the sons of Israel and gave orders concerning the deposition of his bones.[k]

[23]By faith, Moses's parents hid their newborn son for three months because they saw what a fine child he was and they dared defy the decree of the king.[l] [24]By faith, Moses, once he had attained prominence, disdained being called the son of Pharaoh's daughter,[m] [25]choosing instead

---

d. Gen. 17:19; 18:11-14; 21:2

e. Gen. 15:5-6; 22:17; 32:12

f. Gen. 22:1-10

g. Gen. 21:12

h. Our author may be thinking of alternative versions of the sacrifice of Isaac, in which the lad was actually killed, cremated, and rose again to life, reflecting ancient Baal legends. See Shalom Spiegel, *The Last Trial: On the Legends and Lore of the Command to Abraham to Offer Isaac as a Sacrifice,* trans. Judah Goldin (Woodstock, VT: Jewish Lights, 1993), 40-44, 112-18.

i. Gen. 27:27-29, 39-40

j. Gen. 48:31, 47, LXX

k. Gen. 50:24-25

l. Exod. 2:2; 1:22

m. Exod. 2:10

to be ill-treated along with the people of God rather than enjoy sin for a time, [26]considering the reproach of the anointed[n] of greater value than the treasures of Egypt, for he could see his reward off in the distance. [27]By faith, he left Egypt, not because he feared the anger of the king,[o] but he endured as if he could see before him the Unseen One. [28]By faith, he observed the Passover and the sprinkling of blood to protect the firstborn from the one who would have destroyed them.[p] [29]By faith, they passed through the Red Sea as over dry land, though the Egyptians were swallowed up when they took the same risk.[q]

[30]By the faith of Joshua, the walls of Jericho collapsed, having been circled for seven days.[r] [31]By faith, Rahab the prostitute did not perish along with the resisters, having given protection to the spies.[s] [32]And what shall I add? Time will fail me if I begin the stories of Gideon,[t] Barak,[u] Samson,[v] Jephthah,[w] David, too,[x] and Samuel[y] and the prophets, [33]who by faith brought down kingdoms,[z] brought justice,[a] obtained what was promised,[b] shut the mouths of lions,[c] [34]quenched the power of fire,[d] es-

---

n. Here the reference is to Moses himself as the anointed deliverer of Israel.

o. Despite Exod. 2:14-15!

p. Exod. 12:21-30

q. Exod. 14:21-31

r. Josh. 6:12-21

s. Josh. 2:1-21; 6:22-25

t. By faith, Gideon dismissed 31,700 men at the command of God and defeated Midian with only 300 (Judg. 6-8).

u. By faith, Barak heeded the call of Deborah and led Naphtali and Zebulun to destroy all the army of Jabin, king of Hazor, with his 900 chariots of iron (Judg. 4-5).

v. By faith, Samson, when he had been blinded and lost his strength due to the shearing of his locks, prayed to God to avenge him on his tormentors, so that he killed more Philistines in his death than in his life (Judg. 16:28).

w. By faith, Jephthah vowed to give as a burnt offering to the Lord the first one he should meet upon his return if God gave him victory over the Ammonites, and he offered up his daughter (Judg. 11:30-40).

x. By faith, David declined the battle armor of Saul and went out to face Goliath with only a sling and some stones, and with these God gave him victory over the enemy of Israel (1 Sam. 17).

y. By faith, Samuel, when a youth, slept beside the Ark of God and four times heeded the call of God, even when Eli told him he only dreamed, and God established him as both prophet and judge (1 Sam. 3:10-21).

z. Elisha in 2 Kings 9; Jer. 1:10.

a. Elijah in 1 Kings 21:15-24.

b. Elisha in 2 Kings 2:9-14.

caped the mouth of the sword, received strength when weak,[e] became
strong in war,[f] forced foreign armies to surrender, 35 and the women who
received their dead back by resurrection;[g] but others were beaten to
death, refusing to accept deliverance through compromise in order that
they might win a superior deliverance, resurrection.[h] 36 Others were
tested by mockings and scourgings, still more by chains and prison.
37 They were stoned, they were put to the test, they were sawed to pieces,[i]
they died murdered by the sword, they walked about dressed in sheep-
skins and goatskins, being in want, afflicted, ill-treated, 38 heroes of
whom the world was unworthy, wandering over deserts and mountains
and caves and holes in the ground.[j] 39 And all these, though they won
fame through their faith, still did not win what was promised them! God
had foreseen something better concerning us and forestalled them so they
should not be perfected without us.

12

1 Thus, since we are surrounded by such a huge cloud of witnesses
like a stadium audience, let us shed every added weight and the sin that
trips us up and with stamina run the race that stretches before us,
2 looking to the first to run and finish it, *Jesus,*[k] who for the sake of the joy
set before him endured a cross, utterly indifferent to the disgrace of it,
and as a result took his seat at the right of the very throne of God. 3 Think
about one who withstood such opposition to himself by sinners so your
wills do not flag. 4 In your own struggle against sin, you have not yet resisted to the point of bloodshed 5 and you seem to have forgotten the exhortation that addresses you as sons: "My son, do not rebel against the
discipline of Adonai, nor grow discouraged when he reproves you. 6 For
Adonai disciplines every one he loves and he flogs every son he receives."[l]
7 So endure discipline, for God is dealing with you as sons. Show me a son

---

c. Dan. 6:21

d. Shadrach, Meschach, and Abed-Nego in Dan. 3:20-27.

e. Samson in Judg. 16:28.

f. Gideon in Judg. 7.

g. 1 Kings 17:17-24; 2 Kings 4:11-37

h. The seven brothers in 2 Macc. 7; 4 Macc. 1:7-10; chaps. 8-17.

i. Isaiah in *Ascension of Isaiah* 5:1.

j. Faithful Jews and Maccabean resistance fighters in 2 Macc. 5:27; 6:11.

k. The Latin S* omits "Jesus," while a Latin Pseudo-Augustan work has *dominus* instead of "Jesus," reflecting the use of a manuscript lacking the name.

l. Prov. 3:11-12

who is never disciplined by his father! [8]But if you are without discipline, which all sons experience, then you must be a bastard, not a son. [9]After all, we had physical fathers who set us straight and we respected them, didn't we? How much more should we be willing to submit ourselves to the Father of Spirits[m] and live? [10]To be sure, they disciplined us for a short time as they thought best, but he disciplines us for our advantage so we may share in his holiness. [11]No discipline seems pleasant at the moment, rather galling, but later it pays back the peaceable fruit of righteousness to those who are willing to learn from it.

[12]Therefore, straighten out your weary hands and stiffened knees! [13]Make straight tracks for your feet so you don't turn your weak ankle but may cure it instead. [14]Seek peace with everyone and sanctification, without which no one will see the Lord. [15]Be on guard that none of you lapses from the favor of God and that no buried root of bitterness[n] grows up among you and blossoms into an apple of discord, defiling all who eat of it. [16]Beware of any immoral or irreligious man like Esau, who for the sake of one single meal gave up his rights as the firstborn.[o] [17]Remember how afterward, when he wanted to inherit the blessing, it was too late; he was granted no second chance, though he begged for it tearfully.[p]

[18]For you have not drawn near to a tangible mountain belching fire, to darkness and profound gloom, to a cyclone, [19]or to the trumpet blast and a disembodied voice speaking words whose hearers pled that no more be said to them, [20]for they could not bear the command, "If so much as an animal touches the mountain, it shall be stoned."[q] [21]And so frightful was the apparition that Moses himself exclaimed, "I shudder with terror!" [22]But you have drawn near to Mount Zion and to the city of the true God, to a heavenly Jerusalem and myriads of angels, [23]to an assembly and a congregation of the firstborn enrolled in heaven, and to God the universal judge, to spirits of the righteous now finally made perfect,[r] [24]to *Jesus,*[s] the mediator of a new covenant, and to sprinkled blood

m. Cf. "Lord of Spirits" throughout 1 Enoch (47:1-4; 48:2-10; 49:2; 50:2-5; 51:3; etc.).

n. The bitter Tree of Zakkum that grows in hell, whose terrible fruit the damned will eat (Koran 17:60; 37:62ff; 44:43ff; 56:52-53).

o. Gen. 25:29-34

p. Gen. 27:38

q. Exod. 19:12-13

r. These would be the individuals listed in chapter 11.

s. The Latin Codex Augiensis has *deum* instead of Jesus, while papyrus fragment p^{46} has "Jesus Christ" in the nominative, signaling a gloss.

bespeaking better things than Abel's did. [25]See that you do not ignore the
one who speaks. For if those who rebuffed the one who warned them on
earth did not escape, what chance do we have if we ignore the voice
warning us from heaven? [26]His voice then shook the earth, but now he
has promised, saying, "This time, I shall shake not just the earth, but the
sky as well!"[t] [27]Now the phrase "this time" denotes the removal of the
shaken things, that is, created things, in order that the things not being
shaken may remain. [28]For this reason, since we are to receive an unshakable kingdom, let us be gracious and in this manner serve God in a way
well-pleasing to him, with devotion and awe; [29]for indeed, our God is a
devouring fire!

13

[1]Let brotherly love not run short; [2]do not forget to show hospitality,
for by showing hospitality some have unwittingly entertained angels.[u]
[3]Remember the prisoners as if you were chained to them, those ill-
treated as if you were in their body. [4]Let your marriages be such as all
will honor and keep the bed undefiled, for God will judge the immoral[v]
and adulterers. [5]Keep your way of life free from the love of money, being
satisfied with what you have. For he has said, "I will never leave your
side and nothing will make me abandon you."[w] [6]Thus being encouraged,
let us reply, "Adonai is my helper, I will not fear. What can mere mortals
do to me?"[x]

[7]Remember your hegemons who spoke God's message to you. Look-
ing at the result of their conduct, imitate their faith. [8]*Jesus Christ*[y] is the
same yesterday and today and throughout the ages. [9]Do not be carried
away by various strange teachings. For it is good for the heart to be fortified by God's favor, not by foods, which did no good even for those who
walk that path. [10]We have an altar from which those serving the tabernacle lack the right to eat. [11]For whatever animal whose blood is brought
into the Holy of Holies by the archpriest as an offering for sin, their bod-

t. Hag. 2:6

u. Gen. 18-19; Matt. 25:31-46

v. This might well refer to marriages not allowed by the Torah, e.g., between cousins.

w. Deut. 31:6, 8

x. Pss. 118:6

y. Two Latin manuscripts and Ambrose have *iesu christi*, while Ambrose's citations of the verse elsewhere have either *christus* or *iesus*, implying repeated glossing.

ies are incinerated outside the camp. [12]This is why *Jesus,*[z] in order that he might sanctify the people through his own blood, suffered outside the camp.[a] [13]So let us go out to him, outside the camp, bearing his reproach. [14]For we have no permanent city here, but seek the one that is coming. [15]Invoking him, therefore, let us always offer up a sacrifice of praise to God, the appropriate fruit of lips confessing allegiance to his name. [16]But neither forget about doing good and sharing, for these sacrifices are much appreciated by God. [17]Obey your hegemons and submit to them, for they watch over your souls as those who must one day give account of their performance.

The Christian epilogue

[18]Pray for us. We believe our conscience is clear, wishing to behave well in all circumstances. [19]And I beg you to pray much more for us so I may be restored to you all the sooner. [20]Now may the God of peace, the one who led up out of the dead the great shepherd of the sheep[b] covered in the blood of a perpetual covenant, *our Lord Jesus,*[c] [21]improve your skill in every good deed for carrying out his will, bringing to birth in us that which satisfies him *through Jesus-Christ,*[d] to whom be worship throughout ages multiplied by ages! Amen.

[22]And I beg you, brothers, put up with this message of encouragement, for indeed I have written you only briefly. [23]Be advised that our brother Timothy has been released. If I come to see you sooner, I shall come with him. [24]Greet all your hegemons and all the saints. Those who hail from Italy greet you. May God's favor be with all of you.

---

z. One minuscule manuscript and a number of patristic citations read "Christ" instead of "Jesus." Others have *dominus* instead.

a. This is the reading of several textual witnesses, including Papyrus 46 (p^{46}), uncial fragment P 104, and the Bohairic Coptic manuscript (cop^{bo}).

b. The imagery is of Orpheus, who led the dead Eurydice up from the netherworld and, like Lot, lost her by looking back at her. Orpheus was a shepherd, eventually torn apart by crazed Dionysiac maenads. O'Neill divides this section off, noting that without it there is no reference to the resurrection of the anointed, which makes sense if the anointed is the Teacher of Righteousness rather than Jesus. The Teacher of Righteousness was not said to have risen from the dead.

c. Cassiodorus has "Lord Christ."

d. Papyrus 46 inserts αυτο before ποιων; some witnesses (Sinaiticus; uncial fragments A, C*, 0151; minuscule 33*) insert αυτω, while others (minuscules 451, 1912, 2491; Old Latin d) have αυτος. This all implies the use of a text with no prior name.

46.

Melchizedek

The Book of Melchizedek is an apocalypse, meaning an "unveiling," or revelation, like the Greek title of the last book of the New Testament, "The Apocalypse" (a title that still appears in some Bibles). Such books contain accounts of heavenly revelations given to a community in a time of stress or to some chosen person to convey an advantage in achieving salvation. It seems highly unlikely that these are actual records of visions or dreams since they conform to a literary structure with conventions the writer knows his readers will expect, like modern readers expecting certain norms from writers of detective stories or romance novels.

In the Book of Revelation, the prophet John reports visions for the sake of his readers in the seven churches of Asia Minor, whereas in the current book it is the mysterious Old Testament figure Melchizedek who receives the revelations. Melchizedek's job is to entrust these secrets to the Sethian Gnostic sect, whose members, we may presume, were as eager to read this book as were those for whom John wrote his book. It would have been considered holy scripture in the Sethian religion just as the Book of Revelation was to the Christian religion. Jesus sends an angel to speak for him in Revelation, and in Melchizedek's apocalypse, it is an angel named Gamaliel who delivers the message.

All of these are familiar biblical names. Melchizedek was an ancient priest-king of Salem, which is to say the city of Jerusalem before it was renamed by David. In Genesis 14, Melchizedek welcomes Abraham as the latter returns home from a victorious battle. Abraham offers Melchizedek a tenth of his spoils of war, while Melchiz-

edek offers Abraham a sacramental meal of bread and wine. Melchizedek must therefore have been a man of some importance, yet he disappears from the story just as suddenly as he appeared. He is mentioned again in Psalm 110 as the founder of the priesthood in Jerusalem to which the kings of Judah were ordained. Any king in this line is said to be a son of Shahar, goddess of the dawn, suggesting a possible divine origin for Melchizedek, as well, since it was his priesthood the kings entered. Jews were tantalized by such possibilities and began spinning all sorts of theories, some exalting Melchizedek to angelic or divine status. The Epistle to the Hebrews compares him to the immortal Son of God, without beginning of life or end of days. This is reminiscent of the legends and speculations that circulated about the pre-Flood patriarch Enoch, who was said to have risen into heaven without dying, learned the heavenly secrets, related them to his family or disciples back on earth, and acquired a throne alongside the throne of God (2 Enoch 11:35-38). Melchizedek was similarly enshrouded in legend. Some traditions claimed he and Enoch were in fact the same person. For this reason, Melchizedek was a good name for a mystical sect to appropriate for its scriptures. Present-day channelers sometimes claim to be conveying messages from Melchizedek or Seth, which is reminiscent of the Seth-Melchizedek link in our document.

Gamaliel, on the other hand, does not seem to have anything to do with the member of the Sanhedrin of Acts 5:33-40, where he persuades the council not to execute the apostles in case they are true spokesmen of God. This was supposed to be Gamaliel the Great, the famous rabbi of the same period. Either way, what link could there be between this figure and the angel in the Melchizedek apocalypse? Gamaliel was a common enough name. One need only think of the popularity today of the name Jamal, which is the Arabic form, to understand that readers at the time would not have necessarily thought of Rabban Gamaliel when they encountered the name in the Book of Melchizedek.

The book consists of three major parts: (1) a revelation given to Melchizedek, which ends in warning readers not to divulge the secrets to anyone but Sethians in good standing; (2) a section in which Melchizedek undergoes several rituals, including baptism, and offers

praises to the heavenly world, all of which is very likely intended as a pattern to be imitated in the rituals of the Sethians; and (3) more revelations to Melchizedek, concluding with another warning to guard the heavenly mysteries from the unworthy.

The Book of Melchizedek, in the form we have it, is a Gnostic text, more specifically one with a Sethian character, as is evident in the term "children of Seth," referring to the Gnostic elect. The text is peppered with divine names that are trademarks of the Sethian myth. At the same time, other typical features of Gnostic mythology such as the fall of Sophia and, most notably, the Creator-Demiurge do not appear in Melchizedek. Mention of archons and other wicked angelic figures may not be relevant since they are present generally in Jewish apocalyptic thought. One of the most striking features is the rejection of the super-spiritual view that Jesus was an otherworldly phantom. Here the "fleshly" character of the Savior is emphasized: he is begotten "in the flesh," is circumcised, eats and drinks—something ghosts and spirits cannot fake—and truly suffers and is raised from the dead. Such a strong incarnational statement is unparalleled in Gnostic literature. By far, most Gnostics understood the Savior to be a pure spirit, merely projecting a mirage of human form. Therefore, even though there is no doubt that Melchizedek, as we now read it, is a Sethian Gnostic document, it may not originally have been Gnostic; perhaps some later Sethian got hold of it and decided that with a little rewriting here and there it would make a valuable addition to the sect's library. But he neglected to purge the incarnationism.

Neither should we assume that all this interest in Melchizedek grew out of the early Christian reading of Hebrews 7:3. Melchizedek was a figure of considerable fascination, speculation, and even expectation prior to Hebrews. In one of the Dead Sea Scrolls, he is identified with the archangel Michael and is called Elohim, "God," as Seth is in some ancient traditions. It seems the Melchizedekians must have been a kindred sect to the Sethians and perhaps originated out of the same seedbed of Palestinian baptizing sectarianism as the Mandeans, Nazoreans, Simonians, and Dositheans. We can imagine that as time went on and their numbers dwindled, they may have sought to merge with a cousin sect. One way to do this would have been to identify Jesus-

Christ with Melchizedek, just as Genesis 14 seals the merging of worshippers of the hitherto distinct gods Yahve and El Elyon.

We know there were Christians who believed Jesus was Melchizedek. According to Epiphanius, there was a sect in Egypt that identified the two and derived from a second-century founder named Theodotus. Interestingly enough, Theodotus and his followers stressed the genuine humanity of Jesus, just as the book of Melchizedek does. Theodotus's Melchizedekians were not Gnostics, whereas the version of Melchizedek we have here definitely is—all the more reason to suspect the text is a rewrite of an originally non-Gnostic Melchizedekian apocalypse. It is worth considering whether such an Urtext might have been rewritten when a splinter group, forced out of Theodotus's sect, found it hard going it alone and merged with the stronger Gnostic group, from which the text passed into general circulation.

The copy of Melchizedek included in Nag Hammadi Codex IX is the only surviving manuscript of the text, and alas, it is in sorry shape. Only 19 out of the original 745 lines of the Coptic text are complete; another 467 lines are partially preserved, but this means we have less than half of the original text. In such condition, readers are hindered in being able to understand the effect this scriptural document would have had on its ancient readers. They would not have experienced it as a puzzle to be solved or a pile of fragments to be reconstructed. They would have sat down to read and be edified by a continuous text. I have therefore found it worthwhile to try to reconnect the dots, adding what was surely the sort of thing that would have filled the missing spaces. Of course, I have set off my additions by brackets and placed conventional restorations in italics. I have discarded the conventional divisions of page and line numbers for the more natural-seeming chapter-and-verse system.

The Nag Hammadi holograph was written in the Sahidic dialect during the second half of the fourth century (350-400 CE) somewhere in Upper Egypt. The original composition was probably written in Greek in about the third century. If it was based on an earlier non-Gnostic Melchizedek book, the latter could have been written in the century prior to that. All were probably composed in Egypt since Egyptian Christianity often identified Jesus Christ with Melchizedek.

1

[1]Jesus-Christ, the Son *of God,* [sent his angel] from [the pleroma of light unto me, Melchizedek, saying, "I have come from among the] aions *speaking* for each aion, that I might disclose the nature of the aion, what it is, [2]and that I might don friendship and goodness as a garment, O brother [spirit, as I descend secretly among them and pass unnoticed, taking on the appearance of each in every sphere of their habitation, even as Jesus-Christ himself, [3]he who in the last days will at last accomplish] their doom, [and that by subterfuge]. [4]And he will make known to them the truth [they fear, which they did not know, in the form of a mystery which shall nonetheless be known by the wise]: proverbs [and dark sayings] and figures of speech. [5]And at first in parables *and riddles,* [he will speak, and the men of Seth will understand, and thus will he] proclaim them. [6]Death will *shudder* with terror and will grow wroth, not solely he, but indeed his *brother* cosmocrators and archons with him! [7]And likewise the principalities and authorities, the goddesses and the gods, together with the archangels. [8]And in the end, [they will come to know by the preaching of mortals what their heavenly wisdom failed to tell them. And] all of them, [archons,] cosmocrators, [principalities,] all their company, and yet again all the [angels] and all the [planetary spirits, will fear]. [9]They will say [much falsehood] concerning him and concerning [his coming. For they are like the strong man who knows he is in danger of being despoiled by one stronger].[10]And [in their blindness, they] will [despise the] hidden arcana of Jesus-Christ, [which led the sons of Seth to their kingless heritage, as revealed from] out of [the depth of] the All. [11]They will [put him to death by the Law, and because of] this, the lawyers will bury him speedily. They will call him 'impious,' 'lawless,' and 'impure.' [12]And *on* the *third* day, he *will rise from the* dead. [And he shall be seen and marveled at for eighteen months when he rejoins his] *holy disciples.* [13]*And* the Savior *will reveal* to them that higher *world* that imparts life to the *All.* [14]*But* those in the heavens spoke *many* words, together with those who dwell on the earth *and those* under the earth, [and there was much confusion as to which was the true revelation and voice of the Savior. And the voices foretold many things] *which* must happen in his name.

[15]"*Furthermore,* they will say concerning him, that he is unbegotten, though in fact he is begotten; that he does not even eat, though he does eat; that he does not drink, though he drinks; that he is uncircumcised, though he has been circumcised; [16]that he is disincarnate, though he has come in the flesh; that he came not to suffer, though he came for suffer-

ing; that he rose not from the dead, though he did rise from the dead. [17]*But* all the *tribes and* all *the nations* will speak *the truth,* who receive it from *you* yourself, O *Melchizedek,* Holy One, *archpriest,* the perfect hope *and* dispenser of the gifts of life. [18]*I am Gamaliel,* who was *sent* to [instruct and to strengthen] the congregation of the children of Seth, who are exalted above thousands of thousands, even myriads of myriads of the aions, [and to reveal the unutterable, even the] essence of the aions: [abaaiai ababa!] [19]O divine [vessel] of the [light, true] *nature* [of the aions]! O *mother* of the aions, *Barbelo,* O first-born of the aions, glorious Doxomedon[a] Domedon![b] [20]O glorious one, Jesus-Christ, O supreme commanders of the heavenly lights, you *Powers*: Armozel, Oroiael, Daveithe, Eleleth, and you, Light-Man! [21]Immortal aion Piger-Adamas, and you, good god of the blessed worlds, Mirocheirothetou,[c] I invoke you through Jesus-Christ, the Son of God!

[22]"This is he whom I proclaim, inasmuch as the One who truly exists has *appeared among those who* truly exist [in the semblance of one who] does not *exist,* Blessed Abel, *that you might be vouchsafed* the knowledge *of the truth,* [23][namely,] that he hails *from the* race of the archpriest, *which is* lifted up above *thousands of thousands* and *myriads* of myriads of the aions. [24]The opposing *spirits are* ignorant of him and likewise of their own destruction! Not only so, but I am come to *reveal* to you *the* truth that *lies concealed within* the *brethren.* [25]For he included himself *in the* living *sacrifice,* together with your *descendants.* He *presented* them as an *offering to the* All. [26]*For* you shall *not* offer up *cattle for sins* of unbelief *and for* the unwitting lapses *and all the* evil *deeds* which they *will yet* commit. [27][No, Elyon is pleased by contrition, not by butchered carcasses.] *Nor* do they ascend before *the* Father of the All. [28][Nor does] the faith [of the men of Cain suffice unto salvation, seeing it is but the invention of the elemental spirits who will not tread the way of the Father for themselves, nor will they suffer those whose souls turn like the vine to the light, though ignorant of the light. [29]For the faith of the nations is a set of snares and bonds which hold fast the souls who see not past the form of religion to its lack of power to save, so that a promised life brings only death again and again in this world of testings.]

[30]"[Vain is it] to receive *baptism* [here below] in waters [which are but the bile of the cosmocrators]. For *the waters* which are above [purify

a. "king of glory"

b. "lord of the house"

c. "one chosen by the divine hand of fate"

all those] who receive baptism. [31]But do you receive with the water *that baptism* which [appears from above] while he is coming [to offer] knowledge [and blessing and salvation to all those who meet him on the water and invoke the aions in their] *baptism* as they offer [petition and] repentance. [32][They shall likewise drink of the common cup of the common light essence. For that cup is the open mouth of the initiator who speaks the mysteries to awaken the light essence of the Sethians, the true heirs of Piger-Adamas. [33]And of such are none but the sons of Seth worthy, seeing all others are but the heirs of Cain, who seeing darkness call it light and know not the reality thereof. [34]Let him who awakens the knowledge within know well that he belongs upon a farther shore. Let him, by means of these faithful mysteries, commence the ascent of the soul to its origin and on the way] pray for the *spawn of the* archons and the *whole company of* angels, [35]together with *that* immortal seed that flowed *forth from the Father* of the All, [which is] *the* entire [race,] from [Doxamedon, the throne world,] *where he* engendered the *gods and the angels* and the men [of Seth] [36]out of the *seed* all of *the* various *natures,* both *the heavenly and* the earthly [and] *those* [lurking] under *the earth.*

[37]"[For all alike languish under the dreadful burden of the lie. As Adam and Eve in the flesh believed the archons had given them life and light, so had the archons believed the lie of Satan, that they were the very angels of El Elyon. [38]And in the same way did Satan exalt himself as God, in his dark ignorance believing it. Let him who ascends to his soul's home not neglect to petition on their behalf, that light may illumine every corner even of the material cosmos. [39]For though none but the tribe of Seth own it as their birthright, all others may be adopted by grace,] including the nature of the females, yes, [even] among those that are in the [side of the male,] as they were bound with them at first. [40]*But this first man* is *neither* the true Adam *nor* the true Eve. *For when they partook* of the Tree *of Knowledge,* they effortlessly trampled *the cherubim* and the seraphim *despite the flaming circumambient sword.* [41][The aions] saw and [wrested that] which was Adam's [from the covetous grasp of] *the* cosmocrators and [hurled] them out [of the garden] after they had brought forth the spawn of the archons and *their worldly creation,* these belonging to [the divine as to nature, but to the archons as to flesh. [42]And the fleshly counterparts of Adam and Eve lay inert upon the ground. And the true Adam and the true Eve took pity upon them and fed them with the fruit of the Tree of Knowledge, which was even their own light nature. [43]And their images awoke, but the Light-Adam and the Light-Eve were

gone, allowing the fleshly man and woman henceforth to discover for themselves whence had come their light and life. [44]But the archons returned and beheld the wakening forms and boasted themselves as the origin of the] light [within them]. [45]And the *males* and females, those who exist with [the great Seth, are] *concealed* from every nature, *and they will repudiate* the archons [who tricked Adam and accepted] from him [worship]. [46]For [the tribe of Seth] are worthy of [glory and are] *immortal* and *great,* worthy of [acclaim] and [worship] as due to gods and great sons of *men,* [as they seem, who will become the] *disciples* [of him who is in their] invisible *image* and [descends in divers forms] from the *light* that is holy. [47]For [he existed] from the *beginning* [as] a seed [of light].

[48]But I must be silent now, [O Melchizedek,] for that we *are the brothers who* came down from *the* living [light is evident]. [49]They will [seek vengeance upon the company of those of us who share the true knowledge] of Adam, [appearing again in flesh as] *Abel,* Enoch, *Noah,* [and Shem, which is to say] *you,* Melchizedek, *hierophant* of El *Elyon,* [together with] those who [have the form of] women [in the line of Seth. [50]For] these two who have been chosen will *at* no time, nor yet *in* any place, be convicted, at whatever point in history they have been begotten, whether *by* their enemies, by their friends, by strangers, nor by their *own* kin, neither by the *impious* nor by the pious. [51]*All of* the adversary natures will surely plot against them, whether *those that* are seen or those that *are* not *seen,* together with those *who dwell* in the heavens and the dwellers *on* the earth and those that are under the earth. [52]They will wage *war* [against them], every one. For the adversaries, whether in *the heavens or on the earth, or yet hidden beneath the earth*—[the hundred-handed and Gog—will fall. [53]But the children of Seth may neither falter nor fail, for they are the kingless generation]. [54]And as for these in the [earth], every*one* will [meet with ruin]. These will [be shattered] with every blow [on account of their] weaknesses. [55]These will be confined in other forms *and will* be punished. *As for these,* the Savior will take them *away, and* they will overcome everything, *not with* their mouth and words, but by means of the [mighty acts] that will be done for *them. He shall* bring death to naught.

[56]"*These things* which I was charged to reveal, you shall reveal them, too, *even as I have.* But what remains hidden, you are not to reveal *to* any[one] unless *it is revealed* to you to disclose it."

2

[1]And *at once I, Melchizedek,* rose up, and I began to pray to El Elyon

[in order] that I should *rejoice* in him while he *is acting* [on my behalf, even the] true [God; [2]and so] *I said,* "I am *glad* and I [rejoice, O possessor of heaven and earth, at your grace], nor will *I* cease *from this time forth and forever more,* O Father of the *All,* [3]*because* you [have had compassion toward me and] *you have sent the* angel of light, [even mighty Gamaliel,] from among your *aions* [in your own time] *in order to* reveal [the holy arcana]. [4]And when he appeared, he *caused* me *to be raised up* from [the tomb] of ignorance and from bearing fruit unto death to bearing fruit unto life. [5]For I have a mighty name: I am Melchizedek, hierophant of the highest *God.* I *know* that it is I who am *the veritable image of* the true archpriest *of* El Elyon, and [greatest in] this world. [6]For it is no small *thing that* God [was displeased with men] while he [endured their blood offerings]. [7]And what *the angels that dwell upon the* earth [delight in, for which they seek the worship of men], is the *sacrifice* of Abraham, whom death deceived. [8]When he *died,* he chained [others] to the carnal natures that are *leading them astray.* Yet he presented offerings of sheep and cows [and goats. [9]And] I, [too, once] gave them to *death and the angels* and the [hungry] demons, [maws agape, a living] offering [of blood]; [10][but] now I have presented myself to you as a sacrifice, together with those who are mine, to you yourself, O All-Father, and to your beloved, who have emanated from you, who are the holy and *living.* [11]And in obedience to the *perfect* laws, I shall utter my own name as I *now* receive baptism. [12]It shall be, both now and forever, a name renowned among the living holy *names* and now in the [baptismal] *waters,* as well. Amen.

[13]*Holy are you!* Holy are *you*! Holy are you, O *Father of all* who truly exist, as well as [of] those who do not exist, *Blessed Abel,* [precursor of Seth, and blessed] forever and ever. *Amen.*

[14]Holy are *you! Holy are you!* Holy are *you,* [Father Seth, who ever goes before your children] *forever and* ever. *Amen.*

[15]Holy are *you!* Holy are *you! Holy are you, Mother of the* aions, Barbelo, forever and ever. *Amen.*

[16]Holy are you! *Holy are you!* Holy are you, *first*-born of the aions, Doxomedon,[d] *forever* and ever. Amen.

[17]*Holy are you! Holy are you!* Holy are you, immortal aion Piger-Adamas,[e] *forever and ever.* Amen.

---

d. "king of glory"

e. "alien Adam"

[18]*Holy are you! Holy are you!* Holy are you, [dweller in the bosom of the Father,] *first* aion *Harmozel, for*ever and ever. *Amen.*

[19]Holy are you! *Holy are you! Holy are you,* commander, bright star *of the aions,* Oriael, for*ever and ever.* Amen.

[20]Holy are you! *Holy are you! Holy are you,* commander *of the aions,* Light-Man, *Daveithe,* forever *and ever. Amen.*

[21]Holy are you! *Holy are you! Holy are you, supreme commander Eleleth,* [bright star of] *the* aions, *forever and ever.* Amen.

[22][Holy are you! Holy are you! Holy are you, Gamaliel, treasure of God, dispenser of secrets to the sons of men, forever and ever. Amen.]

[23]*Holy are you!* Holy are *you!* Holy are you, good *god of* the *beneficent* words [unspeakable], Mirocheirothetou,[f] *for*ever and ever. *Amen.*

[24]*Holy are* you! *Holy are you! Holy are you,* supreme commander *of the* All, even Jesus-Christ, *forever and ever.* Amen. [I invoke you all!]

[25]Blessed [are they who hold fast this] confession, [who yet do not] confess him before those who now hate us, [26]for [then it becomes a stumbling block of] fear, and [not only of] fear [but of violence that shall] disturb [the ignorant,] surrounding *them* while they are in the place *which has a* great darkness *in it.* [27]*And* many will appear [together] there, [but their true images shall not] *appear.* [28]And [for the time being,] they were clothed with [flesh to suffer the insults of] all and [the persecution of their masters, the archons, who tempt their slaves to murder the illuminati and then require of them sacrifices to atone for it. [29]But blessed are the ones who know and by their knowledge are liable] to provoke disturbances. They gave [the pearls of] their words [to swine, even to those enslaved by Satan and by no means of the flock of Seth. [30] And so they were slain. But their spirits spoke to me from beneath the altar of Elyon.[31] They wept at their folly and for the sin of their murderers, and they said to me, "O great] *Melchizedek, priest* of El Elyon," [but] *they* spoke as though one, *their* mouths united in the All: [32]"Beware lest Satan lead astray your flock with his [carnal] worship *and* [erring] faith *and* [through] his prayers. [33]And [well he knows and cares for those] who *are his,* [the] first-[born of Satan, who dwell where he has his throne]. [34]Little they cared that *your priesthood,* which you perform [and] *which* is from [the beginning, is established for all time] *in the* counsels of [El Elyon]. [35]Satan [planned his own religion, that of the offering of blood and] the sacrifice and his doctrines, which are of the world [and which

f. "one chosen by the hand of divine fate"

weigh down the souls of those who offer them, thinking thereby one day to rise to the heavens. [36]He has given commandments] *which* exist [but] *in* order to lead *astray* [the Jews], and some [to the nations, as well, through the error of Noah, son of Lamech]. [37]And he gave them to [keep, even six hundred] *and* thirteen [commandments]. But throw *him* [over] *that* you might [destroy him], and wait no longer [but act] immediately, O Elyon, [and] *by means of* your right arm, [cast him] *onto the earth.* [38]The [dwellers therein will surely praise you, though for an hour they must suffer his wrath]."

3

[1][And they revealed to me what must transpire with me, how I must enter the world again in the last times, when I shall bear the name above every name, even Jesus-Christ, and shall run afoul of the Jews. [2]For their laws, received from Satan, I will set aside and I will walk the land calling unto and awakening the scattered sheep of the flock of Seth, as from a deep sleep. [3]And all who hear will live. But many will not hear, for they are not of my flock. [4]And I shall hear a voice, as from the heaven] which is above, [and it shall say to me, "The time has come for you to yield in semblance to the Jews and the archons which they serve. [5]And they will imagine themselves to have destroyed you, but they will act in sheer ignorance, doing my will." And so it happened, O Jews. [6]For zeal of your laws, which are of the archons, you arrested me.] And [in your rage,] you struck me, [and outside the Holy City] you cast me [as if already a] corpse. [7]And *you crucified me* from the third hour *of the Sabbath eve* until *the ninth hour.* [8]And after *these things, I arose* from the dead. [And the light returned to my eyes] and I came out of [the tomb and the life of the All came] into me. [9][Then my] eyes *saw* [that those who sought me] *did not* find anyone. [But the angels] greeted *me* [with great joy]. [10]They said to me, "Be *strong, O Melchizedek,* great *hierophant* of El Elyon, *for the archons,* who *are* your *enemies,* waged war, but you have *conquered them and* they did not conquer you. [11]*And you* stood fast and obliterated your enemies, [despoiling them] of their [strongholds, and the rest of your brothers] will rest in any body which is living and holy, [not like] *those who* lifted themselves up against him in [the] flesh. [12][And they shall continue] *with* the sacrifices, laboring on that one which is good, fasting with fasts.

[13]"Reveal these revelations to no one in the flesh since they are incorporeal, unless it is revealed to you to do so." [14]When the brothers, who belong to the generations of life, had said these things, they were assumed into the pleroma above all the heavens. Amen.

47.

The Epistle of Jude

THIS LITTLE EPISTLE IS QUOTED EARLY by Athenagoras the Apologist and Clement of Alexandria and appears in the Muratorian Canon. Origen accepted it but acknowledged that others doubted its authenticity. Didymus of Alexandria defended it against the criticism that it quotes apocryphal books like *1 Enoch* and the *Assumption of Moses*. Then again, Tertullian, a partisan of *1 Enoch,* appreciated Jude because it did quote the disputed book. Eusebius frowned on Jude and included it in his list of "disputed" scriptures. Such reservations about Jude's use of writings of dubious canonical standing are evident in 2 Peter, as well. Second Peter was practically a new version of Jude, one sanitized of the "polluting references" and shielded behind a better apostolic name.

As to Jude's dependence upon *1 Enoch,* it turns out to be much more extensive than one direct quotation. David Persuitte has shown that Jude incorporates adjacent material in a less strict but unmistakable way through allusions and paraphrases. It seems that Jude does with *1 Enoch* what 2 Peter does with Jude!

Who was the author? The name Jude, and variations Judas and Judah, were very common in biblical times. The author calls himself "the brother of James" without further explanation, implying a reference to James the Just, the brother of Jesus. This would make Jude the Judas listed in Mark 6:3 as one of the heirs, the *Desposynoi*, who wielded considerable clout among Jewish Christians. He may even have held a pontifical position after the deaths of James and Simeon bar-Cleophas if he was still alive after their passing. We read in Epiphanius Monachus, Eusebius, and Hegesippus that Domitian was

wary of messianic uprisings and summoned two of Jude's grandsons, Zoker (Zechariah) and Jacob, for interrogation, dismissing them when he saw they were simply poor farmers who cherished no dynastic ambitions. Still, it is likely that in Jewish-Christian circles, Jude would have been a big enough name to be useful as a pseudonym.

It is doubtful that the brother of Jesus himself penned the epistle. The problem is in the apocalyptic section, verses 17-18, where Jude invokes "your apostles" as if they were figures of the past who had foretold the events of Jude's time. He positions himself as a contemporary of the wrong time period. Beyond that, it is unlikely that one of the heirs would so fondly quote the twelve apostles, who were a rival authority group. We must suspect this is a catholicizing document, this time written to paper over the differences among the Jewish-Christian factions, a needful move given the shrinking influence of all of them. As Adolf von Harnack saw long ago, that is the reason for conflating the originally competing lists of resurrection appearances preserved in 1 Corinthians 15:5, 7. Still, the epistle seems early enough, the best conjecture probably being that it comes from the second century.

[1]Jude, a slave of Jesus-Christ and brother of James, to the elect, beloved of God the Father and kept for Jesus-Christ. [2]May mercy, peace,
and love be multiplied for you.

[3]Beloved ones, though very eager to write you on the subject of the
salvation we share, I found it necessary instead to write exhorting you to
struggle on behalf of the faith long ago entrusted to the saints.[a] [4]For certain individuals, the ones anciently assigned this role of damnation, the
impious, are turning the leniency of our God into a pretext for profligacy
and repudiating our sole Despot and Lord, Jesus-Christ. [5]But let me remind you, though I am sure you knew it once, how Adonai, having delivered a whole people out of the land of Egypt, on second thought destroyed those who did not believe. [6]And certain angels, having forsaken
their rightful thrones and deserted their proper homes, he has confined to
adamantine chains in the nether gloom in anticipation of the judgment of

a. This was a standard bit of Hellenistic epistolary rhetoric: to say one had intended to write a letter on a less controversial theme, only to put it aside in order to deal with a more pressing issue.

the great day.[b] 7In similar fashion, Sodom and Gomorrah, together with the neighboring cities, have been exhibited as an example to those who practice prostitution and stray after alien flesh, undergoing fiery vengeance forever. 8In the same way, these hallucinators, too, defile the flesh on the one hand and, on the other, they disdain dominions and blaspheme the Glorious Ones. 9But when Michael, the angel prince, while engaged in dispute with the accuser, laid claim to the body of Moses, even he dared not level blasphemy at him but only said, "May Adonai rebuke you!"[c] 10But these fools, on the one hand, blaspheme realities they do not understand, and on the other, what they do understand, they grasp by instinct like beasts and it is these that corrupt them. 11Woe to them! For they have followed in the footsteps of Cain and abandoned themselves to the mistake of Balaam, seeking wages for prophecy, and perished in Korah's uprising. 12These charlatans are hidden reefs lurking in your agape feasts, joining in the sacred meal impudently, stuffing themselves;[d] clouds betraying the promise of rain and carried away by the wind;[e] trees with no fruit to offer even at the autumn harvest, dying twice and then uprooted;[f] 13crashing waves of the sea, foaming up their own shame; planets leaving regular orbit,[g] for whose ruling spirits the shadows of

b. 1 Enoch 10:12b: "Bind them tight for seventy generations in the caverns of the earth till the day of their judgment ... till the judgment that lasts forever and ever is consummated."

c. Origen (*De Principiis,* 3.2) tells us this story was found in a now-lost pseudepigraphon, *The Assumption of Moses.* The idea seems to be that the accuser claimed Moses on account of his disobedience to God, which had been sufficient to prevent Moses from entering the promised land (Num. 20:7-12). Michael won the dispute and Moses ascended alive into heaven, as Josephus describes (*Antiquities,* 4.8.48). This is why he is available to appear to Jesus at the Transfiguration along with the similarly ascended prophet Elijah (Mark 9:4). The implied scene is similar to that in the *Testament of Amram* where the patriarch beholds in a dream Beliar and Michael fighting over him, based on Zech. 3:1-5. In that passage of Zechariah, v. 2 contains a scribal error. It should read: "And *the angel of* Yahve said to the adversary, 'Yahve rebuke you, O Adversary!'"

d. Jude condemns Gnostic libertines who are docetists, denying the real incarnation of Christ and thus his real presence in the eucharist, which they treat as a mere all-you-can-eat supper.

e. 1 Enoch 2:3: "Behold the summer and the winter, how all the earth is filled with water, and clouds and dew and rain rest upon it."

f. 1 Enoch 3:1: "Observe and behold how all the trees appear as though they had withered and shed all their leaves."

g. 1 Enoch 2:1: "Observe everything taking place in the heavens, how they do not alter their orbits, and the lights which are in the heaven, how they all rise and set in order, each in its season, and transgress not against their assigned order."

darkness have been prepared for ages to come.[h] [14]Enoch, too, in the seventh generation after Adam, prophesied of these troublemakers, saying,

> "Behold! Adonai came with myriads of his holy angels,
> [15]to visit judgment on all people
> and to reprove all the impious
> over all their impious deeds, which they impiously did,
> and over all the nasty things impious sinners spoke against him!"[i]

[16]These types are grumblers and grousers, led along by their own lusts; and their mouths speak arrogant boasts, flattering people to gain advantage.

[17]But you, beloved ones, keep in mind the words previously spoken by the apostles of our Lord, Jesus-Christ, [18]for they warned you: "At the end of time, there will be mockers, obeying their own lusts for impious things." [19]These are the ones who foment schism, natural men bereft of spirit. [20]But you, beloved ones, raise up together the edifice of your most holy faith by praying in the fervor of the Holy Spirit, [21]taking care not to stray outside the love of God, waiting for the mercy of our Lord, Jesus-Christ, the granting of age-abiding life. [22]And take pity on some who are diffident, [23]saving them, yanking them out of the fire.[j] Show others pity mingled with horror, loathing even the semen-stained tunic!

[24]Now to the one capable of keeping you from stumbling and of setting you down safely, all unblemished, facing his splendor, greatly exulting; [25]to the only God, our Savior through Jesus-Christ our Lord, be all worship, greatness, rule and authority before all ages, now and throughout all the ages to come! Amen.

---

h. 1 Enoch 10:4-6: "And again the Lord said to Raphael, 'Bind Azazel hand and foot and pitch him into the darkness … and cover him with darkness, and let him remain there forever and blindfold him to prevent his seeing light.'"

i. 1 Enoch 3:9

j. This allusion to Zech. 3:2 ("Is not this a brand plucked from the fire?") comes from the same verse as the angelic rebuke quoted in Jude 8, showing the writer was well aware of the original source.

48.
The Gospel according to Thomas

A post-narrative gospel

THIS IS THE ONLY SURVIVING EXAMPLE of the sayings gospel genre, though we assume there were others, including the Q Source underlying Matthew and Luke. The Gospel according to Thomas contains bits of stray narrative that serve as set-ups or lead-ins for the sayings that might not have seemed self-explanatory. As Rudolf Bultmann suggested for the apophthegms (pronouncement stories) of the Synoptic Gospels, it seems these narrative lead-ins were secondary additions to cryptic aphorisms, attempts to explain them by supplying some situation for them to address. As such, the framers of the introductory anecdotes might be considered the first form critics, attempting to reconstruct the original context—the *Sitz-im-Leben*—for the brief sayings.

It is nevertheless not quite proper to characterize the Thomas sayings as hanging timelessly in the air with no narrative framework. It is not like the aphorisms collected in the Book of Proverbs. Depending on how one understands the phrase "the living Jesus" at the start of the book, the sayings may represent a primitive example of the "resurrection discourse" genre like in the *Dialogue of the Savior*, *Epistle of the Apostles*, and *Pistis Sophia*.[a] Such books presuppose a Passion and Easter narrative and promise to enlighten readers about the esoteric teachings given to the elite among Jesus' disciples before

a. See Pheme Perkins, *The Gnostic Dialogue: The Early Church and the Crisis of Gnosticism* (NY: Paulist Press, 1980).

his final ascension, the sort of thing hinted at in Acts 1 but not made explicit there. We may read Thomas as a collection of such resurrection teachings.

But does this not conflict with the fact that many of the sayings are variants of those found before Easter in the traditional gospels? Yes and no. Bultmann showed that early Christians made little distinction, such as today's historians like to make, between remembered sayings of a historical Jesus and the inspired oracles of prophets uttering words of wisdom in the name of the risen Lord. In fact, if we press the point further, the plainly non-historical, tendentious, and anachronistic character of so many of the sayings as obviously artificial coinages placed upon the lips of Jesus finally raises the question of whether there was a historical person at all at the root of the whole thing. Virtually all of it sounds ideal, fictive, and more like the words of a dramatic character than a living being.

Thomas who? Why Thomas?

Why should this gospel be connected to the name of Judas Thomas, Judas the twin? Many in early Syrian Christianity supposed Thomas, being after all *some*one's less important twin brother (otherwise the other brother would have been called Didymus, or "ditto"), was actually the twin of Jesus. In fact, Mark 6:3 lists a brother named Judas. But this relationship was often understood to be spiritual and figurative. Thomas was considered to have been the paramount example, if not fictionalized symbol, of a Christian achieving Jesus' own level of spiritual advancement. However, the emerging institutional Catholicism considered this to be impossible, a belief which itself functioned as self-fulfilling prophecy for those catechized in it, thus ensuring the hierarchy would never be out of a job a la the logic of Dostoyevsky's Grand Inquisitor. But there were Christians of many stripes who, with Wesley centuries later, ventured to believe "Christian perfection" was in fact an achievable goal; Thomas stands for this ideal, as certain sayings in this gospel make clear.

Is it Gnostic?

Since Thomas's gospel was discovered among a cache of overtly Gnostic documents at Nag Hammadi, scholars assumed it, too, must

be a Gnostic product. Stevan L. Davies (*The Gospel of Thomas and Christian Wisdom*) and others have since challenged this estimate, pointing out that the esoteric character of Thomas is very mild compared with full-fledged Gnostic texts like *Pistis Sophia*. Though the very genre of a sayings collection, or revelation dialogue, implies a Gnostic milieu for the book's composition, we cannot simply declare it Gnostic when so many of the sayings obviously come from other sources. Some of them do imply Gnostic doctrines like the pre-existence of the soul and implicit reincarnationism, but others inculcate strict Torah observance and extol James the Just as the successor to Jesus. Some hotly repudiate futuristic eschatology, while others plainly teach it. Some teach anti-sexual encratism; others presuppose the Jewish Platonism of Philo. The occasional reference to the "kingdom of the Father," rather than the "kingdom of God," may imply the distinction drawn by Marcionites between Jesus' heavenly Father and the Hebrew Creator God. So Thomas contains materials drawn from various quarters of early Christianity. The earliest popular commentary on Thomas, *The Secret Sayings of the Living Jesus* by Robert M. Grant and David Noel Friedman, assumed a Gnostic composition from the first saying to the last, resulting in such obvious exegetical contortions that the effect was simply to show the futility of the whole enterprise.

Is it independent?

Much ink has been spilled in debates over whether Thomas is dependent on the canonical gospels since there is so much overlap with them. The problem is that the verbal similarities are loose, compared to those between, say, Matthew and Mark or Luke and Mark. The situation is more like that of John and the Synoptics, where the rewriting is considerably freer than in the Matthean/Lukan examples—if there is any dependence. Scholars, including Helmut Koester, Stevan L. Davies, and Stephen J. Patterson, have plausibly argued that Thomas presents us with an independent, often earlier and more authentic version of the sayings we find in Matthew and Luke. The key to the debate is whether a close reading of Thomas's sayings reveals any of the distinctive marks of Matthew's or Luke's redactional style.

That is, we can often pinpoint how and where Matthew and Luke retouched their Markan and Q source materials, so if we were to find in Thomas something that appeared to retain the editorial marks of Matthew or Luke, this would count as evidence that the compiler derived the sayings from those sources, not just from a free-floating oral tradition. If Thomas seems to be quoting Matthew's version of a saying, then Thomas is later than Matthew. In fact, this is what I perceive to be present in the text: there are sufficient signs to indicate Thomas follows Matthew and Luke, at least to my mind. And yet Thomas certainly seems to collect variegated materials, many from out of the oral tradition rather than from written sources, so that we cannot say we have an either/or situation. It must be true that oral tradition about Jesus continued for a long time after the gospels were written, and we learn from Papias that at least some Christians continued to prefer what they considered to be the living voice of apostolic tradition to what they found written down. I think this is reflected in Thomas and that the compiler did three things.

First, he relied upon memory for quotations from Matthew and Luke, having no copy at hand. It would seem that over time, through imprecise memory, the gospel sayings re-entered the oral tradition, not just once but many times. Thomas represents a second written crystallization of some of the gospel sayings. Second, Thomas wrote down various word-of-mouth items, many of them clearly from the Dame Wisdom milieu of Proverbs 7, for instance, and ascribed them to Jesus. Third, he coined a number of sayings himself and redacted or reshaped others.

Is it early?

Those who consider Thomas to be independent of Matthew and Luke tend to date it earlier than others. Koester and Davies both place it around CE 50, earlier than any other surviving gospel. If I am correct, such an early date would be impossible. But there are other reasons for suggesting an early date. First, the Christology is mostly *non-titular* in that it avoids calling Jesus the Son of God, the Son of Man, or even the Christ. For Davies and Patterson, this implies it comes from the dawn of Christianity when devotion to Jesus had not yet

articulated itself in the form of divine titles. In my opinion, it is equally possible the compiler is *reacting to* such titles, programmatically repudiating them out of a Gnostic, Zen-like fear that such titles would serve to make believers substitute a dogma about Jesus for the living one himself. Saying 43 is illustrative of this.

Similarly, scholars have pointed to the supposed lack of futuristic eschatology (the expectation of the end of all things) as a sign of an early date. But the argument is completely secondary to a framework of theories which understand Jesus as having taught the figurative presence of the kingdom as opposed to a literal future coming. In any event, it may be, as I think, that where Thomas repudiates futurism, although inconsistently, he is not innocent of it. Instead, he is reacting against it. I place Thomas late enough for its writers to have seen the world outlast the apocalyptic deadlines set for it, knowing that such timetables could no longer be taken seriously. The kingdom of God could no longer realistically be expected to come from without, so from now on it would be sought within. I would therefore think that Thomas is roughly a contemporary of John, making it a late second-century document.

These are the secret words which the risen Jesus spoke and Didymus Judas Thomas wrote.

1. And he says, "Whoever discovers the interpretation of these words will not taste death."

2. Jesus says, "Let the seeker not give up seeking until he finds, and when he finds, he will be perplexed, and once perplexed, he shall marvel, and he shall rule over all things."

3. Jesus says, "If your leaders tell you, 'Behold, the kingdom is in the sky,' then the birds of the sky will have the advantage over you. If they say to you, 'Behold, the kingdom is in the sea,' then the fish will have the advantage over you. But the kingdom is inside you and it is outside you. If you will only know yourselves, then you will be known and you will know you are the sons of the living Father. But if you do not know yourselves, then you are mired in poverty and you are that poverty."

4. Jesus says, "The man ancient of days will not hesitate to ask a little child of seven days concerning the place of life, and he will live. For many who are first in rank shall become last and they shall become identical."

5. Jesus says, "Recognize what is right in front of you, and what is concealed from you will suddenly be revealed to you."

6. His disciples ask him, saying to him, "Do you want us to fast? And how should we pray? Should we give alms? What diet should we keep?"[b] Jesus says, "Do not lie and do not do what you hate, for everything is observed from heaven. For there is nothing hidden that shall not finally be revealed, and there is nothing covered up that shall remain unexposed."

7. Jesus says, "Blessed is the lion eaten by the man, and the lion will become man; and cursed is that man whom the lion eats, for the lion will become man."[c]

8. And he says, "The man is like a shrewd fisherman who cast his net into the sea. He pulled it up from the sea full of small fish. He found among them a large good fish. That shrewd fisherman threw all the small fish back into the sea. He chose the large fish without a second thought. Whoever has ears to hear, let him hear!"

9. Jesus says, "Behold, the sower went out. He filled his hand with seed and threw. Some seeds fell on the road where the birds lit and gathered them. Others fell on the rock and did not strike root in the earth and did not produce ears. And others fell on the thorns, which choked the seed and the worm ate them. And others fell on good soil and it yielded good fruit, bearing sixty per measure and one hundred twenty per measure."

10. Jesus says, "I have let loose fire upon the world, and behold, I tend it until the world is consumed."

11. Jesus says, "This heaven shall pass away and the one above it shall pass away.[d] And the dead are not alive, and the living shall not die. In the days when you consumed the dead meat, you made it alive. When you consume what is living, what will you do? You will come into the light.[e] On the day when you were one, you became two.[f] But when you have become two, what will you do?"[g]

---

b. There is a mismatch between the disciples' questions and Jesus' answer, the original reply having been displaced to saying 14.

c. In Plato, the lion symbolizes the appetites of the flesh. If reason ("the man") masters it, he gains the benefit of its strength. If reason succumbs to it, his intelligence is bent to the service of his passions. See Howard M. Jackson, *The Lion becomes Man: The Gnostic Leontomorphic Creator and the Platonic Tradition* (Atlanta: Scholars Press, 1985), 203.

d. That is to say that the blue sky and starry vault will be stripped away to reveal the third heaven, where God will sit enthroned for the judgment.

e. Our reading combines the Nag Hammadi text with a Thomas quotation by Hippolytus. The last sentence may have originated as a scribal gloss. See Stevan

12. The disciples say to Jesus, "We know you will depart from us. Who is it who will be great over us?" Jesus says to them, "Wherever you have come from,[h] you will go report to James the Just for whom heaven and earth were prepared."

13. Jesus says to his disciples, "Compare me and tell me what I am like." Simon Peter says to him, "You are like a righteous angel." Matthew says to him, "You are like a philosopher possessed of understanding." Thomas says to him, "Master, my mouth can scarcely frame the words of what you are like!" Jesus says, "I am not your master; because you have drunk, you have become filled from the bubbling spring which I have measured out." He took him aside privately and said three things to him, so when Thomas rejoined his companions, they pressed him, saying, "What did Jesus say to you?" Thomas said to them, "If I tell you even one of the things he said to me, you will pick up stones and hurl them at me—and fire will erupt from the stones and consume you!"

14. Jesus says to them, "If you fast, you will only engender sin for yourselves. And if you pray, you will be damned. If you give alms, you will only do your spirit harm. And if you journey to any land and travel about the region, if they welcome you, eat whatever they set before you. Cure their sick. For what goes into your mouth will not render you profane. Rather, what comes out of your mouth, that is what will render you profane."

15. Jesus says, "When you see him who was not born from woman, fall on your face before him! He is your father."[i]

16. Jesus says, "Perhaps people think I have come to spread peace on the earth, not suspecting I have come to create schisms: fire, sword, war! For there shall be five in a dwelling, and three shall be pitted against two, father versus son and son versus father, and only the solitary will stand fast."

17. Jesus says, "I will give you what eye has never seen, what ear has

---

L. Davies, *The Gospel of Thomas and Christian Wisdom* (NY: Seabury Press, 1983), 75.

f. Gen. 2:21-24, referring here to the encratite Christian view of sex having been the original sin.

g. The answer to this query is that you must seek to "become a single one" by renouncing sex and sex role differences.

h. The reference may be to itinerant brothers returning from their missionary journeys.

i. Adam.

never heard, what hand has never touched, and what has never even occurred to the mind of man!"

18. The disciples say to Jesus, "Tell us our destiny!" Jesus says, "Oh, does that mean you have discovered your origin, that you ask about your destiny? For where your origin is, there too shall be your destiny. Blessed is the one who shall arrive at the beginning, for he shall know the end and he shall not taste death."[j]

19a. Jesus says, "Blessed is he who existed before he came into being."

19b. "If you become my disciples and hear my words, these stones will turn to bread and feed you. For you have five trees in Paradise which are unchanged from summer to winter and their leaves never fall. Whoever knows them will not taste death."[k]

20. The disciples say to Jesus, "Tell us what the kingdom of heaven is like." He says to them, "It is like a mustard seed, smaller than all the rest of the seeds. But when it falls on the tilled earth, it produces a large branch and becomes lodging for the birds of the sky."

21. Mariam says to Jesus, "Who are your disciples like?" He says, "They are like young children who have made a fort for themselves in someone else's field. When the owners of the field come, they will say, 'Get out of our field!' They strip off their clothes in order to vacate it to them and to return their field to them.[l]

"For this reason, I say: If the master of the house is forewarned of the burglar's coming, he will stay awake before he arrives and will forestall his digging through into his house, or his kingdom, to make off with his vessels. You, then, must watch out for the world. Arm yourself with great strength in case the thieves discover a way to get to you because if you know of an opportunity, you can be sure they will find it, too.

---

j. This envisions either a return to celibate, vegetarian, anarchistic Eden living, the goal of encratite Christians, or a postmortem journey of the divine spark to the Pleroma (fullness) from which it was primordially stolen and held captive in the material cosmos. Such salvation could be gained only by the Gnostic elite who understood the secret of their divine origin.

k. We do know these trees: the date palm, fig, cedar, apple, and *thourakion,* each of which yields miraculous abundance according to the *Apocalypse of John, the Lord's Brother,* included in Pseudo-Chrysostom's *Encomium on John the Baptist.*

l. Their fleshly bodies are part of the material cosmos of the Demiurge and his archons. Salvation requires the abandonment of both, beginning with asceticism and monastic isolation here and now.

"Let there be among you a man of discernment like the one who, seeing the fruit was ripe, came quickly with his sickle in his hand and reaped it. Whoever has ears to hear, let him hear!"

22. Jesus saw children being nursed. He says to his disciples, "These nursing children are like those who enter the kingdom." They say to him, "Are we, then, to become children in order to enter the kingdom?" Jesus says to them, "When you make the two sexes one, and when you make the inner reality as the outer appearance and the outer body as the inner spirit, and the heaven above as the earth below,[m] and when you make the male and the female into a single one so that the male will no more be male, nor will the female be female, when you make eyes in the place of an eye[n] and a hand in the place of a hand[o] and a foot in the place of a foot,[p] an image in the place of an image,[q] then you shall enter the kingdom."

23. Jesus says, "I shall choose you, one out of a thousand and two out of ten thousand, and they shall stand fast as a single one."

24. His disciples say, "Show us the place where you are, for it is needful for us to seek it." He says to them, "Whoever has ears to hear, let him hear! Within a man of light there is light, and he illuminates the whole world. When he fails to shine, there is darkness."[r]

25. Jesus says, "Love your brother as your own life. Guard him like the pupil of your eye."

26. Jesus says, "You see the speck in your brother's eye but you do not see the beam in your own eye. When you remove the beam from your own eye, then you will see clearly enough to pick the mote out of your brother's eye."

27. Jesus says, "If you do not abstain from the world, you will not

---

m. Matt. 6:10

n. Mark 9:47: new habits, no longer coveting or lusting.

o. Mark 10:43: honest hand labor instead of stealing, as in Eph. 4:28.

p. Mark 9:45: new habits of not trespassing.

q. Mystery religions, like Vajrayana Buddhism today, taught that ritual initiation, followed by strict discipline, nurtured the light body or glory body inside the cocoon of the physical form. Ultimate salvation coincided with the emergence of this divine body of heavenly substance. Cf. 1 Cor. 15:42-55; 2 Cor. 5:1-4; Phil. 3:21.

r. The disciples imagine the risen Christ to be manifesting himself from heaven, where they also hope to arrive one day. He tells them he is the divine light within, if they can but recognize it. Again, the kingdom of heaven is within, not without.

find the kingdom; if you do not observe the seventh day as a Sabbath, you will not see the Father."

28. Jesus says, "I stood there in the middle of the world and in flesh I appeared to them. I found no one among them athirst. And my heart was broken for the human race because they are blind in their minds and do not realize that they have entered the world empty and they are happy enough to leave the world the same way. But now they are in a stupor. When they have snapped out of it, then surely they will repent."

29. Jesus says, "If the flesh has come into existence because of the spirit, what a marvel! But if the spirit exists because of the body, that is the greatest of marvels. But I marvel at how this great wealth has come to dwell in such squalor."

30. Jesus says, "Wherever there are three gathered in the name of God, they are not without God; where there are two or even one, I am with him."[s]

31. Jesus says, "No prophet is welcome in his own village, no physician cures those who know him."

32. Jesus says, "A city erected atop a high mountain and fortified cannot fall to a siege, but then neither can it be hidden."

33. Jesus says, "What you hear whispered in your ear by two different people, preach that from your housetops. For no one kindles a lamp only to place it underneath a bushel, nor does he put it in a hiding place, but he sets it on the lamp stand so all coming in or out may see its light."

34. Jesus says, "If a blind man leads a blind man, both of them end up in the pit."

35. Jesus says, "It is impossible to enter a strong man's dwelling and take it by force without first tying his hands. Then one may pillage the house."

36. Jesus says, "Do not spare a thought from morning till evening or from evening to morning for what you will wear."

37. His disciples say, "When will you be revealed to us and when will we see you return in glory?" Jesus says, "When you are able to take off your clothes without shame and trample them underfoot like innocent children, then you shall be ready to behold the son of the Living One without fear."[t]

---

s. The literal reading, "Where there are three gods, they are gods," must be a copyist error. The present form is from the Oxyrhynchus papyrus fragment of Thomas.

t. Again, Edenic, pre-sexual innocence is prerequisite for salvation.

38. Jesus says, "You have many times desired to hear these words which I speak to you, and you have no one else from whom to hear them. The days are coming when you will seek me and you will not find me, so take advantage while you have it."[u]

39. Jesus says, "The Pharisees and the scribes have received the keys of knowledge, but they have hidden them. They did not enter, nor did they allow entrance to those who wished to. But as for you, become shrewd as serpents and yet naive as doves."

40. Jesus says, "A vine has been planted that the Father did not create.[v] As it is alien to the soil, it will be pulled up by the roots and destroyed."[w]

41. Jesus says, "Whoever has something in his hand, to him shall be given, and whoever is lacking, from him shall be taken even the little he has."

42. Jesus says, "Be as those who pass by."[x]

43. His disciples say to him, "Who are you that you say such things to us?" Jesus says to them, "From what I say to you, you cannot deduce who I am? No, you have become like the Jews, for they love the tree but hate its fruit; again, they love the fruit but hate the tree."

44. Jesus says, "Whoever blasphemes against the Father, it shall be forgiven him, and whoever blasphemes against the Son, it shall be forgiven him, but whoever blasphemes against the Holy Spirit, it shall not be forgiven him, either on earth or in heaven."

45. Jesus says, "They do not gather grapes from thorns, nor do they pick figs from thistles, for these give no fruit. A good man produces good out of his treasure, while a wicked man produces wicked things out of his wicked treasure, which is in his heart, and so speaks evil things. For out of what fills the heart, he brings forth evils."

---

u. Assuming that resurrection dialogues may have been actual records of what channelers of the risen Jesus said in answer to the questions of their gathered hearers, as channelers do today, we might guess that this saying signaled the opening of the question period.

v. In Zoroastrian myth, poison plants, like vermin, are the creation of Ahriman, the evil god or Demiurge. See Luke 10:19.

w. Matt. 15:13

x. Yoga teaches the attitude of detachment, of being a "mere witness" rather than a participant, abstaining from worldly distractions and acting only when necessary and without worldly expectation of a reward. Such "acting without the fruits of action" renders one immune from karma, good or bad, and thus does not oblige one to yet more incarnations in which to be rewarded or punished.

46. Jesus says, "From Adam up to John the Baptist, there is among mortal men none higher than John the Baptist, whose eyes are not blinded.[y] But I have said to you that whoever among you becomes as a child shall experience the kingdom, and he shall become higher than John."

47. Jesus says, "It is impossible for a man to mount two horses at once and stretch two bows, and it is impossible for a servant to serve two masters. If he tries, he will inevitably find himself honoring the one and, by the same act, offending the other. No one drinks old wine and immediately desires to drink new wine. And they avoid putting new wine into old wineskins so as not to burst them, nor do they put old wine into new wineskins, to avoid spoiling it. They do not sew an old patch on a new garment because it would result in a new tear."

48. Jesus says, "If two make peace with each other in this one house, there is nothing they cannot do by joining their forces. They shall say to this mountain, 'Be moved!' and it shall be moved."

49. Jesus says, "Blessed are the solitary and the elect,[z] for you shall find the kingdom because you come from it and shall find your way there again."

50. Jesus says, "If they say to you, 'Where did you originate?' tell them, 'We have come from the light, where the light originated through itself. It arose and it revealed itself in the image of its offspring.' If they say to you, 'Who are you?' say, 'We are his sons, and we are the elect of the living Father.' If they ask you, 'What is the identifying mark of your Father in you?' tell them, 'It is both movement and repose.'"[a]

51. His disciples say to him, "When will the repose of the dead begin? And when will the new world come?"[b] He says to them, "What you look for has already come, but you fail to recognize it."[c]

52. His disciples say to him, "Twenty-four prophets spoke in Israel and every one of them predicted you!" He said to them, "You have disregarded the living, who is right in front of you, to prattle on about the dead!"[d]

---

y. A sign of respect to a superior.

z. See saying 23.

a. This may be advice to Gnostics in case they are discovered and questioned by the bishops (cf. saying 13). However, it more likely concerns the astral journey of the soul after death. The passwords enable the soul to bypass planetary archons who seek to devour those ascending back to the Pleroma.

b. Mark 13:4

c. Luke 17:20-21

d. There are twenty-four books in the Rabbinic canon, the same count as in

53. His disciples say to him, "Is circumcision worthwhile or not?" He says to them, "If it were, men would be born that way automatically. But the true circumcision in spirit has proven completely worthwhile."[e]

54. Jesus says, "Blessed are the poor, for yours is the kingdom of heaven."

55. Jesus says, "Whoever does not hate his father and his mother will not be able to qualify as my disciple, and whoever does not hate his brothers and his sisters and does not pick up his cross in my wake will not prove worthy of me."

56. Jesus says, "Whoever has recognized the world for what it is has found a rotting corpse. And whoever has found it to be a corpse, of him the world is not worthy."

57. Jesus says, "The kingdom of the Father is like a man who had good seed. His enemy came by night and sowed weeds among the good seed. The man did not allow them to pull up the weeds, telling them, "in case you go to uproot the weed and uproot the wheat along with it. For at harvest time, the weeds will appear. That's the time to uproot and burn them."

58. Jesus says, "Blessed is the one who has suffered; he has found the life."

59. Jesus says, "Look upon the Living One as long as you live in case you should die and seek in vain to see him."

60. They see a Samaritan carrying a lamb on his way to Jerusalem.[f] Jesus says to his disciples, "Why does this man carry the lamb with him?" They say to him, "So he may kill it and eat it." He says to them, "As long as it is alive, he will not eat it, but only if he has killed it and it has become a corpse?" They say, "Otherwise he will not be able to do it." He says to them, "As for yourselves, seek a place of repose for yourselves so you do not become a corpse and get eaten."[g]

61a. Jesus says, "Two will rest on a bed: one will die and one will live." Salome says, "Who are you, sir, and whose son? You reclined up-

---

the Protestant Old Testament, but the twelve Minor Prophets are combined into a single book and Samuel, Kings, and Chronicles are not divided in two.

e. Circumcision was the great debate of the early church (Rom. 3:1; Gal. 5:2-12; Acts 15). This saying has been coined by one of the factions to posthumously enlist Jesus on their side.

f. This marks the man as a member of either the Gorothene or the Dosithean sect, both of which were comprised of Samaritans who observed the Jewish calendar of holy days and went to Jerusalem to celebrate.

g. Heb. 4:9-11; Matt. 11:28-30

on my couch and ate from my table." Jesus says to her, "I am he who is from the same, and all things were given to me by my Father." Salome says, "I am your disciple!" Jesus says to her, "Therefore, I say, if one is the same, he will be filled with light, but if he is divided, he will be filled with darkness."

62. Jesus says, "I entrust my mysteries to those who are worthy of my mysteries. What your right hand may do, do not let your left hand know about it."[h]

63. Jesus says, "Once there was a rich man who had great wealth. He said, 'I will invest my money in a farm so I may sow and reap and plant and fill my barns with produce, so I will lack nothing.' So he resolved, and that night he died! Whoever has ears, let him hear!"

64. Jesus says, "A man had professional acquaintances, and when he had finished preparing a banquet he sent his servant to invite the associates. He went to the first and said to him, 'My master invites you.' He said, 'I have some claims against some merchants. They will come to me this evening. I will go to give them my orders. I must request to be excused from the banquet.' He went to another and said to him, 'My master has invited you.' He said to him, 'I have bought a house, and they will need me for the day. I will have no time.' He came to another and said to him, 'My master invites you.' He said to him, 'Wouldn't you know it? My friend is to be married the same day, and I am to cater the reception. I shall not be able to attend. Please have me excused from the banquet.' He went to another and said to him, 'My master invites you.' He said to him, 'I have bought a farm and I am just on my way to collect the rent. I shall not be able to attend. Please have me excused.' The servant returned and said to his master, 'Those you have invited to the banquet have excused themselves.' The master said to his servant, 'Go out to the roads and bring in whomever you find so they may dine!' Tradesmen and merchants shall never enter the places of my Father."

65. He says, "A good man had a vineyard. He entrusted it to sharecroppers to work it and he would receive his share of its fruit from them. When the time came, he sent his servant for them to give him his share of the produce of the vineyard. They grabbed his servant and beat him. They stopped just short of killing him. The servant returned and told his master. His master said, 'They must not have recognized him!' So he sent

---

h. This half of the saying, which in Matt. 6:3 urges secret giving, here means not to betray the secrets of Jesus to the uninitiated, no matter how close you might otherwise be.

another servant, but the sharecroppers beat him, too. Finally the owner sent his son, thinking, 'Surely they will respect my son.' But since those sharecroppers were well aware this one was the heir of the vineyard, they grabbed him and killed him. Whoever has ears to hear, let him hear!"

66. Jesus says, "Show me the stone which the contractors spurned as unsuitable; in fact, it is the very cornerstone!"

67. Jesus says, "Whoever knows all things yet fails to know himself lacks everything."

68. Jesus says, "Blessed are you when you are hated and persecuted, for the place where they persecuted you will be wiped off the map."

69a. Jesus says, "Blessed are those who have suffered in their hearts from persecution;[i] it is these who have truly known the Father."

69b. "Blessed are the hungry, for the belly of him who desires will be filled."

70. Jesus says, "If you bring out what is inside you, what you have will save you. If you do not have it inside you, what you lack will be the death of you."

71. Jesus says, "I shall destroy this house and no one will be able to rebuild it again."[j]

72. A man says to him, "Tell my brothers to divide my father's possessions with me!" He says to him, "O man, who appointed me executor?" He turned to his disciples and said to them, "Surely I am no executor?"

73. Jesus says, "There is so much waiting to be harvested, but how few laborers there are. So plead with the Lord to send laborers into the field!"

74. He says, "Lord, there are many gathered round the cistern, but no one is using it."

75. Jesus says, "Many are standing at the door, but only the solitary will gain entrance to the bridal chamber."[k]

---

i. That is, as opposed to external, physical suffering, more easily shrugged off than the deep wounds of betrayal and the loss of loved ones.

j. Cf. Dhammapada, trans. Irving Babbit, 153-154: "Looking for the maker of this tabernacle, I ran to no avail through a round of many births; and wearisome is birth again and again. But now, maker of the tabernacle, thou hast been seen; thou shalt not rear this tabernacle again. All thy rafters are broken, thy ridge-pole is shattered; the mind approaching the Eternal has attained to the extinction of all desires."

k. The bridal chamber was a Gnostic and Jewish-Christian sacrament in which the initiate encountered his astral self or heavenly twin, guardian angel, or

76. Jesus says, "The kingdom of the Father is like a man who was a merchant who owned much merchandise and found a pearl. That merchant was shrewd: he sold off all his stock so he could buy the single pearl for himself. You, too, seek the treasure that never gives out, which lasts, in a place where no moth approaches to devour and no worm ruins."

77. Jesus says, "I am the light that shines down upon all. I am the All! All things emerged from me, and all reached their goal in me. Split a log and I am revealed. Pick up a stone and you will find me underneath."

78. Jesus says, "What are you doing in the desert? Did you come all the way out here just to see the wind shake the reeds? To gaze on a man clad in silks? Behold, your mortal kings and celebrities are the ones clad in silks, and they will never be able to know the truth."[l]

79. A woman in the crowd calls out to him, "Blessed is the womb that carried you and the breasts that nursed you!" He says to her, "Blessed are those who have heard the commandment of the Father and have truly kept it. That alone abides, for there will be days when you will say, 'Blessed is the womb that never conceived and the breasts that never nursed!'"

80. Jesus says, "Whoever has understood my references to 'the world' has discovered it means 'the body,' and whoever has mastered the body is too good for this world."

81. Jesus says, "Let him who has become rich become king, but let him who has attained true power renounce the throne."

82. Jesus says, "Whoever is near me is near the fire, but whoever is far from me is far from the kingdom."

83. Jesus says, "The images are manifest to human perception, while the light which is within them is hidden in the image of the light of the Father. But he will manifest himself, and then it is his image that will be overshadowed by his light."[m]

84. Jesus says, "When you see your likeness in a mirror, you rejoice. But when you see your prototype images which came into being before

---

the risen Christ. Here Thomas stands for the twin of Jesus who has reached the necessary enlightenment.

l. They came out to hear a prophet who knows the truth, either Jesus himself or John the Baptist.

m. For now, all we see are human forms, made in the image and likeness of God. The divine light itself is concealed within the material human body, itself an image of the light but marred by sin and obscuring more than revealing the light. One day it will shine forth unobstructed from the resurrection body.

you in the mind of the Creator, those which neither die nor are visible to the eye, you will be overwhelmed!"

85. Jesus says, "Adam came into being from a great Power and a great wealth, and still he was not your equal. For if he had been, he would never have tasted death."

86. Jesus says, "Foxes have their burrows and the birds have their nests, but man has no natural place to rest his head."

87. Jesus says, "Wretched is that body which subsists on another body, and wretched is the soul that depends on these two!"[n]

88. Jesus says, "The angels and the prophets will come to you and they will mete out what is due you. And for your part, render to them what you have in your hands. In the meantime, say to yourselves, 'Is today the day they will come and demand what is due them?'"[o]

89. Jesus says, "Why do you wash only the outside of the cup? Don't you realize that the same artisan made both the inside and the outside?"

90. Jesus says, "Come to me, for my yoke is easy to bear and my lordship is lenient, and you shall find repose for yourselves."

91. They say to him, "Tell us who you are so we may make you into a creed." He says to them, "You can assess the appearance of the sky and the earth, but as for him who stands right in front of you, you have failed to recognize him, for you do not grasp the meaning of the present moment!"

92. Jesus says, "Once I told you, 'Seek and you will find.' But those things you asked me in those days, I refused to tell you then. Now the time has come to tell you and you are no longer interested!"[p]

93. "Do not give what is holy to the dogs, for then it will only end up in the dungpile. Do not throw pearls to swine, for they will only make it defiled."[q]

94. Jesus says, "Whoever seeks will find and whoever knocks, the door will swing open for him."

---

n. The saying advocates vegetarianism, the avoidance of eating "dead things."

o. Compressed here is a judgment scene, like in the Koran, where the prophets testify that you knew better because they warned you (Luke 16:31) and guardian angels testify to what they saw you doing (Matt. 18:10). As in the parable of the talents (Matt. 25:14-30), you are called to account for your life and what you have made of it, for which one should live mindfully each day.

p. They have prematurely given up the search, contra saying 2.

q. The advanced teaching of the Gnostic is not to be leaked to a public not ready for it. It will only be exposed to blasphemy and ridicule. What else could

95. Jesus says, "If you have money, do not lend it out at interest. Rather, give it to him from whom you can expect no return."

96. Jesus says, "The kingdom of the Father is like a woman who has taken a pinch of leaven and hidden it in the dough and has made large loaves from it. Whoever has ears, let him hear!"

97. Jesus says, "The kingdom of the Father is like a woman carrying a jar full of meal. While she was walking a distant road, the handle of the jar cracked. The meal trickled out behind her on the road. She was wholly unaware of it, having noticed no accident. Once she arrived at her dwelling, she put the jar down and found it empty!"[r]

98. Jesus says, "The kingdom of the Father is like a man who plans to kill a powerful opponent. He drew his sword in his house and thrust it into the wall to see whether he was strong enough to strike the death blow. Then he killed the powerful man."[s]

99. The disciples say to him, "Your brothers and your mother are waiting outside." He says to them, "Those here who obey the will of my Father, they are my brothers and my mother, for they are those who shall enter the kingdom of my Father."

100. They show Jesus a gold coin and say to him, "Caesar's agents demand taxes from us." He says to them, "Give Caesar's things to Caesar. Give God's things to God. And give me what is mine."[t]

101. "Whoever does not hate his father and his mother, following in my way, will not be able to be a disciple of mine. My natural mother gave me death, but my true Mother gave me the life."

102. Jesus says, "Woe to them, the Pharisees! For they are like a dog sound asleep in the ox trough, who neither eats nor allows the oxen to eat."[u]

103. Jesus says, "Blessed is the man who knows which watch of the night in which the burglars will arrive so he may get up and collect his weapons and be ready for them before they come in."

104. They say to him, "Come, let us observe this day of prayer and fasting." Jesus says, "Oh? Which sin have I committed? Where has sin de-

---

one expect from those not ready? What else could they do with it? It will be your fault, not theirs.

r. If we are not vigilant, our spiritual life steals away on little cat feet!

s. Luke 14:28-33

t. The repentance and commitment the disciple owes Jesus far outweigh petty concerns such as taxation and temple offerings.

u. Socrates uses the same metaphor.

feated me?[v] Wait till the bridegroom emerges from the bridal chamber, signaling the feast is over, then let them fast and let them pray."

105. Jesus says, "Whoever can identify father or mother shall be called the son of a harlot."[w]

106. Jesus says, "When you make the two one, you will become like Adam,[x] and when you say, 'Mountain, be moved!' it will indeed be moved."[y]

107. Jesus says, "The kingdom is like a shepherd with a flock of a hundred sheep. One of them, the largest, wandered off. He left the ninety-nine to themselves while he went in search of the one till he found it. He was exhausted, but he said to the sheep, 'I love you more than ninety-nine!'"

108. Jesus says, "Whoever drinks from my mouth shall become as I am, and I myself will become him. And the hidden things shall at last be revealed to him."[z]

109. Jesus says, "The kingdom is like a man who had a treasure buried in his field without knowing it. When he died, he left it to his son. The son did not know about it either, and once he inherited the field, he sold it. And he who bought it went to it and, while plowing, discovered the treasure. He began lending money to whomever he wished."

110. Jesus says, "Whoever has found the world and become rich, let him renounce the world."[a]

111a. Jesus says, "The sky and the earth will be rolled up like a tent flap before your very eyes, and he who subsists on the living water and bread shall taste neither death nor fear."

---

v. Another version appears in the Gospel according to the Hebrews, where his mother suggests the whole family submit to John's baptism, also a penitential rite.

w. Anything short of spiritual rebirth is tantamount to the most degrading bastardy.

x. Literally, "you will become sons of man," implying a recovery through celibacy of an androgynous state in the image of Adam before he split into male (*ish*) and female (*ishshah*).

y. The Kabbalistic notion of the superhuman power of the pre-Fall Adam Kadmon.

z. This is just what happens to Thomas in saying 13. The spiritual twin of Jesus who is attaining his insight is no more to be counted a mere disciple, but the very equal of Christ, who was not intended to be unique, but rather the firstborn of many brothers and sisters. Thomas stands in for the ideal reader.

a. If the previous parable is taken literally, it is clear this saying tries to correct it.

111b. Jesus says, "Whoever finds himself is too good for this world."

112. Jesus says, "Woe to the flesh which depends upon the soul! Woe to the soul which depends upon the flesh!"[b]

113. His disciples say to him, "When will the kingdom come?" Jesus says, "It will not come in a way you expect. They will not be able to say, 'Look here!' or 'See there!' Rather, the kingdom of the Father is spread out over the earth without anyone recognizing it."

114. Simon Peter says, "Tell Mariam to leave us because women are unworthy of the life." Jesus says, "Behold, I shall lead her to make her male so that she, too, may become a living spirit like you males. For every woman who makes herself male will enter the kingdom of heaven."[c]

---

b. The physical body is doomed; let it not be the focus of one's life, as with the worldlings.

c. In the terminology of Philo, used here, the "male" element is rational, while the "female" is emotional. Passion must be mortified and controlled by reason or salvation is impossible. The female element is thereby degraded, but the saying nonetheless affirms that women are just as capable of discipleship as men. Against the backdrop of the carping of church misogynists, as represented here by Peter, it is a strong statement.

49.

The Gospel of Mary Magdalene

THE TREATMENT OF MARY MAGDALENE in the canonical gospels is analogous to that of John the Baptist. Both are presented in enigmatic and contradictory ways, implying that each was in some way a problem figure. We know the Baptist was the figurehead of a rival sect and that some early Christians vilified him as a false prophet (see the Preaching of Peter), while others (John and Matthew) fictively had him endorse Jesus in an attempt to elevate Christianity over John's sect. Mark gives no hint that John ever knew Jesus as more than a face in the crowd, but he tells us Jesus received John's baptism, presumably as some kind of credential since John was held in such high esteem. The Q source, followed by Luke and Matthew, says John heard of Jesus while languishing in prison and wondered for the first time if this man might be the Coming One he had predicted. Is any of this historical fact? We cannot know. We only know John appears in different ways to reflect different Christian strategies of dealing with him and the sect he represented.

The same seems to be true of Mary Magdalene. She is said to have been delivered of seven demons (Luke 8:2), though we have no story describing it. Later she was said to have been a reformed prostitute. Interestingly enough, there may be a hint of that charge in the gospels. The rabbis (Babylonian Talmud tractate *Hagigah*, 4b) who called her "Mary the hairdresser" (Aramaic, *megaddela*), denoting a brothel madame, may have preserved a slur created by Mary's rivals. The empty tomb stories disagree about what to do with her, implying that some people gave her a role others thought too grand for her. In Mark

16:1-8, Mary sees a young man in the tomb and disobeys his order to tell Peter and others to meet Jesus in Galilee. In Luke 24:1-10, Mary sees two men but obeys a different order. In Matthew 28:1-10, she sees Jesus. The passage in John 20:11-18 seems to preserve a different story which assumed that Mary *alone* saw Jesus before his ascension: Jesus simply has her tell Peter and company *good-bye* for him rather than promising to meet them.

This is our major clue, for here we see a step along a trajectory we can follow through various Gnostic texts in the second and third centuries, including the *Pistis Sophia,* the *Dialogue of the Savior, Little Questions of Mary, Great Questions of Mary, Gospel of Mary, Gospel of Philip,* and others. In these, we seem to find in full flower what is carefully omitted from the more familiar gospel texts: Mary's role as the greatest of the apostles, "the woman who understood the All." It is Mary who claims special resurrection revelations surpassing those of the male disciples.

Mary is a symbolic figurehead for Gnostic and other sects who claimed her as their authorization. She clearly takes the place of the divine consort who resurrects the dying god in various salvation myths, the Christian version of Cybele, Isis, Ishtar, and Anath. But she may represent an early historic apostolic figure, as well. In any case, we must assume her place was important enough that even her enemies could not simply omit her from their own gospels, though they were happy to denounce her as a demoniac and whore, making her little more than Celsus had: an untrustworthy, "hysterical female" whose recorded teachings no one ought to credit.

As the Gospel of Mary has come down to us among the Nag Hammadi library, it is a tantalizing fragment, with about half the text flaked or ripped away. The present anthology is intended to be a collection of scriptures rather than a file of fragments, and in order to provide a reading experience analogous to that of the original readers, I have taken the liberty of conjecturally restoring the missing text. There are plenty of clues about, for instance, what the ascending soul must have seen. As to the initial dialogue between Jesus and the disciples, I have simply filled in typical Gnostic notions that seem naturally to issue from the kind of ideas that do survive in the remaining

text. I feel rather sure the original text must have contained at least this sort of thing. The conjectural text appears within brackets and conventional fill-ins by previous scholars occur in italics.

The Gospel of Mary Magdalene is included under the rubric of the heirs of Jesus for two reasons. First, the text is clearly related to the Gospel of Thomas, himself identified with Judas Thomas, Jesus' twin. Second, as Barbara G. Walker (*The Women's Encyclopedia of Myths and Secrets*) notes, on the bedrock mythic level, Mary Magdalene and Mary, the mother of Jesus, were no doubt the same character, like Cybele, who was both mother and consort of Attis in some versions of that myth. We can still see this in the fact that Talmudic sages made Jesus' mother a prostitute and Christian tradition made Mary Magdalene the same.

I have abandoned the convention of Nag Hammadi specialists who refer to the text by codex, page, and line numbers. Instead, I have supplied chapter and verse divisions of the kind familiar from the Bible.

1

[[1]On the third day after his suffering, the Savior appeared to his disciples, who were all gathered at the Mount of Olives. [2]And when he had quieted their doubts, he began to teach them as follows: "My brothers and sisters, long have I wished to make known to you the deeper truths which you must know if your souls are to find salvation, but till now your ears were prevented from hearing them. [3]For your hearts were one with that world unto which I died and from which I now have been forever raised. [4]And your minds have been raised with me so that they are now able to comprehend what you could not abide hearing before. [5]I have wrested you from the grasp of the archon of this world that you may hear the words a disciple ought to hear from his teacher and a mortal ought to hear from his God."]

2

[[1]And Peter grew bold and asked, "Lord, tell us concerning the Father. Who is he? And why did he send you?" [2]And the Savior answered, "Simon, you are blessed, for you do not suppose you know that which must be a mystery to all flesh. [3]For my Father is not the maker of the world of matter which you see around you, a world that is filled with

death and despair [4]but which, seeing with the fever of the flesh and its desire, mortals deem full of every delight and comfort and so waste their lives in pursuit of illusions. [5]No, all these things only enslave mankind to the material Creator. [6]My Father is exalted high above this one, whence he is called the Most High God. [7]For no one speaks of anything as ‘the highest’ unless there be others below it.]

3

[[1]“And you mortals are partly his creations, in that he has fashioned the body from unclean foulness. [2]But your souls he has stolen from the Light-World of my Father. [3]With them, he has imparted to your flesh what has the appearance of life, being but a shadow of the life you knew in the Pleroma of the Most High. [4]Here you abide in ignorance, never knowing either your origin or your destiny. [5]And for lack of that knowledge, you perish and are reborn into new bodies time and again, so long as the way out is hidden from you. [6]And that is why the Father sent me into the world in the likeness of your flesh, that I might make known these truths to you.”]

4

[[1]Andreas asked, “O Savior, what shall we then make of the things you said to the multitude, which differ not so very greatly from what they have heard from their scribes?” [2]And the Savior answered, “Let them be, Andreas. Some of them may yet discover they harbor the spark of light within them and then they will seek what I tell you now. [3]Others cannot, but my Father loves them, and he has bidden me to impart to them such wisdom as they can grasp to mitigate the harshness of him who created this world and gave the commandments to the legislator. [4]You will find nothing false in them, and yet they are mute as to the salvation of your spirits.”]

5

[[1]Levi asked the Savior, “My Lord, what then of the sufferings you endured and the death you died?” [2]And the Savior answered, “I suffered and I did not suffer. I died and I died not. [3]All the evil archons wrought was to free me of the shameful clothing I had assumed for the sake of my sojourn in this world. [4]I long bade you keep my identity secret, but the Powers knew, and finally they had me crucified, [5]not suspecting they would be the very cause of my deliverance. [6]And the reason I suffered these indignities was for the sake of those without true spirits, [7]that being lifted up, I might draw them away from the Creator and bring them

within the hearing of the news of me that you will proclaim. [8]Many of them shall be called, though few chosen."]

6

[[1]Salome asked him, "What shall be the end of all things, and will only a few be saved?" [2]The Savior replied, "O handmaid of my Father, your curiosity is as great as that of Sophia, who desired to peer behind the veil of the Pleroma. [3]Amen, I tell you: the news of the Kingdom of Light will be preached throughout this sublunar world [4]and in the world below, and those who hear will escape the wheel of death and birth when they die. [5]Their souls shall ascend, and if they are wise, they shall pass by the rulers of the heavenly spheres. [6]And once the elect have been redeemed, the matter that imprisoned them will fall back into the state of virgin clay with no likeness impressed upon it. [7]Finally, all the creation of the Creator will return to lifelessness."]

7

[1][Simon Peter asked,] "Then will matter be destroyed or not?" [2]The Savior replied, "All natures, all forms, all creatures exist both within and alongside each other and they will finally be reduced down to their individual roots. [3]For the nature of matter is reduced to the elements of its particular nature. He who has ears to hear, let him hear." [4]Peter said to him, "Having explained all things to us, tell us this, too: What is the original sin of the world?" [5]The Savior answered, "There is no sin per se; [6]rather, it is you yourselves who make a thing sinful when you perform the acts that partake of adulteration, which alone is properly termed 'sin.' [7]That is why the good came among you, to purify every nature, in order to restore it to its original state." [8]Then he went on, saying, "This is the reason you *grow ill* and die, for [the spirit ever seeks escape from admixture with the body of death of the one who is not yet enlightened]. *He who* understands, let him understand. [9]*Matter gave birth to* a passion without equal, which emerged from an abomination against nature. From this arose a trembling throughout the whole body. [10]That is why I once said to you: 'Be of good cheer!' [11]and if you should grow disheartened, take heart, surrounded by the various forms of being. He who has ears to hear, let him hear."

8

[1]When the Blessed One had thus spoken, he saluted them all, saying, "Peace to you! Receive my peace in your hearts. [2]Watch out that no one lead you astray saying, 'Lo here!' or 'Lo there!' For the Son of Man is

within you! Follow in his path! Whoever seeks him will find him. [3]So go from here and proclaim the news of the kingdom. [4]See that you stipulate no rules beyond those I ordained for you, and do not promulgate a law code like the legislator did so that you will avoid being tied in knots with it." [5]After saying these words, he left them. But they mourned the loss of him [6]and collapsed in tears, asking, "How are we supposed to go to the nations and proclaim the news of the kingship of the Son of Man? [7]If they had no mercy on him, they will hardly spare us."

9

[1]Then Mary rose to her feet, saluted them all, and spoke to her brothers: "Stop your weeping! [2]Do not mourn or waver, for his favor will accompany you to protect you. [3]No, instead, let us extol his greatness, seeing that he has trained us and transformed us into men."[a] [4]When Mary said this, she moved their hearts to repentance and they commenced to discuss what the Savior had said.

10

[1]Peter said to Mary, "Sister, we are aware of how the Savior loved you more than any other woman. [2]Tell us the things the Savior said that you remember, the things you know but we do not, that we have never heard." [3]Mary answered them, saying, "What is hidden from you, I will surely disclose to you." [4]And she commenced to speak to them these words: "I," she said, "even I, beheld the Lord in a vision, and I said to him, 'Lord, I behold you today in a vision!' [5]He answered and said to me, 'Blessed are you for not quailing at the sight of me! For where the mind is, there too will be the treasure.' [6]I answered him, 'Lord, how does the visionary see the vision: with the soul or with the spirit?' [7]The Savior answered, saying, 'It is not with the soul that one sees, nor yet through the spirit, but by the mind which *lies* between the two. This is *what* sees the vision, and it is [by that means I am speaking with you now, Mary.']

11

[[1]"And I asked him, 'O Lord, we know that you will leave us to ascend to the realm of light whence you first came. [2]And it is there we wish to join you, that we may no longer be orphans in this world. But we know not the way where you are about to go. [3]Do not hasten to depart without revealing the path to the Father that every soul must tread if it would leave the unwholesome mixing with matter in the day the flesh loosens its

a. Thomas, saying 114

grip.' [4]And the Savior said to me, 'O Mary, I shall show you the way you must go, so in the day when your brothers ask you these things, you will know what is required for salvation, [5]that we may be rejoined in the House of Light on high, whence all the souls of the elect first came. [6]First, know this: the way is simple but not unbarred. It winds through seven heavenly spheres, and each of these is jealously watched by its guardian and toll collector, ever vigilant to receive his due. [7]When I myself descended from the pleromatic light, I disguised myself, donning the likeness and nature of each archon and of his realm so that I passed freely among the denizens thereof. [8]And I changed vesture again and again with each world I passed through, like the actor who changes vesture with every new scene. [9]Presently, as you know, I shall return whence I came and I must strip off each outer layer, even seven bodies, each of a different substance, leaving each robe hanging limp in the hands of the archon ruling each sphere. [10]You and your brothers will not be able to easily evade the craft of the archons. [11]But though they are vigilant, it is no great thing to outwit them, provided one knows which words will overcome them.']

12

[[1]"And withal, he showed me in my vision the soul of one of the redeemed, one knowing of his origin and destiny. [2]That soul arose as a spark from a campfire into the cold night. [3]Having sloughed off the smothering body of flesh, it continued to rise until at length the soul came to the first of the Powers, even him who is named Darkness, who spoke thus to him: 'Proceed no farther, transgressor!' [4]And the soul answered, 'Why? In what have I sinned against you?' [5]And Darkness replied, 'In that my kingdom is a kingdom of darkness and no one who lights the torch of knowledge is permitted here! [6]Now let us extinguish your painful light that all may return to the peaceful sleep of ignorance.' [7]And that soul answered, 'No, O Darkness, but those who sleep your sleep do so only because they are first ignorant of your guile! [8]But of this the Savior has warned me!' And thus did it elude the Power of Darkness, rejoicing to be free from another nature, that of worldly ignorance.]

13

[[1]"After a time, that soul passed into the sphere of the archon Desire, that which causes the natures to mix and which seeks to awaken in the fleeing soul a fondness for those false delights it left behind on earth so that it might return there. [2]And Desire himself was there in an instant, speaking to it, saying, 'Who are you? And whence come you?' [3]And the

soul said, 'I am of the seed of the Living Father and do not belong to this world. [4]Hinder me not, as I seek but to return to the place whence I first came!' Thus he spoke to] it. [5]And Desire said to that soul, 'I never saw you descending, but now I behold you ascending! What makes you lie? You are mine!' [6]The soul replied, saying, 'I saw you, but you did not see me or notice me. You saw nothing but my vesture and you did not know me.' [7]When it had said these words, it fled away in great joy.[b]

[8]"Next it encountered the third Power, which is named Ignorance. It interrogated the soul, and it said, 'Where do you think you are going? [9]Do you deserve to enter heaven? In the chains of wickedness, you are captive. You, a prisoner, dare not judge me!' [10]And the soul replied, 'And who are you to judge me so? I have not condemned you. In truth, I was chained to the flesh, though now I am free. [11]I was not recognized. But I have come to recognize that the All is being deconstructed, both the earthly elements and the heavenly ones.'

[12]"When the soul had triumphed over the third Power, it ascended and beheld the fourth Power, which assumed seven likenesses. [13]The first of the likenesses is Darkness, the second Desire, the third Ignorance, the fourth is the Terror of Death, the fifth is the Reign of the Flesh, the sixth is the deluded 'wisdom' of the flesh, the seventh is the vengeance of Wisdom. [14]These are the Seven Wrathful *Powers*. They question the soul: 'Whence come you, murderer? Where are you headed, space traveler?' [15]For its part, the soul answered, saying, 'What held me captive has indeed been killed and what enveloped me has been defeated, and my desire has been extinguished and ignorance has expired. [16]In the midst of a *world,* I was set free from a world, and freed from a pattern of death; I received deliverance from a heavenly prototype, deliverance from the chain of oblivion which passes away. [17]Henceforward, I shall win my way to that repose where no one speaks of time, of season, of age.'"

---

b. Whence did Gnostics derive the notion they had to battle evil archons and angels on their way to heaven? It is an old piece of eschatology stemming from Babylonian astrology and Mithraism, but it was no doubt made real by the visions of ascetics who, alone in their desert cells, strove mightily against the demons of temptation. We read of such warfare in *The Life of Saint Anthony*, for example. If one faces demonic opposition already in the visionary ascent before death, it is reasonable to assume an externalized version would await the ascending soul afterward. The lore of Merkabah mystics tells us so, too, where visionaries recounted assaults by angels as they sought the throne room of God on high. See Gershom Scholem, *Major Trends in Jewish Mysticism* (NY: Schocken Books, 1973), 50, 51-52.

14

[1]After these words, Mary was quiet.[c] She had reached the end of what the Savior had said to her.[d] [2]But Andreas spoke up, saying to the brothers, "Make what you will of what she has said. [3]I, for one, do not believe the Savior said this. For indeed, these doctrines are full of bizarre notions." [4]Peter answered and said the same thing. He challenged them about the Savior: "Did he really speak with a woman without us knowing it?[e] And in secret? [5]Are we now supposed to change direction and all be taught by her? Did he prefer her to us?" [6]At this, Mary cried and said to Peter, "My brother Peter, what is it you suppose? Do you think I made this up in my imagination? Are you accusing me of lying about the Savior?" [7]Levi answered, saying to Peter, "Peter, you have always had a temper. Now I am watching you fight against the women as if they were our enemies. [8]But if the Savior himself made her worthy,[f] then really who are you to dismiss her? [9]Surely the Savior knows her well. After all, he loved her more than us.[g] [10]Instead, we ought to be ashamed of ourselves and don perfect manhood and secure him for ourselves,[h] [11]as he ordered us, and proclaim the news, promulgating no other rule or law in addition to what the Savior himself said."[i] [12]When [Levi said this, they all mustered their courage] and they commenced to go out to proclaim and *to* announce the news.

---

c. Appropriately, after the mention of eternal silence, Mary herself falls silent.

d. Why did the Savior leave her wondering about the last three Powers? He didn't, since the fourth implicitly encompasses all seven and is dealt with handily.

e. John 4:27

f. Thomas, saying 114

g. Gospel of Philip 63:33-37; 64:1-5a

h. This implies actualizing the Son of Man within, as in 8:15-16.

i. That, of course, is just the issue here: should Mary's surprising revelations be considered part and parcel of the authentic deposit of the Savior's teaching, to which no addition need be made? Or do they represent subsequent teachings someone is trying to smuggle in under the wire? Peter and Andreas think the latter, reflecting the Catholic/Orthodox dismissal of Gnostic revelations as "dangerous supplements" that would supplant what they pretend to complete.

VIII.
The Pauline Circle

50.

The Shepherd of Hermas

THIS GREEK APOCALYPSE WAS composed in two stages. The original version consisted simply of Visions 1-4, where Hermas is instructed by an elderly woman. There is a marked emphasis on the soon-coming end of the world, a concern which seems to fade in the longer, later version where the old woman is replaced by the Angel of Repentance. The original core appears to have been written in the 90s, while the enlarged version must have appeared about 150 CE, at least if the Muratorian Canon is correct in pegging the author as the brother of Roman bishop Pius, who died in or near 154. According to statements in the work itself, the seer was acquainted with Clement of Rome (Vision 2.4.3), to whom several pseudonymous works are attributed. It seems very likely that, even if we accept the author as Pius's brother, the Shepherd of Hermas, too, is pseudonymous. The name Clement appears as a Pauline colleague in Philippians 4:3. Likewise, Hermas is listed among Paul's colleagues in Romans 16:14 in a chapter that likely formed a separate epistle and was later added to Romans. It is plausibly suggested that Hermas was chosen as the seer's name to link the text to Paul's circle. This theory gains force from the fact that apocalypses are generally pseudepigraphical; thus we ought to assume this one is and proceed to ask which Hermas would have been a likely choice as the narrator.

There is a double entendre in the authorial ascription, for the document as a whole is very obviously an attempt to Christianize several prominent aspects of traditional and distinctively Roman religion. For instance, the old woman who plays the standard apocalyptic role of the interpreting angel is a Christian version of the oracular

Sibyl. There was a widespread tendency to Christianize her, just as Jews had done in penning their own Sibylline Oracles. The pythoness in Acts 16:16-18, who attests to Paul's preaching the true way of salvation, is another example of this. The virgins associated with the tower in the Shepherd (Similitudes IX.2.3) are obviously Christian counterparts to Rome's vestal virgins. The whole premise of the book, a humble seer being taken under the wing of a teaching angel called the Shepherd of Repentance, must derive from the Hermetic literature in which a heavenly being appears to reveal divine secrets to a seer. We think especially of *Poimandres*, the "Shepherd of Mankind," who is the god *Hermes*! What we are reading is a piece of Christianized Hermetica. This may explain the odd fact that the name of Jesus is never once mentioned in the text. He is instead called the Son of God, which may be an attempt to give the work the philosophical or mystagogical air of the Hermetic tracts by speaking of the Christian savior in more abstract terms.

There are two major theological items in the Shepherd of Hermas. First is the concern, spanning both earlier and later versions, for salvation of those who commit sins after their baptism. It was thought that baptism covered only the sins committed beforehand and that any Christian must keep himself or herself completely pure—a piece of sectarian enthusiasm now practically unimaginable—with the result that many Christians despaired or else contemplated delaying baptism to the deathbed as Constantine did in order to play it safe. Hermas announces that God has allowed a brief reprieve for repentance. God has gone the second mile, but after that, they are on their own again.

Second, the work offers an astonishing bit of adoptionist Christology we might not have expected to thrive in Rome at so advanced a date: we hear that the original and real Son of God was the Holy Spirit who dwelt in the human Jesus during his ministry and then returned to heaven to plead on Jesus' behalf for the Father to raise him from the dead and adopt him as a fellow heir and second Son of God!

The Shepherd of Hermas was widely regarded as canonical New Testament scripture through the second and third centuries. It appears in the fourth-century Codex Sinaiticus. Eusebius places it among the

category of disputed books which are nonetheless accepted by many. Why was it later rejected? Perhaps because of a growing reluctance to accept revelations of a later date for fear one would otherwise have no excuse for not accepting the oracles of the Paraclete voiced through the Phrygian prophets Montanus, Maximilla, and Priscilla.

1. Visions

First vision

1

[1]The master who raised me sold me to a certain Rhoda in Rome. Many years later, I chanced to meet her again and grew to love her as a sister. [2]After a period of time, I noticed her bathing in the river Tiber, so I offered my hand and helped her out of the water. Seeing her beauty in this way, I thought to myself, "How happy I should be to marry a woman so rich in both beauty and character!" But it only crossed my mind. [3]Some time later, I was on my way to Cumae, admiring the creations of God for their great splendor and power, when I fell asleep mid-stride. Then a spirit seized me and carried me off through a chartless waste impassable to man, the region being filled with precipices and crags carved by rivers. Once I crossed a river, I passed into flat terrain, then fell to my knees, starting to pray to the Lord and confess my sins. [4]Now as I prayed, the sky opened up and I beheld the lady for whom I had felt desire. She greeted me from the sky, saying, "Good morning, Hermas."

[5]I gaped at her and said, "My lady, what are you doing here?"

Then she replied, "I was caught up here in order for me to press home to you your sins in the sight of the Lord."

[6]I said to her, "Are you now accusing me, then?"

"No, I am not," she said, "but listen to what else I have to tell you. God, who lives in the sky and created from nothing everything that exists, then increased and multiplied them for his holy church's benefit, is angry with you because you sinned against me!"

[7]I answered her, "Sin against you? How? Have I ever spoken inappropriately to you? Have I not always revered you like a goddess? Have I not always shown you the respect due a sister? How can you make such false charges against me, my lady, making me out a villain and a pervert?"

[8]She laughed and said to me, "A desire for evil crept into your heart.[a]

a. What was so wrong with his momentary thought? Hermas is already married, as we shortly find out.

No? You do not regard it a sin for an evil desire to creep into the heart of a righteous man? Indeed it is, and a great one at that!" she said. "For a righteous man is one who contemplates only righteous plans. While his purposes remain righteous, his reputation is secure in heaven and he finds the Lord readily responsive in everything he does. But those who contemplate evil plans in their hearts invite death and imprisonment, especially those who claim as their portion this present world and glory in its wealth instead of sticking to the superior goods that are in store.
9Their souls will bitterly reproach them once they see they are in a hopeless plight, having abandoned themselves and their life. But as for you, Hermas, pray to God and he will heal your own sins and those of your household and of all the saints."

2

1When she had spoken her message, at once the skies closed up again and I found myself overwhelmed with horror and sorrow. And I said to myself, "If this sin is on my record, how can I be saved? Or how can I hope to satisfy God for my sins, which must be considerable? How can I begin to beg the Lord to be merciful to me?"

2While I was silently deliberating these questions, I see before me a huge white chair, snow-white like wool, and an elderly lady appeared, wearing shining clothing, holding a scroll in her hands. She took her seat with no one else in sight. She addressed me, "Good morning, Hermas."

Still sorrowful and sobbing, I answered, "Good morning, my lady."

3And she asked me, "What makes you so depressed, Hermas, you who are so patient and good-natured, always with a smile on your face? Why are you frowning and so far from good cheer?"

And I answered her, "Because an excellent lady accused me of sinning against her!"
4Then she said, "Far be it from a slave of God to do such a thing! Nonetheless, you must admit the thought of her did cross your mind. Now for the slaves of God, such a seemingly trivial impulse leads to sin. What a wicked, indeed insane, plan it is to ambush a pious soul that has already been approved by God, to prompt it to desire a wicked act, and all the more if that pious soul happens to be the mild-mannered Hermas, he who shuns every wicked wish, who moreover is full of integrity and sincerity!"

3

1"But this is not why God is mad at you, only to motivate you to convert your children, for they have wronged both the Lord and you, their parents. You are so fond of your children, you could never bring yourself

to rebuke them, and you allowed your children to grow terribly corrupt. This is why the Lord is angry with you. But he is willing to heal all the past sins you committed in your family life. You see, because of their sins and iniquities, you have become contaminated by the concerns of this world. [2]But in his wide mercy, the Lord pitied you and your family and will fortify you and give you a secure place in his glory. Just do not be careless, but take courage and strengthen your family. For just as the blacksmith masters the job he works at by repeated hammering, so does the daily repetition of righteous words defeat all evil. Thus, do not leave off correcting your children, for I am sure that if they do repent wholeheartedly, it is not too late for their names to be added to the ledger of life among the saints." [3]After she said this, she says to me, "Will you listen if I read?"

Then I reply, "Yes, my lady!"

She says to me, "Pay close attention and you will hear the glorious things of God!"

So I listened in rapt attention and wonder at that which I found I could not remember afterwards! For all the words were terrible, beyond human capacity. I did recall the closing words, though, since these were fitting for us and gentle: [4]"Behold the God of hosts, who created the world with his unseen and mighty power and his surpassing wisdom. According to his splendid plan, he adorned his creation with beauty and established the dome of the sky by his powerful command and set the earth afloat upon the waters. By his own wisdom and foresight, he formed his holy church, which he also blessed: see how he even removes the firmament and the mountains it rests on and the hills and the seas, and everything is leveled off for the free travel of his chosen ones so he may keep the promise he made to them with great splendor and celebration, as long as they faithfully keep the commandments of God, which they accepted."

4

[1]When she was done with the lesson and got up from her chair, four youths arrived and bore away the chair, heading away east. [2]Then she called me over and tapped my chest. She asked me, "Did you enjoy my reading?"

And I say to her, "My lady, the closing words were pleasing, to be sure, but the ones before that were very disturbing and hard to take!"

Then she answered me, saying, "These last words are addressed to the righteous, while the former are meant for the gentiles and the rebels."

[3]While she was still speaking to me, two men appeared and took hold of her arms. They, too, left in the direction the chair had gone, east-

ward. And she smiled as she left, and as she was going away she says to me, "Be a man, Hermas!"

Second vision

1

[1]I was again on the road to Cumae in the same season as the previous year, and as I walked, I recollected the vision I had that year. And again, a spirit seizes me and bears me off to the same place as the year before! [2]As soon as I got there, I dropped to my knees and started to pray to the Lord and to praise his name, that he had considered me worthy to be alerted to my previous sins. [3]But once I had risen from prayer, I see in front of me that elderly lady whom I had seen last year, strolling as she read a small scroll. Then she addressed me, "Can you recount these things to the chosen of God?"

I say to her, "Lady, I am not able to memorize so much, but if you give me that small scroll, I can make a copy of it."

"Take it, then," she replied, but be sure you bring it back to me." [4]So I took it and found a suitable spot in the countryside, where I began to transcribe it letter by letter, since I could make nothing of the syllables they formed. When I had completed the letters of the scroll, at once the scroll was seized from my hand, I know not by whom.

2

[1]Fifteen days later, after fasting and begging the Lord, the import of the writing became clear to me, as follows: [2]"Your children, Hermas, have sinned against God and have blasphemed the Lord.[b] By their terrible wickedness, they have betrayed their parents. Indeed, they have achieved the reputation of betrayers of parents, though it gained them nothing. But they went on to add further senseless acts and heedless wickedness to their sins, and in this way they have fulfilled their quota of trespasses. [3]But you tell this news to all your children and to your wife, whom you are henceforth to treat as a sister.[c] For she takes no rest from using her tongue to do evil. But she will stop once she hears this and will receive mercy. [4]After you have communicated this message to all of them, which the Master commanded me to reveal to you, then all their previous sins committed in the past will be forgiven them; yes, and to all the saints who have sinned before today if they whole-heartedly repent and expel ambivalence from their hearts. [5]For the Master swore by his own splendor con-

b. Job 1:4-5

c. 1 Cor. 7:5, 36-38

cerning his chosen ones that since he has set today as the limit, any who commit sin after this shall miss salvation. For there is a limit as to how many times the righteous may repent. The period for repentance is finished as far as the saints are concerned, though it will never be too late for pagans to repent. [6]Thus you are to tell the hegemons of the church to focus their attention on righteousness so they will receive a full reward with great splendor. [7]Thus, you who behave righteously, stand firm and do not waver so you may be admitted among the holy angels. Blessed are you all who endure with equanimity the impending Great Tribulation and all who will refuse to repudiate their prospect of everlasting life! [8]For the Lord swore about his Son that all who repudiated their Lord must forfeit the gift of everlasting life, specifically those who will soon repudiate him in the coming days. Yet, in his great mercy, he has granted clemency to those who repudiated him before."

3

[1]"But, Hermas, you must no more hold a grudge against your children. And no longer allow your sister to do as she pleases if you ever hope to see the children cleansed of their old sins. For if you will only drop your grudge against them, they shall meet with a righteous chastisement. A grudge can eventuate only in death. But you, Hermas, have yourself to blame for your family's transgressions since you did not pay adequate attention to them. You neglected them while tangled up in your own evil dealings. [2]But your saving grace is that you never forsook the true God, plus your integrity and your great self-control. These guarantee your salvation, as long as you persevere in them, as they save everyone who lives in such a manner and who behaves with sincerity and integrity. People like this triumph over all wickedness and go on to enter endless life. [3]Blessed are those who act righteously! They shall never come to ruin! [4]But go and tell Maximus, 'Behold! Tribulation is headed your way, if you think it best to repudiate the Lord a second time! "The Lord is near all who take refuge in him," as it is written in the Book of Eldad and Modat, who prophesied to the people of Israel in the desert.'"[d]

4

[1]Now, brothers, a revelation came to me during sleep by a young man, very handsome, who said to me, "The elderly woman who gave you the scroll: who do you think she is?"

I reply, "The Sibyl."

d. Num. 11:26-27

"You are mistaken," he says. "She is not."

"Then who is she?" I say.

"The church," he says.[e]

I ask him, "Then why is she so old?"

"Because," he says, "she was created before everything else, and it was she for whose benefit the very world was built. That is why she is so old."

[2]After this, I had a vision while at home. The elderly woman appeared and asked whether I had already passed on the scroll to the elders. I told her I had not.

"You did the right thing," she said, "because I have some words to add. Then when I have finished it, you shall publish it among the whole community of the chosen. [3]To that end, you are to make two copies. Send one to Clement, the other to Grapte. Clement shall distribute it in foreign cities; that is his responsibility. Grapte is to instruct the widows and orphans with her copy. But you are to read it to this city, along with the elders who preside over the church."

Third vision

1

[1]Brothers, the third vision I saw was like this: [2]After much fasting and pleading with the Lord to make known to me the revelation he promised me by the words of the old woman I saw, that very night I saw her again and she said to me, "Since you are so insistent and so eager to know everything, come into the country where you stay and I will appear about the fifth hour to show you what you ought to see."

[3]I ask her, "Lady, which part of the country?"

"Wherever you wish," she says. So I thought of a picturesque, secluded spot, but before I could mention the place to her, she told me, "Wherever you go, I will come."

[4]Brothers, I then went into the countryside, calculating the time remaining, and arrived at the place I had chosen to meet her, and I see an ivory couch standing there, and on it lay a linen cushion, upon which was spread a coverlet of finely woven flax.

[5]I was amazed to see things so nicely arranged with no one attending them. A spell of trembling overcame me, alone as I was. My hair prickled and shuddering wracked me! When I regained control of myself, calling

e. Here, as part of Hermas's Christianizing of Roman religion, the church has plainly taken the place of the Sibyl as a female oracle. His revelations represent a variation on the theme of the Christian *Sibylline Oracles*.

to mind the splendor of God, I took courage and knelt to confess my sins to the Lord again, just as I had on that previous occasion.

[6]At last she appeared, accompanied by six young men, the same ones I saw before, and she listened closely as I prayed, confessing my sins to the Lord. Then she touched me and said, "Hermas, haven't you begged enough for forgiveness? Pray for righteousness, too, so you may have enough of it to take a portion to your family." [7]Then she took my hand and helped me to my feet. Leading me to the couch, she told the young men, "Start building." [8]After they left and we were alone, she says to me, "Here, sit down."

I reply, "Lady, as my elder, it is yours to sit first!"

[9]"Do as I ask," she says, "sit down." Then I made to sit to her right, but she prevented me, motioning me to sit to her left instead. As I thought this over, disappointed that she would not let me sit on her right, she says to me, "Are you sad, Hermas? The place on the right is saved for others, namely those who have already proven themselves in God's sight by suffering for the sake of his name. You have far to go before you will qualify to sit among them. But if you maintain your integrity, you will one day sit with them, you and all who have done what they did and suffered as they did."

2

[1]"What did they suffer?" I say.

"Listen," she says. "Floggings, prison, great tribulations, crosses, wild animals, all for the sake of the name! This is why the right side of holiness is properly theirs. It belongs to them and to all who suffer for the name. The left side is for everyone else. Nonetheless, both groups, sitting on the right and on the left, enjoy the same gifts and the same promises, only those on the right enjoy a certain glory. [2]You are indeed eager to join them on the right, but you have yet many shortcomings. And yet you shall be purified from them. Yes, all who do not waver shall be cleansed of the sins committed up till today."

[3]Having said this, she was rising to leave, but I fell at her feet and begged her by the Lord to show me the vision she had promised. [4]Again she took my hand and drew me up and set me down to her left on the couch, herself sitting on the right. She pointed with a shining rod and says to me, "Do you see something great?"

I say to her, "My lady, I see nothing."

She says to me, "Look, don't you see before you a huge tower being built upon the waters with shining white stone blocks?" [5]And now, there

was a tower being built, firmly founded, by her six young attendants. And innumerable other men were hauling stones, some of them from the sea bottom, others from the land, and they were turning them over to the six young men, who took them and used them to build. [6]The stones dredged up from the deep they always inserted into the building as is, for they had already been fitted and they joined neatly with the others, joined so tightly each to its neighbor that no division between them could be seen, so that the tower appeared to be made of a single vast stone. [7]But as for the stones fetched from dry land, some they discarded, while others they applied to the structure. Still others they shattered and threw far away from the tower. [8]There were numerous other stones just scattered about the tower and no one used them in the construction. Some were mildewed, others cracked, some too short, others white and round, unable to fit into the design. [9]And other stones I noticed which, when thrown far from the building, sometimes landed on the path but immediately rolled off it. Others landed in the fire and lay burning. Others fell near the waters but could not quite roll into the water, as if they wanted to but were prevented.

3

[1]When she had shown me all this, she made to hasten on her way. I say to her, "My lady, what is the point of my seeing these things if I don't know what they signify?"

Answering, she said to me, "You are perhaps too curious for your own good! So you want to know the whole meaning of the tower?"

"Yes, my lady, so I may share it with my brothers, so they may rejoice the more to hear it and to realize the extent of the Lord's splendor!"

[2]Then she answered, "Many of them shall hear it, but once they do hear it, some will be glad but others will weep. But even these last will come to be glad if they take it to heart and repent. All right, then, hear the secrets of the tower, for I will reveal all of them to you. And then do not pester me for revelations! For even revelations have an end to them, once they have been fulfilled! Yet I know you: you will not stop begging for revelations, for you are shameless!

[3]"The tower you see under construction is none other than myself, Ecclesia, whom you have seen now and earlier. So ask what you please about the tower, and I will tell you so you may rejoice over it with the saints."

[4]I say to her, "My lady, since you have at last deemed me worthy to receive your revelations, then reveal them!"

Then she answered, "Very well. I will reveal to you everything that words will bear. Just be sure your heart is fixed on God and do not permit your mind to doubt the reality of what you are seeing."

5 I asked her, "Why is the tower built upon water, my lady?"

"I already told you that," she said, "You are persistent, and in that manner you arrive at truth! Hear, then, why the tower is raised up on watery foundations. It is because your life is saved and shall be saved by means of water. But it requires no earthy foundation because the tower is established by the command of the Almighty whose name is glorious and it is shored up by the invisible power of the Master."

4

1 I answered and said to her, "My lady, this is a great marvel! And the six young men building it—who are they, my lady?"

"They are holy angels of God, who were created first of all. The Lord entrusted his creation to their charge to expand and build it and to be the masters of the whole creation. Thus it is by their hands that the tower shall be finished."

2 "And who are the men hauling the stones?"

"They, too, are holy angels of God, but the six are their superiors. Once the erection of the tower is done, all of them equally shall celebrate the completion of the round tower, glorifying God upon its completion."

3 I asked her, "My lady, suppose I wanted to know the point of the stones, their properties, what kind they are?"

She answered me, "It is not because you are the worthiest of men that these things are revealed to you, you know. Among your predecessors, there were individuals more deserving than you, and the revelations really should have been made to them. But so the name of God may be worshipped, it has been revealed to you,[f] and more shall follow, for the sake of the waverers who have second thoughts as to whether these things are true or not. Tell them it is all true and that these visions contain nothing but the truth but all are firm and sound, established on a sure foundation."

5

1 "Now for the stones used in the construction. The white stone blocks that fit together so perfectly, these are the apostles, bishops, teachers, and deacons who lived by the holy standards of God and fulfilled their respective tasks in purity and holiness for the sake of God's chosen,

f. 2 Cor. 12:7

some of them already fallen asleep, others still alive. And it is because they always agreed together, peace prevailing among them as they listened to each other, their joinings fit together perfectly in the tower."

2"All right, but those dredged up from the sea floor and applied to the structure, that fit just as well with the pre-fitted blocks, what about them?"

"They are the ones who have suffered for witnessing to the name of their Lord."

3"And the other stones, the ones brought in from dry land: I would love to know who these are, my lady!"

She answered, "Those that fit into the building without having to be cut, these the Lord has approved because they lived in the righteous state the Lord loves and correctly carried out his commandments."

4"What of the ones brought and added to the building, who are they?"

"These are new converts to the faith, and faithful to it, but they require the angels to warn them to do good since a measure of their old sin still clings to them."

5"Those they spurned and threw away: who are they supposed to be?"

"These have sinned but they want to repent. This is why they were not thrown very far away from the tower. They will be quite useful once they repent. The repentant, so long as they do their repenting while the tower is still under construction, will be strong in faith. But once the building is finished, they have lost their opportunity and are doomed to be castaways. Their only advantage is that they still lie close to the tower."

6

1"But don't you want to know about the ones broken to shards and thrown far away from the tower? These are the lawless sons. They made a pretense of accepting the faith and there was no sin they lacked! Thus they are bereft of salvation, useless for the building because of their wickedness. This is the reason they were shattered and thrown so far, because of the Lord's anger, for they goaded him to wrath. 2But the rest that you saw, the large number piled in heaps, not used for construction, the mildewed ones, knew the truth but did not cling to it, nor remained joined to the saints. This renders them useless."

3"But the cracked ones: who may they be?"

"These are the ones who secretly harbor strife against one another, nor live at peace among themselves. They may appear to have reconciled,

but as each departs, he is already planning betrayal. These are the cracks running through the stones. [4]As for the broken stumps, these have believed and are for the most part righteous, but there remain in them certain forbidden impulses. This is why they appear stunted, imperfect."

[5]"And the white, round stones which didn't fit into the building: who are they, my lady?"

She answered and said to me, "Is there truly no end to your foolish stupidity? How long will you ask questions and fail to grasp anything for yourself?[g] These are the ones who have faith but also possess worldly wealth. When a persecution arises, they renounce their Lord so as not to have their property seized or lose business accounts."

[6]And I replied, asking, "My lady, will they ever be useful for construction?"

"Once deprived of their wealth, which alienates their souls, they will become profitable for God. For just as a round stone must have parts of it chiseled away before it can be fitted among square blocks, so too the ones rich in this world, unless their wealth be cut away, can never be of any use to the Lord. [7]Look at your own case! When you had riches, you were useless, but now you are useful and profitable for everlasting life. Make yourself useful to God, for you yourself have been carved from one of these stones!"

7

[1]"But as to the other stones you saw thrown far away from the tower, falling into the path and back out of it into fields with no paths, these are those who believe initially but then have second thoughts and forsake the true path. Imagining they can find some better route, they go astray and find themselves in a dire predicament, wandering through uncharted regions. [2]But the ones who land in the fire and are charred, these are the ones who rebelled irrevocably against God so that it no longer even crossed their mind to repent, given their constant preoccupation with profligate lust and wicked deeds. [3]And the others, falling near the waters yet prevented from falling in, do you want to know who they are? These are the ones who heard the preaching and asked for baptism in the name of the Lord. But then, when they recall the purity henceforth required of them, they balk and return to follow their evil desires."

---

g. Mark 4:13. Why is Ecclesia so nasty to Hermas, who after all is only a zealous truth-seeker? It is a Socratic device common also to miracle stories: the savior figure seeks to raise the bar to see if the seeker will persevere in the teeth of abuse. See Mark 7:27-30.

[4]With this, she completed the explanation of the tower. [5]But still not satisfied, I pressed more questions, whether there was any opportunity of repentance for these stones that were rejected, that would not fit into the tower: might they not yet find a place in the tower?

"In fact," she said, "they can repent, but they cannot be added to the tower. [6]They shall be added to another structure, a far more modest one, and then only after enduring torments and once they have served the full sentence for their sins. And they shall be released for one reason: they did once participate in the message of righteousness. And then they will be offered the chance to escape their torments if their evil deeds come into their consciences. Otherwise they forfeit salvation because of their stubborn hearts."

8

[1]When, at this point, I finished questioning her about all these things, she says to me, "Would you care to see another sight?" Wanting very much to behold one, I was delighted at the prospect. [2]She looked at me, then smiled broadly and she says to me, "Can you see seven women ringing the tower?"

"I do see them, my lady!" I reply.

"At the Lord's command, this tower is shored up by them. Here are their duties. [3]The first, the woman with powerful hands, is called Faith. By her help, the chosen of God are saved. [4]The second, wearing a tool belt and resembling a man, is Continence, the daughter of Faith. Whoever follows her lives a happy life, for he abstains from every evil act in the belief that if he foregoes every evil desire he shall have everlasting life once he dies."

[5]"And the others, my lady? Who are they?"

"Each is the daughter of the one before. One is named Simplicity, the next Knowledge, the next Sincerity, the next Reverence, the next one Love. When you have mastered all the feats of her mother, you shall have life."

[6]"I would like to know, my lady, what power each possesses."

[7]"Listen, then, to their repertoire of powers. The powers of each are adopted by the others, and they follow each other in their birth order. Faith bears Continence. Continence bears Simplicity. Simplicity bears Sincerity. Sincerity bears Reverence. Reverence bears Knowledge. Knowledge bears Love. Thus their deeds are chaste, reverent, and godly. [8]So whoever serves these women and is strong enough to emulate their deeds wins a place to live in the tower among the saints of God."

[9]Then I asked her about the times and seasons, if the time for everything to be fulfilled is now. But she just shouted, "You fool! Can't you see the tower is still under construction? Whenever the tower is finished, the end will come. But it shall be finished very soon now! Ask me no more questions on this score! This reminder should be enough for you and the saints to renew your spirits. [10]But it was not revealed for your own private benefit, but for you to relate all this to everyone else. [11]When three days are past—for I want to give you time enough to digest what you have seen—I order you, Hermas, to tell all these things, and those to follow, in the hearing of the saints. If they listen and implement them, they will be cleansed from their wickednesses, and you, too."

9

[1]"Listen, my children. I raised you in great integrity, sincerity, and reverence, thanks to the mercy of the Lord, who instilled righteousness in you, so you might be made righteous and holy, pure from all wickedness and perversity. But you will not leave off sinning! [2]Hear me now: settle your differences and show consideration for each other. Help each other. No longer enjoy feasts with meat[h] privately, but share with the needy. [3]For some people weaken the body through their gluttony and injure it. But the flesh of the malnourished is injured by the lack of food to the ruin of their bodies. [4]When you exclude the needy and do not share with them, you are harmed. [5]Remember the judgment to come! As for you who possess more than enough, seek out the hungry while the tower is still unfinished because once it is completed, you will want to do good deeds but there will be no opportunity.[i] [6]You who are proud of your riches! Watch out in case the destitute start to moan and the sound of it ascend as a prayer before the Lord[j] and you, with your fine possessions, be left, locked out of the tower!

[7]"Now I turn to you hegemons of the church, who sit on the dais facing the congregation: do not be like the magicians! The sorcerers conceal their potions in boxes, but you hide your potions and your poisons in your hearts! [8]You are hard-hearted, nor will you purify your hearts or

h. Most people in the Roman Empire got by on a daily diet, year in and year out, of corn porridge.

i. This is a perfect statement of the "interim ethic" of Jesus, as Albert Schweitzer understood it: the end is near, so one cannot invest in the future in a conventional way. Only in helping those in need can one accrue security and merit for when one will most need it: at the Final Judgment.

j. James 5:1-5

mix together the formula of wisdom in a clean-washed heart so you might receive mercy from the Great King. [9]Watch out, then, my children, that these divisions between you not cause you to forfeit your lives! [10]How can you be so eager to teach the chosen of the Lord while you yourselves are so untutored?[k] Then teach each other, reconcile your strife so I may be pleased to come before the Father and report on all of you to him."

10

[1]When she was done speaking to me, the six young men working on the building came and escorted her to the tower. Another four lifted the couch and took it to the tower, too. I saw none of their faces, as they were all facing away from me. [2]As she went, I asked her to explain to me the three forms in which she had appeared to me. She answered me, "You must ask another for these things to be revealed to you." [3]You see, brothers, she appeared to me last year in my first vision as a very old woman sitting on a chair. [4]In the second vision, her face was young looking, but her form and her hair were aged and she spoke to me standing up. And she was more cheerful than at first. [5]But in the third vision, she was completely youthful and ravishingly beautiful, her hair alone seeming elderly, and she was altogether cheerful and sat on a couch. [6]I was desperately curious to have this mystery accounted for. Then I see the elderly woman in a vision one night, saying to me: "Every inquiry requires humility. You must fast and then you will get what you seek from the Lord."

[7]So I did fast all day, and that same night a young man appeared to me and he says to me, "Since you are so eager for my revelations and willing to seek them with fasting, watch out that in the process you don't do yourself physical harm! [8]Surely all these revelations are enough for you! Do you think there are grander revelations available than those you have witnessed already?"

[9]In reply, I say to him, "My lord, I ask only one thing: to understand the whole truth about the three forms in which the aged woman appeared to me."

He answered and said to me, "Are you still without understanding? It must be your ambivalent faith that retards your reason, plus the fact that your heart is not fixed on the Lord!"

[10]I answered and said to him again, "Ah, my lord, that may be so. And so I should like to learn the truth more accurately from you."

---

k. James 3:1; John 3:10

11

[1]"Listen, then," he says, "and you will learn about the threefold form you ask about. [2]Why did she appear to you in the first vision as an elderly woman sitting in a chair? Because your spirit was old and worn out, powerless because of your weakness and ambivalent behavior. [3]Just as the aged, with no hope of renewing their youth, have nothing to look forward to except falling asleep in death, so you, weary with worldly concerns, abandoned yourself to regrets and thought not to leave your anxieties with the Lord. Your spirit was broken and your sorrows prematurely aged you!"

[4]"But why was she sitting in a chair? I have to know, my lord!"

"Because every weak person takes a seat, being too fatigued to stand for long. There you have the significance of the first vision's symbols."

12

[1]"But in the second vision, you beheld her standing, with a more youthful face, more cheerful than previously, but still with aged form and hair. Listen to this parable, too," he says. [2]"Picture an old man, now bereft of all hope because of weakness and poverty, only counting the days till the end of his life. Suddenly he receives an inheritance. He hears the news of it, springs up full of joy, dresses with vigor, and abandons his bed. He stands erect, and his spirit, formerly broken because of old circumstances, is rejuvenated. He sits no more but is emboldened. That is how it was in your own case when you heard the revelation the Lord vouchsafed you. [3]He felt compassion for you and renewed your spirits. You set aside your illnesses and felt new strength coursing through you. You became strong in faith and the Lord was delighted to see you donning your strength. That is why he showed you the construction of the tower. Yes, and he is willing to show you more if you will wholeheartedly pursue harmony."

13

[1]"Now in the third vision, you saw her younger and beautiful and cheerful and of beautiful form. [2]Well, just as one grieving receives good news and at once forgets his worries, thinking only of the news he has heard, and is from then on empowered to do good, his spirit being renewed by the joy he has heard of, so too your spirit has been renewed by virtue of the good things you have seen.[1] [3]And though you saw her reclin-

1. In the Arthurian legends of the chalice of the Last Supper, Percival sees the Grail Bearer in two forms, one repulsive, the other beautiful—a Christianization

ing on a couch, this denotes not infirmity but rather firmness, as the couch is held steady by four legs, just as the world itself is established by means of the four elements.[m] [4]So those who repent fully shall have their youth restored to them and shall be established firmly since they have whole-heartedly repented. There you have the revelation whole and complete. Ask no more about revelations! If anything else remains, it shall be revealed to you in due course."

Fourth vision

1

[1]I saw a fourth vision, brothers, twenty days after the previous vision that came to me, this one an image of the Great Tribulation. [2]I was heading into the countryside via the Campanian Way. From the high road, it is about ten stadia and easy traveling. [3]So as I am walking by myself, I beg the Lord to implement the revelations and visions he vouchsafed to me by means of the holy Ecclesia, for him to fortify me and to grant an opportunity for repentance to his slaves who have tripped up and for his name to be worshipped in gratitude for having shown me his wonders. [4]And as I worshipped and thanked him, a sound like a voice answered me: "Do not hesitate through doubt, Hermas!"

At this, I began to examine myself, asking, "A hesitant faith? Me? How can that be, seeing how firmly the Lord has grounded me and the splendid sights I have seen?" [5]I kept walking for a bit, brothers, until behold, I see a pillar of dust mushrooming, it appeared, to heaven itself! So I began to wonder, "Perhaps cattle are stampeding, raising dust in their wake?" Now it was no more than a single stade away! [6]But as the dust cloud only increased in size, I began to suspect something supernatural was in play. Then the sun broke through a rift in the billowing cloud-

---

of Eriu, goddess and personification of Ireland, who looked like a hag in the winter and was beautiful and young in the spring. Embodying the wasteland, the Grail Bearer appears as the Loathly Damsel. The wasteland's rebirth depends on Percival *asking the right question*: "Whom does one serve with the grail?" In our text, Hermas is desperate to ask the right question about the young and old versions of Ecclesia, a similarly allegorical figure. See Roger Sherman Loomis, *The Grail: From Celtic Myth to Christian Symbol* (NY: Columbia University Press, 1963), 46-64.

m. Charles Taylor, *The Witness of Hermas to the Four Gospels* (London: C. J. Clay and Sons, 1892), 7-12ff, argues that Hermas knew of the canonical gospels, represented by the four legs of the couch and the four elements. Taylor thinks Irenaeus's argument about the four winds and four compass directions must be derived from Hermas. If Taylor is correct, it seems difficult to explain why our author makes so little use of the gospels.

bank, disclosing a huge creature like some marine monster. From its maw spewed flaming locusts![n] The thing was about one hundred feet in length and its head armor-plated like pottery!

[7]I started to panic and to beg the Lord to deliver me from it. And suddenly I remembered what had been said to me: "Do not hesitate through doubt, Hermas!" [8]Once I had donned the armor of faith in the Lord, brothers, and thought back to the powerful deeds he had taught me, I regained my composure and decided to take my chances with the beast. So fierce was the headlong momentum of the thing that its impact might have leveled a city! [9]I approach it, and great monster though it was, it lies down on the ground, stretching and lolling its tongue! Nor did it make a move till I had passed by. [10]And then the beast was seen to have four stripes on its head: black, then the red of fire and blood, then gold, then white.[o]

2

[1]Now after passing the creature and continuing on another thirty feet, behold, a virgin steps up to meet me, all adorned as if emerging from the bridal suite, veiled all in white up to her forehead and wearing both white sandals and a turban. Her hair, too, was white. [2]From my previous

---

n. Rev. 9:1-11; 16:13-14

o. A striking and independent parallel to this vision meets us in the *Puratan Janam-Sakhi*, a compilation of Sikh oral traditions about Guru Nanak reduced to writing about 1650. Here is W. H. McLeod's summary: "Next the Guru and [his disciple] Mardana came to a wilderness where they rested. At God's command Kaliyug came to try to deceive the Guru. To Mardana's inexpressible terror a great darkness fell and trees were swept away. Next there appeared fire with smoke ascending on all sides from four abysses of fire. Black clouds then gathered and rain began to fall. Finally, Kaliyug appeared in the form of a demon giant so tall that the top of its head reached to the heavens. It advanced toward them, but the nearer it came the smaller it grew, until eventually it assumed the form of a man and Kaliyug stood before Guru Nanak in a posture of respect. In the discourse which followed he sought to tempt him with offers of a beautiful palace, of jewels, of women, of the power to work miracles, and finally of temporal sovereignty. All were rejected by the Guru, and Kaliyug finally made his submission and asked for salvation."

See W. H. McLeod, *Guru Nanak and the Sikh Religion* (Delhi: Oxford University Press, 1976), 41. The fearsome Kaliyug is the embodiment of the Kali yuga, the fourth and final yuga, or age, of the cosmic cycle of world-death-and-rebirth. The demon giant symbolically incarnates the vices and temptations of a degenerate age. The parallel with the temptation of Jesus in the desert is evident, too, but the stronger resemblance is to the fourth vision of Hermas, where the terrible denouement of history is also monstrously personified as a test for the saint, who tames him.

visions, I knew her for Ecclesia, and my spirits lifted. She greets me, saying, "Good morning, my good fellow!"

And I returned her greeting: "Good morning to you, my lady!"

[3]As if waiting for me to say more, she said, "Did anything unusual cross your path?"

I answer her, "Indeed, my lady! A giant beast capable of destroying whole populations, but thanks to the power of the Lord and his great mercy, I managed to escape it!"

[4]"A fine escape it was," she says, "because you remembered to leave your worries to God and opened yourself to the Lord, believing that nothing but his great and celebrated name could rescue you! For this reason, the Lord dispatched his angel, Segri, whom he put in charge of all animals, to close its mouth[p] so it would do you no harm. Through your faith, you have escaped a great tribulation, and because you did not quail in the face of so great a creature. [5]Now go and tell the chosen of the Lord about his great deeds! And tell them that this creature is a symbol of the impending Great Tribulation. If you fortify yourselves before it happens, repent of your sins, and incline your hearts wholly to the Lord, you will be able to escape it! But only if your hearts are purified, impeccable—and only if you serve the Lord for the rest of your lives without reproach. Throw your burdens on the Lord's strong back and he will relieve you of them. [6]Put your faith in the Lord, you doubters! What can he not do? He is surely able equally to avert the storm of his wrath from you and to unleash his arsenal of plagues upon you who doubt him! Woe to the one who, hearing these words, disregards them! Better for him had he not been born!"

3

[1]I asked her about the four stripes on the creature's head. She answered me, saying, "Your insatiable curiosity shows itself again!"

"I admit it, my lady, " I said. "Do tell me what these things mean!"

[2]"Listen, then: the black stands for the world you live in. [3]The red of fire and blood presages that this world must perish in fire and blood. [4]The gold stripe refers to you who have fled this world, for just as they test gold by fire to make it useful, so you, too, are to be tested, and those who survive the fire, passing through it successfully, will emerge purified. For as gold casts off its impurities, so you will let go your griefs and troubles and be purified. Then you will be useful in the construction of the

---

p. The text has the angel's name as Thegri, amended by Rendel Harris to "Segri," denoting "the one who shuts" (Hebrew *sagar*). In Dan. 6:22, an angel (no doubt this one) similarly shuts the lion's mouth.

tower. [5]Now the white stripe denotes the coming age in which the chosen of God will have their dwelling, for they shall be spotless and pure through the ages. [6]So do not leave off speaking to the saints. You now know the symbolism even of the Tribulation which is gathering strength like a storm. But do not fear: if you so will it, it shall be nothing. When it comes about, remember how it was predicted."

[7]Once she finished her say, she left, but I did not notice which way she went because I thought I heard a noise and I recoiled in fright, sure now that the creature was returning! [8]*But it was only a man, albeit of great height and with shining clothing.* [9]*With him was another man dressed in the garb of a shepherd. His face appeared sun-bronzed and lined from much care. He had the look as of a stern yet compassionate father.* [10]*The tall man pointed to the other and said, "This is he to whom I am entrusting you for your soul's benefit. You shall see much of him in the coming days and he shall reveal to you all things necessary for your repentance. Hear him, then." And in a moment, both were gone.*[q]

Fifth vision

1

[1]I was praying at home, sitting on the couch, when a man with a radiant face entered, dressed like a shepherd. He has clad in white sheepskin and had a pouch slung over one shoulder, holding a staff in his hand. He saluted me and I returned the greeting. [2]At once, he joined me on the couch and he says to me, "I was sent by the holiest of the angels[r] to stay with you for the rest of your days."

[3]I thought he had come as a test of some sort, and I say to him, "For what purpose? Who are you?" I say, "For I know him in whose care I have been placed."

He says to me, "Do you not recognize me?"

"No," I answer.

"I," he says, "am the Shepherd and you have been placed in my care." [4]Even as he spoke, his appearance began to change[s] and I did recognize him as the same to whom I was assigned. At once I was confused,

q. I have added vv. 8-10 as a conjectural replacement for material required by subsequent events but absent from the manuscripts.

r. See note at Mandate 5.1.7.

s. "Polymorphism," or the ability to change forms at will, is a mark of the purely spiritual mode in which angels exist. In the Apocryphal Acts, Jesus is shown the same way because he, too, lacks real human flesh. To have many forms is to have no real physical form at all.

seized by fear, and completely overwhelmed with anxiety at the wicked and foolish answer I had given him. [5]But he reassured me, saying, "You need not be confused; just fortify yourself with the commandments I will presently give you. For I was assigned," he says, "to reiterate all the things you have already seen, of which the highlights are most important for you. First, copy down my commands and parables, and there will be other things you will need to write as I tell you. The reason I tell you to begin by transcribing the commands and the parables," he says, "is so you may consult them at your leisure and thus grow more adept at keeping them." [6]So I did record the commands and parables as he told me. So when you hear them, if you take them to heart, living by them, you shall inherit all that the Lord has promised you. [7]But if you hear them and dismiss them out of hand, neglecting to repent and continuing to accumulate sins, you shall receive from the Lord all that he has threatened for the ungodly. And all that follows is what the Shepherd, the angel of repentance, told me to write down.

2. The Commandments

First mandate

1

[1]"First, believe that there is but a single God, the one who created and arranged everything, who brought all things over from non-being into being, in whom all things are contained, though nothing can contain him. [2]Believe him, then, and fear! And in your fear, contain yourself. Keep these precepts and you shall throw off the clinging bands of wickedness, donning instead every virtue of the righteous. Keep this commandment and you shall live before God."

Second mandate

1

[1]He says to me, "Hold fast integrity and shun deceit. Be like young children who are innocent of the wickedness that ruins human life. [2]First, spread no evil rumor, neither rejoice in the slanderer's report. If you do, you shall share equally in the guilt of his sin, if you believe the rumor you have heard. If you believe it, you assume another's grudge. And so you will be culpable for the sin of the tale bearer. [3]Slander is an evil demon, eager to be about his work. He is never at home except among factions. If you will abstain from it, you shall succeed with everyone. [4]Be clad in reverence; that way lies nothing to trip you, for all is pleasant and goes smoothly. Spend your labor at a noble occupation, and what you make

from the job God gives you, be willing to share with those in want, drawing no prudential distinctions between worthy and unworthy recipients. Give to everyone, for God wants all to receive of his blessings. [5]It is the recipients whose task it is to give account to God, as to why they accepted it and what they wanted to do with it. Those who accepted help to alleviate real lack need fear no judgment. But those who accept fraudulently will have to answer for it. [6]No guilt can lie with the giver; his one concern was to carry out the task the Lord assigned him, and he has done it with sincerity, making judgments on no one. This service, sincerely rendered, wins glory in the eyes of God. Whoever so ministers will attain to life with God. [7]So see that you keep the command, just as I have relayed it to you, so your own repentance, as well as that of your household, may be found sincere, your hearts pure and without stain."

Third mandate

1

[1]Again he speaks to me: "Cherish truth and allow nothing else to escape your lips so that everyone may see the spirit which God made to live in your flesh is trustworthy, and in this way, praise will redound to the Lord, who lives inside you. For every word of the Lord is true, and no falsehood exists in him. [2]Thus liars have no regard for the Lord and indeed steal from him since they cheat him of the deposit they were allowed. He loaned them a spirit free of lying, but they return to him a lying spirit, having sullied the commandment of the Lord and become thieves." [3]Hearing this, I broke down sobbing. But when he saw me crying, he said, "Why do you weep?"

"Because, my lord, my salvation is in jeopardy!"

"And why is that?" he says.

"Because, my lord," I say, "the truth has always been a foreign language to me! I have lived a life of guile with everyone I met. I disguised my lies as truth and no one ever questioned me. No, everyone trusted me implicitly. Then how, my lord," I asked, "can I hope to have everlasting life, having done all this?"

[4]"Your point is a good one, all right," he says, "You were obliged as God's servant to behave truthfully. The Spirit of Truth should not have to share quarters with any evil scheming and you should not cause grief to a Spirit which is both holy and true."

"My lord," I reply, "your words are inescapably clear!"

[5]"So, then," he says, "you hear my words. Good. Treasure them, then, so that the things you said falsely in your business dealings may

henceforth be true. If from now on you hold to the truth, your reputation may become justified after all. If you adhere to the truth from now on, you will be able to gain everlasting life. And anyone who hears this command and avoids lying, which is an insidious habit, shall live before God."

Fourth mandate

1

[1]"I order you," he says, "to stay pure and not allow so much as a single thought about someone else's wife to cross your mind, nor any thought of prostitution or any such sinful acts, because if you do, you are committing a serious sin. Remember your own wife constantly and you will never stray. [2]For if adulterous desire, or anything of the sort, does creep into your heart, you will go astray and commit sin. For such desire on the part of one of God's slaves is a serious sin, and if anyone actually does the deed, he has achieved death for himself. [3]So see to it! Avoid this desire, for lawlessness has no business entering into the righteous heart, which is a sanctuary."

[4]I ask him, "My lord, allow me a few more questions."

"Go on," he says.

"My lord, suppose a husband has a wife who is devoted to the Lord, yet he discovers she is committing adultery. Is the husband sinning if he continues to live with her?"

[5]"As long as he does not know what is going on, he is not sinning," he says, "but once the husband knows about it, and if the wife does not repent, continuing her affair, her husband, if he stays with her, is only aiding and abetting her in sin and therefore shares her culpability."

[6]"Then what, my lord," I say, "should the husband do in such a case?"

"He must divorce her," he says, "and he must live alone from then on. Because if, after divorcing her, he remarries, he too is committing adultery."

[7]"But, my lord," I say, "what if the wife, once divorced, repents and returns to her husband? Shouldn't he take her back?"

[8]"Very definitely!" he says. "In fact, if the husband refuses to take her back, he is sinning and bringing great guilt upon himself. No, a repentant sinner must be welcomed back, though let no one make a habit of it, for the slaves of God are allowed only one chance to repent. So on the chance she might repent, the husband should hold the door open and not marry again. This is the rule of behavior laid down for husband and wife.

[9]"Not only," he continues, "is it adultery when a man defiles his flesh, but if anyone observes the marriage customs of the gentiles, he is committing adultery. So if any one persists undaunted in this behavior, too, shun him and do not live under the same roof with him. Otherwise you seem to be endorsing his sin. [10]This is why you were urged not to remarry, whether a husband or a wife, since repentance always remains a possibility. [11]My aim," he explained, "is not to provide an excuse for moral looseness[t] but rather to make it possible for the sinner to leave off sinning. And as to the original adultery, there is One who can heal the wounds, he who rules over everything."

2

[1]I prepared to ask him something else and began, "Since the Lord judged me worth the effort of sending you to stay with me forever, let me ask a few more things, since I am so slow of understanding, my mind having been dulled by my previous sins. Help me understand, for I am really quite the fool and comprehend nothing at all."

[2]Answering me, he said, "Repentance is my special jurisdiction and I am pleased to grant understanding to every soul who repents. Indeed, do you not see," he says, "that the very act of repentance, denoting a change in mind, is a new kind of understanding? To repent takes a high degree of understanding," he says. "For an individual first sins, then comes to understand that he has done evil in the Lord's eyes, and the sin he committed plagues his conscience and he repents, forswearing further evil. Henceforth, he does good extravagantly and humbles his soul, torturing it with the memory of his sin. From this, you can see how repentance is a matter of profound self-understanding."

[3]"That is precisely why, my Lord," I say, "that I ask you all these detailed questions: first, because I am such a sinner, and second, because I do not know which deeds I must do to gain everlasting life, for my sins are numerous and of many sorts!"

[4]"You shall have life if you but obey my commands and live by them. In fact, anyone who hears and obeys them shall live with God."

3

[1]"My lord, let me venture to pose another question," I say.

He answers, "Go on."

"I have been told," I say, "some teachers say there is no opportunity

t. Hermas anticipates an objection that Tertullian would certainly raise against this passage.

to repent after the one we availed ourselves of when we went under the waters to obtain absolution of the sins committed up to that point."

[2]He says to me, "You were fortunate to hear such instruction, for that indeed is the way of things. For anyone who has received the absolution of his sins is under the obligation never to sin again but to live in a pure state henceforward. [3]But seeing how you must know everything in complete detail, I will tell you this, too, so that I give no excuse to anyone who may yet come to believe or those who already believe in the Lord. For those who now believe, or who may believe in the future, have only the remission of previous sins, not the luxury of repentance from further sins. [4]But for those who were called before these days, when this rule applies, the Lord has afforded them a chance for repentance. For his gaze penetrates the heart and knows everything in advance, and long ago he recognized both the wicked tendencies of mortals and the many strategies of the accuser, how he would be playing tricks on the slaves of God and would deal treacherously with them. [5]So, full of compassion, the Lord took pity on his creations and granted this opportunity to repent, and he put me in charge of administering it. [6]But I tell you," he says, "if after this solemn and holy amnesty anyone tempted by the accuser commits a sin, he has but a single opportunity to repent. Even if he sins inadvertently, then repents, such repentance will do him no good; it is only with great difficulty he may be saved."

[7]I say to him, "I was restored to life when I heard these words from you in such detail. For now I am clear: if I add no more sins to my record, I shall be saved!"

"You shall indeed," he says, "and anyone else who makes the effort."

4

[1]I questioned him again, saying, "My lord, since you seem willing to put up with me, tell me something else, too."

"Go ahead," he says.

"Suppose, my lord," I ask, "a wife, or perhaps a husband, falls asleep in death and the other remarries, does the one who remarries commit a sin?"

[2]"It is no sin," he says, "but to remain single is the more honorable choice, giving the Lord great delight. But again, to remarry is no sin.

[3]"Remain in a state of purity and holiness, then, and you shall have life with God. Everything I tell you now, and will tell you from now on, be sure you cherish it henceforth, from the time you were entrusted to me, and I will continue to stay in your home. [4]Your previous sins will all be

forgiven, provided you keep my commands and behave according to the state of purity I command."

Fifth mandate

1

[1]"If you cultivate long-suffering and understanding," he says, "you shall be able to defeat all evil deeds and do righteous acts instead. [2]For if you are forbearing, the Holy Spirit who lives in you shall be pure, with no shadow cast over it by another spirit, an evil one. Instead, he shall be delighted to live in a spacious den, satisfied with the vessel that contains him, and shall serve God with rejoicing thanks to the prosperity you are affording him. [3]But whenever any spirit of anger encroaches, the Holy Spirit, who is quite sensitive, is at once affronted, no longer having his domicile to himself; and he begins to look for the exit, for he is choking on the newly foul atmosphere and has not the leisure to minister to the Lord as he wishes, being defiled by that angry temper. For just as the Lord lives comfortably in long-suffering, the accuser thrives in an angry mood. [4]Thus it is quite disadvantageous, even evil, for an individual to have both these spirits dwelling together within him. [5]Take a drop of wormwood and put it into a jar of honey. You will ruin all the honey with the smallest portion of wormwood. Having destroyed the honey's sweetness, the only thing that made it valuable in the first place, you will have made it bitter and thus useless. But if you keep the wormwood separate from the honey, the honey remains sweet and as useful to its owner as ever! [6]You see that long-suffering, too, is sweet, sweeter in fact than honey and very useful to the Lord since he thrives in it. But anger is bitter and useless. So if anger is mixed with long-suffering, long-suffering is befouled and one's prayers for others lose all efficacy."

[7]"I would like to know, my lord," I say, "how an angry temper does its work so as to be on guard against it."

"Yes, truly," he says, "if you fail to protect yourself from it, yourself and your family, you have forfeited all hope. But do guard against it; I will help you. Indeed, every one who has repented whole-heartedly will want nothing to do with it. For I will attend them and guard them, for they were all saved by the holiest of angels."[u]

---

u. This seems to be a reference to Jesus, viewing him as the prince of angels. See Richard N. Longenecker, *The Christology of Early Jewish Christianity*. Studies in Biblical Theology Series (Naperville, IL: Alec R. Allenson, 1970), 26-32.

2

[1]"Hear, then," he says, "how the angry temper does its work, how evil it is, and how it manages to undermine the slaves of God by its wiles and how it tempts them away from righteousness. But it is powerless to mislead those with a robust faith; they are immune to it because the power of the Lord safeguards them. Those it misleads are the ones bereft of faith and the hesitant. [2]For when it chances to spot such a one living in calmness, it insinuates itself deep inside him, and for no particular reason the man or woman grows bitter about mundane affairs, perhaps over favorite foods or something insignificant, about a friend, about giving more expensive gifts and receiving cheaper ones or other such foolishness. All these matters are foolish, pointless, idiotic, and a waste of time for the slaves of God.

[3]"Long-suffering, on the other hand, is grand and strong, with a mighty and robust power, and is successful by expanding to great dimensions, making one delighted, elated, carefree, worshipping God in any circumstances, free from bitterness, ever staying calm and peaceful. Such long-suffering, therefore, is to be found among those with mature faith.

[4]"By contrast, the angry temper starts out foolish, fickle, and stupid. Then foolishness produces bitterness, bitterness gives rise to rage, rage to anger, and from anger spitefulness. Then, since spite is a combination of all these ingredients, it becomes a serious, even fatal, sin. [5]Just imagine all these spirits dwelling in a single vessel, one also inhabited by the Holy Spirit! The vessel simply cannot contain them all and overflows. [6]The sensitive Spirit, thus, being unaccustomed to having to share space with an evil spirit, nor indeed with any harshness, abandons such a one and goes elsewhere for some peace and calm. [7]Then, having been forsaken by the noble Spirit which used to live inside him, that one, now empty, is henceforth infested with evil spirits, irrational in behavior, lurching here and there at the tugging of the evil spirits, completely oblivious and stripped of his former good intentions. This is what happens to everyone who has an angry disposition. [8]Steer clear of the violent temper, absolutely the worst of evil spirits! Instead, don the robe of long-suffering, holding anger, foul temper, and bitterness at arm's length, and you shall be located among the holy ranks whom the Lord loves. Be sure you never let this commandment slide, for if you master it, you will have no trouble keeping all the other commandments I will be giving you. Gain strength from them, draw upon their power, and may everyone be so endowed, every one who wants to live in holiness."

Sixth mandate

1

[1]"I told you in no uncertain terms in my very first commandment," he says, "to hold fast faith, the fear of God, and moderation."

"Indeed you did, my Lord," I say.

"And now I want to explain their powers, too, so you will understand the power and result of each one. For there are two kinds of results. These virtues are required equally of the righteous and the unrighteous. [2]You should trust the righteous but suspect the unrighteous, for the righteous take the straight path, but that of the unrighteous is twisting. You must walk in the straight and even path, avoiding the twisting one. [3]The twisting road has no directions, leads nowhere, and is littered with rocks to trip you. It is bumpy and choked with briars. It is no surprise that it injures those who wander down it. [4]But those traveling upon the straight path enjoy a smooth and unobstructed road. There is nothing to trip them, all is level, and all briars have been rooted out.[v] You see, don't you, how it is to your clear advantage to take this path?"

[5]"Why, I am delighted," I say, "to take this path, my lord!"

"And you shall," he says, "yes, and so will everyone else who inclines his heart to the Lord."

2

[1]"Listen now, and I shall discourse upon faith," quoth he. "Each individual is attended by a pair of angels, one good, the other evil."

[2]"My lord!" I interrupted, "How shall I tell which is impelling me if both constantly hover over me?"

[3]"Listen," he says, "and you will understand how they operate. The angel of righteousness is sensitive, unobtrusive, gentle, and peaceful. As soon as this one comes into your heart, he speaks at once of every noble act and every splendid virtue. When all these things come to mind, you will know it is the good angel with you. You may trust him and his influence.

[4]"Now as to the tokens of the wicked angel, first, he is short-tempered, resentful, and irrational and his deeds are evil, unseating the slaves of God. Whenever, then, he makes an appearance in your heart, recognize him by these deeds."

[5]"My lord, I don't know how to recognize him."

---

v. If this is based on Matt. 7:13-14, where the way to perdition is easy, Hermas may be citing it loosely from memory, picking up the thorns from the adjacent Matt. 7:16.

"Listen," he says, "When you erupt into anger or resentfulness, that is a sure sign of his influence, then a desire for more business and for rich food and drinking binges and fits of alcoholic belligerence and all kinds of inappropriate luxuries, the lust for women, greed, arrogance, and braggadocio, and whatever else of the same sort. When these things come to mind, you will know the angel of wickedness has arrived. [6]So recognize his influence, have nothing to do with him, and never trust him, for his works are evil and disadvantageous for the slaves of God. So now you know the activities of both angels. Understand them and trust the guidance of the angel of righteousness, [7]but have nothing to do with the evil angel, for his instruction is unwholesome in every respect. If the desires of this angel find a place in his heart, even a faithful individual will commit some sin. [8]Likewise, even if a man or a woman is extremely wicked and the deeds of the angel of righteousness infiltrate the heart, the man or woman must do something good. [9]You see, then," he says, "that it is good to yield to the impulses from the angel of righteousness and to say good-bye once and for all to the angel of wickedness. [10]This commandment sets forth what pertains to faith so that you may trust what the angel of righteousness is doing and that, doing the works he urges, you may come to live with God. But make sure you recall that the deeds of the evil angel are troublesome; if you repudiate them, you will live to God."

Seventh mandate

1

[1]"Fear the Lord," he says, "and abide by his commandments. Doing this means you will be strengthened in everything you do and your performance will be peerless. As long as you fear the Lord, you will have success in everything. This is the sort of fear that should grip you, and you will be saved. [2]But do not be afraid of the accuser, for he is impotent. There is no reason to fear the powerless, but if one is immensely powerful, there is good reason to fear his wrath. Whoever has power commands fear, but whoever is weak is despised by everyone. [3]But you should fear the deeds of the accuser, for they are wicked. Insofar as you fear the Lord, you will fear the deeds of the accuser. You will by no means practice them, shunning them instead. [4]Thus, there are two sorts of fear. If you are tempted to do evil, fear the Lord and you will do no such thing. But if you want to do good, fear the Lord and you will be motivated to do it. Therefore, the fear of the Lord can be seen to be potent, great, and splendid. Fear the Lord, then, if you want to live with him, and everyone who abides by his commandments does fear him and shall live with God."

[5]"My lord," I say, "why did you specify that it is 'those who abide by his commandments' who will live with him?"

He answers, "Because anyone may fear the Lord, but not everyone keeps his commandments. Thus, it is only those who add obedience of the commandments to their fear of the Lord who will have life with God. Those who disdain his commandments are bereft of life."

Eighth mandate

1

[1]"I told you," he says, "that the creations of God fall into two categories. Well, self-control is also two-fold because in some things self-control is called for, but in others it is inappropriate."

[2]"How, pray tell, can self-control ever not be called for? Show me, kind sir, what things require self-control and which do not."

"Listen," quoth he, "and I shall show you. You must exercise self-control when it comes to sin so you will not commit it. But do not hold yourself back when it comes to doing good. Go ahead and do it! For if you exercise self-restraint in matters of good and neglect to do it, you are committing a serious sin. But if you show self-restraint in that which is evil and avoid doing it, you have done a great good deed. Be self-controlled, then, in refraining from all evil acts, and do the good."

[3]"What sorts of wickedness, my lord," I ask, "most require settled avoidance and all self-restraint?"

"Mark well, Hermas," he replies. "I have in mind particularly adultery, prostitution, drunken rampages, evil excess, gluttony and anxiety of wealth, boasting, conceit and pride, lying, slander and hypocrisy, ill-will, and all manner of blasphemy. [4]These deeds are the most evil of the deeds people perform during their lives.[w] This is why the slave of God must steer clear and restrain himself, for whoever does not control himself enough to shun these sins cannot live with God. And listen to what follows these sins!"

[5]"Surely, my lord," I exclaim, "there can be no more sins after these!"

"Oh, but there are!" he answers. "Many are the sins from which the slave of God must have sufficient self-restraint to refrain: stealing, lying, swindling, perjury, greed, covetousness, deceiving, conceit, bragging, and anything else of the sort. [6]Don't you think these things are wrong—in-

w. The offenses listed as the most grievous that come to the author's mind show the ascetical character of the work. Hermas is less concerned with general morality than with pious introspection and self-salvation. It is equally obvious that Hermas's angel did not consider prolixity a sin.

deed, seriously wrong for the slaves of God? In all these things anyone who serves God must exercise self-restraint. Be self-controlled then, and abstain from all these things so you may attain unto life with God. Look to get yourself registered among those who restrain themselves when it comes to these things. It is these things from which you must restrain yourself. [7]Now for the things in which you need not exercise self-control. Abandon yourself to every good deed."

[8]"My lord," I interrupt, "reveal to me also the power of goodness so I may do good deeds and keep your commands and, in so doing, perhaps be saved."

"Very well, Hermas," he says, "here are the good deeds that must characterize you and to which you must abandon yourself: [9]first and foremost, faith, then the fear of the Lord, love, peaceableness, righteous words, trustworthiness, patience. Nothing improves on a life marked by these. If one sticks to these and does not cautiously hold himself back from them, he enjoys the bliss of heaven already in this life. [10]Now these are what will surely follow in their wake: attending to the needs of widows, visiting the orphans and the destitute, bribing the guards where the slaves of God are imprisoned, and showing hospitality, since this is a type of philanthropy sorely required from time to time, not insisting on your rights, being peaceful, even being a doormat for the stamping foot, revering the elderly, practicing good deeds, maintaining brotherly affection, absorbing every blow, being imperturbable, resenting no one, encouraging the heartsick, not writing off those fallen from the faith but rather winning them back and reinvigorating them, rebuking sinners, showing leniency for the insolvent and the indigent, and whatever deeds of the same flavor. [11]Do these things sound good to you?" he asks.

"My lord," I reply, "could anything be better?"

"Well, then," he says, "do them, and do not neglect them, and you shall be judged worthy of life. Yes, and this is equally true for everyone who keeps these commandments and lives by them: they too shall have life with God. So keep this commandment. If you practice good deeds and do not neglect them, you shall live with God. Indeed, everyone who keeps these commandments, living by them, shall live with God."

Ninth mandate

1

[1]He says to me, "Get rid of any doubting attitude you may have and do not hesitate to petition God, saying not to yourself, 'I dare not make a request of God and hope for it to be granted, I who have sinned so much

against him.' [2]Do not think that way but incline your heart to the Lord and petition him without wavering and you will experience his boundless compassion; you will know he will never wash his hands of you but will grant your sincere request. [3]For God is not like mortals who bear grudges for past offenses. He is pure of ill-will and has mercy on those he has made. [4]You need only cleanse your heart from all the fleeting trivialities of this life and from those things already mentioned and petition the Lord, and all shall be yours and you shall lack nothing you asked for as long as you request from the Lord without hesitation. [5]But if you do doubt deep down, you can forget about getting anything you asked for. For those who hesitate about God are the ambivalent, who are frustrated with prayer. [6]But those whose faith is total make every request in full confidence in the Lord and they receive because they ask without second thoughts.[x] Every one with ambivalence toward God will have a difficult time being saved unless he repents of it.[y] [7]So purify your mind of ambivalence and clothe yourself in faith, for it is mighty, and believe God that you will receive what you ask for.[z] And if, after you have petitioned the Lord, the answer seems to be running late, do not start doubting just because you have not received your soul's desire immediately. For it must be because of some temptation or trespass you are unaware of that your answer is slow in coming. [8]So do not leave off making your dearest request and you will receive it sooner or later. But if you begin to flag and start doubting as you pray, blame yourself for the result, not him who gives to you. [9]Examine this ambivalence, for it is both wicked and irrational and destroys the faith of many, yes, many who are otherwise strong in faith. For this ambivalence is truly a daughter of the accuser and wreaks terrible havoc among the slaves of God. [10]Therefore, you are to hate ambivalence and defeat it at every turn, putting on the armor of faith that is mighty and dynamic. For faith first promises, then accomplishes, everything, but ambivalence, having no backbone of assurance, fails in every endeavor. [11]I trust, then, that you see," he says, "how faith is a gift come down from the Lord and holds great power, while ambivalence is a worldly spirit sent by the accuser and has no power. As for you, serve the faith that is powerful and stave off the ambivalence that has no power; this way, you shall live with God. Yes, and so will everyone who shares the same resolve."

---

x. James 1:6-8

y. Heb. 11:6

z. Mark 11:24

Tenth mandate

1

[1]"Cast sorrow far away from yourself," he says, "for she is the sister of angry temper and ambivalence."

[2]I reply, "My lord, how are they related? To me, an angry disposition would seem to be one thing, ambivalence something else entirely, and sorrow still a distinct third!"

"What a simpleton you are," he says, "not to see that sorrow is the most evil of spirits and is the deadliest of all to the slaves of God! More than any other spirit, it destroys people and extinguishes the Holy Spirit—though it also winds up saving it."

[3]"My lord," I say, "I confess I am clueless and these parables go right over my head. How can it extinguish and then save? I'm afraid I don't get it!"

[4]"Listen," quoth he. "Those who have never plumbed the depths of truth, nor searched out divine things, but have left it to simple belief, preferring to involve themselves in business matters and getting rich and cultivating friendships with the gentiles and all the various secular concerns, all who apply themselves to these things, I say, fail to grasp the divine parables, for their understanding is obscured by these pursuits and have been spoiled and made fruitless for God. [5]Just as fine vineyards are overtaken by briars and all manner of weeds when they are neglected, so do those who first believe but then become involved in such things as I have listed lose their ability to understand and to make sense of righteousness, which begins to seem naive to them. As soon as they hear someone talk about the nature of God or about truth, their minds return to their business concerns and they understand nothing of what was said. [6]But those who fear God and pursue knowledge of divine being and truth, and who direct themselves to the Lord, see and understand everything they are told more readily because the fear of the Lord is deeply rooted in them. For wherever the Lord lives, there also is profound understanding. So stick with the Lord and you shall understand and make sense of everything."

2

[1]"Listen to me, you idiot," he continues, "and I will explain to you how sorrow extinguishes the Holy Spirit and then goes on to save it. [2]When the doubter undertakes any endeavor and it falls through due to his half-way efforts, he begins to feel sorry for himself and this makes the Holy Spirit dejected and it puts out his fire. [3]Likewise, when an angry disposition takes hold of an individual for any cause and he comes to burn

with resentment, again, he becomes anguished, this time because of his wrathful outburst, and he vows to turn over a new leaf. [4]So you see, this sorrow seems to save him because it made him repent of the evil. So both of these grieve the Holy Spirit, doubtful hesitancy and angry moods. [5]So thrust away from you sadness and don't torment the Holy Spirit who lives inside you; otherwise, he may report you to God and abandon you. [6]For the Spirit of God who was assigned to this mortal flesh will not put up with either sadness or cramped quarters."

3

[1]"So deck yourself out in cheerfulness, which always pleases God and which he approves, and be glad about it. For everyone who is cheerful does good deeds, thinks good thoughts, and disdains sadness, [2]but the sadsack is ever committing sins, poor fellow!

"He commits sin, first, by token of grieving the Holy Spirit; second, by grieving the Holy Spirit he commits transgression in that he does not pray for others or confess to God, as God has commanded his slaves to do. For a sadsack's prayer has never had the energy to rise heavenward and never makes it to the ear of God."

[3]"What," I ask, "stops his prayer from going all the way up?"

"Simply," he answers, "because sadness is located deep in the heart and it mixes with the prayer, polluting it and weighting it down. Just as vinegar ruins the taste of wine if they are mixed in the same jar, the same happens when sadness is mixed with the Holy Spirit: the power of intercession is negated. [4]Therefore, do not tolerate in yourself this sinful sadness and you shall live with God. Yes, and the same goes for everyone who will drive out sorrow from themselves and dress up in complete cheerfulness."

Eleventh mandate

1

[1]One day he pointed out to me some men lounging on a couch and another sitting in a chair. And he asked me, "Do you see those fellows sitting on the couch?"

"Yes, my lord," I reply, "I see them right enough."

"These," he says, "are true believers, but the one by himself on the chair is a pseudo-prophet who drives mad the slaves of God, though only the doubters, not the true believers, naturally. [2]These cowards in the faith sneak off to him as to a fortune teller, asking to know their future. And the pseudo-prophet, utterly bereft of any divine spiritual power, infers

from their questions what it is they want to hear and tells them this. [3]He is empty himself, so he dispenses empty answers to empty clients. Whatever questions he is asked, his answers reflect the emptiness of him who asks. But he does occasionally say something that comes true, and this because the accuser fills him full of his own spirit, hoping by this means to decimate as many of the righteous as he can. [4]But all who are strong in the faith of the Lord, wearing the garment of truth, do not join with such spirits, but steer clear of them. But the doubters who are constantly going back and forth may even themselves practice fortune telling like the gentiles. Thus they magnify their sins by adding idolatry! This is because anyone who goes to a pseudo-prophet for guidance is an idol worshipper and bereft of the truth and irrational to boot. [5]No Spirit given by God ever has to be consulted through a medium; instead, as it has the very power of the Deity, it speaks by itself because it descends from heaven, from the power of the divine Spirit. [6]But the kind of spirit one must consult and that speaks when human beings ask it to is of the earth and temperamental, having no real power. And it is mute until asked a question."

[7]"Then how, my lord," I ask, "are we to tell the true prophet from the false?"

"Listen," he says, "and I will tell you about both kinds, and using what I tell you, you will be able to tell the prophet from the pseudo-prophet. You can tell the one with the divine Spirit by examining how he lives. [8]First, the one with the Spirit from above is mild, peaceful, and unprepossessing, and he refrains from all evil and futile desires for the goods of this temporal world. He treats himself less well than others and will not condescend to supply answers to random questions people fire at him. Nor will he speak by the Spirit in private, for the Holy Spirit does not put himself at the disposal of mortal man. No, the true prophet speaks only when God impels him, whether anyone wants to hear it or not. [9]So when a man who has the divine Spirit enters the congregation of the righteous, of those who believe in the divine Spirit, and those people pray together to God, then the angel of the prophetic spirit who is invisibly linked with him fills the man and he, thus full of the Holy Spirit, speaks to those assembled whatever God wants him to speak. [10]It is in this precise manner, then, that the Spirit of the Deity shall be made manifest. Such is the full extent of the power where the Spirit of the Godhead of the Lord is concerned.

[11]"Now," he continues, "for the truth about the worldly and empty spirit which is powerless and foolish. [12]First, the man who appears en-

dowed with a spirit glorifies himself, demanding the chief seat, and at once he is impudent, brazen, and garrulous, used to many luxuries and other such trivialities. He accepts money for his oracles and if no one pays him, he refuses to prophesy. Do you think a divine Spirit would stoop to insisting on money before prophesying? It is impossible for a prophet of God to act in such a manner. No, the spirit of such prophets is worldly. [13]The next sign is that the pseudo-prophet never seeks out a congregation of the righteous. He steers clear of them, seeking instead those of doubtful faith and those bereft of faith. He prophesies to them off in a corner and swindles them, speaking vacant words such as they desire to hear, for their customers are no less empty. When two empty jars are set down side by side, there is no danger one of them will break; they are in perfect harmony! [14]But if he dares enter a meeting full of the righteous, among whom dwells the Spirit of the Deity, and they begin to pray, the man is emptied. The worldly spirit flees in terror, forsaking him, and he is rendered speechless and completely unhinged, unable to say a single word. [15]If you store jars of wine or of oil in a closet and you include one empty jar, when you go back and empty out the closet, the empty jar will be discovered to be—still empty! So with the vacuous prophets; whenever they venture among the righteous, they are revealed as being just as empty as they always were, beneath their pretense.

[16]"I have now described for you the character and conduct of both types of prophets. So examine anyone who claims to be impelled by the Spirit, looking to his life and behavior. [17]And once you have, trust the utterance of the Spirit that comes from God and is powerful, but put no faith in that empty, worldly spirit, for it is impotent and comes from the accuser. [18]Pay attention to the parable I mean to tell you. Pick up a rock and throw it skyward. Do you think you can reach the heaven? Or take a pump full of water and squirt it up in the air. Can it pierce the sky?"

[19]"My lord," I say, "how could I hope to do so? Both these feats are beyond human capacity."

"Right-o!" he answers. "Just as these things are beyond your ability, so likewise worldly spirits just do not have what it takes. [20]Contrast the power that descends from above. A particle of hail is quite small, yet what pain it causes your hand on impact! Or think of a drop of water that runs off a tile roof and eventually erodes a hole in the pavement below it. [21]You see? Even the tiniest thing that descends from above has great power! No wonder the divine Spirit descending from above is powerful! So trust the Spirit and what his prophets tell you, but ignore the other."

Twelfth mandate

1

[1]He says to me, "Strip yourself of every evil desire and put on the desire for what is good and holy, for once swathed in this desire, you will find you hate the evil desire. You will harness it and direct it as you please. [2]For the desire for evil is wild and it is difficult to tame it. It is terrible, and because of its ferocity, it makes one pay a high price, and this is especially so if the slave of God becomes mixed up with it and does not understand what is overtaking him: he has a terrible price to pay! But it takes its toll even upon those who are not robed in desire for good but are enmeshed in the present life. Evil desire ushers such individuals into the realm of death."

[3]"What kind of deeds," I ask, "result from the evil desire you speak of, my lord, that deliver one to death? Please reveal them to me so I may better avoid them."

"Hear, then, what sort of acts the evil desire employs to bring death to God's slaves!"

2

[1]"Principal among them is a husband's or wife's desire for another lover and for the luxury of riches, for many superfluous treats, for drinks and other fripperies numerous and silly. In fact, every luxury is silly and futile for the slaves of God. [2]Such desires as these, then, are evil and destroy the slaves of God. This evil desire is the accuser's daughter. You, therefore, refrain from the evil desires, and by doing so, you will live with God. [3]But whoever is dominated by them and surrenders to them will be utterly destroyed, for these desires are in themselves fatal! [4]Wrap yourself in the desire for righteousness, and having equipped yourself with the fear of the Lord, stand up to them! The fear of God thrives in good desires. If the evil desire sees you approaching armed with the fear of God and in a defensive posture, it will run away as far as it can, terrified of your weaponry, and you will never see it again. [5]When you receive the victor's wreath for vanquishing it, go to the desire of righteousness and yield to her the prize you were awarded and be her slave, doing whatever she may ask of you. If you serve the good desire and obey her, you shall always be strong enough to overcome the evil desire, to place her in subjection to your will."

3

[1]"My lord," say I, "I would like to know the ways in which I might serve the good desire."

"Listen, then. It is simple enough." he says. "Make a habit of righteousness and moral excellence, trustworthiness and the fear of the Lord, faith and mildness, and all other acts of the same kind. Practicing these, you will show yourself a worthy slave of God and shall merit life with him. Yes, and the same obtains for all who place themselves at the disposal of the good desire: they shall attain to life with God."

[2]Thus he finished the twelve commandments and says to me, "You have these commandments; live by them and urge them on your audience so their repentance may remain pure for the remainder of their days. [3]This ministry I am assigning you, perform it diligently till the end and you shall achieve great things. For those near to repenting will hear you gladly, and they will do as you say. For I will be at your side and I will make them obey you."

[4]I say to him, "My lord, these commandments are great, beautiful, and full of glory. They are strong to rejoice the heart of anyone who is able to keep them. But I wonder if mortal man can keep them, for they are quite severe!"

[5]He answered me, saying, "If you decide they can be kept, it will be easy for you to keep them. They will not seem difficult. But if you begin to doubt it is humanly possible to obey them, you will fail to obey them. [6]But now I tell you: if you neglect them and do not obey them, you shall surely forfeit salvation, you and your children. You will already have rendered a verdict on yourself if you decide they cannot be kept by a mortal."

4

[1]He said all this to me with great fury and I was thrown into confusion. I was terrified of him! His form began to change with a fury that no mortal might endure. [2]But when he saw how completely confused and disturbed I was, he began to speak more kindly to me. He says, "You silly fellow, without understanding and with ambivalent faith! Don't you see the glory of God, how great and powerful and wondrous it is, how he made the world for humanity's benefit and placed all creation under his dominion, delegating all authority to them, that mankind should rule everything under the sky? [3]If, therefore, humanity is the master of all God's creations and rules everything, can't he also master these commandments? Indeed," he says, "anyone who has the Lord in his heart can master every one of these commandments. [4]But any who have the Lord merely on their lips, while their hearts are unrepentant and they remain far from the Lord, to them these commands will prove difficult and impenetrable. [5]So, as for you, O man of empty and fair-weather faith, estab-

lish your Lord firmly in your heart and you will find that nothing is easier than these commandments, nor sweeter nor milder!

6"All you who live by the accuser's commands, about face! It is these that are difficult, bitter, wanton, and unmanagable. And have no fear of the accuser, for he has no power against you. 7For I will be by your side, I the Angel of Repentance, and I am victorious over him. The accuser's only weapon is fear, but his fearsomeness is a paper tiger. Thus, do not waste your fear on him! He will run away in panic!"

5

1I say to him, "My lord, I pray you, listen to me for a few moments."

"Very well," he says, "Say anything you please."

"My lord," I say, "we are anxious to observe God's commandments and there is none who does not petition the Lord to strengthen him in keeping the commandments, to obey them. But the accuser is a formidable foe and defeats us."

2"But he cannot defeat the slaves of God," he says, "if they rely on the Lord whole-heartedly. Oh, he can struggle with them, but he is doomed to defeat. So all you need do is stand up to him and he will be whipped, he will run away with his tail between his legs.[a] The problem is that those," he says, "who are completely empty fear the devil as if he were powerful. 3Picture a man filling large jars with wine, and among them are some empty ones. When he inspects them, he does not bother with the full ones but checks only the empty ones for fear that they will have taken on a sour smell. For full jars will not turn smelly, only empty ones, and then they become useless since they would spoil the taste of any wine afterwards placed in them. 4In the same way, the accuser makes the rounds of the slaves of God to tempt them. All those who are full of faith give him a good fight and he leaves them alone, finding no chink in their armor. So he goes on to the empty ones and readily finds an entry route. He goes right in and works whatever mischief he pleases and they become his obedient slaves."

6

1"But I, the Angel of Repentance, tell you this: Do not fear the accuser, for I was sent," he says, "to assist you who have repented whole-heartedly, to reinforce your faith. 2So have faith in God, you who once gave up hope of your lives because of your sins, because you are only adding to your sins and making your life's burden more unbearable. If you

a. James 4:7

turn whole-heartedly to the Lord and devote the rest of your days to righteousness, serving him correctly as he wants you to, he will cure you of your old sins and you will have the strength to vanquish the efforts of the accuser. But don't be the least impressed by the accuser's threats, for he is hamstrung, limp as the muscles of a corpse. [3]Get this straight: fear the One who is omnipotent, who can deliver and destroy, and obey these commandments and you shall have life with God."

[4]I say to him, "Good sir, now I am invigorated for all the orders of the Lord because of your help! And I have no doubt you will smash all the might of the accuser, and together we shall be his masters and shall prove victorious over all his schemes. And I have good hope, my lord, that I have become capable of keeping those commandments you have issued, as long as the Lord makes me able!"

[5]"You shall indeed keep them," he says, "if the Lord sees that your heart is pure. Yes, and everyone will keep them if they cleanse their hearts of the futile desires of the present world, and they shall live with God."

3. Parables He Told Me

First similitude

1

[1]He says to me, "You are aware that you who serve God are sojourning in a foreign land; your home city is far from here. But if you know your own city, where your home is located, is far away, why do you invest time and money planting fields, designing decorative displays, and constructing fine buildings and living rooms that are totally superfluous—here? [2]Whoever undertakes these efforts for this city must not be planning to return to his own. [3]What a senseless, faithless wretch you are, not to see that all these things are someone else's, owned by another! Suppose the master of this city says to you, 'I want you out of my city! Get out if you refuse to obey my laws!' [4]But you have accumulated farms, homes, and many other possessions. When he expels you, what will you do with the farms, houses, and goods you have accumulated? For the lord of the country is well within his rights to tell you, 'Either you abide by my laws or you get out of my realm!' [5]So what will you do, since you are obliged to obey the laws of your own city? Are you going to repudiate your own ancestral ways and adjust to the laws of this place just so you can keep your fields and other possessions? Consider well! It may not prove advantageous to repudiate your allegiance to your homeland's laws: suppose one day you want to return there. You will be able to ex-

pect no welcome there, only a door slammed in your face. [6]So think again: as a sojourner in a foreign country, just develop the minimum skills necessary to get along there for a while and be prepared to leave at any moment should the ruler deport you for failure to observe the laws of that land. That way, you can make a clean break and return to your own city and cheerfully live by its familiar laws with no harm done. [7]Consider, O slaves of God, have him clearly in mind. Do the deeds God requires of you, remembering both his commandments and his promises to you, and trust him to make good on them as long as you keep his commandments. [8]Therefore, instead of farms, invest in endangered souls, as much as you can, and make your business trips to widows and orphans; do not forget about them.[b] Spend your wealth and the goods you proudly show off, which are on loan to you from God, on investments of this kind, the only ones that pay eternal dividends. [9]This is why your master entrusted you with his goods, for you to take care of these tasks for him.[c] How much better to make investments of this kind, for you will find ample houses and farms awaiting you once you return to your own homeland.[d] [10]This is a kind of luxurious extravagance that is beautiful and wholesome to rejoice in. It issues in joy, not sorrow or anxiety that you may lose them. So do not imitate the gentiles in their spending habits, for it is disadvantageous for you as slaves of God. Use your money in the way that will bring satisfaction in the long run. Nor shall you defile another's property by laying your hands on it, nor covet it, for it is evil to do so. [11]You just stick to your own business and you will be saved."[e]

Second similitude

1

[1]Once as I was walking in a field, my eye fell upon an elm and a vine. I was considering the difference between them and between their fruits when the Shepherd appeared before me, and he says, "What are you thinking so deeply about?"

---

b. James 4:13-16; 1:27

c. Matt. 25:14-30

d. Luke 12:33; Acts of Thomas, 17-24

e. "'Business!' cried the Ghost, wringing its hands again. 'Mankind was my business. The common welfare was my business; charity, mercy, forbearance, and benevolence were, all, my business. The dealings of my trade were but a drop of water in the comprehensive ocean of my business!'" Thus Dickens, in *A Christmas Carol,* makes use of pedagogic spirits in similar fashion.

"I am considering," I reply, "how the elm and the vine are ideally suited to each other."

[2]"These two," he says, "are meant as a symbol for the slaves of God."

"I would be interested in knowing more," I say, "about the symbol encoded in the trees you mention."

"See the elm and the vine?" he asks.

"I do indeed, my lord," I reply.

[3]"This vine," he says, "produces fruit, while the elm is an unfruitful breed. Yet unless the vine climbs up the elm, if it remains spread out on the ground, it cannot produce much fruit. What fruit it does manage to produce soon rots for not being suspended from the tree. But when it loops itself around the trunk, it produces fruit, so to speak, for itself and for the elm. [4]So you see, the elm produces fruit, too—not less than the vine does, but more!"

"More?" I say. "How is that, my lord?"

"Because the vine brings luscious fruit abundantly only when it is suspended from the elm. When left on the ground, its fruit is scant and unwholesome. This parable applies to the slaves of God, poor or rich."

[5]"How so, kind sir?" I say, "Please teach me."

"Listen, then," he says, "A rich man has much wealth but runs short of the things of the Lord as his attention is constantly absorbed in his financial affairs, and he seldom intercedes with or confesses to the Lord. And even such prayers and confessions that do come from him are miserable and stunted and do not register in heaven. Then when the rich man approaches the poor and contributes toward his needs, hoping in this way to gain merit with God, calculating that the poor man is rich when it comes to intercession, that his prayers have great weight with God, the rich man does not hesitate to give the poor whatever he needs. [6]For his part, the poor man, having the rich man for his patron, prays for him, thanking God for his benefactor. And the latter grows even more zealous in his assistance, convinced of his client's clout with God and wanting to keep him in good health so as to keep the prayers on his behalf coming! [7]In this manner, both obtain what they want. The poor makes intercession, something he is rich in. This he pays back to the Lord who loaned it to him. And in the same way, the rich man is turning over to his poor client the money the Lord entrusted him with. And he is doing a very important work as far as God sees the matter, for such a rich man knows the proper use of his money and provides for the poor man out of the Lord's

benevolence fund and properly administers it. [8]So while the casual observer may think the elm produces no fruit, he does not think how, in times of drought, the elm, with its water, nourishes the vine, enabling it to produce fruit twice over: both for itself and for its symbiotic partner, the elm. In the same way, the poor, when they pray on behalf of the rich, are securing their material needs, while the rich in providing for them are seeing to their own spiritual capital.[f] [9]So both are partners in a good endeavor! So whoever does likewise shall not find God has forsaken him, but instead will hear his name read from the roll of the living.[g] [10]Blessed are the rich who realize their wealth is on loan from the Lord. For thus mindful, they shall be able to do something worthwhile."

Third similitude

1

[1]He indicated a stand of many bare trees, and as far as I could tell, they had all alike withered up. And he says to me, "See those trees?"

"Yes, I do, my lord," I respond. "All of them are alike, all withered."

[2]He commented, saying to me, "These trees you see stand for the people living in this world."

"But why, lord, are they all the same and all withered?" I ask.

"Because," he says, "in this world you cannot tell the difference between the righteous and the sinners.[h] For the righteous, this world is perpetual winter and they cannot really thrive. Thus they are not easily told from the sinners among whom they perforce dwell. [3]Just as every winter, the trees all look alike without their leaves to distinguish them as dead or alive, so in the present world you cannot infallibly tell the righteous from the sinners in their similarity."

Fourth similitude

1

[1]Again he called my attention to the trees, but this time some were budding, others shriveled up. And he says to me, "See these trees?"

"I see them, lord. Some are budding, but others are shriveled, right?"

[2]"These trees that bud," he says, "stand for the righteous, destined to live in the coming world, for that world will be perpetual summer for them but deep winter to the sinners. When the Lord's mercy is manifest for all to see, then the slaves of God will also be recognized for what they

f. Matt. 10:41-42

g. Luke 10:20; Rev. 20:12

h. Matt. 13:24-30, 36-43

are. In fact, everyone will be revealed. [3]It is just like summer when all trees fruit and their fruit identifies each one. Even so, the fruits of righteousness will one day become evident and each one will visibly flower in the world. [4]But as for the gentiles and the sinners, they will be like the shriveled trees you saw. Unfruitful in the next world, they shall be spent as kindling, publicly exposed, since their life's habits have been evil. Yes, the sinners shall roast, for they have sinned and not repented. Likewise, the gentiles shall perish screaming in the flames since they were alienated from their creator.[i]

[5]"So be sure you produce fruit, so it may be visible when summer comes.[j] But avoid becoming too busy and you will avoid lapsing into any sin. For those who get too busy also sin quite a bit, preoccupied as they are with their business, ignoring opportunities to serve their Lord. [6]How, pray tell," he adds, "can such a one request anything from the Lord and hope to receive it, seeing he is doing the Lord no good? It is only those who actively serve him whose petitions he grants, but those who do nothing for him get nothing from him. [7]But if one has but simple duties, he has leisure to serve the Lord. His mind is not polluted with mundane concerns and alienated from the Lord.[k] No, he shall serve him well since he maintains a pure focus. [8]So if you do this, you too shall yield fruit to harvest in the next world. Whoever learns this lesson will be fruitful likewise."

Fifth similitude

1

[1]I was seated on a certain mountain fasting and thanking the Lord for all the attention he had paid me, and I suddenly behold the figure of the Shepherd sitting beside me, saying, "What are you doing here so early in the morning?"

"Because, my lord," I say, "I am keeping vigil."

[2]"And what is that?" he asks.

"It refers to my fasting, lord," I reply, scarcely able to believe him truly ignorant of such matters.

"And what is the reason for this fast?" quoth he.

"I have just always done it, lord," I answered, "so I do it now."

[3]"You know nothing of fasting for the Lord!" he says. "And this useless exercise you are wasting your time on is not even a fast!"

---

i. Rom. 1:18-32

j. Matt. 3:8; John 15:1-8

k. 1 Cor. 7:32-34

"Lord," I ask, nonplused, "why do you say that?"

"I am telling you," he says, "that this is no fast, whatever it is you think you are doing here! I will instruct you about true and perfect fasting, which the Lord approves. Listen," he says, [4]"God cares nothing for such a futile fast; with such so-called fasting, you effect nothing good.[l] Instead, undertake a fast like this: [5]live without doing any evil and serve the Lord with an undivided heart, keep his commandments and live by his rules and do not let any wicked lust cross your mind, only believe God. Then, if you do these things and fear him, you will live with God; if you do them, you will complete a fine fast, one God approves of."[m]

2

[1]"Consider this parable about fasting. [2]A certain man had extensive property and many slaves and he developed a portion of his property as a vineyard. Selecting one particular slave as trustworthy, praiseworthy, and esteemed by all, he summoned him and told him, 'You are in charge of the vineyard. Encircle it with a fence, but trouble yourself no further beyond that. Only carry out this order and I will make you a freedman attached to my household.' Then that slave's master departed for a trip abroad.[n] [3]Once he was gone, the slave undertook to fence in the vineyard. Finishing the job, he then noticed the vineyard was choked with weeds. [4]So he deliberated, thinking, 'I have implemented my master's order. I believe I will clear the vineyard, and when I have, it will be much neater. Without the weeds, it will produce more grapes, no longer being choked by the weeds.' So he started to clear the vineyard, and by the time he was done, he had rooted out every weed. The vineyard became immaculately tidy, as well as fruitful, without the blight of choking weeds. [5]After a while, the master of that slave returned and entered the vineyard and was astonished to see it not only fenced about but also cleared of all the choking weeds and with the vines flourishing. He was delighted with his slave, [6]so he summoned his beloved son, his heir, and the friends who advised him and told them what he had ordered the slave to do compared with what he did. And they celebrated with that slave for the glowing report his master had given of him. [7]And he says to them, 'I gave this slave my word that I should free him if he carried out my order. But he did much more to my vineyard than I asked, giving me great joy. It seems only right,

l. Thomas, saying 14

m. Isa. 58:1-5

n. Mark 13:34

then, that I should reward him with more than I originally promised him. Now I propose, in view of his service, to appoint him co-heir along with my son because when a good idea occurred to him, he did not shrug it off but went ahead and implemented it.' [8]Not even his son thought the idea a bad one, and he was happy enough to see the slave made co-heir. [9]A few days afterward, his master gave a feast and sent him a platter of delicacies from his table. But when the slave received it, he took only as much as he needed and shared the rest with his fellow slaves. [10]And when these latter received from him the treats, they were glad and commenced to pray for him to rise even higher in his master's esteem since he had treated them so kindly. [11]His master was told of all this and rejoiced to hear of it. So the master again summoned his friends and his son to inform them what the slave did with the delicacies he had been sent. This made them affirm his plan all the more, to name his slave co-heir with his son."

3

[1]"Lord, I confess I can make nothing of these parables, nor understand them, unless you will be so kind as to explain them to me."

[2]"I will be glad to explain them all to you, Hermas," he says, "and I will make clear to you everything I am talking about. [3]I will reveal to you his commandments. Abide by them and God will be pleased with you and you will find yourself registered in the elite ranks of those who obey his commandments. But if you perform any work above and beyond what God has required, you will have earned yourself far greater glory and God will view you as more splendid than he would have otherwise. So if, while doing your primary duty of keeping God's commands, you add these pieties as well, you shall have ample reason to rejoice, as long as you perform them as I prescribe."

[4]I reply, "My lord, I will certainly do whatever you tell me, for I know you are with me to help me."

"And so will I be," he says, "because your zeal for righteousness is great indeed! I will ever be with all who have such enthusiasm," he says. [5]"As for fasting, it is quite valuable so long as one remembers to keep the Lord's commandments. Fasting, then, ought to be pursued in this way: [6]first, shun any evil speech and desire and cleanse your heart from all worldly ephemera. If you do this, your fast shall be ideal. [7]And this is what you are to do. Having kept all the requirements, see that on the day you fast you have nothing but bread and water. Then figure the price of the meat you would have eaten that day and give it to some widow or orphan or needy soul. This way, by your humbling yourself, the one who

profits by your humiliation may be filled and may intercede for you with the Lord. [8]If you shall undertake to fast along the lines I have suggested to you, you will be offering a sacrifice God will greet and your fasting will be recorded in the heavenly ledger of merit and the service thus rendered will shine with beauty and joy and divine approbation. [9]Observe these things, you and your children and your whole household, and if you do, you shall be blessed. Yes, and everyone who may hear these guidelines and follow them shall likewise be blessed, and whatever boon they seek from the Lord, they shall have it."

4

[1]I beseeched him to explain for me the parable of the property, the master, the vineyard, the slave who fenced in the vineyard, the weeds uprooted from the vineyard, the son, the friends, and the advisors. For I knew these things had some deeper meaning.

[2]But he replied to me, "You are most insistent in pressing your questions! You really shouldn't ask questions in the first place. If I have something to explain to you, I shall explain it."

"But my lord, if you show me something and do not bother to explain it, you have wasted your time since I shall not have understood it! Likewise, if you tell me a parable and neglect to explain it, it is all for nothing."

[3]But again he replied, saying to me, "Anyone who serves God and has his own Lord in his heart asks him for understanding and gets it and can interpret any parable for himself! The message of the Lord conveyed in a parable is communicated to him.[o] But anyone who is slothful and lazy in prayer hesitates to ask the Lord. [4]But the Lord is not grudging and is happy to give to the one who asks him persistently.[p] But you who have been made strong by the holy angel and have obtained from him such facility in prayer and are by no means lazy, why don't you just ask the Lord for insight and receive it from him?"

[5]I answer him, "But, lord, I have you right here with me! Surely it is easiest just to ask you! After all, you are the one showing me these things and talking with me! If I had seen or heard them on my own, I should indeed have asked the Lord what I wanted to know."

5

[1]"Well, I did say you were brazen and persistent," he says, "asking for the solutions to the parables! But since you are so dogged, I will eluci-

o. Mark 4:13

p. James 1:5

date the parable of the property and the rest of it so you may convey it to everyone else. Listen," he says, "and all will become clear to you. [2]The property stands for the present world. The master of it corresponds to the maker of all things, who arranged them just so and brought them to life. The slave is the Son of God.[q] The vines are this people whom he himself planted. [3]The fences are the angels of the Lord who shepherd his people, and the weeds uprooted from the vineyard are the sins of the slaves of God. The treats he sent him from his table are the commandments he issued to his people by the hand of his Son, while the friends and advisers are the eldest among the holy angels.[r] The absence of the master is the time remaining till he arrives."

[4]I ask him, "Lord, all these things are great, mighty, and splendid! Do you really think I could have figured them out?"

"No, of course not," he replies. "No mortal, however expert in understanding, can understand them."

"Now once more, lord," I say, "explain what I am about to ask you."

[5]"Go on," he says, "if you want to know anything."

"Why is the Son of God," I ask, "represented under the form of a slave in this parable?"

6

[1]"In fact," he replies, "the Son of God is not depicted as a slave but is rather pictured as a personage of considerable power and authority."[s]

"Come again?" I remark. "I don't see that at all!"

[2]"Because," he says, "God created the vineyard, or rather established his people, and committed them to his Son. The Son posted the angels to keep watch over them while the Son himself cleansed their sins through many labors and arduous efforts, for no one clears the ground without labor and effort. [3]Then, having purified his people from their sins, he indicated for them the paths to life, handing down to them the law he received from his Father.[t] You see," he continues, "that he is himself Lord of the

q. Phil. 2:7; Mark 10:45; Luke 22:27; John 13:1-5

r. In the Old Testament, Yahve frequently takes counsel with the sons of Elohim: Pss. 89:5-7; Job 1:6; 2:1; 1 Kings 22:19-22; Isa. 6:1-8.

s. We were just told the slave is the Son of God (5:2; cf. 6:2). What we read here is an attempt to correct the parable's adoptionistic Christology, which originally had nothing to do with fasting and pious works of supererogation. The writer, or a redactor, misdirects us to the natural-born son, the Holy Spirit, ignoring the point that the slave is adopted as a second son.

t. Here is a remarkable thing: Hermas has the Son redeem the people first, then give his teaching. This is, of course, the reverse of the order of events in the

people by virtue of authority delegated by his Father. [4]But as for the master seeking the advice of his son and the radiant angels about the slave becoming his heir, listen closely: [5]God sent the Holy Spirit, who existed before the creation and indeed created it, to inhabit a body that pleased him. The body of flesh the Holy Spirit inhabited, therefore, became obedient to the Spirit, conducting itself with honor, holiness, and purity, and without ever, in any fashion, besmirching the Spirit. [6]So when it had finished a life of honor and chastity and had done working with the Spirit, cooperating with it in every possible manner, behaving with courage and boldness, he appointed it as a partner with the Holy Spirit; for the life-work of this body of flesh was pleasing, seeing how, possessing the Holy Spirit, it was not defiled in all its years on earth. [7]So the Lord took the Son as an advisor, along with the resplendent angels, deciding that this body of flesh, too, having rendered irreproachable service to the Spirit, might be granted some place to stay and so it might not look as if its service had been taken for granted. For all mortal flesh that is discovered to be unspoiled and unsullied, and which the Holy Spirit inhabited, can expect a reward. [8]Now you have the interpretation of the parable, too."[u]

7

[1]"I was quite glad, my lord," I say, "to hear this interpretation."

"I'm not done," he says. "Be sure to maintain the purity of this flesh of yours undefiled; that way the Sprit who inhabits it may testify to the fact and your flesh will be saved. [2]Don't ever entertain the thought that your flesh is going to die anyway so you might as well degrade it in some disgusting pursuit.[v] Remember, if you pollute the flesh, you pollute the Holy Spirit, too. And if you pollute the Spirit, you shall forfeit salvation."

[3]"But, lord," I ask, "suppose before someone heard this, while he

---

gospels, where the death and resurrection follow the teaching ministry. While such flexibility with the order might be expected in the parable, which need correspond to the underlying truth only in a general way, one might expect the interpretation to agree with the gospel order, had Hermas known it! Maybe he knew the gospel story in a different form. Or maybe he preserves here a memory that the teaching ascribed to Jesus first appeared in the church in the form of prophecies from the ascended Christ, after the Passion.

u. Despite the redactional denial of it in the generalizing summary line, this is a piece of adoptionist Christology: the original point seems to be that because of his extraordinary righteousness, the human Jesus, channeler for the Spirit of God (this latter being the rightful and original son of God), was deemed after his meritorious death to be worthy of appointment as a second son of God alongside his elder brother, the Holy Spirit.

v. 1 Cor. 6:13-14

was ignorant, he did commit some pollution of the flesh. Can he still be saved?"

"Only God," he replies, "has the ability to cure one's previous works done in ignorance, for all authority is his. You just be sure you keep yourself pure, and the all-powerful Lord, who is all compassion, will take care of your own previous deeds of ignorance as long as, from now on, you avoid polluting your flesh or the Spirit. Since the two are so closely intertwined, the one cannot suffer pollution without the other sharing it. So keep both pure and you shall live with God."

Sixth similitude

1

[1]One day I sat in my house, worshipping God for everything I had seen, and I was contemplating the commandments, how fine they were, how powerful and encouraging and splendid, the means whereby one might save one's soul. And I thought, "I shall certainly be blessed if I live by these commandments, and anyone who does likewise will likewise be blessed!"

[2]As I thought these things, all at once I behold him sitting by me and saying, "What do you mean, 'if'? What makes you dubious about these commandments that I gave you? They are beautiful, not burdensome! Have no doubt, just remember your faith in the Lord and you will have no trouble living by them. Remember, I will reinforce your ability to keep them. [3]These commandments are ideally suited to those who are considering repentance, for if they do not obey them, their repentance is a waste of time. [4]So you who repent, rid yourselves of the wicked deeds of this world, for otherwise the burden of them will crush you. And by assuming every righteous virtue, you shall be able to keep these commandments and to accumulate no further sins. If you add not a single sin, you will leave behind your previous sins. Only live by these commandments of mine and you will live with God. I have already told you these things."

[5]After he had reiterated all this, he says to me, "Up, let us go into the countryside. I want to show you the shepherds and their flocks."

I say, "By all means, my lord!" When we had come to a certain plain, he pointed out one particular young man, a shepherd, wearing a bright saffron cloak. [6]He was feeding a huge number of sheep and they appeared to be plump and playful, cheerfully skipping about here and there. The shepherd himself seemed equally happy about his flock and it showed in the smile on his face as he ran about playing with the sheep.

2

[1]And he said to me, "Do you see this shepherd?"

"Yes, sir, I do."

"Mark well his face," he says, "for this is the angel of self-indulgence and deceit. It is he who smashes the souls of God's slaves and twists them away from the truth, seducing them to their doom by means of unwholesome desires. [2]You see, they forget the commandments of the true God and live amid empty delusions, indulging themselves, and the angel thus ruins them, some of them ending in death, others living in a state of corruption."

[3]I answer him, "Lord, I don't know what you mean by 'death' as opposed to 'corruption.'"

"Listen, then," he says. "The sheep you saw happy and frolicking, these are the ones who have been completely severed from God and have abandoned themselves to the lusts of this present world. There is no chance these will ever turn back and find salvation because the gentiles remember their previous profession of faith and believe themselves still to hold it, so the behavior of these sheep causes the name of God to be blasphemed. These are dead while they live. [4]But the sheep you saw not frolicking but grazing off to the side are the ones who have given in to self-indulgence and delusion but who have not yet blasphemed the Lord. These have merely been corrupted from full allegiance to the truth. There remains some hope that these may yet repent, in which case they may live. Corruption, then, implies a possibility of renewal, but death denotes everlasting destruction."

[5]We went on a little further and he pointed out a tall shepherd who looked like a wild man with only a white goatskin wrapped loosely about him. He wore a sort of pouch across his shoulders and carried a very heavy, gnarled staff as well as a heavy whip. And his face was fixed in a scowl that made me shudder! [6]This shepherd would take certain sheep, merry and plump, that no longer frolicked but wandered over from the young shepherd, and he would place them in a certain area high up and infested with thorns and briars in which their fleece became entangled. [7]And as they took what miserable pasturage they could in such straits, they suffered the more when he would club them with his staff. He drove them about in a panic, allowing them no rest, and these sheep saw no more of their former happy state.

3

[1]Seeing them thus tormented and whipped, I pitied them for their ha-

rassment and torture. [2]I say to the Shepherd with whom I converse, "Sir, who is this callous and sadistic shepherd who feels no compassion for his flock?"

"He is the angel of punishment," he says, "and he is one of the righteous angels, not the fallen ones, and he is in charge of punishment. [3]In this capacity, he takes in hand those who stray from God, walking in the path of life's lusts and delusions, and he metes out punishment as they deserve, fearful punishments individually prescribed."

[4]"I would like to know, lord," I say, "what sort of punishments you mean."

"I mean," he says, "nothing but the natural repercussions of their actions in this life. Some suffer loss, others destitution, others various illnesses, still others eviction, others facing the scorn of those less worthy than themselves, so far have they fallen. And there are many others. [5]For many, unsure of what path to choose, dabble in many endeavors, and as a result, none ever pans out. And then they lament that their efforts bring no success. It never occurs to them that their own ill-advised actions are to blame, but they reproach the Lord instead. [6]Then, after they suffer all sorts of troubles, they are handed over to me for good training and are reinforced in their faith in the Lord and serve him whole-heartedly for the remainder of their days. Once they repent, they cannot help but recall the evil deeds they used to do, and this leads them to extol the greatness of God, confessing his fairness as a judge since they only suffered the just deserts of their actions. And from then on, they serve the Lord with a clean conscience. Moreover, they succeed in all their endeavors, obtaining from the Lord anything they care to ask. Then they worship the Lord for having been consigned to me and they no longer suffer any torments."

4

[1]I ask him, "Kind sir, let me ask you something else."

"What can you have left to ask?" he says.

"I want to know whether," I ask, "those who are self-indulgent and deluded suffer their punishments for the same amount of time they spent in indulgence and delusion."

He answers me, "It is the same amount of time for both."

[2]"Then," I say, "I assume their punishments must be rather trivial. One would think people wallowing in self-indulgence, heedless of God, would receive seven times the punishment."

[3]He replies, "You dunce! You fail to grasp the potency of the torment!"

"Obviously!" I say. "If I had grasped it, would I have asked you to clarify it for me?"

"All right," he says, "then learn the power of both the punishment and the crime. [4]Say the duration of the self-indulgence and deceit is one hour. But a single hour of punishment has the combined force of thirty days. So if one lives indulgently, self-deceived, for one day and he is tortured for a day, that one day seems like an entire year! Therefore, for as many days as one wastes in self-indulgence, he will be tormented for what seems to be an equivalent number of years. You can see, then," he says, "that, though the period of self-indulgence flies by, the time of torment will go on and on."

5

[1]"Lord, since I confess I do not altogether understand about the duration of the delusion and self-indulgence on the one hand and the punishment on the other, I wonder," ask I, "if you might further clarify the matter."

[2]Answering, he rebuked me, "Your stupidity sticks to you like glue, I see! You just will not purify your heart to serve God or surely you would understand these things! Watch out, Hermas, or when your time comes, you will be found to be as thick-headed as you are now! Well, if I must ...! I will explain further what you ask so you may understand the thing. [3]The one who indulges himself in delusion for one day, doing as he pleases, is wrapping himself in awful foolishness and he has no idea of the damage he is doing himself because the next day he will forget all he did the previous day. This is because self-indulgence and delusion leave no memories behind due to the confusion that beclouds one. But when punitive torment battens on an individual for a single day, he feels the penalty, the torture, for the length of a whole year, for punishment and torment have excellent memories. [4]After a long year's worth of torment, he finally remembers the original self-indulgence and deceit and realizes this is why he is suffering so. Thus each one who lives in self-indulgence and delusion is vexed in this manner because, though they are still alive, they have sold themselves to death."

[5]"What sort of self-indulgence is destructive, my lord?" I ask.

"Every act is self-indulgent if one enjoys doing it. The quarrelsome individual indulges himself when he gives vent to his annoyance. The philanderer, the drunk, the rumor-monger, the liar, the skinflint, the swindler, and anyone who does such things, each is giving free rein to his special passion, so his deed is self-indulgent. [6]All such habits are destructive

for the slaves of God, and it is because of these delusions that the ones being punished and tormented suffer so much. [7]But there are also, paradoxically, deeds of self-indulgence that bring salvation! I mean those who indulge their desire to do good because they find it such a joy to do so. This sort of self-indulgence, then, is distinctly advantageous for the slaves of God and brings everlasting life to anyone sharing this happy disposition. But those destructive forms of self-indulgence already mentioned bring only torment and punishment, and if people persist in them without repenting, they have only themselves to blame for the death that will overtake them."

Seventh similitude

1

[1]A few days later, I met him again on that same plain where I had seen the shepherds. He asked me, "What are you looking for?"

"I am here, my lord," I answered him, "to find the shepherd of punishment. I was hoping you might ask him to leave my home, for I am suffering terribly on account of him!"

"Unfortunately, you need the punishment," he explains, "for the glorious angel has so prescribed it for you, because he wants to test you."

"But why?" I ask. "What terrible sin have I committed to be handed over to this angel?"

[2]"Listen, Hermas," he says. "You do have many sins, but you are right: none of them is serious enough to merit consigning you to this angel. The serious sins are those of your family, who have committed tragic iniquity. The glorious angel was outraged at what they did, so he asked that you be tormented for a finite period so they might take the hint and join you in repenting and purifying themselves from all worldly desires. So when they are done repenting and being purified, the punishing angel shall leave you."

[3]I ask him, "Lord, all right, so they have sinned so badly the glorious angel bears them a grudge. But what about me?"

"This is the only way they may be made to suffer, don't you see?" he replies, "You, the head of the household, have to be afflicted because if you come on hard times, they will, too, automatically since they live under the same roof. If you are successful, they will enjoy the benefits and so cannot suffer as they ought."

[4]"But, sir! They have repented wholeheartedly!"

"Yes, I am quite aware of that. Surely, though, you don't imagine the sins of the repentant are instantly forgiven with no time lag? No, the poor

wretch who decides to repent must begin by vexing his own soul, must humble himself in everything he does and endure every sort of misfortune. And if he successfully makes it through, then certainly that One who made all things and lends them strength will take pity and send some healing balm. [5]At least, he will do so if he sees the heart of the penitent is actually clean of every atom of evil. Believe me, it is to your advantage that you and your family be tormented now. But why waste so many words? In any case, you have to take the affliction the angel of the Lord assigned you, the same one who consigned you to me. In fact, you should thank the Lord he considered you worthy to have me tell you about the affliction in advance, since forewarned is forearmed, and you will have an easier time of it since you understand what is happening to you."

[6]I answer him, "My lord, as long as you are with me, I'm sure I will pass through any torment safely."

"I will be at your side," he says, "and I will put in a word with the angel of punishment to see if he will ease up a bit on the affliction. But you will be vexed for a brief while and then your family's fortunes will be restored. Just continue to be humble and to serve the Lord with a clean conscience—you, your children, and the rest of those with you—and live by the commandments I gave you, and this will strengthen and purify your repentance. [7]And if you observe these commandments with your household, all affliction will pass you by. Yes, adversity," he says, "will flee from everyone who is willing to live by these commandments of mine."

Eighth similitude

1

[1]He showed me a tall willow tree spreading its branches out over plains and mountains, and all who bear the name of the Lord have taken refuge beneath the shade of that tree. [2]And beside the willow stood an angel of the Lord, shining and of towering height, wielding a huge sickle with which he was busy hacking branches off the willow. These he gave to the people gathered beneath the tree. What he handed them were small rods, each about a single foot in length. [3]Once everyone had his rod, the angel put down the blade and, lo and behold, the tree was as healthy as I had first seen it! [4]Astonished, I reflected, "Now how can that tree still look healthy after having so many branches cut off?"

The Shepherd told me, "Don't be so surprised the tree stayed healthy after the removal of so many branches. Just wait till you see everything and then it will all make sense."

[5]Next, the angel who had given the people the rods asked for them to

be returned, and in the same order as they had been presented the rods, each was called back and yielded up his rod. The angel of the Lord took each and gave it a close look. [6]Some of the rods looked as if they had withered and had been gnawed by larvae. The angel commanded everyone who had given him such a rod to assemble together in one place. [7]Others had handed in rods that appeared withered, yet not chewed by larvae. These, too, he segregated by themselves. Others turned them in only half-chewed; these, too, were shown their place. [8]Others handed them back half-withered, and these also stood separately. [9]Other rods were half-withered but also cracked. Their owners stood by. [10]Yet others' rods were found to be green yet still cracked, and these people too took their place. [11]Still others had rods that were half-withered, half-green, and they stood by themselves. [12]Others had sticks that were two-thirds green, one-third withered, and these too took their own place. [13]Others yielded up sticks that were two-thirds withered, one-third green, and these gathered together. [14]Others' rods were nearly all green with just a bit on the end withered up. But they were cracked as well, and their owners stood in their designated place. [15]In others only a bit was green with most withered. These people found their place. [16]Others handed in green rods, exactly as the angel had first distributed them. In fact, most handed in their rods in this state, and these pleased the angel very much. These, too, had their own proper place. [17]Others turned in rods that were not only green but had actually budded,[w] and this seemed to delight the angel, too. They were set to one side. [18]Others had rods not only green and budding but even bearing some type of fruit. Their owners were exultant to see their rods appear so. And the angel greatly rejoiced in their case. Then each one's rod was returned to him where he waited to see the outcome.

2

[1]And the angel of the Lord gave orders that crowns be brought. And they were brought, and I saw that they were like laurel wreaths but made of palm fronds. With these, he crowned those whose rods had budded and fruited. He sent them off into the tower. [2]He sent others there, too, namely those who had given him the rods green and budding but without fruit. He impressed a seal upon these. [3]Everyone sent into the tower wore the same white clothing, and it was white as snow. [4]Those whose rods proved identical to the state in which they had received them were sent off with a robe and a seal. [5]When the angel was done, he spoke to the

w. Num. 17:8

Shepherd: "It is time for me to depart, but you are to send the rest inside the walls to the abode each properly deserves. But take a close look at their rods before you dispatch them. Be careful and see that no one slips away from you!" quoth he. "And yet, if any do get past you, I will intercept them at the altar and test them there." Having said these things to the Shepherd, he left.

6After the angel went away, the Shepherd turned to me and says, "Let's plant all these rods to see if any will be able to live!"

I say to him, "Lord, how could these shriveled-up sticks live?"

7He answered, "Remember, this is a willow, a hardy variety of tree. If the rods are planted and get a little water, many of them ought to live. So after we get them planted, let's give them a bit of water, shall we? If any of them do live, I will be glad of it; but if not, at least no one will be able to say my neglect was the reason." 8With this, the Shepherd had me call back each group from its place. Row upon row, they filed by to hand the Shepherd their rods. These the Shepherd gathered and planted in rows, then poured so much water over them that their exposed tops could no longer be seen. 9After watering them, he said to me, "Let's be off now. In a few days we will return and inspect all the rods. He who created this tree desires that every one of those who received rods from the tree should live. And I, too, hope most of these little rods, after they soak up the water, will live."

3

1I say to him, "My lord, do tell me: what is this tree? I am puzzled! With so many branches missing, the tree still looks good; nothing seems to have been cut from it at all. That's what puzzles me!"

2"Listen," he says. "This vast tree extending over plains, mountains, and indeed the whole earth, is the Law of God which is given to the entire world. And this Law is the preaching of the Son of God to the farthest corners of the world. The people in the shade are those who have heard that preaching and put their faith in him. 3The great shining angel is Michael.[x] He is in charge of this people and is their chief. It is his task to implant the Law into believers' hearts, and this is why he examines those to whom it is given, to see if they have obeyed it. 4The rods that each possessed are the Law of God. You see how many of the rods were made use-

x. Elsewhere the great angel appears to be the same as the Son of God. Notice that the Son of God is never given any other name in the document—is never called Jesus.

less, and you will see all those who did not keep the Law as well as the place to which each is variously consigned."

[5]I ask him, "Lord, why did he send some on into the tower but leave the rest for you?"

"Every one," he replies, "who disregarded the Law they received from him, these he passed on to me for repentance. But all those who have already met the Law's requirements by obeying it, he retains under his jurisdiction."

[6]"Who are the ones," I ask, "who were given the victor's wreath and sent into the tower?"

"They are the ones who suffered rather than disobey the Law. [7]But those who returned their rods green and budding, though without fruit, are the ones who, though persecuted on account of the Law, did not actually suffer harm, nor did they apostatize from the Law. [8]Those who handed them back in as green as they received them are serious, righteous persons who conducted themselves with completely pure consciences, keeping the commandments of the Lord, though no occasion arose for them to suffer on account of it. But I will tell you the rest once I have inspected these rods we planted and watered."

4

[1]So in a few days, we returned to the place. The Shepherd took his seat where the angel Michael had sat, while I stood at his side. He says to me, "Tie a loincloth of raw flax around you and serve me." And I did put on a fresh length of rough cloth of raw flax. [2]When he saw me thus dressed and ready to serve him, he says to me, "Call those whose rods are planted here, by groups, in the same order in which they handed in their rods. [3]When this was done, he said to them, "Each of you, find your own rod and bring it to me." [4]The first in line were the ones whose rods had been withered and gnawed, and they remained in the same condition. He told them to stand off in one place. [5]Then came those who had rods that had been withered but not chewed. Some handed them in newly green, while others returned them still withered and chewed by larvae. He ordered those with green rods to their separate place. Those with withered and gnawed rods he directed to join the first group. [6]Then came those whose rods had been half-withered and cracked. Many now had rods green and without cracks. Some even presented them green, budding, and fruiting, just like those who formerly had entered the tower wearing wreaths. Some handed in their rods withered and gnawed, some only withered, and some just as they had been: withered and cracked. These he

directed to various locations, some back with their fellows, others by themselves.

5

[1]Next, the ones who had had green cracked rods handed them back. All had now turned green, and their owners stood together. The Shepherd was delighted with these because they had all changed and lost their cracks. [2]And the people with rods halfway green, the other half withered, handed them in, too. Some of these were now completely green, with others half-withered, others withered and gnawed, and some green and budding. These were divided up and sent to the appropriate groups. [3]Then came those whose rods had been two-thirds green, one-third withered. Many of these were now half-withered, some being both withered and gnawed, others half-withered with cracks, and a few of them green. These were appropriately segregated. [5]Next came those whose rods had been mainly green but with just a bit withered and cracked. Of these, some handed them in newly turned green, others not only green but budding. These, too, went off to join their fellows. [6]Then those approached whose rods had been mainly withered with just a bit remaining green. Now these had turned mostly green, with buds and fruit, while some were completely green. Finding these rods in such prime condition filled the Shepherd with joy. And these returned to their group.

6

[1]After inspecting all the rods, he says to me, "Didn't I tell you this tree does not give up easily? Do you see how many of them repented and were saved?"

"I see, my lord," I say.

"The point," he says, "is for you to see how deep is the mercy of the Lord, how great and splendid, and how he has imparted his Spirit to all who are worthy of repentance."

[2]"But why, my lord," I ask, "didn't they all repent?"

"He allowed repentance to those he could see were ready to become pure and serve him whole-heartedly, but he withheld it from the scheming, evil ones he saw planned only to pretend to repent, since otherwise they would only have made a mockery of the whole thing again."

[3]"Lord," I ask, "now show me the significance of those who turned in their rods, what kind each of them represents and their destined place, so that when they hear this, those who have believed and taken the seal of baptism and have broken it and not kept it intact may come to realize

what they are doing and repent and receive a seal from you[y] and may worship the Lord for taking pity on them and sending them to you to refresh their spirits."

4"Listen," he says, "those whose rods turned out to be withered up and gnawed by larvae are apostates and betrayers of the church, who blasphemed the Lord by the sins they committed and were embarrassed they had ever been baptized with the invocation of his name. These, accordingly, became completely dead to God. You have seen how none of these people ever repent, even when they hear you offer the commandments I gave you. Spiritual life has left these people for good. 5But the ones who turned in withered rods but not larvae-eaten, these are close behind them, for they were hypocrites who introduced far-fetched new teachings to pervert the slaves of God, especially the ones who had lapsed into sin, by telling them they could not repent[z] and convincing them of their moronic teachings.[a] Yet there remains a chance these will repent, 6and in fact, you have seen that many of them have been willing to repent when they hear the commandments I gave you. Yet more will repent. Whoever does not repent will forfeit his life, but whoever has repented has turned good. And it is they who were assigned a dwelling inside the first walls, some even going up into the tower. So you see that repenting of one's sins results in life, while neglecting repentance is fatal."

7

1"But listen to the truth about those who handed back their rods half-withered and cracked. The ones who had rods half-withered are the inveterate doubters. They are neither fully alive nor dead. 2But those who have rods half-withered and cracked are not only doubters but rumor-mongers. They are never at peace even among themselves because they are always perforce fomenting schisms. Yet even such as these are still allowed to repent. As you see, some have repented. And there is still," he says, "hope for the rest of them. 3Every one of their number who has repented has a home inside the tower, though those who procrastinate win only a place inside the walls. And of course those who refuse to change their ways shall surely die.

y. This presumably refers to the second opportunity for repentance announced in Mandate 4.3.4-6.

z. Heb. 6:4-8; 10:26-31

a. It is this severe approach, akin to the Islamic Kharijite heresy that any sin was tantamount to apostasy and unforgivable, that is countered by the doctrine of a second repentance.

4"The ones with the green, cracked rods were seen to have been consistently good and steadfast but suffered from a foolish tendency to vie with one another for pre-eminence and honor.[b] 5But being righteous, these repented and purified themselves as soon as they heard my commandments. Thus they have apartments within the tower. But anyone who lapses back into divisiveness, he will be ejected from the tower and lose his life. 6Everlasting life is only for the ones who observe the commandments of the Lord. And among these commandments, one will find nothing about preeminence or any sort of glory but only long-suffering and a life of humility. In that kind of people, life exists, but death indwells the divisive and outlaws."

8

1"But the ones who turned in their rods half-green, half-withered, you will not be surprised to hear they are mired fast in business affairs and do not associate with the saints. Thus they exist half-alive, half-necrotic. 2But many repented when they heard my commandments. And those who did found a place in the tower. But others paid my commandments no heed at all. They have forfeited their opportunity to repent. Because of their business affairs, they were willing to blaspheme the Lord and to repudiate him.[c] Thus they paid with their lives for the sins they had committed. 3But many of these were only ambivalent.[d] These still have the chance to repent if they are quick about it and they shall be welcome in the tower. If they procrastinate, there shall be found room for them only within the walls, and if they fail altogether to repent, they too shall forfeit their lives.

4"Those who have turned in rods two-thirds of which were green with one-third withered have denied their faith many times over. 5Many of them repented and went on into the tower, but many rebelled absolutely against God, finally forfeiting their souls. Some were ambivalent and troublemakers. Repentance awaits them, but only if they repent quickly and do not continue with what they are doing; otherwise, they too are only gaining death."

9

1"Now as to those who handed back rods two-thirds withered,

---

b. 3 John 9; Mark 9:33-34; 10:35-37; 12:39; Luke14:7-11

c. Mark 8:36. Business lunches were sometimes banquets in pagan temples (see 1 Cor. 10:27). As envisioned in Heb. 10:34, members of outlawed sects might have their property seized, as happened to the Mormons in the American West.

d. Matt. 6:24

one-third green, these were at one time believers but they prospered and gained a secular reputation. They wrapped themselves in pride and grew conceited, forsaking the truth instead of sticking with righteousness, and they associated with one another in the way gentiles do. This way of life appealed to them more, but they did not fall away from God. They maintained their faith, though they did not endeavor to do the deeds appropriate to it. [2]But many did repent and entered the tower. [3]Others had lived too long among the gentiles and became corrupted with their worldly views, abandoned God, and lived identical to the gentiles. Henceforth, these were simply considered as gentiles. [4]But others were hesitant, no longer entertaining much hope of being saved because of the deeds they had performed, while still others were ambivalent and created factions among their own number. For the ones ambivalent because of their deeds, there is still hope, but they must repent soon if they are to live in the tower. But for the ones who do not repent, persisting in their hedonism, death comes close!"

10

[1]"As for those who turned in their rods green, yet with the very tips withered and cracked, they were known always to be righteous, steadfast and splendid before God, but they were marked by a modicum of sin by token of minor desires and trifling grudges against each other. As soon as they heard me speak, most repented immediately and they were assigned rooms in the tower. [2]But some were ambivalent, and of these, some made a great fuss. For these, there is still a chance for repentance because they were always so good, and it is rare for one of them to die.

[3]"But as to those whose rods were returned withered except for a small green bit, these people believed but they acted heedless of the law. And yet, they never renounced God, but were happy to be known as his, and they were glad to offer hospitality to the slaves of God. So once they heard of this second chance to repent, they repented without hesitation, and now they live in virtue and righteousness. Some even gladly undergo persecution, hoping to make up for their former deeds. All these shall find their place in the tower."

11

[1]Once he had finished explaining all the rods, he says to me: "Go now, urging everyone to repent, and they shall live with God, for the Lord, being merciful, sent me to offer repentance to everyone, though some hardly deserve it on account of their behavior. But since he is long-suffering, the Lord wants all who were called through his Son to be saved."

[2]I say to him, "Lord, I hope that all who hear these words will repent! And I cannot help thinking that, once each is confronted with his own record and feels the fear of God, he will in fact repent."

[3]He answered me, saying, "All who whole-heartedly cleanse themselves from all the wicked works mentioned heretofore and add no more to their old sins shall gain from the Lord a cure for their old sins, unless of course they are ambivalent about these commandments, and they shall live with God. [4]As for you, abide by my commandments and live!" [5]Once he had finished explaining all this to me, he says to me, "There is more, but I will tell you the rest after you have had a few days to absorb this."

Ninth similitude

1

[1]Once I had recorded the commandments and parables of the Shepherd, the angel of repentance, he came to me and told me, "I want to show you all those things shown you by the Holy Spirit speaking in the form of Ecclesia. For that Spirit is the Son of God. [2]Because when you were still weaker, less spiritual, revelation was not made to you by means of an angel. But once you were prepared by the Spirit, greatly strengthened to the point where you could actually see an angel, then eventually the construction of the tower was revealed to you by Ecclesia. You were given instruction in a fine and becoming manner, as by a virgin, but now you are taught by an angel, though it is the same Spirit, [3]and yet you need to learn everything in more detail from me. This is what the glorious angel had in mind when he assigned me to live in your house, so you might see everything full strength, not being frightened by anything, as for some time now."

[4]Then he spirited me away to Arcadia, to a particular domed mountain where he set me down on the top and showed me the wide plain, as well as a dozen mountains, all quite different-looking, scattered throughout the plain. [5]The first mountain was sooty black, the second denuded of foliage, the third covered with thickets of thorns and briars, [6]the fourth with foliage half shriveled up, with the top of the grass green but withered down by the roots. Some of it had withered up as if from the sun scorching it. [7]The fifth mountain was blanketed in green grass and was craggy. The sixth mountain was cleft all over with gullies, some of them containing foliage, but the grass was not very lush and looked withered. [8]The seventh mountain had bright, healthy foliage and the whole mountain moved with life. Cattle and all varieties of birds fed there, and the more they fed, the more lush did the vegetation grow! The eighth mountain

abounded in springs, and every sort of creature of the Lord drank of those mountain springs. [9]The ninth mountain was completely devoid of water, a total desert. It swarmed with wild animals and venomous reptiles deadly to human beings. The tenth mountain sported huge trees and was draped in shadow and sheep lay down beneath the shade and grazed. [10]The eleventh mountain was densely covered with woods and its trees were very fruitful, laden with numerous varieties of fruit so luscious that anyone seeing them would be tempted to pick some and eat it. The twelfth mountain was completely white and looked very pleasant. And the mountain was very beautiful in its own right.

2

[1]And at the center of the plain, he pointed out a huge white rock rising up from the plain. This rock rose higher than the mountains and it was square-based and large enough to contain within itself the entire world! [2]The rock was ancient and a gateway had been carved from it. But it looked to me as if the gateway had been carved only recently. The gate's polished finish gleamed brighter than the sun itself. I stood amazed at how bright it was! [3]Twelve virgins stood around this gate. The four stationed at the four corners were the most beautiful, though indeed all were quite stunning. The eight stood in pairs between the ones posted at the corners. [4]They were dressed in linen tunics and belted in a becoming fashion.[e] Their right shoulders were bare, as if they would be carrying something. They were prepared for some task and looked eager to be about it.

[5]After seeing these things, I was amazed at the degree of splendor of the things I was seeing. Once again, I was puzzled about the virgins: they appeared so delicate, yet they were stationed like men and seemed ready to hold up the heavenly dome. [6]And the Shepherd said to me, "Why ponder such questions? Why be puzzled and make yourself gloomy? If there are matters you cannot understand, don't try to, if you are wise. Instead, ask the Lord for wisdom to understand them. [7]You cannot see what is behind you, but you see only what is in front of you. What you cannot see, let it alone and don't trouble yourself about it![f] But the things you can

e. This is how Hermas knows they are virgins. Like Vestal Virgins, Christian prophesying virgins wore distinctive garb, including some sort of belts believed to abet their prophetic powers, as in the (possibly Montanist) *Testament of Job* 46:7-9; 47:1-11; 48:1-3; 50:1-3; 51:1-4; and in the story underlying Acts 21:9-11, where it would have been Philip's prophetic daughters who wore the oracular belt. See Robert M. Price, *The Widow Traditions in Luke-Acts: A Feminist-Critical Scrutiny*, SBL Dissertation Series 155 (Atlanta: Scholars Press, 1997), 61-70.

f. Pss. 139:6

see, work on mastering them and do not be curious about the rest. I will explain to you every vision I show you. So take a look at the rest."

3

[1]I witnessed the arrival of six men. They were tall and splendid in appearance—and all identical! These summoned a great crowd of others, all of whom were also tall, good-looking, and mighty. The six commanded them to construct a tower above the gateway. And as the workers got busy, running to and fro over the area, a great hubbub arose. [2]The virgins urged these men on to finish the tower quickly. Next, the virgins held out their hands as if expecting to be given something by the men. [3]The six foremen ordered that stones be fetched from the sea bottom for the construction of the tower. And up from the depths came ten stones, square and polished. [4]And the six men called the virgins and told them to take the stones to be used in construction and bring them through the gateway and hand them to the builders of the tower. [5]So the virgins stacked the first ten stones one atop the other, then together carried them as if they were a single stone.

4

[1]And in the same order in which they had first stood around the gateway, they now carried the stones. Those who seemed strongest stooped down to carry the weight of the corners, while the less robust stooped to support the bottom on the sides of the stone. In this manner, they transported all of them. They took them right through the gate as directed, handing them to the men to add to the tower. The men took the stones and fitted them. [2]The tower was being erected upon the huge rock above the gate. The ten stones, once fitted together, covered the whole top of the rock. And these would serve as the foundation for the tower. It and the gate would support the whole weight of the tower. [3]After these ten stones were placed, the virgins brought in another twenty-five, again raised up from the deep, and these too were placed in the tower. Next, thirty-five stones were brought and added to the structure. These were followed by another forty stones, all used in the construction. Four rows constituted the tower's foundation. [4]Then there was a hiatus in bringing any stones and the workmen took a break. Then the six men gave orders again for the workmen to bring more stones for construction, this time from the mountains. [5]Thus they arrived from all the mountains and were accordingly variously colored. The men cut them evenly and passed them on to the virgins, who transported them through the gate and left them for use in the construction And once the various stones had been fitted into the

structure, lo and behold, they all turned white and identical, having lost their original hues. [6]But there were some stones delivered not by the virgins but by the workmen and not brought in through the gate, and these did not turn white but retained their original color. These stones looked jarringly out of place, [7]so the six supervisors, seeing the problem, ordered that these stones be replaced and dumped back into the pit they came from. [8]And they tell the ones carrying the stones in, "Stop bringing the stones all the way to the construction site, will you? Just leave them near the tower for the virgins to pick up and tote through the gate and hand over to the builders. For if the stones are carried through the gate by anyone but the virgins, they cannot change color. Don't waste your efforts!"

5

[1]And the building was finished that same day, except that the tower was not quite finished, for it was planned to rise to an even greater height. But the project was called to a halt. And the six men told the construction workers to go home and rest for a bit. But they said nothing about a rest to the virgins. So I guessed that the women had been posted to guard the tower. [2]So after everyone went on break, I ask the Shepherd, "Why, my lord, were they unable to finish the tower?"

"The tower," he says, "cannot be completed until the sponsor of the project comes to inspect it, to see if any stones are unsound and need to be replaced. The tower is being constructed according to his specifications."

[3]"I would like to know, lord," I ask, "the significance of the construction of the tower, of the rock and the gate, the mountains, the virgins, and the stones from the deep which needed no cutting and were fitted into the tower just as they were. [4]Why were ten stones fitted into the building first, then twenty-five, then thirty-five, then forty? And what is the symbolic meaning of the stones that were added but then had to be replaced, then were dumped back where they came from? Satisfy my mind on this score, please, sir."

[5]"If you are not asking out of idle curiosity," he says, "then I will tell you. In a few days, we will return here and you will see the outcome of all this and you will understand all the parables accurately."

[6]And a few days later, we did come back and he says to me, "Let's head for the tower because the owner of the tower is coming to look it over." So we came to the tower, but no one was there except the virgins. [7]And the Shepherd asked them if the master of the tower had arrived yet. And they told him the owner should soon arrive to examine the building.

6

[1]Behold, after a little while, I observe a party of many men, and at the center of the crowd walked a man of such gigantic stature as to dwarf even the tower! [2]The six men who had overseen the construction of the tower flanked him, three on either side. All the workmen accompanied him, together with many other retainers, each of whom shone with light. The virgins stationed around the tower ran up to him and kissed him, then walked at his side as he circled the tower, examining it. [3]So minutely did he inspect it that he touched each individual stone. He carried a rod and tapped every stone in the structure. [4]And with each tap, a stone might turn sooty black or mildewed or cracked or broken off short. Others became neither black nor white. Still others assumed an asymmetrical shape, no longer fitting in with the adjacent stones. Others were marked with many spots. Such was the appearance of the various stones he discovered as being unsound for the structure. [5]So he ordered all these removed from the tower and stacked beside the tower and others to be brought in to replace them. [6]The builders asked him from which mountain he preferred they obtain the replacement stones. But he ruled out getting them from the mountains, preferring a place closer at hand. [7]So they started digging in the plain itself and there they brought to light stones bright and square, though some were too rounded. And the virgins took all the stones that could be mined from the plain and carried them through the gate. [8]The square stones were cut and inserted where the others had been removed. The round ones, they did not fit into the building because it was too difficult to reshape them. It took too long to work on them, so they were piled beside the tower as though perhaps they might be chiseled into shape later. They were too bright just to discard.

7

[1]After all this work was finished, the radiant man who was master of the tower called over the Shepherd and gave him all the round stones piled beside the tower, which had been excluded from it. And he said to him, [2]"Polish these stones with great care, my man; and use them in garnishing the tower, at least those which can be made to fit in somewhere. As for the rest, throw them as far as you can from the tower." [3]After leaving him with these orders, he left again, accompanied by his entourage. And the virgins returned to their posts around the tower.

[4]I ask the Shepherd, "How can these stones go into the tower since they were already rejected from it? What has changed?"

In answer, he tells me, "See these stones?"

"I do, lord," I reply.

"I myself will apply the chisel to most of them," he says, "and when I am done, believe me, they will fit in with the others!"

[5]"Lord, I fail to see," I ask. "They are smaller as it is, being rounded. How can cutting off what mass they have allow them to fit in with larger stones?"

He answers me this way: "All the ones found to be small will be placed in the inner wall of the tower, and they shall use the rest to plug the gaps left in the outer wall. And they will have the means to bind the two." [6]With this, he suggests to me, "Let's be off now, and after a couple of days we will come back and polish the stones and fit them into the building. For everything on the site must be cleaned up or the master may appear suddenly and find the area surrounding the tower a mess. This will infuriate him and these stones will not go into the tower, after all. And I will look careless to my master."

[7]So after two days had passed, we returned to the place and he says to me, "Come, let's examine the stones to see which are fit to be added to the structure."

I agreed. "Yes, lord. I am ready."

8

[1]We started with the black stones, and they proved to be no different from their previous state. So the Shepherd gave orders that they be removed and put off to one side. [2]Then he examined the mildewed stones, picking up several, chiseling them, and ordering the virgins to pick them up and apply them to the structure. And the virgins took them and fitted them into place in the midsection. And the remainder of these, he had them put over with the black ones, for these too had turned black. [3]Then he turned his eye on the cracked ones. He was able to work on a number of these, and the chips flew. Then he called the virgins and told them to take them to the building. They put them near the outer wall because they turned out to be more solid. But the rest of the cracked stones were too far gone, vitiated. Thus, they were discarded altogether. [4]Next, he looked over the stumpy stones, and many turned out to have turned black, some seriously cracked. These, too, were dumped on the discard heap. But the remainder he polished and shaped and directed to be used in the building. The virgins accordingly took them to the tower but applied them to the middle, seeing that they were a bit weak. [5]Then he looked over the ones that were half-white, half-black, many of which had now turned completely black, and he had them taken to join the rest in the rubbish pile.

But the virgins took the rest for the construction, as they had turned all white. Having proven solid, they were used in the outer wall to reinforce the slightly weaker stones that were in the middle, and not one of them was too small to do the job as I had feared.

[6]Next, he turned to those rejected before as too harsh and rough. A few were discarded since they could not be chiseled: they were too dense. But the rest were chiseled and applied to the middle of the building, being a bit weak. [7]Then he examined the spotted stones, finding that a few had blackened, and these he dumped with the others. But the rest looked bright and solid and the virgins were able to fit them into the building on the outside, given their strength.

9

[1]When he came at last to the round stones, he asked me, "Hermas, what do you propose we do with these stones?"

I answered, "How should I know, sir?"

"So you notice nothing about them?"

[2]"Lord," I protest, "I know nothing of the builder's art. I am no mason, nor do I know how they do what they do."

"But don't you see how round they are?" he asks. "And if I wanted to square them, don't you see how much I would have to strike off them? And yet we have to use some of them in the construction."

[3]"If it has to be, lord," I say, "then what's the use of fretting over it? Just choose some and get to work!"

So he picked the largest and brightest of them and applied the chisel. When he had finished the labor, the virgins picked them up and fitted them into the outer wall of the building. [4]But the rest of them were picked up and returned to the plain from which they had been taken. They were not simply discarded, however. "Because," he explained, "the tower is not quite finished yet and we may still need them. And the master is keen, if at all possible, for these to be used somewhere in the tower, they are so bright." [5]So he summoned a dozen women, this time dressed in black and with beautiful figures and loose hair hanging about their shoulders, one of which was exposed. I thought these women had something of a wild appearance. The Shepherd commanded them to pick up the stones that had been flung far from the building and to return them to the respective mountains they had come from. [6]They seemed happy to comply and carried the stones back to their origin points. And once all the stones had been removed, not one left on the construction site, the Shepherd said to me, "Let's, you and I, circle the tower and make sure there are no flaws

left in it." So I joined him in his circuit. [7]And when the Shepherd beheld just how beautifully the tower had been constructed, he was quite delighted. Indeed, the tower was so well built that when I saw it, I momentarily wished it was my own. It looked as if it had been carved from a single massive stone, so perfect were the joinings. The detailing appeared to have been sculpted from the natural rock. In truth, one would have thought it made from a single stone!

10

[1]As for me, as I accompanied him, I was thrilled to behold such a fine spectacle. And the Shepherd said to me, "Go and fetch me some plaster and modeling clay so I can fill in and smooth over all the gaps between the stones, for the tower's round surface must appear perfectly smooth!" [2]So I did as he asked and brought him these materials. "If you work with me, we will be done in no time," he said. So he filled in all the gaps between the building stones and ordered the area surrounding the tower to be swept clean. [3]The virgins took brooms and swept, removed all rubbish from the tower, and applied water wherever needed. At last, the site of the tower had been made tidy and attractive. [4]The Shepherd tells me, "Now it is all cleaned up! Whenever the Lord arrives to inspect the tower, he will find no reason to blame us." Having said so, he wanted to leave. [5]But I seized him by his shoulder pouch and began to command him in the name of the Lord to explain what he had shown me. He says to me, "I am very busy just now, Hermas, but a little later I will be happy to explain everything to you. Wait for me here."

[6]I ask him, "Lord, have you any instructions for me while I wait here by myself?"

"But you are not alone!" he says. "These virgins are here with you."

"Introduce me to them, in that case," I say.

So the Shepherd called them over and says to them, "I know this man well. Please keep him company until I return." Then he left, [7]leaving me alone with the virgins. They turned out to be very convivial companions, quite friendly to me, especially the four most beautiful.

11

[1]The virgins say to me, "The Shepherd is not coming today."

"Then what should I do?" I ask.

"Wait for him," they advise, "till evening falls, and if he shows up then, he will talk with you. But if he does not come, you will remain with us until he does."

[2]I reply, "I will wait for him till evening, but if he hasn't come by

then, I believe I will go back home and try him again early tomorrow morning."

But they answered and said to me, "You were entrusted to us. You cannot leave us!"

3"Er ... then where should I stay?" I ask.

"You shall spend the night with us!" they say. "But don't worry! You shall be as a brother, not a husband. For you are our brother, and from now on, we will live with you, for we love you dearly." But I was acutely uncomfortable at the prospect of staying with them. 4All the more so once the one who seemed to be their leader began to kiss me and hug me. When the others saw this, they joined in the kissing and grabbed my hand, leading me around behind the tower to have fun with me. 5All of a sudden, I saw that I had become like a young man again. So I began to join in the play. Some of them started to dance, others to sing. As for me, I kept quiet and merely walked around the tower with them, happy to be with them. 6But when evening came and I wanted to leave for home, they would not hear of it and kept me there. So I spent the night in their company, sleeping beside the tower. 7The virgins took off their linen tunics and laid them out on the ground[g] and had me lie down between them. But all they did was pray. And I, too, prayed without interruption. I remained with them till the second hour of the morning.

8Finally the Shepherd arrived and asks the virgins, "Did you harm him?"

"Ask him!" they reply.

I say to him, "Lord, it was a delight to stay with them."

"What did you have for dinner?" he asks.

"I dined sumptuously all night on the words of the Lord."

"And you say they treated you well?" he asks.

"Indeed, sir," I reply.

9"Now," he says, "what do you want to hear first?"

"Why not start at the beginning with what you showed me first, my lord?" I reply. "I ask, lord, that you explain things to me in the same order I question you."

"I shall interpret for you," he says, "just as you wish, then. I shall hide nothing at all from you."

12

1"First, then, lord, tell me this. What is the meaning of the rock and the gate?"

g. Thomas, sayings 21, 37

"The rock," he says, "as well as the gate, stand for the Son of God."

"Then why, lord," I ask, "was the rock ancient but the gate recently carved?"

"Listen, you blockhead," he says, "and perhaps you will understand. [2]The Son of God predates his whole creation, which is why he could serve as the Father's consultant in the creation process. This is why he is depicted as something ancient."

"But the gate, sir, why should it be recent?" I ask.

[3]"Because," he says, "he was revealed to the world only in the last days before the fulfillment of all things. This is why the gate was shown as new, and through it the saved enter into the kingdom of God. [4]Did you notice that the stones brought through the gate were used in the tower, while those that entered some other way were discarded?"

"Yes, sir, I did."

"In the same way," he explained, "no one enters into the kingdom of God unless he first receives the name of his Son. [5]For if you want to enter any city and the city has a single gate in its perimeter wall, can you go in some other way than that one gate?"

"How else, sir?" I say.

"So if you can enter that city only through the one gate, it should be no surprise," he says, "that no one can enter the kingdom of God except by the name of the Son he so loves. [6]Did you notice," he asks, "the great crowd at work building the tower?"

"I did, my lord." I answer.

"They," he says, "are all radiant angels. With such does the Lord surround himself. But the gate itself is the Son of God; that is the only entrance to the Lord. No one may come into his presence except by his Son. [7]Did you see the six men with the shining powerful man at their center, the one who walked around the tower examining it?"

"I saw him, all right," I say.

[8]"The shining man," he says, "is the Son of God, and those six are his bodyguard, all shining angels who flank him on the right and on the left. Not even any of these radiant angels may come into God's presence apart from him. Whoever declines to bear his name is forever barred from the kingdom of God."

13

[1]"But the tower itself," I ask, "what is it?"

"The tower?" he says. "Why, the tower is the church, of course!"

[2]"And these virgins—who are they?"

"They are," he says, "holy spirits. And no one in the kingdom of God can be found dressed in any other style than wearing the garment of these spirits.[h] If you receive only the name but do not receive the garment from them, it does you no good. For these virgins are Powers of the Son of God. So if you bear his name and lack his power, it is futile for you to carry his name at all. [3]And the stones you saw being discarded, these carried the name but never clothed themselves with the costume of the virgins."

"What, my lord," I ask, "is the peculiar nature of their costume?"

"The names themselves constitute their garments. Whoever takes the name of the Son of God should take their names as well. Even the Son himself carries the names of these virgins![i] [4]Every stone you witnessed entering into the construction of the tower, handed in by them and waiting their turn to be part of the building, has been swathed in the power of these virgins. [5]This is why the tower looks as if it had been carved from a single stone of one piece with the rock beneath it. In the same way, those who have believed in the Lord through his Son and dress themselves in these spirits shall become one body and one soul, their clothing all the same color. But all those who carry the names of the virgins have their abode inside the tower.

[6]"Those stones, lord," I ask, "that were discarded, what was wrong with them? After all, they did pass through the gate and were put into the construction of the tower by the hands of the virgins!"

"Since nothing escapes your interest," he says, "and you do not let up in your inquiry, here is the significance of the stones that were thrown away. [7]These were people who received the name of the Son of God and even received the power of these virgins. They were strengthened when they received these spirits. They served God and shared one spirit and one body. They thought alike and behaved nobly. [8]But after a while, they yielded to the seductions of those women you saw dressed in black, bare-shouldered with loose hair, beautiful and shapely. Seeing them, they lusted after them. They clothed themselves in the power of these women, stripping off the power of the virgins. [9]Then they were ejected from God's house and handed over to these women. All those who saw through the beauty of these women remained safely in the house of God. There you have the meaning of the stones that were thrown away."

---

h. Matt. 22:11-14

i. Isa. 11:2

14

[1]"Suppose, my lord," I ask, "that these men, in their wretched condition, were to repent and forsake their lust for these women and go back to the virgins to live by their power and do the deeds they love? Couldn't they enter the house of God?"

[2]"They shall indeed enter," he says, "if they reject the deeds these women tempt them to and again apply the power of the virgins and live as they do. And this is also the reason for the temporary halt in construction, to allow a chance for these to repent, in which case they might enter the tower; but if they neglect repentance, then others will take their place and they shall at last be shut out of the tower."

[3]I thanked God for all these things, that he showed such mercy on all who invoke his name and dispatched the angel of repentance to us who had sinned against him, rejuvenating our spirits and restoring our salvation when we were already destroyed, with no hope of everlasting life. [4]"Now, lord, if you please," I ask, "tell me why the tower is not built on the plain but on top of the rock and the gate."

"You must be altogether devoid of brains and comprehension!" he says.

"My lord, I must question you precisely because I lack the requisite understanding!" I say. "All these things are too vast, too dazzling, too complex for mortal understanding. Otherwise, what is the point of issuing divine revelations at all?"

[5]"Very well. Listen," he says, "The name of the Son of God is a profound mystery, upholding the entire cosmos. If, therefore, the whole creation is upheld by the Son, what would you infer as to those whom he calls, who bear the name of the Son of God and live by his commandments? [6]Do you see what sort of individuals he supports? Namely, those who bear his name whole-heartedly. He himself has become their foundation and he is glad to uphold them because they are not embarrassed to be known as his."

15

[1]"What about the virgins and the women dressed in black? Can you give me their names?"

"These," he says, "are the names of the strongest virgins, the ones who stand at the corners. [2]First is Faith, second Continence, third Power, and fourth Long-suffering. And the others, standing between them, are called Integrity, Guilelessness, Purity, Cheerfulness, Truth, Understanding, Concord, and Love. Whoever bears these names and that of the Son

of God shall be qualified to enter the kingdom of God. [3]Here, too, are the names of the women dressed in black. Here, too, four are more powerful than the others: first Unbelief, second Intemperance, third Disobedience, and fourth Deceit. Their followers are known as Sadness, Wickedness, Wantonness, Irascibility, Falsehood, Folly, Slander, and Hatred. Any slave of God who bears these names shall only see the kingdom of God without entering into it."

[4]"Now for the stones, lord," I ask, "that were dredged up from the deep and fitted into the building, who are they supposed to be?"

"The initial ten, making up the foundation," he says, "are the first generation of faith. The twenty-five that followed them are the second generation of the righteous. The thirty-five are God's prophets and his slaves. The forty are apostles and teachers of the message of the Son of God."

[5]"Then why, my lord," I ask, "did the virgins hand in these, too, for the construction of the tower and carry them through the gate?"

[6]"Because these men," he says, "were the first to bear the spirits the virgins represent, and the one was never separated from the other, the spirits from the men, nor the men from the spirits. No, the spirits remained with them till they fell asleep. Had these spirits not accompanied them, they would not have been found useful for the tower's construction."

16

[1]"Show me more, lord," I ask.

"What more do you want to know?" he says.

"Why, sir," I ask, "did the stones have to come up from the deep? And why were they added to the building even though they already possessed those spirits?"

[2]"It was required of them," he explained, "to come up through water in order to be made alive; otherwise, they would never have been able to enter into the kingdom of God. They had to repudiate the deadness of their worldly life by means of baptism. [3]So these, too, who had fallen asleep in death took the baptismal seal of the Son of God and entered into the kingdom of God. Before a man receives the name of God, he is dead, but upon receiving the seal, he casts off his living death and starts to live again. [4]So the seal is the water: they descend into the water dead and come up out of it alive. Thus this seal was preached to them, too, and they appropriated it in order to enter into the kingdom of God."

[5]"Why, my lord," I ask, "did the forty stones likewise ascend from the sea even though they must already have had the seal?"

"Simply," he says, "because these, the apostles and teachers, who preached the name of the Son of God, after they fell asleep in the power and faith of the Son of God continued preaching, only now to those who had fallen asleep before them,[j] and it was they who gave them the seal through preaching. 6This is why they descended into the water and rose up with them again, the only difference being that these, the apostles, went down alive, while the rest who had earlier fallen asleep went down dead and came up alive. 7So by means of the apostles, the ancients were rekindled to life and became enlightened as to the saving name of the Son of God. This is also why they came up with them and were placed alongside them into the construction of the tower and were, like them, fitted in without needing to be cut to size. For they were righteous and completely pure when they fell asleep, lacking only this seal. Now you know the meaning of these details, too."

"So I do, my lord!" I say.

17

1"Next, sir, if you would just explain to me the significance of the mountains. Why do they have various forms, each different from the others?"

"Listen," he says, "these dozen mountains correspond to the tribes inhabiting the whole earth. It was to these the apostles preached the Son of God."

2"But that still does not explain, sir, why they differ so, each one with a distinct appearance," I object.

"Listen further," he says. "These dozen tribes populating the entire world are twelve nations, and they are very diverse in understanding and intelligence, as diverse as you observed the mountains to be. Such is the variety among the nations' mental faculties and their mentalities. And I will show you the habitual behavior of each one."

3"Just a moment, lord," I say, "tell me why the stones taken from the mountains, all being so different, became bright white once inserted into the tower—in fact identical to the stones from the sea-floor?"

4"That is because," he explained, "all the nations under heaven, as soon as they heard and believed the message of the Son, were called by the name of God. Having taken his seal, they had from then on a single understanding and attitude. They received a single faith and a single love and they assumed the spirits of the virgins along with the name of the Son of God. Thus the materials of the tower became monochrome, dazzling

j. 1 Pet. 3:19; Gospel of Peter 9

white like the sun. [5]However, after they entered together, fusing into one body, some polluted themselves and were expelled from the commonwealth of the righteous and reverted to their original state, actually worse!"

18

[1]"How could they become worse, my lord," I ask, "seeing they had in the interval come to know God?"

"One who does not know God," he says, "can be expected to do evil and he will naturally be punished for his wrong-doing. But if one has come to know God well, he is under special obligation no longer to do evil, but to do good. [2]Now if the one sworn to good does wrong instead, is he not even more culpable than the poor wretch who has never met God? Therefore, those ignorant of God who commit sin are condemned to die. But those who have known God and witnessed his great deeds and commit sin despite this are in line for a double penalty: everlasting death. This is way the Church of God is purified. [3]As you witnessed some stones being dislodged from their places in the tower and consigned to evil spirits, these people, too, shall be expelled, resulting in a single body of the purified, just as the finished tower, once the defective stones were removed, appeared to be carved from a single stone. The same thing will happen to the Church of God after she has been purified, just as the tower appeared to be unitary once it had been cleansed and all the wicked, the hypocrites, blasphemers, waverers, and all who commit all sorts of evil are expelled! [4]When these are gone, the Church of God shall exist as a single body with a single mentality, mind, faith, and love. And at last the Son of God will rejoice and be delighted with them because it will mean he has received his people back in their proper pure condition."

"These truths are great and glorious, lord," I say. [5]"But, sir, I ask you again, show me the power and the actions of each mountain so every soul that puts its faith in the Lord, when it hears this explanation, may worship his great and wondrous and dazzling name."

"Listen, then," he replies, "to the secret of the various mountains and the twelve nations."

19

[1]"Believers of this kind come from the first mountain, the black one: those who now revolt and blaspheme against the Lord and inform on the slaves of God.[k] They have no hope of repentance, only death awaits

k. See Acts 26:11. The point seems to be that they cave in to persecution, saving their skins by renouncing Christ and "naming names" of other Christians.

them. This is why they are represented as black, for their kind is lawless.

[2]"From the second mountain, the bald one, the believers are of this variety: hypocrites and tutors of wickedness. These, like the previous ones, have borne no righteous fruit. Just as their mountain is stripped of vegetation, these have the name of the Son of God but they are bereft of faith, and the truth, though once planted in them, produces no fruit. They still have a chance for repentance, but they must act quickly. If they put it off, they will find themselves joining the previous group in death."

[3]"Lord," I ask, "why is repentance held out for these but not for the former type? I can see little difference between their actions!"

"This is why repentance is still possible for them," he answers. "They never blasphemed the Lord or turned the slaves of God in to the authorities. The love of money lured them into hypocrisy and they taught such worldly compromise to others as realistic. And make no mistake: they will pay for that. Yet the plan is for them to repent since they are at least innocent of blasphemy or betrayal."

20

[1]"The believers from the third mountain, the one choked with thorns and briars, are like this: some are rich and others are absorbed in business dealings. The briars represent the rich, while the thorns stand for those tangled up in business dealings. [2]These latter join the slaves of God but then wander away, choked by their professional concerns. But the rich join the slaves of God only reluctantly, fearing they will be asked to contribute something. Such as these will be able to enter into the kingdom of God only with difficulty.[1] Just as it is hard to tread among thistles with bare feet, so will it be hard for these to enter into the kingdom of God. [4]But for all these, repentance is an urgent need, that they should go back and try to do some of the good they previously neglected. So if they will repent and do what good they still can, they shall live with God. But if they continue in their present course, they shall be handed over to those women who will not hesitate to put them to death."

21

[1]"Those who believed and came from the fourth mountain, the one thickly grown with vegetation, green toward the top and withered down toward the roots, some scorched by the sun, they are like this: the ambivalent waverers and those who confess the Lord with their mouths, having hearts devoid of his presence. [2]Thus their foundations are crumbling and

1. Mark 10:23

weak. Only their words are alive, their deeds moribund. Such individuals hover somewhere between life and death. This makes them like the waverers, who are neither decidedly green nor withered, and these too are neither exactly alive nor yet dead. [3]Just as their grass shriveled when exposed to the sun, so too the waverers, as soon as they hear that tribulation is on its way, give in to cowardice and yield to persecutors' demands that they sacrifice to idols and revile the name of the Lord. [4]Such people count neither as among the living nor among the dead. Yet even these shall be able to have life if they repent at once. But if they don't—well, they are already in the clutches of those women who stand ready to relieve them of their lives."

22

[1]"And from the fifth mountain, blanketed with verdure but with a rough surface, believers such as these come: steadfast but slow learners, bull-headed and dedicated to gratifying their own desires. They want to know everything but in fact know nothing at all! [2]Because they were so stubborn, understanding stood apart from them and a foolish irrationality crept into them. They flatter themselves as understanding and want to be known as teachers, albeit self-credentialled ones, all the while being totally irrational. [3]Thanks to this proud-heartedness, many have elevated themselves and become empty shells. Stubbornness and unjustified conceit are two names for a very powerful demon. Many such braggarts were thrown aside, but some thought better of it and renewed their belief, submitting themselves to those who really did possess understanding, learning to rue their own previous pig-headedness. [4]Yes, and anyone else in this category is offered the same opportunity to repent. After all, they never really turned evil, just silly and stupid. So if they repent, they will live with God; but if they don't, they shall not be able to escape the company of the wild women who have dreadful plans for them!"

23

[1]"As for those who believed from the sixth mountain, the one cut by gullies big and small, with shriveled foliage in the gullies, they are like this: [2]those with small rifts who maintain petty grudges, and their mutual bickerings cause their faith to shrivel. But many saw what they were doing and repented readily enough. And no doubt, the rest will repent, too, as soon as they hear my commandments, for their bickerings are trivial and it won't take much for them to repent. [3]But those represented by the large crevices seem determined to backslide and to cherish grudges against each other. These were the ones you saw thrown away at once

from the tower and excluded from its construction. Only with difficulty will people like this gain life. [4]Remember, God our Lord, who reigns over all things and has power over all creation, holds no grudge against those who own up to their sins. He is satisfied with that. So how dare a sinful mortal hold a grudge against his fellow as though he were in a position to destroy or to save him?[m] [5]I, the Angel of Repentance himself, tell you this: all of you who hold such an extravagant belief, get rid of it! Repent! For then the Lord will cure your own previous sins, if you just cleanse yourself of this demon. But if not, you shall be fed to him!"

24

[1]"And from the seventh mountain, the one with green and waving foliage, the whole bursting with life, all kinds of cattle grazing and birds feeding on the mountain's greenery which only grew more luxurious—those who believed are like this: [2]they were always straightforward, sincere, and happy, holding no grudges, always delighted to see their fellow slaves of God, clothed in the Holy Spirit of these virgins, showing compassion on everyone, providing for the needs of the poor out of their own pockets, neither making their recipients feel bad nor having second thoughts. [3]When the Lord observed their simple integrity and their complete childlike freshness,[n] he gave their labors success and showed his favor on them in all their endeavors. [4]So I, the very Angel of Repentance, tell you, whom God favors, stay just as you are now until the end and you will never lack descendants. For the Lord has proven your righteousness and registered you among us angels, and all your children will live with the Son of God, for you are full of his Spirit."

25

[1]"From the eighth mountain that abounds in springs of water, from which all God's creatures slake their thirst, those who believed are of this kind: [2]apostles and teachers who made proclamation through the whole earth and who taught the message of the Lord with gravity and purity, never trimming the truth in the interests of evil desires, but always living righteously and by the truth as one would expect from those who have received the Holy Spirit. Thus, people like this will freely associate with the angels."

26

[1]"Now from the ninth mountain, covered with desert, crawling with

---

m. Matt. 18:23-35

n. Mark 10:15; Matt. 18:3-4

venomous reptiles and wild animals, the believers are of this type: [2]the ones with spots are deacons who did a poor job in office and enriched themselves from the pittance widows and orphans had to live on.[o] They charged money for services they were obliged to offer for free.[p] And if they continue catering to their evil desires, they are moribund and bereft of any hope of life. But if they change their ways and fulfill their ministerial duties in a pure manner, it may be possible they will escape death.

[3]"But the mildewed ones are people who repudiated their Lord and made no attempt to turn back to him. No, having become parched desert, they make no effort to associate with the slaves of God but remain isolated and so obliterate their own souls. [4]Picture a lone vine in the middle of a hedge. If the gardener fails to notice it and never clears out the surrounding weeds, it will become ruined because of the weeds. It, too, begins to grow wild and loses its value to its owner. That is the situation of these people who have abandoned themselves to despair and become useless to their Lord, growing rank like weeds. [5]Repentance seeks them out, unless of course they turn out to have truly repudiated the faith from the heart. If one turns out to have genuinely rejected the Lord, not as a forced gesture during persecution, I do not know whether he still has any chance for repentance. [6]Nor am I referring to present-day circumstances, that one may repudiate his Lord and expect to receive a chance to repent. It is now too late for anyone who henceforth denies his Lord to be saved. But for those who denied long ago, repentance does seem to be possible for them.[q] But if one does want to repent, now is the time to do it before the tower is finished. But if he doesn't, he will be destroyed and put to death by the women in black.

[7]"As for the stunted stones, these are the perfidious and the gossips. They are also symbolized as the wild animals you saw on the mountain. Just as wild animals fatally poison their prey with deadly venom, so do the insidious words of a gossip have power to poison one to death. [8]They are broken off stumps as regards their stunted faith, retarded because of their deep-seated habits. Nonetheless, some did repent and were saved. The rest who are in this category can still be saved provided they, too, re-

o. Mark 12:40

p. 2 Kings 5:15-27

q. Here is the newly promulgated second repentance: one more chance for old sinners who assumed they had forfeited salvation; but it is not to be an indulgence, allowing the commission of new sins.

pent. But if they don't, they shall meet death at the hands of those women who now hold them in their power."[r]

27

[1]"From the tenth mountain, where trees shelter sheep, those who believed are like this: [2]hospitable bishops who gladly and sincerely are always ready to roll out the red carpet for the slaves of God whenever they may chance to arrive. These people were always and unceasingly happy to shelter the needy and the widows under their jurisdiction, conducting themselves with moral purity at all times. [3]Thus they themselves shall be given everlasting shelter by the Lord.[s] Those who have performed such alms shine like stars in the sight of God, and a place among the angels waits for them even now, as long as they keep serving the Lord until the end."

28

[1]"From the eleventh mountain with the heavily-laden fruit trees, loaded with all varieties of fruit, those who believed are like this: [2]those who suffered for the sake of the name, who were wholeheartedly willing to suffer and let go their lives."

[3]"But why, sir," I say, "do all the trees have fruit, but some are more luscious than others? What distinction is symbolized in this?"

"Just this," he replies. "All who ever suffered for the name shine like stars in God's sight, and their sins are all negated because of their suffering for the Son of God. Now as to why their fruits vary, some being more excellent than others, [4]those with superior glory in God's eyes are the ones who were tortured but still did not deny the faith when dragged before the magistrates, but were glad to suffer. Theirs is the superlative fruit. But others turned coward, paralyzed with indecision, deliberating whether it might not be better to recant but finally decided to accept suffering. Their fruits are less impressive because the thought of denial entered their minds, for such a thought is itself evil, even if not implemented: that a slave should repudiate his lord. [5]If you dare toy with such a notion, beware! Do not allow it to take root in your heart or you will die vis-à-vis God! But you who suffer on behalf of the name, worship God for it! He

---

r. Here and elsewhere, we must suspect the author has in mind the wild-women devotees of Dionysus, the bacchae or maenads, who in ecstatic trance might tear animals or hapless humans (Orpheus, Pentheus) limb from limb. The women wore animal skins.

s. Luke 16:9

has esteemed you worthy of bearing the name and all your sins will be expunged for it. [6]So consider yourself blessed! Moreover, know that you have performed a great thing if you suffer for the sake of God. The Lord rewards you with everlasting life, though perhaps you did not realize it. Your sins burdened you, and if you had not suffered for the name, your sins would have made you die vis-à-vis God. [7]I say these words to those of you who hesitate between denial and confession: confess his lordship or you will be consigned to prison. [8]If the gentiles punish any slave of theirs that denies his master's ownership, what do you think the Lord will do to you, he who is omnipotent over everything? So eject all such thoughts of denial from your mind and you will live forever with God."

29

[1]"And from the twelfth mountain, the white one, those who believed are like this: they are innocent as infants and no deceitfulness has infiltrated their hearts. They are yet ignorant of evil but remained like infants their whole lives. [2]This sort of person will certainly live in the kingdom of God because in no particular did they ever defile the commandments of God, remaining innocent and sharing the same outlook as long as they lived. [3]Whoever will continue this way," he says, "and will be like guileless infants, will receive a degree of glory unmatched even by those already described! All infants shine forth in the eyes of God and have the preeminence in his estimation. Blessed are you, then, all who have shunned wickedness and have clothed yourself in innocence. You above all shall live with God!"

[4]When he was done explaining the parables of the mountains, I say to him, "My lord, please explain to me next the stones dug from the plain and inserted into the building in place of the stones taken out of the tower, as well as the round ones which were placed inside the structure and those that remained round."

30

[1]"All right," he says, "here is the truth of these things, too. The stones harvested from the plain and placed in the structure of the tower to replace the discarded ones are the very roots of the white mountain. [2]When the believers from the white mountain proved to be without guile, the master of the tower requisitioned these fine stones from the mountain roots to be used in the tower construction. He knew that if these stones were used, they should retain their brightness. None would turn black. [3]By contrast, had he used stones taken from the various other mountains, he would have to go through the whole inspection process all over again.

But all these have turned out to be white, both they who have believed already and those who are to believe hereafter: they are of the same kind. Blessed are these, the innocent!

[4]"Now as for the round, bright stones: all these likewise come from the white mountain. Why are they round? Their wealth has clouded and shadowed their grasp of the truth, but just slightly. They never left God behind, nor did any evil speech ever escape their lips, only fair and virtuous talk such as comes from the truth. [5]So when the Lord took stock of their minds and saw they could still prefer the truth and also remain good, he ordered that their material possessions be stripped from them, yet not completely, so they might have something left with which to feed the needy and might in this way come to live with God. After all, they do come from good stock. This is why they have been chiseled just a bit before being added to the tower."

31

[1]"But the rest of the stones, scattered around the site and not used in the construction, they have not yet received the seal. They have been replaced because of their near-spherical shape. [2]This temporal world and the ephemera of their possessions have to be chiseled away from them before they can fit into the kingdom of God. And it is necessary that they enter the kingdom of God, for the Lord has officially pronounced this blessing on all these innocent ones. Not one of these shall perish. Yes, even if one of them may have been tempted by the most evil of devils to commit some sin, he shall quickly, by reflex, turn back to the Lord. [3]I, the Angel of Repentance, pronounce all of you blessed, whoever among you is as innocent as an infant, because God deems your lot good and honorable. [4]Beyond this, I urge you all, whoever has received this seal of baptism, to maintain innocence and not to cherish a grudge. Do not persist in your momentary wickedness, nor wallow in the resentful memory of an offense, but join as one spirit with your fellows and heal these sinful divisions; root them out from among you so the owner of the flocks may be glad over his sheep. [5]For glad will he be if he finds everything well, but if he discovers half the flock scattered, woe to those shepherds! [6]If the shepherds themselves are found to be scattered, how will they ever be able to give an account of their flocks? Will they claim they were scared off by a bunch of sheep? No one is going to believe that! It is unbelievable that the shepherd could have anything to fear from his flock. He will only have earned a worse punishment because of his transparent lie. And as I am your shepherd, I am very definitely required to give an account of you."

32

[1]"So take yourselves in hand and change your ways while the tower is still under construction. [2]The Lord lives in those who cherish harmony, for he loves peace, but he keeps his distance from the argumentative and those who are sold out to wickedness. Be sure, when the time comes to turn your spirit back in to him who loaned it to you, you give it up safe and sound, just as you received it.[t] [3]Suppose you took a brand new garment to the laundry; naturally, you would expect to get it back in one piece. But if the laundryman handed it back to you ripped to shreds, would you accept it that way? Wouldn't you explode into protests and say, 'What is this? The shirt I brought you was in good shape! Why have you ruined it? It's useless! A handful of rags! How do you expect me to wear this?' Wouldn't you say this to a mere launderer who had done nothing worse than tear a shirt? [4]If you get this upset about a piece of cloth, outraged because you got it back in pieces, what do you think the Lord will have to say to you if he has given you a nice fresh spirit and you have dared return it to him worn out and useless to him? You have defiled it so badly, nothing remains for him but to incinerate it!"

[5]"No doubt," I say, "punishment awaits everyone whom he discovers still cherishing ill-will toward others."

"Be sure you do not disdain his mercy! Instead, worship him for his great long-suffering toward your sins. Fortunately for you, he is very different from you mortals with your grudges. So make an effort to repent if you know what is good for you!"

33

[1]"Everything written here, I, the Shepherd, the Angel of Repentance, have declared to the slaves of God. So if you will believe my words and take them to heart and live by them, improving your behavior, you shall be able to attain everlasting life. But if you persist in evil and in ill-will, know this: none such shall live with God. I have now told you everything I was commanded to tell you."

[2]The Shepherd asked me, "Are you done with all your questions?"

And I answered, "Yes, lord."

"I am amazed that you neglected to ask me about the shape of the stones in the building when we had to fill up the space for them!"

So I said, "I forgot, my lord!"

[3]"Here is the answer, then," he says. "These are the ones who have just now heard my commandments and who have applied their hearts

t. Matt. 25:14-30; Luke 12:20

strenuously to repentance. So observing that their repentance was good and sincere and that they would persist in it, he ordered their record of sins to be expunged. These shapes represented their previous sins and they were chiseled away so as no longer to be visible."

Tenth similitude

1

[1]After I had finished copying out the whole of the present book, the angel who had originally consigned me to the Shepherd's care appeared in my house, sitting on the couch with the Shepherd standing to his right. Then he addressed me and spoke as follows: [2]"I placed you and your household under the Shepherd's care so you might enjoy his protection."

"Amen, lord!" I said.

"So if you desire protection from all trouble and cruelty and to succeed in every good deed and word and to wield the full power of righteousness, then live by his commandments which I have given you and you will find yourself able to vanquish all wickedness. [3]For if you observe his commandments, every evil desire and the enticement of this world will yield to you. Beyond this, success will reward your every noble endeavor. Emulate the Shepherd's seriousness and reticence and spread the word that he is held in high honor by the Lord, a dignitary with great authority. Authority over repentance has been delegated to him alone in the whole world! Do you agree that he appears powerful? Yet you seem to disdain the seriousness and moderation he exhibits toward you."

2

[1]My answer: "Ask him yourself, sir, whether from the first day he arrived to live with me I have ever acted unbecomingly and so offended him!"

[2]"Actually, I know," he said, "that you have done nothing untoward, nor are you likely to. I speak to you this way just to make sure you keep up the good work! For he has made a good report to me about you. You must speak all these things to others to bring those who have practiced or will practice repentance to the same attitude you have attained. Then the Shepherd may give me a good report of them, which I will relay to the Lord."

[3]"I, too, my lord," I say, "make known to everyone the mighty feats of the Lord in hopes that all who have sinned in the past, when they hear these tidings, will gladly seize the opportunity to repent and recover their salvation."

[4]"Then carry on in this ministry, Hermas! Complete it to the very last. For anyone who keeps the Shepherd's commandments shall live. Indeed, such a one shall merit great honor with the Lord. But those who do not keep his commands are fleeing from their own salvation to oppose him. Instead of following his commandments, they condemn themselves to death. Each must bear the guilt for his own blood. But I urge you: keep these commandments and you will find the remedy for your sins."

3

[1]"Furthermore, I have assigned these virgins to you, to live with you, for I have observed that they get along well with you. With their assistance, you will be better able to keep the commandments. In fact, it is virtually impossible to obey the commandments without their help, as I think you know by now. I can tell they relish the opportunity to stay with you. I will order them never to leave you alone. [2]Just see that your house remains pure, for they will not dwell in any other. They themselves are clean, chaste, and eager to work and the Lord delights to see them thus occupied. So if they see that your house is pure, they will be glad to stay with you. But if the tiniest particle of defilement appears, they will exit at once. For these virgins cannot abide defilement of any kind."

[3]"Lord," I reply, "I hope to please them so they will be happy to live in my house forever. I hope that, just as the one you previously sent to live with me gave me a good report, these will have nothing negative to report about me."

[4]Turning to the Shepherd, he says, "I can see he is resolved to live as the slave of God and that he will keep these commandments and that he will provide these virgins a clean environment." [5]With this, he again committed me to the Shepherd's care. Calling the virgins, he speaks to them, "Since I can see you are happy enough to live in this fellow's house, I commend to you both himself and his household and I charge you never to abandon his house." And they were glad to hear this.

4

[1]Then he addressed me: "Be sure you shoulder your responsibility for this ministry like a man! Communicate to everyone the mighty deeds of the Lord and you will harvest success in this ministry. Whoever, then, shall obey these commandments shall have a happy life, but whoever neglects them shall not live with God, nor shall he enjoy this life. [2]Exhort every individual who is capable of righteousness not to leave off doing good deeds, for they will surely see the benefit that accrues to them from it. Furthermore, I say that every individual ought to be delivered from

misfortune, for whoever is destitute and daily suffers adversity endures great torment and lack. [3]So whoever lifts up someone from such destitution wins himself great blessing. For anyone tormented by adversity to such a degree is subjugated to a torture equal to that of a man held captive in dungeon chains. Such circumstances lead many who suffer them to commit suicide. If anyone is aware of such suffering on another's part and makes no effort to help him, he commits a very serious sin and becomes responsible for the poor wretch doing away with himself. [4]So do good works, all of you who can claim to have received anything from the Lord; otherwise, while you let them slide, the construction of the tower may be completed without you. Don't you realize it is for your benefit that the construction has been temporarily suspended?[u] If you do not hurry up and do what is right, the tower will reach completion and its door will be bolted against you!"[v]

[5]And when he was done talking to me, he got up from the couch and left, followed by the Shepherd and the virgins. But he said he would be sending the Shepherd and the virgins back to my house shortly.

u. 2 Pet. 3:8-11, 15
v. Matt. 25:1-13

51.

The Acts of Paul and Thecla

THIS WRITING, CELEBRATING THE virgin apostle Thecla, was at first a portion of the Acts of Paul but circulated more widely as an independent unit. There are some dozen Greek manuscripts, Latin manuscripts stemming from four different translations of the Greek original, and Arabic, Slavonic, and Syriac versions. The book appears to be derived from oral traditions or legends of Thecla circulating among the consecrated, charismatic virgins and widows. Thecla's story functioned both as a legitimization myth for women teaching and baptizing and as a recruitment appeal for women to renounce marriage and family and join the order of widows/virgins instead, no matter the difficulties such a stand might entail.[a]

As Dennis R. MacDonald shows,[b] Paul and Thecla draws upon some of the same Pauline oral tradition forming the basis of the Pastoral Epistles, as both mention some of the same characters. Whereas Paul and Thecla presents Paul as a preacher of the encratite celibacy gospel, the Pastorals, lumping together encratism with Gnosticism and Marcionism, turn these legends on their head and make Paul speak against these "heresies" from the Catholic viewpoint.

Of particular interest is the physical description of Paul, which

---

a. See Ross S. Kraemer, "The Conversion of Women to Ascetic Forms of Christianity," *Signs: Journal of Women in Culture and Society* 6 (Winter, 1980); Virginia Burrus, *Chastity as Autonomy: Women in the Stories of Apocryphal Acts* (New York: Edwin Mellen Press,1987).

b. Dennis R. MacDonald, *The Legend and the Apostle: The Battle for Paul in Story and Canon* (Philadelphia: Westminster Press, 1983).

may represent actual memory or perhaps a conventional description of Heracles, who was a moral example in the ancient world.[c]

1

[1]When Paul went up to Iconium after his escape from Antioch, Demas and Hermogenes joined his party. At that time, they were filled with hypocrisy. [2]But Paul could see only the goodness of God, so he did not rebuff them but instead had great love for them. [3]Consequently, he tried to persuade them concerning all the oracles and teachings about Christ as well as the logic of the news of God's well-loved Son, catechizing them in the gnosis of Christ, in the version revealed to him. [4]And a particular man named Onesiphorus heard of Paul's arrival in Iconium. He went out at once to meet him, bringing his wife, Lectra, and his sons, Simmia and Zeno, meaning to invite him to their home. [5]For Titus had given them a description of Paul's appearance, as they had not yet met him in person, knowing him only by reputation. [6]They took the King's Highway to Lystra and stood there waiting for him, trying to match the description Titus had provided with all who passed by. [7]Finally they saw a man approaching, "short in stature, head shaved, legs bowed though athletically formed, deep-set eyes, broken nose, and full of charisma, for sometimes he appears like a man, at other times with the face of an angel." But it was Paul who spotted Onesiphorus and smiled.

[8]And Onesiphorus said, "Hail, servant of the thrice-blessed God!" Paul replied, "May the favor of God rest on you and your family!" [9]But Demas and Hermogenes were stung with envy, and with an elaborate charade of piety, Demas said, "Are we not servants of the blessed God, too? Why did you not salute us?" [10]Onesiphorus answered, "Simply because I did not notice in you that composure that results from inner righteousness. But never mind that! If you are of the same sort as Paul, you shall be welcomed in my household, too."

[11]Then Paul entered the home of Onesiphorus, to the great joy of all who lived there, and they busied themselves in prayer, breaking bread, and listening to Paul preach the message of God about self-control and the resurrection, in this way:

[12]"Blessed are the pure in heart, for they shall behold God!
[13]"Blessed are they who preserve their flesh undefiled, for they shall be the temple of God!

c. Abraham J. Malherbe, *Paul and the Popular Philosophers* (Minneapolis: Fortress Press, 1989), 167-70.

[14]"Blessed are the chaste, for God will reveal himself to them!

[15]"Blessed are they who leave off their worldly pleasures, for they shall be acceptable to God!

[16]"Blessed are those who treat their wives as if they were single, for they shall be transformed into angels of God!

[17]"Blessed are they who tremble at the command of God, for they shall be comforted!

[18]"Blessed are they who keep their baptismal seal inviolate, for they shall meet with no enmity from the Father, Son, and Holy Ghost!

[19]"Blessed are they who pursue the wisdom of Jesus-Christ, for they shall be called the sons of Elyon![d]

[20]"Blessed are they who live by the instructions of Jesus-Christ, for they shall bask in eternal light!

[21]"Blessed are they who, because they love Christ, leave behind the allurements of the world, for they shall judge angels and be installed to the right of Christ and shall not be subject to the bitter verdict of the Last Judgment!

[22]"Blessed are the bodies and souls of consecrated virgins, for they are acceptable to God and shall not forfeit the reward for their consecration; for the promise of their heavenly Father shall prove good to accomplish their salvation in the day of his Son's triumph and they shall enjoy rest forever!"

2

[1]While Paul was preaching this sermon in the community gathered in the house of Onesiphorus, a particular virgin named Thecla, whose mother's name was Theocleia and who was engaged to a man named Thamyris, sat at a particular window in her house. [2]From this window, which was lined up with a window in the house where Paul was, she was able to listen night and day to Paul's sermons about God, charity, faith in Christ, and prayer. [3]Nor was she willing to leave her perch until, very joyfully, she had given herself over to the teachings of the faith. [4]Finally, when she observed many wives and pledged virgins entering to attend Paul, she wished more than anything that she might be counted worthy to appear before him and hear the message of Christ, for she had not yet actually seen Paul in person, only hearing his sermons and that by herself.

[5]But while they were trying to convince her to leave the window, her

d. The sons of Elyon are angels, as in v. 16.

mother summoned Thamyris, who was delighted to come, hoping this meant it was at last time for him to marry her. So he said to Theocleia, "Where is my Thecla?" [6]Theocleia answered, "Thamyris, I have something quite strange to tell you. For a whole three days now, Thecla has been unwilling to budge from the window, even to eat or drink, but is so fixated listening to the clever and bewitching speeches of a particular foreigner that, frankly, Thamyris, I am amazed a young lady of her known modesty will allow herself to be so bamboozled! [7]For that fellow has upset the entire city of Iconium, including your Thecla and others. All the women and the young men are flocking to him to swallow his teaching. In addition to everything else, he tells them there is only one God, who alone deserves worshipping, and that we ought to live in celibacy!

[8]"As bizarre as it is, my daughter Thecla is stuck to that window like an insect in a spider's web, hypnotized by the discourses of Paul, astonishingly eager to hear more and rapt in delight when she does. And so, by listening to what he says, the young lady is seduced. So then, it is up to you to go and speak with her since you are engaged to her." [9]So Thamyris went and greeted her, careful not to startle her, saying, "Thecla, my mate, why do you languish in such a spell? What has affected you so strangely? Turn to Thamyris now and apologize for this silliness." [10]Her mother joined in, speaking to her the same way, saying, "Child, why do you sit in such a daze like someone in shock, making no reply?"

[11]Then they cried many tears, Thamyris having lost his mate, Theocleia having lost her daughter, and the maids having lost their mistress, and the whole family went into mourning. [12]But none of this made the slightest impression on Thecla, not even moving her to turn her head in their direction and acknowledge their presence, for she was still absorbed in the discourses of Paul. [13]Next Thamyris ran out into the street to see just who was going in to hear Paul and coming out from hearing him. And he spotted two men locked in vigorous argument.

He said to them, [14]"Sirs, just what is your business here? And who is that fellow inside, your associate, who bewitches people's senses, both young men and girls, convincing them not to marry but to stay as they are? [15]I swear I'll pay you a considerable amount if you'll just tell me the straight truth about him, for I am the leading citizen here!" [16]Demas and Hermogenes answered, "We cannot tell you exactly who he is, but we do know this much: he cheats young men out of their wives and virgins out of their husbands by teaching there is no chance of a future resurrection unless one remains celibate, not defiling the flesh."

3

[1]Then Thamyris said, "Return to my house with me and refresh yourselves." And it turned out to be quite an extravagant banquet with wine flowing freely and very rich viands. [2]They were shown to a richly laden table and urged by Thamyris to drink freely. It seemed to him but a small expense in view of his love for Thecla and his desire to marry her. [3]Then Thamyris said, "I wish you would tell me about the teachings of Paul so I can understand them. You see, my worry for Thecla is no light one, seeing how she revels in this stranger's discourses; I fear I am in danger of losing my intended wife!"

[4]Then Demas and Hermogenes both had something to answer. Demas said, "Have him brought before Castellius the governor on charges that he attempts to win the people over to the new religion of the Christians. And he will, according to the edict of Caesar, execute him, and by this means you will regain your wife!"

[5]Hermogenes added, "And at the same time, we will be teaching her that the 'resurrection' he talks about has already arrived, that it consists of having children and living again through them. And that we rose again when we came to the realization of God."

[6]Thamyris, once he heard their report, was overcome with burning resentment. [7]And getting up early in the morning, he headed for Onesiphorus's house, accompanied by the magistrates, the jailer, and a large mob, including slaves. And he said to Paul, [8]"You have led the city of Iconium into perversion! Among the victims is Thecla, who is engaged to me, only now she refuses to marry me. Because of this, you are coming with us to Castellius, the governor." [9]And the whole crowd shouted, "Away with this charlatan! He has perverted the minds of our wives and all the people listen to him!"

4

[1]Then Thamyris stood before the judgment seat of the governor, raised his voice, and said the following: [2]"O governor, where this fellow hails from, I do not know. But he is one of those who teach that marriage is illegal. So command him to render you an explanation as to why he propagates such notions." [3]While he was saying this, Demas and Hermogenes whispered, "Say he is a Christian and he will shortly be executed!" [4]But the governor was more deliberate in judgment and addressed Paul, saying, "Who are you? What do you teach? They appear to accuse you of terrible things!"

[5]Paul then raised his voice and said, "Since I am now ordered to set forth my teachings, O governor, I ask your full attention. [6]Very well, I teach that God, who is a vengeful deity, and who has no need for anything except the salvation of his creatures, has sent me to reclaim them from their wickedness and corruptions, from every pleasure and from death, and to persuade them to give up sinning. [7]It was for this purpose that God sent his Son Jesus-Christ, whom I preach, the one on whom I teach people to set their hopes as the only person who had such compassion on this deluded world, so that, O governor, it might not be condemned but instead have faith, the fear of God, acquaintance with religion, and the love of truth. [8]So tell me, if I do nothing more than teach these things which came to me revealed by God, where is my crime?"

[9]When the governor heard this, he ordered Paul to be manacled and detained in prison till he should have sufficient time available to give him more than a cursory hearing. [10]But during the night, Thecla removed her earrings and gave them to the prison door keeper, who opened the doors for her and allowed her in. [11]And when she offered the jailer the present of a silver mirror, she was allowed to go right into the room where they kept Paul. Then she sat down at his feet and listened to him speak of the mighty acts of God. [12]And when it registered on her that Paul was not afraid of having to suffer, but that with God's help he bore himself courageously, her own faith grew so strong that she kissed his chains.

5

[1]Finally, Thecla's absence was discovered and the family, with Thamyris, searched for her in every street once they learned from one of the porter's fellow slaves that she had left during the night. [2]Then they interrogated the porter and he told them she had gone to the prison to visit the stranger. [3]So they went out, following his lead, and that is where they discovered her. And when they left the prison, they raised up a mob and called on the governor to tell him what had happened. [4]Hearing this, he commanded Paul to be brought before his judgment seat. [5]Meanwhile, Thecla still lay on the ground, wallowing in the spot Paul had sat while teaching her. Learning of this, the governor commanded that she also be brought before his judgment seat. She greeted this summons with joy and promptly went.

[6]When Paul was brought there, the mob only shouted all the louder: "He is a medicine show swindler! Let him die!" [7]Despite this, the governor listened delightedly to Paul's discourses about the holy deeds of Christ. And after consulting with a council, he called for Thecla and

asked her, "Why do you refuse to lawfully marry Thamyris according to the custom of the Iconians?"

[8]She stood there motionless, eyes riveted on Paul. Seeing that no reply could be expected, Theocleia, her own mother, shouted, saying, "Let the wicked vixen be burnt! Let her be burnt right in the middle of the amphitheater for spurning Thamyris, to become an example to all women to avoid the same behavior!" [9]At this, the governor was acutely alarmed and commanded that Paul be flogged outside the city and for Thecla to be burnt. [10]So the governor stood up and headed directly for the amphitheater and the whole populace went out to see the tragic spectacle.

[11]But as for Thecla, just as a lamb lost in the desert looks in all directions to find its shepherd, she looked around for Paul. [12]And as she was scanning the crowd, she saw the Lord Jesus assuming the appearance of Paul, and she thought, "Paul has come to see me in my hour of distress!" And she locked her eyes on him, but all at once he ascended into the sky even while her eyes followed him.

[13]Then the young men and women carried in wood and kindling straw for Thecla's pyre. She, dragged to the stake naked, brought tears from the governor quite against his will, for he was surprised to see just how beautiful she was.

[14]And once they had the wood properly arranged, the people shouted, urging her to take her place on it. This she did, after crossing herself. [15]Then some from the crowd ignited the pile, and though the ensuing flame reared up like a wall, it did not touch her. For God took pity on her and caused the ground to split and a cloud overhead to pour down great droughts of rain and hail. This had the effect that many were in danger from the calamity, some being killed, and the fire was extinguished, saving Thecla.[e]

6

[1]Meanwhile, Paul was with Onesiphorus and his wife and children, keeping a fast, holed up in a particular cave along the road from Iconium to Daphne. [2]And after they had fasted for several days, the children said to Paul, "Father, we are hungry, nor have we any money to buy food." This was because Onesiphorus had abandoned all his possessions to follow Paul, with his family. [3]Then Paul took off his cloak and said to the lad, "This ought to fetch something. Go, child, sell it and buy food and bring it back here." [4]But as the boy was paying for the bread, he spotted

e. The flames are a symbol of male lust, from which her commitment to celibacy saved her.

his neighbor, Thecla, and was surprised and he said to her, "Thecla! Where are you headed?" [5]She answered, "I am looking for Paul since I have been rescued from the flames." [6]The boy then said, "I will take you to him, for he is very worried about you. He has been in a state of prayer and fasting for the last six days!"

[7]When Thecla arrived at the cave, she came upon Paul down on his knees, praying as follows: "O Holy Father! O Lord Jesus-Christ! Grant that the fire should not even touch Thecla, but come to her aid, for she belongs to you!" [8]Thecla, standing behind him, shouted this: "O sovereign Lord! Creator of heaven and earth! The Father of your beloved and holy Son, I praise you for rescuing me from the fire so I might see Paul again." [9]Then Paul got up and, when he saw her, said, "O God, who searches the heart, Father of my Lord Jesus-Christ, I praise you for answering my prayer!" [10]And there was forged among them a bond of great affection there in the cave: Paul, Onesiphorus, and all their companions were filled with joy. [11]They had only five bread rolls with scant herbs and water, but in their hardship they comforted one another by reflecting on the holy deeds of Christ.

[12]Then Thecla said to Paul, "If it meets with your approval, I will follow you wherever you go." [13]He replied to her, "Nowadays people frequently indulge in fornication, and with you being so beautiful, I am afraid you would find yourself subject to more serious temptation than the rest and that you might not prove equal to it, in the end giving in." [14]Thecla answered, "You just provide me the seal of Christ and I shall be immune to temptation." [15]Paul answered, "Thecla, be patient a little longer and you shall receive the gift of Christ."

7

[1]Then Paul sent Onesiphorus and his family back to their own home while he took Thecla along with him and headed for Antioch. [2]But as soon as they entered the city, one particular Syrian, a city magistrate named Alexander, whose term of office had been distinguished by many significant civic improvements, took one look at Thecla and immediately fell in love with her. He tried to present Paul with many expensive gifts by way of winning his loyalty. [3]But Paul told him, "I am not acquainted with this woman you speak of, nor does she belong to me."[f] But being a very influential figure in Antioch, he grabbed her right in the middle of the street and kissed her. [4]Thecla would have none of it but looked around

f. Contrary to some scholars, Paul is not a coward in denying Thecla, as Peter did Jesus; he seeks only to shield her.

for Paul and shouted loudly in distress, "Do not molest me, a friendless stranger! Do not molest me, a slave of God! I am one of the leading citizens of Iconium, but I had to leave because I refused to marry Thamyris!" [5]Then she struck back at Alexander, tearing his cloak and knocking his diadem from his head, which made him a comical sight in public. [6]But Alexander, partly because he was obsessed with her, partly because he was so embarrassed at what had happened, took her to the governor, where she admitted readily enough what she had done. He condemned her to be thrown alive to the wild animals.

8

[1]When the people saw this, they said, "The verdicts rendered in this city are unjust!" But Thecla desired to win the favor of the governor only to the extent that she might be kept safe from molestation till the time came for her to be thrown to the animals. [2]So the governor asked if anyone would assume responsibility for her. At once a wealthy widow named Tryphaena, who had just lately lost a daughter, asked if she might have custody of Thecla, and so she took her into her home and began treating her as her own daughter.

[3]Finally the appointed day came when the beasts were to be brought out, and Thecla was delivered to the amphitheater and placed in a cubicle with an extremely fierce lioness, surrounded by a crowd of spectators. [4]Tryphaena had accompanied Thecla and was not surprised to see that the lioness merely licked Thecla's feet. The title card denoting her crime was inscribed, "sacrilege."[g] Then Tryphaena yelled, "O God! How unfair are the sentences in this city!" [5]After the wild animals had been paraded, Tryphaena took Thecla back home and both went to bed. And behold! The daughter of Tryphaena, who was dead, appeared to her mother in a dream, saying, "Mother, let it be known that you have taken this young woman Thecla as your daughter in my place. And ask her to intercede for me, that I might be transferred to a state of bliss." [6]At this, Tryphaena went to Thecla and awoke her, saying with a mournful tone, "My daughter, Falconilla, has appeared to me and directed me to welcome you in her place. So Thecla, I ask you to intercede for my daughter, for her to be transferred to a condition of bliss, to age-long life." [7]Hearing this, Thecla at once prayed to the Lord, saying, "O Lord, God of heaven and earth! Jesus-Christ, you son of Elyon, grant that her daughter Falconilla may live forever!" At this, Tryphaena groaned again,

g. No doubt predicated on her having knocked off Alexander's diadem, featuring some religious symbol.

saying, "What unjust verdicts! What outrageous injustice that such a creature should be thrown to the beasts!"

[8]At dawn the next day, Alexander presented himself at Tryphaena's house and announced, "The governor and the people are waiting. Bring out the criminal!" [9]But Tryphaena attacked him with such violence that he was scared and ran away. Neither dared he have her arrested since Tryphaena belonged to the royal family. As for her, she expressed her sorrow in this way, saying, "Alas! My house is doubly troubled! Nor can anyone relieve me, either of the loss of my daughter or of my failure to save Thecla! But now, O Lord God, it remains with you to come to Thecla's aid."

[10]Even as she prayed, the governor dispatched one of his own officers to pick up Thecla. Tryphaena grasped her hand and went with her, saying, "I accompanied Falconilla to her grave; now I must accompany Thecla to the beasts!"

[11]Hearing this, Thecla cried and prayed, saying, "O Lord God, in whom I trust, in whom I take refuge, reward Tryphaena, who has had compassion for me and guarded my chastity." [12]At these words, a great ruckus arose all over the amphitheater: the animals roared and the people shouted, "Bring in the criminal!" [13]The women, however, shouted, "May the whole city pay the penalty for such crimes! Why not order all of us, O governor, to undergo the same punishment? What a travesty of justice! What a cruel spectacle!" [14]Others said, "The entire city deserves destruction for this vile deed! You might as well kill us all now, O governor! What a cruel spectacle! What a travesty of justice!"[h]

9

[1]At this point, Thecla was taken from Tryphaena, stripped naked, given a mere loincloth to wear, and shoved into the area designated for fighting off the animals. Then they released the lions and bears on her. [2]But a lioness, the fiercest of all, ran to Thecla, dropped down at her feet, and lay there. At this, all the women present shouted their support. [3]Next a she-bear charged at her, but the lioness rose to meet the bear and ripped it to pieces. [4]And a lion, a known man-eater, Alexander's own pet, ran at her, only to be met by the lioness, whereupon the two killed each other. [5]But this gave the women cause for greater worry since the lioness, Thecla's protectress, was now dead. [6]Subsequently, they let loose many other wild animals, but through it all Thecla stood there, hands

h. Thus some of the disastrous earthquakes and epidemics repeatedly devastating Antioch during this period are blamed on Thecla's martyrdom.

lifted up to the sky, praying. When she finished her prayer, she turned around and spotted a pit filled with water and thought, "This is the perfect time for me to be baptized!" [7]So she jumped bodily into the water, saying, "In your name, O my Lord, Jesus-Christ, I baptize myself on this, my last day!"

When the women, with the rest of the people, saw her heading for the pool, they shouted, saying, "Don't dive into the water!" Even the governor himself shouted, horrified that its carnivorous fish would devour such beauty. [8]But in spite of it, Thecla plunged into the water, invoking the name of our Lord, Jesus-Christ. [9]But at once, a cloud of fire enveloped Thecla, the lightning and fire penetrating the water and killing the fish, which then floated to the surface of the pool. Nor could the beasts approach her, nor the people see her nakedness.

[10]But this did not prevent the officials from setting still more ravenous animals on her, calling forth a great lament from the crowd. Some, as if to anoint her for burial, threw handfuls of spikenard, others cassia, others amomum, still others ointment. The amount of ointment was quite large, given the number of people, and the animals lay down upon it quiescent, leaving Thecla unmolested. [11]Then Alexander said to the governor, "I own some terribly fierce bulls! Let's tie her to them!"

The governor, now very uneasy, replied, "Do as you think best." [12]So they tied a cord round Thecla's waist, also binding her feet and tying her to the bulls. They took red-hot pokers and pressed them to the testicles of the bulls in order to torment them into insane fury, hoping they would charge about more madly, flailing Thecla's body behind them till she was dead. [13]The bulls did indeed plunge about headlong, raising the most bloodcurdling racket, but Thecla's shield of flames returned, at once dissolving the cords which attached her to the testicles of the bulls, leaving her standing in the middle of the stage as unmoved as if she had not been bound in the first place.

[14]But through all this, Tryphaena, sitting in the bleachers, fainted and died. This threw terrible dread into the whole city. [15]Even Alexander himself was frightened and petitioned the governor, saying, "I beg you, have mercy on me and the city—release this woman who has prevailed against wild animals![i] Otherwise, both you and I, together with the whole city, will be destroyed. [16]If Caesar should receive a report of today's

i. Her victory over the wild beasts stands transparently for her withstanding the lusts of suitors like Thamyris and Alexander.

events, he will no doubt destroy the city at once, all because Tryphaena, a member of the royal house and a relative of his, sits dead in her seat!"

[17]In answer to this, the governor summoned Thecla from among the animals. He said to her, "Who are you? And what is it about you that not a single one of the animals will touch you?" [18]Thecla answered him, "I am a slave of the true God. And as to my secret, it is simply that I am a believer in his Son, Jesus Christ, in whom God is well pleased. That is why none of the beasts was able to touch me. [19]He alone is the way to age-long salvation and the foundation on which age-long life is built. He is a refuge for those who are distressed, a bulwark for the afflicted, a hope and defense for the hopeless. And briefly, all who do not believe in him shall not live, but will endure age-long death."

[20]Having heard her out, the governor commanded that her clothes be brought and told her, "Put on your clothes."

[21]Thecla answered, "May the God who clothed me in fire when I stood naked among the beasts clothe your soul with salvation's robe in the Day of Judgment!" Then she picked up her clothes and put them on. And the governor at once issued a declaration as follows, "I release to you Thecla, slave of God."

[22]At this, the women shouted in unison with a loud voice and in complete agreement rendered praise to God, saying, "There is only one God and that is the God of Thecla, the one God who has rescued Thecla!" [23]Their voices rang so loudly that the whole city seemed to shake. Even Tryphaena herself heard the happy news and got up again! Then she ran with the crowd to meet Thecla. Embracing her, she said, "Now I believe in a resurrection of the dead! Now I am convinced that my daughter is alive! Therefore, come home with me, my daughter Thecla, and I will have you made my heir." [24]So Thecla accompanied Tryphaena and was occupied there a few days, catechizing her in the message of the Lord, and by this means many of them were converted and great was the joy in the household of Tryphaena.

[25]Still, Thecla wanted to see Paul; she made inquiries and sent word everywhere to find him. When at last the news came that he was in Myra of Lycia, she organized several young men and women. She donned a waistband and male attire, then journeyed to him in Myra of Lycia, and there she found Paul preaching the message of God. And she managed to stand next to him in the crowd.

10

[1]But it came as no small surprise to Paul to see her and her compan-

ions, and at once he supposed some new peril was about to overtake them. [2]Thecla realized this and said to Paul, "I have baptized myself, O Paul, for he who works in you to preach has worked in me to baptize!"[j]

[3]Then Paul took her and led her to the house of Hermes, where Thecla recounted to Paul everything that happened to her in Antioch so that Paul was greatly astounded, and the faith of everyone who heard was reinforced and they prayed for Tryphaena's happiness. [5]For Tryphaena had sent Paul, in Thecla's care, great amounts of money and clothing, too, for the relief of the poor. [4]Then Thecla stood up and said, "I am going to Iconium." Paul answered her, "Go and teach the message of the Lord!"

[6]So Thecla went to Iconium, and when she arrived at the house of Onesiphorus, she fell prostrate on the floor where Paul had sat to preach. Praying tearfully, she rendered to God worship and praise, as follows: [7]"O Lord, the God of this house in which I first received your enlightenment! O Jesus, Son of the true God! You came to my aid before the governor in the fire and among the wild animals! You alone are God forever and ever! Amen!"

[8]Thecla learned that Thamyris was now dead, but her mother still lived. So she visited her mother and asked, "Theocleia, my mother, is it possible you might yet be won to the faith that there is but one Lord, even that God who lives in the skies? If it is great wealth you desire and hoped to receive from marrying me to Thamyris, God will give it to you through me, and if you want your daughter restored to you, here I am!"

[9]She sought to persuade her mother with these and many other words, but her mother put no credence in anything the martyr Thecla said. [10]Thus Thecla came to see she had spoken for nothing and crossed herself, left the house, and went to Daphne. Arriving there, she sought the cave where she had discovered Paul with Onesiphorus. She dropped to the ground and wept before God. [11]When she left from there, she traveled to Seleucia and brought the light of Christ to many. [12]And wherever she went, a bright cloud illumined her path. [13]And after her arrival at Seleucia, she sought lodging outside the city about a furlong distant for fear of those who lived in that city, idolaters all.

[14]And the cloud led her to a mountain called Calamon, also called Rodeon. She remained there many years and endured very many temptations by the accuser, and she came through these in an admirable manner

j. Gal. 2:8; 1 Cor. 1:17

with the support of Christ. [15]After a while, a group of noblewomen heard of the virgin Thecla and journeyed to see her. She instructed them in the revelations of God, with the result that many of them resolved to renounce this world and join her living the monastic life.[k] [16]In this way, a glowing report of Thecla circulated everywhere and she accomplished several cures, with the result that the whole city, as well as neighboring districts, carried their sick to that mountain, and before they could even reach the door of the cave, they were at once cured of whatever ailment afflicted them. [17]The unclean spirits, when driven out, made a noise. Everyone welcomed back their sick, now restored to health, and gave praise to God who had entrusted such power to the virgin Thecla. [18]It came to the point that the doctors of Seleucia were no longer consulted and lost all profit from their business because no one looked to them any more. This filled them with envy and they started to consider what strategy to adopt toward this slave of God.

11

[1]The accuser then put an ill-advised scheme into their minds. As they gathered on an agreed upon date to conspire, they thought it out like this: "This virgin must be a priestess of the great goddess Diana, who grants anything she may request because of her consecrated virginity, which makes her beloved of all the gods. [2]So all we need to do is recruit some local thugs, get them drunk enough, pay them well, and order them to go defile this virgin, promising an even bigger reward once they've done it!" [3]Their thinking was that if they could defile her, the gods would pay her no more notice, nor would Diana cure the sick upon her request. [4]So they put the plan into operation and the fellows went to the mountain, like animals in heat, to the cave, pounding on the door. [5]The holy martyr Thecla, trusting in the God she believed in, opened the door even though she had earlier been informed of their scheme, and she asked them, "Young men, why are you here?"[l]

[6]They answered, "Is there anyone here named Thecla?" She replied,

k. See 1 Tim. 5:16. These consecrated women's communities represent the matrix out of which the Thecla legend arose. She is a symbol of their sisterhood, the order of "virgins" and "widows" who had renounced sexuality to return to Edenic bliss, holiness, and equality with their brothers. Such women's communities were common through the fourth century, led by wealthy patronesses like Melania the Elder and Melania the Younger. They meet us here under names like Tryphaena (cf. Rom. 16:12) and Thecla herself and elsewhere as Dorcas and Tabitha (Acts 9:36-42), among others.

l. Matt. 26:50

"What business do you have with her?" They answered, "We want to have sex with her!" [7]The blessed Thecla replied, "I may be merely an old woman, but I am the slave of my Lord, Jesus-Christ. And you may have vile plans for me, but you will never carry them through!" They answered, "There is no way we will not be able to do with you as we wish!" [8]And as they were saying this, they took hold of her forcibly and were about to violate her when she, with mild composure, said to them, "Young men, I see you are impatient, but just have patience and behold the glory of God." [9]As they held her, she looked skyward, saying, "O most venerable God, beyond all comparison! You who win yourself glory from the fall of your enemies, who rescued me from the fire, and who did not abandon me to Thamyris or to Alexander, who rescued me from the wild animals, who kept me safe in the deep waters, who has come to my aid at every occasion and has brought glory to your name through me! [10]Now rescue me, too, from the hands of these evil, unreasoning men, nor permit them to defile my chastity which I have managed to keep this long in your honor. For I love you, I long for you, I worship you, O Father, Son, and Holy Spirit, for evermore! Amen."

[11]This was followed by a voice issuing forth from the sky, saying, "Do not fear, Thecla, my faithful slave, for I am with you! Just look and behold the path of your escape: there is where you will find your dwelling forever. There you shall look upon God in bliss!" [12]Blessed Thecla looked and saw an opening in the rock large enough for a man to enter, and she did as she was commanded, bravely fleeing the clutches of her tormentors and escaping into the rock. At once, the fissure closed behind her, leaving not so much as a crack where it had opened up. [13]The men stood there utterly dumbfounded at so spectacular a wonder. Unable to keep hold on the slave of God, they managed only to tear off a bit of her veil or perhaps her hood. [14]And even that was granted them by God's permission in order to provide a relic to reinforce the faith of those who should come on pilgrimage to this hallowed spot, as well as to bring blessings by contact for all who in subsequent ages should believe on our Lord, Jesus-Christ, from a chaste heart.

[15]These are the sufferings of her who is ranked first among the martyrs and apostles of God,[m] the virgin Thecla, who came out of Iconium at the

---

m. One must wonder why Thecla is named a martyr at all, given her repeated protection from death. We can assume she suffered a genuine martyrdom, but that in the retelling, her heavenly glory was filtered backward into the tale of her

age of eighteen years. After this, she lived sometimes on the road, sometimes in the cave monastery, seventy-two years. She was ninety years old when the Lord transferred her to his presence. [16]Thus ends her life. [17]The day observed in her honor is the twenty-fourth of September, to the glory of the Father and the Son and the Holy Spirit, now and for evermore. Amen!

---

earthly career, making her already a triumphant saint invulnerable to harm. Did the story once record a terrible death by hooligans who raped the old woman after ambushing her in her cave retreat? The symbolism might seem delicately to suggest that she was sodomized.

52.

The Epistle of Barnabas

THOUGH THE BODY OF THIS EPISTLE bears no name, it has always been attributed to Joseph Barnabas, an important character in Acts, who is also mentioned in 1 Corinthians 9:6 and Galatians 2:1, 9, 13. If one dates the epistle early enough, and some have placed it about 70 CE, others 96-98 CE, it might well be from Barnabas. But there are two reasons for denying it to him. First, there is a clear reference to the Roman Emperor Hadrian's attempt to build a temple to Jupiter in Jerusalem in 130-131 at the time of writing (16:4-5). Second, it is quite possible Barnabas is a fictional character created by Luke to correspond to Naboth (1 Kings 21:1-16) in his story of Stephen. Bar-Nabas could signify the "son of Naboth" or second Naboth (see introduction to chap. 23). In any case, Barnabas is the link between Paul and the Jerusalem apostles who authorized Paul's mission. Barnabas symbolizes that authorization, serving Luke's redactional agenda of having Christianity unfold entirely under the strict and watchful care of the Jerusalem apostles. This is why Luke only ever calls Paul an apostle in company with Barnabas (Acts 14:4, 14), never by himself.

Naturally, our estimate of Barnabas hinges upon what we make of his appearances in 1 Corinthians and Galatians. Is he not mentioned in passing as an historical character there? It depends on our view of the textual integrity of these epistles. For instance, 1 Corinthians appears to be a patchwork of different opinions on matters assembled from divers sources. In particular, the defense of the apostolic practice of receiving compensation from their congregations (1 Cor. 9:3-12a) seems incongruous with the ensuing renunciation of

the same privilege (9:12b-23): no one works so hard to establish the very view he is about to refute. This fragment may be so late that the reference to Barnabas is borrowed from Acts. In addition, Barnabas suddenly becomes Paul's colleague in 1 Corinthians 9, whereas earlier in the epistle his name is conspicuously absent from the list of Paul, Cephas, and Apollos (1:12), which proceeds from a different source. Note, too, that according to Galatians 2:13 and Acts 15:39, Barnabas and Paul must have parted company by the time 1 Corinthians was written if we were to consider it a unitary writing. Yet again, the context of 1 Corinthians 9 contains a completely allegorical note (vv. 9-10) about the Deuteronomic command not to muzzle the ox. The author sneers at the possibility that the commandment had a thing to do with literal oxen. This sounds like the exegesis in the Epistle of Barnabas and may be an insertion from the same writer or source.

As for Galatians 2, all depends on which portions of the text are earlier than Acts and which were rewritten or were added to reply to Acts. It may be that the references to Barnabas are later and dependent upon the earlier source. Barnabas plays the same symbolic, political role in Galatians as in Acts, connecting Paul with Jerusalem authority (Gal. 2:1, 9).[a]

The Epistle of Barnabas originally concluded at the end of chapter 17. What follows is based closely upon either the *Didache,* a first- or second-century church manual from Syria, or an earlier version of it called the *Doctrina*. The later Latin manuscript of St. Petersburg preserves the shorter form, though the fourth-century Greek Codex Sinaiticus already has the addition. Sinaiticus places Barnabas after the Revelation of John, followed by the Shepherd of Hermas. In the late second century, Clement of Alexandria quotes it as scripture, as does his successor, head of the catechetical school of Alexandria, Origen. Codex Claromontanus preserves an Egyptian canon list from around 300 with Barnabas between Jude and the Revelation, but other lists place it in the category of disputed books. Some inferred from the epistle's popularity in Egypt that it was written there, but this is not certain.

---

a. To measure the severance of the connection to Jerusalem, see Gal. 2:13.

The major preoccupation of Paul's mission companion is how scripture should be interpreted. Employing a variety of exegetical means, he argues that God's covenant belongs to Christians, not to the Jews, and that Jews forfeited the covenant when Moses smashed the stone tablets over the golden calf incident. Barnabas shares with Philo of Alexandria, the great first-century Jewish exegete and middle-Platonic philosopher, the old Stoic method of allegorizing scripture, taking specific characters and events as symbolic of general edifying truths, with or without any historical basis. In this manner, Barnabas moralizes many of the ceremonial laws of the Torah, considering it ridiculous that anyone had ever imagined the literal sense of the laws had to be heeded. This tendency was popular among assimilating Diaspora Jews, who also wanted to pay lip-service to their ancestral scriptures without having to preserve ethno-cultural markers that separated them from neighbors and business associates. As long as one got the larger point, they reasoned, why bother going through the charade? Philo himself tried to refute such Jews who, he judged, had taken a good thing too far. For him, the laws must still be kept, with or without the deeper knowledge of their meaning.

Barnabas indulges in typological exegesis, making various Old Testament rites symbolic pointers to a greater reality to come, namely the sacrifice of Christ. Here, as John Dominic Crossan points out in his *The Cross That Spoke: The Origins of the Passion Narrative*, Barnabas is close to the wellspring of interpretation that mined scripture for material to fill out the historically sketchy story of the Passion. Most of what we read in the gospel Passion stories, Crossan reasoned, is based not on historical memory but on creative midrashic transformation of elements from scripture, especially a combination of Zechariah 12:10 ("They shall look upon him whom they have pierced") and the scapegoat ritual in Leviticus 16. Crossan shows how Barnabas preserves fulsome details of the ritual as then practiced, which supplies the germs that grew into features of the Passion. For instance, the purple robe of the mocked Jesus grew out of the scarlet thread that was tied about the horns of a goat, then around the thorn bush to which the goat was tied. The thorns and pointy reeds with which the scapegoat was goaded eventually became the reed scepter

of the mock-king Jesus and the thorns of his crown, the spear that pierced his side, and the nails in his extremities.

But the central argument of Barnabas draws more naturally upon certain Old Testament themes which, reflecting sectarian, caste, or sectional tensions, themselves write off Israel with its rituals and sacrifices and such practices as fasting in favor of pure morality. The text of Psalm 78, written in Judah, repudiates Northern Israel as apostate, superseded by Judah in God's affections. The prophets deny the divine origin of sacrifice laws (Isa. 1:11-12; Jer. 7:22; Hosea 6:6; Mic. 6:6-8). The Third Isaiah redefines fasting in terms of social morality (58:6-7). Levitical choristers who authored certain psalms (Pss. 50; 51:1-17) exalted their compositions as more effective than what Harry Emerson Fosdick called the "butcher shop religion" of the Aaronide priests. Barnabas did not need to take any of this very far out of context, simply connecting with the powerful and recurrent reforming themes found throughout the biblical tradition.

It is interesting to speculate how Barnabas might fit in with the schema of F. C. Baur. Barnabas would seem to be a catholicizing document attempting, as odd as it may sound to us, to vindicate the Old Testament for Christians. Like Justin Martyr, Barnabas thinks Jewish scriptures are about Christian truths, but he thereby argues for retaining them instead of sending them back to Judaism where Marcionites thought they belonged. Here again, the character of "Barnabas" is used the same way as in Acts in order to bring Paul on board for a more moderate position.

1

1Greetings and peace, sons and daughters, in the name of the one who loved us.

2How greatly and extravagantly do I rejoice over your superlative superiority! God decreed for you the blessing and glorification of your spirits, giving you so profound a charismatic gift of the Spirit. 3Because of this, I reassure myself as to my own salvation since I truly see in your own case how plentifully the Lord has poured out the Spirit from his never-failing spring.[b] Thus the sight of you, for which I so long pined, amazed

b. Thomas, saying 13

me! [4]Being reassured on this score and mindful of how much I have learned since last speaking among you,[c] the Lord being my companion along the way of righteousness, I am more than ever obliged to cherish you more than I do my own life because great faith dwells in you as you await everlasting life. [5]So I have decided that if I take the trouble for your sakes to convey some of the knowledge I have gained, I shall be rewarded for having been of service to such superior spirits. Thus I will not delay to dispatch to you a short letter so your knowledge may keep up with your ever-advancing faith!

[6]So then, there are three dogmas of the Lord: the prospect of life, the beginning and end of our faith; righteousness, the beginning and end of judgment; and the love of joy and gladness, the evidence of righteous behavior. [7]For by means of the prophets, the Lord disclosed to us events past and present, plus the foretaste of future events beginning to transpire. And when we mark these things starting to happen one by one, as he said, we must needs offer a richer and deeper sacrifice out of fear of him. [8]But as for the time being, let me show you a few things for you to rejoice over, not condescending like a teacher, but as one of yourselves.

2

[1]In view of the fact that these are decadent times and that the Evildoer himself holds power, we ought to watch ourselves and seek to obey the commands of the Lord. [2]Thus fear and endurance are our supports in faith, and long-suffering and self-control are our allies. [3]While these attitudes remain sacred to the Lord, wisdom, prudence, understanding, and knowledge celebrate with them. [4]For he has made it clear to us through all the prophets that he needs neither sacrifices nor holocausts nor offerings, [5]as in one passage: "'What do all your sacrifices mean to me?' says the Lord. 'I am sick of holocausts and have no desire for the fat of sheep and the blood of bulls and goats when you bring them before me. Who commanded you to offer these things? Do not let me hear your pious footsteps any more! If you offer flour, it will be futile. Incense is abhorrent to me. I can no longer stomach your new moon and Sabbath charades.'"[d] [6]All this he abolished in order to replace it with the new law of our Lord, Jesus-Christ, which frees us from any yoke of constraint and allows for no offerings made by human hands. [7]Again he says to us, "I never com-

c. This comment perhaps denotes that the anti-Jewish typology and allegorization to follow is a doctrinal innovation the author shares with his constituency for the first time.

d. Isa. 1:11-14

manded your ancestors on their way out of Egypt to offer me holocausts and sacrifices! [8]No, this is what I commanded them:[e] 'Each of you, do not harbor malice in your heart against another and do not love a false oath.'"[f] [9]So unless we are stupid, we ought to understand the noble intention of our Father, for he speaks to us in hopes we will not make the same error they did, but instead, we may discern the proper way to make our offering. [10]So then, he addresses us this way: "The fit sacrifice to the Lord is a broken heart."[g] "A sweet-smelling aroma to the Lord is a heart that worships its creator."[h] It is incumbent on us, then, brothers, to make close inquiry about our salvation so as to forestall the Evil One making an insidious entrance into us and pitching us away from our everlasting life.

3

[1]Thus to them, it again says about these matters: "'Why do you fast before me?' says the Lord, 'so that the sound of your wailing is heard today? This is not the fast I prefer,' says the Lord, 'which is for an individual to humble one's soul. [2]You could not make it acceptable to me even if you bent your neck into a hoop! Nor if you made your bed in the ash-heap.'" [3]But for us, it has this to say: "'Look here: this is the kind of fast I approve,' says the Lord: 'snap every chain locked by wickedness! Cancel the terms of unfair contracts! Proclaim amnesty for those flogged for their crimes. Tear up every one-sided contract! Give your bread to the hungry! Should you notice a naked man, clothe him! Give the homeless space in your house! If you spot a man down on his luck, have no contempt for him, neither you nor anyone else in your family. [4]Only then shall the clouds part for you like the sunrise. Your recovery will quickly come to pass. A reputation for righteousness shall precede you and the radiance of God shall surround you.' [5]Then if you cry out, God will listen; before you have finished, he shall say, 'Lo, here I am!' Just repudiate the enslavement of debtors, the accusing finger, the evil whisper, and begin instead to give your bread to the hungry cheerfully and to show compassion on the down and out.'"[i] [6]So then, brothers, he who is long-suffering planned in advance that the people he prepared through his beloved Son should have

e. Jer. 7:22-23a

f. Zech. 8:17

g. Pss. 51:19

h. One manuscript has a note at this point attributing this quotation to the Apocalypse of Adam, but it must be a different work from that which appears in the Nag Hammadi collection.

i. Isa. 58:4b-10a

faith and innocence, and he made this clear to us in advance so we could avoid coming to ruin through conversion to their Torah.

4

[1]It behooves us, then, to take a closer look at the way things are now and to determine those things that are able to save us. So let us make a complete break with all deeds of lawlessness since otherwise they might get us in their power. Let us no longer tolerate the errors prevalent in our time; that way, we will be loved in the time to come. [2]We must permit our souls no opportunity to consort with the wicked and with backsliders, otherwise we may become like them. [3]The final test is close now, as it is written, for Enoch says, "For this reason the Lord has truncated the allotted times and days: to prod his beloved one to hurry up and arrive at his reward."[j] [4]The prophet says this, too: "Ten kingdoms shall hold sway upon earth, and afterward, a little king shall come to the fore and subject three of the kings under the heel of one."[k] [5]Daniel speaks similarly of the same thing: "And I saw the fourth beast, wicked and potent and more violent than all the beasts out of the sea, how ten horns sprang from it, with one more small horn beside them, and how it subdued three of the large horns under one of them."[l] [6]Surely you understand what this means. And I urge you, as a member of your own company, all the more urgently since I love all of you more than my own life: watch yourselves now! Do not drift into the pattern of some people who pile their sins ever higher by holding that the covenant belongs to those others as well as to us! [7]It belongs to us. As for them, why, they lost it as soon as Moses received it. For scripture says: "And Moses was up the mountain forty days and forty nights when he received the covenant from the Lord, stone tables inscribed by the finger of the hand of the Lord."[m] [8]But they preferred idols and forfeited it. For the Lord says this: "Moses! Moses! Get down there at once! Your people, the ones you brought out of the land of Egypt, they have cast off the Torah!"[n] Moses understood what he had to do and threw the two tablets from him and their covenant was voided in order that the covenant of Jesus, his beloved one, should be stamped onto our hearts, pending the revelation of faith in him. [9]I would like to explore this

j. 1 Enoch 89:61-64; 90:17

k. Dan. 7:24

l. Dan. 7:7-8

m. Exod. 32:16

n. Exod. 32:7; Deut. 9:12

theme at much greater length, but I will try to hasten to the point for your sake. It is not pedantry that tempts me but only the desire to omit none of the truths we cherish. So let us be careful in these last days, for a whole lifetime of faith will do us no good unless we stand fast, as behooves God's sons in such a degenerate time, against the outrages destined to come and thus prevent the Black One from finding any point of entry. [10]Let us repudiate all vanity! Let us despise the deeds done along the path of wickedness.

Do not retreat into seclusion as if you had already attained righteousness; instead, come together for everyone's benefit. [11]For the scripture says: "Woe to those who seem prudent to themselves and commend themselves for their insight!"[o] Come and be spiritual, be a temple dedicated to God. As far as we are able, let us "train ourselves rigorously in the fear" of God[p] and let us do our very best to keep his commandments in order that they may be a cause of rejoicing for us and not of mourning. [12]The Lord will judge the earth without partiality. Each individual will be recompensed as his deeds deserve. If he has been good, his righteousness will lead him to everlasting bliss. If he has been evil, the terrible reward of sin lies before him. [13]Let us never take our calling for granted and become complacent about our sins, or the Archon of Evil will gain control of us and dislodge us from the kingdom of the Lord. [14]Think about this, too, my brothers: remember how, even after Israel had witnessed such great signs and wonders, they were nonetheless abandoned—even back then! Let us watch out or we may find in our own case that, as it was written, "many are called but few make the final cut."[q]

5

[1]For this is why the Lord was willing to hand over his flesh to rot, that we should be made holy by the cancellation of sin—that is, through his sprinkled blood. [2]For the scripture about him has partly to do with Israel, partly to do with us, and this is what it says: "He was injured for our trespasses, beaten for our sins; by his flogging we were healed. He was delivered like a sheep to the stockyard and like a lamb looking innocently into the face of its shearer."[r] [3]So it behooves us to give ardent thanks to the Lord that he has provided us knowledge of the past, wisdom for the

o. Isa. 5:21

p. Isa. 33:18

q. Probably already a familiar piece of Christian exhortation, also used in Matt. 20:16; 22:14.

r. Isa. 53:5, 7

present, and that we do not lack understanding for the future. [4]And scripture says, "It is not unjust to spread the net for the birds."[s] This means that an individual deserves to die if he knows the path of righteousness but decides he prefers the way leading off into the dark. [5]Furthermore, my brothers, if the Lord was willing to suffer for our lives even though he is Lord of the whole world, the one God who said before the creation of the world, "Shall we not make humanity in our image, to look like us?"[t] how then did he ever consent to suffer at human hands? [6]Learn this: the prophets who received charisma predicted him; and in order to annihilate death and to reveal the resurrection from the dead, because it had to be manifested in the flesh, he endured suffering [7]in order to make good the promise made to the fathers and to prepare for himself a new people and attest while still on earth that he himself will resurrect the dead and judge them once they rise. [8]Further, while he was teaching Israel and performing such great signs and wonders,[u] he preached to them and loved them ardently. [9]But when he chose from among his followers the apostles to preach his news, he chose the worst sinners of all[v] to prove that he came to call not the righteous but sinners.[w] That is when he revealed himself to be the Son of God. [10]For unless he had come in the flesh,[x] no one could ever have been saved by beholding him. After all, people cannot even look directly at the sun's brilliance, and it is only a created thing sure to perish one day. [11]So then, this is why the Son of God came in the flesh: that he might give the persecutors of the prophets enough rope to finish hanging themselves. [12]It was for this purpose that he endured his suffering. For when God speaks of the punishment of his flesh, they are the ones he blames: "When they strike down their own shepherd, then the sheep of the flock shall be devoured."[y] [13]And he was willing to suffer as

s. Prov. 1:17

t. Gen. 1:26

u. Barnabas, unlike other epistles, knows Jesus as a miracle worker, implying some acquaintance with the developing gospel tradition which had apparently not come to the attention of earlier epistle writers.

v. Barnabas seems to reflect the melding of Paul, "chief of sinners," with the Twelve, a catholicizing tendency that also eventuated in the fictive missionary journeys of the Twelve to all corners of the earth as if they, too, were "apostles to the gentiles."

w. This becomes a saying of Jesus in Mark 2:17.

x. 1 John 4:2

y. Zech. 13:6-7. The same citation will be ascribed to Jesus in Mark 14:27; Matt. 20:31.

he did because he was destined to suffer upon a tree, as the prophet said of him: "Save my life from the sword"[z] and "Nail my flesh, for the synagogues of the wicked have risen against me."[a] [14]And again it says: "Lo, I have surrendered my back to the lash, my cheeks to flogging, and I endure indomitable!"[b]

6

[1]So when he obeyed this commandment, what does it say? "Who is it who takes me to court? Let him accuse me! Who is he who demands satisfaction from me? Let him approach the Lord's servant. [2]Woe to you! For you shall all grow old like a garment and the moth shall devour you."[c] And again, the prophet says he was poised like a heavy stone for crushing: "Lo, I will lay for Zion's foundation a precious stone, chosen as the best, given the honor of being chief cornerstone."[d] [3]What does it say next? "And whoever places his hopes upon it shall live through the ages."[e] Are we then to trust in a stone? Never! What he means is that the Lord fortified his body with strength. For he says: "And he set me as a solid rock."[f] [4]Yet again, the prophet says: "The stone which the builders thought unfit has become the head of the corner."[g] And again, "This is the great and wonderful day which the Lord has appointed."[h] [5]I am perhaps oversimplifying, but because of my loving devotion to you, I want to make sure you understand. [6]So what else does the prophet have to say? "The synagogue of the sinners surrounded me, swarming about me like bees around the honeycomb."[i] And "they cast lots for my clothes."[j] [7]Therefore, since he was destined to be revealed and to suffer in the flesh, his suffering was foretold. For the prophet says about Israel: "Woe to their souls, for they have laid a deadly trap only for themselves, saying, 'Let us tie up the Just One, for he is inconvenient to us.'"[k] [8]What does

z. Pss. 22:40

a. Pss. 119:120

b. Isa. 50:6-7

c. Isa. 50:8-9

d. Isa. 28:16

e. Isa. 50:7

f. Isa. 50:7

g. Pss. 118:22

h. Pss. 118:24

i. Pss. 118:12

j. Pss. 22:18

k. Wisd. of Sol. 2:12

that other prophet, Moses, say to them? "Lo, thus says the Lord God: 'Enter into the good land which the Lord promised to give Abraham, Isaac, and Jacob for an inheritance, a land flowing with milk and honey.'"[l] [9]But what does knowledge say? Read and learn. "Hope," it says, "in that Jesus who will be revealed to you in the flesh." For man is merely earth that suffers, for Adam was created from the surface of the earth. [10]So then, what is the meaning of the words, "into the good land, one flowing with milk and honey"? Blessed be our God, brothers, for he has given us wisdom to discover his secrets! For the prophet utters a parable about the Lord. Who shall understand but one who is wise and learned and loves his Lord? [11]Since, then, he renewed us by the cancellation of sins, he gave us another simile, that we need to have souls like children, as though he were creating us all over again. [12]For when the scripture says that he says to the Son, "Shall we not make humanity in our image, to look like us? Let them rule over the animals of the earth, the birds of the sky, and the fish of the sea,"[m] it is referring to us! And when he witnessed our new-minted beauty, the Lord said, "Increase now and multiply to fill up the earth!"[n] This he said to the Son, too. [13]Now I will show you in what manner he speaks to us. In the last days he made a second creation, and of it the Lord says, "Behold! I make the last things just like the first!"[o] It was to this, then, that the prophet referred when he said, "Go on into a land flowing with milk and honey and rule it!"[p] [14]You see, then, that we have been created anew, as he says again in another prophet: "'Behold,' says the Lord, 'I will extract from them,'" that is, those whom the Lord saw in advance, "'the petrified hearts, and I will transplant into them living hearts of flesh.'"[q] This is because he was planning to reveal himself in the flesh and to live among us. [15]For, my brothers, the dwelling place of our heart is a shrine consecrated to the Lord. [16]The Lord says again, "And with what shall I appear before the Lord my God to worship him?"[r] He says, "I will confess to you in the assembly of my brothers and will sing to you in the middle of the assembly of the

l. Exod. 33:1, 3
m. Gen. 1:26
n. Gen. 1:28
o. Exod. 33:3?
p. Exod. 33:1, 3
q. Ezek. 11:19
r. Pss. 42:2

saints."[s] So we are the ones he brought into the good land. [17]And what is the milk and honey? A child is at first fed with honey, then later with milk. And so we, too, being fed first with faith in the promise and then by the command, shall live and own the earth. [18]And as we have already said, "And let them increase and multiply and rule the fish," etc. So to whom these days is given the rule of animals or fish or birds in the sky? For we must understand that to rule implies authority, enabling one to issue commandments and to dominate. [19]If this is not happening at present, he has told us when it will: once we ourselves have been made mature as heirs of the Lord's testament.

7

[1]Understand this, then, O children of gladness, that the good Lord made everything clear to us in advance so we might come to know him, whom we owe thanks and praise for so many things. [2]So then, if the Son of God, although reigning as Lord and destined to judge the living and the dead, suffered in order to give us life by means of his injuries, we ought to believe that the Son of God could never have suffered except for our sakes. [3]In addition, when he was crucified, he was given vinegar and gall to drink. Listen to how the priests of the temple themselves foretold this. The commandment was written: "Whoever fails to observe the fast shall surely die."[t] The reason the Lord commanded this was that he himself planned to offer the vehicle of the spirit as a sacrifice for our sins in order to make real the image sketched in Isaac's case, who was himself offered upon the altar. [4]So what does he say through the prophet? "And they are to eat the goat which is offered for all their sins during the fast." Please note: "And let all the priests, but no one else, eat the unwashed entrails with vinegar."[u] [5]Why? To show that he had to suffer for them because "you will be giving me gall and vinegar to drink" when I am just about to offer my flesh on behalf of my new people, and that is why you alone shall eat, while everyone else fasts and mourns, wearing hair shirts and ashes. [6]Note what was commanded: "Pick two goats, healthy and identical, and offer them, and have the priest choose one as an offering for sins." [7]But what about the other one? "The other one," it says, "is accursed."[v] See how Jesus is foreshadowed here: [8]"And all of you shall spit

s. Pss. 22:25

t. Lev. 23:29

u. Perhaps a contemporary liturgical rubric not found in scripture.

v. Lev. 16:5ff

on it and goad it with sharp reeds and tie a thread of scarlet wool around its head, and so let it be driven into the desert."[w] And when this is accomplished, the one who brings the goat to the desert drives it out, taking off the thread and hanging it upon the bush called rachia, the tender shoots of which we eat when we find them in the countryside, such sweet fruit coming only from the rachia. [9]Now what is the significance of all this? Stay with me: "The first goat is for the altar, but the second is accursed." Note that the accursed one is crowned because then "they will see him" on that day[x] with a long scarlet robe down to the feet on his body, and they will ask, "Is not this the one we once crucified, rejected, pierced, and spat at? Indeed, it is that one who at that time said he was the Son of God!" [10]But in what way is he comparable to the goat? In this way: "The goats must be identical, fine specimens, and a matched pair" in order that when they see his coming on that day, they may be astonished at the likeness of the goat. Here you see the foreshadowing of Jesus destined for suffering. [11]But why put the wool in the middle of the thorns? It is an image of Jesus situated in the church because anyone who wanted to remove the scarlet wool would suffer considerable pain due to the terrible thorns. He could manage to get it only through pain. This is why he says, "Any who would see me and attain to my kingdom must lay hold of me with pain and suffering."[y]

8

[1]But what do you suppose is symbolized in the commandment given to Israel that those in whom sin has been brought to completion must offer a heifer, kill it and burn it, and that boys are then to take the ashes and put them into vessels and tie scarlet woolen thread onto sticks—again we see the image of the cross and the scarlet wool—and hyssop brush and that the boys must all sprinkle the people with the ashes one by one so that all may be purified from their sins? [2]See how clearly he speaks to you. The calf is none other than Jesus. The sinners who offer it are the ones who brought him to be killed. Then they are no longer men, glorying in their sins. [3]Their places are taken by the boys who sprinkle: they are those who preached to us the forgiveness of sins and the purification of the heart, those he gave the power to preach the news. Of them, there are

w. Another possible liturgical rubric, not from scripture.

x. Zech. 12:10

y. Acts 14:22. It may be that Barnabas's name was chosen for the epistle on the basis of this verse since it sounds so much like what Paul and Barnabas are supposed to have said in this verse of Acts.

twelve, as a testimony to the twelve tribes of Israel. [4]But then why are there only three boys sprinkling? As a nod to Abraham, Isaac, and Jacob, for these three stand high in the esteem of God. [5]But why was the wool placed on the wood? Because the throne of Jesus is on the tree and because those who hope in him shall live unto the ages. [6]But why are the wool and the hyssop associated? Because during his reign, there shall be evil, bitter days in which we shall nonetheless be saved, for whoever has pain in his flesh is treated with the hyssop's bitterness. [7]Accordingly, we can now clearly see the reasons behind all these ceremonies, which however remain obscure to them because they were deaf to the voice of the Lord.

9

[1]When he speaks again about the ears, he says how he circumcised our hearts. For the Lord says through the prophet: "In the hearing of the ear they obey me."[z] And again he says, "Those who are far away shall hear clearly; they shall learn of the things I have done."[a] And "'circumcise your hearts,' says the Lord."[b] [2]Yet again, he says, "Hear, O Israel! Thus says the Lord your God!"[c] And again, the Spirit of the Lord prophesies, "Does anyone here want to live unto the ages? Then let him hear the voice of my servant!"[d] [3]Again, he says, "Hear, O heaven; lend an ear, O earth! For the Lord has spoken these words by way of testimony."[e] And again he says, "Hear the word of the Lord, you rulers of this people."[f] Again he says, "Hear, O children, the voice of one shouting in the desert."[g] So then, he circumcised our hearing so that, unobstructed, we should hear his promise and believe. [4]Not only that: the circumcision in which they trusted for salvation has been abolished! For he made it quite clear that the relevant circumcision was not that of the flesh. But they went off track because an evil angel was misguiding them. [5]He says to them, "Thus says the Lord your God," and here I read a commandment: "'Do not sow among thorns! Be circumcised to your Lord!'"[h] And what does he say?

z. Pss. 18:44
a. Isa. 33:13
b. Jer. 4:4
c. Jer. 7:2-3
d. Pss. 34:13
e. Isa. 1:2
f. Isa. 1:10
g. Isa. 40:2
h. Jer. 4:3-4

"Circumcise the hard shell of your heart and do not grow stubborn!"[i] Notice again: "'Behold,' says the Lord, 'all the nations are uncircumcised as to the foreskin, but this people is uncircumcised as to the heart.'"[j] [6]You might object: "But surely this people received circumcision as a seal of God's covenant." Indeed, but every Syrian, every Arab, every idol priest has been circumcised too! Do these, then, belong to the covenant? In fact, even the Egyptians practice circumcision. [7]So then, beloved children, the full truth of things: Abraham, the first to circumcise, only did so as looking ahead in the Spirit to Jesus and, having received the doctrines, taught by three letters. [8]For it says, "And Abraham circumcised eighteen men of his household plus three hundred."[k] What knowledge was conveyed to him here? Notice that he mentions the eighteen first, then the three hundred. The eighteen is a combination of the letters *iota,* for ten, and *eta,* for eight, and these two are the first two letters spelling "Jesus." The three hundred refers to the cross-shaped tau, which stands for the amnesty offered in the cross. So in the first two letters, he signals Jesus, with the cross in the third. [9]God, who placed the charisma of his teaching into our hearts, knows this is the truth. No one has ever heard a better lesson from me, I can tell you, but I know you are worthy of it!

10

[1]Now when Moses said, "You shall not eat swine, nor the eagle, no hawk, no crow, nor any sea creature lacking scales,"[l] he taught three doctrines in his wisdom. [2]Besides, he tells them in Deuteronomy, "And I will ratify a covenant of my statutes with this people."[m] So then, what God commands is not abstaining from eating this and that; rather, Moses spoke spiritually. [3]In mentioning swine, he intended: you shall not keep company with people who are like swine, meaning people who forget the Lord as soon as they find themselves with abundance and turn to him again only when they lose it. They are just like the pig, which ignores its master while gobbling but cries out to him when hungry, returning to indifferent silence once he is again fed. [4]"Neither shall you eat the eagle nor the hawk nor kite nor crow."[n] He means you shall not associate with such

i. Deut. 10:16

j. Jer. 9:25-26

k. Gen. 17:23-27; 14:14

l. Lev. 11; Deut. 14

m. Deut. 4:1, 5

n. Lev. 11:13-16

men, nor imitate them, for they do not know how to make an honest living but sinfully plunder the possessions of others for whom they lie in wait, though to all eyes they appear to live the life of innocence even while they cast shifty glances about to find a likely target. In this, they resemble carrion birds, which do not kill fresh game for themselves but perch on a branch waiting for the opportunity to snatch up the hard-won prey of others. Such filthy habits end up spreading disease. [5]"You shall not eat," he says, "the lamprey eel, the octopus, or the cuttlefish," but what he really means is not to spend time with and become like those who are completely impious and long since slated to perish, just as these are the only fish under a curse, being condemned to drift in the ocean depths instead of swimming like the rest. [6]"Furthermore, you shall not eat the rabbit."[o] Why? He means you shall not become a pederast or emulate their manner. Every year the rabbit adds new retreats beside the road, collecting as many burrows as it has years. [7]"Furthermore, do not eat the hyena." He means you shall not become an adulterer or a seducer or anything of the sort. Why? Because every year this creature alternates gender, turning from male to female and back again. [8]Furthermore, Moses is right to detest the weasel, because this creature gives birth from its mouth! You shall not, he says, become like those one hears of who transgress the law with their unclean oral acts. Nor shall you associate with any women who remain in an impure state because of the unclean acts they perform orally. [9]Moses received these three doctrines pertaining to food and so spoke of them in spiritual terms, but his contemporaries received them as if they actually referred to food, thanks to their preoccupation with the flesh. [10]David was informed of the same three teachings, and he says, "Blessed is the one who has not followed the directions of the impious," like the mollusks that ooze along the sea floor, "and has not milled about with the scheming sinners" like those who seem to fear the Lord yet sin like the swine "and has not yet found a seat on the bench of the scofflaws" like birds who perch while awaiting their prey.[p] Do you see the point of the teachings about food? [11]Again, Moses says, "Eat the meat of every animal that has a cloven hoof and chews the cud."[q] What on earth can he mean? He assumes that the one being fed knows the one who feeds him and depends on him and is glad to see him. He spoke aptly, then, of the commandment. And what does he mean? To keep company with people who

o. Lev. 11:5

p. Pss. 1:1

q. Lev. 11:3

fear the Lord, with those who deeply contemplate the implications of the teaching they have received, with people who discuss and observe the statutes of the Lord, with those who know that meditation is a happy task and who mull over the commands of the Lord.

But what is the significance of the "cloven hoof" business? Simply that the righteous individual both exists in this world and anticipates the holy age to come. What an able legislator Moses was. [12]But do you really think it was possible for the ancients to understand these secrets? But we have a proper understanding of them and teach the commandments as the Lord intended. To this end, he circumcised our hearing and our hearts so we could make sense of these things.

11

[1]Next let us see if perhaps the Lord took the trouble to signal in advance concerning the water of baptism and the cross. As for the water, it has been written about Israel that she will not receive the baptism that brings amnesty from sins but will devise something else on their own. [2]For the prophet says: "Gape in amazement, O sky! And let the earth shudder even more at this! This people has committed two evils: they have abandoned me, the very spring of life, and they have dug themselves a well of poisoned water. [3]Does my holy mountain Sinai look like some desert crag?"[r] "Now you shall be like fledgling birds, pushed out of the nest and fluttering frantically!"[s] [4]Once more the prophet says: "I will scout out the road ahead and I will flatten the mountains and I will snap the brass gates and splinter iron bars and I will give you hidden treasures, secret and long-unseen, and this will show them I am the Lord God."[t] [5]And: "You shall take refuge in a high cave in a mighty rock. And his stream will not run dry. You shall live to see the king in his splendor and your soul shall contemplate the fear of the Lord."[u] [6]And again through another prophet, he says: "And the one who does these things shall flourish like a tree planted in delta silt; just as it yields fruit in the proper season and its leaf does not fade prematurely, every one of his endeavors, of whatever type, shall succeed. [7]It is just the opposite with the wicked, not at all alike; they are like the chaff which the wind drives away from the face of the ground. For this reason, the wicked will not successfully sue,

r. Jer. 2:12-13

s. Isa. 16:2a

t. Isa. 45:2-3

u. Isa. 33:16-18a

nor will the word of sinners be heeded in the deliberations of the righteous; for the Lord approves the path of the righteous, but the path of the impious leads to ruin."[v] [8]See how he associates the water with the cross. For this is what he means: "Blessed are as many as hoped in the cross and went down under the water." For he speaks of their reward "in the proper season," and when that time comes, he says, he will repay. But as for when, he says, "Their leaves shall not fade," and means that every good word that emerges from your mouth inspired by faith and love shall facilitate the conversion and hope of many. [9]Yet again, another prophet says, "And the land of Jacob was assessed above every land."[w] He means that he is glorifying the container of his Spirit. [10]What does he say next? "And on the right there was a river flowing, out of which beautiful trees grew. Whoever eats of them shall live unto the ages."[x] He means that anyone who hears and believes these teachings shall live unto the ages.

12

[1]In the same way, again he describes the cross through another prophet. This one says: "'And when are all these things to be fulfilled?' says the Lord. 'When the tree shall fall and rise and when blood flows from the stump.'"[y] Here again, you find reference to the cross and to the one destined to be crucified. [2]And he said this another time to Moses when Israel was besieged by foreigners, and in order to remind those who were besieged that they were being given over to death because of their sins, the Spirit suggests to Moses that he make a representation of the cross and of him destined to suffer upon it because, as he says, unless they place their trust in it, they shall endure war forever. This is why Moses placed one shield atop another in the middle of the battle and, as he stood there elevated above everyone else, he kept his arms stretched out, whereupon the tide of the battle turned again in favor of Israel. But if he should let them falter, Israel began again to taste defeat. [3]Why? To show them they had no chance of salvation without trusting in him. [4]Once more he says through another prophet, "I extended my hands all day long to an insolent people, one that disdains my righteous path."[z] [5]Moses makes another representation of Jesus, showing that he had to

v. Pss. 1:3-6

w. Wisd. of Sol. 3:19

x. Ezek. 47:9

y. 4 Ezra 4:33; 5:5

z. Isa. 65:2

suffer and shall himself give life, though they would believe that he had been executed,[a] through the sign given to Israel when they transgressed, for the Lord sent every snake to bite them,[b] and they were dying, appropriately, since the original transgression took place with Eve because of the snake. The sign was given to persuade them they will be consigned to wretched death on account of their transgression. 6Furthermore, Moses' commandment, "You are to take neither carved nor molded image as your God,"[c] notwithstanding, he himself makes one in order to provide an image of Jesus! So Moses fashions a carved serpent and elevates it and summons the people by proclamation. 7So they assembled and begged Moses to offer supplication on their behalf, that they might be healed. But Moses replied, "Any of you who has been bitten, let him now step up to the snake suspended from this tree and let him believe that, though inanimate, it may yet impart life, and he shall be healed immediately."[d] And they did. Here again you see anticipated the greatness of Jesus, for all these things are meaningful in him and symbols for him.[e] 8Again, why do you think Moses says to Joshua, son of Nun, and as a prophet gives him this name,[f] that the people must listen to no one but him? Because the Father was revealing everything about his own Son, Jesus. 9That is why Moses tells Joshua, son of Nun, calling him by this name, when he sends him out for reconnaissance of the land, "Pick up a book and inscribe in it the pronouncement of the Lord: in the last day, the Son of God shall tear up the whole house of Amalek by the roots!"[g] 10Voila! Again, Jesus! Not as son of man this time, but as Son of God, but shown forth in an image of flesh.

Since therefore, they would one day be saying that the Christ is David's descendent, David himself prophesies, foreknowing and seeking to forestall the error of the sinners: "The Lord said to my lord, 'Sit at my right till I make your foes' necks a stool for your feet!'"[h] 11Again, Isaiah

---

a. Does Barnabas hint here at docetism: Jesus only seemed to die? We are reminded of the Preaching of John, 101.

b. Num. 21:6ff

c. Deut. 27:15

d. Num. 21:8-9

e. The typology of Jesus and the bronze serpent becomes attributed to Jesus in John 3:14.

f. Deut. 32:44. His name had been Hosea, lacking the Yahvist prefix.

g. Exod. 17:14 minus the phrase "the Son of God."

h. Pss. 110:1. This argument against the need for Davidic credentials for the

says much the same: "The Lord said to Christ, my lord, 'whose right hand I held,' that the nations should bow in obedience to him, 'And I will shatter the might of kings.'"[i] Notice how David calls him "lord" but does not say "son."

13

[1]Now let us see which of the two peoples is the heir, this one or the former people. Which one is the covenant intended for? Us or them?
[2]Listen to scripture as it speaks about the people: "And Isaac prayed for Rebecca his wife because she was barren, and she conceived after all. Then Rebecca went out to inquire of the Lord, and the Lord said to her, 'Two nations are in your womb, two peoples inside your belly. And one people shall overcome the other, and the greater shall serve the lesser.'"[j]
[3]You need to understand who Isaac stands for, and Rebecca likewise, of whose descendants he has shown that one people is greater than the
other. [4]And in another prophecy, Jacob speaks more clearly to his son Joseph, saying: "Behold, the Lord has not cheated me of your presence.
Bring me your sons to bless." [5]And he brought him Ephraim and Manasseh, expecting that Manasseh, being the older, should receive the blessing of the firstborn. Accordingly, Joseph led him to the right hand of his father, Jacob. But inspired by the Spirit, Jacob glimpsed an image of the people of the future. So what does it say? "And Jacob crossed his arms, placing his right hand on the head of Ephraim, the second, younger son, and gave him the blessing. And Joseph said to Jacob, 'No, Father, put your right hand on the head of Manasseh, for he is my firstborn son!' And Jacob replied to Joseph, 'I know, my son, I know. But the greater is destined to serve the lesser, so this one shall indeed have the blessing.'"
[6]Look which people it is that he ordains as the first and as heir of the cov-
enant. [7]If besides all this, he remembered to do the same in the case of Abraham, then our argument is capped. So what does he say to Abraham, when he alone had yet believed and he counted it as meritorious for him?

---

messiah will become a saying of Jesus in Mark 12:35-37. It stems from a time when Christians, like our author, had no belief that Jesus was descended from David. The apologetical task was to rebut the Jewish belief in a Davidic messiah. When this proved ineffective, Christians must have shifted to the assumption that Jesus was in fact the Davidic heir and then sought to connect the dots between him and David as best they could. The mixed results are on display in Matt. 1:1-17; Luke 3:23-38.

i. Isa. 45:1. Barnabas reads the original phrase "Cyrus, my anointed" as if it meant "my kyrios Christ" ("my lord, the anointed one").

j. Gen. 25:22-23

"Behold, I have made you, Abraham, the father of the nations who believe in God without being circumcised."[k]

14

[1]So much for that. Now let us see if he actually gave them that covenant he swore to the patriarchs. In fact, he did. But they proved unworthy of it, due to their sins. [2]For the prophet says: "And Moses was fasting on Mount Sinai, a total of forty days and forty nights, preparing to receive the covenant of the Lord for the people. So in the Spirit, Moses received from the Lord the two tables inscribed by the finger of the hand of the Lord."[l] And Moses hefted them and made ready to carry them down to share them with the people. [3]"And the Lord said to Moses, 'Moses! Moses! Get down there at once! Those people you brought out of the land of Egypt have broken the Law already!' And when Moses saw they had relapsed into idolatry, he flung them from his hands, and the tablets of the covenant of the Lord were smashed."[m] [4]Moses received it, but they proved unworthy. Now watch how we received it. Moses received it acting as a servant, but the Lord himself gave it to us, the true heirs of the covenant, when he suffered for our sins. [5]And it became clear both that their sorry saga should terminate with their apostasy and that we, through Jesus, the Lord, who inherits the covenant, should receive it. He was destined for this task so that, when he appeared, he might redeem our hearts from darkness. They had been mortgaged to death, consigned to the sin that springs from error. But by his revelation, he made a covenant with us. [6]For it is written that the Father commands him to redeem us from the darkness and to recruit a people uniquely his own. [7]This is why the prophet says: "I, the Lord your God, did summon you to righteousness, and I will guide your hands and I will strengthen you, for I have designated you a covenant sacrifice for the people, a beacon to the nations to open the eyes of the blind, to release the captives from their chains, and the prisoners from their murky cells."[n] From this description, we can see just what we were redeemed from. [8]Again, the prophet says: "'Lo, I have appointed you a beacon for the nations to guide to safety all those coming

k. We find the same sort of appeal to Abraham as the precedent in Galatians and Romans legitimatizing uncircumcised believers, but there is no particular reason to think Barnabas got it there, as he seems to have derived the point from his own exegetical argument.

l. Exod. 24:18

m. Exod. 22:7-19

n. Isa. 42:6-7

from the far reaches of earth.' So says the Lord who redeemed you."[o] [9]Once more, the prophet speaks: "The Spirit of the Lord is upon me because he anointed me to proclaim the news of mercy to the humble. He has sent me to comfort the broken-hearted, to proclaim freedom to the captives and sight for the blind, to announce a year of amnesty from the Lord and a day of recompense, to encourage all who mourn."[p]

15

[1]Moreover, in the ten commandments, which God spoke face to face with Moses upon Mount Sinai, it was set down concerning the Sabbath, "You shall treat the Sabbath of the Lord as holy, with hands undefiled and with a pure heart."[q] [2]In another passage it says, "If my sons observe the Sabbath, then I will bestow my mercy upon them."[r] [3]It is referring to the Sabbath at the beginning of the world: "And God made his handiwork in six days and finished by the seventh, resting that day and consecrating it."[s] [4]Now children, what do you suppose it means, "He finished in six days"? Just this: that the Lord will bring an end to all things in six thousand years, for one of his days equals a thousand of our years. He himself backs me up on this when he says, "Lo, the day of the Lord shall be equal to a thousand years."[t] So then, children, in six days, or rather six thousand years, everything will be completed. [5]"And he rested on the seventh day." This means that when his Son gets here, he will destroy the reign of the Wicked One and will condemn the impious and will rewind the sun, the moon, and the stars, and then he will have a genuine rest on the seventh day. [6]Furthermore he says, "You shall treat it as holy, with hands free of defilement and with a pure heart."[u] So if anyone today, by being pure in heart, has the ability to keep in perfect holiness the day God appointed as holy, then we have been grossly deceived. [7]For the point is rather that we shall indeed keep it holy at that future time when we enjoy the true Sabbath of rest, for then we shall be able to do so, having been made righteous ourselves. Then we shall have at last inherited what was promised and there shall be no more sin and the Lord will have renewed

o. Isa. 49:6-7

p. Isa. 61:1-2

q. Exod. 20:8; Deut. 5:12

r. Jer. 17:24-25

s. Gen. 2:2

t. Pss. 90:4

u. Exod. 20:8 plus Pss. 24:4a?

all things. Then we shall be able to maintain it as holy because we shall have been made holy ourselves. [8]In addition, he says to them, "Your new moon and Sabbath observances I cannot tolerate."[v] Do you see what he is getting at? The present-day Sabbaths are unacceptable to me, unlike the one I have appointed when I will give rest to all things and which will mark the beginning of an eighth day or the start of another cosmos. [9]This is also why we joyfully celebrate that eighth day on which also Jesus rose from the dead and revealed himself, then ascended into heaven.

16

[1]I propose to speak to you also concerning the temple and to show you how those poor wretches went astray when they placed their hopes on a building, as if it could really be a house of God, instead of hoping in the God who made them. [2]For they installed him in the temple almost like the heathen do their idols. But note what the Lord says as he nullifies the whole business: "'Who has measured out the heavens with a ruler or the earth with his outstretched hand? But I have!' says the Lord. 'Heaven is my throne, the earth my footstool. What sort of house do you propose to build for me? What kind of structure could afford me rest?'"[w] It is obvious their plan was doomed from the start. [3]Moreover, he goes on to say: "Lo, the same ones who destroyed this temple shall rebuild it!"[x] [4]This is happening right now. In the war, it was destroyed by the enemy, but at present, the very servants of the enemy are at work rebuilding it. [5]Again, it was revealed that the city, the temple, and the people of Israel were to be handed over. For the scripture says, "And it shall come about in the last days that the Lord will abandon the sheep of his pasture and the sheepfold and their watchtower to destruction."[y] And it happened just as the Lord had said.

[6]Let us next inquire whether a temple of God exists at present. Indeed it does, and we find it where he himself said that he establishes and completes it. For it is written, "And it shall come about when the week is ended that a temple of God shall be splendidly built in the name of the Lord."[z] [7]I infer from this that a temple does exist. Learn then how it is to be built in the name of the Lord. Before we came to believe in God, the

v. Isa. 1:13

w. Isa. 66:1

x. Isa. 49:17 LXX

y. 1 Enoch 89:56

z. Dan. 9:24?

dwelling of our hearts was rotten and weak like an actual structure built by human hands because it was a den of idolatry, a cave of demons, because of the things we did contrary to the will of God. [8]"But it shall be built in the name of the Lord." Now listen carefully so the temple of the Lord may be built splendidly. Learn how it is to be done. When we received amnesty for sins and placed our hopes on the name, we were renewed, being created all over again from scratch. This is why God truly lives inside us, in the dwelling that we constitute. [9]How? By means of his message of faith, the summons of his promise, the wisdom of the commandments, the statutes of the teaching, his prophesying inside us and living inside us, by his opening the door of the temple, that is, our lips, to speak his words, giving us the chance to repent and in this way leading us, former slaves of death, into the unfading temple. [10]For whoever wants to be saved focuses not on the individual who is preaching the news to him but on the one who lives in him and speaks through him. He is amazed at him, never having heard him speak thus with his mouth, nor has he himself ever wanted particularly to hear such speech. Both the speaking and the hearing attest the presence of the divine. The result is a spiritual temple being erected for the Lord.

17

[1]As far as it is possible to provide a simple enough explanation for you, I deeply hope to have neglected nothing essential to your salvation, as I wanted very much to supply everything needful. [2]For if I were to write you about the current situation or what is in store for the future, you would not understand it because I would have to resort to esoteric parables.[a] So this ought to be sufficient.[b]

18

[1]Next let us go on to a new lesson and teaching. There are two ways of teaching and of power, the one of light, the other of darkness. And what a difference exists between the two ways! For above the first, the illuminating angels of God are stationed, while the angels of the adversary patrol the other. [2]The one is Lord from age to age, but the other is the ruler of the current period of iniquity.

19

[1]Here is the way of light: if anyone wants to make his way to the des-

a. That is, the classic cipher-style of apocalypses.

b. The epistle originally ended here.

tined place, let him be conscientious in all he does. For this reason, the required knowledge delivered to us is as follows: [2]You shall love your maker. You shall fear your creator. You shall worship him who redeemed you from death. You shall be guileless at heart and spiritually rich. You shall avoid those who walk the way of death. You shall hate all that displeases God. You shall hate all hypocrisy. You shall not forsake the commandments of the Lord. [3]You shall not promote yourself but shall be humble in your thinking in all matters. You shall not allow yourself to be praised when God deserves the credit. You shall plan no mischief against your neighbor. You shall not allow your soul to be presumptuous. [4]You shall not patronize prostitutes. You shall not commit adultery. You shall not commit pederasty. You shall not cause the living voice of God to abandon your midst by accommodating the unclean acts of men. You shall not show favoritism in judging transgressions. You shall be meek. You shall be silent. You shall take seriously the words of exhortation. You shall not nurse ill will against your neighbor. [5]You shall not waver in doubt. You shall not take the name of the Lord in vain. You shall love your neighbor more than your own life. You shall not get an abortion. You shall not commit infanticide. You shall not neglect to discipline your son or your daughter but shall teach them the fear of God from their youth onward. [6]You shall not covet your neighbor's possessions. You shall not be greedy. You shall not be close friends with snobs but shall spend your time with the humble and the righteous. You shall welcome the testings that come your way as good things, mindful that nothing happens without God's approval. [7]You shall not be ambivalent or garrulous. You shall obey your masters with modesty and fear as if they were an earthly counterpart to God. You shall not give harsh commands to your male or female slave who shares your own hope in the same God. If you do, they will stop fearing the God who is the master of you both. For he came, not to show partiality to the rich, but rather, to call all whom the Spirit prepared to hear. [8]You shall be willing to share everything with your neighbor and shall not insist your goods are your private property. After all, if you share in the eternal riches, why not all the more in the temporal? You shall not be hasty in speech, for you do not know what sort of trouble your mouth can get you into! You shall keep your soul as pure as you possibly can. [9]You shall not be the kind of person who is always reaching his hands out to take but closes them tight when another asks. You shall love like the pupil of your eye all who speak the Lord's message to you. [10]You shall be mindful of the Day of Judgment day and night, and

you shall seek out the company of the saints every day, either doing the work of speaking, making the rounds to exhort one another, working to save souls by spreading the news, or doing good works with your hands to atone for your sins. [11]You shall not hesitate to give, and when you give, you shall not mutter complaints but shall keep in mind who it is who is the ultimate paymaster who passes out rewards. You shall keep the statutes you have received, adding nothing and omitting nothing. You shall loathe and despise evil. You shall give impartial judgment. [12]You shall not start arguments but shall mediate between those who dispute, and reconcile them. You shall confess your sins. You shall not undertake prayer as long as you have an unresolved matter on your conscience. This is the way of light.

20

[1]But the way of the Black One is perverted and full of profanity because it is the way of age-long death with punishment and along it lurk the things that destroy the soul: idol worship, presumption, the arrogance of the powerful, hypocrisy, ambivalence, adultery, murder, theft, pride, transgression, fraud, ill will, selfish isolation, drug use, sorcery, the lack of the fear of God. [2]Those who travel this path are the persecutors of the righteous, haters of the truth, lovers of deception, those ignorant of the reward of righteousness, those who do not cherish the good nor impartial justice, who ignore the plight of the widow and the orphan—staying up all night not in prayer vigils but in dissipation, those to whom meekness and patience are distant strangers, who love self-conceit and seek rewards, who are indifferent to the needs of the poor, unconcerned to ease the working conditions of the wage slave, inclined to evil speech, ignorant of their maker, child murderers, degraders of God's creation, contemptuous of the needy, advocates of the rich, corrupt judges biased against those too poor to bribe them, and completely sinful.

21

[1]It is fitting, then, that whoever has learned the statutes of the Lord, however many there may be of them, should live by them. For whoever does these things shall receive divine splendor in the kingdom of God, but anyone choosing the opposite deeds shall finally vanish along with his deeds. This is why there is a resurrection—so there can be recompense. [2]I urge those occupying high positions, if you will take any well-intended advice from me, do not isolate yourself from people to whom you may do good. Do not fail to help. [3]The day is close at hand when all temporal things shall be destroyed along with the Evil One. "The Lord is at hand,

bringing his reward."[c] [4]I urge you over and over again, remind each other of the laws binding you all. Remain faithful advisers for each other. Purify yourselves of all hypocrisy. [5]Now may God, the Lord of the whole world, grant you wisdom, understanding, prudence, knowledge of his commandments, and patience. [6]And have a receptive attitude toward all that God would teach you, trying to determine what God wants from each of you. And see that you are found faithful on the Day of Judgment. [7]If we share any good memories, meditate on what I have said and remember me so my desire and my vigilance for your welfare may not be frustrated. I beg you, asking you to do me this favor. [8]While you are in the prison of the flesh, do not fall short of any of these commandments but seek diligently to master them, for they are easily worth the effort. [9]This is why I was so eager to write you to the best of my ability, to make you rejoice. May you win salvation, children of love and peace! May the Lord of glory and of all generous favor fortify your spirit!

---

c. Isa. 40:10

53.

The Revelation of Paul

THERE ARE AT LEAST THREE ANCIENT apocalypses ascribed to Paul that we know of. This one, written in Greek in the late second century, translated into Coptic, was discovered at Nag Hammadi. Unlike the other, longer text conventionally called The Apocalypse of Paul, this one makes clear references to the Pauline Epistles. It imaginatively combines Galatians 2:1-2 with 2 Corinthians 12:1-10, identifying the heavenly journey of the latter with the "revelation" of the former. It must also know 1 Corinthians 15:5 since it has Paul going to Jerusalem to meet not "the Pillars" (as in Galatians) but "the twelve." And it is not the earthly Jerusalem to which Paul journeys but its heavenly counterpart. He does not go there in order to seek the approval of his colleagues or rivals, but rather to be acclaimed by them as at least their equal. The use of Pauline Epistles is significant since it shows how Gnostic writers were familiar with them, while Catholic writers shunned them during the second century before Tertullian, Irenaeus, and others sought to co-opt Paulinism by redacting and reinterpreting the epistles. Before then, as Tertullian quipped, Paul had been "the apostle of Marcion and the apostle of the heretics," who were indeed the first to write commentaries on his letters.[a]

Among Paul's heavenly revelations in this document are a vision of the chastisement of damned souls by their prison-guard angels, which is highly reminiscent of passages in the Shepherd of Hermas. But most of the revelation conforms to a prototype, or map, for the ascension of the soul after death. Paul's actions, guided by the Holy

a. See Elaine Pagels, *The Gnostic Paul: Gnostic Exegesis of the Pauline Letters* (Philadelphia: Fortress Press, 1975).

Spirit, furnish an example for the reader to follow. In that respect, like others of the Gnostic apocalypse genre such as the Gospel of Mary Magdalene, the Revelation of Paul serves the same purpose as the Bardo Thödöl, the Tibetan Book of the Dead.

Undoubtedly the most distinctive and astonishing feature of the Revelation of Paul is the complete absence of any reference to Jesus Christ! Paul is the one who is chosen and prepared as a redeemer, who is sent back to earth to save the souls of the elect. It is Paul who has an encounter with the diabolical Demiurge and prevails! There are two possibilities for making sense of this. First, we may have a glimpse here of a Paulinism that had begun to leave the centrality of Jesus behind, as in Colossians 1:24 (cf. 1 Cor. 1:13) where Paul is already a co-redeemer with Christ. In the same vein, the Acts of Paul virtually make Paul a second Christ, having him die, rise from the dead, and ascend from an empty tomb. Second, we might have a fossil stemming from an earlier period attested in 1 Corinthians 1:12, in which Paul was a full competitor to Apollos, Cephas, and Christ, all apostles in their own right—not apostles defined as disciples and successors of Jesus, as in the gospels, but more along the lines of the original apostle conception of Syrian Gnosticism, preserved in Manichaeism and Islam, where the apostle is virtually an incarnation or avatar, a heavenly messenger.[b] Paul and the others would have been subsequently assimilated to Christ and subordinated to him once the Christian sect prevailed, just as John the Baptist was subsequently and fictively drawn into the Christian orbit.

Of these two options, the former is to be preferred since the author knows of texts that presuppose the more familiar picture of Paul, the Christian apostle. Similarly, the salutary mention of other apostles makes best sense as a vestige of the catholicizing attempt to harmonize Paul with his Judaizing rivals. We have to picture an original Paulinism, perhaps to be identified with the faction of Simon Magus, giving way to the Jesus sect for a while and then beginning to separate from it, returning to its focus on Paul, with Paul's Christian associations becoming more and more vestigial. It is simply a question of

b. See Walter Schmithals, *The Office of the Apostle in the Early Church* (Nashville: Abingdon Press, 1969).

where on this arc to place the Revelation of Paul: does it come from a time before the star of Jesus arose over the Pauline horizon or after it began to set?

I have dispensed with the usual division of the text into codex, page, and line divisions beloved of Nag Hammadi scholars in favor of a conventional biblical approach with chapters and verses. Where there are holes in the manuscript, scholars have made various suggestions as to what the original text might have been, which I have preserved in italics, my own reconstructions appearing in brackets.

1

1[Paul had been summoned to the holy city. He met a little child walking by himself along] the road. 2And *he spoke to him,* saying, "*Which* road *shall I take* up to *Jerusalem*?" 3The little child *answered, saying*: "Tell me your name and *I will* show you which road." 4*The little child* knew well enough *who Paul was.* 5He wished only to engage him in conversation by what he said *so as to* find a pretext for talking to him.
6The little child spoke, saying, "I know who you are, Paul! You are the one consecrated ever since his mother's womb.[c] 7I know because I have come to you so you may *go up to Jerusalem* to meet your fellow apostles.[d]
8And this is why you were summoned. I am the Spirit sent to accompany you. Let *your mind awaken, Paul,* with *open eyes!* 9For *we shall enter that* Whole *which contains,* among the *principalities and* these authorities *and* angel princes and powers and the whole race of demons [and archons], the One that manifests bodies to a soul kernel."[e]

2

1And once he had finished these words, he spoke to me again: "Let your mind awaken, Paul, for behold, this mountain upon which you stand is even the mountain of Jericho. 2Here you may know the things hidden amid those that are visible. 3Now it is to the twelve apostles you shall go, for they are chosen spirits and they will salute you." 4He elevated his gaze and beheld them bidding him welcome.

5Then the Holy Spirit, who was speaking to him, snatched him up on

c. Gal. 1:15

d. Gal. 2:1

e. 1 Cor. 15:37. We see this happening in 21:18-21. The one connecting bodies to a soul about to be reincarnated is the one grasping an iron sceptre, 22:2-5.

high, even unto the third heaven,[f] passing beyond unto the fourth heaven.
6The Holy Spirit spoke to him and said, "Behold your image upon the
earth!" And he looked down and espied those who were upon the earth.
7He gazed and beheld those that *swarmed upon* the earth[, how tiny they
were]. 8Then he peered downward and saw the twelve apostles at his right
and at his left down on the earth, with the Holy Spirit leading them on.

9But I saw the celestial entities in the fourth heaven according to their
ranks: I saw angels who looked like gods,[g] angels who retrieved a soul
from the land of the dead.[h] 10They stood it up at the gate of the fourth
heaven. And the angels were flogging it.[i] 11The soul cried out, "What sin
was it that I committed back in the world to deserve this?" 12The toll collector stationed at the fourth heaven answered him, saying, "It was not a
good idea to commit all those lawless acts back in the world of the
dead!"[j] 13That soul replied, "Produce witnesses! Have them identify the
body I occupied when I committed these lawless acts you accuse me of.
14*I beg you* to produce a record of my deeds *to prove these things*."[k]

15And three witnesses[l] appeared. The first spoke up, saying, "Was I
not in the body the second hour *of so-and-so day*? I confronted you until
you erupted into anger *and rage* and envy." 16And the second spoke, saying, "Was I not there in the world? 17I came in at the fifth hour and spotted you, having been looking for you. And see, now I charge you with the
murders you committed!" 18The third spoke, adding, "Did I not approach you at the twelfth hour of the day when the sun was near to going
down? I waited till it was dark for you to finish your crimes." 19When
that soul heard all this, its countenance fell. And then it raised its eyes.
20They threw it down. The soul plunged down till it entered a body made
ready for it. And behold, the witnesses retired.

3

1Then I looked upward and saw the Spirit speaking to me: "Paul,
come! *Follow* me!" 2Then, as I went, the gate swung open and I ascended

---

f. 2 Cor. 12:2

g. These would be the entities the Greeks had taken for gods: the Erinyes, who lash damned souls onward to meet their torment.

h. Notice that the souls are not in the netherworld but closer at hand in the earth's charnel house.

i. 2 Cor. 12:7; Shepherd of Hermas, parable 6, v. 3

j. See note at 20:10.

k. Rev. 20:12

l. The number mandated in the Torah, Deut. 19:15.

to the fifth heaven. [3]And I beheld my fellow apostles *attending me*, with the Spirit accompanying us. [4]And I beheld a great angel in the fifth heaven, clutching a rod of iron in his hand.[m] [5]There were three more angels with him and I gazed into their faces. But they competed with one another, whip in hand, driving the hapless souls on to the judgment. [6]But as for me, I went with the Spirit and the gate opened unto me.

[7]Then we ascended unto the sixth heaven. Again I saw my fellow apostles accompanying me and the Holy Spirit was leading me before them. [8]And I gazed on high to see a great light bathing the sixth heaven. [9]I spoke, addressing the toll collector stationed in the sixth heaven, "Open to me and the Holy Spirit who goes before me!" And he opened *the gate*.

[10]*Then we ascended* unto the seventh *heaven*, where I beheld an old man *whose face radiated* light *and whose raiment* was white.[n] [11]*His throne*, which sits in the seventh heaven, *was* seven times more brilliant than the sun. [12]The old man spoke and addressed me, "Where are you headed, Paul, O blessed one, consecrated from his mother's womb?" [13]I glanced at the Spirit and he was nodding his head, signaling me, "Speak to him." [14]So I answered and said to the old man, "I go to that place whence once I came." [15]And the Old One answered, "Where is it you hail from?" But I replied, "I am descending unto the world of the dead,[o] to lead home the exiles who were captured in the exile in Babylon."[p] [16]That Old One retorted, "Indeed? And how do you think you will get away from me? Behold the principalities and authorities!"

[17]*The* Spirit spoke [to me], saying, "Show him the sign you carry and

---

m. Pss. 2:9; Rev. 12:5

n. He is the One Ancient in Days from Daniel 7:9-10, El Elyon, who is supplanted by Yahve, the One like a Son of Man, when the latter defeats the beasts of the deep (Dan. 7:2-9, 12-14). Once monotheists merged Yahve with his father, El Elyon (cf. Gen. 14:19-20, 22; Deut. 32:8-9), some sought to preserve the original distinction by reducing either Yahve or El Elyon to the subordinate status of the Demiurge/Creator with a higher God above him. Traditional Jewish theology placed God's dwelling in the third, then later the seventh, heaven. Here we meet the Creator/Ancient of Days as the Demiurge, dwelling in the seventh heaven but below the three new superior heavens! See Margaret Barker, *The Great Angel: A Study of Israel's Second God* (London: SPCK, 1992), esp. chapter 9, "The Evidence of the Gnostics," 162-89.

o. See note at 20:10.

p. Eph. 4:8-9. The Babylonian Captivity here stands for the exile of the divine light-sparks in the murky world of matter, the rescue of self-forgetful souls by the Gnostic redeemer.

he must open the gate for you!" [18]So I showed him the sign[q] and he turned his face downward toward his creation and to those who are his attendant authorities. [19]And at once the seventh heaven opened and we ascended unto *the* Ogdoad.[r] [20]And I saw the twelve apostles. They welcomed me, and together we ascended unto the ninth heaven. [21]I greeted all the denizens of the ninth heaven and we ascended even unto the tenth heaven. And I saluted my fellow spirits.

q. Gal. 6:17

r. The eighth heaven.

54.

The Third Epistle to the Corinthians

THE MONOPHYSITE CHURCH OF Armenia has preserved in its canon a fascinating fictive exchange of two letters between Paul and his Corinthian congregation. The texts were widely known elsewhere by virtue of their inclusion in the Acts of Paul, though they seem to be earlier works incorporated into that larger whole—the opposite of the Acts of Paul and Thecla, a subnarrative of the Acts of Paul, which was abstracted and distributed as a separate work. One reason for thinking 3 Corinthians was a separate composition is that there are few references to the familiar Pauline Epistles in the Acts Paul, whereas 3 Corinthians is so densely packed with them, one can practically regard it as a cento of selected phrases and fragments—which is no doubt what it was. Why would anyone compile such a thing? What would one find in 3 Corinthians that was not available at greater length in the Pauline letter corpus? In fact, 3 Corinthians updates Paul's teachings so that he affirms the virgin birth of Jesus, never mentioned in his other epistles, and rejects docetism, something he never quite does in the canonized letters where, indeed, he may be guilty of it himself!

But otherwise, 3 Corinthians limits itself to bits and pieces of other letters precisely because it is intended as a substitute for the original documents which were suspected of subtly propagating heresy since only the so-called heretics had previously used them. Obviously, the attempt to supplant the Pauline Corpus with a smaller sanitized sampler did not work, as it was eventually simply added onto its

predecessors. A more successful maneuver was the addition of the Pastoral Epistles with their associated interpolations into the previous Pauline texts. This way, the texts of Paulinism, which would not just go away, were retained, albeit with ecclesiastical redaction like those padding out Luke and John.

The epistle, and the letter it responds to, survive in Greek in the third-century Bodmer Papyrus and in Armenian, Coptic, and Latin. For late interpolations, omitted here, I have put a dagger (†) in their place to indicate a gap in the traditional versification.

First, we have the letter addressed to Paul. Note that it mentions a pair of heretics, Simon and Cleobias, who are elsewhere (*The Apostolic Constitutions*) said to represent Simonianism and Dositheanism. The two names may represent an attempt to divert attention from Paul's original Jewish-Christian opponents, away from Simon Cephas, also known as Peter, and Simeon bar-Cleophas, Jesus' brother who succeeded James the Just.

Corinthian elders to Paul

[1]Stephanus and the elders with him, Daphnus and Eubulus and Theophilus and Zenon, to Paul. Greetings in the Lord.

[2]There are two men, Simon and Cleobius, lately arrived in Corinth, who are subverting the faith of many with evil words, [3]which you must test. [4]For we have never heard such teaching from you or from the other apostles, [5]but whatever we have received from you or from them we hold to tightly. [6]Since, therefore, the Lord has shown mercy to us in that, you still being present in the flesh, it is not too late to hear these things again from you, [7]if possible either visit us or write to us. [8]For we believe, as it has been revealed to Theonoe, the Lord has delivered you out of the grasp of the Lawless One.

[9]Now what these men say and teach is this: [10]They say we must not use the Prophets, [11]that God is not all-powerful, [12]that there will be no resurrection of the flesh, [13]that humanity was not made by God, [14]that Christ did not appear in the flesh, nor was he born of Mary, [15]and that the world is not the creation of God but of the angels.

[16]For this reason, brother, do your best to visit us so the congregation of the Corinthians may remain free of offense to God and the lunacy of these men may be exposed. Fare well in the Lord's care.

Paul to the Corinthian elders

[1]Paul, a prisoner of Jesus-Christ, to the brothers in Corinth, Greetings!

[2]Finding myself amid many tribulations, I am not surprised that the doctrines of the Evil One are spreading like wildfire. [3]No doubt, my Lord, Jesus-Christ, will speed up his arrival and will put a stop to those who distort his words. [4]For at the start, I delivered to you the doctrines I received from the holy apostles, my predecessors, who accompanied Jesus-Christ at all times, [5]namely, that our Lord Jesus-Christ was born of Mary, who was descended from David according to the flesh, the Holy Spirit having been dispatched from heaven by the Father to her, [6]that he might descend into this world and redeem all flesh with his flesh and raise us up from the dead in the flesh, as he demonstrated in his own case for an example. [7]And because man was formed by his Father, [8]he was the object of searching once he was lost, so he might be vivified by adoption. [9]It was to gain this goal that God Almighty, who created heaven and earth, first sent the prophets to the Jews, to win them away from their sins. [10]For his plan was to save the house of Israel, so he endowed the prophets with a portion of the Spirit of Christ and sent them first to the Jews, and for a long period they preached the true worship of God. [11]But the Prince of Iniquity, desiring to be God, seized them and killed them and chained all flesh by means of evil lusts.

[12]But God Almighty, who is righteous and would not abandon his creation, [13]sent his Spirit into Mary, [14]that Jesus might come into the world [15]in order that the Wicked One should be publicly defeated by the same flesh he had used to introduce death. [16]For using his own body, Jesus-Christ saved all flesh, [17]displaying the temple of righteousness in his own body.[a] [18]In him we are saved.

[19]These men, therefore, are not children of righteousness but children of wrath, selling short the wisdom of God when they aver that the heaven and the earth and all that they contain are not the handiwork of God. [20]They bear a curse, following the doctrine of the serpent. [21]Expel them from your midst and flee from their teaching![†]

[24]And as to their claim that there is to be no resurrection of the flesh, it is true that they can look forward to no resurrection [25]since they do not believe in him who was raised from the dead, [26]for they seem not to realize, O Corinthians, that the seeds of wheat or of other grains are depos-

a. John 2:19-21

ited bare into the soil and decay and rise again by the will of God with bodies newly clothed.[b] 27Nor is it merely that which was planted that rises up again, but a much more fulsome harvest of blessing. 28And if an example taken from seeds does not suffice, 29remember how Jonah, son of Amitai, when he refused to preach to the Ninevites, was ingested by the sea monster,[c] 30and after three days and nights God acknowledged his prayer from out of the bottommost hell so that not a bit of him was digested, not so much as a hair or an eyelash![d] 31How much more likely is it that he would raise you up who have believed in Jesus-Christ, as he himself rose? 32Similarly, a dead man was dumped onto the bones of the prophet Elisha by some Israelites and he arose, both body and soul, bones and spirit.[e] How much more likely is it that you, who have been cast upon the body and bones and spirit of the Lord, will rise again in that day with your flesh intact?[†]

34If, then, you accept any other teaching, let no one give me any trouble, 35as I wear these chains so I may attain Christ and that is why I carry his stigmata on my body,[f] that I may arrive at the resurrection of the dead.[g] 36And anyone who adheres to the creed he accepted from the blessed prophets and the sacred news shall receive his wages from the Lord. 37But anyone who violates these tenets will wind up in the flames along with those who live the same way, 38who are a nest of vipers.[h] 39Reject them in the power of the Lord 40and you will enjoy God's protection, favor, and love.

---

b. 1 Cor. 15:36-37

c. Jonah 1:17-2:10

d. Matt. 10:30

e. 2 Kings 13:21

f. Gal. 6:17

g. Phil. 3:8

h. Matt. 3:7

BIBLIOGRAPHIC ESSAY

Footnoting is little more than name dropping unless the author provides some sort of historical context for the names. That is the goal of the present essay. Who are these people whose names punctuate the text? To answer that question is to provide a summary of the history of New Testament scholarship, and that is by no means a bad idea. As long as the reader keeps in mind that a comprehensive treatment of the subject would require at least another book, this brief overview may be judged adequate to its modest purpose.

New Testament environment

Without considerable information about the cultural environment of the New Testament and early Christianity, little sense can be made of the writings. Fortunately, we know very much about many aspects of that environment. In recent years our understanding of the Jewish religious background has been corrected and refined. Earlier students had often been unwittingly misled by learned tomes like the venerable Alfred Edersheim's *Life and Times of Jesus the Messiah* (1883) into believing that Jesus lived and moved in an atmosphere of classical rabbinical Judaism of the sort on display in the Mishnah and the Tosefta, deposits of Jewish tradition stemming from the second century and later. Jacob Neusner (*Rabbinic Literature and the New Testament,* 1994) and others have helped us see how anachronistic such a picture was. Ironically, Burton L. Mack *(A Myth of Innocence: Mark and Christian Origins,* 1988) and others have also shown that the gospels' picture of Jesus vis-á-vis Judaism is itself anachronistic, recasting the Jesus figure in terms drawn from a generation or two after the time he is usually thought to have lived. Joachim Jeremias (*The Parables of Jesus,* 1947; English 1954) made deep and extensive use of Jewish sources to explicate the likely meaning of the parables of Jesus, but E. P. Sanders (*Jesus and Judaism,* 1985) has

shown again how Jeremias had misconstrued first-century Judaism, creating, for example, unhistorical Pharisee strawmen for gospel readers to hiss at. Hyam Maccoby (*Revolution in Judea,* 1973; *Jesus the Pharisee,* 2003) had more confidence that Jesus-era Pharisaism was substantially the same as late first-century rabbinical Judaism, and this caused him to regard the historical Jesus himself as a Pharisee, albeit with charismatic, radical leanings—something hardly unheard of in their ranks. J. Duncan M. Derrett (*Law in the New Testament,* 1970; *The Making of Mark: The Scriptural Bases of the Earliest Gospel,* 1985) brought to bear on specific gospel anecdotes a wealth of legal lore from both ancient Judaism and other ancient cultures, as well as a sense for how scriptural writers tended to fabricate new texts from old ones.

Perhaps most startling of the newer discoveries was that not even the famous monotheism of rabbinical Judaism had altogether prevailed in the days of Christian origins. Raphael Patai (*The Hebrew Goddess,* 1967) collected much neglected material tending to demonstrate that various figures in Jesus-era Judaism only thinly veiled the surviving goddesses and gods whose worship had been officially terminated but continued nonetheless. The ancient Asherah, Yahweh's bride in the Solomonic Temple for two-thirds of the years it stood, continued on under the aliases of Wisdom, Matronit, the Shekinah, Queen Sabbath, and so on. Philo, too, knew of a female element in the godhead but ameliorated it in philosophical abstraction. Margaret Barker *(The Great Angel: A Study of Israel's Second God,* 1992) ripped away the veil even more violently by her scrutiny of polytheistic and sacerdotal elements still evident in the largely bowdlerized Old Testament and fully visible in Gnosticism, Philo, and Jewish popular religion. She demonstrated that one need hardly repair to mythemes drawn from alien pagan cultures in order to account for the origin of the Trinity or Gnosticism, much less Jesus being God and the Son of God.

But other scholars (Martin Hengel, *Judaism and Hellenism,* 1974) demonstrated how it need not have been an either-or option since even Palestinian, not just Diaspora, Judaism had been thoroughly permeated by Hellenistic culture and religion by New Testa-

ment times. In any event, the possible extent of theological-ritual syncretism became clearer, vindicating to a large degree the approach of an earlier generation of scholars like G. R. S. Mead (*Did Jesus Live One Hundred BC?* 1903; *The Gnostic John the Baptizer,* 1924) and Alvin Boyd Kuhn (*Shadow of the Third Century: A Revaluation of Christianity,* 1949), whose works had been discounted largely because their authors championed one kind or another of esoteric or theosophical spirituality. Their work was erroneously cast aside along with the uncritical mishmash one finds in Madame Blavatsky's *Isis Unveiled* (1877) and *The Secret Doctrine* (1888).

The crucial question about possible Hellenistic influence, still hotly debated by scholars and apologists, is to what degree, if any, early Christians or possibly pre-Christians (those who fed into the Christian stream) borrowed from the Hellenistic mystery religions. These had been agricultural religions, famously described by James Frazer in his magnum opus *The Golden Bough* (1900; 12 vol. ed., 1911-15) in which the annual death and rebirth of vegetation or the waning and waxing of the sun had been symbolized by the death and resurrection of a god, originally the king or queen's consort. As time went by, the external mysteries of nature renewal were reinterpreted and extended to cover the inner rebirth of the spirit as well, leading to rituals of personal initiation which brought either the blessing of the god in this life or that of immortality afterward. Such deities included Adonis, Attis, Baal, Mithras, Osiris, Tammuz, and even Hercules. Usually such initiation included a symbolic rehearsal of the saving sacrifice of the god, followed by sacred meals which sometimes, as with Osiris, offered tokens representing the savior's body and blood. Richard Reitzenstein set forth these parallels in great detail in *Hellenistic Mystery-Religions: Their Basic Ideas and Significance* (1927; English 1978). Though Frazer himself was reluctant to reduce Jesus to merely another "corn king," as C. S. Lewis put it, Gilbert Murray (*Five Stages of Greek Religion,* 1912) and Robert Graves (*The White Goddess,* 1948) saw the connection. Ancient Christians were confronted by these extensive parallels by pagan skeptics who dismissed Christianity as merely more of the same. Their rejoinders, still offered today, were either that Satan knew the real savior would arrive and

planted these "counterfeits" in advance or that the Holy Spirit had planted mythic "anticipations" of the real thing yet to come. Both explanations, far-fetched special pleading as they seem, nonetheless tacitly admit the fact that the Christians came by the mythemes and rituals later than the pagans did. Jonathan Z. Smith (*Drudgery Divine,* 1994; "Dying and Rising Gods," in Mircea Eliade, ed., *Encyclopedia of Religion,* 1986), Bruce M. Metzger, Edwin M. Yamauchi, Ronald M. Sider, and others still argue that Christianity was the source, not the borrower, or that the parallels are more apparent than real, but their arguments either ignore important pre-Christian evidence or exaggerate secondary differences to distract from the genuine and substantial parallels. Hyam Maccoby (*Paul and Hellenism,* 1991; *The Myth-Maker,* 1986; *The Sacred Executioner,* 1983), Richard C. Carrier, and myself (*Deconstructing Jesus,* 2000) defend the notion of Christian borrowing from pagan rivals or, more likely, inheritance from pre-Christian pagan or Canaanite sources.

Another major feature of the religious scene in New Testament times was Jewish Apocalyptic, an offshoot of scribal Judaism. The wisdom lore of the scribes included astrology/astronomy and natural science, circulated among their peers as revelations attributed to ancient scribes Baruch, Enoch, Ezra, Moses, and others. It commonly featured seers on guided tours of heaven or of the future, angelic guides showing them the storehouses of rain, snowflakes, and stars, as well as jails for fallen angels and for mortal sinners awaiting the judgment of the Last Day. Much of the imagery simply regurgitated that of predecessors in the genre, with a new spin here or some new "information" there. Gershom G. Scholem, the twentieth century's greatest authority on Jewish mysticism (*Major Trends in Jewish Mysticism,* 1941; *Jewish Gnosticism, Merkabah Mysticism, and Talmudic Tradition,* 1960; *On the Kabbalah and Its Symbolism,* 1965; *Sabbatai Sevi: The Mystical Messiah,* 1973), showed how visionary mysticism flourished as well in orthodox circles of rabbinic Judaism as within esoteric groups like the Dead Sea Scrolls sect, a thin line separating apocalyptic and Gnosticism; many characteristics long thought to be Greek or Persian in origin had their own roots in Jewish conceptual soil. George Wesley Buchanan compiled a voluminous anthology

(*Revelation and Redemption,* 1978) of Jewish apocalyptic writings which showed even more forcefully how ubiquitous these themes have been through the whole history of Judaism.

Ethelbert Stauffer, in his deceptively mundane-sounding *New Testament Theology* (1955), showed more fully than anyone before or since how much meat might be put on the bones of New Testament allusions if one were prepared to search among the recesses of the considerable apocalyptic and other sectarian literature of the period. Where others had seen only atolls, Stauffer dived deep and came up with a map of the sea bottom from which these peaks arose. Too bad he was a Nazi.

As the Western study of Islam gradually began to free itself from bondage to the apologetics of Muslim savants, it became increasingly clear the degree to which Islam, both in its formative stages and in the logic of its further development, was an extension of the same religious currents that had shaped early Christianity, only to be suppressed in the name of orthodoxy in the fourth century. Tor Andrae (*Mohammed: The Man and His Faith,* 1956) showed how the role of prophet and apostle, applied to Muhammad in Islam, had been passed down from Jewish Christian "heresies" such as the Ebionites and Elchasites, even Gnostics like the Manichaeans. Geo Widengren (*The Great Vohu Manah and the Apostle of God,* 1945; *Mesopotamian Elements in Manichaeism,* 1946; *The Ascension of the Apostle and the Heavenly Book,* 1950) showed how even the Babylonian Marduk had been a dying and rising god and how archaic were the myths that formed the substructure of both Christianity and Islam. Neal Robinson (*Christ in Islam and Christianity,* 1991) looked through the other end of the scope to trace out how the gospel tradition continued to mutate through Islamic commentary and legend mongering to embellish the Jesus story. John Burton (*The Collection of the Qur'an,* 1977) provided helpful analogies for understanding how Christian scripture may have come together in an earlier generation.

Though the interface between New Testament Christianity and the adjacent Mediterranean religions is the most obviously relevant ground for comparison, one must not neglect the wider province of Hellenistic literature. After all, the medium is sometimes the message,

and the early Christians used the same media everyone else at the time did. We miss the obvious because we stand too close to it, and one example is the gospel presentation of Jesus as a divine hero. Traditional theology tells us not to admire Jesus as a hero but to worship him as a savior who humbled himself so we might be exalted. That certainly captures a major New Testament theme, but no Sunday school child has ever missed that the gospels nonetheless depict Jesus as a hero who wins every argument and every open heart, a wielder of super powers who defeats demonic super-villains. The Jesus of the epistles is a savior and a sacrifice, but the Jesus of the gospels comes across as a hero and a paragon. This we have all seen, but scholars studying Hellenistic literature have helped us realize what we are seeing. Clyde Weber Votaw (*The Gospels and Contemporary Biographies in the Greco-Roman World,* 1915; English 1970), Helmut Koester and James M. Robinson (*Trajectories through Early Christianity,* 1971), Theodore J. Weeden *(Mark: Traditions in Conflict,* 1971), and Charles H. Talbert (*What Is a Gospel?* 1977) have shown beyond refutation, against those few who still quixotically hold otherwise, that the gospels are not some new Christian genre (as Rudolf Bultmann had supposed) but are part and parcel of the well-known ancient genre of aretalogy or hero biography. Like others of their kind, the gospel narratives feature the divine annunciation and miraculous conception of their hero, a child prodigy episode, many miracle healings and exorcisms, nature miracles, popular acclaim followed by rejection, death or the threat of it, and miraculous deliverance, followed by assumption into heaven. George W. E. Nickelsburg ("The Genre and Function of the Markan Passion Narrative," 1980) showed how naturally this genre's conventions hybridized with the old Jewish traditional tale of the young Jew, faithful to the Torah amid a pagan world, the object of envy and plotting, finally vindicated by God's providence. Ancient examples included Joseph, Daniel, and Ahikar. Nickelsburg traced the parallel with the gospel Passion narratives, showing once again how familiar the Christian stories would have sounded to new hearers. These scholars are vindicating the case made long ago by Lord Raglan (Fitzroy James Henry Somerset) in his book, *The Hero* (1936), and Otto Ranck in *The Myth of the Birth of the Hero* (1914).

The story of Jesus conforms in whole and in part to the universal Mythic Hero Archetype of which Joseph Campbell made so much, in Jungian fashion, in *The Hero with a Thousand Faces* (1949).

What the Bible was to Judaism and Christianity, Homer's *Iliad* and *Odyssey* were to the ancient Greeks. These books remained alive and larger than life throughout the early Christian period, and it would be surprising if Homer had not exercised at least some influence on the New Testament. Vernon K. Robbins ("By Land and by Sea: The We-Passages and Ancient Sea-Voyages," 1978) solved the long-standing puzzle of the "we" sections of the Book of Acts by reference to Homer. When the Acts narrator occasionally switches from third-person narrative to first-person, does it denote his presence on the scene? Is part of Acts an eye-witness account? Robbins deflated that tire rather neatly by showing that the first-person narrative was simply an ancient Hellenistic literary technique used to increase the vividness of sea-voyage narratives in particular. Sure enough, just about every one of the "we" passages in Acts occurs when the characters are voyaging on the briny deep. Case closed. Those wanting to view the New Testament as historically accurate were disturbed even more by Dennis R. MacDonald (*The Homeric Epics and the Gospel of Mark,* 2000) when he traced so many striking parallels between the Gospel's Jesus epic and Homer's to suggest that Mark had largely Christianized portions of the *Iliad* and the *Odyssey.* Not all are persuaded by every parallel adduced, but some parallels are so pronounced as virtually to prove a significant dependence upon Homer.

Similarly, Lilian Portefaix (*Sisters Rejoice! Paul's Letter to the Philippians and Luke-Acts as Received by First-Century Philippian Women,* 1988) made clear, against more timid earlier scholars who argued merely for "common motifs," that Acts makes extensive use of Euripides' *Bacchae* rather than historical reporting. Robert Eisenman (*James: The Brother of Jesus,* 1997) has made Josephus's use of Acts equally clear. Robbins (*Ancient Quotes and Anecdotes: From Crib to Crypt,* 1989), Burton Mack, Wayne A. Meeks *(The First Urban Christians,* 1983), and Abraham J. Malherbe (*Social Aspects of Early Christianity*, 1983; *Paul and the Popular Philosophers,* 1989) have all identified various New Testament literary forms and tech-

niques with their counterparts in Hellenistic education, for instance showing how school children were assigned to create "pronouncement stories" indicating what Socrates or Diogenes *would have* said on such and such a topic. That is exactly what Bultmann and other earlier form critics had suggested early Christians did, perhaps under prophetic trance, when they produced new sayings of Jesus.

A very different use of Hellenistic literature meets us in the writings of John Boswell (*Early Christianity, Homosexuality, and Social Tolerance*, 1980) and Robin Scroggs (*New Testament and Homosexuality*, 1983). They share the task of trying to make sense of the sketchy, if any, Pauline references to homosexuality. The relevant Greek words appear so seldom in ancient sources that one cannot know exactly what it was Paul meant to condemn when he exiled *arsenokoitai* and *malakoi* from heaven. What did it mean to go "against nature"? Can we shed light on these questions by reviewing what other ancient Greek writers may have said on the subject?

One of the newest divisions of New Testament study is the application to the text of the social sciences, specifically anthropology and sociology. Perhaps the most fundamental, overarching work is that done by sociologists of knowledge Peter L. Berger (*The Sacred Canopy*, 1969) and Thomas V. Luckmann with Berger (*The Social Construction of Reality*, 1967). These books reach deeply into the religious mindset and explain the social dynamics of belief that are so clearly and colorfully on display in the New Testament. How do social identities and loyalties affect whether one will break away and join a new religious movement? What mental strategies are involved in shunning doubt and confessing faith? Do these processes betray intellectual dishonesty or create fortress mentalities? How do polemic and the defense of faith persuade people—when and if they ever do? How is the individual to deal with faceless corporate powers whose yoke one inherits from one's ancestors? Can Christ redeem us from them? What sort of social existence would follow? Berger and Luckmann have shown the very human social and psychological side of theology.

Those denominated "social science critics" of the New Testament work by analogy, seeking to understand long-vanished first-century

communities on the inevitable and necessary assumption that they would have functioned the same way such groups do today. One outstanding example is the work of John G. Gager (*Kingdom and Community,* 1975), who imposes the parameters of a modern Third World Revitalization Movement onto the data of the Gospels to see how well it fits the data. Was Jesus leading a movement to preserve the older Jewish way of life against incursions from Roman Hellenism, as Judah Maccabee did a century and a half earlier? Bruce J. Malina (*The New Testament World,* 1981) compares New Testament data with what present-day peasant sociology tells us about values and roles in Mediterranean societies that have not changed much since biblical times. Do the resultant anthropological paradigms make new sense of some passages? Why, for instance, would Jesus tell people to turn the other cheek? Who could be expected to listen to such advice? Why is the author of 1 Timothy so suspicious of young widows and their possible escapades? What stereotypes make sense of these things? Malina has done an excellent job of bringing much of the underlying "mundane" detail of the New Testament to life.

Two precursors of New Testament sociology and anthropology as practiced today deserve mention: C. F. D. Moule and M. J. Field. The former (*The Birth of the New Testament,* 1962) set his radar to pick up a great deal of "background" data, the things we take for granted when we are busy reading the texts for theology and ethics, and he managed to piece together an amazingly comprehensive reconstruction of what the New Testament Christian communities must have been like economically, socially, and politically. Gerd Theissen (*The Social Setting of Pauline Christianity: Essays on Corinth,* 1982) tried the same sort of experiment, this time with the aid of the tools of sociological analysis, and did the same fine job, bringing to life the churches of the apostolic era. It is instructive to compare his almost mediumistic interrogation of the long-dead Corinthian church with the on-site anthropological research of Felicitas D. Goodman (*Speaking in Tongues: A Cross-Cultural Study of Glossolalia,* 1974) into Mexican Pentecostal congregations. They fit together pretty well.

In *Angels and Ministers of Grace* (1972), Field brought his years of field observation in Arabian and African villages to bear on the

biblical stories of angelic visitations and miraculous births. He wondered if the stories of Sarah, Mrs. Manoah, Elizabeth, and Mary were rooted in the same practice whereby a supposedly barren woman was enabled to bear children after a visit from an itinerant holy man who would sleep with her, impregnating her. The fault was with the husband, not the wife, and the intervention of the holy man ("angel") would save face for the man. Is that what was happening in the Bible?

Francis Watson (*Paul, Judaism, and the Gentiles,* 1986) added a sociological dimension to the current discussion of whether Paul really meant to teach "justification by faith" as understood by Martin Luther. Was he instead trying to negotiate the entrance of one ethnic group into a religious tradition hitherto bound up with another? When he argued that "works of the law" do not avail for salvation, was he really saying that gentile converts need not embrace alien cultural mores? Perhaps it had nothing at all to do with moral behavior versus believing in things.

Early Christian diversity

Walter Kaufman (*The Faith of a Heretic,* 1961) charged that Christian theologians were able to claim biblical warrant for their beliefs only by "gerrymandering" the text, highlighting the portions of the Bible one accepted and tacitly ignoring the others. But not all were quite so blind as to what they were doing. Ernst Käsemann, one of Bultmann's most brilliant disciples, was once asked by the World Council of Churches to write something up on the New Testament canon as the basis for ecumenical unity among the churches. What he turned in ("The Canon of the New Testament and the Unity of the Church," 1951) must have been a disappointment, for he had to be honest and admit that the official canon is itself the greatest impetus to *dis*unity! Every New Testament writer clashes with another. Rival gospel messages collide. Prophets contradict one another. And there is no sectarian or schismatic who cannot find a square yard of the text on which to take his stand! Käsemann's doctoral mentor, the great Rudolf Bultmann, had already demonstrated as much at great length in his masterpiece, *Theology of the New Testament* (1951). Before him, F. C. Baur of Tübingen University had shaken the theological

world by his demonstration of the warring strife that divided the earliest church right down the middle. The trouble is, devout church people do not want to hear such conclusions, preferring to maintain a Sunday school picture of the first-generation church as a model of harmony and sweet concord. Since no church has ever been like that in real life, one might think it would be more useful to study an ancient church beset by its own factionalism to see if we may learn something from their trials and errors. But the radical disunity of the early Christian movement should come as no surprise once we realize how many elements contributed to it from the variegated environment we have just been looking at. Many kinds of pre-Christians became many kinds of Christians.

Serious reckoning with primitive Christian disunity, or "diversity" if one prefers, began with the Tübingen School of Ferdinand Christian Baur and his disciples, including Edward Zeller (*Contents and Origin of the Acts of the Apostles,* 1876), Albrecht Ritschl, Franz Overbeck, Adolf Hilgenfeld, and others. Baur (*Paul: The Apostle of Jesus Christ,* 2 vols., 1873, 1875; *Church History of the First Three Centuries,* 1879) saw that all the canonical New Testament writings presupposed a long-lasting struggle between two major ecclesiastical parties whose figureheads were Paul and Peter. Peter, as well as James, the brother of Jesus, plus the other eleven apostles, spearheaded a nationalistic Jesus religion distinguished initially by hostility to any mission of preaching among the gentiles and later by the insistence that gentile converts join them in faithful Torah observance. These Jewish Christians forged a temporary accord with their rivals, led by Paul, who championed, especially among the gentile "God-fearers" who admired Judaism from the margins of the synagogue without turning proselyte, a gospel requiring only faith in Jesus and baptism in his name. Over time, Pauline Christianity became more and more closely assimilated to the salvation-sacramentalism of the mystery religions until at last Paul could even be described as "the second founder of Christianity." On the Petrine side of the fence, canonical writings included Matthew, James, and Revelation. On the Pauline side were the Pauline epistles, Hebrews, Mark, and John. Once the two sides patched up their differences and emerged into his-

tory as Catholic orthodoxy, the bond was cemented by the production of: the Pastoral Epistles, which made Paul sound safely Catholic; 1 Peter, which remodeled Peter in Pauline terms; 2 Peter, urging a Petrine reinterpretation of Paul; and most of all Luke and Acts, which sought to parallel Peter and Paul in such a way that no fan of either could repudiate the other since God performed the same feats and spoke the same gospel through both. Baur's reconstruction has stood the test of time despite the desperate efforts of J. B. Lightfoot and many subsequent conservative apologists to tear it down. Despite the retrenching efforts of neo-traditionalists, important critics, including Hans-Joachim Schoeps (*Paul,* 1959; *Jewish Christianity,* 1969), Oscar Cullmann (*Peter: Disciple, Apostle, Martyr,* 1953), and to a real but lesser extent Jacob Jervell (*The Unknown Paul,* 1984), have pressed Baur's insights further with new illuminating results.

Bruno Bauer and subsequent admirers, the so-called Dutch Radical critics, would soon shed a whole new light on F. C. Baur's reconstruction by arguing that all the relevant sources were later than Baur had supposed, none of them being genuinely Pauline. What Baur had missed seeing was that the strife between Petrine, Torah-observant Christianity and Pauline, Torah-free Christianity was an allegorical proxy war between two well-known factions of the second century. The Petrinists were, of course, the emerging Roman Catholics who wanted to retain the Jewish Old Testament as part of scripture—not that they were paying much attention to the minutiae of Levitical sacrifice and so forth. The Paulinists had to be Marcionites who exalted Paul and believed Jews and Christians worshiped two separate Gods and that Christians should therefore have their own scriptures and not try to co-opt the Jewish ones. That was the real point of Pauline freedom from the Law. There had never been any real evidence of Pauline Christians in the first century. The Pauline and anti-Pauline texts made much more sense as monuments to second-century struggles and compromises.

Most scholars, even F. C. Baur, did not give the Dutch critics the time of day and thereby missed a valuable puzzle piece. However, Walter Bauer was so keen-eyed that he saw the relevance of Marcionite Christianity for the true shape of Christian diversity in the sec-

ond and third centuries in his great book, *Orthodoxy and Heresy in Earliest Christianity* (1934; English 1971). Bauer was in effect looking at the second-century church to see if anything like F. C. Baur had detected in the first century was going on a century later. If the Dutch Radicals were right, Bauer was looking at the same struggle, only without the allegorical veil of Peter and Paul. It was like reading the apocalyptic cipher account of the Hasmonean struggle in Daniel, then reading Josephus's straightforward version of it in his *Jewish Antiquities*.

At any rate, Walter Bauer looked over the landscape of second-century Christianity, closely examining virtually every scrap of surviving evidence, and what he saw was a world in which numerous competing Christianities existed side by side, a world in which the very word *Christian* might refer not to Catholics but to Marcionites or Gnostics, depending on which form of the faith had taken root first. He showed how Basilidean Gnosticism and Marcionism were the first form of the faith in Edessa, while various forms of Gnosticism constituted the first-fruits of Christianity in Egypt. Asia Minor venerated the apostle Paul as the founder of Gnosticism and Encratism. Catholicism was spreading outward from Rome and would manage to squeeze most everyone out in a century or two. Bauer thus called the bluff of the hitherto prevalent model of church history once set forth by second-century church historian Hegesippus, namely that Jesus had taught pristine Christian doctrine to the twelve apostles, who then taught it to their successors, the bishops of the various mission churches throughout the Mediterranean. This pure version of the faith was thought to have been crystallized in the Apostles' Creed and other summations of "apostolic tradition" supplied by late second-century Catholics like Irenaeus and Tertullian. To disturb the peace, according to the traditional view, Satan had begun to plant heretical doctrines like weeds amid the wheat, whispering blasphemies into the ears, first of Simon Magus, father of all heresies, and then to his successors, including Apelles, Cerdo, and Marcion. Apparently Satan had already made preliminary sorties even in the Pauline churches since Paul, too, had opponents to correct, but the apostle must have been able to put out the fires. Heresy made its big debut and settled in

for the long haul only in the second century, according to the scheme of Hegesippus, repeated by Eusebius, Constantine's court theologian, a couple of centuries later. All this turned out to be revisionist propaganda penned by the theological winners, the church of Constantine's choosing. Scriptures of the kinds of Christianity that lost out were banned and burnt. Luckily the monks of the St. Pachomius monastery in Egypt thought to bury their library instead of destroying it. It was of course the Nag Hammadi collection, unearthed in 1945. Walter Bauer did not yet have these texts available, but they would have strengthened his case many-fold. Those documents attest to whole extinct branches of the Christian evolutionary tree, Christians who believed Jesus was the reincarnation of Seth, the Second Coming of Melchizedek, the reappearance of Zoroaster. A more recent scholar setting forth the elements of the Bauer thesis in his own way is Bart Ehrman (*Lost Christianities,* 2003).

While Walter Bauer's work might be viewed as a re-application of F. C. Baur and Bultmann to second-century Christianity, the team of Helmut Koester and James M. Robinson, both deeply involved with the Nag Hammadi discoveries, turned Walter Bauer's lens back onto the New Testament, seeking to trace trajectories of development back from second-century fruits to first-century origins (*Trajectories through Early Christianity,* 1971). What New Testament elements might have been the most likely stimulation for later Gnosticism? Can we understand aspects of the New Testament better in light of the later developments they may have given rise to? For instance, it appears that a sayings collection like Q, underlying Matthew and Luke, or Thomas, which is a later sayings sampler as I view it, presupposes Christians of some sort who must have venerated Jesus as a revealer rather than a hero or a savior sacrifice. Then might we not infer works like Q represent the seeds of Christian Gnosticism? What became of the hero-worship treatment of Jesus presupposed in all the gospel miracle stories? Perhaps such tales were the stock in trade of itinerant apostles and exorcists whose exploits we find in the second and third centuries under apostolic names in the Acts of Andrew, John, Paul, Peter, and Thomas. Knowing what was going on in the second century may tell us what first-century developments were giv-

ing rise to our New Testament writings. Burton Mack attempted a rough taxonomy of such proto-Christian movements in *A Myth of Innocence* (1988) and *Who Wrote the New Testament? The Origins of the Christian Myth* (1995).

The seemingly pivotal role of Marcion has occasioned considerable scholarly debate. More traditional treatments like Henry Chadwick's *The Early Church* (1967) and Hans von Campenhausen's *The Formation of the Christian Bible* (1972) do not downplay Marcion's vast importance, but his creative role may have been even greater than these fine historians have estimated. R. Joseph Hoffmann (*Marcion: On the Restitution of Christianity,* 1984) has given all the old evidence a new look, placing Marcion a bit earlier historically than most do, while absolving him of some of the crimes he has been charged with, such as anti-Semitism or anti-Judaism. Hoffmann also dissects the Epistle to the Ephesians, showing how much sense it makes (once certain likely interpolations are bracketed) as a rewrite of the original Marcionite Epistle to the Laodiceans. Joseph B. Tyson (*Marcion and Luke-Acts: A Defining Struggle,* 2006) has drawn new attention to the neglected research of John Knox in his *Marcion and the New Testament* (1942), in which he argued that Marcion's original gospel was not a bowdlerized epitome of canonical Luke, as most hold, but was rather a shorter pre-canonical version. The Tübingen School had also held this. Knox also showed the absolutely central significance of Marcion's new Christian scripture as the model which Catholics imitated with their own counter-writings to form the conventional New Testament.

Luke-Acts and the Pastoral Epistles seem to have been major instruments for forging, reinforcing, or memorializing the eventual merging of Petrinism and Paulinism (F. C. Baur) or Catholicism's co-opting of Marcionites (Dutch Radicals and Knox). This fact raises new questions about the authorship of these texts. If Marcion did use a shorter, more original version of Luke than that which appears in the canon, and if Acts is a counter-blast to Marcionism, what becomes of the near-universal consensus that Acts was written as a sequel to Luke by the same author? Robert C. Tannehill (*The Narrative Unity of Luke-Acts,* 2 vols., 1986, 1989) is only the latest of many who have

made good sense of Luke-Acts as a literary and thematic unity. On the other hand, there have long been persistent doubts as to common authorship. Albert C. Clark (*The Acts of the Apostles: A Critical Edition,* 1933) and A. W. Argyle ("The Greek of Luke and Acts," 1974) have both collected vocabulary differences between Luke and Acts that seem to bear no special significance other than as the kind of minor idiosyncrasies separating one author from another. So we have two books with a vast amount in common but with a surprising number of little loose ends. One could make sense of both groupings of data if an earlier original version of Luke (Ur-Lukas) was heavily rewritten by the same writer who composed Acts as a sequel. Henry Cadbury and Kirsopp Lake, in one of their many essays in *Christian Beginnings* (vol. 4, 1933), had noted how the author of Acts appeared to have plucked various odd items from Mark, assuming it to have been his gospel source, and inserted them in Acts instead of Luke. For instance, Luke omits the charge that Jesus threatened to destroy the temple, but Acts ascribes it to Stephen's accusers. If the author of Acts were instead the redactor of a pre-existent Ur-Lukas, it would make a bit more sense to imagine him switching items from Ur-Lukas since it would fit with his wider editorial activity.

Consistent with the theory that the Pastorals and Luke-Acts helped to pad out and counterbalance the Marcionite Pauline canon are the speculations that Luke-Acts and the Pastorals also came from the same author. Stephen G. Wilson (*Luke and the Pastoral Epistles,* 1979) and Jerome D. Quinn ("The Last Volume of Luke: The Relation of Luke-Acts to the Pastoral Epistles," 1978) have credited all three to the same hand. P. N. Harrison (*The Problem of the Pastoral Epistles,* 1921) showed in great detail not only how dissimilar the three Pastorals are to any of the rest of the letters credited to Paul but also how similar they are in concept and wording both to Luke-Acts and to second-century works like 1 Clement, the *Didache,* the Epistle of Barnabas, the Epistle to Diognetus, Ignatius, and Polycarp. Hans von Campenhausen once suggested ("Polycarp von Smyrna und die Pastoralbriefe," 1964) that Polycarp, bishop of Smyrna, was himself the author of the Pastorals. More recently, Stephan Hermann Huller (*Against Polycarp,* 2000) put two and two together, concluding that

Polycarp must be the one who padded out Ur-Lukas and then composed Acts. It makes sense. Huller also seconded Alvin Boyd Kuhn's guess that the Theophilus to whom the author dedicated Luke-Acts was none other than Theophilus of Antioch, Polycarp's fellow bishop. Huller makes the intriguing suggestion that Polycarp was also Bultmann's Ecclesiastical Redactor of John. One more wrinkle: in his neglected essay, "Concerning the So-Called First Letter of Paul to Timothy" (1807), Friedrich Daniel Ernst Schleiermacher showed that 1 Timothy was not the work of whomever had written what we call 2 Timothy and Titus, but that someone else had written it as a combination of the two, superceding the church manual provisions of the earlier works.

As I have already intimated, scholars have found it needful to supplement Walter Bauer's thesis at some points, mainly because of two areas of evidence he either neglected or did not have available. In an appendix to the English translation of Bauer's *Orthodoxy and Heresy,* Georg Strecker sought to fill in the gap left by Bauer's neglect of Jewish Christianity, an artificial term imposed by modern scholars on a collection of groups well known from the second and third centuries including the Ebionites, Elchasites, Nazarenes, and others. Some of these sects had never heard of the virgin birth, others accepted it. Some excoriated Paul and his legacy as that of the Antichrist. Some professed loyalty to Peter, others to James the Just. All pledged fealty to the Mosaic Law, depending on how one interpreted it. Some held that all Jesus-believers must be circumcised, while others merely defended their own right as Jews to continue the practice among their own ranks. Such Jewish Christians continued to thrive in Syria, Palestine, and elsewhere, eventually dying on the vine as they were finally seen as too Christian to attract fellow Jews and too Jewish to attract gentiles who preferred the Torah-free alternative.

Surely the major work to emerge in recent years concerning Jewish Christianity has been Robert Eisenman's *James: The Brother of Jesus,* in which he paints the head of the Jerusalem church as a revolutionary saint in his own right, virtually eclipsing his brother as the head of Jerusalem Christianity, which Eisenman identifies with the Dead Sea Scrolls community. The central drama of the scrolls is the

opposition among the Teacher of Righteousness, the Spouter of Lies, and the Wicked Priest. Eisenman casts James in the role of the Teacher; Ananus, the high priest of the temple, as the Wicked Priest; and Paul as the Spouter of Lies, an apostate from within the community. Barbara Thiering (*Redating the Teacher of Righteousness,* 1979; *The Gospels and Qumran,* 1981; *The Qumran Origins of the Christian Church,* 1983; *Jesus the Man,* 1992) also argues that the Qumran-New Testament link was close, but in her view the Teacher was John the Baptist and the Spouter of Lies was the same as the Wicked Priest, both referring to Jesus. This is not so wild as it seems to her critics, as New Testament scholars have frequently associated John with the Dead Sea Scrolls sect, and ever since D. F. Strauss *(The Life of Jesus Critically Examined,* 1835), many have understood Jesus as having repudiated the sect of John with its dour asceticism. Thiering rightly observes that the typically overblown rhetoric of the scrolls would call someone wicked if he relaxed the sect's standards in order to accept outsiders, such as by eating with publicans and sinners. And while all the Qumran sectarians were considered priests, Jesus, she thinks, wanted to extend the priesthood to all of pious Israel precisely in the manner of the people's prophets of post-exilic Judea (see Paul D. Hanson, *The Dawn of Apocalyptic,* 1979). In their eyes, this would make Jesus the Wicked Priest. Ceslas Spicq (*L'Epitre aux Hebreux,* 1952) argued ingeniously that the Epistle to the Hebrews may have been written to a particular group of Hebrews, namely Qumran Christians. He did not think to identify the two movements as wholes but only thought of some Qumran covenanters joining Christianity. How much more powerful does his argument become if either Eisenman or Thiering is correct!

Hans-Joachim Schoeps is perhaps the premiere interpreter of Jewish Christianity (see his book of that title, 1969). A more recent survey of much of the same ground is Gerd Lüdemann's *Opposition to Paul in Jewish Christianity,* 1989). Richard N. Longenecker *(The Christology of Early Jewish Christianity,* 1970) isolates one major theme of Jewish-Christian theology, detailing its connection with similar motifs among other early Christian parties. Hugh J. Schonfield (*Jesus: A New Biography,* 1939; *The Passover Plot,* 1965; *The*

Pentecost Revolution, 1974; *The Essene Odyssey,* 1984) envisions Jewish Christianity as nationalistic not only in terms of preserving the markers of Jewish ethnicity among the Diaspora but politically as well. When Paul is accused by local Romans of membership in a sect that "turns the world upside down," Schonfield says, they are confusing him with the violence-prone Jewish Christians of Jerusalem. But even Pauline Christianity is, for Schonfield (*Those Incredible Christians,* 1968), rather more Jewish than many would make it, as Schonfield sees intimations of Kabbalistic mysticism in the Prison Epistles (Colossians, Ephesians, Philippians), which other scholars tend to deny Paul and understand as tinged with Hellenistic Gnosticism instead.

Long ago, Gotthold Lessing, advocate of rational religion, published an essay called "New Hypothesis on the Evangelists as Merely Human Historians" (1778), in which he proposed giving the gospels a fresh look, setting aside our accustomed theology and seeing the texts for themselves. That is no easy task, but he reasoned we would be aided by asking how the ancients understood the gospels, reading them with different lenses. Spotlighting Matthew, Lessing noticed that various ancient Jewish Christian sects found Matthew easily compatible with their beliefs, even necessitating them. Other scholars have pressed Lessing's question further, attempting to read some of what F. C. Baur considered Jewish Christian documents from a genuinely Jewish standpoint. For instance, O. Lamar Cope (*Matthew: A Scribe Trained for the Kingdom of Heaven,* 1976) pointed out neglected features of rabbinism in Matthew's text. What, for instance, did Matthew mean by having Jesus answer the rich young ruler, "Why ask me about the good? The good is one" (Matt. 19:17)? Cope shows how the wording reflects rabbinic views tantamount to James 2:10-11, namely that the Torah is an indivisible whole so that it is a mistake to ask which commandant or duty is more important than all others.

George Howard (*Hebrew Gospel of Matthew,* 1995) has extensively analyzed a medieval Hebrew version of Matthew, concluding that it is not, as had been thought, merely a translation made by Jews for Jews to use in debate against Christians but that it has as much of

a claim to be the original as the standard Greek text does, especially since it harbors some odd similarities here and there with the Gospel of Thomas and the Diatessaron. Suppose Matthew, like Josephus, saw to the production of his works in more than one language at a time, anticipating different audiences?

Jane Schaberg (*The Illegitimacy of Jesus,* 1988) compared Matthew's genealogy and nativity story with various Jewish Targums (ancient Aramaic paraphrases of the Bible) and concluded that, contra our Christmastime expectations, Matthew was not even trying to tell us Jesus had been miraculously conceived, only that his dubious origin had afterward been sanctified by God, who had similarly blessed the illicit unions of Bath-Sheba, Rahab, Ruth, and Tamar.

Arlo J. Nau (*Peter in Matthew,* 1992) skillfully peeled back the layers of Matthew, focusing on the gospel's confusing treatment of Peter. He showed convincingly how an earlier redactor had tried to undo Mark's derisive treatment of the apostle, trading the "Get behind me" saying for the "Thou art Peter" blessing, as well as by adding Peter's water-walking alongside Jesus and having Jesus grant Peter the keys of authority. But then a subsequent redactor, less enamored of the ostensible prince of apostles, took Peter back down a peg, restoring the Satan put-down, having Peter sink, and having Jesus give the keys to the twelve collectively. In this way, Nau's stratigraphy lays bare the politics and the evolution of the Jewish-Christian community behind the gospel.

Josephine M. Ford (*Revelation,* Anchor Bible, 1975) took very seriously the primitive, virtually pre-Christian coloring of the Book of Revelation and argued that at least a substantial portion of it was the work of John the Baptist. That would explain the use of the title "Lamb of God" only here, outside of the Fourth Gospel where Jesus is given the title by none other than John the Baptist!

Sam K. Williams (*The Death of Jesus as Saving Event,* 1975) has the distinction of figuring out the transition between Jewish Christianity and gentile Christianity by way of the atonement doctrine. Williams argues that Paul incorporated a previous text or slogan into Romans 3:25-26, one which originally meant that God had decided to accept the faithful martyrdom of Jesus as an unprecedented sacri-

fice on behalf of the repentant gentiles, to provide ritual purity for them so they could, in Christ, join Jews as the people of God. This was all based on the Diaspora Jewish way of understanding Jewish martyr deaths as atoning for whatever sins of the Jews had called forth persecution to purify them. Martyr blood could atone for the martyr's generation. But what of their gentile persecutors? Animal sacrifices had atoned for the sins of Jews—and those of Jewish Christians—but what was there to help the unwashed pagans? God had now decided to accept the blood of Jesus as a sacrificial lamb on their behalf. The irony was, the cross was first thought to be a way of including gentile outsiders into the Christian fold and wound up excluding Jews.

Bauer could not have known of the Nag Hammadi finds, but subsequent scholars have made much of them. Bultmann's student James M. Robinson shepherded the texts into English publication (*The Nag Hammadi Library in English,* 1977), as well as writing numerous incisive articles showing how Gnostic trends in the texts reflected back on conventional New Testament texts. For instance, why does the Gospel of John have several chapters of revelatory dialogue at the Last Supper, unlike the Synoptic Gospels? Robinson recognized a link to the Gnostic dialogue genre represented in Nag Hammadi (e.g., *Apocryphon of James, Dialogue of the Savior*), wherein Jesus gives long post-Easter interviews to the disciples, finally giving them straight answers, no more parables and symbols. Pheme Perkins made these "resurrection press conferences" the special subject of her book, *The Gnostic Dialogue* (1980).

Walter Schmithals (*Gnosticism in Corinth,* 1971; *Paul and the Gnostics,* 1972; *The Apocalyptic Movement,* 1975) found in Nag Hammadi ample confirmation for his view that Gnosticism had preceded Christianity as a form of esoteric Judaism, especially since the texts frequently center on Adam, Melchizedek, Seth, or other ancient Jewish heroes as channels of revelation, Jesus being almost an afterthought. Richard J. Arthur found evidence of Dositheanism in the Gospel of Philip. Jerome K. Isser's monograph, *The Dositheans* (1976), provides good background for Arthur's work, still unpublished.

Catherine Clark Kroeger ("1 Timothy 2:12—A Classicist's View," 1984) argued compellingly that 1 Timothy does not contain a general prohibition of women teaching but rather forbids the propagation of a particular Gnostic version of the Eden story found in *On the Origin of the World* 115:31-116:8, namely that Eve gave life to Adam and that the archons afterward deceived Adam into believing he was first, not Eve.

Simone Petrement (*A Separate God,* 1990) tried to rehabilitate the ancient apologists' contention that Gnosticism began within Christianity as a derivative Christian heresy. Petrement exercised fantastic ingenuity to show in case after case how this or that Gnostic mytheme might possibly have developed out of someone's zany misreading of this or that New Testament text. For instance, why did the Gnostics write of a deity called Adamas, "Man"? Most scholars see a reference to the archaic doctrine of the Primal Man who sacrificed himself to bring about the creation. But Petrement wants to cut off such roots for Christianity, which she would rather see as a novel revelation to the world. So her guess, surely ingenious, is that some idiot reading how Jesus spoke of himself as the Son of Man deduced there must be a God named Man.

Elaine Pagels (*The Gnostic Gospels,* 1979) attempted the same kind of reconstruction ventured by Moule in *Birth of the New Testament,* only she took as her area of inquiry the Nag Hammadi texts and reconstructed what ancient Gnostic communities might have been like. This was crucially important because Pagels was going against the general scholarly tendency of treating these works as if they were some kind of science fiction novels written in social isolation. Of course, they were not; the Gnostic texts, no matter how far-fetched they may strike us, were the testaments of living faith of particular groups of ancient believers. It is important to try to put the hints together and describe such vanished social entities.

David Noel Friedman & Robert M. Grant wrote the earliest exposition (*The Secret Sayings of the Living Jesus,* 1960) of the first Nag Hammadi book to be made public, the Gospel of Thomas. So convinced were the authors of its Valentinian Gnostic tilt, they translated and interpreted its sayings in almost perverse ways to make

them sound as bizarre and as Gnostic as possible. Later works, such as Steven L. Davies's *The Gospel of Thomas and Christian Wisdom* (1983), made it clear Thomas was by no means simply a product of hard-line Gnosticism. Much of what had sounded Gnostic actually partook rather of Philonic speculation and of the Encratite celibacy preaching.

Any consideration of Gnosticism and the New Testament must include notice of John's gospel and its possible Gnostic character. C. H. Dodd's *The Interpretation of the Fourth Gospel* (1953) draws extensive verbal and conceptual parallels between John and Gnosticism but just as much with Hermeticism and other Hellenistic sources. Bultmann's magisterial *The Gospel of John: A Commentary* (1971) leaves no doubt as to the heavily Gnostic character of the Johannine Jesus, furnishing extensive parallel passages which one would hardly know to ascribe to John or to the Mandaeans unless Bultmann told you so. His case seems irrefutable, but so distasteful is the very idea of Gnostic influence on scripture that some prefer any possible alternative to explain the use of terms like "light versus darkness," "spirit versus flesh," and "death versus eternal life." Raymond E. Brown, in his Anchor Bible volumes on John (1966, 1970), argues the Dead Sea Scrolls evidence a similar form of esoteric idiom. But this is no real alternative since, as Bultmann recognized, the Dead Sea Scrolls themselves represent a Gnosticizing form of Judaism—like the Gospel of John itself!

Bultmann also paid attention to source criticism for John, dividing it into three basic documents: a Gnostic discourse collection, a book of signs (miracles), and a Passion narrative. Robert T. Fortna has carried Bultmann's work further (*The Gospel of Signs,* 1970), brilliantly reconstructing the kind of Christian community that must have lain behind the gospel with its "realized eschatology," which is the belief that the kingdom of God had already come in some nonliteral form.

Bultmann took note of the apparent disorder and discontinuities in John, how Jesus starts somewhere and winds up somewhere else without transition, how he seems to start a discourse in one chapter and pick it up without missing a beat in a later one. Bultmann ven-

tured a hypothetical rearrangement of the gospel, assuming its pages had once been scattered and put back together clumsily. Others, convinced of Bultmann's diagnosis but not of his prescription, tried their own hands at rearranging the gospel, including Thomas Cottam (*The Fourth Gospel Rearranged,* 1952) and F. R. Hoare (*The Original Order and Chapters of St. John's Gospel,* 1944).

As to the date of the Gospel, the Tübingen scholars placed it during the mid- to late-second century based on internal evidence. Conservatives rejoiced at the discovery of a papyrus fragment of Johannine text, now called the John Rylands Papyrus, which paleographical experts dated at about 125 CE, implying a date some half a century earlier for the original. Now one of Darrell J. Doughty's students, Alvin Padilla, has cast doubt on that judgment as circular and without adequate manuscript support. Louis J. Martyn (*History and Theology in the Fourth Gospel,* 1968) continued to press for a late first-, early second-century date based on internal references to the expulsion of Christian Jews from the synagogues toward the end of the first century. John A. T. Robinson ("The New Look on the Fourth Gospel," 1957; *Redating the New Testament,* 1976; *The Priority of John,* 1985) argued, largely on the basis of C. H. Dodd's case in *Historical Tradition in the Fourth Gospel* (1963), that John might be as early as the Synoptic Gospels, making use of many of the same oral traditions, just mixing them up into a different formula. Dodd was arguing merely that John might not have been a free creation by the evangelist, but rather based on earlier traditions, albeit much transformed. But Robinson, as well as A. M. Hunter (*According to John,* 1968), argued as if Dodd had placed the entire Gospel of John in the mid-first century and that it should be regarded as a repository of authentic sayings of Jesus. Robinson, the controversial bishop of Woolwich, loved to twit his public by embracing radical liberal theology on the one hand (*Honest to God,* 1963) and conservative critical positions on the other. At any rate, Maurice Casey (*Is John's Gospel True?* 1996) thoroughly demolished Robinson's position on John, as well as a number of other specious recent treatments of the Fourth Gospel.

Only recently have scholars begun to grasp the relevance for New Testament study of the second-century Apocryphal Acts of the Apos-

tles. These novelistic tales of the apostles Andrew and Matthias, John, Paul, Peter, Philip, and Thomas seem to be Christianized versions of the popular Hellenistic novels, as Rosa Söder argued *(Die apokryphen Apostelgeschichten und die romanhafte Literatur der Antike,* 1932). The two groups of texts share common conventions such as travelogues, dangerous sea voyages, providential interventions, apparent deaths, live entombments, and the survival of crucifixion. Ross S. Kraemer ("The Conversion of Women to Ascetic Forms of Christianity," 1980), Virginia Burrus (*Chastity as Autonomy,* 1987), Stevan L. Davies (*The Revolt of the Widows: The Social World of the Apocryphal Acts,* 1980), and Dennis R. MacDonald (*The Legend and the Apostle: The Battle for Paul in Story and Canon,* 1983) all began to realize that the second-century celibacy movement led by Tatian, Marcion, and various Nag Hammadi Gnostic writers had generated much of the underlying material in the Apocryphal Acts, even some of the later New Testament material. While MacDonald traced many traditions in the Pastoral Epistles and the Acts of Paul back to this strict Encratite spirituality, I showed in my book, *The Widow Traditions in Luke-Acts* (1997) that much of the material in Luke-Acts dealing with women, especially prophetic women and charismatic widows, must have stemmed from these circles.

During the renewed consideration of the Apocryphal Acts in the wake of the Nag Hammadi discovery, some began to question the canonical boundaries. Richard I. Pervo *(Profit with Delight: The Literary Genre of the Acts of the Apostles,* 1987) took aim at the supposedly great differences in theology, style, and historical accuracy that Edgar Schneemelcher, editor of *New Testament Apocrypha* (1959), had alleged existed between the canonical Acts and its non-canonical cousins, which Pervo found to be more fabricated than real. Scholarly special pleading for the innate superiority of the canonical material was revealed as a covert type of apologetics. The present volume has grown out of the realization that the old canonical boundaries are arbitrary and unjustifiable.

The historical Jesus

It seems safe to say the quest to excavate the historical Jesus from

beneath the cathedral of Christology that tradition had erected around him was motivated by a desire to free Western culture from the abuses of the institutional church. The name "Jesus Christ" had come to function as a corporate logo. He was an artificial character, like a fictive pitchman created by a company to give a personal face to its advertisements. Jesus was what theology and ecclesiastical politics needed him to be. So beginning with Hermann Samuel Reimarus *(The Aims of Jesus and His Disciples,* portions published by Lessing in 1778), historical critics began to treat the gospel texts as a historian treats any other ancient documents, no longer giving them a pass when they contradicted one another or were at variance with outside sources. Reimarus discerned several layers of contradictory rewriting, and when he focused on what was left over, that which survived scrutiny and could not be explained as church-serving mythology, what was left was a patriotic Jesus who sought to foment a peasant revolt against Rome. The revolution failed, and his disciples, their illusions shattered, decided to cut their losses by using Jesus as the figurehead for a new and lucrative endeavor which became Christianity.

David Friedrich Strauss's mercilessly systematic work is perhaps still the greatest ever written on the gospels, *The Life of Jesus Critically Examined* (1835, 1836). In its closely packed pages, he refuted both orthodox apologists and rationalist harmonizers, winning every round by showing how the gospels collected myths and legends about Jesus rather than historical facts. He left the teachings of Jesus relatively unmolested except he found Jesus could not have said anything attributed to him in John's gospel, which Strauss decided was more of a didactic drama than a piece of history.

Ernest Renan, a former Catholic seminarian, kicked up his own storm with a controversial look at Jesus (*The Life of Jesus,* 1863) as a social and religious reformer who won hearts among the simple multitudes in Galilee but got the cold shoulder from the Judeans of the south. Resorting to miracle-mongering, he won new attention there, but not all of it was positive, and the authorities finished him. Renan's literary engine was powered not by historical gasoline but by novelistic, sentimental ethanol.

Reimarus, Strauss, and Renan were scarcely spokesmen for Chris-

tianity, but many who sought the historical Jesus as Stanley sought Dr. Livingston in Africa were, in fact, committed churchmen who hoped the historical Jesus would prove their ally in renewing and liberalizing both Catholicism and Protestantism. Adolf von Harnack (*What Is Christianity?* 1900) distilled a liberal but non-political Jesus whose message was about God, not about himself. He preached God's fatherhood, the brotherhood of man, and the infinite value of the human soul: God and the soul, the soul and its God. This was the kernel of the gospel message, all else was merely husk and ought to be broken open and cast aside. Roman Catholic Modernist Alfred Loisy fired off a rejoinder (*The Gospel and the Church,* 1903) in which he set forth the theological manifesto of Modernism: the church need not fear biblical criticism and the consequent exposure of the gradual development of dogma in human hands. The gospel as Harnack described it was not the kernel inside the husk but rather the acorn, the subsequent development being the mighty oak. Catholicism was the gospel in its most mature form. However, the Catholic hierarchy saw bad news where Loisy saw glad tidings, so they excommunicated him, and his writings, never truly conservative, now showed their author to be far more historically radical than Harnack had ever thought of being.

Harnack's book was presented as a series of lectures to packed houses early in the morning in Berlin, and his views were popular in America. The great American spokesman for Protestant Liberalism in America was the preacher Harry Emerson Fosdick (*The Modern Use of the Bible,* 1924; *A General Introduction to the Bible,* 1938), a genuine scholar who set forth his creed of Jesus as the ultimate religious personality, a notion inherited from Albrecht Ritschl through his disciples Harnack and Wilhelm Herrmann *(The Communion of the Christian with God,* 1906).

Albert Schweitzer (*The Mystery of the Kingdom of God,* 1914) wrote a still-unmatched survey of research to his day, *The Quest of the Historical Jesus* (1910). Praising both Reimarus and Strauss, he only half shared their theories, advocating his own, one propounded at the same time by Johannes Weiss (*Jesus' Proclamation of the Kingdom of God,* 1892; English 1971), namely that Jesus' message,

though moral and pious at its heart, was thoroughly conditioned by Jesus' belief in the imminent eruption of the final judgment and the kingdom of God. His urging his disciples to liquidate all possessions for the sake of the starving poor, his preaching that men ought to renounce even defensive violence: all was predicated on the belief that the end would soon come, so all bets were off. There was no future to worry about or provide for. In this eleventh hour, one must perform absolute, unconditional righteousness, unmitigated by mundane demands since these were at the very point of vanishing altogether. As it happens, Jesus was disastrously mistaken, but even so, with his fire of religious delusion, he kindled a torch of service to God and man that we still cannot help calling Christlike.

Many followed Schweitzer, at least as far as admitting that Harnack-style liberalism was not the way and that theology mattered to Jesus, even if his theology was not quite the same as ours. With Jesus reclaimed as a sponsor for eschatology, many spoke of the urgency of repentance and demythologized apocalyptic into existentialism. Others doubted Schweitzer's reading of Jesus. Timothee Colani ("The Little Apocalypse of Mark 13," 1864; English 2003) showed how easily one might lift Mark 13:5-31 out of its artificial context to reveal a Jesus who, like Jeremiah, simply predicted the fall of unrepentant Jerusalem to her foes and then confessed he knew not when the sentence would be executed. Only by someone shoe-horning in a later apocalyptic tract did Jesus come to sound like a preacher of the end of the world. C. H. Dodd (*The Parables of the Kingdom,* 1935), followed by John A. T. Robinson (*Jesus and His Coming,* 1957), dissected the kingdom parables of the Synoptic Gospels to show they made sense in the lifetime of Jesus but that they referred to events unfolding in his own ministry, not his own eventual second coming on the clouds.

A greater degree of methodological rigor was added when Jesus researchers adopted the technique of form criticism, or form history, from Old Testament scholar Herman Gunkel (*Genesis,* 1901; English 1997; *An Introduction to the Psalms,* 1933; English 1998). Just as the oracles of the prophets and the folktales of the patriarchs had been transmitted by word of mouth through many centuries, the assump-

tion was that, before being written down, the sayings and stories of Jesus must have flowed along a stream of oral tradition during the years between Jesus and the writing of the gospels. As Schmithals ("The Parabolic Teachings in the Synoptic Traditions," 1997) has pointed out recently, this is all sheer surmise and the alternative is to admit that very much of the gospel materials are free creations by the evangelists and other anonymous Christians before them. In fact, ultra-radical Bruno Bauer had maintained that the Jesus figure was wholly fictitious, a literary invention of Mark the evangelist.

The classical form critics, Rudolf Bultmann (*History of the Synoptic Tradition,* 1931; English 1963), Martin Dibelius (*From Tradition to Gospel,* 1919; English 1934), Karl Ludwig Schmidt (*The Place of the Gospels in the General History of Literature,* 1923; English 2002), and Vincent Taylor (*The Formation of the Gospel Tradition,* 1933), did proceed on the assumption that oral tradition linked Jesus to the gospels, but they were by no means convinced that every bit of that material reached ultimately back to Jesus. In fact, the very nature of certain formal units such as the miracle story were deemed to be products of a secondary stage of composition coincident with the spread of Christianity among gentiles. They tried to imaginatively infer the *Sitz-im-Leben* (life setting) of each pericope—each unit of tradition such as a single miracle story, parable, or aphorism—which sometimes made sense only as a product of debate within the post-Jesus church, say in debate with Pharisees over the new sect's practices or as rationalizations of the gentile mission, something not on the table in Jesus' day. Norman Perrin (*The Kingdom of God in the Teaching of Jesus,* 1963; *Rediscovering the Teaching of Jesus,* 1976), a student of T. W. Manson and Joachim Jeremias, made it his business to trim with systematic rigor the inauthentic sayings of Jesus, crystallizing form-critical assumptions into a set of methodological criteria, foremost among them being the *criterion of dissimilarity.* If a saying attributed to Jesus sounds like some common Jewish or early Christian maxim, then the critic must assume it was borrowed by the Jesus tradition. Of course, it is possible for Jesus to have voiced opinions held in common with his contemporaries, but in that case one has not captured whatever may have been distinctive about him and

his ministry. Perrin and other critics received flack for this technique, which seemed to many, including conservative evangelical New Testament scholars like George Eldon Ladd (*Gospel of the Kingdom,* 1959; *The New Testament and Criticism,* 1966; *The Presence of the Future,* 1974; *A Theology of the New Testament,* 1974) and Gordon D. Fee (*Gospel and Spirit: Issues in New Testament Hermeneutics,* 1991), to be excessively skeptical. Yet the resultant view of Jesus preaching the kingdom of God is almost identical among all three of these scholars.

Martin Noth (*History of Pentateuchal Traditions,* 1948; English 1972), a great Old Testament historian, has contributed another form criterion that ought to be more widely utilized in New Testament studies, namely the *redundancy principle.* Stories portraying someone as bigger than life sometimes mention a name in passing—someone who does not really fill a role in the story. Noth suspects that such narratives originally may have been about the ones who now hug the shadows, whose exploits were mined for material. When we read about Moses *and* the unnamed elders, or Nadab and Abihu, the stories may not have been about Moses at all. This principle can be applied to stories in Acts featuring Paul, with Barnabas as his silent sidekick; the accounts originally may have been about Barnabas alone. Similarly, the story about Peter confronting Simon Magus in Acts 8 may have substituted Peter for Philip, who now lingers at the sidelines.

Form criticism is both an aid to understanding the gospel tradition and for getting back to the historical Jesus. Joachim Jeremias *(The Parables of Jesus,* 1947; English 1954) impressively peeled back layers of reinterpretation on the part of anonymous tradition bearers to reveal what he believed must be the authentic Jesus. In doing so, his successive levels of meaning were laid out in a manner that was both intellectually fascinating and spiritually edifying. Dennis E. Nineham's commentary on Mark remains a classic demonstration of form criticism (*Pelican Commentary on St. Mark,* 1963). In similar fashion, Gerd Theissen, best known for his innovative sociological treatments of the New Testament (*Sociology of Early Palestinian Christianity,* 1978), wrote a lucid, comprehensive, and invaluable guide to

the miracle stories (*The Miracle Stories of the Early Christian Tradition,* 1974; English 1983). Robert Alter (*The Art of Biblical Narrative,* 1981) drew attention in form-critical spirit to certain "type narratives" spanning the Old and New Testaments, familiar scenes with characters and settings that have been juggled and exchanged again and again but whose basic structure survives in various passages. One example is the story of a visiting Hebrew male meeting a potential mate by the well. The man defends the woman's right to the water and asserts his intent to marry her. Such a tale is told of Moses, Eleazer of Damascus, Jesus at Jacob's Well, and so on.

The next great phase of inquiry in gospel studies was that of the redaction critics. These scholars took off from the consensus of gospel source criticism, namely that Mark and Q were compilations of oral tradition and that Matthew and Luke used them as their principle sources. Some redaction critics have questioned this theory of Synoptic relationships, but most of the major works are based on it. Redaction critics compile the tiny verbal changes that later gospel writers seem to have made in rewriting their sources, eventually revealing certain instructive patterns. In this way, the distinctive theological and literary aims of each writer are revealed. Willi Marxsen was one of the pioneers in this field, working on Mark (*Mark: The Evangelist,* 1956; English 1969). Bultmann's student Hans Conzelmann (*The Theology of Saint Luke,* 1953; English 1961) revolutionized the study of Luke in perhaps the most extensive and impressive demonstration of the method and its strengths. Another Bultmann protégé, Günther Bornkamm, with a couple of his own students, Heinz Joachim Held and Gerhard Barth, applied redaction-critical tools to Matthew with profound results (*Tradition and Interpretation in Matthew,* first delivered as papers, 1948-57; English book, 1963). I would count the maverick Michael D. Goulder as an important redaction critic, though he equivocates on the priority of Mark and rejects Q altogether. In *Midrash and Lection in Matthew* (1974), he argues that Matthew redacted and rewrote Markan passages to create a Jewish-Christian lectionary to provide liturgical texts for the five yearly festivals.

The more scholarly research proceeded into the life of Jesus, the

more difficult it became to achieve its goal. On the one hand, the ascendance of literary criticism made the evangelists look more and more like creative authors rewriting the Old Testament into the New (see Randel Helms, *Gospel Fictions,* 1988; Thomas L. Brodie, "Luke the Literary Interpreter," 1981; Wolfgang Roth, *Hebrew Gospel,* 1988; John Dominic Crossan, *Who Killed Jesus?* 1995), and on the other, the plethora of plausible historical Jesus portraits made it difficult, if not impossible, to point with any confidence either to any bank of historically reliable texts or to reconstruct any portrait that is superior to another. Some scholars, with substantial justification, picture the historical Jesus as a kind of Jewish Cynic philosopher. The Cynics' renunciation of livelihood, family, and home in favor of God's gentle rule in nature and living like unassuming birds and animals sounds strikingly like that of Jesus in the Sermon on the Mount. Scholars endorsing this view include Burton Mack (*The Lost Gospel: The Book of Q and Christian Origins,* 1993), Gerald F. Downing (*Cynics and Christian Origins,* 1992; *Christ and the Cynics,* 1988), Crossan (*The Historical Jesus: The Life of a Mediterranean Jewish Peasant,* 1992), and Stephen J. Patterson (*The Gospel of Thomas and Jesus,* 1993).

Others, equally cogent in their presentation, understand Jesus to have been a revolutionary against Rome and its priestly lapdogs in Jerusalem. The first to espouse this view in modern times was Reimarus, but Robert Eisler (*The Messiah Jesus and John the Baptist,* 1931) made a powerful case for the position, as did S.G.F. Brandon (*The Fall of Jerusalem and the Christian Church,* 1951; *Jesus and the Zealots,* 1967). Oscar Cullmann (*Jesus and the Revolutionaries,* 1970) had considerable sympathy for this theory, as did Hyam Maccoby (*Revolution in Judea,* 1973). Maccoby did not think Jesus would necessarily have taken up the sword, but like the Qumran sectarians, Jesus might have expected God to send legions of angels to do the job. Richard A. Horsley (*Bandits, Prophets, and Messiahs,* 1985; *Jesus and the Spiral of Violence,* 1987) takes Jesus to have been a Gandhi-like non-violent resister.

Morton Smith (*Jesus the Magician,* 1978) focused on Jesus' use of contemporary healers' techniques, healing by symbolic gesture, use

of spittle, and so on as evidence that Jesus was, as both his early critics and supporters claimed, a magician. Geza Vermes (*Jesus the Jew*, 1973) is not far from this paradigm when he argues that Jesus was a Galilean Hasid like Hanina ben-Dosa and Honi the Circle-Maker, charismatic sages who took advantage of God's special love for them to win miraculous favors for the people. Harvey Falk (*Jesus the Pharisee*, 1985) and Hyam Maccoby (also *Jesus the Pharisee*, 2003) see Jesus' disputes with the scribes as collegial debates, not bitter polemics between religious enemies. Margaret Barker (*The Risen Lord*, 1996) sees the historical Jesus as a Gnostic visionary and mystagogue who actually said the sort of thing ascribed to him in the Nag Hammadi Gospels.

Many scholars, like Richard J. Arthur and Bart Ehrman (*Jesus, Prophet of the New Millennium*, 1999), still hold the view of Johannes Weiss, Bultmann, Bornkamm and others that Jesus, while not viewing himself as the Messiah, was nonetheless a prophet predicting the imminent coming of the kingdom of God. Many others, however, especially scholars connected with the Jesus Seminar, repudiate any eschatological element in the teaching of Jesus. The Cynic Jesus is an example, but others practically dissolve Jesus into his sayings, or what little remains of them. James Breech (*The Silence of Jesus*, 1983) and Bernard Brandon Scott (*Hear Then the Parable*, 1989) seem to interpret the material in an ahistorical way that perversely lifts the texts out of any context and takes Jesus along with them. They perhaps confuse descriptive exegesis with a kind of postmodern reading of texts a la Jacques Derrida and Paul de Man, with no regard to authorial intent.

Jesus seems to be shrinking to the vanishing point, so it should come as no surprise that there have always been a number of scholars who have decided that Jesus did not exist as a historical person. I have already mentioned Bruno Bauer (*Christ and the Caesars*, 1877; English 1998), who regarded Jesus as a literary invention like John Galt or Superman. Others understood Jesus to be a mythical god who became a legendary figure just like Samson or Hercules, each of whom had been the sun god in the sky but shrank to the slightly more than human proportions of a legendary hero striding the earth. Scholars

espousing this view include Arthur Drews *(The Christ Myth,* 1910), J. M. Robertson (*Pagan Christs,* 1903; *Christianity and Mythology,* 1910), Paul Couchoud (*The Creation of the Christ,* 1939), and William Benjamin Smith (*Ecce Homo,* 1912; *The Birth of the Gospel,* 1957). Their case has basically consisted in the observations that, first, no source outside the Bible mentions Jesus, at least not as a contemporary, only as the reputed founder of Christianity; second, that the authentic epistles of Paul (pretty much all but the Pastorals), earlier than the gospels, make no mention of a human Jesus who was a teacher or even a miracle worker; and third, that the Christian sacramental system of believers ritually dying and rising with their god smacks so heavily of contemporary mystery religions, there is no good reason to treat it as something different.

Bultmann doubted the sanity of any who would deny a historical Jesus, but even he granted that the figure of Jesus had retreated irretrievably behind the stained-glass barrier of myth and dogma. He thought there must ultimately have been Easter morning visions of some kind, but that the resurrection doctrine was the application of mystery-religion notions to Jesus. So one can see Bultmann already flinching from ultra-radicalism, and most critics, notably including Bultmann's own students, tended to retreat further than he did. Bornkamm (*Jesus of Nazareth,* 1956, English 1960), Robinson (*A New Quest of the Historical Jesus,* 1959), Conzelmann (*Jesus,* 1973), Ernst Fuchs (*Studies of the Historical Jesus,* 1964) and Käsemann *(Jesus Means Freedom,* 1969) all participated to varying degrees in a "New Quest" for a true biography. What they were trying to establish was whether there was any continuity between Jesus' own posture of existential openness to God as guarantor of one's future, on the one hand, and the early Christian preaching of Jesus as the agent of God's grace on the other. It was a rather abstruse thing to define, much less to prove, and Van A. Harvey (*The Historian and the Believer,* 1966) scorned the very attempt to "psych out" an ancient figure of the past, especially on such a modicum of biographical evidence as these post-Bultmannians (Morton Smith called them the "Bultmaniacs") admitted they possessed. Nevertheless, it was this New Quest that Robert W. Funk and Crossan sought to take up and

carry forward when they founded the Jesus Seminar in 1982.

Following the lead of Christian apologists, the retrenching ranks of New Testament criticism treated the Christ Myth Theory with universal disdain, no longer bothering to attempt refutations as their predecessors had thought necessary. But it still had lone torch bearers here and there. George A. Wells (*The Jesus of the Early Christians,* 1971; *Did Jesus Exist?* 1975; *The Historical Evidence for Jesus,* 1988; *Who Was Jesus?* 1989; *The Jesus Legend,* 1996; *The Jesus Myth,* 1999) championed the theory, adducing many new arguments and refuting numerous conventional objections. He did not rely upon the parallel between Jesus and the Mystery Cult redeemers but substituted for it the widespread Hellenistic Jewish speculative myth of the personified Wisdom of God, who had visited the earth in an endeavor to teach the human race, only to be rejected and return again to heaven. Philo of Alexandria thought it better to describe this Wisdom (Sophia) as the male Word (Logos), but the idea was the same. He understood the Word of God to have been God's image, his firstborn Son, the heavenly Adam, the cosmic high priest. It is common for scholars to trace the parallels between Jewish Wisdom speculation and New Testament Christology (see Cullmann, *The Christology of the New Testament,* 1959; Reginald H. Fuller, *The Foundations of New Testament Christology,* 1965; M. Jack Suggs, *Wisdom Christology in Matthew's Gospel,* 1970), but Wells argued that the Wisdom myth was not the veneer but the wood. After all, what was left of the Jesus story if the main substructure was taken away, dismissed as embellishment? Embellishment of what?

Barbara G. Walker (*The Women's Encyclopedia of Myths and Secrets,* 1983) returned to a more traditional version of mythicism, dissolving Jesus into the syncretism of the Hellenistic world and its even more archaic antecedents, employing a bold and convincing imaginative vision. Acharya S (*Suns of God,* 2004) rehabilitated the older approach of boiling all mythology down to ancient sun worship and astrology as the only way of accounting for the global, ancient, spontaneous occurrence of the same mythemes, rituals, and symbols. It must have been a way of representing something everyone could see, not needing to borrow from other cultures. Earl

Doherty (*The Jesus Puzzle,* 1999) focused on the Midrashic character of New Testament stories as rewritten versions of Old Testament narratives. He saw that when early Christians claimed Jesus did this or that "according to the scriptures," they meant not merely that they had successfully fished for clever proof texts to make Jesus stories the fulfillment of prophecy, but they discovered what Jesus did by reading the scriptures esoterically to begin with. At first there had been the purely mythic preaching of a divine savior martyred by archons in some unseen heavenly realm, rather like the primordial sacrifice of Purusha, the Primal Man in the Rig Veda. Later on, when it was felt needful to have an historical founder for the Christian religion, various writers ventured guesses as to when he might have lived, just as Herodotus, Plutarch, and others tried to date the presumed "historical Hercules." Some had Jesus crucified under Alexander Jannaeus in 87 BCE, others under Pontius Pilate or Herod Antipas around 30 CE, still others placing his death in the reign of Claudius Caesar—such ambiguity being an odd circumstance if the story were a matter of recent public memory. To supply a biography for him, early scribes plundered the Septuagint for likely stories, changing the hero's name to Jesus.

Margaret Morris (*Jesus Augustus*), Abelard Reuchlin *(The True Authorship of the New Testament,* 1979), Joseph Atwill (*Caesar's Messiah: The Roman Conspiracy to Invent Jesus,* 2005), and Francesco Carotta (*Jesus Was Caesar: On the Julian Origin of Christianity, an Investigative Report,* 2005), and Cliff Carrington have all argued that there was no historical Jesus but that the hero of the gospels is an ironic residue of Roman propaganda on behalf of one or another of the Roman emperors. Paul Tillich wrote (*Systematic Theology,* 3 vols., 1951-63) that even should the acid bath of criticism make us unsure of any and all the facts in his case, there still must have been an historical founder of Christianity, even if his very name should prove not to have been Jesus, because otherwise we cannot account for the appearance of what Tillich called the New Being, the Life in the Spirit, amid human history. In more ways than one, Tillich's words are true. It is finally the theologians' need for Jesus that will secure him as an historical figure.

Paul

One almost suspects that Protestant theologians could afford to throw Jesus to the wolves of criticism as long as one allowed them to retain Paul. He is really their favorite revealer. Yet neither the Pauline writings nor the historical figure is any more secure than Jesus. First, there is the matter of sources available to us. All critical scholars write off the Book of Acts as basically fiction. Philipp Vielhauer ("On the 'Paulinism' of Acts," 1966) showed how the author of Acts misunderstood Paul, at least if the theology of the epistles is anything to go by. But scholars have forgotten Nietzsche's warning that if one has only fiction and no facts, one makes doubly sure not to start thinking of the fiction as fact since it is all one has left. As a result, many critics, disavowing the historical character and utility of Acts, continue to default to it in describing early Christian history. Like Knox (*Chapters in a Life of Paul,* 1950), Gerd Lüdemann *(Paul, Apostle to the Gentiles: Studies in Chronology,* 1984) sets Acts aside and uses only references in the epistles to fix a chronology for Paul's missionary journeys, though he too repairs to Acts to a surprising extent in both *Early Christianity according to the Traditions in Acts* (1989) and *Paul: The Founder of Christianity* (2002).

If Acts is off the table, what sources remain to reconstruct an historical Paul? First, we must decide which of the thirteen epistles that bear his name are really his. We have already seen how the three Pastoral Epistles lost their place in the list, being post-Marcionite propaganda. Ephesians, too, is widely discounted. Edgar J. Goodspeed saw that it must have been intended as a summarizing introduction, sort of an overture to the rest of the Pauline letters, and in fact, it appears to be a patchwork of snippets drawn from them as well as from the Septuagint. Colossians bears marks of later Gnosticism, so many scholars make it a product of a subsequent Pauline School. Second Thessalonians seems to be a later effort to undo the damage caused by the end-of-the-world enthusiasm fostered by First Thessalonians, hence non-Pauline. Most Pauline scholars today, then, work with a canon of seven supposedly authentic Pauline texts: Romans, 1 and 2 Corinthians, Galatians, Philippians, 1 Thessalonians, and Philemon. But in this, they have again flinched from the bold insight of Baur

(Paul: The Apostle of Jesus Christ), who dropped all but the first four in the list, as well as a bit of Romans, as inauthentic. One may understand the reticence of post-Baur scholars as more a matter of a fear of heights than as reflecting weaknesses in Baur's arguments. Philippians is quite as Gnostic as Colossians. First Thessalonians bears marks of competing with its successor as a pseudonymous contender for attention in post-Pauline Thessalonica.

Yet the game of "more radical than thou" was not finished. The Dutch Radicals, latter-day followers of Bruno Bauer, were dismissed as extremists even by F. C. Baur, much as Martin Luther, himself the target of heresy charges, dismissed Caspar Schwenkfeld as a lunatic. For the Dutch scholars, including Allard Pierson and Samuel A. Naber (*Verisimilia,* 1886), A. D. Loman ("Quaestiones Paulinae," 1882, 1883, 1886), Jan Hendrik Scholten (*Contributions to Historical Criticism,* 1882), W. C. van Manen (*Paul,* 3 vols., 1890, 1891, 1896; see his articles in English in the *Encyclopaedia Biblica,* 1899), and Rudolf Steck (*The Letter to the Galatians,* 1888), marshaled astonishing arguments to show that while there had been an historical Paul, none of the extant letters were his, any more than the truckload of Petrine pseudepigrapha can be reasonably credited to that apostle. English-speaking followers of the Dutch Radicals did their best to propagate these opinions outside of Europe, notably L. Gordon Rylands *(A Critical Analysis of the Four Chief Pauline Epistles,* 1929) and Thomas Whittaker *(On the Origins of Christianity,* 1904). Dutch Radicalism has recently been revived in Germany by Hermann Detering (*The Falsified Paul,* 2003) and in America by Conzelmann's student, Darrell J. Doughty ("Pauline Paradigms and Pauline Authority," 1994), and Doughty's student Robert M. Price (*The Amazing Colossal Apostle,* forthcoming 2007).

Whoever may have penned the epistles attributed to Paul, what of their integrity? Are they each consistent and complete documents, products each of a single hand? Or might they be redacted and counter-redacted patchworks? Van Manen thought the latter and Doughty observes the curious reluctance of scholars, accustomed to cutting the gospel traditions into different sources when discontinuities betray redactional seams, to recognize the same phenomena in Pauline

texts. He points out the vast extent to which mainstream commentaries are simply exercises in ingenious harmonization: if Galatians is all the work of one author, how on earth did he intend B to follow from A?

J. C. O'Neill (*Paul's Letter to the Romans,* 1975), William O. Walker Jr. *(Interpolations in the Pauline Letters,* 2001), and Winsome Munro *(Authority in Paul and Peter: The Identification of a Pastoral Stratum in the Pauline Corpus and 1 Peter,* 1983) have no connection to the speculations of Dutch Radicalism, but they have all advanced theories positing significant subsequent additions to Paul's canon of seven genuine epistles, suggesting that even these are not pure. Each author received a hail of criticism from more timid scholars unwilling even to consider the presence of early interpolations without manuscript evidence. Of course, the problem is that we have no manuscripts at all before the Chester Beatty Papyri collection dating from about 300 CE. But Munro and Walker have proposed ample criteria by which to identify interpolations with some probability. O'Neill, on the other hand, learned to recognize a wider significance in what most textual critics dismissed as marginal manuscript anomalies. Busy at a somewhat different project, the industrious Bart Ehrman (*The Orthodox Corruption of Scripture,* 1993) has made new sense of the manuscript variations, demonstrating an anti-heretical redactional tendency on the part of scribes to "fix" favorite texts to which their theological opponents loved to appeal in debate.

Walter Schmithals sternly opposed the Dutch Radicalism espoused by his student Hermann Detering, but his own brilliant work in many ways seems to point to it. For one thing, Schmithals shows how much sense the admonitions and debates in the Pauline texts would make if they were addressing the issues raised by Gnosticism in the second century. But instead, he concludes that Christian Gnosticism was already up and flying in the mid-first century, that it had to be. On the other hand, Schmithals (*Paul and the Gnostics,* 1972) has vivisected several of the epistles into hypothetical fragments of earlier editions, shown to have been clumsily reassembled by half-witted church secretaries long after their first delivery. Yet Schmithals insists that all the fragments were genuinely Pauline.

Among those who work with the sacrosanct seven epistles, assured that they represent substantially what the apostle wrote, we have at least two important and related tendencies, both seemingly spawned by considerations of ecumenical etiquette, though no less likely to be exegetically well-founded for all that. Though many New Testament scholars are not afraid of finding evidence in the New Testament for ancient anti-Semitism or anti-Judaism (see the unflinching scrutiny of Jack T. Sanders in *The Jews in Luke-Acts,* 1987), others seem to want to absolve Paul of this taint in order not to have to answer for it in their own use of the old texts today. Hoping that Paul might be posthumously inducted as a supporter of a "double covenant" theology whereby Christians and Jews respect one another's place before the Almighty, Lloyd Gaston (*Paul and the Torah,* 1987) and John G. Gager (*The Origins of Anti-Semitism,* 1983; *Reinventing Paul,* 2000) argue ingeniously that all Paul says of Jews in the epistles, he says to Jewish Christians, with nothing to say about the status or fate of non-Christian Jews who are no more in his sight than Buddhists.

The twin of this theory is the repudiation of what scholars now call the Lutheran paradigm of justification by grace through faith. Mentioned earlier, this trend, as so many things do, goes back to F. C. Baur, who already saw that the Pauline epistles are not so much concerned with the inability of sinful humans to merit salvation by their own moral deeds as with the freedom of gentile converts from alien cultural mores, those of the Jewish Torah. But as Nietzsche's mad prophet said, it takes a long time for the light, even from the brightest nova, to become visible here across the void. Thus it was generations before Protestant exegetes reinvented this particular wheel. Krister Stendahl (*Paul among Jews and Gentiles,* 1976) started the ball rolling by noticing how Paul's epistles as a whole give no signal of the existential despair he supposedly expressed in Romans 7 over his one-time inability to fulfill the Torah. Elsewhere he boasts of flawless legal piety. So maybe he meant something else in Romans, something that would not comport with Martin Luther's agonizing over how one might gain a clean conscience before God. Maybe Lutheran soteriology was based more on Luther than on Paul. The scholar E. P. Sanders (*Paul, the Law, and the Jewish People,* 1983) argued that

Paul never taught any general human inability to keep the Torah. Instead, he merely "reverse-engineered" a theology from the assumed superiority of Christianity over Judaism. Christianity must have superceded Judaism because Paul had converted from the older faith to the new, and so he had to rationalize his conversion—and everyone else's.

Much remains to be said both of the New Testament, a bottomless abyss of fascination, and of the nearly as interesting history of New Testament scholarship, but I judge the foregoing is sufficient to provide some context for the many unfamiliar names infesting the footnotes of this Pre-Nicene New Testament.

NOTE ON TEXT AND TRANSLATION

For traditional New Testament writings, I worked from the various editions of Nestle's *Novum Testamentum Graece,* although not feeling bound by all the text-critical choices codified in Nestle. Instead, I followed my own historical instincts, recognizing with J. C. O'Neill that sometimes minor readings preserve something closer to the original text than the majority readings. William O. Walker Jr. and Winsome Munro have shown that we cannot simply accept on faith that during the early centuries, for which we have no manuscript evidence at all, documents were preserved without alterations. My feeling is that one does better to engage in educated speculation if the internal evidence points to early interpolations. Odd readings preserved in Old Latin and Old Syriac manuscripts were probably translated from earlier Greek manuscripts than we now have and should carry some weight of seniority when considering how an original passage may have read. Old Testament scholars have long recognized this and have cheerfully given preference to the Greek Septuagint, absent available Hebrew manuscript evidence, again obviously because the Septuagint was translated from earlier manuscripts than we currently possess. The discovery of much earlier Hebrew copies among the Dead Sea Scrolls has justified these choices. Therefore, I have followed the same logic in the case of New Testament versional evidence.

For Barnabas, Hermas, and others, I followed the Greek texts of the Loeb Classical Library editions. For documents written in other languages, I compared available translations to produce what I believe are accurate English paraphrases. I hasten to add that I am not fluent in Arabic, Aramaic, Coptic, Hebrew, or Latin, although I consulted textual commentaries discussing difficulties in texts in these languages. I might have invited other scholars to join me in preparing

translations for these books, but I decided not to because I wanted my own distinctive viewpoint to be reflected throughout the whole collection. In my experience, committee translations tend to be dull and safe. I wanted neither.

INDEX

ROBERT M. PRICE holds doctoral degrees from Drew University in both theology and New Testament. He is currently Professor of Biblical Criticism at the Center for Inquiry Institute in Amherst, New York, and editor of the *Journal of Higher Criticism*. His books include *Deconstructing Jesus*; *Paul as Text: The Apostle and the Apocrypha*; and *The Widow Traditions in Luke-Acts: A Feminist-Critical Scrutiny*. He has published in the *American Rationalist*, *Dialogue*, *Evangelical Quarterly*, *Journal of Psychology and Theology*, *Hervormde Teologiese Studies*, *Reformed Journal*, and elsewhere.

D1559522